Human Resource Management

GAINING A COMPETITIVE ADVANTAGE

Human Resource Management

GAINING A COMPETITIVE ADVANTAGE 11e

RAYMOND A. NOE
The Ohio State University

JOHN R. HOLLENBECK
Michigan State University

BARRY GERHART
University of Wisconsin–Madison

PATRICK M. WRIGHT
University of South Carolina

McGraw Hill Education

HUMAN RESOURCE MANAGEMENT: GAINING A COMPETITIVE ADVANTAGE, ELEVENTH EDITION

Published by McGraw-Hill Education, 2 Penn Plaza, New York, NY 10121. Copyright © 2019 by McGraw-Hill Education. All rights reserved. Printed in the United States of America. Previous editions © 2017, 2015, and 2013. No part of this publication may be reproduced or distributed in any form or by any means, or stored in a database or retrieval system, without the prior written consent of McGraw-Hill Education, including, but not limited to, in any network or other electronic storage or transmission, or broadcast for distance learning.

Some ancillaries, including electronic and print components, may not be available to customers outside the United States.

This book is printed on acid-free paper.

1 2 3 4 5 6 7 8 9 LWI 21 20 19 18

ISBN 978-1-260-07684-4 (bound edition)
MHID 1-260-07684-9 (bound edition)

ISBN 978-1-260-14229-7 (loose-leaf edition)
MHID 1-260-14229-9 (loose-leaf edition)

Brand Manager: *Anke Weeks*
Product Developer: *Jamie Koch*
Content Project Managers: *Rick Hecker; Keri Johnson*
Buyer: *Susan K. Culbertson*
Design: *Matt Backhaus*
Content Licensing Specialists: *Melissa Homer*
Cover Image: *©Rawpixel.com/Shutterstock*
Compositor: *Aptara®, Inc.*

All credits appearing on page or at the end of the book are considered to be an extension of the copyright page.

Chapter opening photo credits (in order of appearance): ©Image Source RF; ©G-stockstudio/Shutterstock.com; AJR_photo/Shutterstock; Andriy Popov/123RF; ©Image Source RF

Library of Congress Cataloging-in-Publication Data

Names: Hollenbeck, John R., author. | Noe, Raymond A., author. | Gerhart, Barry A., author.
Title: Human resource management : gaining a competitive advantage / John R. Hollenbeck, Michigan State University, Raymond A. Noe, The Ohio State University, Berry Gerhart, University of Wisconsin, Madison, Patrick M. Wright, University of South Carolina.
Description: Eleventh Edition. | New York, NY : McGraw-Hill Education, 2018. | Revised edition of Human resource management, 2015.
Identifiers: LCCN 2017040499| ISBN 9781260076844 (hardback : alk. paper) | ISBN 1260076849
Subjects: LCSH: Personnel management—United States. | BISAC: BUSINESS & ECONOMICS / Human Resources & Personnel Management.
Classification: LCC HF5549.2.U5 H8 2018 | DDC 658.3—dc23 LC record available at https://lccn.loc.gov/2017040499

The Internet addresses listed in the text were accurate at the time of publication. The inclusion of a website does not indicate an endorsement by the authors or McGraw-Hill Education, and McGraw-Hill Education does not guarantee the accuracy of the information presented at these sites.

mheducation.com/highered

To my wife, Caroline, and my children,
Ray, Tim, and Melissa
— R. A. N.

To my parents, Harold and Elizabeth, my wife,
Patty, and my children, Jennifer, Marie, Timothy,
and Jeffrey
— J. R. H.

To my parents, Robert and Shirley, my wife,
Heather, and my children, Chris and Annie
— B. G.

To my parents, Patricia and Paul, my wife, Mary,
and my sons, Michael and Matthew
— P. M. W.

ABOUT THE AUTHORS

RAYMOND A. NOE is the Robert and Anne Hoyt Designated Professor of Management at The Ohio State University. He was previously a professor in the Department of Management at Michigan State University and the Industrial Relations Center of the Carlson School of Management, University of Minnesota. He received his BS in psychology from The Ohio State University and his MA and PhD in psychology from Michigan State University. Professor Noe conducts research and teaches undergraduate as well as MBA and PhD students in human resource management, managerial skills, quantitative methods, human resource information systems, training, employee development, performance management, and organizational behavior. He has published over 70 articles and invited chapters and authored, coauthored or edited seven books covering a variety of topics in training and development (training needs, trainee motivation, informal learning, autonomous learning, mentoring), human resource management (recruiting), and organizational behavior (psychological contracts, teams, work and family). Professor Noe has received awards for his teaching and research excellence, including the Ernest J. McCormick Award for Distinguished Early Career Contribution from the Society for Industrial and Organizational Psychology. He is also a fellow of the Society of Industrial and Organizational Psychology and American Psychological Association.

JOHN R. HOLLENBECK holds the positions of University Distinguished Professor at Michigan State University and Eli Broad Professor of Management at the Eli Broad Graduate School of Business Administration. Dr. Hollenbeck received his PhD in Management from New York University in 1984. He served as the acting editor at *Organizational Behavior and Human Decision Processes* in 1995, the associate editor of *Decision Sciences* from 1999 to 2004, and the editor of *Personnel Psychology* from 1996 to 2002. He has published over 90 articles and book chapters on the topics of team decision making and work motivation. According to the Institute for Scientific Information, this body of work has been cited over 4,000 times by other researchers. Dr. Hollenbeck has been awarded fellowship status in both the Academy of Management and the American Psychological Association, and was recognized with the Career Achievement Award by the HR Division of the Academy of Management (2011), the Distinguished Service Contributions Award (2014), and the Early Career Award by the Society of Industrial and Organizational Psychology (1992). At Michigan State, Dr. Hollenbeck has won several teaching awards including the Michigan State Distinguished Faculty Award, the Michigan State Teacher-Scholar Award, and the Broad MBA Most Outstanding Faculty Member.

BARRY GERHART is Professor of Management and Human Resources and the Bruce R. Ellig Distinguished Chair in Pay and Organizational Effectiveness, Wisconsin School of Business, University of Wisconsin-Madison. He has also served as department chair or area coordinator at Cornell, Vanderbilt, and Wisconsin. His research interests include compensation, human resource/human capital strategy, international human resources, and employee retention. Professor Gerhart received his BS in psychology from Bowling Green State University and his PhD in Industrial Relations from the University of Wisconsin-Madison. He has co-authored two books in the area of compensation. He serves on the editorial boards of and has published in the *Academy of Management Journal, Industrial and Labor Relations Review, International Journal of Human Resource Management, Journal of Applied Psychology, Management and Organization Review,* and *Personnel Psychology.* Professor Gerhart is a past recipient of the Heneman Career Achievement Award, the Scholarly Achievement Award, and (twice) the International Human Resource Management Scholarly Research Award, all from the Human Resources Division, Academy of Management. He is a Fellow of the Academy of Management, the American Psychological Association, and the Society for Industrial and Organizational Psychology.

PATRICK M. WRIGHT is Thomas C. Vandiver Bicentennial Chair and the Director of the Center for Executive Succession in the Darla Moore School of Business at the University of South Carolina. Prior to joining USC, he served on the faculties at Cornell University, Texas A&M University, and the University of Notre Dame. Professor Wright teaches, conducts research, and consults in the area of strategic human resource management (SHRM), particularly focusing on how firms use people as a source of competitive advantage and the changing nature of the chief HR officer (CHRO) role. He is the faculty leader for the Cornell ILR Executive Education/NAHR program, "The Chief HR Officer: Strategies for Success," aimed at developing potential successors to the CHRO role. He served as the lead editor on the recently released book, *The Chief HR Officer: Defining the New Role of Human Resource Leaders,* published by Wiley. Professor Wright has published more than 60 research articles in journals as well as more than 20 chapters in books and edited volumes. He recently served as the editor at the *Journal of Management,* has co-edited a special issue of *Research in Personnel and Human Resources Management* titled "Strategic Human Resource Management in the 21st Century," and guest edited a special issue of *Human Resource Management Review* titled "Research in Strategic HRM for the 21st Century." He currently serves as a member on the Board of Directors for the Society for Human Resource Management and the National Academy of Human Resources. He is a former board member of HRPS, SHRM Foundation, and World at Work (formerly American Compensation Association). From 2011 to 2016, he was named by *HRM Magazine* as one of the 20 "Most Influential Thought Leaders in HR."

PREFACE

Our intent is to provide students with the background to be successful HRM professionals, to manage human resources effectively, and to be knowledgeable consumers of HRM products. Managers must be able to identify effective HRM practices to purchase these services from a consultant, to work with the HRM department, or to design and implement them personally. *Human Resources Management: Gaining a Competitive Advantage, 11th edition,* emphasizes how a manager can more effectively manage human resources and highlights important issues in current HRM practice.

Human Resources Management: Gaining a Competitive Advantage, represents a valuable approach to teaching human resource management for several reasons:

- The text draws from the diverse research, teaching, and consulting experiences of four authors who have taught human resource management to undergraduates, traditional day MBA students as a required and elective course, and more experienced managers and professional employees in weekend and evening MBA programs. The teamwork approach gives a depth and breadth to the coverage that is not found in other texts.
- Human resource management is viewed as critical to the success of a business. The text emphasizes how the HRM function, as well as the management of human resources, can help companies gain a competitive advantage.
- The book discusses current issues such as social media, use of nontraditional employment relationships, big data, talent management, diversity, and employee engagement, all of which have a major impact on business and HRM practice.
- Strategic human resource management is introduced early in the book and integrated throughout.
- Examples of how new technologies are being used to improve the efficiency and effectiveness of HRM practices are provided throughout.
- We provide examples of how companies are evaluating HRM practices to determine their value.
- The chapter openers, in-text boxes, and end-of-chapter materials provide questions that provide students the opportunity to discuss and apply HR concepts to a broad range of issues including strategic human resource management, HR in small businesses, ethics and the role of HR in helping companies achieve sustainability, adopt and use technology, adapt to globalization, and practice integrity. This should make the HR classroom more interactive and increase students' understanding of the concepts and their application.

Organization

Human Resource Management: Gaining a Competitive Advantage, 11th edition, includes an introductory chapter (Chapter 1) and five parts.

Chapter 1 provides a detailed discussion of the global, new economy, stakeholder, and work system challenges that influence companies' abilities to successfully meet the needs of shareholders, customers, employees, and other stakeholders. We discuss how the management of human resources can help companies meet the competitive challenges.

Part One includes a discussion of the environmental forces that companies face in attempting to capitalize on their human resources as a means to gain competitive advantage. The environmental forces include the strategic direction of the business, the legal environment, and the type of work performed and physical arrangement of the work.

A key focus of Chapter 2, on strategic human resource management, is to highlight the role that staffing, performance management, training and development, and compensation play in different types of business strategies.

A key focus of Chapter 3, on the legal environment, is to enhance managers' understanding of laws related to sexual harassment, affirmative action, and accommodations for disabled employees. The various types of discrimination and ways they have been interpreted by the courts are discussed.

Chapter 4, on analysis and design of work, emphasizes how work systems can improve company competitiveness by alleviating job stress and by improving employees' motivation and satisfaction with their jobs.

Part Two deals with the acquisition and preparation of human resources, including human resource planning and recruitment, selection, and training.

Chapter 5, on human resource planning and recruitment, illustrates the process of developing a human resource plan. Also, the strengths and weaknesses of staffing options such as outsourcing, use of contingent workers, and downsizing are discussed. Strategies for recruiting talented employees are emphasized.

Chapter 6, on selection and placement, emphasizes ways to minimize errors in employee selection and placement to improve the company's competitive position. Selection method standards such as validity and reliability are discussed in easily understandable terms without compromising the technical complexity of these issues. The chapter discusses selection methods such as interviews and various types of tests (including personality, honesty, and drug tests) and compares them on measures of validity, reliability, utility, and legality.

Chapter 7 discusses the components of effective training systems and the manager's role in determining employees' readiness for training, creating a positive learning environment, and ensuring that training is used on the job. The advantages and disadvantages of different training methods are described, such as e-learning, serious games, and mobile training.

Part Three explores how companies can determine the value of employees and capitalize on their talents through retention and development strategies.

Chapter 8, on performance management, examines the strengths and weaknesses of performance management methods that use ratings, objectives, or behaviors.

Chapter 9, on employee development, introduces the student to how assessment, job experiences, formal courses, and mentoring relationships are used to develop employees.

Chapter 10, on retention and separation, discusses how managers can maximize employee productivity and satisfaction to avoid absenteeism and turnover. The chapter emphasizes the use of employee surveys to monitor job and organizational characteristics that affect satisfaction and subsequently retention.

Part Four covers rewarding and compensating human resources, including designing pay structures (Chapter 11), recognizing individual contributions (Chapter 12), and providing benefits (Chapter 13).

Here we explore how managers should decide the pay rate for different jobs, given the company's compensation strategy and the worth of jobs. The advantages and disadvantages of merit pay, gainsharing, and skill-based pay are discussed. The benefits chapter highlights the different types of employer-provided benefits and discusses how benefit costs can be contained. International comparisons of compensation and benefit practices are provided.

Part Five covers special topics in human resource management, including labor–management relations, international HRM, and strategically managing the HRM function.

Chapter 14, on collective bargaining and labor relations, focuses on traditional issues in labor–management relations, such as union structure and membership, the organizing process, and contract negotiations; it also discusses new union agendas and less adversarial approaches to labor–management relations.

Chapter 15 discusses social and political changes, such as Brexit, on global human resource management. Selecting, preparing, and rewarding employees for foreign assignments is also discussed.

The text concludes with Chapter 16, which emphasizes how HRM practices should be aligned to help the company meet its business objectives. The chapter emphasizes that the HRM function needs to have a customer focus to be effective.

New Feature and Content Changes in This Edition

All examples, figures, and statistics have been updated to incorporate the most recently published human resource data. Each chapter was revised to include current examples, research results, and relevant topical coverage. All of the Exercising Strategy, Managing People, and HR in Small Business end-of-chapter cases are either new or updated. Following are the highlights for each chapter:

Chapter 1

New Opening Vignette: Looks at how Publix's use of human resource practices contributes to its dedication to the dignity, value, and employment security of its associates, which has led to its recognition as a great place to work and shop.

New Boxes:
- Dow Chemical, Novartis, and Mars help improve living conditions and employees skills around the world.
- How Verizon, Best Buy, and Kohl's use social media and apps to enhance HR practices.
- How Sodexo used data to show how gender balance on teams was related to financial performance, employee engagement, and client retention.
- How Amtrak's first-ever chief human capital officer used competencies and behaviors to build integrity and demonstrate integrity, which helped rebuilding HR and provided value to Amtrak's business.
- Iberdrola USA, Boeing, and L'Oreal efforts to prepare employees for global assignments.

New Text Material:
- HR in organizations: budgets, example of the role of HR in companies (Airbnb, Marsh, Juniper Networks, Abbott, Tesla Motors), managers' expectations for the HR function, and the skills needed by HR professionals to contribute to the businesses.
- Companies' use of big data and workforce analytics to identify successful new employees and reduce turnover (Google, Mattress Firm, Credit Suisse).
- Economy data, labor force statistics, occupational and job growth projections, skill shortages, working at home, flexible schedules, nontraditional employment, and the gig economy.

- The role of HR in ensuring product quality and customer service, including examples of HR practices of 2016 Baldrige Award winner Don Chalmers Ford.
- Actions that Alcoa and General Electric are taking to overcome problems finding employees with the necessary skills.
- How Keller Williams Realty facilitates continuous learning.
- Steps that Portsmouth Naval Shipyard is taking to manage change.
- Echo Global Logistics's, Whole Foods's, and Timberlane's efforts to support employee engagement.
- Talent management at BNSF Railway.
- Ammacore's and KPMG's use of nontraditional employment and work arrangements.
- How Blue Apron is developing develop human, social, and intellectual capital.
- Discussion of characteristics and expectations that Generation Z and Millennials bring to the workplace.
- How Coke gives millennial employees a voice in shaping the business.
- Discussion of the role of immigration in the economy; the workforce; and restaurant, roofing, landscaping, and high-tech businesses.
- How Microsoft's approach to diversity focuses on its employees, culture, suppliers, and customers.
- Legal issues and the gig economy (e.g., Uber) and immigration restrictions.
- Growth of global business for companies such as Ford, General Motors, Yum! Brands, McDonalds, and Uber.
- Offshoring jobs in the United States (Rexnord Corporation).
- Use of artificial intelligence and robots (BMW, Airport Guide Robot, Whirpool, H&R Block, and Watson).

Chapter 2

New Opening Vignette: Discusses Amazon's move into traditional brick-and-mortar stores.

New Information: Updated example of Merck's mission and values statement.

New Boxes:
- Companies use ADP's app to help manage pay for gig workers.
- Volkswagen's efforts to develop zero-emission vehicles to enhance its reputation.
- IKEA's expanding parental leave policy.

Chapter 3

New Opening Vignette: Looks into alleged discrimination in pay and hiring practices at Oracle.

New Information:
- Updated figures for different types of discrimination complaints in the United States.
- Description of the potential discrimination and retaliation at Uber.
- Discussion of LGBT issues in the workplace.
- Evidence-based HR about how weight discrimination can impact hiring decisions.

New Boxes:
- Tech companies challenges in increasing workforce diversity.
- Banning head scarves: Discriminatory or not in the European Union?
- The use of a wearable human grasp assist device to reduce repetitive injuries.
- Southwest's decision to end overbooking.

New Text Material:
- Frequency of discrimination cases.

Chapter 4

New Opening Vignette: Analyzes challenges associated with new organizational structures that try and promote teamwork but inadvertently create jobs that can get too large in scope, using Royal DSM as an example.

New Boxes:
- Data from wearable sensors to construct social network patterns that reveal the organizations informal structure.
- The aging of both equipment and workers in Japan are limiting national productivity.
- Chipotle's decentralized decision-making structures create recurrent problems when it comes to standardized food safety practices.
- The International Federation of Association Football (FIFA) has been accused of violating worker rights in Qatar due to the widespread practice of "kafala".
- The dangers associated with working from sedentary position and the push to get people to use "stand-up desks".

New Text Material:
- Portuguese manufacturers successfully compete against low cost Chinese competitors via work processes that promote quality over cost.
- Lean productivity practices promote lower costs, but also reduce the need for labor.
- Workflow analyses often identify the overuse of specific and costly pieces of equipment in the field of medicine.
- Centralized decision-making structures can identify critical customer needs that might be resisted by local managers, such as McDonald's All-day Breakfast.
- Jobs change over time, using the specific example of increased obesity in nursing care contexts and how this led to increased injuries until it was addressed.

Chapter 5

New Opening Vignette: Examines how more restrictive immigration policies regarding immigrants and refugees are creating labor shortages in the area of agriculture and meat processing.

New Boxes:
- Robotic technology still relies very heavily on human intervention using call centers as an example.
- Limits on H1-B visas in the U.S. are creating competitive disadvantages versus Canada in the field of high tech.
- the Trade Adjustment Assistance (TAA) program provides money for training to U.S. workers when their jobs move overseas.
- The increased aggressiveness of workplace raids conducted by Immigration and Customs Enforcement (ICE) office is breaking up families and local communities.
- Recent evidence shows that immigration results in a loss of U.S. jobs in the short term, but in the long term, results in large job gains for the country.

New Text Material:
- Qualcomm used leading indicators and forecasting to avoid a labor surplus that would have been caused by failures at Samsung–one of their primary customers.

- Improvements in technology reduce the need for workers when manufacturing jobs that moved overseas move back to the U.S.
- Changes in American eating habits related to restaurants is causing a shortage of labors for cooks, where turnover rates have soared to 100% in some regions.
- Low cost, online degree programs in the field of law have created a vast over-supply of unemployable lawyers.
- Deloitte is addressing a potential brain drain caused by the imminent retirement of a large cadre of workers.

Chapter 6

New Opening Vignette: Discusses how personnel selection processes in the field of law enforcement make it difficult to weed out police officers with criminal records.

New Boxes:
- Employers in the field of software use programming competitions to cheaply identify gifted programmers from around the world.
- Educational achievements reported by job applicants from some countries like Egypt mean nothing due to corruption in educational institutions.
- Increased use of opioid drugs in some regions of the U.S. make it impossible to hire people for "safety sensitive" jobs.
- "Religious Freedom Bills" are complicating the relationship between some firms and their communities.
- Employment gaps attributed to having children negatively affects some job applicants in certain fields.

New Text Material:
- Recent Supreme Court rulings have expanded the scope of Affirmative Action protections based upon race.
- Age discrimination cases have been expanding in the service sector of the economy as employers try to respond to customer preferences.
- The "Wounded Warriors Project" has helped create job opportunities for Gulf War Era veterans.
- Employers use information from social networking sites to obtain information that might be illegal to obtain in an interview.
- Programming teams at Pinterest are composed one person at a time, where each person added to the team is selected based upon some unique trait or perspective.

Chapter 7

New Opening Vignette: Highlights how GameStop uses an online game-based training program to deal with seasonal hiring and turnover.

New Boxes:
- How Sears is using learning to emphasize continuous learning and try to reinvent itself to survive.
- How Operation Smile and Marriott use language and cultural understanding to enhance global success.
- Central Iowa Works and Aon's use of education and training partnerships to develop workforce skills and meet both business and community needs.
- Janssen Pharmaceuticals use of just-in time technology-driven learning.
- How Pfizer evaluated the effectiveness of a new mobile training app.

New Text Material:
- Knowledge sharing at Defense Acquisition University.
- How Aerospace Corporation and Hilton Worldwide use training in ways that support the business.
- How the design elements of the training programs at Verizon, Farmers Insurance, and General Motors support learning and transfer of training.
- How companies such as PricewaterhouseCoopers, Western Union, Sonic, Cathay Life Insurance, Tata Consultancy Services, and EMC insure managers and peers support, incorporate action plans, and use performance support and communities of practice to enhance employees learning and transfer of training.
- Examples of how companies such as Asurion, EY, IBM, PPD, BNSF Railway, TELUS, ADP, University Health System, and PepsiCo use different training methods including video, serious games, simulations, online learning, social media, blended learning, and action learning.
- Example of how Massive Open Online Courses (MOOCs) are being developed through joint university industry partnership to offer programs and degrees designed to provide employees and companies with high demand skills unavailable in the workforce.
- The training outcomes companies such as The Maryland Transit Administration (MTA) use to evaluate training effectiveness.
- Highlight how Deloitte prepares its employees on global assignments for repatriation.
- Discussion of the difficulties companies in high tech industries are facing to increase the diversity of their workforces.

Chapter 8

New Opening Vignette: Shows the changes that General Electric made to its performance evaluation system to more closely align it with business cycles and the company strategy.

New Boxes:
- How performance management at The Analysis Group includes both how the partner is contributing to the firm's financial health as well as what the partner is doing to insure the future health and growth of the business.
- Highlights how Wells-Fargo overemphasis on performance goals results in driving unethical behavior which is detrimental to customers and the organization.
- The advantages and potential disadvantages of companies (such as Gables Residential, IBM, Uber, and Amazon) use of apps for providing and receiving feedback.
- Shows the data that Cargill is using to monitor the effectiveness of its new performance management system.

New Text Material:
- Recent survey results on the problems with traditional performance appraisal.
- Shows how companies such as Procter & Gamble, and Gables Residential, and FORUM Credit Union are changing their performance management approach to make it more of an ongoing process emphasizing performance conversations and employee development.
- Highlights how companies such as Whirpool are training managers to help increase their effectiveness in performance management.
- Shows how companies including Etsy, Unami Burger, and Intellicare are using peer, customer, and self-ratings in their performance management systems.
- The actions that Kimberly-Clark and Zulily take to avoid the potential problems of the use of performance goals.

- Examples of how companies such as UPS, Florida Hospital Celebration Health, and Shuttle Express are using electronic monitoring, including cameras and wearables to track employees performance.
- Discussion of the need for collaborative, ongoing performance conversations and highlights the questions that managers can use to start them with employees.
- Discusses the role of unconscious bias in performance evaluation and how companies such as Microsoft and Google are using training to reduce its impact.

Chapter 9

New Opening Vignette: Highlights the various methods that 3M uses to develop employees and leaders including development plans, formal education and training, 360-degree assessment, and challenging job experiences.

New Boxes:
- How Voya, a customer-focused financial company with high ethical standards, aligns its financial strategy with a leadership development strategy that supports its culture of continuous improvement and corporate values.
- Cardinal Health's use of a cloud-based system for mentoring.
- CA Technologies evaluation of its Leaders at all Levels program.
- Managers joining non-profit boards to develop skills and benefit the organization.
- How McKinsey and Company is developing leaders for its African business.

New Text Material:
- How Citigroup is using development programs to attract and retain millennials.
- New York Life and BB&T use of assessment for development.
- Companies such as Consigli Construction and Wells-Fargo use of online tools to support development planning and identification of development opportunities.
- Highlight how at Michelin North America the employee, their boss, and the employees career manager have responsibility for development.
- How Procter & Gamble's promotion from within policy is supported by career planning.
- BNY Mellon School of Leadership and Management Development use of formal education programs.
- Blue Cross Blue Shield of Michigan use of 360-degree feedback.
- How VF Corporation and Dow use job experiences for developing skills and competencies.
- Bell and Howell and Haskell's use of job rotation for development.
- Sabbaticals at David Weekly Homes
- Examples of mentoring programs from EMC Corporation, Mariner Finance, Gilbane and Vistage Worldwide.
- How United Health is using reverse mentoring.
- Highlights how companies including Edward Jones, United Shoe Financial Services, The Gates Foundation, and Wide Open West are using and benefiting from coaching.
- Discussion of women's underrepresentation in top management positions.
- The types of programs that companies including General Electric, SAP, and Cisco Systems are using to help women gain the visibility and assignments needed to break the glass ceiling.
- Succession planning at BlueCross Blue Shield of Michigan

Chapter 10

New Opening Vignette: Discusses how the culture at Wells Fargo resulted in unprecedented levels of unethical behavior related to falsifying customer accounts.

New Boxes:
- Employers in the banking industry are eavesdropping on employees' mobile phones in order to prevent fraud and Dodd-Frank violations.
- French employers get around job security provisions by isolating workers that would otherwise be fired.
- The job demands at Amazon are a perfect fit for some workers, but a terrible fit for others, and how this contributes to their culture.
- Problems that some organizations would like to keep secret go "viral" due to social networking sites where stories take on a life of their own.
- The pay gap due to gender plays out among workers – all of whom have obtained the same MBA degree.

New Text Material:
- The paternal culture at Kimberly Clark created problems that could only be fixed by increasing involuntary turnover rates among low performing employees.
- Private equity firms identify and eliminate inefficient work practices and workers at old established companies like Kraft.
- The use of temporary employees at companies like Microsoft create two-tiered work cultures that disrupt teamwork.
- Problems associated with the workforce at United Airlines often spilled over to affect customer service.
- Work-life policies in the investment banking industry are being over-hauled in order to promote a more gender diverse workforce.

Chapter 11

New Opening Vignette: Looks at how companies are increasing pay levels to help them compete for workers in the face of low unemployment rates and to help them improve their customer experience and business strategy execution.

New Boxes:
- Why individuals choose to become gig workers rather than traditional employees.
- Wage and overtime implications for independent contractors or full-time employees.
- Changes in the salary test for exempt employees results in generous pay increases that are not required by law.
- Why companies like Foxconn (which assembles Apple products like the iPhone) are looking beyond China for other production locations and how they balance labor costs, production costs and the need to be close to customers in deciding where to locate.
- How technology advances in automating work may influence how many employees will still be needed for some jobs.
- Why some companies that may no longer need to give pay increases to comply with wage-hour regulations may still do so.

New Text Material:
- New salary test under the Fair Labor Standards Act (and the expected increase in the number of employees eligible for overtime premiums).
- How even employee-friendly companies like the Container Store sometimes must reduce labor costs and their methods.
- The distinction between equality and equity.
- Updated data on total compensation costs and how they differ by industry and country.

- Updated data on CEO compensation and how it compares to worker compensation and to company performance.
- Discussion of gaps in employment law when it comes to gig workers.

Chapter 12

New Opening Vignette: Examines Big Three U.S. automakers move to better control fixed labor costs by using profit sharing payments.

New Boxes:
- Kimberly-Clark's change to raise performance standards and its use of pay for performance and technology to this change.
- The shift from pay based on seniority to pay based on performance in Japan
- Using stock option exchange programs to maintain employee motivation.
- Volkswagen changes executive pay to avoid future scandals like "dieselgate."
- How incentives went awry at Wells Fargo.

New Text Material:
- Streamlined exhibit on the key features of different pay for performance programs.
- New discussion on the importance of not confusing pay for performance (which takes many forms and is pervasive) with individual incentives (which are rare).

Chapter 13

New Opening Vignette: Discusses why balancing work and family in high tech and finance companies is becoming increasingly necessary to attract and retain top talent.

New Boxes:
- Ikea provides (paid) parental leave to all employees, included low paid, part-time, and hourly employees.
- How telemedicine is used to provide health care to under-served areas.
- Using data and technology to improve health care quality and control costs.
- The issues employers need to consider when deciding to have work performed by gig workers versus employees.
- Redesigning the workplace and benefits to attract and retain women employees in India.

New Text Material:
- Update on the number and percentage of people without health insurance in the United States.
- Updates on benefits costs and benefits coverage generally.
- Updates on how companies differentiate themselves by using unique benefits.
- Use of big data to understand usage of health care.
- Incentives and penalties employers can use under the Affordable Care Act to encourage healthy behavior.
- The new fiduciary rule for investment advice.
- Employee preferences for how benefits are communicated.
- Decline in use of defined benefit plans.

Chapter 14

New Opening Vignette: Shows how nonunion workers and their supporters take actions to change work conditions and policies.

New Boxes:
- Nontraditional representation for nonunion employees at Uber.
- How employees use social media apps for union organizing efforts at Walmart and other companies.
- Boeing employees in South Carolina say 'no' to the union.
- Chinese companies encounter labor unions in the United States.

New Text Material:
- Update of what companies are doing to improve garment workers safety in Bangladesh, as well as the role of unions in improving safety.
- New NLRB rulings that facilitate union organizing efforts.
- Updates on union-nonunion differences in wages and benefits.
- The latest data on employer resistance to unions.
- Updates on international differences in union membership and coverage.

Chapter 15

New Opening Vignette: Discusses how potential changes in U.S. trade policy will affect the profit GM earns from its operations in Mexico.

New Boxes:
- Artificial intelligence threatens high-skilled jobs.
- Doing business in Africa has risks and rewards.
- Challenging the influence of national culture on HR practices.
- Las Vegas Sands violations of anti-bribery laws.
- Companies unite to aid refugees in need.

New Text Material:
- *Fortune* global companies and cost-of-living figures.
- New table of expatriate adjustment factors.

Chapter 16

New Opening Vignette: Describes the new HR practices and philosophy at Cisco.

New Boxes:
- Citigroup employs a theologian to help them think about ethics.
- Chief human resource officers can help CEO's overcome their leadership weaknesses.
- Why Hershey's turned down global food company Mondelez's offer to acquire them.
- Connecting charity donors and their beneficiaries using technology.
- Behaviors that are useful for predicting employee turnover.

New Text Material:
- Section on how predictive analytics are being used to identify employees who may leave before they actually leave.
- Discussion of customization of HR through data and technology.

Acknowledgments

As this book enters its 11th edition, it is important to acknowledge those who started it all. The first edition of this book would not have been possible if not for the entrepreneurial spirit of two individuals. Bill Schoof, president of Austen Press, gave us the resources and had the confidence that four unproven textbook writers could provide a new perspective for teaching human resource management. John Weimeister, our former editor, provided us with valuable marketing information, helped us in making major decisions regarding the book, and made writing this book an enjoyable process. Anke Weekes, our current brand manager, continues to provide the same high-quality guidance and support we received from John. We also worked with an all-star development and project management team, including Jamie Koch and Rick Hecker. Their suggestions, patience, gentle prodding, and careful oversight kept the author team focused on providing a high-quality revision while meeting publication deadline.

We would also like to thank the professors who gave of their time to review the text and attend focus groups. Their helpful comments and suggestions have greatly helped to enhance this learning program:

Vondra Armstrong
Pulaski Technical College

Richard Arvey
National University of Singapore

Steve Ash
University of Akron

Carlson Austin
South Carolina State University

Janice Baldwin
The University of Texas at Arlington

Alison Barber
Michigan State University

Kathleen Barnes
University of Wisconsin, Superior

Brian Bartel
Mid-State Technical College

James E. Bartlett, II
University of South Carolina–Columbia

Ron Beaulieu
Central Michigan University

Joan Benek-Rivera
University of Pennsylvania–Bloomsburg

Philip Benson
New Mexico State University

Nancy Bereman
Wichita State University

Chris Berger
Purdue University

Carol Bibly
Triton College

Angela Boston
The University of Texas at Arlington

Wendy Boswell
Texas A&M University

Sarah Bowman
Idaho State University

Charles Braun
University of Kentucky

James Browne
University of Southern Colorado

Ronald Brownie
Purdue University–North Central

Jon Bryan
Bridgewater State College

David Calland
Liberty University

Gerald Calvasina
Southern Utah University

Stacy Campbell
Kennesaw State University

Martin Carrigan
University of Findlay

Georgia Chao
Michigan State University

Fay Cocchiara
Arkansas State University

LeAnne Coder
Western Kentucky University

Walter Coleman
Florida Southern College

Mary Connerley
Virginia Tech University

Donna Cooke
Florida Atlantic University–Davis

Craig Cowles
Bridgewater State College

Susie Cox
McNeese State University

Michael Crant
University of Notre Dame

Shaun W. Davenport
High Point University

Shannon Davis
North Carolina State University

Roger Dean
Washington & Lee University

John Delery
University of Arkansas

Fred Dorn
The University of Mississippi

Jennifer Dose
Messiah College

Tom Dougherty
University of Missouri

Berrin Erdogan
Portland State University

Angela Farrar
University of Nevada–Las Vegas

Dan Farrell
Western Michigan University

Dyanne Ferk
University of Illinois–Springfield

Anne Fiedler
Nova Southeastern University

Robert Figler
University of Akron

Louis Firenze
Northwood University

Art Fischer
Pittsburgh State University

Barry Friedman
State University of New York at Oswego

Cynthia Fukami
University of Denver

Daniel J. Gallagher
University of Illinois–Springfield

Donald G. Gardner
University of Colorado at Colorado Springs

Bonnie Fox Garrity
D'Youville College

David Gerth
Nashville State Community College

Sonia Goltz
Michigan Technological University

Bob Graham
Sacred Heart University

Terri Griffith
Washington University

Ken Gross
University of Oklahoma–Norman

John Hannon
University at Buffalo

Bob Hatfield
Indiana University

Alan Heffner
James Monroe Center

Fred Heidrich
Black Hills State University

Rob Heneman
Ohio State University

Gary Hensel
McHenry County College

Kim Hester
Arkansas State University

Nancy Higgins
Montgomery College–Rockville

Michael Hill
University of Georgia

Wayne Hockwater
Florida State University

Fred Hughes
Faulkner University

Ning Hou
St. Cloud State University

Denise Tanguay Hoyer
Eastern Michigan University

Natalie J. Hunter
Portland State University

Julie Indvik
California State University, Chico

Sanford Jacoby
University of California–Los Angeles

Frank Jeffries
University of Alaska–Anchorage

Roy Johnson
Iowa State University

Gwen Jones
Fairleigh Dickinson University

Gwendolyn Jones
University of Akron

Hank Karp
Hampton University

Gundars Kaupins
Boise State University

Marianne Koch
University of Oregon

James Kolacek
*Palm Beach Atlantic
University*

Tom Kolenko
Kennesaw State College

Elias Konwufine
Keiser University

Beth Koufteros
Texas A&M University

Ken Kovach
George Mason University

Chalmer Labig
*Oklahoma State
University*

Patricia Lanier
*University of Louisiana at
Lafayette*

Vonda Laughlin
Carson-Newman College

Helen LaVan
DePaul University

Renee Lerche
University of Michigan

Nancy Boyd Lillie
University of North Texas

Beth A. Livingston
Cornell University

Karen Locke
William & Mary

Michael Dane Loflin
York Technical College

Susan Madsen
Utah Valley University

Larry Mainstone
Valparaiso University

Ann-Marie Majeskey
Mount Olive College

Liz Malatestinic
Indiana University

Patricia Martina
*University of Texas–San
Antonio*

Nicholas Mathys
DePaul University

Lisa McConnell
Oklahoma State University

Liliana Meneses
*University of Maryland
University College*

Jessica Methot
Rutgers University

Angela Miles
*North Carolina A&T State
University*

Stuart Milne
*Georgia Institute of
Technology*

Barbara Minsky
Troy University

Kelly Mollica
University of Memphis

Jim Morgan
*California State
University–Chico*

Pamela Mulvey
*Olney Central College
Lake Land College*

Gary Murray
Rose State College

David M. Nemi
*Niagara County
Community College*

Millicent Nelson
*Middle Tennessee State
University*

Lam Nguyen
Palm Beach State College

Nhung Nguyen
Towson University

Thomas J. Norman
*California State University–
Dominguez Hills*

Cheri Ostroff
*Teachers College
Columbia*

Teresa Palmer
Illinois State University

Robert Paul
Kansas State University

Tracy Porter
*Cleveland State
University*

Gregory Quinet
*Southern Polytechnic State
University*

Sam Rabinowitz
Rutgers University

David Rahn
*California State
University–Chico*

Jude Rathburn
*University of
Wisconsin–Milwaukee*

Katherine Ready
University of Wisconsin

Herbert Ricardo
Indian River State College

Mike Ritchie
*University of South
Carolina*

Gwen Rivkin
Cardinal Stritch University

Mark Roehling
Michigan State University

Mary Ellen Rosetti
*Hudson Valley Community
College*

Craig J. Russell
University of Oklahoma

Sarah Sanders-Smith
*Purdue University–North
Central*

Miyako Schanely
*Jefferson Community
College*

Robert Schappe
*University of
Michigan–Dearborn*

Jack Schoenfelder
*Ivy Tech Community
College*

Machelle K. Schroeder
*University of
Wisconsin–Platteville*

Joshua Schwarz
Miami University–Ohio

Pat Setlik
Harper College

Christina Shalley
Georgia Tech

Richard Shuey
Thomas More College

Richard Simpson
University of Utah

Romila Singh
*University of
Wisconsin–Milwaukee*

Erika Engel Small
Coastal Carolina University

Mark Smith
*Mississippi Gulf
Coast Community
College–Gulfport*

Scott Snell
University of Virginia

Kris Sperstad
*Chippewa Valley Technical
College*

Howard Stanger
Canisius College

Carol S. Steinhaus
*Northern Michigan
University*

Gary Stroud
Franklin University

Cynthia Sutton
*Indiana University–South
Bend*

Peg Thomas
*Pennsylvania State
University–Behrend*

Steven L. Thomas
Missouri State University

Tom Timmerman
*Tennessee Technology
University*

George Tompson
University of Tampa

J. Bruce Tracey
Cornell University

K. J. Tullis
*University of Central
Oklahoma*

Dan Turban
*University of
Missouri–Columbia*

Linda Turner
Morrisville State College

Linda Urbanski
University of Toledo

William Van Lente
*Alliant International
University*

Charles Vance
*Loyola Marymount
University*

John Varlaro
Johnson & Wales University

Kim Wade
Washington State University

Sheng Wang
*University of
Nevada–Las Vegas*

Renee Warning
*University of Central
Oklahoma*

Bruce Western
*Western Illinois
University*

Lynn Wilson
Saint Leo University

Jenell Wittmer
University of Toledo

George Whaley
San Jose State University

Steve Woods
University of Baltimore

Lin Xiu
*University of
Minnesota–Duluth*

Daniel Yazak
*Montana State
University–Billings*

Ryan D. Zimmerman
Texas A&M University

Raymond A. Noe
John R. Hollenbeck
Barry Gerhart
Patrick M. Wright

connect®

McGraw-Hill Connect® is a highly reliable, easy-to-use homework and learning management solution that utilizes learning science and award-winning adaptive tools to improve student results.

Homework and Adaptive Learning

- Connect's assignments help students contextualize what they've learned through application, so they can better understand the material and think critically.

- Connect will create a personalized study path customized to individual student needs through SmartBook®.

- SmartBook helps students study more efficiently by delivering an interactive reading experience through adaptive highlighting and review.

Connect's Impact on Retention Rates, Pass Rates, and Average Exam Scores

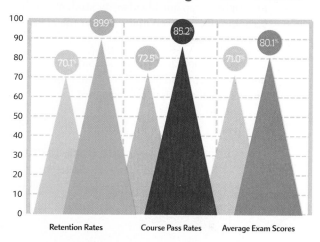

without Connect   with Connect

Over **7 billion questions** have been answered, making McGraw-Hill Education products more intelligent, reliable, and precise.

Using **Connect** improves retention rates by **19.8 percentage points**, passing rates by **12.7 percentage points, and** exam scores by **9.1 percentage points.**

73% of instructors who use **Connect** require it; instructor satisfaction **increases** by 28% when **Connect** is required.

Quality Content and Learning Resources

- Connect content is authored by the world's best subject matter experts, and is available to your class through a simple and intuitive interface.

- The Connect eBook makes it easy for students to access their reading material on smartphones and tablets. They can study on the go and don't need internet access to use the eBook as a reference, with full functionality.

- Multimedia content such as videos, simulations, and games drive student engagement and critical thinking skills.

Robust Analytics and Reporting

- Connect Insight® generates easy-to-read reports on individual students, the class as a whole, and on specific assignments.

- The Connect Insight dashboard delivers data on performance, study behavior, and effort. Instructors can quickly identify students who struggle and focus on material that the class has yet to master.

- Connect automatically grades assignments and quizzes, providing easy-to-read reports on individual and class performance.

©Hero Images/Getty Images

Impact on Final Course Grade Distribution

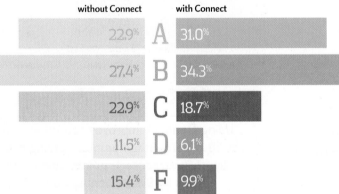

without Connect		with Connect
22.9%	A	31.0%
27.4%	B	34.3%
22.9%	C	18.7%
11.5%	D	6.1%
15.4%	F	9.9%

More students earn **As** and **Bs** when they use **Connect**.

Trusted Service and Support

- Connect integrates with your LMS to provide single sign-on and automatic syncing of grades. Integration with Blackboard®, D2L®, and Canvas also provides automatic syncing of the course calendar and assignment-level linking.

- Connect offers comprehensive service, support, and training throughout every phase of your implementation.

- If you're looking for some guidance on how to use Connect, or want to learn tips and tricks from super users, you can find tutorials as you work. Our Digital Faculty Consultants and Student Ambassadors offer insight into how to achieve the results you want with Connect.

www.mheducation.com/connect

CONNECT INSTRUCTOR LIBRARY

INSTRUCTOR'S MANUAL

The Instructor's Manual contains notes, answers to the discussion questions, additional questions and exercises, teaching suggestions, and answers to the end-of-chapter case questions.

TEST BANK

The test bank has been revised and updated to reflect the content of the new edition of the book. Each chapter includes multiple-choice, true/false, and essay questions.

VIDEOS

Human Resource Management Videos offer clips on HRM issues for each chapter of this edition. You'll find a video produced by the SHRM Foundation, entitled "Once the Deal Is Done: Making Mergers Work." Three videos specifically address employee benefits: "GM Cuts Benefits and Pay," "Sulphur Springs Teachers," and "Google Employee Perks." Other videos available for this edition include "E-Learning English" for the chapter on employee development and "Recession Job Growth" for the chapter on HR planning and recruitment.

POWERPOINT

This presentation program features detailed slides for each chapter.

MCGRAW-HILL CAMPUS

McGraw-Hill Campus is a new one-stop teaching and learning experience available to users of any learning management system. This institutional service allows faculty and students to enjoy single sign-on (SSO) access to all McGraw-Hill Higher Education materials, including the award-winning McGraw-Hill Connect platform, from directly within the institution's website. With McGraw-Hill Campus, faculty receive instant access to teaching materials (e.g., eBooks, test banks, PowerPoint slides, animations, learning objects, etc.), allowing them to browse, search, and use any instructor ancillary content in our vast library at no additional cost to instructor or students.

MCGRAW-HILL AND BLACKBOARD

The Best of Both Worlds

McGraw-Hill Higher Education and Blackboard have teamed up. What does this mean for you?

1. **Your life, simplified.** Now you and your students can access McGraw-Hill's Connect™ and Create™ right from within your Blackboard course—all with one single sign-on. Say goodbye to the days of logging in to multiple applications.

2. **Deep integration of content and tools.** Not only do you get single sign-on with Connect™ and Create™, you also get deep integration of McGraw-Hill content and content engines right in Blackboard. Whether you're choosing a book for your course or building Connect™ assignments, all the tools you need are right where you want them—inside Blackboard.

3. **Seamless gradebooks.** Are you tired of keeping multiple gradebooks and manually synchronizing grades into Blackboard? We thought so. When a student completes an integrated Connect™ assignment, the grade for that assignment automatically (and instantly) feeds your Blackboard grade center.

4. **A solution for everyone.** Whether your institution is already using Blackboard or you just want to try Blackboard on your own, we have a solution for you. McGraw-Hill and Blackboard can now offer you easy access to industry-leading technology and content, whether your campus hosts it, or we do. Be sure to ask your local McGraw-Hill representative for details.

MCGRAW-HILL CUSTOMER CARE CONTACT INFORMATION

At McGraw-Hill, we understand that getting the most from new technology can be challenging. That's why our services don't stop after you purchase our products. You can e-mail our product specialists 24 hours a day to get product-training online. Or you can search our knowledge bank of frequently asked questions on our support website. For customer support, call 800-331-5094 or visit www.mhhe.com/support. One of our technical support analysts will be able to assist you in a timely fashion.

BRIEF CONTENTS

CONTENTS

Human Resource Management: Gaining a Competitive Advantage

LEARNING OBJECTIVES

After reading this chapter, you should be able to:

LO 1-1   Discuss the roles and activities of a company's human resource management function. *page 5*

LO 1-2   Discuss the implications of the economy, the makeup of the labor force, and ethics for company sustainability. *page 17*

LO 1-3   Discuss how human resource management affects a company's balanced scorecard. *page 29*

LO 1-4   Discuss what companies should do to compete in the global marketplace. *page 45*

LO 1-5   Identify how social networking, artificial intelligence, and robotics is influencing human resource management. *page 50*

LO 1-6   Discuss human resource management practices that support high-performance work systems. *page 54*

LO 1-7   Provide a brief description of human resource management practices. *page 56*

Publix: HR Practices Result in Happy Employees and Customers

Publix is a leader in the supermarket industry. As the largest employee-owned grocery store chain in the United States, Publix employs over 189,000 people in the Southeast, with over 1,100 store locations, eight distribution centers, and ten manufacturing facilities. Publix is a great place to work and to shop. Publix has been recognized as one of *Fortune* magazine's "100 Best Companies to Work For" for nineteen consecutive years and as one of *Fortune*'s "100 Best Workplaces for Millennials." The company has also received numerous awards for customer service and satisfaction. Publix's mission is to be the world's premier quality food retailer. Publix strives to do so through its commitment to providing customers with value; its intolerance of waste; its dedication to the dignity, value, and employment security of its associates; its devotion to stewardship for stockholders; and its involvement in the communities in which Publix stores operate.

Publix employees are extremely loyal. The average store manager has been with Publix for over twenty-five years, and over 24,000 associates have been with the company for more than thirty years. Its voluntary turnover rate is 5%, compared to the retail industry average of 65%. Other supermarket chains such as Whole Foods and Safeway have recently laid off employees, but Publix has never laid off an employee in its history. In fact, rather than closing or consolidating stores, as its competitors have done, Publix continues to grow through opening new stores.

What accounts for Publix's business success and makes it a great place to work? Its human resource management practices play an important role in ensuring that employees are satisfied and motivated at work and committed to the company. One management practice is to help all associates in identifying and moving along their career path. Computers are located in offices and breakrooms of every store to make it easy for associates to access training courses. Associates receive training on standards for customer service, cleanliness, safety, teamwork, merchandising, waste intolerance, and a drug-free work environment. Publix has a generous tuition reimbursement program that supports employees who want to earn a college degree to expand their career opportunities. Supporting employees' development and career growth is the Publix policy to promote from within to fill all store manager positions and most department manager positions. Publix does this to ensure that managers are aware of company standards, best practices, and culture. Any current associate interesting in moving into a management role can register their interest by completing what is called an ROI. The ROI helps managers understand associates' career ambitions and match their skills to job openings. Typically, more than 60,000 associates complete ROIs each year, with more than 9,500 promoted into positions leading to management and 2,100 promoted into management positions. Associates who become managers must move to a different store than the one in which they worked. This practice ensures that management talent is spread across the company, and it also helps employees create new personal and professional networks.

Another management practice is to give associates the opportunity to become an owner of Publix. Any associate who stays with Publix for more than a year and works more than 1,000 hours is granted shares of company stock that are worth between 8% and 12% of their annual pay. Once in the plan, they can buy additional stock through a paycheck deduction. From 1974 through 2015, the stock has provided an average annual return of nearly 17%.

CONTINUED

Beyond holding stock, being a true owner requires an understanding of how you are doing and receiving rewards for your accomplishments. Publix makes sure its associates receive frequent feedback, and good performance is linked to raises. New employees have "check-ins" with their manager every thirty, sixty, and ninety days. After six months, associates qualify for their first raise and are eligible for future raises every six months. Full- and part-time associates receive an annual holiday bonus, which is uncommon in the retail industry. Full-time associates receive two weeks' pay, and salaried associates receive a full month's pay. Finally, Publix supports its associates' efforts to give back to the communities where they live and work. Publix and its associates contribute more than $36 million a year and hours of volunteer work to charitable organizations such as the United Way, Special Olympics, March of Dimes, Children's Miracle Network, and Food for All.

SOURCES: Based on www.corporatepublix.com, visited February 22, 2017; C. Tkaczyk, "My Five Days of Bleeding Green," *Fortune,* March 15, 2016, pp. 166–76; "Publix Super Markets Inc.," http://reviews.greatplacetowork.com/publix-super-markets-inc, accessed February 8, 2017.

Introduction

Competitiveness
A company's ability to maintain and gain market share in its industry.

Publix illustrates the key role that human resource management plays in determining the survival, effectiveness, and competitiveness of U.S. businesses. **Competitiveness** refers to a company's ability to maintain and gain market share in its industry. Publix's human resource management practices are helping support the company's business strategy and provide services the customer values. The value of a product or service is determined by its quality and how closely the product fits customer needs.

Competitiveness is related to company effectiveness, which is determined by whether the company satisfies the needs of stakeholders (groups affected by business practices). Important stakeholders include stockholders, who want a return on their investment; customers, who want a high-quality product or service; and employees, who desire interesting work and reasonable compensation for their services. The community, which wants the company to contribute to activities and projects and minimize pollution of the environment, is also an important stakeholder. Companies that do not meet stakeholders' needs are unlikely to have a competitive advantage over other firms in their industry.

Human resource management (HRM)
The policies, practices, and systems that influence employees' behavior, attitudes, and performances.

Human resource management (HRM) refers to the policies, practices, and systems that influence employees' behavior, attitudes, and performance. Many companies refer to HRM as involving "people practices." Figure 1.1 emphasizes that there are several important HRM practices. The strategy underlying these practices needs to be considered to maximize their influence on company performance. As the figure shows, HRM practices include analyzing and designing work, determining human resource needs (HR planning), attracting potential employees (recruiting), choosing employees (selection), teaching employees how to perform their jobs and preparing them for the future (training and development), rewarding employees (compensation), evaluating their performance (performance management), and creating a positive work environment (employee relations). The HRM practices discussed in this chapter's opening highlighted how effective HRM practices support business goals and objectives. That is, effective HRM practices are strategic! Effective HRM has been shown to enhance company performance by contributing to employee and customer satisfaction, innovation, productivity, and development of a favorable reputation in the firm's community.[1] The potential role of HRM in company performance has been recognized only recently.

We begin by discussing the roles and skills that a human resource management department and/or managers need for any company to be competitive. The second section of

Figure 1.1

Human Resource Management Practices

the chapter identifies the competitive challenges that U.S. companies currently face, which influence their ability to meet the needs of shareholders, customers, employees, and other stakeholders. We discuss how these competitive challenges are influencing HRM. The chapter concludes by highlighting the HRM practices covered in this book and the ways they help companies compete.

What Responsibilities and Roles Do HR Departments Perform?

Only recently have companies looked at human resource management as a means to contribute to profitability, quality, and other business goals through enhancing and supporting business operations.

Table 1.1 shows the responsibilities of human resource departments. How much should companies budget for HR and how many HR professionals should a company employ? One study estimates that HR budgets on average are $2,936 per employee.[2]

High-impact HR teams have one staff person per 64 employees, spend more than the average HR budget per employee ($4,434 on average per employee), and employ a higher percentage of HR specialists than more compliance-driven and basic HR organizations.

High-impact HR functions are more integrated with the business, skilled at helping managers in attracting, building, engaging, and retaining talented employees. They can adapt quickly to business needs and workforce changes, identify and promote talent from within the company, and are continuously trying to identify what motivates employees to help them grow and develop. Also, high-impact HR functions ensure that they are continuously building the talent and skills of HR professionals necessary to help the company meet new competitive challenges. The greater cost-per-employee of high-impact HR functions is offset by the greater savings resulting from reduced turnover and increased levels of employee engagement.

The HR department is solely responsible for outplacement, labor law compliance, record keeping, testing, unemployment compensation, and some aspects of benefits administration. The HR department is most likely to collaborate with other company functions on

LO 1-1

Discuss the roles and activities of a company's human resource management function.

Table 1.1
Responsibilities of HR Departments

FUNCTION	RESPONSIBILITIES
Analysis and design of work	Job analysis, work analysis, job descriptions
Recruitment and selection	Recruiting, posting job descriptions, interviewing, testing, coordinating use of temporary employees
Training and development	Orientation, skills training, development programs, career development
Performance management	Performance measures, preparation and administration of performance appraisals, feedback and coaching, discipline
Compensation and benefits	Wage and salary administration, incentive pay, insurance, vacation, retirement plans, profit sharing, health and wellness, stock plans
Employee relations/labor relations	Attitude surveys, employee handbooks, labor law compliance, relocation and outplacement services
Personnel policies	Policy creation, policy communications
Employee data and information systems	Record keeping, HR information systems, workforce analytics, social media, Intranet and Internet access
Legal compliance	Policies to ensure lawful behavior; safety inspections, accessibility accommodations, privacy policies, ethics
Support for business strategy	Human resource planning and forecasting, talent management, change management, organization development

SOURCES: Based on Bureau of Labor Statistics, U.S. Department of Labor, "Human Resources Specialists," *Occupational Outlook Handbook, 2016–17 Edition,* https://www.bls.gov/ooh/business-and-financial/human-resources-specialists.htm, accessed February 9, 2017; SHRM-BNA Survey No. 66, "Policy and Practice Forum: Human Resource Activities, Budgets, and Staffs, 2000–2001," *Bulletin to Management,* Bureau of National Affairs Policy and Practice Series, June 28, 2001 (Washington, DC: Bureau of National Affairs).

employment interviewing, performance management and discipline, and efforts to improve quality and productivity. Large companies are more likely than small ones to employ HR specialists, with benefits specialists being the most prevalent. Other common specializations include recruitment, compensation, and training and development.[3]

Many different roles and responsibilities can be performed by the HR department, depending on the size of the company, the characteristics of the workforce, the industry, and the value system of company management. The HR department may take full responsibility for human resource activities in some companies, whereas in others it may share the roles and responsibilities with managers of other departments such as finance, operations, or information technology. In some companies the HR department advises top-level management; in others the HR department may make decisions regarding staffing, training, and compensation after top managers have decided relevant business issues.

One way to think about the roles and responsibilities of HR departments is to consider HR as a business within the company with three product lines. Figure 1.2 shows the three product lines of HR. The first product line, administrative services and transactions, is the traditional product that HR has historically provided. The newer HR products—business partner services and the strategic partner role—are the HR functions that top managers want HR to deliver.

To ensure that HR is business focused, Walgreens's HR professionals are paired with functional leaders.[4] The HR field organization works to develop strategic talent plans for each business and helps implement important initiatives such as succession planning, change management, organizational design, and culture and leadership development.

Figure 1.2

HR as a Business with Three Product Lines

Administrative Services and Transactions: Compensation, hiring, and staffing • Emphasis: Resource efficiency and service quality	**Business Partner Services:** Developing effective HR systems and helping implement business plans, talent management • Emphasis: Knowing the business and exercising influence—problem solving, designing effective systems to ensure needed competencies	**Strategic Partner:** Contributing to business strategy based on considerations of human capital, business capabilities, readiness, and developing HR practices as strategic differentiators • Emphasis: Knowledge of HR and of the business, competition, the market, and business strategies

SOURCE: Adapted from Figure 1, "HR Product Lines," in E. E. Lawler, "From Human Resource Management to Organizational Effectiveness," *Human Resource Management* 44 (2005), pp. 165–69.

The HR director at TAMKO Building Products Inc. helped align the company's HR function to business needs.[5] She noticed that inexperienced HR professionals were spending too much time on transactional duties such as payroll and benefits administration. She wanted them to focus on supplying managers with skilled, well-trained employees and meaningful data. She revised their training to ensure that they understood the industry and the skills that the company needed for continued success. She urged her staff to be proactive (rather than reactive) about offering HR solutions to help managers avoid or solve workplace problems. The team responded by identifying and implementing a new time-and-attendance tracking system, a virtual onboarding and orientation process, and a leadership development program.

Strategic Role of the HRM Function

The amount of time that the human resource management function devotes to administrative tasks is decreasing, and its roles as a strategic business partner, change agent, and employee advocate are increasing.[6] HR managers face two important challenges: shifting their focus from current operations to strategies for the future and preparing non-HR managers to develop and implement HR practices.[7] To ensure that HRM contributes to the company's competitive advantage, many HR departments are organized on the basis of a shared service model. The shared service model can help control costs and improve the business relevance and timeliness of HR practices. A **shared service model** is a way to organize the HR function that includes centers of expertise or excellence, service centers, and business partners.[8] Centers of expertise or excellence include HR specialists in areas such as staffing or training who provide their services companywide. Service centers are a central place for administrative and transactional tasks such as enrolling in training programs or changing benefits that employees and managers can access online. Business partners are HR staff members who work with business-unit managers on strategic issues such as creating new compensation plans or development programs for preparing high-level managers. Walgreens provides employee relations, recruiting, and HR data services through a shared services team.[9] Walgreens introduced a website,

Shared service model
A way to organize the HR function that includes centers of expertise or excellence, service centers, and business partners.

myHR, that employees can access to get answers to their questions about benefits, HR policies, and talent management. It provides confidential personalized information that is easy for employees to access. We will discuss the shared service model in more detail in Chapter 16.

The role of HRM in administration is decreasing as technology is used for many administrative purposes, such as managing employee records and allowing employees to get information about and enroll in training, benefits, and other programs. The availability of the Internet has decreased the HRM role in maintaining records and providing self-service to employees.[10] **Self-service** refers to giving employees online access to, or apps that provide, information about HR issues such as training, benefits, compensation, and contracts; enrolling online in programs and services; and completing online attitude surveys. The shift to self-service means that HR can focus more time on consulting with managers on important employee issues and less time on day-to-day transactional tasks. For example, U.S. Bancorp implemented the PeopleSoft 9.1 human capital management system, which allows managers to review or approve basic personnel actions such as terminations, relocations, and salary changes.[11] As managers became more comfortable with the system, they were given control over transactions such as approving bonuses, reviewing résumés, and evaluating job candidates. Managers were initially resistant to take on duties that previously were handled by HR staff, but they accepted the change because it enabled them to execute transactions more quickly and gave them more access to workforce data they could use for decision making. HR professionals now have more time to work with managers on ensuring the right employee development plans are in place, evaluating workforce needs due to retirements or growth, and ensuring their organizational structures are efficient and effective.

Many companies are also contracting with HR service providers to conduct important but administrative HR functions such as payroll processing, as well as to provide expertise in strategically important practice areas such as recruiting. **Outsourcing** refers to the practice of having another company (a vendor, third party, or consultant) provide services. The most commonly outsourced activities include those related to benefits administration (e.g., flexible spending accounts, health plan eligibility status), relocation, and payroll. The major reasons that company executives choose to outsource HR practices include cost savings, increased ability to recruit and manage talent, improved HR service quality, and protection of the company from potential lawsuits by standardizing processes such as selection and recruitment.[12] ADP, Hewitt, IBM, and Accenture are examples of leading outsource providers.

Goodyear Tire and Rubber Company reenergized its recruitment and hiring practices through outsourcing recruiting practices.[13] The recruiting outsource provider worked with the company to understand its culture, its history, and its employees' recruitment experiences. The recruiting outsourcing service provider was able to help Goodyear streamline the recruiting process by providing hiring managers with online access to create new job requisitions, providing interview feedback, scheduling interviews, generating customized job offer letters, and gaining a real-time perspective on job candidates' progress in the recruitment process. Goodyear recognized several benefits from outsourcing recruitment, including improving the timeliness of job offers, increasing the diversity and quality of new hires, and reducing turnover.

Traditionally, the HRM department (also known as "personnel" or "employee relations") was primarily an administrative expert and employee advocate. The department took care of employee problems, made sure employees were paid correctly, administered labor contracts, and avoided legal problems. The HRM department ensured that employee-related issues did not interfere with the manufacturing or sales of products or services.

Self-service
Giving employees online access to human resources information.

Outsourcing
An organization's use of an outside organization for a broad set of services.

Human resource management was primarily reactive; that is, HR issues were a concern only if they directly affected the business. That still remains the case in many companies that have yet to recognize the competitive value of HRM, or among HR professionals who lack the competencies and skills or understanding needed to anticipate problems and contribute to the business strategy. However, other companies believe that HRM is important for business success and therefore have expanded the role of HRM as a change agent and strategic partner.

A discussion group of company HR directors and academic thought-leaders reported that increasingly HR professionals are expected to lead efforts focused on talent management and performance management.[14] Also, HR professionals should take the lead in helping companies attract, develop, and retain talent in order to create the global workforces that companies need to be successful. HR professionals have to be able to use and analyze data to make a business case for ideas and problem solutions. In many companies, top HR managers report directly to the CEO, president, or board of directors to answer questions about how people strategies drive value for the company. For example, at Marsh, an insurance brokerage and risk management company, the chief human resources officer (CHRO) is a true strategic partner with the CEO.[15] The CHRO is included in meetings with the company's CEO and chief financial officer (CFO). In these meetings the company's financial performance and talent reviews are discussed. The group works to identify how people issues affect the business. For example, the group recently discussed and implemented a new compensation plan for Marsh's sales force. The CHRO contributed to the discussion (and the business) by considering whether the sales compensation plan was motivating the right behaviors and positively influencing the financial results of the business.

Consider how HRM has supported the business at Juniper Networks and Abbott.[16] Juniper Networks, a networking technology company that had become successful by introducing a new router, was a major innovator in the computer network industry. But Juniper found that, despite its success, it needed to reinvent its business strategy and grow. To help reinvent its business strategy and structure, Juniper's HR team had conversations with 150 senior company leaders, including the company chairman, and 100 other managers located around the world. During these conversations, the HR team asked the leader or manager questions about important environmental challenges facing Juniper, how the challenges affected the leader's or manager's team, what most excited them about Juniper's business strategy and execution of that strategy, and key business concerns. The conversations helped identify that Juniper had too many business priorities, leaders tended to avoid conflict, and work was overly complex, making it difficult to provide customers with the best solutions. As a result of the conversations, product lines have been streamlined and the company adopted a simpler and more integrated business structure. For example, across the company, any decision can be made by six people.

Abbott spun off a new company, AbbVie, which focused on pharmaceutical research and development, while keeping consumer-oriented health care products such as Ensure nutrition shakes. Spin-offs are new companies that are created from the parent company with a specialized focus on one aspect of the business market. They are expected to be worth more as independent businesses than as part of a larger business. Human resource issues such as retaining talent, making sure employees are enthusiastic and motivated, and making sure employees are in the right roles in the new company are important for the success of spin-offs. The CHRO for AbbVie, who worked for Abbott, was faced with the challenging and complex assignment of helping to get the new company established. Specifically, he worked with other executives to create the new organizational structure, logo, and branding campaign. Also, he worked on people issues such as making sure the reasons for the spin-off were communicated, to reduce employees' fear and anxiety; deciding which employees would join the new company and determining their job assignments; and developing a new compensation and benefits plan. The success of his efforts were one of the reasons the combined value of Abbott and AbbVie has nearly doubled since 2013.

The structure and responsibilities of HR departments are likely to continue to change in the future to ensure that they remain strategic. Some companies, such as Airbnb, are beginning to recognize that the employee experience is critical for keeping employees happy and committed to the company. Happier employees are more likely to work hard to satisfy customers, which helps the company grow and prosper.[17] To maximize the employee experience, Airbnb combined three separate HR groups (talent, recruiting, and "Ground Control") into one group. Airbnb's top HR officer's title is chief employee experience officer (CEEO). At Airbnb, human resources involves marketing, communications, real estate, and social responsibility, in addition to traditional HR functions. The CEEO's responsibilities go beyond the traditional HR functions such as talent management, and compensation to include workplace design and facilities, food, global citizenship, and the network of community managers who interact daily with Airbnb employees. For example, Airbnb's airy, open workplace includes small lockers for employees to charge their devices, which provides more room for a conference room, couches, nap spaces, communal tables, and small spaces for employees to have conversations with their peers. Numerous cafes are available where employees can eat or collaborate on projects. Also, human resources helps employees give back to the communities where Airbnb operates by encouraging four hours a month of individual volunteering as well as by participating in larger events such as painting a homeless shelter or cooking meals for hospital patients' families.

Table 1.2 provides several questions that managers can use to determine if HRM is playing a strategic role in the business. If these questions have not been considered, it is highly unlikely that (1) the company is prepared to deal with competitive challenges or (2) HRM is being used strategically to help a company gain a competitive advantage. The bottom line for evaluating the relationship between HRM and the business strategy is to consider this question: "What is HRM doing to ensure that the right people with the right skills are doing the right things in the jobs that are important for the execution of the business strategy?"[18] We will discuss strategic HRM in more detail in Chapter 2.

Some companies that want managers to have more accountability for employees, believe that traditional HR departments are unnecessary because they inhibit innovation by creating unnecessary and inefficient policies and procedures.[19] In these companies,

Table 1.2

Questions to Ask: Is HRM Playing a Strategic Role in the Business?

1. What is HRM doing to provide value-added services to internal clients?
2. Do the actions of HRM support and align with business priorities?
3. How are you measuring the effectiveness of HRM?
4. How can we reinvest in employees?
5. What HRM strategy will we use to get the business from point A to point B?
6. From an HRM perspective, what should we be doing to improve our marketplace position?
7. What's the best change we can make to prepare for the future?
8. Do we react to business problems or anticipate them in advance?

SOURCES: Based on A. Halcrow, "Survey Shows HR in Transition," *Workforce*, June 1988, p. 74; P. Wright, *Human Resource Strategy: Adapting to the Age of Globalization* (Alexandria, VA: Society for Human Resource Management Foundation, 2008); J. Mundy, "Be a Strategic Performance Consultant," *HR Magazine*, March 2013, pp. 44–46.

important payroll, benefits, and other HR processes are automated or outsourced. For example, managers at Ruppert Landscape, which has 900 employees working in different markets across the United States, perform HR responsibilities such as recruiting employees and explaining the company's retirement plan. Its managers spend about 5% of their time on human resources. The CEO feels that local managers are in a better position to understand and solve employee problems than is an HR professional located in the company's Maryland headquarters. However, there are many advantages to having HR professionals and an HR department. Managers often lack the specialized knowledge necessary to understand employment laws and how to identify potential employees, determine skills and salaries for positions, and develop current employees. HR professionals can create systems to avoid legal liability, counsel employees, and coach managers on how to identify, retain, and develop talent.

Consider the role of HRM at Tesla Motors, an automotive company with all of the characteristics of a high-tech company.[20] Tesla builds cars, manufactures electric powertrains for other car companies, operates car-charging stations around the world, and sells its cars directly to customers. The luxurious Model S has won numerous awards, and Tesla recently introduced Model 3, a more affordable sedan, and Model X, a sport-utility vehicle. The role of HRM at Tesla is to support the business by finding and helping to retain the most talented employees and ensure they understand and believe in the company's fast-paced culture, which requires long workdays and constant change. They do this in several different ways. The HR team seeks talented employees who have a positive, self-starting attitude and have tried to improve processes in the areas in which they have worked. They encourage employee referrals because they have found that their best employees attract other high performers who fit the company's culture. To find talent to fill a robotics team, the HR staffing team looked beyond the traditional sources, such as other automakers, and instead focused on robotics competitions at colleges and industries, such as biotechnology, that employ robotic-programming specialists. Human resources worked with employees from legal, security, and environmental health and safety departments and a small group of employees from company stores and the factory to develop an employee handbook. The handbook, known as the "anti-handbook handbook," captures in just four pages written in a conversational style what Tesla stands for and what it is like to work there.

For example, the employee attendance policy emphasizes that employees should be the kind of person their work team can rely on. Emphasis is placed on employees being at work when they are supposed to be, because the team can't get things done if employees are absent. Human resources supports Tesla's emphasis on open communications through the "Answer Bar" at its Freemont, California, factory. At the Answer Bar employees can walk up to HR staffers and ask questions they have about benefits or the company. Tesla encourages employees to use the Answer Bar to provide personal feedback. This allows Tesla to quickly make changes when new employee programs are introduced. Human resources has developed training that meets company and employee needs for *just-in-time learning,* that is, learning that is meaningful, is short, holds employees' attention, and is provided when needed. For example, factory employees can use their smartphones next to their workstations to scan codes that allow them to view short tutorial videos on job tasks.

Tesla regularly surveys employees to get a feel for employees' levels of enthusiasm. What separates Telsa's use of the surveys from many other companies is that it quickly shares survey results with employees, provides them with access to the data, and requires managers to hold action planning sessions with employees and identify one change the team will make based on the discussion of results. Tesla also has shown that more positive survey results translate into business results: less employee absenteeism, less turnover, and fewer safety issues and increased profitability and productivity.

HRM may be the most important lever for companies to gain a competitive advantage over both domestic and foreign competitors. We believe this is because HRM practices are directly related to companies' success in meeting competitive challenges. These challenges and their implications for HRM are discussed later in the chapter.

DEMONSTRATING THE STRATEGIC VALUE OF HRM: HR ANALYTICS AND EVIDENCE-BASED HR

For HRM to contribute to business goals, there is increasing recognition that data must be used to answer questions such as "Which practices are effective?" and "Which practices are cost effective?" and to project the outcomes of changes in practices on employees' attitudes, behavior, and company profits and costs. This helps show that time and money invested in HR programs are worthwhile and that human resources is as important to the business as finance, marketing, and accounting. **Evidence-based HR** refers to the demonstration that HR practices have a positive influence on the company's bottom line or key stakeholders (employees, customers, community, shareholders). Evidence-based HR requires the use of HR or workforce analytics. **HR or workforce analytics** refers to the practice of using quantitative methods and scientific methods to analyze big data.

Big data refers to information merged from HR databases, corporate financial statements, employee surveys, and other data sources to make evidence-based HR decisions and show that HR practices influence the organization's bottom line, including profits and costs.[21] Several companies have used workforce analytics to analyze big data to help improve HR practices.[22] Google was one of the first companies to use analytics to improve its workforce. Google created algorithms or equations to identify which job candidates were most likely to succeed. It also produced algorithms to review applications that were rejected. This helped Google hire engineers who its normal application screening process would have missed.

Mattress Firm evaluates job applicants based on their online assessments of 39 behavioral, cognitive, and cultural traits. The job applicants' characteristics are compared against a benchmark of strong-performing employees. The analytics are then used to hire new salespeople. Based on two years of hiring and sales data, the company found that the salespeople hired were 80% less likely to leave and sold 11% more products than others who were hired but not recommended by the analytics.

Credit Suisse has a department of HR analysts who specialize in using workforce data to help reduce turnover. This can provide substantial cost savings to the company. For example, if the turnover rate for the company's 46,600 employees could be reduced by 1% per year, it could save $100 million! Each year, eight different pieces of data, including employees' performance ratings, their bosses' performance ratings, their yearly changes in compensation, and the length of time they have been in a job without a promotion, are used to identify who is likely to leave. The analysis provides reports for managers showing the turnover risk of their employees, which they can use to decide how to prevent them from leaving. For example, managers can use this information to recommend a raise, a promotion, or access to development training or opportunities for high-performing employees they don't want to lose.

Because evidence-based HR and analytics are important for showing the value of HR practices and how they contribute to business strategy and goals, throughout each chapter of the book we provide examples of companies' use of workforce analytics to make evidenced-based HR decisions or to evaluate HR practices.

Evidence-based HR
Demonstrating that HR practices have a positive influence on the company's bottom line or key stakeholders (employees, customers, community, shareholders).

HR or workforce analytics
The practice of using data from HR databases and other data sources to make evidence-based HR decisions.

Big data
Information merged from a variety of sources, including HR databases, corporate financial statements, and employee surveys, to make evidence-based HR decisions and show that HR practices can influence the organization's bottom line.

POSITION	SALARY
Top HR executive	$240,206
Global HR manager	121,095
Management development manager	117,114
Health and safety manager	101,872
Employee benefits manager	95,244
HR manager	95,267
Mid-level labor relations specialist	83,974
Campus recruiter	64,725
Entry-level HRIS specialist	54,233
HR generalist	51,180
Entry-level compensation analyst	56,267
Entry-level employee training specialist	48,286

Table 1.3
Median Salaries for
HRM Positions

SOURCE: Based on data from Salary Wizard, http://swz.salary.com, accessed February 23, 2017.

THE HRM PROFESSION: POSITIONS AND JOBS

There are many different types of jobs in the HRM profession. Table 1.3 shows various HRM positions and their salaries. A survey conducted by the Society for Human Resource Management (SHRM) to better understand what HR professionals do found that the primary activities involve performing the HR generalist role (providing a wide range of HR services); fewer HR professionals are involved in the HR function at the executive level of the company, training and development, HR consulting, and administrative activities.[23] Projections suggest that overall employment in HR-related positions is expected to grow by 9% between 2014 and 2024, faster than the average for all occupations in the United States. [24]

Salaries for HR professionals vary according to position, level of experience, training, location, and firm size. As you can see from Table 1.3, some positions involve work in specialized areas of HRM, like recruiting, training, or labor and industrial relations. HR generalists usually make between $41,000 and $65,500 depending on their experience and education level. HR generalists perform a wide range of activities including recruiting, selection, training, labor relations, and benefits administration. HR specialists work in one specific functional area such as training or compensation. Although HR generalists tend to be found in smaller companies, many mid- to large-size companies employ HR generalists at the plant or business levels and HR specialists at the corporate, product, or regional levels. Most HR professionals chose human resources as a career because they found it appealing as a career, they wanted to work with people, or they were asked by chance to perform HR tasks and responsibilities.[25]

EDUCATION AND EXPERIENCE

The HR profession will likely continue to be in transition in the near future.[26] A large number of HR professionals who will be retiring soon have held mainly administrative roles with little previous formal education in HRM. As is currently the case for many HR professionals, the new generation of HR professionals will likely have a four-year college degree and many will have completed a graduate HR degree. Business is typically the field of study (human resources or industrial relations), although some HR professionals have degrees in the social sciences (economics or psychology), the humanities, or law.

Those who have completed graduate work have master's degrees in HRM, business management, industrial organizational psychology, or a similar field. Human resource professionals can be expected to have both strategic and tactical roles. For example, a senior HR role will likely involve developing and supporting the company culture, employee recruitment, retention and engagement, succession planning, and designing the company's overall HR strategy. Junior HR roles will handle all of the transactions related to paperwork, benefits and payroll administration, answering employee questions, and data management.

Professional certification demonstrating that an individual has gained foundational knowledge in human resources is available through the Human Resources Certification Institute (HRCI) or SHRM.[27] Only 12% of U.S. HR professionals hold certification. One reason for the low level of certification is that many companies value education and/or experience more than certification when hiring for HR positions. As a result, professional certification in HRM is less common than membership in professional associations. A well-rounded educational background will likely serve a person well in an HRM position. As one HR professional noted, "One of the biggest misconceptions is that it is all warm and fuzzy communications with the workers. Or that it is creative and involved in making a more congenial atmosphere for people at work. Actually it is both of those some of the time, but most of the time it is a big mountain of paperwork which calls on a myriad of skills besides the 'people' type. It is law, accounting, philosophy, and logic as well as psychology, spirituality, tolerance, and humility."[28]

COMPETENCIES AND BEHAVIORS

Many experts acknowledge that top-level HR professionals are generalists who have expertise in benefits, compensation, and labor relations and focus on important issues such as employee engagement and managing company culture.[29] However, they lack business acumen, the expertise in relating human resources to real-world business needs. That is, they don't know how key decisions are made and are unable to determine why employees or parts of the company fail to meet performance goals. This is congruent with the belief of companies' top HR leaders that developing the skills of professionals working in human resources is an urgent need.[30] Less than 10% of HR leaders believe that their functional teams have the skills needed to help companies meet their current competitive challenges. Consider the requirements that Netflix wanted when it was looking for a new HR director.[31] Netflix wanted someone who puts business first, customers second, and talent third. It did not want a change agent, organizational development practitioner, a SHRM certificate, or a people person. HR professionals should consider themselves as business people, not morale boosters. They need to be able to consider key questions, such as "What's good for the company?" "How do we communicate that to employees?" and "How can we help every employee understand what is meant by high performance?"

HR professionals need to have the nine competencies shown in Figure 1.3. These are the most recent competencies developed by SHRM, based on a literature review, input from over 1,200 HR professionals, and a survey of over 32,000 respondents.[32] The full version of the competency model, which can be found on the SHRM website (**www.shrm.org**), provides more detailed information on the competencies, behaviors, and standards for proficiency for HR professionals at entry, mid, senior, and executive career stages. Demonstrating these competencies can help HR professionals show managers that they are capable of helping the HR function create value, contribute to the business strategy, and shape the company culture. They also help the HR department

Figure 1.3

Competencies and Example Behaviors for HR Professionals

SOURCE: Based on SHRM Competency Model, Society for Human Resource Management, 2012, www.shrm.org, accessed February 9, 2017.

effectively and efficiently provide the three HR products discussed earlier and shown in Figure 1.2. These competencies and behaviors show that although the level of expertise required may vary by career level, all HR professionals need to have a working knowledge of strategic business management, HR planning, development, compensation and benefits, risk management (safety, quality, etc.), labor relations, HR technology, evidence-based decision making, and global human resources. HR professionals need to be able to interact and coach employees and managers, yet engage in ethical practice through maintaining confidentiality and acting with integrity. Providing support for the usefulness and validity of the SHRM competency model, research shows that HR professionals who have a higher level of proficiency on the SHRM competencies do perform better in their jobs.[33]

Many top-level managers and HR professionals believe that the best way to develop employees who have the competencies needed to be effective in an HR role is to train them or insure they have on-the-job experiences that help them understand the business and the role of HRM in it. For example, an HR leader at Rivermark Community Credit Union developed skills in reading and interpreting financial data by spending time with the CFO.[34] This has allowed her to contribute more in senior-level leader meetings.

Both Garden City Group and General Motors use job experiences for insuring that current and aspiring HR professionals have the competencies they need to meet both employees and managers needs.[35] Also, these opportunities help build relationships both in the HR department and across locations. Garden City rotates HR professionals through each of its office locations and encourages its staff to shadow other HR professionals working in different functional areas. To develop future HR leaders General Motors has two specialized HR career paths: a manufacturing path and a corporate path. In the manufacturing path, employees who already work for General Motors but want to work in HR spend a year each working in labor relations, as a business partner, and in a production group. Similarly, the corporate path offered for HR interns include a labor relations assignment as well as a year assignment in global compensation and benefits and either talent acquisition or talent management. Participants in both career paths are matched with mentors who can provide personal insight and advice. Also, participants in both tracks have opportunities to attend training, presentations from speakers outside the company, and forums with senior leaders.

The primary professional organization for HRM is the Society for Human Resource Management. SHRM is the world's largest HRM association, with more than 285,000 professional and student members throughout the world. If you are interested in human resources, you should join SHRM. The organization provides education and information services, conferences and seminars, government and media representation, certification, and online services and publications (such as *HR Magazine*). You can visit SHRM's website at **www.shrm.org**.

Competitive Challenges Influencing Human Resource Management

Sustainability
The ability of a company to make a profit without sacrificing the resources of its employees, the community, or the environment. Based on an approach to organizational decision making that considers the long-term impact of strategies on stakeholders (e.g., employees, shareholders, suppliers, community).

Stakeholders
The various interest groups who have relationships with and, consequently, whose interests are tied to the organization (e.g., employees, suppliers, customers, shareholders, community).

Three competitive challenges that companies now face will increase the importance of human resource management practices: the challenge of sustainability, the global challenge, and the technology challenge. These challenges are shown in Figure 1.4.

As you will see in the following discussion, these competitive challenges are directly linked to the HR challenges that companies are facing, including developing, attracting, and retaining talented employees; finding employees with the necessary skills; and breaking down cultural barriers to create a global company.[36]

COMPETING THROUGH SUSTAINABILITY

Traditionally, sustainability has been viewed as one aspect of corporate social responsibility related to the impact of the business on the environment.[37] However, we take a broader view of sustainability. **Sustainability** refers to the company's ability to meet its needs without sacrificing the ability of future generations to meet their needs.[38] Organizations pursuing a sustainable strategy pursue the "triple bottom line": economic, social, and environmental benefits. Company success is based on how well the company meets the needs of its stakeholders. **Stakeholders** refers to shareholders, the community, customers, employees, and all of the other parties that have an interest in seeing that the

Competing through Sustainability	**Competing through Globalization**	**Competing through Technology**
• Deal with the workforce and employment implications of the economy • Understand and enhance the value of intangible assets and human capital • Meet the needs of stakeholders: shareholders, customers, employees, and the community • Emphasize customer service and quality • Recognize and capitalize on the demographics and diversity of the workforce • Deal with legal and ethical issues	• Entering international markets • Offshoring & reshoring	• Consider social networking • Use HRIS, mobile devices, cloud computing, and HR dashboards • Consider High-performance work systems and virtual teams

U.S. Business Competitiveness

Figure 1.4

Competitive Challenges Influencing U.S. Companies

company succeeds. Sustainability includes the ability to deal with economic and social changes, practice environmental responsibility, engage in responsible and ethical business practices, provide high-quality products and services, and put in place methods to determine if the company is meeting stakeholders' needs; that is, HR systems that create the skills, motivation, values, and culture that help the company achieve its triple bottom line and ensure long-term benefits for the organization's stakeholders.

LO 1-2
Discuss the implications of the economy, the makeup of the labor force, and ethics for company sustainabilility

Deal with the Workforce and Employment Implications of the Economy

The economy has important implications for HRM. Some key statistics about the economy and the workforce are shown in Table 1.4 and we will discuss their implications in greater detail below. These include the structure of the economy, aging of the workforce, and growth in professional and service occupations. Growth in professional and service occupations means that skill demands for jobs have changed, with knowledge becoming more valuable. Not only have skill demands changed, but remaining competitive in a global economy requires demanding work hours and changes in traditional employment patterns. The creation of new jobs, aging employees leaving the workforce, slow population growth, and a lack of employees who have the skills needed to perform the high-demand jobs means that companies need to give more attention to HR practices that influence their ability to attract and retain employees.

Table 1.4
Highlights of Employment Projections to 2024

- The labor force is expected to increase by 8 million, reaching 164 million.
- Today, 93% of U.S. jobs are nonagriculture wage and salary jobs: 12% are in goods-producing industries (mining, construction, manufacturing); 81% are in service-providing industries; and 1.3% in agriculture, forestry, fishing, and hunting. The distribution of jobs across industries is projected to be similar in 2024.
- 46.5 million job openings are expected, with more than three-fourths resulting from the need to replace workers who retire or leave an occupation.
- The median age of the workforce will increase to 42.4 years.
- Health care support and practitioner occupations are projected to be the fastest-growing occupational groups and contribute the most new jobs (one out of four new jobs).

SOURCE: M. Toossi, "Labor Force Projections to 2024: The Labor Force Is Growing, but Slowly," *Monthly Labor Review*, December 2015, from https://www.bls.gov/opub/mlr/, accessed May 3, 2017; A. Hogan and B. Roberts, "Occupational Employment Projections to 2024," *Monthly Labor Review*, December 2015, from https://www.bls.gov/opub/mlr/, accessed May 3, 2017; Bureau of Labor Statistics, "Employment Projections: Replacement Needs," from https://www.bls.gov/emp/ep_table_110.htm, accessed February 10, 2017; R. Henderson, "Industry Employment and Output Projections to 2024," *Monthly Labor Review*, December 2015, from https://www.bls.gov/opub/mlr/, accessed May 3, 2017.

The economy is steady but has some issues.[39] Overall, in January 2017, U.S. businesses appeared to have gained confidence to add jobs and expand, partly in response to President Donald Trump's promises to reduce regulations and cut taxes and also because of a sense of economic stability. For 2016, real GDP increased 1.6%, which was less than occurred in 2015. The increase in real GDP in 2016 reflected increases in consumer spending, residential investment, state and local government spending, exports, and federal government spending. The stock market reached record highs at the start of 2017: The Dow Jones Industrial Average exceeded 20,000.

In April 2017, the labor market was at or close to full employment, with the unemployment rate remaining below 5%. The labor force participation rate, the percentage of those with or actively seeking jobs, remained near a four-year low of 62.9%. The economy added almost 2.2 million jobs in 2016, but this represents the smallest gain since 2012. Further, many of these jobs were low-paying jobs in the retail, hospitality, restaurant, and health care sectors. If the Federal Reserve Bank follows through on its planned three interest rate increases in 2017, this could likely slow hiring.

For some workers, wages began to grow as unemployment dropped. For example, hourly wages rose 4.4% in 2016 for restaurant workers and bartenders in the leisure and hospitality sector. Skilled job candidates in high-demand fields such as information technology received competing offers with increasing pay. However, hourly wage growth for production and nonsupervisory employees and education and health care workers was smaller. Regardless of wage growth, because consumer-price inflation was low, workers lost less of what they earned due to the rising costs of goods and services.

In the business cycle that followed the recession of 2009, labor productivity growth was at its lowest point since the early 1980s. Labor productivity is based on a comparison of the amount of goods and services produced with the number of labor hours used to produce them. Labor productivity growth is important because if the economy is able to produce more goods and services for the same amount of work, this leads to improvements in employees' wages and increases in leisure time for workers and profits and capital gains for business, all of which contribute to improvements in our standards of living.

The United States had a trade deficit of over $502 billion in 2016, the largest in four years.[40] The deficit means that the United States imports more products than it exports to the rest of the world. The value of imports and exports with Canada and Mexico covered by the North American Free Trade Agreement (NAFTA) are somewhat comparable. But the value of U.S. imports from China and other fast-developing Asian countries such as Vietnam and Malaysia is considerable more than the value of goods exported. President Trump has said that stimulating economic growth and supporting U.S. jobs is critical, especially for helping working-class Americans. One way to try to stimulate economic growth and protect and create new jobs is to reduce the trade deficit through tariffs on imports, new legislation, and the renegotiation or cancellation of trade deals such as NAFTA and the Trans-Pacific Partnership (TPP), which involved 12 countries (the United States, Japan, Mexico, Canada, Australia, New Zealand, Vietnam, Peru, Chile, Malaysia, Singapore, and Brunei). However, the relationship between trade, economic growth, and employment is complex, influenced by such factors as currency exchange rates and government spending and taxation. In fact, the United States has had trade deficits during periods of economic expansion and recession, and under high and low employment.

The current economic period has several implications for HRM. Companies are using HR practices to enhance labor productivity by improving the design of work and the use of technology, upskilling employees through training, and managing performance and compensation to incentivize and motivate workers to work smarter and harder. Although companies are looking to add new employees to expand operations, replace retiring employees, or keep up with increased demand for their products and services, many may be unable to find new employees with the skills they need.[41]

Also, valuable high-performing employees may be looking to change jobs for higher wages or better career opportunities. As a result, companies are having problems attracting and retaining talented employees. Many are increasing wages, paying for benefits, and providing training as part of the solution. For example, one Wendy's franchise owner raised his store's average pay by almost $1 per hour; in addition, he provides $500 referral bonuses to employees who find new hires and offers employees more flexible work schedules.[42] The availability of workers with the right skill set is a key factor that many companies, such as Salesforce.com and Cisco, are using to determine in which city or region to open new offices.

In addition to raising pay, companies are focusing on learning.[43] For example, Starbucks has focused on learning as a way to attract and retain employees and show it is committed to their success. The Starbucks College Achievement Plan covers employees' tuition to earn an online bachelor's degree from Arizona State University. Employees can choose from 60 undergraduate degree programs. The only requirements are that employees must work at least 20 hours per week for three consecutive months; be U.S.-based working in support centers, plants, or at any company-operated store (including Teavana, Evolution Fresh, and Seattle's Best Coffee stores); and not yet have a bachelor's degree. Employees have no commitment to remain at Starbucks after they graduate. EJ Ajax Metalforming Solutions posts a skills matrix on a bulletin board where all employees can see it. The skills matrix lists employees' skill levels and all machines and tasks required within a department. This shows employees available training opportunities they can request from their supervisors. The currently lower unemployment rate is especially affecting the ability of small businesses to find qualified employees with the skills they need. As a result, many are spending more time training workers. For example, precision tool maker Mountz Inc. now spends about 36 hours each year on training, compared to six to eight hours three years ago.

HR programs and the HR function are under pressure to relate to their company's business strategy and show a return on investment. Customer focus needs to be included in all HRM practices. New technology means that administrative and transactional HR activities will be delivered via technology, creating less need for HR professionals to provide these activities. The aging workforce, combined with reduced immigration because of security concerns, may lead employers to focus more on retraining employees or encouraging older, skilled workers to delay retirement or work part time.[44]

Labor Force and Employment Characteristics.   Table 1.4 highlights employment projections to 2024. Our discussion of employment projections is based on the work done by the U.S. Bureau of Labor Statistics.[45] Population is the most important factor in determining the size and composition of the labor force. The labor force is expected to grow to almost 164 million by 2024. The size of the labor force will increase, but it is growing more slowly than in previous decades primarily because of the declining growth rate of the population. The labor force will continue to age with more people from the Baby Boomer generation (born between 1946 and 1964) entering retirement age or having already left the workforce.

Because the U.S. population is expected to become increasingly diverse, so is the U.S. workforce. The growth rate of women in the labor force will be faster than the growth rate for men. Immigration is an important force in population and workforce growth and diversity. Traditionally, Hispanic and Asian men have high labor force participation. All racial and ethnic groups, except non-Hispanic whites, are expected to grow by 2024; the share of non-Hispanic whites is expected to decline. With the fastest population growth of all racial and ethnic groups, Hispanics are projected to make up nearly 20% of the labor force (the diversity and aging of the workforce is discussed in more detail later in this chapter).

The importance of the service sector in the U.S. economy is emphasized by considering industry and occupational employment rates and future projections. In all, 80% of jobs are in the service sector. Currently, the largest percentages of jobs are found in health care and social assistance, leisure and hospitality, state and local government, professional and business services, and retail trade. Most of the employment growth will be in the health care and social assistance sector, which will account for over one-third of projected job growth through 2024. The construction industry is expected to add the largest number of jobs by 2024 but not back to prerecession levels.[46]

Table 1.5 provides examples of the largest percentage growth in jobs from 2014 to 2024. Of the 15 fastest growing occupations, over half are related to health care (such as occupational therapy assistants, home health aides, nurse practitioners, and physical therapists). The growth in health care reflects the inpatient and outpatient medical care that is needed for the aging U.S. population.

All major occupations are projected to gain jobs between 2014 and 2024 except production occupations, and farming, fishery, and forestry. Six industries are projected to have decreases in employment—manufacturing; federal government; agriculture; forestry, fishing, and hunting; information; and utilities. This loss of jobs and workers is due to several factors including technological improvements, which means fewer workers are needed; global competition; industry consolidation; cost-cutting and more efficient work processes; and decrease in the number of workers who want to work in these occupations.

Education plays an important role in meeting occupational or job requirements and in employee earnings.[47] A minimum level of education is not required for approximately 31% of U.S. jobs. But, 22% of jobs require some form of training such as a certificate or license. Further, 11 of the 15 fastest-growing occupations require some level of postsecondary education and have higher median weekly earnings than the national average. Today, the median weekly earnings for jobs requiring a high school diploma is $678,

OCCUPATION	EMPLOYMENT CHANGE 2014–2024		MOST SIGNIFICANT EDUCATION OR TRAINING
	NUMBER (IN THOUSANDS)	PERCENT	
Wind turbine service technicians	9	100	Some college, no degree
Occupational therapy assistants	47	43	Associate degree
Physical therapy assistants	111	41	Associate degree
Physical therapists aides	69	39	High school diploma or equivalent
Home health aides	1,262	38	No formal educational requirement
Commercial divers	6	37	Postsecondary nondegree award
Nurse practitioners	172	35	Master's degree
Physical therapists	283	34	Doctoral or professional degree
Statisticians	40	34	Master's degree
Ambulance drivers and attendants, except emergency medical technicians	26	33	High school diploma or equivalent

Table 1.5
Examples of the Occupations with the Largest Growth in Jobs

SOURCE: Based on Bureau of Labor Statistics, "Employment Projections: 2014–2024 Summary," News Release, December 8, 2015, www.bls.gov/emp, accessed February 23, 2017.

compared to $738 for those who have some college but no degree, $798 for an associate degree, $1,137 for a bachelor's degree, and $1,730 for a professional degree. The discrepancy in earnings is expected to continue in the future.

Despite the availability of unemployed and underemployed workers and new high school and college graduates, companies are having a difficult time finding employees with the right skills. Several studies illustrate how the skills deficit is influencing companies and identify what skills are in short supply.[48] Although many businesses plan to hire new employees, they are concerned that they will not be able to find the talent needed to capitalize on investments they are making in new technology and other strategic capabilities. Skills deficits are not limited to any one business sector, industry, or job. Nearly half of CEOs of U.S. businesses believe that a significant skills gap exists that will result in loss of business, loss of revenue, decreased customer satisfaction, or a delay in new products or services. The Manufacturing Institute found that 80% of manufacturers report a moderate or serious shortage of qualified applicants for skilled and highly skilled production positions. One estimate is that 60% of manufacturing job openings in the next 10 years are likely to be unfilled due to the lack of employees with the necessary skills. The Organisation for Economic Co-operation and Development (OECD) found that the United States ranked 21 out of 23 countries in math and 17 out of 19 countries in problem solving. But skills deficits are not just a problem facing U.S. companies. They are occurring around the world. For example, in Italy and Spain nearly 3 out of 10 adults perform at or below the lowest proficiency level in literacy and numerical ability. One study found that, regardless of their education level, only half the companies surveyed rated new employees as adequately prepared for work. Companies' greatest basic skills needs were in reading, writing, and math. Many employers also feel that they are having a difficult time finding employees with the right "soft skills" such as work ethic, teamwork, and communications that they believe are more important for success on the job than job-specific or "hard skills" such as blueprint reading or writing. Interpersonal skills, the ability to learn, creativity, and problem solving are especially important in the service economy because employees have responsibility for the final product or service provided. There is especially a shortage of employees with skills in science, technology, engineering, and math (STEM skills).

Companies are partnering with unions, elementary and secondary schools, and colleges and universities to develop the necessary skills needed in today's workforce.[49] As the aluminum manufacturer Alcoa works with Airbus to provide 3-D-printed titanium fuselage parts for commercial airlines, it needs more workers with technical skills focused on 3-D printing. To meet this need, Alcoa has quadrupled its internships in the past three years at its Technology Center in New Castle, Pennsylvania. The company is also partnering with a community college to train 60 students for jobs. Some companies are even choosing to locate new plants close to college towns, where they have access to employees with the skill sets they need and the opportunity to collaborate on research that has business implications. For example, General Electric (GE) chose to locate a plant that would use 3-D printing to make products in Auburn, Alabama (home of Auburn University). General Electric picked Auburn because it could find and train technicians needed to operate the printers and work with the university on research products focused on understanding the properties of the powder used in the printers in order to improve product consistency. Auburn University bought the same 3-D printer that GE uses so that students can learn how to use the machine. Recognizing the future growth potential of the 3-D printing industry, Auburn University and the city of Auburn, Alabama, are hopeful that they can attract other 3-D printer manufacturers and suppliers and vendors.

Understand and Enhance the Value Placed on Intangible Assets and Human Capital

Intangible assets
A type of company asset that includes human capital, customer capital, social capital, and intellectual capital.

Today more and more companies are interested in using intangible assets and human capital as a way to gain an advantage over competitors. A company's value includes three types of assets that are critical for the company to provide goods and services: financial assets (cash and securities), physical assets (property, plant, equipment), and intangible assets. Table 1.6 provides examples of intangible assets. **Intangible assets** include human capital, customer capital, social capital, and intellectual capital. Intangible assets are equally or even more valuable than financial and physical assets, but they are difficult to duplicate or imitate.[50] By one estimate, up to 75% of the source of value in a company is in intangible assets.[51]

Intangible assets have been shown to be responsible for a company's competitive advantage. Human resource management practices such as training, selection, performance management, and compensation have a direct influence on human and social capital through influencing customer service, work-related know-how and competence, and work relationships.

Blue Apron, a company that delivers the fresh ingredients and cooking instructions its customers need to prepare delicious meals, puts a great deal of effort into developing human capital, social capital, and customer capital.[52] Blue Apron hosts a wine happy hour that brings customers together to help build friendships, facilitate networking, and introduce wines the company is selling that month as part of its meal delivery subscription.

Table 1.6

Examples of
Intangible Assets

Human capital
- Tacit knowledge
- Education
- Work-related know-how
- Work-related competence

Customer capital
- Customer relationships
- Brands
- Customer loyalty
- Distribution channels

Social capital
- Corporate culture
- Management philosophy
- Management practices
- Informal networking systems
- Coaching/mentoring relationships

Intellectual capital
- Patents
- Copyrights
- Trade secrets
- Intellectual property

SOURCES: Based on L. Weatherly, *Human Capital: The Elusive Asset* (Alexandria, VA: SHRM Research Quarterly, 2003); E. Holton and S. Naquin, "New Metrics for Employee Development," *Performance Improvement Quarterly* 17 (2004), pp. 56–80; M. Huselid, B. Becker, and R. Beatty, *The Workforce Scorecard* (Boston: Harvard University Press, 2005).

Full-time employees attend an annual camping trip, which often involves visiting a farm to see where its ingredients are grown. Blue Apron provides leadership training programs for every level of manager within the company. The training programs focus on how managers want to develop as leaders, how they can help their employees develop, and how to lead across the organization.

Intangible assets have been shown to be related to a company's financial performance, productivity, and innovation.[53] The American Society for Training and Development found that companies that invested the most in training and development had a shareholder return 86% higher than companies in the bottom half and 46% higher than the market average.

One way companies try to increase intangible assets is through attracting, developing, and retaining knowledge workers. **Knowledge workers** are employees who contribute to the company not through manual labor, but through what they know about customers or a specialized body of knowledge. Employees cannot simply be ordered to perform tasks; they must share knowledge and collaborate on solutions. Knowledge workers contribute specialized knowledge that their managers may not have, such as information about customers. Managers depend on them to share information. Knowledge workers have many job opportunities. If they choose, they can leave a company and take their knowledge to a competitor. Knowledge workers are in demand because companies need their skills and jobs requiring them are growing (see Table 1.5).

Emphasize Empowerment and Continuous Learning. To completely benefit from employees' knowledge requires a management style that focuses on developing and empowering employees. **Empowering** means giving employees responsibility and authority

Knowledge workers
Employees who own the intellectual means of producing a product or service.

Empowering
Giving employees the responsibility and authority to make decisions.

to make decisions regarding all aspects of product development or customer service.[54] Employees are then held accountable for products and services; in return, they share the rewards and losses of the results. For empowerment to be successful, managers must be trained to link employees to resources within and outside the company (people, websites, etc.), help employees interact with their fellow employees and managers throughout the company, and ensure that employees are updated on important issues and cooperate with each other. Employees must also be trained to understand how to use the Web, e-mail, and other tools for communicating, collecting, and sharing information.

Learning organization
An organization whose employees are continuously attempting to learn new things and apply what they have learned to improve product or service quality.

As more companies become knowledge-based, it's important that they promote continuous learning at the employee, team, and company levels. A **learning organization** embraces a culture of lifelong learning, enabling all employees to continually acquire and share knowledge. Improvements in product or service quality do not stop when formal training is completed.[55] Employees need to have the financial, time, and content resources (courses, experiences, development opportunities) available to increase their knowledge. Managers take an active role in identifying training needs and helping to ensure that employees use training in their work. Also, employees should be actively encouraged to identify problems, make decisions, continuously experiment, and improve.

Keller Williams Realty, which focuses on buying and selling residential and commercial real estate, emphasizes continuous learning both to attract new real estate agents and to help all agents boost their sales, which means the company makes profits and they earn more money.[56] Learning is accessible for agents anywhere and anytime via KW Connect, a learning platform that includes all of the company's training programs and materials, as well as user-generated content from top real-estate professionals. For example, KW Connect includes videos, audio files, and links, a feature that allows learners to follow top executives and agents and receive notifications when they post new content, a question-and-answer forum, user ratings and comments for all content that helps identify the best ideas, and a searchable calendar that allows agents to sign up for over 250,000 instructor-led training classes. Top agents provide videos explaining how they deal with common real estate challenges. Office managers can create custom content for new agents or other groups.

Change
The adoption of a new idea or behavior by a company.

Adapt to Change. **Change** refers to the adoption of a new idea or behavior by a company. Technological advances, changes in the workforce or government regulations, globalization, and new competitors are among the many factors that require companies to change. Change is inevitable in companies as products, companies, and entire industries experience shorter life cycles.[57] This has played a major role in reshaping the employment relationship.[58] New or emergent business strategies that result from these changes cause companies to merge, acquire new companies, grow, and in some cases downsize and restructure. This has resulted in changes in the employment relationship. Companies demand excellent customer service and high productivity levels. Employees are expected to take more responsibility for their own careers, from seeking training to balancing work and family. In exchange for top performance and working longer hours without job security, employees want companies to provide flexible work schedules, comfortable working conditions, more autonomy in accomplishing work, training and development opportunities, and financial incentives based on how the company performs. Employees realize that companies cannot provide employment security, so they want employability—that is, they want their company to provide training and job experiences to help ensure that employees can find other employment opportunities. The HRM challenge is how to build a committed, productive workforce in economic conditions that offer opportunity for financial success but can also quickly turn sour, making every employee expendable.

Consider how Portsmouth Naval Shipyard embraced the need to change.[59] It was performing poorly compared to other government-run shipyards in the United States. Submarine maintenance and upgrades took longer to complete and were more costly than they should have been. Employees, managers, and the unions recognized the need to change or otherwise risk the shipyard closing and its business going to other government or for-profit shipyards. They collectively developed a "Declaration of Excellence," which included the values, beliefs, and attitudes that employees should strive to achieve. It represented a commitment to excellence for employees and the entire shipyard to try to achieve every day. To help facilitate positive changes in operations, whiteboards were placed around the shipyard to provide a way for employees to write down ideas for improving safety and suggestions for changing work processes to save time and money. Ideas were reviewed and implemented by a joint labor–management committee. The change effort continues, but so far results have been positive. Portsmouth has moved from the bottom to the top of government rankings for cost and time of maintenance and ship upgrades.

Maximize Employee Engagement. **Employee engagement** refers to the degree to which employees are fully involved in their work and the strength of their commitment to their job and the company.[60] How do we know if an employee is engaged? An engaged employee is passionate about his or her work, is committed to the company and its mission, and works hard to contribute. Engagement survey results show that approximately 32% of US employees are engaged in their work, 51% are not engaged, and 17% are actively disengaged.[61] Actively disengaged employees cost the United States billions of dollars every year in lost productivity.

Perhaps the best way to understand engagement is to consider how companies measure employee engagement. Companies measure employees' engagement levels with attitude or opinion surveys. Although the types of questions asked on these surveys vary from company to company, research suggests the questions generally measure 10 common themes shown in Table 1.7. As you probably realize after reviewing the themes shown in Table 1.7, employees' engagement is influenced by how managers treat employees as well as HR practices such as recruiting, selection, training and development, performance management, work design, and compensation.

Consider how Echo Global Logistics, Whole Foods, and Timberlane support employee engagement.[62] Echo Global Logistics uses a Facebook-like application to allow employees to provide positive feedback and badges to other employees. The application gives

Employee engagement
The degree to which employees are fully involved in their work and the strength of their job and company commitment.

Pride in employer
Satisfaction with employer
Satisfaction with the job
Opportunity to perform challenging work
Recognition and positive feedback for contributions
Personal support from manager
Effort above and beyond the minimum
Understanding the link between one's job and the company's mission
Prospects for future growth with the company
Intention to stay with the company

Table 1.7
Common Themes of Employee Engagement

SOURCE: Based on R. Vance, *Employee Engagement and Commitment* (Alexandria, VA: Society for Human Resource Management, 2006); T. Lytle, "The Engagement Challenge," *HR Magazine*, October 2016, pp. 52–58.

employees the ability to use sayings in their feedback to each other that reflect Echo's values such as "Bring Your Own," which refers to employees bringing their best effort to work. The use of the sayings as part of employees' feedback to each other has resulted in their more seriously paying attention to the company values. The application also has a survey function that can be used to measure employee engagement and track improvements. The surveys can be administered weekly or even daily, which allows the company to take fast action to implement necessary improvements. The surveys ask employees to indicate their level of agreement with statements such as, "I can see a link between my performance and total compensation," "Echo operates by strong values and ethics," and "There is good teamwork across departments." Whole Foods supports engagement by allowing employee teams to make recommendations about whether new hires should be hired permanently at the end of their probationary period. Timberlane uses results from a test of employees' preferences to match them with the tasks they are most interested in and comfortable performing.

Talent management
Attracting, retaining, developing, and motivating highly skilled employees and managers.

Manage Talent. **Talent management** refers to the systematic planned strategic effort by a company to use bundles of HRM practices—including acquiring and assessing employees, learning and development, performance management, and compensation—to attract, retain, develop, and motivate highly skilled employees and managers. This means recognizing that all HR practices are interrelated, are aligned with business needs, and help the organization manage talent to meet business goals. For example, at Qualcomm, a San Diego company, talent management is organized around core values that emphasize recruiting smart, motivated employees and creating a work environment that allows them to innovate, execute, partner, and lead.[63] When Qualcomm wanted to introduce technology for its performance management process, HR generalists worked together with organizational development and information technology specialists to ensure that what employees were being evaluated on (performance management) and what employees were paid and rewarded for (compensation and rewards) were aligned. Managers were trained to use the performance management system and now focus on identifying employee skills gaps to identify opportunities to improve performance.

Survey results suggest that having opportunities for career growth, learning, and development, and performing exciting and challenging work are some of the most important factors in determining employees' engagement and commitment to their current employer.[64] As the economy improves, high-achieving employees may be looking to leave companies if they do not feel they have adequate opportunities to develop or move to positions in which they can best utilize their skills.

Consider how YUM! Brands and BNSF manage talent.[65] All corporate employees at YUM! Brands are provided with a midyear development plan and reviews of their skills from their boss and peers to help them identify their strengths and weaknesses. Managers provide the coaching necessary to help the employees set short- and long-term career goals and identify training and development activities. BNSF, the largest freight railroad in North America, recognizes that developing and promoting talent from within the company is critical for business success because of the technical nature of the work, the complicated operating environment, and the company's desire to maintain its strong culture. BNSF uses programs and processes to develop its internal talent, including an internship and management training program that starts with college and graduate school hires, regular department-level discussions of top talent and talent movement, and development plans matched to each employees' development needs and desired career path. The emphasis on talent has paid off: 38% of the company's top talent received a development move or promotion and 96% of its top 500 leadership positions have been filled with internal talent.

Consider Nontraditional Employment and the Gig Economy. More companies are moving away the traditional employment model based on full-time workers to increasingly rely on nontraditional employment. **Nontraditional employment** includes the use of independent contractors, freelancers, on-call workers, temporary workers, and contract company workers. Studies estimate that between 20% and 35% of the total U.S. workforce is engaged in nontraditional employment, including those who have a full-time job (what is called "moonlighting").[66] Companies that rely primarily on nontraditional employment to meet service and product demands are competing in the **gig economy.**[67] Although many companies will continue to rely on a traditional employment model using full- and part-time employees, 40% believe they will use a nontraditional model (independent contractors, project-based or freelance need-based work) in the next decade.

What does nontraditional employment look like? Often, a website or mobile app is used to assign work, and the worker sets his or her own schedule. Because these workers do not work for a company, they do not have taxes withheld from their earnings, they do not have to receive minimum wage or overtime pay, and they are not eligible for worker's compensation and unemployment insurance. Examples of companies that rely on the gig economy include transportation services Uber and Lyft and food-delivery services such as Caviar. Nontraditional employment has benefits and disadvantages for both individuals and employers.[68]

More workers in nontraditional employment relationships are choosing these arrangements. Nontraditional employment can benefit both individuals and employers. More and more individuals don't want to be attached to any one company. They want the flexibility to work when and where they choose. They may want to work fewer hours to better balance work and family responsibilities. Also, individuals who have been downsized may choose nontraditional employment while they are seeking full-time employment. From the company perspective, it is easier to add temporary employees when they are needed and easier to terminate their employment when they are not needed. Part-time workers can be a valuable source of skills that current employees may not have and are needed for a specific project that has a set completion date. Part-time workers can be less expensive than permanent employees because they do not receive employer health benefits or participate in pension plans. Employing part-time workers such as interns allows the company to determine if the worker meets performance requirements and fits in with the company culture, and if so, the company may then decide to offer the employee a permanent position. For example, Ammacore's workers install cabling and perform electronic troubleshooting for the company's clients.[69] Ammacore uses a third-party vendor to screen and verify credentials of technicians it uses. A community manager communicates with the technicians before, during, and after a project to ensure they have the information they need. Using a service provided by the third-party vendor, the company rates the technicians' timeliness, performance, and reliability. The technicians rate Ammacore on the timeliness of the payment for their services and communication during the project. Technicians who perform well receive small bonuses. Ammacore depends on receiving good ratings from technicians to attract talented technicians. Some technology companies such as Honeywell have relied on crowdsourcing using services such as Topcoder and Amazon's Mechanical Turk to find scientists and software engineers who have the skills not found in the company's employees to solve problems, create apps, or write code. Alphabet Inc., the parent company of Google, has equal numbers of full-time and temporary and contract workers who test self-driving cars, manage projects, review legal documents, and do other jobs. Nontraditional employment also has potential disadvantages. These include concerns about work quality, inability to maintain the company culture or team environment, and legal liability.[70]

Nontraditional employment
Includes the use of independent contractors, freelancers, on-call workers, temporary workers, and contract company workers.

Gig economy
Companies who rely primarily on nontraditional employment to meet service and product demands

Provide Flexibility to Help Employees Meet Work and Life Demands.   The globalization of the world economy and the development of e-commerce have made the notion of a 40-hour work week obsolete. Survey results show that 46% of employees work more than 45 hours per week.[71] As a result, companies need to be staffed 24 hours a day, seven days a week. Employees in manufacturing environments and service call centers are being asked to move from 8- to 12-hour days or to work afternoon or midnight shifts. Similarly, professional employees face long hours and work demands that spill over into their personal lives. Notebook computers, smartphones, and smartwatches bombard employees with information and work demands. In the car, on vacation, on planes, and even in the bathroom, employees can be interrupted by work demands. More demanding work results in greater employee stress, less satisfied employees, loss of productivity, and higher turnover—all of which are costly for companies.

One study found that because of work demands 75% of employees report not having enough time for their children, and 61% report not having enough time for their husbands or wives. However, only half of employees in the United States strongly agree that they have the flexibility they need to successfully manage their work and personal or family lives.[72] Many companies are recognizing the benefits that can be gained by both the company and employees through providing flexible work schedules, allowing work-at-home arrangements, protecting employees' free time, and more productively using employees' work time.[73] The benefits include the ability to have an advantage in attracting and retaining talented employees, reduced stress resulting in healthier employees, and a rested workforce that can maximize the use of their skills. It is estimated that 24% of all workers do some or all of their work at home. [74] Some 23 million workers worked at home on an average day in 2016. Employees in managerial, business, and financial operations and professional occupations are most likely to do some or all of their work at home.

KPMG offers employees the option of working part time while keeping their benefits yet not ruining their chances for promotion.[75] Almost all KPMG employees have used the company's work/life benefits, which also include job sharing, working at home, and paid leaves for parents and unpaid leaves for a career break at some point. Employees are encouraged to discuss their use of work/life benefits with their managers and team members to ensure that their personal needs as well as the client's needs are met. The World Wildlife Fund (WWF) gives its 6,200 employees every other Friday off but requires them to work 70 hours over nine days. Despite this requirement, employees like the benefit and it matches WWF's conservation mission by reducing employee commuting and the use of electricity in the office. Diebold was able to attract top executives who didn't want to relocate to Ohio by allowing them to work remotely.[76] They spend at least a few days a month in Ohio, but otherwise they work from their home offices and travel to meet with their staffs and customers. Phone calls, e-mails, and teleconferences every Monday are used to ensure that the executives stay up to date on current company issues.

The use of nontraditional work employment and work-at-home has resulted in the development of co-working sites or shared offices where diverse workers such as designers, artists, freelancers, consultants, and other independent contractors pay a daily or monthly fee for a guaranteed work space.[77] Co-working sites are equipped with desks, Internet, and conferences rooms, and some even provide couches for relaxing and free coffee and beer. Co-working sites help independent contractors and employees who work at home, travel, or telecommute and who have feelings of isolation, enabling them to collaborate and interact, providing a more professional working atmosphere than coffee shops, and helping to decrease traffic and pollution.

Meet the Needs of Stakeholders: Shareholders, Customers, Employees, and Community

As we mentioned earlier, company effectiveness and competitiveness are determined by whether the company satisfies the needs of stakeholders. Stakeholders include stockholders (who want a return on their investment), customers (who want a high-quality product or service), and employees (who desire interesting work and reasonable compensation for their services). The community, which wants the company to contribute to activities and projects and minimize pollution of the environment, is also an important stakeholder.

Demonstrate Performance to Stakeholders: The Balanced Scorecard. The **balanced scorecard** gives managers an indication of the performance of a company based on the degree to which stakeholder needs are satisfied; it depicts the company from the perspective of internal and external customers, employees, and shareholders.[78] The balanced scorecard is important because it brings together most of the features that a company needs to focus on to be competitive. These include being customer-focused, improving quality, emphasizing teamwork, reducing new product and service development times, and managing for the long term.

The balanced scorecard differs from traditional measures of company performance by emphasizing that the critical indicators chosen are based on the company's business strategy and competitive demands. Companies need to customize their balanced scorecards based on different market situations, products, and competitive environments.

The balanced scorecard should be used to (1) link human resource management activities to the company's business strategy and (2) evaluate the extent to which the HRM function is helping the company meet its strategic objectives. Communicating the scorecard to employees gives them a framework that helps them see the company's goals and strategies, how these goals and strategies are measured, and how they influence the critical indicators. Measures of HRM practices primarily relate to productivity, people, and process.[79] Productivity measures involve determining output per employee (such as revenue per employee). Measuring people includes assessing employees' behavior, attitudes, or knowledge. Process measures focus on assessing employees' satisfaction with people systems within the company. People systems can include the performance management system, the compensation and benefits system, and the development system. To show that HRM activities contribute to a company's competitive advantage, managers need to consider the questions shown in Table 1.8 and be able to identify critical indicators or metrics related to human resources. As shown in the last column of Table 1.8, critical indicators of HR practices primarily relate to people, productivity, and process.

For example, at ConocoPhillips, the balanced scorecard for top executives includes costs, health and safety, production, and resource replacement.[80] ConocoPhillips has also developed scorecards for operational-level activities such as safety. Some physicians employed by OhioHealth, a hospital system, receive up to 10% of their pay based on a balanced scorecard consisting of quality, service, financial performance, and employee engagement.[81]

Demonstrate Social Responsibility. Increasingly, companies are recognizing that social responsibility can help boost a company's image with customers, gain access to new markets, and help attract and retain talented employees. Companies thus try to meet shareholder and general public demands that they be more socially, ethically, and environmentally responsible. For example, Bill Gates, former CEO and Microsoft Corporation founder, has improved Microsoft's corporate reputation through his personal involvement in a charitable foundation dedicated to using science and technology to improve lives around the world.

Balanced scorecard
A means of performance measurement that gives managers a chance to look at their company from the perspectives of internal and external customers, employees, and shareholders.

LO 1-3
Discuss how human resource management affects a company's balanced scorecard.

Table 1.8
The Balanced Scorecard

PERSPECTIVE	QUESTIONS ANSWERED	EXAMPLES OF CRITICAL BUSINESS INDICATORS	EXAMPLES OF CRITICAL HR INDICATORS
Customer	How do customers see us?	Time, quality, performance, service, cost	Employee satisfaction with HR department services Employee perceptions of the company as an employer
Internal	What must we excel at?	Processes that influence customer satisfaction, availability of information on service, and/or manufacturing processes	Training costs per employee, turnover rates, time to fill open positions
Innovation and learning	Can we continue to improve and create value?	Improve operating efficiency, launch new products, continuous improvement, empowering of workforce, employee satisfaction	Employee/skills competency levels, engagement survey results, change management capability
Financial	How do we look to shareholders?	Profitability, growth, shareholder value	Compensation and benefits per employee, turnover costs, profit per employee, revenue per employee

SOURCE: Based on K. Thompson and N. Mathys, "The Aligned Balanced Scorecard," *Organizational Dynamics* 37 (2008), pp. 378–393; B. Becker, M. Huselid, and D. Ulrich, *The HR Scorecard: Linking People, Strategy, and Performance* (Boston: Harvard Business School Press, 2001).

Coca-Cola is involved in an initiative focused on women's economic empowerment throughout the world by providing business skills training, access to financing, and networking and mentoring.[82] The initiative is helping millions of women around the world to build their businesses, support their families, and build their communities.

Companies are realizing that helping to protect the planet can also save money.[83] International Paper, a global paper and packaging company, has focused on reducing the amount of manufacturing waste sent to landfills.[84] It has reduced solid waste to landfills by 11% since 2010, and its goal is to reduce manufacturing waste to landfills to 30% by 2020. It has done so by collecting and selling the by-products of its manufacturing to other companies to make solvents, soaps, lubricants, paint thinners, and other products. Dow Chemical has sustainability goals that include the use of sustainable chemistry, reducing energy usage, and publishing safety evaluations for all of its products.[85]

The "Competing through Sustainability" box highlights the sustainable business practices of several companies.

Emphasize Customer Service and Quality

Companies' customers judge quality and performance. As a result, customer excellence requires attention to product and service features as well as to interactions with customers. Customer-driven excellence includes understanding what the customer wants and anticipating future needs. Customer-driven excellence includes reducing defects and errors, meeting specifications, and reducing complaints. How the company recovers from defects and errors is also important for retaining and attracting customers.

Due to increased availability of knowledge and competition, consumers are very knowledgeable and expect excellent service. This presents a challenge for employees who

Socially Responsible Programs Help Improve the World

Sustainability is an important part of many companies' business strategy. Dow's leadership development program, Leadership in Action, is part of Dow's approach to meeting the world's basic needs by matching its employees with organizations that need support for sustainable development projects, especially in business growth areas for Dow. In 2016, 40 Dow employees worked in teams on six projects with partners from nongovernmental organizations in Cebu, Philippines. The projects included branding and packaging for meat and dairy products, assessing water quality and helping to rehabilitate Tinago Creek which runs through the city, and increasing crop production through better farming practices.

The pharmaceutical company Novartis is actively involved in improving health care for pregnant women in Africa. Many health centers lack necessary medical supplies, and health care workers often do not have the medical expertise needed to help women with pregnancy complications. A new program was started in Ethiopia, called New Life & New Hope, to improve maternal and child health and to reduce mortality associated with childbirth. The program sponsored basic emergency obstetric and newborn care training for 80 midwives, affecting the care of approximately 40,000 pregnant women in the Addis Ababa area.

The Mars Ambassador Program provides employees with the opportunity to share their expertise and develop skills by spending up to six weeks supporting projects managed by organizations such as the Rainforest Alliance or the World Wildlife Federation, or to work with local communities. For example, one Mars Ambassador team spent a week in Puerto Rico rebuilding an animal shelter. The local community benefited by being able to provide better care and quality of life for the animals. The employees learned how to work on a team in challenging situations. Another team worked with students in Bucharest, Romania, to design and implement an energy audit for their school, which resulted in cost savings and energy conservation.

DISCUSSION QUESTION

1. How does a company's sustainability efforts help the company attract, retain, and develop employees? Explain your answer.

SOURCES: Based on "Dow Chemical's New Formula for Global Leaders," *Chief Learning Officer*, April 2015, pp. 42–43, 49; "Leadership in Action: Phillipines 2016," www.dow.com, accessed February 20. 2017; "Our Work in Africa," www.novartis.com, accessed February 20, 2017; D. Moss, "One Sweet Job," *HR Magazine*, October 2016, pp. 43–45; "Mars Ambassador Program," www.marsgcc.com, accessed February 16, 2017.

---

interact with customers. The way in which clerks, sales staff, front-desk personnel, and service providers interact with customers influences a company's reputation and financial performance. Employees need product knowledge and service skills, and they need to be clear about the types of decisions they can make when dealing with customers.

To compete in today's economy, whether on a local or global level, companies need to provide a quality product or service. If companies do not adhere to quality standards, their ability to sell their product or service to vendors, suppliers, or customers will be restricted. Some countries even have quality standards that companies must meet to conduct business there. **Total quality management (TQM)** is a companywide effort to continuously improve the ways people, machines, and systems accomplish work.[86] Core values of TQM include the following:[87]

- Methods and processes are designed to meet the needs of internal and external customers.
- Every employee in the company receives training in quality.

Total quality management (TQM)
A cooperative form of doing business that relies on the talents and capabilities of both labor and management to continually improve quality and productivity.

- Quality is designed into a product or service so that errors are prevented from occurring rather than being detected and corrected.
- The company promotes cooperation with vendors, suppliers, and customers to improve quality and hold down costs.
- Managers measure progress with feedback based on data.

Malcolm Baldrige National Quality Award
An award established in 1987 to promote quality awareness, to recognize quality achievements of U.S. companies, and to publicize successful quality strategies.

ISO 9000:2015
A series of quality assurance standards developed by the International Organization for Standardization in Switzerland and adopted worldwide.

Malcolm Baldrige National Quality Award. One way that companies can improve the quality of their products or services is through competing for the **Malcolm Baldrige National Quality Award** or gaining certification in the **ISO 9000:2015** standards. The Baldrige award, created by public law, is the highest level of national recognition for quality that a U.S. company can receive. To become eligible for the Baldrige, a company must complete a detailed application that consists of basic information about the firm as well as an in-depth presentation of how it addresses specific criteria related to quality improvement.[88] The categories and point values for the Baldrige Award are found in Table 1.9. The award is not given for specific products or services. Organizations can compete for the Baldrige Award in one of several categories, including manufacturing, service, small business, education, health care, and nonprofit. The Baldrige Award is given annually in each of the categories with a total limit each year of 18 awards. All applicants for the Baldrige Award undergo a rigorous examination process that takes from 300 to 1,000 hours. Applications are reviewed by an independent board of about 400 examiners who come primarily from the private sector. One of the major benefits of applying for the Baldrige Award is the feedback report from the examining team noting the company's strengths and areas for improvement.[89]

The Baldrige Award winners usually excel at HR practices. For example, consider Don Chalmers Ford, a 2016 small business award winner.[90] Don Chalmers Ford is an independent Ford Motor automobile dealer with 182 employees in Rio Rancho, New Mexico. Don Chalmers has been nationally recognized by Ford Motors for customer satisfaction and market share 13 times over the past 17 years. This has been accomplished by only 4% of U.S. Ford dealerships. In the past four years, its dealership profits increased by 13%, exceeding Ford's national dealership benchmark by over 8%. In addition to analyzing its service and sales processes on a daily, weekly, and monthly basis to identify opportunities for improvement, Don Chalmers's HR practices support the dealership's commitment to quality. To retain sales consultants, new employees are mentored by senior leaders to ensure they understand the business strategy and that their role is aligned with the company's core values. This resulted in a 71% employee retention rate in 2015, which is 45% higher than the national average for Ford's non-luxury-brand dealerships. To help meet the needs of its diverse workforce, Don Chalmers provides a free on-site wellness clinic staffed with a nurse practitioner, for employees and their families. To engage employees, Don Chalmers management provides employees with monthly status reports on its operations and business plans, and the senior leadership team regularly discusses customer satisfaction and provides performance feedback. Employees are encouraged to submit ideas for improvement, and senior leaders review, discuss, and implement them.

ISO (International Organization for Standardization) 9000 Standards. ISO (International Organization for Standardization), a network of national standards institutes including 160 countries with a central governing body in Geneva, Switzerland, is the world's largest developer and publisher of international standards.[91] The ISO develops standards related to management, as well as a wide variety of other areas including education, music, ships, and even the protection of children. ISO standards are voluntary, though countries may decide to adopt ISO standards in their regulations, in which case they may become a requirement to compete in the market.

Leadership	**120**
How senior executives create and sustain vision, values, and mission; promote legal and ethical behavior; create a sustainable company; and communicate with and engage the workforce.	
Measurement, Analysis, and Knowledge Management	**90**
How the company selects, gathers, analyzes, uses, manages, and improves its data, information, and knowledge assets	
Strategic	**85**
How the company sets strategic direction, how it determines action plans, how it changes strategy and action plans if required, and how it measures progress	
Workforce	**85**
How the company develops and utilizes the workforce to achieve high performance; how the company engages, manages, and develops the potential of the workforce in alignment with company goals	
Operations	**85**
How the company designs, manages, and improves work systems and work processes to deliver customer value and achieve company success and sustainability	
Results	**450**
How the company performs and improves in key business areas (product, service, and supply quality; productivity; operational effectiveness and related financial indicators; environmental, legal, and regulatory compliance); the company's level of ethical and social responsibility	
Customer	**85**
The company's knowledge of the customer, customer service systems, current and potential customer concerns, and customer satisfaction and engagement	
Total Points	**1,000**

Table 1.9
Categories and Point Values for the Malcolm Baldrige National Quality Award Examination

SOURCE: Based on National Institute of Standards and Technology (NIST), "2017–2018 Criteria for Performance Excellence and Point Values," Baldridge Excellence Framework, January 2017, www.nist.gov/baldridge.

The ISO 9000 is a family of standards related to quality (ISO 9000, ISO 9001, ISO 9004, and ISO 19011). The ISO 9000 quality standards address what the company does to meet regulatory requirements and the customer's quality requirements while striving to improve customer satisfaction and continuous improvement. The standards represent an international consensus on quality management practices. ISO 9000:2015 (2015 is the most recent version) has been adopted as the quality standard in nearly 170 countries, meaning that companies have to follow the standards to conduct business in those countries. The quality management standards of the ISO 9000 are based on eight quality management principles, including customer focus, leadership, employee engagement, a process approach, a systems approach to management, continuous improvement, using facts to make decisions, and establishing mutually beneficial relationships with suppliers. ISO 9001:2008 is the most comprehensive standard because it provides a set of requirements for a quality management system for all organizations both private and public. The ISO 9001:2015 has been implemented by over 1 million organizations around the world. ISO 9004 provides a guide for companies that want to improve.

Why are standards useful? Customers may want to check that the product they ordered from a supplier meets the purpose for which it is required. One of the most efficient ways to do this is when the specifications of the product have been defined in an International Standard. That way, both supplier and customer are on the same wavelength, even if they are based in different countries, because they are both using the same references. Many products require testing for conformance with specifications or compliance with safety or other regulations before they can be put on many markets. In addition, national legislation may require such testing to be carried out by independent bodies, particularly when the products concerned have health or environmental implications. One example of an ISO standard is on the back cover of this book and nearly every other book. On the back cover is something called an ISBN. ISBN stands for International Standard Book Number. Publishers and booksellers are very familiar with ISBNs, because they are the method through which books are ordered and bought. Try buying a book on the Internet, and you will soon learn the value of the ISBN—there is a unique number for the book you want! And it is based on an ISO standard.

Six Sigma process
A system of measuring, analyzing, improving, and controlling processes once they meet quality standards.

Six Sigma In addition to competing for quality awards and seeking ISO certification, many companies are using the Six Sigma process and lean thinking. The **Six Sigma process** refers to a process of measuring, analyzing, improving, and then controlling processes once they have been brought within the narrow Six Sigma quality tolerances or standards. The objective of Six Sigma is to create a total business focus on serving the customer, that is, to deliver what customers really want when they want it. Six Sigma involves highly trained employees known as Champions, Master Black Belts, Black Belts, and Green Belts who lead and teach teams that are focusing on an ever-growing number of quality projects. The quality projects focus on improving efficiency and reducing errors in products and services. The Six Sigma quality initiative has produced more than $5 billion in benefits for General Electric. For example, introducing the Six Sigma quality initiative at GE meant going from approximately 35,000 defects per million operations—which is average for most companies, including GE—to fewer than four defects per million in every element of every process GE businesses perform—from manufacturing a locomotive part to servicing a jet engine, or reinventing radiation technology used in health care.[92]

Lean thinking
A way to do more with less effort, equipment space, and time, but still provide customers what they need and want.

Lean Thinking & Process Improvement. Training is an important component of quality programs because it teaches employees statistical process control and how to engage in "lean thinking." **Lean thinking** is a way to do more with less effort, time, equipment, and space, but still provide customers what they need and want. Part of lean thinking includes training workers in new skills or how to apply old skills in new ways so that they can quickly take over new responsibilities or use new skills to help fill customer orders. Baylor Health Care System wanted to decrease waste and improve patient satisfaction and outcomes through implementing lean thinking and process improvements in several of its hospitals.[93] This included training employees on how to make changes to work processes. Lean thinking and process improvement supported by training provided significant value. For example, the corporate supply management team eliminated two-thirds of the time required to complete contracts, developed a decision tree for different types of projects, and reduced errors, saving $10 million. A hospital readmission team redesigned the patient discharge process to reduce the chances of patients returning within 30 days. They realized a 44% decrease in readmissions over a six-month period, which improved the quality of life for patients and Baylor's ability to receive Medicare/ Medicaid payments from the government.

Table 1.10
Examples of HR Practices That Enhance Customer Service

Wegmans
Has given $100 million in scholarships to more than 32,000 employees. Senior managers sit side-by-side with employees, listening in on phones in the company's call center.

Asana
Gives employees a $10,000 allowance for computers and office décor, which employees can use to purchase mini-refrigerators, headphones, and ergonomic chairs. Asana also offers free yoga classes and in-house chefs prepare and serve three meals every day.

Google
Provides employees with food service, fitness centers, bicycle repairs, and napping pods.

Unilever
The Agile Working Program allows employees to work any hours, anywhere they want. Office cubicles have been replaced with collaborative work spaces with small, shared work pods. The new work areas are designed to provide a comfortable environment by including televisions, foosball tables, and treadmills.

Delaware North Companies
Uses tests that assess job candidates' personality and work styles to ensure they have the friendliness, curiosity, and ability to multitask, which customer service representatives need to help customers plan vacations.

Cadillac
Performance of repair technicians is carefully monitored to ensure they are not repeating mistakes in repairs. Dealers who maintain good customer service ratings based on customer surveys receive cash rewards.

Ricoh USA
Service employees participate in several training programs focused on communications skills and listening skills, telephone etiquette, and technical printing technologies. The programs are delivered via e-learning, face-to-face, and virtual instruction.

SOURCES: Based on Ricoh USA, Inc., "Services Team Annual Recognition Program," *Training*, January/February 2017, pp. 98–99; "Learn and Grow," www.wegmans.com, accessed March 1, 2017; www.asana.com, accessed Match 1, 2017; L. Weber, "To Get a Job, New Hires Are Put to the Test," *Wall Street Journal*, April 15, 2015, pp. A1, A10; R. Feintzeig, "Meet Silicon Valley's Little Elves," *Wall Street Journal*, November 21, 2014, pp. A1, A10; W. Bunch, "Unleashing the Workforce," *Human Resource Executive*, November 2012, pp. 14–17; J. McGregor, "Customer Service Champs," *BusinessWeek*, March 5, 2007, pp. 52–64.

In addition to developing products or providing services that meet customer needs, one of the most important ways to improve customer satisfaction is to improve the quality of employees' work experiences. Research shows that satisfied employees are more likely to provide high-quality customer service. Customers who receive high-quality service are more likely to be repeat customers. As Table 1.10 shows, companies that are recognized as providing elite customer service emphasize state-of-the-art HR practices, including rigorous employee selection, employee loyalty, training, and keeping employees satisfied by offering generous benefits.

Recognize and Capitalize on the Demographics and Diversity of the Workforce

A company's performance on the balanced scorecard is influenced by the characteristics of its labor force. The labor force of current employees is often referred to as the **internal labor force**. Employers identify and select new employees from the external labor market

Internal labor force
Labor force of current employees.

External labor market
Persons outside the firm who are actively seeking employment.

through recruiting and selection. The **external labor market** includes persons actively seeking employment. As a result, the skills and motivation of a company's internal labor force are influenced by the composition of the available labor market (the external labor market). The skills and motivation of a company's internal labor force determine the need for training and development practices and the effectiveness of the company's compensation and reward systems.

Important changes in the demographics and diversity of the workforce are projected. First, the average age of the workforce will increase. Second, the workforce will become more diverse in terms of gender, race, and generations. Third, immigration will continue to affect the size and diversity of the workforce.

Aging of the Workforce. The labor force will continue to age, and the proportion of workers age 55 and older will grow from 22% to 25% by 2024.[94] Figure 1.5 compares the distribution of the age of the workforce in 2014 to that projected for 2024. The labor force participation of those 55 years and older is expected to grow because older individuals are leading healthier and longer lives than in the past, providing the opportunity to work more years; the high cost of health insurance and decrease in health benefits causes many employees to keep working to keep their employer-based insurance or to return to work after retirement to obtain health insurance through their employer; and the trend toward pension plans based on individuals' contributions to them rather than years of service provides an incentive for older employees to continue working. The aging labor force means companies are likely to employ a growing share of older workers— many in their second or third career. Older people want to work, and many say they plan a working retirement. Despite myths to the contrary, worker performance and learning are not adversely affected by aging.[95] Older employees are willing and able to learn new technology. An emerging trend is for qualified older workers to ask to work part time or for only a few months at a time as a means to transition to retirement. Employees and companies are redefining the meaning of retirement to include second careers as well as part-time and temporary work assignments. An aging workforce means that employers will increasingly face HRM issues such as career plateauing, retirement planning, and retraining older workers to avoid skill obsolescence. Companies will struggle with how to control the rising costs of benefits and health care. Companies face competing challenges with older workers. Companies will have to ensure that older workers are not discriminated against in hiring, training, and workforce reduction decisions. At the same time, companies will want to encourage retirement and make it financially and psychologically acceptable.

Figure 1.5
Comparison of the Age Distribution of the 2014 and 2024 Labor Forces

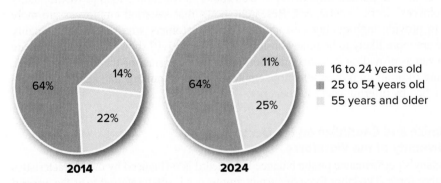

2014   2024

16 to 24 years old
25 to 54 years old
55 years and older

SOURCE: Bureau of Labor Statistics, "Employment Projections, 2014–2024," News Release, www.bls.gov, accessed February 9, 2017.

Many companies are offering special programs to capitalize on older employees' skills and accommodate their needs.[96] CVS/pharmacy has stores in every region of the United States. CVS created its Snowbirds Program to allow older employees to move among locations according to their preferences. This is especially important for older employees who spend winters in the southern states and summer in the northern states. Over 1,000 employees, including retail clerks, pharmacists, and managers, have participated in the program.

Scripps Health has equipped patient rooms with lifts to help all employees, but especially older workers, providing assistance to move patients from beds to wheelchairs, help them to sit up, and change their position in bed. The National Institutes of Health (NIH) has two phased-retirement programs that allow employees to choose to gradually transition to retirement by reducing hours or a trial-retirement program that allows retirees to return to work within one year of retiring in case they decide they aren't ready to leave the workforce. This helps ease their transition out of the job and workplace but provides them time to share their knowledge and help train other employees to take their jobs.

The Multigenerational Workforce. Because employees are working longer, the workforce now has five generations, each one with unique characteristics and characteristics similar to the others. Table 1.11 shows the year born, nicknames, and ages represented for each generation. Consider some of the attributes that are believed to characterize each generation.[97] For example, Generation Z, born after 1995, have started to graduate from college and are already part of the workforce. They are digital natives, more attached to mobile phones and tablets for learning and connecting with others than are Millennials. Generation Z may be more entrepreneurial than other generations and more interested in meaningful work than money. They likely lack basic job skills because they were unable to get jobs during the recession when they were teenagers. With Baby Boomers retiring, this generation will have many job and career opportunities. Generation Z wants a work environment in which they can get instant communications and access to answers.

Millennials grew up with diversity in their schools and were coached, praised, and encouraged for participation rather than accomplishment by their Baby Boomer parents. Millennials are characterized as being optimistic, willing to work and learn, eager to please, self-reliant, globally aware, and valuing of diversity and teamwork. They are also believed to have high levels of self-esteem. Millennials are a highly educated and technologically connected group who approach the workplace with the mentality, "What's in it for me?" They are the generation most likely to switch jobs and be on the lookout for new opportunities. Millennials want to understand how they fit in with their jobs, teams, and companies. They look for work that fuels their sense of purpose and makes them feel important. They do not feel close ties to their jobs or the brands to which they give their money.

YEAR BORN	GENERATION	AGES
1925–45	Traditionalists Silent Generation	>72
1946–64	Baby Boomers	53–72
1965–80	Generation X	37–52
1981–95	Millennials Generation Y Echo Boomers	22–36
1996	Generation Z	<21

Table 1.11
Generations in the Workforce

Generation Xers grew up during a time when the divorce rate doubled, the number of women working outside the home increased, and the personal computer was invented. They were often left on their own after school (latchkey kids). They value skepticism, informality, and practicality; seek work/life balance; and dislike close supervision. They tend to be impatient and cynical. They have experienced change all of their lives (in terms of parents, homes, and cities).

Baby Boomers, the "Me" generation, marched against the "establishment" for equal rights and an end to the Vietnam War. They value social conscientiousness and independence. They are competitive, hard working, and concerned with the fair treatment of all employees. They are often considered to be workaholics and rigid in conforming to rules. Traditionalists grew up during the Great Depression and lived during World War II. They tend to value frugality, are patriotic and loyal, adhere to rules, are loyal to employers, and take responsibility and sacrifice for the good of the company.

Members of each generation may have misperceptions of each other, causing tensions and misunderstanding in the workplace.[98] For example, Generation Xers who will be managing Generation Z employees may become irritated by having to answer Generation Z employees' questions about why they are expected to perform a job a certain way, and by their employees' preference for instant feedback and praise when they get work completed. Millennials may think Generation X managers are bitter, jaded, abrasive, uninterested in them, and poor delegators. In turn, their Generation X managers consider Millennials too needy for attention, demanding, and overly self-confident. Millennials might believe that Baby Boomers are too rigid and follow company rules too closely. They believe employees in the older generations have been too slow in adopting social media tools and overvalue tenure rather than knowledge and performance. Traditionalists and Baby Boomers believe that Millennials don't have a strong work ethic because they are too concerned with work/life balance. Also, members of the younger generations may resent Baby Boomers and Traditionalists who are working longer before retiring, blocking promotions and career moves.

Although generational differences likely exist, members of the same generation are no more alike than members of the same gender or race. This means that you should be cautious in attributing differences in employee behaviors and attitudes to generational differences or expecting all employees of a generation to have similar values. Research suggests that the generations of employees have similarities as well as differences.[99] Although differences in work ethic have been found among Baby Boomers, Generation Xers, and Millennials, Millennial employees are more similar than different from other generations in their work beliefs, job values, and gender beliefs. Most employees view work as a means to more fully use their skills and abilities, meet their interests, and allow them to live a desirable lifestyle. They also value work/life balance, meaning flexible work policies are necessary to allow them to choose where and when work is performed.

Consider how Coke gives Millennial employees a voice in shaping the business, which in turn helps engage and retain them.[100] Millennial Voices, an employee group, helps recruit and retain top talent by creating a more entrepreneurial culture. Millennial Voices has provided valuable insights about the business and consumers. For example, they have influenced new technology pilots and on-campus recycling initiatives, employee benefits packages, flexible work policies, and a reverse mentoring program.

A Workforce of Mixed Gender, Race, and Nationality.   As Figure 1.6 shows, by 2024 the workforce is expected to be 77% white, 13% African American, 6% Asian, and 4% other groups, which includes individuals of multiple racial origin, American Indian, Alaskan Native or Native Hawaiian, and other Pacific Islanders.[101] The diversity of the

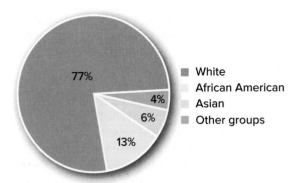

Figure 1.6
The U.S. Workforce,
2024

- White
- African American
- Asian
- Other groups

77%

4%

6%

13%

SOURCE: BUREAU of Labor Statistics, "Employment Projections, 2014–2024," News Release, www.bls.gov, accessed February 9, 2017.

workforce is expected to increase by 2024. As a result of different fertility rates and differences in immigration patterns, racial and ethnic groups will show different trends in labor force growth.

Immigration contributes to the diversity of the U.S. population and workforce. Many U.S. industries including high-technology, meatpacking, construction, farming, and service rely on immigrants to perform jobs requiring physical labor or skills not readily available in the U.S. workforce. Although a common belief is that most immigrants have rudimentary skills, the percentage of highly skilled immigrants now exceeds the percentage of low-skilled immigrants.

There is an ongoing debate in the U.S. government about the role of both legal and illegal immigration in terrorism and the reduction of job opportunities for U.S. citizens. Over 40 million people living in the United States were born in other countries, and approximately an equal number have a foreign-born parent. More than 1 million immigrants come to the United States each year, and 6 out of 10 are relatives of U.S. citizens.[102] Mexico, India, and China are the leading countries of birth for lawful permanent residents or "green card" recipients, who may live and work anywhere in the United States. Another 14% come on work-related visas, some of which are available only for workers with exceptional qualifications in science, business, or the arts. The U.S. government also provides temporary visas to a limited number of highly educated workers, allowing them to work in the country for a set period of time but not to remain as immigrants. Approximately 70,000 persons have been admitted to the United States each year since 2008 as refugees (persecuted persons) from countries including Iraq, Somalia, Bhutan, Burma, China, Egypt, and Syria. Once they pass screening and are resettled in the United States, they are eligible for employment.

One key question is what is the proper amount of legal immigration into the United States that is needed to meet our economic needs? One study suggests that immigrants have helped the U.S. economy over the long term and have had little impact on wages or employment levels of U.S.-born employees.[103] In recent years, Immigration and Customs Enforcement (ICE) has focused its efforts on auditing employers to ensure they are not employing undocumented immigrants. The focus on identifying and deporting illegal immigrants is likely to continue with the added involvement of state and local law enforcement.[104] Regardless, many companies would face severe hardship if they were forced to no longer rely on immigrants. A low unemployment rate means that many employers are struggling to fill both full-time and seasonal skilled and unskilled jobs.[105] For example, the King of Texas Roofing Company has turned down projects worth millions of dollars because it can't hired enough roofers, who come primarily from Mexico. Thousands of

Mexican workers and other immigrants are needed to pick citrus crops in Florida, work in restaurants such as Tacoliscious in San Francisco, and do landscaping in Colorado. Apple, Google, and other high-tech companies rely on the U.S. visa program to provide foreign employees with specialized skills needed to design software and new products, skills in short supply among U.S. workers.

The implications of the changing labor market for managing human resources are far-reaching. Managing diversity involves many different activities, including creating an organizational culture that values diversity, ensuring that HRM systems are bias-free, facilitating higher career involvement of women, promoting knowledge and acceptance of cultural differences, ensuring involvement in education both within and outside the company, and dealing with employees' resistance to diversity.[106] Table 1.12 presents ways that managing cultural diversity can provide a competitive advantage. How diversity issues are managed has implications for creativity, problem solving, retaining good employees, and developing markets for the firm's products and services. To successfully manage a diverse workforce, managers must develop a new set of skills, including the following:

1. Communicating effectively with employees from a variety of cultural backgrounds
2. Coaching and developing employees of different ages, educational backgrounds, ethnicities, physical abilities, and races
3. Providing performance feedback based on objective outcomes rather than values and stereotypes that work against women, minorities, and disabled persons by prejudging these persons' abilities and talents
4. Creating a work environment that makes it comfortable for employees of all backgrounds to be creative and innovative
5. Recognizing and responding to generational issues[107]

Diversity is important for tapping all employees' creative, cultural, and communication skills and using those skills to provide a competitive advantage as shown in Table 1.12.

Consider Microsoft's approach to diversity, which focuses on its employees, culture, suppliers, and customers.[108] To find the best and brightest employees, Microsoft has expanded the universities, conferences, and events from which it recruits new employees, to include the National Society of Black MBAs, the National Society of Hispanic MBAs, Out and Equal, and Recruit Military Expo. To support universities' and high schools' information technology curriculum and to develop opportunities for women and minorities, the company has formed partnerships with traditionally women's schools, historically black colleges and universities, and Hispanic-serving institutions. Also, through its DigiGirlz program and Blacks at Microsoft Minority Student Day, the company exposes diverse high school students to the high-tech work world. A diverse culture is supported several ways. Current employees can participate in resource groups including those for parents, Asians, Blacks, Hispanics and Latinos, women, the LBGTQ community, and the physically challenged. Training courses on topics such as managing diversity, how to build an inclusive culture, and understanding unconscious bias are available for all employees and managers. Microsoft offers flexible work policies to help employees balance work and life. These include resource and referral services as well as generous maternity and paternity leave policies. On the customer side, Microsoft has spent more than $2 billion with suppliers that are minority, women, or veteran owned, or owned by persons with disabilities. Also, Microsoft is developing technology that contributes to diversity by removing barriers between people. For example, the Kinect Sign Language Translator eliminates communication barriers by enabling speech–to–sign language translation.

The bottom line is that to gain a competitive advantage, companies must harness the power of the diverse workforce. These practices are needed not only to meet employee

1. Cost argument	As organizations become more diverse, the cost of a poor job in integrating workers will increase. Those who handle this well will thus create cost advantages over those who don't.
2. Employee attraction and retention argument	Companies develop reputations on favorability as prospective employers for women and ethnic minorities. Those with the best reputations for managing diversity will win the competition for talent. As the labor pool shrinks and changes composition, this edge will become increasingly important.
3. Marketing argument	The insight and cultural sensitivity that diverse employees bring to the marketing effort should help the company enter new markets and develop products and services for diverse populations.
4. Creativity argument	Diversity of perspectives and less emphasis on conformity to norms of the past improves the level of creativity.
5. Problem-solving argument	Heterogeneity in decisions and problem-solving groups potentially produces better decisions through a wider range of perspectives and more thorough critical analysis of issues.
6. System flexibility argument	Greater flexibility to react to changes in customer preferences and tastes (i.e., reactions should be faster and cost less).

Table 1.12
How Managing Cultural Diversity Can Provide a Competitive Advantage

SOURCES: A. C. Homan, C. Buengeler, R. A. Eckhoff, W. P. van Ginkel, and S. C. Voelpel. "The Interplay of Diversity Training and Diversity Beliefs on Team Creativity in Nationality Diverse Teams," *Journal of Applied Psychology* 100 (2015), pp. 1456–67; M. E. Mor Barak, *Managing Diversity: Toward a Globally Inclusive Workplace*, 3rd ed. (Thousand Oaks, CA: Sage, 2013); T. H. Cox and S. Blake, "Managing Cultural Diversity: Implications for Organizational Competitiveness," *Academy of Management Executive*, 5 (1991), pp. 45–56; N. Lockwood, *Workplace Diversity: Leveraging the Power of Difference for Competitive Advantage* (Alexandria, VA: Society for Human Resource Management, 2005).

needs but also to reduce turnover costs and ensure that customers receive the best service possible. The implication of diversity for HR practices will be highlighted throughout this book. For example, from a staffing perspective, it is important to ensure that tests used to select employees are not biased against minority groups. From a work design perspective, employees need flexible schedules that allow them to meet nonwork needs. From a training perspective, it is clear that all employees need to be made aware of the potential damaging effects of stereotypes. From a compensation perspective, new benefits such as elder care and day care need to be included in reward systems to accommodate the needs of a diverse workforce.

EVIDENCE-BASED HR

Rohini Anand, global chief diversity officer at Sodexo, a food services and facilities management company, collected, analyzed, and shared data showing the value of her work. She conducted a study of the company's 50,000 managers showing that gender balance on teams significantly related to improved financial performance, employee engagement, and client retention. She found that teams with a male–female ratio of between 40% and 60% delivered the best results. As a result of Anand's study, Sodexo's CEO has set a goal that by 2025 at least 40% of Sodexo's 1,400 senior leaders will be women (a total of 560 women leaders). To ensure that goal is reached, 10% of senior leaders' bonuses are based on their yearly progress toward that goal.

SOURCE: Based on J. Simons, "Workplace Diversity Efforts Get a Reboot," *Wall Street Journal,* February 15, 2017, p. B5.

Consider Legal and Ethical Issues

Legal Issues. There will likely be development and debate of new and current employment laws and regulations, as well as increased emphasis on enforcing specific aspects of current laws and regulations such as those related to immigrant employment.[109] There are likely to be more challenges of sex and race discrimination because of lack of access to training and development opportunities that are needed for promotions to better-paying jobs or higher-level management positions. Eliminating discrimination against veterans and people with disabilities, especially among federal contractors, is likely. This is especially likely due to the expanded definition of disability under the Americans with Disabilities Act to include cancer, diabetes, epilepsy, and intellectual disabilities.

As a result of the growing gig economy, more legal challenges related to whether workers are misclassified as independent contractors rather than full-time employees (who are eligible for overtime pay, unemployment, and worker's compensation) are likely. Such a case was brought against ride-sharing services Uber and Lyft in California and Massachusetts and settled out of court, but cases in other states are likely.[110] However, given the current political environment, it is also possible that government regulations might loosen the distinction between full-time employment and independent contractors, creating a middle ground that could, for example, allow companies to contribute to employees' health care costs without having to pay for overtime.

Universal health care coverage will continue to be debated in Congress. The plan they decide on will affect the availability of health care for employees, the conditions and dependents that will be covered, and out-of-pocket charges and employer costs. Regardless, in their efforts to reduce employee health care insurance costs, companies will continue to offer incentives for employees to participate in wellness programs and providing penalties if they do not. Wellness programs typically include smoking cessation, exercise, dieting, and submitting to biometric screening tests (e.g., blood tests) to detect illness or risk of illness such as heart attacks. However, wellness programs are coming under scrutiny. The Equal Employment Opportunity Commission has issued preliminary rules about when the penalties or rewards related to participating in wellness programs are too extreme and may violate the Americans with Disabilities Act.

Under the Trump administration, immigration will come under increased scrutiny, to protect both national security and American jobs. Scrutiny of companies that employ unlawful immigrants or abuse laborers will face significant penalties. Companies can face criminal charges if immigration and customs officials can show that they knowingly employed undocumented and illegal immigrants. The number of company audits conducted by ICE has increased over the past several years, resulting in over $10 million in fines.

The number of workers eligible to enter the United States under different visa programs may be reconsidered, and employers may have to pay a fine or tariff for employing foreign workers. Bans on immigration from countries suspected of harboring terrorists are possible. Legislation affecting immigration will be fiercely debated because of its potential impact on business and the diversity of the United Sates. For example, leaders in many companies, but especially those in technology industries such as Apple, Microsoft, and Facebook, have been the most vocal to criticize legislation intended to reduce the possibility of terrorist attacks by banning people from seven Muslim-majority countries (Iran, Iraq, Libya, Somalia, Sudan, Syria, and Yemen) from entering the United States.[111] Their criticisms are based on their personal perspective, business needs, and business values. The leaders personally believe that immigration has always played and will continue to play an important role in the United States. Many businesses, even those not necessarily in the technology industry, need skilled foreign talent to fill engineering roles, help design innovative products and services, and create new business start-ups. Finally, most companies, such as Coca-Cola and Ford Motors, have core values that include respect for all people and commitment to diversity and inclusion which run counter to the ban.

The publication of classified documents by WikiLeaks, Wall Street insider trading probes, and data breaches of employee data have resulted in companies more carefully scrutinizing data-security practices and increased concerns about protecting intellectual property. For example, a Boeing employee who could not format a spreadsheet sent it to his spouse for help, causing a security breach that could have exposed ID numbers, accounting codes, and Social Security numbers for 36,000 employees.[112] Data-security concerns will likely influence HR practices related to performance management such as the use of electronic monitoring and surveillance of knowledge workers. We may see more litigation related to employee privacy rights and intellectual property rights as a result of companies terminating employees or taking disciplinary action against them for data-security breaches, discussing employment practices using social media, or sharing or stealing intellectual property for personal gain. Also, issues regarding the confidentiality and security of employees' health care information will receive more attention as companies provide employees with wearables (such as Fitbits) and apps as part of wellness initiatives to track what they eat and drink, their heart rate, and physical activity. Employers who provide employees with wearables as part of wellness programs are not allowed by health privacy laws to view any single employee's health statistics.

Ethical Issues. Many organizations have engaged in serious ethical misconduct, including General Motors (failure to fix and notify customers about faulty ignition switches), the U.S. Department of Veterans Affairs (concealed patient wait times), the U.S. Secret Service (security breaches involving partying and prostitutes), and Takata (installed faulty airbags). Many decisions related to managing human resources are characterized by uncertainty. **Ethics** can be considered the fundamental principles of right and wrong by which employees and companies interact.[113] These principles should be considered in making business decisions and interacting with clients and customers. Ethical, successful companies can be characterized by four principles shown in Figure 1.7.[114] First, in their relationships with customers, vendors, and clients, these companies emphasize mutual benefits. Second, employees assume responsibility for the actions of the company. Third, such companies have a sense of purpose or vision that employees value and use in their day-to-day work. Finally, they emphasize fairness; that is, another person's interests count as much as their own. HR and business decisions should be ethical, but that is not always the case. A recent survey of employees found that 41% had witnessed some form of unethical conduct at their workplace.[115] This probably helps explain public perception of business ethics: 32% rated business executives' honesty and ethics standards as low or very low.[116] It is important to note that *ethics* refers to behavior that is not clearly right or wrong. *Compliance* means that the company is not violating legal regulations. But a company can be compliant and still have employees engaging in unethical practices.

The **Sarbanes-Oxley Act of 2002** sets strict rules for corporate behavior and sets heavy fines and prison terms for noncompliance: Organizations are spending millions of dollars each year to comply with regulations under the Sarbanes-Oxley Act, which imposes criminal penalties for corporate governing and accounting lapses, including retaliation against whistle-blowers who report violations of Securities and Exchange Commission (SEC) rules.[117] These Due to Sarbanes-Oxley and SEC regulations that impose stricter standards for disclosing executive pay, corporate boards are paying more attention to executive pay

Ethics
The fundamental principles of right and wrong by which employees and companies interact.

Sarbanes-Oxley Act of 2002
A congressional act passed in response to illegal and unethical behavior by managers and executives. The act sets stricter rules for business, especially related to accounting practices—including requiring more open and consistent disclosure of financial data and the CEO's assurance that the data are completely accurate—and provisions that affect the employee–employer relationship (e.g., development of a code of conduct for senior financial officers).

Figure 1.7

Principles of Ethical Companies

as well as issues such as leadership development and succession planning.[118] This has resulted in an increase in the number of HR executives and individuals with HR expertise who are being asked to serve on corporate boards to provide data and analysis. For example, a CEO or chief financial officer (CFO) who falsely represents company finances may be fined up to $1 million and/or imprisoned for up to 10 years. The penalty for willful violations is up to $5 million and/or 20 years of imprisonment. Sarbanes-Oxley requires CEOs and CFOs to certify corporate financial reports, prohibits personal loans to officers and directors, and prohibits insider trading during pension fund blackout periods.[119] A "blackout" is any period of more than three consecutive business days during which the company temporarily stops 50% or more of company plan participants or beneficiaries from acquiring, selling, or transferring an interest in any of the company's equity securities in the pension plan. The law also requires retention of all documents relevant to a government investigation. Because of the burden it places on companies the Sarbanes-Oxley Act will be carefully scrutinized, and perhaps changed by Congress or President Trump.

Sarbanes-Oxley has a number of provisions that directly affect the employer–employee relationship.[120] Whistleblowers are individuals who have turned in the company or one or more of its officers for an illegal act. The act prohibits retaliation against whistle-blowers and government informants. The act also requires that publicly traded companies disclose whether they have a code of ethics.[121] Other federal guidelines such as the Federal Acquisition Regulation also require or provide incentives to encourage all businesses to adopt codes of conduct, train employees on these codes, and create effective ways to audit and report ethical and unethical behavior. This means that companies, with human resources taking the lead, should develop codes of conduct that clearly define ethics and professional responsibility. HR professionals, along with other top-level managers, usually play a key role in helping conduct ethics audits, develop ethical codes of conduct, and respond to ethics violations. Guidelines for disciplinary actions for employees guilty of unethical behavior and conduct need to be developed. Managers and employees will need to be trained on ethics policies to ensure that business processes and procedures are correctly followed. HR professionals will need to document the fact that employees have received these policies and have attended training to ensure their compliance with the law. Because of the potential liability for retaliation in the context of discrimination and harassment, policies should include assurances that an employee will not be retaliated against for making a complaint or for serving as a witness. Executive compensation programs will need to be monitored to ensure that the program is in compliance with provisions related to personal loans and the sale of pension funds during blackout periods.

Consider the policies and practices that companies are using to help ensure an ethical workplace.[122] Dimension Data's employees participate in a half-day ethics program discussing how they would respond to different ethical dilemmas that occur at work. Southern Company invited a convicted felon to speak to employees about how a good person can violate ethics. Before his conviction, which resulted in a five-year prison term, the felon was CFO for a health care company. Eaton Corporation includes its ethics principles on its website. Examples of the company's principles include obeying the law, avoiding conflicts of interest, acting with integrity, protecting assets and information, and respecting human rights. Eaton Corporation's employees receive regular training on how to apply ethical principles to their daily work. The Global Ethics and Compliance Office provides ethics training programs and communications designed to ensure that Eaton's ethics and values are integrated into its business practices on a consistent basis around the world. Xerox conducts regular ethics surveys, which ask employees if they have experienced an ethics violation. To receive promotions, managers are expected to take an active role in supporting Xerox's ethics strategy. Managers review their previous year's performance, create action plans as to how they plan to improve the ethics policy (such as with more training or better communications), and are expected to chair their local ethics committee. All employees are encouraged to report ethics violations or questions to the ethics office; they can do so face-to-face, using an ethics hotline, or by sending them to an e-mail address. Xerox's high ethical standards have won it recognition as one of the world's most ethical companies. This has helped Xerox to recruit high-quality employees, especially in global locations where business decisions are not transparent to employees and ethics are frequently violated.

Human resource managers must satisfy three basic standards for their practices to be considered ethical.[123] First, HRM practices must result in the greatest good for the largest number of people. Second, employment practices must respect basic human rights of privacy, due process, consent, and free speech. Third, managers must treat employees and customers equitably and fairly.

To call attention to the important role of ethics in the workplace, throughout the book we include "Integrity in Action" boxes that highlight the good (and bad) decisions related to ethical HR practices made by company leaders and managers. The "Integrity in Action" box in this chapter shows how the chief human capital officer at Amtrak changed the HR function and helped revitalize the business.

COMPETING THROUGH GLOBALIZATION

Companies are finding that to survive they must compete in international markets as well as fend off foreign corporations' attempts to gain ground in the United States. To meet these challenges, U.S. businesses must develop global markets, use their practices to improve global competitiveness, and better prepare employees for global assignments.

Every business must be prepared to deal with the global economy. Global business expansion has been made easier by technology. The Internet allows data and information to be instantly accessible and sent around the world. The Internet, e-mail, social networking, and video conferencing enable business deals to be completed between companies thousands of miles apart.

LO 1-4
Discuss what companies should do to compete in the global marketplace.

INTEGRITY IN ACTION

HR is Not Just a Back-Office Function

Barry Melnkovic became Amtrak's first-ever chief human capital officer in 2016. His challenge was to energize and reshape an HR function that was broken. Human resources at Amtrak was primarily transactional, was reactive rather than proactive, lacked incentives to attract top talent, and had very costly employee benefits. Multiple audits had found major deficiencies in HR structure, programs, and processes.

Melnkovic didn't just come up with his own solutions and try to implement them. He spent hours and days traveling on trains discussing with employees and customers their experiences with Amtrak, asking for ideas about how Amtrak could improve, and familiarizing himself with the numerous jobs necessary for trains to run on time and safely (by doing some of them himself). His vision was to implement a Human Capital Strategic Plan. To do so he traveled to host meetings with Amtrak board members, managers, and employees to describe and educate others about his plan and get their input. His ideas included making sure human resources was involved in strategy development and execution, creating a more results-driven culture, and redoing Amtrak's rewards structure.

Many observers were skeptical that Melnkovic could bring about much-needed changes. Within the HR function, he made the tough decision to replace HR team members with others who were more "bottom-line focused" and were motivated to make a difference. He created a new role to focus specifically on human capital issues such as performance management and succession planning. He created a team—including himself, the CEO, and leaders from operations, information technology, marketing, and sales—to apply lean and Six Sigma techniques to spark continuous improvement in the company. This resulted in reducing the time to fill vacant positions and speeding up processes through which employees file for family and medical leave. Also, the HR function became the only department at Amtrak to receive ISO certification. Melnkovic also created a learning council with company leaders that helped design a customer experience training program designed to improve Amtrak's customers' experience. Finally, he worked with his HR team to change compensation and benefits. He introduced incentives for nonunion employees based on their performance as well as yearly awards to recognize individual and team achievements. Previously, company and individual performance were not considered in annual wage increases. He changed pension and retiree health plans that will save Amtrak more than $1.4 billion over 20 years. These changes were not popular with employees, but to help alleviate concerns, Melnkovic visited numerous Amtrak locations to explain the changes, listen to employees, and answer questions. He followed up his visits with webinars, notes to employees, and other corporate communications.

DISCUSSION QUESTIONS

1. What competencies and behaviors shown in Figure 1.3 were most important for Melnkovic's success in rebuilding human resources and providing value to Amtrak's business?
2. How did he build credibility and demonstrate integrity? Explain your answer.

SOURCE: Based on M. McGraw, "Back on Track," *Human Resource Executive,* October 2016, 14–16, www.careers.amtrak.com, accessed March 1, 2017.

Globalization is not limited to any particular sector of the economy, product market, or company size.[124] Companies without international operations may buy or use goods that have been produced overseas, hire employees with diverse backgrounds, or compete with foreign-owned companies operating within the United States.

Businesses around the world are attempting to increase their competitiveness and value by increasing their global presence, often through mergers and acquisitions.

Entering International Markets

Many companies are entering international markets by exporting their products overseas, building manufacturing facilities or service centers in other countries, entering into alliances with foreign companies, and engaging in e-commerce. One estimate is that developing economies and emerging markets such as those found in the BRIC nations (Brazil, Russia, India, and China) are responsible for 19% of the world's economy.[125] Other countries such as Indonesia, Malaysia, Kenya, Colombia, and Poland have a growing middle class, strong infrastructure, business-friendly regulations, and stable governments and are likely new emerging markets. The importance of globalization is seen in recent hiring patterns of large U.S. multinational corporations that have increased their overseas workforces, particularly in Asia.[126] China is the world's largest auto market, with over 21 million cars sold in 2015. German brands Audi, BMW, and Mercedes-Benz are the top-selling luxury brands in China, but U.S. automakers are trying to take away some of their market share.[127] Ford Motor's Lincoln brand opened 3 showrooms in China in 2014, and by the end of 2016 they planned to have 60. Lincoln discovered that the customer focus was lacking in the Chinese market. So they hired Mandarin Oriental staff to train showroom salespeople in customer service. General Motors opened a Cadillac factory in Shanghai, its first plant built to support the brand in China. The plant can produce over 150,000 Cadillacs each year, including a sedan that it plans to export to the United States. General Motors anticipates that luxury car sales could reach 3.5 million vehicles each year by 2020, making China one of the world's largest market for luxury cars. Yum! Brands, parent company of KFC, Pizza Hut, and Taco Bell, has over 7,000 stores in China. Globally, Yum! Brands opened over 2,000 restaurants in 2016, with 600 of those in China, contributing over 50% of the company's profits.

Global companies are struggling to find and retain talented employees, especially in emerging markets. Companies are moving into China, India, eastern Europe, the Middle East, Southeast Asia, and Latin America, but the demand for talented employees exceeds supply. Also, companies often place successful U.S. managers in charge of overseas operations, but these managers lack the cultural understanding necessary to attract, motivate, and retain talented employees. To cope with these problems, companies are taking actions to better prepare their managers and their families for overseas assignments and to ensure that training and development opportunities are available for global employees. Cross-cultural training prepares employees and their families to understand the culture and norms of the country they are being relocated to and to return to their home country after the assignment. Cross-cultural training is discussed in Chapter 7. For example, McDonald's has designated Russia as its high-growth market, with more than a dozen restaurants in Siberian towns and plans to open more.[128] When a new McDonald's opened in Tomsk, it served 6,000 customers in the first day of operations. McDonald's global sales in 2016 were the strongest in five years, while the U.S. market was struggling. To train future managers in store operations, leadership, and staff management skills needed for global expansion to be successful, McDonald's has seven Hamburger Universities in the United States and abroad, including campuses in Oak Brook, Illinois; Sydney; Munich; London; Tokyo; São Paulo; and Shanghai. All provide training materials and tools in different languages and cultures.

To successfully compete with its Indian rival, Ola, Uber is challenged to recruit and train a million new drivers in India, where most people have never driven or own a car, and few potential drivers understand English or how to use an app.[129] The stakes are huge given the market size: India has 1.2 billion people. Uber has recruited Indians driving taxis, buses, and rickshaws; private drivers working for companies and families; and individuals who have never driven before. To be successful in India, Uber has to teach new drivers how to speak politely, dress well, and follow traffic rules. They have to check to ensure recruits have necessary licenses and other documents, teach them how to use the Uber app, and learn about online banking so that they can see if they have been paid. Uber also helps drivers lease automobiles. Uber currently has 400,000 drivers, but it wants to add 1 million in the next two years.

IBM obtains more than two-thirds of its revenue from outside the United States and is seeking to build team leadership in order to compete in emerging markets around the world. IBM's Corporate Service Program has donated the time and service of about 600 employees for over 1,000 projects in countries such as Turkey, Romania, Ghana, Vietnam, the Philippines, and Tanzania.[130] The goal of the program is to develop a leadership team that learns about the needs and culture of these countries while providing valuable community service. For example, eight IBM employees from five countries traveled to Timisoara, Romania. Each employee was assigned to help a different company or nonprofit organization. One software-development manager helped GreenForest, a manufacturer of office, hotel, school, and industrial furniture, reach its goal of cutting costs and becoming more efficient by recommending computer equipment and systems needed to increase production and exports to western Europe. Another employee worked with a nonprofit organization that offers services to disabled adults. Besides benefiting the companies, the employees have also found that the experience has helped them understand cultural differences, improve their communication and teamwork skills, and gain insights on global marketing and strategy. The "Competing through Globalization" box shows how several global companies are preparing employees for global assignments.

Offshoring and Reshoring

Offshoring
A special case of outsourcing, in which the jobs that move leave one country and go to another.

Offshoring refers to the exporting of jobs from developed countries, such as the United States, to countries where labor and other costs are lower. India, Canada, China, Russia, Ireland, Mexico, Brazil, and the Philippines are some of the destination countries for offshored jobs. Why are jobs offshored?[131] The reasons given for offshoring factory and other jobs often include lower labor costs and the availability of a skilled workforce with a strong work ethic. For example, Rexnord Corporation plans to close its industrial bearings factory in Indiana and move the jobs to Mexico in order to save $30 million annually.[132] Rexford still employs more than half of the company's workforce in the United States and has operations in Europe, Asia, and Africa.

Reshoring
Moving jobs from overseas to the United States.

However, rather than offshoring work, **reshoring**, or the return of jobs to the United States, is becoming more common. There are several reasons for this, including higher product shipping costs, fear of supply chain disruptions due to natural disasters and political instability, quality concerns, and customer preference for U.S.-made products.[133] Also, rising labor costs in some countries, such as China, are becoming more comparable to those in the United States. Finally, some countries' local standards for safety, health, and working conditions may be substantially lower than those in the United States, resulting in negative publicity and turning off potential customers. For example, Hanesbrands has added workers to a plant in North Carolina.[134] Socks are knitted there and then sent to a plant in El Salvador that sews, dyes, and packages the socks. Although El Salvador has the advantage on labor costs, electricity costs in North Carolina are much lower. Also, having plants in both places provides a backup in case of problems. Peds Legwear also makes socks in North Carolina, allowing the company to avoid import taxes, cut shipping costs, and respond faster to shifts in demand. Plus, selling socks made in the United States was a major reason Walmart contracted with the company.

Effectiveness in Global Business Requires More Than Just a First-Class Ticket

For companies that conduct business around the world, employees need to go beyond just understanding cultural differences. Employees have to adapt and adjust their behavior to effectively work and live in the host culture. This means that employees and their families need to be prepared for international assignments. Iberdrola USA, a global company with 5,000 U.S. employees, is in the electricity transmission and generation business. Iberdrola sends U.S. employees to work at its locations in Mexico, Scotland, Brazil, and Britain and other European Union countries. Also, it brings employees to the United States to work for two to three years.

To prepare employees for international assignments, Iberdrola pays training consultants $1,500 to $3,000 per day to teach employees language and cultural basics, such as understanding preferences for personal space. The company also

has an exchange program in which children of U.S. employees temporarily stay with host families overseas and vice versa.

At Boeing, the aerospace company with employees in 28 countries, employees and their families going on an international assignment are provided with one-on-one cultural sensitivity training and orientation. Boeing also provides "lunch and learn" cultural talks and rotation programs that allow overseas staff to work up to nine months in the United States.

For companies with a global presence, developing global leaders who can be effective with employees from different cultures and countries is essential to their success. Qualcomm, the semiconductor and telecommunications company, helps leaders prepare for global assignment by matching them with a mentor who has expertise about the country where the job is located. L'Oreal, known for its cosmetics,

asks its leaders to complete a cultural assessment that gives them information about how their leadership style would be seen in different countries. L'Oreal uses this assessment to provide experiential-based learning, such as overseas assignments and serving on a project team including members from around the world.

DISCUSSION QUESTIONS

1. What should be included in programs designed to prepare employees for global assignments?
2. Would this preparation differ for business leaders? Explain.
3. Why is it important for employees' families to receive training, too?

SOURCE: Based on B. Hassell, "Are You Developing Global Leaders?" *Chief Learning Officer*, August 2016, 26–31, 52; A. Whyte, "How to Develop Global Leaders Early," *Chief Learning Officer*, August 2015, 38–41, 47; R. Chebium, "A Common Language: Training across Borders," *HR Magazine*, January/February 2015, pp. 52–58.

COMPETING THROUGH TECHNOLOGY

Technology has reshaped the way we play, shop, communicate, and plan our lives, and where we work. Consider these statistics: Roughly 84% of U.S. households have a computer (desktop, laptop, tablet, or smartphone) and 75% have Internet access. Some 60% visit Google during the week, and 43% have a Facebook page.[135] Most of us (especially Americans) are so attached to our smartphones for access to apps, social media, and the Internet that the devices are with us day and night: 41% check their phone a few times each hour, and 40% report they would feel significant anxiety if their smartphone went missing for a day. Using Facebook, Twitter, LinkedIn, and other social networking tools available on the Internet accessed through smartphones, notebooks, or personal computers, companies can connect with job candidates and employers can connect with friends, family, and co-workers.

Consider Applications of Social Networking, Artificial Intelligence, and Robotics

LO 1-5
Identify how social networking, artificial intelligence, and robotics is influencing human resource management.

Advances in sophisticated technology along with reduced costs for the technology are changing many aspects of human resource management. Specifically, companies are using or considering using social networking, artificial intelligence, and robotics.

Social networking
Websites and blogs that facilitate interactions between people.

Social Networking. Technological advances in electronics and communications software have made possible mobile technology such as personal digital assistants (PDAs), iPads, and iPods and enhanced the Internet by developing enhanced capability for social networking. **Social networking** refers to websites such as Facebook, Twitter, and LinkedIn, and wikis and blogs that facilitate interactions between people usually around shared interests. Table 1.13 shows some of the potential issues that can be addressed by using social networking.[136] In general, social networking facilitates communication, decentralized decision making, and collaboration. Social networking can be useful for connecting to customers and valuable for busy employees to share knowledge and ideas with their peers and managers with whom they may not have much time to interact face-to-face on a daily basis. Employees, especially young Millennial or Generation Y workers, have used social networking tools for much of their lives and see them as valuable tools for both their work and nonwork lives.

Despite the potential advantages of social networking, many companies are uncertain whether they should embrace it.[137] They fear that social networking will result in employees wasting time or offending or harassing their co-workers. Other companies believe that the benefits of using social networking for HR practices and allowing employees to access social networks at work outweigh the risks. They trust employees to use social networking productively and are proactive in developing policies about personal use and training employees about privacy settings and social network etiquette. They realize that employees will likely check their Twitter, Facebook, or LinkedIn accounts but ignore it

Table 1.13
Potential Uses of Social Networking

ISSUES	USE
Loss of expert knowledge due to retirement	Knowledge sharing, capturing, and storing
Employee engagement	Collect employees' opinions, chat with employees
Identify and promote employee expertise	Create online expert communities
Promote innovation and creativity	Encourage participation in online discussions
Reinforce learning	Share best practices, applications, learning, points, links to articles and webinars
Employees need coaching and mentoring	Interact with mentors and coaching peers
Need to identify and connect with promising job candidates	Share job openings, respond to candidates' questions, cultivate a pool of potential employees

SOURCES: Based on L. McFarland and R. Ployhart, "Social Media: A Contextual Framework to Guide Research and Practice," *Journal of Applied Psychology* 100 (2015), pp. 1653–77; D. Robb, "Cultivating Connections," *HR Magazine*, September 2014, pp. 65–66; M. McGraw, "Managing the Message," *Human Resource Executive*, December 2014, pp. 16–18; P. Brotherson, "Social Networks Enhance Employee Learning," *T + D*, April 2011, pp. 18–19; M. Derven, "Social Networking: A Frame for Development," *T + D*, July 2009, pp. 58–63; M. Weinstein, "Are You Linked In?" *Training*, September/October, 2010, pp. 30–33.

unless it is interfering with completing their work. In some ways, social networking has become the electronic substitute for daydreaming at one's desk or walking to the break room to socialize with co-workers.

Artificial Intelligence & Robotics. Artificial intelligence, robotics, tracking systems, radio frequency identification, and nanotechnology are transforming work.[138] Technology has also made it easier to monitor environmental conditions and employees and operate equipment. Driverless cars, self-driving trucks at iron ore mines that need no human operators, and computers that perform legal research are recent advances in automation.

Artificial intelligence is a technology that simulates human thinking It works through queries that allow it to learn from data over time so that it can identify trends and patterns that influence future searches and suggestions. Artificial intelligence is in use at home and in the workplace.[139] Artificial intelligence has provided us with personal assistants such as Apple's Siri or Amazon's Alexa that we can give orders to, such as to make a purchase or play your favorite music. In the workplace, IBM has teamed up its artificial intelligence (called Watson) with H&R Block to help clients prepare their tax returns and maximize their tax refunds. Watson has also been used in health care to provide cancer diagnoses, the law profession to conduct legal research, and in service industries to answer customers' questions.

Artificial intelligence
Technology that can think like a human

Robots are being used in service in manufacturing.[140] Heasy, a robot with eyes, can help you find your way through a hotel or resort. Airport Guide Robot can answer airline passengers' questions in English, Chinese, Japanese, and Korean; scan a ticket; and give directions. Robots at Whirpool's dryer factory snap pictures to scan defects. At BMW's auto plant they help install doors and windshields. On the shop floor, robots can work alongside employees, freeing them from having to perform repetitive, physically demanding tasks so that they can perform more important and knowledge-intensive work. Robots can help companies save money because they can work more efficiently and lower labor costs, but they still can't perform many important tasks. For example, unlike humans, robots have been unable to make the distinctions between fabric types and weights and irregular clothes sizes that are needed to neatly fold clothes.

Wearables are just beginning to be developed and used for training and performance support solutions. Wearable Intelligence provides smart eyewear technology and camera technology that gives employees hands-free, voice-activated access to procedures and checklists and live access to experts using tablet computers. These technologies allow data and live video sharing, the opportunity to review best-practice videos before or during the performance of complex procedures and operations, and real-time notifications and alerts.[141] For example, an operator who might be working on a remote oil rig or a surgeon in a sterile operating room can share live video with experts and get their advice needed to fix a broken valve or complete a medical procedure, while remaining focused on the equipment or patient. To understand whether personal interactions between employees made a difference, Bank of America asked call center employees to wear badges that contained sensors to record their movements and tone of their conversations.[142] The data showed that the most productive employees belonged to cohesive teams and they spoke frequently to their peers. To get employees to interact more, the bank scheduled employees for group breaks. Productivity increased more than 10% as a result.

Use HRIS, Mobile Devices, Cloud Computing, and HR Dashboards

Companies continue to use human resource information systems to store large quantities of employee data including personal information, training records, skills, compensation

Human resource information system (HRIS)
A system used to acquire, store, manipulate, analyze, retrieve, and distribute information related to human resources.

Mobile devices
Equipment such as smartphones and tablet computers that provide employees with any-time, anywhere access to HR applications and other work-related information.

Cloud computing
A computing system that provides information technology infrastructure over a network in a self-service, modifiable, and on-demand model.

HR dashboard
HR metrics such as productivity and absenteeism that are accessible by employees and managers through the company intranet or human resource information system.

rates, absence records, and benefits usages and costs. A **human resource information system (HRIS)** is a computer system used to acquire, store, retrieve, and distribute information related to a company's human resources.[143] An HRIS can support strategic decision making, help the company avoid lawsuits, provide data for evaluating policies and programs, and support day-to-day HR decisions. Hilton Worldwide is giving managers access to talent data so that they can integrate it with business data to make more effective and strategic decisions about talent and performance.[144] This allows managers to perform workforce planning by seeing the gaps between workforce projections and available supply of staff or projected turnover and modeling different scenarios.

Mobile devices refer to smartphones and tablet computers. Mobile devices are increasingly being used to provide employees with anytime and anywhere access to HR applications and other work-related information. For example, at Rackspace, employees can use their devices to check their pay stubs, bonus reports, and time cards, and share knowledge.[145] At Biogen, salespersons can access e-learning modules on their tablets. PepsiCo has a mobile-accessible career site. In the first year of using the recruitment app, the company found 150 job candidates who started an employment application each month. The "Competing through Technology" box shows how Verizon is using social networking tools and mobile devices to support its products and provide customer service through employee training, collaboration, and performance support.

"Cloud computing" allows companies to lease software and hardware and employees don't even know the location of the computers, databases, and applications they are using (they are in the "cloud"). **Cloud computing** refers to a computing system that provides information technology infrastructure over a network in a self-service, modifiable, and on-demand model.[146] In fact, many companies have moved their HRIS to the cloud or are considering doing so in the next few years.[147] Clouds can be delivered on-demand via the Internet (public cloud) or restricted to use by a single company (private cloud). Cloud computing gives companies and their employees access to applications and information from mobile devices rather than relying solely on personal computers. It also allows groups to work together in new ways, can make employees more productive by allowing them to more easily share documents and information, and provides greater access to large company databases. This means that tools for conducting workforce analytics using metrics on turnover, absenteeism, and performance, as well as social media and collaboration tools such as Twitter, blogs, Google documents, and YouTube videos will be more easily accessible and available for use. Cloud computing also can make it easier for employees to access training programs from a variety of vendors and educational institutions. Siemens has a cloud computing system for its more than 400,000 employees who work in 190 countries. This allowed Siemens to standardize its global recruitment and development processes into a single system using the cloud.[148]

More sophisticated systems extend management applications to decision making in areas such as compensation and performance management. Managers can schedule job interviews or performance appraisals, guided by the system to provide the necessary information and follow every step called for by the procedure.[149] One of the most important uses of Internet technology is the development of HR dashboards. An **HR dashboard** is a series of indicators or metrics that managers and employees have access to on the company intranet or HRIS. The HR dashboard provides access to important HR metrics for conducting workforce analytics. HR dashboards are important for determining the value of HR practices and how they contribute to business goals. As a result, the use of dashboards is critical for evidence-based HR discussed earlier in the chapter. For example, Cisco Systems views building talent as a priority, so it has added to its dashboard of people measures a metric to track how many people move and the reasons why.[150] This allows Cisco to identify divisions that are developing new talent.

Connectiveness and Mobility Enhance HR Practices

Verizon uses social networking tools and mobile devices to train employees, interact with customers, and support new products and devices. Device Blog, Device Forums, and Learning Communities help ensure that employees are ready to support customers when new products and devices are introduced to the market; they also engage Verizon's multigenerational workforce and facilitate peer-to-peer learning. Device Blog makes available information and updates on wireless devices, FAQs (frequently asked questions), how-to-videos, and troubleshooting tips. Device Forums enable retail employees to learn from peers and product manufacturers. Employees can ask each other questions, share issues, post tips, make suggestions, and access product experts. Learning Communities are accessed through the Device Blog. They include video blogs, message boards, links to online training modules, and product demonstrations. In addition to these tools, employees have access to My Network for collaborating with their peers,

knowledge and document sharing, and creating working groups. Some instructors also use it for posting supplemental content for learners to use.

Best Buy uses an app-based training tool known as Gravity. Gravity allows employees to use any smart device to scan a product's UPS or QR code, which provides access to short training videos and important product information.

Employees at retailer Kohl's post messages, photographs, and videos using Twitter (#lifeatkohls), Instagram, and Facebook. Postings brag about taking part in community events, and videos show employees at work demonstrating their folding skills or merchandise displays. In stores and distribution centers, large video screens scroll these postings. This openness to employees using social media runs counter to many companies' viewpoint that it can cause problems for the company's image, wastes time at work, and can bring legal challenges such as union organizing or the posting of trade secrets. But through listening sessions designed to

help develop a plan to help Kohl's return to its days as a thriving retailer, Millennial employees expressed that they wanted to talk more on Facebook and Twittter about what they did at work. Recognizing that engaging these employees was important for providing customers with a better shopping experience as well as enhancing the brand image, Kohl's created a more open social media policy. Social media has connected employees to each other, creating a greater community feel; allowed managers to better understand what employees were thinking and doing; and gotten the brand in front of consumers.

DISCUSSION QUESTION
1. What are some of the potential disadvantages of using social networks and mobile devices for HR practices?

SOURCES: Based on "Best Buy: Gravity," *Training*, January/February 2017, p. 102; W. Bunch, "Social Turnaround," *Human Resource Executive*, November 2016, p. 12–15; J. Salopek, "Good Connections," *T + D*, October 2014, pp. 48–50.

Consider High-Performance Work Systems and Virtual Teams

New technology causes changes in skill requirements and work roles and often results in redesigning work structures (e.g., using work teams).[151] **High-performance work systems** maximize the fit between the company's social system (employees) and its technical system.[152] For example, computer-integrated manufacturing uses robots and computers to automate the manufacturing process. The computer allows the production of different products simply by reprogramming the computer. As a result, laborer, material handler, operator/assembler, and maintenance jobs may be merged into one position. Computer-integrated manufacturing requires employees to monitor equipment

High-performance work systems
Work systems that maximize the fit between employees and technology.

LO 1-6
Discuss human resource management practices that support high-performance work systems.

and troubleshoot problems with sophisticated equipment, share information with other employees, and understand the relationships between all components of the manufacturing process.[153]

Besides changing the way that products are built or services are provided within companies, technology has allowed companies to form partnerships with one or more other companies. **Virtual teams** refer to teams that are separated by time, geographic distance, culture, and/or organizational boundaries and that rely almost exclusively on technology (e-mail, Internet, videoconferencing) to interact and complete their projects. Virtual teams can be formed within one company whose facilities are scattered throughout the country or the world. A company may also use virtual teams in partnerships with suppliers or competitors to pull together the necessary talent to complete a project or speed the delivery of a product to the marketplace. For example, Art & Logic software developers all work remotely from across the United States and Canada from home offices, rented office space, or at a co-working facility.[154] Their clients represent a diverse set of industries, including education, aerospace, music technology, consumer electronics, entertainment, and financial services. The project teams work on the most unusual and difficult problems, which developers at other companies have failed to solve. Art & Logic tries to accommodate the unique schedule and work-style requirements of its developers, but its work is highly collaborative within project teams. Every project consists of at least a project manager/developer and has a maximum of five to seven developers. Teams use Google Apps for Business for sharing documents and communicating (both within the team and with clients).

Virtual teams
Teams that are separated by time, geographic distance, culture, and/or organizational boundaries and rely exclusively on technology for interaction between team members.

Human resource management practices that support high-performance work systems are shown in Table 1.14. The HRM practices involved include employee selection, work design, training, compensation, and performance management. These practices are designed to give employees skills, incentives, knowledge, and autonomy. Research studies suggest that high-performance work practices are usually associated with increases in productivity and long-term financial performance.[155] Research also suggests that it is more effective to improve HRM practices as a whole, rather than focus on one or two isolated practices (such as the pay system or selection system).[156] There may be a best HRM system, but whatever the company does, the practices must be aligned with each other and be consistent with the system if they are to positively affect company performance.[157] We will discuss this alignment in more detail in Chapters 2 and 16.

Employees often have responsibility for hiring and firing team members and can make decisions that influence profits. As a result, employees must be trained in principles of employee selection, quality, and customer service. They need to understand financial data so that they can see the link between their performance and company performance.

In high-performance work systems, previously established boundaries between managers and employees, employees and customers, employees and vendors, and the various functions within the company are abandoned. Employees, managers, vendors, customers, and suppliers work together to improve service and product quality and to create new products and services. Line employees are trained in multiple jobs, communicate directly with suppliers and customers, and interact frequently with engineers, quality experts, and employees from other functions.

Consider how HRM practices support high-performance work systems at both small and large companies.[158] HindlePower is a manufacturer of battery chargers. Most of HindlePower's 75 employees work in the factory as assemblers. There is no time clock. Employees do not need to punch in or out and there are no rules for time off.

Table 1.14
How HRM Practices
Support High-
Performance Work
Systems

Staffing	• Employees participate in selecting new employees, e.g., peer interviews.
Work design	• Employees understand how their jobs contribute to the finished product or service.
	• Employees participate in planning changes in equipment, layout, and work methods.
	• Work may be organized in teams.
	• Job rotation is used to develop skills.
	• Equipment and work processes are structured and technology is used to encourage flexibility and interaction between employees.
	• Work design allows employees to use a variety of skills.
	• Decentralized decision making, reduced status distinctions, information sharing.
	• Increased safety.
Training	• Ongoing training emphasized and rewarded.
	• Training in finance and quality control methods.
Compensation	• Team-based performance pay.
	• Part of compensation may be based on company or division financial performance.
Performance management	• Employees receive performance feedback and are actively involved in the performance improvement process.

SOURCES: Based on K. Birdi, C. Clegy, M. Patterson, A. Robinson, C. Stride, T. Wall, and S. Wood, "The Impact of Human Resource and Operational Management Practices on Company Productivity: A Longitudinal Study," *Personnel Psychology* 61 (2008), pp. 467–501; A. Zacharatos, J. Barling, and R. Iverson, "High Performance Work Systems and Occupational Safety," *Journal of Applied Psychology* 90 (2005), pp. 77–93; S. Way, "High Performance Work Systems and Intermediate Indicators of Performance within the U.S. Small Business Sector," *Journal of Management* 28 (2002), pp. 765–85; M. A. Huselid, "The Impact of Human Resource Management Practices on Turnover, Productivity, and Corporate Financial Performance," *Academy of Management Journal* 38 (1995), pp. 635–72.

Employees don't abuse the policy—hours in the factory consistently reach 97% to 100% of full time. Hindle established a program called the Professional Manufacturing Team, which pairs training with employee involvement in designing more efficient processes. The training includes 25 to 30 courses customized for each production line. Employees are responsible for completing all of the courses, and when they do they are designated as a manufacturing professional. Employees are also involved in decisions that go beyond training. For example, employees redesigned a production line resulting in an additional 150,000 units produced per week. At the Chrysler Dundee Engine plant, hourly employees rotate jobs and shifts, giving the company greater flexibility and employees more family time. The plant's culture emphasizes problem solving and the philosophy that anyone can do anything, anytime, anywhere. Every employee is either a team member or a team leader. Job candidates have to make it through a difficult screening process that includes testing, evaluation of how they perform in team activities, and interviews with managers and team leaders. Rotating jobs helps keep employees motivated and reduces injuries. Team leaders and engineers are expected on the shop floor as part of six-person teams. Large electronic screens hanging from the plant ceiling provide alerts of machinery parts that are ending their lifespan and need to be replaced before they malfunction. A performance management system, accessible on personal computers, alerts employees to delays or breakdowns in productivity. Employees are empowered to fix problems—not just managers or engineers.

Meeting Competitive Challenges through HRM Practices

LO 1-7
Provide a brief description of human resource management practices.

We have discussed the sustainability, globalization, and technology challenges U.S. companies are facing. We have emphasized that management of human resources plays a critical role in determining companies' success in meeting these challenges. HRM practices have not traditionally been seen as providing economic value to the company. Economic value is usually associated with equipment, technology, and facilities. However, HRM practices have been shown to be valuable. Compensation, staffing, training and development, performance management, and other HRM practices are investments that directly affect employees' motivation and ability to provide products and services that are valued by customers. Research has shown that companies that attempt to increase their competitiveness by investing in new technology and becoming involved in the quality movement also invest in state-of-the-art staffing, training, and compensation practices.[159] Figure 1.8 shows examples of HRM practices that help

Figure 1.8

Examples of How HRM Practices Can Help Companies Meet Competitive Challenges

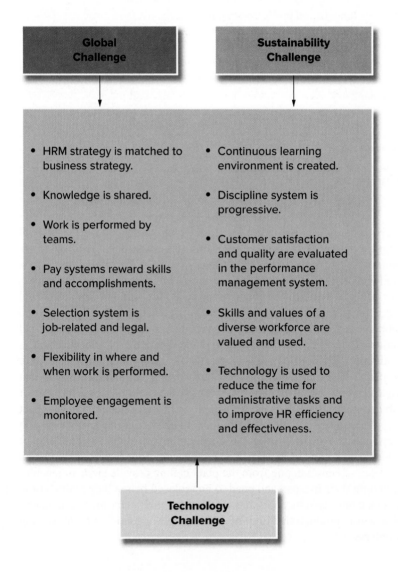

Dimensions of HRM Practices

| Managing the human resource environment | Acquiring and preparing human resources | Assessment and development of human resources | Compensating human resources | Competitiveness |

Figure 1.9

Major Dimensions of HRM Practices Contributing to Company Competitiveness

companies deal with the three challenges. For example, to meet the sustainability challenge, companies need to identify through their selection processes whether prospective employees value customer relations and have the levels of interpersonal skills necessary to work with fellow employees in teams. To meet all three challenges, companies need to capitalize on the diversity of values, abilities, and perspectives that employees bring to the workplace.

HRM practices that help companies deal with the competitive challenges can be grouped into the four dimensions shown in Figure 1.9. These dimensions include the human resource environment, acquiring and preparing human resources, assessment and development of human resources, and compensating human resources. In addition, some companies have special issues related to labor–management relations, international human resource management, and managing the human resource function.

Managing the Human Resource Environment

Managing internal and external environmental factors allows employees to make the greatest possible contribution to company productivity and competitiveness. Creating a positive environment for human resources involves the following:

- Linking HRM practices to the company's business objectives—that is, strategic human resource management
- Ensuring that HRM practices comply with federal, state, and local laws
- Designing work that motivates and satisfies employees as well as maximizes customer service, quality, and productivity

Acquiring and Preparing Human Resources

Customer needs for new products or services influence the number and type of employees that businesses need to be successful. Terminations, promotions, and retirements also influence human resource requirements. Managers need to predict the number and type of employees needed to meet customer demands for products and services. Managers must also identify current or potential employees who can successfully deliver products and services. This area of HRM deals with the following:

- Identifying human resource requirements—that is, human resource planning, recruiting employees, and selecting employees
- Training employees to have the skills needed to perform their jobs

Assessment and Development of Human Resources

Managers need to ensure that employees have the necessary skills to perform current and future jobs. As we discussed earlier, because of new technology and the quality movement, many companies are redesigning work so that it is performed by teams. As a result, managers and employees may need to develop new skills to succeed in a team environment. Companies need to create a work environment that supports employees' work and nonwork activities. This area of HRM addresses the following:

- Measuring employees' performance
- Preparing employees for future work roles and identifying employees' work interests, goals, values, and other career issues
- Creating an employment relationship and work environment that benefits both the company and the employee

Compensating Human Resources

Besides interesting work, pay and benefits are the most important incentives that companies can offer employees in exchange for contributing to productivity, quality, and customer service. Also, pay and benefits are used to reward employees' membership in the company and attract new employees. The positive influence of new work designs, new technology, and the quality movement on productivity can be damaged if employees are not satisfied with the level of pay and benefits or believe pay and benefits are unfairly distributed. This area of HRM includes the following

- Creating pay systems
- Rewarding employee contributions
- Providing employees with benefits

Special Issues

In some companies, employees are represented by a labor union. Managing human resources in a union environment requires knowledge of specific laws, contract administration, and the collective bargaining process.

Many companies are globally expanding their business through joint ventures, mergers, acquisitions, and establishing new operations. Successful global expansion depends on the extent to which HRM practices are aligned with cultural factors as well as management of employees sent to work in another country. Human resource management practices must contribute to organizational effectiveness.

Human resource management practices of both managers and the human resource function must be aligned and contribute to the company's strategic goals. The final chapter of the book explains how to effectively integrate human resource management practices.

Organization of This Book

The topics in this book are organized according to the four areas of human resource management and special issues. Table 1.15 lists the chapters covered in the book.

The content of each chapter is based on academic research and examples of effective company practices. Each chapter includes examples of how the HRM practice covered in the chapter helps a company gain a competitive advantage by addressing sustainability, global, and technological challenges. Also, each chapter includes an example of a company that demonstrates how HR practices add value (evidence-based HR).

Table 1.15
Topics Covered in
This Book

A LOOK BACK

HRM at Publix

One of Publix's core values, "Dedicated to the dignity, value and employment security of our associates" drives its management and human resources practices, which in turn leads to happy employees, satisfied customers, and a positive "bottom line."

QUESTIONS

1. Which of Publix's HR practices do you think are most important for its success? Why?
2. Could promotion from within have disadvantages for Publix? Explain why?
3. Would Publix's HR practices be successful in other industries such as health care or manufacturing? Explain.
4. Do Publix's HR practices give it an advantage over its competitors? Why or why not?

SUMMARY

This chapter introduced the roles and activities of a company's human resource management function and emphasized that effective management of human resources can contribute to a company's business strategy and competitive advantage. Human resources can be viewed as having three product lines: administrative services, business partner services, and strategic services. To successfully manage human resources, individuals need personal credibility, business knowledge, understanding of the business strategy, technology knowledge, and the ability to deliver HR services. Human resource management practices should be evidence-based, that is, based on data showing the relationship between the practice and business outcomes related to key company stakeholders (customers, shareholders, employees, community). In addition to contributing to a company's business strategy, HR practices are important for helping companies deal with sustainability, global, and technology challenges. The sustainability challenges are related to the economy, the characteristics and expectations of the labor force, how and where work is done, the value placed on intangible assets and human capital, and meeting stakeholder needs (ethical practices, high-quality products and

services, return to shareholders, and social responsibility). Global challenges include entering international markets, immigration, and offshoring. Technology challenges include using new technologies to support flexible and virtual work arrangements; high-performance work systems; and implementing and using social networks, wearables, human resource information systems, artificial intelligence, and mobile devices.

The chapter concludes by showing how the book is organized. The book includes four topical areas: the human resource environment (strategic HRM, legal, analysis and design of work), acquisition and preparation of human resources (HR planning and recruitment, selection, training), assessment and development of human resources (performance management, development, separation and retention), compensation of human resources (pay structures, recognizing employee contributions with pay, benefits), and special topics (collective bargaining and labor relations, managing human resources globally, and strategically managing the HR function). All of the topical areas are important for companies to deal with the competitive challenges and contribute to business strategy.

KEY TERMS

Competitiveness, 4
Human resource management (HRM), 4
Shared service model, 7
Self-service, 8
Outsourcing, 8
Evidence-based HR, 12
HR or workforce analytics, 12
Big data, 12
Sustainability, 16
Stakeholders, 16
Intangible assets, 22
Knowledge workers, 23
Empowering, 23

Learning organization, 24
Change, 24
Employee engagement, 25
Talent management, 26
Nontraditional employment, 27
Gig economy, 27
Balanced scorecard, 29
Total quality management (TQM), 31
Malcolm Baldrige National Quality Award, 32
ISO 9000:2015, 32
Six Sigma process, 34
Lean thinking, 34
Internal labor force, 35

External labor market, 36
Ethics, 43
Sarbanes-Oxley Act of 2002, 43
Offshoring, 48
Reshoring, 48
Social networking, 50
Artificial intelligence, 51
Human resource information system (HRIS), 52
Mobile devices, 52
Cloud computing, 52
HR dashboard, 52
High-performance work systems, 53
Virtual teams, 54

DISCUSSION QUESTIONS

1. Traditionally, human resource management practices were developed and administered by the company's human resource department. Some companies are abandoning or don't have HR departments. Why is this occurring? Is it

a good idea for companies not to have an HR department or HR professionals? Explain your position.
2. Staffing, training, compensation, and performance management are important HRM functions. How can

each of these functions help companies succeed in meeting the sustainability challenge, the global challenge, and the technology challenge?

3. What are intangible assets? How are they influenced by HRM practices?

4. What is evidence-based HR? Why might an HR department resist becoming evidence based?

5. What types of big data would you collect and analyze to understand why an employer was experiencing a high turnover rate?

6. Which HR practices can benefit by the use of social collaboration tools like Twitter and Facebook? Identify the HR practices and explain the benefits gained.

7. Do you agree with the statement "Employee engagement is something companies should be concerned about only if they are making money"? Explain.

8. This book covers four HRM practice areas: managing the human resource environment, acquiring and preparing human resources, assessment and development of human resources, and compensating human resources. Which area do you believe contributes most to helping a company gain a competitive advantage? Which area do you believe contributes the least? Why?

9. What is the balanced scorecard? Identify the four perspectives included in the balanced scorecard. How can HRM practices influence the four perspectives?

10. Is HRM becoming more strategic? Explain your answer.

11. What is sustainability? How can HR practices help a company become more socially and environmentally conscious?

12. Explain the implications of each of the following labor force trends for HRM: (1) aging workforce, (2) diverse workforce, (3) skill deficiencies.

13. What role do HRM practices play in a business decision to expand internationally?

14. What might a quality goal and high-performance work systems have in common in terms of HRM practices?

15. What disadvantages might result from outsourcing HRM practices? From employee self-service? From increased line manager involvement in designing and using HR practices?

16. What factors should a company consider before reshoring? What are the advantages and disadvantages of reshoring?

SELF-ASSESSMENT EXERCISE

connect

Do You Have What It Takes to Work in HR?

Instructions: Read each statement and circle *yes* or *no*.

Yes No 1. I have leadership and management skills I have developed through prior job experiences, extracurricular activities, community service, or other noncourse activities.

Yes No 2. I have excellent communications, dispute resolution, and interpersonal skills.

Yes No 3. I can demonstrate an understanding of the fundamentals of running a business and making a profit.

Yes No 4. I can use spreadsheets and the World Wide Web, and I am familiar with information systems technology.

Yes No 5. I can work effectively with people of different cultural backgrounds.

Yes No 6. I have expertise in more than one area of human resource management.

Yes No 7. I have a willingness to learn.

Yes No 8. I listen to issues before reacting with solutions.

Yes No 9. I can collect and analyze data for business solutions.

Yes No 10. I am a good team member.

Yes No 11. I have knowledge of local and global economic trends.

Yes No 12. I demonstrate accountability for my actions.

Scoring: The greater the number of yes answers, the better prepared you are to work as an HR professional. For questions you answered *no*, you should seek courses and experiences to change your answers to *yes*—and better prepare yourself for a career in HR!

SOURCE: Based on B. E. Kaufman, "What Companies Want from HR Graduates," *HR Magazine*, September 1994; SHRM Elements for HR Success Competency Model, 2012, from www.shrm.org, March 21, 2012.

EXERCISING STRATEGY

Zappos Faces Competitive Challenges

Zappos, based in Las Vegas, is an online retailer with the initial goal of trying to be the best website for buying shoes by offering a wide variety of brands, styles, colors, sizes, and widths. The Zappos.com brand has grown to offer shoes, handbags, eyewear, watches, and accessories for online purchase. The company's goal is to provide the best service online, not just in shoes but in any product category. Zappos believes that the speed with which a customer receives an online purchase plays a critical role in how that customer thinks about shopping online again in the future, so the company is focusing on making sure the items get delivered to its customers as quickly as possible.

Zappos CEO Tony Hsieh has shaped the company's customer-service-focused culture, brand, and business strategy around 10 core values:

Deliver WOW through service.
Embrace and drive change.
Create fun and a little weirdness.
Be adventurous, creative, and open-minded.
Pursue growth and learning.
Build open and honest relationships with communication.
Build a positive team and family spirit.
Do more with less.
Be passionate and determined.
Be humble.

"Deliver WOW through service" means that call center employees need to provide excellent customer service. Call center employees encourage callers to order more than one size or color because shipping and return shipping is free. They are also encouraged to use their imaginations to meet customer needs.

Zappos has received many awards for its workplace culture and practices, including being frequently recognized in *Fortune* magazine's annual rankings of the 100 Best Companies to Work For. The job of human resources at Zappos is more than just a rule enforcer. HR's job is to protect the culture and to educate employees. HR focuses on interactions with managers and employees to understand what they need from HR (HR is even invited to attend work teams' happy hours). Zappos's employment practices help perpetuate its company culture. Only about 1 out of 100 applicants passes a hiring process that is equally weighted on job skills and on the potential to work in Zappos's culture. Some managers at Zappos believe that if you want to get a job the most important value to demonstrate is "be humble" including a focus on "we" instead of "I." Job candidates are interviewed for cultural fit and a willingness to change and learn. For example, they observe whether job candidates talk at lunch

with others or just the person they think is making the hiring decision. The HR team uses unusual interview questions—such as, How weird are you? and What's your theme song?—to find employees who are creative and have strong individuality. Zappos provides free lunch in the cafeteria (cold cuts) and a full-time life coach (employees have to sit on a red velvet throne to complain), managers are encouraged to spend time with employees outside of the office, and any employee can reward another employee a $50 bonus for good performance. Call center employees can use an online scheduling tool that allows them to set their own hours, and they can earn more pay if they work during hours with greater customer demand. Most of the over 1,500 employees at Zappos are hourly. Every new hire undergoes four weeks of training, during which the company culture must be committed to memory, and spends two weeks dealing with customers by working the telephones. New recruits are offered $2,000 to leave the company during training to weed out individuals who will not be happy working at the company. Zappos provides free breakfast, lunch, snacks, coffee, tea, and vending machine snacks. Work is characterized by constant change; a loud, open office environment; and team interactions. Employees at Zappos move around. For example, call center employees can bid for different shifts every month.

To reinforce the importance of the 10 core values, Zappos's performance management system asks managers to evaluate how well employees' behaviors demonstrate the core values such as being humble or expressing their personalities. To evaluate task performance, managers are asked to regularly provide employees with status reports on such things as how much time they spend on the telephone with customers. The status reports and evaluations of the core values are informational or used to identify training needs. Zappos also believes in helping others understand what inspired the company culture. The company created the Zappos.com library, which provides a collection of books about creating a passion for customer service, products, and local communities. These books can be found in the front lobby of Zappos offices and are widely read and discussed by company employees.

Corporate culture is more than a set of values, and it is maintained by a complex web of human interactions. At Zappos, the liberal use of social media including blogs and Twitter facilitates the network that links employees with one another and with the company's customers. Zappos takes the pulse of the organization monthly, measuring the health of the culture with a happiness survey. Employees respond to such unlikely questions as whether they believe that the company has a higher purpose than profits, whether their own role has meaning, whether they feel in control of their career path, whether they consider their coworkers to be like family and friends, and whether they are happy in their jobs. Results from the survey are broken down by department, and opportunities for development are identified and acted upon. For example, when it was clear from the survey that one department had veered off course and felt isolated from the rest of the organization, a program was instituted that enabled individuals in the group to learn more about how integral their work was. To keep the company vibrant, CEO Tony Hsieh spent $350 million to develop a neighborhood in downtown Las Vegas, which is the home of Zappos.com's new headquarters. Hsieh wants to provide employees with a great place to work as well as to live and socialize.

Recently, Zappos adopted a management philosophy, holocracy, which gives employees the freedom and responsibility to decide how to get their work done and eliminated people managers. Hsieh's intent was to allow employees to act more like entrepreneurs and help stimulate new ideas, bring their full selves to work, and have a purpose beyond making money, all of which he believes will benefit the business. Employees work in teams or "circles" rather than as individuals, and team membership can change. However, employees are finding the new management system confusing and requiring them to spend more time in meetings. Also, they wonder how they will earn raises and advance their careers without management jobs. In all, 210 employees found the new philosophy so dissatisfying that they took three months of severance pay and left the company. Zappos is changing its recruitment process to ensure that its new hires are comfortable with holocracy's self-management style.

Despite this setback, other companies are trying to learn from Zappos's practices. Zappos Insights is a department within Zappos created to share the Zappos culture with other companies. Zappos Insights provides programs about building

a culture (3-Day Culture Camp), its WOW service philosophy (School of WOW), the power of a coaching-based culture (Coaching Event), how the HR function protects the culture and how its programs support it (People Academy), and custom programs. The cost to attend these programs ranges from $2,000 to $6,000 for each attendee.

QUESTIONS

1. Zappos seems to be well-positioned to have a competitive advantage over other online retailers. What challenges discussed in Chapter 1 pose the biggest threat to Zappos's ability to maintain and enhance its competitive position? How can HRM practices help Zappos meet these challenges?

2. Do you think that employees of Zappos have high levels of engagement? Why?

3. Which of Zappos's 10 core values do you believe that HR practices can influence the most? The least? Why? For each of the core values, identify the HR practices that are related to it. Explain how the HR practices you identified are related to the core values.

4. How might the change to the holocracy management style undermine Zappos's core values and cause employees to have lower levels of engagement?

SOURCES: Based on www.zappos.com, accessed February 17, 2017; E. Bernstein, J. Bunch, N. Canner, and M. Lee, "Beyond the Holocracy Hype," *Harvard Business Review,* July/August 2016, pp. 38–49; J. Reingold, "The Zappos Experiment," *Fortune,* March 15, 2016, pp. 206–14; *The Columbus Dispatch,* April 6, 2015, p. C3; "Zappos Insights," www.zapposinsights.com, accessed March 1, 2017; D. Richard, "At Zappos, Culture Pays," *Strategy + Business,* August 2010, p. 60, www.strategybusiness.com, accessed March 25, 2013; K. Gurchick, "Delivering HR at Zappos," *HR Magazine,* June 2011; R. Pyrillis, "The Reviews Are In," *Workforce Management,* May 2011, pp. 20–25; J. O'Brien, "Zappos Knows How to Kick It," *Fortune,* February 2, 2009, pp. 55–66; R. Silverman, "Going Bossless Backfires at Zappos," *Wall Street Journal,* May 21, 2015, pp. A1, A10.

MANAGING PEOPLE

Marriott: HR Practices Result in Engaged Employees and Satisfied Customers

If you have traveled, you probably have seen or stayed at a Marriott hotel. But did you know that Marriott owns few hotels? Most are owned by real estate partners, and Marriott manages or franchises them. Marriott is doing well in a competitive industry. Its 2014 revenue and net income ($13.8 billion, and $753 million, respectively) were at record levels. Marriott reported net income totaled $244 million in the fourth quarter of 2016, a 21 percent increase over 2015 fourth quarter net income. To stay relevant in the hotel industry, Marriott has added new properties around the world and is reinventing itself to appeal to tastes of the new Millennial generation of travelers. Marriott purchased Starwood Hotels

and Resorts and has added three new brands, Moxy Hotels, for budget-conscious travelers, and AC Hotels and Edition brand for more sophisticated travelers. Also, Marriott is changing room design to reflect Millennials's tastes and preferences: big comfortable beds, large televisions, large public lounges, and instead of traditional room service, online ordering and food delivery.

How Marriott manages its employees plays a key role in its financial performance and customer satisfaction. Its practices are based on the principle "Take care of associates and they will take care of customers." "We put people first" is one of Marriott's core values. Marriott has been on

Fortune magazine's "Best Companies to Work For" list for all 18 years the list has been in existence, a distinction shared by only 11 other companies, including Publix, Whole Foods, Nordstrom, and REI. The company has more than 200,000 employees who work in hotel properties around the world. The work isn't necessarily sexy or sophisticated. Most employees, who are known as "associates," work helping guests, serving meals, and cleaning rooms. Housekeepers represent the largest category of associates, and 85% of associates earn an hourly wage. Despite the routine nature of the work and demanding customers, associates often refer to their co-workers as "family," and many stay in their jobs for many years. Marriott's general manager's tenure is 25 years—much greater than the industry average. More than 10,000 employees have worked at Marriott more than 20 years.

Marriott emphasizes hiring friendly people who can learn through training. For hourly associates, the company screens for interpersonal skills, dependability, and positive disposition. Employees' opinions matter. At every hotel, each shift starts with a 15-minute meeting during which employees share updates and get motivated for the day's work. The meetings often include stretching, music, and dancing. Employee benefits also contribute to making Marriott a desirable company to work for. The benefits include flexible scheduling; an employee assistance phone number; health care benefits for hourly employees if they work 30 hours a week; and discounts on room rates for employees, families, and friends. Employees working at company headquarters have access to a gym, a dry cleaners, a gift store, and day care. The company holds a celebration of excellence each year that recognizes outstanding employees who are flown in for the event. The best benefit may be the opportunity that all employees have to grow their careers.

Many top executives started as hourly employees working as housekeepers, waiters, sales people, or security guards. Employees are given opportunities to explore career paths and learn through job experiences. Mentoring from senior employees is common. Bill Marriott, the company's executive chairman and CEO for 40 years until stepping down, believes happy employees result in lower costs. Happy employees mean Mariott has lower turnover and less need to train and orient replacement employees, and an experienced workforce provides better customer service. Marriott regularly surveys its employees to measure their engagement. The results show that in hotels where employee engagement is higher, customers who experienced a problem were more satisfied with the solution.

QUESTIONS

1. Which HR practices do you believe are the most critical for Marriott to maintain and grow its competitive advantage? Explain why.
2. Would Marriott have been successful without its current HR practices? Explain.
3. Can companies in other industries such as health care, manufacturing, or research and development adopt Marriott's value and practices and have similar success? Explain why or why not.
4. What other types of HR practices should Marriott consider adopting that would appeal to its growing number of Millennial employees?

SOURCE: Based on L. Gallagher, "Why Employees Love Marriott," *Fortune*, March 15, 2015, pp. 112–118; company website, "Careers" and "About Marriott: Core Values and Heritage," www.marriott.com, accessed February 28, 2017; "Marriott International Reports Fourth Quarter 2016 Results" February 15, 2017 from http://news.marriott.com/2017/02/marriott-international-reports-fourth-quarter-2016-results/ accessed May 3, 2017.

HR IN SMALL BUSINESS

Network Is the Key to HRM at 1Collision

The typical auto body shop used to be a small, independent business that dealt directly with car owners or the local claims adjuster at an owner's insurance company. Today, however, more shops are part of a chain or join a network of shops. One reason is that insurers prefer to direct work to a few companies, rather than many small shops. Another is that a larger organization can support shops with functions such as human resource management. In fact, the two advantages build on each other: Joining a successful network brings in more business, which requires more employees, which requires more sophisticated HR practices.

Milwaukee-based 1Collision Network has seized on these opportunities by emphasizing HRM along with

marketing to consumers and insurance companies. The more than 20 shops that have joined 1Collision Network use its online software to carry out the tasks of signing up new employees and enrolling all employees in benefits such as health insurance and retirement savings plans.

Jim Keller, 1Collision's president, says many shops find recruiting new employees to be a particular challenge. The network has employees who work full time on providing shops with support for recruiting qualified technicians.

The network also supports performance management and training. It works with an outside service provider to apply key performance indicators, using them to identify areas in which coaching can help the shop improve. For training,

1Collision works with equipment suppliers to identify training requirements and necessary certifications. Then 1Collision makes arrangements to have the instruction delivered to the shops in its network. The network also promotes learning through peer meetings in which the shops share lessons from experience.

QUESTIONS

1. Give examples of 1Collision's HRM professionals providing the competencies of (a) HR technical expertise and practice and (b) critical evaluation.

2. How might HRM support from the 1Collision Network make an auto body shop more competitive than if it relied on the shop manager to handle human resource management? In other words, how might this support contribute to business success?

SOURCES: 1Collision Network, "Body Shop Partners," http://1collision .com; Brian Albright, "Strength in Numbers," *Auto Body Repair Network,* October 2015, pp. 36–38; Stacey Phillips, "Growing Trend of Collision Repair Networks Led to Formation of 1Collision Network," *Autobody News,* September 14, 2015, http://www.autobodynews.com.

NOTES

1. J. T. Delaney and M. A. Huselid, "The Impact of Human Resource Management Practices on Perceptions of Organizational Performance," *Academy of Management Journal* 39 (1996), pp. 949–69; R. E. Ployhart, J. A. Weekley, and J. Ramsey, "The Consequences of Human Resources Stocks and Flows: A Longitudinal Examination of Unit Service Orientation and Unit Effectiveness," *Academy of Management Journal* 52 (2009), pp. 996–1015; Y. Kim and R. E. Ployhart, "The Effects of Staffing and Training on Firm Productivity and Profit Growth before, during, and after the Great Recession" *Journal of Applied Psychology* 99 (2014), pp. 361–89; R. Ployhart and T. Moliterno, "Emergence of the Human Capital Resource: A Multilevel Model," *Academy of Management Review* 36 (2011), pp. 127–50; B. Campbell, R. Coff, and D. Kryscynski, "Rethinking Sustained Competitive Advantage from Human Capital," *Academy of Management Review* 37 (2010), pp. 376–395: T. Crook, S. Todd, J. Combs, D. Woehr, and D. Ketchen, Jr., "Does Human Capital Matter? A Meta-Analysis of the Relationship between Human Capital and Firm Performance," *Journal of Applied Psychology* 96 (2011), pp. 443–56.

2. K. O'Leonard, "A Breed Apart," *Human Resource Executive,* January/February 2015, p. 38.

3. SHRM-BNA Survey No. 66, "Policy and Practice Forum: Human Resources Activities, Budgets, and Staffs: 2000–2001," *Bulletin to Management,* Bureau of National Affairs Policy and Practice Series, June 28, 2001 (Washington, DC: Bureau of National Affairs); Bureau of Labor Statistics, U.S. Department of Labor, "Human Resources Specialists," *Occupational Outlook Handbook, 2016–17 Edition,* https://www.bls.gov/ooh/business-and-financial/human-resources-specialists.htm, accessed February 9, 2017

4. G. Tucker, "HR at the Corner of People and Strategy," *HR Magazine,* May 2014, pp. 42–44.

5. R. Zeidner, "Rebuilding HR," *HR Magazine,* May 2015, pp. 26–34.

6. A. Halcrow, "Survey Shows HRM in Transition," *Workforce,* June 1998, pp. 73–80; J. Laabs, "Why HR Can't Win Today," *Workforce,* May 1998, pp. 62–74; C. Cole, "Kodak Snapshots," *Workforce,* June 2000, pp. 65–72; W. Ruona and S. Gibson, "The Making of Twenty-First Century HR: An Analysis of the Convergence of HRM, HRD, and OD," *Human Resource Management* 43 (2004), pp. 49–66.

7. J. Bersin, "What's in Store for HR in 2015," *HR Magazine,* January/February 2015, pp. 32–51; T. Starner, "An HR Exodus," *HR Executive,* May 2014, p. 13; T. Henneman, "Is HR at Its Breaking Point?" *Workforce Management,* April 2013, pp. 28–32; C. Gibson, I. Ziskin, and J. Boudreau, "What Is the Future of HR?" *Workforce,* January 2014, pp. 30–33, 48; M. McGraw, "What's Keeping HR Up at Night," *Human Resource Executive,* September 2013, pp. 32–36.

8. R. Grossman, "Saving Shared Services," *HR Magazine,* September 2010, pp. 26–31.

9. Tucker, "HR at the Corner of People and Strategy."

10. S. Greengard, "Building a Self-Service Culture That Works," *Workforce,* July 1998, pp. 60–64.

11. D. Zielinski, "Making the Most of Manager Self-Service," *HR Magazine,* December 2013, pp. 51–55.

12. K. Kramer, "Industrial-Organizational (I-O) Psychology's Contribution to Strategic Human Resources Outsourcing (HRO): How Can We Shape the Future of HR?" *The Industrial-Organizational Psychologist,* January 2011, pp. 13–20.

13. B. Roberts, "Outsourcing in Turbulent Times," *HR Magazine,* November 2009, pp. 42–47; The Right Thing, "The Goodyear Tire and Rubber Company Discovers Key to Successful Outsourcing Partnerships," *Workforce Management,* March 2011, p. S2.

14. Society for Human Resource Management, "Future Insights: Top Ten Trends Affecting the Workplace and the HR Profession According to SHRM Special Expertise Panels," 2016, www.shrm.org, accessed February 14, 2017; SHRM Foundation Leadership Roundtable, "What's Next for HR?" November 12, 2010, www.shrm.org, accessed March 21, 2013.

15. R. Charan, D. Barton, and D. Carey, "People Before Strategy: A New Role for the CHRO," *Harvard Business Review,* July–August 2015, pp. 63–71.

16. J. Boudreau, and S. Rice, "Bright, Shiny Objects and the Future of HR," *Harvard Business Review,* July/August 2015, pp. 72–78; W. Bunch, "Split Decision," *Human Resource Executive,* September 2015, pp. 14–16.

17. W. Bunch, "the (other) Airbnb experience", *Human Resource Executive* (July/August 2016): 14-16; J. Meister & K. Mulcahy, "The future workplace experience" (New York: McGraw-Hill, 2017).

18. P. Wright, *Human Resource Strategy: Adapting to the Age of Globalization* (Alexandria, VA: Society for Human Resource Management Foundation, 2008).

19. L. Weber and R. Feintzeig, "Is It a Dream or a Drag? Companies without HR," *Wall Street Journal*, March 9, 2014, pp. B1, B7; Henneman, "Is HR at Its Breaking Point?"

20. From Tesla website , www.tesla.com, accessed February 9, 2017; K. Kazmierczak, "Tesla Motors–Growing Rapidly and Strategically," Human Capital Institute, March 19, 2015, http://www.hci. org/blog/tesla-motors-growing-rapidly-and-strategically, accessed February 9, 2017; S. Alexander, "How Tesla Engages Its Employees to Drive Business Results," *Modern Workforce,* September 11, 2015, https://www.geteverwise.com/human-resources/how-tesla-engages-its-employees-to-drive-business-results/, accessed February 9, 2017; A. McIlvaine, "Powering a Revolution," *HR Executive*, July/August 2014, pp. 14–17.

21. J. Ramirez, "The Anticipators", *Human Resource Executive,* May 2016, pp. 14–17; E. Frauenheim, "Numbers Game," *Workforce Management*, March 2011, pp. 20–21; P. Gallagher, "Rethinking HR," *Human Resource Executive*, September 2, 2009, pp. 1, 18–23.

22. C. Fleck, "An Algorithm for Success," *HR Magazine,* June 2016, pp. 130–35.

23. L. Claus and J. Collison, *The Maturing Profession of Human Resources: Worldwide and Regional View* (Alexandria, VA: Society for Human Resource Management, 2005).

24. Bureau of Labor Statistics, U.S. Department of Labor, *Occupational Outlook Handbook, 2016–17 Edition*, "Human Resources Specialists," www.bls.gov/ooh/business-and-financial/human-resources-specialists.htm, accessed February 9, 2017.

25. Ibid; E. Krell, "Become a Master of Expertise and Credibility," *HR Magazine*, May 2010, pp. 53–63.

26. T. Starner, "An HR Exodus," *HR Executive*, May 2014, p. 13.

27. S. Greengard, "The Debate over HR Credentials," *Workforce*, June 2016, pp. 40–43, 48.

28. J. Wiscombe, "Your Wonderful, Terrible HR Life," *Workforce*, June 2001, pp. 32–38.

29. R. Charan, "It's Time to Split HR," *Harvard Business Review*, July/August 2014, p. 34; Henneman, "Is HR at Its Breaking Point?"

30. P. Cappelli, "Why We Love to Hate HR . . . and What HR Can Do about It," *Harvard Business Review,* July/August 2015, pp. 54–61; D. Meinert, "Reskilling HR among Top Challenges Facing Companies," *HR Magazine*, May 2014, p. 18.

31. P. McCord, "How Netflix Reinvented HR," *Harvard Business Review*, January/February 2014, pp. 71–76; Henneman, "Is HR at Its Breaking Point?"

32. Society for Human Resource Management, SHRM Elements for HR Success Competency Model, www.shrm.org, accessed March 21, 2012; R. Zeidner, "Rebuilding HR," *HR Magazine*, May 2015, pp. 26–34.

33. K. Strobel, "Competency Proficiency Predicts Better Job Performance," *HR Magazine*, October 2014, p. 67.

34. Zeidner, "Rebuilding HR."

35. J. Arnold, "Building strength through cross-training", *HR Magazine* (April 2017: 50–55.

36. K. Frasch, "Engagement Still Keeping HR Awake," *Human Resource Executive,* April 2016, p. 21; J. Benz et al., "Happy New HR: Nine Thought Leaders Map Out Everything You Need to Know and Do in 2016 and Beyond," *HR Magazine,* December 2015/January 2016, pp. 28–44; M. McGraw, "*Engagement Is Still the Issue*," *Human Resource Executive*, March 2017, p. 36.

37. A. Jones, "Evolutionary Science, Work/Life Integration, and Corporate Responsibility," *Organizational Dynamics* 32 (2002), pp. 17–31; S. Ladika, "The Responsible Way," *Workforce Management*, July 2013, pp. 24–29.

38. E. Cohen, S. Taylor, and M. Muller-Camen, *HRM's Role in Corporate Social and Environmental Sustainability* (Alexandria, VA: SHRM Foundation, 2012); WCED, *Our Common Future* (Oxford: Oxford University Press, 1987), A. A. Savitz, *The Triple Bottom Line* (San Francisco: Jossey-Bass, 2006); S. Hart and S. Milstein, "Creating Sustainable Value," *Academy of Management Executive* 17 (2003), pp. 56–67.

39. From Bureau of Economic Analysis, "GDP Increases in Fourth Quarter," January 27, 2017, https://www.bea.gov/newsreleases/ national/gdp/gdphighlights.pdf, accessed February 9, 2017; L. Mutakani, "U.S. Jobless Claims Near 43-Year Low; Wholesale Inventories Surge," http://www.reuters.com/article/us-usa-economy-unemployment-idUSKBN15O1MF, accessed February 9, 2017; Bureau of Labor Statistics, "The Employment Situation–January 2017," Economic News Release, February 3, 2017; E. Morath and B. Leubsdorf, "Wage Growth Ticks Higher," *Wall Street Journal,* January 7, 2017, pp. A1, A2; J. Mitchell, "Jobs, Wage Picture Gives Fed Room on Raising Rates," *Wall Street Journal*, February 4, 2017, pp. A1, A2; S. Sprague, "Below Trend: The U.S. Productivity Slowdown since the Great Recession," Beyond the Numbers, Bureau of Labor Statistics, 6 (January 2017); E. Morath, "Jobless Rate Falls in Sign of Revival", *Wall Street Journal*, Saturday/Sunday May 6-7, 2017, pp. A1&A2; Bureau of Labor Statistics, "Labor Force Characteristics From the Current Population Survey, May 9, 2017, from https://data.bls. gov/timeseries/LNS11300000, accessed May 9, 2017.

40. B. Leubsdorf, "Trade Deficit at Its Widest in Four Years," *Wall Street Journal,* February 8, 2017, p. A2; J. Meltzer and M. Solis, *The High Cost of Protectionism* (Washington, DC: Brookings Institution, February 7, 2017), https://www.brookings.edu/blog/order-from-chaos/2017/02/07/the-high-costs-of-protectionism/, accessed February 9, 2017.

41. Deloitte Development LLC, "The Skills Gap in US Manufacturing, 2015 and Beyond," www.manufacturinginstitute.org, accessed February 14, 2017; D. Meinert, "Manufacturing Magnets," *HR Magazine,* November 2015, pp. 45–50; "Good to Grow: 2014 US CEO Survey," pwc.com, accessed February 20, 2015; J. Mitchell, "Job Market Rebounds after a Chill," *Wall Street Journal*, May 9, 2015, pp. A1–A2.

42. L. Patton, "The Latest Shortage: Fast Food Workers" from https://www.bloomberg.com/news/articles/2017-01-11/ headhunters-throwing-cash-at-people-who-know-how-to-flip-burgersast-Food Workers, accessed May 3, 2017; L. Weber, "Firms Flock to Cities with Top Talent," *Wall Street Journal,* April 13, 2016, p. B11.

43. "Starbucks College Achievement Plan," from www.starbucks. com, accessed February 14, 2017; Meinert, "Manufacturing Magnets"; J. Sparshott, "Job Training Ramps Up at Smaller Firms," *Wall Street Journal*, February 3, 2017, p. A2.

44. Society for Human Resource Management, "Business and Human Capital Challenges Today and in the Future," December 9, 2015, www.shrm.org, accessed February 14, 2017; "2015 State of Talent Management Research Report," *Human Resources Executive*, February 10, 2015, www.hreonline.com.

45. Bureau of Labor Statistics, "Employment Projections: 2012–2022," News Release, www.bls.gov, accessed February 25, 2015; D. Sommers and J. Franklin, "Overview of Projections to 2020," *Monthly Labor Review*, January 2012, pp. 3–20.

46. Based on Bureau of Labor Statistics, "Employment Projections: 2014–2024 Summary," News Release, December 8, 2015, www.bls.gov/emp, accessed February 23, 2017.

47. Bureau of Labor Statistics, "Employment Projections: Earnings and Unemployment Rates by Educational Attainment, 2015,"

www.bls.gov/emp/ep_chart_001.htm, accessed February 10, 2017; Bureau of Labor Statistics, "Occupational Requirements Survey Summary," December 1, 2016, from www.bls.gov/ors, accessed February 17, 2017.

48. Deloitte Development LLC, "Upskilling Manufacturing: How Technology Is Disrupting America's Industrial Labor Force," in *The Skills Gap in US Manufacturing: 2015 and Beyond,* www.pwc.com, accessed February 14, 2017; Meinert, "Manufacturing Magnets"; Organisation for Economic Co-operation and Development (OECD), "Skilled for Life? Key Findings from the Survey of Adult Skills," http://skills.oecd.org, accessed February 20, 2015; "Good to Grow: 2014 US CEO Survey"; P. Gaul, "Nearly Half of U.S. Executives Are Concerned About Skills Gap," *T + D,* February 2014, p. 18; "2014 Accenture Manufacturing Skills & Training Study," www.themanufacturinginstitute.org, accessed March 2, 2015; "Survey of Adult Skills," www.manufacturinginstitute.org, accessed February 14, 2017; J. Casner-Lotto, E. Rosenblum, and M. Wright, *The Ill-Prepared U.S. Workforce* (New York: The Conference Board, 2009).

49. L. Putre, "Building a Better Advanced Manufacturing Workforce," *Industry Week,* May 17, 2016, www.industryweek.com, accessed February 14, 2017; B. Davis, "Antidote to Malaise: College Towns," *Wall Street Journal,* December 13, 2016, pp. A1, A10.

50. J. Barney, *Gaining and Sustaining a Competitive Advantage* (Upper Saddle River, NJ: Prentice Hall, 2002).

51. L. Weatherly, *Human Capital: The Elusive Asset* (Alexandria, VA: SHRM Research Quarterly, 2003).

52. G. Tucker, "HR in the Age of Disruption," *HR Magazine,* September 2016, pp. 68–73.

53. L. Bassi, J. Ludwig, D. McMurrer, and M. Van Buren, *Profiting from Learning: Do Firms' Investments in Education and Training Pay Off?* (Alexandria, VA: American Society for Training and Development, September 2000); S. Sung and J. Choi, "Do Organizations Spend Wisely on Employees? Effects of Training and Development Investments on Learning and Innovation in Organizations," *Journal of Organizational Behavior* 35 (2014), pp. 393–412; H. Aguinis and K. Kraiger, "Benefits of Training and Development for Individuals, Teams, Organizations, and Society," *Annual Review of Psychology* 60 (2009), pp. 451–74.

54. T. J. Atchison, "The Employment Relationship: Untied or Re-Tied," *Academy of Management Executive* 5 (1991), pp. 52–62.

55. D. Senge, "The Learning Organization Made Plain and Simple," *Training and Development Journal,* October 1991, pp. 37–44.

56. L. Freifeld, "Keller Williams Realty's View from the Top," *Training,* January/February 2017, pp. 26–30.

57. *SHRM Workplace Forecast* (Alexandria, VA: Society for Human Resource Management, 2013).

58. J. O'Toole and E. Lawler III, *The New American Workplace* (New York: Palgrave McMillan, 2006); R. Hoffman, B. Casnocha, and C. Yeh, "Tours of Duty: The New Employer-Employee Compact," *Harvard Business Review,* June 2013, pp. 48–58.

59. W. Dougan, "Organization Evolution Requires Successful Change," *TD,* December 2015, pp. 60–65.

60. R. Vance, *Employee Engagement and Commitment* (Alexandria, VA: Society for Human Resource Management, 2006).

61. A. Adkins, "Employee Engagement in U.S. Stagnant in 2015," Gallup, January 16, 2016, http://www.gallup.com/poll/188144/employee-engagement-stagnant-2015.aspx, accessed February 16, 2017.

62. L. Stevens, "Engagement Tools," *Human Resource Executive,* June 16, 2016, pp. 36–37; T. Lytle, "The Engagement Challenge," *HR Magazine,* October 2016, pp. 52–58.

63. M. Ciccarelli, "Keeping the Keepers," *Human Resource Executive,* January/February 2011, pp. 1, 20–23.

64. P. Cappelli, "Talent Management for the Twenty-First Century," *Harvard Business Review,* March 2008, pp. 74–81; "Towers Watson 2014 Global Talent Management and Rewards Study," *HR Magazine,* April 2015, p. 54.

65. M. Weinstein, "BNSF Railway Is on the Right Training Track," *Training,* January/February 2017, pp. 42–44; Lytle, "The Engagement Challenge."

66. Freelancers Union & Elance-oDesk , "Freelancing in America: 2016," www.freelancersunion.org, accessed February 15, 2017; Bureau of Labor Statistics, "Contingent and Alternative Employment Arrangements, February 2005," www.bls.gov, accessed February 28, 2017.

67. A. Sussman and J. Zumbrun, "'Gig' Economy Spreads Broadly," *Wall Street Journal,* March 26, 2016, pp. A1, A2; Bloomberg BNA, "The Gig Economy: HR's Role in Navigating the On-Demand Workforce," January 2016, https://www.bna.com/gig-economy-hrs-m57982067661/.

68. J. Wald, "The Benefits or Lack Thereof of the 'Gig'," *Workforce,* August 2016, pp. 22–25.

69. L. Weber, "The End of Employees," *Wall Street Journal,* February 3, 2017, pp. A1, A10; A. McIlvaine, "The Contingent Quandary," *Human Resource Executive,* November 2015, pp. 14–16.

70. E. Frauenheim, "Creating a New Contingent Culture," *Workforce Management,* August 2012, pp. 34–39.

71. Gallup, "Work and Workplace," August 3–7, 2016, www.gallup.com, accessed February 17, 2017.

72. C. Patton, "On the Frontier of Flexibility," *Human Resource Executive,* May 2, 2009, pp. 48–51.

73. A. Fox, "Achieving Integration," *HR Magazine,* April 2011, pp. 42–47; P. Marinova, "Who Works from Home and When," February 28, 2013, www.cnn.com; C. Suddath, "Work-from-Home Truths, Half-Truths, and Myths," *Bloomberg Businessweek,* March 4–March 10, 2013, p. 75; R. Silverman and Q. Fottrell, "The Home Office in the Spotlight," *Wall Street Journal,* February 27, 2013, p. B6; N. Shah, "More Americans Working from Home Remotely," *Wall Street Journal,* April 6, 2013, p. A3.

74. Bureau of Labor Statistics, "American Time Use Survey", (June 24, 2016), from www.bls.gov/tus, accessed February 17, 2017; Gallup, "Work and Workplace, (August 3-7, 2016), from www.gallup.com, accessed February 17, 2017.

75. T. Agovino, "Tinkering with Time," *HR Magazine,* February 2017, pp. 46–52; "Rewards and Benefits," www.kpmg.com, accessed February 17, 2017.

76. C. Hymowitz, "Diebold's new executive suite", *Bloomberg BusinessWeek* (August 10-August 23, 2015) 21–24.

77. R. Feintzeig, "WeWork Courts More Corporate Clients", *Wall Street Journal,* August 16, 2016, pp. B1, B2; A. Fox, "At Work in 2020," *HR Magazine,* January 2010, pp. 18–23.

78. R. S. Kaplan and D. P. Norton, "The Balanced Scorecard—Measures That Drive Performance," *Harvard Business Review,* January–February 1992, pp. 71–79; R. S. Kaplan and D. P. Norton, "Putting the Balanced Scorecard to Work," *Harvard Business Review,* September/October 1993, pp. 134–47.

79. S. Bates, "The Metrics Maze," *HR Magazine,* December 2003, pp. 50–55; D. Ulrich, "Measuring Human Resources: An Overview of Practice and a Prescription for Results," *Human Resource Management* 36 (1997), pp. 303–20.

80. SAS Institute, "Customer Success: SAS Helps ConocoPhillips Norway Focus on Performance and Control Costs," www.sas.com, accessed April 24, 2012.

81. B. Sutherly, "Doctor Pay Still Based on Volume," *The Columbus Dispatch*, March 24, 2013, pp. A1 and A9.

82. Coca-Cola, 2015–2016 Sustainability Update, "Women's Economic Empowerment," www.coca-colacompany.com, accessed February 20, 2017.

83. D. Stanford, "Sustainability Meets the Profit Motive," *Bloomberg Businessweek*, April 4–April 10, 2011, pp. 25–26.

84. International Paper, "Company Overview 2015," www.internationalpaper.com, accessed February 20, 2017.

85. "Dow 2015 Sustainability Report" www. dow.com, accessed February 20, 2017; Ladika, "The Responsible Way."

86. J. R. Jablonski, *Implementing Total Quality Management: An Overview* (San Diego: Pfeiffer, 1991).

87. R. Hodgetts, F. Luthans, and S. Lee, "New Paradigm Organizations: From Total Quality to Learning World-Class," *Organizational Dynamics*, Winter 1994, pp. 5–19.

88. National Institute of Standards and Technology (NIST), Baldrige Performance Excellence Program, "Baldrige Frequently Asked Questions," www.nist.gov/baldrige, accessed April 8, 2011.

89. A. Pomeroy, "Winners and Learners," *HR Magazine*, April 2006, pp. 62–67.

90. National Institute of Standards and Technology, "Don Chalmers Ford, Malcolm Baldrige National Quality Award 2016 Award Recipient, Small Business," November 17, 2016, www.nist. gov/baldrige/don-chalmers-ford, accessed February 13, 2017.

91. "ISO in One Page," "Quality Management Principles," "ISO 9000 Essentials," and "Management and Leadership Standards," International Organization for Standardization, www. iso.org, accessed April 9, 2011.

92. General Electric Company website, "What Is Six Sigma?" www.ge.com, accessed February 13, 2017; Shmula, "GE and Six Sigma: The Beginning of a Beautiful Relationship," www. shmula.com, accessed March 1, 2017.

93. "Baylor Health Care System: Lean and Process Improvement Training," *Training*, January/February 2014, p. 106.

94. Bureau of Labor Statistics, "Employment Projections, 2014–2024," News Release, www.bls.gov, accessed February 9, 2017.

95. S. Milligan, "Wisdom of the Ages," *HR Magazine*, November 2014, pp. 22–27; C. Paullin, *The Aging Workforce: Leveraging the Talents of Mature Employees* (Alexandria, VA: The SHRM Foundation, 2014); N. Lockwood, *The Aging Workforce* (Alexandria, VA: Society for Human Resource Management, 2003).

96. J. Ramirez, "Betting on Older Workers," *Human Resource Executive*, June 16, 2016, pp. 14–16; Milligan, "Wisdom of the Ages"; V. Giang, "The Fifty Best Employers for Older Workers," *Business Insider*, accessed April 14, 2015, www.businessinsider.com; S. Hewlett, L. Sherbin, and K. Sumberg, "How Gen Y & Boomers Will Reshape Your Agenda," *Harvard Business Review*, July/August 2009, pp. 71–76.

97. A. Adkins, "What Millennials Want From Work and Life," www.gallup.com, May 11, 2016, accessed February 20, 2017; S. Gale, "Forget Millennials: Are You Ready for Generation Z?", *Chief Learning Officer,* July 2015, pp. 38–48; K. Tyler, "New Kids on the Block," *HR Magazine*, October 2013, pp. 35–40; Milligan, "Wisdom of the Ages"; Hewlett, Sherbin, and Sumberg, "How Gen Y & Boomers Will Reshape Your Agenda"; A. Fox, "Mixing It Up" *HR Magazine*, May 2011, pp. 22–27; K. Ball and G. Gotsill, *Surviving the Baby Boomer Exodus* (Boston, MA: Cengage, 2011).

98. J. Meriac, D. Woehr, and C. Banister, "Generational Differences in Work Ethic: An Examination of Measurement Equivalence across Three Cohorts," *Journal of Business and Psychology*, 25 (2010), pp. 315–24; K. Real, A. Mitnick, and W. Maloney, "More Similar than Different: Millennials in the U.S. Building Trades," *Journal of Business and Psychology*, 25 (2010), pp. 303–13.

99. T. Lennon, "Managing a Multi-generational Workforce: The Myths vs. the Realities," 2015, www.haygroup.com, accessed February 20, 2017; S. Lyons and L. Kuron, "Generational Differences in the Workplace: A Review of the Evidence and Directions for Future Research," *Journal of Organizational Behavior* 35 (2013), pp. 139–57; J. Deal, D. Altman, and S. Rogelberg, "Millennials at Work: What We Know and What We Need to Do (If Anything)," *Journal of Business and Psychology*, 25 (2010), pp. 191–99.

100. Coca-Cola Company, "2015 Highlights," April 27, 2016, www. coca-colacompany.com/stories/2015-highlights, accessed February 14, 2017.

101. Bureau of Labor Statistics, "Employment Projections, 2014–2024," News Release, www.bls.gov, accessed February 9, 2017.

102. N. Mossaad, "U.S. Lawful Permanent Residents: 2014," Annual Flow Report, April 2016, U.S. Department of Homeland Security, Office of Immigration Statistics, www.dhs.gov, accessed February 12, 2017; N. Mossaad, "Refugees and Asylees: 2014," Annual Flow Report, April 2016, U.S. Department of Homeland Security, Office of Immigration Statistics, www.dhs.gov, accessed February 12, 2017.

103. J. Sparshott, "Immigration Study Sees More Pros Than Cons," *Wall Street Journal*, September 23, 2016, p. A2; National Academies of Science, Engineering, and Medicine, *The Economic and Fiscal Consequences of Immigration* (Washington, DC: National Academies Press, 2016).

104. L. Meckler, "U.S. sets hard line on illegal immigrants", *Wall Street Journal* (February 22, 2017): A1 & A6.

105. L. Meckler, "H-1B's Future Causes Rift," *Wall Street Journal,* February 10, 2017, p. B4; M. Trottman, "Clash Erupts over Seasonal-Worker Visas," *Wall Street Journal,* February, 26, 2016, p. A3; L. Meckler and L. Stevens, "White House Takes on Working Visas," *Wall Street Journal*, February 1, 2017; M. Jordan and S. Perez, "Employers' Lament: Too Few Immigrants," *Wall Street Journal*, November 25, 2016, pp. A1, A9.

106. B. Groysberg and K. Connolly, "Great Leaders Who Make the Mix Work," *Harvard Business Review*, September 2013, pp. 68–76; K. Jones, E. King, J. Nelson, D. Geller, and L. Bowes-Sperry, "Beyond the Business Case: The Ethical Perspective on Diversity Training," *Human Resource Management*, January–February 2013, pp. 55–74; T. H. Cox and S. Blake, "Managing Cultural Diversity: Implications for Organizational Competitiveness," *The Executive* 5 (1991), pp. 45–56.

107. Groysberg and Connolly, "Great Leaders Who Make the Mix Work"; M. Loden and J. B. Rosener, *Workforce America!* (Homewood, IL: Business One Irwin, 1991); N. Lockwood, *Workplace Diversity: Leveraging the Power of Difference for Competitive Advantage* (Alexandria, VA: Society for Human Resource Management, 2005).

108 J. Robinson, "Culture-Change Agents," *Human Resource Executive*, September 16, 2016, pp. 10–12; "The Business of Inclusion," www.microsoft.com, accessed February 20, 2017.

109. S. Sipek, "Wearing Your Health on Your Sleeve," *Workforce*, August 2014, p. 16; C. Donham, "Legal Considerations," *Workforce*, August 2014, p. 47; L. Weber, "EEOC Issues Proposal for Wellness Programs," *Wall Street Journal*, April 17, 2015, p. B5; M. Mihelich, "Sacred Ground for Lawsuits," *Workforce*,

April 2014, pp. 18–19; J. Hyman, "Any Headway on Headware?" *Workforce*, November 2013, p. 27; M. Mihelich, "The Expanded Definition of Disability," *Workforce*, February 2014, pp. 20–21; J. Palazzolo, "Family-Leave Lawsuits Take Off," *Wall Street Journal*, August 9–10, 2014, p. A3; R. Grossman, "No Federal Regulatory Relief in Sight," *HR Magazine*, February 2013, pp. 24–25.

110. L. Weber, "Uber Settlement with Drivers Meets Dissent," *Wall Street Journal,* June 2, 2016, p. B3; C. Duhigg, "How Trump Might Become a Workplace Disrupter," *New York Times,* February 22, 2017.

111. S. Jakab, C. Grant, and D. Gallagher, "Why Travel Curb Irks Executives," *Wall Street Journal,* January 31, 2017, p. B12; J. Nicas, "Executives Say Move Hurts High Tech Workers," *Wall Street Journal,* January 30, 2017, p. A4; D. Paletta and N. Hong, "Migrant Order Faces New Challenges," *Wall Street Journal,* January 31, 2017, pp. A1, A5.

112. A. Wright, "Boeing Insider Data Breach Serves as Reminder for HR," www.shrm.org, accessed March 10, 2017.

113. M. Pastin, *The Hard Problems of Management: Gaining the Ethics Edge* (San Francisco: Jossey-Bass, 1986); T. Thomas, J. Schermerhorn, Jr., and J. Dienhart, "Strategic Leadership of Ethical Behavior in Business," *Academy of Management Executive* 18 (2004), pp. 56–66.

114. Ibid; J. Robinson, "Balancing Act," *Human Resource Executive,* December 2016, pp. 14–16.

115. D. Meinert, "Creating an Ethical Culture," *HR Magazine*, April 2014, pp. 22–27.

116. Gallup, "Honesty/Ethics in Professions," December 2015, www.gallup.com, accessed February 20, 2017.

117. K. Gurchiek, "Sarbanes-Oxley Compliance Costs Rising," *HR Magazine*, January 2005, pp. 29, 33.

118. R. Grossman, "HR and the Board," *HR Magazine*, January 2007, pp. 52–58.

119. J. Segal, "The 'Joy' of Uncooking," *HR Magazine* 47 (2002).

120. D. Buss, "Corporate Compasses," *HR Magazine* 49 (2004), pp. 126–32.

121. E. Krell, "How to Conduct an Ethics Audit," *HR Magazine*, April 2010, pp. 48–50.

122. "Global Ethics & Compliance," www.eaton.com, accessed February 20, 2017; D. Meinert, "Creating an Ethical Culture," *HR Magazine*, April 2014, pp. 22–27; A. McIlvaine, "Ethical Champions," *Human Resource Executive*, November 2014, pp. 14–16.

123. G. F. Cavanaugh, D. Moberg, and M. Velasquez, "The Ethics of Organizational Politics," *Academy of Management Review* 6 (1981), pp. 363–74.

124. "Manufacturing: Engine of US Innovation," *National Association of Manufacturing*, October 4, 2006, www.nam.org, accessed January 21, 2009.

125. I. Bremmer, "The New World of Business," *Fortune*, February 1, 2015, pp. 86–92.

126. D. Wessel, "Big U.S. Firms Shift Hiring Abroad," *Wall Street Journal*, April 19, 2011, pp. B1, B2.

127. B. Einhorn, "Can Lincoln and Caddy Find Fans in China?" *BloombergBusinessWeek*, April 7, 2016, pp. 21–22.

128. J. Marson, "McDonald's Puts Down Stakes in Siberia," *Wall Street Journal*, January 24, 2017, p. B6.

129. N. Purnell, "Uber Taps Novice Drivers," *Wall Street Journal,* December 27, 2016, p. B4.

130. IBM Corporate Service Corps, www.ibm.com/ibm/responsibility/corporateservicecorps/programdetails.html, accessed February 13, 2017; IBM Corporation, "2015 Corporate Responsibility Report," June 2016, www.ibm.com/ibm/responsibility/2015/assets/downloads/IBM_2015_CR_report.pdf, accessed February 13, 2017; C. Hymowitz, "IBM Combines Volunteer Service, Teamwork to Cultivate Emerging Markets," *Wall Street Journal*, August 4, 2008, p. B6.

131. J. Schramm, "Offshoring," *Workplace Visions* 2 (Alexandria, VA: Society for Human Resource Management, 2004); P. Babcock, "America's Newest Export: White Collar Jobs," *HR Magazine* 49 (4) 2004, pp. 50–57.

132. A. Tangel, "For some manufacturers, Mexico still the best move", *Wall Street Journal* February 9, 2017, A1.

133. J. Hagerty and M. Magnier, "Companies Tiptoe Back Toward 'Made in America,'" *Wall Street Journal*, January 14, 2015, pp. A1, A12.

134. J. Hagerty, "Decimated U.S. Industry Pulls Up Its Socks," *Wall Street Journal*, December 26, 2014, p. B6.

135. U.S. Census Bureau, "Census Bureau's American Community Survey Provides New State and Local Income, Poverty, Health Insurance Statistics," www.census.gov, accessed February 27, 2015; L. Morales, "Nearly Half of Americans Are Frequent Internet Users," January 2, 2009, www.gallup.com; L. Morales, "Google and Facebook Users, Skew Young, Affluent and Educated," February 17, 2011, www.gallup.com; F. Newport, "Most US Smartphone Owners Check Phone at Least Hourly," July 9, 2015, www.gallup.com; and L. Saad, "Nearly Half of Smartphone Users Can't Imagine Life without It," July 13, 2015, www.gallup.com, accessed February 20, 2017.

136. M. Derven, "Social Networking: A Frame for Development," *T + D*, July 2009, pp. 58–63; J. Arnold, "Twittering and Facebooking While They Work," *HR Magazine*, December 2009, pp. 53–55.

137. C. Goodman, "Employers Wrestle with Social-Media Policies," *The Columbus Dispatch*, January 30, 2011, p. D3.

138. W. Cascio and R. Montealegre, "How Technology Is Changing Work and Organizations," *Annual Review of Organizational Psychology and Organizational Behavior*, 3 (2016), pp. 349–75; J. Bersin, "Transformative Tech: A Disruptive Year Ahead," *HR Magazine,* February 2017, pp. 29–36; G. Colvin, "In the Future, Will There Be Any Work Left for People to Do?" *Fortune*, June 2, 2014; T. Aeppel, "Jobs and the Clever Robot," *Wall Street Journal*, February 25, 2015, pp. A1, A10.

139. S. Gale, "Ready or Not, the Future Is Now," *Chief Learning Officer,* March 2017, pp. 20–21; J. Stern, "Alexa, Stop Bringing Chaos to Anyone with a Similar Name," *Wall Street Journal,* January 27, 2016, pp. A1, A8; "Are You Leaving Money on the Table? H&R Block with Watson Can Help," www.ibm.com, accessed February 20, 2017.

140. N. Olivarez-Giles, "Robots with Skills and Charm," *Wall Street Journal,* January 6, 2017, p. B4; A. Tangel, "Latest Robots Lend an Arm," *Wall Street Journal,* November 9, 2016, pp. B1, B4.

141. K. Everson, "Special Report: Learning Is All in the Wrist," *Chief Learning Officer*, accessed March 18, 2015, www.clomedia.com; company website, "About" and "Products," www.wearableintelligence.com, the website for Wearable Intelligence, accessed April 21, 2015.

142. R. Silverman, "Tracking Sensors Invade the Workplace," *Wall Street Journal*, March 7, 2013, pp. B1, B2.

143. M. J. Kavanaugh, H. G. Guetal, and S. I. Tannenbaum, *Human Resource Information Systems: Development and Application* (Boston: PWS-Kent, 1990).

144. A. Abbatiello, "The Digital Override," *Workforce*, May 2014, pp. 36–39.

145. D. Zielinski, "The Mobilization of HR Tech," *HR Magazine*, February 2014, pp. 30–36.

146. A. McAfee, "What Every CEO Needs to Know about the Cloud," *Harvard Business Review*, November 2011, pp. 124–132; B. Roberts, "The Grand Convergence," *HR Magazine*, October 2011, pp. 39–46; M. Paino, "All Generations Learn in the Cloud," *Chief Learning Officer*, September 28, 2011, http://blog.clomedia.com, accessed October 11, 2011.

147. "HR Heads to the Cloud," *Human Resource Executive,* September 2016, p. 16.

148. M. Charney, "Five Reasons Why Cloud Computing Matters for Recruitment and Hiring," *Monster.com*, http://hiring.monster.com, accessed May 17, 2015; D. Shane, "A Human Giant," *InformationAge*, accessed May 17, 2015, http://www.information-age.com.

149. L. Weatherly, "HR Technology: Leveraging the Shift to Self-Service," *HR Magazine*, March 2005.

150. N. Lockwood, *Maximizing Human Capital: Demonstrating HR Value with Key Performance Indicators* (Alexandria, VA: SHRM Research Quarterly, 2006).

151. P. Choate and P. Linger, *The High-Flex Society* (New York: Knopf, 1986); P. B. Doeringer, *Turbulence in the American Workplace* (New York: Oxford University Press, 1991).

152. J. A. Neal and C. L. Tromley, "From Incremental Change to Retrofit: Creating High-Performance Work Systems," *Academy of Management Executive* 9 (1995), pp. 42–54.

153. K. A. Miller, *Retraining the American Workforce* (Reading, MA: Addison-Wesley, 1989).

154. B. Reynolds, "Twenty-Six Companies That Thrive on Remote Work," *Flex Jobs*, www.flexjobs.com, accessed March 3, 2015; company website, www.artandlogic.com, accessed March 3, 2015; "Working at Art & Logic," www.artandlogic.com/careers, accessed July 1, 2015.

155. M. A. Huselid, "The Impact of Human Resource Management Practices on Turnover, Productivity, and Corporate Financial Performance," *Academy of Management Journal* 38 (1995), pp. 635–72; U.S. Dept. of Labor, *High-Performance Work Practices and Firm Performance* (Washington, DC: U.S. Government Printing Office, 1993); J. Combs, Y. Liu, A. Hall, and D. Ketchen, "How Much Do High-Performance Work Practices Matter? A Meta-analysis of Their Effects on Organizational Performance," *Personnel Psychology* 59 (2006), pp. 501–28.

156. B. Becker and M. A. Huselid, "High-Performance Work Systems and Firm Performance: A Synthesis of Research and Managerial Implications," in *Research in Personnel and Human Resource Management* 16, ed. G. R. Ferris (Stamford, CT: JAI Press, 1998), pp. 53–101; A. Zacharatos, J. Barling, and R. Iverson, "High Performance Work Systems and Occupational Safety," *Journal of Applied Psychology* 90 (2005), pp. 77–93.

157. B. Becker and B. Gerhart, "The Impact of Human Resource Management on Organizational Performance: Progress and Prospects," *Academy of Management Journal* 39 (1996), pp. 779–801.

158. Company website, www.hindlepower.com, accessed May 17, 2015; P. Fehrenbach, "HindlePower's Pro Shop: Greatness Within," *Industry Week*, June 3, 2014; ProQuest eLibrary, http://elibrary.bigchalk.com; J. Juski, "The Value of Labor," *Industry Week*, November 2013, pp. 24–26; A. Wlazelek, "HindlePower Inc.: Manufacturing without a Time Clock," *Morning Call* (Lehigh Valley, PA), March 4, 2103, http://articles.mcall.com; "Dundee Engine Plant, Michigan: The Former GEMA Factory," www.allpar.com, accessed February 23, 2017; Fiat Chrysler Automobiles (FCA), "Dundee Engine Plant," January 2017, http://media.fcanorthamerica.com/, accessed February 23, 2017; J. Marquez, "Engine of Change," *Workforce Management*, July 2006, pp. 20–30.

159. S. A. Snell and J. W. Dean, "Integrated Manufacturing and Human Resource Management: A Human Capital Perspective," *Academy of Management Journal* 35 (1992), pp. 467–504; M. A. Youndt, S. Snell, J. W. Dean Jr., and D. P. Lepak, "Human Resource Management, Manufacturing Strategy, and Firm Performance," *Academy of Management Journal* 39 (1996), pp. 836–66.

CHAPTER

2

Strategic Human Resource Management

LEARNING OBJECTIVES

After reading this chapter, you should be able to:

LO 2-1   Describe the differences between strategy formulation and strategy implementation. *page 76*

LO 2-2   List the components of the strategic management process. *page 77*

LO 2-3   Discuss the role of the HRM function in strategy formulation. *page 78*

LO 2-4   Describe the linkages between HRM and strategy formulation. *page 81*

LO 2-5   Discuss the more popular typologies of generic strategies and the various HRM practices associated with each. *page 86*

LO 2-6   Describe the different HRM issues and practices associated with various directional strategies. *page 93*

Amazon: From Digital to Brick-and-Mortar?

Amazon.com's Internet-based business model created havoc in the retail industry. Beginning with selling books online, then music, then just about anything, the company cut into traditional retailers' markets and margins. Built on a business model that created profits through selling high volume at a low margin, and doing so with very little physical assets, it quickly became the 800-pound gorilla every retailer had to face. Those that have survived have done so by trying to develop their own online presence while maintaining their brick-and-mortar operations.

Now Amazon is attacking them on their traditional turf: the brick-and-mortar store. The company recently unveiled a grocery store called "Amazon Go." The plans are to open more than 2,000 of these grocery stores, which would put them on a par with Kroger Co., which has around 2,800 locations in 35 states. These stores will be multi-functioning, with curbside pickup capability, in-store shopping, and even delivery.

One potential format would be like a convenience store, but one that eliminates checkouts, cash registers, and lines. Customers scan their phones upon entering the store, and using artificial-intelligence-powered technology, Amazon can

©seastock/shutterstock.com

determine what customers took from the shelves, charge them for the items, and send a receipt. Another format would resemble the traditional 30,000–40,000 square foot grocery store where customers pick the fresh selections they like and also order other items via touch-screen to be delivered later.

SOURCE: L. Stevens and S. Khadeeja, "Amazon Working on Several Grocery Store Formats, Could Open More Than 2,000 Locations," *Wall Street Journal,* December 5, 2016, https://www.wsj.com/articles/amazon-grocery-store-concept-to-open-in-seattle-in-early-2017-1480959119.

Introduction

As the Amazon example illustrates, business organizations exist in an environment of competition. They can use a number of resources to compete with other companies. These resources are physical (such as plant, equipment, technology, and geographic location), organizational (the structure; planning, controlling, and coordinating systems; and group relations), and human (the experience, skill, and intelligence of employees). It is these resources under the control of the company that provide competitive advantage.[1]

The goal of strategic management in an organization is to deploy and allocate resources in a way that gives it a competitive advantage. As you can see, two of the three classes of resources (organizational and human) are directly tied to the human resource management function. As Chapter 1 pointed out, the role of human resource management is to ensure that a company's human resources provide a competitive advantage. Chapter 1 also pointed out some of the major competitive challenges that companies face today. These challenges require companies to take a proactive, strategic approach in the marketplace.

To be maximally effective, the HRM function must be integrally involved in the company's strategic management process.[2] This means that human resource managers should (1) have input into the strategic plan, both in terms of people-related issues and in terms of the ability of the human resource pool to implement particular strategic alternatives; (2) have specific knowledge of the organization's strategic goals; (3) know what types of employee skills, behaviors, and attitudes are needed to support the strategic plan; and (4) develop programs to ensure that employees have those skills, behaviors, and attitudes.

We begin this chapter by discussing the concepts of business models and strategy and by depicting the strategic management process. Then, we discuss the levels of integration between the HRM function and the strategic management process in strategy formulation. Next, we review some of the more common strategic models and, within the context of these models, discuss the various types of employee skills, behaviors, and attitudes, and the ways HRM practices aid in implementing the strategic plan. Finally, we discuss the role of HR in creating competitive advantage.

What Is a Business Model?

A business model is a story of how the firm will create value for customers and, more important, how it will do so profitably. We often hear or read of companies that have "transformed their business model" in one way or another, but what that means is not always clear. To understand this, we need to grasp a few basic accounting concepts.

First, fixed costs are generally considered the costs that are incurred regardless of the number of units produced. For instance, if you are producing widgets in a factory, you have the rent you pay for the factory, depreciation of the machines, the utilities, the property taxes, and so on. In addition, you generally have a set number of employees who work a set number of hours with a specified level of benefits, and although you might be able to vary these over time, on a regular basis you pay the same total labor costs whether your factory runs at 70% capacity or 95% capacity.

Second, you have a number of variable costs, which are those costs that vary directly with the units produced. For instance, all of the materials that go into the widget might cost a total of $10, which means that you have to charge at least $10 per widget, or you cannot even cover the variable costs of production.

Third is the concept of "contribution margins," or margins. Margins are the difference between what you charge for your product and the variable costs of that product. They are called contribution margins because they are what contributes to your ability to cover your fixed costs. So, for instance, if you charged $15 for each widget, your contribution margin would be $5 ($15 price − $10 variable cost).

Fourth, the gross margin is the total amount of margin you made and is calculated as the number of units sold times the contribution margin. If you sold 1,000,000 units, your gross margin would then be $5,000,000. Did you make a profit? That depends. Profit refers to what is left after you have paid your variable costs and your fixed costs. If your gross margin was $5,000,000, and your fixed costs were $6,000,000, then you lost $1,000,000.

GM'S ATTEMPT TO SURVIVE

Let's look at how a business model plays out with the recent challenges faced by General Motors (GM). Critics of GM talk about the fact that GM has higher labor costs than its foreign competitors. This is true, but misleading. GM's average hourly wage for its existing workforce is reasonably competitive. However, the two aspects that make GM uncompetitive are its benefit costs (in particular, health care) and, most important, the cost of its legacy workforce.

A legacy workforce describes the former workers (i.e., those no longer working for the company) to whom the firm still owes financial obligations. GM and the United Automobile Workers (UAW) union have negotiated contracts over the years that provide substantial retirement benefits for former GM workers. In particular, retired GM workers have defined benefit plans that guarantee a certain percentage of their final (preretirement) salary as a pension payment as long as they live; in addition, the company pays for their health insurance. The contract specifies that workers are entitled to retire at full pension after 30 years of service.

This might have seemed sustainable when the projections were that GM would continue growing its sales and margins. However, since the 1970s, foreign competitors have been eating away at GM's market share to the extent that GM's former 50% of the market has shrunk to closer to 20%. Since the 2008 economic crisis, the market itself has been shrinking, leaving GM with a decreasing percentage of a decreasing market. For instance, in December of 2005, GM sold 26% of the cars in the global market, but by 2015 that market share had shrunk to 11.2%.[3] Thus, in addition to the legacy workforce, GM had a significant number of plants with thousands of employees that were completely unnecessary, given the volume of cars GM can produce and sell.[4]

If you look at Figure 2.1, you'll see that the solid lines represent the old GM business model, which was based on projections that GM would be able to sell 4 million units at a reasonably high margin, and thus completely cover its fixed costs to make a strong profit. However, the reality was that its products didn't sell at the higher prices, so to try to sell 4 million vehicles, GM offered discounts, which cut into its margins. When GM ended up selling only 3.5 million vehicles, and those were sold at a lower margin, the

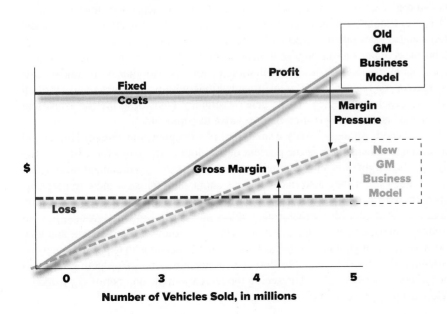

Figure 2.1

An Illustration of a Business Model for GM

company could not cover its fixed costs, resulting in a $9 billion loss in 2008 (this is illustrated by the dotted blue line in the figure). So, when GM refers to the "redesigned business model," what it is referring to is a significant reduction in fixed costs (through closing plants and cutting workers) to get the fixed-cost base low enough (the dotted brown line) to remain profitable while selling fewer cars at lower margins (again, the dotted blue line).

One can easily see how, given the large component that labor costs are to most companies, reference to business models almost inevitably leads to discussions of labor costs. These can be the high cost associated with current unionized employees in developed countries within North America or Europe or, in some cases, the high costs associated with a legacy workforce. For instance, the Big Three automakers have huge numbers of retired or laid-off workers for whom they still have the liability of paying pensions and health care benefits. This is a significant component of their fixed-cost base, which makes it difficult for them to compete with other automakers that either have fewer retirees to cover or have no comparable costs because their home governments provide pensions and health care. In fact, this changing business model at GM has driven it to locate more manufacturing outside of the United States. The "Competing through Globalization" box describes how one firm has moved manufacturing to Mexico as a way to lower its labor costs.

What Is Strategic Management?

LO 2-1
Describe the differences between strategy formulation and strategy implementation.

Many authors have noted that in today's competitive market, organizations must engage in strategic planning to survive and prosper. Strategy comes from the Greek word *strategos,* which has its roots in military language. It refers to a general's grand design behind a war or battle. In fact, *Webster's New American Dictionary* defines strategy as the "skillful employment and coordination of tactics" and as "artful planning and management."

Strategic management is a process, an approach to addressing the competitive challenges an organization faces. It can be thought of as managing the "pattern or plan that integrates an organization's major goals, policies, and action sequences into a cohesive whole."[5] These strategies can be either the generic approach to competing or the specific adjustments and actions taken to deal with a particular situation.

First, business organizations engage in generic strategies that often fit into some strategic type. One example is "cost, differentiation, or focus."[6] Another is "defender, analyzer, prospector, or reactor."[7] Different organizations within the same industry often have different generic strategies. These generic strategy types describe the consistent way the company attempts to position itself relative to competitors.

However, a generic strategy is only a small part of strategic management. The second aspect of strategic management is the process of developing strategies for achieving the company's goals in light of its current environment. Thus, business organizations engage in generic strategies, but they also make choices about such things as how to scare off competitors, how to keep competitors weaker, how to react to and influence pending legislation, how to deal with various stakeholders and special interest groups, how to lower production costs, how to raise revenues, what technology to implement, and how many and what types of people to employ. Each of these decisions may present competitive challenges that have to be considered. For instance, the "Competing through Technology" box describes how ADP, seeing the increase in the number of gig workers, has developed a product to help them manage their own HR processes.

COMPETING THROUGH GLOBALIZATION

Lowering Costs through Offshoring

Companies often build facilities in overseas locations to capitalize on lower labor costs, and then close down their facilities in the United States, essentially moving those jobs (but not those people) to the new location. Rexnord Corporation, a supplier of power transmission components, recently announced that it was closing its industrial bearings factory in Indiana and moving the manufacturing to Mexico. Rexnord expects to save $30 million annually by moving the plant.

Rexnord employs 350 people at the plant, most of whom will lose their jobs. The workers are worried about finding jobs that match their current $25 per hour rate, and about whether or not they will be able to pay their car, mortgage, and tuition payments. The company is currently asking workers to train their Mexican replacements. Although it not required and, in fact, Rexnord pays extra to those who are willing to do so, the request does not sit well with current workers. Machinist Tim Mathis, who has worked there for 12 years says, "That's a real kick in the ass to be asked to train your replacement. To train the man that's going to eat your bread."

DISCUSSION QUESTIONS

1. Is it legitimate for firms to move jobs from the United States to other countries to lower labor costs?
2. How do you feel about having soon-to-be-displaced workers training their replacements?

SOURCE: A. Tangel, "Companies Plow Ahead with Moves to Mexico, Despite Trump's Pressure," *Wall Street Journal,* February 8, 2017, https://www.wsj.com/articles/rexnord-plows-ahead-with-mexico-plans-despite-trumps-pressure-1486555201/.

Strategic management is more than a collection of strategic types. It is a process for analyzing a company's competitive situation, developing the company's strategic goals, and devising a plan of action and allocation of resources (human, organizational, and physical) that will increase the likelihood of achieving those goals. This kind of strategic approach should be emphasized in human resource management. HR managers should be trained to identify the competitive issues the company faces with regard to human resources and think strategically about how to respond.

Strategic human resource management (SHRM) can be thought of as "the pattern of planned human resource deployments and activities intended to enable an organization to achieve its goals."[8] For example, many firms have developed integrated manufacturing systems such as advanced manufacturing technology, just-in-time inventory control, and total quality management in an effort to increase their competitive position. However, these systems must be run by people. SHRM in these cases entails assessing the employee skills required to run these systems and engaging in HRM practices, such as selection and training, that develop these skills in employees.[9] To take a strategic approach to HRM, we must first understand the role of HRM in the strategic management process.

Strategic human resource management (SHRM)
A pattern of planned human resource deployments and activities intended to enable an organization to achieve its goals.

Strategy formulation
The process of deciding on a strategic direction by defining a company's mission and goals, its external opportunities and threats, and its internal strengths and weaknesses.

COMPONENTS OF THE STRATEGIC MANAGEMENT PROCESS

The strategic management process has two distinct yet interdependent phases: strategy formulation and strategy implementation. During **strategy formulation**, the strategic planning groups decide on a strategic direction by defining the company's mission and goals, its external opportunities and threats, and its internal strengths and weaknesses. They then generate various strategic alternatives and compare those alternatives' ability

LO 2-2
List the components of the strategic management process.

Strategy implementation
The process of devising structures and allocating resources to enact the strategy a company has chosen.

to achieve the company's mission and goals. During **strategy implementation**, the organization follows through on the chosen strategy. This consists of structuring the organization, allocating resources, ensuring that the firm has skilled employees in place, and developing reward systems that align employee behavior with the organization's strategic goals. Both of these strategic management phases must be performed effectively. This process does not happen sequentially. As we will discuss later with regard to emergent strategies, this process entails a constant cycling of information and decision making. Figure 2.2 presents the strategic management process.

In recent years organizations have recognized that the success of the strategic management process depends largely on the extent to which the HRM function is involved.[10]

LINKAGE BETWEEN HRM AND THE STRATEGIC MANAGEMENT PROCESS

The strategic choice really consists of answering questions about competition—that is, how the firm will compete to achieve its mission and goals. These decisions consist of addressing the issues of where to compete, how to compete, and with what to compete, which are described in Figure 2.3.

Although these decisions are all important, strategic decision makers often pay less attention to the "with what will we compete" issue, resulting in poor strategic decisions. For example, PepsiCo in the 1980s acquired the fast-food chains of Kentucky Fried Chicken, Taco Bell, and Pizza Hut ("where to compete" decisions) in an effort to increase its customer base. However, it failed to adequately recognize the differences between its existing workforce (mostly professionals) and that of the fast-food industry (lower skilled people and high schoolers) as well as its ability to manage such a workforce. This was one reason that PepsiCo, in 1998, spun off the fast-food chains. In essence, it had made a decision about where to compete without fully understanding what resources would be needed to compete in that market.

Boeing illustrates how failing to address the "with what" issue resulted in problems in its "how to compete" decisions. When the aerospace firm's consumer products division entered into a price war with Airbus Industrie, it was forced to move away from its traditional customer service strategy toward emphasizing cost reduction.[11] The strategy was a success on the sales end as Boeing received large numbers of orders for aircraft from firms such as Delta, Continental, Southwest, and Singapore Airlines. However, it had recently gone through a large workforce reduction (thus, it didn't have enough people to fill the orders) and did not have the production technology to enable the necessary increase in productivity. The result of this failure to address "with what will we compete" in making a decision about how to compete resulted in the firm's inability to meet delivery deadlines and the ensuing penalties it had to pay to its customers. The end result is that after all the travails, for the first time in the history of the industry, Airbus sold more planes than Boeing in 2003. Luckily, Boeing was able to overcome this stumble, in large part because of a number of stumbles on the part of its chief rival, Airbus. However, Boeing has faced difficulties as its new Dreamliner was grounded because of fires starting in the wiring.

ROLE OF HRM IN STRATEGY FORMULATION

LO 2-3
Discuss the role of the HRM function in strategy formulation.

As the preceding examples illustrate, often the "with what will we compete" question presents ideal avenues for HRM to influence the strategic management process. This might be through either limiting strategic options or forcing thoughtfulness among the executive team regarding how and at what cost the firm might gain or develop the human

Figure 2.2

A Model of the Strategic Management Process

HR for the Gig Worker

The gig economy continues to grow with an estimated 55 million people working as freelancers such as drivers for Lyft or Uber, artists on Etsy, or hairdressers who rent a chair in a salon. One major challenge such workers face is how to calculate retirement contributions, tax deductions, or other tasks that are done automatically for employees. Such tasks comprise much of the administrative role that HR functions play in organizations.

In response, Automatic Data Processing (ADP), the payroll processor has entered this market. It traditionally performed back-office functions for companies and provided software that company employees could use to look at paystubs or other data housed in the company's information system. However, ADP is now working on an app to help gig workers do many of the things that company employees have done for them. For instance, the app links to their bank accounts. Whenever a company like Uber deposits pay, the app calculates the taxes the worker must set aside and provides an alert. ADP hopes to build in additional functionality to help gig workers access health care insurers or retirement managers and help them choose the best providers.

DISCUSSION QUESTION

1. Do you think ADP's strategy of reaching out to gig workers will be effective? Why or why not?

SOURCE: K. Nash, "ADP Building Mobile App for Gig Workers," *Wall Street Journal*, December 5, 2016, http://blogs.wsj.com/cio/2016/12/05/adp-building-mobile-app-for-gig-workers/.

resources (people) necessary for such a strategy to be successful. For example, HRM executives at PepsiCo could have noted that the firm had no expertise in managing the workforce of fast-food restaurants. The limiting role would have been for these executives to argue against the acquisition because of this lack of resources. Alternatively, they might have influenced the decision by educating top executives as to the costs (of hiring, training, and so on) associated with gaining people who had the right skills to manage such a workforce.

A firm's strategic management decision-making process usually takes place at its top levels, with a strategic planning group consisting of the chief executive officer, the chief financial officer, the president, and various vice presidents. However, each component of the process involves people-related business issues. Therefore, the HRM function needs to be involved in each of those components. One recent study of 115 strategic business units within *Fortune* 500 corporations found that 49–69% of the companies had some link between HRM and the strategic planning process.[12] However, the level of linkage varied, and it is important to understand these different levels.

Figure 2.3

Strategy—Decisions about Competition

1. Where to compete?
   In what market or markets (industries, products, etc.) will we compete?
2. How to compete?
   On what criterion or differentiating characteristic(s) will we compete? Cost? Quality? Reliability? Delivery?
3. With what will we compete?
   What resources will allow us to beat our competition?
   How will we acquire, develop, and deploy those resources to compete?

SOURCE: Adapted from K. Golden and V. Ramanujam, "Between a Dream and a Nightmare: On the Integration of the Human Resource Function and the Strategic Business Planning Process," *Human Resource Management* 24 (1985), pp. 429–51.

Figure 2.4
Linkages of Strategic Planning and HRM

Four levels of integration seem to exist between the HRM function and the strategic management function: administrative linkage, one-way linkage, two-way linkage, and integrative linkage.[13] These levels of linkage will be discussed in relation to the different components of strategic management. The linkages are illustrated in Figure 2.4.

Administrative Linkage

In administrative linkage (the lowest level of integration), the HRM function's attention is focused on day-to-day activities. The HRM executive has no time or opportunity to take a strategic outlook toward HRM issues. The company's strategic business planning function exists without any input from the HRM department. Thus, in this level of integration, the HRM department is completely divorced from any component of the strategic management process in both strategy formulation and strategy implementation. The department simply engages in administrative work unrelated to the company's core business needs.

LO 2-4
Describe the linkages between HRM and strategy formulation.

One-Way Linkage

In one-way linkage, the firm's strategic business planning function develops the strategic plan and then informs the HRM function of the plan. Early in the history of SHRM, people believed this level of integration constituted strategic HRM—that is, the role of the HRM function is to design systems and/or programs that implement the strategic plan. Although one-way linkage does recognize the importance of human resources in implementing the strategic plan, it precludes the company from considering human resource issues while formulating the strategic plan. This level of integration often leads to strategic plans that the company cannot successfully implement.

Two-Way Linkage

Two-way linkage allows for consideration of human resource issues during the strategy formulation process. This integration occurs in three sequential steps. First, the strategic planning team informs the HRM function of the various strategies the company is considering. Then HRM executives analyze the human resource implications of the various strategies, presenting the results of this analysis to the strategic planning team.

Finally, after the strategic decision has been made, the strategic plan is passed on to the HRM executive, who develops programs to implement it. The strategic planning function and the HRM function are interdependent in two-way linkage.

Integrative Linkage

Integrative linkage is dynamic and multifaceted, based on continuing rather than sequential interaction. In most cases the HRM executive is an integral member of the senior management team. Rather than using an iterative process of information exchange, companies with integrative linkage have their HRM functions built in to the strategy formulation and implementation processes. It is this role that we will discuss throughout the rest of this chapter.

Thus, in strategic HRM, the HRM function is involved in both strategy formulation and strategy implementation. The HRM executive gives strategic planners information about the company's human resource capabilities, and these capabilities are usually a direct function of the HRM practices.[14] This information about human resource capabilities helps top managers choose the best strategy because they can consider how well each strategic alternative would be implemented. Once the strategic choice has been determined, the role of HRM changes to the development and alignment of HRM practices that will give the company employees having the necessary skills to implement the strategy.[15] In addition, HRM practices must be designed to elicit actions from employees in the company.[16] One recent study found that strategic HR functions were positively related to firm performance, but only when those firms had structures and systems in place to leverage the input of their employees.[17] In the next two sections of this chapter, we show how HRM can provide a competitive advantage in the strategic management process.

Strategy Formulation

Five major components of the strategic management process are relevant to strategy formulation.[18] These components are depicted in Figure 2.5. The first component is the organization's mission. The mission is a statement of the organization's reason for being; it usually specifies the customers served, the needs satisfied and/or the values received by the customers, and the technology used. The mission statement is often accompanied by a statement of a company's vision and/or values. For example, Table 2.1 illustrates the mission and values of Merck & Co., Inc.

An organization's **goals** are what it hopes to achieve in the medium- to long-term future; they reflect how the mission will be operationalized. The overarching goal of most profit-making companies in the United States is to maximize stockholder wealth. But companies have to set other long-term goals in order to maximize stockholder wealth.

External analysis consists of examining the organization's operating environment to identify the strategic opportunities and threats. Examples of opportunities are customer markets that are not being served, technological advances that can aid the company, and labor pools that have not been tapped. Threats include potential labor shortages, new competitors entering the market, pending legislation that might adversely affect the company, and competitors' technological innovations.

Internal analysis attempts to identify the organization's strengths and weaknesses. It focuses on the quantity and quality of resources available to the organization—financial, capital, technological, and human resources. Organizations have to honestly and accurately assess each resource to decide whether it is a strength or a weakness. For instance, after Volkswagen got caught using technologies to mask the emissions in some of its

Goals
What an organization hopes to achieve in the medium- to long-term future.

External analysis
Examining the organization's operating environment to identify strategic opportunities and threats.

Internal analysis
The process of examining an organization's strengths and weaknesses.

Figure 2.5
Strategy Formulation

HR input

SOURCE: Adapted from K. Golden and V. Ramanujam, "Between a Dream and a Nightmare," *Human Resource Management* 24 (1985), pp. 429–51.

vehicles when being tested, its reputation clearly took a hit. The "Integrity in Action" box describes how Volkswagen is trying to restore its reputation through investing in developing zero-emissions vehicles.

External analysis and internal analysis combined constitute what has come to be called the SWOT (strengths, weaknesses, opportunities, threats) analysis. Table 2.2 shows an example of a SWOT analysis for Google. After going through the SWOT analysis, the strategic planning team has all the information it needs to generate a number of strategic alternatives. The strategic managers compare the ability of each alternative to attain the organization's strategic goals; then they make their **strategic choice**. The strategic choice is the organization's strategy; it describes the ways the organization will attempt to fulfill its mission and achieve its long-term goals.

Strategic choice
The organization's strategy; the ways an organization will attempt to fulfill its mission and achieve its long-term goals.

Many of the opportunities and threats in the external environment are people related. With fewer and fewer highly qualified individuals entering the labor market, organizations compete not just for customers but also for employees. It is HRM's role to keep close tabs on the external environment for HR–related opportunities and threats, especially those directly related to the HRM function: potential labor shortages, competitor wage rates, government regulations affecting employment, and so on. For example, as discussed in Chapter 1, U.S. companies are finding that more and more high school graduates lack the basic skills needed to work, which is one source of the "human capital shortage."[19] However, not recognizing this environmental threat, many companies have encouraged the exit of older, more skilled workers while hiring less skilled younger workers who require basic skills training.[20]

Table 2.1
Merck & Co.'s
Mission and Values

MISSION STATEMENT
To discover, develop and provide innovative products and services that save and improve lives around the world.
Values:
Improving Life
We embrace our quest to tackle health challenges because we are inspired by the differences we can make in the lives of people around the world.
Ethics and Integrity
We are committed to the highest standards of ethics and integrity. We are responsible to our customers, to Merck employees, to the environments we inhabit, and to the societies we serve worldwide.
Innovation
We are dedicated to the highest level of scientific excellence. We strive to identify the most critical needs of consumers and customers, and through continuous innovation we challenge ourselves to meet those needs.
Access to Health
We aspire to improve the health and wellness of people around the world by expanding access to our medicines and vaccines.
Diversity and Teamwork
Our ability to excel depends on the integrity, knowledge, imagination, skill, diversity and teamwork of our employees.

SOURCE: Courtesy of Merck.

Table 2.2
SWOT Analysis for
Google, Inc.

STRENGTHS	WEAKNESSES
Expanding liquidity	Issues with Chinese government
Operational efficiency	Dependence on advertising segment
Broad range of services portfolio	Losses at YouTube

OPPORTUNITIES	THREATS
Growing demand for online video	Weak economic outlook
Growth in Internet advertising market	Invalid clicks
Inorganic growth	Microsoft–Yahoo! deal

SOURCE: GlobalData.

An analysis of a company's internal strengths and weaknesses also requires input from the HRM function. Today companies are increasingly realizing that their human resources are one of their most important assets. In fact, one estimate is that over one-third of the total growth in U.S. gross national product (GNP) between 1943 and 1990 was the result of increases in human capital. A company's failure to consider the strengths and weaknesses of its workforce may result in its choosing strategies it is not capable of pursuing.[21] However, some research has demonstrated that few companies have achieved this level of linkage.[22] For example, one company chose a strategy of cost reduction through technological improvements. It built a plant designed around a computer-integrated manufacturing

INTEGRITY IN ACTION

From Hidden Emissions to Zero Emissions: Volkswagen's Correction

Recent revelations surfaced regarding how Volkswagen deceived regulators and consumers by using technology to sense when a vehicle's emissions were being tested and to emit lower amounts than when not tested. They have paid hefty fines to the government and consumers, and suffered significant reputational loss.

However, the company has now committed over $2 billion in investments in the United States to develop and promote zero-emissions vehicles. Called Electrify America LLC, this company has as its main goal to install charging stations for electric vehicles in a number of metropolitan areas. Most of the investment will be in California, where electric vehicles have the highest volume sales. Simultaneously, Volkswagen is working on developing electric vehicles that they expect to begin selling in 2020. Investing in both electric vehicles and charging stations may demonstrate Volkswagen's commitment to the environment.

DISCUSSION QUESTION

1. Do you think Volkswagen's efforts to develop zero-emissions vehicles will be effective in restoring the company's reputation? Why or why not?

SOURCE: A. Roberts, "Volkswagen Forms U.S. Unit for Zero-Emission Vehicles," *Wall Street Journal*, February 7, 2017, https://www.wsj.com/articles/volkswagen-forms-u-s-unit-for-zero-emission-vehicles-1486497992.

system with statistical process controls. Although this choice may seem like a good one, the company soon learned otherwise. It discovered that its employees could not operate the new equipment because 25% of the workforce was functionally illiterate.[23]

Thus, with an integrative linkage, strategic planners consider all the people-related business issues before making a strategic choice. These issues are identified with regard to the mission, goals, strengths, weaknesses, opportunities, and threats, leading the strategic planning team to make a more intelligent strategic choice. Although this process does not guarantee success, companies that address these issues are more likely to make choices that will ultimately succeed.

Recent research has supported the need to have HRM executives integrally involved in strategy formulation. One study of U.S. petrochemical refineries found that the level of HRM involvement was positively related to the refinery manager's evaluation of the effectiveness of the HRM function.[24] A second study of manufacturing firms found that HRM involvement was highest when top managers viewed employees as a strategic asset and associated them with reduced turnover.[25] However, both studies found that HRM involvement was unrelated to operating unit financial performance.

Research has indicated that few companies have fully integrated HRM into the strategy formulation process.[26] As we've mentioned before, companies are beginning to recognize that in an intensely competitive environment, managing human resources strategically can provide a competitive advantage. Thus, companies at the administrative linkage level will either become more integrated or face extinction. In addition, companies will move toward becoming integratively linked in an effort to manage human resources strategically.

It is of utmost importance that all people-related business issues be considered during strategy formulation. These issues are identified in the HRM function. Mechanisms or structures for integrating the HRM function into strategy formulation may help the strategic planning team make the most effective strategic choice. Once that strategic choice is determined, HRM must take an active role in implementing it. This role will be discussed in the next section.

Strategy Implementation

LO 2-5
Discuss the more popular typologies of generic strategies and the various HRM practices associated with each.

After an organization has chosen its strategy, it has to execute that strategy—make it come to life in its day-to-day workings. The strategy a company pursues dictates certain HR needs. For a company to have a good strategy foundation, certain tasks must be accomplished in pursuit of the company's goals, individuals must possess certain skills to perform those tasks, and these individuals must be motivated to perform their skills effectively.

The basic premise behind strategy implementation is that "an organization has a variety of structural forms and organizational processes to choose from when implementing a given strategy," and these choices make an economic difference.[27] Five important variables determine success in strategy implementation: organizational structure; task design; the selection, training, and development of people; reward systems; and types of information and information systems.

As we see in Figure 2.6, HRM has primary responsibility for three of these five implementation variables: task, people, and reward systems. In addition, HRM can directly affect the two remaining variables: structure and information and decision processes. First, for the strategy to be successfully implemented, the tasks must be designed and grouped into jobs in a way that is efficient and effective.[28] In Chapter 4 we will examine how this can be done through the processes of job analysis and job design. Second, the HRM function must ensure that the organization is staffed with people who have the necessary knowledge, skill, and ability to perform their part in implementing the strategy. This goal is achieved primarily through recruitment, selection and placement, training, development, and career management—topics covered in Chapters 5, 6, 7, and 9. In addition, the HRM function must develop performance management and reward systems that lead employees to work for and support the strategic plan. The specific types of performance management systems are covered in Chapter 8, and the many issues involved in developing reward systems are discussed in Chapters 11, 12, and 13. In other words, the role of the HRM function becomes one of (1) ensuring that the company has the proper number of employees with the levels and

Figure 2.6
Variables to Be Considered in Strategy Implementation

types of skills required by the strategic plan[29] and (2) developing "control" systems that ensure that those employees are acting in ways that promote the achievement of the goals specified in the strategic plan.[30]

In essence, this is what has been referred to as the "vertical alignment" of HR with strategy. Vertical alignment means that the HR practices and processes are aimed at addressing the strategic needs of the business. But the link between strategy and HR practices is primarily through people. For instance, as IBM moved from being a manufacturer of personal computers to being a fully integrated service provider, the types of people it needed changed significantly. Instead of employing thousands of workers in manufacturing or assembly plants, IBM increasingly needed software engineers to help write new "middleware" programs, and an army of consultants who could help their corporate customers to implement these systems. In addition, as IBM increasingly differentiated itself as being the "integrated solutions" provider (meaning it could sell the hardware, software, consulting, and service for a company's entire information technology needs), employees needed a new mindset that emphasized cooperating across different business divisions rather than running independently. IBM's more recent transformation into the "smarter planet" increasingly relies on the use of "big data" to provide insights. Thus, with each change in strategy comes a change in the kinds of skills, employees, and behaviors required to execute that strategy effectively.

How does the HRM function implement strategy? As Figure 2.7 shows, it is through administering HRM practices: job analysis and design, recruitment, selection systems, training and development programs, performance management systems, reward systems, and labor relations programs. The details of each of these HRM practices are the focus of the rest of this book. However, at this point it is important to present a general

Figure 2.7
Strategy
Implementation

overview of the HRM practices and their role in strategy implementation. We then discuss the various strategies companies pursue and the types of HRM systems congruent with those strategies. First we focus on how the strategic types are implemented; then we discuss the HRM practices associated with various directional strategies.

HRM PRACTICES

The HRM function can be thought of as having six menus of HRM practices, from which companies can choose the ones most appropriate for implementing their strategy. Each of these menus refers to a particular functional area of HRM: job analysis and design; recruitment and selection; training and development; performance management; pay structure, incentives, and benefits; and labor and employee relations.[31] These menus are presented in Table 2.3.

Table 2.3
Menu of HRM
Practice Options

Job Analysis and Design		
Few tasks	↔	Many tasks
Simple tasks	↔	Complex tasks
Few skills required	↔	Many skills required
Specific job descriptions	↔	General job descriptions
Recruitment and Selection		
External sources	↔	Internal sources
Limited socialization	↔	Extensive socialization
Assessment of specific skills	↔	Assessment of general skills
Narrow career paths	↔	Broad career paths
Training and Development		
Focus on current job skills	↔	Focus on future job skills
Individual orientation	↔	Group orientation
Train few employees	↔	Train all employees
Spontaneous, unplanned	↔	Planned, systematic
Performance Management		
Behavioral criteria	↔	Results criteria
Developmental orientation	↔	Administrative orientation
Short-term criteria	↔	Long-term criteria
Individual orientation	↔	Group orientation
Pay Structure, Incentives, and Benefits		
Pay weighted toward salary and benefits	↔	Pay weighted toward incentives
Short-term incentives	↔	Long-term incentives
Emphasis on internal equity	↔	Emphasis on external equity
Individual incentives	↔	Group incentives
Labor and Employee Relations		
Collective bargaining	↔	Individual bargaining
Top-down decision making	↔	Participation in decision making
Formal due process	↔	No due process
View employees as expense	↔	View employees as assets

SOURCES: Adapted from R. S. Schuler and S. F. Jackson, "Linking Competitive Strategies with Human Resource Management Practices," *Academy of Management Executive* 1 (1987), pp. 207–19; and C. Fisher, L. Schoenfeldt, and B. Shaw, *Human Resource Management*, 2nd ed. (Boston: Houghton Mifflin, 1992).

Job Analysis and Design

Companies produce a given product or service (or set of products or services), and the manufacture of these products requires that a number of tasks be performed. These tasks are grouped together to form jobs. **Job analysis** is the process of getting detailed information about jobs. **Job design** addresses what tasks should be grouped into a particular job. The way that jobs are designed should have an important tie to the strategy of an organization because the strategy requires either new and different tasks or different ways of performing the same tasks. In addition, because many strategies entail the introduction of new technologies, this affects the way that work is performed.[32]

In general, jobs can vary from having a narrow range of tasks (most of which are simplified and require a limited range of skills) to having a broad array of complex tasks requiring multiple skills. In the past, the narrow design of jobs has been used to increase efficiency, while the broad design of jobs has been associated with efforts to increase innovation. However, with the advent of total quality management (TQM) methods and a variety of employee involvement programs such as quality circles, many jobs are moving toward the broader end of the spectrum.[33]

Employee Recruitment and Selection

Recruitment is the process through which the organization seeks applicants for potential employment. **Selection** refers to the process by which it attempts to identify applicants with the necessary knowledge, skills, abilities, and other characteristics that will help the company achieve its goals. Companies engaging in different strategies need different types and numbers of employees. Thus, the strategy a company is pursuing will have a direct impact on the types of employees that it seeks to recruit and select.[34]

Employee Training and Development

A number of skills are instilled in employees through training and development. **Training** refers to a planned effort to facilitate the learning of job-related knowledge, skills, and behavior by employees. **Development** involves acquiring knowledge, skills, and behavior that improve employees' ability to meet the challenges of a variety of existing jobs or jobs that do not yet exist. Changes in strategies often require changes in the types, levels, and mixes of skills. Thus, the acquisition of strategy-related skills is an essential element of the implementation of strategy. For example, many companies have recently emphasized quality in their products, engaging in TQM programs. These programs require extensive training of all employees in the TQM philosophy, methods, and often other skills that ensure quality.[35]

Through recruitment, selection, training, and development, companies can obtain a pool of human resources capable of implementing a given strategy.[36]

Performance Management

Performance management is used to ensure that employees' activities and outcomes are congruent with the organization's objectives. It entails specifying those activities and outcomes that will result in the firm's successfully implementing the strategy. For example, companies that are "steady state" (not diversified) tend to have evaluation systems that call for subjective performance assessments of managers. This stems from the fact that those above the first-level managers in the hierarchy have extensive knowledge about how the work should be performed. By contrast, diversified

Job analysis
The process of getting detailed information about jobs.

Job design
The process of defining the way work will be performed and the tasks that will be required in a given job.

Recruitment
The process of seeking applicants for potential employment.

Selection
The process by which an organization attempts to identify applicants with the necessary knowledge, skills, abilities, and other characteristics that will help it achieve its goals.

Training
A planned effort to facilitate the learning of job-related knowledge, skills, and behavior by employees.

Development
The acquisition of knowledge, skills, and behaviors that improve an employee's ability to meet changes in job requirements and in client and customer demands.

Performance management
The means through which managers ensure that employees' activities and outcomes are congruent with the organization's goals.

Figure 2.8

Percentage of Objectives Identified in Individual Performance Plans That Are Tied to Each Strategic Imperative

Strategic Imperative	Business A	Business B	International	Investment	Finance	Legal	IT	HR&S	Enterprise
Achieve superior medical performance	10.5%	12.5%	2.7%	7.6%	3.1%	2.7%	11.4%	2.1%	10.0%
Effectively serve our customers	24.7%	27.2%	36.7%	12.2%	10.3%	27.2%	18.9%	19.5%	23.7%
Create great products and services	5.6%	6.1%	10.1%	9.8%	5.0%	10.1%	15.3%	8.9%	6.9%
Create a winning environment	27.7%	29.7%	30.1%	29.9%	30.3%	33.7%	22.4%	39.4%	27.7%
Establish a cost advantage	31.5%	24.5%	20.5%	40.5%	51.3%	26.3%	32%	30.0%	31.7%
Total	100%	100%	100%	100%	100%	100%	100%	100%	100%

companies are more likely to use quantitative measures of performance to evaluate managers because top managers have less knowledge about how work should be performed by those below them in the hierarchy.[37]

Similarly, executives who have extensive knowledge of the behaviors that lead to effective performance use performance management systems that focus on the behaviors of their subordinate managers. However, when executives are unclear about the specific behaviors that lead to effective performance, they tend to focus on evaluating the objective performance results of their subordinate managers.[38]

An example of how performance management can be aligned with strategy is provided in Figure 2.8. This comes from a firm in the health care industry whose strategy consisted of five "strategic imperatives," or things that the company was trying to accomplish. In this company all individuals set performance objectives each year, and each of their objectives had to be tied to at least one of the strategic imperatives. The senior VP of HR used the firm's technology system to examine the extent to which each business unit or function was focused on each of the imperatives. The figure illustrates the percentage of objectives that were tied to each imperative across the different units. This analysis allowed the company to determine if the mix of objectives was right enterprisewide as well as within each business unit or function.

Pay Structure, Incentives, and Benefits

The pay system has an important role in implementing strategies. First, a high level of pay and/or benefits relative to that of competitors can ensure that the company attracts and retains high-quality employees, but this might have a negative impact on the company's overall labor costs.[39] Second, by tying pay to performance, the company can elicit specific activities and levels of performance from employees.

In a study of how compensation practices are tied to strategies, researchers examined 33 high-tech and 72 traditional companies. They classified them by whether they were in a growth stage (greater than 20% inflation-adjusted increases in annual sales) or a maturity stage. They found that high-tech companies in the growth stage used compensation systems that were highly geared toward incentive pay, with a lower percentage of total pay devoted to salary and benefits. By contrast, compensation systems among mature companies (both high-tech and traditional) devoted a lower percentage of total pay to incentives and a higher percentage to benefits.[40]

Labor and Employee Relations

Whether companies are unionized or not, the general approach to relations with employees can strongly affect their potential for gaining competitive advantage.

Companies can choose to treat employees as an asset that requires investment of resources or as an expense to be minimized.[41] They have to make choices about how much employees can and should participate in decision making, what rights employees have, and what the company's responsibility is to them. The approach a company takes in making these decisions can result in it either successfully achieving its short- and long-term goals or ceasing to exist.

Recent research has begun to examine how companies develop sets of HRM practices that maximize performance and productivity. For example, one study of automobile assembly plants around the world found that plants that exhibited both high productivity and high quality used "HRM best practices," such as heavy emphasis on recruitment and hiring, compensation tied to performance, low levels of status differentiation, high levels of training for both new and experienced employees, and employee participation through structures such as work teams and problem-solving groups.[42] Another study found that HRM systems composed of selection testing, training, contingent pay, performance appraisal, attitude surveys, employee participation, and information sharing resulted in higher levels of productivity and corporate financial performance, as well as lower employee turnover.[43] Finally, a recent study found that companies identified as some of the "best places to work" had higher financial performances than a set of matched companies that did not make the list.[44] Similar results have also been observed in a number of other studies.[45]

In addition to the relationship between HR practices and performance in general, in today's fast-changing environment, businesses have to change quickly, requiring changes in employees' skills and behaviors. In one study the researchers found that the flexibility of HR practices, employee skills, and employee behaviors were all positively related to the firm's financial performance, but only the skill flexibility was related to cost efficiency.[46] Although these relationships are promising, the causal direction has not yet been proven. For instance, effective HR practices should help firms perform better, but it is also true that highly profitable firms can invest more in HR practices.[47] The research seems to indicate that although the relationship between practices and performance is consistently positive, we should not go too far out on a limb arguing that increasing the use of HRM practices will automatically result in increased profitability.[48]

STRATEGIC TYPES

As we discussed earlier, companies can be classified by the generic strategies they pursue. These generic "strategies" are not what we mean by a strategic plan. They are merely similarities in the ways companies seek to compete in their industries. Various typologies have been offered, but we focus on the two generic strategies proposed by Porter: cost and differentiation.[49]

According to Michael Porter of Harvard Business School, competitive advantage stems from a company's being able to create value in its production process. Value can be created in one of two ways. First, value can be created by reducing costs. Second, value can be created by differentiating a product or service in such a way that it allows the company to charge a premium price relative to its competitors. This leads to two basic strategies. According to Porter, the "overall cost leadership" strategy focuses on becoming the lowest cost producer in an industry. This strategy is achieved by constructing efficient large-scale facilities, by reducing costs through capitalizing on the experience curve, and by controlling overhead costs and costs in such areas as research and development, service, sales force, and advertising. This strategy provides above-average returns within an industry, and it tends to bar other firms' entry into the industry because the firm can lower its prices below competitors' costs.

The "differentiation" strategy, according to Porter, attempts to create the impression that the company's product or service is different from that of others in the industry. The perceived differentiation can come from creating a brand image, from technology, from offering unique features, or from unique customer service. If a company succeeds in differentiating its product, it will achieve above-average returns, and the differentiation may protect it from price sensitivity. For instance, Dell Computer Company built its reputation on providing the lowest cost computers through leveraging its supply chain and direct selling model. However, recently they have seen share eroding as the consumer market grows and HP has offered more differentiated, stylish-looking computers sold through retail outlets where customers can touch and feel them. In addition, Apple has differentiated itself through its own operating system that integrates well with peripheral devices such as the iPad and iPhone. In both cases, these companies can charge a premium (albeit higher for Apple) over Dell's pricing.[50]

HRM NEEDS IN STRATEGIC TYPES

Although all of the strategic types require competent people in a generic sense, each of the strategies also requires different types of employees with different types of behaviors and attitudes. As we noted earlier, different strategies require employees with specific skills and also require these employees to exhibit different "role behaviors."[51] **Role behaviors** are the behaviors required of an individual in his or her role as a jobholder in a social work environment. These role behaviors vary on a number of dimensions. Additionally, different role behaviors are required by the different strategies. For example, companies engaged in a cost strategy require employees to have a high concern for quantity and a short-term focus, to be comfortable with stability, and to be risk averse. These employees are expected to exhibit role behaviors that are relatively repetitive and performed independently or autonomously.

Thus, companies engaged in cost strategies, because of the focus on efficient production, tend to specifically define the skills they require and invest in training employees in these skill areas. They also rely on behavioral performance management systems with a large performance-based compensation component. These companies promote internally and develop internally consistent pay systems with high pay differentials between superiors and subordinates. They seek efficiency through worker participation, soliciting employees' ideas on how to achieve more efficient production.

By contrast, employees in companies with a differentiation strategy need to be highly creative and cooperative; to have only a moderate concern for quantity, a long-term focus, and a tolerance for ambiguity; and to be risk takers. Employees in these companies are expected to exhibit role behaviors that include cooperating with others, developing new ideas, and taking a balanced approach to process and results.

Thus, differentiation companies will seek to generate more creativity through broadly defined jobs with general job descriptions. They may recruit more from outside, engage in limited socialization of newcomers, and provide broader career paths. Training and development activities focus on cooperation. The compensation system is geared toward external equity, as it is heavily driven by recruiting needs. These companies develop results-based performance management systems and divisional–corporate performance evaluations to encourage risk taking on the part of managers.[52]

Role behaviors
Behaviors that are required of an individual in his or her role as a jobholder in a social work environment.

EVIDENCE-BASED HR

A study of HRM among steel mini-mills in the United States found that mills pursuing different strategies used different systems of HRM. Mills seeking cost leadership tended to use control-oriented HRM systems that were characterized by high centralization, low participation, low training, low wages, low benefits, and highly contingent pay, whereas differentiator mills used "commitment" HRM systems, characterized as the opposite on each of those dimensions. A later study from the same sample revealed that the mills with the commitment systems had higher productivity, lower scrap rates, and lower employee turnover than those with the control systems.

SOURCE: J. Arthur, "The Link between Business Strategy and Industrial Relations Systems in American Steel Mini-Mills," *Industrial and Labor Relations Review* 45 (1992), pp. 488–506.

DIRECTIONAL STRATEGIES

As discussed earlier in this chapter, strategic typologies are useful for classifying the ways different organizations seek to compete within an industry. However, it is also necessary to understand how increasing size (growth) or decreasing it (downsizing) affects the HRM function. For example, the top management team might decide that they need to invest more in product development or to diversify as a means for growth. With these types of strategies, it is more useful for the HRM function to aid in evaluating the feasibility of the various alternatives and to develop programs that support the strategic choice.

Companies have used four possible categories of directional strategies to meet objectives.[53] Strategies emphasizing market share or operating costs are considered "concentration" strategies. With this type of strategy, a company attempts to focus on what it does best within its established markets and can be thought of as "sticking to its knitting." Strategies focusing on market development, product development, innovation, or joint ventures make up the "internal growth" strategy. Companies with an internal growth strategy channel their resources toward building on existing strengths. Those attempting to integrate vertically or horizontally or to diversify are exhibiting an **"external growth" strategy**, usually through mergers or acquisitions. This strategy attempts to expand a company's resources or to strengthen its market position through acquiring or creating new businesses. Finally, a "divestment," or downsizing, strategy is one made up of retrenchment, divestitures, or liquidation. These strategies are observed among companies facing serious economic difficulties and seeking to pare down their operations. The human resource implications of each of these strategies are quite different.

Concentration Strategies

Concentration strategies require that the company maintain the current skills that exist in the organization. This requires that training programs provide a means of keeping those skills sharp among people in the organization and that compensation programs focus on retaining people who have those skills. Appraisals in this strategy tend to be more behavioral because the environment is more certain, and the behaviors necessary for effective performance tend to be established through extensive experience.

LO 2-6
Describe the different HRM issues and practices associated with various directional strategies.

External growth strategy
An emphasis on acquiring vendors and suppliers or buying businesses that allow a company to expand into new markets.

Concentration strategy
A strategy focusing on increasing market share, reducing costs, or creating and maintaining a market niche for products and services.

Internal Growth Strategies

Internal growth strategy
A focus on new market and product development, innovation, and joint ventures.

Internal growth strategies present unique staffing problems. Growth requires that a company constantly hire, transfer, and promote individuals, and expansion into different markets may change the necessary skills that prospective employees must have. In addition, appraisals often consist of a combination of behaviors and results. The behavioral appraisal emphasis stems from the knowledge of effective behaviors in a particular product market, and the results appraisals focus on achieving growth goals. Compensation packages are heavily weighted toward incentives for achieving growth goals. Training needs differ depending on the way the company attempts to grow internally. For example, if the organization seeks to expand its markets, training will focus on knowledge of each market, particularly when the company is expanding into international markets. By contrast, when the company is seeking innovation or product development, training will be of a more technical nature, as well as focusing on interpersonal skills such as team building. Joint ventures require extensive training in conflict resolution techniques because of the problems associated with combining people from two distinct organizational cultures.

Mergers and Acquisitions

Increasingly we see both consolidation within industries and mergers across industries. For example, Procter and Gamble's acquisition of Gillette represented a consolidation, or a reduction in the number of firms within the industry. By contrast, Citicorp's merger with Travelers Group to form Citigroup represented firms from different industries (pure financial services and insurance) combining to change the dynamics within both. Whatever the type, one thing is for sure—mergers and acquisitions are on the increase, and HRM needs to be involved.[54] In addition, these mergers more frequently consist of global mega-mergers, in spite of some warnings that these might not be effective.

According to a report by the Conference Board, "people issues" may be one of the major reasons that mergers do not always live up to expectations. Some companies now heavily weigh firm cultures before embarking on a merger or acquisition. For example, prior to acquiring Value Rx, executives at Express Scripts Inc. interviewed senior executives and middle managers at the potential target firm in order to get a sense of its culture.[55] In spite of this, fewer than one-third of the HRM executives surveyed said that they had a major influence in how mergers are planned, yet 80% of them said that people issues have a significant impact after the deals are finalized.[56]

In addition to the desirability of HRM playing a role in evaluating a merger opportunity, HRM certainly has a role in the actual implementation of a merger or acquisition. Training in conflict resolution is also necessary when companies engage in an external growth strategy. All the options for external growth consist of acquiring or developing new businesses, and these businesses often have distinct cultures. Thus, many HRM programs face problems in integrating and standardizing practices across the company's businesses. The relative value of standardizing practices across businesses must be weighed against the unique environmental requirements of each business and the extent of desired integration of the two firms. For example, with regard to pay practices, a company may desire a consistent internal wage structure to maintain employee perceptions of equity in the larger organization. In a recent new business developed by IBM, the employees pressured the company to maintain the same wage structure as IBM's main operation. However, some businesses may function in environments where pay practices are driven heavily by market forces. Requiring these businesses to adhere to pay practices in other environments may result in an ineffective wage structure.

Downsizing

Of increasing importance to organizations in today's competitive environment is HRM's role in **downsizing** or "rightsizing." The number of organizations undergoing downsizing increased significantly from the third to the fourth quarter of 2008, and although this trend has slowed, layoffs are still significant (see Figure 2.9).[57] In fact, some of these layoffs are due to outright bankruptcies because firms simply did not have sustainable business models. In addition, even as the economy has grown, layoffs continue in companies that face challenging environments. For instance, by partway through 2016, Macy's announced 4,350 job cuts, Microsoft 4,700 job cuts, Intel 12,000 job cuts, Halliburton 15,200 job cuts, and Walmart 17,500 job cuts.[58] A recent review of the downsizing literature noted that downsizing tends to fall short of meeting companies' financial and organizational objectives, and has negative effects on employee morale and productivity.[59] The "Competing through Sustainability" box describes how, rather than downsizing, IKEA has been trying to increase its retention through expanding its parental leave policies in the United States.

One would have great difficulty ignoring the massive "war for talent" that went on during the late 1990s, particularly with the notable dot-com craze. Firms during this time sought to become "employers of choice," to establish "employment brands," and to develop "employee value propositions" as ways to ensure that they would be able to attract and retain talented employees.

Downsizing
The planned elimination of large numbers of personnel, designed to enhance organizational effectiveness.

Figure 2.9

Layoff Events and Separations 2009–2013

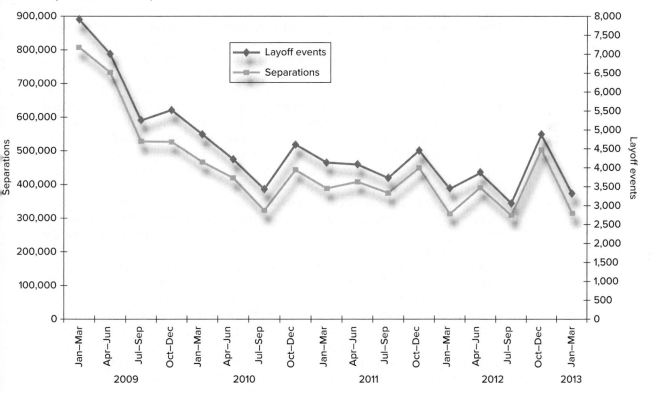

SOURCE: U.S. Department of Labor, Bureau of Labor Statistics, "Mass Layoffs Summary," May 13, 2013, www.bls.gov/news.release/mslo.nr0.htm.

COMPETING THROUGH SUSTAINABILITY

IKEA Helps Parents

In its home country of Sweden, IKEA's employees receive 68 weeks of paid parental leave to both mothers and fathers. However, until recently, IKEA employees in the United States received only five days of paid time off. In addition, mothers could take disability-related pay for up to eight weeks after the birth of their baby.

Recently IKEA announced that it was expanding its parental leave for all employees (salaried and hourly) with at least one year of tenure. Under its new policy,

employees will receive full pay for the first six weeks and half pay for the next six weeks. Those with tenure of at least three years are eligible for the same levels of pay for eight weeks and eight weeks, respectively.

Lars Petersson, the head of IKEA's U.S. operations says, "We can't say when or how, but we're convinced there will be a big payback. We know a workforce that has an opportunity to spend time with family and friends and particularly to welcome a new

child will be happier and therefore do a better job."

DISCUSSION QUESTIONS

1. What traits help promote a company as an employer of choice?
2. Do you think IKEA will be viewed as an employer of choice? Why or why not?

SOURCE: L. Weber, "IKEA Broadens U.S. Parental Leave," *Wall Street Journal*, December 6, 2016, https://www.wsj.com/articles/ ikea-broadens-u-s-parental-leave-coverage- 1481001301.

The dynamic economic conditions requiring firms to constantly churn their workforces means that one important question facing firms is, How can we develop a reputation as an employer of choice, and engage employees to the goals of the firm, while laying off a significant portion of our workforce? How firms answer this question will determine how they can compete by meeting the stakeholder needs of their employees.

In spite of the increasing frequency of downsizing, research reveals that it is far from universally successful for achieving the goals of increased productivity and increased profitability. For example, Table 2.4 illustrates the results of a survey conducted by the American Management Association (AMA), indicating that only about one-third of the companies that went through downsizings actually achieved their goal of increased profits. Another survey by the AMA found that over two-thirds of the companies that downsize repeat the effort a year later.[60] Also, research by the consulting firm Mitchell & Company found that companies that downsized during the 1980s lagged the industry average stock price in 1991.[61] Thus, it is important to understand the best ways of managing downsizings, particularly from the standpoint of HRM.

Downsizing presents a number of challenges and opportunities for HRM.[62] In terms of challenges, the HRM function must "surgically" reduce the workforce by cutting only the workers who are less valuable in their performance. Achieving this is difficult because the best workers are most able (and often willing) to find alternative employment and may leave voluntarily prior to any layoff. For example, in 1992 General Motors and the UAW agreed to an early retirement program for individuals between the ages of 51 and 65 who had been employed for 10 or more years. The program provided those who agreed to retire their full pension benefits, even if they obtained employment elsewhere, and as much as $13,000 toward the purchase of a GM car.[63] As mentioned earlier in the chapter, this is part of GM's labor cost problem.

DESIRED OUTCOME	PERCENTAGE THAT ACHIEVED DESIRED RESULT
Reduced expenses	46%
Increased profits	32
Improved cash flow	24
Increased profits	22
Increased return on investment	21
Increased competitive advantage	19
Reduced bureaucracy	17
Improved decision making	14
Increased customer satisfaction	14
Increased sales	13
Increased market share	12
Improved product quality	9
Technological advances	9
Increased innovation	7
Avoidance of a takeover	6

Table 2.4
Effects of Downsizing on Desired Outcomes

SOURCE: From *Wall Street Journal* by News Corporation; Dow Jones & Co, June 6, 1991. Reproduced with permission of Dow Jones & Company via Copyright Clearance Center.

Early retirement programs, although humane, essentially reduce the workforce with a "grenade" approach. This type of reduction does not distinguish between good and poor performers but rather eliminates an entire group of employees. In fact, recent research indicates that when companies downsize by offering early retirement programs, they usually end up rehiring to replace essential talent within a year. Often the company does not achieve its cost-cutting goals because it spends 50–150% of the departing employees' salaries in hiring and retraining new workers.[64]

Another HRM challenge is to boost the morale of employees who remain after the reduction; this topic is discussed in greater detail in Chapter 5. Survivors may feel guilt over keeping their jobs when their friends have been laid off, or they may envy their friends who have retired with attractive severance and pension benefits. Their reduced satisfaction with and commitment to the organization may interfere with work performance. Thus, the HRM function must maintain open communication with remaining employees to build their trust and commitment rather than withholding information.[65] All employees should be informed of the purpose of the downsizing, the costs to be cut, the duration of the downsizing, and the strategies to be pursued. In addition, companies going through downsizing often develop compensation programs that tie the individual's compensation to the company's success. Employee ownership programs often result from downsizing, and gainsharing plans such as the Scanlon plan (discussed in Chapter 12) as a way to incent employees to cut costs because it will benefit them monetarily.

In spite of these challenges, downsizing provides opportunities for HRM. First, it often allows the company to "get rid of dead wood" and make way for fresh ideas. In addition, downsizing is often a unique opportunity to change an organization's culture. In firms characterized by antagonistic labor–management relations, downsizing can force the parties to cooperate and to develop new, positive relationships.[66] Finally, downsizing can demonstrate to top-management decision makers the value of the company's human resources to its ultimate success. The role of HRM is to effectively manage the process in a way that makes this value undeniable. We discuss the implications of downsizing as a labor force management strategy in Chapter 5.

STRATEGY EVALUATION AND CONTROL

A final component to the strategic management process is that of strategy evaluation and control. Thus far we have focused on the planning and implementation of strategy. However, it is extremely important for the firm to constantly monitor the effectiveness of both the strategy and the implementation process. This monitoring makes it possible for the company to identify problem areas and either revise existing structures and strategies or devise new ones. In this process we see emergent strategies appear as well as the critical nature of human resources in competitive advantage.

The Role of Human Resources in Providing Strategic Competitive Advantage

Thus far we have presented the strategic management process as including a step-by-step procedure by which HRM issues are raised prior to deciding on a strategy and then HRM practices are developed to implement that strategy. However, human resources can provide a strategic competitive advantage in two additional ways: through emergent strategies and through enhancing competitiveness.

EMERGENT STRATEGIES

Having discussed the process of strategic management, we also must distinguish between intended strategies and emergent strategies. Most people think of strategies as being proactive, rational decisions aimed toward some predetermined goal. The view of strategy we have presented thus far in the chapter focuses on intended strategies. Intended strategies are the result of the rational decision-making process used by top managers as they develop a strategic plan. This is consistent with the definition of strategy as "the pattern or plan that integrates an organization's major goals, policies, and action sequences into a cohesive whole."[67] The idea of emergent strategies is evidenced by the feedback loop in Figure 2.2.

Most strategies that companies espouse are intended strategies. For example, when Howard Schultz founded Starbucks, he had the idea of creating a third place (between work and home) where people could enjoy traditional Italian-style coffee. He knew that the smell of the coffee and the deeper, darker, stronger taste would attract a new set of customers to enjoy coffee the way he thought it should be enjoyed. This worked, but as Starbucks grew, customers began asking if they could have nonfat milk in their lattes, or if they could get flavor shots in their coffees. Schultz swore that such things would essentially pollute the coffee and refused to offer them. Finally, after repeated requests from his store managers who kept hearing customers demanding such things, Schultz finally relented.[68]

Emergent strategies, by contrast, consist of the strategies that evolve from the grassroots of the organization and can be thought of as what organizations actually do, as opposed to what they intend to do. Strategy can also be thought of as "a pattern in a stream of decisions or actions."[69] For example, when Honda Motor Company first entered the U.S. market with its 250-cc and 350-cc motorcycles in 1959, it believed that no market existed for its smaller 50-cc bike. However, the sales on the larger motorcycles were sluggish, and Japanese executives running errands around Los Angeles on Honda 50s attracted a lot of attention, including that of a buyer with Sears, Roebuck. Honda found a previously undiscovered market as well as a new distribution outlet (general retailers) that it had not planned on. This emergent strategy gave Honda a 50% market share by 1964.[70]

The distinction between intended and emergent strategies has important implications for human resource management.[71] The new focus on strategic HRM has tended to focus primarily on intended strategies. Thus, HRM's role has been seen as identifying for top management the people-related business issues relevant to strategy formulation and then developing HRM systems that aid in the implementation of the strategic plan.

However, most emergent strategies are identified by those lower in the organizational hierarchy. It is often the rank-and-file employees who provide ideas for new markets, new products, and new strategies. HRM plays an important role in facilitating communication throughout the organization, and it is this communication that allows for effective emergent strategies to make their way up to top management. For example, Starbucks' Frappuccino was a drink invented by one of the store employees in California; Starbucks leaders (including Schultz) thought it was a terrible idea. They fought it in a number of meetings, but the employee kept getting more and more information supporting her case for how much customers seemed to like it. The leaders finally gave the go-ahead to begin producing it, and it has become a $1 billion a year product, and one that has contributed to the Starbucks brand.[72]

ENHANCING FIRM COMPETITIVENESS

A related way in which human resources can be a source of competitive advantage is through developing a human capital pool that gives the company the unique ability to adapt to an ever-changing environment. Recently managers have become interested in the idea of a "learning organization," in which people continually expand their capacity to achieve the results they desire.[73] This requires the company to be in a constant state of learning through monitoring the environment, assimilating information, making decisions, and flexibly restructuring to compete in that environment. Companies that develop such learning capability have a competitive advantage. Although certain organizational information-processing systems can be an aid, ultimately the people (human capital) who make up the company provide the raw materials in a learning organization.[74]

Thus, the role of human resources in competitive advantage should continue to increase because of the fast-paced change characterizing today's business environment. It is becoming increasingly clear that even as U.S. automakers have improved the quality of their cars to compete with the Japanese, these competitors have developed such flexible and adaptable manufacturing systems that they can respond to customer needs more quickly.[75] This flexibility of the manufacturing process allows the emergent strategy to come directly from the marketplace by determining and responding to the exact mix of customer desires. It requires, however, that the company have people in place who have the skills to similarly adapt quickly.[76] As Howard Schultz says, "If people relate to the company they work for, if they form an emotional tie to it and buy into its dreams, they will pour their heart into making it better. When employees have self-esteem and self-respect they can contribute so much more; to their company, to their family, to the world."[77] This statement exemplifies the increasing importance of human resources in developing and maintaining competitive advantage.[78]

A LOOK BACK

Amazon's Brick-and-Mortar Move

Amazon's foray into brick-and-mortar seems to go completely against the company's traditional business model. The Amazon Go model focuses on selling lower margin items, many of which have potential to spoil. It requires significant investment in facilities and people to stock shelves and fulfill orders. However, Amazon is betting that even with these deviations, it can still outperform traditional grocery stores in terms of profitability.

QUESTIONS

1. Do you think this is a good strategic move by Amazon? Why or why not?
2. What kinds of people issues does this strategy entail? Do you think Amazon is equipped to manage this kind of workforce?
3. How do you think traditional grocers like Kroger Co. will react to Amazon's entry into their market?

SUMMARY

A strategic approach to human resource management seeks to proactively provide a competitive advantage through the company's most important asset: its human resources. Although human resources are the most important asset, they are also usually the single largest controllable cost within the firm's business model. The HRM function needs to be integrally involved in the formulation of strategy to identify the people-related business issues the company faces. Once the strategy has been determined, HRM has a profound impact on the implementation of the plan by developing and aligning HRM practices that ensure that the company has motivated employees with the necessary skills. Finally, the emerging strategic role of the HRM function requires that HR professionals in the future develop business, professional–technical, change management, and integration competencies. As you will see more clearly in later chapters, this strategic approach requires more than simply developing a valid selection procedure or state-of-the-art performance management systems. Only through these competencies can the HR professional take a strategic approach to human resource management.

KEY TERMS

Strategic human resource management (SHRM), 77
Strategy formulation, 77
Strategy implementation, 78
Goals, 82
External analysis, 82
Internal analysis, 82

Strategic choice, 83
Job analysis, 89
Job design, 89
Recruitment, 89
Selection, 89
Training, 89
Development, 89

Performance management, 89
Role behaviors, 92
External growth strategy, 93
Concentration strategy, 93
Internal growth strategy, 94
Downsizing, 95

DISCUSSION QUESTIONS

1. Pick one of your university's major sports teams (like football or basketball). How would you characterize that team's generic strategy? How does the composition of the team members (in terms of size, speed, ability, and so on) relate to that strategy? What are the strengths and weaknesses of the team? How do they dictate the team's generic strategy and its approach to a particular game?
2. Do you think that it is easier to tie human resources to the strategic management process in large or in small organizations? Why?
3. Consider one of the organizations you have been affiliated with. What are some examples of human resource practices that were consistent with that organization's

strategy? What are examples of practices that were inconsistent with its strategy?
4. How can strategic management within the HRM department ensure that HRM plays an effective role in the company's strategic management process?
5. What types of specific skills (such as knowledge of financial accounting methods) do you think HR professionals will need in order to have the business, professional–technical, change management, and integrative competencies necessary in the future? Where can you develop each of these skills?
6. What are some of the key environmental variables that you see changing in the business world today? What impact will those changes have on the HRM function in organizations?

SELF-ASSESSMENT EXERCISE

Additional assignable self-assessments available in Connect.

Think of a company you have worked for, or find an annual report for a company you are interested in working for. (Many companies post their annual reports on their website.) Then answer the following questions.

QUESTIONS

1. How has the company been affected by the trends discussed in this chapter?

2. Does the company use the HR practices recommended in this chapter?
3. What else should the company do to deal with the challenges posed by the trends discussed in this chapter?

EXERCISING STRATEGY

Southwest Airlines Comes of Age

Southwest Airlines has perennially been considered a model of how an innovative strategy combined with strong culture and a strong relationship between management and employees can lead to business success. The company was founded in 1967 and was built on low costs, labor harmony, simplicity, and rapid expansion. Although labor strife seems endemic to the airline industry, Southwest always stood up for its workforce, which seemed unflinchingly committed to the company's success.

However, as the company has expanded and grown older, the original strategy seems to be in peril. Mergers among the major airlines such as American/US Airways, United/Continental, and Delta/Northwest have enabled them to reduce their cost structures and come closer to Southwest on price. In addition, ultra-discount airlines, such as Spirit Airlines, can undercut Southwest on price. Finally, airlines like

JetBlue and Virgin America compete for Southwest's traditional middle-class customers.

While Southwest faces a number of competitive and technological challenges, its labor costs stand front and center. Because Southwest is not expanding as fast, the company cannot hire as many new employees at the lowest rungs of the wage scale. With 83% of its workforce unionized, Southwest now seeks to negotiate wage freezes and tighten rules on sick time. In addition, the airline wants to hire more part-time workers and has floated the idea of outsourcing a number of jobs.

Employees pine for the former CEO and co-founder, Herb Kelleher, who was beloved by employees. Says Randy Barnes, a union representative for the ramp workers, "Ever since Herb . . . left, this has been more of a corporation and less of a family."

Southwest Airlines' challenges face every company sooner or later. Although firm success can be sustained for a number of years, at some point competition begins to take its toll. In addition, with changes in leadership (Herb Kelleher retired from the CEO role and handed it off to Gary Kelly in 2004), it is difficult to maintain the same strong culture. This has profound effects on how people must be managed to sustain success amid a changing competitive landscape.

In spite of these challenges, Southwest's performance remains strong. The airline made a record $2.24 billion in profits in 2016. In addition, the airline will continue to expand internationally, providing new opportunities for revenue growth.

QUESTIONS

1. What do you think has made Southwest Airlines so successful?
2. What do you think are the major challenges facing Southwest?
3. How would a strategic approach to HRM help Southwest successfully address these challenges?

SOURCES: Based on T. Maxon, "Southwest Airlines Tops $1 Billion in Annual Profits for First Time," *Dallas Morning News*, January 22, 2015, http://aviationblog.dallasnews.com; J. Nicas and S. Carey, "Southwest Airlines, Once a Brassy Upstart, Is Showing Its Age," *The Wall Street Journal*, April 1, 2014, www.wsj.com.

MANAGING PEOPLE

How Should Dell Respond to the HP Challenge?

Dell Computers was founded by Michael Dell in his college dormitory room. It quickly became one of the fastest growing businesses in history, an almost unparalleled success story. By 2005 Dell had become the largest manufacturer of PC's, primarily focusing on the B2B market. This was achieved by creating a "Direct" model that allowed companies to buy customized computers directly from Dell, cutting out the margins previously captured by middlemen such as CDW. The creation of Dell's "Premier Pages" website made it easy for corporate customers to easily place orders for large numbers of computers configured exactly as they wanted. The direct model also allowed Dell be better manage its supply chain, reducing both the inventory of components as well as finished products.

However, by 2007 HP had surpassed Dell in PC sales. After having tried to imitate the Dell model, in 2005 HP hired Todd Bradley to turn the business around. Instead of fighting Dell in internet and phone sales where Dell was strong, Mr. Bradley decided to focus on its strength, retail stores, where Dell was completely absent, and where individual customers, the fastest growing segment, made most of their purchases. He noted that PCs "aren't just a commodity that you run out and buy on the internet. People are going to want to touch it and feel it and understand how it connects." He also began advertising campaigns using celebrities such as hip-hop mogul Jay-Z to talk about how they used their HP laptops.

In talking with retailers, he found that they complained about late deliveries and incomplete deliveries. So, he focused on fixing the logistical problems and consolidated 30 manufacturing plants into 23. This enabled HP to reduce both the time and cost of building PCs, and reducing late deliveries by 30%. HP's margins grew to 4.8% in the second quarter of 2007 from 3.6% a year earlier while Dell's fell to 6.5% from 6.7% a year earlier.

Finally, he built better relationships with the retailers. He pushed products such as touch-screen PCs that would garner attention from customers. He also helped retailers to design products exclusive to their stores, enabling them to differentiate their products from competitors. He worked with them to be able to create customized imprints. For instance, working with Best Buy, HP created a silver and white laptop, softer colors aimed at female customers.

Thus, in 2007 Dell gave up its title as the largest producer of PCs. In addition, as the consumer market continued to grow at a much faster rate than the corporate market, Dell was ill-positioned to reverse this trend.

QUESTIONS

1. What are the major competitive and strategic challenges Dell needs to deal with if it is to regain a position of strength within the industry?
2. What can HR do to help Dell re-establish its position as the leader in PCs? Assume you just got on the elevator with Michael Dell and want to explain how HR will aid him in regaining its pre-eminent position. What will you tell him in the 1-2 minutes you have?

SOURCE: Lawton, C. (June 4, 2007) How HP regained its lead over Dell. *Wall Street Journal* http://online.wsj.com/article_print/SB118092117687623314.

HR IN SMALL BUSINESS

Radio Flyer Rolls Forward

The mid-2000s were a difficult time for Radio Flyer, a private business famous for its little red wagons. After spending hundreds of thousands of dollars to develop what they hoped was a hit, managers realized their idea wouldn't fly, so they killed it. And in the same year, management decided the company could no longer afford to build wagons in the United States.

First, the development flop: Thomas Schlegel, vice president for product development, thought he had a winner with an idea for a collapsible wagon to be called Fold 2 Go Wagon. It would be a fun product that parents could fold up and toss into the back of a minivan for a trip to the park or other outings. The problem was, a collapsing toy that children sit inside is difficult to make both functional and safe. The costs were excessive.

When Schlegel ended the project, he feared his reputation might suffer as well. But CEO Robert Pasin assured Schlegel that failure was acceptable as long as the company could learn from it. The value placed on learning became something that Schlegel capitalized on as his team applied what they learned to the development of a new success, the Twist Trike and a new model of its wagons called the Ultimate Family Wagon. Furthermore, Pasin expanded that one experience into a teaching opportunity. He invites new employees to join him for breakfasts, during which he recalls the incident as a way to reinforce the company's commitment to innovation and learning.

The story of Radio Flyer's need to outsource manufacturing has what some might see as a less-happy ending. Looking at the numbers, management determined that it would have to close its factory in Chicago and lay off about half of its workforce. Manufacturing moved to a factory in China. Pasin describes the effort as "an incredibly difficult time."

The company's effort with its remaining U.S. employees focused on building morale. These efforts include creating ideas for employees to have fun and pursue their passions, with events such as the Radio Flyer Olympics, during which employees compete in silly contests like tricycle races. More seriously, teams of employees tackle issues that they care about. The wellness committee put together a cash benefit that pays employees up to $300 for participating in health-related activities such as weight-loss counseling or running races. Another committee brought together employees concerned about the environment. They assembled a campaign aimed at persuading employees to reduce their carbon footprint.

In caring for the U.S. employees, Radio Flyer hasn't forgotten the ones in China. The company tries to maintain similar levels of benefits and engagement among the four dozen employees in its China office.

QUESTIONS

1. How could a human resource manager help Radio Flyer get the maximum benefit from the motivational efforts described in this case?
2. Do you think outsourcing would be harder on employees in a small company such as Radio Flyer than in a large corporation? Why or why not? How could HRM help to smooth the transition?
3. What additional developments described in this chapter could help Radio Flyer live out the high value it places on learning and innovation?

SOURCES: Company website, www.radioflyer.com, accessed May 24, 2015; "Best Places to Work 2015 in Chicago: #7 Radio Flyer," *Crain's Chicago Business*, www.chicagobusiness.com, accessed May 24, 2015; J. Scanlon, "Radio Flyer Learns from a Crash," *Bloomberg Businessweek*, www.businessweek.com, accessed May 24, 2015.

NOTES

1. J. Barney, "Firm Resources and Sustained Competitive Advantage," *Journal of Management* 17 (1991), pp. 99–120.
2. L. Dyer, "Strategic Human Resource Management and Planning," in *Research in Personnel and Human Resources Management*, ed. K. Rowland and G. Ferris (Greenwich, CT: JAI Press, 1985), pp. 1–30.
3. http://marketrealist.com/2016/03/general-motors-global-market-share-falling/
4. P. Ingrassia, "GM's Plan: Subsidize Our 48-Year-Old Retirees," *Wall Street Journal*, February 19, 2009, http://online.wsj.com/article/SB123500874299418721.html; S. Terlep and N. King, "Bondholders Say GM's Plan Fails to Tackle Issues," *Wall Street Journal*, February 19, 2009, http://online.wsj.com/article/SB123500467245718075.html?mod=testMod.
5. J. Quinn, *Strategies for Change: Logical Incrementalism* (Homewood, IL: Richard D. Irwin, 1980).
6. M. Porter, *Competitive Strategy: Techniques for Analyzing Industries and Competitors* (New York: Free Press, 1980).
7. R. Miles and C. Snow, *Organizational Strategy, Structure, and Process* (New York: McGraw-Hill, 1978).
8. P. Wright and G. McMahan, "Theoretical Perspectives for Strategic Human Resource Management," *Journal of Management* 18 (1992), pp. 295–320.

9. D. Guest, "Human Resource Management, Corporate Performance and Employee Well-Being: Building the Worker into HRM," *Journal of Industrial Relations* 44 (2002), pp. 335–58; B. Becker, M. Huselid, P. Pinckus, and M. Spratt, "HR as a Source of Shareholder Value: Research and Recommendations," *Human Resource Management* 36 (1997), pp. 39–47.

10. P. Boxall and J. Purcell, *Strategy and Human Resource Management* (Basingstoke, Hants, U.K.: Palgrave MacMillan, 2003).

11. F. Biddle and J. Helyar, "Behind Boeing's Woes: Chunky Assembly Line, Price War with Airbus," *Wall Street Journal,* April 24, 1998, pp. A1, A16.

12. K. Martell and S. Carroll, "How Strategic Is HRM?" *Human Resource Management* 34 (1995), pp. 253–67.

13. K. Golden and V. Ramanujam, "Between a Dream and a Nightmare: On the Integration of the Human Resource Function and the Strategic Business Planning Process," *Human Resource Management* 24 (1985), pp. 429–51.

14. P. Wright, B. Dunford, and S. Snell, "Contributions of the Resource-Based View of the Firm to the Field of Strategic HRM: Convergence of Two Fields," *Journal of Management* 27 (2001), pp. 701–21.

15. J. Purcell, N. Kinnie, S. Hutchinson, B. Rayton, and J. Swart, *Understanding the People and Performance Link: Unlocking the Black Box* (London: CIPD, 2003).

16. P. M. Wright, T. Gardner, and L. Moynihan, "The Impact of Human Resource Practices on Business Unit Operating and Financial Performance," *Human Resource Management Journal* 13, no. 3 (2003), pp. 21–36.

17. H. Kim and K. Sung-Choon, "Strategic HR Functions and Firm Performance: The Moderating Effects of High-Involvement Work Practices," *Asia Pacific Journal of Management* 30, no. 1 (2013), pp. 91–113.

18. C. Hill and G. Jones, *Strategic Management Theory: An Integrated Approach* (Boston: Houghton Mifflin, 1989).

19. W. Johnston and A. Packer, *Workforce 2000: Work and Workers for the Twenty-First Century* (Indianapolis, IN: Hudson Institute, 1987).

20. "Labor Letter," *Wall Street Journal,* December 15, 1992, p. A1.

21. P. Wright, G. McMahan, and A. McWilliams, "Human Resources and Sustained Competitive Advantage: A Resource-Based Perspective," *International Journal of Human Resource Management* 5 (1994), pp. 301–26.

22. P. Buller, "Successful Partnerships: HR and Strategic Planning at Eight Top Firms," *Organizational Dynamics* 17 (1988), pp. 27–42.

23. M. Hitt, R. Hoskisson, and J. Harrison, "Strategic Competitiveness in the 1990s: Challenges and Opportunities for U.S. Executives," *The Executive* 5 (May 1991), pp. 7–22.

24. P. Wright, G. McMahan, B. McCormick, and S. Sherman, "Strategy, Core Competence, and HR Involvement as Determinants of HR Effectiveness and Refinery Performance." Paper presented at the 1996 International Federation of Scholarly Associations in Management, Paris, France.

25. N. Bennett, D. Ketchen, and E. Schultz, "Antecedents and Consequences of Human Resource Integration with Strategic Decision Making." Paper presented at the 1995 Academy of Management Meeting, Vancouver, BC, Canada.

26. Golden and Ramanujam, "Between a Dream and a Nightmare."

27. J. Galbraith and R. Kazanjian, *Strategy Implementation: Structure, Systems, and Process* (St. Paul, MN: West, 1986).

28. B. Schneider and A. Konz, "Strategic Job Analysis," *Human Resource Management* 27 (1989), pp. 51–64.

29. P. Wright and S. Snell, "Toward an Integrative View of Strategic Human Resource Management," *Human Resource Management Review* 1 (1991), pp. 203–25.

30. S. Snell, "Control Theory in Strategic Human Resource Management: The Mediating Effect of Administrative Information," *Academy of Management Journal* 35 (1992), pp. 292–327.

31. R. Schuler, "Personnel and Human Resource Management Choices and Organizational Strategy," in *Readings in Personnel and Human Resource Management,* 3rd ed., ed. R. Schuler, S. Youngblood, and V. Huber (St. Paul, MN: West, 1988).

32. J. Dean and S. Snell, "Integrated Manufacturing and Job Design: Moderating Effects of Organizational Inertia," *Academy of Management Journal* 34 (1991), pp. 776–804.

33. E. Lawler, *The Ultimate Advantage: Creating the High Involvement Organization* (San Francisco: Jossey-Bass, 1992).

34. J. Olian and S. Rynes, "Organizational Staffing: Integrating Practice with Strategy," *Industrial Relations* 23 (1984), pp. 170–83.

35. G. Smith, "Quality: Small and Midsize Companies Seize the Challenge—Not a Moment Too Soon," *BusinessWeek,* November 30, 1992, pp. 66–75.

36. J. Kerr and E. Jackofsky, "Aligning Managers with Strategies: Management Development versus Selection," *Strategic Management Journal* 10 (1989), pp. 157–70.

37. J. Kerr, "Strategic Control through Performance Appraisal and Rewards," *Human Resource Planning* 11 (1988), pp. 215–23.

38. Snell, "Control Theory in Strategic Human Resource Management."

39. B. Gerhart and G. Milkovich, "Employee Compensation: Research and Practice," in *Handbook of Industrial and Organizational Psychology,* 2nd ed., ed. M. Dunnette and L. Hough (Palo Alto, CA: Consulting Psychologists Press, 1992), pp. 481–569.

40. D. Balkin and L. Gomez-Mejia, "Toward a Contingency Theory of Compensation Strategy," *Strategic Management Journal* 8 (1987), pp. 169–82.

41. S. Cronshaw and R. Alexander, "One Answer to the Demand for Accountability: Selection Utility as an Investment Decision," *Organizational Behavior and Human Decision Processes* 35 (1986), pp. 102–18.

42. P. MacDuffie, "Human Resource Bundles and Manufacturing Performance: Organizational Logic and Flexible Production Systems in the World Auto Industry," *Industrial and Labor Relations Review* 48 (1995), pp. 197–221; P. McGraw, "A Hard Drive to the Top," *U.S. News & World Report* 118 (1995), pp. 43–44.

43. M. Huselid, "The Impact of Human Resource Management Practices on Turnover, Productivity, and Corporate Financial Performance," *Academy of Management Journal* 38 (1995), pp. 635–72.

44. B. Fulmer, B. Gerhart, and K. Scott, "Are the 100 Best Better? An Empirical Investigation of the Relationship between Being a 'Great Place to Work' and Firm Performance," *Personnel Psychology* 56 (2003), pp. 965–93.

45. J. E. Delery and D. H. Doty, "Modes of Theorizing in Strategic Human Resource Management: Tests of Universalistic, Contingency and Configurational Performance Predictions," *Academy of Management Journal* 39 (1996), pp. 802–83; D. Guest, J. Michie, N. Conway, and M. Sheehan, "Human Resource Management and Corporate Performance in the UK," *British Journal of Industrial Relations* 41 (2003), pp. 291–314; J. Guthrie, "High Involvement Work Practices, Turnover, and Productivity: Evidence from New Zealand," *Academy of Management Journal* 44 (2001), pp. 180–192; J. Harter, F. Schmidt,

and T. Hayes, "Business-Unit-Level Relationship between Employee Satisfaction, Employee Engagement, and Business Outcomes: A Meta-analysis," *Journal of Applied Psychology* 87 (2002), pp. 268–79; Watson Wyatt, Worldwide, "Human Capital Index®: Human Capital as a Lead Indicator of Shareholder Value" (2002).

46. M. Bhattacharya, D. Gibson, and H. Doty, "The Effects of Flexibility in Employee Skills, Employee Behaviors, and Human Resource Practices on Firm Performance," *Journal of Management* 31 (2005), pp. 622–40.

47. D. Guest, J. Michie, N. Conway, and M. Sheehan, "Human Resource Management and Corporate Performance in the UK," *British Journal of Industrial Relations* 41 (2003), pp. 291–314; P. Wright, T. Gardner, L. Moynihan, and M. Allen, "The HR–Performance Relationship: Examining Causal Direction," *Personnel Psychology* 58 (2005), pp. 409–76.

48. P. Wright, *No Strategy: Adaptive to the Age of Globalization* (Arlington, VA: SHRM Foundation, 2008).

49. M. Porter, *Competitive Advantage* (New York: Free Press, 1985).

50. C. Lawton, "How HP Reclaimed Its PC Lead over Dell," June 2007; "Can Dell's Turnaround Strategy Keep HP at Bay?" September 2007, *Knowledge@Wharton,* http://knowledge.wharton.upenn.edu/article.cfm?articleid51799.

51. R. Schuler and S. Jackson, "Linking Competitive Strategies with Human Resource Management Practices," *Academy of Management Executive* 1 (1987), pp. 207–19.

52. R. Miles and C. Snow, "Designing Strategic Human Resource Management Systems," *Organizational Dynamics* 13, no. 1 (1984), pp. 36–52.

53. A. Thompson and A. Strickland, *Strategy Formulation and Implementation: Tasks of the General Manager,* 3rd ed. (Plano, TX: BPI, 1986).

54. J. Schmidt, *Making Mergers Work: The Strategic Importance of People* (Arlington, VA: SHRM Foundation, 2003).

55. G. Fairclough, "Business Bulletin," *Wall Street Journal,* March 5, 1998, p. A1.

56. P. Sebastian, "Business Bulletin," *Wall Street Journal,* October 2, 1997, p. A1.

57. U.S. Department of Labor, Bureau of Labor Statistics, "Mass Layoffs Summary," May 13, 2013, www.bls.gov/news.release/mslo.nr0.htm.

58. Challenger, Gray and Christmas, "2016 July Job Cut Report: Cuts Jump 19 Percent to 45,346," https://www.challengergray.com/press/press-releases/2016-july-job-cut-report-cuts-jump-19-percent-45346.

59. M. Hansson, and F. Gandolfi, "Causes and Consequences of Downsizing: Towards an Integrative Framework," *Journal of Management & Organization* 17, no. 4 (2010), pp. 498–521.

60. S. Pearlstein, "Corporate Cutback Yet to Pay Off," *Washington Post,* January 4, 1994, p. B6.

61. K. Cameron, "Guest Editor's Note: Investigating Organizational Downsizing—Fundamental Issues," *Human Resource Management* 33 (1994), pp. 183–88.

62. W. Cascio, *Responsible Restructuring: Creative and Profitable Alternatives to Layoffs* (San Francisco: Berrett-Koehler, 2002).

63. N. Templin, "UAW to Unveil Pact on Slashing GM's Payroll," *Wall Street Journal,* December 15, 1992, p. A3.

64. J. Lopez, "Managing: Early-Retirement Offers Lead to Renewed Hiring," *Wall Street Journal,* January 26, 1993, p. B1.

65. A. Church, "Organizational Downsizing: What Is the Role of the Practitioner?" *Industrial–Organizational Psychologist* 33, no. 1 (1995), pp. 63–74.

66. N. Templin, "A Decisive Response to Crisis Brought Ford Enhanced Productivity," *Wall Street Journal,* December 15, 1992, p. A1.

67. Quinn, *Strategies for Change.*

68. H. Schultz and D. Yang, *Pour Your Heart Into It* (New York: Hyperion, 1987).

69. R. Pascale, "Perspectives on Strategy: The Real Story behind Honda's Success," *California Management Review* 26 (1984), pp. 47–72.

70. Templin, "A Decisive Response to Crisis."

71. P. Wright and S. Snell, "Toward a Unifying Framework for Exploring Fit and Flexibility in Strategic Human Resource Management," *Academy of Management Review* 23, no. 4 (1998), pp. 756–72.

72. H. Behar, *It's Not about the Coffee: Lessons for Putting People First from a Life at Starbucks* (New York: Penguin Group, 2007).

73. T. Stewart, "Brace for Japan's Hot New Strategy," *Fortune,* September 21, 1992, pp. 62–76.

74. B. Dunford, P. Wright, and S. Snell, "Contributions of the Resource-Based View of the Firm to the Field of Strategic HRM: Convergence of Two Fields," *Journal of Management* 27 (2001), pp. 701–21.

75. C. Snow and S. Snell, *Staffing as Strategy,* vol. 4 of *Personnel Selection* (San Francisco: Jossey-Bass, 1992).

76. T. Batten, "Education Key to Prosperity—Report," *Houston Chronicle,* September 7, 1992, p. 1B.

77. Schultz and Yang, *Pour Your Heart Into It.*

78. G. McMahan, University of Texas at Arlington, personal communications.

CHAPTER

3

The Legal Environment: Equal Employment Opportunity and Safety

LEARNING OBJECTIVES

After reading this chapter, you should be able to:

LO 3-1   Identify the three branches of government and the role each plays in influencing the legal environment of human resource management. *page 108*

LO 3-2   List the major federal laws that require equal employment opportunity and the protections provided by each of these laws. *page 109*

LO 3-3   Discuss the roles, responsibilities, and requirements of the federal agencies responsible for enforcing equal employment opportunity laws. *page 117*

LO 3-4   Identify the three theories of discrimination under Title VII of the Civil Rights Act and apply these theories to different discrimination situations. *page 120*

LO 3-5   Identify behavior that constitutes sexual harassment, and list things that an organization can do to eliminate or minimize it. *page 133*

LO 3-6   Discuss the legal issues involved with preferential treatment programs. *page 136*

LO 3-7   Identify the major provisions of the Occupational Safety and Health Act (1970) and the rights of employees that are guaranteed by this act. *page 140*

ENTER THE WORLD OF BUSINESS

Discrimination at Oracle?

The U.S. Department of Labor recently filed suit against Oracle Corp., alleging that the company is discriminating in pay and hiring practices. Interestingly, the discrimination they allege is in favor of whites for pay, and Asians in hiring.

As a government contractor with millions of dollars in contracts, Oracle faces significant risks if it is found guilty. Government contractors are prohibited from discriminating in any employment decision on the basis of race, color, sex, sexual orientation or gender identity, or national origin, and is required to take affirmative actions with regard to these characteristics. The government alleges that Oracle prefers hiring Asians over non-Asians in its product development and other technical jobs. At the same time, the government alleges that Oracle pays Caucasian male employees more than female, African American, and Asian employees.

Oracle, not surprisingly, denies the claim. An Oracle spokeswoman stated, "Oracle values diversity and inclusion, and is a responsible equal opportunity and affirmative action employer. Our hiring and pay decisions are nondiscriminatory and made based on legitimate business factors including experience and merit."

So who is correct? The government relies on statistical analyses showing differences in average pay or hiring rates. Oracle claims those differences are due to legitimate business factors. In this chapter we will explore how statistical analyses may signal potential discrimination and what legitimate business factors companies can use to defend themselves.

SOURCE: A. Steele and S. Green, S. "U.S. Sues Oracle, Alleging Salary and Hiring Discrimination," *Wall Street Journal,* January 18, 2017, https://www.wsj.com/articles/u-s-sues-oracle-alleging-salary-and-hiring-discrimination-1484768488.

Introduction

In Chapter 1, we discussed the environment of the human resource management function, and we noted that several environmental factors affect an organization's HRM function. One is the legal environment, particularly the laws affecting the management of people. As the potential troubles at Oracle suggest, legal issues can cause serious problems for a company's success and survival. In this chapter, we first present an overview of the U.S. legal system, noting the different legislative bodies, regulatory agencies, and judicial bodies that determine the legality of certain HRM practices. We then discuss the major laws and executive orders that govern these practices.

One point to make clear at the outset is that managers often want a list of "dos and don'ts" that will keep them out of legal trouble. They rely on rules such as "Don't ever ask a female applicant if she is married" without understanding the "why" behind these rules. Clearly, certain practices are illegal or inadvisable, and this chapter will provide some valuable tips for avoiding discrimination lawsuits. However, such lists are not compatible with a strategic approach to HRM and are certainly not the route to developing a competitive advantage. They are simply mechanical reactions to the situations. Our goal is to provide an understanding of how the legislative, regulatory, and judicial systems work to define equal employment opportunity law. Armed with this understanding, a manager is better prepared to manage people within the limits imposed by the legal system. Doing so effectively is a source of competitive advantage. Doing so ineffectively results in competitive disadvantage. Rather than viewing the legal system as a constraint, firms that embrace the concept of diversity can often find that they are able to leverage the differences among people as a tremendous competitive tool.

The Legal System in the United States

LO 3-1
Identify the three branches of government and the role each plays in influencing the legal environment of human resource management.

The foundation for the U.S. legal system is set forth in the U.S. Constitution, which affects HRM in two ways. First, it delineates a citizen's constitutional rights, on which the government cannot impinge.[1] Most individuals are aware of the Bill of Rights, the first 10 amendments to the Constitution; but other amendments, such as the Fourteenth Amendment, also influence HRM practices. The Fourteenth Amendment, called the equal protection clause, states that all individuals are entitled to equal protection under the law.

Second, the Constitution established three major governing bodies: the legislative, executive, and judicial branches. The Constitution explicitly defines the roles and responsibilities of each of these branches. Each branch has its own areas of authority, but these areas have often overlapped, and the borders between the branches are often blurred.

LEGISLATIVE BRANCH

The legislative branch of the federal government consists of the House of Representatives and the Senate. These bodies develop laws that govern many HRM activities. Most of the laws stem from a perceived societal need. For example, during the civil rights movement of the early 1960s, the legislative branch moved to ensure that various minority groups received equal opportunities in many areas of life. One of these areas was employment, and thus Congress enacted Title VII of the Civil Rights Act. Similar perceived societal needs have brought about labor laws such as the Occupational Safety and Health Act, the Employee Retirement Income Security Act, the Age Discrimination in Employment Act, and, more recently, the Americans with Disabilities Act of 1990 and the Civil Rights Act of 1991.

EXECUTIVE BRANCH

The executive branch consists of the president of the United States and the many regulatory agencies the president oversees. Although the legislative branch passes the laws, the executive branch affects these laws in many ways. First, the president can propose bills to Congress that, if passed, would become laws. Second, the president has the power to veto any law passed by Congress, thus ensuring that few laws are passed without presidential approval—which allows the president to influence how laws are written.

Third, the regulatory agencies, under the authority of the president, have responsibility for enforcing the laws. Thus, a president can influence what types of violations are pursued. For example, many laws affecting employment discrimination are enforced by the Equal Employment Opportunity Commission under the Department of Justice. During President Jimmy Carter's administration, the Department of Justice brought a lawsuit against the Birmingham, Alabama, fire department for not having enough black firefighters. This suit resulted in a consent decree that required blacks to receive preferential treatment in hiring and promotion decisions. Two years later, during Ronald Reagan's administration, the Department of Justice sided with white firefighters in a lawsuit against the city of Birmingham, alleging that the preferential treatment required by the consent decree discriminated against white firefighters.[2]

Fourth, the president can issue executive orders, which sometimes regulate the activities of organizations that have contracts with the federal government. For example, Executive Order 11246, signed by President Lyndon Johnson, required all federal contractors and subcontractors to engage in affirmative action programs designed to hire and promote women and minorities within their organizations. Fifth, the president can influence the Supreme Court to interpret laws in certain ways. When particularly sensitive cases come before the Court, the attorney general's office, representing the executive branch, argues for certain preferred outcomes. For example, one court case involved a white female schoolteacher who was laid off from her job in favor of retaining a black schoolteacher with equal seniority and performance with the reason given as "diversity." The white woman filed a lawsuit in federal court and the George H. W. Bush administration filed a brief on her behalf, arguing that diversity was not a legitimate reason to use race in decision making. She won in federal court, and the school district appealed. The Bill Clinton administration, having been elected in the meantime, filed a brief on behalf of the school district, arguing that diversity was a legitimate defense.

Finally, the president appoints all the judges in the federal judicial system, subject to approval from the legislative branch. This affects the interpretation of many laws.

JUDICIAL BRANCH

The judicial branch consists of the federal court system, which is made up of three levels. The first level consists of the U.S. District Courts and quasi-judicial administrative agencies. The district courts hear cases involving alleged violations of federal laws. The quasi-judicial agencies, such as the National Labor Relations Board (or NLRB, which is actually an arm of the executive branch, but serves a judicial function), hear cases regarding their particular jurisdictions (in the NLRB's case, disputes between unions and management). If neither party to a suit is satisfied with the decision of the court at this level, the parties can appeal the decision to the U.S. Courts of Appeals. These courts were originally set up to ease the Supreme Court's caseload, so appeals generally go from the federal trial level to one of the 13 appellate courts before they can be heard by the highest level, the Supreme Court. The Supreme Court must grant certiorari before hearing an appealed case. However, this is not usually granted unless two appellate courts have come to differing decisions on the same point of law or if the case deals with an important interpretation of constitutional law.

The Supreme Court serves as the court of final appeal. Decisions made by the Supreme Court are binding; they can be overturned only through legislation. For example, Congress, dissatisfied with the Supreme Court's decisions in certain cases such as *Wards Cove Packing v. Atonio,* overturned those decisions through the Civil Rights Act of 1991.[3]

Having described the legal system that affects the management of human resources, we now explore some laws that regulate HRM activities, particularly equal employment opportunity laws. We first discuss the major laws that mandate equal employment opportunity in the United States. Then we examine the agencies involved in enforcing these laws. This leads us into an examination of the four theories of discrimination, with a discussion of some relevant court cases. Finally, we explore some equal employment opportunity issues facing today's managers.

Equal employment opportunity (EEO)
The government's attempt to ensure that all individuals have an equal opportunity for employment, regardless of race, color, religion, sex, age, disability, or national origin.

Equal Employment Opportunity

Equal employment opportunity (EEO) refers to the government's attempt to ensure that all individuals have an equal chance for employment, regardless of race, color, religion, sex, age, disability, or national origin. To accomplish this, the federal government has used constitutional amendments, legislation, and executive orders, as well as the court decisions that interpret these laws. (However, equal employment laws are not the same in all countries.) The major EEO laws we discuss are summarized in Table 3.1.

LO 3-2
List the major federal laws that require equal employment opportunity and the protections provided by each of these laws.

Table 3.1

Summary of Major EEO Laws and Regulations

ACT	REQUIREMENTS	COVERS	ENFORCEMENT AGENCY
Thirteenth Amendment	Abolished slavery	All individuals	Court system
Fourteenth Amendment	Provides equal protection for all citizens and requires due process in state action	State actions (e.g., decisions of government organizations)	Court system
Civil Rights Acts (CRAs) of 1866 and 1871 (as amended)	Grants all citizens the right to make, perform, modify, and terminate contracts and enjoy all benefits, terms, and conditions of the contractual relationship	All individuals	Court system
Equal Pay Act of 1963	Requires that men and women performing equal jobs receive equal pay	Employers engaged in interstate commerce	Equal Employment Opportunity Commission (EEOC)
Title VII of the CRA of 1964	Forbids discrimination based on race, color, religion, sex, or national origin	Employers with 15 or more employees working 20 or more weeks per year; labor unions; and employment agencies	EEOC
Age Discrimination in Employment Act of 1967	Prohibits discrimination in employment against individuals 40 years of age and older	Employers with 15 or more employees working 20 or more weeks per year; labor unions; employment agencies; federal government	EEOC
Rehabilitation Act of 1973	Requires affirmative action in the employment of individuals with disabilities	Government agencies; federal contractors and subcontractors with contracts greater than $2,500	Office of Federal Contract Compliance Programs (OFCCP)
Pregnancy Discrimination Act	Prohibits discrimination on the basis of pregnancy, childbirth, or related medical conditions	Employers with more than 15 employees	EEOC
Americans with Disabilities Act of 1990	Prohibits discrimination against individuals with disabilities	Employers with more than 15 employees	EEOC
Civil Rights Act of 1991	Prohibits discrimination (same as Title VII)	Same as Title VII, plus applies Section 1981 to employment discrimination cases	EEOC
Executive Order 11246	Requires affirmative action in hiring women and minorities	Federal contractors and subcontractors with contracts greater than $10,000	OFCCP

CONSTITUTIONAL AMENDMENTS

Thirteenth Amendment

The Thirteenth Amendment of the Constitution abolished slavery in the United States. Though one might be hard-pressed to cite an example of race-based slavery in the United States today, the Thirteenth Amendment has been applied in cases where the discrimination involved the "badges" (symbols) and "incidents" of slavery.

Fourteenth Amendment

The Fourteenth Amendment forbids the states from taking life, liberty, or property without due process of law and prevents the states from denying equal protection of the laws. Passed immediately after the Civil War, this amendment originally applied only to discrimination against blacks. It was soon broadened to protect other groups such as immigrants and Asian Americans, and more recently it has been applied to the protection of whites in allegations of reverse discrimination. In *Bakke v. California Board of Regents*, Alan Bakke alleged that he had been discriminated against in the selection of entrants to the University of California at Davis medical school.[4] The university had set aside 16 of the available 100 places for "disadvantaged" applicants who were members of racial minority groups. Under this quota system, Bakke was able to compete for only 84 positions, whereas a minority applicant was able to compete for all 100. The Court ruled in favor of Bakke, noting that this quota system had violated white individuals' right to equal protection under the law.

One important point regarding the Fourteenth Amendment is that it is applicable only to "state actions." This means that only the decisions or actions of the government or of private groups whose activities are deemed state actions can be construed as violations of the Fourteenth Amendment. Thus, one could file a claim under the Fourteenth Amendment if one were fired from a state university (a government organization) but not if one were fired by a private employer.

CONGRESSIONAL LEGISLATION

Reconstruction Civil Rights Acts (1866 and 1871)

The Thirteenth Amendment eradicated slavery in the United States, and the Reconstruction Civil Rights Acts were attempts to further this goal. The Civil Rights Act passed in 1866 was later broken into two statutes. Section 1982 granted all persons the same property rights as white citizens. Section 1981 granted other rights, including the right to enter into and enforce contracts. Courts have interpreted Section 1981 as granting individuals the right to make and enforce employment contracts. The Civil Rights Act of 1871 granted all citizens the right to sue in federal court if they felt they had been deprived of some civil right. Although these laws might seem outdated, they are still used because they allow the plaintiff to recover both compensatory and punitive damages.

In fact, these laws came to the forefront in a Supreme Court case: *Patterson v. McLean Credit Union*.[5] The plaintiff had filed a discrimination complaint under Section 1981 for racial harassment. After being hired by McLean Credit Union, Patterson failed to receive any promotions or pay raises while she was employed there. She was also told that "blacks work slower than whites." Thus, she had grounds to prove discrimination and filed suit under Section 1981, arguing that she had been discriminated against in the making and enforcement of an employment contract. The Supreme Court ruled that this situation did not fall under Section 1981 because it did not involve the making and enforcement of contracts. However, the Civil Rights Act of 1991 amended this act to include the making, performance, modification, and termination of contracts, as well as all benefits, privileges, terms, and conditions of the contractual relationship.

Equal Pay Act of 1963

The Equal Pay Act, an amendment to the Fair Labor Standards Act, requires that men and women in the same organization who are doing equal work must be paid equally. The act defines *equal* in terms of skill, effort, responsibility, and working conditions. However, the act allows for reasons why men and women performing the same job might be paid differently. If the pay differences are the result of differences in seniority, merit, quantity or quality of production, or any factor other than sex (such as shift differentials or training programs), then differences are legally allowable.

Title VII of the Civil Rights Act of 1964

Title VII is the major legislation regulating equal employment opportunity in the United States. It was a direct result of the civil rights movement of the early 1960s, led by such individuals as Dr. Martin Luther King Jr. To ensure that employment opportunities would be based on character or ability rather than on race, Congress wrote and passed Title VII, which President Lyndon Johnson signed into law.

Title VII states that it is illegal for an employer to "(1) fail or refuse to hire or discharge any individual, or otherwise discriminate against any individual with respect to his compensation, terms, conditions, or privileges of employment because of such individual's race, color, religion, sex, or national origin, or (2) to limit, segregate, or classify his employees or applicants for employment in any way that would deprive or tend to deprive any individual of employment opportunities or otherwise adversely affect his status as an employee because of such individual's race, color, religion, sex, or national origin." The act applies to organizations with 15 or more employees working 20 or more weeks a year that are involved in interstate commerce, as well as state and local governments, employment agencies, and labor organizations.

Age Discrimination in Employment Act of 1967

Passed in 1967 and amended in 1986, the Age Discrimination in Employment Act (ADEA) prohibits discrimination against employees over the age of 40. The act almost exactly mirrors Title VII in terms of its substantive provisions and the procedures to be followed in pursuing a case.[6] As with Title VII, the Equal Employment Opportunity Commission (EEOC) is responsible for enforcing this act.

The ADEA was designed to protect older employees when a firm reduces its workforce through layoffs. By targeting older employees, who tend to have higher pay, a firm can substantially cut labor costs. Recently, firms have often offered early retirement incentives, a possible violation of the act because of the focus on older employees. Early retirement incentives require employees to sign an agreement waiving their rights to sue under the ADEA. Courts have tended to uphold the use of early retirement incentives and waivers as long as the individuals were not coerced into signing the agreements, the agreements were presented in a way that the employees could understand, and the employees were given enough time to make a decision.[7]

However, age discrimination complaints make up a large percentage of the complaints filed with the EEOC, and the number of complaints continues to grow whenever the

Figure 3.1

Age Discrimination Complaints, 1991–2014

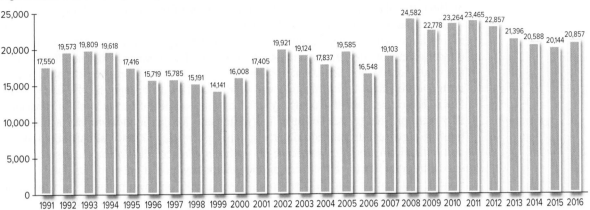

SOURCE: Equal Employment Opportunity Commission, "Age Discrimination in Employment Act (Charges Filed with EEOC)," https://www.eeoc.gov/eeoc/statistics/enforcement/adea.cfm.

economy is slow. For example, as we see in Figure 3.1, the number of cases increased during the early 1990s, when many firms were downsizing, but then decreased as the economy expanded. The number of complaints increased again as the economy began slowing in 2000 and with the recession in 2008. These trends often stem from firms seeking to lay off older (and thus higher-paid) employees when they are downsizing.

These cases can be costly; most are settled out of court, but such settlements run from $50,000 to $400,000 per employee.[8] In one case, Schering-Plough Corporation fired 35-year employee Fred Maiorino after he twice failed to accept an early retirement offer made to all sales representatives. After hearing testimony that Maiorino's boss had plastered his file with negative paperwork aimed at firing him, rather than trying to help him improve his performance, the jurors unanimously decided he had been discriminated against because of his age. They awarded him $435,000 in compensatory damages and $8 million in punitive damages.[9]

Rehabilitation Act of 1973

The Rehabilitation Act covers executive agencies and contractors and subcontractors that receive more than $2,500 annually from the federal government. It requires them to engage in affirmative action for individuals with disabilities. Congress designed this act to encourage employers to actively recruit qualified individuals with disabilities and to make reasonable accommodations to allow them to become active members of the labor market. The Employment Standards Administration of the Department of Labor enforces this act.

Vietnam Era Veteran's Readjustment Assistance Act of 1974

Similar to the Rehabilitation Act, the Vietnam Veteran's Readjustment Assistance Act requires federal contractors and subcontractors to take affirmative action toward employing Vietnam veterans (those serving between August 5, 1964, and May 7, 1975). The Office of Federal Contract Compliance Programs (OFCCP), discussed later in this chapter, has authority to enforce this act.

Pregnancy Discrimination Act

The Pregnancy Discrimination Act is an amendment to Title VII of the Civil Rights Act of 1964. It makes illegal discrimination on the basis of pregnancy, childbirth, or related medical conditions as a form of unlawful sex discrimination. An employer cannot refuse to hire a pregnant woman because of her pregnancy; a pregnancy-related condition; or the prejudices of co-workers, clients, or customers. For instance, in a recent court case, the retail store Motherhood Maternity, a Philadelphia-based maternity clothes retailer, settled a pregnancy discrimination and retaliation lawsuit brought by the EEOC. The EEOC had charged that the company refused to hire qualified female applicants because they were pregnant. As a result of the settlement, Motherhood Maternity agreed to a three-year consent decree requiring them to pay plaintiffs $375,000, adopt and distribute an antidiscrimination policy specifically prohibiting discrimination on the basis of pregnancy, train its Florida employees on the new policy, post a notice of resolution of the lawsuit, and provide twice-a-year reports to the EEOC on any pregnancy discrimination complaints.[10]

In addition, regarding pregnancy and maternity leave, employers may not single out pregnancy-related conditions for special procedures to determine an employee's ability to work, and if an employee is temporarily unable to perform during her pregnancy, the employer must treat her the same as any temporarily disabled employees. The act also requires that any health insurance must cover expenses for pregnancy-related conditions on the same basis as costs for other medical conditions. Finally, pregnancy-related benefits cannot be limited to married employees, and if an employer provides any benefits to workers on leave, they must also provide the same benefits for those on leave for pregnancy-related conditions.

Recently the EEOC filed suit against HCS Medical Staffing, Inc., for allegedly discriminating against a pregnant employee and then firing her while she was on maternity leave. According to the EEOC's suit, owner Charles Sisson engaged in escalating negative comments about the upcoming maternity leave of HCS bookkeeper Roxy Leger. He allegedly insisted that Leger's pregnancy was a joke, described her maternity leave as "vacation," and insisted that maternity leave should be no longer than two days. Sisson then allegedly terminated Leger, who had no prior negative comments on her work performance, seven days after she gave birth by cesarean section.[11]

Civil Rights Act of 1991

The Civil Rights Act of 1991 (CRA 1991) amends Title VII of the Civil Rights Act of 1964, Section 1981 of the Civil Rights Act of 1866, the Americans with Disabilities Act, and the Age Discrimination in Employment Act of 1967. One major change in EEO law under CRA 1991 has been the addition of compensatory and punitive damages in cases of discrimination under Title VII and the Americans with Disabilities Act. Before CRA 1991, Title VII limited damage claims to equitable relief such as back pay, lost benefits, front pay in some cases, and attorneys' fees and costs. CRA 1991 allows compensatory and punitive damages when intentional or reckless discrimination is proven. Compensatory damages include such things as future pecuniary loss, emotional pain, suffering, and loss of enjoyment of life. Punitive damages are meant to discourage employers from discriminating by providing for payments to the plaintiff beyond the actual damages suffered.

Recognizing that one or a few discrimination cases could put an organization out of business, thus adversely affecting many innocent employees, Congress has put limits on the amount of punitive damages. Table 3.2 depicts these limits. As can be seen, damages

EMPLOYER SIZE	DAMAGE LIMIT
14 to 100 employees	$ 50,000
101 to 200 employees	$ 50,000
201 to 500 employees	200,000
More than 500 employees	300,000

Table 3.2
Maximum Punitive Damages Allowed under the Civil Rights Act of 1991

range from $50,000 to $300,000 per violation, depending on the size of the organization. Punitive damages are available only if the employer intentionally discriminated against the plaintiff(s) or if the employer discriminated with malice or reckless indifference to the employee's federally protected rights. These damages are excluded for an employment practice held to be unlawful because of its disparate impact.[12]

The addition of damages to CRA 1991 has had two immediate effects. First, by increasing the potential payoff for a successful discrimination suit, it has increased the number of suits filed against businesses. Second, organizations are now more likely to grant all employees an equal opportunity for employment, regardless of their race, sex, religion, or national origin. Many organizations have felt the need to make the composition of their workforce mirror the general population to avoid costly lawsuits. This act adds a financial incentive for doing so.

Americans with Disabilities Act of 1990

One of the most far-reaching acts concerning the management of human resources is the **Americans with Disabilities Act (ADA)**. This act protects individuals with disabilities from being discriminated against in the workplace. It prohibits discrimination based on disability in all employment practices such as job application procedures, hiring, firing, promotions, compensation, and training—in addition to other employment activities such as advertising, recruitment, tenure, layoff, leave, and fringe benefits. We will cover its various stipulations individually.

The ADA defines a disability as a physical or mental impairment that substantially limits one or more major life activities, a record of having such an impairment, or being regarded as having such an impairment. The first part of the definition refers to individuals who have serious disabilities—such as epilepsy, blindness, deafness, or paralysis—that affect their ability to perform major life activities such as walking, seeing, performing manual tasks, learning, caring for oneself, and working. The second part refers to individuals who have a history of disability, such as someone who has had cancer but is currently in remission, someone with a history of mental illness, and someone with a history of heart disease. The third part of the definition, "being regarded as having a disability," refers, for example, to an individual who is severely disfigured and is denied employment because an employer fears negative reactions from others.[13]

Thus, the ADA covers specific physiological disabilities such as cosmetic disfigurement and anatomical loss affecting the neurological, musculoskeletal, sensory, respiratory, cardiovascular, reproductive, digestive, genitourinary, hemic, or lymphatic systems. In addition, it covers mental and psychological disorders such as mental retardation, organic brain syndrome, emotional or mental illness, and learning disabilities. However, conditions such as obesity, substance abuse, eye and hair color, and lefthandedness are not covered.[14]

Americans with Disabilities Act (ADA)
A 1990 act prohibiting individuals with disabilities from being discriminated against in the workplace.

In addition, the Americans with Disabilities Act Amendments Act (ADAAA), effective January 1, 2009, broadened the scope of who is considered to be an individual with a disability. It states that the definition of disability should be broadly construed and that the "question of whether an individual's impairment is a disability under the ADA should not demand extensive analysis." The Supreme Court had interpreted the term "substantially limited" in a major life activity to require the individual to be "significantly restricted," but the ADAAA states that this is too high a standard and directs the EEOC to revise its regulations to set a lower standard. Also, regarding the term "regarded as disabled," previously employers could avoid liability by showing that the impairment did not substantially limit a major life activity. However, the ADAAA states that an employee can prove he or she was subjected to an illegal act "because of an actual or perceived physical or mental impairment whether or not the impairment limits or is perceived to limit a major life activity." In fact, in response to the ADAAA, the EEOC has clarified and somewhat redefined *disability*. According to their most recent guidelines, a disability is defined along three so-called prongs: a physical or mental impairment that "substantially limits one or more major life activity"; a record or past history of such an impairment; and/or being "regarded as" having a disability by an employer whether you have one or not, usually in terms of hiring, firing, or demotion. In essence, a person is considered disabled not only if he or she cannot *do* something but also if he or she has a medical condition, whether or not it impairs functioning.[15]

EXECUTIVE ORDERS

Executive orders are directives issued and amended unilaterally by the president. These orders do not require congressional approval, yet they have the force of law. Two executive orders directly affect HRM.

Executive Order 11246

President Johnson issued this executive order, which prohibits discrimination based on race, color, religion, sex, and national origin. Unlike Title VII, this order applies only to federal contractors and subcontractors. Employers receiving more than $10,000 from the federal government must take affirmative action to ensure against discrimination, and those with contracts greater than $50,000 must develop a written affirmative action plan for each of their establishments within 120 days of the beginning of the contract. The OFCCP enforces this executive order.

Although this order requires contractors to take affirmative action, many companies seek, on their own, to develop more diverse workforces. When they do so, they are proud to broadcast this. However, creating a diverse workforce is often difficult, particularly in the science, technology, engineering, and mathematics (STEM) fields, as is illustrated in the "Competing through Sustainability" box.

Executive Order 11478

President Richard Nixon issued Executive Order 11478, which requires the federal government to base all its employment policies on merit and fitness, and specifies that race, color, sex, religion, and national origin should not be considered. (The U.S. Office of Personnel Management is in charge of enforcement.) The order also extends to all contractors and subcontractors doing $10,000 worth of business with the federal government. (The relevant government agencies are responsible for ensuring that contractors and subcontractors comply with the order.)

COMPETING THROUGH SUSTAINABILITY

Do We Really Want to Report This?

Most companies seek to increase the diversity of their workforce, and some find it more difficult than others. Because of a historic lack of women and minorities in the STEM (science, technology, engineering, and mathematics) fields, many tech companies face serious challenges in increasing the diversity of their workers.

In 2013, Tracy Chou, then a software engineer at Pinterest, started the trend for tech companies to report their diversity numbers. She revealed that only 11 out of 89 engineers at Pinterest were women and asked other companies to report their numbers. Companies such as Twitter, Salesforce.com, and eBay began issuing diversity reports. In 2016, a number of these companies began to shift from reporting their current diversity to reporting their *goals* for diversity. This shift is partly due to the fact that a number of companies have shown little change in diversity. If companies show little change, "there is a risk in sending the message that the company doesn't care about diversity," said Ellen Pao, a former tech executive who works with Project Include.

Twitter hoped to increase female representation in engineering jobs to 16% from 13% in 2015 and to increase minority representation in these jobs to 9% from 6%. For 2016, Pinterest hopes to hire 30% female and 8% underrepresented minorities into its full-time engineering roles. Pinterest's head of diversity and inclusion, Candice Morgan, said, "If we miss a goal, it means we need longer to figure out the complexities needed to move the needle and make sure we do it right."

DISCUSSION QUESTION

1. Do you think it is helpful for companies to report their diversity, even when they are not achieving their goals? Why or why not?

SOURCE: G. Wells, "Tech Companies Delay Diversity Reports to Rethink Goals," *Wall Street Journal*, December 5, 2016, https://www.wsj.com/articles/tech-companies-delay-diversity-reports-to-rethink-goals-1480933984.

Enforcement of Equal Employment Opportunity

LO 3-3
Discuss the roles, responsibilities, and requirements of the federal agencies responsible for enforcing equal employment opportunity laws.

As discussed previously, the executive branch of the federal government bears most of the responsibility for enforcing all EEO laws passed by the legislative branch. In addition, the executive branch must enforce the executive orders issued by the president. The two agencies responsible for the enforcement of these laws and executive orders are the **Equal Employment Opportunity Commission (EEOC)** and the Office of Federal Contract Compliance Programs, respectively.

EQUAL EMPLOYMENT OPPORTUNITY COMMISSION (EEOC)

An independent federal agency, the EEOC is responsible for enforcing most of the EEO laws, such as Title VII, the Equal Pay Act, and the Americans with Disabilities Act. The EEOC has three major responsibilities: investigating and resolving discrimination complaints, gathering information, and issuing guidelines.

Equal Employment Opportunity Commission (EEOC)
The government commission established to ensure that all individuals have an equal opportunity for employment, regardless of race, color, religion, sex, age, disability, or national origin.

Investigation and Resolution

Individuals who feel they have been discriminated against must file a complaint with the EEOC or a similar state agency within 180 days of the incident. Failure to file a complaint within the 180 days results in the case's being dismissed immediately, with certain exceptions, such as the enactment of a seniority system that has an intentionally discriminatory purpose. For instance, the Lilly Ledbetter Fair Pay Act signed by President Barack Obama was crafted in direct response to the 180-day window. Ledbetter had been an area manager at the Goodyear Tire and Rubber plant in Alabama from 1979 to 1998, during which time she received lower raises than male employees. The differences were such that by the end of her career she was making $6,700 less per year than her male counterparts, and because pension payments were related to the salary at the time of retirement, she received smaller pension payments. When she filed the lawsuit, the Supreme Court ruled that the illegal acts were the pay raise decisions themselves (which fell far outside the 180-day window); Ledbetter wanted to argue that every time she received a pension check lower than her peers it served as an act of discrimination. Thus, Congress passed the act specifying that an "illegal act" occurs when (1) a discriminatory compensation decision is adopted; (2) an employee becomes subject to the decision; or (3) an employee is affected by its application, including each time compensation is paid.

Once the complaint is filed, the EEOC takes responsibility for investigating the claim of discrimination. The complainant must give the EEOC 60 days to investigate the complaint. If the EEOC either does not believe the complaint to be valid or fails to complete the investigation, the complainant may sue in federal court. If the EEOC determines that discrimination has taken place, its representatives will attempt to provide a reconciliation between the two parties without burdening the court system with a lawsuit. Sometimes the EEOC enters into a consent decree with the discriminating organization. This decree is an agreement between the agency and the organization that the organization will cease certain discriminatory practices and possibly institute additional affirmative action practices to rectify its history of discrimination.

If the EEOC cannot come to an agreement with the organization, it has two options. First, it can issue a "right to sue" letter to the alleged victim, which certifies that the agency has investigated and found validity in the victim's allegations. Second, although less likely, the agency may aid the alleged victim in bringing suit in federal court.

Information Gathering

The EEOC also plays a role in monitoring the hiring practices of organizations. Each year, organizations with 100 or more employees must file a report (EEO-1) with the EEOC that provides the number of women and minorities employed in nine different job categories. The EEOC computer analyzes these reports to identify patterns of discrimination that can then be attacked through class-action suits.

Issuance of Guidelines

A third responsibility of the EEOC is to issue guidelines that help employers determine when their decisions are violations of the laws enforced by the EEOC. These guidelines are not laws themselves, but the courts give great deference to them when hearing employment discrimination cases.

For example, the *Uniform Guidelines on Employee Selection Procedures* is a set of guidelines issued by the EEOC, the Department of Labor, the Department of Justice, and the U.S. Civil Service Commission.[16] This document provides guidance on the ways an organization should develop and administer selection systems so as not to violate Title VII. The courts often refer to the *Uniform Guidelines* to determine whether a company has engaged in discriminatory conduct or to determine the validity of the procedures it used to validate a selection system. Another example: Since the passage of the ADA, employers have been somewhat confused about the act's implications for their hiring procedures. Therefore, the EEOC issued guidelines in the *Federal Register* that provided more detailed information regarding what the agency will consider legal and illegal employment practices concerning disabled individuals. Although companies are well advised to follow these guidelines, it is possible that courts will interpret the ADA differently from the EEOC. Thus, through the issuance of guidelines, the EEOC gives employers directions for making employment decisions that do not conflict with existing laws.

OFFICE OF FEDERAL CONTRACT COMPLIANCE PROGRAMS (OFCCP)

The OFCCP is the agency responsible for enforcing the executive orders that cover companies doing business with the federal government. Businesses with contracts for more than $50,000 cannot discriminate in employment based on race, color, religion, national origin, or sex, and they must have a written affirmative action plan on file.

These plans have three basic components.[17] First, the **utilization analysis** compares the race, sex, and ethnic composition of the employer's workforce with that of the available labor supply. For each job group, the employer must identify the percentage of its workforce with a given characteristic (e.g., female) and identify the percentage of workers in the relevant labor market with that characteristic. If the percentage in the employer's workforce is much less than the percentage in the comparison group, then that minority group is considered to be "underutilized."

Second, the employer must develop specific **goals and timetables** for achieving balance in the workforce concerning these characteristics (particularly where underutilization exists). Goals and timetables specify the percentage of women and minorities that the employer seeks to have in each job group and the date by which that percentage is to be attained. These are not to be viewed as quotas, which entail setting aside a specific number of positions to be filled only by members of the protected class. Goals and timetables are much more flexible, requiring only that the employer have specific goals and take steps to achieve those goals. In fact, one study that examined companies with the goal of increasing black employment found that only 10% of them actually achieved their goals. Although this may sound discouragingly low, it is important to note that these companies increased their black employment more than companies that set no such goals.[18]

Third, employers with federal contracts must develop a list of **action steps** they will take toward attaining their goals to reduce underutilization. The company's CEO must make it clear to the entire organization that the company is committed to reducing underutilization, and all management levels must be involved in the planning process. For example, organizations can communicate job openings to women and minorities through publishing the company's affirmative action policy, recruiting at predominantly female or minority schools, participating in programs designed to increase employment opportunities for underemployed groups, and removing unnecessary barriers to employment. Organizations must also take affirmative steps toward hiring Vietnam veterans and individuals with disabilities.

The OFCCP annually audits government contractors to ensure that they actively pursue the goals in their plans. These audits consist of (1) examining the company's affirmative action plan and (2) conducting on-site visits to examine how individual employees perceive the company's affirmative action policies. If the OFCCP finds that the contractors or subcontractors are not complying with the executive order, then its representatives may notify the EEOC (if there is evidence that Title VII has been violated), advise the Department of Justice to institute criminal proceedings, request that the secretary of labor cancel or suspend any current contracts, and forbid the firm from bidding on future contracts. This last penalty, called debarment, is the OFCCP's most potent weapon.

Utilization analysis
A comparison of the race, sex, and ethnic composition of an employer's workforce with that of the available labor supply.

Goals and timetables
The part of a written affirmative action plan that specifies the percentage of women and minorities that an employer seeks to have in each job group and the date by which that percentage is to be attained.

Action steps
The part of a written affirmative action plan that specifies what an employer plans to do to reduce underutilization of protected groups.

Having discussed the major laws defining equal employment opportunity and the agencies that enforce these laws, we now address the various types of discrimination and the ways these forms of discrimination have been interpreted by the courts in a number of cases.

Types of Discrimination

LO 3-4
Identify the three theories of discrimination under Title VII of the Civil Rights Act and apply these theories to different discrimination situations.

How would you know if you had been discriminated against? Assume that you have applied for a job and were not hired. How do you know if the organization decided not to hire you because you are unqualified, because you are less qualified than the individual ultimately hired, or simply because the person in charge of the hiring decision "didn't like your type"? Discrimination is a multifaceted issue. It is often not easy to determine the extent to which unfair discrimination affects an employer's decisions.

Legal scholars have identified three theories of discrimination: disparate treatment, disparate impact, and reasonable accommodation. In addition, there is protection for those participating in discrimination cases or opposing discriminatory actions. In the act, these theories are stated in very general terms. However, the court system has defined and delineated these theories through the cases brought before it. A comparison of the theories of discrimination is given in Table 3.3.

Table 3.3
Comparison of Discrimination Theories

	TYPES OF DISCRIMINATION		
	DISPARATE TREATMENT	**DISPARATE IMPACT**	**REASONABLE ACCOMMODATION**
Show intent?	Yes	No	Yes
Show intent?	Individual is a member of a protected group, was qualified for the job, and was turned down for the job, and the job remained open	Statistical disparity in the effects of a facially neutral employment practice	Individual has a belief or disability, provided the employer with notice (request to accommodate), and was adversely affected by a failure to be accommodated
Employer's defense	Produce a legitimate, non-discriminatory reason for the employment decision or show bona fide occupational qualification (BFOQ)	Prove that the employment practice bears a manifest relationship with job performance	Job-relatedness and business necessity, undue hardship, or direct threat to health or safety
Plaintiff's rebuttal	Reason offered was merely a "pretext" for discrimination	Alternative procedures exist that meet the employer's goal without having disparate impact	
Monetary damages	Compensatory and punitive damages	Equitable relief (e.g., back pay)	Compensatory and punitive damages (if discrimination was intentional or employer failed to show good-faith efforts to accommodate)

DISPARATE TREATMENT

Disparate treatment exists when individuals in similar situations are treated differently and the different treatment is based on the individual's race, color, religion, sex, national origin, age, or disability status. If two people with the same qualifications apply for a job and the employer decides whom to hire based on one individual's race, the individual not hired is a victim of disparate treatment. In a disparate treatment case, the plaintiff must prove that there was a discriminatory motive—that is, that the employer intended to discriminate.

Whenever individuals are treated differently because of their race, sex, or the like, there is disparate treatment. For example, if a company fails to hire women with school-age children (claiming the women will be frequently absent) but hires men with school-age children, the applicants are being treated differently based on sex. Another example would be an employer who checks the references and investigates the conviction records of minority applicants but does not do so for white applicants. Why are managers advised not to ask about marital status? Because in most cases, a manager will either ask only the female applicants or, if the manager asks both males and females, he or she will make different assumptions about females (such as "She will have to move if her husband gets a job elsewhere") and males (such as "He's very stable"). In all these examples, notice that (1) people are being treated differently and (2) there is an actual intent to treat them differently.[19]

For instance, the Timken Company agreed to a $120,000 settlement over a sex and disability discrimination suit. In 2007, Carmen Halloran applied for a full-time position at Timken, after having worked at the facility as a part-time process associate for four years. The EEOC alleged that the company refused to hire Halloran because managers believed that Halloran, who is the mother of a disabled child, would be unable to work full time and care for her disabled child. They also alleged that this decision was based on an unfounded gender stereotype that the mother of a disabled child would necessarily be the primary caregiver because they did hire men with disabled children. "The EEOC is committed to fighting discrimination in the workplace," said Lynette A. Barnes, regional attorney for the EEOC's Charlotte District Office. "Employers must be careful not to apply stereotypes against women based on perceptions that they must always be the primary caregivers and therefore are unreliable employees."[20]

To understand how disparate treatment is applied in the law, let's look at how an actual court case, filed under disparate treatment, would proceed.

Disparate treatment
A theory of discrimination based on different treatment given to individuals because of their race, color, religion, sex, national origin, age, or disability status.

The Plaintiff's Burden

As in any legal case, the plaintiff has the burden of proving that the defendant has committed an illegal act. This is the idea of a "prima facie" case. In a disparate treatment case, the plaintiff meets the prima facie burden by showing four things:

1. The plaintiff belongs to a protected group.
2. The plaintiff applied for and was qualified for the job.
3. Despite possessing the qualifications, the plaintiff was rejected.
4. After the plaintiff was rejected, the position remained open and the employer continued to seek applicants with similar qualifications, or the position was filled by someone with similar qualifications.

Although these four elements may seem easy to prove, it is important to note that what the court is trying to do is rule out the most obvious reasons for rejecting the plaintiff's claim (for example, the plaintiff did not apply or was not qualified, or the position was already filled or had been eliminated). If these alternative explanations are ruled out, the court assumes that the hiring decision was based on a discriminatory motive.

The Defendant's Rebuttal

Once the plaintiff has made the prima facie case for discrimination, the burden shifts to the defendant. The burden is different depending on whether the prima facie case presents only circumstantial evidence (there is no direct evidence of discrimination such as a formal policy to discriminate, but rather discriminatory intent must be inferred) or direct evidence (a formal policy of discrimination for some perceived legitimate reason). In cases of circumstantial evidence, the defendant simply must produce a legitimate, nondiscriminatory reason, such as that, although the plaintiff was qualified, the individual hired was more qualified.

Bona fide occupational qualification (BFOQ)
A job qualification based on race, sex, religion, and so on that an employer asserts is a necessary qualification for the job.

However, in cases where direct evidence exists, such as a formal policy of hiring only women for waitress jobs because the business is aimed at catering to male customers, then the defendant is more likely to offer a different defense. This defense argues that, for this job, a factor such as sex or religion was a **bona fide occupational qualification (BFOQ)**. For example, if one were hiring an individual to hand out towels in a women's locker room, being a woman might be a BFOQ. However, there are very few cases in which sex qualifies as a BFOQ, and in these cases it must be a necessary, rather than simply a preferred, characteristic of the job.

UAW v. Johnson Controls, Inc., illustrates the difficulty in using a BFOQ as a defense.[21] Johnson Controls, a manufacturer of car batteries, had instituted a "fetal protection" policy that excluded women of childbearing age from a number of jobs in which they would be exposed to lead, which can cause birth defects in children. The company argued that sex was a BFOQ essential to maintaining a safe workplace. The Supreme Court did not uphold the company's policy, arguing that BFOQs are limited to policies that are directly related to a worker's ability to do the job.

Interestingly, some factors are by no means off-limits when it comes to discrimination. For instance, a survey by *Newsweek* of 202 hiring managers revealed that almost 60% said that qualified, yet unattractive, applicants face a harder time getting hired. In addition, two-thirds believe that managers hesitate before hiring qualified, but overweight, candidates.[22]

The Plaintiff's Rebuttal

If the defendant provides a legitimate, nondiscriminatory reason for its employment decision, the burden shifts back to the plaintiff. The plaintiff must now show that the reason offered by the defendant was not in fact the reason for its decision but merely a "pretext" or excuse for its actual discriminatory decision. This could entail providing evidence that white applicants with similar qualifications to the plaintiff have often been hired while black applicants with similar qualifications were all rejected. To illustrate disparate treatment, let's look at the first major case dealing with disparate treatment, *McDonnell Douglas Corp. v. Green.*

This Supreme Court case was the first to delineate the four criteria for a prima facie case of discrimination. From 1956 to 1964, Green had been an employee at McDonnell Douglas, a manufacturing plant in St. Louis, Missouri, that employed about 30,000 people. In 1964, he was laid off during a general workforce reduction.

While unemployed, he participated in some activities that the company undoubtedly frowned upon: a "lock-in," where he and others placed a chain and padlock on the front door of a building to prevent the employees from leaving; and a "stall-in," where a group of employees stalled their cars at the gates of the plant so that no one could enter or leave the parking lot. About three weeks after the lock-in, McDonnell Douglas advertised for qualified mechanics, Green's trade, and he reapplied. When the company rejected his application, he sued, arguing that the company didn't hire him because of his race and because of his persistent involvement in the civil rights movement.

In making his prima facie case, Green had no problem showing that he was a member of a protected group, that he had applied for and was qualified for the job (having already worked in the job), that he was rejected, and that the company continued to advertise the position. The company's defense was that the plaintiff was not hired because he participated in the lock-in and the stall-in. In other words, the company was merely refusing to hire a troublemaker.

The plaintiff responded that the company's stated reason for not hiring him was a pretext for discrimination. He pointed out that white employees who had participated in the same activities (the lock-in and the stall-in) were rehired, whereas he was not. The court found in favor of the plaintiff.

This case illustrates how similarly situated individuals (white and black) can be treated differently (whites were hired back whereas blacks were not) with the differences in treatment based on race. As we will discuss later, most plaintiffs bring cases of sexual harassment under this theory of discrimination, sexual harassment being a situation in which individuals are treated differently because of their sex.

Mixed-Motive Cases

In a mixed-motive case, the defendant acknowledges that some discriminatory motive existed but argues that the same hiring decision would have been reached even without the discriminatory motive. In *Hopkins v. Price Waterhouse*, Ann Hopkins was an accountant who had applied for partnership in her firm. Although she had brought in a large amount of business and had received high praise from her clients, she was turned down for a partnership on two separate occasions. In her performance reviews, she had been told to adopt more feminine dress and speech and received many other comments that suggested gender-based stereotypes. In court, the company admitted that a sex-based stereotype existed but argued that it would have come to the same decision (not promoted Hopkins) even if the stereotype had not existed.

One of the main questions that came out of this case was, Who has the burden of proof? Does the plaintiff have to prove that a different decision would have been made (that Hopkins would have been promoted) in the absence of the discriminatory motive? Or does the defendant have to prove that the same decision would have been made?

According to CRA 1991, if the plaintiff demonstrates that race, sex, color, religion, or national origin was a motivating factor for any employment practice, the prima facie burden has been met, and the burden of proof is on the employer to demonstrate that the same decision would have been made even if the discriminatory motive had not been present. If the employer can do this, the plaintiff cannot collect compensatory or punitive damages. However, the court may order the employer to quit using the discriminatory motive in its future employment decisions.

EVIDENCE-BASED HR

Weight discrimination, that is, making decisions based on negative stereotypes about people who are perceived as overweight, is not illegal and has been described as the last acceptable form of discrimination. A recent study used experts to rate male and female CEOs regarding their weight. These ratings suggested that 5–22% of top female CEOs in the United States are overweight and approximately 5% are obese, and that 45–61% of male CEOs are overweight and approximately 5% are obese. Compared to the general U.S. population, overweight and obese women are significantly underrepresented among top female CEOs. Compared to the population, these results show that overweight and obese female CEOs are underrepresented, overweight male CEOs are overrepresented, and obese male CEOs are underrepresented. In other words, weight discrimination occurs at the highest levels in organizations, and it impacts women more negatively than men.

SOURCE: Patricia V. Roehling, Mark V. Roehling, Jeffrey D. Vandlen, Justin Blazek, William C. Guy, (2009) "Weight discrimination and the glass ceiling effect among top US CEOs", *Equal Opportunities International*, Vol. 28 Iss: 2, pp. 179–196

DISPARATE IMPACT

Disparate impact
A theory of discrimination based on facially neutral employment practices that disproportionately exclude a protected group from employment opportunities.

The second type of discrimination is called **disparate impact**. It occurs when a facially neutral employment practice disproportionately excludes a protected group from employment opportunities. A facially neutral employment practice is one that lacks obvious discriminatory content yet affects one group to a greater extent than other groups, such as an employment test. Although the Supreme Court inferred disparate impact from Title VII in the *Griggs v. Duke Power* case (discussed later in this section), it has since been codified into the Civil Rights Act of 1991.

There is an important distinction between disparate impact and disparate treatment discrimination. For there to be discrimination under disparate treatment, there has to be intentional discrimination. Under disparate impact, intent is irrelevant. The important criterion is that the consequences of the employment practice are discriminatory.

For example, if, for some practical reason, you hired individuals based on their height, you may not have intended to discriminate against anyone, yet using height would have a disproportionate impact on certain protected groups. Women tend to be shorter than men, so fewer women will be hired. Certain ethnic groups, such as those of Asian ancestry, also tend to be shorter than those of European ancestry. Thus, your facially neutral employment practice will have a disparate impact on certain protected groups.

This is not to imply that simply because a selection practice has disparate impact, it is necessarily illegal. Some characteristics (such as height) are not equally distributed across race and gender groups; however, the important question is whether the characteristic is related to successful performance on the job. To help you understand how disparate impact works, let's look at a court proceeding involving a disparate impact claim.

The Plaintiff's Burden

In a disparate impact case, the plaintiff must make the prima facie case by showing that the employment practice in question disproportionately affects a protected group relative to the majority group. To illustrate this theory, let's assume that you are a manager who has 60 positions to fill. Your applicant pool has 80 white and 40 black applicants.

You use a test that selects 48 of the white and 12 of the black applicants. Is this a disparate impact? Two alternative quantitative analyses are often used to determine whether a test has adverse impact.

The **four-fifths rule** states that a test has disparate impact if the hiring rate for the minority group is less than four-fifths (or 80%) of the hiring rate for the majority group. Applying this analysis to the preceding example, we would first calculate the hiring rates for each group:

$$\text{Whites} = 48/80 = 60\%$$
$$\text{Blacks} = 12/40 = 30\%$$

Then we would compare the hiring rate of the minority group (30%) with that of the majority group (60%). Using the four-fifths rule, we would determine that the test has adverse impact if the hiring rate of the minority group is less than 80% of the hiring rate of the majority group. Because it is less (i.e., 30%/60% = 50%, which is less than 80%), we would conclude that the test has adverse impact. The four-fifths rule is used as a rule of thumb by the EEOC in determining adverse impact.

The **standard deviation rule** uses actual probability distributions to determine adverse impact. This analysis uses the difference between the expected representation (or hiring rates) for minority groups and the actual representation (or hiring rate) to determine whether the difference between these two values is greater than would occur by chance. Thus, in our example, 33% (40 of 120) of the applicants were blacks, so one would expect 33% (20 of 60) of those hired to be black. However, only 12 black applicants were hired. To determine if the difference between the expected representation and the actual representation is greater than we would expect by chance, we calculate the standard deviation (which, you might remember from your statistics class, is the standard deviation in a binomial distribution):

$$\sqrt{\text{Number hired} \times \frac{\text{Number of minority applicants}}{\text{Number of total applicants}} \times \frac{\text{Number of nonminority applicants}}{\text{Number of total applicants}}}$$

or in this case:

$$\sqrt{60 \times \frac{40}{120} \times \frac{80}{120}} = 3.6$$

If the difference between the actual representation and the expected representation (20 − 12 = 8 in this case) of blacks is greater than 2 standard deviations (2 × 3.6 = 7.2 in this case), we would conclude that the test had adverse impact against blacks, because we would expect this result less than 1 time in 20 if the test were equally difficult for both whites and blacks.

The *Wards Cove Packing Co. v. Atonio* case involved an interesting use of statistics. The plaintiffs showed that the jobs in the cannery (lower-paying jobs) were filled primarily with minority applicants (in this case, American Eskimos). However, only a small percentage of the noncannery jobs (those with higher pay) were filled by nonminorities. The plaintiffs argued that this statistical disparity in the racial makeup of the cannery and noncannery jobs was proof of discrimination. The federal district, appellate, and Supreme Courts all found for the defendant, stating that this disparity was not proof of discrimination.

Once the plaintiff has demonstrated adverse impact, he or she has met the burden of a prima facie case of discrimination.[23]

Four-fifths rule
A rule that states that an employment test has disparate impact if the hiring rate for a minority group is less than four-fifths, or 80 %, of the hiring rate for the majority group.

Standard deviation rule
A rule used to analyze employment tests to determine disparate impact; it uses the difference between the expected representation for minority groups and the actual representation to determine whether the difference between the two is greater than would occur by chance.

Defendant's Rebuttal

According to CRA 1991, once the plaintiff has made a prima facie case, the burden of proof shifts to the defendant, who must show that the employment practice is a "business necessity." This is accomplished by showing that the practice bears a relationship with some legitimate employer goal. With respect to job selection, this relationship is demonstrated by showing the job relatedness of the test, usually by reporting a validity study of some type, to be discussed in Chapter 6. For now, suffice it to say that the employer shows that the test scores are significantly correlated with measures of job performance.

Measures of job performance used in validation studies can include such things as objective measures of output, supervisor ratings of job performance, and success in training.[24] Normally, performance appraisal ratings are used, but these ratings must be valid for the court to accept the validation results. For example, in *Albemarle Paper v. Moody*, the employer demonstrated that the selection battery predicted performance (measured with supervisors' overall rankings of employees) in only some of the 13 occupational groups in which it was used. In this case, the court was especially critical of the supervisory ratings used as the measure of job performance. The court stated, "There is no way of knowing precisely what criteria of job performance the supervisors were considering."[25]

Plaintiff's Rebuttal

If the employer shows that the employment practice is the result of some business necessity, the plaintiff's last resort is to argue that other employment practices could sufficiently meet the employer's goal without adverse impact. Thus, if a plaintiff can demonstrate that selection tests other than the one used by the employer exist, do not have adverse impact, and correlate with job performance as highly as the employer's test, then the defendant can be found guilty of discrimination. Many cases deal with standardized tests of cognitive ability, so it is important to examine alternatives to these tests that have less adverse impact while still meeting the employer's goal. At least two separate studies reviewing alternative selection devices such as interviews, biographical data, assessment centers, and work sample tests have concluded that none of them met both criteria.[26] It seems that when the employment practice in question is a standardized test of cognitive ability, plaintiffs will have a difficult time rebutting the defendant's rebuttal.

To illustrate how this process works, let's look at the *Griggs v. Duke Power* case.[27] Following the passage of Title VII, Duke Power instituted a new system for making selection and promotion decisions. The system required either a high school diploma or a passing score on two professionally developed tests (the Wonderlic Personnel Test and the Bennett Mechanical Comprehension Test). A passing score was set so that it would be equal to the national median for high school graduates who had taken the tests.

The plaintiffs met their prima facie burden showing that both the high school diploma requirement and the test battery had adverse impacts on blacks. According to the 1960 census, 34% of white males had high school diplomas, compared with only 12% of black males. Similarly, 58% of white males passed the test battery, whereas only 6% of blacks passed.

Duke Power was unable to defend its use of these employment practices. A company vice president testified that the company had not studied the relationship between these employment practices and the employees' ability to perform the job. In addition, employees already on the job who did not have high school diplomas and had never taken the tests were performing satisfactorily. Thus, Duke Power lost the case.

It is interesting to note that the court recognized that the company had not intended to discriminate, mentioning that the company was making special efforts to help undereducated employees through financing two-thirds of the cost of tuition for high school training. This illustrates the importance of the consequences, as opposed to the motivation, in determining discrimination under the disparate impact theory.

PATTERN AND PRACTICE

In class-action pattern and practice lawsuits, plaintiffs attempt to show three things. First, they show some statistical disparities between the composition of some group within the company compared to some other relevant group. For instance, in a discrimination case brought against Walmart (*Dukes v. Walmart*), the plaintiff's lawyers pointed to two comparative statistics as evidence of discrimination. First, they compared the female representation in the nonmanagerial (63.4%) and managerial (33.6%) employee groups. They also compared the female representation in the managerial group (again, 33.6%) with that in their top 20 competitors (56.5%). They also calculated that hourly female workers were paid, on average, $1,100 less per year than men and salaried women received $14,500 less. However, Walmart disputed the list of comparison companies, arguing that if a broader group were used, reflecting Walmart's wide geographic footprint and variety of products offered, it did not differ from that group. The company also argued that if it had claimed its highest-level hourly-wage supervisors as "managers" on its EEO-1 forms, as many of the comparison companies do, the entire disparity disappeared. Walmart also noted that of the applicants for managerial positions, only 15% were female, and of those promoted, 18% were female. Finally, regarding pay, Walmart's experts suggested that the plaintiff's pay comparisons did not account for crucial factors such as the number of hours worked or whether the work was night-shift work, which pays more. Their analyses suggested that when pay was compared at the department level, where pay decisions are determined, 92.8% of all stores showed no statistically significant pay disparities, and that of the remainder, 5.2% showed disparities favoring men whereas 2.0% showed disparities favoring women.

Second, plaintiffs try to show that individual acts of intentional discrimination suggest that the statistical disparity is a function of the employer's larger culture. In the *Dukes* case, the plaintiffs argued that at Monday morning meetings of high-level Sam's Club executives, female store employees were referred to as "Janie Q's," and that this continued even after a woman executive complained that she found the term demeaning.

Finally, plaintiffs usually try to make the case that the promotion and/or pay procedures leave too much discretion to managers, providing the avenue through which their unconscious biases can play a part. In the *Dukes* case, the plaintiffs brought in expert witnesses to argue that the performance management processes were extremely subjective, and that male managers have subconscious tendencies to favor male over female employees.

REASONABLE ACCOMMODATION

Reasonable accommodation presents a relatively new theory of discrimination. It began with regard to religious discrimination but has been both expanded and popularized with the passage of the ADA. Reasonable accommodation differs from the other two theories in that rather than simply requiring an employer to refrain from some action, reasonable accommodation places a special obligation on an employer to

Reasonable accommodation Making facilities readily accessible to and usable by individuals with disabilities.

affirmatively do something to accommodate an individual's disability or religion. This theory is violated when an employer fails to make reasonable accommodation, where that is required, to a qualified person with a disability or to a person's religious observation and/or practices.

Religion and Accommodation

Often individuals with strong religious beliefs find that some observations and practices of their religion come into direct conflict with their work duties. For example, some religions forbid individuals from working on the sabbath day when the employer schedules them for work. Others might have beliefs that preclude them from shaving, which might conflict with a company's dress code. Although Title VII forbids discrimination on the basis of religion, just like race or sex, religion also receives special treatment requiring employers to exercise an affirmative duty to accommodate individuals' religious beliefs and practices. As Figure 3.2 shows, the number of religious discrimination complaints has dropped consistently over the past few years but began to rise again in 2016.

In cases of religious discrimination, an employee's burden is to demonstrate that he or she has a legitimate religious belief and provided the employer with notice of the need to accommodate the religious practice, and that adverse consequences occurred due to the employer's failure to accommodate. In such cases, the employer's major defense is to assert that to accommodate the employee would require an undue hardship.

Examples of reasonably accommodating a person's religious obligations might include redesigning work schedules (most often accommodating those who cannot work on their sabbath), providing alternative testing dates for applicants, not requiring union membership

Figure 3.2

Religious Discrimination Complaints, 2000–2016

SOURCE: Equal Employment Opportunity Commission, "Religion-Based Charges (Charges Filed with EEOC)," https://www.eeoc.gov/eeoc/statistics/enforcement/religion.cfm.

Is Banning Head Scarves Discriminatory?

A number of religions suggest or require certain aspects of dress for their adherents. For instance, Orthodox Jewish men are to wear yarmulkes, initiated male and female Sikhs are to cover their hair with turbans, and Muslim women are to cover their heads with a head scarf. This is where the trouble began in Europe recently.

Both general immigration policy as well as the large number of refugees from war-torn Syria and its surrounding countries have resulted in a large influx of Muslims. London-based security firm G4S PLC had employed a female receptionist at their office in Belgium for three years. She began wearing an Islamic head scarf, but the company would not let her do so. She filed a complaint through the European Union's court system, and the EU's top court sided with the company, arguing that the prohibition of head scarves did not constitute "direct discrimination based on religion or belief." Although such a prohibition might indirectly discriminate against employees of particular religions, it "may be objectively justified by a legitimate aim."

DISCUSSION QUESTION

1. Do you think companies should be able to ban religious clothing such as head scarves? Why or why not?

SOURCE: E. Peker, "EU Court Rules Companies Can Bar Muslim Head Scarf," *Wall Street Journal*, March 14, 2017, https://www.wsj.com/articles/eu-court-private-companies-can-bar-muslim-head-scarf-1489494938.

and/or allowing payment of "charitable contributions" in lieu of union dues, or altering certain dress or grooming requirements. Although an employer is required to make a reasonable accommodation, it need not be the one that is requested by the employee.[28]

In one case, Walmart agreed to settle with a former employee who alleged that he was forced to quit in 1993 after refusing to work on Sunday. Walmart agreed to pay the former employee unspecified damages, to instruct managers on employees' rights to have their religious beliefs accommodated, and to prepare a computer-based manual describing employees' rights and religious harassment.[29]

Following the 9/11 terrorist attacks, a number of cases sprang up with regard to discrimination against Muslims, partly accounting for the significant increase in religious discrimination complaints in 2002. In one case, the EEOC and Electrolux Group settled a religious accommodation case brought by Muslim workers from Somalia. The Islamic faith requires Muslims to offer five prayers a day, with two of these prayers offered within restricted time periods (early morning and sunset). Muslim employees alleged that they were disciplined for using an unscheduled break traditionally offered to line employees on an as-needed basis to observe their sunset prayer. Electrolux worked with the EEOC to respect the needs of its Muslim workers without creating a business hardship by affording them with an opportunity to observe their sunset prayer.[30]

Religious discrimination continues to be an issue around the globe. The "Competing through Globalization" box provides an example of how the European Union has limited the religious freedom of employees by enabling companies to ban religious attire in the workplace.

Religion and accommodation also bring up the question of what to do when different rights collide. For instance, John Nemecek had been a respected business professor at Spring Arbor University for 15 years, when administrators at the evangelical college in Michigan began to take issue with some of his behavior. After he began wearing earrings and makeup and asking friends to call him "Julie," Nemecek found himself demoted and then fired because his womanly appearance violated "Christian behavior." In 2004, a doctor diagnosed Nemecek with a "gender identity disorder," in which a person identifies with a gender different from the one assigned at birth based on physical characteristics. Soon after, the school began taking away some of his responsibilities, and then issued him a contract revoking his dean's post, reassigning him to a non-tenure-track role in which he would work from home, teaching online. It also required him not to wear any makeup or female clothing or to display any outward signs of femininity when visiting campus. Gayle Beebe, the university's president, said, "We felt through a job reassignment we could give him the space to work on this issue." Nemecek signed the contract but then violated it by showing up on campus with earrings and makeup on four separate occasions. Nemecek filed a complaint with the EEOC, and the university then declined to renew his contract. Nemecek, whose Baptist church also asked him to leave the congregation, said of the university, "Essentially, they're saying they can define who is a Christian. I don't agree that our biology determines our gender."[31]

Disability and Accommodation

As previously earlier, the ADA made discrimination against individuals with disabilities illegal. However, the act itself states that the employer is obligated not just to refrain from discriminating but also to take affirmative steps to accommodate individuals who are protected under the act.

Under disability claims, the plaintiff must show that she or he is a qualified applicant with a disability and that adverse action was taken by a covered entity. The employer's defense then depends on whether the decision was made without regard to the disability or in light of the disability. For example, if the employer argues that the plaintiff is not qualified, then it has met the burden, and the question of reasonable accommodation becomes irrelevant.

If, however, the decision was made "in light of" the disability, then the question becomes one of whether the person could perform adequately with a reasonable accommodation. This leads to three potential defenses. First, the employer could allege job relatedness or business necessity through demonstrating, for example, that it is using a test that assesses ability to perform essential job functions. However, the question then arises of whether the applicant could perform the essential job functions with a reasonable accommodation. Second, the employer could claim an undue hardship to accommodate the individual. In essence, this argues that the accommodation necessary is an action entailing significant difficulty or expense. Finally, the employer could argue that the individual with the disability might pose a direct threat to his or her own or others' health or safety in the workplace. This requires examining the duration of the risk, the nature and severity of potential harm, the probability of the harm occurring, and the imminence of the potential harm. For instance, Walmart was sued by one of its employees, a fitting room attendant who had cerebral palsy and was confined to a wheelchair. The employee requested to use a grabber and a shopping cart to help her pick up and hold clothes. However, a manager prevented her from using both and then implemented progressive discipline, ending in the attendant's termination.[32]

What are some examples of reasonable accommodation with regard to disabilities? First, an employer might provide readily accessible facilities such as ramps and/or elevators for disabled individuals to enter the workplace. Second, job restructuring might include eliminating marginal tasks, shifting these tasks to other employees, redesigning job procedures, or altering work schedules. Third, an employer might reassign a disabled employee to a job with essential job functions he or she could perform. Fourth, an employer might accommodate applicants for employment who must take tests by providing alternative testing formats, providing readers, or providing additional time for taking the test. Fifth, readers, interpreters, or technology to offer reading assistance might be given to a disabled employee. Sixth, an employer could allow employees to provide their own accommodation such as bringing a guide dog to work.[33] Most accommodations are inexpensive. A study by Sears, Roebuck & Co. found that 69% of all accommodations cost nothing; 29% cost less than $1,000; and only 3% cost more than $1,000.[34]

EVIDENCE-BASED HR

As information technology becomes more and more ubiquitous in the workplace, some researchers have begun to explore the implications for people with disabilities. Researchers at the Yang-Tan Institute on Employment and Disability at Cornell University recently reviewed the accessibility of 10 job boards and 31 corporate e-recruiting websites using Bobby 3.2, a software program designed to check for errors that cause accessibility concerns. They found that none of the job boards and only a small minority of the e-recruiting sites met the Bobby standards.

In phase 2 of the study, the researchers surveyed 813 HR professionals who were members of the Society for Human Resource Management (SHRM). Between 16% and 46% of the HR professionals were familiar with six of the most common assistive technologies to adapt computers for disabled individuals (screen magnifiers, speech recognition software, video captioning, Braille readers/displays, screen readers, guidelines for web design). In addition, only 1 in 10 said they knew that their firm had evaluated the websites for accessibility to people with disabilities.

This study indicates that, although firms may not have any intention of discriminating against people with disabilities, the rapid expansion of information technology combined with an inattention to and/or lack of education regarding accessibility issues may lead them to do so unintentionally.

SOURCE: S. Bruyere, S. Erickson, and S. VanLooy, "Information Technology and the Workplace: Implications for Persons with Disabilities," *Disability Studies Quarterly* 25, no. 2 (2005), www.dsq-sds.org.

Retaliation for Participation and Opposition

Suppose you overhear a supervisor in your workplace telling someone that he refuses to hire women because he knows they are just not cut out for the job. Believing this to be illegal discrimination, you face a dilemma. Should you come forward and report this statement? Or if someone else files a lawsuit for gender discrimination, should you testify on behalf of the plaintiff? What happens if your employer threatens to fire you if you do anything?

Title VII of the Civil Rights Act of 1964 protects you. It states that employers cannot retaliate against employees for either "opposing" a perceived illegal employment practice or "participating in a proceeding" related to an alleged illegal employment practice. Opposition refers to expressing to someone through proper channels that you believe that an illegal employment act has taken place or is taking place. Participation refers to actually testifying in an investigation, hearing, or court proceeding regarding an illegal employment act. Clearly, the purpose of this provision is to protect employees from employers' threats and other forms of intimidation aimed at discouraging the employees from bringing to light acts they believe to be illegal.

Southwest Ends Overbooking

United Airlines took tremendous heat amid public outcry after it had airport police forcibly remove passenger David Dao from a plane because it had overbooked the flight. Airlines overbook flights to protect them from flying with empty seats when passengers do not show up. The goal is to maximize revenue. However, many passengers do not like the practice. In particular, if not enough passengers voluntarily give up their seats in exchange for whatever compensation the airline offers, some passengers are involuntarily denied access to the overbooked flight.

Southwest Airlines recently announced that it will no longer overbook its flights. The company's past practice had been to overbook flights by only one passenger, which does not sound like much. However, in 2016, Southwest had to "reaccommodate" over 15,000 passengers, more than United, American, and Delta, combined.

Southwest CEO Gary Kelly noted, "I never get complaints from our customers about overbooking." However, he added that "for quite some time we have been challenging ourselves to make the traveling experience better for our customers. That's one of the pain points we'd like to eliminate."

DISCUSSION QUESTION

1. Do you think Southwest's decision will increase customer satisfaction? Why or why not?

SOURCE: D. Cameron, "Southwest to End Overbooking on Flights by June," *Wall Street Journal*, April 27, 2017, https://www.wsj.com/articles/southwest-to-end-overbooking-on-flights-by-june-1493320790.

The EEOC filed suit against Dillard's, a major department store chain, for firing a business manager as retaliation for filing a discrimination charge. In 2008, Shontel Mayfield filed a charge with the EEOC in which she alleged that Dillard's management had discriminated against her because of her race. She had begun working for Dillard's in July 2001, and earned a promotion to business manager of the Estee Lauder counter in 2006. However, in September 2008, Mayfield complied with a Jefferson County, Texas, mandatory evacuation order and evacuated the area in advance of Hurricane Ike. She returned to Jefferson County consistent with the directives of the county's "disaster declarations." After Mayfield returned to work, she was told that she was being fired for the stated reason of "excessive absenteeism." On her termination paperwork, she was accused of having "failed to maintain verbal communication concerning her absences with either the store manager or the operations manager." Yet telephone records showed that Mayfield placed numerous calls to Dillard's "disaster recovery" number, as well as to the cellular telephones of the store manager and the operations manager during the evacuation period.[35]

These cases can be extremely costly for companies because they are alleging acts of intentional discrimination, and therefore plaintiffs are entitled to punitive damages. For example, a 41-year-old former Allstate employee who claimed that a company official told her that the company wanted a "younger and cuter" image was awarded $2.8 million in damages by an Oregon jury. The jury concluded that the employee was forced out of the company for opposing age discrimination against other employees.[36]

In one case, Target Corporation agreed to pay $775,000 to a group of black workers who charged that, at one store, the company condoned a racially hostile work environment exemplified by inappropriate comments and verbal berating based on race. When one of the black employees objected to this treatment, he was allegedly retaliated against, forcing him to resign.[37]

This does not mean that employees have an unlimited right to talk about how racist or sexist their employers are. The courts tend to frown on employees whose activities result in a poor public image for the company unless those employees had attempted to use the organization's internal channels—approaching one's manager, raising the issue with the HRM department, and so on—before going public.

In today's environment, firms face cell phones as the greatest whistle-blower. Millions of people have seen video of the forcible removal of United Airlines passenger David Dao. The "Integrity in Action" box describes how Southwest Airlines is avoiding such problems by no longer overbooking their flights.

Current Issues Regarding Diversity and Equal Employment Opportunity

Because of recent changes in the labor market, most organizations' demographic compositions are becoming increasingly diverse. A study by the Hudson Institute projected that 85% of the new entrants into the U.S. labor force over the next decade will be females and minorities.[38] Integrating these groups into organizations made up predominantly of able-bodied white males will bring attention to important issues like sexual harassment, affirmative action, and the "reasonable accommodation" of employees with disabilities.

LO 3-5
Identify behavior that constitutes sexual harassment, and list things that an organization can do to eliminate or minimize it.

SEXUAL HARASSMENT

A number of recent allegations of sexual harassment have made it into the news. For instance, now-retired Uber CEO Travis Kalanick announced that Uber will begin an "urgent investigation" following a former female engineer's blog post alleging systemic sexual harassment. The engineer, Susan Fowler, says her manager propositioned her for sex during her first day on the job. When she complained, she was told he would not be punished because he was a "high performer" and this was his first offense. However, she later spoke to other women whom the manager had also propositioned and each of them had been told it was his "first offense." Kalanick has instructed Uber's chief HR officer to conduct the investigation because "what's described here is abhorrent & against everything we believe in."[39]

In spite of the big headlines, the number of sexual harassment charges filed has been decreasing since 2010, as we see in Figure 3.3.

Figure 3.3
Sexual Harassment Charges, 2010–2016

SOURCE: Equal Employment Opportunity Commission, "Charges Alleging Sex-Based Harassment (Charges Files with EEOC)," https://www.eeoc.gov/eeoc/statistics/enforcement/sexual_harassment_new.cfm.

Table 3.4
EEOC Definition of Sexual Harassment

Unwelcome sexual advances, requests for sexual favors, and other verbal or physical contact of a sexual nature constitute sexual harassment when

1. Submission to such conduct is made either explicitly or implicitly a term or condition of an individual's employment,

2. Submission to or rejection of such conduct by an individual is used as the basis for employment decisions affecting such individual, or

3. Such conduct has the purpose or effect of unreasonably interfering with an individual's work performance or creating an intimidating, hostile, or offensive working environment.

SOURCE: EEOC guideline based on the Civil Rights Act of 1964, Title VII.

Sexual harassment refers to unwelcome sexual advances (see Table 3.4). It can take place in two basic ways. "Quid pro quo" harassment occurs when some kind of benefit (or punishment) is made contingent on the employee's submitting (or not submitting) to sexual advances, such as the situation with Uber. For example, a male manager tells his female secretary that if she has sex with him, he will help her get promoted, or he threatens to fire her if she fails to do so; these are clearly cases of quid pro quo sexual harassment.

The *Bundy v. Jackson* case illustrates quid pro quo sexual harassment.[40] Sandra Bundy was a personnel clerk with the District of Columbia Department of Corrections. She received repeated sexual propositions from Delbert Jackson, who was at the time a fellow employee (although he later became the director of the agency). She later began to receive propositions from two of her supervisors: Arthur Burton and James Gainey. When she raised the issue with their supervisor, Lawrence Swain, he dismissed her complaints, telling her that "any man in his right mind would want to rape you," and asked her to begin a sexual relationship with him. When Bundy became eligible for a promotion, she was passed over because of her "inadequate work performance," although she had never been told that her work performance was unsatisfactory. The U.S. Court of Appeals found that Bundy had been discriminated against because of her sex, thereby extending the idea of discrimination to sexual harassment.

A more subtle, and possibly more pervasive, form of sexual harassment is a "hostile working environment." This occurs when someone's behavior in the workplace creates an environment that makes it difficult for someone of a particular sex to work. Many plaintiffs in sexual harassment lawsuits have alleged that men ran their fingers through the plaintiffs' hair, made suggestive remarks, and physically assaulted them by touching their intimate body parts. Other examples include having pictures of naked women posted in the workplace, using offensive sexually explicit language, or using sex-related jokes or innuendoes in conversations.[41]

For instance, in the aforementioned situation at Uber, the engineer claimed that a manager bought leather jackets for more than 120 men but not six women because there were not enough to get a similar bulk discount. Fowler was told that "if we wanted leather jackets, we women needed to find jackets that were the same price as the bulk-order price of the men's jackets."

When she threatened to go to HR, her manager threatened to fire her. "I told him that was illegal, and he replied that he had been a manager for a long time, he knew what was illegal, and threatening to fire me for reporting things to HR was not illegal." When she reported the situation to HR, the managers there told her retaliation is illegal, but then they did nothing in response to the threat.[42]

These types of behaviors are actionable under Title VII because they treat individuals differently based on their sex. In addition, although most harassment cases involve male-on-female harassment, any individual can be harassed. For example, male employees at Jenny Craig alleged that they were sexually harassed, and a federal jury found that a male employee had been sexually harassed by his male boss.[43]

In another example, Ron Clark Ford of Amarillo, Texas, agreed to pay $140,000 to six male plaintiffs who alleged that they and others were subjected to a sexually hostile work environment and different treatment by male managers because of their gender. Evidence gathered showed that the men were subjected to lewd, inappropriate comments of a sexual nature, and had their genitals and buttocks grabbed against their will by their male managers. The defendants argued that the conduct was "harmless horseplay."[44]

Finally, Babies 'R' Us agreed to pay $205,000 to resolve a same-sex suit. The lawsuit alleged that Andres Vasquez was subjected to a sexually hostile working environment and was the target of unwelcome and derogatory comments as well as behavior that mocked him because he did not conform to societal stereotypes of how a male should appear or behave.[45]

Sexual harassment charge filings with the EEOC by men increased to 16.6% of all filings in 2016, up from 10% of filings in 1994. Although the commission does not track same-sex, male-on-male charges, anecdotal evidence shows that most harassment allegations by men are against other men.

There are three critical issues in these cases. First, the plaintiff cannot have "invited or incited" the advances. Often the plaintiff's sexual history, whether she or he wears provocative clothing, and whether she or he engages in sexually explicit conversations are used to prove or disprove that the advance was unwelcome. However, in the absence of substantial evidence that the plaintiff invited the behavior, courts usually lean toward assuming that sexual advances do not belong in the workplace and thus are unwelcome. In *Meritor Savings Bank v. Vinson*, Mechelle Vinson claimed that during the four years she worked at a bank she was continually harassed by the bank's vice president, who repeatedly asked her to have sex with him (she eventually agreed) and sexually assaulted her.[46] The Supreme Court ruled that the victim's voluntary participation in sexual relations was not the major issue, saying that the focus of the case was on whether the vice president's advances were unwelcome.

A second critical issue is that the harassment must have been severe enough to alter the terms, conditions, and privileges of employment. Although it has not yet been consistently applied, many courts have used the "reasonable woman" standard in determining the severity or pervasiveness of the harassment. This consists of assessing whether a reasonable woman, faced with the same situation, would have reacted similarly. The reasonable woman standard recognizes that behavior that might be considered appropriate by a man (like off-color jokes) might not be considered appropriate by a woman.

The third issue is that the courts must determine whether the organization is liable for the actions of its employees. In doing so, the court usually examines two things. First, did the employer know about, or should he or she have known about, the harassment? Second, did the employer act to stop the behavior? If the employer knew about it and the behavior did not stop, the court usually decides that the employer did not act appropriately to stop it.

Sexual harassment suits can be quite costly for companies. For instance, Aaron's Inc., the furniture rental company, faced a sexual harassment suit filed by a female employee who claimed that her manager groped her, exposed himself to her, and sexually assaulted her.

COMPETING THROUGH TECHNOLOGY

Better Watch What You E-mail at Work

The world's largest executive search firm, Korn Ferry, has found itself entangled in a messy legal dispute over its dismissal of a top executive, but e-mail may reveal an even messier set of details. Robert Damon, the company's former executive chairman of the Americas, says that he lost over $1.7 million in deferred compensation when he was fired in retaliation for complaining to the board of directors about how CEO Gary Burnison treated a number of female colleagues. An outside investigator who explored the allegations of Burnison's treatment of women did suggest to the directors that they hire a coach to teach him

"how to lawfully behave in the workplace."

However, the company denies all the allegations. "Mr. Damon's complaint is an attempt to deflect the real reason for his termination," said Michael Distefano, Korn Ferry's chief marketing officer. "He was terminated with cause of inappropriate personal behavior, flagrant violations of company policies, and material breaches of his own employment arrangements."

Although the case has yet to be resolved, technology may point to a particular outcome. In a court filing, Korn Ferry alleges Damon used his company e-mail "to solicit and arrange for

meetings with at least 20 different call girls and escorts." In addition, Korn Ferry says he used his company e-mail "to receive and distribute photographs of nude and semi-nude women."

DISCUSSION QUESTION

1. In this era of mobile technology and social media, should the fired senior executive have understood the implications of using his company e-mail account for inappropriate behavior?

SOURCES: J. S. Lublin, "Korn/Ferry Says It Fired Former Executive for Allegedly Soliciting Escorts," *Wall Street Journal*, April 9, 2015; J. S. Lublin, "Former Korn/Ferry Executive Alleges Retaliation," *Wall Street Journal*, April 1, 2015.

She contacted a company harassment hotline but was never called back. She also alleged that she was denied a promotion for complaining about the alleged assault. In 2011, a jury awarded the employee $95 million, a significant sum given that Aaron's profits had been $118 million the previous year.[47]

To ensure a workplace free from sexual harassment, organizations can follow some important steps. First, the organization can develop a policy statement that makes it clear that sexual harassment will not be tolerated in the workplace. Second, all employees, new and old, can be trained to identify inappropriate workplace behavior. Third, the organization can develop a mechanism for reporting sexual harassment that encourages people to speak out. Fourth, management can prepare to take prompt disciplinary action against those who commit sexual harassment as well as appropriate action to protect the victims of sexual harassment.[48] The "Competing through Technology" box describes how e-mails helped to demonstrate how a leader was behaving inappropriately and possibly illegally at search firm Korn Ferry.

AFFIRMATIVE ACTION AND REVERSE DISCRIMINATION

LO 3-6
Discuss the legal issues involved with preferential treatment programs.

Few people would disagree that having a diverse workforce in terms of race and gender is a desirable goal, if all individuals have the necessary qualifications. In fact, many organizations today are concerned with developing and managing diversity. To eliminate discrimination in the workplace, many organizations have affirmative action programs to increase minority representation. Affirmative action was originally conceived as a way of taking extra effort to attract and retain minority employees. This was typically done by extensively recruiting minorities on college campuses, advertising in minority-oriented publications, and providing educational and training opportunities to minorities.[49] However, over the years, many organizations have resorted to quota-like hiring to ensure that their workforce composition mirrors that of the labor market. Sometimes these organizations act voluntarily; in other cases, the quotas are imposed by the courts or by the EEOC. Whatever the impetus for these hiring practices, many white and/or male individuals have fought against them, alleging what is called reverse discrimination.

An example of an imposed quota program is found at the fire department in Birmingham, Alabama. Having admitted a history of discriminating against blacks, the department entered into a consent decree with the EEOC to hold 50% of positions at all levels in the fire department open for minorities, even though minorities made up only 28% of the relevant labor market. The result was that some white applicants were denied employment or promotion in favor of black applicants who scored lower on a selection battery. The federal court found that the city's use of the inflexible hiring formula violated federal civil rights law and the constitutional guarantee of equal protection. The appellate court agreed, and the Supreme Court refused to hear the case, thus making the decision final.

Ricci v. DeStefano is another case that was appealed to the Supreme Court regarding the potential for reverse discrimination based on a situation in New Haven, Connecticut. In this case, a professional consulting firm developed a firefighter test specifically eliminating questions that had adverse impact against minority members (based on pilot study testing). However, when the test was given, no blacks made the promotion list, so the city simply ignored the test and promoted no one. White and Hispanic firefighters who would have been on the promotion list sued, stating that the failure to use the test results discriminated against them because of their race. The district and appellate courts ruled that because no blacks were promoted either (because there were no promotions), there had been no discrimination.

The entire issue of affirmative action should evoke considerable attention and debate over the next few years. Although most individuals support the idea of diversity, few argue for the kinds of quotas that have to some extent resulted from the present legal climate. In fact, one survey revealed that only 16% of the respondents favored affirmative action with quotas, 46% favored it without quotas, and 28% opposed all affirmative action programs. One study found that people favor affirmative action when it is operationalized as recruitment, training, and attention to applicant qualifications but oppose it when it consists of discrimination, quotas, and preferential treatment.[50]

OUTCOMES OF THE AMERICANS WITH DISABILITIES ACT

The ADA was passed with the laudable goals of providing employment opportunities for the truly disabled who, in the absence of legislation, were unable to find employment. Certainly, some individuals with disabilities have found employment as a result of its passage. However, as often occurs with legislation, the impact is not necessarily what was intended. First, there has been increased litigation. The EEOC reports that since 2010 an average of over 26,000 complaints have been filed each year. Approximately 50% of the complaints filed have been found to be without reasonable cause. For example, in one case a company fired an employee for stealing from other employees and bringing a loaded gun to work. The fired employee sued for reinstatement under the ADA, claiming that he was the victim of a mental illness and thus should be considered disabled.[51]

A second problem is that the kinds of cases being filed are not based on the rights that Congress intended to protect. Although the act was passed because of the belief that discrimination against individuals with disabilities occurred in the failure to hire them,

52.2% of the claims deal with firings, 28.9% with failure to make reasonable accommodation, and 12.5% with harassment. Only 9.4% of the complaints allege a failure to hire or rehire.[52] In addition, although the act was passed to protect people with major disabilities such as blindness, deafness, lost limbs, or paralysis, these disabilities combined account for a small minority of the disabilities claimed. As we see in Table 3.5, the biggest disability category is "other," meaning that the plaintiff claims a disability that is not one of the 35 types of impairment listed in the EEOC charge data system. The second largest category is "being regarded as disabled" accounting for 13.4% of all charges, followed by "back impairment" claims at 8.8%. As an example, a fired employee sued IBM asking for $5 million in damages for violation of the Americans with Disabilities Act. The employee had been fired for spending hours at work visiting adult chat rooms on his computer. He alleged that his addiction to sex and the Internet stemmed from trauma experienced by seeing a friend killed in 1969 during an army patrol in Vietnam.[53]

Finally, the act does not appear to have had its anticipated impact on the employment of Americans with disabilities. According to the Bureau of Labor Statistics, only 17.5 percent of people with disabilities are employed, compared to 65 percent of the general population.[54,55]

For these reasons, Congress has explored the possibility of amending the act to more narrowly define the term *disability*.[56] The debate continues regarding the effectiveness of the ADA.

LGBT ISSUES

Society, in general, and most large businesses have developed much more inclusive attitudes toward lesbian, gay, bisexual, and transgender (LGBT) individuals. Most large companies state that they do not discriminate on the basis of sexual orientation, and many have opened up benefit packages to same-sex partners of their employees, even prior to the *Obergefell* Supreme Court decision legalizing same-sex marriage. However, the state of employment law has not completely caught up yet.

The Equality Act of 2017 was proposed in Congress after earlier versions failed to pass. The act would amend Title VII of the Civil Rights Act (along with some other federal laws) to include sexual orientation and gender identity as protected categories. However, the legislation is unlikely to pass in the foreseeable future. Thus, much of the activity surrounding these protections has been through the court system, making the argument that sexual orientation should be covered by Title VII. For instance, in a recent case heard by the Seventh Circuit Court of Appeals, Kimberly Hively alleged that she was not hired full time and was dismissed from her part-time teaching role at Ivy Tech because she is a lesbian. In essence, she argued that the application of stereotypes such as those regarding the sex of a person's partner are illegal sex discrimination.

In an 8–3 decision, the Seventh Circuit agreed with this logic. One of the concurring judges, Diane Wood, wrote, "Any discomfort, disapproval, or job decision based on the fact that the complainant—woman or man—dresses differently, speaks differently, or dates or marries a same-sex partner, is a reaction purely and simply based on sex. That means that it falls within Title VII's prohibition against sex discrimination." However, the Seventh Circuit's Diane Sykes argued in her dissenting opinion that this does not qualify as sex discrimination: "We are not authorized to infuse the text with a new or unconventional meaning or to update it to respond to changed social, economic, or political conditions.... It's understandable that the court is impatient to protect lesbians and gay men from workplace discrimination without waiting for Congress to act. Legislative change is arduous and can be slow to come. But we're not authorized to

Table 3.5
Sample of Complaints Filed under the ADA

	2000	2001	2002	2003	2004	2005	2006	2007	2008	2009	2010	2011	2012	2013	2014
Number of complaints	15,864	16,470	15,964	15,377	15,576	14,893	15,575	17,734	19,453	21,451	25,165	25,742	26,379	25,957	25,369
% dealing with*															
Asthma	2.0%	1.6%	1.6%	1.6%	1.5%	1.6%	1.7%	1.0%	1.7%	1.6%	1.7%	1.9%	1.6%	1.5%	1.4%
Back impairment	10.2	9.3	9.5	8.6	8.0	8.4	8.1	8.3	9.3	9.9	9.7	8.2	8.9	8.7	8.8
Cancer	2.7	2.8	2.9	2.9	2.8	2.7	3.2	3.3	3.6	3.7	3.9	4.4	4.4	4.7	4.4
Diabetes	4.1	4.3	4.7	4.8	4.7	4.5	4.8	5.1	5.6	5.5	5.4	4.6	4.2	4.7	5.0
Hearing	3.1	2.9	3.2	3.1	3.4	3.2	3.3	3.0	3.3	3.3	3.1	3.2	3.4	3.4	3.7
Vision	2.3	2.3	2.6	2.6	2.5	2.3	2.3	2.5	2.6	2.2	2.3	2.5	2.4	2.4	2.2
Heart	3.3	3.6	4.0	3.7	3.5	3.3	3.4	3.7	3.8	3.8	4.2	4.0	3.7	4.0	3.9
Regarded as disabled	13.7	12.8	13.7	16.8	18.2	17.4	17.2	17.7	16.7	14.1	12.8	13.0	13.1	13.8	13.4
Drug addiction	0.6	0.5	0.6	0.6	0.5	0.3	0.5	0.5	0.7	0.6	0.5	.5	.5	0.4	0.3
Anxiety	3.4	3.4	4.1	3.5	2.4	2.2	2.2	2.8	4.5	5.3	5.3	4.5	5.1	5.5	5.8
Depression	6.5	6.1	6.7	6.3	2.9	5.4	6.6	5.5	6.1	6.5	6.3	6.6	6.8	6.3	6.4
Other	22.2	22.3	23.7	18.1	12.3	14.7	15.7	16.4	20.2	24.4	26.3	29.8	30.3	29.0	32.1

*Not all complaints are listed.
SOURCE: Equal Employment Opportunity Commission, "ADA Charge Data by Impairment/Bases—Receipts," www.eeoc.gov, accessed May 26, 2015.

amend Title VII by interpretation." Because the Eleventh Circuit Court, in a similar case, concluded that sexual orientation did not qualify for protection as sex discrimination, it appears that the issue remains unresolved until either Congress passes a law or the Supreme Court rules in a way that clarifies whether or not sexual orientation and gender identity are protected categories.[57]

Employee Safety

LO 3-7
Identify the major provisions of the Occupational Safety and Health Act (1970) and the rights of employees that are guaranteed by this act.

In March 2005, officials at the BP refinery in Texas City, Texas, were aware that repairs needed to be done on some of the equipment in an octane-boosting processing unit. On March 23, knowing that some of the key alarms were not working, managers authorized a start-up of the unit. The start-up resulted in the deadliest petrochemical accident in 15 years, killing 15 people and injuring an additional 170.[58]

Like equal employment opportunity, employee safety is regulated by both the federal and state governments. However, to fully maximize the safety and health of workers, employers need to go well beyond the letter of the law and embrace its spirit. With this in mind, we first spell out the specific protections guaranteed by federal legislation and then discuss various kinds of safety awareness programs that attempt to reinforce these standards.

THE OCCUPATIONAL SAFETY AND HEALTH ACT (OSHA)

Occupational Safety and Health Act (OSHA)
The 1970 law that authorizes the federal government to establish and enforce occupational safety and health standards for all places of employment engaging in interstate commerce.

Although concern for worker safety would seem to be a universal societal goal, the **Occupational Safety and Health Act (OSHA)**—the most comprehensive legislation regarding worker safety—did not emerge in the United States until the early 1970s. At that time, there were roughly 15,000 work-related fatalities every year.

OSHA authorized the federal government to establish and enforce occupational safety and health standards for all places of employment engaging in interstate commerce. The responsibility for inspecting employers, applying the standards, and levying fines was assigned to the Department of Labor. The Department of Health and Human Services was assigned responsibility for conducting research to determine the criteria for specific operations or occupations and for training employers to comply with the act. Much of this research is conducted by the National Institute for Occupational Safety and Health (NIOSH).

Employee Rights under OSHA

General duty clause
The provision of the Occupational Safety and Health Act that states an employer has an overall obligation to furnish employees with a place of employment free from recognized hazards.

The main provision of OSHA states that each employer has a general duty to furnish each employee a place of employment free from recognized hazards that cause or are likely to cause death or serious physical harm. This is referred to as the **general duty clause**. Some specific rights granted to workers under this act are listed in Table 3.6. The Department of Labor recognizes many specific types of hazards, and employers are required to comply with all the occupational safety and health standards published by NIOSH.

A recent example is the development of OSHA standards for occupational exposure to blood-borne pathogens such as the AIDS virus. These standards identify 24 affected industrial sectors, encompassing 500,000 establishments and 5.6 million workers. Among other features, these standards require employers to develop an exposure control plan (ECP). An ECP must include a list of jobs whose incumbents might be exposed to blood, methods for implementing precautions in these jobs, postexposure follow-up plans, and procedures for evaluating incidents in which workers are accidentally infected.

Table 3.6
Rights Granted to Workers under the Occupational Safety and Health Act

Employees have the right to
1. Request an inspection.
2. Have a representative present at an inspection.
3. Have dangerous substances identified.
4. Be promptly informed about exposure to hazards and be given access to accurate records regarding exposures.
5. Have employer violations posted at the work site.

Although NIOSH publishes numerous standards, regulators clearly cannot anticipate all possible hazards that could occur in the workplace. Thus, the general duty clause requires employers to be constantly alert for potential sources of harm in the workplace (as defined by the standards of a reasonably prudent person) and to correct them. For example, managers at Amoco's Joliet, Illinois, plant realized that over the years some employees had created undocumented shortcuts and built them into their process for handling flammable materials. These changes appeared to be labor saving but created a problem: Workers did not have uniform procedures for dealing with flammable products. This became an urgent issue because many of the experienced workers were reaching retirement age, and the plant was in danger of losing critical technical expertise. To solve this problem, the plant adopted a training program that met all the standards required by OSHA. That is, it conducted a needs analysis highlighting each task new employees had to learn and then documented these processes in written guidelines. New employees were given hands-on training with the new procedures and were then certified in writing by their supervisor. A computer tracking system was installed to monitor who was handling flammable materials, and this system immediately identified anyone who was not certified. The plant met requirements for both ISO 9000 standards and OSHA regulations and continues to use the same model for safety training in other areas of the plant.[59]

OSHA is responsible for inspecting businesses, applying safety and health standards, and levying fines for violations. OSHA regulations prohibit notifying employers of inspections in advance.

SOURCE: www.OSHA.gov

Many companies have also explored the use of technologies as a way to increase occupational safety and health. The "Competing through Technology" box describes one new technology that can reduce repetitive motion injuries and help others to better perform jobs requiring grip strength.

OSHA Inspections

OSHA inspections are conducted by specially trained agents of the Department of Labor called compliance officers. These inspections usually follow a tight "script." Typically, the compliance officer shows up unannounced. For obvious reasons, OSHA's regulations prohibit advance notice of inspections. The officer, after presenting credentials, tells the employer the reasons for the inspection and describes, in a general way, the procedures necessary to conduct the investigation.

An OSHA inspection has four major components. First, the compliance officer reviews the employer's records of deaths, injuries, and illnesses. OSHA requires this kind of record keeping from all firms with 11 or more full- or part-time employees. Second, the officer, typically accompanied by a representative of the employer (and perhaps by a representative of the employees), conducts a "walkaround" tour of the

Robo-Grip to the Rescue!

Often jobs that require repetitive motions consistently throughout the day can create fatigue, inflammation, and even carpal tunnel syndrome. However, Robo-Glove, developed by NASA and General Motors is "a wearable human grasp assist device, to help reduce the grasping force needed by an individual to operate tools for an extended time or when performing tasks having repetitive motion."

This tool, which provides an assisted grip, can help older workers, who sometimes lose strength as they age. However, it may also be useful for Millennials, who lack the grip strength of past generations. For instance, in 1985, men aged 20–24 averaged 121 pounds of force in their right hand and 105 pounds in their left hand. Today's men of that age average 101 and 99 pounds for their right and left hands, respectively. In addition, women of this age have lost 10 pounds of grip strength over the same time period.

DISCUSSION QUESTIONS
1. Do you think technologies like Robo-Grip can reduce injuries?
2. What other advantages do they provide?

SOURCE: D. Lechner, "Technology Continues Aim at Improving Workplace Safety — But at What Cost?" October 26, 2016, http://info. ergoscience.com/employer-blog/technology-continues-aim-at-improving-workplace-safety-but-at-what-cost.

employer's premises. On this tour, the officer notes any conditions that may violate specific published standards or the less specific general duty clause. The third component of the inspection, employee interviews, may take place during the tour. At this time, any person who is aware of a violation can bring it to the attention of the officer. Finally, in a closing conference, the compliance officer discusses the findings with the employer, noting any violations. The employer is given a reasonable time frame in which to correct these violations. If any violation represents imminent danger (that is, could cause serious injury or death before being eliminated through the normal enforcement procedures), the officer may, through the Department of Labor, seek a restraining order from a U.S. district court. Such an order compels the employer to correct the problem immediately.

Citations and Penalties

If a compliance officer believes that a violation has occurred, he or she issues a citation to the employer that specifies the exact practice or situation that violates the act. The employer is required to post this citation in a prominent place near the location of the violation—even if the employer intends to contest it. Nonserious violations may be assessed up to $7,000 for each incident, but this penalty may be adjusted downward if the employer has no prior history of violations or if the employer has made a good-faith effort to comply with the act. Serious violations of the act or willful, repeated violations may be fined up to $70,000 per incident. Fines for safety violations are never levied against the employees themselves. The assumption is that safety is primarily the responsibility of the employer, who needs to work with employees to ensure that they use safe working procedures.

In addition to these civil penalties, criminal penalties may also be assessed for willful violations that kill an employee. Fines can go as high as $20,000, and the employer or agents of the employer can be imprisoned. Criminal charges can also be brought against anyone who falsifies records that are subject to OSHA inspection or anyone who gives advance notice of an OSHA inspection without permission from the Department of Labor.

Table 3.7
Workplace Illnesses and Injuries

NONFATAL INJURIES AND ILLNESSES, PRIVATE INDUSTRY	FATAL WORK-RELATED INJURIES
Total recordable cases: 2,905,900 in 2015	Total fatal injuries (all sectors): 4,836 in 2015
Cases involving days away from work: 902,200 in 2015	Roadway incidents (all sectors): 1,264 in 2015
Median days away from work: 8 in 2015	Falls, slips, trips (all sectors): 800 in 2015
Cases involving sprains, strains, tears: 324,700 in 2015	Homicides (all sectors): 417 in 2015
Cases involving injuries to the back: 155,740 in 2015	
Cases involving falls, slips, trips: 238,610 in 2015	

SOURCE: Bureau of Labor Statistics, www.bls.gov.

The Effect of OSHA

OSHA has been unquestionably successful in raising the level of awareness of occupational safety. Table 3.7 presents recent data on occupational injuries and illnesses. Yet legislation alone cannot solve all the problems of work site safety.[60] Many industrial accidents are a product of unsafe behaviors, not unsafe working conditions. Because the act does not directly regulate employee behavior, little behavior change can be expected unless employees are convinced of the standards' importance.[61] This has been recognized by labor leaders. For example, Lynn Williams, then president of the United Steelworkers, noted, "We can't count on government. We can't count on employers. We must rely on ourselves to bring about the safety and health of our workers."[62]

Because conforming to the statute alone does not necessarily guarantee safety, many employers go beyond the letter of the law. In the next section we examine various kinds of employer-initiated safety awareness programs that comply with OSHA requirements or, in some cases, exceed them.

SAFETY AWARENESS PROGRAMS

Safety awareness programs go beyond compliance with OSHA and attempt to instill symbolic and substantive changes in the organization's emphasis on safety. These programs typically focus either on specific jobs and job elements or on specific types of injuries or disabilities. A safety awareness program has three primary components: identifying and communicating hazards, reinforcing safe practices, and promoting safety internationally.

Safety awareness programs
Employer programs that attempt to instill symbolic and substantive changes in the organization's emphasis on safety.

Identifying and Communicating Job Hazards

Employees, supervisors, and other knowledgeable sources need to sit down and discuss potential problems related to safety. The **job hazard analysis technique** is one means of accomplishing this.[63] With this technique, each job is broken down into basic elements, and each of these is rated for its potential for harm or injury. If there is consensus that some job element has high hazard potential, this element is isolated and potential technological or behavioral changes are considered.

Job hazard analysis technique
A breakdown of each job into basic elements, each of which is rated for its potential for harm or injury.

Technic of operations review (TOR)
Method of determining safety problems via an analysis of past accidents.

Another means of isolating unsafe job elements is to study past accidents. The **technic of operations review (TOR)** is an analysis methodology that helps managers determine which specific element of a job led to a past accident.[64] The first step in a TOR analysis is to establish the facts surrounding the incident. To accomplish this, all members of the work group involved in the accident give their initial impressions of what happened. The group must then, through group discussion, reach a consensus on the single, systematic failure that most contributed to the incident as well as two or three major secondary factors that contributed to it.

An analysis of jobs at Burger King, for example, revealed that certain jobs required employees to walk across wet or slippery surfaces, which led to many falls. Specific corrective action was taken based on analysis of where people were falling and what conditions led to these falls. Now Burger King provides mats at critical locations and has generally upgraded its floor maintenance. The company also makes slip-resistant shoes available to employees in certain job categories.[65]

Communication of an employee's risk should take advantage of several media. Direct verbal supervisory contact is important for its saliency and immediacy. Written memos are important because they help establish a "paper trail" that can later document a history of concern regarding the job hazard. Posters, especially those placed near the hazard, serve as a constant reminder, reinforcing other messages.

In communicating risk, it is important to recognize two distinct audiences. Sometimes relatively young or inexperienced workers need special attention. Research by the National Safety Council indicates that 40% of all accidents happen to individuals in the 20–29 age group and that 48% of all accidents happen to workers during their first year on the job.[66] The employer's primary concern with respect to this group is to inform them. However, the employer must not overlook experienced workers. Here the key concern is to remind them. Research indicates that long-term exposure to and familiarity with a specific threat lead to complacency.[67] Experienced employees need retraining to jar them from complacency about the real dangers associated with their work. This is especially the case if the hazard in question poses a greater threat to older employees. For example, falling off a ladder is a greater threat to older workers than to younger ones. More than 20% of such falls lead to a fatality for workers in the 55–65 age group, compared with just 10% for all other workers.[68] Although most of this discussion has focused on workplace safety, technology has increasingly enabled and encouraged workers to work at home off the clock.

Reinforcing Safe Practices

One common technique for reinforcing safe practices is implementing a safety incentive program to reward workers for their support and commitment to safety goals. Initially, programs are set up to focus on improving short-term monthly or quarterly goals or to encourage safety suggestions. These short-term goals are later expanded to include more wide-ranging, long-term goals. Prizes are typically distributed in highly public forums (like annual meetings or events). These prizes usually consist of merchandise rather than cash because merchandise represents a lasting symbol of achievement. A good deal of evidence suggests that such programs are effective in reducing injuries and their cost.[69]

Whereas the safety awareness programs just described focus primarily on the job, other programs focus on specific injuries or disabilities. Lower back disability (LBD), for example, is a major problem that afflicts many employees. LBD accounts for approximately 25% of all workdays lost, costing firms nearly $30 billion a year.[70] Human resource managers can take many steps to prevent LBD and rehabilitate those who are

Table 3.8
A 10-Step Program for Reducing Eye-Related Injuries

1. Conduct an eye hazard job analysis.
2. Test all employees' vision to establish a baseline.
3. Select protective eyewear designed for specific operations.
4. Establish a 100% behavioral compliance program for eyewear.
5. Ensure that eyewear is properly fitted.
6. Train employees in emergency procedures.
7. Conduct ongoing education programs regarding eye care.
8. Continually review accident prevention strategies.
9. Provide management support.
10. Establish written policies detailing sanctions and rewards for specific results.

SOURCE: From T. W. Turrif, "NSPB Suggests 10-Step Program to Prevent Eye Injury," *Occupational Health and Safety* 60 (1991), pp. 62–66. Copyright © Media Inc. Reprinted with permission.

already afflicted. Eye injuries are another target of safety awareness programs. The National Society to Prevent Blindness estimated that 1,000 eye injuries occur every day in occupational settings.[71] A 10-step program to reduce eye injuries is outlined in Table 3.8. Similar guidelines can be found for everything from chemical burns to electrocution to injuries caused by boiler explosions.[72]

Promoting Safety Internationally

Given the increasing focus on international management, organizations also need to consider how to best ensure the safety of people regardless of the nation in which they operate. Cultural differences may make this more difficult than it seems. For example, a study examined the impact of one standardized corporation-wide safety policy on employees in three different countries: the United States, France, and Argentina. The results of this study indicated that the same policy was interpreted differently because of cultural differences. The individualistic, control-oriented culture of the United States stressed the role of top management in ensuring safety in a top-down fashion. However, this policy failed to work in Argentina, where the collectivist culture made employees feel that safety was everyone's joint concern; therefore, programs needed to be defined from the bottom up.[73]

At the beginning of this section, we discussed a horrific accident at BP's Texas City refinery. After examining the causes of the explosion, the U.S. Chemical Safety and Hazard Investigation Board asked BP to set up an independent panel that would focus on overseeing radical changes in BP's safety procedures. This panel was tasked with investigating the safety culture at BP along with the procedures for inspecting equipment and reporting near-miss accidents. The panel's charter is not just to oversee the Texas City refinery, but also to look at the safety practices in refineries that BP has acquired over the years.[74]

A LOOK BACK

Discrimination at Oracle?

At the outset of this chapter, we discussed how the Department of Labor uses statistical analyses to show evidence of discrimination and quoted an Oracle spokeswoman explaining that any differences in pay and hiring practices are based on legitimate business factors. So, how will this case play out?

Interestingly, we may never know. The case was brought by the Obama administration's Labor Department near the end of his term. Oracle allegedly refused to comply with a number of requests for employment and pay data, delaying the process. Now that the Trump administration has taken over, no one knows whether or not the new Labor Department appointees will want to continue the case.

SUMMARY

Viewing employees as a source of competitive advantage results in dealing with them in ways that are ethical and legal as well as providing a safe workplace. An organization's legal environment—especially the laws regarding equal employment opportunity and safety—has a particularly strong effect on its HRM function. HRM is concerned with the management of people, and government is concerned with protecting individuals. One of HRM's major challenges, therefore, is to perform its function within the legal constraints imposed by the government. Given the multimillion-dollar settlements resulting from violations of EEO laws (and the moral requirement to treat people fairly regardless of their sex or race) as well as the penalties for violating OSHA, HR and line managers need a good understanding of the legal requirements and prohibitions in order to manage their businesses in ways that are sound, both financially and ethically. Organizations that do so effectively will definitely have a competitive advantage.

KEY TERMS

Equal employment opportunity (EEO), 109
Americans with Disabilities Act (ADA), 115
Equal Employment Opportunity Commission (EEOC), 117
Utilization analysis, 119
Goals and timetables, 119

Action steps, 119
Disparate treatment, 121
Bona fide occupational qualification (BFOQ), 122
Disparate impact, 124
Four-fifths rule, 125
Standard deviation rule, 125
Reasonable accommodation, 127

Occupational Safety and Health Act (OSHA), 140
General duty clause, 140
Safety awareness programs, 143
Job hazard analysis technique, 143
Technic of operations review (TOR), 144

DISCUSSION QUESTIONS

1. Disparate impact theory was originally created by the court in the *Griggs* case before finally being codified by Congress 20 years later in the Civil Rights Act of 1991. Given the system of law in the United States, from what branch of government should theories of discrimination develop?

2. Disparate impact analysis (the four-fifths rule, standard deviation analysis) is used in employment discrimination cases. The National Assessment of Education Progress conducted by the U.S. Department of Education found that among those aged 21–25, (1) 60% of whites, 40% of Hispanics, and 25% of blacks could locate information in a news article or almanac; (2) 25% of whites, 7% of Hispanics, and 3% of blacks could decipher a bus schedule; and (3) 44% of whites, 20% of Hispanics, and 8% of blacks could correctly determine the change they were due from the purchase of a two-item restaurant meal. Do these tasks (locating information in a news article, deciphering a bus schedule, and determining correct change) have adverse impact? What are the implications?

3. Many companies have dress codes that require men to wear suits and women to wear dresses. Is this discriminatory according to disparate treatment theory? Why or why not?

4. Cognitive ability tests seem to be the most valid selection devices available for hiring employees, yet they also have adverse impact against blacks and Hispanics. Given the validity and adverse impact, and considering that race norming is illegal under the Civil Rights Act of 1991, what would you say in response to a recommendation that such tests be used for hiring?

5. How might the ADA's reasonable accommodation requirement affect workers such as law enforcement officers and firefighters?

6. The reasonable woman standard recognizes that women have different ideas than men of what constitutes appropriate behavior. What are the implications of this distinction? Do you think it is a good or bad idea to make this distinction?

7. Employers' major complaint about the ADA is that the costs of making reasonable accommodations will reduce their ability to compete with businesses (especially foreign ones) that do not face these requirements. Is this a legitimate concern? How should employers and society weigh the costs and benefits of the ADA?

8. Many people have suggested that OSHA penalties are too weak and misdirected (aimed at employers rather than employees) to have any significant impact on employee safety. Do you think that OSHA-related sanctions need to be strengthened, or are existing penalties sufficient? Defend your answer.

SELF-ASSESSMENT EXERCISE

Mc Graw Hill Education **connect**

Additional assignable self-assessments available in Connect.

Take the following self-assessment quiz. For each statement, circle T if the statement is true or F if the statement is false.

WHAT DO YOU KNOW ABOUT SEXUAL HARASSMENT?

1. A man cannot be the victim of sexual harassment. T F

2. The harasser can only be the victim's manager or a manager in another work area.   T F

3. Sexual harassment charges can be filed only by the person who directly experiences the harassment. T F

4. The best way to discourage sexual harassment is to have a policy that discourages employees from dating each other.   T F

5. Sexual harassment is not a form of sex discrimination. T F

6. After receiving a sexual harassment complaint, the employer should let the situation cool off before investigating the complaint.   T F

7. Sexual harassment is illegal only if it results in the victim being laid off or receiving lower pay.   T F

EXERCISING STRATEGY

Sexism at Kleiner Perkins Caufield & Byers

Silicon Valley firms are notorious for their masculine cultures, and how they treat women has long been a sensitive issue. In fact, a 2014 Babson College study revealed that women comprise only 6% of venture capitalists. A recent discrimination case against venture capital firm Kleiner Perkins Caufield & Byers illustrates this problem.

Ellen Pao filed a $16 million discrimination suit against the firm, alleging sex discrimination and retaliation. She alleged that the firm's leaders failed to promote her and provide her with choice assignments following an affair with one of the firm's partners, Ajit Nazre, in 2006. She said that after the affair ended, Nazre made life difficult, alleging, "He would cut me out of e-mails, take me off e-mail threads. He would not invite me to meetings."

On the other hand, the firm paints a picture of a woman scorned. An attorney hired to examine her claims said that she was "not truthful about the relationship with Ajit Nazre" and suggested that the affair was consensual and that she had wanted a deeper relationship.

During the trial, Pao testified that for Valentine's Day another male partner gave her a book of erotic poems. She told some of the partners that the firm would benefit from better human resources policy and training.

Ellen Pao lost her discrimination case against Kleiner Perkins. Although her allegations carried credibility, the firm successfully argued that the decisions it took with regard to her were based on poor performance and poor relationships with co-workers. A number of witnesses described her as passive-aggressive, generally ineffective, and disloyal. In the trial, Pao was accused of being both too aggressive and too timid. "You have this needle that you have to thread, and sometimes it feels like there's no hole in the needle," she said. "From what I've heard from women, they do feel like there's no way to win. They can't be aggressive and get this opportunity without being treated like they've done something wrong."

QUESTIONS

1. Do you think that all discrimination is overt and obvious, or does it often happen due to implicit mindsets? Explain.
2. How can firms ensure that all employees have a fair chance at promotions and pay raises, and that these decisions are not determined by implicit discrimination?

SOURCE: J. Elder, "Kleiner Accuser Testifies on Sexism," *Wall Street Journal*, March 9, 2015.

MANAGING PEOPLE

Uber Life after Kalanick?

Earlier in the chapter we referred to the challenge Uber faced in response to a former female engineer's blog alleging that Uber had created a very discriminatory and sexist environment. However, that may have been the least of Uber's problems.

Earlier in 2017 CEO Travis Kalanick was caught on video berating an Uber driver. Kalanick attempted to minimize this public relations disaster by confessing that he needed to "grow up" and get "leadership help." He was seeking to hire a Chief Operating Officer (COO) to provide such leadership and help manage the company. However, after interviewing a number of potential COO's, Uber was unsuccessful at hiring one, in part because many did not find the proposition of reporting to Kalanick. Many said they would not take the job if Kalanick remained as CEO.

This vacancy created an even greater executive-level staffing challenge as Uber had lost some of its most important executives over the previous year. The leaders of operations, marketing, finance, communications and self-driving car development had all left either through resignation or firing. In fact, Jeff Jones had been hired away from his chief marketing officer role at Target to become president of ride-sharing. However, Jones left after six months saying in a

written statement "that the beliefs and approach to leadership that have guided my career are inconsistent with what I saw and experienced at Uber."

In June of 2017 the board of directors at Uber asked for and received Kalanick's resignation as CEO. He will remain on the board because of his significant holdings of Uber's stock, but will no longer exert any operational control over the organization.

So, now Uber has no CEO, no CFO, no COO and a number of other c-suite jobs vacant. In addition, the recent Covington report chastised Uber for creating an extremely dysfunctional culture.

QUESTIONS

1. Do you think CEO's should be fired for not having a good leadership style, even if the company seems to be performing well? Why or why not?
2. Given the large number of problems facing Uber, what should the focus be on solving first, second, and third?

SOURCES: https://www.wsj.com/articles/how-uber-backers-orchestrated-kalanicks-ouster-as-ceo-1498090688; https://www.wsj.com/articles/uber-president-of-ride-sharing-jeff-jones-resigns-1489961810

HR IN SMALL BUSINESS

Company Fails Fair-Employment Test

Companies have to comply with federal as well as state and local laws. One company that didn't was Professional Neurological Services (PNS), which was cited by the Chicago Commission on Human Relations when it discriminated against an employee because she is a parent. Chicago is one of a few cities that prohibit this type of discrimination.

The difficulties began with employee Dena Lockwood as soon as she was interviewing for a sales position with PNS. The interviewer noticed that Lockwood made a reference to her children, and he asked her if her responsibilities as a parent would "prevent her from working 70 hours a week." Lockwood said no, but the job offer she received suggests that the interviewer had his doubts. According to Lockwood's later complaint, female sales reps without children routinely were paid a $45,000 base salary plus a 10% commission. Lockwood was offered $25,000 plus the 10% commission. Lockwood negotiated and eventually accepted $45,000 plus 5%, with a promise to increase the commission rate to 10% when she reached sales of $300,000. She was also offered five vacation days a year; when she objected, she was told not to worry.

Lockwood worked hard and eventually reached her sales goal. Then the company raised the requirement for the higher commission rate, and the situation took a turn for the worse. Lockwood's daughter woke up one morning with pink-eye, a highly contagious ailment. Lockwood called in to reschedule a meeting for that day, but her manager told her not to bother; she was being fired. When Lockwood asked why, the manager said "it just wasn't working out."

She went to the Chicago Human Relations Commission for help. The commission investigated and could find no evidence of performance-related problems that would justify her dismissal. Instead, the commission found that Lockwood was a victim of "blatant" discrimination against employees with children and awarded her $213,000 plus attorney's fees—a hefty fine for a company with fewer than 50 employees. PNS stated that it would appeal the decision.

QUESTIONS

1. Why do you think "parental discrimination" was the grounds for this complaint instead of a federally protected class? Could you make a case for discrimination on the basis of sex? Why or why not?
2. How could Professional Neurological Services have avoided this problem?
3. Imagine that the company has called you in to help it hold down human resources costs, including costs of lawsuits such as this one. What advice would you give? How can the company avoid discrimination and still build an efficient workforce?

SOURCES: Courtney Rubin, "Single Mother Wins $200,000 in Job Bias Case," *Inc.*, January 25, 2010; and Ameet Sachdev, "She Took a Day Off to Care for Sick Child, Got Fired," *Chicago Tribune*, January 24, 2010, NewsBank, http://infoweb.newsbank.com.

NOTES

1. J. Ledvinka, *Federal Regulation of Personnel and Human Resource Management* (Boston: Kent, 1982).
2. *Martin v. Wilks*, 49 FEP Cases 1641 (1989).
3. *Wards Cove Packing Co. v. Atonio*, FEPC 1519 (1989).
4. *Bakke v. Regents of the University of California*, 17 FEPC 1000 (1978).
5. *Patterson v. McLean Credit Union*, 49 FEPC 1814 (1987).
6. J. Friedman and G. Strickler, *The Law of Employment Discrimination: Cases and Materials*, 2nd ed. (Mineola, NY: Foundation Press, 1987).
7. "Labor Letter," *Wall Street Journal*, August 25, 1987, p. 1.
8. J. Woo, "Ex-Workers Hit Back with Age-Bias Suits," *Wall Street Journal*, December 8, 1992, p. B1.
9. W. Carley, "Salesman's Treatment Raises Bias Questions at Schering-Plough," *Wall Street Journal*, May 31, 1995, p. A1.
10. Equal Employment Opportunity Commission, "Maternity Store Giant to Pay $375,000 to Settle EEOC Pregnancy Discrimination and Retaliation Lawsuit," January 8, 2017, www.eeoc.gov/press/1-8-07.html.
11. Equal Employment Opportunity Commission, "EEOC Sues Milwaukee Medical Staffing Agency for Pregnancy Discrimination," April 27, 2011, www.eeoc.gov/eeoc/newsroom/release/4-27-11b.cfm.
12. Special feature issue: "The New Civil Rights Act of 1991 and What It Means to Employers," *Employment Law Update* 6 (December 1991), pp. 1–12.
13. "ADA: The Final Regulations (Title I): A Lawyer's Dream/An Employer's Nightmare," *Employment Law Update* 16, no. 9 (1991), p. 1.
14. "ADA Supervisor Training Program: A Must for Any Supervisor Conducting a Legal Job Interview," *Employment Law Update* 7, no. 6 (1992), pp. 1–6.
15. https://www.eeoc.gov/eeoc/history/35th/thelaw/ada.html
16. Equal Employment Opportunity Commission, "Uniform Guidelines on Employee Selection Procedures," *Federal Register* 43 (1978), pp. 38290–315.
17. Ledvinka, *Federal Regulation of Personnel*.
18. R. Pear, "The Cabinet Searches for Consensus on Affirmative Action," *New York Times*, October 27, 1985, p. E5.
19. *McDonnell Douglas v. Green*, 411 U.S. 972 (1973).
20. Equal Employment Opportunity Commission, "The Timken Company to Pay $120,000 to Settle EEOC Gender and Disability Discrimination Suit," April 29, 2011, www.eeoc.gov/eeoc/newsroom/release/4-29-11.cfm.
21. *UAW v. Johnson Controls, Inc.* 499 U.S. 187 (1991).
22. M. O'Brien, "Ugly People Need Not Apply?" *HR Executive*, September 16, 2010, p. 12.
23. Special feature issue: "The New Civil Rights Act of 1991," pp. 1–6.
24. *Washington v. Davis*, 12 FEP 1415 (1976).
25. *Albemarle Paper Company v. Moody*, 10 FEP 1181 (1975).
26. R. Reilly and G. Chao, "Validity and Fairness of Some Alternative Employee Selection Procedures," *Personnel Psychology* 35 (1982), pp. 1–63; J. Hunter and R. Hunter, "Validity and Utility of Alternative Predictors of Job Performance," *Psychological Bulletin* 96 (1984), pp. 72–98.
27. *Griggs v. Duke Power Company*, 401 U.S. 424 (1971).
28. B. Lindeman and P. Grossman, *Employment Discrimination Law* (Washington, DC: BNA Books, 1996).
29. M. Jacobs, "Workers' Religious Beliefs May Get New Attention," *Wall Street Journal*, August 22, 1995, pp. B1, B8.
30. Equal Employment Opportunity Commission, "EEOC and Electrolux Reach Voluntary Resolution in Class Religious Accommodation Case," September 24, 2003, www.eeoc.gov/press/9-24-03.

31. S. Sataline, "Who's Wrong When Rights Collide?" *Wall Street Journal*, March 6, 2007, p. B1.

32. "Manager's Failure to Accommodate Creates Liability for Store," *Disability Compliance Bulletin*, January 15, 2009.

33. Lindeman and Grossman, *Employment Discrimination Law*.

34. J. Reno and D. Thornburgh, "ADA—Not a Disabling Mandate," *Wall Street Journal*, July 26, 1995, p. A12.

35. Equal Employment Opportunity Commission, "Dillard's Sued by EEOC for Retaliation," April 28, 2011, www.eeoc.gov/eeoc/newsroom/release/4-28-11.cfm.

36. Woo, "Ex-Workers Hit Back."

37. Equal Employment Opportunity Commission, "Target Corp. to Pay $775,000 for Racial Harassment: EEC Settles Suit for Class of African American Employees; Remedial Relief Included," January 26, 2007, www.eeoc.gov/press/1-26-07.html.

38. W. Johnston and A. Packer, *Workforce 2000* (Indianapolis, IN: Hudson Institute, 1987).

39. Toppo, G. Uber CEO calls for investigation of sexual harassment claims. *USA Today*. http://www.usatoday.com/story/tech/2017/02/19/uber-ceo-investigation-sexual-harassment/98142146/ (accessed 2.20.17)

40. *Bundy v. Jackson*, 641 F.2d 934, 24 FEP 1155 (D.C. Cir., 1981).

41. L. A. Graf and M. Hemmasi, "Risqué Humor: How It Really Affects the Workplace," *HR Magazine*, November 1995, pp. 64–69.

42. X. Author, "Article Title," *Source Publication*, Month ##, ####, URL.

43. B. Carton, "At Jenny Craig, Men Are Ones Who Claim Sex Discrimination," *Wall Street Journal*, November 29, 1995, p. A1; "Male-on-Male Harassment Suit Won," *Houston Chronicle*, August 12, 1995, p. 21A.

44. Equal Employment Opportunity Commission, "Texas Car Dealership to Pay $140,000 to Settle Same-Sex Harassment Suit by EEOC," October 28, 2002, www.eeoc.gov/press/10-28-02.

45. Equal Employment Opportunity Commission, "Babies 'R' Us to Pay $205,000, Implement Training Due to Same-Sex Harassment of Male Employee," January 15, 2003, www.eeoc.gov/press/1-15-03.

46. *Meritor Savings Bank v. Vinson* 477 U.S. 57 (1986).

47. R. Patrick, "Verdict: Jury Awards $95 Million in Fairview Heights Sex Harassment Suit," *St. Louis Post-Dispatch*, June 10, 2011, www.stltoday.com/news/local/crime-and-courts/jury-awardsmil...icle_6f46fa47-3a8b-5266-b094-b95910d51c46.html.

48. R. Paetzold and A. O'Leary-Kelly, "The Implications of U.S. Supreme Court and Circuit Court Decisions for Hostile Environment Sexual Harassment Cases," in *Sexual Harassment: Perspectives, Frontiers, and Strategies*, ed. M. Stockdale (Beverly Hills, CA: Sage); R. B. McAfee and D. L. Deadrick, "Teach Employees to Just Say 'No'!" *HR Magazine*, February 1996, pp. 586–89.

49. C. Murray, "The Legacy of the 60's," *Commentary*, July 1992, pp. 23–30.

50. D. Kravitz and J. Platania, "Attitudes and Beliefs about Affirmative Action: Effects of Target and of Respondent Sex and Ethnicity," *Journal of Applied Psychology* 78 (1993), pp. 928–38.

51. J. Mathews, "Rash of Unintended Lawsuits Follows Passage of Disabilities Act," *Houston Chronicle*, May 16, 1995, p. 15A.

52. C. Bell, "What the First ADA Cases Tell Us," *SHRM Legal Report* (Winter 1995), pp. 4–7.

53. J. Fitzgerald, "Chatty IBMer Booted," *New York Post*, February 18, 2007.

54. Source: https://www.bls.gov/news.release/disabl.nr0.htm

55. National Organization on Disability, *2006 Annual Report*, www.nod.org.

56. K. Mills, "Disabilities Act: A Help, or a Needless Hassle," *B/CS Eagle*, August 23, 1995, p. A7.

57. https://www.usnews.com/news/business/articles/2017-04-05/gay-rights-organizations-hail-court-ruling-as-game-changer

58. C. Cummins and T. Herrick, "Investigators Fault BP for More Lapses in Refinery Safety," *Wall Street Journal*, August 18, 2005, p. A3.

59. V. F. Estrada, "Are Your Factory Workers Know-It-All?" *Personnel Journal*, September 1995, pp. 128–34.

60. R. L. Simison, "Safety Last," *Wall Street Journal*, March 18, 1986, p. 1.

61. J. Roughton, "Managing a Safety Program through Job Hazard Analysis," *Professional Safety* 37 (1992), pp. 28–31.

62. M. A. Verespec, "OSHA Reform Fails Again," *Industry Week*, November 2, 1992, p. 36.

63. R. G. Hallock and D. A. Weaver, "Controlling Losses and Enhancing Management Systems with TOR Analysis," *Professional Safety* 35 (1990), pp. 24–26.

64. H. Herbstman, "Controlling Losses the Burger King Way," *Risk Management* 37 (1990), pp. 22–30.

65. L. Bryan, "An Ounce of Prevention for Workplace Accidents," *Training and Development Journal* 44 (1990), pp. 101–2.

66. J. F. Mangan, "Hazard Communications: Safety in Knowledge," *Best's Review* 92 (1991), pp. 84–88.

67. T. Markus, "How to Set Up a Safety Awareness Program," *Supervision* 51 (1990), pp. 14–16.

68. J. Agnew and A. J. Saruda, "Age and Fatal Work-Related Falls," *Human Factors* 35 (1994), pp. 731–36.

69. R. King, "Active Safety Programs, Education Can Help Prevent Back Injuries," *Occupational Health and Safety* 60 (1991), pp. 49–52.

70. J. R. Hollenbeck, D. R. Ilgen, and S. M. Crampton, "Lower Back Disability in Occupational Settings: A Review of the Literature from a Human Resource Management View," *Personnel Psychology* 45 (1992), pp. 247–78.

71. T. W. Turriff, "NSPB Suggests 10-Step Program to Prevent Eye Injury," *Occupational Health and Safety* 60 (1991), pp. 62–66.

72. D. Hanson, "Chemical Plant Safety: OSHA Rule Addresses Industry Concerns," *Chemical and Engineering News* 70 (1992), pp. 4–5; K. Broscheit and K. Sawyer, "Safety Exhibit Teaches Customers and Employees about Electricity," *Transmission and Distribution* 43 (1992), pp. 174–79; R. Schuch, "Good Training Is Key to Avoiding Boiler Explosions," *National Underwriter* 95 (1992), pp. 21–22.

73. M. Janssens, J. M. Brett, and F. J. Smith, "Confirmatory Cross-Cultural Research: Testing the Viability of a Corporation-wide Safety Policy," *Academy of Management Journal* 38 (1995), pp. 364–82.

74. Cummins and Herrick, "Investigators Fault BP."

LEARNING OBJECTIVES

After reading this chapter, you should be able to:

LO 4-1 Analyze an organization's structure and work-flow process, identifying the output, activities, and inputs in the production of a product or service. *page 155*

LO 4-2 Understand the importance of job analysis in strategic human resource management. *page 169*

LO 4-3 Choose the right job analysis technique for a variety of human resource activities. *page 176*

LO 4-4 Identify the tasks performed and the skills required in a given job. *page 177*

LO 4-5 Understand the different approaches to job design. *page 178*

LO 4-6 Comprehend the trade-offs among the various approaches to designing jobs. *page 178*

ENTER THE WORLD OF BUSINESS

New Organizational Structures: Teeming with Teaming

"Years ago, people just kind of did their tasks in front of them. Work was much more about what I did to accomplish something. Now it's much more about who did I work with so we could accomplish things together." These are the word of Hugh Welsh, an executive for the North American branch of Royal DSM, a global science-based company active in the areas of health and nutrition. Welsh is the general counsel for Royal DSM; however, he holds several other job titles in the company, and across his many roles, he has over 100 direct and indirect employees who report to him.

Welsh is not alone, in this regard, because organizations are increasingly organizing work around teams that create many more opportunities and challenges when it comes to managing workplace relationships. A recent survey of 7,000 managers from over 130 countries conducted by Deloitte Consulting indicates that over half of the companies surveyed had either restructured work around teams or were in the process of doing so. The goal of this revolutionary change in the nature of work is to break down former functional silos and increase speed of operations by creating cross-discipline teams that manage their own group processes with a minimum amount of hierarchical micro-management. John Chambers, executive chairman and former CEO of the electronics firm Cisco notes this need for speed, arguing that "we compete against market transitions, not competitors, and transitions that used to take seven years now take one or two."

However, as anyone who ever worked in agriculture can tell you, silos have their uses, and the same Deloitte survey also indicates that only 20% of managers feel they have the teamwork skills necessary to coordinate and motivate all the members of all the teams of which they are a part. Indeed, not everyone has the teamwork skills necessary to work effectively in these kinds of organizations, even when the structure of interteam relationships is clear. More critically, however, only 12% of managers working in team-based structures feel they have a solid understanding of all the social networks embedded in their organization. The fluid nature of these loose networks makes them hard to understand even for people with strong interpersonal skills, and the process of directly linking people with specialized talents to every team that needs them runs the risk of creating role overload that prevents any work from being done.

Organizations moving to a team-based structure are finding that creating the right balance between effective and timely collaboration, on the one hand, and the ability to execute one's primary job, on the other hand, is easy to mishandle. Hugh Welsh's skills as a general counsel make him potentially valuable to many different teams, but he notes that during a recent trip to the company's headquarters in the Netherlands, he scrambled from one meeting to the next, mainly making "token appearances" at each before rushing off to more meetings. "I said to myself, 'what the hell am I doing? This is crazy. I'm not making meaningful contributions to the business'."

SOURCES: R. Feintzeig, "So Busy at Work, No Time to Do the Job," *Wall Street Journal,* June 28, 2016; P. Schumpeter, "Team Spirit," *The Economist,* March 23, 2016; C. Duhigg, "How to Build a Perfect Team." *Wall Street Journal,* February 28, 2016.

Introduction

In Chapter 2, we discussed the processes of strategy formulation and strategy implementation. Strategy formulation is the process by which a company decides how it will compete in the marketplace; this is often the energizing and guiding force for everything it does. Strategy implementation is the way the strategic plan gets carried out in activities of organizational members. We noted five important components in the strategy implementation process, three of which are directly related to the human resource management function and one of which we will discuss in this chapter: the task or job. For example, in the vignette that opened this chapter, the way the work was structured at Royal DSM created excessive demands for collaboration and often made it difficult for some people to execute their own jobs. Although team-based structures can help promote flexibility and speed of operations, the limits of an individual's capacity for ever-increasing collaboration have to be recognized.

Many central aspects of strategy formulation address how the work gets done, in terms of individual job design as well as the design of organizational structures that link individual jobs to each other and the organization as a whole. The way a firm competes can have a profound impact on the ways jobs are designed and how they are linked via organizational structure. In turn, the fit between the company's structure and environment can have a major impact on the firm's competitive success.

If a company decides to compete on cost, and hence hire low-cost offshore labor, the jobs have to be designed so that they can be performed by minimally skilled people who will require little training. The organization in this case needs to have a centralized structure so that low-level workers are not forced into making too many decisions and the workers should work independently to prevent errors from cascading through the system. In contrast, if the organization is going to compete by differentiating its product, and hence hiring high-wage labor, it has to design the jobs in a different way.

For example, when shoe manufacturers in Portugal saw that they were losing sales to cheaper Chinese competitors, they completely revamped their work processes to emphasize higher quality shoes that would support higher prices. Well-trained and well-paid employees worked with expensive, state-of-the-art technology like high-speed waterjet cutters to produce small batches of high-end shoes that were sold to luxury designers. Portuguese shoes are now second only to those made in Italy when it comes to export price—$32 a pair, compared to $4 for China.[1]

Throughout this chapter, we provide examples of the kinds of decisions that need to be made with regard to how organizations should be structured and to the jobs that exist within these organizations, so that you can learn how these choices affect a number of outcomes. This includes not just quantity and quality of production, but also outcomes like coordination; innovation; and worker attraction, motivation, and retention. In many cases, there are trade-offs associated with the choices, and the more you know about these trade-offs, the better decisions you can make in terms of making your team or organization more competitive.

It should be clear from the outset of this chapter that there is no "one best way" to design jobs and structure organizations. The organization needs to create a fit between its environment, competitive strategy, and philosophy, on the one hand, and its jobs and organizational design, on the other. Failing to design effective organizations and jobs has important implications for competitiveness. Many years ago, some people believed that the difference between U.S. auto producers and their foreign competitors could be traced to American workers; however, when companies like Toyota and Honda came into the United States and demonstrated clearly that they could run profitable car companies with American workers, the focus shifted to processes and organization. Now many U.S. car companies are making a comeback, which can be traced at least in part to more effective design of the work.[2]

This chapter discusses the analysis and design of work and, in doing so, lays out considerations involved in making informed decisions about how to create and link jobs. The chapter is divided into three sections, the first of which deals with "big picture" issues related to work-flow analysis and organizational structure. The remaining two sections deal with more specific, lower level issues related to job analysis and job design.

The fields of job analysis and job design have extensive overlap, yet in the past they have been treated differently. Job analysis has focused on analyzing existing jobs to gather information for other HRM practices such as selection, training, performance appraisal, and compensation. Job design, by contrast, has focused on redesigning existing jobs to make them more efficient or more motivating to jobholders. Thus, job design has had a more proactive orientation toward changing the job, whereas job analysis has had a passive, information-gathering orientation.

Work-Flow Analysis and Organization Structure

Work-flow design is the process of analyzing the tasks necessary for the production of a product or service, prior to allocating and assigning these tasks to a particular job category or person. Only after we thoroughly understand work-flow design can we make informed decisions regarding how to initially bundle various tasks into discrete jobs that can be executed by a single person.

Organization structure refers to the relatively stable and formal network of vertical and horizontal interconnections among jobs that constitute the organization. Only after we understand how one job relates to those above (supervisors), below (subordinates), and at the same level in different functional areas (marketing versus production) can we make informed decisions about how to redesign or improve jobs to benefit the entire organization.

Finally, work-flow design and organization structure have to be understood in the context of how an organization has decided to compete. Both work-flow design and organization structure can be leveraged to gain competitive advantage for the firm, but how one does this depends on the firm's strategy and its competitive environment.

LO 4-1
Analyze an organization's structure and work-flow process, identifying the output, activities, and inputs in the production of a product or service.

WORK-FLOW ANALYSIS

All organizations need to identify the outputs of work, to specify the quality and quantity standards for those outputs, and to analyze the processes and inputs necessary for producing outputs that meet the quality standards. This conception of the work-flow process is useful because it provides a means for the manager to understand all the tasks required to produce a number of high-quality products as well as the skills necessary to perform those tasks. This work-flow process is depicted in Figure 4.1.

Analyzing Work Outputs

Every work unit—whether a department, a team, or an individual—seeks to produce some output that others can use. An output is the product of a work unit and this is often an identifiable object such as a jet engine blade, a forklift, or a football jersey. However, an output can also be a service, such as an airline that transports you to some destination, a housecleaning service that maintains your house, or a babysitter who watches over your children.

Figure 4.1

Developing a Work–Unit Activity Analysis

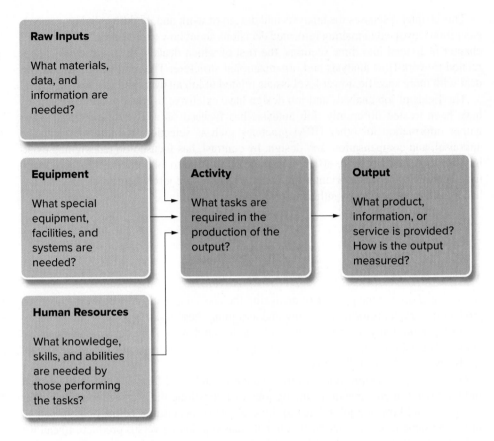

We often picture an organization only in terms of the product that it produces, and then we focus on that product as the output. Merely identifying an output or set of outputs is not sufficient. Once these outputs have been identified, it is necessary to specify standards for the quantity or quality of these outputs. In many cases, the number and nature of the outputs chosen create challenges for how to efficiently process the inputs in order to generate the outputs. For example, recently McDonald's restaurants added many new items to its menus, including oatmeal, snack wraps, and lattes in order to appeal to a wider array of consumers. In fact, the number of menu items at McDonald's swelled to 121 items in 2014, compared to just 85 in 2007. Not surprisingly, this results in slower service, and McDonald's also recorded its worst speed-of-performance metrics that same year. Managers often referred to the McWrap specifically as a "showstopper" that required many of the workers to look up a series of instructions in order to execute a single order.[3]

Analyzing Work Processes

Once the outputs of the work unit have been identified, it is possible to examine the work processes used to generate the output. The work processes are the activities that members of a work unit engage in to produce a given output. Every process consists of operating procedures that specify how things should be done at each stage of the development of the product. These procedures include all the tasks that must be performed in the production of the output. The tasks are usually broken down into those performed by each person in the work unit. Of course, in many situations where the work that needs to be done is highly complex, no single individual is likely to have all the required skills. In these situations, the work may be assigned to a team, and as we saw in our opening vignette, team-based job design is becoming increasingly popular in contemporary organizations. In addition to providing a wider set of skills, team members can back each other up, share work when any member becomes overloaded, and catch each other's errors.

For example, although the job of driving a truck used to be an individual job, increasingly teams of drivers are assigned to trucks in order to keep the big rigs—which reflect a major capital investment—moving 24 hours a day. U.S. regulations limit the number of hours truck drivers can operate to 11 hours a day, but by swapping drivers at the end of a shift, teams can carry goods more than twice the distance than can be accomplished by drivers working alone.[4]

The use of teams can also be seen in the field of medicine, where team-based care is increasingly becoming the norm. Rather than a single one-on-one doctor–patient relationship, many medical services are delivered by a team that might include a nurse practitioner, a physician's assistant, a clinical pharmacist, and a variety of technicians who work alongside the primary physician. Part of this is a result of the increased workload created by the Affordable Care Act as well as the decreased number of general practitioners minted by medical schools. As noted by Kirsten Meisinger, a supervising physician who oversees an 11-person team, "I can't possibly do everything that needs to be done for all of our patients as a single human being." The main challenge with team-based work design is to make sure that there is effective coordination and communication between team members to make sure patients do not fall through the cracks or miss some important treatment due to a weak "hand-off."[5]

Still, these kinds of errors are less likely to happen when people are working face-to-face in teams relative to when the hand-off is a depersonalized electronic exchange from one functional unit to another. Avoiding errors attributed to faulty work procedures is critical because routine medical errors are the third leading cause of death in the United States, trailing only heart disease and cancer.[6]

Teams are not a panacea. For teams to be effective, it is essential that the level of task interdependence (how much they have to cooperate) matches the level of outcome interdependence (how much they share the reward for task accomplishment).[7] That is, if work is organized around teams, team bonuses rather than individual pay raises need to play a major role in terms of defining rewards. In addition, some members of teams may lean too much on the other team members and fail to develop their own skills or take responsibility for their own tasks; even in teams it is critical to establish individual accountability of behavior.[8] Indeed, it often takes only one member to seriously disrupt a team and create lasting problems. For example, individuals who chronically show up late for team meetings waste the time of those who show up on time, and this one single act of poor teamwork creates more lasting damage than not even showing up for the meeting at all.[9]

There is a great deal of value in studying work-flow processes and this is best illustrated when private equity groups come in and buy a failing company at a low price, revamp the work-flow process, and then sell the company again at a higher price. Private equity groups employ efficiency experts who try to wring out every ounce of waste in production operations. When efficiency experts first visit a company, they are looking for three different kinds of waste: (1) movement that creates no value, (2) the overburdening of specific people or machines, and (3) inconsistent production that creates excessive inventories. Typically armed with stopwatches, clipboards, and flowcharts, efficiency experts prowl the manufacturing floor for waste that would not be detected by

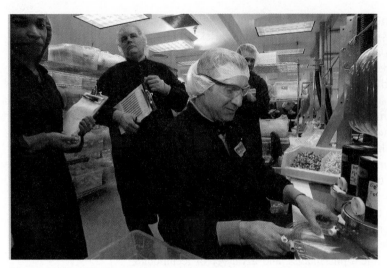

©Andrew Ford/ConMed Corporation

This job may look tedious or possibly even uninteresting. Considering how to engage employees in seeing the benefits of their work outside of the lab is an important way to motivate them through their day.

most managers. More often than not, this leads to a reduction in headcount because improved procedures dramatically streamline operations. As Justin Hillenbrand, an executive at Monomoy Capital Partners, notes, "You could have the best CEO in the world, but in a manufacturing company, profits are made on the floor."[10]

Organizations often work hard to minimize overstaffing via lean production techniques. *Lean production* refers to processes developed in Japan, but then adopted worldwide, emphasizing manufacturing goods with a minimum amount of time, materials, money—and most important—people. Lean production tries to leverage technology, along with small numbers of flexible, well-trained, and skilled personnel in order to produce more custom-based products at less cost. This can be contrasted with more traditional "batch work" methods, where large groups of low-skilled employees churn out long runs of identical mass products that are stored in inventories for later sale. In lean production systems, there are fewer employees to begin with, and the skill levels of those employees are so high that the opportunity to cuts costs by laying off employees is simply less viable.

Indeed, a paradox of the most recent recession in 2008–2009 was how small many of the layoffs in the manufacturing sector of the economy were given the huge drop in production levels. For example, 14 months into the recession of 2000, manufacturers cut 9.5% of their employees in response to a *2% cut* in production. In contrast, 14 months into the most recent recession, the same 9.5% of employees were laid off in response to a *12% cut* in production. If the same ratio of job cuts to production cuts from the year 2000 held in the year 2009, this would have resulted in an astounding layoff rate of over 50% of manufacturing employees. Many observers have attributed the lower "job cut–to–production cut" ratio in the most recent recession to the use of job redesign initiatives that emphasize lean production over more traditional approaches.

Although lean design is great for employers, it is not always great for workers. For example, one side effect of this increased level of efficiency is that when the economy did bounce back, this was accomplished with much less new hiring relative to what was experienced in prior recessions. This left a permanent dent in the number of U.S. manufacturing jobs because many of those jobs were never going to come back due to the more efficient design of work processes.[11]

Analyzing Work Inputs

The final stage in work-flow analysis is to identify the inputs used in the development of the work unit's product. As shown in Figure 4.1, these inputs can be broken down into the raw materials, equipment, and human skills needed to perform the tasks. *Raw materials* consist of the materials that will be converted into the work unit's product.

Organizations that try to increase efficiency via lean production techniques often try to minimize the stockpile of inputs via "just-in-time" inventory control procedures. Indeed, in some cases, inventories are being abandoned altogether, and companies at the edge of the lean production process do not even manufacture any products until customers place an order for them. For example, surgical device maker CONMED used to forecast demand for their products one to two months ahead, and when those forecasts turned out to be inaccurate they would either lose sales or stockpile inventories. Today, because the length of time it takes to produce their devices has decreased from 6 weeks to 48 hours, they do not even manufacture any products that are not already sold. The impact of this can be seen at CONMED's plant in Utica, New York, where a $93,000 inventory that used to take up 3,300 square feet on the factory floor has been all but eliminated. This allowed the company to take back lost sales from Chinese competitors that, despite their lower labor costs, face the costs of long lead times, inventory pile-ups, quality problems, and transportation costs. As David Johnson, vice president for global operations at CONMED notes, "If more U.S. companies deploy these job design methods we can compete with anybody and still provide security to our workforce."[12]

However, there are also downsides to "just-in-time" inventory management practices. Specifically, the efficiency gained from maintaining an inventory measured in days rather than weeks creates a lack of flexibility. An example of this can be seen in the aftermath of the earthquake that struck northern Japan in 2011. This region of Japan was home to a number of suppliers who had to unexpectedly halt all production overnight on March 22. This disruption rippled through the entire global economy that relied on "just-in-time" practices when organizations as varied as Boeing, General Motors, John Deere, Hewlett-Packard, and Dell had to halt their own production lines after running out of inputs. As one analyst noted, "If supply is disrupted in this situation, there's nowhere to get inputs."[13]

Equipment refers to the technology and machinery necessary to transform the raw materials into the product. Although most of the early software programs were designed to free human operators from many mundane tasks, such as an autopilot function on an airplane or a computer-aided design program for an architect, new software is increasingly capable of analysis and decision making. Thus, rather than "up-skilling" the work, many programs "de-skill" the work, and over time, people who use it become less self-reliant. For example, one study found that the more pilots relied on autopilot when flying, the less able they were to react to emergencies in a training simulator. Some observers attributed the medical community's slow reaction to the Ebola breakout to medical diagnosing software that was not sensitive to detecting highly rare and complex events. As one physician noted, "Medical software is no replacement for basic history-taking, examination skills, and critical thinking."[14]

In general, the amount of money that an organization invests in equipment is calculated in terms of the amount of "capital spending per worker," and some labor economists in the United States are concerned that this form of investment has not kept pace with what is needed to compete against international competition. For example, 2014 marked the fifth year in a row that the U.S. economy showed no growth in capital spending per worker, and not coincidentally, this year also witnessed a severe drop in worker productivity. Even though profits are up, U.S. employers are not investing in equipment but instead are using their funds to pay stock dividends or support stock buyback programs. Thus, the average age of equipment in U.S. plants is 7.4 years old—the highest figure in 20 years.[15] Still, as is evident in the "Competing through Globalization" box, modernization in Japan is lagging what we see in the United States.

Growing Old Together in Japan

At Osaka Machine Tool, one piece of equipment, the Spiramatic Jigmill Horizontal Boring Mill, made by the DeVlieg Machine Company in Michigan over 50 years ago, is still in operation. This one piece of equipment is emblematic of the decaying equipment infrastructure in Japan that many people believe is holding back the country's national competitiveness when it comes to manufacturing. As noted by one of Japan's chief economic analyst, Toshihiro Nagahama, "Facilities and equipment getting creaky isn't good for our economy and Japanese companies are falling behind our foreign rivals."

The average age of facilities and equipment in Japan is over 15 years and according to a 2016 survey conducted by the Bank of Japan, manufacturers in that country plan to increase capital spending by just 1%. Many years of economic stagnation and deflation in Japan prompted companies to restrain from domestic spending on equipment, and even when the economy started to turn around, companies used those profits to invest in shifting production to facilities outside of Japan where labor costs were lower. Over the years, this failure to reinvest in local manufacturing has taken a toll on the country's manufacturing infrastructure.

Moreover, the aging of Japan's equipment is made even more problematic by its aging workforce. Japan is already home to world's oldest manufacturing workforce, with over 12% of factory workers over 65 years of age. The average age of company owners is also at an all-time high of 59.2 years old, versus 54 years in 1990. Many of these owners operate small companies that serve as suppliers to larger companies like Toyota, Nissan, Canon, and Panasonic. About two-thirds of them lack any formal succession plan for when the proprietors retire or die. In 2016, over 25,000 Japanese firms shut down voluntarily by owners who could not find successors. This translates into a trickle-up effect that could ripple through the economy when these companies have to seek overseas contractors, which results in a further hollowing out of these industries. This is definitely the case at Osaka Machine Tool, where there is only one employee at the company old enough to even operate the Spiramatic—the company's 70-year-old chairman, Katumi Takata, who plans or retiring at the end the year.

DISCUSSION QUESTIONS

1. How does this example illustrate the trade-offs that have to be made between short-term and long-term investment at both the organizational level and the national level?

2. Ironically, although the average age of Japan's equipment is very high, that country is also home to many advanced robotic factories. How might investments in robotic technology be leveraged to change Japan's competitive position in the world?

SOURCES: K. Ujikane and M. Horie, "In Japan, Older Workers Work Older Machines," *Businessweek,* April 21, 2015, pp. 21–22; E. Warnock, "Numbers of Japanese Elders in Workforce Soars," *Wall Street Journal,* November 28, 2016; "Japan's Aging Population Has Business Owners Struggling to Find Successors," *Reuters,* October 3, 2016.

Of course, sometimes a work-flow analysis points to the fact that employees are using some specific piece of equipment too much. For example, cardiac telemetry is performed with equipment that lets a clinician monitor the heart for abnormal rhythms. At Christiana Care hospitals, administrators knew that these machines were being used by many physicians even when it was not considered necessary. To reduce routine use of this machine, the electronic ordering system was redesigned so that physicians could not order the tests by simply checking a box. A physician could still override the system and "write it in," but he or she had to take this one extra step. The results a year later showed that use of telemetry fell by 70%, costs were reduced by over $13,000, and there was no negative effect on patients. Nader Najafi, the University of California at San Francisco professor who led the study, noted, "It is remarkable to achieve such a substantial reduction in the use of such a resource without significantly increased adverse outcomes."[16]

The final input in the work-flow process is the *human skills* and efforts necessary to perform the tasks. Obviously, the human skills consist of the workers available to the company. Generally speaking, in terms of human skills, work should be delegated to the lowest-cost employee who can do the work well, and in some cases this principle is violated when too much emphasis is placed on reducing headcount. For example, between 2009 and 2011, the U.S. economy wiped out close to 1 million office and administrative support positions. Although this might seem a reasonable place to cut costs, does it really make financial sense to have C-level executives booking their own travel, completing routine paperwork, loading toner into the copier, and screening 500 e-mails a day, 400 of which are spam? For an executive making $1 million a year, an $80,000 assistant needs to increase that person's productivity by only 8% for the company to break even.[17]

ORGANIZATION STRUCTURE

Whereas work-flow design provides a longitudinal overview of the dynamic relationships by which inputs are converted into outputs, organization structure provides a cross-sectional overview of the static relationships between individuals and units that create the outputs. Organization structure is typically displayed via organizational charts that convey both vertical reporting relationships and horizontal functional responsibilities.

Dimensions of Structure

Two of the most critical dimensions of organization structure are centralization and departmentalization. **Centralization** refers to the degree to which decision-making authority resides at the top of the organizational chart as opposed to being distributed throughout lower levels (in which case authority is *decentralized*). **Departmentalization** refers to the degree to which work units are grouped based on functional similarity or similarity of work flow.

For example, a school of business could be organized around functional similarity so that there would be a marketing department, a finance department, and an accounting department, and faculty within these specialized departments would each teach their area of expertise to all kinds of students. Alternatively, one could organize the same school around work-flow similarity, so that there would be an undergraduate unit, a graduate unit, and an executive development unit. Each of these units would have its own marketing, finance, and accounting professors who taught only their own respective students and not those of the other units.

Structural Configurations

Although there are an infinite number of ways to combine centralization and departmentalization, two common configurations of organization structure tend to emerge in organizations. The first type, referred to as a *functional structure*, is shown in Figure 4.2. A functional structure, as the name implies, employs a functional departmentalization scheme with relatively high levels of centralization. High levels of centralization tend to go naturally with functional departmentalization because individual units in the structures are so specialized that members of the unit may have a weak conceptualization of the overall organization mission. Thus, they tend to identify with their department and cannot always be relied on to make decisions that are in the best interests of the organization as a

Centralization
The degree to which decision-making authority resides at the top of the organizational chart.

Departmentalization
The degree to which work units are grouped based on functional similarity or similarity of work-flow.

Figure 4.2

The Functional Structure

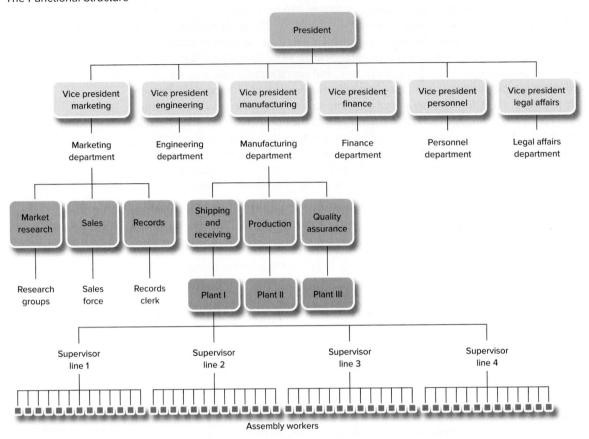

SOURCE: Adapted from J. A. Wagner and J. R. Hollenbeck, *Organizational Behavior: Securing Competitive Advantage,* 3rd ed. (New York: Prentice Hall, 1998).

whole. In addition, the opportunity for finger pointing and conflict between subunits that fundamentally do not understand the work that other subunits do creates the need for a centralized decision-making mechanism to manage potential disputes.[18]

For example, some observers believed that one of the major problems with the failed launch of the HealthCare.gov website meant to support the administration of the Affordable Care Act was that the structure of the system that employed highly functionalized groups for different elements of the website were not tightly linked to a centralized authority system. In testimony before the U.S. Congress, each contractor responsible for one part of the system pointed the finger of blame at some other contractor, and the central administration seemed unable to convey who they thought was accountable for what. At one point, the congressional committee became so frustrated with the lack of clarity on who in the central administration made key decisions that they forced people at the contracting agencies to name specifically who talked to whom on what date.[19]

Alternatively, a second common configuration is a *divisional structure*, three examples of which are shown in Figures 4.3, 4.4, and 4.5. Divisional structures combine a divisional departmentalization scheme with relatively low levels of centralization. Units in these structures act almost like separate, self-sufficient, semi-autonomous

Figure 4.3

Divisional Structure: Product Structure

SOURCE: Adapted from J. A. Wagner and J. R. Hollenbeck, *Organizational Behavior: Securing Competitive Advantage,* 3rd ed. (New York: Prentice Hall, 1998).

Figure 4.4

Divisional Structure: Geographic Structure

SOURCE: Adapted from J. A. Wagner and J. R. Hollenbeck, *Organizational Behavior: Securing Competitive Advantage,* 3rd ed. (New York: Prentice Hall, 1998).

organizations. The organization shown in Figure 4.3 is divisionally organized around different products; the organization shown in Figure 4.4 is divisionally organized around geographic regions; and the organization shown in Figure 4.5 is divisionally organized around different clients.

Regardless of how subunits are formed, many organizations try to keep the size of each subunit small enough that people within the subunit feel like they can make a difference and feel connected to others. People within very large subunits experience reduced feelings of individual accountability and motivation, which hinders organizational performance. Research suggests that these types of problems start to manifest themselves once a group exceeds 150 people; hence, many organizations try to limit subunits to this specific size. For example, W.L. Gore and Associates,

Figure 4.5

Divisional Structure: Client Structure

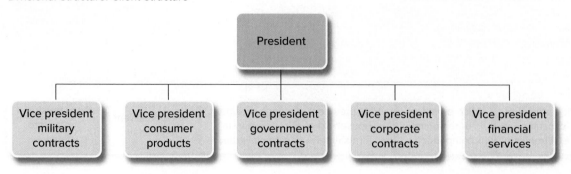

SOURCE: Adapted from J. A. Wagner and J. R. Hollenbeck, *Organizational Behavior: Securing Competitive Advantage,* 3rd ed. (New York: Prentice Hall, 1998).

the company that makes Gore-Tex and other innovative materials, typically will break up a division once its size exceeds this number, splitting it in two and opening a new physical office.[20]

Because of their work-flow focus, their semi-autonomous nature, and their proximity to a homogeneous consumer base, divisional structures tend to be more flexible and innovative. They can detect and exploit opportunities in their respective consumer bases faster than the more centralized functionally structured organizations. Indeed, because decision making in functional structures occurs at a level far from the shop floor or customer interface, there can sometimes be a disconnect between the perceived needs of those working on the front lines and upper management. For example, earlier we noted how the expansion of menus at McDonald's was causing problems for franchise owners. As one owner noted, "If more of the corporate people would spend their lunch hour and work the line and in the kitchen, we wouldn't be in the position we're in today. They kept expanding the menu; we knew this was only making the problem worse."[21]

By contrast, it is also the case that some strategic decisions made at corporate headquarters are more informed by wider trends in the industry that may not be recognizable by those on the front lines. For example, back at McDonald's, the local operators offered stiff resistance to the decision to offer "all-day breakfast" because, again, this was expanding the menu.[22] However, that decision was based on wide-ranging market surveys conducted at the corporate level, and that program turned out to be a huge success for all.[23] All of this again points to the fact that there is no one best way to design the organization's structure, and that the key is to make sure the structure is aligned with the competitive strategy.

In fact, when highly functional structures that are really built for efficiency and cost containment try to compete via speed and flexibility, serious problems can ensue. This is perfectly illustrated in the "fast fashion" industry. Historically, retailers launched new styles at the beginning of each season, and it often took a full year for a design concept to go from the drawing board to the store floor. Although last-minute changes could be made, these were typically costly and cut into margins at a rate that offset the value of the change. However, chains such as H&M and Zara are rewriting the rules of the fashion industry and increasingly introducing new styles every month as part of the push for "fast fashion."[24] The only problem with this practice, however, is that many people feel that it can be accomplished only via the exploitation of workers in small, emerging, third-world labor markets. It might not seem like such a major request to shift an order from 20,000 blue blouses to 10,000 blue blouses and 10,000 red blouses. However, quick shifts in operations like this, when not accompanied by changes in order delivery dates, cause plant managers in emerging economies to pump up worker hours and take short-cuts with maintenance that create major safety issues.

These problems have surfaced most clearly in Bangladesh, a country that has been at the forefront of the fast-fashion industry after surging wages in China sent retailers looking for cheaper and more accommodating manufacturers.

In some extreme cases, small divisions may not even be supervised by a formal manager, and the employees may self-manage. For example, Valve Corporation, a video-game producer located in Bellevue, Washington, touts itself as a "boss-free" company where decisions regarding hiring, firing, and pay are made by the employees themselves, who are organized into teams. The teams tend to vote on most decisions, or in some cases, due to experience or expertise, one or two people will emerge as leaders for specific projects. Typically this type of leadership emergence occurs in a way that is supported by the team. As one employee notes, "It absolutely is less efficient up front, but once you have the organization behind it, the buy-in and the execution happen quickly."[25] Zappos, the Amazon-owned shoe retailer, also employs what it calls a "bossless" company, and its experience too suggests that this nontraditional structure requires a great deal of time to learn. The orientation program as Zappos that teaches new employees the self-motivation and collaboration skills needed to be successful at the company takes four weeks, that is, unless you are late on the first day, in which case you are fired on the spot.[26]

A good example of the interplay of alternative structures can be seen in recent developments in the computer industry. Historically, the computer industry started with large and divisionally structured companies, like IBM, that over time splintered off into increasingly smaller and functionally specialized organizations. Technology companies focused narrowly on hardware *or* software *or* data storage *or* IT consulting services, but no one company was interested in providing all of these services. The thought was that specialization would boost efficiency and technical innovation. Indeed, as one analyst noted, "Today, a typical corporate computer system might be assembled by Accenture PLC with data storage systems from EMC Corporation and computers from Hewlett-Packard that use chips from Intel Corporation to run Oracle software."

However, Oracle announced that it was going to reverse that trend with the purchase of Sun Microsystems, making the company both a software producer and a hardware manufacturer. Oracle now plans on selling complete systems made of chips, computers, storage devices, and software—highlighting a competitive strategy based on the idea that corporate customers are tired of assembling and integrating different technological components from multiple suppliers. In similar moves, Hewlett-Packard announced just a few months later that it was going to purchase Electronic Data Systems, thus entering the data storage industry; and Apple announced it was making a move to enter the semiconductor chip business by buying chip maker P.A. Semi.[27]

The temptation toward this type of "vertical integration" can be strong because one of the virtues of divisional structures is that they allow one to control all aspects of an entire business, making one's former supplier part of the team, as opposed to an unpredictable element of the business environment. Vertical integration also tends to generate large-scale operations that would not naturally evolve organically from smaller organizations, and with size comes some degree of power. Indeed, Oracle's CEO, Larry Ellison, directly invoked the old 1960s IBM model by stating, "We want to be T. J. Watson's IBM, which was the greatest company in the history of enterprise in America because its hardware and software ran most companies."[28] Time will tell whether this strategy is effective, or like the old IBM, whether Oracle will learn that there are real limits associated with divisional structures as well.

Divisional structures are not very efficient because of the redundancy associated with each group carrying its own functional specialists. Also, divisional structures can "self-cannibalize" if the gains achieved in one unit come at the expense of another unit. For example, Kinko's stores were structured divisionally with highly decentralized control. Each manager could set his or her own price and has had autonomy to make his or her own decisions. The drawback to this structure was lack of coordination in the sense that every Kinko's store considered every other Kinko's store a competitor; they vied against each other for work, and they bid against each other competing on price."[29] These problems eventually led to the demise of the company when it was taken over by FedEx, restructured, and renamed FedEx Office and Print Shops.[30]

Lack of coordination caused by decentralized and divisional structures can be especially problematic with new and emerging organizations that do not have a great deal of history or a firmly established culture. Higher levels of centralization and more functional design of work make it easier in this context to keep everyone on the same page while the business builds experience.[31] Decentralized and divisional structures can also create problems if the stand-alone divisions start making decisions that are overly risky or out of line with the organization's larger goals. This can be particularly problematic when the organization is trying to manage a universal brand image with demands for standardized practices across many far-flung units. For example, as you can see from the "Competing through Sustainability" box, Chipotle experienced this exact problem when it came to local sourcing decisions regarding its ingredients.

Another example can be seen in the experience at Procter and Gamble (P&G), where each separate division had been given control over its own research and development budget. During tough economic times, each separate unit began to reduce expenditures on R&D in an effort to tighten their budgets and meet short-term profit goals. The cumulative effect of all of these short-term independent decisions was that, as a company, P&G was underinvesting in R&D, and a dearth of new and innovative products harmed the company's long-term competitiveness. Then-CEO Bob McDonald stepped in and centralized the R&D function so that the majority of researchers worked in a single unit and reported to a single authority, Jorge Mesquita. The hope was to leverage the research talent that was spread across the divisions and consolidate them into a single unit focused on more radical breakthroughs rather than incremental innovations.[32]

Alternatively, functional structures are very efficient, with little redundancy across units, and they provide little opportunity for self-cannibalization or for rogue units running wild. Also, although the higher level of oversight in centralized structures tends to reduce the number of errors made by lower-level workers, when errors do occur in overly centralized systems, they tend to cascade through the system as a whole more quickly and can, therefore, be more debilitating. Moreover, these structures tend to be inflexible and insensitive to subtle differences across products, regions, or clients.

Functional structures are most appropriate in stable, predictable environments, where demand for resources can be well anticipated and coordination requirements between jobs can be refined and standardized over consistent repetitions of activity. This type of structure also helps support organizations that compete on cost, because efficiency is central to making this strategy work. Divisional structures are most appropriate in unstable, unpredictable environments, where it is difficult to anticipate demands for resources, and coordination requirements between jobs are not consistent over time. This type of structure also helps support organizations that compete on differentiation or innovation, because flexible responsiveness is central to making this strategy work.

Of course, designing an organizational structure is not an either–or proposition, and some research suggests that "middle-of-the-road" options that combine functional and divisional elements are often best. For example, most organizations take a "mixed"

Chipotle's Decentralized Decision-Making Structure Can Make You Sick

Chipotle Mexican Grill had a winning formula for luring customers and investors with the promise of healthy fast food, achieved in an environmentally sustainable manner. At the core of its business strategy was the decentralized nature of decision making, which meant franchise managers had the freedom to make their own decisions regarding local sourcing of ingredients. Unlike national burger chains such as McDonald's and Burger King, which rely on a small number of huge beef and potato suppliers chosen by corporate headquarters, Chipotle's 2,000 restaurants rely on decentralized supply-chain decisions that involve hundreds of small, local independent farmers. This was a distinguishing element of the company's competitive strategy, and it was one of the main factors that made it a darling of the "farm-to-table" segment of the market.

All of this changed, however, in December 2015, when the organization was upended by a breakout of *E. coli* bacterial poisoning at many of its restaurants. The outbreak affected over 250 people from a variety of locations in Oregon, Washington, California, Minnesota, and Massachusetts and required the chain to close over 40 restaurants. Typically, outbreaks such as this are isolated incidents, but when one chain is struck in so many different regions at the same time, customers and investors begin to think that something was going wrong systematically. Many people came to believe that the decentralized nature of the decisions regarding ingredients was simply too loose when it came to strict quality control. Sales dropped by 16% soon after the outbreaks, and the company's stock price closed 22% lower in the wake of the scandal. As one industry analyst noted, "This strikes deeper at their brand, because so much of their story is based on the quality of their ingredients."

The problems associated with quality control related to food safety is just part of the issue, however, when it comes to the decentralized nature of the decision making at Chipotle. Another challenge is finding local suppliers that can adhere to the company's high standards for produce that is responsibly grown and meat that does not contain any antibiotics. According to the company, 95% of U.S.- raised pork fails to meet its standards, and these standards are more difficult and expensive to meet in some locations than in others. Chipotle has often struggled to keep its chains regularly stocked with pork, and *carnitas* has been an off-and-on item at roughly 33% of its stores for years. Some people may have issues with the big burger chains when it comes to their centralized decision-making processes regarding ingredient sources and how this affects their product, but you never see burgers and fries pulled from their menus.

DISCUSSION QUESTIONS

1. In what ways does this example illustrate the virtues and liabilities of alternative organizational structures when it comes to centralization and standardization?

2. What are some of the disadvantages of centralized structures that might make it more difficult for the big burger chains to be successful?

SOURCES: C. Giammona and L. Patton, "Small Suppliers, Big Problems," *Businessweek,* December 14, 2015; P. R. Lamonica, "Will Chipotle Ever Recover from Its E. coli Woes?" *CNN Money Online,* September 22, 2016; P. Wahba, "Chipotle's E. Coli Hangover Lingers as Sales Plunge Again," *Fortune Magazine Online,* July 21, 2016.

approach to how they structure the HR function. Typically, there is a subunit called a shared service center that is highly centralized and handles all the major routine transactional tasks such as payroll. There is also a center of excellence subunit that houses specialized expertise in the area of training or labor relations, which is centralized but separate from the shared service center. Finally, there is a third decentralized subunit that acts as business partner to other subunit leaders on talent management or succession planning. This three-pronged structure has elements that strive to achieve efficiency when it comes to routine tasks, specialization when it comes to complex tasks, and flexibility when it comes to supporting each separate business unit.[33]

Structure and the Nature of Jobs

Finally, moving from big-picture issues to lower-level specifics, the type of organization structure also has implications for the design of jobs. Jobs in functional structures need to be narrow and highly specialized. Workers in these structures (even middle managers) tend to have little decision-making authority or responsibility for managing coordination between themselves and others. In contrast, the steel producer Nucor is structured divisionally; production at its 30 minimill plants has doubled almost every two years, and profit margins have pushed beyond 10% largely because of its flat, divisional structure. At Nucor, individual plant managers have wide autonomy in how to design work at their own mills. Nucor plants sometimes compete against each other, but the CEO makes sure that the competition is healthy and that best practices are distributed throughout the organization as fast as possible, preventing any long-term sustainable advantage to any one plant. Moreover, the profit-sharing plan that makes up the largest part of people's pay operates at the organizational level, which also promotes collaboration among managers who want to make sure that every plant is successful. Thus, after taking over a new mill for the first time, one new plant manager got a call or visit from every other manager, offering advice and assistance. As the new manager noted, "It wasn't idle politeness. I took them up on it. My performance impacted their paycheck."[34]

Nucor employs just four levels of management and operates a headquarters of just 66 people, compared to one of its competitors, U.S. Steel, which has over 20 levels and 1,200 people at its headquarters. This gives Nucor a long-term sustainable competitive advantage, which it has held for close to 15 years. Sales at Nucor grew from $4.5 billion in 2000 to over $13 billion in 2006. During the same period, U.S. Steel's volume decreased by 6%. This has translated into success for both investors (roughly 400% return on investment in a five-year period) and workers, whose wages average $100,000 a year, compared to $70,000 a year at U.S. Steel. As one industry analyst notes, "In terms of a business model, Nucor has won this part of the world," and much of that victory can be explained by its superior structure and process for managing work.[35]

The choice of structure also has implications for people who would assume the jobs created in functional versus divisional structures. For example, managers of divisional structures often need to be more experienced or high in cognitive ability relative to managers of functional structures.[36] The relatively smaller scope and routine nature of jobs created in centralized and functional structures make them less sensitive to individual differences between workers.

Taller structures also have implications for organizational culture in terms of ethics and accountability. For example, in a highly public scandal, Putnam Investments was fined $110 million for engaging in "market timing," that is, jumping quickly in and out of funds in order to take advantage of momentary market inefficiencies. This is considered an unethical practice within the industry because it increases fund expenses which, in turn, harms long-term investors. Many long-term investors left the organization, some of whom had more than $800 million being managed by Putnam.

According to Putnam insiders, the organization's tall and narrow organizational structure created a situation in which too many people were managing other people and telling them what they had to do to get promoted. Because the only way to earn more money at

Putnam was to climb the corporate ladder, too much pressure was put on managers and employees alike to boost short-term results in order to attract the attention of those high above. The culture was one where people tended to ask "What is the fine for this?" instead of "What does this do to help my clients?" When new CEO Ed Haldeman was brought in to repair the damage, one of his first steps was to remove hundreds of sales-people, and then flatten the structure. The goal was to attract a different kind of employee, who would be less interested in short-term gains and hierarchical promotions handed out by others and more interested in establishing personal long-term relationships with customers and more collaborative relationships with colleagues. In Haldeman's words, "To retain and attract the best people, it's necessary to provide them with autonomy and independence to make their own decisions."[37]

In the next two sections, we cover specific approaches for analyzing and designing jobs. Although all of these approaches are viable, each focuses on a single, isolated job. These approaches do not necessarily consider how that single job fits into the overall work flow or structure of the organization. Whereas the Putnam Investments example shows how a firm moved from a functional structure to a divisional structure, Eli Lilly changed its structure in just the opposite direction, and this reinforces our general principle that there is no "one best way" when it comes to organizational structure. Without this big-picture appreciation, we might redesign a job in a way that might be good for that one job but out of line with the work flow, structure, or strategy of the organization.

For example, because patents for well-established drugs run out after a set time period, a company like Eli Lilly can survive only by inventing new products before the time bomb represented by their older drugs goes off. Faced with the prospect of losing the patent on its $5 billion a year schizophrenia medication, Zyprexa, this company restructured operations in a functional direction in order to create new products more quickly and efficiently. For example, all persons who were responsible for converting molecules into medicine were taken out of their home departments and placed under one roof in the new Development Center for Excellence.

This group of intensely focused specialists, who were all working together for the first time, came up with an innovative new method for launching and testing drugs. This group took a formerly sequential two-stage process for determining general effectiveness and then the optimal dosage, and converted it into a single-stage process in which multiple dose levels were tested all at once and compared to each other. This process shaved 14 months off the process of developing a new drug for diabetes and was then generalized to other therapeutic causes.[38]

Job Analysis

Job analysis refers to the process of getting detailed information about jobs. It is important for organizations to understand and match job requirements and people to achieve high-quality performance. This is particularly true in today's competitive marketplace.

Job analysis
The process of getting detailed information about jobs.

LO 4-2
Understand the importance of job analysis in strategic human resource management.

THE IMPORTANCE OF JOB ANALYSIS

Job analysis is the building block of everything that human resource managers do. Almost every human resource management program requires some type of information that is gleaned from job analysis: work redesign, human resource planning, selection, training and development, performance appraisal, career planning, and job evaluation.

Work Redesign. As previously discussed, job analysis and job design are interrelated. Often a firm will seek to redesign work to make it more efficient or effective. To redesign the work, detailed information about the existing job(s) must be available. In addition, redesigning a job will, in fact, be similar to analyzing a job that does not yet exist.

Human Resource Planning. In human resource planning, managers analyze an organization's human resource needs in a dynamic environment and develop activities that enable a firm to adapt to change. This planning process requires accurate information about the levels of skill required in various jobs to ensure that enough individuals are available in the organization to meet the human resource needs of the strategic plan.

Selection. Human resource selection identifies the most qualified applicants for employment. To identify which applicants are most qualified, it is first necessary to determine the tasks that will be performed by the individual hired and the knowledge, skills, and abilities the individual must have to perform the job effectively. This information is gained through job analysis.

Training and Development. Almost every employee hired by an organization will require training. Some training programs may be more extensive than others, but all require the trainer to have identified the tasks performed in the job to ensure that the training will prepare individuals to perform their jobs effectively.

Performance Appraisal. Performance appraisal deals with getting information about how well each employee is performing in order to reward those who are effective, improve the performance of those who are ineffective, or provide a written justification for why the poor performer should be disciplined. Through job analysis, the organization can identify the behaviors and results that distinguish effective performance from ineffective performance.

Career Planning. Career planning entails matching an individual's skills and aspirations with opportunities that are or may become available in the organization. This matching process requires that those in charge of career planning know the skill requirements of the various jobs. This allows them to guide individuals into jobs in which they will succeed and be satisfied.

Job Evaluation. The process of job evaluation involves assessing the relative dollar value of each job to the organization to set up internally equitable pay structures. If pay structures are not equitable, employees will be dissatisfied and quit, or they will not see the benefits of striving for promotions. To put dollar values on jobs, it is necessary to get information about different jobs to determine which jobs deserve higher pay than others.

THE IMPORTANCE OF JOB ANALYSIS TO LINE MANAGERS

Job analysis is clearly important to the HR department's various activities, but why it is important to line managers may not be as clear. There are many reasons. First, managers must have detailed information about all the jobs in their work group to understand the work-flow process. Second, managers need to understand the job requirements to make intelligent hiring decisions. Very seldom do employees get hired by the HR department without a manager's input. Third, a manager is responsible for ensuring that each individual is performing satisfactorily (or better). This requires the manager to evaluate how well each person is performing and to provide feedback to those whose performance needs improvement. Finally, it is also the manager's responsibility to ensure that the work is being done safely, know where potential hazards might manifest themselves and create a climate where people feel free to interrupt the production process if dangerous conditions exist.[39]

For example, in 2016, Donald Blankenship, the CEO of Massey Energy Company was fined $250,000 and sentenced to a year in prison for conspiring to violate federal safety standards when it came to running mining operations. Prosecutors in this case argued that Blankenship created a culture at the organization that placed financial performance ahead of safety standards, and that this contributed to the deaths of 29 miners after an explosion in the Upper Big Branch Mine in Appalachia.[40]

In contrast, some observers were shocked when Alcoa's new CEO Paul O'Neill's opening remarks at his first shareholders' meeting were focused on pointing out the nearest emergency exits in the building. However, O'Neill's emphasis on safety and work processes actually ended up making him one of the best CEOs in history. After he took over at Alcoa, O'Neill changed reporting procedures so that any time an employee got hurt, the department head in that unit had to develop a plan detailing how work processes were going to be changed to make sure the same accident did not happen again. Executives who failed to embrace this new standard routine were fired. As a result of this new policy, each department head had to become intimately familiar with work processes, which ultimately led to many conversations with lower-level workers who had great ideas not only for shoring up safety but also for streamlining workflow. Eventually, even as safety was improving, costs came down, quality went up, and productivity skyrocketed.[41]

Of course, one problem with trying to make job analysis fulfill so many different purposes is that the best job analysis for one objective may not be the best job analysis for another. For example, a job description that is based on a job analysis performed for recruitment purposes needs to be short and attract attention to applicants who may not spend a great deal of time reading an advertisement. In contrast, a job description that is based on a job analysis used as part of a performance management program needs to be detailed enough to tease out the strengths and weaknesses of a job incumbent who may have been observed over a full year. Thus, a company may perform multiple job analyses for a single job or derive multiple job descriptions from a single job analysis. Sodexo USA, a food and facilities management company, does exactly this and has "dual documents" for over 900 different jobs.[42]

JOB ANALYSIS INFORMATION

Nature of Information

Two types of information are most useful in job analysis: job descriptions and job specifications. A **job description** is a list of the tasks, duties, and responsibilities (TDRs) that a job entails. TDRs are observable actions. For example, a clerical job requires the jobholder to type. If you were to observe someone in that position for a day, you would certainly see some typing. When a manager attempts to evaluate job performance, it is most important to have detailed information about the work performed in the job (that is, the TDRs). This makes it possible to determine how well an individual is meeting each job requirement. Table 4.1 shows a sample job description. On the one hand, job descriptions need to be written broadly because overly restrictive descriptions make it easy for someone to claim that some important task, perhaps unforeseen, "is not my job." On the other hand, lack of specificity can result in disagreement and conflict between people about the essential elements of what the job entails.[43] Thus, it is critical to strike an effective balance between breadth and specificity when constructing job descriptions.

Job description
A list of the tasks, duties, and responsibilities (TDRs) that a job entails.

Table 4.1
A Sample Job Description

Job Title: Maintenance Mechanic
General Description of Job: General maintenance and repair of all equipment used in the operations of a particular district. Includes the servicing of company vehicles, shop equipment, and machinery used on job sites.

1. *Essential Duty (40%): Maintenance of Equipment*
   Tasks: Keep a log of all maintenance performed on equipment. Replace parts and fluids according to maintenance schedule. Regularly check gauges and loads for deviances that may indicate problems with equipment. Perform nonroutine maintenance as required. May involve limited supervision and training of operators performing maintenance.
2. *Essential Duty (40%): Repair of Equipment*
   Tasks: Requires inspection of equipment and a recommendation that a piece be scrapped or repaired. If equipment is to be repaired, mechanic will take whatever steps are necessary to return the piece to working order. This may include a partial or total rebuilding of the piece using various hand tools and equipment. Will primarily involve the overhaul and troubleshooting of diesel engines and hydraulic equipment.
3. *Essential Duty (10%): Testing and Approval*
   Tasks: Ensure that all required maintenance and repair has been performed and that it was performed according to manufacturer specifications. Approve or reject equipment as being ready for use on a job.
4. *Essential Duty (10%): Maintain Stock*
   Tasks: Maintain inventory of parts needed for the maintenance and repair of equipment. Responsible for ordering satisfactory parts and supplies at the lowest possible cost.

Nonessential Functions
Other duties as assigned.

Job specification
A list of the knowledge, skills, abilities, and other characteristics (KSAOs) that an individual must have to perform a job.

A **job specification** is a list of the knowledge, skills, abilities, and other characteristics (KSAOs) that an individual must have to perform the job. *Knowledge* refers to factual or procedural information that is necessary for successfully performing a task. A *skill* is an individual's level of proficiency at performing a particular task. *Ability* refers to a more general enduring capability that an individual possesses. Finally, *other characteristics* might be personality traits such as one's achievement motivation or persistence. Thus, KSAOs are characteristics of people that are not directly observable; they are observable only when individuals are carrying out the TDRs of the job. If someone applied for the clerical job mentioned earlier, you could not simply look at the individual to determine whether he or she possessed typing skills. However, if you were to observe that individual typing something, you could assess the level of typing skill. When a manager is attempting to fill a position, it is important to have accurate information about the characteristics a successful jobholder must have. This requires focusing on the KSAOs of each applicant.

Sources of Job Analysis Information

In performing the job analysis, one question that often arises is, Who should be responsible for providing the job analysis information? Whatever job analysis method you choose, the process of job analysis entails obtaining information from people familiar with the job. We refer to these people as *subject-matter experts* because they possess deep knowledge of the job.

In general, it will be useful to go to the job incumbent to get the most accurate information about what is actually done on the job. This is especially the case when it is difficult to monitor the person who does the job. The ratings of multiple job incumbents that are doing the same job do not always agree, however, especially if the job is complex and does not involve standardized equipment or tight scripts for customer contact.[44] Thus, you will also want to ask others familiar with the job, such as supervisors, to look over the information generated by the job incumbent. This serves as a check to determine whether what is being done is congruent with what is supposed to be done in the job.

Job incumbents are also useful when one is trying to assess the informal social network that exists within the formal organizational structure. That is, although the formal organizational structure suggests who *should* be talking to whom from a top-down normative perspective, an analysis of a company's social structure shows who really is talking to whom from a bottom-up descriptive perspective. In fact, one example of the growing field of business analytics deals with people analytic programs that show who is talking to whom on a day-to-day basis via self-report surveys or e-mail trails or from data derived from wearable sensors.

In many cases, social networks develop due to limitations in the formal structure when people realize they need to interact with some person in a way that was not anticipated by a formal organizational designer. Once alerted to this need, formal planners may wish to reconfigure the formal structure to reflect the needs identified by the informal, emergent social structure.[45] For example, Figure 4.6 shows a social network among the division leaders within an organization that produces scientific equipment. In this figure, the blue dots represent engineers engaged in production, the green dots represent scientists engaged in design, the black dots represent administrative support personnel, and the red dots represent the top management team. The lines in this figure denote who frequently interacts with whom on a face-to-face basis.

Unlike formal structures designed in a top-down fashion that tend to embrace symmetry and balance, social networks are much more organic and seemingly chaotic. These pictures are an important supplement to the formal organizational chart, however, because they often point out individuals who are more central to the organization than one might think given their job description and the formal chart.[46] In Figure 4.6, individuals like 4605, 7219, 2727, and 7389 are important "boundary spanners" across the units, whereas 3417, 2776, 1471, and 6367 do not even seem closely tied to members of their own units. It is easy for organizations to underestimate the importance of these informal boundary spanners, and the loss of any one of these individuals is likely to have a much more negative impact on the organization than the loss of individuals who are social outliers.

For these and many other reasons, organizations are increasingly complementing depictions of their formal structure with depictions of these informal structures, and these pictures, more often than not, rely on self-reports.[47] However, as the "Competing though Technology" box shows, Bluetooth signals coming from wearable sensors can accomplish the same goal, and indeed, the social network depicted in Figure 4.6 was based on data from wearable sensors and not self-reports. By relying on relational data captured automatically and continuously via this technology, one can obtain monthly, weekly, and even daily social network depictions that, due to their organic nature, are more volatile than formal organizational charts. In many cases, informal structures arise as adaptations to problems with formal structures, and over time, the formal structure may be changed so that it conforms more closely to the informal structure.

Figure 4.6

Social Network within an Organization

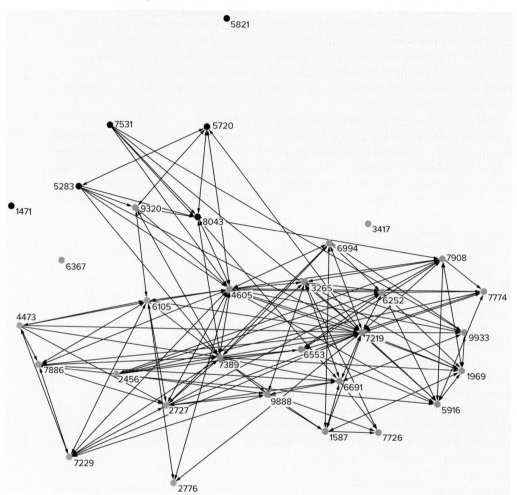

In contrast to cases where some communication link develops between people in order to meet a legitimate need to get the job done, a close examination of the social network in other cases uncovers individuals who overcommunicate for no good reason related to the work and, hence, waste their time and the time of others. For example, one company that analyzed its e-mail communications found one executive who generated so many e-mails that it took the equivalent of 10 people working full time just to read the e-mails sent by this one person. An analysis of these e-mails suggested that few of the people who were being sent the communications really needed e-mails from this person to do their job. An intervention directed at "fixing" this part of the social network increased the efficiency of a large number of people.[48]

One conclusion that can be drawn from this research is that incumbents may provide the most accurate estimates of the actual time spent performing job tasks, and who really has to talk to whom. However, supervisors may be a more accurate source of information about the importance of job duties. Incumbents also seem more accurate in terms of assessing safety-related risk factors associated with various aspects of work, and in general, the

Wearing Your Social Network on Your Sleeve

As we saw in the vignette that opened this chapter, organizations are increasingly relying on team-based structures where people come together to collaborate in a nearly spontaneous manner. These social networks often become more important than the formally designed organizational chart, but their emergent nature does not mean that they do not need to be actively managed. Managing such fluid multiteam systems can be a challenge, however, even when it comes to just understanding the basic emergent structure that characterizes who tends to work with whom over extended periods. Although surveys can be used to obtain self-reported linkages like those needed to generate illustrations of social networks, such as that depicted in Figure 4.6, these self-reports are often biased, and even when they are not, it has been impossible to visualize and depict these emergent team-based structures at a more granular level on an hourly or daily basis.

However, recent developments in the use of Bluetooth technology for detecting co-location and collaboration are revolutionizing the ability to generate real-time and temporally bracketed project-based

collaboration patterns. Originally developed to link devices, new applications of Bluetooth technology allow organizations to detect the degree to which any two individuals are co-located within a specified distance at any one moment in time. The Bluetooth device is essentially a wearable sensor that is miniaturized to the point that it can be worn within clothing and, hence, is totally unobtrusive. Unlike self-reports that may overestimate or underestimate collaboration patterns, Bluetooth signals create an accurate and objective record of who was working face-to-face at any point in time. Although face-to-face communication is not the only way that people collaborate, research shows that this is the best method for the exchange of complex, nonroutine, or private information. As a result, continuously streaming Bluetooth data can be used to depict the most critical social networks within the organization.

The value of collecting this information has to be weighed against the privacy protection rights of employees, and to date, the technology is advancing at a much more rapid rate relative to a full understanding of the ethical implications of this data collection method. For example,

many employers have used GPS monitoring to keep track of workers who perform their jobs offsite, and several court cases have reinforced the right of employees to expect privacy from electronic monitoring when off duty. However, the strongest social networks are those characterized by close friendship ties that often do transcend normal working hours. As this technology advances, it will be important to strike the right balance between managing the social network and invading the privacy of those embedded in such networks.

DISCUSSION QUESTIONS

1. What kind of self-report biases might be eliminated by objective measures of collaboration like Bluetooth?
2. In what sense might the social networks captured via Bluetooth also be inaccurate, and what biases might this new technology create?

SOURCES: T. D. Chaffin, R. Heidl, J. R. Hollenbeck, R. Calantone, M. Howe, C. Voorhees, and A. Yu, A., "The Promise and Perils of Wearable Sensors in Organizational Research," *Organizational Research Methods,* 20 (2017), pp. 3–31; P. F. Gorder, "Computers in Your Clothes? A Milestone for Wearable Electronics," *News Room,* Ohio State University Online, April 13, 2016; R. Greenfield "Testing Workers Digital Privacy Protections," *Businessweek,* May 25, 2015, pp. 33–34.

farther one moves up the organizational hierarchy, the less accurate the risk assessments.[49] Although job incumbents and supervisors are the most obvious and frequently used sources of job analysis information, other sources, such as customers, can be helpful, particularly for service jobs. Finally, when it comes to analyzing skill levels, external job analysts who have more experience rating a wide range of jobs may be the best source.[50]

JOB ANALYSIS METHODS

LO 4-3

Choose the right job analysis technique for a variety of human resource activities.

There are various methods for analyzing jobs and no "one best way." In this section, we discuss two methods for analyzing jobs: the Position Analysis Questionnaire (PAQ) and the Occupational Information Network (O*NET). Although most managers may not have time to use each of these techniques in the exact manner suggested, the two provide some anchors for thinking about broad approaches, task-focused approaches, and person-oriented approaches to conducting job analysis.

Position Analysis Questionnaire (PAQ)

We lead off this section with the PAQ because this is one of the broadest and most well-researched instruments for analyzing jobs. Moreover, its emphasis on inputs, processes, relationships, and outputs is consistent with the work-flow analysis approach discussed at the beginning of this chapter (Figure 4.1).

The PAQ is a standardized job analysis questionnaire containing 194 items.[51] These items represent work behaviors, work conditions, and job characteristics that can be generalized across a wide variety of jobs. They are organized into six sections:

1. *Information input*—Where and how a worker gets information needed to perform the job.
2. *Mental processes*—The reasoning, decision making, planning, and information-processing activities that are involved in performing the job.
3. *Work output*—The physical activities, tools, and devices used by the worker to perform the job.
4. *Relationships with other persons*—The relationships with other people required in performing the job.
5. *Job context*—The physical and social contexts where the work is performed.
6. *Other characteristics*—The activities, conditions, and characteristics other than those previously described that are relevant to the job.

The job analyst is asked to determine whether each item applies to the job being analyzed. The analyst then rates the item on six scales: extent of use, amount of time, importance to the job, possibility of occurrence, applicability, and special code (special rating scales used with a particular item). These ratings are submitted to the PAQ headquarters, where a computer program generates a report regarding the job's scores on the job dimensions.

Research has indicated that the PAQ measures 12 overall dimensions of jobs (listed in Table 4.2) and that a given job's scores on these dimensions can be very useful. The PAQ database has linked scores on certain dimensions to scores on subtests of the General Aptitude Test Battery (GATB). Thus, knowing the dimension scores provides some guidance regarding the types of abilities that are necessary to perform the job. Obviously, this technique provides information about the work performed in a format that allows for comparisons across jobs, whether those jobs are similar or dissimilar. Another advantage of the PAQ is that it covers the work context as well as inputs, outputs, and processes.

Knowledge of work context is important because in many cases, one can predict absenteeism and turnover from the nature of the surroundings in which the work takes place, and some people are more resilient than others when it comes to dealing with adverse environments. In addition, if one knows that the job includes adverse working conditions, providing additional levels of peer support and supervisor support might be required to help people cope.[52] In contrast, work spaces that are designed in ways that people find pleasing can often help overcome other aspects of a job that are generally seen as less desirable.[53]

Decision/communication/general responsibilities
Clerical/related activities
Technical/related activities
Service/related activities
Regular day schedule versus other work schedules
Routine/repetitive work activities
Environmental awareness
General physical activities
Supervising/coordinating other personnel
Public/customer/related contact activities
Unpleasant/hazardous/demanding environment
Nontypical work schedules

Table 4.2
Overall Dimensions
of the Position
Analysis
Questionnaire

The Occupational Information Network (O*NET)

The *Dictionary of Occupational Titles* (DOT) was born during the 1930s and served as a vehicle for helping the new public employment system link the demand for skills and the supply of skills in the U.S. workforce. Although this system served the country well for more than 60 years, it became clear to officials at the U.S. Department of Labor that jobs in the new economy were so qualitatively different from jobs in the old economy, that the DOT no longer served its purpose. Technological changes in the nature of work, global competition, and a shift from stable, fixed manufacturing jobs to a more flexible, dynamic, service-based economy were quickly making the system obsolete.[54]

For all these reasons, the Department of Labor abandoned the DOT in 1998 and developed an entirely new system for classifying jobs referred to as the Occupational Information Network, or O*NET. Instead of relying on fixed job titles and narrow task descriptions, the O*NET uses a common language that generalizes across jobs to describe the abilities, work styles, work activities, and work context required for various occupations that are more broadly defined (e.g., instead of the 12,000 jobs in the DOT, the O*NET describes only 1,000 occupations).[55] Although it was developed to analyze jobs in the U.S. economy, research suggests that the ratings tend to be transportable across countries. That is, if one holds the job title constant (e.g., first-line supervisor, office clerk, computer programmer), the ratings of the job tend to be the same even if the job is located in a different country.[56]

The O*NET was also designed to help job seekers. For example, the O*NET seems particularly well suited to describing the literacy requirements associated with alternative jobs. Thus, individuals who want to improve their ability to find employment can obtain from the O*NET relatively accurate information about what jobs they are qualified for given their current literacy level. They can also see how much their literacy skills would have to improve if they wanted to apply for higher-level jobs characterized by higher levels of complexity.[57]

DYNAMIC ELEMENTS OF JOB ANALYSIS

Although we tend to view jobs as static and stable, in fact, jobs tend to change and evolve over time. Those who occupy or manage the jobs often make minor, cumulative adjustments to the job that try to match either changing conditions in the environment or personal preferences for how to conduct the work.[58] Indeed, although there are numerous sources for error in the job analysis process,[59] most inaccuracy is likely to result from job descriptions simply being outdated. For this reason, in addition to statically defining the job, the job analysis process must also detect changes in the nature of jobs.

LO 4-4
Identify the tasks performed and the skills required in a given job.

For example, although working in a nursing home has always been a stressful occupation mentally, changes over time in the nature of the patients has dramatically increased requirements related to pure physical strength. The percentage of morbidly obese patients has increased from less than 15% in 2000 to over 25% in 2015, which has led to an unprecedented spike in staff injuries related to heavy lifting because, in many cases, this aspect of the job was not reflected in outdated job descriptions.[60]

Indeed, in today's world of rapidly changing products and markets, some people have begun to question whether the concept of "the job" is simply a social artifact that has outlived its usefulness. Indeed, many researchers and practitioners are pointing to a trend referred to as "dejobbing" in organizations. This trend consists of viewing organizations as a field of work needing to be done rather than a set of discrete jobs held by specific individuals. For example, HR director Scott Pitasky notes that, at Amazon, "a person might be in the same 'job,' but three months later be doing completely different work."[61] This means Amazon puts more emphasis on broad worker specifications ("entrepreneurial and customer-focused") than on detailed job descriptions ("C++ programming") that may not be descriptive one year down the road.

Job Design

LO 4-5
Understand the different approaches to job design.

So far we have approached the issue of managing work in a passive way, focusing only on understanding what gets done, how it gets done, and the skills required to get it done. Although this is necessary, it is a very static view of jobs, in that jobs must already exist and that they are already assumed to be structured in the one best way. However, a manager may often be faced with a situation in which the work unit does not yet exist, requiring jobs within the work unit to be designed from scratch. Sometimes work loads within an existing work unit are increased, or work-group size is decreased while the same work load is required. Finally, sometimes the work is not being performed in the most efficient manner. In these cases, a manager may decide to change the way that work is done in order for the work unit to perform more effectively and efficiently. This requires redesigning the existing jobs.

Job design
The process of defining the way work will be performed and the tasks that will be required in a given job.

Job design is the process of defining how work will be performed and the tasks that will be required in a given job. **Job redesign** refers to changing the tasks or the way work is performed in an existing job. To effectively design jobs, one must thoroughly understand the job as it exists (through job analysis) and its place in the larger work unit's work-flow process (work-flow analysis). Having a detailed knowledge of the tasks performed in the work unit and in the job, a manager then has many alternative ways to design a job. This can be done most effectively through understanding the trade-offs between certain design approaches.

Job redesign
The process of changing the tasks or the way work is performed in an existing job.

Research has identified four basic approaches that have been used among the various disciplines (such as psychology, management, engineering, and ergonomics) that have dealt with job design issues.[62] All jobs can be characterized in terms of how they fare according to each approach; thus a manager needs to understand the trade-offs of emphasizing one approach over another. The Work Design Questionnaire (WDQ), a specific instrument that reliably measures these and other job design characteristics, is available for use by companies wishing to comprehensively assess their jobs on these dimensions.[63]

LO 4-6
Comprehend the trade-offs among the various approaches to designing jobs.

MECHANISTIC APPROACH

The mechanistic approach has roots in classical industrial engineering. The focus of the mechanistic approach is identifying the simplest way to structure work that maximizes efficiency. This most often entails reducing the complexity of the work to provide more human resource efficiency—that is, making the work so simple that anyone can be trained quickly and easily to perform it. This approach focuses on designing jobs around the concepts of task specialization, skill simplification, and repetition.

For example at Chili's Restaurants, cooks used to cut up vegetables, meats, and other ingredients as part of preparing a meal. To increase efficiency, the organization decided to break this job into two smaller parts: one job, called "prep cook," involves coming in the morning to cut up the ingredients, and the second job, "line cook," involves using these prepared ingredients to assemble the final meal.[64]

Scientific management was one of the earliest and best-known statements of the mechanistic approach.[65] According to this approach, productivity could be maximized by taking a scientific approach to the process of designing jobs. Scientific management first sought to identify the "one best way" to perform the job. Once the best way to perform the work is identified, workers should be selected based on their ability to do the job, they should be trained in the standard "one best way" to perform the job, and they should be offered monetary incentives to motivate them to work at their highest capacity.

The scientific management approach was built upon in later years, resulting in a mechanistic approach that calls for jobs to be designed so that they are very simple. By designing jobs in this way, the organization reduces its need for high-ability individuals and thus becomes less dependent on individual workers. Individuals are easily replaceable—that is, a new employee can be trained to perform the job quickly and inexpensively.

Many jobs structured this way are performed in developing countries where there is a large supply of low-skilled labor and relatively lax legal guidelines regarding safety standards. For example, manufacturing silicon chips involves a process that exposes workers to a large number of carcinogens that are regulated less heavily in Asia than in the United States; hence, chip production has largely moved overseas.[66] As one might expect, this includes a host of "low-tech" manufacturing and assembly jobs, but increasingly this also involves "digital factory jobs."[67]

In some cases, jobs designed via mechanistic practices result in work that is so simple that a child could do it, and this is exactly what can happen in some undeveloped countries. This can lead to a backlash against companies that benefit from this unethical practice, and increasingly, organizations are taking the lead in preventing these kinds of practices. For example, when it learned that Uzbekistan cotton growers were using child labor to pick their crops, Walmart used its power to force them to abandon this practice. Working with other large U.S. retailers, Walmart took the lead to create the first system for tracking where cotton came from and organized a boycott against Uzbekistan, which quickly acquiesced to the corporate giant's pressure, freeing the children to return to school.[68] At the time, almost everyone else perceived that Walmart was a corporate villain and bully, assaulting workers, the environment, and consumers. Over the course of his tenure as the Walmart CEO, H. Lee Scott dramatically reversed this perception, and now Walmart is routinely listed as one of the most sustainable and corporately responsible organizations in the United States.[69]

MOTIVATIONAL APPROACH

The motivational approach to job design has roots in organizational psychology and management literature and, in many ways, emerged as a reaction to mechanistic approaches to job design. It focuses on the job characteristics that affect psychological meaning and motivational potential, and it views attitudinal variables (such as satisfaction) as the most important outcomes of job design. The prescriptions of the motivational approach focus on increasing the meaningfulness of jobs through such interventions as job enlargement, job enrichment, and the construction of jobs around socio-technical systems.[70]

A model of how job design affects employee reactions is the Job Characteristics Model.[71] According to this model, jobs can be described in terms of five characteristics. *Skill variety* is the extent to which the job requires a variety of skills to carry out the tasks. *Task identity* is the degree to which a job requires completing a "whole" piece of work from beginning to end. *Autonomy* is the degree to which the job allows an individual to make decisions about the way the work will be carried out. *Feedback* is the extent to which a person receives from the work itself clear information about performance effectiveness. *Task significance* is the extent to which the job has an important impact on the lives of other people. Although all five characteristics are important, the belief that the task is significant because performing it well leads to outcomes one values may be the most critical motivational aspect of work.[72] This can often be enhanced by making it clear to the worker how his or her job affects other people, whether they be customers, co-workers, or society in general.[73]

Job design interventions emphasizing the motivational approach tend to focus on increasing the meaningfulness of jobs. Much of the work on job enlargement (broadening the types of tasks performed), job enrichment (empowering workers by adding more decision-making authority to jobs), and self-managing work teams has its roots in the motivational approach to job design. Not all workers respond positively to enriched jobs like these because it requires some degree of flexibility and responsiveness to other people, but with the right workers, interventions such as these have been found to have dramatic effects on employee motivation.[74] Indeed, relatively elaborate theories have been developed that link specific personality traits to specific job characteristics; thus, to some degree, creating meaningful work requires matching the right type of person to the right type of task.[75]

In some cases, even work that may not be that interesting can be made significant by clarifying the link between what workers do and the outcomes of their work, perhaps far down the chain. For example, working in a call center trying to drum up contributions to a university's scholarship fund is boring, routine work that, more often than not, leads to rejection for employees. However, one experiment conducted in this setting found that after introducing the workers to scholarship recipients whose lives were changed by their awards, productivity among the call center team increased over 150%.[76] Helping workers see the meaningfulness of their jobs can be very motivational, and it is easy to lose this "line of sight" on a day-to-day basis if it is not reinforced.

BIOLOGICAL APPROACH

Ergonomics
The interface between individuals' physiological characteristics and the physical work environment.

The biological approach to job design comes primarily from the sciences of biomechanics (i.e., the study of body movements), work physiology, and occupational medicine, and it is usually referred to as *ergonomics*. **Ergonomics** is concerned with examining the interface between individuals' physiological characteristics and the physical work environment. The goal of this approach is to minimize physical strain on the worker by structuring the physical work environment around the way the human body works. It therefore focuses on outcomes such as physical fatigue, aches and pains, and health complaints. Any job that creates a significant number of injuries is a target for ergonomic redesign.

The biological approach has been applied in redesigning equipment used in jobs that are physically demanding. Such redesign is often aimed at reducing the physical demands of certain jobs so that anyone can perform them. In addition, many biological interventions focus on redesigning machines and technology, such as adjusting the height of the computer keyboard to minimize occupational illnesses (like carpal tunnel syndrome). The design of chairs and desks to fit posture requirements is very important in many office jobs and is another example of the biological approach to job design.

Although providing comfortable, ergonomically designed chairs is certainly laudable, recent research suggests that getting employees out of their chairs is also critically important when it comes to health outcomes. That is, the evidence is becoming increasingly clear that merely sitting for long periods can be damaging to employees. From an evolutionary perspective, the human body was designed to move, and long stretches of sedentary behavior are at odds with this design. For example, people who are above the mean in "time spent sitting" have a 24% greater risk of developing colon cancer, a 32% higher risk of endometrial cancer, and a 21% increased risk of lung cancer, even when one controls for the amount of physical exercise that people get when they are not sitting. Thus, office redesign programs that involve the introduction of treadmill desks or stand-up desks are becoming increasingly common elements of design, and some organizations are trying to make standing, rather than sitting, the default position for performing jobs.[77] However, as the "Evidence-Based HR" box illustrates, too much time standing can also be problematic when it comes to ergonomics.

EVIDENCE-BASED HR

One critical ergonomic element associated with work is the degree to which the work requires one to sit. In terms of safety, nothing would seem less dangerous than sitting in a comfortable chair all day, but in fact, research has long recognized that sedentary behavior, when taken to excess, is highly problematic for one's health. Sitting for long durations triggers physiological changes in the body that are associated with cardiovascular disease and diabetes, and, sadly, regular exercise after work does not seem to ameliorate these problems. Numerous interventions have been investigated to help reduce the problems caused by sitting, one of which is the stand-up desk.

Unfortunately, the most recent evidence suggests that standing too long also is associated with negative health outcomes. Excessive standing causes people to lean in odd directions, resulting in musculoskeletal problems, back problems, foot problems, carotid artery disease, and even varicose veins. Ergonomic science is now homing in on the precise formula for mixing sitting, standing, and light activity while at work for a standard eight-hour day. The current evidence suggests that the best mix includes two to four hours of standing and roughly 15 episodes of light activity (two minutes each) spread throughout the day, but that few workers are able to maintain the discipline required for this balance without some technical aid, such as sensors to remind them when to do what for how long a period.

SOURCES: S. Reddy, "The Price We Pay for Sitting Too Much," *Wall Street Journal*, September 28, 2015; C. Paddock, "Prolonged Standing Can Cause Health Problems Too," *Medical News Today*, July 15, 2015.

In addition to the direct effects of these kinds of interventions on worker well-being, such programs also have a positive psychological effect on workers by emphasizing an organizational climate that values safety and health.[78] That is, in addition to changes in design, some organizations try to instill a safety culture by giving each and every employee the power to report, or better yet, stop any worker who engages in unsafe behavior. At Chevron, for example, any worker within its headquarters office in San Ramon, California, can halt an activity he or she deems unsafe by taking out a small white "stop work" card. Thus, in terms of decision-making authority, each person has the

INTEGRITY IN ACTION

Workers' Rights Groups Give FIFA a Red Card

The International Federation of Association Football (FIFA) is the governing body for world soccer. Although many sports fans may be familiar with the scandal surrounding FIFA when it comes to on-the-field issues, this organization is also coming under heavy ethical scrutiny when it comes to off-the-field activity related to labor practices. Specifically, in the run-up for the 2022 World Cup that will be held in Qatar, FIFA has been cited by human rights groups for its treatment of migrant construction workers, most of whom hail from Bangladesh, India, Nepal, and the Philippines.

At the heart of the problems in Qatar is the system known as *kafala,* under which employers sponsor migrant workers. In most cases, the workers within this system have to pay up to one year's salary to handlers in their home country to get a job in the Gulf, but then they fall into debt when they learn that they were lied to about their actual wage. To pay off the original debt, workers have to take out loans at up to 30%, in effect, making them indentured servants. Because the workers need permission from their employer to return to their home country, the *kafala* system borders on modern-day slavery.

The powerlessness that workers experience when it comes to pay and mobility is compounded by their unsafe working conditions. One study estimated that as many as 4,000 workers could die prior to the 2022 games. This number was based on an earlier study of the number of deaths associated with a similar project—the construction of several new embassies in Qatar over a three-year period.

Although the *kafala* system was clearly not invented by U.S. firms, many American companies such as Bechtel, AECOM, and CH2M are involved in building the World Cup sites. Although technically these migrant laborers do not work directly for these organizations, thousands of them are employed by local subcontractors that the U.S. firms manage and oversee. Sunjeev Bery, an Amnesty International official who has studied the situation has noted that "companies and employers have a responsibility to prevent abuses even if they do not directly contribute to them," and this theme seems to be resonating back in the states. U.S. Senator Jerry Moran (R-Kansas), the chairman of the Senate Commerce Subcommittee on Consumer Protection, stated that "FIFA's culture of corruption is turning a blind eye to significant human rights violations and the tragic loss of lives." Given that the World Cup is likely to generate well over $4 billion in total revenue for FIFA, the need to "cut corners on cost" when it comes to labor like this is hard to defend ethically.

DISCUSSION QUESTION

1. Although sports entertainment is certainly a major industry when it comes to making profits, historically, outside a few professional sports, the industry has been loath to pay athletes and coaches their fair share of the revenue—often relying on an amateurism model. What might explain this mindset, and how is it related to the nature of the work?

SOURCES: B. Meier, "Labor Scrutiny for FIFA as a World Cup Rises in the Qatar Desert," *New York Times,* July 15, 2015; J. Montague, "Qatars Workers Cup," *New York Times,* April 24, 2016; A. Brennan, "FIFA and Qatar, A Money Story," *Forbes,* January 31, 2017.

power to identify and correct safety lapses regardless of where they reside on the formal organizational chart.[79] Indeed, in workplaces where safety is a major concern—such as working on a nuclear submarine—there may be hundreds of rules that new employees have to memorize prior to being able to start on the job.[80] Unfortunately, not all organizations necessarily share the same culture committed to employee health and well-being. Indeed, as the "Integrity in Action" box illustrates, some cultures place a greater emphasis on cost containment than on employee working conditions. In the Middle East, this culture has a name: *kafala.*

PERCEPTUAL–MOTOR APPROACH

The perceptual–motor approach to job design has roots in human-factors literature. Whereas the biological approach focuses on physical capabilities and limitations, the perceptual–motor approach focuses on human mental capabilities and limitations. The goal is to design jobs in a way that ensures they do not exceed people's mental capabilities and limitations. This approach generally tries to improve reliability, safety, and user reactions by designing jobs to reduce their information-processing requirements. In designing jobs, one looks at the least capable worker and then constructs job requirements that an individual of that ability level could meet. Similar to the mechanistic approach, this approach generally decreases the job's cognitive demands.

Recent changes in technological capacities hold the promise of helping to reduce job demands and errors, but in some cases, these developments have made the problem worse. The term "absence presence" has been coined to refer to the reduced attentive state that one might experience when simultaneously interacting with multiple media. For example, someone might be talking on a cell phone while driving a car, or surfing the Internet while attending a business meeting, or checking e-mail while preparing a presentation. In all these cases, the new technology serves as a source of distraction from the primary task, reducing performance and increasing the opportunities for errors.[81] In this case, the source of distraction is mental, not physical. Hence, ergonomic interventions aimed at reducing physical barriers are likely to be largely ineffective. For example, holding a stressful conversation while driving in heavy traffic is dangerous regardless of whether one is using a "hands-free" device or not. It is the mental strain, not the physical challenge, that makes this a hazardous activity.[82] Research shows that on complex tasks, even very short interruptions can break one's train of thought and derail performance. Thus, e-mail servers that have a feature that signals the arrival of each incoming message might best be turned off if the job incumbent cannot resist the temptation this creates to interrupt ongoing activity.[83]

In addition to external disruptions, information-processing errors are also increased in any context that requires a "hand-off" of information from one person to another. Indeed, as we noted earlier, problems with hand-offs have become a major concern in the field of medicine. As Mike Leonard, physician leader for patient safety at Kaiser's Colorado Permanente Medical Group, notes, "In almost all serious avoidable episodes of patient harm, communication failures play a central role." This would include information that fails to get handed off from nurses, doctors, and medical technicians to one another (e.g., the results of the most recent test that was handed to the attending doctor does not get handed to the attending nurse) or information that fails to get handed off from one work shift to another (e.g., a patient who has already received medication from one shift gets it again from the next shift). Problems between shifts are especially likely due to fatigue and burnout, which may be present at the end of a shift for workers in stressful jobs.[84]

Increasingly, hospitals are borrowing the "SBAR" method, originally developed in commercial and military aviation as a means to hand off an airplane moving through different people's airspace, to standardize communication protocols at the hand-off point in medical contexts. SBAR stands for situation, background, assessment, and recommendation, which constitute the four components of every successful hand-off. That is, in a few seconds, the person handing off the patient needs to get control of the situation by demanding the listener's attention (situation), then relay enough information to establish the context or the problem (background), then give an overall evaluation of the condition (assessment), and finally make a specific suggestion about the next best course of action (recommendation). At one hospital that introduced this procedure, the rate of adverse events (i.e., unexpected medical problems that cause harm) was reduced by more than half, from 90 to 40 for every 1,000 patients receiving treatment.[85]

In many cases, team-based work design is a central component in terms of strategy and competitive advantage. In fact, even industries like apparel and clothing—where U.S. manufacturing was written-off for dead—are experiencing a renaissance due to team-based work design. For example, Boathouse Sports, a manufacturer of jerseys, uniforms, and jackets in Philadelphia, Pennsylvania, relies on flexible manufacturing teams and finds its own unique competitive advantage in adaptively responding to small orders, and then delivering results with the kind of speed that simply cannot be matched by offshore producers. Even though Boathouse prices are 10–15% higher, they can deliver on most small orders in four weeks, compared to Chinese manufacturers, which would take over eight weeks. Indeed, the high cost of shipping expenses due to the recent spike in oil prices is even cutting into the price differential. Thus, although some observers have suggested that global competition is eliminating high-wage manufacturing jobs where workers have a strong voice in how the work gets accomplished, in many corners of the economy, high-priced and empowered workers are more than earning their own way.[86]

A LOOK BACK

Promoting Collaboration at Work

This chapter opened with a vignette that illustrated how the formal design of an organization's structure trickles down to affect the ability of individuals to effectively execute their roles. Well-intentioned efforts to decentralize authority and promote collaboration, when left unchecked, can result in confusion and role overload that harms the organization's ability to accomplish its mission. We also showed throughout the chapter numerous methods and examples of how organizations can effectively design work and create jobs in which duties are clear, the work is meaningful, and workers are protected from unsafe conditions.

QUESTIONS

1. The analysis of work-flow design traditionally starts at the end of the process, with the final product or service that is to be rendered. One then works back to determine the best process for this, and then determines the appropriate inputs. If an employer wants to commit to processes that highlight the role of effective collaboration and teamwork, how could the process of work-flow design play out and how might the results be different than if the organization was committed to processes aimed at promoting individual autonomy?

2. Although there are advantages and disadvantages to different structural configurations, why might it be more difficult to change one's structure in some directions than others? Specifically, how are the HR challenges associated with moving from centralized and functional structures to decentralized and divisional structures different from the challenge of moving in the other direction?

3. We have seen throughout this chapter that many of the ways to reduce the cost of getting jobs done come at some price to workers who have to do those jobs. What can be done to promote a more just, fair, humane, and sustainable workforce in all corners of the world? Does the competitive nature of product or labor markets mean that "nice guys always finish last?"

SUMMARY

The analysis and design of work is one of the most important components to developing and maintaining a competitive advantage. Strategy implementation is virtually impossible without thorough attention devoted to work-flow analysis, job analysis, and job design. Managers need to understand the entire work-flow process in their work unit to ensure that the process maximizes efficiency and effectiveness. To understand this process, managers also must have clear,

detailed information about the jobs that exist in the work unit, and the way to gain this information is through job analysis. Equipped with an understanding of the work-flow process and the existing job, managers can redesign jobs to ensure that the work unit is able to achieve its goals while individuals within the unit benefit from the various work outcome dimensions such as motivation, satisfaction, safety, health, and achievement. This is one key to competitive advantage.

KEY TERMS

Centralization, 161
Departmentalization, 161
Job analysis, 169

Job description, 171
Job specification, 172
Job design, 178

Job redesign, 178
Ergonomics, 180

DISCUSSION QUESTIONS

1. Assume you are the manager of a fast-food restaurant. What are the outputs of your work unit? What are the activities required to produce those outputs? What are the inputs?
2. Based on Question 1, consider the cashier's job. What are the outputs, activities, and inputs for that job?
3. Consider the "job" of college student. Perform a job analysis on this job. What are the tasks required in the job? What are the knowledge, skills, and abilities necessary to perform those tasks? What environmental trends or shocks (like computers) might change the job, and how would that change the skill requirements?
4. Discuss how the following trends are changing the skill requirements for managerial jobs in the United States: (a)

increasing use of computers, (b) increasing international competition.
5. Why is it important for a manager to be able to conduct a job analysis? What are the negative outcomes that would result from not understanding the jobs of those reporting to the manager?
6. What are the trade-offs between the different approaches to job design? Which approach do you think should be weighted most heavily when designing jobs?
7. For the cashier job in Question 2, which approach to job design was most influential in designing that job? In the context of the total work-flow process of the restaurant, how would you redesign the job to more heavily emphasize each of the other approaches?

SELF-ASSESSMENT EXERCISE

Additional assignable self-assessments available in Connect.

The chapter described how the Department of Labor's Occupational Information Network (O*NET) can help employers. The system was also designed to help job seekers. To see if you think this new system meets the goal of promoting "the effective education, training, counseling, and employment needs of the American workforce," visit O*NET's website at https://www.onetonline.org/.

Look up the listing for your current job or dream job. List the skills identified for that job. For each skill, evaluate how well your own experiences and abilities enable you to match the job requirements.

EXERCISING STRATEGY

Orion and UPS: Plotting a Strategy for Efficiency and Savings

On average, one single UPS driver can log over 200 miles and make over 120 stops every day. When you multiply this times thousands of drivers who work five or six days a week for a year, then you begin to see how even very small improvements in efficiency can generate huge sums of money when it comes to saving on gas and vehicle wear and tear. To the CEO of this business, small things can mean a lot. If you can reengineer a process, the gains can be greater than you think. In fact, UPS can save $50 million a year by just reducing the aggregated travel distance for its average driver by just one mile.

This is critical to UPS because it competes directly with FedEx, but unlike FedEx, which employs a private contractor model and delivers mainly to businesses, UPS manages a high-wage union workforce that delivers mainly to widely scattered households. The problem with planning the best route each day, however, is that there are literally over a billion options. If you were to have each driver plan his or her own route, there would be wide variability in their decisions, and the odds that any one of them might come up with the optimal path are—for all intents and purposes—zero.

This is where the computer program "Orion" comes in. Orion is a 1,000-page algorithm that tries to mathematically determine the optimal route for making those 120 stops every day for UPS drivers. Working like a GPS system on steroids, Orion continually updates a driver's schedule and automatically vectors the vehicle based on two criteria: optimum efficiency and consistency. This latter criterion, consistency, is one of the features that make Orion different from most purely mathematical optimizing programs. The program recognizes that both human operators and customers place a great deal of value on consistency; thus, it sacrifices some degree of pure efficiency in order to create a comfortable routine in terms of delivery times and routes.

QUESTIONS

1. Can you think of any other industries or jobs in which a program like Orion might have value, and is this a product or service that you believe UPS could market to other companies?
2. What role does the company's CEO play in establishing the competitive strategy and how does this "trickle down," when it comes to the organization's structure and culture?
3. What are some of the major difficulties associated with trying to change an unethical culture, and is it realistic for a new CEO to think he or she can change the culture without terminating a large number of upper-level managers?

SOURCES: S. Rosenbush and L. Stevens, "At UPS, the Algorithm is the Driver," *Wall Street Journal*, February 16, 2015; D. Zax, "Brown Down: UPS Drivers versus UPS Algorithms," *Fast Company Online*, January 3, 2013.

MANAGING PEOPLE

The Role of GM's Structure in a Product Recall

Organizations exist in order to allow people to accomplish goals and missions that would far outstrip what could ever be done by a single person working alone. Large, complex missions have to be broken down into smaller parts that can be executed by individuals whose contributions can then be integrated together. Unfortunately, when the structure created by this process is ineffective, this means that organizations can also do more harm than could ever be done by a single person working alone. Nowhere was this more evident than in the 2014 recall of 2.7 million General Motor (GM) vehicles in response to failures in the ignition system that resulted in the death or injury of over 500 customers, in addition to financial losses of over $400 million.

Two specific problems associated with the structure of GM contributed to the ignition system disaster. First, the structure created functional silos in which people who worked on one aspect of the cars rarely spoke to people who worked in other functional areas. For example, the switch problem was, in part, a result of a single engineer who redesigned a faulty part but failed to renumber it. Since it was not renumbered, when the part moved through other divisions down through the line, those divisions all thought they were working on the original part. Then, when reports of cars stalling began rolling in, this was treated as a customer satisfaction problem, not a safety issue or a design flaw. Thus, the personnel who were monitoring customer satisfaction never talked to the personnel in design, who were not even aware of the problem until it was too late.

A second problem with GM's structure was that it was not at all clear who had decision-making authority for different decisions, and people at lower levels of the organization were reluctant to take responsibility for problems or pass bad news up the organizational chart. An external investigation of the incident conducted by the U.S. Attorney General's Office revealed that many people were aware of the problem as far back as 2001, but these individuals either said nothing or pointed the finger of blame at other units, and so no one actually did anything to solve the problem. In fact, when the Attorney General's Office asked one worker who knew about the problem if "fixing the problem was part of your job description," the person simply answered no. The report from the Attorney General's Office specifically noted that "no single person owned any decision related to the ignition switch problem."

The ignition switch problem was one of the first to fall on the desk of GM's new CEO, Mary Barra, who vowed to fix the structural problems that contributed to this costly incident. Barra noted that "we used to have an organizational structure built around parts—the body, the interior, the electrical structure, and unfortunately, that created a situation in which people were expert in this or that without recognizing people don't buy this or that—they buy a car and we've got to pull it together, and people have to talk." She also noted that GM would be "restructuring operations to prioritize safety." This was accomplished by creating a system of "czars" who had specific decision-making authority that cut across functional units and who all reported to a single new vice president of global safety.

QUESTIONS

1. The analysis of work-flow design traditionally starts at the end of the process, with the final product or service to be rendered. One then works backward to determine the best process for this, and then determines the appropriate inputs. If an employer like GM wants to commit to processes that highlight the role of safety, how could the process of work-flow design play out, and how might the results be different than if the organization was committed to processes aimed at reducing costs?

2. In this case, GM employed a traditional centralized structure with strong functional silos. The vignette that opened this chapter suggested that many organizations are now employing team-based structures that cut across functions. How might this approach have helped prevent some of the problems illustrated in this case?

SOURCES: R. Foroohar, "Mary Barra's Bumpy Ride," *Time*, October 6, 2014, pp. 33–38; T. Higgens and N. Summers, "GM Recalls: How General Motors Silenced a Whistle-Blower," *Bloomberg Business Week*, June 14, 2014; P. Valdes-Dalpena and T. Yellin, "Steps to a Recall Nightmare," CNNMoney.com, May 21, 2014.

HR IN SMALL BUSINESS

Blink UX Takes a Hard Look at Work Design

The main human resource challenge that faced Blink UX was related to the company's small size. As a research and digital-product design firm specializing in user experience (UX), Blink offers meaningful work to talented professionals. Its employees—researchers and designers with master's and doctorate degrees—enable the firm's client businesses to improve how they interact with their customers online. But with only a few dozen employees, the Seattle-based firm offered limited opportunities for career growth. Blink's founder and CEO, Karen Clark Cole, tried to hire people who would stay and contribute until retirement, but employees would leave after a few years when they saw no opportunities for advancement.

Clark Cole took a hard look at the way work was structured. Employees were assigned to project teams. Project directors controlled the decisions related to their projects, which sometimes caused team members to focus more on satisfying their director. The director was left to ensure that the team focused on clients' needs.

Though this setup had allowed Blink to build an expanding client base and great reputation, Clark Cole realized it was holding back the full potential of her firm's people. So she eliminated the lines of authority; now each employee takes responsibility for satisfying clients. Employees also are asked to choose specialty areas in which to become experts. A team called the GROW group (with rotating membership) meets each week to assign employees to fill roles on projects, aiming to ensure employees get assigned to roles that will help them develop their careers as well as use their areas of expertise to provide great service and creative solutions.

Yet another round of change is in the works. After several years of rapid growth in revenues, Blink UX is preparing to expand into several new branch offices. As Clark Cole ramps up the hiring process to staff those offices, she needs to be careful that new employees can function well in a culture that values learning, flexibility, and the ability to take the perspective of others, including clients and end users.

QUESTIONS

1. As described, is Blink UX's redesigned approach to teamwork an example of a structure based on function or one based on customers? How well does this structure fit the company's goals for employee empowerment?

2. Does the example of job redesign at Blink UX sound most like an example of job enlargement, job rotation, or job enrichment? Explain your answer.

SOURCES: "America's Best Small Companies 2016: Blink UX," *Forbes,* http://www.forbes.com; Karen Clark Cole, "Blink UX Named One of *Forbes* Magazine's Best Small Companies in America!" Blink UX blog, February 4, 2016, http://blinkux.com; Adam Worcester, "For Blink's Karen Clark Cole, UX Is a Tidal Wave of Opportunity," *BizWomen*, December 1, 2015, http://www.bizjournals.com; Amber Johnson, "Creating a Business That's Optimized for Personal Growth and a Thriving Culture: Blink UX," blog of the Benedictine University Center for Values-Driven Leadership, March 13, 2014, http://www.cvdl.org.

NOTES

1. N. Leiber, "Portuguese Shoemakers Get Fancy," *Businessweek*, September 7, 2015, pp. 45–46.
2. B. Snavely, "Fiat Chrysler Returns to $101.2 Million Profit in Q1," *USA Today*, April 29, 2015, www.usatoday.com.
3. J. Jargon, "McDonald's Menu Problem: It's Supersized," *Wall Street Journal*, December 3, 2014.
4. L. Chao, "Trucker Teams Drive to the Rescue of Online Shipping," *Wall Street Journal*, December 26, 2015, www.wsj.com.
5. L. Landro, "The Doctor's Team Will See You Now," *Wall Street Journal*, February 17, 2014.
6. J. Christensen, "Medical Errors May Be the Third Leading Cause of Death in the U.S.," CNN.com, May 3, 2016.
7. G. S. Van der Vegt, B. J. M. Emans, and E. Van de Vliert, "Patterns of Interdependence in Work Teams: A Two-Level Investigation of the Relations with Job and Team Satisfaction," *Personnel Psychology* 54 (2001), pp. 51–70.
8. C. M. Barnes, J. R. Hollenbeck, D. T. Wagner, D. S. DeRue, J. D. Nahrgang, and K. M. Schwind, "Harmful Help: The Costs of Backing-up Behaviors in Teams," *Journal of Applied Psychology* 93 (2008), pp. 529–39.
9. S. Shellenbarger, "Don't Be the Office Schedule Wrecker," *Wall Street Journal*, www.wsj.com, July 7, 2015.
10. B. Greeley, "We're from Private Equity and We're Here to Help," *Businessweek*, April 30, 2012, pp. 55–59.
11. E. Porter, "The Mirage of a Return to Manufacturing Greatness," *New York Times*, April 26, 2016, https://www.nytimes.com/2016/04/27/business/economy/the-mirage-of-a-return-to-manufacturing-greatness.html.
12. P. Engardio, "Lean and Mean Gets Extreme," *Bloomberg Businessweek*, March 23, 2009, pp. 60–62.
13. T. Black, "Downsides of Just-in-Time Inventory," *Bloomberg Businessweek*, March 28, 2011, pp. 17–18.
14. N. Carr, "Automation Makes Us Dumb, *Wall Street Journal*, November 21, 2014.
15. M. Phillips and P. Coy, "Choosing Profits over Productivity," *Bloomberg Businessweek*, May 19, 2014, pp. 12–13.
16. J. Whalen, "Hospitals Cut Costs by Getting Doctors to Stick to Guidelines," *Wall Street Journal*, September, 22, 2014.
17. S. Kolhatkar, "Where Have All the Secretaries Gone?" *Businessweek*, April 8, 2013, pp. 67–69.
18. S. Grobart, "Hooray for Hierarchy," *Businessweek*, January 14, 2013, p. 74.
19. A. Schatz, "Contractors Point Fingers over Health Care Website," *Wall Street Journal*, October 24, 2013.
20. D. Bennett, "The Dunbar Number," *Businessweek*, January 10, 2013, pp. 53–56.
21. B. Gruley and L. Patton, "The franchises are not lovin' it. *Businessweek*, September 16, 2015, pp. 64–69.
22. J. Chung, "The Franchises Are Not Lovin' It," *Businessweek*, September 16, 2015, pp. 64–69.
23. J Jargon, "All Day Breakfast is a Pick-Me-up for McDonalds," *Wall Street Journal*, www.wsj.com, January 25, 2016.
24. K. Akter, "The Bloodshed Behind Our Cheap Clothes," CNN.com, May 3, 2013.
25. R. E. Silverman, "Who's the Boss? There Isn't One," *Wall Street Journal*, June 13, 2012.
26. R. Greenfield, "The Future Is Bossless," *Businessweek*, December, 7, 2016, p. 63.
27. A. Vance, A. H.P.'s , "Bet in Buying E.D.S. Seems a Winner." *New York Times Online*. September 22, 2009.
28. B. Worthen, C. Tuna, and J. Scheck, "Companies More Prone to Go Vertical," *Wall Street Journal*, November 30, 2009, pp. A1, A16.
29. T. Neff and J. Citrin, "You're in Charge: Now What?" *Fortune*, January 24, 2005, pp. 109–20.
30. P. Orfalea and A. Marsh, *Copy This!: How I Turned Dyslexia, ADHD, and 100 Square Feet into a Company Called Kinko's* (New York: Workman Publishing, 2007).
31. W. D. Sine, H. Mitsuhashi, and D. A. Kirsch, "Revisiting Burns and Stalker: Formal Structure and New Venture Performance in Emerging Economic Sectors," *Academy of Management Journal* 49 (2006), pp. 121–32.
32. J. E. Ellis, "At P&G, the Innovation Well Runs Dry," *Businessweek*, September 12, 2012, pp. 24–26.
33. T. Henneman, "Is HR at Its Breaking Point," *Workforce Management*, April 2013, pp. 28–33.
34. P. Glader, "It's Not Easy Being Lean," *Wall Street Journal*, June 19, 2006, pp. B1, B3.
35. N. Byrnes, "The Art of Motivation," *BusinessWeek*, May 1, 2006, pp. 57–62.
36. J. R. Hollenbeck, H. Moon, A. Ellis, B. West, D. R. Ilgen, L. Sheppard, C. O. Porter, and J. A. Wagner, "Structural Contingency Theory and Individual Differences: Examination of External and Internal Person–Team Fit," *Journal of Applied Psychology* 87 (2002), pp. 599–606.
37. J. A. Marquez, "Taking a Longer View," *Workforce Management*, May 21, 2006, pp. 18–22.
38. A. Weintraub and M. Tirrell, "Eli Lilly's Drug Assembly Line," *Businessweek*, February 25, 2010, pp. 34–35.
39. D. A. Hofmann, F. P. Morgeson, and S. J. Gerras, "Climate as a Moderator of the Relationship between Leader–Member Exchange and Content-Specific Citizenship: Safety Climate as an Exemplar," *Journal of Applied Psychology* 88 (2003), pp. 170–78.
40. A. Blinder, "Donald Blankenship Sentenced to a Year in Prison in Mine Safety Case, *New York Times*, April 6, 2016, https://www.nytimes.com/2016/04/07/us/donald-blankenship-sentenced-to-a-year-in-prison-in-mine-safety-case.html.
41. M. Rosenwald, "Bound by Habit," *Businessweek*, March 19, 2012, pp. 106–7.
42. L. Weber, "Help Wanted—on Writing Job Descriptions," *Wall Street Journal*, October 2, 2013.
43. E. C. Dierdorf and F. P. Morgeson, "Effects of Descriptor Specificity and Observability on Incumbent Work Analysis Ratings," *Personnel Psychology* 62 (2009), pp. 601–28.
44. P. Lievens, J. I. Sanchez, D. Bartram, and A. Brown, "Lack of Consensus among Competency Ratings of the Same Occupation: Noise or Substance," *Journal of Applied Psychology* 95 (2010), pp. 562–71.
45. C. Mims, "In 'People Analytics,' You're Not a Human, You're a Data Point," *Wall Street Journal*, February 16, 2015.
46. J. R. Hollenbeck and B. Jamieson, "Human Capital, Social Capital, and Social Network Analysis: Implications for Strategic Human Resource Management," *Academy of Management Perspectives,* 29 (2015), pp. 370–385.
47. R. McMillan, "Social Networking Comes (at Last) to the Workplace," *Wall Street Journal*, March 14, 2016, www.wsj.com.

48. S. Shellenbarger, "Stop Wasting Everyone's Time," *Wall Street Journal*, December 2, 2014.

49. A. K. Weyman, "Investigating the Influence of Organizational Role on Perceptions of Risk in Deep Coal Mines," *Journal of Applied Psychology* 88 (2003), pp. 404–12.

50. L. E. Baranowski and L. E. Anderson, "Examining Rater Source Variation in Work Behavior to KSA Linkages," *Personnel Psychology* 58 (2005), pp. 1041–54.

51. E. McCormick and R. Jeannerette, "The Position Analysis Questionnaire," in *The Job Analysis Handbook for Business, Industry, and Government* (New York: Wiley, 1988), pp. 880–901.

52. M. Biron and P. Bamberger, "Aversive Workplace Conditions and Abseteeism: Taking Referent Group Norms and Supervisor Support into Account," *Journal of Applied Psychology*, 97 (2012), pp. 901–12.

53. C. Coleman, "How to Create a Workplace People Never Want to Leave," *Businessweek*, April 11, 2013, p. 51.

54. N. G. Peterson, M. D. Mumford, W. C. Borman, P. R. Jeanneret, and E. A. Fleishman, *An Occupational Information System for the 21st Century: The Development of O*NET* (Washington, DC: American Psychological Association, 1999).

55. N. G. Peterson, M. D. Mumford, W. C. Borman, P. R. Jeanneret, E. A. Fleishman, K. Y. Levin, M. A. Campion, M. S. Mayfield, F. P. Morgenson, K. Pearlman, M. K. Gowing, A. R. Lancaster, M. B. Silver, and D. M. Dye, "Understanding Work Using the Occupational Information Network (O*NET): Implications for Practice and Research," *Personnel Psychology* 54 (2001), pp. 451–92.

56. P. J. Taylor, W. D. Li, K. Shi, and W. C. Borman, "The Transportability of Job Information across Countries," *Personnel Psychology* 61 (2008), pp. 69–111.

57. C. C. Lapolice, G. W. Carter, and J. W. Johnson, "Linking O*NET Descriptors to Occupational Literacy Requirements Using Job Component Validation," *Personnel Psychology* 61 (2008), pp. 405–441.

58. M. K. Lindell, C. S. Clause, C. J. Brandt, and R. S. Landis, "Relationship between Organizational Context and Job Analysis Ratings," *Journal of Applied Psychology* 83 (1998), pp. 769–76.

59. F. P. Morgeson and M. A. Campion, "Social and Cognitive Sources of Potential Inaccuracy in Job Analysis," *Journal of Applied Psychology* 82 (1997), pp. 627–55.

60. S. Varney, "Rising Obesity Rates Put Strain on Nursing Homes," *New York Times*, December 14, 2015, https://www.nytimes.com/2015/12/15/health/rising-obesity-rates-put-strain-on-nursing-homes.html.

61. S. Caudron, "Jobs Disappear When Work Becomes More Important," *Workforce*, January 2000, pp. 30–32.

62. M. Campion and P. Thayer, "Development and Field Evaluation of an Interdisciplinary Measure of Job Design," *Journal of Applied Psychology* 70 (1985), pp. 29–34.

63. F. P. Morgeson and S. E. Humphrey, "The Work Design Questionnaire (WDQ): Developing and Validating a Comprehensive Measure for Assessing Job Design and the Nature of Work," *Journal of Applied Psychology* 91 (2006), pp. 1312–39.

64. J. Jargon, "Chili's Feels Heat to Pare Costs," *Wall Street Journal*, January 28, 2011, pp. B8.

65. F. Taylor, *The Principles of Scientific Management* (New York: W. W. Norton, 1967) (originally published in 1911 by Harper & Brothers).

66. Simpson, "Samsung's War at Home," *Bloomberg Businessweek*, April 10, 2014, pp. 60–65.

67. B. Helm, "Life on the Web's Factory Floor," *BusinessWeek*, May 22, 2006, pp. 70–71.

68. M. Gunther, "Wal-Mart: A Bully Benefactor," CNNMoney.com, December 5, 2008, p. 1.

69. L. Delevevigne, "Surprising Corporate Do-gooders," CNNMoney.com, January 20, 2009, p. 1.

70. R. Griffin and G. McMahan, "Motivation through Job Design," in *OB: The State of the Science*, ed. J. Greenberg (Hillsdale, NJ: Lawrence Erlbaum Associates, 1993).

71. R. Hackman and G. Oldham, *Work Redesign* (Boston: Addison-Wesley, 1980).

72. A. M. Grant, "The Significance of Task Significance," *Journal of Applied Psychology* 93 (2007), pp. 108–24.

73. A. M. Grant, E. M. Campbell, G. Chen, K. Cottone, D. Lapedia, and K. Lee, "Impact and Art of Motivation Maintenance: The Effects of Contact with Beneficiaries on Persistence Behavior," *Organizational Behavior and Human Decision Processes* 103 (2007), pp. 53–67.

74. F. W. Bond, P. E. Flaxman, and D. Bunce, "The Influence of Psychological Flexibility on Work Redesign: Mediated Moderation of a Work Reorganization Intervention," *Journal of Applied Psychology* 93 (2008), pp. 645–54.

75. M. R. Barrick, M. K. Mount, and N. Li, "The Theory of Purposeful Work Behavior: The Role of Personality, Higher-Order Goals, and Job Characteristics," *Academy of Management Review* 38 (2013), pp. 132–153.

76. B. Schwartz, "Rethinking Work," *New York Times*, August 28, 2015, https://www.nytimes.com/2015/08/30/opinion/sunday/rethinking-work.html.

77. A. Park, "Stand Up for Yourself," *Time*, September 8, 2014, pp. 22–23.

78. S. Mewman, M. A. Griffen, and C. Mason, "Safety in Work Vehicles: A Multilevel Study Linking Safety Values and Individual Predictors to Work-related Driving Crashes," *Journal of Applied Psychology* 93 (2008), pp. 632–44.

79. R. Feintzieg and A. Berzon, "Safety Cops Patrol the Office for High Heels," *Wall Street Journal*, July 27, 2014.

80. J. E. Barnes, "Life on a Navy Sub Relies on Rules: Some Dead Serious, Others Completely Ridiculous," *Wall Street Journal*, May 1, 2014.

81. D. K. Berman, "Technology Has Us So Plugged into Data, We Have Turned Off," *Wall Street Journal*, November 10, 2003, pp. A1–A2.

82. M. Beck, "What Cocktail Parties Teach Us," *Wall Street Journal*, April 22, 2012.

83. J. Baker, "From Open Doors to Gated Communities," *BusinessWeek*, September 8, 2003, p. 36.

84. L. E. LaBlanc, J. J. Hox, W. B. Schaufell, T. W. Taris, and M. C. W. Peters, "Take Care! The Evaluation of a Team-Based Burnout Intervention Program for Oncology Health Care Providers," *Journal of Applied Psychology* 92 (2007), pp. 213–27.

85. L. Landro, "Hospitals Combat Errors at the 'Hand-Off,'" *Wall Street Journal*, June 28, 2006, pp. D1, D2.

86. M. N. Leiber, "Suddenly, Made in the USA Looks like a Strategy," *Businessweek*, March 28, 2011, pp. 57–58.

CHAPTER

5

Human Resource Planning and Recruitment

LEARNING OBJECTIVES

After reading this chapter, you should be able to:

LO 5-1   Discuss how to align a company's strategic direction with its human resource planning. *page 193*

LO 5-2   Determine the labor demand for workers in various job categories. *page 194*

LO 5-3   Discuss the advantages and disadvantages of various ways of eliminating a labor surplus and avoiding a labor shortage. *page 196*

LO 5-4   Describe the various recruitment policies that organizations adopt to make job vacancies more attractive. *page 212*

LO 5-5   List the various sources from which job applicants can be drawn, their relative advantages and disadvantages, and the methods for evaluating them. *page 214*

LO 5-6   Explain the recruiter's role in the recruitment process, the limits the recruiter faces, and the opportunities available. *page 219*

Biting the Hand That Feeds You?

California's Central Valley is home to some of the nation's most fertile farmland. Over six million people live in the area, and the fields bring in $35 billion a year in revenue. It is a bustling region in a state that provides the United States with more of its food than any other state. However, in 2016, large portions of the annual crop rotted in the fields because employers were not able to find workers to harvest the wide variety of produce grown in the valley. In general, California's agricultural economy reported lost production across the board of 8–10% that year, and some individual growers lost over 25% of their crop due to labor shortages caused by crackdowns on illegal workers from Mexico.

Farther east, meat producers in the U.S. Midwest also experienced similar problems with labor shortages that limited production. Already burned by hiring illegal immigrants in prior years, only to watch them be deported, meat producers changed their strategy 10 years earlier and turned to a new supply of labor—refugees—to solve their chronic labor shortage problem. U.S. regulations allow refugees to work as soon as they arrive in the country, and over the years, the share of immigrant labor in Midwest slaughterhouses has grown to 35%. This strategy was upended in 2017, when U.S. policy placed restrictions on refugees entering the country, cutting this supply of labor in half. Like produce, meat is a commodity that needs to be processed in a timely fashion; thus, labor shortages also threaten the viability of this segment of the economy, worth $29 billion.

The common element to the problems plaguing these two industries is that the nature of the work is so undesirable that no native-born Americans would be willing to take these jobs. The work is physically demanding and conducted either in the scorching hot sun or within freezing ice coolers at very low pay. However, the strategies of relying on illegal workers and refugees to plug this labor gap are becoming increasingly untenable, leaving the human resource management professionals in these industries struggling to meet the demand for labor.

H2-A visas are temporary visas issued strictly to farmworkers, and back in California, employers are trying to get the government to raise the number of H2-As, but they are running into stiff political opposition. This has also been the experience of large meat producers, which have been unable to get relief from the limits on refugees, many of which come from predominantly Muslim countries such as Somalia. Joseph Pezzini, now CEO of Ocean Mist farms, notes that when it comes to feeding the nation, "labor has always been an important part of what we do, but there were other resources issues that would take center stage like safety or water. But now the highest priority issue is the availability of labor."

SOURCES: C. Dickerson and J. Medina, "California Farmers Backed Trump, but Now Fear Losing Field Workers," *New York Times,* February 9, 2017; K. Gee and J. Bunge, "Tighter Refugee Rules Seen Squeezing Meat Companies," *Wall Street Journal,* January 28, 2017, www.wsj.com; "Big Meat Braces for a Labor Shortage," *Businessweek,* February 8, 2017, pp. 19–21; I. Brat, "On U.S. Farms, Fewer Hands for the Harvest," *Wall Street Journal,* August 12, 2015, www.wsj.com.

Introduction

Human resource managers are at the forefront of the worldwide war for competitive advantage. Organizations need to find the best set of workers for meeting their strategic objectives, attract those workers to their companies, and then get them to stay long enough to obtain some return on their investment. As our opening vignette shows, the failure to secure a sufficient supply of labor is crippling certain industries like agriculture and meat processing. Throughout this chapter, we will highlight other job categories where the demand for labor is outstripping the supply and what employers are trying to do to secure the workers they need. We will also examine occupations characterized by an over-supply of labor and what workers can do to make sure that the talents they develop fit the needs of the current labor market. Employers who are able to tap in to the best pool of talent for executing their own unique competitive strategy gain a competitive advantage over their rivals that is often sustainable for a long period.

The purpose of this chapter is to examine factors that influence the supply and demand for labor and, in particular, to focus on what HR managers can do in terms of planning and executing policies that give their firms competitive advantage in a dynamic environment. Although our focus is at the firm level, nations also compete in labor markets, and when a country begins to see most of its human talent emigrate, this type of "brain drain" can have a devastating impact on national competitiveness. For example, in Iran, 40% of the top graduates in undergraduate science and technology programs leave the country to attend graduate school in Europe and the United States, and then, upon matriculation, 90% never return to Iran.[1] Thus, the war for talent takes place at both the organizational level and the national level, and later in this chapter we will highlight some of the countries that are winning and losing this war.

Two of the major ways that societal trends and events affect employers are through (1) consumer markets, which affect the demand for goods and services, and (2) labor markets, which affect the supply of people to produce goods and services. In some cases, the market might be characterized by a labor shortage. In other cases, there might be a surplus of labor. Reconciling the difference between the supply and demand for labor presents a challenge for organizations, and how they address this challenge will affect their overall competitiveness.

There are three keys to effectively utilizing labor markets to one's competitive advantage. First, companies must have a clear idea of their current configuration of human resources. In particular, they need to know the strengths and weaknesses of their present stock of employees. Second, organizations must know where they are going in the future and be aware of how their present configuration of human resources relates to the configuration that will be needed. Third, where there are discrepancies between the present configuration and the configuration required for the future, organizations need programs that will address these discrepancies.

This chapter looks at tools and technologies that can help an organization develop and implement effective strategies for leveraging labor market "threats" into opportunities to gain competitive advantage. In the first half of the chapter, we lay out the steps that go into developing and implementing an HR plan. Through each section, we focus especially on recent trends and practices (like downsizing, employing temporary workers, and outsourcing) that can have a major impact on the firm's bottom line and overall reputation. In the second half of the chapter, we familiarize you with the process by which individuals find and choose jobs and the role of personnel recruitment in reaching these individuals and shaping their choices.

The Human Resource Planning Process

An overview of human resource planning is depicted in Figure 5.1. The process consists of forecasting, goal setting and strategic planning, and program implementation and evaluation. We discuss each of these stages in the next sections of this chapter.

FORECASTING

The first step in the planning process is **forecasting,** as shown in the top portion of Figure 5.1. In personnel forecasting, the HR manager attempts to ascertain the supply of and demand for various types of human resources. The primary goal is to predict areas within the organization where there will be future labor shortages or surpluses.

Forecasting, on both the supply and demand sides, can use either statistical methods or judgmental methods. Statistical methods are excellent for capturing historic trends in a company's demand for labor, and under the right conditions they give predictions that are much more precise than those that could be achieved through subjective judgments of a human forecaster. However, many important events that occur in the labor market have no historical precedent; hence, statistical methods that work from historical trends are of little use in such cases. With no historical precedent, one must rely on the pooled subjective judgments of experts, and their "best guesses" might be the only source from which to make inferences about the future. Typically, because of the complementary strengths and weaknesses of the two methods, companies that engage in human resource planning use a balanced approach.

An example of the forecasting process can be seen at Qualcomm, one of the world's biggest suppliers of chips for mobile phones. Qualcomm products handle cellular communications and computing in smartphones, and although one might think there is a never-ending demand for these types of chips, Qualcomm's analysis of the market in 2015 suggested that there was going to be an over-supply of its product in the future.

LO 5-1
Discuss how to align a company's strategic direction with its human resource planning.

Forecasting
The attempts to determine the supply of and demand for various types of human resources to predict areas within the organization where there will be future labor shortages or surpluses.

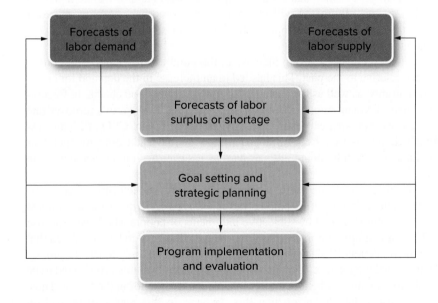

Figure 5.1

Overview of the Human Resource Planning Process

Samsung was the biggest buyer for Qualcomm's chips; however, Samsung's share of the cell phone market was shrinking, causing future collateral damage at Qualcomm. In addition, smaller upstarts like MediaTek were cutting into Qualcomm's share of the market, and then Samsung announced it was going to start manufacturing its own chips for its new Galaxy S6. According to Qualcomm's forecast, the company was likely to produce far too many chips for the market if it failed to take preventive steps, one of which included a workforce reduction of 155 people.[2]

Determining Labor Demand

LO 5-2
Determine the labor demand for workers in various job categories.

Typically, demand forecasts are developed around specific job categories or skill areas relevant to the organization's current and future state. Once the job categories or skills are identified, the planner needs to seek information that will help predict whether the need for people with those skills or in that job category will increase or decrease in the future. For example, due to the aging population in the United States, elder care is one of the fast-growing industries; thus, there is likely to be a high demand for workers with skills that suit this work. In contrast, the advent of e-mail, the Internet, and text messaging means that the demand for postal carriers is headed in the opposite direction.[3] Organizations differ in the sophistication with which such forecasts are derived.

At the most sophisticated level, an organization might have statistical models that predict labor demand for the next year given relatively objective statistics on leading indicators from the previous year. A **leading indicator** is an objective measure that accurately predicts future labor demand. For example, although the relationship between oil prices and demand for rig workers is well known, the drop in oil prices in 2015, attributed to the rapid growth of the fracking industry, came as a surprise to many. Hence, over 100,000 workers had to be laid off when this industry confronted an unanticipated change in demand.[4] Then, when the industry made a comeback in 2017, rather than hire back all of the workers, many firms in the industry turned to labor-saving automation that largely replaced the "roustabouts" who, in the past, performed the task of connecting hundreds of drill pipes. Sites that used to employ 20 workers now can be managed with 5, and the 15 jobs eliminated will probably never come back. As one manager noted, "It used to be that you had a toolbox full of wrenches and tubing benders, but now, your main tool is a laptop."[5]

Leading indicator
An objective measure that accurately predicts future labor demand.

Similarly, statistics suggest a strong increase in the numbers of people eating out at U.S. restaurants, relative to the past. This has led to an increase in the demand for cooks at high-end restaurants, as well as for managers of low-level fast-food chains. In December 2016, the unemployment rate was at 4.7%, a 10-year low. This led to a turnover rate among restaurant workers that exceeded 100% a year. Gregg Flynn, CEO of Flynn Restaurant Group, which runs Taco Bell, Applebee's, and Panera Bread Company, spoke for many in this industry when he noted, "It's as hard as it's ever been to attract and retain great people."[6]

Statistical planning models are useful when there is a long, stable history that can be used to reliably detect relationships among variables. However, these models almost always have to be complemented by subjective judgments of people who have expertise in the area. There are simply too many one-time changes that have to be considered that cannot be captured accurately in statistical models. For example, only a decade ago, no one would have heard the job title "cloud computing engineer," yet this is projected to be one of the fast-growing areas when it comes to the demand for labor in the future. Thus, there are no historical data for a job like this. Experts in this area rely instead on subjective judgments; hence, Robert Patrick, vice president for marketing at Hewlett-Packard, confidently predicts that "the clouds skill gap is the single biggest barrier to the future adoption of cloud infrastructures."[7]

Determining Labor Supply

Once a company has projected labor demand, it needs to get an indicator of the firm's labor supply. Determining the internal labor supply calls for a detailed analysis of how many people are currently in various job categories (or who have specific skills) within the company. This analysis is then modified to reflect changes in the near future caused by retirements, promotions, transfers, voluntary turnover, and terminations.

As in the case of labor demand, projections for labor supply can be derived either from historical statistical models or through judgmental techniques. One type of statistical procedure that can be employed for this purpose involves transitional matrices. **Transitional matrices** show the proportion (or number) of employees in different job categories at different times. Typically these matrices show how many people move in one year from one state (outside the organization) or job category to another state or job category.

Table 5.1 shows a transitional matrix for a hypothetical manufacturer, focusing on seven job categories. Although these matrices look imposing at first, they are easy to read and use in determining the internal labor supply. A matrix like the one in this table can be read in two ways. First, we can read the rows to answer the question "Where did people in this job category in 2013 go by 2016?" For example, 70% of those in the clerical job category (row 7) in 2013 were still in this job category in 2016, and the remaining 30% had left the organization. For the production assembler job category (row 6), 80% of those in this position in 2013 were still there in 2016. Of the remaining 20%, half (10%) were promoted to the production manager job category, and the other half (10%) left the organization.

A transitional matrix can also be read from top to bottom (in the columns) to answer the question "Where did the people in this job category in 2016 come from (i.e., where were they in 2013)?" Again, starting with the clerical job (column 7), 70% of the 2016 clerical positions were filled by people who were also in this position in 2013, and the remaining 30% were external hires (they were not part of the organization in 2013). In the production assembler job category (column 6), 80% of those occupying this job in 2016 occupied the same job in 2013, and the other 20% were external hires.

Transitional matrix
A matrix showing the proportion or number of employees in different job categories at different times.

2013	2016							
	(1)	(2)	(3)	(4)	(5)	(6)	(7)	(8)
(1) Sales manager	.95							.05
(2) Sales representative	.05	.60						.35
(3) Sales apprentice		.20	.50					.30
(4) Assistant plant manager				.90	.05			.05
(5) Production manager				.10	.75			.15
(6) Production assembler					.10	.80		.10
(7) Clerical							.70	.30
(8) Not in organization	.00	.20	.50	.00	.10	.20	.30	

Table 5.1
A Hypothetical Transitional Matrix for an Auto Parts Manufacturer

Matrices such as these are extremely useful for charting historical trends in the company's supply of labor. More important, if conditions remain somewhat constant, they can also be used to plan for the future. For example, if we believe that we are going to have a surplus of labor in the production assembler job category in the next three years, then we see that by simply initiating a freeze on external hires, the ranks of this position will be depleted by 20% on their own. Similarly, if we believe that we will have a labor shortage in the area of sales representatives, the matrix informs us that we may want to (1) decrease the amount of voluntary turnover in this position, since 35% of those in this category leave every three years, (2) speed the training of those in the sales apprentice job category so that they can be promoted more quickly than in the past, and/or (3) expand external recruitment of individuals for this job category, since the usual 20% of job incumbents drawn from this source may not be sufficient to meet future needs.

As with labor demand, historical precedents for labor supply may not always be reliable indicators of future trends, and there are often one-time unforeseen events that shock that system. For example, in the nuclear energy field, the near meltdown of three nuclear power plants in Fukushima, Japan, following the earthquake and tsunami that rocked that region in 2011 had an immediate effect on students enrolling in nuclear engineering programs across the world. Many students stopped enrolling in those programs or switched to other fields of study, suggesting that, in the future, the supply of young people with this set of skills is likely to be much lower than it is today.[8]

Determining Labor Surplus or Shortage

LO 5-3
Discuss the advantages and disadvantages of various ways of eliminating a labor surplus and avoiding a labor shortage.

Once forecasts for labor demand and supply are known, the planner can compare the figures to ascertain whether there will be a labor shortage or labor surplus for the respective job categories. When this is determined, the organization can determine what it is going to do about these potential problems. For example, in the construction industry in 2015, a shortage of skilled laborers meant that many real estate developers had to cut back on building plans or had these plans delayed an inordinate amount of time because of the inability to find workers with specific skills. In Denver, Shea Homes had plans and funding to build 325 homes but could not execute these plans because the company could not find workers to fit and install cabinets, as well as heating, ventilation, and air conditioning installers.[9]

This problem was compounded in 2017 when tighter rules on immigration cut the number of workers in the home building trades even further. Many of those employed in the construction trades are immigrants, including 50% of drywall and ceiling tile installers, 40% of roofers, and 60% of plasterers and stucco workers. Like the agricultural and meat-procession industries that we saw in the opening vignette, this is another industry that has relied on low-cost labor that has been rocked by labor shortages. Svenda Gudell, the chief economist at real estate tracker Zillow noted, "When you ask builders, 'why aren't you building more?' labor shortages are at the top of their list."[10]

In contrast, the Bureau of Labor Statistics estimates that during the decade ending in 2020, the U.S. economy will create roughly 70,000 lawyer positions, while U.S. law schools are matriculating over 25,000 graduates a year. This translates into a labor surplus of 180,000 lawyers with little or nothing to do.[11] Some observers have noted that smaller, private, and less reputable law schools have contributed to this problem. Kyle McEntee, executive director of the advocacy group Law School Transparency notes, "People are not being helped by going to these schools. The debt is really high, bar passage rates are horrendous, employment is horrendous."[12] In any event, the longer one has to adjust to these kinds of surpluses and shortages, the easier the adjustment; thus, forecasting is a critical strategic human resource activity.

GOAL SETTING AND STRATEGIC PLANNING

The second step in human resource planning is goal setting and strategic planning, as shown in the middle of Figure 5.1. The purpose of setting specific quantitative goals is to focus attention on the problem and provide a benchmark for determining the relative success of any programs aimed at redressing a pending labor shortage or surplus. The goals should come directly from the analysis of labor supply and demand and should include a specific figure for what should happen with the job category or skill area and a specific timetable for when results should be achieved.

Once these goals are established, the firm needs to choose from the many different strategies available for redressing labor shortages and surpluses. Table 5.2 shows some of the options for a HR planner seeking to reduce a labor surplus. Table 5.3 shows some options available to the same planner intent on avoiding a labor shortage.

This stage is critical because the many options available to the planner differ widely in their expense, speed, effectiveness, amount of human suffering, and revocability (how easily the change can be undone). For example, if the organization can anticipate a labor surplus far enough in advance, it may be able to freeze hiring and then just let natural attrition adjust the size of the labor force. If successful, an organization may be able to avoid layoffs altogether, so that no one has to lose a job. Similarly, with enough advance warning, if an organization can anticipate a labor shortage for some job category like "cook," it might be able to work with a local community college to provide scholarships to students who are willing to learn those skills in return for committing to work for that employer in the future.

Unfortunately for many workers, in the past decade the typical organizational response to a surplus of labor has been downsizing, which is fast but high in human suffering. The human suffering caused by downsizing has both an immediate and a

OPTION	SPEED	HUMAN SUFFERING
1. Downsizing	Fast	High
2. Pay reductions	Fast	High
3. Demotions	Fast	High
4. Transfers	Fast	Moderate
5. Work sharing	Fast	Moderate
6. Hiring freeze	Slow	Low
7. Natural attrition	Slow	Low
8. Early retirement	Slow	Low
9. Retraining	Slow	Low

Table 5.2
Options for Reducing an Expected Labor Surplus

OPTION	SPEED	REVOCABILITY
1. Overtime	Fast	High
2. Temporary employees	Fast	High
3. Outsourcing	Fast	High
4. Retrained transfers	Slow	High
5. Turnover reductions	Slow	Moderate
6. New external hires	Slow	Low
7. Technological innovation	Slow	Low

Table 5.3
Options for Avoiding an Expected Labor Shortage

long-term element. In the short term, the lack of pay, benefits, and meaningful work has negative implications for financial, physical, and psychological aspects of individuals, causing bankruptcies, illnesses, and depression. Then, even if one can survive these immediate problems, in the long term, an extended bout of unemployment (e.g., lasting over six months) can stigmatize the individual, thus reducing future opportunities.

In particular, in job categories where skills are perishable and need to be updated continually, many laid-off workers will take any work within their area—even unpaid volunteer work—to prevent a gap in their employment history.[13] However, after very long periods of unemployment, people may give up looking for work altogether. This can often create a confusing message, as in 2014, when the unemployment rate improved, not because more people were finding work (and hence boosting the numerator of that index), but because people stopped looking for work (and hence reduced the denominator of that index).[14] The typical organizational response to a labor shortage has been either hiring temporary employees or outsourcing, responses that are fast and high in revocability. Given the pervasiveness of these choices, we will devote special subsections of this chapter to each of these options.

Downsizing

Downsizing
The planned elimination of large numbers of personnel, designed to enhance organizational effectiveness.

We define **downsizing** as the planned elimination of large numbers of personnel designed to enhance organizational effectiveness. Although one tends to think of downsizing as something that a company turns to in times of recession or when facing bouts of poor performance, in fact, many companies that are doing quite well still downsize their workforce regularly for strategic reasons. For example, although Microsoft was doing fine in 2014, it still laid off 18,000 workers in the phone and tablet divisions after the purchase of Nokia left the company with a surplus of workers in those areas.[15] Similarly, Hewlett-Packard cut 16,000 jobs that same year and used the roughly $1 billion in savings to invest more heavily in cloud computing services.[16]

Surveys indicate three major reasons that organizations engage in downsizing. First, many organizations are looking to reduce costs, and because labor costs represent a big part of a company's total costs, this is an attractive place to start.

An example of this can be seen in 2017 as Boeing announced plans to downsize to cut costs. John Hamilton, the company's vice president of engineering noted, "We continue to operate in an environment characterized by fewer sales opportunities and tough competition, and the decision to reduce the number of 777 jets underscores that environment and what we need to do to help Boeing win."[17] This is a clear example of projections of reduced sales triggering cost-cutting downsizing moves.

Second, in some organizations, the introduction of new technologies or robots reduces the need for a large number of employees. This places the focus of competition on who can produce the best robots, and when it comes to this battle, Japanese manufacturers seem to be far ahead of their rivals. Japanese companies such as Fanuc and Kawasaki Heavy Industries produce over 50% of the world's working robots.[18] However, as the "Competing through Technology" box shows, there still may be room for human workers, even in the field of artificial intelligence.

Although not employing robots per se, General Electric's new battery manufacturing plant in Schenectady, New York, shows how new technology can destroy jobs. The entire 200,000-square-foot facility requires only 370 workers, only 200 of which are actually on the shop floor. The plant manager runs the entire operation, including lights, heat, inventory, purchasing, and maintenance from an iPad that is linked to

COMPETING THROUGH TECHNOLOGY

A Person Pretending to be a Robot Pretending to be a Person

Although many observers have predicted that robots will eventually replace human workers engaged in simple tasks, the process of "training one's replacement" is often a time-consuming and aggravating project for the humans involved. For example, Willie Calvin was a 24-year-old graduate from the University of Chicago who was anxious to work in the growing field of artificial intelligence (AI). Willie took a job with x.ai, to work with an AI personal assistant called "Amy." Amy works with your online calendar and takes over many routine tasks for you, including scheduling meetings and sending reminders of meetings to co-workers. Amy sounds incredibly like a real person, which can be attributed mainly to Willie —the human pretending to be a robot.

Willie would sit in front of a computer screen 12 hours a day, listening in on Amy's communications, clicking and editing the robot's right and wrong answers to customer requests and intervening directly when Amy was not up to the task at hand. "It was either really boring or incredibly frustrating. It was a weird combination of the exact same thing over and over again and really frustrating single cases of a person demanding something we couldn't provide." Willie's experience is not unique, and many people in the field have similar complaints when it comes to the artificial nature of AI.

For example, the people working for GoButler, a do-anything service that takes requests via text messages, were literally called "heroes," because almost nothing was automated when the service first started. GoButler's heroes typically multitasked up to a half-dozen requests at one time, and in the words of one employee, "People felt a bit overworked and under-appreciated." Indeed, although the day may eventually come when AI products replace human workers, that day could not come fast enough for Willie Calvin. He eventually quit x.ai, noting, "The work was too taxing."

DISCUSSION QUESTIONS

1. How can employers design jobs like the ones currently dominating the AI field that are more interesting for workers?
2. Although AI is a high-tech field, why might workers who are interested in AI be the worst source of recruits for the work as currently designed?

SOURCES: R. Miller and S. Chandra, "Robots Will Take All the Jobs? Not so Fast," *Businessweek*, January 12, 2017, p. 16; E. Huet, "The Humans Hiding Behind the Chabots," *Businessweek*, April 18, 2006, pp. 34–35; T. Moss, "Robots on Track to Bump Humans From Call-Center Jobs," *Wall Street Journal*, June 21, 2016.

wireless sensors embedded in the batteries themselves. As Prescott Logan, the general manager of the plant, states, "It is not about low cost labor but high technology. We are listening directly to what our batteries are telling us and then thinking about ways to monetize that."[19] In general, new technologies often displace workers, and in today's modern manufacturing plants, a small number of highly skilled workers can run a plant that in previous generations required hundreds of low-skilled laborers whose jobs will never come back.[20]

Third, many firms downsized for economic reasons by changing the location where they do business. Some of this shift was from one region of the United States to another—in particular, many organizations moved from the Northeast, the Midwest, and California to the South and the mountain regions of the West. In other cases, jobs moved from one country to another, resulting in downsizing in the country that exports the jobs. For example, most garment jobs left the United States over 20 years ago, but in the intervening period, these same jobs have moved over and over again, from India to China to Bangladesh and now, most recently, to Africa. In addition to the lure of low worker wages ($20 a month), Africa is able to produce its own cotton, and its expanse of open space allows companies to build single-level plants that are cheaper and safer relative to the multilevel structures in Bangladesh.[21]

Although downsizing has an immediate effect on costs, much of the evidence suggests that it has negative effects on long-term organizational effectiveness, especially for some types of firms. Also, the negative effects of downsizing seem to be exacerbated in service industries characterized by high levels of customer contact. For example, in the five-year period between 2009 and 2013, Walmart added over 450 new stores to its portfolio, but at the same time, reduced headcount by over 20,000 people. The average number of employees per store dropped from 343 to 301, which resulted in a workforce that was spread too thinly across the large stores. This in turn resulted in longer checkout lines, less support to customers who needed help, and difficulty keeping the shelves stocked. One former Walmart customer, Tim White, noted, "You wait 20, 25 minutes for someone to help you, and then, the person who comes was not trained in that area. And, even though the long checkout lines were irritating, the No. 1 reason I gave up on Walmart was its prolonged, horrible, maddening inability to keep items in stock."[22]

Still, many employers engage in this tactic, so it is important to understand what goes into an effective versus an ineffective downsizing campaign. There seem to be a number of reasons for the failure of most downsizing efforts to live up to expectations in terms of enhancing firm performance. First, although the initial cost savings are a short-term plus, the long-term effects of an improperly managed downsizing effort can be negative. Downsizing not only leads to a loss of talent, but in many cases it also disrupts the social networks needed to promote creativity and flexibility.[23] For example, many observers have attributed the slow public health response to the Ebola outbreak in 2014 to cuts made at local agencies. City, county, and state health departments cut 60,000 jobs in the six-year period from 2008 to 2014, which included the elimination of programs that might have prevented health care workers like those in Dallas from catching the disease from their own patients. Reversing this process in an area that relies on skilled employees is difficult. As one industry expert noted, "You may be able to buy equipment quickly but you can't buy trained personnel quickly."[24]

Second, many downsizing campaigns let go of people who turn out to be irreplaceable assets. In fact, one survey indicated that in 80% of the cases, firms wind up replacing some of the very people who were let go. In other cases, firms bring back the specific people who were let go, often at a higher salary. In fact, the term *boomerang employee* has been coined to refer to this increasingly used source of recruits. Several companies such as Procter & Gamble, JC Penney, Nike, PepsiCo, and Toys "R" Us have tapped former executives to lead their management team. These individuals come in knowing the company well, but they also bring a new perspective achieved by having success at some other venture. More than a traditional outsider, boomerang executives have a sense of what changes will and will not take hold at their old company.[25]

A third reason downsizing efforts often fail is that employees who survive the purges often become narrow minded, self-absorbed, and risk averse. Motivation levels drop off because any hope of future promotions—or even a future—with the company dies out. Many employees also start looking for alternative employment opportunities.[26] The negative publicity associated with a downsizing campaign can also hurt the company's image in the labor market, making it more difficult to recruit employees later. Especially in an age of blogs and text messaging, the once-private practice of laying off employees is becoming increasingly transparent, and any organizational mistake that gets made in the process is likely to become highly public.[27]

The key to a successful downsizing effort is to avoid indiscriminate across-the-board reductions, and instead perform surgical strategic cuts that not only reduce costs but also improve the firm's competitive position. For example, at the State University of New York, $50 million was saved across the system via a series of cuts that consolidated many senior administrative positions. The same practice cut $70 million at the University of California at Berkeley, and $5 million at the University of Kansas. These cuts were specifically targeted at "administrative bloat" revealed by research that showed that the number of employees hired by colleges to administer people and programs rose 50% faster than the number of professors in the preceding 12 years. The size of the instructional and research staff was left as is, and the evidence suggests that student outcomes were not affected at all by such cuts.[28]

Early Retirement Programs and Buyouts

Another popular means of reducing a labor surplus is to offer an early retirement program. As shown in Figure 5.2, the average age of the U.S. workforce is increasing. Although many Baby Boomers are approaching traditional retirement age, early indications are that this group has no intention of retiring any time soon.[29] Several forces fuel the drawing out of older workers' careers. First, the improved health of older people in general, in combination with the decreased physical labor in many jobs, has made working longer a viable option. Second, this option is attractive for many workers because they fear Social Security will be cut, and many have skimpy employer-sponsored pensions that may not be able to cover their expenses. Third, age discrimination legislation and the outlawing of mandatory retirement ages have created constraints on organizations' ability to unilaterally deal with an aging workforce.

Finally, many employers are increasingly concerned about losing the wealth of experience that older workers bring to their companies. Although historically Baby Boomers made up the largest share of the U.S. population and Generation X made up the largest share of the workforce, in 2016, for the first time, both of these generational groups trailed Millennials on both of these statistics. Rather than sponsoring early retirement

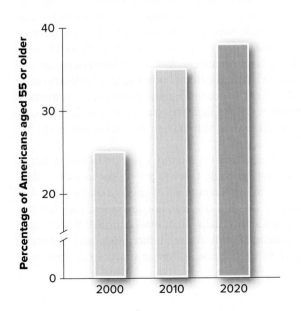

Figure 5.2

Aging of the U.S. Population, 2000–2020

programs, many organizations such as Deloitte Consulting are trying to keep older workers on board longer in order to help train the next generation of leaders. Deloitte forecasts that, in a just a few years, there will be no Baby Boomers left in its leadership ranks. To prevent the permanent loss of implicit knowledge embodied in these workers, Deloitte pairs them with Millennial managers to create synergistic pairs that are greater than the sum of their parts. As one participant in this program noted, "Millennials bring data and analytics but boomers have experience that they can rely on when the data isn't sufficient."[30]

Although an older workforce has some clear advantages for employers in terms of experience and stability, it also poses problems. First, older workers are sometimes more costly than younger workers because of their higher seniority, higher medical costs, and higher pension contributions. For example, at Toyota's plant in Georgetown, Kentucky, veteran workers earn $26 an hour, compared to $16 an hour for new hires. In an effort to shift the workforce from high-paid to low-paid workers, Toyota offered retirement incentives to 2,000 workers at the plant. Each worker could get a lump-sum payment equal to two weeks of pay for every year of service, up to a maximum of 25 years, plus eight weeks' additional pay. In return for taking the buyout, workers would agree to retire on a fixed schedule that prevents all the workers from retiring at once.[31]

Second, because older workers typically occupy the best-paid jobs, they sometimes block the advancement of younger workers. This is frustrating for the younger workers and leaves the organization in a perilous position whenever the older workers decide to retire. Indeed, although a weak economy hurts the prospects of all workers, the impact is especially hard on young people who have limited work experience and skills. In many cases, the first place companies pull back when hiring is with entry-level jobs critical to young employees who are trying to start their careers. For example, the number of recruiters that require two or more years' experience for first-line management positions rose by 30% from 2009 to 2014. In addition, the demand for bottom-rung professional positions such as loan officer, insurance underwriter, and credit analyst has dropped substantially over the same time period.[32]

In the face of such demographic pressures, many employers try to induce voluntary attrition among their older workers through early retirement incentive programs. Although some research suggests that these programs do induce attrition among lower-performing older workers, to a large extent, such programs' success is contingent on accurate forecasting. For example, in Japan, many workers continue to work well beyond the country's official retirement age of 60. Fortunately, Japan's private employers can force employees to retire at 60 if they wish, and workers often accept lower wages in order to stay on. Thus, Komatsu, the world's second largest construction equipment manufacturer, rehires 90% of its retirees at 40% of their past pay. In the United States, by contrast, people cannot be forced into retirement and have to be coaxed out of the job with an incentive package.[33]

For example, the *Washington Post* offered workers roughly a year and a half in salary, and this offer seemed in line with what it generally takes to get people to leave voluntarily. Interestingly, while the *Post* was cutting the number of employees, the *New York Times* decided to reduce pay levels by roughly 3% and not lay off or buy out any employees. Rather than seeing size as a liability, then–executive editor Bill Keller saw it as a source of unique competitive advantage for the *Times* (in fact, the largest newsroom in the country), describing his stock of employees as "the engine of our long term success."[34]

Temporary Workers and Independent Contractors

Whereas downsizing has been a popular method for reducing a labor surplus, hiring temporary workers and outsourcing have been the most widespread means of eliminating a labor shortage. The number of temporary employees in the United States swelled from 4.5 million in 1997 to 28 million in 2014.[35] Temporary employment afforded firms the flexibility needed to operate efficiently in the face of swings in the demand for goods and services. In fact, a surge in temporary employment often preceded a jump in permanent hiring and was often a leading indicator that the economy was expanding. However, that no longer seems to be the case. Employers today seem to appreciate the flexibility that comes with hiring temporary employees and like being able to match quick changes in consumer demands for products and services with quick changes in the supply of labor.

In addition to flexibility, hiring temporary workers offers several other advantages:

- The use of temporary workers frees the firm from many administrative tasks and financial burdens associated with being the "employer of record."
- Small companies that cannot afford their own testing programs often get employees who have been tested by a temporary agency.
- Many temporary agencies train employees before sending them to employers, which reduces training costs and eases the transition for both the temporary worker and the company.
- Because the temporary worker has little experience in the host firm, the person brings an objective perspective to the organization's problems and procedures that is sometimes valuable.

Although it may seem ironic, many employers wind up trying to hire excellent temporary workers for full-time jobs after some period of time. Note, however, that there is usually a fee that has to be paid for permanently "stealing" a temporary employee from a temp agency. Still, some temp agencies have "temp-to-full-time programs" that try to promote this goal for workers who want to be full-time employees. The client in this case is encouraged to make a job offer to the employee within a predetermined time period, should the match seem like a good one. According to the American Staffing Association, 74% of temporary workers decide to become temporary employees because it's a way to get a full-time job.[36]

Steven Berkenfeld, an investment banker who specializes in this area, sums up the feeling of many employers when he says that, when it comes to needing more labor, the key questions are, "Can I automate it? If not, can I outsource it? If not, can I give it to an independent contractor?"[37] Few jobs make it through that obstacle course, and for many contemporary organizations, hiring a real employee is the last resort.

It is useful to distinguish between temporary workers, who are part of a large employment agency and are more or less rented by the primary employer, and independent contract workers, who are more or less freelancers and not part of any organization. Independent contractors are unattached individuals who agree to do specific tasks for specific time periods as part of a written contract between the worker and the employer. Rather than shifting the burden to be the "employer of record" from the employer to a temporary agency, in this case, virtually all the burden associated with this distinction falls on the worker himself or herself.

There has been an unprecedented increase in the use of contract workers like this in recent years, fueled in part by the ability of mobile apps to link employers to workers without the need to go through any other intermediary. In addition, the demonstrated success associated with this business model achieved by companies like Uber, Instacart,

TaskRabbit, and Handy have made this option even more attractive to employers, and the number of individuals working as part of this form of employment grew by 10 million people from 2005 to 2015.[38] In fact, the term *gig economy* has been coined to characterize this shift in the supply of labor.

Although many individuals prefer the autonomy, freedom, and flexibility associated with being an independent contractor, for many workers, this option is chosen only as a last resort. Independent contracting jobs rarely provide any job security, health benefits, or retirement support, and many of the jobs are poorly paid. In Spain, over 90% of the job growth in that country experienced in the 2012–2015 period was attributed to such jobs, often referred to as *trabajo basura,* or "garbage work."[39] Governments and labor organizations in both the United States and the European Union, have been worried about this trend in employment and are studying ways to help protect workers who are part of such arrangements.[40] In the meantime, Uber recently agreed to settle a class-action lawsuit for $84 million brought by its drivers, who argued that they were misclassified as independent contractors. Uber also agreed to give drivers more warning before being deactivated and that they could no longer block drivers who turned down rides too frequently.[41]

Outsourcing, Offshoring, and Immigration

Whereas a temporary employee can be brought in to manage a single job, in other cases a firm may be interested in getting a much broader set of services performed by an outside organization; this is called **outsourcing.** Outsourcing is a logical choice when a firm simply does not have certain expertise and is not willing to invest time and effort into developing it. For example, rather than hire an MBA full time, some companies may decide just to "rent one" for a short, specific project. In fact, a group of Harvard MBAs started a new firm called HourlyNerd to meet just this growing need. Businesses pay $75–$100 an hour for specific one-time tasks like pricing a new product or valuating a business that requires a short dose of expertise.[42] Similarly, in the area of research and development, generic labs have sprung up that allow companies to perform experiments and product testing that may require expensive equipment that is better to rent than own. For example, Emerald Therapeutics provides these kinds of services for small pharmaceutical companies that may have big ideas but limited infrastructure to test such ideas. Emerald rents out both its expensive machinery and talented technicians, thus essentially creating a virtual research and development division for a small company that could never develop this capacity internally.[43]

Ironically, companies increasingly outsource many of their HRM tasks to outside vendors that specialize in efficiently performing many of the more routine administrative tasks associated with this function. Cost savings in this area are easily obtained because rather than purchase and maintain their own specialized hardware and software, as well as specialized staff to support such systems, companies can time-share the facilities and expertise of a firm that focuses on this technology. HR outsourcing firms often focus on health care or financial/retirement programs because these areas are subject to heavy government regulation. These regulations are often changing and demand a great deal of paperwork that is best left to experts who focus single-mindedly on these tasks.[44] The hope is that this frees up HR managers to focus on more strategic issues.[45]

In other cases, outsourcing is aimed at simply reducing costs by hiring less expensive labor to do the work, and, more often than not, this means moving the work outside the country. **Offshoring** is a special case of outsourcing, in which the jobs that move leave one

---

Outsourcing
An organization's use of an outside organization for a broad set of services.

Offshoring
A special case of outsourcing, in which the jobs that move leave one country and go to another.

COMPETING THROUGH SUSTAINABILITY

Disabled by Foreign Competition: The TAA Program

Van Buren County in Arkansas has gone through a tough economic stretch. One company that manufactured electrical cable moved all its jobs to Mexico, a second company that processed poultry shut its doors after failing to find sufficient labor, and a third company was wiped out by a tornado. However, in addition to the county's financial troubles, the numbers on disability insurance would also suggest that the country has experienced a catastrophe when it comes to physical injuries. Over 11% of Van Buren County's residents were on disability in 2016.

Arkansas is not alone. Along with Missouri, Appalachia, and rural areas of the Deep South, it is part of what has become known as the "American Disability Belt," where some counties have experienced disability rates of over 20%. The average for the United States as a whole in 2016 was 5.2%, but this is still twice as high as the rate in 1990. Research shows that one of the primary

transfers of federal funds to states affected by jobs displaced by foreign competition is in the form of disability insurance claims made by people who cannot find new jobs. Thus, disability payments become a form of long-term unemployment insurance for individuals who might have endured some amount of pain in order to work a physically demanding job, but then apply for disability when that job disappears.

Many experts now question the degree to which this is sustainable, given all the other pressures on the federal budget. Attention has begun to shift to other federal programs, such as the Trade Adjustment Assistance (TAA) program. TAA is a program offered by the Labor Department to provide money for training to U.S. workers when their jobs move overseas. TAA is not a panacea and has its own problems. For example, it is still a small program, it does not help workers who lose their jobs due to automation, training

opportunities have to be locally available, and retrained workers often find new jobs at lower wages. Still, it can help sustain a community. For example, when Alcoa shut down two plants in Washington state, the TAA program helped buffer two towns that might otherwise have faced a fate similar to Van Buren County's.

DISCUSSION QUESTIONS

1. What other steps might the government take to help individuals find new work when they are displaced by foreign trade?
2. Should employers who move jobs overseas be compelled to contribute to programs like TAA, or should this responsibility just fall on regular taxpayers?

SOURCES: T. Black and I. Cota, "The Disabled American Worker," *Businessweek*, December 9, 2016, pp. 24–26; B. Leubsdorf, "The Recession's Economic Trauma Has Left Enduring Scars," *Wall Street Journal*, May 9, 2016; "How Do You Solve Kevin's Problem: You Put a Backpack on Him," *Businessweek*, May 16, 2016, pp. 35–36.

country and go to another. This kind of job migration has always taken place; however, rapid technological changes have made the current trends in this area unprecedented. Offshoring is controversial because although it may help a company's bottom line, it harms many citizens who lose their jobs and then look to their government for relief.

The United States has lost over five million manufacturing jobs to China since the mid-1990s, and a great deal of political pressure is being placed on companies to "reshore" this work.[46] For example, Walmart created a program called the Reshoring Initiative that had a goal of spending $250 billion over 10 years on domestically produced goods. On the one hand, this program was successful, in that it did shift production away from China and back to the United States. However, when this production came back to the United States, much of the work was automated; thus, far fewer jobs were created relative to those lost originally.[47] Most experts believe that the only way to achieve a significant increase in the number of new jobs for workers displaced by offshoring is through retraining. The "Competing through Sustainability" box describes one such program.

This political pressure regarding outsourcing may seem problematic for U.S. employers, but still, if effectively managed, firms that offshore certain aspects of work gain an undeniable competitive advantage over their rivals. Ignoring this source of advantage is self-defeating and akin to putting one's head in the sand. For example, Levi-Strauss tried for years to compete against other low-cost jeans manufacturers who offshored their labor. However, after years of one plant shutdown after another, the firm finally gave up and closed down all of its U.S. manufacturing plants. The move, which many people saw as inevitable, was long overdue, and had it been made earlier, the company might have been able to avoid losing over $20 million.[48]

When making the decision to offshore some product or service, organizations should consider several critical factors. Many companies that failed to look before they leaped onto the offshoring bandwagon have been disappointed by their results. Quality control problems, security violations, and poor customer service experiences have in many cases wiped out all the cost savings attributed to lower wages, and more. For example, in 2014, meat supplier OSI Group Inc., a main supplier of beef and chicken to restaurants such as McDonald's, Yum Brands, and Burger King, was fined when inspectors discovered that meat processed in Shanghai, China, was repackaged and sold long after the legally mandated sell-by dates. Sheldon Lavin, the CEO of the company, had to go public after this incident and stated, "I will not try to defend or explain it. It was terribly wrong, and I am appalled that it ever happened in a company that I own." This incident threatened the long-term relationship between OSI and the many restaurants that it supplied, and in some cases, those relationships came to an end.[49]

As another example, problems with the development of Boeing's 787 Dreamliner, a project that is three years overdue and billions of dollars over budget, have been attributed to both the amount and type of work that was offshored. With respect to the amount of outsourced work, the 787 had more foreign content (30%) than any plane Boeing ever built (the average is 5%), and many of the component parts manufactured by far-flung suppliers did not fit together very well. In terms of the nature of the work, Boeing took on final assembly of the plane, but this is the activity that provided the least amount of value added. Jim Albaugh, then the company's chief of aviation, admitted, "We gave too much work to people that had never really done this before, and then we didn't provide the oversight that was necessary. In hindsight, we spent a lot more money than we ever would have spent if we tried to keep many of the key technologies closer to Boeing. The pendulum swung too far."[50]

If one cannot take the work overseas, but still wishes to tap into less-expensive global talent to fill a labor shortage, then one might simply bring foreign workers into the country. Immigration has always been a vital part of the American economy, and many foreign workers are happy to leave their homes and pursue their own American dream.[51] However, entrance of foreign workers into the United States to fill jobs is federally regulated, so there are limits to what can be accomplished here. Employers wishing to hire foreign workers need to help them secure work visas and show that there are no qualified Americans who could do the same work.[52]

The vignette that opened this chapter illustrates the complications of using immigrant labor in low-skill jobs in the agriculture and meat processing industries. Employers that fail to secure the required H2-A visas for such workers expose themselves to raids by immigration officials, which, as the "Integrity in Action" box demonstrates, can cause a great deal of human suffering.

Whereas H2-A visas deal with agricultural workers and other lower-skill jobs, H1-B visas deal with high-skill jobs. The barriers that the U.S. government has put in place to limit H1-B visas—with the current ceiling of 85,000 visas a year—are

Enforcing Immigration Law: As Cold as ICE?

Guadalupe Garcia de Rayos was an undocumented worker whose parents brought her into the United States illegally in the mid-1990s, when she was 14 years old. Guadalupe, now the mother of two young children, worked in a large waterpark in a suburb of Phoenix. In 2008, Guadalupe was arrested for using a fake Social Security card to secure her job, and although she was not deported at that time, she was required to check in regularly with her local Immigration and Customs Enforcement (ICE) office. This was a routine activity for her for the past nine years; however, in 2017, this visit was anything but routine. Guadalupe was arrested and immediately deported back to Mexico, tearing apart her family and creating one new job opening at the waterpark.

Although this was considered an isolated incident, later that month, ICE agents staged a series of raids on employers in several cities including Los Angeles, Austin, Atlanta, and Chicago, as well as on employers in small towns in North Carolina, Florida, Texas, and Virginia. ICE officials insisted that the raids netted a large number of individuals convicted of violent crimes, but the widespread nature of the enforcement actions also swept up a large number of workers who were not convicted of any serious crime.

Many observers considered the series of raids as part of the effort by the Trump administration to meets its goal of three million deportations by the end of the year. This is an ambitious goal, and no one would argue against the idea of removing violent criminals from the country. Still, the goal is so high that many people believe this number can be reached only by arresting individuals with no criminal history, and they question the ethical implications of tearing apart families headed by people who present no real threat to their communities. John Sandweg, a former acting director of ICE, noted that people like Guadalupe "are the low hanging fruit in the system: non-dangerous undocumented immigrants with families. Those people don't hide. Criminals hide." This was certainly true of Guadalupe, and recalling his mother's original arrest in 2008, her son Angel noted, "I was in 2nd grade. I never forgot that night. I've lived in fear of losing my mother every night since then."

DISCUSSION QUESTIONS

1. What is the moral responsibility of employers for ensuring that they are not harboring illegal workers who pose a threat to their communities?
2. Some "sanctuary cities," such as Los Angeles and Austin, refuse to enforce federal laws that they feel target nondangerous undocumented people living in their communities. What are the ethical implications of these cities refusing to enforce federal laws?

SOURCES: F. Santos, "She Showed Up Yearly to Meet Immigration Agents. Now They've Deported Her," *New York Times*, February 8, 2017; L. Rein, "Federal Agents Conduct Immigration Enforcement Raids in at Least Six States," *Reuters*, February 11, 2017; A. Chozick, "Raids of Illegal Immigrants Bring Harsh Memories, and Strong Fears," *New York Times*, January 2, 2017.

designed to protect American jobs, but many people believe this has had the opposite effect on the economy. Research suggests that every immigrant hired by a tech company creates an additional five jobs.[53] Recognizing this fact, Canada has loosened its visa requirements and reached out to U.S. employers to move their operations north of the border. Many tech companies, including Microsoft, Amazon, Facebook, and Salesforce.com, have taken the Canadians up on this offer and are building spacious new facilities in Vancouver. As a representative for Microsoft stated, "The U.S. laws clearly did not meet our needs, and thus we have to look to other places."[54]

Indeed, the limits on bringing foreign labor into the United States are particularly problematic for high-tech companies. The growth of these firms has not been matched by a growing number of students with the advanced skills in mathematics and the sciences that these firms need. Thus, employers like Microsoft and Oracle have aggressively lobbied the government to ease these restrictions.[55] These efforts paid off in 2013 when a new immigration bill was approved by the Senate Judiciary Committee. This new law provided access to a green card to any foreign worker with a job in the United States and an advanced degree in math, science, engineering, or technology.[56] A green card allows a non-U.S. citizen to live and work in the United States on a permanent basis. Although many employers saw this as a step in the right direction, as we noted earlier, this did not stop companies from expanding their presence in Canada in 2014.

Still, outside the high-tech industry, there are different feelings about the value of this kind of free trade in the United States. A 2016 survey found that over 80% of Americans wanted to see more restrictions on both foreign goods and foreign workers; hence, there is some conflict between the needs of employers and would-be employees when it comes to this issue.[57] The "Evidence-Based HR" box provides some data on this issue with respect to short- and long-term effects of immigration.

EVIDENCE-BASED HR

Given the current national focus on immigration and employment, one of the most important questions to answer is, "Do the benefits of immigration offset the costs?" The answer to this question depends very much on your time frame. According to a study by the National Academy of Sciences, Engineering, and Medicine, the first generation of newcomers cost governments more than they contribute. Those total annual costs run about $57 billion and fall disproportionately on state and local governments because of the costs associated with the education of immigrant families. In addition, those local costs are not offset by taxes because first-generation immigrants earn less money, and state and local tax rates tend to be low.

In contrast, the second generation of immigrants earns more money and pays more taxes. Most of this benefit goes to the federal government, however, because federal taxes are the largest share of a person's personal tax burden. The value of immigrants at this point is a net plus of roughly $30 billion a year. The big payoff, however, occurs in the third generation, when immigrant families contribute $223 billion to the government. This report concluded that immigration is "integral to the nation's economic growth" because immigrants bring new ideas and add to a labor force that would be shrinking without them.

SOURCE: J. Preston, "Immigrants Aren't Taking American's Jobs, New Study Finds," *New York Times,* September 26, 2016, https://www.nytimes.com/2016/09/22/us/immigrants-arent-taking-americans-jobs-new-study-finds.html.

Altering Pay and Hours

Companies facing a shortage of labor may be reluctant to hire new full-time or part-time employees. Under some conditions, these firms may have the option of trying to garner more hours out of the existing labor force. Despite having to pay workers time-and-a-half for overtime production, employers see this as preferable to hiring and training new employees—especially if they are concerned that current demand for products or services may not extend to the future. Also, for a short time at least, many workers enjoy the added compensation. However, over extended periods, employees experience stress and frustration from being overworked in this manner. Historically, in the United States, overtime pay was granted only to hourly workers or workers earning less than $24,000 a year, but a law passed in 2016 expanded overtime pay to any worker earning less than $50,000 a year. This significantly increased the number of workers eligible for overtime pay and was aimed primarily at employers who might be misclassifying exempt workers in an attempt to avoid paying overtime.[58]

In the face of a labor surplus, organizations can sometimes avoid layoffs if they can get their employees to take pay cuts. In general, wages tend to be "sticky" in the sense that employers are reluctant to cut someone's pay, and the data suggest that this holds true even during economic recession and depressions.[59] Still, some employers have gone this route recently. For example, Hewlett-Packard cut salaries between 3% and 20% and reduced their contributions to 401(k) plans in the face of the last recession, and many other firms engaged in the same sort of practices.[60] Alternatively, one can avoid layoffs and hold the pay rate constant but reduce the number of hours of all the workers. For example, when business at the Bristol, Rhode Island, plastics manufacturer Saint-Gobain slowed in 2012, none of the workers were laid off, but many had their hours cut by 40%. This would have resulted in a major cut in pay for the workers, except for a state government program that helped Saint-Gobain pay 70% of the lost wages in return for the company keeping the workers on the payroll. The state would have wound up paying a similar amount in unemployment compensation, but this program allowed the company to hold on to experienced employees for when the economy turned around. These kinds of "work share" programs have always been popular in Europe but are now starting to be seen in the United States.[61]

When a cut in hours is targeted at salaried workers rather than hourly workers, this is called a *furlough*. For example, in 2016, roughly 10,000 workers at Honeywell were furloughed for one week. The program was an attempt to reduce costs necessary because of slow economic growth and decreased U.S. defense spending.[62] Furloughs are perceived as a good strategy to use when the employer has an immediate need to conserve money and protect cash flow, but also believes that need will be short term and the employees involved have skills that make them hard to replace in the long term.[63]

Furloughs are controversial because, unlike most hourly workers who go home after the assembly line stops running, the work of most white-collar professionals simply piles up when they leave the office for extended periods of time. Indeed, when furloughs were instituted at Arizona State University and the University of Maryland, most of the professional workers came to work anyway, meaning that the furloughs were actually pay cuts, not reductions in hours. Furloughs are also controversial because they hit higher-paid employees harder than lower-paid employees, and if these pay differences were a result of some type of pay-for-performance system, this means that the best employees take the biggest hit.

PROGRAM IMPLEMENTATION AND EVALUATION

The programs developed in the strategic planning stage of the process are put into practice in the program-implementation stage, shown at the bottom of Figure 5.1. A critical aspect of program implementation is to make sure that some individual is held accountable for achieving the stated goals and has the necessary authority and resources to accomplish this goal. It is also important to have regular progress reports on the implementation to be sure that all programs are in place by specified times and that the early returns from these programs are in line with projections. The final step in the planning process is to evaluate the results. This evaluation consists of comparing results to goals, as well as an "after-action-review" of what worked or failed to work when it came to accomplishing goals.

THE SPECIAL CASE OF AFFIRMATIVE ACTION PLANNING

Human resource planning is an important function that should be applied to an organization's entire labor force. It is also important to plan for various subgroups within the labor force. For example, affirmative action plans forecast and monitor the proportion of various protected group members, such as women and minorities, that are in various job categories and career tracks. The proportion of workers in these subgroups can then be compared with the proportion that each subgroup represents in the relevant labor market. This type of comparison is called a **workforce utilization review.** This process can be used to determine whether there is any subgroup whose proportion in the relevant labor market is substantially different from the proportion in the job category.

Workforce utilization review
A comparison of the proportion of workers in protected subgroups with the proportion that each subgroup represents in the relevant labor market.

If such an analysis indicates that some group—for example, African Americans—makes up 35% of the relevant labor market for a job category but that this same group constitutes only 5% of the actual incumbents in that job category in that organization, then this is evidence of underutilization. Underutilization could come about because of problems in selection or from problems in internal movement, and this could be seen via the transitional matrices discussed earlier in this chapter. Interestingly, recent workforce utilization reviews with respect to women show that this subpopulation of the workforce has been faring well when it comes to employment. A record 67.5 million women were working in 2013 and whereas women regained all the jobs they lost in the last recession, the same was not true of men, whose labor force participation rates are at an all-time low. Much of this can be attributed to the fact that women work in industries with strong job growth and low wages, such as health care, education, hospitality, and retail, whereas men tend to work in construction and manufacturing—industries that were struggling until very recently.[64]

One exception, however, is in the field of software development. Only 15% of software engineers in Silicon Valley are women, a proportion that is far short of their general participation rate.[65] The proportion is even lower for African Americans, who represent just 1% of software engineers versus a 13% general participation rate. These figures would support the inference that these groups are underutilized, and many firms are trying to respond to this situation with one program or another. For example, Google has sent several workers to predominantly African American colleges like Howard University to help cultivate future coders.[66]

These kinds of affirmative action programs are often controversial because many nonminorities see them as unfair.[67] However, when the evidence provided from a workforce utilization review makes it clear that a specific minority group has been historically underrepresented because of past discrimination, and that increasing the level of representation will benefit workforce diversity and competitiveness, then these kinds of programs are easier to justify to all involved.[68] Organizations need to realize, however, that affirmative action plans need to be complemented with communication programs that clearly spell out the needs and benefits that these programs bring to the organization and the larger society.[69]

America's Got Talent: But Still Needs More H1-B Visas

In the global war for talent, one measure of success is the number of Nobel Prizes awarded to citizens from different countries. Four countries are clearly winning in this war; however, these countries are increasingly accomplishing this via immigrants rather than native-born citizens. Specifically, over 30% of Nobel Prizes awarded in the last 30 years have gone to immigrants, and more than 50% of those went to immigrants working in the U.S. Indeed, over 50% of U.S. startups worth over 1 billion were founded by an immigrant. Although trailing the U.S. on this metric, Great Britain, Australia, and Canada are the other three clear winners in this competition, whereas India, China, and the Philippines are the clearest losers when it comes to this international brain drain.

The U.S.'s ability to maintain this status, however, is increasingly threatened by changes in immigration policies that may restrict the flow of talent into the county. In the vignette that opened this chapter we focused the labor shortage in some low skilled jobs in the agricultural and meat processing industries and how this has recently been exacerbated by changes in U.S. immigration policy and policing. Increasing the number of H2-A temporary visas that allow temporary employment to farmworkers was seen as one solution to this problem, but when it comes to highly skilled workers, it is the H1-B visa program that matters most. H1-B visas allow highly skilled workers in areas where there are shortages of labor to work in the country for three years.

Recent changes in immigration policies and a shortage of such visas, however, are leaving human resource managers in high tech fields struggling to fill critical jobs. This, plus the general perception that the U.S. is increasingly unfriendly toward foreign workers is considered a major threat to employers such as Google, Amazon, Microsoft and Facebook who alone employ over 100,000 people who are part of the H1-B program. Facebook CEO Mark Zuckenberg spoke for many in the industry when he stated that "we need to keep this country safe, but we should do that by focusing on people who actually pose a threat."

DISCUSSION QUESTIONS

1. How does the increased difficulty of working in the U.S. create exploitable opportunities for countries like India, China and the Philippines when it comes to plugging their brain drain?
2. What can a country like the U.S. do to decrease its reliance on immigration to fill high tech jobs?

SOURCES: A. Creighton, "Four Nations are Winning the Global War for Talent," *The Wall Street Journal Online,* www.wsj.com, October 18, 2016; M. Jordan, "Demand for H1-B Skilled Worker Visas Forces Agency into Lottery," *The Wall Street Journal Online,* www.wsj.com, April 7, 2016; E. Huet and G. DeVynck, "America's Got No Talent," *Businessweek,* November 21, 2016, pp 32–33; "Google Criticizes Impact on Staff of Trump Immigration Order," *The Wall Street Journal Online,* www.wsj.com, January 28, 2017.

The Human Resource Recruitment Process

As the first half of this chapter shows, it is difficult to always anticipate exactly how many (if any) new employees will have to be hired in a given year in a given job category. The role of human resource recruitment is to build a supply of potential new hires that the organization can draw on if the need arises. Thus, **human resource recruitment** is defined as any practice or activity carried on by the organization with the primary purpose of identifying and attracting potential employees. It thus creates a buffer between planning and actual selection of new employees, which is the topic of our next chapter.

Human resource recruitment
The practice or activity carried on by the organization with the primary purpose of identifying and attracting potential employees.

Figure 5.4

Overview of the
Individual Job
Choice–
Organizational
Recruitment Process

Job Choice

The goal of the recruiting is not simply to generate large numbers of applicants. If the process generates a sea of unqualified applicants, the organization will incur great expense in personnel selection, but few vacancies will actually be filled. This problem of generating too many applicants is often promulgated by the use of wide-reaching technologies like the Internet to reach people.

The goal of personnel recruitment is not to finely discriminate among reasonably qualified applicants, either. Recruiting new personnel and selecting new personnel are both complex processes. Organizations explicitly trying to do both at the same time will probably not do either well. For example, research suggests that recruiters provide less information about the company when conducting dual-purpose interviews (interviews focused on both recruiting and selecting applicants).[70] Also, applicants apparently remember less information about the recruiting organization after dual-purpose interviews.[71]

In general, as shown in Figure 5.4, all companies have to make decisions in three areas of recruiting: (1) personnel policies, which affect the kinds of jobs the company has to offer; (2) recruitment sources used to solicit applicants, which affect the kinds of people who apply; and (3) the characteristics and behaviors of the recruiter. These, in turn, influence both the nature of the vacancies and the nature of the people applying for jobs in a way that shapes job choice decisions.

PERSONNEL POLICIES

LO 5-4
Describe the various
recruitment policies
that organizations
adopt to make job
vacancies more
attractive.

Personnel policies is a generic term we use to refer to organizational decisions that affect the nature of the vacancies for which people are recruited. If the research on recruitment makes one thing clear, it is that characteristics of the vacancy are more important than recruiters or recruiting sources when it comes to predicting job choice.

Internal versus External Recruiting: Job Security

One desirable feature of a vacancy is that it provides ample opportunity for advancement and promotion. One organizational policy that affects this is the degree to which the company "promotes from within"—that is, recruits for upper-level vacancies internally rather than externally. Promote-from-within policies make it clear to applicants that there are opportunities for advancement within the company. These opportunities spring not just from the first vacancy but from the vacancy created when a person in the company fills that vacancy.

For example, Cisco Systems uses a program called Talent Connection to help identify internal candidates for jobs within the organization that have traditionally been staffed by outsiders. About half of Cisco's 65,000 employees have created profiles that are stored in the program, and these can be easily searched for matches when a new opening becomes available. Mark Hamberlin, then vice president for global staffing at Cisco, noted that the program "saved the company millions of dollars in search firm fees and other recruiting costs while at the same time, employee satisfaction with career development has risen by 20%."[72]

Although these programs are popular with employees because they increase job security and promotion opportunities, there are two downsides. First, this type of program sometimes upsets current managers of employees who are recruited away. Many of these employees are top performers in their current units, and some managers bristle at the loss of these individuals.[73] Second, bringing in recruits from external sources often helps spur creativity and innovation. For example, in 2016, Carnival Cruise Line changed its recruiting procedures from hiring industry insiders to bringing in employees who had close to zero experience with cruises. Although these novices do have to be surrounded by some experts in the area, they often came up with new and lucrative ideas, such as volunteer public service cruises where social-conscious passengers got off the boat and helped local villages build housing. This was a new niche in the market that no one steeped in cruise culture was likely to see.[74]

In addition to using promote-from-within policies and internal recruiting sources, employers can promote perceptions of job security and long-term commitment to the organization through due process policies. **Due process policies** formally lay out the steps an employee can take to appeal a termination decision. Organizational recruiting materials that emphasize due process, rights of appeal, and grievance mechanisms send a message that job security is high; employment-at-will policies suggest the opposite. **Employment-at-will policies** state that either party in the employment relationship can terminate that relationship at any time, regardless of cause. Companies that do not have employment-at-will provisions typically have extensive due process policies. Research indicates that job applicants find companies with due process policies more attractive than companies with employment-at-will policies.[75]

Extrinsic and Intrinsic Rewards

Because pay is an important job characteristic for almost all applicants, companies that take a "lead-the-market" approach to pay—that is, a policy of paying higher-than-current-market wages—have a distinct advantage in recruiting. A lead-the-market strategy does not just mean that the organizations raise wages relative to what they have done in the past; instead, they raise wages faster than the competition. When pay rates are already rising, as was the case in 2015, when the average pay rate was rising 2.5% a year, this requires moves larger than the going rate of change.[76]

For example, Matt Noon, owner of Noon Turf Care, a fast-growing start-up with 50 employees and $4 million in revenue, struggled to find any experienced telemarketing employees when he was paying $25,000 per year for the position. When he changed that figure to $45,000 per year, he was able to hire four highly qualified individuals who more than made up for the pay difference when it came to generating additional revenue.[77] Pay can also make up for a job's less desirable features—for example, paying higher wages to employees who have to work midnight shifts. These kinds of specific shift differentials and other forms of more generic compensating differentials will be discussed in more detail in later chapters that focus on compensation strategies. We note here that "lead" policies make

Due process policies
Policies by which a company formally lays out the steps an employee can take to appeal a termination decision.

Employment-at-will policies
Policies stating that either an employer or an employee can terminate the employment relationship at any time, regardless of cause.

any given vacancy more attractive to applicants. For example, because the perception is that Walmart may not be the nation's best employer to work for, the company raised wages 24% for workers across the board in 2015 in order to help recruit new workers.[78]

There are limits to what can be done in terms of using pay to attract people to certain jobs, however. For example, the U.S. Army cannot compete on pay, because as General Michael Rochelle, then head of army recruiting, noted, "We can't get started down a slippery slope where we are depending on money to lure people in. The reality is that while we have to remain at least competitive, we're never going to be able to pay as much as the private sector." To offset this disadvantage in extrinsic financial rewards, the army has to rely on more intrinsic rewards related to patriotism and personal growth opportunities that people associate with military service.

For example, because cyberwar is an increasingly large element within the field of national defense, the military needs coders and software engineers that are already in high demand in the private sector. Although the military cannot match pay with the private sector, it can leverage intrinsic motivation related to serving one's country and learning new skills. Many of the military's cyber warriors are "homegrown" and trained specialists who come from other jobs such as mechanics.[79]

Image Advertising

Organizations often advertise specific vacancies (discussed in the next section). Sometimes, however, organizations advertise just to promote themselves as a good place to work in general. Image advertising is particularly important for companies in highly competitive labor markets that perceive themselves as having a bad image. Indeed, research evidence suggests that the impact of company image on applicant reactions ranks second only to the nature of the work itself.[80]

For example, in a different context, in the wake of the Jerry Sandusky sex scandal at Pennsylvania State University, the school found it increasingly difficult to recruit out-of-state students. As one accepted student from Chicago noted, "The reputation of Penn State has taken a hit lately." Recruiting out-of-state students is critical to Penn State because it receives just 6% of its revenues from the state, and nonresidents pay up to $12,000 more per year relative to Pennsylvanians. Thus, when out-of-state students' enrollments fell from 36% to 24%, this was a major hit to revenue. To make up for this reputational damage, Penn State lowered admissions standards and accepted over 4,000 more nonresidents relative to the years prior to the scandal.[81]

Even though it does not provide information about any specific job, image advertising is often effective because job applicants develop ideas about the general reputation of the firm (i.e., its brand image), and then this spills over to influence their expectations about the nature of specific jobs or careers at the organization.[82] These perceptions then influence the degree to which the person feels attracted to the organization, especially if there appears to be a good fit between the traits of the applicant and the traits that describe the organization.[83] Applicants seem particularly sensitive to issues of diversity and inclusion in these types of advertisements; hence, organizations that advertise their image need to ensure that the actors in their advertisements reflect the broad nature of the labor market constituencies to which they are trying to appeal, in terms of race, gender, and culture.

LO 5-5
List the various sources from which job applicants can be drawn, their relative advantages and disadvantages, and the methods for evaluating them.

RECRUITMENT SOURCES

The sources from which a company recruits potential employees are a critical aspect of its overall recruitment strategy. The type of person who is likely to respond to a job advertised on the Internet may be different from the type of person who responds to an ad in the classified section of a local newspaper. In this section, we examine the different sources from which recruits can be drawn, highlighting the advantages and disadvantages of each.

Internal versus External Sources

We discussed internal versus external sources of recruits earlier in this chapter and focused on the positive effects that internal recruiting can have on recruits' perceptions of job security. We discuss this issue again here but with a focus on how using internal sources affects the kinds of people who are recruited.

In general, relying on internal sources offers a company several advantages. First, it generates a sample of applicants who are well known to the firm. Second, these applicants are relatively knowledgeable about the company's vacancies, which minimizes the possibility of inflated expectations about the job. Third, it is generally cheaper and faster to fill vacancies internally. Finally, inside hires often outperform outsiders, especially when it comes to filling jobs at the top end of the hierarchy. When one examines what happens at the top of the organization, the evidence is quite clear that outsiders often struggle to adapt to their new role. For example, when it comes to tenure, CEOs hired from outside the company average four years prior to departing, compared to five years for insiders. In addition, when it comes to being forced out, 35% of outsider CEOs get ousted after less than three years, compared to 19% for insiders. Finally, in terms of return on investment, companies with an internally hired CEO outperformed those headed by an outsider by 4.4%.[84]

With all these advantages, you might ask why any organization would ever employ external recruiting methods. There are several good reasons why organizations might decide to recruit externally. First, for entry-level positions and perhaps even for some specialized upper-level positions, there may not be any internal recruits from which to draw. Second, bringing in outsiders may expose the organization to new ideas or new ways of doing business. Using only internal recruitment can result in a workforce whose members all think alike and who therefore may be poorly suited to innovation.

Finally, recruiting from outside sources is a good way to strengthen one's own company and weaken one's competitors at the same time. In fact, having one's employees "poached" by another company can be so devastating that companies go to great lengths, perhaps even illegal or unethical lengths, to prevent this from happening. For example, in the constant war for talent in Silicon Valley, poaching the best programmers away from one's competition is a common strategy, and "cold calling" is the central tactic employed to execute that strategy. *Cold calling* refers to the practice in which recruiters from one company call an employee of some other company who has the skills they need and try to get that person to switch sides. Thus, rather than search for new employees among those that do not have jobs and are looking for work, cold callers search the pool of people who have jobs and are not looking for work. Obviously, to move a person who is basically happy and not looking for work costs money, and this can lead to bidding wars that drive up salaries and employers' costs.

One tempting way for organizations to avoid this outcome is to come to agreements where they all refrain from trying to hire employees away from each other. For example, when an employee at Adobe (whose CEO at the time was Bruce Chizen) received a cold call from a recruiter at Apple, an Adobe HR executive sent an e-mail to the cold caller stating that "Bruce and Steve Jobs have an agreement that we are not to solicit ANY Apple employees and vice versa." In another e-mail, after receiving a telephone call from Jobs regarding a cold call to Apple originating at Google, then CEO Eric Schmidt fired off an e-mail to his HR staff that stated, "I believe we have a policy of no recruiting from Apple." Schmidt told his HR unit to "get this stopped and let me know why it is happening."[85]

As tempting as this kind of agreement might be, however, this way of "competing" is actually considered "anticompetitive," and the e-mails described above were at the center of an antitrust lawsuit filed against Apple, Google, Adobe, and Intel. The lawsuit charged these firms with colluding to restrict the free movement of labor and fix wages. These companies eventually agreed to an out-of-court settlement of $20 million to workers who were affected by this policy.[86]

Direct Applicants and Referrals

Direct applicants

People who apply for a job vacancy without prompting from the organization.

Referrals

People who are prompted to apply for a job by someone within the organization.

Direct applicants are people who apply for a vacancy without prompting from the organization. **Referrals** are people who are prompted to apply by someone within the organization. These two sources of recruits share some characteristics that make them excellent sources from which to draw.

First, many direct applicants are to some extent already "sold" on the organization. Most of them have done some homework and concluded that there is enough fit between themselves and the vacancy to warrant their submitting an application. This process is called *self-selection*. A form of aided self-selection occurs with referrals. Many job seekers look to friends, relatives, and acquaintances to help find employment, and evoking these social networks can greatly aid the job search process for both the job seeker and the organization. Current employees (who are knowledgeable of both the vacancy and the person they are referring) do their homework and conclude that there is a fit between the person and the vacancy; they then sell the person on the job.

In the war for talent, some employers who try to entice one new employee from a competitor will often try to leverage that one person to try to entice even more people away. The term *liftout* has been coined for this practice of trying to recruit a whole team of people. For example, when Mike Mertz was recruited as the new chief executive at Optimus, a computer servicing outfit, within hours of leaving his former employer, he in turn recruited seven other former colleagues to join Optimus. Liftouts are seen as valuable because in recruiting a whole intact group, as Mertz noted, "You get the dynamics of a functioning team without having to create that yourself."[87] The team chemistry and coordination that often takes years to build is already in place after a liftout, and this kind of speed provides competitive advantage. Of course, having a whole team lifted out of your organization is devastating, because customers are frequently next to leave, following the talent rather than standing pat; hence, firms have to work hard to make sure they can retain their critical teams.

Electronic Recruiting

The growth of the information superhighway has opened up new vistas for organizations trying to recruit talent. There are many ways to employ the Internet, and increasingly organizations are refining their use of this medium. Obviously, one of the easiest ways to get into "e-cruiting" is to simply use the organization's own web page to solicit applications. By using their own web page, organizations can highly tune their recruitment message and focus on specific people. For example, the interactive nature of this medium allows individuals to fill out surveys that describe what they are looking for and what they have to offer the organizations. These surveys can be "graded" immediately, and recruits can be given direct feedback about how well they are matched for the organization. Indeed, customizing e-recruiting sites to maximize their targeted potential for helping people effectively match their own values with the organization's values, and their skills with the demands of the job, is probably their best feature.[88] The value of steering recruits to company websites is so high that many employers will pay to have their sites rise to the top of the list in particular search engines when certain terms are entered.

For example, PricewaterhouseCoopers (PwC) struck a deal with the career networking site LinkedIn so that if any student from one of the 60 schools from which it recruits does a search of accounting-related jobs, PwC pops up first and is listed as "the featured job." PwC also gets space on the page to promote the organization that includes videos of current employees extolling the virtues of working at that company.[89] Other companies pay LinkedIn roughly $8,000 a year for the opportunity to search among its 187 million profiles, and some, such as Adobe, fill roughly half of their jobs via LinkedIn alone.[90]

Of course, smaller and less well-known organizations may not attract any attention to their own websites; thus, for them this is not a good option. A second way for organizations to use the web is to interact with the large, well-known job sites such as Craigslist, Monster.com or LinkedIn. These sites attract a vast array of applicants, who submit standardized résumés that can be searched electronically using key terms. Applicants can also search for companies in a similar fashion. The biggest downside to these large sites, however, is their sheer size and lack of differentiation.

Social networking sites such as Facebook are yet another avenue for employers to reach out to younger workers in their own environments. Facebook does not allow employers to create pages as members, but it does allow them to purchase pages in order to create what is called a "sponsored group." Ernst & Young's sponsored group page has been joined by more than 5,000 Facebook users, who can access information about the company and chat with recruiters from the company in a blog-like manner.[91] Unlike more formal media, the conversations held here are very informal and serve as an easy first step for potential recruits to take in their relationship with the company. New entrants to this market, like the site BranchOut, take this informal format even further and allow its members to rate other workers in a "Hot or Not" format. That is, users are shown the pictures of two of their Facebook friends and then asked to choose which one they would rather work with. Scores accumulate over time, and founder Rick Marini suggests that "it provides a realistic, crowd sourced assessment of a candidate that recruiters might find hard to come by on their own."[92]

As with any new and developing technology, all of these approaches present some unique challenges. From an employer's perspective, the interactive, dynamic, and unpredictable nature of blogs and social networking sites means that sometimes people who have negative things to say about the organization join in on the conversations, and this can be difficult to control. The biggest liability from the applicant's perspective is the need to protect his or her identity, because this medium has also been a haven for identity thieves, who post false openings in the hope of getting some applicant to provide personal information.[93]

Public and Private Employment Agencies

The Social Security Act of 1935 requires that everyone receiving unemployment compensation be registered with a local state employment office. These state employment offices work with the United States Employment Service (USES) to try to ensure that unemployed individuals eventually get off state aid and back on employer payrolls. To accomplish this, agencies collect information from the unemployed about their skills and experiences.

Employers can register their job vacancies with their local state employment office, and the agency will attempt to find someone suitable using its computerized inventory of local unemployed individuals. The agency makes referrals to the organization at no charge, and these individuals can be interviewed or tested by the employer for potential vacancies. Because of certain legislative mandates, state unemployment offices often have specialized "desks" for minorities, handicapped individuals, and Vietnam-era veterans. Thus, this is an excellent source for employers who feel they are currently underutilizing any of these subgroups.

Public employment agencies serve primarily the blue-collar labor market; private employment agencies perform much the same service for the white-collar labor market. Unlike public agencies, however, private employment agencies charge the organization for the referrals. Another difference between private and public employment agencies is that one doesn't have to be unemployed to use a private employment agency. One special type of private employment agency is the so-called executive search firm. These agencies are often referred to as *headhunters* because, unlike the other sources we have examined, they operate almost exclusively with people who are currently employed. Dealing with executive search firms is sometimes a sensitive process because executives may not want to advertise their availability for fear of their current employer's reaction.

Many organizations have shifted away from private employment agencies in the past few years and focus more on using their own internal recruiters to staff openings. For example, Time Warner filled thousands of senior positions from 2005 to 2012 but used an outside agency only once. Instead, like roughly 25% of the Fortune 500 companies, Times Warner has created a head of executive recruitment to do the work formerly done by private agencies. At Time Warner, this person oversees a 30-person team where each person handles 10–15 placements at a time. This unit saved Time Warner over $100 million in search firm fees and filled each job in roughly 100 days, compared to 170 days associated with a private agency.[94]

Colleges and Universities

Most colleges and universities have placement services that seek to help their graduates obtain employment. Indeed, on-campus interviewing is the most important source of recruits for entry-level professional and managerial vacancies. Organizations tend to focus especially on colleges that have strong reputations in areas for which they have critical needs (chemical engineering, public accounting, or the like). For example, colleges with strong reputations in the areas of science, technology, engineering, and mathematics (STEM) have been inundated with employers desperate to find workers with these skills. Research estimates that the demand for these workers is going to rise 15% between now and 2022. As we saw earlier in our box on H1-B visas, U.S. colleges and universities, while remaining the best source for this talent, still struggle to supply the total demand.[95]

Many employers have found that to effectively compete for the best students, they need to do more than just sign up prospective graduates for interview slots. One of the best ways to establish a stronger presence on a campus is with a college internship program. These kinds of programs allow an organization to get early access to potential applicants and to assess their capacities directly. These programs also allow applicants to gain firsthand experience with the employer, so that both parties can make well-informed choices about fit with relatively low costs and commitment.[96]

In some of the toughest labor markets, employers have bypassed colleges and gone straight to high schools. Online coding tutorials and collaborative web communities have made it possible for many high school students to develop their own applications well before they reach the age to go to college. If these apps become successful, then the coder who created them immediately draws attention from recruiters. For example, Facebook recruited Michael Saymen when he was just 16 years old after they learned that the game he built using Facebook's development tools had attracted more than 500,000 players.[97]

Evaluating the Quality of a Source

Because there are few rules about the quality of a given source for a given vacancy, it is generally a good idea for employers to monitor the quality of all their recruitment sources. One means of accomplishing this is to develop and compare yield ratios for each source. Yield ratios express the percentage of applicants who successfully move from one stage of the recruitment and selection process to the next. Comparing yield ratios for different sources helps determine which is best or most efficient for the type of vacancy being investigated.

Table 5.4 shows hypothetical yield ratios and cost-per-hire data for five recruitment sources. For the job vacancies generated by this company, the best two sources of recruits are local universities and employee referral programs. Newspaper ads generate the largest number of recruits, but relatively few of these are qualified for the position. Recruiting at nationally renowned universities generates highly qualified applicants, but relatively few of them ultimately accept positions. Finally, executive search firms generate a small list of highly qualified, interested applicants, but this is an expensive source compared with other alternatives.

RECRUITERS

The last part of the model presented in Figure 5.4 that we will discuss is the recruiter. Many applicants approach the recruiter with some degree of skepticism. Knowing that it is the recruiter's job to sell them on a vacancy, some applicants may discount what the recruiter says relative to what they have heard from other sources (like friends, magazine articles, and professors). For these and other reasons, recruiters' characteristics and behaviors seem to have less impact on applicants' job choices than we might expect.

LO 5-6
Explain the recruiter's role in the recruitment process, the limits the recruiter faces, and the opportunities available.

Table 5.4
Hypothetical Yield Ratios for Five Recruitment Sources

	RECRUITING SOURCE				
	LOCAL UNIVERSITY	RENOWNED UNIVERSITY	EMPLOYEE REFERRALS	NEWSPAPER AD	EXECUTIVE SEARCH FIRMS
Résumés generated	200	400	50	500	20
Interview offers accepted	175	100	45	400	20
Yield ratio	87%	25%	90%	80%	100%
Applicants judged acceptable	100	95	40	50	19
Yield ratio	57%	95%	89%	12%	95%
Accept employment offers	90	10	35	25	15
Yield ratio	90%	11%	88%	50%	79%
Cumulative yield ratio	90/200	10/400	35/50	25/500	15/20
	45%	3%	70%	5%	75%
Cost	$30,000	$50,000	$15,000	$20,000	$90,000
Cost per hire	$333	$5,000	$428	$800	$6,000

Recruiter's Functional Area. Most organizations must choose whether their recruiters are specialists in human resources or experts at particular jobs (supervisors or job incumbents). Some studies indicate that applicants find a job less attractive and the recruiter less credible when he is a personnel specialist.[98] This does not completely discount personnel specialists' role in recruiting, but it does indicate that such specialists need to take extra steps to ensure that applicants perceive them as knowledgeable and credible.

Recruiter's Traits. Two traits stand out when applicants' reactions to recruiters are examined. The first, which could be called "warmth," reflects the degree to which the recruiter seems to care about the applicant and is enthusiastic about her potential to contribute to the company. The second characteristic could be called "informativeness." In general, applicants respond more positively to recruiters who are perceived as warm and informative. These characteristics seem more important than such demographic characteristics as age, sex, or race, which have complex and inconsistent effects on applicant responses.[99] In addition, timing seems to play a role as well, in the sense that recruiters have a bigger impact early in the job search process, but then give way to job and organizational characteristics when it comes down to the applicant's final decision.[100]

Recruiter's Realism. Perhaps the most well-researched aspect of recruiting deals with the level of realism that the recruiter incorporates into his message. Because the recruiter's job is to attract candidates, there is some pressure to exaggerate the positive features of the vacancy while downplaying the negative features. Applicants are highly sensitive to negative information. However, if the recruiter goes too far in a positive direction, the candidate can be misled and lured into taking the job under false pretenses.

Many studies have looked at the capacity of "realistic job previews" to circumvent this problem and help minimize early job turnover. On the whole, the research indicates that realistic job previews do lower expectations and can help reduce future turnover in the workforce.[101] Certainly, the idea that one can go overboard in selling a vacancy to a recruit has merit. However, the belief that informing people about the negative characteristics of the job will totally "inoculate" them to such characteristics seems unwarranted, based on the research conducted to date.[102] Thus, we return to the conclusion that an organization's decisions about personnel policies that directly affect the job's attributes (pay, security, advancement opportunities, and so on) will probably be more important than recruiter traits and behaviors in affecting job choice.

Enhancing Recruiter Impact. Although research suggests that recruiters do not have much influence on job choice, this does not mean recruiters cannot have an impact. Organizations can take steps to increase the impact that recruiters have on those they recruit. First, recruiters can provide timely feedback. Applicants react very negatively to delays in feedback, often making unwarranted attributions for the delays (such as, the organization is uninterested in my application).[103] Second, recruiting can be done in teams rather than by individuals. As we have seen, applicants tend to view line personnel (job incumbents and supervisors) as more credible than personnel specialists, so these kinds of recruiters should be part of any team. However, personnel specialists have knowledge that is not shared by line personnel (who may perceive recruiting as a small part of their "real" jobs), so they should be included as well.

A LOOK BACK

Addressing Labor Shortages and Surpluses: Exploring Your Options

We opened this chapter with a story of how labor shortages in some industries, such as agriculture and meat processing, are so severe that without illegal immigrants and refugees, the work comes to a halt. We also saw how some companies are relying on outsourcing and offshoring of work, whereas others are relying more on local talent to compete in today's fast-moving economy. Still, there are advantages and disadvantages to recruiting workers from different sources, and we highlighted the strengths and weaknesses of alternative methods for addressing a labor shortage or a labor surplus.

QUESTIONS

1. Discuss the advantages and disadvantages of hiring local workers versus offshoring versus bringing in immigrant labor? How does the nature of the product market affect what you might do in the labor market?
2. Assume you have a well-established company that is facing a labor surplus in some job category. Why might it be in your best interest to use some method other than layoffs to reduce this surplus, and in what sense are your options here a function of how well you did in terms of forecasting labor demand and supply?
3. Discuss the advantages and disadvantages of promoting workers from within your own firm versus going outside the firm to bring in external hires. How does the nature of the business situation affect this decision?

SUMMARY

Human resource planning uses labor supply and demand forecasts to anticipate labor shortages and surpluses. It also entails programs that can be utilized to reduce a labor surplus (such as downsizing and early retirement programs) and eliminate a labor shortage (like bringing in temporary workers or expanding overtime). When done well, human resource planning can enhance the success of the organization while minimizing the human suffering resulting from poorly anticipated labor surpluses or shortages. Human resource recruiting is a buffer activity that creates an applicant pool that the organization can draw from in the event of a labor shortage that is to be filled with new hires. Organizational recruitment programs affect applications through personnel policies (such as promote-from-within policies or due process provisions) that affect the attributes of the vacancies themselves. They can also impact the nature of people who apply for positions by using different recruitment sources (like recruiting from universities versus advertising in newspapers). Finally, organizations can use recruiters to influence individuals' perceptions of jobs (eliminating misconceptions, clarifying uncertainties) or perceptions of themselves (changing their valences for various work outcomes).

KEY TERMS

Forecasting, 193
Leading indicator, 194
Transitional matrix, 195
Downsizing, 198

Outsourcing, 204
Offshoring, 204
Workforce utilization review, 210
Human resource recruitment, 211

Due process policies, 213
Employment-at-will policies, 213
Direct applicants, 216
Referrals, 216

DISCUSSION QUESTIONS

1. Discuss the effects that an impending labor shortage might have on the following three subfunctions of human resource management: selection and placement, training and career development, and compensation and benefits. Which subfunction might be affected most heavily? In what ways might these groups develop joint cooperative programs to avert a labor shortage?
2. Discuss the costs and benefits associated with statistical versus judgmental forecasts for labor demand and labor supply. Under what conditions might either of these techniques be infeasible? Under what conditions might both be feasible, but one more desirable than the other?
3. Some companies have detailed affirmative action plans, complete with goals and timetables, for women and minorities, and yet have no formal human resource plan for the organization as a whole. Why might this be the case? If you were a human resource specialist interviewing with this company for an open position, what would this practice imply for the role of the human resource manager in that company?
4. Recruiting people for jobs that entail international assignments is increasingly important for many companies. Where might one go to look for individuals interested in these types of assignments? How might recruiting practices aimed at these people differ from those one might apply to the "average" recruit?
5. Discuss the relative merits of internal versus external recruitment. What types of business strategies might best be supported by recruiting externally, and what types might call for internal recruitment? What factors might lead a firm to decide to switch from internal to external recruitment or vice versa?

SELF-ASSESSMENT EXERCISE

Mc Graw Hill Education connect®

Additional assignable self-assessments available in Connect.

Most employers have to evaluate hundreds of résumés each week. If you want your résumé to have a good chance of being read by prospective employers, you must invest time and energy not only in its content but also in its appearance. Review your résumé and answer yes or no to each of the following questions.

1. Does it avoid typos and grammatical errors?
2. Does it avoid using personal pronouns (such as I and me)?
3. Does it clearly identify what you have done and accomplished?
4. Does it highlight your accomplishments rather than your duties?
5. Does it exceed two pages in length?
6. Does it have correct contact information?
7. Does it have an employment objective that is specific and focuses on the employer's needs as well as your own?
8. Does it have at least one-inch margins?
9. Does it use a maximum of two typefaces or fonts?
10. Does it use bullet points to emphasize your skills and accomplishments?
11. Does it avoid use of underlining?
12. Is the presentation consistent? (Example: If you use all caps for the name of your most recent workplace, do you do that for previous workplaces as well?)

The more "yes" answers you gave, the more likely your résumé will attract an employer's attention and get you a job interview!

EXERCISING STRATEGY

Is the Demand for On-Demand Labor About to Shift?

When they discuss their business model, representatives for Uber always focus on the software application that links would-be riders with would-be drivers, and hence, quickly and seamlessly connects a specific demand for labor with a specific supply of labor. The success of this business model is undeniable in the sense that, even though it has been in existence for only five years, the company has expanded to more than 300 cities and is now valued at over $50 billion.

The number of people who drive for Uber all over the world is difficult to estimate, but the company states that it has 26,000 drivers in New York City, 15,000 in London, 10,000 in Paris, and 20,000 in Chengdu, China, alone.

Beyond the software application, though, a big part of Uber's success can be attributed to the fact that all of the labor employed in this case is low paid, has no job security, and is provided no benefits. In the United States, for example, many Uber drivers enjoy the flexibility that this work provides, but the fact is that they are paid far less than the minimum wage, especially when expenses and vehicle depreciation are taken into account. The company can get away with this because the drivers are classified as "independent contractors" rather than "traditional employees." This classification has been challenged in several instances, however, and in June 2015, the California Labor Commissioner's Office ruled that Uber drivers should be classified as traditional employees.

This finding has huge implications because Uber is just one of many "on-demand" companies that rely on this ever-increasing business model for managing workers. This is the same model that is employed by Uber's number-one rival, Lyft, as well as companies such as Instacart, which delivers groceries; Handy, which provides cleaning services; Task-Rabbit, which does odd jobs; and Mechanical Turk, which provides a broad range of services. Some observers have even suggested that this freelance model of employment is the next wave of the future. As one labor economist noted, "The $40-an-hour-manufacturing job is not going to come back, but the $25 local services job represents a viable alternative."

Few of these jobs actually pay at this rate, however, and the generally high level of worker discontent has made some of these companies reconsider their business model. For example, Instacart announced—the week after the California ruling—that it was reclassifying its workers as employees. Instacart ran a trial experiment with this reclassification in Boston the year before and concluded that "this change improved the quality and efficiency of order picking and made for a better customer experience." Apparently, the customer services advantages of a more traditional supply of labor outweighed the cost savings associated with the on-demand labor supply.

QUESTIONS

1. Do you believe contract work like what one sees at Uber is the wave of the future, or do you think that eventually it will be difficult to find people willing to take such jobs?
2. How does technology shape the ability of organizations to employ contract workers in unprecedented ways?

SOURCES: L. Weber and R. E. Silverman, "On-Demand Workers: We Are Not Robots," *Wall Street Journal*, January 27, 2015; M. Isaac and N. Singer, "California Says Uber Driver Is Employee, not a Contractor," *New York Times*, June 17, 2015; S. A. O'Brien, "The Uber Effect: Instacart Moves Away from Contract Workers," CNNMoney.com, June 22, 2015.

MANAGING PEOPLE

Beyond the Ethics of Representation: The Business Case for Diversity at the CIA

One could argue that there are ethical issues associated with any government agency in which the representation of minorities is far below the proportion of those groups in the general set of citizens served by the agency. However, when it comes to the Central Intelligence Agency (CIA), the role of diversity is mission critical. Some outside critics blamed the agency's lack of preparedness for the September 11 terrorist attacks on a lack of creative and "out-of-the-box" thinking on the part of agency staff, who were mainly older white Americans whose main experience dealt with fighting the Soviet Union. But even the agency's then current director, John Brennan, noted that when it comes to a lack of diversity, "I think it has not allowed us to optimize the capabilities we have, and allows us to fall prey to groupthink."

When a 2015 workforce utilization review charged the agency with failure to recruit, hire, and promote African American employees, Brennan had to get out in front of the agency and "make the business case for diversity." According to the utilization report, although nonwhites comprise 30% of the U.S. population, over 90% of the agency's senior leadership positions are held by whites. Brennan, who is white, stressed that this problem went well beyond the politics of this issue and had a direct impact on the agency's

ability to accomplish its mission, emphasizing that "individuals who look like me, they're not going to be able to operate clandestinely in many parts of the world."

To address this issue, the CIA set a goal to make sure that minorities would make up 30% of leadership positions at the agency within three years. Although the agency had made and broken this promise before, Brennan said, "We're not kidding, this is real this time," and he backed up this statement with a formal plan making it clear that the performance evaluations of senior managers were going to be based on how well they met the diversity goals he set.

QUESTIONS

1. How does the unique nature of the work conducted by the CIA make diversity a critical consideration?
2. How does the unique nature of the CIA's current workforce and the agency's history make diversity difficult to achieve?

SOURCES: D. Paletta, "CIA Launches New Effort to Diversify Workforce," *Wall Street Journal*, June 30, 2015; J. Donovan, "CIA Failing to Recruit and Promote Minorities, Study Finds," *New York Times*, June 30, 2015; E. Perez, "CIA Lagging in Recruiting, Promoting Minorities, Study Finds," CNN.com, June 30, 2015.

HR IN SMALL BUSINESS

For Personal Financial Advisors, a Small Staffing Plan with a Big Impact

Robert J. Reed has been a financial planner since 1978 and received his certified financial planner designation in 1981. In 1999, he hired Lucy Banquer, a former legal secretary, to work as his assistant and the only employee at his firm, Personal Financial Advisors LLC in Covington, Louisiana. At that point, human resource planning wasn't on Reed's radar at all.

But around 2005, Reed began to act on a desire to have a more complete plan for his firm's growth. He determined that he wanted the business to grow from about $400,000 in annual revenues to become a million-dollar firm by 2012. That was a realistic goal, but not one he could achieve with only the support of Banquer. Although Banquer does an excellent job of fielding client phone calls and answering questions, Reed needed to bring in more financial expertise to serve more clients.

Typically, a financial-planning firm like Reed's expands by hiring an entry-level advisor to handle routine tasks while learning on the job until he or she can take on clients independently. But Reed didn't simply take the usual path; he considered what role he wanted for himself in his firm as it grew. Reed realized that the part he excelled at and loved most was managing the investments, not the presentations to clients, and that he wanted the firm to grow in a way that would free more time for him to spend with his family, not expand his hours to supervise others. As Reed defined the scope of his own desired job, he clarified what he wanted from his next employee: a certified financial planner who had experience plus an interest in all the planning and advising tasks *except* investment management.

With that strategy in mind, Reed began the search for another planner to work with him. After about eight months of recruiting, Reed met Lauren Gadkowski, who was running her own advisory firm in Boston but preparing to relocate to Baton Rouge to be with her future husband, Lee Lindsay. Reed wanted his new financial planner to operate independently, so he agreed to the idea of her office being in Baton Rouge, about a 45-minute drive from his, and he let her determine how often she would need to visit the Covington office.

Reed stuck to his plan: Lauren Lindsay quickly began working with Reed's larger clients and introduced herself as their main contact with the firm. After sitting in on a few meetings to satisfy himself that he had made a good hiring decision, Reed shifted his efforts to managing the investments. About 10% of the clients indicated they would prefer to maintain their working relationship with Reed. Lindsay took over the remaining 90% as well as the new clients she has brought into the firm since joining it.

Reed's decision to focus on investment management has paid off for Personal Financial Advisors, giving the firm better-than-average performance on its investments even as revenues have climbed. And with Lindsay on board to handle client contact, Reed became able to follow the more traditional path to further growth by hiring an associate financial planner, David Hutchinson, in 2008. In contrast to Lindsay, Hutchinson is still preparing to become a certified financial planner, but he has an educational background in financial planning and experience as an investment broker.

QUESTIONS

1. Is a company ever too small to need to engage in human resource planning? Why or why not? Discuss whether you think Robert Reed planned his hiring strategy at an appropriate time in the firm's growth.
2. Using Table 5.3, review the options for avoiding a labor shortage, and discuss how well the options besides new hires could have worked as ways for Reed to reach his goals for growth. As you do so, consider qualities of a financial-planning business that might be relevant (for example, direct client contact and the need for confidentiality).
3. Suppose that when Reed was seeking to hire a certified financial planner, he asked you for advice on where to recruit this person. Which sources would you suggest, and why?

SOURCES: Angie Herbers, "Letting Go," *Investment Advisor*, June 2009, pp. 96–97; Personal Financial Advisors, "Why Choose Us?", corporate website, http://www.mypfa.com.

NOTES

1. G. Motevalli, "Iran's Latest Headache: A Brain Drain," *Bloomberg Businessweek*, May 18, 2014, pp. 18–19.
2. D. Clark and C. Dulaney, "Qualcomm to Cut 15% of Workforce," *Wall Street Journal*, July 22, 2015.
3. E. Morath, "Which Fields Hold Jobs of the Future? Low Paying Ones Mostly," *Wall Street Journal*, January 9, 2014.
4. D. Molinski, "Oil Layoffs Hit 100,000 and Counting," *Wall Street Journal*, April 14, 2015.
5. D. Wethe, "Drilling Is Back, What about the Workers?" *Businessweek*, January 30, 2017, pp. 14–15.
6. L. Patton, "The Latest Shortage," Fast-food Workers," *Businessweek*, January 16, 2017.

7. G. Beach, "The Dog Fight for Tech Talent," *Wall Street Journal*, August 18, 2014, http://blogs.wsj.com.

8. J. Johnsson, "A Labor Shortage for U.S. Nuclear Power Plants," *Businessweek*, July 11, 2013, pp. 50–51.

9. K. Hudson, "Labor Shortage Bests Home Builders," *Wall Street Journal*, May 1, 2014.

10. C. Kirkham, "Trump Immigration Rules Likely to Exacerbate Home Builders' Labor Shortfall," *Wall Street Journal*, www.wsj.com, January 28, 2017.

11. P. M. Barrett, "Big Law: The Future," *Businessweek*, May 2, 2013, pp. 53–58.

12. N. Scheiber, "An Expensive Law Degree and Nowhere to Use It," *New York Times,* June 17, 2016.

13. T. R. Homan and Z. Tracer, "The Long-Term Jobless Are Being Left Behind," *Bloomberg Businessweek*, August 9, 2010, pp. 53–54.

14. G. Hubbard, "The Unemployment Puzzle: Where Have All the Workers Gone?" *Wall Street Journal*, April 4, 2014.

15. S. Ovide, "Microsoft to Cut Up to 18,000 Jobs," *Wall Street Journal*, July 17, 2014.

16. S.E. Ante, "H-P Slashes up to 16,000 More Jobs," *Wall Street Journal*, May 22, 2014.

17. D. Gates, "Boeing Plans Buyouts, Layoffs for Engineers in First of Three Cuts for 2017," *Seattle Times*, January 10, 2017.

18. B. Bremner, "Japan Releases a Robot Revolution," *Businessweek*, May 28, 2015.

19. R. Foroohar and B. Shaparito, "Made in the USA," *Time*, April 11, 2013, pp. 22–29.

20. C. Kenny, "Factory Jobs Are Gone, Get over It." *Businessweek*, February 2, 2014, pp. 12–13.

21. C. Passareillo and S. Kapner, "Search for Ever Cheaper Garment Factories Leads to Africa," *Wall Street Journal*, July 8, 2015.

22. R. Dudley, "What Good Are Low Prices if the Shelves Are Empty," *Businessweek*, April 1, 2013, pp. 23–24.

23. P. P. Shaw, "Network Destruction: The Structural Implications of Downsizing," *Academy of Management Journal* 43 (2000), pp. 101–12.

24. J. Tozzi and B. Greeley, "Making It Up as We Go," *Businessweek*, October 26, 2014, pp. 27–28.

25. J. S. Lublin, "How to Be a Good Boss—The Second Time Around," *Wall Street Journal*, January 9, 2014.

26. C. O. Trevor and A. J. Nyberg, "Keeping Your Headcount When All About You Are Losing Theirs: Downsizing, Voluntary Turnover Rates, and the Moderating Role of HR Practices," *Academy of Management Journal* 51 (2008), pp. 259–76.

27. E. Frauenheim, "Technology Forcing Firms to Shed More Light on Layoffs," *Workforce Management*, January 19, 2009, pp. 7–8.

28. D. Belkin, "Colleges Trim Staffing Bloat," *Wall Street Journal*, December 25, 2013.

29. J. Marquez, "The Would-be Retirees," *Workforce Management*, November 3, 2008, pp. 24–28.

30. J. Green, "Chowing Down on Boomers' Brains," *Businessweek*, January 21, 2016, pp 19–20.

31. M. Ramsey, "Toyota Offers U.S. Workers Retirement Incentives," *Wall Street Journal*, November 30, 2012.

32. L. Weber and M. Korn, "Where Did All the Entry Level Jobs Go?" *Wall Street Journal*, August 5, 2014.

33. K. Matsuyama, "In Japan, Retirees Go on Working," *Businessweek*, September 3, 2012, pp. 14–15.

34. R. Adams, "New York Times Will Cut Salaries; Washington Post to Offer Buyouts," *Wall Street Journal*, March 26, 2009, p. C1.

35. M. Zuckerman, "The Full-Time Scandal of Part-Time America," *Wall Street Journal*, July 13, 2014.

36. B. Smith, "Hiring Temporary Employees," *Entrepreneur*, February 25, 2013.

37. L. Weber, "The End of Employees," *Wall Street Journal*, February 7, 2017.

38. N. Irwin, "With 'Gigs' Instead of Jobs, Workers Bear New Burdens," *New York Times*, March 31, 2016.

39. C. Matlack and N. Leiber, "Empleado Ymiserable," *Businessweek*, July 4, 2015.

40. J. Eidelson, "Unionize Me," *Businessweek,* January 16, 2017.

41. S. Riordan, "An Uber Shakedown," *Wall Street Journal*, April 24, 2016.

42. E. Zlomek, "Why Hire an MBA When You Can Rent One," *Bloomberg Businessweek*, October 24, 2013, pp. 60–62.

43. A. Vance, "Emerald Therapeutics: Biotech Lab for Hire," *Bloomberg Business*, July 3, 2014.

44. E. Newcomer, "This Time, It's HR Getting Fired," *Businessweek*, May 21, 2015.

45. F. Hanson, "Special Report: Mid-Market Outsourcing," *Workforce Management*, February 12, 2007, pp. 23–26.

46. N. E. Boudette, "Ford Criticized by Trump, Cancels Plans to Build Mexican Plant," *New York Times,* January 3, 2017.

47. S. Pettypiece, "This Owl Won't Save American Jobs," *Businessweek*, July 26. 2016, pp. 14–15.

48. P. McDougall, "Bored of the USA?: 'Made in America' Jeans Maker Levi Strauss to Move 500 Jobs Offshore," *International Business Times*, November 13, 2014.

49. L. Burkitt and J. Bunge, "Meat Supplier's CEO Apologizes for China Unit," *Wall Street Journal*, July 23, 2014.

50. M. Hiltzik, "787 Dreamliner Teaches Boeing a Costly Lesson on Outsourcing," *Los Angeles Times*, February 15, 2013, p. B1.

51. K. Weise, "Send Us Your Educated Masses," *Bloomberg Businessweek*, May 23, 2013, p. 30.

52. J. Light, "Labor Shortage Persists in Some Fields," *Wall Street Journal*, February 7, 2013, p. C1.

53. M. L. Slaughter, "How America Loses a Job Every 43 Seconds," *Wall Street Journal*, March 25, 2014.

54. K. Weise, "How to Hack a Visa Limit," *Bloomberg Businessweek*, June 1, 2014.

55. E. Dwoskin, "Want to Move a Worker to the U.S.? Good Luck," *Businessweek*, June 18, 2012, pp. 27–28.

56. E. Werner, "Unlimited Visas Could Boost Tech," *Lansing State Journal*, May 27, 2013, p. 5B.

57. P. Coy, "An Inconvenient Myth about Free Trade," *Businessweek*, May 31, 2016, p. 6–7.

58. D. J. Boudreaux and L. Palagashilivi, "Working Overtime to Avoid the Truth," *Wall Street Journal*, April 7, 2016.

59. B. Greeley, "The Incredible Stickiness of Wages," *Bloomberg Businessweek*, April 10, 2015.

60. C. Tuna, "Looking for More Tools to Trim Costs," *Wall Street Journal*, February 23, 2013, p. B4.

61. L. Woellert, "Half the Hours, Most of the Pay," *Businessweek*, January 31, 2013, pp. 23–24.

62. R. Randazza, "Honeywell Employees Told to Take Furloughs," *Arizona Republic*, May 25, 2016.

63. C. Tuna, "Weighing Furlough vs. Layoff," *Wall Street Journal*, April 13, 2009, p. B6.

64. J. House, "Women Reach Milestone in Job Market," *Wall Street Journal*, November 17, 2013.

65. C. Suddath, "Girl Code," Businessweek, May 13, 2015.

66. V. Vara, "Why Doesn't Silicon Valley Hire Black Coders," *Businessweek*, January 21, 2016, pp. 40–45.

67. G. Shteynberg, L. M. Leslie, A. P. Knight,, and D. M. Mayer, "But Affirmative Action Hurts Us! Race-Related Beliefs Shape Perceptions of White Disadvantage and Policy Unfairness," *Organizational Behavior and Human Decision Processes* 115 (2013), pp. 1–12.

68. D. A. Harrison, D. A. Kravitz, D. M. Mayer, L. M. Leslie, and D. Lev-Arey, "Understanding Attitudes toward Affirmative Action Programs in Employment: Summary and Meta-analysis of 35 Years of Research," *Journal of Applied Psychology* 91 (2006), pp. 1013–36.

69. I. Hideg and J. L. Michela, "Overcoming Negative Reactions of Nonbeneficiaries of Employment Equity: The Effect of Participation in Policy Formulation," *Journal of Applied Psychology* 96 (2013), pp. 363–76.

70. C. K. Stevens, "Antecedents of Interview Interactions, Interviewers' Ratings, and Applicants' Reactions," *Personnel Psychology* 51 (1998), pp. 55–85.

71. A. E. Barber, J. R. Hollenbeck, S. L. Tower, and J. M. Phillips, "The Effects of Interview Focus on Recruitment Effectiveness: A Field Experiment," *Journal of Applied Psychology* 79 (1994), pp. 886–96.

72. D. Schwabel (2012).The power within: Why internal recruiting and hiring are on the rise. *Time Magazine Online,* Augsut 15, 2012.

73. R. E. Silverman and L. Weber, "An Inside Job: More Firms Opt to Recruit from Within," *Wall Street Journal*, May 29, 2012.

74. C. Palmeri, "Carnival Rocks the Boat," *Businessweek*, November 12, 2015, pp. 22–23.

75. C. M. Harold, B. C. Holtz, B. K. Griepentrog, L. M. Brewer, and S. M. Marsh, "Investigating the Effects of Applicant Justice Perceptions on Job Offer Acceptance," *Personnel Psychology*, 69 (2016), pp. 199–227.

76. J. Smialek and R. Miller, "Wages Bounce Back," *Businessweek*, November 12, 2015, pp. 16–18.

77. E. Maltby and S. E. Needleman, "Small Firms Seek Skilled Workers but Can't Find Any," *Wall Street Journal*, July 25, 2012.

78. P. Ziobro and M. Calia, "Wal-Mart Plans to Boost Pay of U.S. Workers," *Wall Street Journal*, February 9, 2015.

79. J. Robertson and M. Riley, "Drop and Give Me 20 Lines of Code," *Businessweek*, July 9, 2015.

80. D. S. Chapman, K. L. Uggerslev, S. A. Carroll, K. A. Piasentin, and D. A. Jones, "Applicant Attraction to Organizations and Job Choice: A Meta-analytic Review of the Correlates of Recruiting Outcomes," *Journal of Applied Psychology* 90 (2005), pp. 928–44.

81. A. Athavaley, R. Bachman, K. Maher, and J. W. Miller, "Selling Students on Penn State," *Wall Street Journal*, January 31, 2012.

82. C. Collins and C. K. Stevens, "The Relationship between Early Recruitment-Related Activities and the Application Decisions of New Labor Market Entrants: A Brand Equity Approach to Recruitment," *Journal of Applied Psychology* 87 (2002), pp. 1121–33.

83. B. W. Swider, R. D. Zimmerman, and M. R. Barrick, "Searching for the Right Fit: Development of Person-Organization Fit Perceptions during the Recruitment Process," *Journal of Applied Psychology* 100 (2015), pp. 880–93.

84. L. Kwoh, "Chief Executives Hired Internally Outlast, Outperform Their Rivals," *Wall Street Journal*, May 29, 2012.

85. S. Lynch, "Google and Apple Are Safe from an Anti-Poaching Lawsuit, but Maybe Not for Long," *Silicon Valley Business Journal*, April 5, 2013, www.bizjournals.com.

86. J. Elder, "Tech Companies Agree to Settle Wage Suit," *Wall Street Journal*, April 24, 2014.

87. J. McGregor, "I Can't Believe They Took the Whole Team," *Businessweek*, December 18, 2006, pp. 120–22.

88. B. Dineen and R. A. Noe, "Effects of Customization on Applicant Decisions and Applicant Pool Characteristics in a Web-based Recruiting Context," *Journal of Applied Psychology* 94 (2009), pp. 224–34.

89. "PwC Pays for Priority," *Wall Street Journal*, October 4, 2010, p. B6.

90. O. Kharif, "Finding Job Candidates Who Aren't Looking," *Businessweek*, December 17, 2012, pp. 41–42.

91. E White, "Ernst & Young Reaches Out to Recruits on Facebook," *Wall Street Journal*, January 8, 2007, p. B5.

92. S. Berfield, "Dueling Your Facebook Friends for a New Job," *Bloomberg Businessweek*, March 7, 2013, pp. 35–36.

93. D. Mattioli, "Who's Reading On-Line Resumes? Identity Crooks," *Wall Street Journal*, October 17, 2006, p B9.

94. J. S. Lublin, "More Executive Recruiting Shifts In-House," *Wall Street Journal*, October 9, 2012.

95. M. V. Rafter, "Recruiting Down to a Science," *Workforce*, January 2016, pp. 36–39.

96. H. Zhao and R. C. Liden, "Internship: A Recruitment and Selection Perspective," *Journal of Applied Psychology* 96 (2011), pp. 221–29.

97. S. Frier, "OMG, Best Summer Ever," *Bloomberg Businessweek*, July 20, 2014, pp. 31–32.

98. M. S. Taylor and T. J. Bergman, "Organizational Recruitment Activities and Applicants' Reactions at Different Stages of the Recruitment Process," *Personnel Psychology* 40 (1984), pp. 261–85.

99. L. M. Graves and G. N. Powell, "The Effect of Sex Similarity on Recruiters' Evaluations of Actual Applicants: A Test of the Similarity–Attraction Paradigm," *Personnel Psychology* 48 (1995), pp. 85–98.

100. K. L. Uggerslev, N. E. Fassina, and D. Kraichy, "Recruiting Through the Stages: A Meta-Analytic Test of Predictors of Applicant Attraction at Different Stages of the Recruiting Process," *Personnel Psychology* 65 (2012), pp. 597–660.

101. J. M. Phillips, "The Effects of Realistic Job Previews on Multiple Organizational Outcomes: A Meta-analysis," *Academy of Management Journal* 41 (1998), pp. 673–90.

102. J. M. Phillips and S. M. Gully, "Multilevel and Strategic Recruiting: Where Have We Been and Where Can We Go from Here?" *Journal of Management* 41 (2015), pp. 1416–45; P. G. Irving and J. P. Meyer, "Reexamination of the Met-Expectations Hypothesis: A Longitudinal Analysis," *Journal of Applied Psychology* 79 (1995), pp. 937–49.

103. W. J. Becker, T. Connolly, and J. E. Slaughter, "The Effect of Job Offer Timing on Offer Acceptance, Performance, and Turnover," *Personnel Psychology* 63 (2010), pp. 223–41.

6 Selection and Placement

LEARNING OBJECTIVES

After reading this chapter, you should be able to:

LO 6-1   Establish the basic scientific properties of personnel selection methods, including reliability, validity, and generalizability. *page 230*

LO 6-2   Discuss how the particular characteristics of a job, an organization, or an applicant affect the utility of any test. *page 240*

LO 6-3   Describe the government's role in personnel selection decisions, particularly in the areas of constitutional law, federal laws, executive orders, and judicial precedent. *page 242*

LO 6-4   List the common methods used in selecting human resources. *page 247*

LO 6-5   Describe the degree to which each of the common methods used in selecting human resources meets the demands of reliability, validity, generalizability, utility, and legality. *page 247*

Policing Hiring Practices in the Field of Law Enforcement

William Melendez had quite a long criminal record—for a policeman. Melendez worked as part of the police force in Garden City, Michigan. In his 15 years as an officer there, he was involved in over a dozen lawsuits alleging various forms of misconduct, including the use of excessive force, planting evidence, making arrests without probable cause, and wrongful death. In one 1996 case, Melendez shot and killed an unarmed motorist whom he had made lie down by the side of the road during a traffic stop. The city settled with the deceased man's family for $1 million in a plea deal that allowed Melendez to avoid prison. Although this information was in the public record, that did not stop Melendez from landing a new job in Inkster, Michigan, a few years later. In 2016, he was arrested again when released video showed him dragging a man out of his car and beating him unconscious—after stopping him for running a stoplight. Inkster, like Garden City, also settled out of court, awarding the beaten motorist $1.4 million.

In the wake of controversies over recent cases like this one—as well as other nationally publicized police brutality cases in New York City, Baltimore, Chicago, Seattle, and Ferguson, Missouri—many people are beginning to ask questions about how police officers are selected and why some "bad apples" are allowed to move from one jurisdiction to another, despite clearly questionable employment histories. Indeed, a study conducted by the *Wall Street Journal* followed for seven years the cases of roughly 3,500 officers who lost their jobs due to arrests or convictions and found that over 10% of this group was still working in law enforcement.

Part of problem can be traced to the difficulty of finding people willing to do this dangerous work, as well as the difficulty associated with obtaining the information needed to make better hiring decisions. Although some states have formal decertification lists containing the names of officers who were fired for criminal acts, some do not. Moreover, the decertification process varies widely between states that have such lists. Georgia, for example, decertified close to 6,000 officers in the past nine years, whereas Pennsylvania decertified less than 30 over the same time period. Finally, although it may seem remarkable, there is no national registry that aggregates these state-level data that one could search when making a hiring decision. As a result, decertified cops are able to move from state to state.

The lack of standardization and subjective nature of selection decisions in law enforcement is now a focus of national scrutiny. After the killing of Michael Brown in Ferguson, a national commission was created to collect, maintain, and distribute decertification data to all states. The goal is to make it easier for those making hiring decisions to isolate officers with troubled pasts and keep them off the streets. For this information to be useful, however, it has to be combined with the creation of a different culture that will promote the use of that information. When Gregory Gaskin, the Inkster police chief who hired William Melendez, was asked whether he had read the prehiring investigation report dealing with Melendez's background, he simply responded, "Well, I read it, but as far as significance, I didn't think much of it."

SOURCES: L. Radnofsky, Z. Elinson, J. R. Emshwiller, and G. Fields, "Why Some Problem Cops Don't Lose Their Badges," *Wall Street Journal,* December 30, 2016; J. Dawsey and P. Shallwani, "Police Work to Balance Crime Fighting with Protecting Citizen's Rights," *Wall Street Journal,* June 14, 2015; F. Speilman, "Emanual Opens the Door to Relaxing Police Hiring Standards," *Chicago Sun Times*, December 14, 2016.

Introduction

Any organization that intends to compete through people must take the utmost care with how it chooses organizational members. These decisions have a critical impact on the organization's ability to compete, as well as on each and every job applicant's life. Organizations have to strive to make sure that the decisions they make with respect to who gets accepted or rejected for jobs promote the best interests of the company and are fair to all parties involved. Poorly informed decisions like the ones we saw at the beginning of this chapter harm everyone who comes into contact with such organizations.

Although the vignette that opened this chapter focused on the police, similar concerns apply to job applicants who go on to commit other crimes. For example, the terrorist who killed 49 people in an Orlando nightclub, Omar Mateen, had been hired by the global security firm G4S, which issued him one of the weapons used in the fatal attack. G4S blamed this hiring decision on "a clerical error." The question then becomes whether one would trust their security needs to a company that would make such an egregious mistake with an otherwise simple background check.[1]

Selecting the best talent is critical to the competitiveness of organizations, as well as to that of the nations within which they are embedded. The United States has always been a magnet for talent from other nations, and this country grew economically powerful through the contributions of many people who emigrated here from other countries. Some observers have suggested the United States is losing its edge in this regard, however, and that "this is America's most serious long-term threat."[2] That is, social and economic inequality, racial and ethnic bias, growing political intolerance, and a failing educational system are contributing to a state of reverse migration, where highly trained professionals who came to this country are now leaving the United States in larger percentages than those coming in. Innovation and economic growth are fueled by people, and the firms or countries that bring in the best people will be the ones that compete most successfully.

The purpose of this chapter is to familiarize you with ways to minimize errors in employee selection and placement and, in doing so, improve your company's competitive position. We focus first on five standards that any selection method should meet. Then we evaluate several common selection methods that meet those standards.

Selection Method Standards

LO 6-1
Establish the basic scientific properties of personnel selection methods, including reliability, validity, and generalizability.

Personnel selection is the process by which companies decide who will or will not be allowed into organizations. Several generic standards should be met in any selection process. We focus on five: (1) reliability, (2) validity, (3) generalizability, (4) utility, and (5) legality. The first four build off each other in the sense that the preceding standard is often necessary but not sufficient for the one that follows. This is less the case with legal standards. However, a thorough understanding of the first four standards helps us understand the rationale underlying many legal standards.

RELIABILITY

Much of the work in personnel selection involves measuring characteristics of people to determine who will be accepted for job openings. For example, we might be interested in applicants' physical characteristics (like strength or endurance), their cognitive abilities (such as spatial memory or verbal reasoning), or aspects of their personality (like their decisiveness or integrity). Many people have inaccurate stereotypes about how these kinds of characteristics may be related to factors such as race, sex, age, or ethnic background; therefore, we need to get past these stereotypes and measure the actual attributes directly.[3] For example, with respect to jobs in the field of public safety, research employing fake résumés sent to employers found that white applicants with a criminal background were more likely to be hired than African American applicants with no criminal record but identical on all other attributes.[4]

One key standard for any measuring device is its reliability. We define **reliability** as the degree to which a measure is free from random error. If a measure of some supposedly stable characteristic such as intelligence is reliable, then the score a person receives based on that measure will be consistent over time and in different contexts.

Reliability
The consistency of a performance measure; the degree to which a performance measure is free from random error.

Estimating the Reliability of Measurement

Most measurement in personnel selection deals with complex characteristics like intelligence, integrity, and leadership ability. However, to appreciate some of the complexities in measuring people, we will consider something concrete in discussing these concepts: the measurement of height. For example, if we were measuring an applicant's height, we might start by using a 12-inch ruler. Let's say the first person we measure turns out to be 6 feet, $1^1/_4$ inches tall. It would not be surprising to find out that someone else measuring the same person a second time, perhaps an hour later, found this applicant's height to be 6 feet, $^3/_4$ inches. The same applicant, measured a third time, maybe the next day, might be measured at 6 feet, $1^1/_2$ inches tall.

As this example makes clear, even though the person's height is a stable characteristic, we get slightly different results each time he is assessed. This means that each time the person is assessed, we must be making slight errors. If we used a measure of height that was not as reliable as a ruler—for example, guessing someone's height after seeing her walk across the room—we might see an even greater amount of unreliability in the measure. Thus *reliability* refers to the measuring instrument (a ruler versus a visual guess) rather than to the characteristic itself.

We can estimate reliability in several different ways, and because most of these rely on computing a correlation coefficient, we will briefly describe and illustrate this statistic. The *correlation coefficient* is a measure of the degree to which two sets of numbers are related. The correlation coefficient expresses the strength of the relationship in numerical form. A perfect positive relationship (as one set of numbers goes up, so does the other) equals $+1.0$; a perfect negative relationship (as one goes up, the other goes down) equals -1.0. When there is no relationship between the sets of numbers, the correlation equals .00. Although the actual calculation of this statistic goes beyond the scope of this book, it will be useful for us to conceptually examine the nature of the correlation coefficient and what this means in personnel selection contexts.

When assessing the reliability of a measure, for example, we might be interested in knowing how scores on the measure at one time relate to scores on the same measure at another time. Obviously, if the characteristic we are measuring is supposedly stable (like intelligence or integrity) and the time period is short, this relationship should be strong. If it were weak, then the measure would be inconsistent—hence, unreliable. This is called assessing *test–retest reliability*. Note that the time period between measurements is important when it comes to interpreting test–retest reliability. The assumption is that the characteristic being measured is not changing; hence, any change from Time 1 to Time 2 is treated as an error. When the time period becomes too long, this increases the chance that the characteristic itself is changing. For example, if one is measuring personality traits, the evidence suggests that people become more conscientious, more introverted, and more emotionally stable as they get older. These are not age stereotypes but rather scientifically documented facts about the instability of certain personality traits over extended periods of time.[5]

Plotting the two sets of numbers on a two-dimensional graph often helps us to appreciate the meaning of various levels of the correlation coefficient. Figure 6.1, for example, examines the relationship between student scholastic aptitude in one's junior and senior years in high school, where aptitude for college is measured in three ways: (1) via scores on the SAT (formerly known as the Scholastic Aptitude Test), (2) via ratings from a high school counselor on a 1-to-100 scale, and (3) via tossing dice. In this plot, each number on the graphs represents a person whose scholastic aptitude is assessed twice (in the junior and senior years), so in Figure 6.1a, 1 represents a person who scored 1580 on the SAT in the junior year and 1500 in the senior year; 20 represents a person who scored 480 in the junior year and 620 in the senior year.

Figure 6.1a shows a very strong relationship between SAT scores across the two years. This relationship is not perfect in that the scores changed from one year to the next but not by a great deal. Turning to Figure 6.1b, we see that the relationship between the high school counselors' ratings across the two years, while still positive, is not as strong. That is, the counselors' ratings of individual students' aptitudes for college are less consistent over the two years than are the students' test scores. This might be attributable to the fact the counselor's rating during the junior year was based on a smaller number of observations relative to the ratings made during senior year. Finally, Figure 6.1c shows a worst-case scenario, where the students' aptitudes are assessed by tossing two six-sided dice. As you would expect, the random nature of the dice means that there is virtually no relationship between scores taken in one year and scores taken the next. Although no one would seriously consider tossing dice to be a measure of aptitude, research shows that the correlation of overall ratings of job applicants' suitability for jobs based on unstructured interviews is very close to .00. Thus, one cannot assume a measure is reliable without checking its reliability directly. Novices in

Figure 6.1a

Measurements of a Student's Aptitude

Figure 6.1b

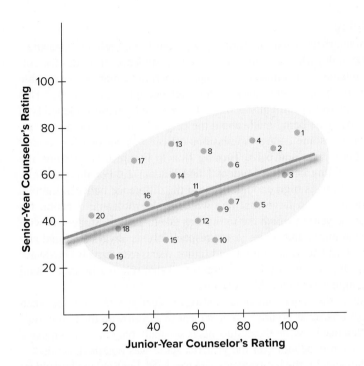

measurement are often surprised at exactly how unreliable many human judgments turn out to be. Thus, much of the science that deals with selection tries to go beyond subjective human judgments. So for example, if one wants to really know how extraverted a person is, a sociometric badge that records the number, length, and nature of this person's communication patterns across time is likely to provide more reliable test–retest data relative to the subjective perceptions of a former supervisor or interviewer who met the person just once.[6]

Figure 6.1c

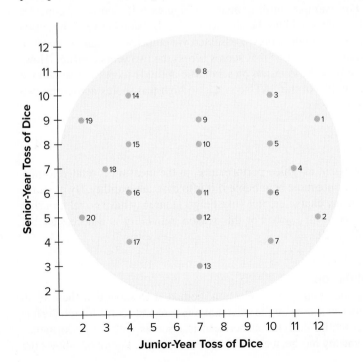

Standards for Reliability

Regardless of what characteristic we are measuring, we want highly reliable measures. Thus, in the previous example, when it comes to measuring students' aptitudes for college, the SAT is more reliable than counselors' ratings, which in turn are more reliable than tossing dice. But in an absolute sense, how high is high enough—.50, .70, .90? This is a difficult question to answer specifically because the required reliability depends in part on the nature of the decision being made about the people being measured.

For example, let's assume some college admissions officer was considering several students depicted in Figures 6.1a and 6.1b. Turning first to Figure 6.1b, assume the admissions officer was deciding between Student 1 and Student 20. For this decision, the .50 reliability of the ratings is high enough because the difference between the two students' counselors' ratings is so large that one would make the same decision for admissions regardless of the year in which the rating was taken. That is, Student 1 (with scores of 100 and 80 in the junior and senior years, respectively) is always admitted and Student 20 (with scores of 12 and 42 for junior and senior years, respectively) is always rejected. Thus, although the ratings in this case are not all that reliable in an absolute sense, their reliability is high enough for this decision.

By contrast, let's assume the same college admissions officer was deciding between Student 1 and Student 2. Looking at Figure 6.1a, it is clear that even with the highly reliable SAT scores, the difference between these students is so small that one would make a different admissions decision depending on the year the score was obtained. Student 1 would be selected over Student 2 if the junior-year score was used, but Student 2 would be chosen over Student 1 if the senior-year score was used. Thus, even though the reliability of the SAT exam is high in an absolute sense, it is not high enough for this decision. Under these conditions, the admissions officer needs to find some other basis for making the decision regarding these two students (like high school GPA or rank in graduating class).

Although these two scenarios clearly show that no specific value of reliability is always acceptable, they also demonstrate why, all else being equal, the more reliable a measure is, the better. For example, turning again to Figures 6.1a and 6.1b, consider Student 9 and Student 14. One would not be able to make a decision between these two students based on scholastic aptitude scores if assessed via counselors' ratings, because the unreliability in the ratings is so large that scores across the two years conflict. However, one would be able to base the decision on scholastic aptitude scores if assessed via the SAT, because the reliability of the SAT scores is so high that scores across the two years point to the same conclusion.

VALIDITY

Validity
The extent to which a performance measure assesses all the relevant—and only the relevant—aspects of job performance.

We define **validity** as the extent to which performance on the measure is related to performance on the job. A measure must be reliable if it is to have any validity. By contrast, we can reliably measure many characteristics (like height) that may have no relationship to whether someone can perform a job. For this reason, reliability is a necessary but insufficient condition for validity.

Criterion-Related Validation

Criterion-related validity
A method of establishing the validity of a personnel selection method by showing a substantial correlation between test scores and job-performance scores.

One way of establishing the validity of a selection method is to show that there is an empirical association between scores on the selection measure and scores for job performance. If there is a substantial correlation between test scores and job-performance scores, **criterion-related validity** has been established. For example, Figure 6.2 shows the relationship between 2014 scores on the SAT and 2015 freshman grade point average (GPA). In this example, there is roughly a .50 correlation between the SAT and GPA. This .50 is referred to as a *validity coefficient*. Note that we have used the correlation coefficient to assess both reliability and validity, which may seem somewhat confusing. The key distinction is that the correlation reflects a reliability estimate when we are attempting to assess the same characteristic twice (such as SAT scores in the junior and senior years), but the correlation coefficient reflects a validity coefficient when we are attempting to relate one characteristic (SAT) to performance on some task (GPA).

Criterion-related validity studies come in two varieties. **Predictive validation** seeks to establish an empirical relationship between test scores taken *prior* to being hired and eventual performance on the job. Because of the time and effort required to conduct a predictive validation study, many employers are tempted to use a different design. **Concurrent validation** assesses the validity of a test by administering it to people already on the job and then correlating test scores with existing measures of each person's performance. For example, the testing company Infor measures 39 behavioral, cognitive, and cultural traits among job applicants and then compares their scores on those dimensions with the top performers in the company. The assumption is that if high performers in the company score high on any trait, then the company should use scores on this trait to screen new hires.[7] Figure 6.3 compares the two types of validation study.

Despite the extra effort and time needed for predictive validation, it is superior to concurrent validation for a number of reasons. First, job applicants (because they are seeking work) are typically more motivated to perform well on the tests than are current employees (who already have jobs). Thus, job applicants are more tempted to fake responses in order to look good relative to current jobholders. Second, current employees have learned many things on the job that job applicants have not yet learned. Therefore, the correlation between test scores and job performance for current employees may not be the same as the correlation between test scores and job performance for

Predictive validation
A criterion-related validity study that seeks to establish an empirical relationship between applicants' test scores and their eventual performance on the job.

Concurrent validation
A criterion-related validity study in which a test is administered to all the people currently in a job and then incumbents' scores are correlated with existing measures of their performance on the job.

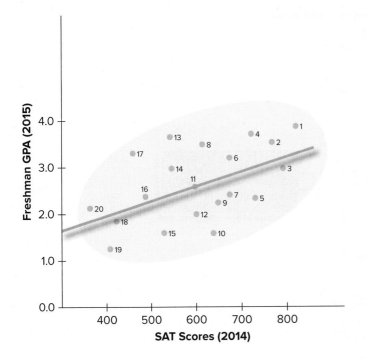

Figure 6.2

Relationship between 2014 SAT Scores and 2015 Freshman GPA

less knowledgeable job applicants. Third, current employees tend to be homogeneous—that is, similar to each other on many characteristics. Thus, on many of the characteristics needed for success on the job, most current employees will show restriction in range. This restricted range makes it hard to detect a relationship between test scores and job-performance scores because few of the current employees will be very low on the characteristic one is trying to validate. For example, if emotional stability is required for a nursing career, it is quite likely that most nurses who have amassed five or six years' experience will score high on this characteristic. Yet to validate a test, one needs both high test scorers (who should subsequently perform well on the job) and low test scorers (who should perform poorly on the job). Thus, although concurrent studies can sometimes help one to anticipate the results of predictive studies, they do not serve as substitutes.

Obviously, we would like our measures to be high in validity; but as with the reliability standard, we must also ask, how high is high enough? When trying to determine how much validity is enough, one typically has to turn to tests of statistical significance. A test of statistical significance answers the question, "Assuming that there is no true

Figure 6.3

Graphic Depiction of Concurrent and Predictive Validation Designs

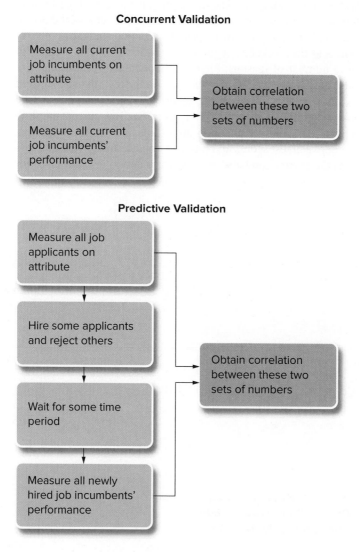

SAMPLE SIZE	REQUIRED CORRELATION
5	.75
10	.58
20	.42
40	.30
80	.21
100	.19

Table 6.1
Required Level of Correlation to Reach Statistical Significance as a Function of Sample Size

relationship between the predictor and the criterion, what are the odds of seeing a relationship this strong by chance alone?" If these odds are very low, then one might infer that the results from the test were in fact predicting future job performance.

Table 6.1 shows how big a correlation between a selection measure and a measure of job performance needs to be to achieve statistical significance at a level of .05 (that is, there is only a 5 out of 100 chance that one could get a correlation this big by chance alone). Although it is generally true that bigger correlations are better, the size of the sample on which the correlation is based plays a large role as well. Because many of the selection methods we examine in the second half of this chapter generate correlations in the .20s and .30s, we often need samples of 80 to 90 people. A validation study with a small sample (such as 20 people) is almost doomed to failure from the start. Fortunately, advances in the ability to process "big data" via cloud-based analytics is greatly expanding the ability to find valid predictors of future job performance. For example, in the past, when it came to staffing its call centers, Xerox Corporation always looked for applicants who had done the job before. This seemed like a reasonable approach to take until the company assessed the empirical relationship between experience, on the one hand, and performance and turnover, on the other hand, and learned that experience did not matter at all. Instead, what really separated winners and losers in this occupation was their personality. People who were creative tended to perform well and stay on the job for a long time, whereas those who were inquisitive tended to struggle with the job and leave well before the company ever recouped its $5,000 investment in training.

Xerox now leaves all hiring for its nearly 500,000 call center jobs to a computer software algorithm that tirelessly looks for links between responses to personality items and a highly specific set of job outcomes. The program was developed by Evolv, Inc., and rather than relying on interviewer judgments that might be subject to personal biases, the Evolv program puts applicants through a battery of tests and personality items, then tracks their outcomes at the company over time. The algorithm is continually adjusting itself with the accumulation of ever more data, all in an effort to develop a statistical model that describes the ideal call center employee.[8]

Evolv is just one player in an expanding industry that seeks to use big data to help companies find and retain the best employees. Globally, spending on this sort of talent management software rose 15% in just one year to an estimated value of $3.8 billion, and the competition for this business is intense. For example, in 2011 alone, IBM purchased Kenexa for $1.3 billion, Oracle acquired Taleo for $1.9 billion, and SAP bought SuccessFactors for $3.4 billion.[9]

Content Validation

When sample sizes are small, an alternative test validation strategy, content validation, can be used. **Content validation** is performed by demonstrating that the questions or problems posed by the test are a representative sample of the kinds of situations or problems

Content validation
A test-validation strategy performed by demonstrating that the items, questions, or problems posed by a test are a representative sample of the kinds of situations or problems that occur on the job.

that occur on the job. A test that is content valid exposes the job applicant to situations that are likely to occur on the job, and then tests whether the applicant currently has sufficient knowledge, skills, or abilities to handle such situations.

Many of the new simulations that organizations are using are essentially computer-based role-playing games, where applicants play the role of the job incumbent, confronting the exact types of people and problems real-live job incumbents would face. The simulations are just like traditional role-playing games (e.g., "The Sims"), and the applicant's reactions and behaviors are scored to see how well they match with what one would expect from the ideal employee. For example, if one is considering applicants for a wait staff job at a restaurant, the game *Wasabi Waiter*, designed by Knack.it, allows the employer to watch how the applicant responds to finicky customers, uppity receptionists, emotionally unstable chefs, and other predictably challenging situations that are likely to take place in a busy establishment.[10] Because the content of these tests so closely parallels the content of the job, one can safely make inferences from one to the other. For example, as the "Competing through Technology" box shows, in the field of computer programming, employers see the skills needed to win international software code problem-solving competitions as highly related to the skills necessary to perform well on the job. Although criterion-related validity is established by empirical means, content validity is achieved primarily through a process of expert judgment.

The ability to use content validation in small-sample settings makes it generally more applicable than criterion-related validation. However, content validation has two limitations. First, one assumption behind content validation is that the person who is to be hired must have the knowledge, skills, or abilities at the time he or she is hired. Second, because subjective judgment plays such a large role in content validation, it is critical to minimize the amount of inference involved on the part of judges. Thus, the judges' ratings need to be made with respect to relatively concrete and observable behaviors.

GENERALIZABILITY

Generalizability
The degree to which the validity of a selection method established in one context extends to other contexts.

Generalizability is defined as the degree to which the validity of a selection method established in one context extends to other contexts. Thus, the SAT may be a valid predictor of someone's performance (e.g., as a measure of someone's GPA in an undergraduate program), but, does this same test predict performance in graduate programs? If the test does not predict success in this other situation, then it does not "generalize" to this other context.

There are two primary "contexts" over which we might like to generalize: different situations (jobs or organizations) and different samples of people. Just as reliability is necessary but not sufficient for validity, validity is necessary but not sufficient for generalizability.

It was once believed, for example, that validity coefficients were situationally specific—that is, the level of correlation between test and performance varied as one went from one organization to another, even though the jobs studied seemed to be identical. Subsequent research has indicated that this is largely false. Rather, tests tend to show similar levels of correlation even across jobs that are only somewhat similar (at least for tests of intelligence and cognitive ability). Correlations with these kinds of tests change as one goes across widely different kinds of jobs, however. Specifically, the more complex the job, the higher the validity of many tests. It was also believed that tests showed differential subgroup validity, which meant that the validity coefficient for any test–job performance pair was different for people of different races or genders. This belief was also refuted by subsequent research, and, in general, one finds very similar levels of correlations across different groups of people.[11]

COMPETING THROUGH TECHNOLOGY

Computer Programming as a Sport and Work Sample

Although many Americans probably are aware of who is in the top 10 when it comes to college football and basketball, they may not be aware of who is ranked number one by separate rating agencies Topcoder and Codeforces in the field of software programming. The answer is Gennedy Korotkevich, a 21-year-old Belarusian who has been competing in international coding events since he was in second grade. Korotkevich has won more Facebook Hacker Cups and Google Code Jam trophies than any other contestant in history, and earns over $250,000 a year through his participation in a wide variety of sport programming competitions.

For those who are unaware of the fast-growing sport of computer programming, an important warning—these contests do not make for riveting television. In most of the contests, roughly two dozen competitors, who made their way to the finals by topping a thousand or so others in preliminary events online, rarely move from their workstations as they tackle five standardized puzzles that have to be solved

quickly with code that is as efficient as possible. Still, many employers study the results from these events looking to hire both winners and losers because they view this as a highly valid work sample test. Vladimer Novakovski, then vice president for engineering at Addepar, a software provider in the investment industry, noted, "Every time I hire someone who is good in these contests, they have crushed the job. They tend to be fast, accurate, and into getting things done."

The demographics at these competitions are hardly diverse. At the most recent Hacker Cup, all of the final 25 contestants were young white males and hailed from just three geographic regions: the United States, China, and Eastern Europe. The United States dominated sport programming early in the history of these events, winning 17 out of 20 International Collegiate Programming Contests between 1977 and 1997. Since 1997, however, the United States has not won a single competition. This can be traced to the fact that, relative to

China and Eastern Europe, winning these competitions is not that highly valued among U.S. colleges and universities. Scott Wu, one of the top sport programmers from China, sums this up well, noting that "if you do well in these competitions in China or Russia, you don't even have to apply to college. In the U.S., kids who do very well are still getting turned down from Harvard." That may be true, but clearly employers in the industry are well aware of those ranked in the top 100—including Gennedy Korotkevich.

DISCUSSION QUESTIONS

1. Why might having citizens who perform well in sport coding competitions not only help a country's economy but also be helpful to national security?
2. What can be done to enhance the involvement of woman and minorities in contests such as these?

SOURCES: A. Vance, "The Jocks of Computer Code Do It for the Job Offers," *Businessweek*, September 25, 2015, pp. 31–33; B. Poucher, "Behind the Scenes at the International Collegiate Programming Contest," *Forbes*, July 1, 2016.

Because the evidence suggests that test validity often extends across situations and subgroups, *validity generalization* stands as an alternative for validating selection methods for companies that cannot employ criterion-related or content validation. Validity generalization is a three-step process. First, the company provides evidence from previous criterion-related validity studies conducted in other situations that shows that a specific test (such as a test of emotional stability) is a valid predictor for a specific job (like nurse at a large hospital). Second, the company provides evidence from job analysis to document that the job it is trying to fill (nurse at a small hospital) is similar in all major respects to the job validated elsewhere (nurse at a large hospital). Finally, if the company can show that it uses a test that is the same as or similar to that used in the validated setting, then one can "generalize" the validity from the first context (large hospital) to the new context (small hospital).

UTILITY

LO 6-2

Discuss how the particular characteristics of a job, an organization, or an applicant affect the utility of any test.

Utility

The degree to which the information provided by selection methods enhances the effectiveness of selecting personnel in real organizations.

Utility is the degree to which the information provided by selection methods enhances the bottom-line effectiveness of the organization. In general, the more reliable, valid, and generalizable the selection method is, the more utility it will have. However, many characteristics of particular selection contexts enhance or detract from the usefulness of given selection methods, even when reliability, validity, and generalizability are held constant.

Figures 6.4a and 6.4b, for example, show two different scenarios where the correlation between a measure of extroversion and the amount of sales revenue generated by a sample of sales representatives is the same for two different companies: Company A and Company B. Although the correlation between the measure of extroversion and sales is the same, Company B derives much more utility or practical benefit from the measure. That is, as indicated by the arrows proceeding out of the boxes (which indicate the people selected), the average sales revenue of the three people selected by Company B (Figure 6.4b) is $850,000, compared to $780,000 from the three people selected by Company A (Figure 6.4a).

The major difference between these two companies is that Company B generated twice as many applicants as Company A. This means that the selection ratio (the percentage of people selected relative to the total number of people tested) is quite low for Company B (3/20) relative to Company A (3/10). Thus, the people selected by Company B have higher amounts of extroversion than those selected by Company A; therefore, Company B takes better advantage of the relationship

Figure 6.4a

Utility of Selecting on Extroversion Scores When Selection Ratio Is High

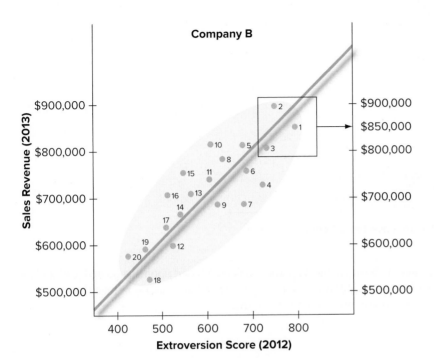

Figure 6.4b

Utility of Selecting on Extroversion Scores When Selection Ratio Is Low

between extroversion and sales. Thus, the utility of any test generally increases as the selection ratio decreases, as long as the additional costs of recruiting and testing are not excessive.

Many other factors relate to the utility of a test. For example, the value of the product or service produced by the job incumbent plays a role: The more valuable the product or service, the more value there is in selecting the top performers. For example, in a high-tech company, there is tremendous value associated with a great team of software engineers with a proven record of working productively together to create innovative products. If a company tried to hire total strangers without this kind of track record and build a team from scratch, it might take years to see any value from a set of individual hires. Thus, many organizations in this industry are willing to pay top dollar to hire entire intact teams. The term "acqui-hire" is used in this industry to describe this practice, and in some cases, large companies are willing to pay up to $5 million to bring an independent team into their fold. Ashley Vandy, an HR director at Facebook, notes, "We are always looking for talent, and these deals are one way to bring great teams to Facebook."[12]

Most individual differences take on the form of a *normal distribution*. In other words, most people are in the middle, followed by a smaller group of people who are a little bit above or below the mean, followed by an even smaller group of outliers far above and below the mean. This belief in the normal distribution has traditionally been extended to people's beliefs about job performance, even though little evidence has been collected to test this belief. However, a study examining over 600,000 entertainers, politicians, amateur athletes, professional athletes, and scientists has challenged this idea and instead suggests that job performance follows a *power law distribution*. Figure 6.5 shows how a distribution that follows a power law differs dramatically from a normal distribution, in the sense that there are few high performers and a large group of potentially poor performers. The implication of these findings for utility analysis is important because it implies that the dollar value of a "highly productive worker" (e.g., someone who is one

Figure 6.5

Comparing a Normal Distribution (Red Curve) to a Power Law (Blue Shading)

standard deviation above the mean, perhaps selected based upon a validated test) and an "average worker" (e.g., at the mean, perhaps selected at random) is much greater than one would expect if the distribution were normal.[13]

LEGALITY

LO 6-3

Describe the government's role in personnel selection decisions, particularly in the areas of constitutional law, federal laws, executive orders, and judicial precedent.

The final standard to which any selection method should adhere is *legality*. All selection methods should conform to existing laws and existing legal precedents. For example, Kentucky Fried Chicken requires its workers to wear slacks, and was charged with discrimination when it refused to allow Sheila Silver, a Pentecostal Christian, to wear a long dress at work, which was what her religion required. In a similar case, with a different religion, the New York City Police Department was charged with violating the religious rights of a Muslim officer whose religion-required beard violated the department's appearance code.[14] These are hardly isolated incidents in the sense that cases based on religious discrimination have skyrocketed recently. According to the Equal Employment Opportunity Commission (EEOC), in 2013 alone, over 3,700 religious discrimination claims were brought against employers.[15]

In both of these cases, the law upheld the religious beliefs of the job applicant against requirements posed by the employer. In other cases, recent legislation, falling under the heading of "religious freedom" bills, has attempted to defend the religious beliefs of business owners, allowing companies to discriminate against certain groups. As you can see from the "Integrity in Action" box, these new laws are controversial and are being opposed by many large employers.

Employers who are taken to court for illegal discrimination experience high costs associated with litigation, settlements, and awards, and also suffer potential damage to their social reputations as good employers, making recruitment more difficult. Moreover, although the threat of litigation is ever present, this is especially a problem during economic recessions, when it is difficult to find a job. The number of discrimination cases filed with the EEOC set a record of over 100,000 in 2011 alone.[16] These kinds of suits are costly to defend, and even if the company prevails in a court of law, it may not prevail in the court of public opinion.

This is exactly what happened to Chick-fil-A. Even though the firm had never been charged with any form of employment discrimination, when the president of the company made disparaging comments regarding gay marriage in 2012, there was an immediate negative backlash against "hate chicken" that harmed sales. Even worse, it threatened

INTEGRITY IN ACTION

Employers Unite to Fight "Religious Freedom" Bills

Almost all organizations that care about ethics have a mission statement and a values statement that they adhere to with religious fervor. However, in some contexts, this comes into conflict with legislation that, in an effort to protect freedom of religion, contradicts those values. For example, across the United States, a large number of states have introduced "religious freedom" bills that allow employers to discriminate against lesbian, gay, bisexual, and transgender (LGBT) applicants and employees. Supporters of these bills argue that the practices in which LGBT individuals engage run counter to the religious beliefs held by some business owners, and that the values of the LGBT community should not be forced on those employers.

Indiana was one of the first states to pass a religious freedom bill, and although that bill was later repealed, it sparked numerous similar efforts in other regions. The Bureau of Labor Statistics reports that antigay discrimination is legal in 28 states that, as a whole, comprise over 50% of the workforce. According to the Human Rights Campaign, over 200 new bills deemed hostile to gay and transgender individuals are under consideration in 33 states.

Many employers who view such legislation as running counter to their own values are collaborating to fight or prevent future laws. In the beginning, employers took a divide-and-conquer strategy to this battle, in which different companies led in different regions. For example, Eli Lilly and Salesforce.com spearheaded efforts in Indiana, Disney has led efforts in Georgia, and MGM Resorts has focused on Mississippi, all because they had substantial operations in those regions. However, a more integrated approach is now being adopted so that companies do not have to take a reactive, "whack-a-mole" approach to impending legislation. As one of the employers stated, "Equality is a core value, and where we see negative legislation we have to take a stand. We want to be a spark for others to get involved in areas and states that are considering these types of legislation."

DISCUSSION QUESTIONS

1. How can one reconcile the religious values espoused by some business owners with the values of LGBT employees, or is this strictly a zero-sum game?

2. Why is the effort to thwart religious freedom bills sponsored primarily by large employers, and is there any way to reconcile the values of large employers and small employers on this issue?

SOURCE: J. Green and Tim Higgens, "LGBT Inc." *Businessweek,* April 27, 2016, pp. 26–28; J. Eidelson, "Sweet Cakes with a Bitter Aftertaste," *Businessweek,* May 30, 2016, pp. 29–30; J. Green, "At Work and Out of the Closest in the Heartland," *Businessweek,* March 6, 2017, pp. 22–23.

the company's expansion plans and strategy to move into northern and urban areas. The mayor of Boston went so far as to send a letter to the company urging it to back down from plans to locate in Boston, and he was quoted in the *Boston Herald* saying that "he would make it very difficult" for the restaurant to come to town. Chicago mayor Rahm Emanuel chimed in and stated that "Chick-fil-A's values are not Chicago's values," and protest movements in New York City and San Francisco were organized to oppose expansion into those areas. All of this happened even though no one ever presented any evidence or even charged the company with discriminating against gay customers or job applicants.[17]

Federal Legislation

Three federal laws form the basis for a majority of the suits filed by job applicants: the Civil Rights Act of 1991, the Age Discrimination in Employment Act of 1967, and the Americans with Disabilities Act of 1990 (all discussed in Chapter 3).

Civil Rights Act of 1991.   An extension of the Civil Rights Act of 1964, the Civil Rights Act of 1991 protects individuals from discrimination based on race, color, sex, religion, and national origin with respect to hiring as well as compensation and working conditions.

First, it defines employers' explicit obligation to establish the business necessity of any neutral-appearing selection method that has had adverse impact on groups specified by the law. This is typically done by showing that the test has significant criterion-related or content validity. If the employer cannot show such a difference, which the research suggests will be difficult, then the process may be ruled illegal. Ironically, for example, the Consumer Finance Protection Bureau (CFPB) that was created as part of the Dodd-Frank Act, which regulates banks and financial institutions to specifically prevent discrimination in loan practices, discovered that its own promotion policies created adverse impact. An investigation into the CFPB's promotion policies found that 21% of the agency's white employees received the highest performance rating compared with just 10% of the African American employees and 9% of Hispanic employees. Since this rating was used to make promotion decisions, it became a neutral-appearing employment practice that created adverse impact and thus had to be justified.[18]

Second, the 1991 act allows the individual filing the complaint to have a jury decide whether he or she may recover punitive damages (in addition to lost wages and benefits) for emotional injuries caused by the discrimination. This can generate large financial settlements as well as poor public relations that can hinder the organization's ability to compete.

Finally, the 1991 act explicitly prohibits the granting of preferential treatment to minority groups. Preferential treatment is often attractive because many of the most valid methods for screening people, especially cognitive ability tests and work sample tests, often are high in adverse impact.[19] For example, as we saw earlier in the "Competing through Technology" box, although software coding sport competitions help organizations uncover talented programmers, almost all of the tournament champions tend to be white males. Thus, there is somewhat of a trade-off in terms of selecting the highest scorers on validated tests, on the one hand, and creating diversity in the workforce, on the other hand.[20]

One potential way to "have your cake and eat it too" is to simply rank the scores of different races or gender groups within their own groups, and then take perhaps the top 10% of scorers from each group, instead of the top 10% that would be obtained if one ignored race or gender. Many observers feel that this practice is justified because it levels the playing field in a context where bias works against African Americans. However, the 1991 act specifically outlaws this practice (sometimes referred to as *race norming*). Adjusting scores in this way has been found to have a number of negative effects, not only on the attitudes of white males who claim it causes reverse discrimination but also on the proposed beneficiaries of such preferential treatment.[21]

Two Supreme Court cases show that policies that may be construed as promoting preferential treatment will not stand up in court. In the first case, voters in the state of Michigan backed an initiative that made it illegal to engage in affirmative action for minorities when it came to admissions to Michigan colleges. Because the majority of voters in this state were white, this initiative was challenged because of legal precedents that protect minorities from being targeted for unfair treatment through the political process. That is, taken to an extreme, if a majority of members of a state were white, it would not be permissible for them to support a ballot initiative that would prevent minorities from attending college at all, since doing so would be patently unfair. The challenge to the Michigan initiative claimed that its effect was close to this extreme, but the challenge was struck down by the Supreme Court, which decided that the electorate was acting within its rights.[22] The Court did not necessarily say that affirmative action was illegal in this case, but rather that it was fair for the general electorate to impose its will in this way, which leaves colleges that are trying to promote diversity scrambling for other alternatives, one of which took place at the University of Texas.[23]

The Supreme Court case that involved the University of Texas illustrates how difficult it can be to achieve diversity goals while still upholding merit-based selection and avoiding perceptions of reverse discrimination. Specifically, in order to increase the percentage of African American and Hispanic students in the UT system, the school made it a policy to accept the top 10% of the graduating class of every high school. Because many high schools in Texas tend to be segregated by race and ethnicity, this policy worked somewhat like race norming in ensuring that members of every group found their way into college; so far, so good.[24]

To push the diversity gains even further, though, the admissions officers at UT noted that many African American students in affluent suburban schools often were rejected for admission, even though they had higher test scores than African American students from urban schools. When the school tried to reach out and accept those students, however, this policy was challenged. In 2016, a divided Supreme Court upheld the legality of the UT affirmative action program. Writing for the 4–3 majority, Justice Anthony Kennedy stated that "the university is entitled considerable deference in defining the type of institution it wished to be, including intangible characteristics, such as student body diversity that might be central to the university's identity and educational mission.[25]

Whereas the issue at the heart of the UT case dealt with the underrepresentation of African American students, a separate issue deals with what to do when neutral-appearing selection methods create a situation where some minority group might exceed its representation in the general population. For example, at many of the nation's most prestigious universities, the percentage of Asian American students has remained at 15–20% for the past 20 years, even though the Asian American population has doubled in that time period. The 15–20% rate is still within the bounds of the general rate for this group in the population, but this can be achieved only by capping the number of admitted Asian American students to a fixed quota. Thus, according to one study, an Asian American would have to score 140 points higher than whites on the SAT, 270 points higher than Hispanics, and 450 points higher than African Americans, in order to have the same chance at admission to many of the nation's leading universities. Clearly, balancing the need for both diversity and meritocracy will always be challenging whenever one group underperforms or overperforms on some test used to make decisions.[26]

Rather than employing race norming, employers can partially achieve both goals of maximizing predicted future performance and diversity in several ways. First, aggressive recruiting of members of protected groups allows an employer to generate a larger pool of protected group members, and, by being highly selective within this larger group, the scores of admitted applicants will more closely match those of all the other groups.[27] Second, as we will see later in this chapter, different selection methods have different degrees of adverse impact, and multistage selection batteries that use different methods at different stages can also help.[28]

Finally, one common approach that does not seem to work is to abandon the kinds of compliance-driven, evidenced-based workforce utilization reviews discussed in Chapter 5, in favor of softer, "inclusion" initiatives that express the generic value of diversity but fail to document goals and timetables statistically. Some organizations treat diversity more like a marketing campaign than an HR initiative, and it is not uncommon to see companies that won awards for their "inclusion programs," such as Texaco and Bank of

America, also later convicted of illegal discrimination. Some observers have noted that there is an almost complete overlap of the lists of the top 50 companies for inclusion and the top 50 companies for advertising expenditures, and the need to complement style with substance cannot be overlooked in this critical area.[29] The simple truth is that the best predictors of whether a firm becomes truly diverse and avoids litigation is whether (1) there is a specific person (e.g., a diversity compliance officer) whose sole job is to monitor hiring statistics, (2) this person has the power to change hiring practices, and (3) this person is held strictly accountable in his or her own performance appraisal for achieving quantifiable results.[30]

Age Discrimination in Employment Act of 1967. Court interpretations of the Age Discrimination in Employment Act mirror those of the Civil Rights Act, in that if any neutral-appearing practice happens to have adverse impact on those over age 40, then the burden of proof shifts to the employer, who must show business necessity to avoid a guilty verdict.

For example, the Texas Roadhouse restaurant company was sued for discrimination based on this law. Whereas 20% of servers nationally are over the age of 40, this was true for less than 2% of Texas Roadhouse employees. The suit was brought by a 40-year-old woman who applied for a job at a Texas Roadhouse restaurant in Palm Bay, Florida, and was told there were no openings. A few days later, she learned that one of her daughter's friends interviewed after she did and got a job offer. Despite this incident and the larger data on under-utilization, the chain defended its action by stating that it needed younger workers to reflect its brand image and attract more customers.[31] This appeal to brand image and customer preference has a long history as a "business necessity" defense, but it rarely seems to prevail in court.[32]

This act does not protect younger workers (thus, there is never a case for "reverse discrimination" here), and like the most recent Civil Rights Act, it allows for jury trials and punitive damages. This act outlaws almost all "mandatory retirement" programs (company policies that dictate that everyone who reaches a set age must retire).

Americans with Disabilities Act (ADA) of 1990. The ADA protects individuals with physical and mental disabilities (or with a history of the same), and requires that employers make "reasonable accommodation" to disabled individuals whose handicaps may prevent them from performing essential functions of the job as currently designed. "Reasonable accommodation" could include restructuring jobs, modifying work schedules, making facilities accessible, providing readers, or modifying equipment. The ADA does not require an organization to hire someone whose disability prevents him or her from performing either critical or routine aspects of the job, nor does it require accommodations that would cause "undue hardship."

There is some degree of political pressure to increase the hiring of disabled workers, and in 2014, the Department of Labor issued new rules aimed at government contractors that decreed they should set a goal of having 7% of their workforce be composed of disabled employees. Thus, if you are applying for a job with a government contractor, you need to check a box that asks whether or not you are disabled. The ruling was controversial because many disabled workers, especially those with nonobvious physical impairments or mental impairments, are unlikely to check that box. This means that some employers may be meeting the goal but are not able to show it because of applicants' reluctance to check the box.[33]

One source of disabled workers that employers are increasingly tapping in to is the pool of Gulf War era veterans. This pool of potential workers was highly under-utilized by employers as recently as 2011, when the unemployment rate for this group was well over 30%. That proportion has since dropped to less than 10%. Although part of the drop is attributable to a general improvement in the labor market, some of it is also due to the efforts of programs like the Wounded Warrior Project, which seeks to help disabled veterans find jobs in the private sector. For example, this group led efforts to reclassify the idiosyncratic codes for technical skills used in the military to the codes used by the Department of Labor's O*NET system (see Chapter 4 for a description of O*NET). This made it much easier for veterans to translate their skills into terms more broadly used in the private sector.[34]

Types of Selection Methods

In the first half of this chapter, we laid out the five standards by which to judge selection measures. In this half of the chapter, we examine the common selection methods used in various organizations and discuss their advantages and disadvantages in terms of these standards.

LO 6-4
List the common methods used in selecting human resources.

INTERVIEWS

A selection interview has been defined as "a dialogue initiated by one or more persons to gather information and evaluate the qualifications of an applicant for employment." The selection interview is the most widespread selection method employed in organizations, and there have been literally hundreds of studies examining their effectiveness.[35]

Unfortunately, the long history of research on the employment interview suggests that, without proper care, it can be unreliable, low in validity, and biased against a number of different groups. Moreover, interviews are relatively costly because they require at least one person to interview another person, and these persons have to be brought to the same geographic location. Finally, in terms of legality, the subjectivity embodied in the process, as well as the opportunity for unconscious bias effects, often makes applicants upset, particularly if they fail to get a job after being asked apparently irrelevant questions. In the end, subjective selection methods like the interview must be validated by traditional criterion-related or content-validation procedures if they show any degree of adverse impact.

Fortunately, more recent research has pointed to a number of concrete steps that one can employ to increase the utility of the personnel selection interview. First, HR staff should keep the interview structured, standardized, and focused on accomplishing a small number of goals. That is, they should plan to come out of each interview with quantitative ratings on a small number of dimensions that are observable (like interpersonal style or ability to express oneself) and avoid ratings of abilities that may be better measured by tests (like intelligence). In addition to coming out of the interview with quantitative ratings, interviewers should also have a structured note-taking system that will aid recall when it comes to justifying the ratings.

Selection interviews should be focused totally on rating and ranking applicants, and even though it may be tempting to accomplish other goals like recruiting the candidate, this temptation needs to be resisted.[36] As we saw in Chapter 5, recruitment interviews should be kept separate from selection interviews because these types of dual-purpose interviews tend to fail on both scores. Then, after a sufficient amount of time to obtain performance evaluation data, interviewers should get normative feedback on which of the employees that they selected performed well versus poorly so that they can learn from past experience.[37]

LO 6-5
Describe the degree to which each of the common methods used in selecting human resources meets the demands of reliability, validity, generalizability, utility, and legality.

Table 6.2
Examples of Experience-Based and Future-Oriented Situational Interview Items

Experience-based	
Motivating employees:	"Think about an instance when you had to motivate an employee to perform a task that he or she disliked but that you needed to have done. How did you handle that situation?"
Resolving conflict:	"What was the biggest difference of opinion you ever had with a co-worker? How did you resolve that situation?"
Overcoming resistance to change:	"What was the hardest change you ever had to bring about in a past job, and what did you do to get the people around you to change their thoughts or behaviors?"
Future-oriented	
Motivating employees:	"Suppose you were working with an employee who you knew greatly disliked performing a particular task. You needed to get this task completed, however, and this person was the only one available to do it. What would you do to motivate that person?"
Resolving conflict:	"Imagine that you and a co-worker disagree about the best way to handle an absenteeism problem with another member of your team. How would you resolve that situation?"
Overcoming resistance to change:	"Suppose you had an idea for a change in work procedures that would enhance quality, but some members of your work group were hesitant to make the change. What would you do in that situation?"

Situational interview
An interview procedure where applicants are confronted with specific issues, questions, or problems that are likely to arise on the job.

When it comes to content, interviewers should ask questions dealing with specific situations that are likely to arise on the job, and use the responses to determine what the person is likely to do in those situations. These types of **situational interview** items have been shown to have high predictive validity.[38] Situational judgment items come in two varieties, as shown in Table 6.2. Some items are "experience based" and require the applicant to reveal an experience he or she had in the past when confronting the situation. Other items are "future oriented" and ask what the person is likely to do when confronting a certain hypothetical situation in the future. Research suggests that both types of items can show validity but that experience-based items often outperform future-oriented ones. Experience-based items also appear to reduce some forms of impression management, such as ingratiation, better than future-oriented items.[39]

It is also important to use multiple interviewers who are trained to avoid many of the subjective errors that can result when one human being is asked to rate another. For example, at Google, there were definite concerns with demographic similarity bias in interviews, because their own analysis of local data was suggesting that managers were hiring people who seemed just like them.

©Digital Vision RF/Getty Images

When more than one person is able to interview a candidate for a position, there is significant advantage in removing any errors or biases that a single individual might make in choosing the correct person for the job. In today's technological world, it is becoming easier for multiple people to give their input in an interview by watching a video-recording or listening via conference call if they cannot be there in person.

To eliminate this problem, Google now compiles elaborate files for each candidate, and then has all interviews conducted by groups rather than individuals. Laszlo Bock, then vice president for Google's People Operations, noted that "we do everything to minimize the authority and power of the lone manager in making hiring decisions that are going to affect the entire company."[40] Many companies find that a good way to get "multiple eyes" on an applicant is to conduct digitally taped interviews, and then send the digitized files (rather than the applicants) around from place to place. Some employers find that the lack of true interaction that can take place in videos limits their value; hence, the use of face-to-face interactive technology like Skype is also on the rise.[41]

Regardless of the medium, anyone who will be conducting an employment interview needs to be trained, and a relatively small amount of money spent on training up front (in the $3,000–$30,000 range) can save major expenses later in the process if it prevents a lawsuit or a poor hiring decision that harms the organization.[42] The goal of most training programs is to limit the subjectivity of the process, and research suggests that it is best to ask interviewers to be "witnesses" of facts that can later be integrated via objective formulas, as opposed to being "judges" allowed to idiosyncratically weigh how various facts should be combined to form the final recommendation.[43]

REFERENCES, APPLICATION BLANKS, AND BACKGROUND CHECKS

Just as few employers would think of hiring someone without an interview, nearly all employers also use some method for getting background information on applicants before an interview. This information can be solicited from the people who know the candidate through reference checks.

The evidence on the reliability and validity of reference checks suggests that these are, at best, weak predictors of future success on the job. The main reason for this low validity is that the evaluations supplied in most reference letters are so positive that it is hard to differentiate applicants. This problem with reference letters has two causes. First, the applicant usually gets to choose who writes the letter and can thus choose only those writers who think the highest of her abilities. Second, because letter writers can never be sure who will read the letters, they may justifiably fear that supplying damaging information about someone could come back to haunt them. Thus, it is clearly not in the past employers' interest to reveal too much information beyond job title and years of service.

Another problem with reference checks is that applicants do not always tell the truth when it comes to listing their references. In fact, 30% of the companies that check references find false or misleading references on applications. Michael Erwin, a career advisor at CareerBuilder, notes, "For some reason, people think companies aren't going to check their references and therefore they think they can get away with all sorts of fabrications. In reality, 80% of companies do in fact check references prior to offering someone an interview or prior to making an offer.[44]

In addition to outside references, employers can also collect background information from the applicants themselves. The evidence on the utility of biographical information collected directly from job applicants is much more positive relative to hand-picked references.[45] The low cost of obtaining such information significantly enhances its utility, especially when the information is used in conjunction with a well-designed, follow-up interview that complements, rather than duplicates, the biographical information bank.

Where Diplomas Signify Nothing

Nineteen-year-old Mariam Malak was full of hope when it came time to hear the results of her exam performance. In previous years, she had received almost perfect scores, and she already had a growing reputation as one of Egypt's top high school students. She was looking to advance her reputation with this most recent test so that she could pursue her dream of becoming a doctor. When Malak could not find her name at the top of the list, she was confused, and when she was told she scored a zero on not just one of the tests—but seven—she fainted. After being hospitalized briefly, she appeared in tears on Egyptian television and accused the school of swapping out her tests with the tests of another student who had bribed the school to make the switch.

The Ministry of Education in Egypt was long suspected by many to be a highly corrupt organization, and Malak quickly became a heroine and national symbol of all that is wrong with that agency. Over 30,000 people posted messages of support on Facebook, and on an "I believe Mariam Malak" Twitter feed. Many of these contributors recounted their own experiences of victimization at the hands of the Ministry of Education. Eventually, the Egyptian prime minister intervened on Malak's behalf, and several celebrities offered to pay her tuition to medical school at a foreign university.

Although this story eventually turned out fine for Malak, corruption in schools of education throughout the world does serious harm to students and the countries in which they reside. In terms of the students, since only the rich can afford to bribe officials, this cements income inequality and prevents upward mobility among a nation's most deserving citizens. Economically, it harms the country because lack of faith in the educational system means that foreign employers are much more likely to staff openings with expatriates instead of local nationals. Finally, and most critically, the related problem of fake degrees means that the holders of those documents may not have the skills needed do the tasks required by their jobs. For example, in Russia, the administrators at the Pirogov National Research Medical University all were fired when it was learned that half of the graduating class were "ghost students" who simply paid $14,000 for their degrees. After the scandal, the school's new rector, Andrei Kamkin, noted, "We realized the dangers of letting ignorant and uneducated people pretend to be doctors."

DISCUSSION QUESTIONS

1. Individuals working in education in many parts of the world are poorly paid. Do you believe that corruption and bribery would be reduced if these people were better paid?
2. What are some steps employers can use to determine whether a degree from a foreign school was legitimately earned?

SOURCES: M. Noman, "Mariam Malak: The Star Pupil Who Scored Zero on All Her Exams," BBC.com, September 6, 2015; K. Desouki, "Top Female Student Takes on Corruption in Egypt after Scoring Zero on Exams," *Guardian*, September 9, 2015; C. Matlack, "Buying a Diploma Is Easy if You Can Pay Up," *Businessweek*, October 1, 2015.

One of the most important elements of biographical information deals with educational background. In some cases, employers are looking for specialized educational backgrounds reflected in functional degrees such as business or nursing or engineering, but in other cases, employers are just looking for critical-thinking and problem-solving skills that might be associated with any college degree.[46] As the "Competing through Globalization" box indicates, this information is not always valid for applicants whose education was received from certain regions of the world, and thus one cannot always accept a degree at face value.

This focus on education is attributed to the nature of the economy, which increasingly demands people with high levels of education. Indeed, it is ironic that despite relatively high levels of employment, many employers find it impossible to find people with the skills they need.[47] The term *education gap* has been coined to capture the difference between the average years of education required in a job listing in a given area, and the average years of education in that same area. For the nation as a whole, the education gap runs at about 5%, but in some cities, like Las Vegas, the gap exceeds 10%. Areas that have larger education gaps experience much higher rates of unemployment and are usually the last to show signs of job recovery during an economic expansion.[48]

Again, as with the interview, the biggest concern with the use of biographical data is that applicants who supply the information may be motivated to misrepresent themselves. Résumé fraud is on the rise, and one survey indicated that roughly 45% of job applications that were audited contained some amount of inaccurate material. To prevent embarrassing episodes, many employers hire outside companies to do background checks on employees.

For example, when Steve Masiello applied for a position coaching basketball at the University of South Florida, a routine background check revealed that he had lied on his application when he stated that he had earned a degree in communications from the University of Kentucky in 2000. This came as an embarrassment to Masiello's current employer, Manhattan College, which also required a college degree for any top coaching position but apparently never checked on this when they hired Masiello.[49] A similar failure to conduct a routine background check was partially to blame for the 2015 jailbreak at the Clinton Correctional Facility in New York, where an employee helped two convicted murderers escape.[50] An investigation in the wake of this incident revealed widespread lapses and failures to conduct adequate background checks at the prison.[51]

PHYSICAL ABILITY TESTS

Although automation and other advances in technology have eliminated or modified many physically demanding occupational tasks, many jobs still require certain physical abilities or psychomotor abilities. In these cases, tests of physical abilities may be relevant not only to predicting performance but also to predicting occupational injuries and disabilities.[52] There are seven classes of tests in this area: ones that evaluate (1) muscular tension, (2) muscular power, (3) muscular endurance, (4) cardiovascular endurance, (5) flexibility, (6) balance, and (7) coordination.[53]

The criterion-related validities for these kinds of tests for certain jobs, such as firefighting, are quite strong.[54] Unfortunately, these tests, particularly the strength tests, are likely to have an adverse impact on some applicants with disabilities and many female applicants. For example, roughly two-thirds of all males score higher than the highest-scoring female on muscular tension tests.[55] This difference between the sexes in physical strength was once used to legally bar women from certain jobs in the military; however, this is no longer the case, and all jobs within the U.S. military were opened up to women in 2015.[56]

There are two key questions to ask in deciding whether to use these kinds of tests. First, is the physical ability essential to performing the job, and is it mentioned prominently enough in the job description? Neither the Civil Rights Act nor the ADA requires employers to hire individuals who cannot perform essential job functions, and both accept a written job description as evidence of the essential functions of the job. Second, is there a probability that failure to adequately perform the job would result in some risk to the safety or health of the applicant, co-workers, or clients? The "direct threat" clause of the ADA makes it clear that adverse impact against those with disabilities is warranted under such conditions.

Invoking this clause can sometimes cause controversy, as in 2014, when United Parcel Service (UPS) cited this clause to support the decision to fire a pregnant worker because she could not lift packages weighing more than 20 pounds. UPS was sued, because it routinely made accommodations for injured employees, and the same woman who was fired for being pregnant would have been accommodated had she hurt her back. UPS eventually settled out of court and eliminated this policy, probably as much for public relations reasons as for any other factor related to business necessity.[57] An important lesson to learn from litigation that involves terminating pregnant women (or placing them on unpaid leave) is that letters from medical personnel to companies need to be very specific when it comes to laying out what duties can and cannot be performed at different stages of the pregnancy. Form letters or letters that are too general in nature are often interpreted in the least favorable light for the employee by employers looking to save money or reduce their exposure to risk.[58] In general, as one can see from the "Evidence-Based HR" box, being explicit about all aspects of motherhood is critical when women are trying to balance life and work.

EVIDENCE-BASED HR

Regardless of one's race, sex or national origin, the one incontrovertible thing we all have in common is that we all have a mother. Thus, we all might be concerned to learn that employers tend to have a bias when it comes to hiring anyone whose résumé shows an employment gap—including job applicants who take time off to raise children. Thus, the question becomes, What can a woman who has made this choice do to overcome this bias? Clearly, the laws against gender discrimination prohibit employers from broaching the topic, but what does the evidence suggest happens when moms self-disclose this information?

One study that addressed this question asked 3,000 people to choose among two job applicants with similar work histories who each had a 10-year employment gap. One of the applicants explained that the gap was explicitly attributable to child rearing and the other was silent on the topic. Those who self-disclosed were 35% more likely to get the job, relative to those who offered no explanation at all. Some observers have suggested that this study misses the point, in that discrimination at early stages of the employment process would eliminate both candidates; however, all agree that if one can get to the interview stage, it is better to explicitly disclose. As the researchers noted, "Given how strong the evidence is against mothers, women should seize hold of the situation rather than cede interpretation to an employer who cannot explicitly ask the question."

SOURCE: P. Cohen, "A Child Care Gap in the Résumé: Whether to Explain or Not," *New York Times,* May 19, 2016.

Cognitive ability tests
Tests that include three dimensions: verbal comprehension, quantitative ability, and reasoning ability.

Verbal comprehension
Refers to a person's capacity to understand and use written and spoken language.

Quantitative ability
Refers to the speed and accuracy with which one can solve arithmetic problems of all kinds.

Reasoning ability
Refers to a person's capacity to invent solutions to many diverse problems.

COGNITIVE ABILITY TESTS

Cognitive ability tests differentiate individuals based on their mental rather than physical capacities. Cognitive ability has many different facets, although we will focus only on three dominant ones. **Verbal comprehension** refers to a person's capacity to understand and use written and spoken language. **Quantitative ability** concerns the speed and accuracy with which one can solve arithmetic problems of all kinds. **Reasoning ability**, a broader concept, refers to a person's capacity to invent solutions to many diverse problems.

Some jobs require only one or two of these facets of cognitive ability. Under these conditions, maintaining the separation among the facets is appropriate. However, many jobs that are high in complexity require most, if not all, of the facets; hence, one general test is often as good as many tests of separate facets. Highly reliable commercial tests measuring these kinds of abilities are widely available, and they are generally valid predictors of job performance in many different kinds of contexts, including widely different countries.[59] The validity of these kinds of tests is related to the complexity of the job, however, in that one sees higher criterion-related validation for complex jobs than for simple jobs.

One of the major drawbacks to these tests is that they typically have adverse impact on some minority groups. Indeed, the size of the differences is so large that some observers have advocated abandoning these types of tests for making decisions regarding who will be accepted for certain schools or jobs. This is somewhat ironic in that these standardized tests were originally designed to be anti-elitist and to help identify talented individuals who may not be high in socioeconomic status but were still very bright by objective standards. However, over time, the tests have become a major hurdle to many disadvantaged groups by restricting their college opportunities and thus are now perceived as elitist due to their adverse impact on minorities.[60]

The notion of race norming, mentioned earlier, was born of the desire to use these high-utility tests in a manner that avoided adverse impact. Although race norming was made illegal by amendments to the Civil Rights Act, some people have advocated the use of banding both to achieve the benefits of testing and to minimize its adverse impact. The concept of *banding* suggests that similar groups of people whose scores differ by only a small amount all be treated as having the same score. Then, within any band, preferential treatment is given to minorities. Most observers feel preferential treatment of minorities is acceptable when scores are tied, and banding simply broadens the definition of what constitutes a tied score. Like race norming, banding is controversial, especially if the bands are set too wide.[61]

As with all the selection measures we have seen so far, a concern is that applicants may be tempted to cheat in order to score well on whatever instrument is used to make selection decisions. Cheating on tests is hardly a new phenomenon, however. What is new is the degree to which the use of computerized testing and social networking has changed the nature and scope of cheating. The term *question harvesting* has been coined to capture the process whereby test takers use advanced technology to download questions or capture images of questions with digital cameras or other devices while taking a test, and then transmit the content of the test wirelessly to people outside the testing facility, who then post the questions for future test takers.[62] Cheating scandals such as these become particularly controversial when allegations are based on nationality. For example, the evidence of wrongdoing with respect to test scores reported from China and South Korea grew so large in 2014 that the Educational Testing Service withheld the scores for applicants from these countries until all the allegations could be sorted out.[63]

PERSONALITY INVENTORIES

Whereas ability tests attempt to categorize individuals relative to what they can do, personality measures tend to categorize individuals by what they are like. The number of firms employing personality tests as screens has ballooned over the years, from just 26% in 2000 to just under 60% in 2014.[64] Research suggests that there are five major dimensions of personality, known as the "Big Five": (1) extroversion, (2) adjustment, (3) agreeableness, (4) conscientiousness, and (5) openness to experience. Table 6.3 lists each of these with a corresponding list of adjectives that fit each dimension.

Table 6.3

The Five Major Dimensions of Personality Inventories

1.	Extroversion	Sociable, gregarious, assertive, talkative, expressive
2.	Adjustment	Emotionally stable, nondepressed, secure, content
3.	Agreeableness	Courteous, trusting, good-natured, tolerant, cooperative, forgiving
4.	Conscientiousness	Dependable, organized, persevering, thorough, achievement-oriented
5.	Openness to experience	Curious, imaginative, artistically sensitive, broad-minded, playful

Although it is possible to find reliable, commercially available measures of each of these traits, the evidence for their validity and generalizability is mixed at best.[65] For example, conscientiousness, which captures the concepts of self-regulation and self-motivation, is one of the few factors that displays any validity across a number of different job categories, and many real-world managers rate this as one of the most important characteristics they look for in employees. People who are high in conscientiousness tend to show very good self-control when pursuing work goals and are especially adept at overcoming challenges and obstacles, relative to people low in this trait.[66]

Instead of showing strong direct and positive correlations with future performance across all jobs, the validity coefficients associated with personality measures tend to be job specific. For example, extroverts tend to excel in jobs likes sales or politics because these jobs demand gregariousness and assertiveness, two of the central features shared by all extroverts. In contrast, introverts are better at studying and working in isolation, and hence they are best at jobs like accountant or research scientist because these jobs demand patience and vigilance. Extroverts tend to enjoy working in team-oriented environments more than introverts, but this does not always spill over into performance differences for engaging in teamwork.[67] Both extroverts and introverts can become effective leaders, although they achieve effectiveness in different ways. Extroverts tend to be top-down, autocratic and charismatic leaders who motivate followers by getting them emotionally engaged. In contrast, effective introverted leaders tend to be more bottom-up, participative leaders who listen to empowered employees and then engineer reward structures so that people are working toward their own self-interests.[68]

One important element of staffing in team-based structures, however, relates to how the selection of one team member influences the requirements associated with other team members.[69] In some cases, organizations might try to select people who have similar values and personality traits in order to create a strong team culture. When there is a strong team culture, everyone shares the same views and traits, promoting harmony and cohesiveness.[70] In other cases, people putting together a team go out of their way to make sure that the people on the team have different values and personalities. The hope here is that a diversity of opinion promotes internal debate and creativity. For example, at Pinterest, programming teams are put together one person at a time, and each new person added to the team is evaluated and selected based on some unique trait or perspective they might bring to the team that is not already there.[71]

The concept of "emotional intelligence" is also important in team contexts and has been used to describe people who are especially effective in fluid and socially intensive contexts. Emotional intelligence is traditionally conceived of as having five aspects: (1) self-awareness (knowledge of one's strengths and weaknesses), (2) self-regulation (the ability to keep disruptive emotions in check), (3) self-motivation (the ability to motivate oneself and persevere in the face of obstacles), (4) empathy (the ability to sense and read emotions in others), and (5) social skills (the ability to manage the emotions of other people).[72] Relative to standard measures of ability and personality, there has not been a great deal of scientific research on emotional intelligence, and critics have raised both theoretical and empirical questions about the construct. Theoretically, some critics have argued that the construct is overly broad and confuses aspects of perception, ability, and temperament that are best conceptualized as separate processes.[73] Empirically, the data seem to suggest that if one holds constant the scores on the variables captured by the five-factor model of personality and scores on tests of cognitive ability, there is little, if any, added predictive power attributable to emotional intelligence.[74]

Regardless of the nature of the context, the validity for almost all of the Big Five factors in terms of predicting job performance also seems to be higher when the scores are not obtained from the applicant but are instead taken from other people.[75] The lower validity associated with self-reports of personality can be traced to three factors. First, people sometimes lack insight into what their own personalities are actually like (or how they are perceived by others), so their scores are inaccurate or unreliable.

Second, people's personalities sometimes vary across different contexts. Thus, someone may be very conscientious when it comes to social activities such as planning a family wedding or a fraternity party, but less conscientious when it comes to doing a paid job. Thus, contextualized measures that add the term "at work" to standard personality items often perform better as predictors than standard noncontextualized measures. On average, "contextualizing" measures on personality tests in this manner can boost their average validity coefficient from around .10 to .25.[76] Third, with some traits like ability, validity coefficients are higher when one uses a curvilinear prediction instead of just a straight linear prediction. That is, with a trait like emotional stability, the best job performers often score in the middle range, and for a lot of jobs, both being too nervous and being too calm can be problematic.[77] This kind of curvilinear effect is rarely found with ability measures, in the sense that people who are "overqualified" on ability typically perform at the highest levels with evidence of a drop-off at extreme levels.[78]

In addition, although some negative emotions are almost always unhelpful when it comes to job performance, other negative emotions have positive motivational implications for some jobs. For example, hopelessness and despair have been called "empty" emotions because they promote inactivity. In contrast, emotions like anger and guilt often spur people to engage in additional effort or make needed changes in their approach to life and work that are adaptive.[79]

Finally, one factor that also limits the validity of personality items is that, unlike cognitive ability scores, applicants find it easier to fake traits by providing socially desirable responses to questions. Research suggests that when people fill out these inventories when applying for a job, their scores on conscientiousness and emotional stability are much higher relative to when they are just filling out the same questionnaires anonymously for research purposes.[80] In addition to being "fake-able," some of the items that tap emotional stability start to get close to categories of mental illness that reflect protected groups according to the ADA, and some applicants have legally challenged these sorts of screening devices on that score.[81] Also, if people fail a personality test and then take the same test again in the future, their scores seem to increase dramatically.[82]

Several steps can be used to try to reduce faking. For example, if employers simply warn applicants that they are going to cross-check the applicants' self-ratings with other people, this seems to reduce faking.[83] Also, the degree to which people can fake various personality traits is enhanced with questionnaires, and one sees much less faking of traits when interviewers are assessing the characteristics.[84] All of this reinforces the idea that it is better to obtain this information from people other than the job applicant, and that it is better to use this information to reject low scorers but not necessarily hire all higher scorers on the basis of self-reports alone.[85]

Finally, technologies are now being developed to create objective measures of traits from "digital traces" that people leave on the world. For example, software has been developed to track people's "likes and dislikes" on Facebook, and then link these to the traits captured by the Big Five framework. Research shows that computer algorithms that process these data can generate an estimated score on the five traits that converges with self-reports better than what can be obtained from co-workers, friends, or even close relatives.

WORK SAMPLES

Work-sample tests attempt to simulate the job in a prehiring context to observe how the applicant performs in the simulated job. For example, at Compose, Inc., a cloud-based storage firm in California, all applicants are brought in on one day to work on "mock projects" that simulate the actual work. The identities of the applicants are kept secret, and those making the hiring decision make it based solely on the work produced without ever meeting the candidates personally or studying their résumés.[86]

The degree of fidelity in work samples can vary greatly. In some cases, applicants respond to a set of standardized hypothetical case studies and role-play how they would react to certain situations.[87] Often these standardized role-plays employ interactive video technology to create "virtual job auditions."[88] Simulations involving video-based role-plays seem to be more engaging and display higher levels of predictive validity relative to paper-and-pencil approaches.[89] In other cases, the job applicants are brought to the employers' location and perform the job for a short time period as part of a "job tryout."[90]

In some cases, as we saw earlier, employers will sponsor competitions in which contestants (who at this point are not even considered job applicants) vie for attention by going head-to-head in solving certain job-related problems. These sorts of competitions have been common in some industries like architecture and fashion design, but their use is spreading across many other business contexts. These competitions tend to be cost effective in generating a lot of interest, and some have attracted as many as 1,000 contestants who bring their talents to bear on specific problems faced by the employing organization.[91] Competitions are particularly well-suited for assessing and "discovering" young people who may not have extended track records or portfolios to evaluate. For example, "hackathons," that is, competitions between computer programmers, were once only held on campuses with college students. Today, however, these contests are increasingly being won by high school dropouts who bypassed college altogether to focus exclusively on programming and application development using web-based tools generally accessible to a wider audience.[92]

With all these advantages of work-sample tests come two drawbacks. First, by their very nature the tests are job specific, so generalizability is low. Second, partly because a new test has to be developed for each job and partly because of their nonstandardized formats, these tests are relatively expensive to develop. It is much more cost effective to purchase a commercially available cognitive ability test that can be used for a number of different job categories within the company than to develop a test for each job.

In the area of managerial selection, work-sample tests are typically the cornerstone in assessment centers. Generically, the term **assessment center** is used to describe a wide variety of specific selection programs that employ multiple selection methods to rate

Assessment center
A process in which multiple raters evaluate employees' performance on a number of exercises.

either applicants or job incumbents on their managerial potential. Someone attending an assessment center would typically experience work-sample tests such as an in-basket test and several tests of more general abilities and personality. Because assessment centers employ multiple selection methods, their criterion-related validity tends to be quite high. Assessment centers seem to tap a number of different characteristics, but problem-solving ability and interpersonal skills stand out as probably the two most important skills tapped via this method.[93] However, many observers have argued that it is the exercises themselves—through their value as work samples—that explain why assessment centers have such high criterion-related validity, rather than their ability to tap generic underlying traits and skills.[94]

HONESTY TESTS AND DRUG TESTS

Many problems that confront society also exist within organizations, which has led to two new kinds of tests: honesty tests and drug-use tests. Many companies formerly employed polygraph tests, or lie detectors, to evaluate job applicants, but this changed with the passage of the Polygraph Act in 1988. This act banned the use of polygraphs in employment screening for most organizations. However, it did not eliminate the problem of theft by employees. As a result, the paper-and-pencil honesty-testing industry was born.

Paper-and-pencil honesty tests come in a number of different forms. Some directly emphasize questions dealing with past theft admissions or associations with people who stole from employers. Other items are less direct and tap more basic traits such as social conformity, conscientiousness, or emotional stability.[95] A large-scale independent review of validity studies suggests they can predict both theft and other disruptive behaviors. However, the reported correlations tend to be much higher when the research studies were conducted by test publishers who market the tests, relative to outside, objective parties with a less obvious conflict of interest. Thus, it is always a good idea for organizations to check the predictive accuracy of these kinds of tests for themselves and not rely solely on the results reported by test publishers.[96]

As is the case with measures of personality, some people are concerned that people confronting an honesty test can fake their way to a passing score. The evidence suggests that people instructed to fake their way to a high score (indicating honesty) can do so. However, it is not clear that this affects the validity of the predictions made using such tests. That is, it seems that despite this built-in bias, scores on the test still predict future theft. Thus, the effect of the faking bias is not large enough to detract from the test's validity.[97]

As with theft, there is a growing perception of the problems caused by drug use among employees. The major controversies surrounding drug tests involve not their reliability and validity but whether they represent an invasion of privacy, an unreasonable search and seizure, or a violation of due process. Urinalysis and blood tests are invasive procedures, and accusing someone of drug use is a serious matter. Still, due to incidents like the 2015 suicide crash of a Germanwings airliner in Europe, the balance of power in the "privacy versus safety" debate for testing is changing in the direction of increased testing (see the "Managing People" section at the end of this chapter).

Employers considering the use of drug tests would be well advised to make sure that their drug-testing programs conform to some general rules. First, these tests should be administered systematically to all applicants for the same job. Second, testing seems more defensible for jobs that involve safety hazards associated with failure to perform.[98] Test results should be reported to the applicant, who should be allowed an avenue of

Pains of Staffing "Safety-Sensitive" Jobs Need to Be Treated

Things were going fine at the job fair sponsored by JCB, a heavy-equipment manufacturing company near Savannah, Georgia. The company was expanding and offered the highly coveted, high- paying manufacturing jobs everyone wants. The room was full of potential applicants, many of whom were highly experienced and needed work. However, half the room emptied out when it was announced that the hiring process involved a drug test. The speed of the exit was so fast that it almost seemed like half the people in the room heard a fire alarm that could not be heard by the other half of the people in the room.

This is not an isolated incident. Across the United States, employers are finding it increasingly difficult to find workers who can pass a drug test. Drug testing is mandated by federal law for many occupations classified as "safety-sensitive" jobs regulated by the Department of Transportation, such as truck drivers, pilots, ship captains, and train engineers. It is also a widespread

practice among employers for whom it is not mandated. When drug-testing legislation was introduced in 1988, close to 15% of people tested positive for illegal drugs. Compared to that figure, the rate today is still low, at about 5%. However, the rate has increased steadily from a low of less than in 2% in 2002. Moreover, the rate is higher in certain occupations and regions of the country. For instance, the rate for those working in the mining and construction industries is 18%, and the states of Colorado and Washington have the highest rates in the nation. Indeed, Jesse Russow, owner of Avalanche Roofing & Exteriors in Colorado Springs, says that "to find a roofer or painter who can pass a drug test is unheard of."

The federal government estimates that, by 2020, mental and substance abuse disorders are likely to surpass physical disease as the major cause of disability in the United States and that this may be a problem when it comes to staffing safety-sensitive jobs. Most of the problem is attributed to marijuana,

which is sold legally in some states, such as Colorado. However, opioids such as oxycodone and hydrocodone are increasingly the drugs most likely to derail job seekers. Although employee assistance programs (EAPs) can help workers once they are hired, the problem today is getting workers in the door, rather than running for the exits.

DISCUSSION QUESTIONS

1. What factors might be contributing to higher rates of illicit drug use among job applicants in the United States, and are any of those factors under the control of employers?

2. Are some drugs "worse than others" when it comes to safety-sensitive jobs, and how should alcohol consumption be treated by employers when it comes to hiring?

SOURCES: J. Calmes, "Hiring Hurdle: Finding Workers Who Can Pass a Drug Test," *New York Times,* May 17, 2016; S. Sipek, "There's a Miner Problem, Not a Minor Problem," *Workforce,* March 2016, p. 17; L. Weber, "Greater Share of Workers Testing Positive for Illicit Drugs," *Wall Street Journal,* September 14, 2016.

appeal (and perhaps retesting). Tests should be conducted in an environment that is as unintrusive as possible, and results from those tests should be held in strict confidence. Also, when testing current employees, the program should be part of a wider organizational program that provides rehabilitation counseling.[99]

Finally, companies that employ drug testing also have to recognize the changing legal status for drugs like marijuana. Indeed, as the "Competing through Sustainability" box shows, failure to loosen the requirements for drug-testing results has made it hard for some employers to hire any workers. Marijuana is currently legal for medicinal or recreational use in 29 states and the District of Columbia, and many employers are backing off requirements associated with marijuana. Ironically, one such employer is the Federal Bureau of Investigation (FBI), which noticed that many of the young applicants best skilled for tracking down cyber crimes also have a history of marijuana use. James Comey, then the director of the FBI, suggested the agency may have to loosen its no-tolerance policy for marijuana in order to attract this talent. Comey notes, "I have to hire a great workforce to compete with cyber criminals and some of the best kids want to smoke weed on the way to the interview."[100] Thus, the quest for deriving competitive advantage from one's workforce sometimes takes odd twists.

A LOOK BACK

Policing the Police

The decisions that organizations make regarding who is going to be part of the organization and who is going to be turned away are some of the most important decisions that firms will make in terms of gaining a competitive advantage. These decisions also have a major impact on the lives of individuals and organizational outcomes for all jobs. As we saw in the chapter' opening vignette, this is especially critical in the public safety sector. The importance of these decisions means that they have to be based on empirically validated procedures. They cannot be left to idiosyncratic judgments of untrained individuals who, confronting a labor shortage in the jobs they are trying to fill, may make hasty, ill-informed decisions. This chapter has summarized hundreds of years of research and demonstrated a large and varied set of tactics that firms can use to make the right decisions when it comes to the selection process.

QUESTIONS

1. Based on this chapter, what are the best methods of obtaining information about job applicants?
2. What are the best characteristics to look for in applicants, and how does this depend on the nature of the job?
3. If you could use only two of the methods described in this chapter and could assess only two of the characteristics discussed, which would you choose, and why?

SUMMARY

In this chapter, we examined the five critical standards with which all personnel selection methods should conform: reliability, validity, generalizability, utility, and legality. We also looked at nine different selection methods currently used in organizations and evaluated each with respect to these five standards. Table 6.4 summarizes these selection methods and can be used as a guide in deciding which test to use for a specific purpose. Although we discussed each type of test individually, it is important to note in closing that there is no need to use only one type of test for any one job. Indeed, managerial assessment centers use many different forms of tests over a two- or three-day period to learn as much as possible about candidates for important executive positions. As a result, highly accurate predictions are often made, and the validity associated with the judicious use of multiple tests is higher than that for tests used in isolation.

Table 6.4
A Summary of Personnel Selection Methods

METHOD	RELIABILITY	VALIDITY	GENERALIZABILITY	UTILITY	LEGALITY
Interviews	Low when unstructured and when assessing nonobservable traits	Low if unstructured and nonbehavioral	Low	Low, especially because of expense	Low because of subjectivity and potential interviewer bias; also, lack of validity makes job-relatedness low
Reference checks	Low, especially when obtained from letters	Low because of lack of range in evaluations	Low	Low, although not expensive to obtain	Those writing letters may be concerned with charges of libel
Biographical information	High test–retest, especially for verifiable information	High criterion-related validity; low in content validity	Usually job specific, but have been successfully developed for many job types	High; inexpensive way to collect vast amounts of potentially relevant data	May have adverse impact; thus often develop separate scoring keys based on sex or race
Physical ability tests	High	Moderate criterion-related validity; high content validity for some jobs	Low; pertain only to physically demanding jobs	Moderate for some physical jobs; may prevent expensive injuries and disability	Often have adverse impact on women and people with disabilities; need to establish job-relatedness
Cognitive ability tests	High	Moderate criterion-related validity; content validation inappropriate	High; predictive for most jobs, although best for complex jobs	High; low cost and wide application across diverse jobs in companies	Often have adverse impact on race, especially for African Americans, though decreasing over time
Personality inventories	High	Low to moderate criterion-related validity for most traits; content validation inappropriate	Low; few traits predictive for many jobs, except conscientiousness	Low, although inexpensive for jobs where specific traits are relevant	Low because of cultural and sex differences on most traits, and low job-relatedness in general
Work-sample tests	High	High criterion and content validity	Usually job specific, but have been successfully developed for many job types	High, despite the relatively high cost to develop	High because of low adverse impact and high job-relatedness
Honesty tests	Insufficient independent evidence	Insufficient independent evidence	Insufficient independent evidence	Insufficient independent evidence	Insufficient history of litigation, but will undergo scrutiny
Drug tests	High	High	High	Expensive, but may yield high payoffs for health-related costs	May be challenged on invasion-of-privacy grounds

KEY TERMS

Reliability, 231
Validity, 234
Criterion-related validity, 234
Predictive validation, 235
Concurrent validation, 235

Content validation, 237
Generalizability, 238
Utility, 240
Situational interview, 248
Cognitive ability tests, 252

Verbal comprehension, 252
Quantitative ability, 252
Reasoning ability, 252
Assessment center, 256

DISCUSSION QUESTIONS

1. We examined nine different types of selection methods in this chapter. Assume that you were just rejected for a job based on one of these methods. Obviously, you might be disappointed and angry regardless of what method was used to make this decision, but can you think of two or three methods that might leave you most distressed? In general, why might the acceptability of the test to applicants be an important standard to add to the five we discussed in this chapter?

2. Video-recording applicants in interviews is becoming an increasingly popular means of getting multiple assessments of that individual from different perspectives. Can you think of some reasons why video-recording interviews might also be useful in evaluating the interviewer? What would you look for in an interviewer if you were evaluating one on video?

3. Distinguish between concurrent and predictive validation designs, discussing why the latter is preferred over the former. Examine each of the nine selection methods discussed in this chapter and determine which of these would have their validity most and least affected by the type of validation design employed.

4. Some observers have speculated that, in addition to increasing the validity of decisions, employing rigorous selection methods has symbolic value for organizations. What message is sent to applicants about the organization through hiring practices, and how might this message be reinforced by recruitment programs that occur before selection and by training programs that occur after selection?

SELF-ASSESSMENT EXERCISE

Additional assignable self-assessments available in Connect.

Reviews of research about personality have identified five common aspects of personality, referred to as the Big Five personality traits. Find out which are your most prominent traits. Read each of the following statements, marking "Yes" if it describes you and "No" if it does not.

1. In conversations, I tend to do most of the talking.
2. Often people look to me to make decisions.
3. I am a very active person.
4. I usually seem to be in a hurry.
5. I am dominant, forceful, and assertive.
6. I have a very active imagination.
7. I have an active fantasy life.
8. How I feel about things is important to me.
9. I find it easy to feel myself what others are feeling.
10. I think it's interesting to learn and develop new hobbies.
11. My first reaction is to trust people.
12. I believe that most persons are basically well intentioned.
13. I'm not crafty or shy.
14. I'd rather not talk about myself and my accomplishments.
15. I'd rather praise others than be praised myself.
16. I come into situations being fully prepared.
17. I pride myself on my sound judgment.
18. I have a lot of self-discipline.
19. I try to do jobs carefully so that they don't have to be done again.
20. I like to keep everything in place so that I know where it is.
21. I enjoy performing under pressure.
22. I am seldom sad or depressed.
23. I'm an even-tempered person.
24. I am levelheaded in emergencies.
25. I feel I am capable of coping with most of my problems.

The statements are grouped into categories. Statements 1–5 describe extroversion; 6–10, openness to experience; 11–15, agreeableness; 16–20, conscientiousness; and 21–25, emotional stability. The more times you wrote "Yes" for the statements in a category, the more likely you are to have the associated trait.

EXERCISING STRATEGY

U.S. Supreme Court Makes a Fashion Statement

Samantha Elauf was a mere 17 years old when she began a journey that would take her all the way to the U.S. Supreme Court. Like many 17 year olds, Elauf liked to spend her time hanging out at the local mall. She loved to shop, watch movies, and above all eat at her favorite sushi restaurant. Thus, when she needed money and decided to apply for a part-time job, she sought out employment within the mall at the local Abercrombie & Fitch clothing store. Everything seemed to go well in her interview, but in the end, Elauf was denied employment because of what she was wearing—a simple black head scarf. Elauf is a Muslim American, and wearing such a scarf was required by her religious beliefs.

In terms of competitive advantage, Abercrombie & Fitch has tried to carve out a unique retail niche by promoting what it calls a "classic East Coast collegiate style." Promoting this image is paramount to the company from top to bottom, and this includes young people who work on the sales floor. This is not a unique characteristic of Abercrombie & Fitch, and virtually all modern retailers maintain what is called a "looks policy" that is used to reinforce their brand image. The problem with some of these policies, however, is that the looks being reinforced are not nearly as diverse as the nation as a whole. In this case, an employee wearing a hijab, which apparently is not part of the Abercrombie & Fitch looks policy, put the company's brand image strategy in conflict with laws that prevent religious discrimination in hiring.

In general, there are three categories of religious discrimination in the workplace, and two of them are central parts of this case. First, it is illegal to make employment decisions based on someone's faith or lack of faith. Second, it is illegal

to harass someone at work because of the person's religion. Third, it is illegal to fail to make reasonable accommodations to meet an employee's religious beliefs, unless such accommodations create an undue hardship for the employer. The first and third categories came into play in this case. Lawyers for Abercrombie & Fitch argued, however, that Elauf never explicitly stated in the interview that she wore the hijab for religious reasons; hence, "they had no idea that she was Muslim."

In the end, the Supreme Court sided with Elauf 8–1, and Justice Antonin Scalia noted explicitly, "This is really easy." Allowing Muslim employees to wear the hijab was considered a very reasonable accommodation and not a factor that could be used to deny someone employment. Although this may have been an easy call in Elauf's favor in the United States, in other countries it would have been an easy call for Abercrombie & Fitch's side. For example, in France, the law actually prohibits people from wearing overt signs of religion, including the hijab; hence, Elauf would have not fared so well had the trial been held in Europe.

QUESTIONS

1. What does accommodation mean in this context, and how does one test for what is reasonable?
2. How does a company's brand image potentially set up the company for failure when it comes to fair hiring practices?

SOURCES: A. Liptak, "Muslim Denied Job over Head Scarf Wins in Supreme Court," *New York Times*, June 1, 2015; "A Muslim Woman Beats Abercrombie and Fitch," *Washington Post*, June 1, 2015; J. Smith, "European Court Upholds French Veil Ban," *BBC News*, July 1, 2014.

MANAGING PEOPLE

Privacy and Public Safety Collide on Germanwings Flight 9525

Germanwings Flight 9525 was well on its journey to Dusseldorf, Germany, from Barcelona, Spain, when it crashed into the French Alps, killing all 149 people on board. Although every plane crash is a tragedy, two facts stood out in this case that made it especially tragic. First, the co-pilot, Andreas Lubitz, intentionally flew the plane into the mountains as part of a suicide attempt. Lubitz had locked the cockpit door after the pilot left and then ignored

pleas from the rest of his crew while he crashed the plane. Second, prior to being hired at Germanwings, Lubitz had been treated repeatedly for mental illness and suicidal tendencies.

News of these two facts spurred a major debate regarding the selection of pilots, especially as it relates to uncovering evidence of mental illness. In the United States, health professions are legally required to report on any patients who are likely to engage in conduct that would result in serious harm to themselves or others. However, in Germany, the law emphasizes privacy, and the laws of that country bar doctors from revealing any medical information on their patients. German laws place responsibility for reporting mental health problems on the individual, and the belief is that forcing mental health officials to "out" their patients merely drives mental illness underground. People with problems will not come forward for treatment for fear of losing their jobs if they are reported.

Clearly, this system broke down in the Andreas Lubitz case. In fact, investigators found a doctor's note in his apartment that would have excused him from work for a time period that included the day of the fatal crash, but this note was never shared with his employer. Thus, Germanwings claimed that it had no knowledge of Lubitz's condition either before or after he was hired. The question becomes, Should

it have? And will regulators and consumers allow this practice to continue in the future or demand changes in how Europe balances privacy rights against public safety?

QUESTIONS

1. German and U.S. laws clearly differ on the role of public reporting of mental illness. Which side do you think has the better argument, and how should a society balance privacy rights and public safety?
2. When does the public's right to know trump the individual's right to privacy?

SOURCES: N. Kulish and M. Eddy, "Germanwings Co-pilot Was Treated for 'Suicidal Tendencies,' Authorities Say," *New York Times*, March 30, 2015; S. Meichtry and R. Wall, "Germanwings Investigation to Focus on How Industry Vets Psychological Backgrounds of Pilots," *Wall Street Journal*, March 31, 2015; E. Goode, "Role of Illness in Germanwings Crash Raises Worry about Stigma," *New York Times*, March 30, 2015.

HR IN SMALL BUSINESS

Kinaxis Chooses Sales Reps with Personality

Kinaxis, a software company headquartered in Ottawa, Ontario, sells to clients around the world. Its specialty is software for supply chain management—all the processes and relationships through which companies obtain supplies as needed and get their products to customers on time and at minimal cost. This is a sophisticated type of product, tailored to a company's specific needs. Therefore, Kinaxis depends on salespeople who understand how businesses work, who listen carefully to identify needs, and who provide excellent customer service to maintain long-term business relationships.

Recently, Bob Dolan, vice president for sales at Kinaxis, needed to hire a sales team to serve clients in North America. The company had just one salesperson serving the continent, and Dolan wanted to add four more. He received about 100 résumés and wanted to select from these. He started by reviewing the résumés against job requirements and selected 20 candidates for a first round of interviews. The interview process helped Dolan cut the list of candidates in half, so he needed another way to narrow his options.

Dolan decided his next step would be personality testing. He hired a firm called Opus Productivity Solutions to administer a test called PDP ProScan to the remaining 10 candidates. In addition, Dolan himself took the test and had his current sales rep do the same. The existing salesperson was doing an excellent job, so the results of his test could help Dolan and Opus pinpoint the characteristics of someone likely to succeed in sales at Kinaxis. Based on analysis of all

the results, Opus created a benchmark of traits associated with success in the job.

Representatives from Opus also discussed the test results with each candidate, giving each one a chance to disagree with the scores. No one did. Dolan observed that all the candidates scored high in assertiveness and extroversion—not surprising for people in sales. In addition, two of them scored above the benchmark in conformity and below the benchmark in dominance. Those results suggested to Dolan that these candidates might be so eager to please that they would be quick to give in to whatever customers requested—a pattern that could become costly for the company. Dolan eliminated those two candidates.

That meant Dolan still had eight candidates to fill four positions. He asked each one to give him the names of major accounts he or she had signed up in the previous two years. Four candidates were able to come up with three or four large clients. Those were the candidates Dolan hired.

Since then, Dolan says his experience with personality testing has only reinforced his belief that this selection method helps Kinaxis identify the best candidates. For example, one sales rep had scored low on "pace," indicating that the individual might lack the patience needed for the slow cycles required to close a sale of a complex software system. Dolan hoped the issue could be overcome if he provided enough coaching, but in fact, the sales rep sometimes behaved impatiently, annoying prospects. After three years of trying to help him grow into the job, Dolan laid him off.

The company's commitment to careful selection is expressed on its website: "As a growing and determined company, we're always looking for people eager to push the limits of each day of what's possible." Kinaxis was recently named one of Canada's top employers for young people.

QUESTIONS

1. What selection methods did Bob Dolan use for hiring salespeople? Did he go about using these methods in the best order? What, if anything, would you change about the order of the methods used?

2. What were the advantages to Kinaxis of using personality tests to help select sales representatives? What were the disadvantages?

3. Given the information gathered from the selection methods, what process did Dolan use to make his selection decision? What improvements can you recommend to this process for decisions to hire sales reps in the future?

SOURCES: Susan Greco, "Personality Testing for Sales Recruits," *Inc.*, March 1, 2009; Kinaxis website, Corporate Overview and Careers pages, www.kinaxis.com.

NOTES

1. K. Maher, "Security Firm That Employed Orlando Killer Says It Made 'Clerical Error' in Evaluation Documents," *Wall Street Journal*, June 19, 2016.
2. V. Wadhwa, "America's Immigrant Brain Drain," *BusinessWeek*, March 16, 2009, p. 68.
3. D. Nishi, "Tackling Stereotypes before Your Job Interview," *Wall Street Journal*, August 2, 2014.
4. P. Coy, "Will the Jobs Boom End Too Soon," *Businessweek*, December 3, 2015, p. 15.
5. E. Bernstein, "Personality Research Says Change in Major Traits Occurs Naturally," *Wall Street Journal*, April 22, 2014.
6. B. Weber, "Gender Bias by the Numbers," *Bloomberg Businessweek*, January 30, 2014.
7. E. Gray, "Do You Understand Why Stars Twinkle?" *Time*, June 22, 2015.
8. J. Walker, "Meet the New Boss: Big Data," *Wall Street Journal*, September 20, 2012.
9. D. Cormier-Smith, "AkzoNobel Selects Oracle Talent Management Cloud Services for Its Recruiting Needs," *Wall Street Journal*, April 10, 2013.
10. A. Ito, "Hiring in the Age of Big Data," *Bloomberg Businessweek*, November 13, 2013, pp. 40–41.
11. F. Schmidt, H. Le, I. S. Oh, and J. Shaffer, "General Mental Ability, Job Performance, and Red Herrings: Responses to Osterman, Hauser, and Schmitt," *Academy of Management Perspectives* 21 (2007), pp. 64–76.
12. S. E. Needleman, "Start-Ups Get Snapped Up for Their Talent," *Wall Street Journal*, September 12, 2012.
13. E. O'Boyle and H. Aguinis, "The Best and the Rest: Revisiting the Norm of Normality of Individual Performance," *Personnel Psychology* 65 (2012), pp. 79–119.
14. A. Southall, "Muslim Officer Sues New York Police Department over No Beard Policy," *New York Times*, June 22, 2016.
15. M. Mihelich, "Sacred Grounds—for Lawsuits," *Workforce*, April 2014, pp. 18–19.
16. M. Trottman, "Charges of Bias at Work Hit Record," *Time*, January 29, 2012, p. 7.
17. D. Bennett, "Deep Fried Civil War," *Bloomberg Businessweek*, August 2, 2012, pp. 62–64.
18. R. L. Lubin, "When 'Disparate Impact' Bites Back," *Wall Street Journal*, March 9, 2014.
19. P. Roth, P. Bobko, L. McFarland, and M. Buster, "Work Sample Tests in Personnel Selection: A Meta-analysis of Black-White Differences in Overall Exercise Scores," *Personnel Psychology* 61 (2008), pp. 637–61.
20. R. E. Ployhart and B. C. Holtz, "The Diversity-Validity Dilemma: Strategies for Reducing Racioethnic and Sex Group Differences and Adverse Impact in Selection," *Personnel Psychology* 61 (2008), pp. 153–72.
21. G. Flynn, "The Reverse Discrimination Trap," *Workforce*, June 2003, pp. 106–7.
22. J. Bravin, "Supreme Court Upholds Michigan's Affirmative Action Ban," *Wall Street Journal*, April 22, 2014.
23. T. Lewin, "Colleges Seek New Paths to Diversity After Court Ruling," *New York Times*, April 22, 2014.
24. E. Zlomik, "An End Run around Affirmative Action Bans," *Bloomberg Businessweek*, April 23, 2012, p. 52.
25. J. Bravin, "Supreme Court Upholds Affirmative Action in University Admissions," *Wall Street Journal*, June 23, 2016.
26. A. Lam, "White Students' Unfair Advantage in Admissions," *Wall Sreet Journal*, January 30, 2017.
27. D. A. Newman and J. S. Lyon, "Recruitment Efforts to Reduce Adverse Impact: Targeted Recruiting for Personality, Cognitive Ability and Diversity," *Journal of Applied Psychology* 94 (2009), pp. 298–317.
28. D. M. Finch, B. D. Edwards, and J. C. Wallace, "Multistage Selection Strategies: Simulating the Effects of Adverse Impact and Expected Performance for Various Predictor Combinations," *Journal of Applied Psychology* 94 (2009), pp. 318–40.
29. F. Hanson, "Diversity of a Different Color," *Workforce Management*, June 2010, pp. 21–24.
30. L. T. Cullen, "The Diversity Delusion," *Time*, May 2007, p. 45.
31. P. G. Lee, "No Place for Old Waiters at Texas Roadhouse," *Businessweek*, September 28, 2015, pp. 23–24.
32. C. A. Liptak, "Muslim Denied Job over Head Scarf Wins in Supreme Court," *Wall Street Journal*, June 1, 2015.
33. L. Weber, "Are You Disabled? Your Boss Needs to Know," *Wall Street Journal*, March 18, 2014.
34. M. Phillips, "From War Zone to Workplace," *Businessweek*, November 25, 2015, pp. 18–19.
35. R. A. Posthuma, F. R. Morgeson, and M. A. Campion, "Beyond Employment Interview Validity: A Comprehensive Narrative

Review of Recent Research and Trends over Time," *Personnel Psychology* 55 (2002), pp. 1–81.

36. A. Wilhelmy, M. Kleinmann, C. J. Konig, K. G. Melchers, and D. M. Truxillo, "How and Why Do Interviewers Try to Make Impressions on Applicants? A Qualitative Study," *Journal of Applied Psychology* 101 (2016), pp. 313–32.

37. C.J. Hartwell and M.A. Campion, "Getting on the Same Page: The Effect of Normative Feedback Interventions on Structured Interview Ratings," *Journal of Applied Psychology* 101 (2016), pp. 757–78.

38. M. A. McDaniel, F. P. Morgeson, E. B. Finnegan, M. A. Campion, and E. P. Braverman, "Use of Situational Judgment Tests to Predict Job Performance: A Clarification of the Literature," *Journal of Applied Psychology* 86 (2001), pp. 730–40.

39. A. P. J. Ellis, B. J. West, A. M. Ryan, and R. P. DeShon, "The Use of Impression Management Tactics in Structured Interviews: A Function of Question Type?" *Journal of Applied Psychology* 87 (2002), pp. 1200–8.

40. A. Bryant, "Google's Quest to Build a Better Boss," *New York Times*, March 12, 2011, p. C1.

41. A. Dizik, "Wooing Job Recruiters with Video Resumes," *Wall Street Journal*, May 2010, p. D4.

42. L. Weber, "Now Hiring? Tips for Conducting Interviews," *Wall Street Journal*, December 4, 2012.

43. J. S. Lublin, "What Won't You Do for a Job," *Wall Street Journal*, June 2, 2009, p. B1.

44. C. Suddath, "Imaginary Friends," *Bloomberg Businessweek*, January 21, 2013, p. 66.

45. M. R. Barrick and R. D. Zimmerman, "Reducing Voluntary Turnover through Selection," *Journal of Applied Psychology* 90 (2005), pp. 159–66.

46. M. Korn, "Wealth of Waste? Rethinking the Value of a Business Major," *Wall Street Journal*, April 5, 2012.

47. V. L. Chien and J. Berman, "Companies Are Hiring, Just Not You," *Bloomberg Businessweek*, August 15, 2011, pp. 10–11.

48. C. Dougherty, "Gap Hurts Job Hunters," *Wall Street Journal*, August 29, 2012.

49. K. Darcy, "Manhattan: Steve Masiello on Leave," *ESPN*, March 26, 2014.

50. R. Sanchez, G. Botelho, and F. Karimi, "New York Prison Employee Arraigned for Allegedly Helping Killers Escape," *CNN*, June 12, 2015, www.cnn.com.

51. M. Schwirtz and M. Winerip, "Warning Signs Overlooked in Hiring for New York City Jails," *New York Times*, January 15, 2015.

52. M. Barnekow-Bergkvist, U. Aasa, K. A. Angquist, and H. Johansson, "Prediction of Development of Fatigue during a Simulated Ambulance Work Task from Physical Performance Tests," *Ergonomics* 47 (2004), pp. 1238–50.

53. J. Hogan, "Structure of Physical Performance in Occupational Tasks," *Journal of Applied Psychology* 76 (1991), pp. 495–507.

54. N. D. Henderson, "Predicting Long-Term Firefighter Performance from Measures of Cognitive Ability and Physical Ability Measures," *Personnel Psychology* 63 (2010), pp. 999–1039.

55. J. Hogan, "Physical Abilities," in *Handbook of Industrial & Organizational Psychology*, 2nd ed., ed. M. D. Dunnette and L. M. Hough (Palo Alto, CA: Consulting Psychologists Press, 1991).

56. M. Rosenbert and D. Phillips, "All Combat Roles Now Open to Women, Defense Secretary Says," *New York Times*, December 3, 2015.

57. Editorial Board, "Women Who Work," *New York Times*, November 30, 2014.

58. C. St. Louis, "Doctor's Notes for Pregnant Employees Can Backfire, Experts Warn," *New York Times*, July 8, 2015.

59. J. F. Salagado, N. Anderson, S. Moscoso, C. Bertua, and F. De Fruyt, "International Validity Generalization of GMA and Cognitive Abilities: A European Community Meta-Analysis," *Personnel Psychology* 56 (2003), pp. 573–605.

60. P. Coy, "The SAT Is Elitist, Unfair, Out of Date, or All of the Above," *Bloomberg Businessweek*, October 7, 2013.

61. M. A. Campion, J. L. Outtz, S. Zedeck, F. S. Schmidt, J. E. Kehoe, K. R. Murphy, and R. M. Guion, "The Controversy over Score Banding in Personnel Selection: Answers to 10 Key Questions," *Personnel Psychology* 54 (2001), pp. 149–85.

62. C. McWhirter, "High Tech Cheaters Pose Test Threat," *Wall Street Journal*, June 10, 2013.

63. E. Barber, "Chinese and South Korean SAT Students Face Nervous Wait after Scores Delayed," *Time*, October 30, 2014.

64. L. Weber, "Today's Personality Tests Raise the Bar for Job Seekers," *Wall Street Journal*, April 14, 2015.

65. F. P. Morgeson, M. A. Campion, R. L. Dipboye, J. R. Hollenbeck, K. R. Murphy, and N. Schmitt, "Reconsidering the Use of Personality Tests in Personnel Selection Contexts," *Personnel Psychology* 60 (2007), pp. 683–729.

66. L. Winerman, "What Sets High Achievers Apart?" *Monitor on Psychology*, December 2013, pp. 28–31.

67. R. Pyrillis, "Searching for Solace," *Workforce*, November, 2014, pp. 41–43.

68. B. Walsh, "The Upside of Being an Introvert (and Why Extroverts Are Over-rated)," *Time*, February 6, 2012, pp. 40–45.

69. S. E. Humphrey, J. R. Hollenbeck, C. J. Meyer, and D. R. Ilgen, "Trait Configurations in Self-managed Teams: A Conceptual Examination of the Use of Seeding for Maximizing and Minimizing Trait Variance in Teams," *Journal of Applied Psychology* 92 (2007), pp. 885–92.

70. A. Hedger, "Employee Screening: Common Challenges, Smart Solutions," *Workforce Management*, March 17, 2008, pp. 39–46.

71. E. Huet, "In the Land of the Blind Hire," *Businessweek*, January 23, 2017, pp. 27–28.

72. D. Goleman, "Sometimes, EQ Is More Important Than IQ," *CNN.com*, January 14, 2005, p. 1.

73. R. D. Roberts, G. Mathews, and M. Zeidner, "Emotional Intelligence: Muddling through Theory and Measurement," *Industrial and Organizational Psychology* 3 (2010), pp. 140–44.

74. D. L. Joseph and D. A. Newman, "Emotional Intelligence: An Integrative Meta-analysis and Cascading Model," *Journal of Applied Psychology* 95 (2010), pp. 54–78.

75. J. M. Hunthausen, D. M. Truxillo, T. N. Bauer, and L. B. Hammer, "A Field Study of Frame of Reference Effects on Personality Test Validity," *Journal of Applied Psychology* 88 (2003), pp. 545–51.

76. J. A. Shaffer and J. E. Postlewaite, "A Matter of Context: A Meta-analytic Investigation of the Relative Validity of Contextualized and Non-contextualized Personality Measures," *Personnel Psychology*, 65 (2012), pp. 445–494.

77. H. Le, I. S. Oh, S. B. Robbins, R. Ilies, E. Holland, and P. Westrick, "Too Much of a Good Thing? Curvilinear Relationship between Personality Traits and Job Performance," *Journal of Applied Psychology* 96 (2011), pp. 113–33.

78. B. Erdogan, T. N. Bauer, J. M. Peiro, and D. M. Truxillo, "Over-Qualified Employees: Making the Best of a Potentially Bad Situation for Individuals and Organizations," *Industrial and Organizational Psychology* 4 (2011), pp. 215–32.

79. E. Bernstein, "Why You Need Negative Thoughts," *Wall Street Journal*, August 22, 2016.

80. S. A. Birkland, T. M. Manson, J. L. Kisamore, M. T. Brannick, and M. A. Smith, "Faking on Personality Measures," *International Journal of Selection and Assessment* 14 (December 2006), pp. 317–35.
81. L. Weber and E. Dwoskin, "Are Personality Tests Fair?" *Wall Street Journal*, September 29, 2014.
82. J. P. Hausknecht, "Candidate Persistence and Personality Test Practice Effects: Implications for Staffing System Management," *Personnel Psychology* 63 (2010), pp. 299–324.
83. N. L. Vasilopoulos, J. M. Cucina, and J. M. McElreath, "Do Warnings of Response Verification Moderate the Relationship between Personality and Cognitive Ability?" *Journal of Applied Psychology* 90 (2005), pp. 306–22.
84. C. H. Van Iddekinge, P. H. Raymark, and P. L. Roth, "Assessing Personality with a Structured Employment Interview: Construct-Related Validity and Susceptibility to Response Inflation," *Journal of Applied Psychology* 90 (2005), pp. 536–52.
85. R. Mueller-Hanson, E. D. Heggestad, and G. C. Thornton, "Faking and Selection: Considering the Use of Personality from Select-In and Select-Out Perspectives," *Journal of Applied Psychology* 88 (2003), pp. 348–55.
86. R. Feintzeig, "The Boss Doesn't Want Your Resume, *Wall Street Journal*, January 5, 2016.
87. C. Palmeri, "Putting Managers to the Test," *BusinessWeek*, November 20, 2006, p. 82.
88. C. Winkler, "Job Tryouts Go Virtual: Online Job Simulations Provide Sophisticated Candidate Assessments," *HR Magazine*, September 2006, pp. 10–15.
89. M. S. Christian, B. D. Edwards, and J. C. Bradley, "Situational Judgment Tests: Constructs Assessed and a Meta-analysis of Their Criterion-Related Validities," *Personnel Psychology* 63 (2010), pp. 83–117.
90. E. White, "Walk a Mile in My Shoes," *Wall Street Journal*, January 16, 2006, p. B3.
91. K. Maher, "Win in a Competition, Land on Square That Offers Job," *Wall Street Journal*, June 1, 2004, p. B10.
92. S. Leckhart, "The Hackathon Fast Track, From Campus to Silicon Valley," *New York Times*, April 6, 2015.
93. T. Oliver, P. Hausdorf, F. Lievens, and P. Conlon, "Interpersonal Dynamics in Assessment Center Exercises: Effects of Role Player Portrayed Disposition," *Journal of Management* 42 (2016), pp. 1992–2017.
94. D. J. Jackson, G. Michaelides, C. Dewberry, and Y. J. Kim, "Everything That You Have Ever Been Told about Assessment Center Ratings Is Confounded," *Journal of Applied Psychology* 101 (2016), pp. 976–994.
95. J. E. Wanek, P. R. Sackett, and D. S. Ones, "Toward an Understanding of Integrity Test Similarities and Differences: An Item-Level Analysis of Seven Tests," *Personnel Psychology* 56 (2003), pp. 873–94.
96. C. H. Van Iddekinge, P. L. Roth, P. H. Raymark, and H. N. Odle-Dusseau, "The Criterion-Related Validity of Integrity Tests: An Updated Meta-analysis, *Journal of Applied Psychology*, 97 (2012), pp. 499–530.
97. M. R. Cunningham, D. T. Wong, and A. P. Barbee, "Self-Presentation Dynamics on Overt Integrity Tests: Experimental Studies of the Reid Report," *Journal of Applied Psychology* 79 (1994), pp. 643–58.
98. M. E. Paronto, D. M. Truxillo, T. N. Bauer, and M. C. Leo, "Drug Testing, Drug Treatment, and Marijuana Use: A Fairness Perspective," *Journal of Applied Psychology* 87 (2002), pp. 1159–66.
99. K. R. Murphy, G. C. Thornton, and D. H. Reynolds, "College Students' Attitudes toward Drug Testing Programs," *Personnel Psychology* 43 (1990), pp. 615–31.
100. C. Levinson, "Comey: FBI 'Grappling' with Hiring Policy Concerning Marijuana," *Wall Street Journal*, May 20, 2014.

Training

LEARNING OBJECTIVES

After reading this chapter, you should be able to:

Learning through Gaming at GameStop

GameStop, a retailer of new and used video games, consumer electronics, and wireless services, has 18,000 employees in more than 6,600 locations worldwide. GameStop customers can get games there that aren't available anywhere else, and the company allows customers to buy, sell, or trade old games and electronics, unlike many of its competitors. GameStop serves a variety of customers, from five year olds and their parents who are looking for Nintendo games, to adult gamers who want to buy the latest gaming equipment. Most GameStop employees (called game-associates) hold part-time, entry-level jobs that require them to work several shifts during the week. Most new employees who join GameStop are expert gamers, have expertise about the technology and trends influencing the gaming market, and were loyal customers themselves. GameStop believes the gaming experience and gaming passion of its employees differentiate it from big-box retailers that also sell games.

Training is especially important for GameStop because of the business realities of normal turnover and seasonal hiring. Game-associates often leave for other jobs or opportunities such as going back to school. During the holiday season, the company hires and needs to train up to 25,000 temporary employees. Although only approximately 15% of these temporary employees become full-time employees, even if they never work for GameStop again, they are still potential customers. Training helps ensure new employees provide consistent customer service, which translates into satisfied customers and return business. As a result, GameStop's training doesn't focus on teaching employees about video games but instead emphasizes how to interact with customers and understand their gaming needs. Also, the training helps employees become ambassadors for the company by sharing their knowledge and passion for gaming with customers.

The Level Up program is an online game-based training program that enables employees to complete training on their own time and at their own pace, scoring points and earning badges based on achieving different skills and advancing to the next level. Learning missions require trainees to read documents, watch videos, and take quizzes. No mission is longer than 30 minutes. Training content varies based on the employees' needs, allows them to log in and out of training at any time, and allows them to skip content they already know. As they earn points to complete levels, the next level of learning is unlocked, giving them access to new badges and learning missions. In addition to preparing new game-associates, the Level Up program provides training for more experienced game-associates who may be more interested in a retail career and want to gain the knowledge and skills necessary to become assistant managers and store managers. To support online learning, all managers complete a train-the-trainer program designed to help them mentor and coach all employees, but especially seasonal hires. Managers learn how to explain the customer service process, create opportunities for new hires to "shadow" them, and provide feedback when trainees make mistakes.

The results for Level Up have been positive. Customer surveys show high levels of satisfaction, employees feel prepared to do their jobs, and managers like having the ability to easily track employees' training progress.

SOURCES: Based on S. Gale, "'Tis the Season to Be Training," *Chief Learning Officer,* April 2016, pp. 58, 60, 65; M. McGraw, "Staying Power," *Human Resource Executive,* January/February 2015, pp. 39–41; "About Us," www.gamestop.com, accessed March 13, 2017.

Introduction

As the chapter opener shows, training contributes to GameStop's focus on its employees and customers. Training helps GameStop's employees develop skills they need to succeed in their current jobs and develop for future positions. From GameStop's perspective, training is strategic because it leads to consistent service that attracts and retains customers, high-quality associates, and positive revenues. GameStop recognizes that there is stiff competition for consumers who are purchasing games and electronics—success requires smart, motivated employees who can delight customers.

Why is the emphasis on strategic training important? Companies are in business to make money, and every business function is under pressure to show how it contributes to business success or it may face spending cuts and even outsourcing. To contribute to a company's success, training activities should help the company achieve its business strategy. (Consider how GameStop's training helped the company manage the challenges of associate turnover and seasonal hiring.)

There is both a direct and an indirect link between training and business strategy and goals. Training can help employees develop skills needed to perform their jobs, which directly affects the business. Giving employees opportunities to learn and develop creates a positive work environment, which supports the business strategy by attracting talented employees as well as motivating and retaining current employees.

Why do GameStop and many other companies believe that an investment in training can help them gain a competitive advantage? Training can

- Increase employees' knowledge of foreign competitors and cultures, which is critical for success in foreign markets
- Help ensure that employees have the basic skills needed to work with new technology, such as robots and computer-assisted manufacturing processes
- Help employees understand how to work effectively in teams to contribute to product and service quality
- Ensure that the company's culture emphasizes innovation, creativity, and learning
- Ensure employment security by providing new ways for employees to contribute to the company when their jobs change, their interests change, or their skills become obsolete
- Prepare employees to accept and work more effectively with each other, particularly with minorities and women[1]

In this chapter, we emphasize the conditions through which training practices can help companies gain competitive advantage and how managers can contribute to effective training and other learning initiatives. We begin by discussing a systematic and effective approach to training design. Next, we review training methods and training evaluation. The chapter concludes with a discussion of special training issues including cross-cultural preparation, managing diversity, and orienting and socializing employees.

LO 7-1
Discuss how training, informal learning, and knowledge management can contribute to continuous learning and companies' business strategy.

Training: Its Role in Continuous Learning and Competitive Advantage

As we discussed in Chapter 1, intangible assets, including human capital, customer capital, social capital, and intellectual capital, help companies gain competitive advantage. Recognizing that formal training, informal learning, and knowledge management are important for the development of intangible assets, many companies now consider

Figure 7.1
Key Features of
Continuous Learning

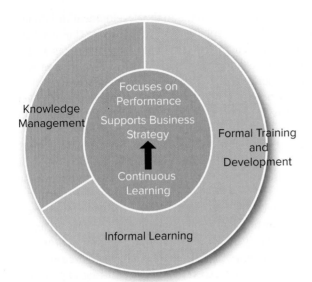

training one part of a larger emphasis on continuous learning. Figure 7.1 shows that formal training and development, informal learning, and knowledge management are the key features of a continuous learning philosophy that focuses on performance and supports the business strategy. **Continuous learning** refers to a learning system that requires employees to understand the entire work system; they are expected to acquire new skills, apply them on the job, and share what they have learned with other employees.[2]

Training refers to a planned effort by a company to facilitate employees' learning of job-related competencies, knowledge, skills, and behaviors. The goal of training is for employees to master the knowledge, skills, and behaviors emphasized in training and apply them to their day-to-day activities. Traditionally, companies have relied on formal training through a course, a program, or an event to teach employees the knowledge, skills, and behaviors they need to successfully perform their jobs. **Formal training** refers to training and development programs, courses, and events that are developed and organized by the company. Typically employees are required to attend or complete these programs, which can include face-to-face training programs (such as instructor-led courses) as well as online programs. U.S. companies make substantial investments in formal training. One estimate is that U.S. organizations spend over $70 billion on formal employee training and development.[3] We will discuss employee development in Chapter 9.

Despite companies' significant investments in formal training and development activities, informal learning is also important for facilitating knowledge and skill acquisition.[4] **Informal learning** refers to learning that is learner initiated, involves action and doing, is motivated by an intent to develop, and does not occur in a formal learning setting.[5] Informal learning occurs without an instructor, and its breadth, depth, and timing are controlled by the employee. It occurs on an as-needed basis and may involve an employee learning alone or through face-to-face or technology-aided social interactions. Informal learning can occur through many different ways, including casual unplanned interactions with peers, e-mail, informal mentoring, or company-developed or publicly available social networking websites such as Twitter or Facebook. The application of social media from a marketing strategy to a learning strategy and the availability of Web 2.0 technologies such as social networks, microblogs, and wikis give employees easy access to social learning through collaboration and sharing with one or two or more people.[6] One estimate is that informal learning may account for up to 75% of learning within organizations.

Continuous learning
A learning system that requires employees to understand the entire work process and expects them to acquire new skills, apply them on the job, and share what they have learned with other employees.

Training
A planned effort to facilitate the learning of job-related knowledge, skills, and behavior by employees.

Formal training
Training and development programs and courses that are developed and organized by the company.

Informal learning
Learning that is learner initiated, involves action and doing, is motivated by an intent to develop, and does not occur in a formal learning setting.

Both formal training and informal learning contribute to the development of intangible assets but especially human capital. Human capital includes knowledge (know what), advanced skills (know how), system understanding and creativity (know why), as well as motivation to deliver high-quality products and services (care why).[7] One reason why informal learning may be especially important is that it may lead to the effective development of *tacit* knowledge, which can be contrasted with *explicit* knowledge.[8] **Explicit knowledge** refers to knowledge that is well documented, easily articulated, and easily transferred from person to person. Examples of explicit knowledge include processes, checklists, flowcharts, formulas, and definitions. Explicit knowledge tends to be the primary focus of formal training. **Tacit knowledge** refers to personal knowledge based on individual experiences that make it difficult to codify. It is best acquired through informal learning. The characteristics of the formal training environment may limit the extent to which tacit knowledge can be acquired, such as the relatively short duration of classroom or online training and limited opportunities for practice. Thus, informal learning is central to the development of tacit knowledge. Well-designed formal training programs can help employees acquire explicit knowledge. But to acquire tacit knowledge employees need to interact with peers, colleagues, and experts and have learning experiences that are not usually found in formal training. Informal learning does not replace formal training. Formal training is still needed to prepare employees for their jobs and help them progress to future positions. Informal learning complements training by helping employees gain tacit knowledge that formal training cannot provide.

Knowledge management refers to the process of enhancing company performance by designing and implementing tools, processes, systems, structures, and cultures to improve the creation, sharing, and use of knowledge.[9] Knowledge management contributes to informal learning.

The Defense Acquisition University (DAU) is a corporate university of the U.S. Department of Defense, providing training to military and federal civilian staff and federal contractors.[10] DAU provides a knowledge sharing system giving staff and contractors access to searchable regulations, performance support tools, and communities of practice. The system includes an online encyclopedia of common defense acquisition topics organized as articles. Each article contains a definition and a brief narrative and includes links to policy, guidance, tools, practices, and training. Employees and contractors are able to interact and share lessons learned and experiences, which helps support job performance, avoid the duplication of effort, and advance the connection of people and ideas. This knowledge sharing system helped to significantly reduce the price of surveillance aircraft, which saved the military $630 million.

It is important for all aspects of continuous learning, including formal training and development, informal learning, and knowledge management, to contribute to and support the business strategy. Continuous learning needs to address performance issues that lead to improved business results. To do so requires that the emphasis on continuous learning aligns with the business strategy; has visible support from senior managers and involves leaders as instructors and teachers; creates a culture or work environment that encourages learning; provides a wide range of learning opportunities including training, informal learning, knowledge management, and employee development; uses traditional methods and innovative technologies to design and deliver learning; and measures the effectiveness and overall business impact of learning.[11]

Consider how Jiffy Lube embraces a continuous learning philosophy that supports the business strategy.[12] Jiffy Lube's strategic goals focus on developing growth opportunities for franchisees and providing a world-class customer experience. Jiffy Lube's customer value proposition is that every driver deserves to be free from the anxiety of

---

Explicit knowledge
Knowledge that is well documented and easily transferred to other persons.

Tacit knowledge
Knowledge based on personal experience that is difficult to codify.

Knowledge management
The process of enhancing company performance by designing and using tools, systems, and cultures to improve creation, sharing, and use of knowledge.

keeping his or her vehicle in excellent shape. This requires that service technicians be knowledgable about and able to provide high quality and necessary services to drivers. At Jiffy Lube this means that service technicians need to be trained and certified. Training is provided through Jiffy Lube University (JLU). Its estimated that employees participated in more than two million learning hours in the previous two years. Learning for employees and franchisees is offered using face-to-face and virtual instruction, as well as online self-paced modules. JLU evaluates the success of learning efforts many ways, including through learner feedback, franchisee surveys, the number of training courses completed, earned certifications, and customer service scores from mystery shoppers.

Jiffy Lube recognizes the value of continuous learning and informal learning. Recently, every employee, including the company president, was required to complete courses at JLU plus spend at least one day at a Jiffy Lube service center. The courses included orientation and safety and training for the courtesy technician, upper bay technician, customer service advisor, and team lead positions. Jiffy Lube also has established partnerships with colleges to allow service center employees to transfer credits from courses earned through JLU to earn an undergraduate certificate in management foundations. Learners and managers can access an online roadmap, which shows how training is helping them advance their careers. Also, recognizing that its service center employees typically are 18–25 year olds who are actively involved in social media, Jiffy Lube provides video cameras so that store employees can capture best practices and ideas. These videos have focused on customer service, team building, operational excellence, and safety. Jiffy Lube trainers edit the videos and make them available to all employees on YouTube.

Designing Effective Formal Training Activities

A key characteristic of training activities that contribute to competitiveness is that they are designed according to the instructional design process.[13] **Training design process** refers to a systematic approach for developing training programs. Instructional System Design (ISD) and the ADDIE model (analysis, design, development, implementation, evaluation) are two specific types of training design processes you may know. Figure 7.2 presents the six stages of this process, which emphasizes that effective training practices involve more than just choosing the most popular or colorful training method.

The first stage is to assess needs to determine if training is needed. Stage 2 involves ensuring that employees have the readiness for training and that they have the motivation and basic skills to master training content. Stage 3 addresses whether the training session (or the learning environment) has the factors necessary for learning to occur. Stage 4 focuses on ensuring that trainees apply the content of training to their jobs. This requires support from managers and peers for the use of training content on the job as well as getting the employee to understand how to take personal responsibility for skill improvement. Stage 5 involves choosing a training method. As we will see in this chapter, a variety of training methods are available ranging from traditional on-the-job training to newer technologies such as social media. The key is to choose a training method that will provide the appropriate learning environment to achieve the training objectives. Stage 6 is evaluation—that is, determining whether training achieved the desired learning outcomes and/or financial objectives.

The training design process should be systematic yet flexible enough to adapt to business needs. Different steps may be completed simultaneously. Also, feedback from each

LO 7-2
Explain the role of the manager in identifying training needs and supporting training on the job.

Training design process
A systematic approach for developing training programs.

Figure 7.2
The Training Process

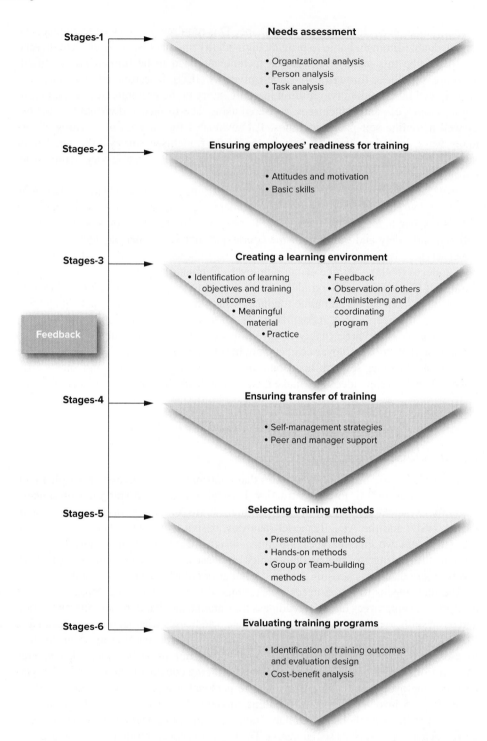

Stages-1 — **Needs assessment**
- Organizational analysis
- Person analysis
- Task analysis

Stages-2 — **Ensuring employees' readiness for training**
- Attitudes and motivation
- Basic skills

Stages-3 — **Creating a learning environment**
- Identification of learning objectives and training outcomes
- Meaningful material
- Practice
- Feedback
- Observation of others
- Administering and coordinating program

Feedback

Stages-4 — **Ensuring transfer of training**
- Self-management strategies
- Peer and manager support

Stages-5 — **Selecting training methods**
- Presentational methods
- Hands-on methods
- Group or Team-building methods

Stages-6 — **Evaluating training programs**
- Identification of training outcomes and evaluation design
- Cost-benefit analysis

stage in the process can be useful for the other stages. For example, if transfer of training is difficult, then the learning environment should overemphasize practice and feedback. Keep in mind that designing training unsystematically will reduce the benefits that can be realized. For example, choosing a training method before determining training needs or ensuring employees' readiness for training increases the risk that the method chosen will not be the most effective one for meeting training needs. Also, training may not even be necessary and may result in a waste of time and money. Employees may have the knowledge, skills, or behavior they need but simply not be motivated to use them. In the next several sections, we discuss important aspects of the training design process.

NEEDS ASSESSMENT

The first step in the instructional design process, **needs assessment**, refers to the process used to determine if training is necessary. Figure 7.3 shows the causes and outcomes resulting from needs assessment. As the figure illustrates, many different "pressure points" suggest that training is necessary. These pressure points include performance problems, new technology, internal or external customer requests for training, job redesign, new legislation, changes in customer preferences, new products, or employees' lack of basic skills as well as support for the company's business strategy (e.g., growth, global business expansion). Training is not always the correct solution to a pressure point. Consider, for example, a delivery truck driver whose job is to deliver anesthetic gases to medical facilities. The driver mistakenly hooks up the supply line of a mild anesthetic to the supply line of a hospital's oxygen system, contaminating the hospital's oxygen supply. Why did the driver make this mistake, which is clearly a performance problem? The driver may have done this because of a lack of knowledge about the appropriate line hookup for the anesthetic, anger over a requested salary increase that his manager recently denied, or mislabeled valves for connecting the gas supply. Only the lack of knowledge can be addressed by training. The other pressure points require addressing issues related to the consequence of good performance (pay system) or the design of the work environment.

Needs assessment typically involves organizational analysis, person analysis, and task analysis.[14] Organizational analysis considers the context in which training will occur. That is, **organizational analysis** involves determining the business appropriateness of training, given the company's business strategy, its resources available for training, and support by managers and peers for training activities.

Person analysis helps identify who needs training. **Person analysis** involves (1) determining whether performance deficiencies result from a lack of knowledge, skills, or abilities (a training issue) or from a motivational or work-design problem; (2) identifying

LO 7-3
Conduct a needs assessment.

Needs assessment
The process used to determine if training is necessary.

Organizational analysis
A process for determining the business appropriateness of training.

Person analysis
A process for determining whether employees need training, who needs training, and whether employees are ready for training.

Figure 7.3

The Needs Assessment Process

Reasons or "pressure points"   What is the context?

- Legislation
- Lack of basic skills
- Poor performance
- New technology
- Customer requests
- New products
- Higher performance standards
- New jobs
- Business growth or contraction
- Global business expansion

Organization analysis

Task analysis

Person analysis

Who needs training?

In what do they need training?

Outcomes

- What trainees need to learn
- Who receives training
- Type of training
- Frequency of training
- Buy-versus-build training decision
- Training versus other HR options such as selection or job redesign
- How training should be evaluated

Task analysis
The process of identifying the tasks, knowledge, skills, and behaviors that need to be emphasized in training.

who needs training; and (3) determining employees' readiness for training. **Task analysis** includes identifying the important tasks and knowledge, skills, and behaviors that need to be emphasized in training for employees to complete their tasks.

In practice, organizational analysis, person analysis, and task analysis are usually not conducted in any specific order. However, because organizational analysis is concerned with identifying whether training fits with the company's strategic objectives and whether the company wants to devote time and money to training, it is usually conducted first. Person analysis and task analysis are often conducted at the same time because it can be difficult to determine whether performance deficiencies are a training problem without understanding the tasks and the work environment.

What outcomes result from a needs assessment? As shown in Figure 7.3, needs assessment shows who needs training and what trainees need to learn, including the tasks in which they need to be trained plus knowledge, skill, behavior, or other job requirements. Needs assessment helps determine whether the company will purchase training from a vendor or consultant or develop training using internal resources.

MasTec is a construction company that engineers, procures, constructs, and maintains the infrastructures for electric transmission and distribution, oil and natural gas pipelines, and communications companies.[15] The company wanted to develop an online learning management system through which employees could access training and development courses. MasTec conducted a needs assessment to identify questions such as what technology and functionality were needed to support new training programs and to identify unique employee needs. As a result, the development team started by conducting a shareholder analysis. This involved considering who would be involved in the process, understanding how to partner with them, and what type of information they could offer. This further involved meeting with safety team leaders, trainers, and construction crew members; observing employees performing their jobs; and attending existing training classes. The team recorded every need and request made throughout this process. As a result of this analysis, they identified four goals for the learning management system. These goals included increased accessibility of training content; increased flexibility and variety in how training was delivered and completed; improved process for registering employees for training; and reporting tools that make training requirements, participation, and completion visible to employees, their managers, and the employee development group.

Organizational Analysis

Three factors need to be considered before choosing training as the solution to any pressure point: the support of managers and peers for training activities, the company's strategy, and the training resources available.

Support of Managers and Peers. Various studies have found that peer and manager support for training is critical. The key factors for success are a positive attitude among peers and managers about participation in training activities; managers' and peers' willingness to tell trainees how they can more effectively use knowledge, skills, or behaviors learned in training on the job; and the availability of opportunities for the trainees to use training content in their jobs.[16] If peers' and managers' attitudes and behaviors are not supportive, then employees are not likely to apply training content to their jobs.

Company Strategy. In Chapter 2, we discussed the importance of business strategy for a company to gain a competitive advantage, and earlier in this chapter we discussed how Jiffy Lube relies on learning to support the company's mission and strategy. As Figure 7.1 highlights, training should help companies achieve their business strategy. Table 7.1 shows possible strategic initiatives and their implications for training practices.

STRATEGIC TRAINING AND DEVELOPMENT INITIATIVES	IMPLICATIONS
Improve customer service	• Ensure that employees have product and service knowledge • Ensure that employees have skills needed to interact with customers • Ensure that employees understand their roles and decision-making authority
Improve employee engagement	• Ensure that employees have opportunities to develop • Ensure that employees understand career opportunities and personal growth opportunities • Ensure that training and development addresses employees' needs in current job as well as growth opportunities
Enhance innovation and creativity	• Capture insight and information from knowledgeable employees • Logically organize and store information • Provide methods to make information available (e.g., resource guides, websites) • Dedicate physical space to encourage teamwork, collaboration, creativity, and knowledge sharing
Growth in global markets	• Prepare high potential managers to take over global leadership positions • Prepare expatriates to function cross-culturally • Train local workforce in company culture

Table 7.1

Examples of Strategic Initiatives and Their Implications for Training Practices

SOURCE: Based on S. Tannenbaum, "A Strategic View of Organizational Training and Learning," in *Creating, Implementing and Managing Effective Training and Development*, ed. K. Kraiger (San Francisco: Jossey-Bass, 2002), pp. 10–52.

It is important to identify the prevailing business strategy and goals to ensure that (1) the company allocates enough of its budget to training, (2) employees receive training on relevant topics, and (3) employees get the right amount of training.[17] Consider how training at Hilton Worldwide supports the business.[18] Hilton Worldwide is faced with the business challenge of using technology to create operational efficiency and engage with its hotel guests from when they book their stay to when they check-out. Training plays a key role in supporting Hilton's strategy to use technology to help increase its market share. More than 80,000 front desk staff and managers in 4,400 hotels had to become familiar with Digital Check-in, an app that customers can use to make reservations, choose their room, and check in with their mobile devices. Hilton used a blended training approach that included short games, job aids, and quick reference guides, which are available using a computer or smartphone. Front desk employees and managers have to achieve a 100% score to complete the training. So far, 67,000 have done so. The use of technology for training delivery and instruction meshes nicely with the use of the innovative Digital Check-in app.

The "Integrity in Action" box highlights how one business leader is using training to help employees and contribute to a turnaround strategy.

Training Resources. The company must determine whether it has the budget, time, and expertise for training. For example, if the company is installing computer-based manufacturing equipment in one of its plants, it has three possible strategies to have computer-literate employees. First, the company can use technical experts on staff to train all affected employees. Second, the company may decide that it is more cost effective to identify computer-literate employees by using tests and work samples and replace or reassign employees who lack the necessary skills. Third, if it lacks time or expertise, the company may decide to purchase training from an outside consultant or organization.

Table 7.2 provides examples of questions to ask vendors and consultants to help evaluate whether they can meet the company's training needs.

Person Analysis

Person analysis helps the manager identify whether training is appropriate and which employees need training. In certain situations, such as the introduction of a new technology or service, all employees may need training. However, when managers, customers, or employees identify a problem (usually as a result of a performance deficiency), it is often unclear whether training is the solution.

Table 7.2
Questions to Ask
Vendors and
Consultants

- How do your products and services fit our needs?
- How much and what type of experience does your company have in designing and delivering training?
- What are the qualifications and experiences of your staff?
- Can you provide demonstrations or examples of training programs you have developed?
- Can you provide references from clients for whom you worked?
- What evidence do you have that your programs work?
- How long will it take to develop the training program?
- How much will your services cost?
- What instructional design methods do you use?
- What about recurring costs, such as those related to administering, updating, and maintaining the training program?
- Do you provide technical support?

SOURCES: Adapted from R. Zemke and J. Armstrong, "Evaluating Multimedia Developers," *Training*, November 1996, pp. 33–38; B. Chapman, "How to Create the Ideal RFP," *Training*, January 2004, pp. 40–43; M. Weinstein, "What Vendors Wished You Knew," *Training*, February 2010, pp. 122–125.

A major pressure point for training is poor or substandard performance—that is, when a gap exists between employees' current performance and their expected performance. Poor performance is indicated by customer complaints, low performance ratings, or on-the-job accidents or unsafe behavior. Another potential indicator of the need for training is if the job changes so that current performance levels need improvement or employees must complete new tasks.

For managers to determine if training is needed to address a performance problem, they must analyze characteristics of the performer, input, output, consequences, and feedback.[19] This can be done by assessing whether

1. The performance problem is important and has the potential to cost the company a significant amount of money from lost productivity or customers.
2. Employees do not know how to perform effectively. Perhaps they received little or no previous training or the training was ineffective (person characteristics).
3. Employees cannot demonstrate the correct knowledge or behavior. Perhaps they were trained but they infrequently or never used the training content (knowledge, skills, etc.) on the job (input problem).
4. Performance expectations are clear (input) and there are no obstacles to performance such as faulty tools or equipment (output).
5. There are positive consequences for good performance, whereas poor performance is not rewarded. For example, if employees are dissatisfied with their compensation, their peers or a union may encourage them to slow down their pace of work (consequences).
6. Employees receive timely, relevant, accurate, constructive, and specific feedback about their performance (feedback).
7. Other solutions such as job redesign or transferring employees to other jobs are too expensive or unrealistic.

If employees lack the knowledge and skill to perform and the other factors are satisfactory, then training is likely the effective solution. If employees have the knowledge and skill to perform, but input, output, consequences, or feedback are inadequate, then training may not be the best solution. For example, if poor performance results from faulty equipment, training cannot solve this problem, but repairing the equipment will. If poor performance results from a lack of feedback, then employees may not need training, but their managers may need training on how to give performance feedback.

Task Analysis

A task analysis identifies the conditions in which tasks are performed. The conditions include identifying equipment and the environment the employee works in, time constraints (deadlines), safety considerations, or performance standards. Task analysis results in a description of work activities, including tasks performed by the employee and the knowledge, skills, and abilities required to successfully complete the tasks. A *job* is a specific position requiring the completion of specific tasks. A *task* is a statement of an employee's work activity in a specific job. The four steps in a task analysis are (1) identifying the job(s) to be analyzed; (2) developing a list of tasks performed on the job; (3) validating or confirming the tasks; and (4) identifying the knowledge, skills, abilities, and other factors (e.g., equipment, working conditions) needed to successfully perform each task.[20]

For example, consider how KLA-Tencor conducted a needs assessment for its service engineers.[21] KLA-Tencor supplies process controls and equipment to the semiconductor industry. KLA-Tencor service engineers need to diagnose and repair its customers' complex machines that use advanced laser, optical, and robotic technologies. The engineers need to main proficiency in their current skills as well as add new skills to keep pace with new technology used in the company's equipment. This is critical for KLA-Tencor to quickly solve equipment problems, which if unresolved, can result in millions of dollars of lost revenue for its customers. Providing effective service is critical for the company to keep current customers and develop new business. In fact, one of the company's values is "indispensable" (the others values are perseverance; drive to be better; high performance teams; and honest, forthright, and consistent).

KLA-Tencor uses a skills management process (the "right people, right knowledge" process) to monitor its workforce skills and use this information to change its training programs. The process involves developing a task list, training on the task, practicing on-the-job training to gain certification, and conducting an annual skills assessment. To conduct the skills assessment, KLA-Tencor sent a survey to all of its more than 1,000 service engineers. For each task, the engineers were asked to rate their capability of doing the task on a scale from "I don't know how" to "I can teach it to others." Also, they were asked to evaluate how frequently they performed the task, from "never" to "more than two times per year." Based on their responses, they were assigned a training task. More than 200 courses were created to train the engineers. To ensure that the training was completed, both engineers and their managers were held accountable. This helped the company to achieve a 95% completion rate within one year after training was assigned. The skills assessment data were also used to identify gaps in current training, resulting in more than 2,000 changes in courses and certification programs. The skills assessment is done annually to ensure that service engineers' skills keep up to date with new technology and products.

Readiness for training
Employee characteristics that provide them with the desire, energy, and focus necessary to learn from training.

Motivation to learn
The desire of the trainee to learn the content of a training program.

LO 7-4
Evaluate employees' readiness for training.

ENSURING EMPLOYEES' READINESS FOR TRAINING

The second stage in the training design process is to evaluate whether employees are ready for training. **Readiness for training** refers to employee characteristics that provide employees with the desire, energy, and focus necessary to learn from training. The desire, energy, and focus is referred to as **motivation to learn**.[22] Various research studies have shown that motivation to learn is related to knowledge gain, behavior change, or skill acquisition in training programs.[23] Table 7.3 presents factors that influence motivation to learn and the actions that strength them. Motivation to learn influences mastery of all types of training content, including knowledge, behavior, and skills. Managers need to ensure that employees' motivation to learn is as high as possible. They can do this by ensuring employees' self-efficacy; understanding the benefits of training; being aware of training needs, career interests, and goals; understanding work environment characteristics; and ensuring employees' basic skill levels.

Table 7.3
Factors That Influence Motivation to Learn

FACTOR	DESCRIPTION	ACTIONS TO ENHANCE OR IMPROVE
Self-efficacy	Employee belief that they can successfully learn content of the training program	Show employees their peers' training success. Communicate that purpose of training is to improve, not identify, area of incompetence. Communicate purpose and activities involved in training. Emphasize that learning is under their personal control.
Benefits or consequences of training	Job-related, personal, career benefits that can result from attending training	Communicate realistic short- and long-term benefits from training.
Awareness of training needs	Knowledge of skill strengths and weaknesses	Communicate why they were asked to attend training program. Share performance appraisal information. Encourage trainees to complete self-evaluation of all strengths and weaknesses. Give employees input on the choice of training to attend.
Work environment	Proper tools and equipment, materials, supplies, budget time; managers' and peers' willingness to provide feedback and reinforce use of training content	Give employees opportunities to practice skills and apply them to their work. Encourage employees to provide feedback to each other. Encourage trainees to share training experiences and situations where use of training content was beneficial. Acknowledge use of training content in their work. Provide resources necessary for training content to be used in their work.
Basic skills	Cognitive ability, reading and writing skills	Ensure trainees have prerequisite skills needed for understanding and learning training content. Provide remedial training. Use video or other visual training methods. Modify training program to meet trainees' basic skill levels.
Goal orientation	Goals held by employees in a learning situation	Create a learning goal orientation by deemphasizing competition between trainees; allowing trainees to make errors and to experiment with new knowledge, skills, and behavior during training; and setting learning goals.
Conscientiousness	Tendency to be reliable, hardworking, self-disciplined, and persistent	Communicate need for learning.

SOURCES: Based on J. Colquitt, J. LePine, and R. Noe, "Toward an Integrative Theory of Training Motivation: A Meta-Analytic Path Analysis of 20 Years of Research," *Journal of Applied Psychology* 85 (2000), pp. 678–707; R. Noe and J. Colquitt, "Planning for Impact Training: Principles of Training Effectiveness," in K. Kraiger (ed.), *Creating, Implementing, and Managing Effective Training and Development* (San Francisco: Jossey-Bass, 2002), pp. 53–79.

CREATING A LEARNING ENVIRONMENT

Learning permanently changes behavior. For employees to acquire knowledge and skills in the training program and apply this information in their jobs, the training program must include specific learning principles. Educational and industrial psychologists and instructional design specialists have identified several conditions under which employees learn best.[24] Table 7.4 shows the events that should take place for learning to occur in the training program and their implications for instruction.

Table 7.4
Conditions for Learning and Their Importance

CONDITIONS FOR LEARNING	IMPORTANCE AND APPLICATION TO TRAINING
Need to know why they should learn	Employees need to understand the purpose or objectives of the training program to help them understand why they need training and what they are expected to accomplish.
Meaningful training content	Motivation to learn is enhanced when training is related to helping learner (such as related to current job tasks, problems, enhancing skills, or dealing with jobs or company changes). The training context should be similar to the work environment.
Opportunities for practice	Trainees need to demonstrate what is learned (knowledge, skill, behavior) to become more comfortable using it and to commit it to memory. Let trainees choose their practice strategy.
Feedback	Feedback helps learners to modify behavior or skill, or to use knowledge to meet objectives. Video, other trainees, and the trainer are useful feedback sources.
Observe, experience, and interact with training content, other learners, and the instructor	Adults learn best by doing. They can gain new perspectives and insights by working with others and can learn by observing the actions of models or by sharing experiences with each other in communities of practice or through social networking. Interacting with and manipulating content through reading or using tools that allow for building ideas and solving problems, such as worksheets and online interactions, is helpful.
Good program coordination and administration	Eliminate distractions that could interfere with learning, such as cell phone calls. Make sure the room is properly organized, comfortable, and appropriate for the training method (e.g., movable seating for team exercises). Trainees should receive announcements of the purpose of training, place, hour, and any pretraining materials such as cases or readings.
Commit training content to memory	Facilitate recall of training content after training. Examples include using concept maps showing relationships among ideas, using multiple types of review (writing, drawing, role-plays), teaching key words, providing a visual image, or asking trainees to reflect on what they learned. Limit instruction to manageable units or chunks that don't exceed memory limits; review and practice over multiple days (overlearning). Use short quizzes or other activities to help trainees retrieve what they learned and emphasize its importance.

SOURCES: Based on R. M. Gagne, "Learning Processes and Instruction," *Training Research Journal* 1 (1995/1996), pp. 17–28; M. Knowles, *The Adult Learner*, 4th ed. (Houston: Gulf, 1990); A. Bandura, *Social Foundations of Thought and Action* (Englewood Cliffs, NJ: Prentice Hall, 1986); E. A. Locke and G. D. Latham, *A Theory of Goal Setting and Task Performance* (Englewood Cliffs, NJ: Prentice Hall, 1990); B. Mager, *Preparing Instructional Objectives*, 2nd ed. (Belmont, CA: Lake, 1984); B.J. Smith and B. L. Delahaye, *How to Be an Effective Trainer*, 2nd ed. (New York: Wiley, 1987); K. A. Smith-Jentsch, F. G. Jentsch, S. C. Payne, and E. Salas, "Can Pretraining Experience Explain Individual Differences in Learning?" *Journal of Applied Psychology* 81 (1996), pp. 110–16; H. Nuriddin, "Building the Right Interaction," *T + D*, March 2011, pp. 32–35; R. Feloni, "This Simple Daily Exercise Boosts Employee Performance," *Business Insider India*, www.businessinsider.in.com; G. Di Stefano, F. Gino, G. Pisano, and B. Staats, "Learning by Thinking: How Reflection Aids Performance," Harvard Business School Working Paper, 14-093 (March 25, 2014); M. Plater, "Three Trends Shaping Learning," *Chief Learning Officer*, June 2014, pp. 44–47; A. Kohn, "Use It or Lose It," *T + D*, February 2015, pp. 56–61; J. Karpicke and Henry Roediger III, "The Critical Importance of Retrieval for Learning" *Science*, February 2008, pp. 966–68; A. Paul, "Microlearning 101", *HR Magazine* (May 2016): 36–42.

Consider how several companies are creating a positive learning environment using a variety of training methods.[25] In a training program designed to prepare employees to perform technical installation and maintenance roles, Verizon uses training labs with live circuits and equipment and a practice field with telephone poles. To maintain and update learning, small chunks of learning content and questions are sent to the learner's computer or smartphone. Correct answers to the questions are reinforced and incorrect answers require the learner to review the learning content. Employees can use a social media platform to share learning, ask questions, connect with other trainees, and access resources. Also, Verizon uses a train-the-trainer program to ensure that trainers involved in face-to-face instruction are able to create a positive learning environment. In the program known as TEACH (technician, educator, advisor, coach, host), trainers complete 100 hours of training over several weeks. SuperValu, a supermarket chain, uses Web-based training that emphasizes microlearning or breaking training content into small chunks of information that employees can easily commit to memory. Training might include a short video or brief online modules that employees can work on at their own pace.

ENSURING TRANSFER OF TRAINING

Transfer of training refers to on-the-job use of knowledge, skills, and behaviors learned in training. As Figure 7.4 shows, transfer of training is influenced by manager support, peer support, opportunity to use learned capabilities, technology support, and self-management skills. As we discussed earlier, learning is influenced by the learning environment (such as meaningfulness of the material and opportunities for practice and feedback) and employees' readiness for training (e.g., their self-efficacy and basic skill level). If no learning occurs in the training program, transfer is unlikely.

Transfer of training
The use of knowledge, skills, and behaviors learned in training on the job.

Manager Support

Manager support refers to the degree to which trainees' managers (1) emphasize the importance of attending training programs and (2) stress the application of training content to the job. Table 7.5 shows what managers should do to support training.

PricewaterhouseCoopers (PwC) partners and senior-level leaders delivered more than 90% of the training hours to employees.[26] All senior partners and the company's U.S. chairman completed more than 66 hours of training in technical and interpersonal skills. Then, demonstrating the importance that PwC places on learning and to develop employees as leaders, they led formal training sessions as well as provided informal coaching.

The greater the level of manager support, the more likely that transfer of training will occur.[27] The basic level of support that a manager should provide is acceptance, that is, allowing trainees to attend training. The highest level of support is to participate in training

Manager support
The degree to which trainees' managers emphasize the importance of attending training programs and stress the application of training content to the job.

Figure 7.4

Work Environment Characteristics Influencing Transfer of Training

Table 7.5
How Managers Can
Support Training

- Understand the content of the training.
- Know how training relates to what you need employees to do.
- In performance appraisals, evaluate employees on how they apply training to their jobs.
- Support employees' use of training when they return to work.
- Ensure that employees have the equipment and technology needed to use training.
- Prior to training, discuss with employees how they plan to use training.
- Recognize newly trained employees who use training content.
- Give employees release time from their work to attend training.
- Explain to employees why they have been asked to attend training.
- Give employees feedback related to skills or behavior they are trying to develop.
- If possible, be a trainer.

SOURCES: Based on S. Bailey, "The Answer to Transfer," *Chief Learning Officer*, November 2014, pp. 33–41; R. Hewes, "Step by Step," *T + D*, February 2014, pp. 56–61; R. Bates, "Managers as Transfer Agents," in E. Holton III and T. Baldwin (eds.), *Improving Learning Transfer in Organizations* (San Francisco: Jossey-Bass, 2003), pp. 243–70; A. Rossett, "That Was a Great Class, but . . ." *Training and Development*, July 1997, p. 21.

Action plan
A document summarizing what the trainee and manager will do to ensure that training transfers to the job.

as an instructor (teaching in the program). Managers who serve as instructors are more likely to provide lower-level support functions such as reinforcing use of newly learned capabilities, discussing progress with trainees, and providing opportunities to practice. Managers can also facilitate transfer through use of action plans. An **action plan** is a written document that includes the steps that the trainee and manager will take to ensure that training transfers to the job. The action plan includes (1) a goal identifying what training content will be used and how it will be used (project, problem); (2) strategies for reaching the goal, including resources needed; (3) strategies for getting feedback (such as meetings with the manager); and (4) expected outcome (what will be different?). The action plan includes a schedule of specific dates and times when the manager and trainee agree to meet to discuss the progress being made in using learned capabilities on the job.

To help ensure learning and transfer of training, Western Union's Guide.Performance. Succeed (GPS) program requires leaders to get involved in helping to develop their employees' skills by setting clear expectations, providing regular real-time feedback, and holding their employees and themselves accountable for meeting talent development goals.[28] At Sonic Automotive, an automotive retailer, after trainees complete interactive instructor-led training, they are asked to identify an opportunity to use their new skills at their store. Their action plan has to be developed within 7 days and implemented within 45 days.[29]

At a minimum, special sessions should be scheduled with managers to explain the purpose of the training and to set expectations that they will encourage attendance at the training session, provide practice opportunities, reinforce use of training, and follow up with employees to determine their progress in using newly acquired capabilities.

Peer Support

Support network
Trainees who meet to discuss their progress in using learned capabilities on the job.

Transfer of training can also be enhanced by creating a support network among the trainees.[30] A **support network** is a group of two or more trainees who agree to meet and discuss their progress in using learned capabilities on the job. This could involve face-to-face meetings or communications via e-mail, Twitter, or other social networking tools. For example, EMC, a company that provides IT storage hardware solutions, provided newly hired technical support engineers with an online tool that makes it easy to have conversations and ask peers questions about concepts covered in their training.[31] Trainees can share successful experiences in using training content on the job; they can also discuss how they obtained resources needed to use training content or how they coped with a work environment that interfered with use of training content.

Websites or electronic newsletters might be used to show how trainees are dealing with transfer of training issues. Available to all trainees, the newsletter or website might feature interviews with trainees who were successful in using new skills or provide tips for using new skills. Managers may also provide trainees with a mentor—a more experienced employee who previously attended the same training program. The mentor, who may be a peer, can provide advice and support (such as how to find opportunities to use the learned capabilities).

Opportunity to Use Learned Capabilities

Opportunity to use learned capabilities (**opportunity to perform**) refers to the extent to which the trainee is provided with or actively seeks experience with newly learned knowledge, skills, and behaviors from the training program.[32] Opportunity to perform is influenced by both the work environment and trainee motivation. One way trainees can use learned capabilities is through assigned work experiences (problems or tasks) that require their use. The trainees' manager usually plays a key role in determining work assignments. Opportunity to perform is also influenced by the degree to which trainees take personal responsibility to actively seek out assignments that allow them to use newly acquired capabilities. Trainees given many opportunities to use training content on the job are more likely to maintain learned capabilities than trainees given few opportunities.[33]

> **Opportunity to perform**
> The trainee is provided with or actively seeks experience using newly learned knowledge, skills, or behavior.

Technological Support: Performance Support and Knowledge Management Systems

Performance support systems are computer applications that can provide, as requested, skills training, information access, and expert advice.[34] Performance support may be used to enhance transfer of training by giving trainees an electronic information source that they can refer to as needed as they attempt to apply learned capabilities on the job.

For example, Cathay Life Insurance provides its sales agents with iPads that include several different apps (applications created specifically for smartphones and tablet computers) designed to support what they have learned and to give them access to additional training they might need.[35] One app helps arrange sales schedules and self-assess their performance. Another app is a selling tool that allows agents to display insurance plans for clients and process claims online. Learning is also facilitated by an app that agents can use to access multimedia courses and short videos. Managers can provide advice and arrange for refresher training based on data generated by the agents' use of the apps.

As discussed earlier in the chapter, many companies are using knowledge management systems to improve the creation, sharing, and use of knowledge. The National Aeronautics and Space Administration (NASA) needs to manage knowledge to ensure its missions are successful.[36] At NASA, knowledge management means sharing solutions and expertise across employees, teams, projects, programs, centers, and missions. This includes scientific, engineering, and technical knowledge and business processes as well as know-how including techniques and procedures. To manage knowledge, NASA uses online tools including collaboration sites, video and document libraries, search and tagging tools, case studies and publications, processes to identify and retain lessons learned, knowledge networks, and social exchanges such as forums and workshops.

Knowledge management systems often include communities of practice. **Communities of practice** are groups of employees who work together, learn from each other, and

> **Performance support systems**
> Computer applications that can provide (as requested) skills training, information access, and expert advice.

> **Communities of practice**
> Groups of employees who work together, learn from each other, and develop a common understanding of how to get work accomplished.

develop a common understanding of how to get work accomplished. Tata Consultancy Services, a global information technology services, consulting, and business services organization provides employees with communities of practice on its social collaboration platform.[37] The communities include Eminence, for sharing new ideas, success stories, and trends in technology; Learners Enablers community, where employees share their expertise and availability to help others; and Culturesque, which offers cultural quizzes on countries where the company does business.

Self-Management Skills

Training programs should prepare employees to self-manage their use of new skills and behaviors on the job.[38] Specifically, within the training program, trainees should set goals for using skills or behaviors on the job, identify conditions under which they might fail to use them, identify the positive and negative consequences of using them, and monitor their use of them. Also, trainees need to understand that it is natural to encounter difficulty in trying to use skills on the job; relapses into old behavior and skill patterns do not indicate that trainees should give up. Finally, because peers and supervisors on the job may be unable to reward trainees using new behaviors or to provide feedback automatically, trainees need to create their own reward system and ask peers and managers for feedback.

As you should have realized by now, learning and transfer of training are closely related. If training does not facilitate learning there is nothing to transfer to the job. Similarly, if employees do learn, transfer of training will not occur if the work environment does not support or actively discourages applying what was learned. Consider how Farmers Insurance and General Motors training gets learners actively involved and helps to ensure transfer of training.[39] Farmers CE-It's Up to Me training includes four online modules and two-minute videos with supporting worksheets that allow employees to observe customer interactions, identify their impact on the interaction, and determine how they can improve the experience. Managers hold team meetings to discuss the training after trainees complete the online modules and watch the short videos. General Motors' district manager training includes face-to-face instruction; experiences in dealer operations, customer call centers, and after-sales centers; self-directed training and mentoring from more experienced district managers; and opportunities to share what they learned with other trainees.

LO 7-5
Discuss the strengths and weaknesses of presentation, hands-on, and group training methods.

SELECTING TRAINING METHODS

A number of different methods can help employees acquire new knowledge, skills, and behaviors. Figure 7.5 provides an overview of the use of training methods across companies of all sizes. The instructor-led classroom remains the most frequently used training method. However, the use of online learning, mobile learning, social learning, and blended learning (i.e., a combination of approaches) for training continues to increase. Expectations are that this trend with continue.

One estimate is that nearly 40% of executives plan to use tablets such as the iPad in their new training and development initiatives.[40] These devices are expected to be used for learning and performance support but also for coaching and mentoring employees, mobile gaming, and microblogging (e.g., Twitter).

Regardless of the training method, for training to be effective it needs to be based on the training design model shown in Figure 7.2. Needs assessment, a positive learning environment, and transfer of training are critical for training program effectiveness. The "Competing through Globalization" box shows how globalization affects the choice of training methods.

Language and Cultural Understanding: The Foundation for Global Success

English is still the most common language used for business, but Mandarin Chinese, French, and Arabic are becoming increasingly important. Providing employees working globally with language training is difficult because it requires time and instructor-led courses to learn a new language, but virtual instruction, online coursework, and mobile apps are making it easier to do so. It's also important for language training to match employees proficiency level and to insure that they are exposed to language and phrases that apply to their jobs. For example, doctors and nurses working for Operation Smile provide dental surgery for children in developing countries. They don't have time to learn all of the nuances of the country's language where they will be working but need to be able to

use some phrases such as "Don't worry" or "Open" and "Close".

Communicating in another language is necessary but not sufficient for global effectiveness. Employees need to be willing to learn (and admit what they don't know) about local religion, education, and government systems and cultural appreciation is critical. Cultural appreciation means taking the time to build relationships and build trust. For example, Marriott International is preparing employees to take management positions based on its plans to expand its presence in Asia and the Middle East. Marriott recognizes that understanding cultural context and human connection is important for running international properties. Its Elevate program provides a year of training in owner relations, sales and revenue management,

brand, customer focus, finance and crisis communications, human resources, and intercultural communications. Training is delivered through classroom instruction, webinars, mentoring, and employees participate in peer forums. Groups of 30 to 40 employees from more than fifty-five countries take the training together.

DISCUSSION QUESTION

1. Which training method or combination of methods would be best to use for language training and cultural knowledge and appreciation? Explain why.

SOURCES: C. Curry, "Prepare for Arrival", TD (May 2016): 30–35; S. Shullman & L. Kelly-Radford, "Global Leaders Embrace Difference", *Chief Learning Officer* (May 2015): 26–28, 48; K. Everson, "Learning in Translation", *Chief Learning Officer* (May 2015): 38–41.

Percentage of training hours delivered by each method

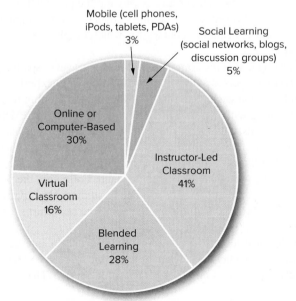

Figure 7.5

Overview of Use of Training Methods

SOURCE: "2016 Training Industry Report," *Training*, November/December 2016, pp. 28–41.

Presentation methods
Training methods in which trainees are passive recipients of information.

Presentation Methods

Presentation methods refer to methods in which trainees are passive recipients of information. Presentation methods include traditional classroom instruction, distance learning, and audiovisual training. They can include the use of personal computers, smartphones, and tablet computers such as iPads. These methods are ideal for presenting new facts, information, different philosophies, and alternative problem-solving solutions or processes.

Instructor-Led Classroom Instruction. Classroom instruction typically involves having the trainer lecture a group. In many cases, the lecture is supplemented with question-and-answer periods, discussion, or case studies. Classroom instruction remains a popular training method despite new technologies such as interactive video and computer-assisted instruction. Traditional classroom instruction is one of the least expensive, least time-consuming ways to present information on a specific topic to many trainees. The more active participation, job-related examples, and exercises that the instructor can build in to traditional classroom instruction, the more likely trainees will learn and use the information presented on the job.

Distance Learning. Distance learning is used by geographically dispersed companies to provide information about new products, policies, or procedures as well as skills training and expert lectures to field locations.[41] Distance learning features two-way communications between people.[42] First, it can include teleconferencing. **Teleconferencing** refers to synchronous exchange of audio, video, and/or text between two or more individuals or groups at two or more locations. Trainees attend programs in facilities in which they can communicate with trainers (who are at another location) and other trainees using the telephone or personal computer. Second, distance learning can include a virtual classroom. A third type of distance learning also includes individualized, personal computer–based training.[43] Employees participate in training anywhere they have access to a personal computer. This can also include **webcasting**, which involves face-to-face instruction provided online through live broadcasts. Course material, including video, can be distributed using the company's intranet. Trainers and trainees interact using e-mail, bulletin boards, and conferencing systems. Distance learning can also allow trainees to respond to questions posed during the training program using a keypad.

Teleconferencing
Synchronous exchange of audio, video, or text between individuals or groups at two or more locations.

Webcasting
Classroom instruction provided online via live broadcasts.

Distance learning usually includes a link so that trainees viewing the presentation can call in questions and comments to the trainer. Also, satellite networks allow companies to link up with industry-specific and educational courses for which employees receive college credit and job certification.

An advantage of distance learning is that the company can save on travel costs. It also allows employees in geographically dispersed sites to receive training from experts who would not otherwise be available to visit each location. For example, for training its tax professionals, EY combines e-learning with a virtual classroom (described in more detail later in the chapter) and face-to-face instruction.[44] The virtual classroom courses are 30 minutes long. In the first 10 minutes, online polling is used to test participants' understanding of key concepts covered in the e-learning course. The trainer is encouraged to help clarify any key concepts that the participants don't understand. Following the polling, participants work in five- or six-person virtual teams on case studies. Next, participants attend the live, face-to-face class in which they complete income tax returns using EY's processes and technology.

The major disadvantage of distance learning is the potential for lack of interaction between the trainer and the audience. To help ensure that distance learning is effective, a high degree of interaction between trainees and the trainer is necessary.[45] That's why establishing a communications link between employees and the trainer is important. Also, on-site instructors or facilitators should be available to answer questions and moderate question-and-answer sessions.

Audiovisual Training. Audiovisual training includes the use of overheads, slides, and video. It has been used for improving communication skills, interviewing skills, and customer service skills and for illustrating how procedures (such as welding) should be followed. Learners may not be required to attend a class. They can work independently, using materials in workbooks or on the Internet. PowerPoint or other presentation software and video or audio clips can also be used to show learning points, real-life experiences, and examples. For example, Asurion provides device insurance, warranties, and support services for cell phones, consumer electronics, and home appliances.[46] Asurion's development team creates and provides employees with videos explaining the features and selling points of new products. These videos help employees learn how to deal with customers' questions and concerns about new products.

©JETTA Productions/Getty Images

Mobile technology is useful not only for entertainment but also for employees who travel and need to be in touch with the office. Smartphones, tablets, and other digital devices also give employees the ability to listen to and participate in training programs at their leisure.

Audiovisual training can easily be made available on desktop computers, smartphones, and tablet computers. These devices allow users to access the materials at any time or place. They also allow instruction to include video clips, podcasts, charts and diagrams, learning points, and lectures. This helps facilitate learning by appealing to a variety of the users' senses and by both communicating and demonstrating knowledge, skills, and behaviors.

For example, sales representatives at Coca-Cola Bottling Company Consolidated (CCBCC) are responsible for business development and customer relationships.[47] Most of their time is spent traveling to meet customer needs or visiting prospects for new business. To help sales reps better manage their workload and meet their sales quotas, CCBCC developed an online learning program. Sales reps can use an iPad to access an app that links to the program's content as well as videos on key concepts and action planning templates. The program's content covers how to get work done, how to work smart, and how to handle information overload. The app also includes editable PDF files that allow sales reps working with their managers during on-the-job coaching sessions to create and update action plans. The app is frequently used by sales reps, and its use has contributed to a 20% increase in daily sales calls.

The use of audiovisual training has a number of advantages. First, users have control over the presentation. They can review, slow down, or speed up the lesson, which permits flexibility in customizing the session depending on trainees' expertise. Second, trainees can be exposed to equipment, problems, and events that cannot be demonstrated easily in a classroom. Another advantage is that learners get a consistent presentation.

Most problems from these methods result from having too much content for the trainee to learn, overuse of humor or music, and drama that distracts from the key learning points.[48]

Hands-on Methods

Hands-on methods are training methods that require the trainee to be actively involved in learning. Hands-on methods include on-the-job training, simulations, business games and case studies, behavior modeling, interactive video, and Web-based training. These methods are ideal for developing specific skills, understanding how skills and behaviors can be transferred to the job, experiencing all aspects of completing a task, and dealing with interpersonal issues that arise on the job.

Hands-on methods Training methods that require the trainee to be actively involved in learning.

On-the-job training (OJT)
Peers or managers training new or inexperienced employees who learn the job by observation, understanding, and imitation.

On-the-Job Training. **On-the-job training (OJT)** refers to new or inexperienced employees learning through observing peers or managers performing the job and trying to imitate their behavior. OJT can be useful for training newly hired employees, upgrading experienced employees' skills when new technology is introduced, cross-training employees within a department or work unit, and orienting transferred or promoted employees to their new jobs.

OJT takes various forms, including apprenticeships and internships (discussed later in this section). OJT is an attractive training method because, compared to other methods, it needs less investment in time or money for materials, trainers' salaries, or instructional design. Managers or peers who are job knowledge experts are used as instructors. OJT must be structured to be effective. Table 7.6 shows the principles of structured OJT.

Apprenticeship
A work-study training method with both on-the-job and classroom training.

Apprenticeship is a work-study training method with both OJT and classroom training. To qualify as a registered apprenticeship program under state or federal guidelines, at least 144 hours of classroom instruction and 2,000 hours, or one year, of on-the-job experience are required.[49] Apprenticeships can be sponsored by individual companies or by groups of companies cooperating with a union. The majority of apprenticeship programs are in the skilled trades, such as plumbing, carpentry, electrical work, and bricklaying.

The hours and weeks that must be devoted to completing specific skill units are clearly defined. OJT involves assisting a certified tradesperson (a journeyman) at the work site. The on-the-job training portion of the apprenticeship follows the guidelines for effective on-the-job training.[50]

A major advantage of apprenticeship programs is that learners can earn pay while they learn. This is important because programs can last several years. Learners' wages usually increase automatically as their skills improve. Also, apprenticeships are usually effective learning experiences because they involve learning why and how a task is performed in classroom instruction provided by local trade schools, high schools, or

Table 7.6
Principles of On-the-Job Training

PREPARING FOR INSTRUCTION

1. Break down the job into important steps.
2. Prepare the necessary equipment, materials, and supplies.
3. Decide how much time you will devote to OJT and when you expect the employees to be competent in skill areas.

ACTUAL INSTRUCTION

1. Tell the trainees the objective of the task and ask them to watch you demonstrate it.
2. Show the trainees how to do it without saying anything.
3. Explain the key points or behaviors. (Write out the key points for the trainees, if possible.)
4. Show the trainees how to do it again.
5. Have the trainees do one or more single parts of the task and praise them for correct reproduction (optional).
6. Have the trainees do the entire task and praise them for correct reproduction.
7. If mistakes are made, have the trainees practice until accurate reproduction is achieved.
8. Praise the trainees for their success in learning the task.

SOURCES: Based on W. J. Rothwell and H. C. Kazanas, "Planned OJT Is Productive OJT," *Training and Development Journal*, October 1990, pp. 53–55; P. J. Decker and B. R. Nathan, *Behavior Modeling Training* (New York: Praeger Scientific, 1985).

COMPETING THROUGH SUSTAINABILITY

Partnerships Provides Skills and Jobs

Central Iowa Works (CIW) is a partnership between employers and workers, public and private funding sources, and relevant community partners. The purpose of CIW is to close the skills gap from both employers' and job seekers' perspectives. For employers, CIW helps them to recruit and hire qualified workers for jobs in central Iowa. Job seekers get trained and hired for real jobs with opportunities for career advancement. CIW works in partnership with energy and financial services companies to provide apprenticeship programs. After participating in classroom training and paid work experiences that are part of an apprenticeship program (sometimes called "earn as you learn"), employees have the skills they need for entry-level jobs. Companies benefit by finding better trained employees who are likely to be motivated and less likely to leave the company.

Electric power companies are facing a daunting workforce shortage due to the retirement of utility workers in the next several years. Utility companies are collaborating with colleges and labor unions to develop and promote online education and other types of training to ensure that the utility industry has a workforce with the necessary skills. For example, one partnership is with Bismark State College to provide apprentices with foundational skills needed to understand electrical systems, electrical components, and transformers. In the Electric Power Technology Program, apprentices take online courses developed by industry experts as part of their required technical instruction. These courses are designed specifically to support necessary on-the-job learning as part of the apprenticeship program.

Aon's mission is to empower economic and human possibility.

Aon is partnering with the City Colleges of Chicago Harold Washington College to offer apprenticeship programs in insurance, technology, or human resources. During an apprenticeship, students are regular, full-time Aon employees, working in real jobs. Aon supports the apprentices by providing a paid tuition benefit and work hours that allow them to pursue an associate degree. Students spend about 20 hours in class and 20 hours working each week for two years.

DISCUSSION QUESTION

1. How do employers, job seekers, educational institutions, and local communities benefit from apprenticeship programs?

SOURCES: Central Iowa Works, www. centraliowaworks.org, accessed March 13, 2017; L. Schroeder, "The New Face of Apprenticeships," *Chief Learning Officer,* August 2016, pp. 44–47; Aon plc, "Aon Apprenticeship Program," www. aoncampus.com, accessed March 13, 2017.

community colleges. Apprenticeships also usually result in full-time employment for trainees when the program is completed. From the company's perspective, apprenticeship programs meet specific business needs and help to attract talented employees. The "Competing through Sustainability" box shows how employers, communities, and educational institutions are partnering to develop apprenticeships.

There are several potential disadvantages of apprenticeship programs. One is that there is no guarantee that jobs will be available when the program is completed. Another disadvantage is that employers may not hire apprentices because they believe apprentices are narrowly trained in one occupation or with one company, and program graduates may have only company-specific skills and may be unable to acquire new skills or adapt their skills to changes in the workplace.

An **internship** is on-the-job learning sponsored by an educational institution or is part of an academic program. Students are placed in paid positions where they can gain experiences related to their area of study. For example, Ford, Whirlpool, and Rolls-Royce use interns in human resources and engineering positions. If interns perform well, many companies offer them full-time positions after they complete their studies.

Internship
On-the-job learning sponsored by an educational institution, or part of an academic program.

Simulation
A training method that represents a real-life situation, allowing trainees to see the outcomes of their decisions in an artificial environment.

Simulations. A **simulation** is a training method that represents a real-life situation, with trainees' decisions resulting in outcomes that mirror what would happen if they were on the job. Simulations, which allow trainees to see the impact of their decisions in an artificial, risk-free environment, are used to teach production and process skills as well as management and interpersonal skills. Simulations are used for training pilots, cable installers, and call center employees.

IBM uses a simulation to train security teams how to handle cyberattacks.[51] The staging area is similar to a flight simulator but with room for two dozen people. Video panels cover the front wall and racks of computer servers located below the floor simulate the data stream of a company's network. One simulation involves a phishing e-mail sent to an HR representative. The hackers took data before the information technology crew could determine the source of the computer breach. After news of the breach leaked to the press, U.S. government agencies started an investigation. As the simulation developed, the security team discovered that the hackers had also changed the company's financial data before its quarterly report. Security teams have to learn to deal with the pressure the breach created, identify what was stolen, take steps to notify the appropriate persons and agencies, and secure the breach.

Virtual reality
Computer-based technology that provides trainees with a three-dimensional learning experience. Trainees operate in a simulated environment that responds to their behaviors and reactions.

One way to enhance simulations is through virtual reality. **Virtual reality** is a computer-based technology that provides trainees with a three-dimensional (3D) learning experience. Using specialized equipment or viewing the virtual model on the computer screen, trainees move through the simulated environment and interact with its components.[52] Technology is used to stimulate multiple senses of the trainee.[53] Devices relay information from the environment to the senses. For example, audio interfaces, gloves that provide a sense of touch, treadmills, or motion platforms are used to create a realistic, artificial environment. Devices also communicate information about the trainee's movements to a computer. These devices allow the trainee to experience the perception of actually being in a particular environment. BNSF Railway uses virtual reality for training employees on how to conduct a brake safety inspection.[54] Employees take the role of avatars in a 3D simulation in which they perform brake inspections on rail cars. The simulation includes all of the important parts that have to be examined in a proper inspection, including air hoses, angle cocks, and hand brakes. In the simulation, BNSF includes all defects that can occur but cannot be incorporated in on-the-job training for safety reasons or because they would be difficult to demonstrate. The program improves employees' ability to both identify and correct malfunctions.

Avatars
Computer depictions of humans that can be used as imaginary coaches, co-workers, and customers in simulations.

Avatars refer to computer depictions of humans that are being used as imaginary coaches, co-workers, and customers in simulations.[55] Typically, trainees see the avatar throughout the training course. For example, PPD is a global contract research organization with staff in 47 countries that is involved in drug discovery, development, life-cycle management, and laboratory services. PPD uses a virtual 3D learning environment to deliver its clinical foundations program.[56] Learners use a virtual simulated environment and realistic avatars to talk, send messages, watch and interact with presentations and video content, take notes, and access the Internet. This simulated environment is accessible from anywhere in the world. PPD also uses virtual clinical spaces including pharmacies, nurses rooms, and surgical spaces for training. PPD found that virtual training improved the cost-effectiveness and speed of training, as well as employees' accessibility to it. Among trainees who participated in virtual programs, 80% preferred it to classroom training, and 95% believed they were more engaged than in traditional instruction.

As you can see from the examples, simulations can be effective for several reasons.[57] First, trainees can use them on their desktop, eliminating the need to travel to a central training location. Second, simulations are meaningful, get trainees involved in learning, and are emotionally engaging (they can even be fun). This helps increase employees' willingness to practice, retain, and improve their skills. Third, simulators provide a consistent message of what needs to be learned; trainees can work at their own pace; and, compared to face-to-face instruction, simulators can incorporate more situations or problems that a trainee might encounter. Fourth, simulations can safely put employees in situations that would be dangerous in the real world. Fifth, simulations have been found to result in positive outcomes such as training being completed in a shorter time compared to traditional training courses, and providing a positive return on investment. Disadvantages of simulations include their cost and need for constant updating. This is because simulators must have elements identical to those found in the work environment. The simulator needs to respond exactly as the equipment (or customer) would under the conditioned response given by the trainee.[58]

Games and Case Studies. Situations that trainees study and discuss (case studies) and games in which trainees must gather information, analyze it, and make decisions are used primarily for management skill development. There are many sources of case studies, including Harvard Business School and the Darden Business School at University of Virginia.

Games can be played face-to-face or accessed through apps or notebook computers. **Serious games** refer to games in which the training content is turned into a game but has business objectives.[59] "Gamification" means that game-based strategies are applied to e-learning programs. The chapter opener described how GameStop uses games for learning and highlighted how they can enhance learning. Games enhance learning by providing a fun way to learn, use leaderboards to increase learners' motivation by capitalizing on their competitiveness, and incorporate levels that require learners to demonstrate they are competent in prerequisite knowledge and skills (by achieving certain scores) before learning more challenging knowledge and skills.

Games stimulate learning because participants are actively involved and they mimic the competitive nature of business. The types of decisions that participants make in games include all aspects of management practice, including labor relations (such as agreement in contract negotiations), marketing (the price to charge for a new product), and finance (financing the purchase of new technology). A realistic game or case may stimulate more learning than presentation methods (such as classroom instruction) because it is more meaningful.

For example, KLA-Tencor uses case studies as part of a program known as the Situation Room to help managers learn how to deal with common leadership problems.[60] A group of between 8 and 20 managers get together face-to-face or virtually each month for one year and read one of twelve 350- to 400-word case studies. Each case is based on a real situation or problem that occurred at KLA-Tencor. The situation needs to be broad enough for most managers to have experienced the situation, issue, or problem, but specific enough to be useful. After they read the case, the managers are given three minutes to write their response to the situation. Participants share their responses and their peers provide feedback. If a peer doesn't like the response, he or she can provide an alternative. When all participants have shared their responses, four teams are formed and they are given "homework." After the first session, participants are expected to meet for an hour in their teams to review content, models, methodology, or tools that they have been exposed to in prior courses. Based on this review, they are asked to respond to the situation. During the next session, participants share their prepared responses and discuss them. Based on what they learned from the two sessions, participants are asked to prepare a personal response focusing on how they will handle this situation if they encounter

Serious games
Games in which the training content is turned into a game but has business objectives.

it on their job. The outcomes of the sessions are documented on the company's knowledge management system so that practices can be shared with other managers facing similar challenges.

CMS Energy uses an online game (the Resolver) to teach employees about conflicts of interest.[61] For example, employees understand that accepting bribes is illegal, but they might not understand all of the different types of bribes. In the game, players interact with different characters and make decisions. Each decision they make affects different people, including colleagues, friends, and family members. Those affected by each decision discuss how the player's decision affects them. Teams of five employees are formed to compete against each other. During game play, the team format facilitates conversations and questions among team members about ethics and conflicts of interest. When the competition ends, team members can see how they rank against others on an online leaderboard. This stimulates further employee conversations about how they responded to the scenarios and what they should have done differently to earn more points.

Cases may be especially appropriate for developing higher-order intellectual skills such as analysis, synthesis, and evaluation. These skills are often required by managers, physicians, and other professional employees. Cases also help trainees develop the willingness to take risks given uncertain outcomes, based on their analysis of the situation. To use cases effectively, the learning environment must let trainees prepare and discuss their case analyses. Also, face-to-face or electronic communication among trainees must be arranged. Because trainee involvement is critical for the effectiveness of the case method, learners must be willing and able to analyze the case and then communicate and defend their positions.

Behavior Modeling.　Research suggests that behavior modeling is one of the most effective techniques for teaching interpersonal skills.[62] Each training session, which typically lasts four hours, focuses on one interpersonal skill, such as coaching or communicating ideas. Each session presents the rationale behind key behaviors, a video of a model performing key behaviors, practice opportunities using role-playing, evaluation of a model's performance in the video, and a planning session devoted to understanding how the key behaviors can be used on the job. In the practice sessions, trainees get feedback regarding how closely their behavior matches the key behaviors demonstrated by the model. The role-playing and modeled performance are based on actual incidents in the employment setting in which the trainee needs to demonstrate success.

LO 7-6
Explain the potential advantages of e-learning for training.

E-learning
Instruction and delivery of training by computers through the Internet or company intranet.

E-Learning.　**E-Learning,** *computer-based training, online learning,* and *Web-based training* refer to instruction and delivery of training by computer through the Internet or the Web.[63] To enhance learning, these training methods can include and integrate the following into instruction: text; interaction using simulations and games; video; collaboration using blogs, wikis, and social networks; and hyperlinks to additional resources. In some types of computer-based training, content is provided using standalone software with no connection to the Internet. Trainees can still interact with the training content, answer questions, and choose responses regarding how they would behave in certain situations, but they cannot collaborate with other learners.

Online learning, e-learning, and Web-based training all include delivery of instruction using the Internet or Web. The training program can be accessed using a password through the public Internet or the company's private intranet. There are many potential features that can be included in online learning to help trainees learn and transfer training to their jobs. For example, online programs that use video may make it an interactive experience for trainees. That is, trainees watch the video and have the opportunity to use the keyboard or touch the screen to answer questions, respond with how they would act in certain situations, or identify the steps they would take to solve a problem. Interactive video is especially valuable for helping trainees learn technical or interpersonal skills.

For example, e-learning offered by the U.S. Office of Disease Prevention and Health Promotion uses modeling through simulated conversations and interactions with patients to train health care providers how to provide high-quality patient care.[64] They can take on different roles such as a busy nurse working as a pain management professional at her practice. Trainees can make choices about how to respond to patients' questions, get feedback on their choice, and learn from their mistakes.

Effective e-learning is grounded on a thorough needs assessment and complete learning objectives. **Repurposing** refers to directly translating an instructor-led, face-to-face training program online. Online learning that merely repurposes an ineffective training program will remain ineffective. Unfortunately, in their haste to develop online learning, many companies are repurposing bad training. The best e-learning combines the advantages of the Internet with the principles of a good learning environment. Effective online learning takes advantage of the Web's dynamic nature and ability to use many positive learning features, including linking to other training sites and content through the use of hyperlinks, and allowing the trainee to collaborate with other learners. Online learning also gives the learner control over the pace of learning, exercises, and the use of links to other material and peer and expert networks. Online learning allows activities typically led by the instructor (presentations, visuals, slides), trainees (discussion, questions), and group interaction (discussion of application of training content) to be incorporated into training without trainees or the instructor having to be physically present in a training room. Effective online learning gives trainees meaningful content, relevant examples, and the ability to apply content to work problems and issues. Also, trainees can practice and receive feedback through problems, exercises, assignments, and tests.

Massive open online courses (MOOCs) are a new type of e-learning. **Massive open online courses (MOOCs)** is learning that is designed to enroll large number of learners (massive); is free and accessible to anyone with an Internet connection (open); takes place online using videos of lectures, interactive course work including discussion groups, and wikis (online); and has specific start and completion dates, quizzes and assessment, and exams (courses).[65] MOOCs cover a wide variety of subject matter including chemistry, math, physics, computer science, philosophy, mythology, health policy, cardiac arrest and resuscitation, and even poetry. Popular providers of MOOCs include Coursera, edX (nonprofit founded by Harvard and MIT), and Udacity (a for-profit company founded by a Stanford University Research professor and founder of Google X Labs). The courses are often developed in partnership with colleges and universities and, recently, private companies. For example, Georgia Tech, Udacity, and AT&T worked together to create a MOOC designed to offer a master's degree in computer science.[66] Udacity and AT&T created MOOC courses for nanodegrees, which provide AT&T's programmers with the opportunity to take a a series of courses that prepare them for high-technology specializations such as software engineering, coding, or Web development. This helps the programmers prepare themselves with the skills need for emerging jobs. The MOOC also benefits AT&T by providing employees with the STEM skills they need to compete against companies such as Google and Amazon, or risk going out of business.

MOOCs have several advantages and disadvantages.[67] Their low cost, accessibility, and wide range of topics make them attractive to learners. They include many features that facilitate learning and transfer: Learning is interactive, learner controlled, involves social interaction, and emphasizes application. Learning happens through engaging short

Repurposing
Directly translating instructor-led training online.

Massive open online courses (MOOCs)
Online learning designed to enroll large numbers of learners who have access to the Internet and composed of interactive course-work including video lectures, discussion groups, wikis, and assessment quizzes.

Janssen Pharmaceuticals Just-in Time Technology-Driven Learning

The Janssen Pharmaceutical Companies of Johnson & Johnson develop and sell drugs to treat and cure diseases such as cancer, Alzheimer's, and HIV. Salespeople need to learn about drugs and other products before they can sell them to doctors, pharmacies, and hospitals. The faster that salespeople are trained on new drugs, the sooner that patients can gain access to them. Because they are located around the world and often on the road, salespeople don't have the time to learn in a classroom environment. To facilitate a culture of learning, Janssen relies on digital resources that enable employees to access

information on products when and where they need it. For example, before the company introduced a new diabetes drug, it had to train 2,000 salespeople in less than two months. Using a virtual classroom, Janssen was able to provide training four days after the drug received government approval.

Other sales training has been delivered using iPads and other mobile devices. This training includes video case studies and podcasts. Janssen also provides employees with a performance support tool, known as YouLearn, that allows them to acquire skills and knowledge on their own time. Janssen helps to ensure that technology-delivered

learning is in sync with the employees and the company's learning needs through in-person coaching and development planning. Managers are required to have at least five development conversations with employees each year, and each employee completes an individual development plan.

DISCUSSION QUESTIONS

1. Does Janssen's use of technology for training support a continuous learning strategy?
2. Transfer of training? Explain why or why not.

SOURCE: F. Kalman, "Janssen Pharmaceuticals: Ahead of the Curve," *Chief Learning Officer,* June 2016, pp. 32–33; Janssen Pharmaceuticals, "About Us," www.janssen.com.

lectures combined with interaction with course materials, other students, and the instructor. It emphasizes applying knowledge and skills using role-plays, cases, and projects. It is semi-synchronous, meaning learners receive the same assignments, video lectures, readings, quizzes, and discussions, but they can complete the coursework on their own time. Also, many MOOCs offer college credit or certificates of completion, which provide incentives for learning and formal acknowledgement. However, despite claims that MOOCs will revolutionize training and education, they have significant disadvantages. Those who enroll in MOOCs tend to interact with them less over time, dropping off after the first two weeks of the course; course completion rates are low (10–20%), and most students who complete the courses don't take the credential exam. MOOCs may also be inappropriate for courses where synchronous or real-time collaboration or interaction is needed.

Many companies are using tablets such as the iPad for training because of their ease of use, colorful easy-to-read display, ability to connect to the Web, access to social media, and availability of powerful apps. Apps are primarily being used to supplement training, manage the path or sequence of training, and help employees maintain training records.[68] For example, PwC provides employees with an app that enables them to access course materials, complete course prerequisites, and access materials on an as-needed basis.[69] In 2015 more than 9,000 pieces of content were accessed and more than 36,000 hours of learning were completed by employees on their mobile devices.

The "Competing through Technology" box highlights how technology is used to deliver and support training for salespeople who work in many different locations.

Blended Learning. Many companies are moving to a hybrid, or blended, learning approach because of the limitations of e-learning related to technology (e.g., insufficient bandwidth, lack of high-speed Web connections), trainee preferences for face-to-face contact with instructors and other learners, and employees' inability to find unscheduled time during their workday to devote to learning from their desktops. **Blended learning** refers to combining technology methods, such as e-learning, simulations, or social media, with face-to-face instruction, for delivery of learning content and instruction. ADP's training program for new hires includes one week of in-person workshops, eight simulations, and collaborative, self-paced online learning.[70] This allows for the new hires to spend more time on hands-on training (which includes online virtual instructor-led classes focused on product training), working with their mentor, and networking with their peers.

Learning Management Systems. A **learning management system (LMS)** refers to a technology platform that can be used to automate the administration, development, and delivery of all of a company's training programs. An LMS can provide employees, managers, and trainers with the ability to manage, deliver, and track learning activities.[71] LMSs are becoming more popular for several reasons. An LMS can help companies reduce travel and other costs related to training, reduce time for program completion, increase employees' accessibility to training across the business, and provide administrative capabilities to track program completion and course enrollments. An LMS allows companies to track all of the learning activity in the business. For example, Keller Williams Realty's KWConnect is a central place for all of the company's training programs and materials.[72] It also includes user-generated content from its agents and leaders, who can upload videos, audio files, and links; a question-and-answer forum where agents can ask questions and provide answers; and a searchable calendar that employees can use to find and register for instructor-led training classes.

Group- or Team-Building Methods

Group- or team-building methods are training methods designed to improve team or group effectiveness. Training is directed at improving the trainees' skills as well as team effectiveness. In group-building methods, trainees share ideas and experiences, build group identity, understand the dynamics of interpersonal relationships, and get to know their own strengths and weaknesses and those of their co-workers. Group techniques focus on helping teams increase their skills for effective teamwork. All involve examination of feelings, perceptions, and beliefs about the functioning of the team; discussion; and development of plans to apply what was learned in training to the team's performance in the work setting. Group-building methods fall into three categories: experiential programs, team training, and action learning.

Experiential Programs. **Experiential programs** involve gaining conceptual knowledge and theory; taking part in a behavioral simulation or activity; analyzing the activity; and connecting the theory and activity with on-the-job or real-life situations.[73]

For experiential training programs to be successful, several guidelines should be followed. The program needs to tie in to a specific business problem. The trainees need to be moved outside their personal comfort zones but within limits so as not to reduce trainee motivation or ability to understand the purpose of the program. Multiple learning modes should be used, including audio, visual, and kinesthetic. When preparing activities for an experiential training program, trainers should ask trainees for input on the program goals. Clear expectations about the purpose, expected outcomes, and trainees'

Blended learning
Delivering content and instruction with a combination of technology-based and face-to-face methods.

Learning management system (LMS)
Technology platform that automates the administration, development, and delivery of a company's training program.

Group- or team-building methods
Training methods that help trainees share ideas and experiences, build group identity, understand the dynamics of interpersonal relationships, and get to know their own strengths and weaknesses and those of their co-workers.

Experiential programs
Training programs in which trainees gain knowledge and theory, participate in behavioral simulations, analyze the activity, and connect the theory and activity with on-the-job situations

role in the program are important. Finally, training programs that include experiential learning should be linked to changes in employee attitudes, behaviors, and other business results.

DaVita HealthCare Partners provides kidney-related health care services such as dialysis.[74] DaVita contracted with a training provider to develop a three-hour experiential learning activity that would be collaborative; have a sense of purpose; and reinforce the company's values of teamwork, fulfillment, and fun. The goals of the program were to understand the importance of their work, understand how team members relate to patients and to each other, and how to address challenges. The activity started with a discussion of the importance of communicating and collaborating for successful teamwork on the job. Employees were divided into three member teams and given the task of building prosthetic hands that would be donated to organizations serving amputees. Building the prostheses provided an opportunity for the achievement of the program's goals. The employees built more than 14,000 prostheses during the three-hour activity. The activity concluded with a discussion of ways to apply what they learned to their jobs at DaVita.

Adventure learning
Learning focused on the development of teamwork and leadership skills by using structured outdoor activities.

Adventure learning, a type of experiential program, develops teamwork and leadership skills using structured outdoor activities.[75] Adventure learning appears to be best suited for developing skills related to group effectiveness, such as self-awareness, problem solving, conflict management, and risk taking. Adventure learning may involve strenuous, challenging physical activities such as dogsledding or mountain climbing. It can also use structured individual and group outdoor activities such as climbing walls, going through rope courses, making trust falls, climbing ladders, and traveling from one tower to another using a device attached to a wire that connects the two towers.

For example, 20 coders, marketing executives, and product team members from RealScout left their office and spent a day in the California mountains learning survival skills such as constructing shelters, purifying water, and starting a fire without matches.[76] The program cost $2,000, in addition to the $7,000–$10,000 lost by shutting down the business for the day. RealScout executives believed the benefits of the adventure would outweigh its costs. They believed it helps develop stronger teams, allows employees to better know each other even if they don't work together on a daily basis, and gives employees a fun experience that will aid in retention.

Adventure learning can also include demanding activities that require coordination and place less of a physical strain on team members. For example, Cookin' Up Change is one of many team-building courses offered around the United States by chefs, caterers, hotels, and cooking schools.[77] These courses have been used by companies such as Honda and Microsoft. The underlying idea is that cooking classes help strengthen communication and networking skills by requiring team members to work together to create a multiple-course meal. Each team has to decide who does what kitchen tasks (e.g., cooking, cutting, cleaning) and who prepares the main course, salads, or dessert. Often team members are required to switch assignments in the middle of preparation to see how the team reacts to change.

For adventure learning programs to succeed, the exercises should be related to the types of skills that participants are expected to develop. Also, after the exercises, a skilled facilitator should lead a discussion about what happened in the exercise, what was learned, how the exercise relates to the job situation, and how to set goals and apply what was learned on the job.[78]

Does adventure learning work? Participants often report that they gained a greater understanding of themselves and the ways they interact with their co-workers. One key to the success of an adventure learning program may be the insistence that whole work groups participate together so that group dynamics that inhibit effectiveness can emerge and be discussed.

The physically demanding nature of adventure learning and the requirement that trainees often have to touch each other in the exercises may increase the company's risk for negligence claims due to personal injury, intentional infliction of emotional distress, and invasion of privacy. Also, the Americans with Disabilities Act (discussed in Chapter 3) raises questions about requiring employees with disabilities to participate in physically demanding training experiences.

Team Training. Team training coordinates the performance of individuals who work together to achieve a common goal. Such training is an important issue when information must be shared and individuals affect the overall performance of the group. For example, in the military as well as the private sector (think of nuclear power plants or commercial airlines), much work is performed by crews, groups, or teams. Success depends on team performance, coordination of individual activities to make decisions, and readiness to deal with potentially dangerous situations (like an overheating nuclear reactor).

Team training strategies include cross-training and coordination training.[79] In **cross-training**, team members understand and practice each other's skills so that members are prepared to step in and take another member's place. **Coordination training** trains the team in how to share information and decisions to maximize team performance. Coordination training is especially important for commercial aviation and surgical teams, who monitor different aspects of equipment and the environment but must share information to make the most effective decisions regarding patient care or aircraft safety and performance. **Team leader training** refers to training of the team manager or facilitator. This may involve training the manager on how to resolve conflict within the team or how to help the team coordinate activities or other team skills.

For example, United Airlines had its supervisors "lead" ramp employees in attending Pit Instruction & Training (Pit Crew U), which focuses on the preparation, practice, and teamwork of NASCAR pit crews. United used the training to develop standardized methods to safely and efficiently unload, load, and send off its airplanes.[80] Pit Instruction & Training, located outside of Charlotte, North Carolina, has a quarter-mile race track and a pit road with places for six cars. The school offers programs to train new racing pit crews, but most of its business comes from companies interested in having their teams work as safely, efficiently, and effectively as NASCAR pit crews. The training was part of a multimillion-dollar investment that includes updating equipment and providing luggage scanners. The purpose of the training is to reinforce the need for ramp teams to be orderly and communicate, to help standardize tasks of ramp team members, to help shorten the time an airplane is serviced at the gate, and to improve morale.

The keys for safety, speed, and efficiency for NASCAR pit crews is that each member knows what tasks to do (change tires, use an air gun, add gasoline, clean up spills) and, when the crew has finished servicing the race car, moves new equipment into position anticipating the next pit stop. The training involved the ramp workers actually working as pit crews. They learn how to handle jacks, change tires, and fill fuel tanks on race cars. They are video-recorded and timed just like real pit crews. They receive feedback from professional pit crew members who work on NASCAR teams and trainers. Also, the training requires them to deal with circumstances they might encounter on the job. For one pit stop, lug nuts had been sprinkled intentionally in the area where the car stops to see if the United employees would notice them and clean them up. On their jobs, ramp employees are responsible for removing debris from the tarmac so that it doesn't get sucked into jet engines or harm equipment. For another pit stop, teams had to work with fewer members, as sometimes occurs when ramp crews are understaffed due to absences.

Cross-training
Training in which team members understand and practice each other's skills so that members are prepared to step in and take another member's place should he or she temporarily or permanently leave the team.

Coordination training
Training a team in how to share information and decision-making responsibilities to maximize team performance.

Team leader training
Training of the team manager or facilitator.

Action learning
Training in which teams work on an actual business problem, commit to an action plan, and are accountable for carrying out the plan.

Action Learning. In **action learning**, teams or work groups get an actual business problem, work on solving it and commit to an action plan, and are accountable for carrying out the plan.[81] Typically, action learning involves between 6 and 30 employees; it may also include customers and vendors. There are several variations on the composition of the group. In one variation, the group includes a single customer for the problem being dealt with. Sometimes the groups include cross-functional team members (members from different company departments) who all have a stake in the problem. Or the group may involve employees from multiple functions who all focus on their own functional problems, each contributing to helping solve the problems identified. Action learning is often part of quality improvement processes such as Six Sigma training and Kaizen. *Kaizen*, the Japanese word for improvement, is one of the underlying principles of lean manufacturing and total quality management (lean thinking is discussed in Chapter 1).

Consider how University Health System and PepsiCo used action learning to solve important and complex business problems.[82] At University Health System, nine cross-functional teams of managers who otherwise would not work together worked on separate business problems. These problems included how to increase patient satisfaction, reduce billing errors, and enhance inventory control. Each team was asked to present its solution to what was called the Shark Tank—three senior executives and the CEO for pediatric services, who served as "sharks." As each team presented their ideas, the sharks provided coaching and feedback. The problem solutions helped University Health System save millions of dollars and improved patient satisfaction. PepsiCo employed action learning when it wanted to train managers to take a global perspective on the company's strategy. Leslie Teichgraeber, who led the training programs, observed that most managers were familiar only with their local or national markets. So she assembled teams of managers from various locations and assigned each team to solve problems related to business needs that had been identified by the heads of their units. At the end of nine months, they presented their ideas to PepsiCo executives.

LO 7-7
Design a training session to maximize learning.

ADVICE FOR SELECTING A TRAINING METHOD

Given the large number of available training methods, the task of choosing one may seem difficult. One way to choose a training method is to compare methods. The first step in choosing a method is to identify the type of learning outcome the training is to influence. These outcomes include verbal information, intellectual skills, cognitive strategies, attitudes, motor skills, or some combination. Training methods may influence one or several learning outcomes.

There is considerable overlap between learning outcomes across the training methods. Group-building methods are unique because they focus on individual as well as team learning (e.g., improving group processes). One of the group-building methods (e.g., experiential learning, team training, action learning) would be appropriate if the goal is to improve the effectiveness of groups or teams. Second, comparing the presentation methods to the hands-on methods illustrates that most hands-on methods provide a better learning environment and transfer of training than do the presentation methods.

E-learning or blended learning can be an effective training method for geographically dispersed trainees. E-learning and other technology-driven training methods have higher development costs, but travel and housing cost savings will likely offset development costs over time. A blended learning approach can take advantage of the positive features of both face-to-face and technology-based instruction. For example, Nationwide Mutual Insurance uses several different methods to train new agents.[83] An interactive game is used to help agents understand the life cycle of an insurance policy. It includes an animated simulation using different customer profiles. New agents watch and listen to experienced agents interacting and communicating with customers both face-to-face and over the phone. They also engage in self-directed learning, including calling competitors to get an insurance quote and evaluating their experience.

A final but important consideration is the training budget. If the budget for developing new training methods is limited, then structured on-the-job training is a good choice. It is a relatively inexpensive yet effective hands-on method. Hands-on methods that facilitate transfer of training, such as simulators, are feasible with a larger budget.

Evaluating Training Programs

Training evaluation can provide useful information, including the program's strengths and weaknesses, identifying which learners benefited most and least from participating, determining the program's financial benefits and costs, and allowing the comparison of the benefits and costs of different programs.

Examining the outcomes of a program helps in evaluating its effectiveness. These outcomes should be related to the program objectives, which help trainees understand the purpose of the program. **Training outcomes** can be categorized as cognitive outcomes, skill-based outcomes, affective outcomes, results, and return on investment.[84] Table 7.7 shows the types of outcomes used in evaluating training programs and what is measured and how it is measured.

The Maryland Transit Administration (MTA) uses several outcomes to evaluate the effectiveness of new bus operator training.[85] At the completion of training, new bus operators complete surveys asking about their satisfaction with the instructor, course

LO 7-8
Choose appropriate evaluation design and training outcomes based on the training objectives and evaluation purpose.

Training outcomes
A way to evaluate the effectiveness of a training program based on cognitive, skill-based, affective, and results outcomes.

OUTCOME	WHAT IS MEASURED	HOW MEASURED	EXAMPLE
Cognitive outcomes	• Acquisition of knowledge	• Pencil-and-paper tests • Work sample	• Safety rules • Electrical principles • Steps in appraisal interview
Skill-based outcomes	• Behavior • Skills	• Observation • Work sample • Ratings	• Jigsaw use • Listening skills • Coaching skills • Airplane landings
Affective outcomes	• Motivation • Reaction to program • Attitudes	• Interviews • Focus groups • Attitude surveys	• Satisfaction with training • Beliefs regarding other cultures
Results	• Company payoff	• Observation • Data from information system or performance records	• Absenteeism • Accidents • Patents
Return on investment	• Economic value of training	• Identification and comparison of costs and benefits of the program	• Dollars

Table 7.7
Outcomes Used in Evaluating Training Programs

content, and training environment (affective outcome). Written exams are used to assess new bus operators' knowledge of how to operate the vehicle (cognitive outcomes). Training instructors ride along with new bus operators during their 90-day probationary period following completion of training. Using a checklist, they observe the extent to which the new bus operators engage in 60 safe behaviors, including keeping both hands on the steering wheel and looking both directions when they approach the intersection between two streets (skill-based outcome). Finally, bus driver accident data collected in MTA's learning management system are used as a results outcome. The accident data helped establish the return on investment of the training. The total accident claims paid out in 2015 were $560,000, far less than the $3 million paid out in 2012.

Which training outcomes measure is best? The answer depends on the training objectives. For example, if the instructional objectives identified business-related outcomes such as increased customer service or product quality, then results outcomes should be included in the evaluation. Both reaction and cognitive outcomes are usually collected before the trainees leave the training site. As a result, these measures do not help determine the extent to which trainees actually use the training content in their jobs (transfer of training). Skill-based, affective, and results outcomes measured following training can be used to determine transfer of training—that is, the extent to which training has changed behavior, skills, or attitudes or directly influenced objective measures related to company effectiveness (such as sales).

Evaluation Designs

As shown in Table 7.8, a number of different evaluation designs can be applied to training programs. Table 7.8 compares each evaluation design on the basis of who is involved (trainees and/or a comparison group that does not receive training), when outcome measures are collected (pretraining, posttraining), the costs, the time needed to conduct the evaluation, and the strength of the design for ruling out alternative explanations for the results (e.g., are improvements due to factors other than the training?). In general, designs that use pretraining and posttraining measures of outcomes and include a comparison group reduce the risk that factors other than training itself are responsible for the evaluation results. This builds confidence to use the results to make decisions. The trade-off is that evaluations using these designs are more costly and time consuming to conduct than evaluations not using pretraining or posttraining measures or comparison groups.

Table 7.8
Comparison of Evaluation Designs

DESIGN	GROUPS	MEASURES PRETRAINING	POSTTRAINING	COST	TIME	STRENGTH
Posttest only	Trainees	No	Yes	Low	Low	Low
Pretest/posttest	Trainees	Yes	Yes	Low	Low	Medium
Posttest only with comparison group	Trainees and comparison	No	Yes	Medium	Medium	Medium
Pretest/posttest with comparison group	Trainees and comparison	Yes	Yes	Medium	Medium	High
Time series	Trainees	Yes	Yes, several	Medium	Medium	Medium

For example, if a manager is interested in comparing the effectiveness of two programs—that is, determining how much outcomes (knowledge, affect, skills, behavior, results) have changed as a result of one program compared to another—then a pretest/posttest design is necessary. Consider how Mountain America Credit Union evaluated the effectiveness of a revised sales training program.[86] Mountain America tracked the average monthly sales of 30 new employees during their first two months of employment. Ten of the 30 employees attended training before it was revised (they called this the Traditional Group). Twenty employees attended the program after it was revised (the Express Group). The revised program included more interactions with a variety of customers with different needs. Monthly sales were compared between the Express Group and the Traditional Group. The average number of sales in the Express Group exceeded the average number of sales in the Traditional Group in both the first (11.4 versus 3.5 average) and second months (34.83 versus 5.5) of employment.

Many companies are interested in determining the financial benefits of learning, including training courses and programs, and development activities (see Chapter 9). One way to do this is by determining return on investment (ROI). **Return on investment (ROI)** refers to the estimated dollar return from each dollar invested in learning. Keep in mind that ROI is not a substitute for outcomes that also provide an indication of the success or usefulness of learning, such as trainees' reactions, knowledge acquisition, or behavior change. Also, ROI is best suited for outcomes that can be quantified, such as quality, accidents, or turnover. Otherwise, you will have to make an educated guess about the value of the outcome. For example, how do you value increased leadership skills?

Return on investment
Refers to the estimated dollar return from each dollar invested in learning.

Determining the Financial Benefits of Learning

To make an ROI analysis, follow these steps:[87]

1. Identify outcomes (e.g., quality, accidents).
2. Place a value on the outcomes.

EVIDENCE-BASED HR

Each of Pfizer's 2,500 medical sales representatives in India uses an iPad for communicating with the customer and reporting sales. Pfizer developed and launched Roket, a mobile learning app, to increase the sales competencies of the medical representatives. Roket's key features include access to videos and reading materials; quizzes on training content as well as a leaderboard, which allows the sales reps to compete against each other to see who gets the highest quiz score; video sharing; and built-in coaching forms that sales reps' managers used to provide an application-of-training score at the end of a joint sales trip with a sales rep. Pfizer found that utilization of the app was good: 66% of the sales reps use the app each week, and 42% use it more than three times each week. Sales proficiency scores were based on weighting quiz scores by 40% and application score by 60%. Using a time series design in which outcome measures are collected at several different points in time following training, Pfizer found that sales reps' proficiency scores increased 24% over a 16-week period. Also, the number of coaching sessions managers held with sales reps that focused on how they could improve their application scores increased 29%.

SOURCE: Based on S. Ramachandran, "From Idle Time to Time to Learn," *TD*, December 2015, pp. 22–25.

3. Determine the change in performance after eliminating other potential influences on training results.
4. Obtain an annual amount of benefits (operational results) from training by comparing results after training to results before training (in dollars).
5. Determine the training costs (direct costs + indirect costs + development costs + overhead costs + compensation for trainees).
6. Calculate the total savings by subtracting the training costs from benefits (operational results).
7. Calculate the ROI by dividing benefits (operational results) by costs. The ROI gives an estimate of the dollar return expected from each dollar invested in training.

ROI can be measured and communicated based on a percentage or a ratio. For example, assume that a new safety training program results in a decline of 5% in a company's accident rate. This provides a total annual savings (the benefit) of $150,000 in terms of lost workdays, material and equipment damage, and workers' compensation costs. The training program costs $50,000 to implement (including both direct and indirect costs). To calculate the ROI, you need to subtract the training costs from the benefits, divide by the costs, and multiply by 100. That is, ROI = [(150,000 – 50,000) ÷ 50,000] × 100% = 200%. The ROI for this program is 200%. Another way to think about ROI is to consider it as a ratio based on the return for every dollar spent. In this example, the company gained a net benefit of $2 for every dollar spent. This means the ROI is 2:1. Tata Consultancy Service, a global information technology services company headquartered in India, measures ROI for its technology training programs.[88] To calculate the ROI, revenues earned as a result of training are calculated based on the billing rates of participants who attend the training and use the new skills. Then, training costs are subtracted from the revenues. ROI for the technical programs is 483%.

LO 7-9
Design a cross-cultural preparation program.

Special Training Issues

To meet the competitive challenges of sustainability, globalization, and technology discussed in Chapter 1, companies must successfully deal with several special training issues. The special training issues include preparing employees to work in different cultures abroad, managing workforce diversity, and orienting and socializing new employees.

CROSS-CULTURAL PREPARATION

Expatriate
Employee sent by his or her company to manage operations in a different country.

As we mentioned in Chapter 1, companies today are challenged to expand globally. Because of the increase in global operations, employees often work outside their country of origin or work with employees from other countries. An **expatriate** works in a country other than his or her country of origin. The most frequently selected locations for expatriate assignments include the United States, China, Africa, and India.[89] At Ernst & Young, about 2,600 of over 167,000 employees are on an international assignment at any one time, including 270 Americans in 30 countries (e.g., Brazil, China, India, Russia, and South Africa).[90] Many U.S. companies are using expatriate assignments as a training tool. For example, employees who want top management positions, such as chief financial officer, need to understand how cultural norms and the political environment influence the movements in currencies and commodities in order to build effective global financial plans.[91]

We discuss international human resource management in detail in Chapter 15. Here the focus is on understanding how to prepare employees for expatriate assignments. **Cross-cultural preparation** educates employees (expatriates) and their families who are to be sent to a foreign country. To successfully conduct business in the global marketplace, employees must understand the business practices and the cultural norms of different countries.

Steps in Cross-Cultural Preparation

To succeed overseas, expatriates (employees on foreign assignments) need to be

1. Competent in their areas of expertise
2. Able to communicate verbally and nonverbally in the host country
3. Flexible, tolerant of ambiguity, and sensitive to cultural differences
4. Motivated to succeed; able to enjoy the challenge of working in other countries; and willing to learn about the host country's culture, language, and customs
5. Supported by their families[92]

One reason U.S. expatriates often fail is that companies place more emphasis on developing employees' technical skills than on preparing them to work in other cultures. This has resulted in failed overseas assignments, which means companies don't fully capitalize on business opportunities and incur costs for replacing employees who leave the company after returning to the United States.[93] Research suggests that the comfort of an expatriate's spouse and family is the most important determinant of whether the employee will complete the assignment.[94] Studies have also found that personality characteristics are related to expatriates' desire to terminate the assignment and performance in the assignment.[95] Expatriates who were extroverted (outgoing), agreeable (cooperative and tolerant), and conscientious (dependable, achievement oriented) were more likely to want to stay on the assignment and perform well. This suggests that cross-cultural training may be effective only when expatriates' personalities predispose them to be successful in assignments in other cultures. The key to a successful foreign assignment is a combination of training and career management for the employee and family.

Predeparture Phase

Before departure, employees need to receive language training and an orientation to the new country's culture and customs. It is critical that the family be included in orientation programs.[96] Expatriates and their families need information about housing, schools, recreation, shopping, and health care facilities in the areas where they will live. Expatriates also must discuss with their managers how the foreign assignment fits into their career plans and what types of positions they can expect upon return.

Cross-cultural training methods include presentational techniques, such as lectures that expatriates and their families attend on the customs and culture of the host country, immersion experiences, or actual experiences in the home country in culturally diverse communities.[97] Sodexo provides instructor-led courses for its global leaders on how to build a globally competent workforce and how to develop trust, collaborate, and communicate effectively across cultures.[98] Sodexo also provides research summaries, TED talks, and articles on topics such as managing global virtual teams and communication across culture that company leaders can access from the company's intranet. Experiential exercises allow expatriates to spend time with a family from the ethnic group of the host country while still in the United States. At Advanced Micro Devices an Indian trainer took 20 managers on a two-week immersion trip, during which the group traveled to

New Delhi, Bangalore, and Mumbai, meeting with business persons and government officials.[99] The program required six months of planning, including providing the executives with information on foods to eat, potential security issues, and how to interact in business meetings. For example, Indians prefer a relatively indirect way into business discussions, so the managers were advised to discuss current events and other subjects before talking business.

Research suggests that the degree of difference between the United States and the host country (cultural novelty), the amount of interaction with host country citizens and host nationals (interaction), and the familiarity with new job tasks and work environment (job novelty) all influence the "rigor" of the cross-cultural training method used.[100] Hands-on and group-building methods are most effective (and most needed) in assignments with a high level of cultural and job novelty that require a good deal of interpersonal interaction with host nationals.

On-Site Phase

On-site training involves continued orientation to the host country and its customs and cultures through formal programs or through a mentoring relationship. Expatriates should be encouraged to develop social relationships both inside and outside of the workplace.[101] Expatriates and their families may be paired with an employee from the host country who helps them understand the new, unfamiliar work environment and community.[102] Companies are also using the Web to help employees on expatriate assignments get answers to questions.[103] Expatriates can use a website to get answers to questions such as, How do I conduct a meeting here? or What religious philosophy might have influenced today's negotiation behavior? Knowledge management software allows employees to contribute, organize, and access knowledge specific to their expatriate assignment.

A major reason employees refuse expatriate assignments is that they can't afford to lose their spouse's income or are concerned that their spouse's career could be derailed by being out of the workforce for a few years.[104] Some "trailing" spouses decide to use the time to pursue educational activities that could contribute to their long-term career goals. But it is difficult to find these opportunities in an unfamiliar place. GlaxoSmithKline's International Service Center, which handles all of its relocations from or to the United States, offers a buddy system for spouses to connect with others who have lived in the area for the past several years.[105] General Motors offers career continuation services, which reimburse spouses $2,500 each year during the expatriate assignment for maintaining professional licenses or certifications. The World Bank manages a dedicated Internet site for expatriates where spouses can post résumés and ask for job leads.

Repatriation Phase

Repatriation
The preparation of expatriates for return to the parent company and country from a foreign assignment.

Repatriation prepares expatriates for return to the parent company and country from the foreign assignment. Expatriates and their families are likely to experience high levels of stress and anxiety when they return because of the changes that have occurred since their departure. Employees should be encouraged to self-manage the repatriation process.[106] Before they go on the assignment they need to consider what skills they want to develop and the types of jobs that might be available in the company for an employee with those skills. Because the company changes and colleagues, peers, and managers may leave while the expatriate is on assignment, they need to maintain contact with key company and industry contacts. Otherwise, on return the employees' reentry shock will be heightened when they have to deal with new colleagues, a new job, and a company culture that may have changed. This includes providing expatriates with company newsletters and community newspapers and ensuring that they receive personal and work-related mail from the United States while they are on foreign assignment. Employees and their families sometimes have to readjust to a lower standard of living in the United States than they had in the foreign country, where they may have enjoyed maid service, a limousine, private schools, and clubs. Salary and other compensation arrangements should be worked out well before employees return from overseas assignments.

Aside from reentry shock, many expatriates decide to leave the company because the assignments they are given upon returning to the United States have less responsibility, challenge, and status than their foreign assignments.[107] For example, consider how Deloitte prepares employees for repatriation.[108] At Deloitte, approximately 100 employees return to the United State from a foreign assignment each year. To make the repatriation process easier for employees and their families, Deloitte provides checklists and videos that discuss responsibilities at each stage of the process. These resources are available on Deloitte's intranet and are accessible worldwide using a smartphone or computer. Expats have designated mentors as well as global mobility advisers who can offer advice by phone or videoconference. Deloitte addresses potential concerns that expats may have about their skills and experience being underutilized in their job when they return home by having managers and employees discuss their expectations before and during their overseas assignment. These conversations include discussions about possible career paths.

MANAGING WORKFORCE DIVERSITY AND INCLUSION

Diversity can be considered to be any dimension that differentiates one person from another.[109] For example, at Verizon, diversity means embracing differences and variety including age, ethnicity, education, sexual orientation, work style, race, gender, and more. **Inclusion** refers to creating an environment in which employees share a sense of belonging, mutual respect, and commitment from others so that they can perform their best work.[110] Inclusion allows companies to capitalize not only on the diversity of their employees but also on their customers, suppliers, and community partners.

Diversity training refers to learning efforts designed to change employee attitudes about diversity or to develop skills needed to work with a diverse workforce. However, training alone is insufficient to capitalize on the strengths of a diverse workforce.[111] **Managing diversity and inclusion** involves creating an environment that allows all employees to contribute to organizational goals and experience personal growth. This environment includes access to jobs as well as fair and positive treatment of all employees. The company must develop employees who are comfortable working with people from a wide variety of ethnic, racial, and religious backgrounds. Managing diversity may require changing the company culture. It includes the company's standards and norms about how employees are treated, competitiveness, results orientation, innovation, and risk taking. The value placed on diversity is grounded in the company culture.

For example, companies in high-tech industries are struggling with how to increase the diversity of their workforces.[112] Google recognized that its high-tech workforce lacked diversity. Its workforce was 83% male, and in terms of race or ethnicity, only 2% were Latino and 1% African American. To increase the diversity of its workforce, Google is spending more time recruiting at historically black colleges and universities, among other efforts. To increase the number of women in technology firms, Facebook and Pinterest are experimenting with requiring that at least one woman or underrepresented minority be interviewed for available positions. Cisco is increasing the diversity of its

LO 7-10
Develop a program for effectively managing diversity.

Inclusion
Creating an environment in which employees share a sense of belonging, mutual respect, and commitment with others so that they can perform their best work.

Diversity training
Refers to learning efforts that are designed to change employees' attitudes about diversity and/or develop skills needed to work with a diverse workforce.

Managing diversity and inclusion
The process of creating an environment that allows all employees to contribute to organizational goals and experience personal growth.

hiring teams by ensuring that at least one interviewer that job candidates meet is of the same ethnicity or gender as the candidate. Cisco has found that this practice has significantly increased the chances that candidates from underrepresented groups will be hired for the position.

Diversity may enhance performance when organizations have an environment that promotes learning from diversity. Research shows that diversity training can impact cognitive (acquiring knowledge), affective (attitudes), and behavioral outcomes.[113] Diversity training is most effective when it is part of a larger effort to manage diversity and inclusion rather than a standalone program. This means that a company will see the success of its diversity efforts only if it makes a long-term commitment to managing diversity. Successful diversity requires that it be viewed as an opportunity for employees to (1) learn from each other how to better accomplish their work, (2) be provided with a supportive and cooperative organizational culture, and (3) be taught leadership and process skills that can facilitate effective team functioning. Diversity is a reality in labor and customer markets and is a social expectation and value. Managers should focus on building an organizational environment, on human resource practices, and on managerial and team skills that capitalize on diversity. As you will see in the discussion that follows, managing diversity requires difficult cultural change, not just slogans on the wall.

Consider Sodexo's diversity effort.[114] Sodexo is the leading food and facilities management company in the United States, Canada, and Mexico, daily serving 10 million customers. Employees in 80 countries representing 128 nationalities connect with customers on a daily basis. A policy of inclusion is not an option or a choice—it is a business necessity. Sodexo is focused on gender representation, generational opportunities in the workplace, people with disabilities, and ethnic minority representation. As a result, diversity and inclusion are core elements of the business strategy. Sodexo believes that diversity and inclusion is a fundamental business objective focused on employees (e.g., work culture, recruitment, talent development, work–life effectiveness), customers, clients, and shareholders (e.g., supplier diversity, cross-market diversity council, diversity consulting), and communities (e.g., Sodexo Foundation, Community Partners). For example, some of the company's objectives include understanding and living the business case for diversity and inclusion; increasing awareness of how diversity relates to business challenges; creating and fostering a diverse work environment by developing management practices that drive hiring, promotion, and retention of talent; engaging in relationship management and customer service to attract and retain diverse clients and customers; and partnering with women and minority businesses to deliver food and facility management services. Diversity and inclusion are core competencies at Sodexo. Diversity and inclusion are part of employees' training and managers' annual performance review. The new employee orientation emphasizes Sodexo's values and expectations regarding diversity and inclusion.

Sodexo separates equal employment opportunity (EEO) and legal compliance training from diversity training. At Sodexo, diversity training is part of the managing diversity strategy. Every three years, employees are required to take EEO and affirmative action refresher courses. Top management is also involved in and committed to managing diversity. The senior executives program includes ongoing classroom training that is reinforced with community involvement, sponsoring employee groups, and mentoring diverse employees. Executives are engaged in learning the business case for diversity and are personally held accountable for the company's diversity agenda. The one-day Spirit of Inclusion session, mandatory for all managers, focuses on building awareness and skills around diversity and inclusion. Sodexo's diversity training involves learning labs focused on skill building and diversity awareness. Examples of these learning labs include Generations in the Workplace, Disability Awareness Training, Cross-Cultural Communications, and Improving Team Effectiveness through Inclusion. The company's learning and development team develops customized learning solutions for different functions and work teams. For example, a course related to selling to a diverse client base was developed and offered to the sales force, and a cross-cultural communication program was provided for recruiters.

In addition to diversity training activities, Sodexo has six employee network groups—such as the African American Leadership Forum; People Respecting Individuality, Diversity, and Equality (PRIDE); Honoring Our Nation's Finest with Opportunity and Respect (HONOR); and the Intergenerational Network Group (i-Gen). These network groups provide forums for employees to build a sense of community, learn from each other, develop their careers, and share input and ideas to support the company's diversity efforts. Sodexo's Champions of Diversity program rewards and recognizes employees who advance diversity and inclusion.

To emphasize the importance of diversity for the company, at Sodexo each manager has a diversity scorecard that evaluates his or her success in recruitment, retention, promotion, and development of all employees. The scorecard includes both quantitative goals as well as evaluation of behaviors such as participating in training, mentoring, and doing community outreach. A proportion of a manager's pay bonus is determined by success in these areas.

Sodexo has found that its diversity training and efforts to manage diversity are positively affecting the business in several different ways. Its mentoring program has led to increased productivity, engagement, and retention of women and people of color. There was an estimated return on investment of $19 for every dollar spent on the program. Sodexo has found that gender-balanced teams—those with 40–60% women in management—outperform nonbalanced teams on measures of global engagement, brand awareness, client retention, and positive profit and growth. Sodexo also has been awarded several new business contracts and retained clients because of its involvement in managing diversity. Sodexo has been recognized for its diversity and inclusion efforts, which helps attract talented employees by signaling that the company cares about the well-being of all of its employees. For example, Sodexo continues to receive recognition for its efforts, earning a top ranking on the DiversityInc 2016 Top 50 Companies for Diversity, marking its eighth consecutive year being recognized as a top 10 company. Sodexo is also recognized as a top company for executive women and ranked among the top 10 companies for Latinos, blacks, global diversity, and people with disabilities. Most effective programs to manage diversity, such as Sodexo's, include the key components shown in Table 7.9.

As should be apparent from this discussion, successful diversity programs involve more than just an effective training program. They require an ongoing process of culture change that includes top management support, a position in charge of managing diversity (chief diversity officer), as well as diversity policies and practices in the areas of recruitment and hiring, training and development, and administrative structures, such as conducting diversity surveys and evaluating managers' progress on diversity goals.[115] They also focus on enhancing diversity and inclusion with suppliers, vendors, and in the communities where the company conducts business. For example, ABB North America recently created a chief diversity and inclusion officer position reporting directly to the CEO.[116] This sends a message that diversity is supported and creates a position responsible for managing diversity and inclusion and establishing metrics to track progress.

Table 7.9
Key Components
of Effective Diversity
Management
Programs

Top Management Support
- Make the business case for diversity.
- Include diversity as part of the business strategy and corporate goals.
- Participate in diversity programs, and encourage all managers to attend.
- Ensure that the composition of the executive management team mirrors the diversity of the workforce.

Recruitment and Hiring
- Ask search firms to identify wider arrays of candidates.
- Enhance the interviewing, selection, and hiring skills of managers.
- Expand college recruitment at historically minority colleges.

Talent Identification and Development
- Form a partnership with internship programs that target minority students for management careers.
- Establish a mentoring process.
- Refine the company's global succession planning system to improve identification of talent.
- Improve the selection and development of managers and leaders to help ensure that they are capable of maximizing team performance.
- Ensure that all employees, especially women and minorities, have access to management development and leadership programs.

Employee Support
- Form resource groups or employee network groups, including employees with common interests, and use them to help the company develop business goals and understand the issues they are concerned with (e.g., Asian Pacific employees, women, gays, lesbians, transgender employees, Native Americans, veterans, Hispanics).
- Celebrate cultural traditions, festivities, and holidays.
- Make work/life balance initiatives (such as flextime, telecommuting, and eldercare) available to all employees.

Fair Treatment
- Conduct extensive diversity training.
- Implement an alternative dispute resolution process.
- Include women and minorities on all human resources committees throughout the company.

Manager Accountability
- Link managers' compensation to their success in meeting diversity goals and creating openness and inclusion in the workplace.
- Use employee attitude or engagement surveys to track employees' attitudes on inclusion, fairness, opportunities for development, work/life balance, and perceptions of the company culture.
- Implement 360-degree feedback for all managers and supervisors.

Relationships with External Stakeholders
- Increase marketing to diverse communities.
- Provide customer service in different languages.
- Broaden the company's base of suppliers and vendors to include businesses owned by minorities and women.
- Provide scholarships and educational and neighborhood grants to diverse communities and their members.

SOURCES: Based on F. Dobbins and A. Kalev, "Why Diversity Programs Fail," *Harvard Business Review,* July/August 2016, pp. 52–60; B. Groysberg and K. Connolly, "Great Leaders Who Make the Mix Work," *Harvard Business Review,* September 2013, pp. 68–76; K. Bezrvkova, K. Jehn, and C. Spell, "Reviewing Diversity Training: Where Have We Been and Where Should We Go?" *Academy of Management Learning & Education* 11 (2012), pp. 207–227; R. Anand and M. Winters, "A Retrospective View of Corporate Diversity Training from 1964 to the Present," *Academy of Management Learning & Education* 7 (2008), pp. 356–72; C. Chavez and J. Weisinger, "Beyond Diversity Training: A Social Infusion for Cultural Inclusion," *Human Resource Management* 47 (2008), pp. 331–50.

ONBOARDING OR SOCIALIZATION

Onboarding, or socialization, refers to the process of helping new hires adjust to social and performance aspects of their new jobs.[117] This process is important to help employees adjust to their jobs by establishing relationships to increase satisfaction; clarifying goals and expectations to improve performance; and providing feedback, coaching, and follow-up activities to reduce turnover. Although onboarding programs vary widely across companies, effective onboarding involves the four steps shown in Figure 7.6. It does include understanding mundane tasks such as completing tax forms and knowing how to complete time sheets or travel reimbursement forms, but it goes beyond compliance. Effective onboarding includes enhancing new hires' self-confidence and their feeling socially comfortable and accepted by their peers and manager; ensuring that new hires understand their role and job expectations, responsibilities, and performance requirements; and helping them "fit in" to and understand the company culture. Effective onboarding is related to many important outcomes for the employee and the company, including higher job satisfaction, organizational commitment, lower turnover, higher performance, reduced stress, and career effectiveness.[118]

Table 7.10 shows the characteristics of effective onboarding programs. In particular, effective onboarding programs actively involve the new employee. Several companies offer onboarding programs that include these characteristics. For example, Genscape changed its onboarding program because it was based too much on new hires completing paperwork and allowed little time for personal interaction.[119] Genscape now uses an online portal to reduce the time spent completing paperwork and increase the opportunity for more personal interaction during onboarding. The online portal allows new employees to complete forms, but they can also virtually meet the company's HR team, watch a welcome message from the CEO, review their benefit choices, and learn about the company's values.

Booz Allen Hamilton's onboarding program involves face-to-face and online activities to enhance the effectiveness of the process. Booz Allen Hamilton, a strategy and

Onboarding
Refers to the process of helping new hires adjust to social and performance aspects of their new jobs.

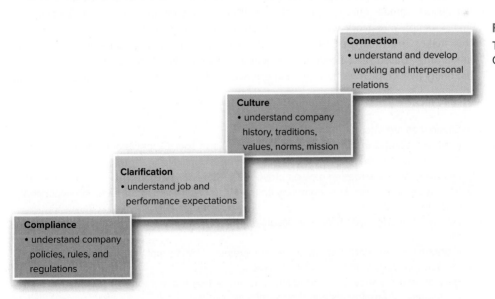

Figure 7.6
The Four Steps in Onboarding

Connection
• understand and develop working and interpersonal relations

Culture
• understand company history, traditions, values, norms, mission

Clarification
• understand job and performance expectations

Compliance
• understand company policies, rules, and regulations

SOURCE: Based on T. Bauer, *Onboarding New Employees: Maximizing Success* (Alexandria, VA: SHRM Foundation, 2010); G. Chao, A. O'Leary-Kelly, S. Wolf, H. Klein, and P. Gardner, "Organizational Socialization: Its Content and Consequences," *Journal of Applied Psychology* 79 (1994), pp. 730–43.

technology consulting company, revised its onboarding program to reduce the time it took for new employees to become productive, make them feel good about working for the company, and develop knowledge regarding the company culture and core values.[120] The program, which spans 12 months, includes learning activities and events organized into three phases. The first phase, known as Engage, is designed to motivate and prepare new hires for their first year. Engage spans two to three weeks. It includes learning activities that actively involve the new hires, including working in cross-functional teams with members from different offices and levels. New hires can use their laptops to explore online resources for career planning and development. Teams of three new hires each begin to compete in a simulated year-long client project. They have access to an experienced employee who can provide insights and examples of how he or she has worked with clients over time. Also, senior company leaders deliver welcome messages and lead discussions on how to succeed at the company.

The second phase of the Booz Allen Hamilton onboarding program, Equip, begins the new hires' second week and continues through their first six months. Equip provides employees with the skills, behaviors, and tools they need for success at the company. It includes 30-, 60-, and 90-day meetings with their manager, a series of e-newsletters, and a detailed onboarding tool kit designed to reinforce and build on what they learned in the first phase of the program. The third and final phase, Excel, emphasizes professional development, relationship building, and acceptance of the company's values. Excel covers the seven-month period through the end of the new hires' first year of employment. The employees' first annual performance review occurs at the end of Excel.

Booz Allen Hamilton's new hires also have access to and are encouraged to use the company's social media and knowledge management tool, the Onboarding Community, to discover and share information via blogs and to take part in online activities and access resources that support the onboarding program. As a result of the program, turnover for new employees who have been with the company six months or less has been reduced by 4%. Also, new employees' time to productivity has been reduced, saving the company millions of dollars in lost revenue.

Shape Corp. designs, engineers, manufactures, and tests metal and plastic products that absorb impact energy and protect vehicles, their occupants, and pedestrians.[121] Shape's employees work with cutting torches, welders, grinders, and other machinery. This makes it critical that Shape's orientation program focuses on safety as well as onboarding. Based on a needs assessment using employee focus groups, Shape found that many new employees had little experience working in manufacturing and had begun

Table 7.10
Characteristics of Effective Onboarding Programs

Employees are encouraged to ask questions.
Program includes information on both technical and social aspects of the job.
The employee manager has some onboarding responsibility.
Debasing or embarrassing new employees is avoided.
Employees learn about the company culture, history, language, products, services, and customers.
Follow-up of employee progress occurs at different points up to one year after joining the company.
Program involves participation, active involvement, and formal and informal interaction between new hires and current employees.
Relocation assistance is provided (such as house hunting or information sessions on the community for employees and their significant others).

working prior to any training or orientation. As result, the orientation was changed from one day to four days for all new employees, followed by a six-day manufacturing technician training course for employees working in manufacturing. The new orientation includes speakers, plant tours, an introduction to the company's mentoring program and the employee's mentor, Web-based training, and instructor-led safety training. If employees fail the manufacturing technology training course, they are not allowed to work in manufacturing and may be terminated. The orientation program has been implemented globally with 1,800 employees in their native languages. Shape continually revises the program content based on focus groups that meet semiannually. As a result of the orientation program, injury rates have decreased 75% among employees who have worked one year or less at Shape. The program provides employees with the knowledge they need to perform their jobs, improves their safety awareness, and helps them develop relationships at work that enhance their socialization.

A LOOK BACK

GameStop

The Level Up program that GameStop uses for training is an online game-based training program that enables employees to complete training on their own time and at their own pace, scoring points and earning badges based on achieving different skills and advancing to the next level.

QUESTIONS

1. Does Level Up support GameStop's business? Explain.
2. Do you think that online game-based learning like Level Up needs to be supplemented with some type of face-to-face training or coaching? Why or why not?
3. What features of game-based learning such as Level Up contribute to its effectiveness as a training method? Explain why.

SUMMARY

Technological innovations, new product markets, and a diverse workforce have increased the need for companies to reexamine how their training practices contribute to learning. In this chapter, we discussed a systematic approach to training, including needs assessment, design of the learning environment, consideration of employee readiness for training, and transfer-of-training issues. We reviewed numerous training methods and stressed that the key to successful training was to choose a method that would best accomplish the objectives of training. We also emphasized how training can contribute to effectiveness by establishing a link with the company's strategic direction and demonstrating through cost–benefit analysis how training contributes to profitability. Cross-cultural preparation and managing diversity are two relevant training issues, given companies' needs to capitalize on global markets and a diverse workforce. Onboarding or socialization is critical for helping new hires feel comfortable and connected in their new job.

KEY TERMS

Continuous learning, 271
Training, 271
Formal training, 271

Informal learning, 271
Explicit knowledge, 272
Tacit knowledge, 272

Knowledge management, 272
Training design process, 273
Needs assessment, 275

DISCUSSION QUESTIONS

1. Noetron, a retail electronics store, recently invested a large amount of money to train sales staff to improve customer service. The skills emphasized in the program include how to greet customers, determine their needs, and demonstrate product convenience. The company wants to know whether the program is effective. What outcomes should it collect? What type of evaluation design should it use?

2. "Melinda," bellowed Toran, "I've got a problem, and you've got to solve it. I can't get people in this plant to work together as a team. As if I don't have enough trouble with the competition and delinquent accounts, now I have to put up with running a zoo. It's your responsibility to see that the staff gets along with each other. I want a human relations training proposal on my desk by Monday." How would you determine the need for human relations training? How would you determine whether you actually had a training problem? What else could be responsible for the situation?

3. Assume you are general manager of a small seafood company. Most training is unstructured and occurs on the job. Currently, senior fish cleaners are responsible for teaching new employees how to perform the job. Your company has been profitable, but recently wholesale fish dealers that buy your product have been complaining about the poor quality of your fresh fish. For example, some fillets have not had all the scales removed and abdomen parts remain attached to the fillets. You have decided to change the on-the-job training received by the fish cleaners. How will you modify the training to improve the quality of the product delivered to the wholesalers?

4. A training needs analysis indicates that managers' productivity is inhibited because they are reluctant to delegate tasks to their subordinates. Suppose you had to decide between using adventure learning and a lecture using a virtual classroom for your training program. What are the strengths and weaknesses of each technique? Which would you choose? Why? What factors would influence your decision?

5. To improve product quality, a company is introducing a computer-assisted manufacturing process into one of its assembly plants. The new technology is likely to modify jobs substantially. Employees will also be required to learn statistical process control techniques. The new technology and push for quality will require employees to attend numerous training sessions. More than 50% of the employees who will be affected by the new technology completed their formal education more than 10 years ago. Only about 5% of the company's employees have used the tuition reimbursement benefit. How should management maximize employees' readiness for training?

6. A training course was offered for maintenance employees in which trainees were supposed to learn how to repair and operate a new, complex electronics system. On the job, maintenance employees were typically told about a symptom experienced by the machine operator and were asked to locate the trouble. During training, the trainer would pose various problems for the maintenance employees to solve. He would point out a component on an electrical diagram and ask, "What would happen if this component was faulty?" Trainees would then trace the circuitry on a blueprint to uncover the symptoms that would appear as a result of the problem. You are receiving complaints about poor troubleshooting from maintenance supervisors of employees who

have completed the program. The trainees are highly motivated and have the necessary prerequisites. What is the problem with the training course? What recommendations do you have for fixing this course?

7. What factors contribute to the effectiveness of e-learning training programs?

8. Choose a job you are familiar with. Design a new employee onboarding program for that job. Explain how your program contributes to effective socialization.

9. What features of games motivate learning, especially for Millennials?

10. Why might employees prefer blended learning to training using only iPads?

11. What learning condition do you think is most necessary for learning to occur? Which is least critical? Why?

12. What can companies do to encourage informal learning?

13. List and discuss the steps in cross-cultural preparation.

SELF-ASSESSMENT EXERCISE

Additional assignable self-assessments available in Connect.

In this chapter, we discussed the need for learners to be motivated so that training will be effective. What is your motivation to learn? Find out by answering the following questions.

Read each statement and indicate how much you agree with it, using the following scale:

1. I try to learn as much as I can from the courses I take.   5 4 3 2 1
2. I believe I tend to learn more from my courses than other students do.   5 4 3 2 1
3. When I'm involved in courses and can't understand something,   5 4 3 2 1
   I consider it a challenge and try harder to learn.

5 = Strongly agree
4 = Somewhat agree
3 = Neutral
2 = Somewhat disagree
1 = Strongly disagree

Add up your points across the three statements. Your points could range from 3 to 15. What's your score? The higher your score the greater your motivation to learn.

EXERCISING STRATEGY

Formal and Self-Directed Learning at LinkedIn

LinkedIn is the world's largest professional network on the Internet, with more than 450 million members. LinkedIn strives to create economic opportunity for every person in the world and strives to helps its employees transform themselves by developing their knowledge and skills. Transformation and collaboration are key parts of LinkedIn's culture. At LinkedIn, onboarding includes a New Hire Roadmap, which provides a weekly list of things that new employees have to do to become productive during their first 30 days on the job. The Transformation Plan gives employees the opportunity to improve in their current job and consider their future career. At LinkedIn, 70% of the way that employees learn is self-directed. That is, employees access information when they need it, in the context of how they perform their job or how they want to move in their career. Most content is available online. Through LearnIn, employees can search for relevant learning content. Thirty percent of learning includes classroom training and working in teams to solve real problems. For example, a month-long program called Conscious

Business focuses on effective collaboration, improving work relationships, problem solving, and acting with integrity. Employees learn through interacting in teams, watching videos, completing knowledge checks, and engaging in practice activities that involve genuine business situations. They share ideas using discussion boards and meet weekly with a facilitator to discuss what they have learned.

QUESTIONS

1. Is LinkedIn's approach to training strategic? Why or why not?

2. At LinkedIn, 70% of training is informal and self-directed and 30% is formal, including classroom training and working in teams. Do you think this is the right mix for LinkedIn? Why? Should all companies adopt the same mix? Why or why not?

SOURCES: Based on K. Whitney, "Dreaming Big to Make Learning Happen," *Chief Learning Officer*, March 2016, pp. 22–23; "About Us," www.linkedin.com; "3 Reasons LinkedIn Is an Awesome Place to Work," http://theundercoverrecruiter.com/linkedin-culture/.

MANAGING PEOPLE

Learning Helps Agents Succeed at Keller Williams

At Keller Williams, the largest real estate franchise in North America, the vision is to be the real estate company of choice for agents, franchisees, and customers. Keller Williams strives to train its agents better than any other company in the world so that they can delight customers, build their business, and have financial success. Just as location is a key factor in attracting buyers to purchase a home or commercial property, training is a reason for Keller Williams' ability to reach its business goals, which include adding 8,000 agents, increasing agents' commissions by 20%, and ensuring that over 90% of its franchise offices are profitable. Keller Williams' CEO believes that training is critical for the company to attract new agents because it helps them quickly become productive, resulting in sales and commissions. Training involves both online and classroom instruction where learning occurs through interacting with instructors and coaching and opportunities for agents to collaborate, which helps them learn from each other by sharing knowledge and practices. Keller Williams' commitment to training and its role in the success of the business was recognized by the top ranking it received in back-to-back years in *Training* magazine's Top 125. The company earned the distinction of being ranked number 1 in 2017 and 2015 and number 2 in 2014.

Keller Williams has several different training programs that support agents and the business. Business Objective: A Life By Design (BOLD) is a seven-week training program during which agents are taught mindset exercises and language techniques, and in which they participate in lead-generation activities. The course focuses on personal well-being as well as business skills. During some classes in the program, agents engage in "real play," calling customers with instructors providing guidance and support. This allows the agents to generate business while learning. BOLD graduates have increased sales volumes by 80%, closed sales by 86%, and increased commissions by 118%, compared to agents who haven't taken the program.

Mega Agent Expansion (MAE) helps top-performing agents understand how and when to expand into new markets. MAE includes instructor-led classes, webinars, expert interviews, productivity resources, and coaching. The program helps participants understand all aspects of expanding their business, including how to centralize lead generation and administration and develop a workable business plan. They have access to a social media network for learning and sharing as well as monthly opportunities to ask questions of Keller Williams' top expansion agents. Growth Initiative (GI) is a distance learning and consulting program that trains managers how to effectively recruit and retain agents. The program includes weekly one-hour seminars; requires managers to make two recruiting appointments each day, five days a week; and helps managers share best practices through an online community and a dedicated Facebook page.

In addition to its training programs, Keller Williams invested in building a training and education center at its corporate headquarters in Austin, Texas. The center manages all aspects of learning and develops new courses, learning tools, and videos. Recently, the center developed apps that provide short training opportunities that agents can access anytime and anywhere through their smartphone, laptop, or notebook.

Keller Williams doesn't just invest time and money into training; it also takes steps to ensure its effectiveness. To keep training standards high and improve learning, every trainer and instructor must take several train-the-trainer courses before they can teach any courses. Different types of evaluation data are collected and shared with agents and managers. Because all training is voluntary, one measure of its value is participation. This includes tracking how much time employees spend in training (82 average per-person hours of formal, planned training) and the number of employees and franchisees trained each year in instructor-led courses (100,000) and online courses (26,000). The return on investment of many courses is calculated. For example, BOLD costs $799 per student, but the average agent who participated in the course earned an additional $55,000 for the year. Keller Williams also tracks metrics such as the average days a property is on the market. Keller Williams' average days on the market is lower than its competitors, providing evidence that training is helping agents close deals quicker and provide better service.

QUESTIONS

1. What are the advantages and disadvantages of the blended learning approach used at Keller Williams?
2. Is Keller Williams' training strategic? Explain your answer.
3. What other data could Keller William collect to evaluate its training programs?

SOURCES: L. Freifeld, "Keller Williams Realty's View from the Top," *Training*, January/February 2017, pp. 26–32; L. Freifeld, "Keller Williams Is at Home at No. 1," *Training*, January/February 2015, pp. 28–34; L. Freifeld, "Keller Williams Is on the Move," *Training*, January/February 2014, pp. 40–42.

HR IN SMALL BUSINESS

Zeigler Automotive Group Drives Growth by Training Its People

In 2004, the Zeigler Automotive Group was four dealerships and a president, Aaron Zeigler, with a desire to expand. Along with aggressive hiring, Zeigler's plan would require a training program to build skills and alignment with the company's values. A solid training program is a lure for ambitious salespeople, because recruiters can show that it will help them develop their selling skills and perhaps move into management. Furthermore, the largest dealership networks have formal training programs, and Zeigler wanted to compete for talent with them.

The company built training that combines classroom instruction with videos. Today all the salespeople and service advisers are expected to watch three training videos every day from an online library of more than 2,000, which are categorized by level of complexity. Each video runs five to seven minutes and features a presentation by Aaron Zeigler; the director of talent development, Mike Van Ryn; or an outside training specialist. After watching each one, the employees take a quiz to check their understanding. Van Ryn and Zeigler employ video instruction because the format is flexible, allowing employees to learn as their schedule permits. When they meet for classroom training, which happens every month or two, they drill down deeper into topics. Usually, this involves a guest speaker at headquarters, with the presentation shared in other locations via videoconferencing.

In addition to the daily training, new hires participate in an orientation program. The main feature of this training is a six-hour class, which covers teamwork, customer service, and the company's history. Other training brings together selected teams of employees targeted for promotion to management positions. They meet every other month at headquarters in Kalamazoo, Michigan, to study financial statements and learn other management skills.

One measure of the success of the training is that employee turnover in 2014 was just 7%, far down from more than 25% ten years earlier. Also, sales per employee per month are higher than they had been before the company started using the high-frequency video approach to learning. Furthermore, the company is meeting its president's ambition to expand. It now has more than 20 dealerships in four states, with a workforce that includes hundreds of salespeople and service advisers.

QUESTIONS

1. Imagine you were helping Zeigler and Van Ryn prepare a needs assessment for training. Using examples from the information provided, what information would you include in the needs assessment?
2. What training methods is Zeigler Automotive Group using? What other methods would you recommend it use? Give reasons for your recommendations.

SOURCES: Zeigler Automotive Group, "Careers," http://www.zeigler.com; Al Jones, "Kalamazoo-Based Zeigler Buys More Car Dealerships in Chicago Area," MLive, January 21, 2016, http://mlive.com; Jon McKenna, "Training Helps Sustain Michigan Dealership Group's Evolution into a Substantial Corporate Player," CBT Automotive Network, December 1, 2015, http://cbtnews.com; Arlena Sawyers, "Getting Schooled in the Car Dealership Business," *Automotive News*, June 1, 2015, https://www.autonews.

NOTES

1. E. Salas and J. A. Cannon-Bowers, "The Science of Training: A Decade of Progress," *Annual Review of Psychology* 52 (2002), pp. 471–99; R. Noe, *Employee Training and Development*, 7th ed. (New York: McGraw-Hill Irwin, 2015); H. Aguinis and K. Kraiger, "Benefits of Training and Development for Individuals, Teams, Organizations, and Society," *Annual Review of Psychology* 60 (2009), pp. 451–74.
2. R. Noe, A. Clarke, and H. Klein, "Learning in the Twenty-First Century Workplace", *Annual. Review of Organizational Psychology & Organizational Behavior* 1 (2014), pp. 245–75; U. Sessa and M. London, *Continuous Learning in Organizations* (Mahwah, NJ: Lawrence Erlbaum, 2006); M. London, "Lifelong Learning: Introduction," in M. London (ed.), *The Oxford Handbook of Lifelong Learning* (New York: Oxford University Press, 2011), pp. 3–11.
3. "2016 Training Industry Report", *training* (November/December 2016): 28–41.
4. J. Roy, "Transforming Informal Learning into a Competitive Advantage," *T + D*, October 2010, pp. 23–25; P. Galagan, "Unformal, the New Normal," *T + D*, September 2010, pp. 29–31.
5. S. I. Tannenbaum, R. Beard, L. A. McNall, and E. Salas, "Informal Learning and Development in Organizations," in S. W. J. Kozlowski and E. Salas (eds.), *Learning, Training, and Development in Organizations* (New York: Routledge, 2010), pp. 303–32; D. J. Bear, H. B. Tompson, C. L. Morrison, M. Vickers, A. Paradise, M. Czarnowsky, M. Soyars, and K. King, *Tapping the Potential of Informal Learning. An ASTD Research Study* (Alexandria, VA: American Society for Training and Development, 2008).
6. T. Bingham and M. Conner, *The New Social Learning* (Alexandria, VA: ASTD Press, 2010).
7. J. Quinn, P. Andersen, and S. Finkelstein, "Leveraging Intellect," *Academy of Management Executive* 10 (1996), pp. 7–39;

R. Ployhart and T. Moliterno, "Emergence of the Human Capital Resource: A Multilevel Model," *Academy of Management Review* 36 (2011), pp. 127–50; B. Campbell, R. Coff, and D. Kryscynski, "Rethinking Sustained Competitive Advantage from Human Capital," *Academy of Management Review* 37 (2012), pp. 376–95; T. Crook, S. Todd, J. Combs, D. Woehr, and D. Ketchen, Jr., "Does Human Capital Matter? A Meta-Analysis of the Relationship between Human Capital and Firm Performance," *Journal of Applied Psychology* 96 (2011), pp. 443–56.

8. I. Nonaka and H. Takeuchi, *The Knowledge-Creating Company: How Japanese Companies Create the Dynamics of Innovation* (New York: Oxford University Press, 1995).

9. S. E. Jackson, M. A. Hitt, and A. S. Denisi, eds., *Managing Knowledge for Sustained Competitive Advantage: Designing Strategies for Effective Human Resource Management* (San Francisco: Jossey-Bass, 2003); A. Rossett, "Knowledge Management Meets Analysis," *Training and Development*, May 1999, pp. 63–68; R. Davenport, "Why Does Knowledge Management Still Matter?" *T + D* 59 (2005), pp. 19–23.

10. B. Hassell, "DAU Helps Its Learners Every Day," *Chief Learning Officer* (June 2016), pp. 28–29; "DAU Online Resources: An Overview," www.dau.mil, accessed March 13, 2017.

11. M. Weinstein, "Long-Range Learning Plans," *Training*, November/December 2010, pp. 38–41; L. Miller, *2014 State of the Industry* (Alexandria, VA: American Society for Training & Development, 2014); "2014's Very Best Learning Organizations," *T + D*, October 2014, pp. 34–98.

12. "Training Top 125 2017 Top 10 Hall of Fame: Jiffy Lube International, Inc.," *Training*, January/February 2017, p. 54; L. Freifeld, "Jiffy Lube's *Training* Drive," *Training*, January/February 2013, pp. 34–37; M. Weinstein, "Jiffy-Lube Greases the Wheels of Success," *Training*, January/February 2015, pp. 36–38; L. Freifeld, "Jiffy-Lube Revs Up to No. 1," *Training*, January/February 2014, pp. 30–38.

13. R. Noe, *Employee Training and Development*, 7th ed. (New York: Irwin/McGraw-Hill, 2015).

14. Ibid; E. A. Surface, "Training Needs Assessment: Aligning Learning and Capability with Performance Requirements and Organizational Objectives," in *The Handbook of Work Analysis: Methods, Systems, Applications and Science of Work Measurement in Organizations*, ed. M. A. Wilson, W. Bennett, S. G. Gibson, & G. M. Alliger (New York: Routledge Academic, 2012), pp. 437–62.

15. J. Congemi, "MasTec Tackles the LMS," *Training*, July/August 2014, pp. 52–54.

16. J. B. Tracey, S. I. Tannenbaum, and M. J. Kavanaugh, "Applying Trained Skills on the Job: The Importance of the Work Environment," *Journal of Applied Psychology* 80 (1995), pp. 239–52; E. Holton, R. Bates, and W. Ruona, "Development of a Generalized Learning Transfer System Inventory," *Human Resource Development Quarterly* 11 (2001), pp. 333–60; E. Helton III and T. Baldwin, eds., *Improving Learning Transfer in Organizations* (San Francisco: Jossey-Bass, 2003); J. S. Russell, J. R. Terborg, and M. L. Powers, "Organizational Performance and Organizational Level Training and Support," *Personnel Psychology* 38 (1985), pp. 849–63.

17. S. Gale, "Speak Your CEOs Language," *Chief Learning Officer*, February 2016, pp. 26–29; S. Tannenbaum, "A Strategic View of Organizational Training and Learning," in *Creating, Implementing, and Managing Effective Training and Development*, ed. K. Kraiger (San Francisco: Jossey-Bass, 2002), pp. 10–52.

18. J. Salopek, "No Vacancy", *T + D*, October 2016, pp. 38–40.

19. C. Reinhart, "How to Leap over Barrier to Performance," *Training and Development*, January 2000, pp. 20–29; G. Rummter and K. Morrill, "The Results Chain," *T + D*, February 2005, pp. 27–35; O. Rummter, "In Search of the Holy Performance Grail," *Training and Development*, April 1996, pp. 26–31.

20. C. E. Schneier, J. P. Guthrie, and J. D. Olian, "A Practical Approach to Conducting and Using Training Needs Assessment," *Public Personnel Management,* Summer 1988, pp. 191–205; I. Goldstein, "Training in Organizations," in *Handbook of Industrial/Organizational Psychology*, 2nd ed., ed. M. D. Dunnette and L. M. Hough (Palo Alto, CA: Consulting Psychologists Press, 1991), vol. 2, pp. 507–619.

21. Company website, "Careers: About Us," www.kla-tencor.com, accessed February 25, 2015; "KLA-Tencor Corporation: Right People, Right Knowledge," *Training*, January/February 2015, pp. 56–57.

22. R. A. Noe, "Trainees' Attributes and Attitudes: Neglected Influences on Training Effectiveness," *Academy of Management Review* 11 (1986), pp. 736–49.

23. T. T. Baldwin, R. T. Magjuka, and B. T. Loher, "The Perils of Participation: Effects of Choice on Trainee Motivation and Learning," *Personnel Psychology* 44 (1991), pp. 51–66; S. I. Tannenbaum, J. E. Mathieu, E. Salas, and J. A. Cannon-Bowers, "Meeting Trainees' Expectations: The Influence of Training Fulfillment on the Development of Commitment, Self-Efficacy, and Motivation," *Journal of Applied Psychology* 76 (1991), pp. 759–69.

24. D. Rock, "Your Brain on Learning", *Chief Learning Officer*, May 2015, pp. 30–48; A. Beninghof, "Pathways to Retention," TD, June 2015, pp. 21–22; C. E. Schneier, "Training and Development Programs: What Learning Theory and Research Have to Offer," *Personnel Journal*, April 1974, pp. 288–93; M. Knowles, "Adult Learning," in *Training and Development Handbook*, 3rd ed., ed. R. L. Craig (New York: McGraw-Hill, 1987), pp. 168–79; R. Zemke and S. Zemke, "30 Things We Know for Sure about Adult Learning," *Training*, June 1981, pp. 45–52; B. J. Smith and B. L. Delahaye, *How to Be an Effective Trainer*, 2nd ed. (New York: Wiley, 1987).

25. "Verizon," *TD,* October 2016, p. 65; "Verizon: Emergency Work Assignment Training," *Training*, January/February 2016, p. 56; A. Paul, "Microlearning 101," *HR Magazine*, May 2016, pp. 36–42.

26. S. Sipek, "Learning Is Doing at PwC," *Chief Learning Officer*, June 2016, pp. 38–39.

27. S. Bailey, "The Answer to Transfer," *Chief Learning Officer*, November 2014, pp. 33–41; R. Hewes, "Step by Step," *T + D*, February 2014, pp. 56–61; E. Holton III and T. Baldwin, eds, *Improving Learning Transfer in Organizations* (San Francisco: Jossey-Bass, 2003); J. M. Cusimano, "Managers as Facilitators," *Training and Development* 50 (1996), pp. 31–33.

28. S. Gale, "Taking Leadership in a New Direction at Western Union," *Chief Learning Officer*, March 2017, pp. 54, 56.

29. M. Weinstein, "Sonic Automotive Revs Its Leadership Engine," *Training,* January/February 2017, pp. 46–50.

30. C. M. Petrini, ed., "Bringing It Back to Work," *Training and Development Journal*, December 1990, pp. 15–21.

31. R. Emelo, "Shift Your Focus With Modern Mentoring," *TD*, September 2015, pp. 36–41.

32. Ford, Quinones, Sego, and Sorra, "Factors Affecting the Opportunity to Perform Trained Tasks on the Job."

33. M. A. Quinones, J. K. Ford, D. J. Sego, and E. M. Smith, "The Effects of Individual and Transfer Environment Characteristics

on the Opportunity to Perform Trained Tasks," *Training Research Journal* 1 (1995/96), pp. 29–48.

34. G. Stevens and E. Stevens, "The Truth about EPSS," *Training and Development* 50 (1996), pp. 59–61; J. Ford and T. Meyer, "Advances in Training Technology: Meeting the Workplace Challenges of Talent Development, Deep Specialization, and Collaborative Learning," in M. Coovert and L. Thompson, eds., *The Psychology of Workplace Technology* (New York: Routledge, 2014), pp. 43–76.

35. J. Salopek, "Mobile and Social Learning Attracts, Equips Young Insurance Agents," *TD*, October 2016, pp. 42–44.

36. E. Hoffman and J. Boyle, "Managing Mission Knowledge at NASA," *T + D*, July 2014, pp. 50–55.

37. "Tata Consultancy Services," *TD*, October 2016, p. 47.

38. R. D. Marx, "Relapse Prevention for Managerial Training: A Model for Maintenance of Behavior Change," *Academy of Management Review* 7 (1982), pp. 433–41; G. P. Latham and C. A. Frayne, "Self-Management Training for Increasing Job Attendance: A Follow-up and Replication," *Journal of Applied Psychology* 74 (1989), pp. 411–16.

39. "Farmers Insurance: CE-It's Up to Me," *Training*, January/February 2017, pp. 58–59; "General Motors Sales, Service, & Marketing Division: District Manager New Hire Learning Journey," *Training*, January/February 2017, p. 97.

40. B. Mirza, "Social Media Tools Redefine Learning," *HR Magazine*, December 2010, p. 74; L. Patel, "The Rise of Social Media," *T + D*, July 2010, pp. 60–61; J. Meister, E. Kaganer, and R. Von Feldt, "2011: The Year of the Media Tablet as a Learning Tool," *T + D*, April 2011, pp. 28–31.

41. "Putting the Distance into Distance Learning," *Training*, October 1995, pp. 111–18.

42. D. Picard, "The Future Is Distance Training," *Training*, November 1996, pp. s3–s10.

43. A. F. Maydas, "On-Line Networks Build the Savings into Employee Education," *HR Magazine*, October 1997, pp. 31–35.

44. "EY: Tax 1 Blended Program," *Training*, January/February 2016, p. 57.

45. T. Byham and A. Lang, "Avoid These 10 Pitfalls of Virtual Classrooms," *Chief Learning Officer*, May 2014, pp. 18–21; C. Huggett, "Make Virtual Training a Success," *T + D*, January 2014, pp. 40–45.

46. "Asurion," *TD*, October 2016, p. 80.

47. C. Tate, "Mobile Masters," *T + D*, April 2013, pp. 22–24.

48. R. B. Cohn, "How to Choose a Video Producer," *Training*, July 1996, pp. 58–61.

49. Commerce Clearing House, Inc., *Orientation–Training* (Chicago, IL: Personnel Practices Communications, Commerce Clearing House, 1981), pp. 501–905; K. Tyler, "The American Apprentice," *HR Magazine*, November 2013, pp. 33–36; S. Wartenberg, "No Snow Days," *The Columbus Dispatch*, February 22, 2015, pp. D1, D3; L. Weber, "Here's One Way to Solve the Skills Gap," *Wall Street Journal*, April 28, 2014, p. R3.

50. A. H. Howard III, "Apprenticeships," in *The ASTD Training and Development Handbook*, pp. 803–13; Tyler, "The American Apprentice."

51. M. Riley, "Training Companies to Handle a Hack", *Bloomberg BusinessWeek* (November 23, 2016) from www.bloomberg.com, accessed March 17, 2017.

52. N. Adams, "Lessons from the Virtual World," *Training*, June 1995, pp. 45–48.

53. Ibid.

54. "BNSF Railway: Virtual Power Brake Law (VPBL)," *Training*, January/February 2017, p. 102.

55. J. Borzo, "Almost Human," *Wall Street Journal*, May 24, 2004, pp. R1, R10; J. Hoff, "My Virtual Life," *BusinessWeek*, May 1, 2006, pp. 72–78.

56. "PPD: Virtual Clinical Foundations Program 2.0," *Training*, January/February 2016, p. 106; "About Us," www.ppdi.com, accessed March 14, 2017; P. Harris, "Avatars Rule," *T + D*, October 2013, pp. 60–61.

57. Cornell, "Better than the Real Thing?"; E. Frauenheim, "Can Video Games Win Points as Teaching Tools?" *Workforce Management*, April 10, 2006, pp. 12–14; S. Boehle, "Simulations: The Next Generation of e-Learning," *Training*, January 2005, pp. 22–31; Borzo, "Almost Human"; T. Sitzmann, "A Meta-Analytic Examination of the Instructional Effectiveness of Computer-Based Simulation Games," *Personnel Psychology* 64 (2011), pp. 489–528.

58. L. Freifeld, "Solid Sims," *Training*, October 2007, p. 48.

59. B. Roberts, "Gamification: Win, Lose or Draw", *HR Magazine* (May 2014): 28-35; T. Sitzmann, "A meta-analytic investigation of the instructional effectiveness of computer-based simulation games" *Personnel Psychology* 64 (2011): 489–528.

60. "KLA-Tencor: The Situation Room," *Training*, September/October 2014, pp. 60–61.

61. "CMS Energy: Tackling Conflicts with 'The Resolver,'" *Training*, September/October 2014, p. 46.

62. G. P. Latham and L. M. Saari, "Application of Social Learning Theory to Training Supervisors through Behavior Modeling," *Journal of Applied Psychology* 64 (1979), pp. 239–46.

63. M. Rosenberg, *E-learning Strategies for Delivering Knowledge in the Digital age* (New York: McGraw-Hill, 2001); "What Is Web-Based Training?" from www.clark.net/pub/nractive/ft.html; R. Johnson and H. Gueutal, *Transforming HR through Technology* (Alexandria, VA: SHRM Foundation, 2010).

64. L. Harris and E. Squire, "Bedside Manners," *T + D*, December 2015, pp. 48–52.

65. S. Herring, "MOOCs Come of Age," *T + D*, January 2014, pp. 46–49.

66. L. Maxey, "An Investment in MOOCs Pays Off in Talent", *Chief Learning Officer* (March 2017: 16; J. Donovan & C. Benko, "AT&T's Talent Overhaul", *Harvard Business Review* (October 2016): 68–73.

67. M. Weinstein, "Managing MOOCs," *Training*, September/October 2014, pp. 26–28; R. Grossman, "Are Massive Open Online Courses in Your Future?" *HR Magazine*, August 2013, pp. 30–36; J. Meister, "How MOOCs Will Revolutionize Corporate Learning and Development," *Forbes,* August 20, 2013; C. Straumsheim, "Confirming the MOOC Myth," *Inside Higher Ed*, December 6, 2013, www.insidehighered.com; K. Jordan, "MOOC Completion Rates: The Data," http://www.katyjordan.com/MOOCproject.html; M. Chafkin, "Uphill Climb," *Fast Company*, December 2013/January 2014, pp. 146–56.

68. G. Dutton, "There's an App for That!" *Training*, September/October 2011, pp. 36–37.

69. S. Sipek, "Learning Is Doing at PwC," *Chief Learning Officer*, June 2016, pp. 38–39.

70. "ADP, LLC: ADP National Accounts Implementation – Reduced Time to Competency", *Training* (January/February 2016): 102–103.

71. "Learning Management Systems: An Executive Summary," *Training*, March 2002, p. 4; S. Castellano, "The Evolution of the LMS," *T + D*, November 2014, p. 14.

72. L. Freifeld, "Keller Williams Realty's View from the Top," *Training*, January/February 2017, pp. 26–28, 30.

73. D. Brown and D. Harvey, *An Experiential Approach to Organizational Development* (Englewood Cliffs, NJ: Prentice Hall, 2000); J. Schettler, "Learning by Doing," *Training,* April 2002, pp. 38–43; G. Kranz, "From Fire Drills to Funny Skills," *Workforce Management,* May 2011, pp. 28–32.

74. "Lending a Hand," *T + D,* December 2013, p. 72.

75. R. J. Wagner, T. T. Baldwin, and C. C. Rowland, "Outdoor Training: Revolution or Fad?" *Training and Development Journal,* March 1991, pp. 51–57; C. J. Cantoni, "Learning the Ropes of Teamwork," *Wall Street Journal,* October 2, 1995, p. A14.

76. R. Greenfield, "Startup vs. Wild," *Bloomberg Businessweek,* December 3, 2015.

77. D. Mishev, "Cooking for the Company," *Cooking Light,* August 2004, pp. 142–47.

78. P. F. Buller, J. R. Cragun, and G. M. McEvoy, "Getting the Most Out of Outdoor Training," *Training and Development Journal,* March 1991, pp. 58–61.

79. J. Cannon-Bowers and C. Bowers, "Team Development and Functioning," in *APA Handbook of Industrial and Organizational Psychology,* ed. S. Zedeck (Washington, DC: American Psychological Association, 2011), vol. 1, pp. 597–650; L. Delise, C. Gorman, A. Brooks, J. Rentsch, and D. Steele-Johnson, "The Effects of Team Training on Team Outcomes: A Meta-Analysis," *Performance Improvement Quarterly* 22 (2010), pp. 53–80.

80. S. Carey, "Racing to Improve," *Wall Street Journal,* March 24, 2006, pp. B1, B6.

81. P. Froiland, "Action Learning," *Training,* January 1994, pp. 27–34.

82. "University Health System," *TD,* October 2016, p. 77; Sarah Sipek, "A Global Vision: Leading PepsiCo's Learning Evolution," *Chief Learning Officer,* March 2015, pp. 22–25.

83. "Nationwide Mutual Insurance Company: Fast-Start for Agents," *Training,* January/February 2015, p. 107.

84. K. Kraiger, J. K. Ford, and E. Salas, "Application of Cognitive, Skill-Based, and Affective Theories of Learning Outcomes to New Methods of Training Evaluation," *Journal of Applied Psychology* 78 (1993), pp. 311–28; J. J. Phillips, "ROI: The Search for Best Practices," *Training and Development,* February 1996, pp. 42–47; D. L. Kirkpatrick, "Evaluation of Training," in *Training and Development Handbook,* 2nd ed., ed. R. L. Craig (New York: McGraw-Hill, 1976), pp. 18-1 to 18–27.

85. C. Denault, "MTA: Why the Kirkpatrick Model Works for US," *Chief Learning Officer,* November/December 2016, pp. 60–61.

86. "Mountain America Credit Union: Flow Philosophy Training," *Training,* January/February 2015, p. 103.

87. J. Phillips, P. Phillips, and R. Ray, "Derive Hard Numbers from Soft Skills," *TD,* September 2015, pp. 54–59; J. J. Phillips, *Handbook of Training Evaluation and Measurement Methods,* 2nd ed. (Houston, TX: Gulf Publishing, 1991); J. Phillips and P. Phillips, "Moving from Evidence to Proof," *T + D,* August 2001, pp. 34–39.

88. P. Harris, "Short Can Be Oh, So Sweet," *T + D,* October 2013, pp. 66–69.

89. I. Speizer, "Rolling through the Downturn," *Workforce Management,* August 11, 2008, pp. 31–37.

90. S. Ladika, "Lost in Translation," *Workforce Management,* May 2013, pp. 30–33.

91. K. Johnson, "Career Booster for CFOs: A Stint Abroad," *Wall Street Journal,* February 10, 2015, p. B7.

92. W. A. Arthur Jr. and W. Bennett Jr., "The International Assignee: The Relative Importance of Factors Perceived to Contribute to Success," *Personnel Psychology* 48 (1995), pp. 99–114; G. M. Spreitzer, M. W. McCall Jr., and Joan D. Mahoney, "Early Identification of International Executive Potential," *Journal of Applied Psychology* 82 (1997), pp. 6–29.

93. J. Robinson, "Coming Home," *Human Resource Executive,* September 2, 2016, pp. 39–40, 42; R. Feintzeig, "After Stints Abroad, Re-entry Can Be Hard," *Wall Street Journal,* September 18, 2013, p. B6.

94. J. S. Black and J. K. Stephens, "The Influence of the Spouse on American Expatriate Adjustment and Intent to Stay in Pacific Rim Overseas Assignments," *Journal of Management* 15 (1989), pp. 529–44; M. Shaffer and D. A. Harrison, "Forgotten Partners of International Assignments: Development and Test of a Model of Spouse Adjustment," *Journal of Applied Psychology* 86 (2001), pp. 238–54.

95. M. Shaffer, D. A. Harrison, H. Gregersen, J. S. Black, and L. A. Ferzandi, "You Can Take It with You: Individual Differences and Expatriate Effectiveness," *Journal of Applied Psychology* 91 (2006), pp. 109–25; P. Caligiuri, "The Big Five Personality Characteristics as Predictors of Expatriate's Desire to Terminate the Assignment and Supervisor-Rated Performance," *Personnel Psychology* 53 (2000), pp. 67–88.

96. E. Dunbar and A. Katcher, "Preparing Managers for Foreign Assignments," *Training and Development Journal,* September 1990, pp. 45–47.

97. J. S. Black and M. Mendenhall, "A Practical but Theory-Based Framework for Selecting Cross-Cultural Training Methods," in *Readings and Cases in International Human Resource Management,* ed. M. Mendenhall and G. Oddou (Boston: PWS-Kent, 1991), pp. 177–204.

98. Sodexo, "2016 Global Diversity and Inclusion Report," www.sodexousa.com, accessed March 14, 2017.

99. P. Tam, "Culture Course," *Wall Street Journal,* May 25, 2004, pp. B1, B12.

100. S. Ronen, "Training the International Assignee," in *Training and Development in Organizations,* ed. I. L. Goldstein (San Francisco: Jossey-Bass, 1989), pp. 417–53.

101. H. Ren, M. Shaffer, D. Harrison, C. Fu, and K. Fodchuk, "Reactive Adjustment or Proactive Embedding? Multistudy, Multiwave Evidence for Dual Pathways to Expatriate Retention," *Personnel Psychology* 67 (2014), pp. 203–39.

102. P. R. Harris and R. T. Moran, *Managing Cultural Differences* (Houston, TX: Gulf, 1991).

103. J. Carter, "Globe Trotters," *Training,* August 2005, pp. 22–28.

104. C. Solomon, "Unhappy Trails," *Workforce,* August 2000, pp. 36–41.

105. C. Patton, "Coming to America," *Human Resource Executive,* January/February 2012, pp. 22, 26–29.

106. H. Lancaster, "Before Going Overseas, Smart Managers Plan Their Homecoming," *Wall Street Journal,* September 28, 1999, p. B1; A. Halcrow, "Expats: The Squandered Resource," *Workforce,* April 1999, pp. 42–48.

107. Harris and Moran, *Managing Cultural Differences.*

108. J. Robinson, "Coming Home," *Human Resource Executive,* September 2, 2016, pp. 39–40, 42.

109. H. Dolezalek, "The Path to Inclusion," *Training,* May 2008, pp. 52–54.

110. E. McKeown, "Quantifiable Inclusion Strategies," *T + D,* October 2010, p. 16.

111. F. Dobbins and A. Kalev, "Why Diversity Programs Fail," *Harvard Business Review,* July/August (2016), pp. 52–60; S. E. Jackson and Associates, *Diversity in the Workplace: Human Resource Initiatives* (New York: Guilford, 1992).

112. L. Gellman and G. Wells, "Progress Is Hampered for Women in Tech Jobs," *Wall Street Journal*, March 23, 2016, p. B1; M. O'Brien, "Diversity Chief Helping Google Play Catch-Up," *Columbus Dispatch*, March 16, 2015, p. C4.

113. K. Bezrukova, C. Spell, J. Perry, and K. Jehn, "A Meta-Analytical Integration of over 40 Years of Research on Diversity Training Evaluation," *Psychological Bulletin* 142 (2016), pp. 1227–74.

114. "Corporate Responsibility," www.sodexousa.com; "Report Highlights Diversity and Inclusion as a Core Component of Sodexo Business Growth Strategy," February 6, 2017, www.sodexousa.com; "2016 Global Diversity and Inclusion Report," www.sodexousa.com; M. Landel, "How We Did It... SODEXO's CEO on Smart Diversification," *Harvard Business Review*, March 2015, pp. 41–44; R. Emelo, "Peer Collaboration Enhances Diversity and Inclusion," *T + D*, December 2014, pp. 48–52. R. Anand and M. Winters, "A Retrospective View of Corporate Diversity Training from 1964 to the Present," *Academy of Management Learning & Education*, 7 (2008), pp. 356–72; Dolezalek, "The Path to Inclusion."

115. C. T. Schreiber, K. F. Price, and A. Morrison, "Workforce Diversity and the Glass Ceiling: Practices, Barriers, Possibilities," *Human Resource Planning* 16 (1994), pp. 51–69; K. Bezrvkova, K. Jehn, and C. Spell, "Reviewing Diversity Training: Where Have We Been and Where Should We Go?" *Academy of Management Learning and Education* 11 (2012), pp. 207–227; B. Groysberg and K. Connolly, "Great Leaders Who Make the Mix Work," *Harvard Business Review*, September 2013, pp. 68–76.

116. Groysberg and Connolly, "Great Leaders Who Make the Mix Work."

117. T. Bauer, *Onboarding New Employees: Maximizing Success* (Alexandria, VA: SHRM Foundation, 2010); T. Bauer and B. Erdogan, "Delineating and Reviewing the Role of Newcomer Capital in Organizational Socialization," *Annual Review of Organizational Psychology and Organizational Behavior* 1 (2014), pp. 439–57.

118. H. Klein and N. Weaver, "The Effectiveness of Organizational-Level Orientation Program in the Socialization of New Hires," *Personnel Psychology* 23 (2000), pp. 47–66; C. Wanberg, J. Kammeyer-Mueller, "Predictors and Outcomes of Proactivity in the Socialization Process," *Journal of Applied Psychology* 85 (2000), pp. 373–85; T. Bauer, T. Bodner, B. Erdogan, D. Truxillo, and J. Tucker, "Newcomer Adjustment during Organizational Socialization: A Meta-analytic Review of Antecedents, Outcomes, and Methods," *Journal of Applied Psychology* 92 (2007), pp. 707–21; D. Allen, "Do Organizational Socialization Tactics Influence Newcomer Embeddedness and Turnover?" *Journal of Management* 32 (2006), pp. 237–56; J. Kammeyer-Mueller, C. Wanberg, A. Rubenstein, and Z. Song, "Support, Undermining, and Newcomer Socialization: Fitting in During the First 90 Days," *Academy of Management Journal* 56 (2013), pp. 1104–24.

119. D. Robb, "New-Hire Onboarding Portals Provide a Warmer Welcome," *HR Magazine*, December 2015/January 2016, pp. 58–60.

120. D. Milliken, "Poised for Discovery," *T + D*, August 2011, pp. 70–71.

121. R. Weiss, "Inside Story: A New Orientation Program for New Employees," Association for Talent Development, www.astd.org.

CHAPTER

8 Performance Management

LEARNING OBJECTIVES

After reading this chapter, you should be able to:

The New Face of Performance Management

General Electric (GE) recognized that its performance evaluation system needed to be revamped to more closely align with business cycles and company strategy. Businesses no longer have clear and specific annual product cycles—projects are shorter term, their requirements tend to change frequently, and it's difficult to accurately set goals or plan tasks. GE's strategic refocus on taking risks, testing new ideas with customers, and making mistakes along the way represents a significant change from the company's historical focus on perfection through conforming to standards and eliminating defects. GE is striving to become an innovation-driven company with employees who can more quickly and cheaply develop products. GE's five core values have been changed to reflect the new strategy: "Expertise" and "clear thinker" have been replaced with "learn and adapt to win and "stay lean to go fast." CEO and chairman of the board Jeff Immelt recognized the importance of developing a performance management system that supports the strategy. According to Immelt, "We took a new look at performance rankings. We will always reward our best people and fire those who don't perform. But the centerpiece of GE today are purposeful, high-performance teams dedicated to winning together. What we require is a strong sense of mutual accountability. Each leader depends on the other to 'do their job' in pursuit of valuable outcomes for customers and investors. Our leaders get rewarded—or fired—based on how well they perform for each other. A simple culture requires transparency around performance."

GE's old performance management system for salaried employees required a formal performance evaluation at the end of the year. Employees were asked to complete a self-evaluation, managers read them and provided their own evaluation, and then the managers provided an overall rating for each employee ranging from a low "unsatisfactory" to a high "role model." Employees' pay raises and promotions were tied to these ratings. The old system took as long as five months to complete, which meant that employees would receive performance feedback too late to change their behavior or seek help.

GE's new performance management system encourages managers to evaluate employees on their understanding of customers' needs and how quickly they test and confirm their assumptions about new products and solutions. Each employee has a series of short-term performance goals or priorities. Managers and employees have performance conversations throughout the year (known as "touchpoints") to review progress toward these goals, and they have a brief summary meeting at the end of the year. Employees are encouraged to give and seek performance feedback from their peers (and their managers) at any time. To help facilitate the feedback process, GE developed PD@ GE, a mobile app that allows constructive messages and praise to be provided under separate categories. Feedback received via the app can be gathered into a performance summary. Employees are encouraged to attend team meetings that include a facilitator to provide feedback to their managers. The team is expected to hold the manager accountable for changing their behavior through regular progress meetings.

The culture change supported by the new performance management system is awkward but progressing. Employees are becoming less reluctant about providing constructive messages to

CONTINUED

their managers. Managers are still trying to get employees to adopt new behaviors and be more comfortable testing underdeveloped ideas and product prototypes with customers. Performance management continues to evolve. One of the key issues is how to make promotion and pay decisions without basing them on ranking employees or an overall performance rating.

SOURCES: R. Silverman, "GE Tries to Reinvent the Employee Review, Encouraging Risks," *Wall Street Journal*, June 8, 2016, pp. B1, B6; R. Silverman, "GE Scraps Staff Ratings to Spur Feedback," *Wall Street Journal*, July 27, 2016, p. B8; *GE 2016 Annual Report*, www.ge.com, accessed March 2, 2017; M. Weinstein, "Annual Review Under Review," *Training*, July/August 2016, pp. 22–29; M. Schoenberger, "The Risk of Reviews," *Wall Street Journal*, October 28, 2015, p. R5; "How GE Renews Performance Management from Stack Rankings to Continuous Feedback," from http://blog.impraise.com, accessed March 2, 2017; P. Cappelli and A. Tavis, "The Performance Management Evolution," *Harvard Business Review*, October 2016, pp. 58–67.

Introduction

Companies that seek competitive advantage through employees must be able to manage the behavior and results of all employees. Traditionally, the formal performance appraisal system was viewed as the primary means for managing employee performance. Performance appraisal was an administrative duty performed by managers and was primarily the responsibility of the human resource function. Managers now view performance appraisal as an annual ritual—they quickly complete the form and use it to catalog all the negative information they have collected on an employee over the previous year. Because they may dislike confrontation and feel that they don't know how to give effective evaluations, some managers spend as little time as possible giving employees feedback. Not surprisingly, most managers and employees dislike performance appraisals. "Time-consuming," "frustrating," "dread," "burden," and "pain" are some of the words that come to employees' minds when giving or receiving performance reviews.[1] Reasons for these reactions include the lack of consistency of use of performance appraisals across the company; the inability to differentiate among performance levels; the inability of the appraisal system to help employees build their skills and competencies; excessive time burdens on managers to complete evaluations; and performance discussions that were limited to only once or twice a year and tended to be backward rather than future focused.[2]

Some people have argued that all performance appraisal systems are flawed to the point that they are manipulative, abusive, autocratic, and counterproductive. However, doing away with performance reviews entirely has been found to lead to lower-quality performance conversations between managers and employees and a decrease in employee engagement. This occurs because, without reviews, managers have difficulty explaining to employees how they have performed and what they need to do to improve.[3] It is important to realize that the criticisms voiced about annual performance appraisals shown in Table 8.1 are not the result of evaluating employee performance. Rather, they result from how the performance management system is developed and used. If done correctly, performance management can provide valuable benefits to both employees and the company. As a result, many companies, including GE (discussed in the chapter opener), Eli Lilly, Adobe, Dell, New York Life, Microsoft, Intel, and Gap, have changed their performance management systems. In fact, one estimate is that more than one-third of U.S. companies are now using performance management systems that encourage more frequent manager–employee performance conversations, reducing or eliminating formal evaluation meetings, and moving away from overall performance ratings. These new systems help meet all employees' need for feedback, coaching, and development opportunities, but especially Millennials, who represent a significant part of the workforce.

Performance management
The means through which managers ensure that employees' activities and outcomes are congruent with the organization's goals.

We believe that performance appraisal is only one part of the broader process of performance management. We define **performance management** as the process through which managers ensure that employees' activities and outputs are congruent with the organization's goals. Performance management is central to gaining competitive advantage.

Table 8.1
Examples of Problems with Traditional Annual Performance Reviews

"The annual performance review is dead. Progressive HR leaders are realizing they need continuous real time feedback and solutions" —CEO of Glint
"Over time the rating system has become a huge obstacle. The employee would see their rating first and then the whole review evolved into a discussion of Why this? Why not that? It was no longer driving performance." —Executive VP for Global HR at Expedia
"There is a lot of pain in performance management." —Senior Consultant for Towers Watson
"[M]ainstream management is embedded in, and relies on, a culture of domination . . . the performance review is the biggest hammer management has." —Samuel A. Culbert, author of *Get Rid of the Performance Review*
"In a traditional performance review, the employee listens until he hears the rating and then tunes out because he's doing the calculation in his head about how that will affect his bonus." —Senior VP of Human Resources for Motorola Solutions

SOURCES: D. Wilkie, "Is the Annual Performance Review Dead," *HR Magazine,* October 2015, pp. 11–12; E. Goldberg, "Performance Management Gets Social," *HR Magazine,* August 2014, pp. 35–38; J. Ramirez, "Rethinking the Review," *Human Resource Executive,* July/August 2013, pp. 16–19; V. Liberman, "Performance Management: To Get Results Stop Measuring People by Them," *The Conference Board Review,* Summer 2013, pp. 57–63; S. Culbert, *Get Rid of the Performance Review* (New York: Business Plus, 2010).

Our performance management system has three parts: defining performance, measuring performance, and feeding back performance information. First, a performance management system specifies which aspects of performance are relevant to the organization, primarily through job analysis (discussed in Chapter 4). Second, it measures those aspects of performance through **performance appraisal**, which is only one method for managing employee performance. Third, it provides feedback to employees through **performance feedback** sessions so that they can adjust their performance to the organization's goals. Performance feedback is also fulfilled through tying rewards to performance via the compensation system (such as through merit increases or bonuses), a topic to be covered in Chapters 11 and 12.

In this chapter, we examine a variety of approaches to performance management. First, we provide a brief summary of current performance management practices. Next, we present a model of performance that helps us examine the system's purposes. Then we discuss specific approaches to performance management and the strengths and weaknesses of each. We also look at various sources of performance information. The errors resulting from subjective assessments of performance are presented, as well as the means for reducing those errors. Then we discuss some effective components to performance feedback. Finally, we address components of a legally defensible performance management system.

Performance appraisal
The process through which an organization gets information on how well an employee is doing his or her job.

Performance feedback
The process of providing employees information regarding their performance effectiveness.

The Practice of Performance Management

Several recent surveys of human resource professionals suggest that most companies' performance management practices require annual paper-driven reviews that include both behaviors and business goals.[4] Although many companies use performance management to manage employee performance and make pay decisions, less than 25% of the companies use performance management to help manage talent through identifying training needs and developing leadership talent. Another finding is that 66% of companies use the same performance management system across all levels of the organization. Unfortunately, although performance management is a prevalent practice, it is often not valued or used effectively. Some 70% of companies believe that they need to improve their performance management practices—one of the major reasons is that managers lack the skills needed to coach employees and provide timely and actionable feedback. Further, 50% of employees are surprised by the ratings they receive, and 90% of those employees are unhappy because they expected a higher rating. Finally, 95% of managers are dissatisfied with way their company conducts performance reviews.

Many HR professionals don't believe that yearly performance evaluations are useful: 90% of HR leaders believe the process does not provide accurate information. More than half (53%) gave their organizations a grade of C+ to B, another one-fifth (21%) chose a C, and only 2% gave their organizations an A in performance management.

The Process of Performance Management

LO 8-1
Identify the major parts of an effective performance management process.

Although performance management does include the once- or twice-a-year formal appraisal or evaluation meeting, effective performance management is a process, not an event. Figure 8.1 shows the performance management process. As shown in the process model, providing feedback and the formal performance evaluation are important, but they are not the only important parts of an effective performance management process that contributes to the company's competitive advantage.[5] Also, visible CEO and senior management support for the system are necessary. This ensures that the system is used consistently across the company, appraisals are completed on time, and giving and receiving performance feedback is an accepted part of the company culture.

The first two steps of the performance management process involve identifying what the company is trying to accomplish (goals or objectives) and a set of key performance dimensions that represent critical factors or drivers that influence the goals or objectives, and then developing performance measures for the key performance dimensions.[6] The first step in the performance management process starts with understanding and identifying important performance outcomes or results. Typically, these outcomes or results benefit customers, the employee's peers or team, and the organization itself. The company's and department's or team's strategy, mission, and values play an important part in determining these outcomes. Chapter 2 pointed out that most companies pursue some type of strategy to reach revenue, profit, and market share goals. Divisions, departments, teams, and employees must align their goals and behaviors, and choose to engage in activities that help achieve the organization's strategy and goals. The second step of the process involves understanding the process (or how) to achieve the goals established in the first step. This includes identifying measurable goals, behaviors, and activities that will help employees achieve the performance results. The goals, behaviors, and activities should be measurable so that the manager and the employee can determine if they have been achieved. The goals, activities, and behaviors should be part of the employee's job description.

The third step in the process, organizational support, involves providing employees with training, necessary resources and tools, and frequent feedback communication between employees and managers focusing on accomplishments as well as issues and challenges influencing performance. For effective performance management, managers and employees have to value feedback and regularly exchange it. Managers need to make time to provide feedback as well as train in how to give and receive it. The fourth step

Figure 8.1

Model of the Effective Performance Management Process

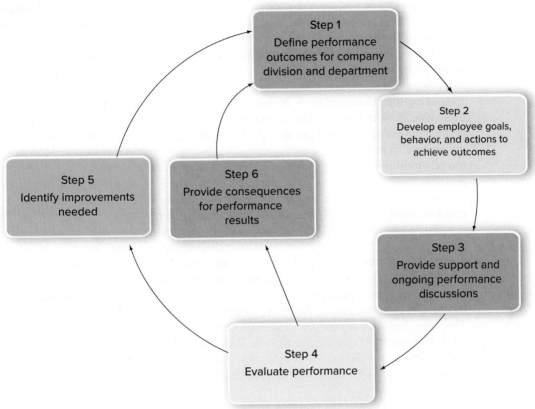

SOURCES: Based on E. Pulakos, R. Hanson, S. Arad, and N. Moye, "Performance Management Can Be Fixed: An On-the-Job Experiential Learning Approach for Complex Behavior Change," *Industrial and Organizational Psychology*, March 2015, pp. 51–76; E. Pulakos, R. Mueller-Hanson, R. O'Leary, and M. Meyrowitz, *Building a High-Performance Culture: A Fresh Look at Performance Management* (Alexandria, VA: SHRM Foundation, 2012); H. Aguinis, "An Expanded View of Performance Management," in J. W. Smith and M. London (eds.), *Performance Management* (San Francisco: Jossey-Bass, 2009), pp. 1–43; J. Russell and L. Russell, "Talk Me through It: The Next Level of Performance Management," *T + D,* April 2010, pp. 42–48.

involves performance evaluation, that is, when the manager and the employee discuss and compare the targeted performance goals and supporting behaviors with the actual results. This typically involves the annual or biannual formal performance review. As we will see later in the chapter, there are many ways to help make this formal review more of a performance conversation designed to identify and discuss opportunities to improve and less of a one-way evaluation by the manager. One way to make the formal evaluation more effective is for managers to engage in frequent performance conversations with employees rather than wait for the formal annual review.

The final steps of the performance management cycle involve the employee and the manager identifying what the employee (with help from the manager) can do to capitalize on performance strengths and address weaknesses (step 5) and providing consequences for achieving (or failing to achieve) performance outcomes (step 6). This includes identifying training needs; adjusting the type or frequency of feedback the manager provides to the employee; clarifying, adjusting, or modifying performance outcomes; and discussing behaviors or activities that need improvement or relate to new priorities based on changes or new areas of emphasis in organizational or department goals. Achieving performance results may relate to compensation (salary increases, cash bonuses), recognition, promotion, development opportunities, and continued employment. This depends on the purposes the company decides on for the performance management system (see the section "Purposes of Performance Management").

What employees accomplish (or fail to accomplish) and the consequences of those accomplishments (or lack thereof) help shape changes in the organizational business strategy and performance goals and the ongoing performance management process. Evaluating the effectiveness of the performance management system is necessary to determine needed changes. This could include gathering comments about managers' and employees' concerns about the system, analyzing rating data to determine if they are being affected by rating errors, reviewing objectives for their quality, and studying the relationship between employees meeting objectives and department and organizational results.

For example, Procter & Gamble changed its performance management approach to make it more of an ongoing process emphasizing performance conversations and employee development.[7] There are four phases in the performance management process. The first phase, Prioritize, focuses on setting challenging and achieving goals based on the employees' most meaningful work. The next phase, Evaluation, involves managers and employees discussing what and how results were achieved during the year. In the third phase, Assess, managers consider employees' growth potential. The final stage, Know and Grow, emphasizes discussing and determining employees' development plans. The conversations that managers and employees need to have are critical for the success of performance management. As a result, Procter & Gamble developed coaching videos and workshops to help managers learn how to conduct effective performance conversations and serve as coaches to help employees develop.

Purposes of Performance Management

LO 8-2
Discuss the three general purposes of performance management.

The purposes of performance management systems are of three kinds: strategic, administrative, and developmental.

STRATEGIC PURPOSE

First and foremost, a performance management system should link employee activities with the organization's goals. One of the primary ways strategies are implemented is through defining the results, behaviors, and, to some extent, employee characteristics that are necessary for carrying out those strategies, and then developing measurement and feedback systems that will maximize the extent to which employees exhibit the characteristics, engage in the behaviors, and produce the results.

Performance management is critical for companies to execute their talent management strategy, that is, to identify employees' strengths and weaknesses, drive employee engagement, link employees to appropriate training and development activity, and reward good performance with pay and other incentives. Also, performance management practices can relate positively to companies' financial success.[8] For example, among business executives who believe their companies are excellent or very good at performance management, 76% of their companies experienced a revenue increase. In contrast, 30% of companies that were less effective in performance management experienced a decline in revenues, and 20% performed more poorly than their competitors.

ADMINISTRATIVE PURPOSE

Organizations use performance management information (performance appraisals, in particular) in many administrative decisions: salary administration (pay raises), promotions, retention–termination, layoffs, and recognition of individual performance.[9] Despite the importance of these decisions, however, many managers, who are the source of the information, see the performance appraisal process only as a necessary evil they must go through to fulfill their job requirements. They feel uncomfortable evaluating others and feeding those evaluations back to the employees. Thus, they tend to rate everyone high or at least rate them the same, making the performance appraisal information relatively useless. For example, one manager stated, "There is really no getting around the fact that whenever I evaluate one of my people, I stop and think about the impact—the ramifications of my decisions on my relationship with the guy and his future here. . . . Call it being politically minded, or using managerial discretion, or fine-tuning the guy's ratings, but in the end, I've got to live with him, and I'm not going to rate a guy without thinking about the fallout."[10]

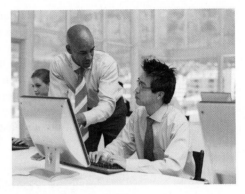

©Stockbyte/Getty images RF

Performance management is critical for executing a talent management system and involves one-on-one contact with managers to ensure that proper training and development are taking place.

DEVELOPMENTAL PURPOSE

A third purpose of performance management is to develop employees. When employees are not performing as well as they should, performance management seeks to improve their performance. The feedback given during a performance evaluation process often pinpoints the employee's weaknesses. Ideally, however, the performance management system identifies not only any deficient aspects of the employee's performance but also the causes of these deficiencies—for example, a skill deficiency, a motivational problem, or some obstacle holding the employee back.

Managers are often uncomfortable confronting employees with their performance weaknesses. Such confrontations, although necessary to the effectiveness of the work group, often strain everyday working relationships. Giving high ratings to all employees enables a manager to minimize such conflicts, but then the developmental purpose of the performance management system is not fully achieved.[11] Development doesn't just focus on poor performers. Development also involves helping good performers get the training and other opportunities they need to enhance their skill set and advance their careers.

Texas Roadhouse revamped the performance management system for 500 employees at the company's corporate headquarters.[12] Under the previous system, managers were having a hard time understanding the meaning of an overall rating of three on a five-point scale. For some managers a "three" meant that an employee was doing a good job, while for others it meant that the employee was merely "average." The new system eliminated the rating and replaced it with a process called GPS, which stands for growth, plan, and support. The objective of GPS is to encourage managers to have frequent performance conversations with employees and for employees to take more responsibility for their performance and development. A month before the anniversary of their hiring date, employees are reminded to have GPS meetings with their managers to discuss their career goals and the resources they need to perform successfully. HR provides a discussion guide to help managers and employees have an effective conversation. Also, in the old performance management system, managers tended to spend more time working with poor performers, who represented less than 10% of employees. GPS emphasizes the need to spend similar amounts of time in performance conversations with good and high-performing employees. This means more frequent meetings with employees who need to improve but also having discussions with high performers, the top talent in the company, about how training and development opportunities can help them further develop their skills and reach their career goals.

An important step in performance management is to develop the measures by which performance will be evaluated. We next discuss the issues involved in developing and using different measures of performance.

Performance Measures Criteria

In Chapter 4 we discussed how, through job analysis, one can analyze a job to determine exactly what constitutes effective performance. Once the company has determined, through job analysis and design, what kind of performance it expects from its employees, it needs to develop ways to measure that performance. This section presents the criteria underlying job performance measures. Later sections discuss approaches to performance measurement, sources of information, and errors.

Although people differ about criteria to use to evaluate performance management systems, we believe that five stand out: strategic congruence, validity, reliability, acceptability, and specificity.

STRATEGIC CONGRUENCE

Strategic congruence
The extent to which the performance management system elicits job performance that is consistent with the organization's strategy, goals, and culture.

Strategic congruence is the extent to which a performance management system elicits job performance that is congruent with the organization's strategy, goals, and culture. If a company emphasizes customer service, then its performance management system should assess how well its employees are serving the company's customers. Strategic congruence emphasizes the need for the performance management system to guide employees in contributing to the organization's success. This requires systems flexible enough to adapt to changes in the company's strategic posture. The "Competing through Globalization" box shows the important role of performance management in developing a global business.

Many companies use critical success factors (CSFs) or key performance indicators (KPIs) in their performance management systems.[13] CSFs are factors in a company's business strategy that give it a competitive edge. Companies measure employee behavior that relates to attainment of CSFs, which increases the importance of these behaviors for employees. Employees can be held accountable and rewarded for behaviors that directly relate to the company attaining the CSFs.

Brinker International Inc., known for Chili's restaurants, used to have 40 KPIs, but employees were confused about what performance outcomes were expected. Brinker reduced the number of KPIs from 40 to 4. The focus on a smaller number of KPIs helped motivate and focus employees, resulting in a return of 20% to shareholders, lowered turnover, and increased employee engagement survey scores.

One challenge that companies face is how to measure customer loyalty, employee satisfaction, and other nonfinancial performance areas that affect profitability. To effectively use nonfinancial performance measures managers need to do the following:[14]

- Develop a model of how nonfinancial performance measures link to the company's strategic goals. Identify the performance areas that are critical to success.

Timely and Future-Focused Feedback Helps Ensure Travel Customers Are Satisfied around the World

Expedia Inc. is an online travel company with more than 200 travel websites in over 75 countries. Expedia wanted employees to receive more ongoing real-time feedback, which they could use to change their performance, rather than limiting performance conversations to the past-focused feedback they received during their formal performance review. As a result, Expedia eliminated performance ratings and instead changed the emphasis to providing employees with ongoing feedback.

The new emphasis in Expedia's Passport to Performance performance management program meant that managers were required to have weekly or at least biweekly conversations with employees that were focused on their performance, development, and career path along with completing a formal midyear review. For this shift in focus to be effective, managers needed

training on how to provide feedback in specific, behavior-based language that employees could understand. Expedia's training consisted of providing managers with an overview of the new performance management system, helping them understand how to give feedback, and understanding the link between performance conversations and compensation decisions. Expedia also provided training for employees so that they understood the new performance management system and how they could use it to benefit their development and career. For example, in the training focused on how to provide feedback, managers were told to stop using adjectives such as "be proactive" and instead use verbs to describe the behavior they wanted to see in employees such as "thinking through what could happen and planning before something becomes an emergency." Effective performance was now

based on business goals and desired behaviors.

Both managers and employees feel the new performance management system is an improvement. For example, an employee survey found that over 40% reported that it had more focus on performance strengths and areas for improvement, 70% believed it had a good discussion of future-focused topics including business results and behaviors, and 61% felt the program improved how Expedia manages performance.

DISCUSSION QUESTION

1. One of the criteria used to evaluate a performance management system is development. How would you evaluate Expedia's Passport to Performance program according to this criterion? Explain your evaluation.

SOURCES: Based on "No Performance Ratings," www.lifeatexpedia.com; K. Kuehner-Hubert, "Passport to Performance," *Chief Learning Officer,* July 2013, pp. 42–47; J. Ramirez, "Rethinking the Review," *Human Resource Executive,* July/August 2013, pp. 16–19.

- Using already existing databases, identify data that exist on key performance measures (e.g., customer satisfaction, employee satisfaction surveys). If data are not available, identify a performance area that affects the company's strategy and performance. Develop measures for those performance areas.
- Use statistical and qualitative methods for testing the relationship between the performance measures and financial outcomes. Regression and correlation analysis as well as focus groups and interviews can be used. For example, studies show that employees' involvement, satisfaction, and enthusiasm for work are significantly related to business performance, including customer satisfaction, productivity, and profitability.[15]
- Revisit the model to ensure that the nonfinancial performance measures are appropriate and determine whether new measures should be added. This is important to understand the drivers of financial performance and to ensure that the model is appropriate as the business strategy and economic conditions change.

- Act on conclusions that the model demonstrates. For example, Sears found that employee attitudes about the supervision they received and the work environment had a significant impact on customer satisfaction and shareholder results. As a result, Sears invested in managerial training to help managers do a better job of holding employees accountable for their jobs while giving them autonomy to perform their roles.[16]
- Audit whether the actions taken and the investments made produced the desired result.

Most companies' appraisal systems remain constant over a long time and through a variety of strategic emphases. However, when a company's strategy changes, its employees' behavior needs to change, too.[17] The fact that appraisal systems often do not change may account for why many managers see performance appraisal systems as having little impact on a firm's effectiveness.

VALIDITY

Validity

The extent to which a performance measure assesses all the relevant—and only the relevant—aspects of job performance.

Validity is the extent to which a performance measure assesses all the relevant—and only the relevant—aspects of performance. This is often referred to as *content validity*. For a performance measure to be valid, it must not be deficient or contaminated. As you can see in Figure 8.2, one of the circles represents "true" job performance—all the aspects of performance relevant to success in the job. On the other hand, companies must use some measure of performance, such as a supervisory rating of performance on a set of dimensions or measures of the objective results on the job. Validity is concerned with maximizing the overlap between actual job performance and the measure of job performance (the green portion in the figure).

A performance measure is deficient if it does not measure all aspects of performance (the brown portion in the figure). An example is a system at a large university that assesses faculty members based more on research than teaching, thereby relatively ignoring a relevant aspect of performance.

A contaminated measure evaluates irrelevant aspects of performance or aspects that are not job related (the gold portion in the figure). The performance measure should seek to minimize contamination, but its complete elimination is seldom possible. An example of a contaminated measure is the use of actual sales figures for evaluating salespeople across very different regional territories. Often sales are highly dependent upon the territory (number of potential customers, number of competitors, economic conditions) rather than the actual performance of the salesperson. A salesperson who works harder and better than others might not have the highest sales totals because the territory simply does not have as much sales potential as others. Thus, these figures alone would be a measure that is strongly affected by things beyond the control of the individual employee.

Figure 8.2

Contamination and Deficiency of a Job Performance Measure

Job performance measure

Actual, or "true," job performance

Contamination   Validity   Deficiency

RELIABILITY

Reliability refers to the consistency of a performance measure. One important type of reliability is *interrater reliability:* the consistency among the individuals who evaluate the employee's performance. A performance measure has interrater reliability if two individuals give the same (or close to the same) evaluations of a person's job performance. Evidence seems to indicate that most subjective supervisory measures of job performance exhibit low reliability.[18] With some measures, the extent to which all the items rated are internally consistent is important (*internal consistency reliability*).

In addition, the measure should be reliable over time (*test–retest reliability*). A measure that results in drastically different ratings depending on when the measures are taken lacks test–retest reliability. For example, if salespeople are evaluated based on their actual sales volume during a given month, it would be important to consider their consistency of monthly sales across time. What if an evaluator in a department store examined sales only during May? Employees in the lawn and garden department would have high sales volumes, but those in the men's clothing department would have somewhat low sales volumes. Clothing sales in May are traditionally lower than in other months. One needs to measure performance consistently across time.

Reliability
The consistency of a performance measure; the degree to which a performance measure is free from random error.

ACCEPTABILITY

Acceptability refers to whether the people who use a performance measure accept it. Many elaborate performance measures are extremely valid and reliable, but they consume so much of managers' time that they refuse to use it. Alternatively, those being evaluated by a measure may not accept it.

Acceptability is affected by the extent to which employees believe the performance management system is fair. As Table 8.2 shows, there are three categories of perceived fairness: procedural, interpersonal, and outcome fairness. The table also shows specifically

Acceptability
The extent to which a performance measure is deemed to be satisfactory or adequate by those who use it.

FAIRNESS CATEGORY	IMPORTANCE FOR PERFORMANCE MANAGEMENT SYSTEM	IMPLICATIONS
Procedural fairness	Development	• Give managers and employees opportunity to participate in development of system • Ensure consistent standards when evaluating different employees • Minimize rating errors and biases
Interpersonal fairness	Use	• Give timely and complete feedback • Allow employees to challenge the evaluation • Provide feedback in an atmosphere of respect and courtesy
Outcome fairness	Outcomes	• Communicate expectations regarding performance evaluations and standards • Communicate expectations regarding rewards

Table 8.2
Categories of Perceived Fairness and Implications for Performance Management Systems

SOURCE: Adapted from S. W. Gilliland and J. C. Langdon, "Creating Performance Management Systems That Promote Perceptions of Fairness," in *Performance Appraisal: State of the Art in Practice,* ed. J. W. Smither. Copyright © 1998 by Jossey-Bass, Inc. This material is used by permission of John Wiley & Sons, Inc.

how the performance management system's development, use, and outcomes affect perceptions of fairness. In developing and using a performance management system, managers should take the steps shown in the column labeled "Implications" in Table 8.2 to ensure that the system is perceived as fair. Research suggests that performance management systems that are perceived as unfair are likely to be legally challenged, be used incorrectly, and decrease employee motivation to improve.[19]

SPECIFICITY

Specificity
The extent to which a performance measure gives detailed guidance to employees about what is expected of them and how they can meet these expectations.

Specificity is the extent to which a performance measure tells employees what is expected of them and how they can meet these expectations. Specificity is relevant to both the strategic and developmental purposes of performance management. If a measure does not specify what an employee must do to help the company achieve its strategic goals, then it does not achieve its strategic purpose. Additionally, if the measure fails to point out employees' performance problems, it is almost impossible for the employees to correct their performance.

Deloitte's performance management system for its project teams meets most of the criteria for a good performance management system.[20] Deloitte's goals are to recognize, observe, and motivate performance through the annual compensation decision, the project performance snapshot, and the weekly performance conversations. Deloitte's client needs tend to involve both short- and long-term projects that are too complex for any one employee to have the expertise needed to carry them out. So to meet its clients' needs Deloitte relies on employee teams. These teams include a team leader and employees who each bring a different skill set. To evaluate each team member's performance Deloitte asks team leaders to answer four questions. These questions ask if the leader would award the person the highest possible compensation increase and bonus (measures overall performance and unique value to the organization), always want them on their team (measures ability to work well with others), and if the person is a risk for low performance (identifies problems that might harm the customer), and is ready for promotion today (measures potential). These four questions each represent a specific performance dimension (pay, teamwork, poor performance, promotion) that is relevant to Deloitte's project teams. The team leaders were chosen as the raters because they were in the best position to see the performance of team members and in their role must make subjective judgments. The questions were used after they were tested to see if they differentiated ineffective from effective team members and were correlated with other performance outcomes measured in other ways such as engagement surveys.

For short-term projects, team member evaluations occur at the end of each project, and longer-term project evaluations occur quarterly. To ensure that the evaluations are driving team performance and are accepted by team members, every team leader has to check in with each team member once each week. During these conversations team leaders discuss expectations, review priorities, and provide feedback on recent work. Team members are encouraged to initiate check-ins because team leaders may otherwise forget to have the discussions because they have many demands on their time. Once each quarter, Deloitte's business leaders use the evaluations to review a group of employees, such as those with critical skills or who are eligible for promotion, to discuss the actions that need to be taken to develop that group. The questions provide input into compensation decisions made at the end of the year by business leaders who also consider the difficulty of project assignments and other contributions team members have made to Deloitte.

Approaches to Measuring Performance

An important part of effective performance management is establishing how we evaluate performance. This is difficult to do because performance is complex—it includes how employees perform their individual work tasks as well as contribute to teams and behave in ways that support their peers and the company.[21] What is considered effective performance and when and how it is measured likely varies across positions. For example, in sales positions, results such as number of sales might be more important than behaviors, whereas the opposite may be true in management positions. In this section, we explore different ways to evaluate performance: the comparative approach, the attribute approach, the behavioral approach, the results approach, and the quality approach. We also evaluate these approaches against the criteria of strategic congruence, validity, reliability, acceptability, and specificity. As you will see, all of these approaches have strengths and weaknesses. As a result, many companies' performance evaluations use a combination of approaches.

LO 8-4
Discuss the five approaches to performance management, the specific techniques used in each approach, and the way these approaches compare with the criteria for effective performance management systems.

There is no one best approach to measuring performance. But to effectively contribute to organizational business strategy and goals and motivate employees, effective performance evaluation systems should measure both what gets accomplished (objectives) and how it gets accomplished (behaviors). Regardless of the approach used, the key is to provide employees with accurate and timely feedback about their performance, emphasize frequent performance discussions between managers and employees rather than one-way manager-led conversations, and simplify appraisal forms, For example, Gables Residential has found that encouraging managers and employees to have informal performance conversations (rather than manager-driven one-way communications about performance) throughout the year in combination with an annual formal performance review improves employee engagement and development.[22] Gables changed its appraisal form so that it focuses more on highlighting employees' achievements and development needs and less on evaluating past performance. The form is used in the annual formal performance review to facilitate performance discussions and to encourage managers to coach employees on how to better capitalize on their strengths. Employees are also encouraged to ask their managers to help them develop in areas they want they to improve.

Figure 8.3 shows an example of a performance management system that evaluates behavior and results. The results (project development) are linked to the goals of the business. The performance standards include behaviors that the employee must demonstrate to reach the results. The system provides feedback to the employee and holds both the employee and the manager accountable for changing behavior.

THE COMPARATIVE APPROACH

The comparative approach to performance measurement requires the rater to compare an individual's performance with that of others. This approach usually uses some overall assessment of an individual's performance or worth and seeks to develop some ranking of the individuals within a work group. At least three techniques fall under the comparative approach: ranking, forced distribution, and paired comparison.

Ranking

Simple ranking requires managers to rank employees within their departments from highest performer to poorest performer (or best to worst). *Alternation ranking*, by contrast, consists of a manager looking at a list of employees, deciding who is the best employee, and crossing that person's name off the list. From the remaining names, the manager decides who the worst employee is and crosses that name off the list—and so forth.

Figure 8.3

Example of a Performance Management System That Includes Behavior and Results

Accountabilities and Key Results	Performance Standards	Interim Feedback	Actual Results	Performance Rating	Areas for Development	Action
Key result areas that the employee will accomplish during the review period. Should align with company values, business goals, and job description.	How the key result area will be measured (quality, cost, quantity). Focus on work methods and accomplishments.	Employee and manager discuss performance on an ongoing basis.	Review actual performance for each key result.	Evaluate performance on each key result. 1 = Outstanding 2 = Highly effective 3 = Acceptable 4 = Unsatisfactory	Specific knowledge, skills, and behaviors to be developed that will help employee achieve key results.	What employee and manager will do to address development needs.
Project Development Manage the development of project scope, cost estimate studies, and schedules for approval.	Develop preliminary project material for approval within four weeks after receiving project scope. Eighty percent of new projects receive approval. Initial cost estimates are within 5% of final estimates.	Preliminary project materials are developed on time.	By end of year, approvals were at 75%, 5% less than standard.	3	Increase knowledge of project management software.	Read articles, research, and meet with software vendors.

Ranking has received specific attention in the courts. As discussed in Chapter 3, in the *Albemarle v. Moody* case, the validation of the selection system was conducted using employee rankings as the measure of performance. The Court stated, "There is no way of knowing precisely what criteria of job performance that supervisors were considering, whether each supervisor was considering the same criteria—or whether, indeed, any of the supervisors actually applied a focused and stable body of criteria of any kind."[23]

Forced Distribution

The *forced distribution* method also uses a ranking format, but employees are ranked in groups. This technique requires the manager to put certain percentages of employees into predetermined categories. Most commonly, employees are grouped into three, four, or five categories, usually of unequal size, indicating the best workers, the worst workers, and one or more categories in between. The insurance company American International Group (AIG) uses a forced distribution system in which AIG employees are ranked on a scale from 1 to 4.[24] Based on this system, only 10% of employees receive the top ranking of "1," 20% of employees receive a ranking of "2," 50% of employees receive a ranking of "3," and 20% receive the lowest ranking of "4." Employees with higher rankings receive much more year-end incentive pay such as bonuses than those with lower rankings (employees ranked in the top 10% will get much greater bonuses compared to their peers). The CEO advocated the implementation of the forced distribution system to ensure that the company is paying the best people for their performance and to better differentiate poor from high performers. The company had previously used ranking systems but found that over half of employees were evaluated as high performers.

Advocates of these systems say that they are the best way to identify high-potential employees who should be given training, promotions, and financial rewards and to identify the poorest performers who should be helped or asked to leave. Top-level managers at many companies have observed that despite corporate performance and return to shareholders being flat or decreasing, compensation costs have continued to spiral upward and performance ratings continue to be high. They question how there can be such a disconnect between corporate performance and employees' evaluations and compensation. Forced distribution systems provide a mechanism to help align company performance and employee performance and compensation. Employees in the bottom 10% cause performance standards to be lowered, influence good employees to leave, and keep good employees from joining the company.

A forced distribution system helps managers tailor development activities to employees based on their performance. For example, as shown in Table 8.3, poor performers are given specific feedback about what they need to improve in their job and a timetable is set for their improvement. If they do not improve their performance, they are dismissed. Top performers are encouraged to participate in development activities such as job experiences, mentoring, and completion of leadership programs, which will help prepare them for top management positions. The use of a forced distribution system is seen as a way for companies to increase performance, motivate employees, and open the door for new talent to join the company to replace poor performers.[25]

Advocates say these systems force managers to make hard decisions about employee performance based on job-related criteria, rather than to be lenient in evaluating employees. Critics, by contrast, say the systems in practice are arbitrary, erroneously assume that employees' performance can be best summarized by a normal distribution, may be illegal, and cause poor morale.[26] For example, one work group might have 20% poor performers while another might have only high performers, but the process mandates that 10% of

Table 8.3
Performance and
Development Based
on Forced
Distribution and
Ranking

RANKING OR DISTRIBUTION CATEGORY	PERFORMANCE AND DEVELOPMENT PLAN
A Above average Exceptional A1 performer	• Accelerate development through challenging job assignments • Provide mentor from leadership team • Recognize and reward contributions • Praise employee for strengths • Consider leadership potential • Nominate for leadership development programs
B Average Meets expectations Steady performer	• Offer feedback on how B can become a high performer • Encourage development of strengths and improvement of weaknesses • Recognize and reward employee contributions • Consider enlarging job
C Below expectations Poor performance	• Give feedback and agree upon what specific skills, behavior, and/or results need to be improved, with timetable for accomplishment • Move to job that better matches skills • Ask to leave the company

SOURCES: Based on B. Axelrod, H. Handfield-Jones, and E. Michaels, "A New Game Plan for C Players," *HBR*, January 2002, pp. 80–88; A. Walker, "Is Performance Management as Simple as ABC?" *T + D*, February 2007, pp. 54–57; T. De Long and V. Vijayaraghavan, "Let's Hear It for B Players," *HBR*, June 2003, pp. 96–102.

employees be eliminated from both groups. Also, in many forced distribution systems, an unintended consequence is that the bottom category tends to consist of minorities, women, and people over 40 years of age, causing discrimination lawsuits (we discuss legal issues affecting performance management later in the chapter). Finally, it is difficult to rank employees into distinctive categories when criteria are subjective or when it is difficult to differentiate employees on the criteria (such as teamwork or communications skills).

Research simulating different features of a forced system and other factors that influence company performance (e.g., voluntary turnover rate, validity of selection methods) suggests that forced distribution rating systems can improve the potential performance of a company's workforce.[27] The majority of improvement appears to occur during the first several years the system is used, mainly because of the large number of poorly performing employees who are identified and fired. Forced ranking is ethical as long as the system is clearly communicated, the system is part of a positive dimension of the organization's culture (innovation, continuous improvement), and the employees have the chance to appeal decisions.

Despite the potential advantages of forced choice systems, the potential negative side effects on morale, teamwork, recruiting, and shareholder perceptions should be considered before adopting such a system. Many companies are emphasizing the linkage between employees' performance and their development plan without using a forced distribution or ranking system. For example, Microsoft is no longer requiring its managers to evaluate its employees against one another and rank them on a scale from 1 to 5.[28] The system was abandoned because many employees complained that it resulted in unfair rankings, power struggles between managers over which of their employees could receive the more favorable rankings, and aggressive competition between employees. Also, the system was inconsistent with Microsoft's strategic emphasis on teamwork.

Paired Comparison

The *paired comparison* method requires managers to compare every employee with every other employee in the work group, giving an employee a score of 1 every time he or she is considered the higher performer. Once all the pairs have been compared, the manager computes the number of times each employee received the favorable decision (i.e., counts up the points), and this becomes the employee's performance score.

The paired comparison method tends to be time consuming for managers and will become more so as organizations become flatter with an increased span of control. For example, a manager with 10 employees must make 45 ($10 \times {}^9/_2$) comparisons. However, if the group increases to 15 employees, 105 comparisons must be made.

Evaluating the Comparative Approach

The comparative approach to performance measurement is an effective tool in differentiating employee performance; it virtually eliminates problems of leniency, central tendency, and strictness. This is especially valuable if the results of the measures are to be used in making administrative decisions such as pay raises and promotions. In addition, such systems are relatively easy to develop and in most cases easy to use; thus, they are often accepted by users.

One problem with these techniques, however, is their common failure to be linked to the strategic goals of the organization. Although raters can evaluate the extent to which individuals' performances support the strategy, this link is seldom made explicit. In addition, because of the subjective nature of the ratings, their validity and reliability depend on the raters themselves. Some firms use multiple evaluators to reduce the biases of any individual, but most do not. At best, we could conclude that their validity and reliability are modest.

These techniques lack specificity for feedback purposes. Based only on their relative rankings, individuals are completely unaware of what they must do differently to improve their ranking. This puts a heavy burden on the manager to provide specific feedback beyond that of the rating instrument itself. Finally, many employees and managers are less likely to accept evaluations based on comparative approaches. Evaluations depend on how employees' performance relates to that of other employees in a group, team, or department (normative standard) rather than on absolute standards of excellent, good, fair, and poor performance.

THE ATTRIBUTE APPROACH

The attribute approach to performance management focuses on the extent to which individuals have certain attributes (characteristics or traits) believed desirable for the company's success. The techniques that use this approach define a set of traits—such as initiative, leadership, and competitiveness—and evaluate individuals on them.

Graphic Rating Scales

The most common form that the attribute approach to performance management takes is the *graphic rating scale*. Table 8.4 shows a graphic rating scale used in a manufacturing company. As you can see, a list of traits is evaluated by a five-point (or some other number of points) rating scale. The manager considers one employee at a time, circling the number that signifies how much of that trait the individual has. Graphic rating scales can provide a number of different points (a discrete scale) or a continuum along which the rater simply places a check mark (a continuous scale).

Table 8.4
Example of a Graphic Rating Scale

The following areas of performance are significant to most positions. Indicate your assessment of performance on each dimension by circling the appropriate rating.

PERFORMANCE DIMENSION	RATING				
	DISTINGUISHED	EXCELLENT	COMMENDABLE	ADEQUATE	POOR
Knowledge	5	4	3	2	1
Communication	5	4	3	2	1
Judgment	5	4	3	2	1
Managerial skill	5	4	3	2	1
Quality performance	5	4	3	2	1
Teamwork	5	4	3	2	1
Interpersonal skills	5	4	3	2	1
Initiative	5	4	3	2	1
Creativity	5	4	3	2	1
Problem solving	5	4	3	2	1

Mixed-Standard Scales

Mixed-standard scales were developed to get around some of the problems with graphic rating scales. To create a mixed-standard scale, we define the relevant performance dimensions and then develop statements representing good, average, and poor performance along each dimension. These statements are then mixed with the statements from other dimensions on the actual rating instrument. An example of a mixed-standard scale is presented in Table 8.5.

As we see in the table, the rater is asked to complete the rating instrument by indicating whether the employee's performance is above (+), at (0), or below (−) the statement. A special scoring key is then used to score the employee's performance for each dimension. Thus, for example, an employee performing above all three statements receives a 7. If the employee is below the good statement, at the average statement, and above the poor statement, a score of 4 is assessed. An employee below all three statements is given a rating of 1. This scoring is applied to all the dimensions to determine an overall performance score.

Note that mixed-standard scales were originally developed as trait-oriented scales. However, this same technique has been applied to instruments using behavioral rather than trait-oriented statements as a means of reducing rating errors in performance appraisal.[29]

Evaluating the Attribute Approach

Attribute-based performance methods are quite easy to develop and are generalizable across a variety of jobs, strategies, and organizations. In addition, if much attention is devoted to identifying those attributes relevant to job performance and carefully defining them on the rating instrument, they can be as reliable and valid as more elaborate measurement techniques.

Table 8.5
An Example of a
Mixed-Standard
Scale

Three traits being assessed:
  Initiative (INTV)
  Intelligence (INTG)
  Relations with others (RWO)

Levels of performance in statements:
  High (H)
  Medium (M)
  Low (L)

Instructions: Please indicate next to each statement whether the employee's performance is above (+), equal to (0), or below (−) the statement.

INTV	H	1.	This employee is a real self-starter. The employee always takes the initiative and his/her superior never has to prod this individual.	+
INTG	M	2.	While perhaps this employee is not a genius, s/he is a lot more intelligent than many people I know.	+
RWO	L	3.	This employee has a tendency to get into unnecessary conflicts with other people.	0
INTV	M	4.	While generally this employee shows initiative, occasionally his/her superior must prod him/her to complete work.	+
INTG	L	5.	Although this employee is slower than some in understanding things, and may take a bit longer in learning new things, s/he is of average intelligence.	+
RWO	H	6.	This employee is on good terms with everyone. S/he can get along with people even when s/he does not agree with them.	−
INTV	L	7.	This employee has a bit of a tendency to sit around and wait for directions.	+
INTG	H	8.	This employee is extremely intelligent, and s/he learns very rapidly.	−
RWO	M	9.	This employee gets along with most people. Only very occasionally does s/he have conflicts with others on the job, and these are likely to be minor.	−

Scoring Key:

	STATEMENTS			SCORE
	HIGH	MEDIUM	LOW	
	+	+	+	7
	+	+	+	6
	+	+	+	5
	−	0	+	4
	−	−	+	3
	−	−	0	2
	−	−	−	1

Example score from preceding ratings:

	STATEMENTS			SCORE
	HIGH	MEDIUM	LOW	
Initiative	+	+	+	7
Intelligence	0	+	+	6
Relations with others	−	−	0	2

However, these techniques fall short on several of the criteria for effective performance management. There is usually little congruence between the techniques and the company's strategy. These methods are used because of the ease in developing them and because the same method (list of traits, comparisons) is generalizable across any organization and any strategy. In addition, these methods usually have vague performance standards that are open to different interpretations by different raters. Because of this, different raters often provide extremely different ratings and rankings. The result is that both the validity and reliability of these methods are usually low. This can lead to legal challenges. For example, the validity of graphic rating scales was questioned in the *Brito v. Zia* case.[30] In this case, Spanish-speaking employees had been terminated as a result of their performance appraisals. These appraisals consisted of supervisors' rating subordinates on a number of undefined dimensions such as volume of work, quantity of work, job knowledge, dependability, and cooperation. The court criticized the subjective appraisals and stated that the company should have presented empirical data demonstrating that the appraisal was significantly related to actual work behavior.

Virtually none of these techniques provides any specific guidance on how an employee can support the company's goals or correct performance deficiencies. In addition, when raters give feedback, these techniques tend to elicit defensiveness from employees. For example, how would you feel if you were told that on a five-point scale, you were rated a "2" in maturity? Certainly you might feel somewhat defensive and unwilling to accept that judgment, as well as any additional feedback. Also, being told you were rated a "2" in maturity doesn't tell you how to improve your rating.

THE BEHAVIORAL APPROACH

The behavioral approach to performance management attempts to define the behaviors an employee must exhibit to be effective in the job. The various techniques define those behaviors and then require managers to assess the extent to which employees exhibit them. We discuss three techniques that rely on the behavioral approach.

Behaviorally Anchored Rating Scales

A *behaviorally anchored rating scale (BARS)* is designed to specifically define performance dimensions by developing behavioral anchors associated with different levels of performance.[31] An example of a BARS is presented in Figure 8.4. As you can see, the performance dimension has a number of examples of behaviors that indicate specific levels of performance along the dimension.

To develop a BARS, we first gather a large number of critical incidents that represent effective and ineffective performance on the job. These incidents are classified into performance dimensions, and the ones that experts agree clearly represent a particular level of performance are used as behavioral examples (or anchors) to guide the rater. The manager's task is to consider an employee's performance along each dimension and determine where on the dimension the employee's performance fits using the behavioral anchors as guides. This rating becomes the employee's score for that dimension.

Behavioral anchors have advantages and disadvantages. They can increase interrater reliability by providing a precise and complete definition of the performance dimension. A disadvantage is that they can bias information recall—that is, behavior that closely approximates the anchor is more easily recalled than other behavior.[32] Research has also demonstrated that managers and their subordinates do not make much of a distinction between BARS and trait scales.[33]

Figure 8.4
Task-BARS Rating
Dimension: Patrol
Officer

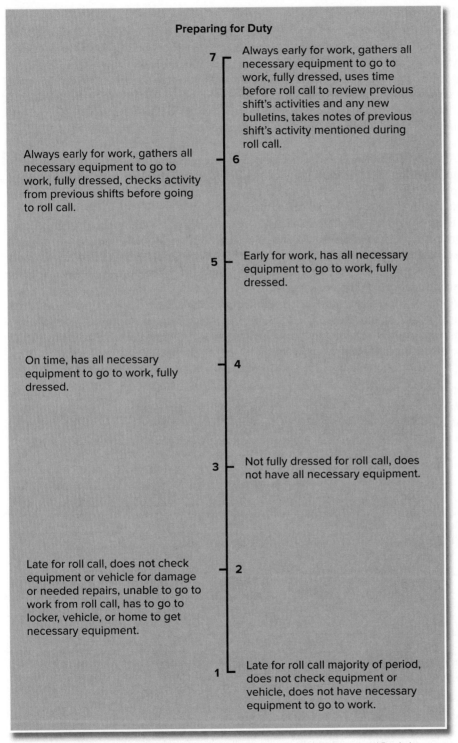

Preparing for Duty

7 — Always early for work, gathers all necessary equipment to go to work, fully dressed, uses time before roll call to review previous shift's activities and any new bulletins, takes notes of previous shift's activity mentioned during roll call.

Always early for work, gathers all necessary equipment to go to work, fully dressed, checks activity from previous shifts before going to roll call.

6 —

5 — Early for work, has all necessary equipment to go to work, fully dressed.

On time, has all necessary equipment to go to work, fully dressed.

4 —

3 — Not fully dressed for roll call, does not have all necessary equipment.

Late for roll call, does not check equipment or vehicle for damage or needed repairs, unable to go to work from roll call, has to go to locker, vehicle, or home to get necessary equipment.

2 —

1 — Late for roll call majority of period, does not check equipment or vehicle, does not have necessary equipment to go to work.

SOURCE: Adapted from R. Harvey, "Job Analysis," in *Handbook of Industrial & Organizational Psychology,* 2nd ed., ed. M. Dunnette and L. Hough (Palo Alto, CA: Consulting Psychologists Press, 1991), p. 138.

Behavioral Observation Scales

A *behavioral observation scale* (*BOS*) is a variation of a BARS. Like a BARS, a BOS is developed from critical incidents.[34] However, a BOS differs from a BARS in two basic ways. First, rather than discarding a large number of the behaviors that exemplify effective or ineffective performance, a BOS uses many of them to more specifically define all the behaviors that are necessary for effective performance (or that would be considered ineffective performance). Instead of using, say, 4 behaviors to define 4 levels of performance on a particular dimension, a BOS may use 15 behaviors. An example of a BOS is presented in Table 8.6.

A second difference is that rather than assessing which behavior best reflects an individual's performance, a BOS requires managers to rate the frequency with which the employee has exhibited each behavior during the rating period. These ratings are then averaged to compute an overall performance rating.

The major drawback of a BOS is that it may require more information than most managers can process or remember. A BOS can have 80 or more behaviors, and the manager must remember how frequently an employee exhibited each of these behaviors over a 6- or 12-month rating period. This is taxing enough for one employee, but managers often must rate 10 or more employees.

A direct comparison of BOS, BARS, and graphic rating scales found that both managers and employees prefer BOS for differentiating good from poor performers, maintaining objectivity, providing feedback, suggesting training needs, and being easy to use among managers and subordinates.[35]

Competency Models

Competencies are sets of skills, knowledge, abilities, and personal characteristics that enable employees to successfully perform their jobs.[36] A **competency model** identifies and provides descriptions of competencies that are common for an entire occupation,

Competencies
Sets of skills, knowledge, and abilities and personal characteristics that enable employees to perform their jobs.

Competency model
Identifies and provides a description of competencies that are common for an entire occupation, organization, job family, or specific job.

Table 8.6
An Example of a Behavioral Observation Scale (BOS) for Evaluating Job Performance

Teamwork						
(1) Works with team members to achieve common goals.						
Almost Never	1	2	3	4	5	Almost Always
(2) Seeks input from team members.						
Almost Never	1	2	3	4	5	Almost Always
(3) Communicates work due date changes to team members.						
Almost Never	1	2	3	4	5	Almost Always
(4) Listens to team members concerns.						
Almost Never	1	2	3	4	5	Almost Always
(5) Participates in team meetings.						
Almost Never	1	2	3	4	5	Almost Always
(6) Helps team members with their work						
Almost Never	1	2	3	4	5	Almost Always

Total = _____

Below Adequate	Adequate	Full	Excellent	Superior
6—10	11—15	16—20	21—25	26—30

Scores are set by management.

organization, job family, or a specific job. Competency models can be used for performance management. However, one of the strengths of competency models is that they are useful for a variety of HR practices including recruiting, selection, training, and development. Competency models can be used to help identify the best employees to fill open positions, and as the foundation for development plans that allow the employee and the manager to target specific strengths and development areas.

Table 8.7 shows the competency model that Luxottica Retail, known for premium, luxury, and sports eyewear sold through LensCrafters, Sunglass Hut, and Pearle Vision, developed for its associates in field and store positions.[37] The competency model includes leadership and managerial, functional, and foundational competencies. The goal was to define and identify competencies that managers could use for hiring, performance management, and training. Also, competencies would help associates identify and develop the skills they need to apply for different jobs.

To effectively use competency models for performance evaluation they must be up-to-date, drive business performance, be job related (valid), be relevant (or customized) for all of the company's business units, and provide sufficient detail to make an accurate assessment of employees' performance. At Luxottica Retail, developing competencies started with meetings with business leaders to understand their current and future business strategies. Business drivers were identified and questionnaires, focus groups, and meetings with managers and associates were used to identify important competencies and examples of behaviors related to each. To ensure they are relevant, competencies across business units and brands are reviewed every four or five years or whenever a major change in jobs or business strategy occurs. Also, the weighting given to each set of competencies in the performance evaluation is reviewed to ensure that they are appropriate (e.g., what weights

Table 8.7
Luxottica Retail's
Competency Model

Leadership and Managerial
Leadership
Coach and develop others
Motivate others
Foster teamwork
Think strategically

Functional
Global perspective
Financial acumen
Business key performance indicators

Foundational
Critical thinking
Foster open communications
Build relationships and interpersonal skills
Develop and manage oneself
Adaptability and flexibility
Customer focus
Act with integrity
Diversity and multiculturalism
Drive and commitment

SOURCE: From C. Spicer, "Building a Competency Model," *HR Magazine*, April 2009, pp. 34–36. Reprinted with permission of Society for Human Resource Management.

should be given to the functional skills). Depending on their relevance for a specific job, various combinations of these competencies are used for evaluating associates' performances. Associates are rated for each competency on a scale from 1 to 5, with "5" meaning the employee far exceeds expectations. HR, training and development, and operations teams worked together to define the levels of each competency, that is, what does it mean and what does the competency look like when an employee is rated "meets expectations" versus "below expectations"? This was necessary to ensure that managers are using a similar frame of reference when they evaluate associates using the competencies.

Evaluation of the Behavioral Approach

The behavioral approach can be very effective. It can link the company's strategy to the specific behavior necessary for implementing that strategy. It provides specific guidance and feedback for employees about the performance expected of them. Most of the techniques rely on in-depth job analysis, so the behaviors that are identified and measured are valid. Because those who will use the system develop the measures, the acceptability is also often high. Finally, with a substantial investment in training raters, the techniques are reasonably reliable.

The major weaknesses have to do with the organizational context of the system. Although the behavioral approach can be closely tied to a company's strategy, the behaviors and measures must be continually monitored and revised to ensure that they are still linked to the strategic focus. This approach also assumes that there is "one best way" to do the job and that the behaviors that constitute this best way can be identified. One study found that managers seek to control behaviors when they perceive a clear relationship between behaviors and results. When this link is not clear, they tend to rely on managing results.[38] The behavioral approach might be best suited to less complex jobs (where the best way to achieve results is somewhat clear) and least suited to complex jobs (where there are multiple ways, or behaviors, to achieve success).

THE RESULTS APPROACH

The results approach focuses on managing the objective, measurable results of a job or work group. This approach assumes that subjectivity can be eliminated from the measurement process and that results are the closest indicator of one's contribution to organizational effectiveness.[39] We examine three performance management systems that use results: the use of objectives, the balanced scorecard, and the productivity measurement and evaluation system.

The Use of Objectives

The use of objectives is popular in both private and public organizations.[40] In a results-based system, the top management team first defines the company's strategic goals for the coming year. These goals are passed on to the next layer of management, and these managers define the goals they must achieve for the company to reach its goals. This goal-setting process cascades down the organization so that all managers set goals that help the company achieve its goals.[41] These goals are used as the standards by which an individual's performance is evaluated.[42]

For example, a company goal might be to increase sales by 6% in the next year. This goal is linked to the sales team goal of achieving $500,000 in new sales. As a result of the team goal, the individual salesperson's goal is to achieve $100,000 in new sales this year, which represents a 10% improvement in sales over the previous year.

KEY RESULT AREA	OBJECTIVE	% COMPLETE	ACTUAL PERFORMANCE
Loan portfolio management	Increase portfolio value by 10% over the next 12 months	90	Increased portfolio value by 9% over the past 12 months
Sales	Generate fee income of $30,000 over the next 12 months	150	Generated fee income of $45,000 over the past 12 months

Table 8.8
An Example of an Objectives Measure of Job Performance

Results-based systems have three common components.[43] They require setting effective goals. The most effective goals are SMART goals. That is, the goals are specific (clearly stated, defining the result to be achieved), measurable (compared to a standard), attainable (difficult but achievable), relevant (linked to organizational success factors or goals), and timely (measured in deadlines, due dates, cycles, or schedules). Different types of measurements can be used for goals or objectives, including timeliness (e.g., responds to requests within 12 hours), quality (report provided clear information with no revisions necessary), quantity (increased sales by 25%), or financial metrics (e.g., reduced purchasing costs by 10%). An example of objectives used in a financial services firm is presented in Table 8.8. Goals are not usually set unilaterally by management but with the managers' and subordinates' participation. And the manager gives objective feedback throughout the rating period to monitor progress toward the goals.

Research on objectives has revealed two important findings regarding their effectiveness.[44] Of 70 studies examined, 68 showed productivity gains, while only 2 showed productivity losses, suggesting that objectives usually increase productivity. Also, productivity gains tend to be highest when there is substantial commitment to the objectives program from top management: an average increase of 56% when commitment was high, 33% when commitment was moderate, and 6% when commitment was low.

Clearly, use of an objectives system can have a positive effect on an organization's performance. Considering the process through which goals are set (involvement of staff in setting objectives), it is also likely that use of an objectives system effectively links individual employee performance with the firm's strategic goals. Evaluation of objectives, based on results or business-based metrics, removes the subjectivity from the evaluation process—employees either meet the objectives or they do not.

Table 8.9 shows how to best use objectives or goals in performance management. Waiting for goals to cascade down from company leaders, to division, function, and their team, takes too much time and employees have a difficult time understanding how their goals are related to company goals (line of sight). As a result, employees should set goals that as much as possible are linked to organizational goals. Goals should be SMART but also meaningful.[45] Rewards and incentives are best for motivating employees to achieve performance goals in jobs in which the results are easily measured and under employees' control. Goals typically focus just on results, not on behaviors, values, or how things get done. If you want employees to behave in certain ways (or avoid behaving in certain ways) in achieving goals, you need to ensure that your performance management system includes evaluation of behaviors. Otherwise, for example, a goal emphasis on sales might cause employees to mislead customers and treat their peers poorly. The "Competing through Sustainability" box shows how the use of objectives can result in undesirable outcomes for a company's stakeholders.

Table 8.9
Best Practices in
Goal Setting

1. Employees and managers should discuss and set no more than three to five goals.
2. Goals should be brief, meaningful, challenging, and include the results the employee is expected to achieve.
3. The time frame for goal achievement should be related to when they are expected to be accomplished.
4. The relationship between goals and rewards should be appropriate.
5. Goals should be "linked up" rather than "cascaded down." This means that functions, teams, and employees should set their own goals that are related to company goals.

SOURCES: Based on R. Hanson and E. Pulakos, *Putting the "Performance" Back in Performance Management* (Alexandria, VA: Society for Human Resource Management, 2015); R. Noe and L. Inks, *It's about People: How Performance Management Helps Middle Market Companies Grow Faster* (Columbus, OH: National Center for the Middle Market, Ohio State University Fisher College of Business, GE Capital, 2014): D. Grote, *How to Be Good at Performance Appraisals* (Boston, MA: Harvard University Press, 2011); A. Fox, "Put Plans into Action," *HR Magazine*, April 2013, pp. 27–31.

Balanced Scorecard

Some companies use the balanced scorecard to measure performance (we discussed the use of the balanced scorecard in Chapter 1). The balanced scorecard includes four perspectives of performance, including financial, customer, internal or operations, and learning and growth (see Table 1.8 in Chapter 1). The financial perspective focuses on creating sustainable growth in shareholder value, the customer perspective defines value for customers (e.g., service, quality), the internal or operations perspective focuses on processes that influence customer satisfaction, and the learning and growth perspective focuses on the company's capacity to innovate and continuously improve. Each of these perspectives is used to translate the business strategy into organizational, managerial, and employee objectives. Employee performance is linked with the business strategy through communicating and educating employees on the elements of the balanced scorecard, translating strategic objectives into measures for departments and employees, and linking rewards to performance measures.[46] Employees need to know the corporate objectives and how they translate into objectives for each business unit, and then develop their own and team objectives that are consistent with the business unit and company objectives. Effective balanced scorecards allow employees to understand the business strategy by looking only at the scorecard and the strategy map (the cause-and-effect relationships among the measures).

For example, for the customer perspective of the balanced scorecard, an airline might have on-time performance as a critical success factor.[47] Gate agents, ground crews, maintenance, and scheduling represent groups of employees who affect on-time performance. Gate agents have four roles that can influence boarding speed including check-in timeliness, effectively dealing with connections, flight documentation, and the boarding process. Gate agents' performance in these four roles should be evaluated because they influence key performance indicators related to on-time performance including cost savings, customer satisfaction, customer losses, and operational costs.

Productivity Measurement and Evaluation System (ProMES)

The main goal of the Productivity Measurement and Evaluation System (ProMES) is to motivate employees to improve team or company-level productivity.[48] It is a means of measuring and feeding back productivity information to employees.

Team members try to map the relationship between specific outcomes and productivity and the relationships between effect and performance, performance and outcomes, and

Wells Fargo: Boosting Sales Damages Stakeholders

Wells Fargo has historically been admired by its customers as a solid financial lender that avoided the problems that plagued other banks during the financial crisis of 2007-2009. But regulators found that employees opened as many as two million deposit and credit card accounts without customers' knowledge. Employees created fake accounts, invented personal identification numbers, and moved funds between customers' accounts without authorization. To make things worse, Wells Fargo terminated employees because they either refused to participate in such aggressive cross-selling practices or reported these activities to the company's ethics hotline or human resources.

The aggressive cross-selling practices were motivated by extremely challenging performance objectives linked to incentives that rewarded employees and their managers for sales of products like checking accounts and credit cards. These objectives were based on Wells Fargo's business model, which depended on selling additional products to its customers who had checking and savings accounts. Many bank branch managers monitored employees' progress toward meeting sales goals hourly, and sales numbers from bank branches were reported to higher-level managers as frequently as seven times each day. Managers asked employees who failed to meet their sales objectives if they could get closer to hitting their goals by opening accounts for their family members or friends. Cross-selling benefits the bank because customers who have more products are not likely to change banks.

As a result of this scandal, Wells Fargo's reputation was tarnished, it likely lost potential customers, senior management and employees responsible were fired, and the company had to pay $185 million in fines. It has since shifted away from objectives and incentives based on cross-selling products to objectives based on customer service, customer usage, and growth in account balances. Mary Mack, the new CEO, is working hard to rebuild customers' trust.

DISCUSSION QUESTION

1. What could Wells Fargo have done in its performance management system that might have prevented the sales objectives from having a negative impact on its key stakeholders?

SOURCES: Based on E. Glazer, "Wells Fargo Shakes Up Retail Unit," *Wall Street Journal*, March 10, 2017, p. B9; E. Glazer, "Wells Revamps Pay after Scandal," *Wall Street Journal*, January 7–8, 2016, pp. B1–B2; E. Glazer, C. Rexrode, and A. Andriotis, "Wells Fargo's Next Job: Fixing Its Mess," *Wall Street Journal*, December 28, 2016, pp. A1, A8; E. Glazer, "Wells Chief Quits under Attack," *Wall Street Journal*, October 13, 2016, pp. A1, A2; E. Glazer, "Customers Continue Pullback from Wells," *Wall Street Journal*, December 17–18, 2016, p. B4; E. Glazer, "Wells Fargo Tripped By Its Sales Culture," *Wall Street Journal*, September 16–17, 2016, pp. A1, A8; A. Beck, "Wells's Questionable Cross-Sales," *Wall Street Journal*, September 10–11, 2016, p. B12.

outcomes relationship to satisfaction of employee needs. ProMES consists of four steps. First, people in an organization identify the products, or the set of activities or objectives, the organization expects to accomplish. The organization's productivity depends on how well it produces these products. At a repair shop, for example, a product might be something like "quality of repair." Second, the staff defines indicators of the products. Indicators are measures of how well the products are being generated by the organization. Quality of repair could be indicated by (1) return rate (percentage of items returned that did not function immediately after repair) and (2) percentage of quality-control inspections passed. Third, the staff establishes the contingencies between the amount of the indicators and the level of evaluation associated with that amount. Fourth, a feedback system is developed that provides employees and work groups with information about their specific level of performance on each of the indicators. An overall productivity score can be computed by summing the effectiveness scores across the various indicators.

Figure 8.5

Increases in Productivity for a Repair Shop Using ProMES Measures

SOURCE: P. Pritchard, S. Jones, P. Roth, K. Stuebing, and S. Ekeberg, "The Evaluation of an Integrated Approach to Measuring Organizational Productivity," *Personnel Psychology,* 42, (1989), pp. 69–115. Used by permission.

Research thus far strongly suggests that ProMES is effective in increasing productivity. (Figure 8.5 illustrates the productivity gains in the repair shop described previously.) The research also suggests the system is an effective feedback mechanism. However, users found it time consuming to develop the initial system.

Evaluation of the Results Approach

The results approach minimizes subjectivity, relying on objective, quantifiable indicators of performance. Thus, it is usually highly acceptable to both managers and employees. Another advantage is that it links an individual's results with the organization's strategies and goals.

However, there are a number of challenges in using objective performance measures. Objective measurements can be both contaminated and deficient—contaminated because they are affected by things that are not under the employee's control and deficient because not all the important aspects of job performance are amenable to objective measurement. For example, consider how an economic recession can influence sales goals or, for a teacher, parental support for studying can influence student's achievement test scores. Another disadvantage is that individuals may focus only on aspects of their performance that are measured, neglecting those that are not. For example, if the large majority of employees' goals relate to productivity, it is unlikely they will be concerned with customer service. One study found that objective performance goals led to higher performance but that they also led to helping co-workers less.[49] It is important to identify if goals should be set at the individual, team, or department level. Setting employees' objectives may not be appropriate if work is team based. Individual objectives may undermine behaviors related to team success such as sharing information and collaboration. A final disadvantage is that, although results measures provide objective feedback, the feedback may not help employees learn how they need to change their behavior to increase their performance. If baseball players are in a hitting slump, simply telling them that their batting average is .190 may not motivate them to raise it. Feedback focusing on the exact behavior that needs to be changed (like taking one's eye off the ball or dropping one's shoulder) would be more helpful.[50]

Kimberly-Clark and Zulily take specific actions to deal with the challenges in using objectives.[51] At Kimberly-Clark, salaried employees use an online tool to set goals and report their progress, record accomplishments or mistakes, and ask for and give feedback to peers or employees at levels above or below them. The online tool collects the feedback, which can be viewed by the employee's manager. It also stores data on employees' strengths, development needs, and performance ratings, and an assessment of their turnover risk. The CEO reviews senior managers' performance plans each year to make sure their goals are challenging and align with the businesses goals. At Zulily, employees can set their own goals and review their managers' and senior leaders' goals every quarter to see what they are focused on, ask questions, and help align their goals with the direction the company is going.

THE QUALITY APPROACH

Thus far we have examined the traditional approaches to measuring and evaluating employee performance. Fundamental characteristics of the quality approach include a customer orientation, a prevention approach to errors, and continous improvement. Improving customer satisfaction is the primary goal of the quality approach. Customers can be internal or external to the organization. A performance management system designed with a strong quality orientation can be expected to do the following:

- Emphasize an assessment of both person and system factors in the measurement system
- Emphasize that managers and employees work together to solve performance problems
- Involve both internal and external customers in setting standards and measuring performance
- Use multiple sources to evaluate person and system factors[52]

Based on this chapter's earlier discussion of the characteristics of an effective performance management system, it should be apparent to you that these characteristics are not just unique to the quality approach but are characteristics of an effective appraisal system.

Advocates of the quality approach believe that most U.S. companies' performance management systems are incompatible with the quality philosophy for a number of reasons:

1. Most existing systems measure performance in terms of quantity, not quality.
2. Employees are held accountable for good or bad results to which they contribute but do not completely control.
3. Companies do not share the financial rewards of successes with employees according to how much they have contributed to them.
4. Rewards are not connected to business results.[53]

Sales, profit margins, and behavioral ratings are often collected by managers to evaluate employees' performance. These are person-based outcomes. An assumption of using these types of outcomes is that the employee completely controls them. However, according to the quality approach, these types of outcomes should not be used to evaluate employees' performance because they do not have complete control over them (i.e., they are contaminated). For example, for salespeople, performance evaluations (and salary increases) are often based on attainment of a sales quota. Salespeople's abilities and motivations are assumed to be directly responsible for their performance. However, quality approach advocates argue that better determinants of whether a salesperson reaches the quota are "systems factors" (such as competitors' product price changes) and economic conditions (which are not under the salesperson's control).[54] Holding employees accountable for outcomes affected by systems factors is believed to result in dysfunctional behavior, such as falsifying sales reports, budgets, expense accounts, and other performance measures, as well as lowering employees' motivation for continuous improvement.

Quality advocates suggest that the major focus of performance evaluations should be to provide employees with feedback about areas in which they can improve. Two types of feedback are necessary: (1) subjective feedback from managers, peers, and customers about the personal qualities of the employee and (2) objective feedback based on the work process itself using statistical process control methods.

At Just Born, the company that makes Peeps and Mike and Ike candy, the performance management process is designed with a strong quality orientation.[55] The performance management system is designed to facilitate employee improvement (a forward-looking approach) rather than focus entirely on what the employee has accomplished during the past year. Also, managers and employees are encouraged to work together to solve performance problems.

The performance management system is part of the company's broader people development system (PDS), which is designed to ensure that learning and development align with business strategy and drive business results while ensuring employees have the skills needed to succeed in their current and future jobs. The PDS includes the performance management process, learning and career development processes, and a succession planning process. Information from each of these systems is shared to ensure that employees are developing the skills needed for their current jobs through training and on-the-job experiences, as well as preparing for their future career interests. Just Born's performance management system starts with a planning meeting between the employee and his or her manager. At this meeting, the employee's role and strategic goals of the department are discussed. The manager and the employee agree on up to four personal objectives that will help the department meet its objectives and the employee achieve the specific deliverables described in the job description. Two competencies that the employee needs to deliver or improve on are identified. The manager and the employee work together to develop a learning plan to help the employee gain the competencies. During the year, the employee and the manager meet to discuss the progress in meeting the deliverables and improving the competencies. Pay decisions made at the end of each fiscal year are based on the achievement of performance objectives and learning goals.

Just Born also uses the Wow . . . Now improvement process, a customized Kaizen process to improve business processes and results. The Wow . . . Now improvement process includes teaching employees how to identify improvement opportunities, collect data, make improvements, measure results, and, based on the results, refine practices. Kaizen, the Japanese word for improvement, is one of the underlying principles of lean manufacturing and total quality management (we discussed lean thinking in Chapter 1). **Kaizen** refers to practices participated in by employees from all levels of the company that focus on continuous improvement of business processes.[56] As the Wow . . . Now improvement process illustrates, Kaizen involves considering a continuous cycle of activities including planning, doing, checking, and acting (PDCA).

Kaizen
Practices participated in by employees from all levels of the company that focus on continuous improvement of business processes.

Statistical process control techniques are important in the quality approach. These techniques provide employees with an objective tool to identify causes of problems and potential solutions. These techniques include process-flow analysis, cause-and-effect diagrams, Pareto charts, control charts, histograms, and scattergrams. *Process-flow analysis* identifies each action and decision necessary to complete work, such as waiting on a customer or assembling a television set. Process-flow analysis is useful for identifying redundancy in processes that increase manufacturing or service time. In *cause-and-effect diagrams*, events or causes that result in undesirable outcomes are identified. Employees try to identify all possible causes of a problem. The feasibility of the causes is not evaluated, and as a result, cause-and-effect diagrams produce a large list of possible causes. A *Pareto chart* highlights the most important cause of a problem. In a Pareto chart, causes are listed in decreasing order of importance, where *importance* is usually defined as the frequency with which that cause resulted in a problem. The assumption of Pareto analysis is that the majority of problems are the result of a small number of causes. Figure 8.6 shows a Pareto chart listing the reasons managers give for not selecting current employees for a job vacancy. *Control charts* involve collecting data at multiple points in time. By collecting data at different times, employees can identify what factors contribute to an outcome and when they tend to occur. Figure 8.7 shows the percentage of employees hired internally for a company for each quarter between 2013 and 2015. Internal hiring increased dramatically during the third quarter of 2014. The use of control charts helps employees understand the number of internal candidates who can be expected to be hired each year. Also, the control chart shows that the amount of internal hiring conducted during the third quarter of 2014 was much larger than normal. *Histograms* display distributions of large sets of data. Data are grouped into a smaller number of categories or classes. Histograms are useful for understanding the amount of variance between an outcome and the expected value or average outcome.

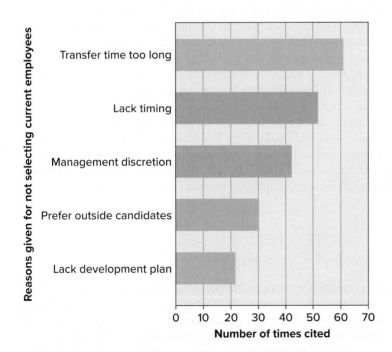

Figure 8.6
Pareto Chart

Figure 8.7
Control Chart

SOURCE: Based on Clara Carter, *HR Magazine.* Copyright 1992.

Scattergrams show the relationship between two variables, events, or different pieces of data. Scattergrams help employees determine whether the relationship between two variables or events is positive, negative, or zero.

Evaluation of the Quality Approach

LO 8-5
Choose the most effective approach to performance measurement for a given situation.

The quality approach relies primarily on a combination of the attribute and results approaches to performance measurement. However, traditional performance appraisal systems focus more on individual employee performance, whereas the quality approach adopts a systems-oriented focus.[57] Many companies may be unwilling to completely abandon their traditional performance management system because it serves as the basis for personnel selection validation, identification of training needs, or compensation decisions. Also, the quality approach advocates evaluation of personal traits (such as cooperation), which are difficult to relate to job performance unless the company has been structured into work teams.

In summary, organizations can take five approaches to measuring performance: comparative, attribute, behavioral, results, and quality. Table 8.10 summarizes the various approaches to measuring performance based on the criteria we set forth earlier and illustrates that each approach has strengths and weaknesses. As a result, effective performance evaluations involve a combination of approaches including assessment of objectives and behaviors.

Choosing a Source for Performance Information

LO 8-6
Discuss the advantages and disadvantages of the different sources of performance information.

Whatever approach to performance management is used, it is necessary to decide whom to use as the source of the performance measures. Each source has specific strengths and weaknesses. We discuss five primary sources: managers, peers, direct reports, self, and customers. Many companies include manager and self-assessment of performance. This helps facilitate a conversation about performance during the appraisal meeting and on a more frequent basis.

Table 8.10
Evaluation of Approaches to Performance Measurement

	CRITERIA				
APPROACH	STRATEGIC CONGRUENCE	VALIDITY	RELIABILITY	ACCEPTABILITY	SPECIFICITY
Comparative	Poor, unless manager takes time to make link	Can be high if ratings are done carefully	Depends on rater, but usually no measure of agreement used	Moderate; easy to develop and use but resistant to normative standard	Very low
Attribute	Usually low; requires manager to make link	Usually low; can be fine if developed carefully	Usually low; can be improved by specific definitions of attributes	High; easy to develop and use	Very low
Behavioral	Can be quite high	Usually high; minimizes contamination and deficiency	Usually high	Moderate; difficult to develop, but accepted well for use	Very high
Results	Very high	Usually high; can be both contaminated and deficient	High; main problem can be test–retest—depends on timing of measure	High; usually developed with input from those to be evaluated	High regarding results, but low regarding behaviors necessary to achieve them
Quality	Very high	High, but can be both contaminated and deficient	High	High; usually developed with input from those to be evaluated	High regarding results, but low regarding behaviors necessary to achieve them

MANAGERS

Managers are the most frequently used source of performance information. It is usually safe to assume that supervisors have extensive knowledge of the job requirements and that they have had adequate opportunity to observe their employees—in other words, that they have the ability to rate their employees. In addition, because supervisors have something to gain from the employees' high performance and something to lose from low performance, they are motivated to make accurate ratings.[58] Finally, feedback from supervisors is strongly related to performance and to employee perceptions of the accuracy of the appraisal if managers attempt to observe employee behavior or discuss performance issues in the feedback session.[59]

Whirpool's performance management system involves setting and aligning goals with the business strategy, providing feedback and engaging in performance conversations, and evaluating progress toward the goals.[60] Whirpool found that its managers were spending too much time on evaluating goal progress, which took time away from aligning goals and providing feedback and having performance conversations, the most important parts of the performance management process. To help managers reallocate their time, Whirpool provided them with coaching and development resources. The "Manager Minute" consisted of videos, blogs, and discussion forums provided by

LO 8-7
Choose the most effective source(s) for performance information for any situation.

Whirlpool's leaders that offered tips, advice, and stories to inspire managers to become great at managing their employees' performance. Seventy-three percent of the managers reported they were using the Manager Minute for advice and were acting on it.

Problems with using supervisors as the source of performance information can occur in particular situations. In some jobs, for example, the supervisor does not have an adequate opportunity to observe the employee performing his job duties. For example, in outside sales jobs, the supervisor does not have the opportunity to see the salesperson at work most of the time. This usually requires that the manager occasionally spend a day accompanying the salesperson on sales calls. However, on those occasions, the employee will be on his or her best behavior, so there is no assurance that performance that day accurately reflects performance when the manager is not around.

Also, some supervisors may be so biased against a particular employee that to use the supervisor as the sole source of information would result in less-than-accurate measures for that individual. Favoritism is a fact of organizational life, but it is one that must be minimized as much as possible in performance management.[61] Thus, the performance evaluation system should seek to minimize the opportunities for favoritism to affect ratings. One way to do this is not to rely on only a supervisor's evaluation of an employee's performance.

PEERS

Another source of performance information is the employee's co-workers. Peers are an excellent source of information in a job such as law enforcement, where the supervisor does not always observe the employee. Peers have expert knowledge of job requirements, and they often have the most opportunity to observe the employee in day-to-day activities. Also, peers are often in the best position to praise and recognize each other's performance on a daily basis. Peer evaluations can be even more motivating than managers' evaluations because, unlike managers, peers are not expected to provide feedback.

For example, at Etsy, employees can request feedback from their peers and direct reports.[62] Feedback providers can choose to give their comments anonymously, and feedback receivers have the choice to seek training or coaching from an HR business partner or manager. Technology has made it easier for employees to seek feedback from their peers and managers (and to provide it). See the "Competing through Technology" box later in the chapter for more on some apps that fill this role.

Peers also bring a different perspective to the evaluation process, which can be valuable in gaining an overall picture of the individual's performance. In fact, peers have been found to provide extremely valid assessments of performance in several different settings.[63]

One disadvantage of using peer ratings is the potential for friendship to bias ratings.[64] Little empirical evidence suggests that this is often a problem, however. Another disadvantage is that when the evaluations are made for administrative decisions, peers often find the situation of being both rater and ratee uncomfortable. When these ratings are used only for developmental purposes, however, peers react favorably.[65]

DIRECT REPORTS

Upward feedback
A performance appraisal process for managers that includes subordinates' evaluations.

Direct reports are employees who report to a manager. Direct reports are an especially valuable source of performance information when managers are evaluated. Direct reports often have the best opportunity to evaluate how well a manager treats employees. **Upward feedback** refers to appraisals that involve collecting subordinates' evaluations of a manager's behavior or skills. To attract and keep talented employees, Dell Inc., the Texas-based computer company, recently took steps to focus not only on financial goals but also on making the company a great place to work.[66] Dell uses upward

- Even if I were offered a comparable position with similar pay and benefits at another company, I would stay at Dell.
- I receive ongoing feedback that helps me to improve my performance.
- My manager/supervisor supports my efforts to balance my work and personal life.
- My manager/supervisor is effective at managing people.
- I can be successful at Dell and still retain my individuality.

SOURCE: Based on A. Pomeroy, "Agent of Change," *HR Magazine,* May 2005, pp. 52–56.

feedback to help sustain its "culture code" and develop its leaders. To be a successful leader at Dell requires humility: having confidence in your ability, being willing to take on challenges, but always welcoming feedback. Managers are rated by their employees on semiannual "Tell Dell" surveys. Managers who receive less than 50% favorable scores on five questions receive less favorable compensation, bonus, and promotion opportunities and are required to take additional training. Table 8.11 shows the five questions. Managers are expected to work continuously to improve their scores. Their goal is to receive at least 75% favorable ratings from employees on the five questions. One study found that managers viewed receiving upward feedback more positively when receiving feedback from subordinates who were identified, but subordinates preferred to provide anonymous feedback. When subordinates were identified, they inflated their ratings of the manager.[67]

One problem with subordinate evaluations is that they give subordinates power over their managers, thus putting the manager in a difficult situation.[68] This can lead to managers' emphasizing employee satisfaction over productivity. However, this happens only when administrative decisions are based on these evaluations. As with peer evaluations, it is a good idea to use subordinate evaluations only for developmental purposes. To assure subordinates that they need not fear retribution from their managers, it is necessary to use anonymous evaluations and at least three subordinates for each manager.

SELF

Although self-ratings are not often used as the sole source of performance information, they can still be valuable.[69] Obviously, individuals have extensive opportunities to observe their own behavior, and they usually have access to information regarding their results on the job. Intelicare Direct's You in Review is a self-assessment that asks employees to describe their successes and failures and to grade themselves.[70] They are required to present their assessment to their manager in writing but also in creative ways such as with videos, collages, or slide decks. Similarly, the manager has to provide feedback following the same requirements. You in Review enables employees to highlight accomplishments that their manager may be unaware of or have forgotten. This helps the manager provide a more complete performance evaluation. Since starting You in Review, the company has seen a significant increase in productivity immediately following feedback, which did not occur with their traditional, manager-led performance evaluations.

One problem with self-ratings, however, is a tendency toward inflated assessments. Research has found that self-ratings for personal traits as well as overall performance ratings tend to be lenient, compared to ratings from other sources.[71] This stems from two sources. If the ratings are going to be used for administrative decisions (e.g., for pay raises), it is in the employees' interests to inflate their ratings. Ample evidence in the social psychology literature indicates that individuals attribute their poor performance to external causes, such as a co-worker who they think has not provided them with timely information. Although self-ratings are less inflated when supervisors provide frequent performance feedback, it is not advisable to use them for administrative purposes.[72] The best use of self-ratings is as a prelude to the performance feedback session to get employees thinking about their performance and to focus discussion on areas of disagreement.

CUSTOMERS

Many companies are involving customers in their evaluation systems. One writer has defined *services* this way: "Services is something which can be bought and sold but which you cannot drop on your foot."[73] Because of the unique nature of services—the product is often produced and consumed on the spot—supervisors, peers, and subordinates often do not have the opportunity to observe employee behavior. Instead, the customer is often the only person present to observe the employee's performance and thus is the best source of performance information.

Most companies in service industries use customer evaluations of employee performance. Marriott Corporation provides a customer satisfaction card in every room and mails surveys to a random sample of customers after their stay in a Marriott hotel. Whirlpool's Consumer Services Division requires service technicians to ask customers to use their notebook computer to complete a survey immediately after they have serviced their appliances. Umami Burger restaurants provide three jars for customers to evaluate their experience: happiness with service (green), average feelings (yellow), and below expectations (red).[74] Customers are asked to toss a chip in the jar that best matches their experience. This provides Umami's managers with immediate feedback every time a customer places a chip in a jar, as well as cumulative feedback on customer experiences during the day. They can use this feedback to discuss with the restaurant team what's working and what needs to be fixed.

Using customer evaluations of employee performance is appropriate in two situations.[75] The first is when an employee's job requires direct service to the customer or linking the customer to other services within the company. Second, customer evaluations are appropriate when the company is interested in gathering information to determine what products and services the customer wants. That is, customer evaluations serve a strategic goal by integrating marketing strategies with human resource activities and policies. Customer evaluations collected for this purpose are useful for both evaluating the employee and helping to determine whether changes in other HRM activities (such as training or the compensation system) are needed to improve customer service.

The weakness of customer surveys is their expense, particularly if printing, postage, telephone, and labor are involved. On-site surveys completed using handheld computers help eliminate these expenses.

In conclusion, the best source of performance information often depends on the particular job. One should choose the source or sources that provide the best opportunity to observe employee behavior and results. Often, eliciting performance information from a variety of sources results in a performance management process that is accurate and effective. In fact, one recent popular trend in organizations is called **360-degree appraisal**.[76] This technique consists of having multiple raters (boss, peers, subordinates, customers) provide input into a manager's evaluation. The major advantage of the technique is that it provides a means for minimizing bias in an otherwise subjective evaluation technique. It has been used primarily for strategic and developmental purposes and is discussed in greater detail in Chapter 9.[77] Netflix doesn't use annual performance

360-degree appraisal
A performance appraisal process for managers that includes evaluations from a wide range of persons who interact with the manager. The process includes self-evaluations as well as evaluations from the manager's boss, subordinates, peers, and customers.

INTEGRITY IN ACTION

Taking the Long-Term View on Performance

Martha Samuelson, president and CEO of the Analysis Group, determines the firm's partners' compensation based on extensive discussions of the types of contributions each makes to the firm. The Analysis Group provides economic, financial, and strategy consulting to law firms, corporations, and government agencies. The Analysis Group has 11 offices and 19 different practice areas. Rather than using profitability metrics as a performance measure that puts the offices in competition with each other, Samuelson considers Analysis Group as one firm. This creates a culture of collaboration that makes it easier for the partners to work together and helps build their commitment to the firm.

An important aspect of performance management is the self-evaluation that every partner completes. The self-evaluation summarizes each partner's accomplishments for the year, including business sold and who they hired and mentored. This reflects a performance emphasis on both how the partner is contributing to the firm's financial health as well as what the partner is doing to ensure the future health and growth of the business. Meetings are held throughout the year to discuss each person's contributions and identify their development objectives. There have been mismatches between how an individual's performance is evaluated and his or her pay. This occurs when individuals are not getting a direct and honest message about their performance. Usually, additional discussions with the individual resolve disagreements, but sometimes partners have decided to leave the firm.

Samuelson admits that early in her career she tended to avoid difficult conversations about where employees needed to improve. But she learned that it is better to address problems directly with employees, give them a chance to change, and reward them for doing so.

DISCUSSION QUESTION

1. Is using self-appraisals appropriate for measuring employee performance at Analysis Group? Why or why not?

SOURCE: Based on M. Samuelson, "How I Did It. . .Analysis Group's CEO on Managing with Soft Metrics," *Harvard Business Review*, November 2015, pp. 43–45; Analysis Group website, www.analysisgroup.com, accessed March 7, 2017.

reviews but instead uses informal 360-degree reviews.[78] Employees are asked to identify things that their peers should start, stop, and continue doing. The reviews are not anonymous, and many teams hold the reviews face-to-face. Netflix's use of 360-degree appraisals fits into the company's performance culture that emphasizes that performance should be discussed simply and honestly. The "Integrity in Action" box shows how Analysis Group's choice of source for performance information was based on the company's culture and desired employee behavior.

Use of Technology in Performance Management

Technology is influencing performance management systems in three ways. First, many companies are moving to Web-based online paperless performance management systems. These systems help companies ensure that performance goals across all levels of the organization are aligned, they provide managers and employees with greater access to performance information, and they provide tools for understanding and using the performance management process.[79]

LO 8-8
Discuss the potential advantages of social performance management and electronic monitoring for performance management.

Apps Make Giving and Receiving Feedback Quick and Easy

IBM's Checkpoint app allows employees to set short-term performance goals and managers to provide feedback on their progress. Employees and managers at Mozilla can use an app to send each other colorful "badges" to recognize good performance. The badges include slogans such as "you rock" or "kicking butt." Also, employees can receive feedback and coaching from peers and managers by posting short questions about their performance, such as "What did you think about my speech?" Uber uses an app that includes sensors in a driver's smartphone to detect when the driver moves or touches his or her phone, such as during texting. The app also tracks when drivers speed, cut corners, or brake severely. The purpose of the app is to help drivers improve by

providing them with more detailed data than the ratings they receive from customers. The data also provide a record that can protect them from groundless customer complaints.

The availability of apps used to ask for and give feedback may not always be positive. Amazon's Anytime Feedback Tool can be used secretly by office workers to praise or critique their colleagues. The peer evaluations can be submitted to members of the management team at any time, using the company's internal directory. Many workers used the app in a dysfunctional way. They described making agreements with colleagues to comment negatively on the same co-worker or to heap high praise on each other. Some employees felt sabotaged by the negative

comments from unidentified colleagues. In some cases, the negative comments were copied directly into employees' performance reviews (known as "the full paste.").

DISCUSSION QUESTION

1. Does the use of apps for feedback help or hinder performance management? Explain.

SOURCE: Based on H. Clancy, "How Am I Doing?" *Fortune*, March 1, 2017, p. 34; D. MacMillan, "Uber to Monitor Actions by Drivers in Safety Push," *Wall Street Journal*, June 30, 2016; M. Weinstein, "Annual Review under Review," *Training*, July/August 2016, pp. 22–29; C. Zillman, "IBM Is Blowing Up Its Annual Performance Review," *Fortune*, February 1, 2016; B. Hassell, "IBM's New Checkpoint Reflects Employee Preferences," *Workforce*, April 2016, p. 12; J. Kantor and D. Streitfeld, "Inside Amazon: Wrestling Big Ideas in a Bruising Workplace," *New York Times*, August 16, 2015, p. A1; E. Goldberg, "Performance Management Gets Social," *HR* Magazine, August 2014, pp. 35–38.

Social performance management
Social media and micro-blogs similar to Facebook, LinkedIn, and Yammer that allow employees to quickly exchange information, talk to each other, provide coaching, and receive feedback and recognition in the form of electronic badges.

Second, social media tools similar to Facebook and Twitter are increasingly being used to deliver timely feedback. **Social performance management** refers to systems similar to Facebook, LinkedIn, and Yammer and apps that allow employees to quickly exchange information, talk to each other, provide coaching, and receive recognition. Social performance management is especially valued by Millennials and Generation Z employees, who want more frequent feedback about their performance. This preference has been reinforced by their having grown up connecting to others through social networking via smartphones and computers.[80] Baby Boomers may be more likely to believe that feedback involves judgment, compared to younger generations, who see feedback as an opportunity to learn, but high performers of all ages are likely to seek and value feedback. As emphasized in the effective performance management model (see Figure 8.1), performance feedback is a critical part of the performance management process that should not be limited to quarterly, midyear, or annual formal performance evaluations. Also, peers and co-workers can often give more timely and accurate feedback and recognition than busy managers. The "Competing through Technology" box describes how apps are being used in performance management.

Third, companies are relying on electronic tracking and monitoring systems to ensure that employees are working when and how they should be and to block access to certain websites (such as those containing pornographic images). These systems include handprint and fingerprint recognition systems, global positioning systems (GPS), software that can track employees using smartphones and notebook computers, and wearables.

For example, at the New York law firm Akin & Smith LLC, paralegals, receptionists, and clerks clock in by placing their finger on a sensor kept at a secretary's desk. The managing partners believe the system improves productivity and keeps everyone honest, holding them to their lunch times.[81]

In the trucking industry, drivers are monitored continually.[82] An onboard computer records whether the driver is on or off duty, documents the driver's gas mileage, and tells him or her where to get gas. If the truck stops while the driver is on duty, he or she is asked to provide an explanation. The electronic monitoring system built in to the computer tells the driver which route to follow and records even slight deviations from the route due to traffic or accidents. UPS uses a computer analysis program to monitor its delivery drivers. This helps them avoid wasting time and fuel on left-hand turns on their routes. It also helps promote driver safety by documenting seat belt usage and how many feet a driver backs up, which is a dangerous maneuver. Shuttle Express company vans are equipped with cameras, which allows the company to determine if accidents are the driver's fault.

Memorial Care, a nonprofit hospital group, keeps detailed data on the extent to which doctors order immunizations and mammograms and reduce blood sugar levels in diabetes patients.[83] In its hospitals, the company tracks the extent to which patients experience complications and hospital readmissions, as well as the cost of services. Doctors are graded as green, yellow, or red based on how well they are performing compared to their peers. The data collected are discussed with individual doctors as well as clinics. For example, at one clinic, all of the numbers exceeded the standards except for cervical cancer screenings. Some patients were getting Pap smears more often than the recommended guideline of every three years. The clinic doctors discussed the results and identified that the high rate of Pap smears was due to tests being ordered by gynecologists outside the group who also saw Memorial Care patients and to the resistance that some patients at low risk for cancer had to not getting annual Pap smears. To persuade these patients and reduce the number of Pap smears, one doctor hung cervical cancer guidelines on the wall of the exam room.

Companies are using software that analyzes employees' computers and creates a profile.[84] Over time the software is able to create a baseline of normal behavior, including where they log in, what programs and databases they use, and which external websites they browse. It also provides a score for users (a risk score) based on what dangers they may pose to the company, such as stealing data or new product designs or viewing pornography. Software called Scout can be used to evaluate the content of employees' e-mail and other communications. The software scans for variations in language usage in the e-mails such as an increase in the use of phrases such as "medical bills" or "missed payments," which may mean the employee is at an increased risk for stealing.

Wearables allow us to track our sleep, steps, and exercise levels. Companies offer health-tracking wearables to employees as part of wellness programs designed to reduce health care costs. For example, IBM and Appirio distribute Fitbits to employees to encourage them to exercise and maintain a healthy lifestyle.[85] Appirio used data from the Fitbits to negotiate a reduction in premiums from the company's health insurance provider. Wearables can also be used to track our movements and personal interactions.[86] For example, at Florida Hospital Celebration Health, nurses and patient care technicians wear badges with sensors that allow tracking of their visits to patients' rooms and nurses' stations. The tracking helped the hospital determine that nurses were spending more time finding medicines that were understocked at certain nursing stations. The monitoring helped the hospital improve its supply procedures.

Despite the potential increased productivity and efficiency benefits that can result from these systems, they still present privacy concerns.[87] Critics argue that these systems threaten to reduce the workplace to an electronic sweatshop in which employees are treated as robots that are monitored to maximize productivity for every second they are at work. Also, electronic monitoring systems threaten employees' rights and dignity to work without being monitored.

Some critics argue that electronic tracking systems are needlessly surveilling and tracking employees when there is no reason to believe that anything is wrong. Good managers know what their employees are doing, and electronic systems should not be a substitute for good management. Critics also argue that such systems result in less productivity and motivation, demoralize employees, and create unnecessary stress. A mentality is created that employees always have to be at their desks to be productive. Wearable devices have the potential to gather a much broader range of information than other types of monitoring technology. But most employees don't know what data are being collected, and health and personal data collected by a wearable are not necessarily private or secure. The EEOC requires participation in company wellness programs linked to health insurance plans to be voluntary. But, even if the adoption of wearables is optional, employees may feel pressure to participate and resent the need to do so.

However, electronic monitoring can ensure that time is not abused, it can improve scheduling, and it can help motivate workers and improve performance.[88] To avoid the potential negative effects of electronic monitoring, managers must communicate to employees why they are being monitored. Monitoring can also be used as a way for more experienced employees to coach less experienced employees.

REDUCING RATER ERRORS, POLITICS, AND INCREASING RELIABILITY AND VALIDITY OF RATINGS

LO 8-9
Distinguish types of rating errors, and explain how to minimize each in a performance evaluation.

Research consistently reveals that humans have tremendous limitations in processing information. Because we are so limited, we often use "heuristics," or simplifying mechanisms, to make judgments, whether about investments or about people.[89] These heuristics, which appear often in subjective measures of performance, cause unconscious bias, which can lead to rater errors and incorrect attributions or reasons we use to explain an employee's performance. **Unconscious bias** is a judgment outside of our consciousness that affects decisions based on background, culture, and personal experience. We are all subject to unconscious bias. For example, research has found that, compared to men, women receive two and one-half times more feedback about having an aggressive communication style.[90] Also, men tend to receive more feedback linked to a business outcome than do women. It doesn't matter whether the manager conducting the performance evaluation was a man or a woman.

Unconscious bias
A judgment outside of our consciousness that affects decisions based on background, culture, and personal experience.

Table 8.12 shows the different types of rating errors. The "similar to me" error is based on stereotypes the rater has about how individuals with certain characteristics are expected to perform.[91] Leniency, strictness, and central tendency are known as distributional errors because the rater tends to use only one part of the rating scale.

Appraisal politics
A situation in which evaluators purposefully distort a rating to achieve personal or company goals.

Appraisal politics refer to evaluators purposefully distorting a rating to achieve personal or company goals. Research suggests that several factors promote appraisal politics. These factors are inherent in the appraisal system and the company culture. Appraisal politics are most likely to occur when raters are accountable to the employee being rated, there are competing rating goals, and a direct link exists between performance appraisal and highly desirable rewards. Also, appraisal politics are likely to occur if top executives tolerate distortion or are complacent toward it, and if distortion strategies are part of "company folklore" and are passed down from senior employees to new employees.

Table 8.12
Typical Rater Errors

RATER ERROR	DESCRIPTION
Similar to me	Individuals who are similar to us in race, gender, background, interest, beliefs, and the like receive higher ratings than those who are not.
Contrast	Ratings are influenced by comparison between individuals instead of an objective standard (e.g., employee receives lower-than-deserved ratings because he or she is compared to outstanding peers).
Leniency	Rater gives high ratings to all employees regardless of their performance.
Strictness	Rater gives low ratings to all employees regardless of their performance.
Central tendency	Rater gives middle or average ratings to all employees despite their performance.
Halo	Rater gives employee high ratings on all aspects of performance because of an overall positive impression of the employee.
Horns	Rater gives employee low ratings on all aspects of performance because of an overall negative impression of the employee.

There are four approaches to reducing rating errors.[92] They include rater error training, frame-of-reference training, unconscious bias training, and calibration meetings. *Rater error training* attempts to make managers aware of rating errors and helps them develop strategies for minimizing those errors.[93] These programs consist of having the participants view video-recorded vignettes designed to elicit rating errors such as "contrast." They then make their ratings and discuss how the error influenced the ratings. Finally, they get tips to avoid committing those errors. This approach has been shown to be effective for reducing errors, but there is evidence that reducing rating errors can also reduce accuracy.[94]

Rater accuracy training, also called *frame-of-reference training*, attempts to emphasize the multidimensional nature of performance and to get raters to understand and use the same idea of high, medium, and low performance when making evaluations. This involves providing examples of performance for each dimension and then discussing the actual or "correct" level of performance that the example represents.[95] Accuracy training seems to increase accuracy, provided that the raters are held accountable for ratings, job-related rating scales are used, and raters keep records of the behavior they observe.[96]

In addition to these approaches many companies, such as Microsoft, Google, Facebook, and Dow Chemical, are requiring employees to participate in training programs to reduce the potential influence of unconscious bias in performance evaluations and other work-related decisions (e.g., promotions).[97] These training programs focus on making employees aware of unconscious bias and reducing its impact by slowing down decision making and carefully considering reasons behind and language used in judgments.

An important way to help ensure that performance is evaluated consistently across managers and to reduce the influence of unconscious bias, rating errors, and appraisal politics is to hold calibration meetings.[98] **Calibration meetings** provide a way to discuss employees' performance with the goal of ensuring that similar standards are applied to their evaluations. These meetings include managers responsible for conducting

Calibration meetings
A way to discuss employees' performance with the goal of ensuring that similar standards are applied to their evaluations.

performance appraisals and their managers; they are facilitated by an internal HR representative or an external consultant. In the meetings, each employee's performance rating and the manager's reasons for the ratings are discussed. Managers have the opportunity to discuss the definition of each performance rating and ask questions. The calibration meetings help managers identify if their ratings are too positive or negative or tend to be based on employees' most recent performance. Managers are more likely to provide accurate evaluations that are well documented when they know they may have to justify them in a calibration meeting. Calibration meetings can also help eliminate politics by discussing how performance ratings relate to business results. To minimize appraisal politics, managers also should keep in mind the characteristics of a fair appraisal system, shown in Table 8.2. Thus, managers should also do the following:

- Build top management support for the appraisal system and actively discourage distortion
- Give raters some latitude to customize performance objectives and criteria for their ratees
- Recognize employee accomplishments that are not self-promoted
- Provide employees with access to information regarding which behaviors are desired and acceptable at work
- Encourage employees to actively seek and use feedback to improve performance
- Make sure that constraints such as the budget do not drive the process
- Make sure that appraisal processes are consistent across the company
- Foster a climate of openness to encourage employees to be honest about weaknesses[99]

Performance Feedback

LO 8-10
Conduct an effective performance feedback session.

Once the expected performance has been defined and employees' performances have been measured, it is necessary to feed that performance information back to the employees so that they can correct any deficiencies. The performance feedback process is complex and provokes anxiety for both the manager and the employee.

Few of us feel comfortable sitting in judgment of others. The thought of confronting others with what we perceive to be their deficiencies causes most of us to shake in our shoes. If giving negative feedback is painful, receiving it can be excruciating—thus the importance of the performance feedback process.

THE MANAGER'S ROLE IN AN EFFECTIVE PERFORMANCE FEEDBACK PROCESS

If employees are not made aware of how their performance is not meeting expectations, their performance will almost certainly not improve. In fact, it may get worse. Effective managers provide specific performance feedback to employees in a way that elicits positive behavioral responses. Because of the importance of performance feedback for an effective performance management system, many companies are training managers on how to provide feedback. For example, Lubrizol Corporation, a chemical manufacturer based in Wickliffe, Ohio, requires that managers enroll in a two-day training course designed to help them provide meaningful feedback.[100] The company's goal is to become recognized as the best developer of people. The training course focuses on how managers give feedback, who they need help from, and how they can hold themselves accountable. To contribute to the effectiveness of a performance management system through providing effective feedback, managers should consider the recommendations in this section.[101]

Feedback Should Be Given Frequently, Not Once a Year. There are three reasons for this. First, managers have a responsibility to correct performance deficiencies immediately on becoming aware of them. If performance is subpar in January, waiting until December to appraise the performance could mean an 11-month productivity loss. Second, a major determinant of the effectiveness of a feedback session is the degree to which the subordinate is not surprised by the evaluation. An easy rule to follow is that employees should receive such frequent performance feedback that they already know almost exactly what their formal evaluation will be. Third, many employees, especially Millennials, want more frequent and candid performance feedback from managers beyond what is provided once or twice a year during their formal performance review.[102]

Consider how FORUM Credit Union encourages employees to seek feedback and managers to provide it.[103] FORUM Credit Union uses formal check-ins to help managers provide and employees receive more frequent feedback. Each quarter, employees are sent a questionnaire that asks them to respond to four or five questions. The completed questionnaire is sent to the employee's manager, who reviews it and schedules a meeting to discuss the answers. Some managers have monthly meetings with employees, but at a minimum quarterly manager–employee conversations are required.

Create the Right Context for the Discussion. Managers should choose a neutral location for the feedback session. The manager's office may not be the best place for a constructive feedback session because the employee may associate the office with unpleasant conversations. Managers should describe the meeting as an opportunity to discuss the role of the employee, the role of the manager, and the relationship between them. Managers should also acknowledge that they would like the meeting to be an open dialogue.

Ask the Employee to Rate His or Her Performance before the Session. Having employees complete a self-assessment before the feedback session can be very productive. It requires employees to think about their performance over the past rating period, and it encourages them to think about their weaknesses. Although self-ratings used for administrative decisions are often inflated, there is evidence that they may actually be lower than supervisors' ratings when done for developmental purposes. Another reason a self-assessment can be productive is that it can make the session go more smoothly by focusing discussion on areas where disagreement exists, resulting in a more efficient session. Finally, employees who have thought about past performance are more able to participate fully in the feedback session.

Have Ongoing, Collaborative Performance Conversations. Managers should use a "problem-solving" or collaborative approach to work with employees to solve performance problems in an atmosphere of respect and encouragement. When employees participate in the feedback session, they are consistently satisfied with the process. (Recall the discussion of fairness earlier in this chapter.) Participation includes allowing employees to voice their opinions of the evaluation, as well as to discuss performance goals and development needs.

Moving to an ongoing collaborative performance conversation is necessary to reduce the anxiety, uncertainty, and feelings of lack of fairness and control that employees typically experience in a manager-driven "tell-and-sell" or "tell-and-listen" approach.[104] One study found that, other than satisfaction with one's supervisor, participation was the single most important predictor of satisfaction with the feedback session.[105] Table 8.13 provides examples of questions that managers can use to start a collaborative ongoing performance conversation with their employees.

Table 8.13
Examples of
Questions That Start
a Collaborative,
Ongoing Performance
Conversation

- What's working?
- Where did you get stuck?
- How can I help?
- What have you learned?
- What would you do differently next time?
- What skills would you like to develop?
- What would you like to discuss today?
- What do you think the next steps are?
- When can I check-in with you next?

SOURCE: Based on M. Buckingham, "Out With the Old In With. . .," *TD*, August 2016, pp. 44–48; "Goodyear Performance Management Optimization Case Study," presented on September 6, 2016, to MHR 4328 Performance Management class, The Ohio State University.

Recognize Effective Performance through Praise. One usually thinks of performance feedback sessions as focusing on the employee's performance problems. This should never be the case. The purpose of the session is to give accurate performance feedback, which entails recognizing effective performance as well as poor performance. Praising effective performance provides reinforcement for that behavior. It also adds credibility to the feedback by making it clear that the manager is not just identifying performance problems.

Focus on Solving Problems. A common mistake that managers make in providing performance feedback is to try to use the session as a chance to punish poorly performing employees by telling them how utterly lousy their performance is. This only reduces the employees' self-esteem and increases defensiveness, neither of which will improve performance.

To improve poor performance, a manager must attempt to solve the problems causing it. This entails working with the employee to determine the actual cause and then agreeing on how to solve it. For example, a salesperson's failure to meet a sales goal may be the result of lack of a proper sales pitch, lack of product knowledge, or stolen sales by another salesperson. Each of these causes requires a different solution. Without a problem-solving approach, however, the correct solution might never be identified.

Focus Feedback on Behavior or Results, Not on the Person. One of the most important things to do when giving negative feedback is to avoid questioning the employee's worth as a person. This is best accomplished by focusing the discussion on the employee's behaviors or results, not on the employee. Saying, "You're screwing up! You're just not motivated!" will bring about more defensiveness and ill feelings than saying, "You did not meet the deadline that you agreed to because you spent too much time on another project."

Minimize Criticism. Obviously, if an individual's performance is below standard, some criticism must take place. However, an effective manager should resist the temptation to reel off a litany of offenses. Having been confronted with the performance problem, an employee often agrees that a change is in order. However, if the manager continues to come up with more and more examples of low performance, the employee may get defensive.

Agree to Specific Goals and Set a Date to Review Progress. The importance of goal setting cannot be overemphasized. It is one of the most effective motivators of performance.[106] Research has demonstrated that it results in increased satisfaction, motivation to improve, and performance improvement.[107] Besides setting goals, the manager must also set a specific follow-up date to review the employee's performance toward the goal. This provides an added incentive for the employee to take the goal seriously and work toward achieving it.

EVIDENCE-BASED HR

At Cargill, performance management has deemphasized the annual performance meeting or completion of a complex appraisal form. Instead, Cargill's performance management process, known as Everyday Performance Management, emphasizes that managers and employees need to have daily, ongoing performance conversations. The performance management process focuses on setting goals that get results and adjusting those goals as the business changes, continuously improving performance, and building strong manager–employee relationships. There still is a year-end performance review, but it is a discussion without performance ratings. Employee development is seen as a critical part of performance management. Survey data collected one year after Everyday Performance Management was implemented showed that 85% of employees reported they had ongoing performance discussions with their manager, 69% received useful developmental feedback, and 70% felt valued as a result of ongoing discussions with their manager.

SOURCES: Based on CEB, "Why Cargill Excels at Performance Management," https://www.cebglobal.com/blogs/everyday-performance-management-at-cargill-a-best-practice-case-study/; E. Pulakos, R. Hanson, S. Arad, and N. Moye, "Performance Management Can Be Fixed: An On-the-Job Experiential Learning Approach for Complex Behavior Change," *Industrial and Organizational Psychology*, March 2015, pp. 51–76; "Cargill China-Fostering and Rewarding Success-Performance Management," http://www.cargill.com.cn/en/careers/fostering-rewarding-success/performance-management/index.jsp.

What Managers Can Do to Diagnose Performance Problems and Manage Employees' Performance

As we emphasized in the previous section, employees need performance feedback to improve their current job performance. As we discuss in Chapter 9, performance feedback is also needed for employees to develop their knowledge and skills for the future. In addition to understanding how to effectively give employees performance feedback, managers need to be able to diagnose the causes of performance problems and take actions to improve and maintain employee performance. For example, giving performance feedback to marginal employees may not be sufficient to improve their performance.

LO 8-11
Identify the cause of a performance problem.

DIAGNOSING THE CAUSES OF POOR PERFORMANCE

Many different reasons can cause an employee's poor performance. For example, poor performance can be due to lack of employee ability, misunderstanding of performance expectations, lack of feedback, or the need for training an employee who does not have the knowledge and skills needed to meet the performance standards. When diagnosing the causes of poor performance, it is important to consider whether the poor performance is detrimental to the business. That is, is poor performance critical to completing the job, and does it affect business results? If it is detrimental, then the next step is to conduct a performance analysis to determine the cause of poor performance. The different factors that should be considered in analyzing poor performance are shown in Figure 8.8. For example, if an employee understands the expected level of performance, has been given sufficient feedback, understands the consequences, but lacks the knowledge and skills

Figure 8.8

Factors to Consider
in Analyzing Poor
Performance

Input

Does the employee recognize what he or she is supposed to do?

Are the job flow and procedures logical?

Do employees have the resources (tools, equipment, technology, time) needed for
successful performance?

Are other job demands interfering with good performance in this area?

Employee Characteristics

Does the employee have the necessary skills and knowledge?

Does the employee know why the desired performance level is important?

Is the employee mentally, physically, and emotionally able to perform at the
expected level?

Feedback

Has the employee been given information about his or her performance?

Is performance feedback relevant, timely, accurate, specific, and understandable?

Performance Standard/Goals

Do performance standards exist?

Does the employee know the desired level of expected performance?

Does the employee believe she or he can reach the performance standard?

Consequences

Are consequences (rewards, incentives) aligned with good performance?

Are the consequences of performance valuable to the employee?

Are performance consequences given in a timely manner?

Do work-group or team norms encourage employees not to meet
performance standards?

SOURCES: Based on G. Rummler, "In Search of the Holy Performance Grail," *Training and Development,* April 1996,
pp. 26–31; C. Reinhart, "How to Leap over Barriers to Performance," *Training and Development,* January 2000, pp.
20–24; F. Wilmouth, C. Prigmore, and M. Bray, "HPT Models: An Overview of the Major Models in the Field," *Performance Improvement* 41 (2002), pp. 14–21.

needed to meet the performance standard, this suggests that the manager may want to
consider training the employee to improve performance, moving the employee to a different job that better fits that person's skills, or discharging the employee and making
sure that selection methods to find a new employee measure the level of knowledge and
skills needed to perform the job.

After conducting the performance analysis, the manager should meet with the
employee to discuss the results, agree to the next steps that the manager and employee
will take to improve performance (e.g., training, providing resources, giving more

feedback), discuss the consequences of failing to improve performance, and set a time line for improvement. This type of discussion is most beneficial if it occurs more frequently than the quarterly or yearly performance review, so that performance issues can be dealt with quickly, before they have adverse consequences for the company (and the employee). In the next section, we discuss the actions that should be considered for different types of employees.

ACTIONS FOR MANAGING EMPLOYEES' PERFORMANCE

Table 8.14 shows actions for the manager to take with four different types of employees. As the table highlights, managers need to take into account employees' ability, motivation, or both in considering ways to improve performance. To determine an employee's level of ability, a manager should consider if he or she has the knowledge, skills, and abilities needed to perform effectively. Lack of ability may be an issue if an employee is new or the job has changed recently. To determine employees' level of motivation, managers need to consider if employees are doing a job they want to do and if they feel they are being appropriately paid or rewarded. A sudden negative change in an employee's performance may indicate personal problems.

Employees with high ability and motivation include likely good and outstanding performers (*solid performers*). Table 8.14 emphasizes that managers should not ignore employees with high ability and high motivation. Managers should provide

Table 8.14
Ways to Manage Employees' Performance

	ABILITY	
	HIGH	**LOW**
MOTIVATION High	**Solid performers** • Reward good performance • Identify development opportunities • Provide honest, direct feedback	**Misdirected effort** • Coaching • Frequent performance feedback • Goal setting • Training or temporary assignment for skill development • Restructured job assignment
Low	**Underutilizers** • Give honest, direct feedback • Provide counseling • Use team building and conflict resolution • Link rewards to performance outcomes • Offer training for needed knowledge or skills • Manage stress levels	**Deadwood** • Withholding pay increases • Demotion • Outplacement • Firing • Specific, direct feedback on performance problems

SOURCES: Based on M. London, *Job Feedback* (Mahwah, NJ: Lawrence Erlbaum Associates, 1997), pp. 96–97; H. Aguinis and E. O'Boyle, Jr., "Star Performers in the Twenty-First Century," *Personnel Psychology* 67 (2014), pp. 313–50; D. Grote, *How to Be Good at Performance Appraisals* (Boston: Harvard University Press, 2011).

development opportunities to keep them satisfied and effective. Some individuals who are outstanding or good performers may be candidates for leadership positions within the company. They will need challenging development experiences and exposure to different aspects of the business. We discuss development experiences in Chapter 9. Other employees may not desire positions with managerial responsibility. These employees need development opportunities to help keep them engaged in their work and to avoid obsolescence.

Finally, there are different reasons why employees are considered poor performers (see Table 8.14). Poor performance resulting from lack of ability but not motivation (*misdirected effort*) may be improved by skill development activities such as training or temporary assignments. Managers with employees who have the ability but lack motivation (*underutilizers*) need to consider actions that focus on interpersonal problems or incentives. These actions include making sure that incentives or rewards that the employee values are linked to performance and making counseling available to help employees deal with personal problems or career or job dissatisfaction. Chronic poor performance by employees with low ability and motivation (*deadwood*) indicates that outplacement or firing may be the best solution.

Many companies use a performance improvement plan to try to improve poorly performing employees.[108] A **performance improvement plan (PIP)** refers to a plan that describes the performance changes that a poorly performing employee needs to make in a specified time period or face termination. In a PIP, a manager needs to be specific about both the changes the employee is expected to make and the time frame for doing so. The manager is expected to try to help the employee improve his or her performance through coaching, training, and feedback. If the desired changes are not made in the expected time frame, the employee is notified that he or she will be fired if job performance does not improve in another time period, typically 30–60 days.

Performance tends to vary over time due to changes in tasks, assignments, and business goals.[109] As a result, managers should consider the categories shown in Table 8.14 but give employees the chance to change. One way to do this is to have frequent performance conversations with employees, which helps them recognize the need to either change or maintain their performance. Actively managing employees by setting expectations, making project assignments based on their skills and interests, and holding employees accountable for their performance makes a difference.

Performance pmprovement plan (PIP)
A plan that describes the performance changes that a poorly performing employee needs to make in a specified time period or face termination.

Developing and Implementing a System That Follows Legal Guidelines

We now discuss the legal issues and constraints affecting performance management. Because performance measures play a central role in administrative decisions such as promotions, pay raises, and discipline, employees who sue an organization over these decisions ultimately attack the measurement systems on which the decisions were made. Two types of cases have dominated: discrimination and unjust dismissal.

In discrimination suits, the plaintiff often alleges that the performance measurement system unjustly discriminated against the plaintiff because of age, race, gender, or national origin. Many performance measures are subjective, and we have seen that individual biases can affect them, especially when those doing the measuring harbor racial or gender stereotypes.

In *Brito v. Zia*, the Supreme Court essentially equated performance measures with selection tests.[110] It ruled that the *Uniform Guidelines on Employee Selection Procedures* apply to evaluating the adequacy of a performance appraisal instrument. This ruling presents a challenge to those involved in developing performance measures, because a substantial body of research on race discrimination in performance rating has demonstrated that both white and black raters give higher ratings to members of their own racial group, even after rater training.[111] There is also evidence that the discriminatory biases in performance rating are worse when one group makes up a small percentage of the work group. When the vast majority of the group is male, females receive lower ratings; when the minority is male, males receive lower ratings.[112]

In the second type of suit, an unjust dismissal suit, the plaintiff claims that the dismissal was for reasons other than those the employer claims. For example, an employee who works for a defense contractor might blow the whistle on the company for defrauding the government. If the company fires the employee, claiming poor performance, the employee may argue that the firing was, in fact, because of blowing the whistle on the employer—in other words, that the dismissal was unjust. The court case will likely focus on the performance measurement system used as the basis for claiming the employee's performance was poor. Unjust dismissal also can result from terminating for poor performance an employee who has a history of favorable reviews and raises. This may occur especially when a new evaluation system is introduced that results in more experienced older employees receiving unsatisfactory reviews. Rewarding poor performers or giving poor performers positive evaluations because of an unwillingness to confront a performance issue undermines the credibility of any performance management system. This makes it difficult to defend termination decisions based on a performance appraisal system.

For example, Baltimore-based MRA Systems, Inc., a subsidiary of General Electric, paid $130,000 to settle an age discrimination lawsuit.[113] An employee received a lower performance rating, despite his successful job performance, because of his age, which was 61. In addition, MRA Systems had to provide at least two hours of mandatory training on federal laws prohibiting employment discrimination to all managers, supervisors, and other employees who participate in the performance evaluation process or assignment decisions. The EEOC sued Wisconsin Plastics, Inc. (WPI), a metal and plastic products manufacturer, for violating federal law by firing several Hmong and Hispanic employees because of their national origin.[114] WPI fired the Hmong and Hispanic employees based on 10-minute observations that marked them down for their English skills even though those skills were not needed to perform their jobs. The fired employees had received satisfactory ratings on their annual performance evaluations.

Because of the potential costs of discrimination and unjust dismissal suits, an organization needs to determine exactly what the courts consider a legally defensible performance management system. Based on reviews of such court decisions, we offer the following characteristics of a system that will withstand legal scrutiny:[115]

1. The system should be developed by conducting a valid job analysis that ascertains the important aspects of job performance. The requirements for job success should be clearly communicated to employees.
2. The system should be based on either behaviors or results; evaluations of ambiguous traits should be avoided. Also, performance discussions should focus on work behavior and results other than questioning potential underlying reasons for behavior and results, such as a physical or mental disability.
3. Raters should be trained in how to use the system rather than simply given the materials and left to interpret how to conduct the appraisal.

4. There should be some form of review by upper-level managers of all the performance ratings, and there should be a system for employees to appeal what they consider to be an unfair evaluation.
5. The organization should provide some form of performance counseling or corrective guidance to help poor performers improve their performance before being dismissed. Both short- and long-term performance goals should be included.
6. Multiple raters should be used, particularly if an employee's performance is unlikely to be seen by only one rating source such as a manager or customer. At a minimum, employees should be asked to comment on their appraisals. There should be a dialogue between the manager and the employee.
7. Performance evaluations need to be documented.

A LOOK BACK

GE's Revised Performance Management System

GE's new performance management system emphasizes setting short-term performance goals, encourages frequent performance conversations between managers and their employees, and includes a brief end of year summary meeting during which performance is discussed. Employees can use a mobile app to provide feedback to their manager and peers.

QUESTIONS

1. Which of the three purposes of performance management (strategic, administrative, development) are new performance management systems like GE's best suited for? Explain.
2. What are the advantages and potential disadvantages of encouraging peers to provide feedback using apps?
3. If a company is considering developing a performance management system similar to GE's, what should it do to support the system's effectiveness?

SUMMARY

Measuring and managing performance is a challenging enterprise and one of the keys to gaining competitive advantage. Performance management systems serve strategic, administrative, and developmental purposes—their importance cannot be overstated. A performance measurement system should be evaluated against the criteria of strategic congruence, validity, reliability, acceptability, and specificity. Measured against these criteria, the comparative, attribute, behavioral, results, and quality approaches have different strengths and weaknesses. Thus, deciding which approach and which source of performance information are best depends on the job in question. Effective managers need to be aware of the issues involved in determining the best method or combination of methods for their particular situations. In addition, once performance has been measured, a major component of a manager's job is to provide frequent informal as well as formal feedback during performance evaluations in a way that results in improved performance rather than defensiveness and decreased motivation. Technologies can be potentially useful in streamlining the performance management process and providing employees with feedback and other information, which can motivate them to perform effectively. Managers should take action based on the causes for poor performance: ability, motivation, or both. Managers must be sure that their performance management system can meet legal scrutiny, especially if it is used to discipline or fire poor performers.

KEY TERMS

Performance
  management, 324
Performance appraisal, 325
Performance feedback, 325
Strategic congruence, 330
Validity, 332
Reliability, 333

Acceptability, 333
Specificity, 334
Competencies, 344
Competency model, 344
Kaizen, 352
Upward feedback, 356
360-degree appraisal, 358

Social performance
  management, 360
Unconscious bias, 362
Appraisal politics, 362
Calibration meetings, 363
Performance improvement plan
  (PIP) 370

DISCUSSION QUESTIONS

1. What are examples of administrative decisions that might be made in managing the performance of professors? Developmental decisions?
2. What would you consider the strategy of your university (e.g., research, undergraduate teaching, graduate teaching, a combination)? How might the performance management system for faculty members fulfill its strategic purpose of eliciting the types of behaviors and results required by this strategy?
3. What do you think is the most important step shown in the model of the effective performance management process? Justify your answer.
4. What sources of performance information would you use to evaluate faculty members' performance?
5. Why are companies changing their performance management systems? Is this a good idea? Why?
6. Think of the last time you had a conflict with another person, either at work or at school. Using the guidelines for performance feedback, how would you provide effective performance feedback to that person?

7. Explain what fairness has to do with performance management.
8. Why might a manager unintentionally distort performance ratings or the reasons used to explain an employee's performance? What would you recommend to minimize this problem?
9. Can electronic monitoring of performance ever be acceptable to employees? Explain.
10. Customer satisfaction surveys completed after a service call show that a call center representative is having difficulty answering customers' questions about their cell phone bills. How would you diagnose the cause of this performance problem? Explain.
11. How can the use of apps benefit the performance management process? How can they detract from it?
12. What would you do to ensure that a results or objective focus of performance management is effective?

SELF-ASSESSMENT EXERCISE

Mc Graw Hill Education connect®

Additional assignable self-assessments available in Connect.

How do you like getting feedback? To test your attitudes toward feedback, take the following quiz. Read each statement, and write A next to each statement you agree with. If you disagree with the statement, write D.

_____ 1. I like being told how well I am doing on a project.
_____ 2. Even though I may think I have done a good job, I feel a lot more confident when someone else tells me so.
_____ 3. Even when I think I could have done something better, I feel good when other people think well of me for what I have done.
_____ 4. It is important for me to know what people think of my work.

_____ 5. I think my instructor would think worse of me if I asked him or her for feedback.
_____ 6. I would be nervous about asking my instructor how she or he evaluates my behavior in class.
_____ 7. It is not a good idea to ask my fellow students for feedback; they might think I am incompetent.
_____ 8. It is embarrassing to ask other students for their impression of how I am doing in class.
_____ 9. It would bother me to ask the instructor for feedback.
_____ 10. It is not a good idea to ask the instructor for feedback because he or she might think I am incompetent.

_____ 11. It is embarrassing to ask the instructor for feedback.

_____ 12. It is better to try to figure out how I am doing on my own, rather than to ask other students for feedback.

For statements 1–4, add the total number of As: _____

For statements 5–12, add the total number of As: _____

For statements 1–4, the greater the number of As, the greater your preference for and trust in feedback from others. For statements 5–12, the greater the number of As, the greater the risk you believe there is in asking for feedback.

How might this information be useful in understanding how you react to feedback in school or on the job?

SOURCES: Based on D. B. Fedor, R. B. Rensvold, and S. M. Adams, "An Investigation of Factors Expected to Affect Feedback Seeking: A Longitudinal Field Study," *Personnel Psychology* 45 (1992), pp. 779–805; S. J. Asford, "Feedback Seeking in Individual Adaptation: A Resource Perspective," *Academy of Management Journal* 29 (1986), pp. 465–87.

EXERCISING STRATEGY

Keeping Annual Reviews

Although other companies are eliminating annual performance evaluations, Facebook is not. Focus groups and a survey that Facebook conducted found that 87% of employees wanted to keep performance ratings. As a result, Facebook decided to keep its traditional performance management system involving ratings. Facebook conducts performance reviews every six months based on self-evaluations and insights provided by an employee's manager and peers. The reviews are conducted every six months to account for the quickly changing nature of the business.

Facebook takes several steps to ensure that its system is fair and transparent, and that it focuses on development. Evaluaters are asked to provide ratings on specific performance dimensions, such as technical contributions, before they make their overall performance rating. Peers' evaluations are shared with each other and their managers. Managers are trained to stay up to date on employees' projects and provide employees with feedback and help, if necessary. Managers attend meetings and discuss their direct reports, defending and advocating for them and considering their peer evaluations. The goal of these meetings is to reduce the effect of individual managers being hard or easy evaluaters. After the managers write their performance reviews, they examine them for bias (e.g., if words such as *aggressive* or *abrasive* are used more often to describe women and result in lower evaluations). The overall performance ratings are then converted directly into compensation decisions using a formula. This allows managers to focus on making accurate performance evaluations rather than on having to painstakingly deliberate about compensation.

Facebook has eliminated the problem of employees being categorized as excellent, good, or poor employees from one year to the next, whether they deserve it or not by using stretch goals (what they call 50-50 goals). These goals are challenging: There is an equal chance that employees will or will not reach these goals. As a result, employees have a chance of just one in three that they will receive the same overall performance rating each year.

QUESTIONS

1. Why do you think Facebook's employees wanted to keep rather than abandon performance ratings? Do you think performance ratings are necessary? Why or why not?
2. Consider Figure 8.1. What else could Facebook do to improve the effectiveness of its performance management process?
3. Which part of Facebook's performance management process contributes most to its effectiveness? Explain.

SOURCE: L. Goler, G. Gale, and A. Grant, "Let's Not Kill Performance Evaluations," *Harvard Business Review*, November 2016, pp. 90–94; R. Feloni, "Facebook's HR Chief Explains How the Company Does Performance Reviews," *Business Insider,* February 5, 2016.

MANAGING PEOPLE

Helping to Encourage Frequent and Productive Performance Conversations

Adobe Systems Inc. provides multimedia and creativity software products including Photoshop, Adobe Acrobat, and Adobe Acrobat Reader. Adobe was experiencing an increase in turnover, which it discovered was related to employees' dissatisfaction with the performance review process, a lack of recognition, and the lack of regular feedback about their performance. Like other companies, Adobe used a performance review system in which managers provided an overall rating of each employee on a scale from 1 to 4, based on how the employee's performance compared to that of other employees. This created a competitive work environment, rather than the collaborative one that Adobe values. Each year after employees received their reviews, HR saw a spike in voluntary turnover, which was especially concerning because Adobe was losing good employees.

To improve performance management, Adobe decided to abandon annual ratings and introduced a new system called the Check-In. The Check-In emphasizes ongoing feedback. Instead of managers discussing performance with employees only during the formal performance review, as tended to occur in the old system, Check-In encourages managers and employees to have informal performance discussions at least every other month. Managers are asked to focus performance discussions around employees' performance objectives or goals and what resources they need to succeed. Also, employees' career development needs are part of the conversations. Managers are given complete freedom to decide how often and in what ways they want to set goals and provide feedback. The discussion is future focused. That is, both the employee and the manager consider what to change to increase the likelihood that performance will be effective. Employees are evaluated on the basis of how they have performed against their goals rather than how they compare to other employees. More frequent performance feedback is especially important to Millennial employees, who are used to real-time communications through texting and postings.

Managers no longer have to complete lengthy performance evaluation forms and submit them to HR. HR's role is to provide managers with consulting and tools to help with performance discussions rather than policing to see if reviews are completed or discussions have occurred. Both managers and employees can access a resource center that provides materials about coaching, giving feedback, and personal and professional development. For example, managers might use the resource center to help them with tough performance conversations such as those involving giving employees difficult feedback. HR relies on what is known as a skip-level process to ensure that performance discussions are occurring throughout the year. This means that the manager's own boss holds the manager accountable for having performance discussions. The boss asks employees if discussions are occurring and if they have a development plan.

There are several indications that Check-In is effective. HR includes questions about performance management on its annual employee survey. Survey results show that 80% of employees responded that they had regular performance meetings with their managers and felt supported by them. Since Check-In was introduced, voluntary turnover has decreased by 25%. Also, it is estimated that Check-In saves Adobe managers 80,000 hours each year that were previously spent completing employee performance evaluation forms.

QUESTIONS

1. What steps should managers take to ensure that performance discussions are effective?
2. What are the benefits and potential disadvantages of more frequent performance discussions between managers and employees?
3. Which purpose of performance management will be more difficult to achieve for companies like Adobe that decide to abandon ranking or rating employee performance?

SOURCES: Based on R. Feintzeig, "The Trouble with Grading Employees," *Wall Street Journal*, April 22, 2015, pp. B1, B7; D. Meinert, "Reinventing Reviews," *HR Magazine*, April 2015, pp. 36–40; J. Ramirez, "Rethinking the Review," *Human Resource Executive*, July/August 2013, pp. 16–19.

HR IN SMALL BUSINESS

Retrofit's Mobile Performance Management

Retrofit offers a combination of a mobile app and personal coaching to help people achieve and maintain a healthy weight. It serves companies looking to improve the health of their workforces and health care organizations seeking to promote healthy lifestyles in their patient populations. Individuals also can sign up for Retrofit's service. Participants use the mobile app to track their food consumption, physical activity, hours of sleep, and weight. They and their coach monitor their progress on a dashboard, and the coach uses the performance data to provide personalized coaching via online video connections.

As an employer of almost 50 people, Chicago-based Retrofit applies similar features—ease of use, mobile technology, and frequent feedback—to its performance management system. Originally, the company started out requiring twice-yearly performance appraisals, but it recently replaced that system by introducing an app called TINYpulse Perform.

Employees work with their managers to enter goals into Perform. When a manager observes goal-related performance to rate, he or she simply opens the app and swipes right for meeting expectations, up for exceeding expectations, or down for falling short. Employees and managers also can enter comments and post supporting documents such as e-mails in praise of an employee's work. At the end of the year, the performance data are available on the app to represent a year's worth of efforts and outcomes for each employee.

According to Catalina Andrade, director of employee happiness at Retrofit, the app supports a goal of making reviews "instantaneous." Managers and employees are less likely to forget about achievements or problems they want to discuss, because they quickly record the information right after these events occur. That efficiency supports Retrofit's expectation that managers will discuss performance with their employees at least twice a month. The expectation of frequent feedback, in turn, aims to support employee engagement and what the company's vice president of human resources calls Retrofit's "culture of health and happiness."

QUESTIONS

1. What methods for measuring performance would be most suitable for the system Retrofit is using? Why?

2. What advice would you give managers at Retrofit to help them deliver performance feedback effectively when they meet with their employees?

SOURCES: Retrofit website, https://www.retrofitme.com, accessed March 9, 2017; Alexia Elajalde-Ruiz, "Annual Reviews Scrapped for Real-Time Feedback," *Chicago Tribune,* April 24, 2016; "Retrofit Signals Growth: Corporate Weight Management Company Announces Talent Acquisition," news release, March 3, 2015, http://www.prweb.com; John Pletz, "Retrofit Bulks Up Corporate Weight-Loss Effort with BSwift," *Crain's Chicago Business,* August 26, 2014, http://www.chicagobusiness.com.

NOTES

1. A. Bradley, "Taking the Formality out of Performance Reviews," *T + D,* June 2010, p. 18; R. Pyrillis, "The Reviews Are In," *Workforce Management,* May 2011, pp. 20–25.
2. P. Cappelli and A. Tavis, "The Performance Management Evolution," *Harvard Business Review,* October 2016, pp. 58–67; M. Laff, "Performance Management Gives a Shaky Performance," *T + D,* September 2007, p. 18; A. Fox, "Curing What Ails Performance Reviews," *HR Magazine,* January 2009, pp. 52–56.
3. J. Wolper, "The Ever Evolving Workplace", *TD* (December 2016): 40-44; CEB, "The Real Impact of Removing Performance Ratings on Employee Performance", May 12, 2016, from www.cebglobal.com, accessed March 8, 2017.
4. V. Fludd, "Performance Management for Managers," *TD,* March 2016, p. 12; "Performance Reviews: Love'em or Hate'em," *TD,* February 2016, p. 18; C. Schoenberger, "The Risk of Reviews," *Wall Street Journal,* October 28, 2015, p. R5; M. Weinstein, "Annual Review under Review," *Training,* July/August 2016, pp. 22–29; D. Wilke, "Is the Annual Performance Review Dead?" *HR Magazine,* October 2015, pp. 11–12; National Center for the Middle Market, R. A. Noe, and L. W. Inks, *It's About People: How Performance Management Helps Middle Market Companies Grow Faster* (Columbus, OH: National Center for the Middle Market, Ohio State University Fisher College of Business, GE Capital, October 2014); J. Ramirez, "Rethinking the Review," *Human Resource Executive,* July/August 2013, pp. 16–19; "SHRM Survey Findings: HR Professionals' Perceptions about Performance Management Effectiveness," October 14, 2014, from www.shrm.org, accessed April 27, 2015.
5. L. Goler, G. Gale, and A. Grant, "Let's Not Kill Performance Evaluations," *Harvard Business Review,* November 2016, pp. 90–94; E. Pulakos, R. Hanson, S. Arad, and N. Moye, "Performance Management Can Be Fixed: An On-the-Job Experiential Learning Approach for Complex Behavior Change, *Industrial and Organizational Psychology,* March 2015, pp. 51–76; E. Pulakos, *Performance Management* (Oxford, U.K.: Wiley-Blackwell, 2009); H. Aguinis, "An Expanded View of Performance Management," in J. W. Smith and M. London (eds.), *Performance Management* (San Francisco: Jossey-Bass, 2009), pp. 1–43; J. Russell and L. Russell, "Talk Me through It: The Next Level of Performance Management," *T + D,* April 2010, pp. 42–48; J. Dahling and A. O'Malley, "Supportive Feedback Environments Can Mend Broken

Performance Management Systems," *Industrial and Organizational Psychology* 4 (2011), pp. 201–3; E. Pulakos and R. O'Leary, "Why Is Performance Management Broken?" *Industrial and Organizational Psychology* 4 (2011), pp. 146–64; E. Mone, C., Eisinger, K. Guggenheim, B. Price, and C. Stine, "Performance Management at the Wheel: Driving Employee Engagement in Organizations," *Journal of Business & Psychology* 26 (2011), pp. 205–12.
6. J. Harbour, "The Three 'Ds' of Successful Performance Measurement: Design, Data, and Display," *Performance Improvement* 50 (February 2011), pp. 5–12.
7. M. McGraw, "Creating Coaches," *Human Resource Executive,* September 2015, pp. 52–53.
8. R. Noe and L. Inks, *It's about People: How Performance Management Helps Middle Market Companies Grow Faster* (Columbus, OH: National Center for the Middle Market, Ohio State University Fisher College of Business, GE Capital, 2014).
9. P. Cappelli and M. Conyon, "What Do Performance Appraisals Do? *National Bureau of Economic Research Working Paper Series,* July 2016, www.nber.org/papres/w22400; J. Cleveland, K. Murphy, and R. Williams, "Multiple Uses of Performance Appraisal: Prevalence and Correlates," *Journal of Applied Psychology* 74 (1989), pp. 130–35.
10. C. Longenecker, "Behind the Mask: The Politics of Employee Appraisal," *Academy of Management Executive* 1 (1987), p. 183.
11. M. Beer, "Note on Performance Appraisal," in *Readings in Human Resource Management,* ed. M. Beer and B. Spector (New York: Free Press, 1985).
12. D. Meinert, "Reinventing Reviews," *HR Magazine,* April 2015, pp. 36–40.
13. C. G. Banks and K. E. May, "Performance Management: The Real Glue in Organizations," in *Evolving Practices in Human Resource Management,* ed. A. Kraut and A. Korman (San Francisco: Jossey-Bass, 1999), pp. 118–45; R. Connors and T. Smith, "Want Results? Fix Accountability," *Chief Learning Officer,* February 2015, pp. 44–46.
14. C. D. Ittner and D. F. Larcker, "Coming Up Short on Nonfinancial Performance Measurement," *Harvard Business Review,* December 2003, pp. 88–95.
15. J. K. Harter, F. Schmidt, and T. L. Hayes, "Business-Unit-Level Relationships between Employee Satisfaction, Employee Engagement, and Business Outcomes: A Meta-analysis," *Journal of Applied Psychology* 87 (2002), pp. 268–79.

16. A. J. Rucci, S. P. Kim, and R. T. Quinn, "The Employee-Customer-Profit Chain at Sears," *Harvard Business Review*, January/February 1998, pp. 82–97.

17. R. Schuler and S. Jackson, "Linking Competitive Strategies with Human Resource Practices," *Academy of Management Executive* 1 (1987), pp. 207–19.

18. L. King, J. Hunter, and F. Schmidt, "Halo in a Multidimensional Forced-Choice Performance Evaluation Scale," *Journal of Applied Psychology* 65 (1980), pp. 507–16.

19. B. R. Nathan, A. M. Mohrman, and J. Millman, "Interpersonal Relations as a Context for the Effects of Appraisal Interviews on Performance and Satisfaction: A Longitudinal Study," *Academy of Management Journal* 34 (1991), pp. 352–69; M. S. Taylor, K. B. Tracy, M. K. Renard, J. K. Harrison, and S. J. Carroll, "Due Process in Performance Appraisal: A Quasi-experiment in Procedural Justice," *Administrative Science Quarterly* 40 (1995), pp. 495–523; J. M. Werner and M. C. Bolino, "Explaining U.S. Courts of Appeals Decisions Involving Performance Appraisal: Accuracy, Fairness, and Validation," *Personnel Psychology* 50 (1997), pp. 1–24.

20. M. Buckingham and A. Goodall, "Reinventing Performance Management," *Harvard Business Review*, April 2015, pp. 40–50.

21. A. DeNisi and K. Murphy, "Performance Appraisal and Performance Management: 100 Years of Progress?" *Journal of Applied Psychology*, January 26, 2017; J. Campbell and B. Wiernik, "The Modeling and Assessment of Work Performance," *Annual Review of Organizational Psychology and Organizational Behavior* 2 (2015), pp. 47–74.

22. Weinstein, "Annual Review under Review."

23. *Albemarle Paper Company v. Moody*, 10 FEP 1181 (1975).

24. S. Ng and J. Lublin, "AIG Pay Plan: Rank and Rile," *Wall Street Journal*, February 11, 2010, p. R8.

25. S. Bates, "Forced Ranking," *HR Magazine*, June 2003, pp. 63–68; A. Meisler, "Deadman's Curve," *Workforce Management*, July 2003, pp. 44–49; M. Lowery, "Forcing the Issue," *Human Resource Executive* (October 16, 2003), pp. 26–29; J. Welch, "Rank and Yank, That's Not How It's Done," *Wall Street Journal*, November 15, 2013, p. A15.

26. Ibid; P. Cappelli, "Why Managers Should Stop Thinking of A, B, and C Players," *Wall Street Journal*, February 21, 2017, pp. R5, R7; E. O'Boyle, Jr. and H. Aguinis, "The Best and the Rest: Revisiting the Norm of Normality of Individual Performance," *Personnel Psychology* 65 (2010), pp. 79–119.

27. S. Scullen, P. Bergey, and L. Aiman-Smith, "Forced Choice Distribution Systems and the Improvement of Workforce Potential: A Baseline Simulation," *Personnel Psychology* 58 (2005), pp. 1–32.

28. S. Ovide and R. Feintzeig, "Microsoft Abandons Dreaded 'Stack,'" *Wall Street Journal*, November 13, 2013, pp. B1, B5.

29. F. Blanz and E. Ghiselli, "The Mixed Standard Scale: A New Rating System," *Personnel Psychology* 25 (1973), pp. 185–99; K. Murphy and J. Constans, "Behavioral Anchors as a Source of Bias in Rating," *Journal of Applied Psychology* 72 (1987), pp. 573–77.

30. *Brito v. Zia Co.*, 478 F.2nd 1200 (10th Cir 1973).

31. P. Smith and L. Kendall, "Retranslation of Expectations: An Approach to the Construction of Unambiguous Anchors for Rating Scales," *Journal of Applied Psychology* 47 (1963), pp. 149–55.

32. Murphy and Constans, "Behavioral Anchors"; M. Piotrowski, J. Barnes-Farrel, and F. Esrig, "Behaviorally Anchored Bias: A Replication and Extension of Murphy and Constans," *Journal of Applied Psychology* 74 (1989), pp. 823–26.

33. U. Wiersma and G. Latham, "The Practicality of Behavioral Observation Scales, Behavioral Expectation Scales, and Trait Scales," *Personnel Psychology* 39 (1986), pp. 619–28.

34. G. Latham and K. Wexley, *Increasing Productivity through Performance Appraisal* (Boston: Addison-Wesley, 1981).

35. Wiersma and Latham, "The Practicality of Behavioral Observation Scales, Behavioral Expectation Scales, and Trait Scales."

36. M. Campion, A. Fink, B. Ruggeberg, L. Carr, G. Phillips, and R. Odman, "Doing Competencies Well: Best Practices in Competency Modeling," *Personnel Psychology* 64 (2011), pp. 225–62; J. Shippmann, R. Ash, M. Battista, L. Carr, L. Eyde, B. Hesketh, J. Kehow, K. Pearlman, and J. Sanchez, "The Practice of Competency Modeling," *Personnel Psychology* 53 (2000), pp. 703–40; A. Lucia and R. Lepsinger, *The Art and Science of Competency Models* (San Francisco: Jossey-Bass, 1999).

37. C. Spicer, "Building a Competency Model," *HR Magazine*, April 2009, pp. 34–36.

38. S. Snell, "Control Theory in Strategic Human Resource Management: The Mediating Effect of Administrative Information," *Academy of Management Journal* 35 (1992), pp. 292–327.

39. T. Patten Jr., *A Manager's Guide to Performance Appraisal* (New York: Free Press, 1982).

40. M. O'Donnell and R. O'Donnell, "MBO—Is It Passe?" *Hospital and Health Services Administration* 28, no. 5 (1983), pp. 46–58; T. Poister and G. Streib, "Management Tools in Government: Trends over the Past Decade," *Public Administration Review* 49 (1989), pp. 240–48.

41. E. Locke and G. Latham, *A Theory of Goal Setting and Task Performance* (Englewood Cliffs, NJ: Prentice Hall, 1990).

42. S. Carroll and H. Tosi, *Management by Objectives* (New York: Macmillan, 1973).

43. G. Odiorne, *MBO II: A System of Managerial Leadership for the 80's* (Belmont, CA: Pitman, 1986); E. Pulakos, *Performance Management* (Oxford, England: Wiley-Blackwell, 2009).

44. R. Rodgers and J. Hunter, "Impact of Management by Objectives on Organizational Productivity," *Journal of Applied Psychology* 76 (1991), pp. 322–26.

45. V. Liberman, "Performance Management: To Get Results Stop Measuring People by Them," *The Conference Board Review*, Summer 2013, pp. 57–63.

46. R. S. Kaplan and D. P. Norton, "Using the Balanced Scorecard as a Strategic Management System," *Harvard Business Review*, July/August 2007, pp. 150–161.

47. W. Schiemann, "Aligning Performance Management with Organizational Strategy, Values, and Goals," in J. W. Smither and M. London (eds.), *Performance Management* (San Francisco: Jossey-Bass, 2009), pp. 45–87.

48. R. Pritchard, S. Jones, P. Roth, K. Stuebing, and S. Ekeberg, "The Evaluation of an Integrated Approach to Measuring Organizational Productivity," *Personnel Psychology* 42 (1989), pp. 69–115; R. Pritchard, M. Harrell, D. DiazGranados, and M. Guzman, "The Productivity Measurement and Enhancement System: A Meta-Analysis," *Journal of Applied Psychology* 93 (2008), pp. 340–67.

49. P. Wright, J. George, S. Farnsworth, and G. McMahan, "Productivity and Extra-Role Behavior: The Effects of Goals and Incentives on Spontaneous Helping," *Journal of Applied Psychology* 78, no. 3 (1993), pp. 374–81.

50. Latham and Wexley, *Increasing Productivity through Performance Appraisal*.

51. L. Weber, "At Kimberly-Clark, 'Dead Wood' Workers Have Nowhere to Hide," *Wall Street Journal*, August 22, 2016,

pp. A1, A10; G. Tucker, "HR in the Age of Disruption," *HR Magazine*, September 2016, pp. 69–73.

52. R. L. Cardy, "Performance Appraisal in a Quality Context: A New Look at an Old Problem," in *Performance Appraisal: State of the Art in Practice*, ed. J. W. Smither (San Francisco: Jossey-Bass, 1998), pp. 132–62.

53. E. C. Huge, *Total Quality: An Executive's Guide for the 1990s* (Homewood, IL: Richard D. Irwin, 1990): see Chapter 5, "Measuring and Rewarding Performance," pp. 70–88; W. E. Deming, *Out of Crisis* (Cambridge, MA: MIT Center for Advanced Engineering Study, 1986).

54. M. Caroselli, *Total Quality Transformations* (Amherst, MA: Human Resource Development Press, 1991); Huge, *Total Quality*.

55. M. Sallie-Dosunmu, "Born to Grow," *T + D*, May 2006, pp. 33–37.

56. A. Brunet and S. New, "Kaizen in Japan: An Empirical Study," *International Journal of Production and Operations Management* 23 (2003), pp. 1426–46.

57. D. E. Bowen and E. E. Lawler III, "Total Quality-Oriented Human Resource Management," *Organizational Dynamics* 21 (1992), pp. 29–41.

58. R. Heneman, K. Wexley, and M. Moore, "Performance Rating Accuracy: A Critical Review," *Journal of Business Research* 15 (1987), pp. 431–48.

59. T. Becker and R. Klimoski, "A Field Study of the Relationship between the Organizational Feedback Environment and Performance," *Personnel Psychology* 42 (1989), pp. 343–58; H. M. Findley, W. F. Giles, and K. W. Mossholder, "Performance Appraisal and Systems Facets: Relationships with Contextual Performance," *Journal of Applied Psychology* 85 (2000), pp. 634–40.

60. WorldatWork, "Performance Management at Whirlpool," www.youtube.com/user/WorldatWorkTV, accessed March 6, 2017.

61. L. Axline, "Performance Biased Evaluations," *Supervisory Management*, November 1991, p. 3.

62. G. Tucker, "HR in the Age of Disruption," *HR Magazine*, September 2016, pp. 69–73.

63. K. Wexley and R. Klimoski, "Performance Appraisal: An Update," in *Research in Personnel and Human Resource Management* (vol. 2), ed. K. Rowland and G. Ferris (Greenwich, CT: JAI Press, 1984).

64. F. Landy and J. Farr, *The Measurement of Work Performance: Methods, Theory, and Applications* (New York: Academic Press, 1983).

65. G. McEvoy and P. Buller, "User Acceptance of Peer Appraisals in an Industrial Setting," *Personnel Psychology* 40 (1987), pp. 785–97.

66. "Our Culture Code" and "How We Lead Matters," www.dell.com, accessed March 8, 2017; C. A. Pomeroy, "Agent of Change," *HR Magazine*, May 2005, pp. 52–56.

67. D. Antonioni, "The Effects of Feedback Accountability on Upward Appraisal Ratings," *Personnel Psychology* 47 (1994), pp. 349–56.

68. K. Murphy and J. Cleveland, *Performance Appraisal: An Organizational Perspective* (Boston: Allyn & Bacon, 1991).

69. J. Bernardin and L. Klatt, "Managerial Appraisal Systems: Has Practice Caught Up with the State of the Art?" *Public Personnel Administrator*, November 1985, pp. 79–86.

70. Weinstein, "Annual Review under Review."

71. H. Heidemeier and K. Moser, "Self-Other Agreement in Job Performance Rating: A Meta-analytic Test of a Process Model," *Journal of Applied Psychology* 94 (2008), pp. 353–70.

72. R. Steel and N. Ovalle, "Self-Appraisal Based on Supervisor Feedback," *Personnel Psychology* 37 (1984), pp. 667–85; L. E. Atwater, "The Advantages and Pitfalls of Self-Assessment in Organizations," in J. Smither (ed.) *Performance Appraisal: State of the Art in Practice* (San Francisco: Jossey-Bass, 1998) pp. 331–65.

73. E. Gummerson, "Lip Services—A Neglected Area of Service Marketing," *Journal of Services Marketing* 1 (1987), pp. 1–29.

74. Weinstein, "Annual Review under Review."

75. J. Bernardin, B. Hagan, J. Kane, and P. Villanova, "Effective Performance Management: A Focus on Precision, Customers, and Situational Constraints," in *Performance Appraisal: State of the Art in Practice*, ed. J. W. Smither (San Francisco: Jossey-Bass, 1998), pp. 3–48.

76. R. Hoffman, "Ten Reasons You Should Be Using 360-Degree Feedback," *HR Magazine*, April 1995, pp. 82–84.

77. S. Sherman, "How Tomorrow's Best Leaders Are Learning Their Stuff," *Fortune*, November 27, 1995, pp. 90–104; W. W. Tornow, M. London, and Associates, *Maximizing the Value of 360-Degree Feedback* (San Francisco: Jossey-Bass, 1998); D. A. Waldman, L. E. Atwater, and D. Antonioni, "Has 360-Degree Feedback Gone Amok?" *Academy of Management Executive* 12 (1988), pp. 86–94.

78. P. McCord, "How Netflix Reinvented HR," *Harvard Business Review*, January/February 2014, pp. 71–76.

79. J. Farr, J. Fairchild, and S. Cassidy, "Technology and Performance Appraisal," in *The Psychology of Workplace Technology*, ed. M. Coovert and L. Thompson (New York: Routledge, 2014), pp. 77–98.

80. A. Adkins, "What Millennials Want from Work and Life," www.gallup.com, May 11, 2016; A. Williams, "Move over Millennials: Here Comes Generation Z," *New York Times*, September 18, 2015, p. ST1.

81. K. Maher, "Big Employer Is Watching," *Wall Street Journal*, November 4, 2003, pp. B1, B6.

82. B. Morris, "Meet the Truck Driver of 2013," *Wall Street Journal*, November 14, 2013, pp. B1, B6; L. Katz, "Big Employer Is Watching," *HR Magazine*, June 2015, pp. 67–74.

83. A. Mathews, "Big Data's New Prescription: Tracking Doctors at Work," *Wall Street Journal*, July 12, 2013, pp. 11, A10.

84. D. Lawrence, "Tracking the Enemy Within," *Bloomberg Businessweek*, March 16–March 22, 2015, pp. 39–41.

85. C. Farr, "Fitbit At Work," *FastCompany*, May 2016, pp. 27–30.

86. D. Brin, "Wearable Worries," *HR Magazine*, June 2016, pp. 138–140.

87. Katz, "Big Employer Is Watching"; Brin, "Wearable Worries"; "Should Companies Monitor Their Employees Social Media," *Wall Street Journal*, May 12, 2014, pp. R1, R2.

88. D. Bhave, "The Invisible Eye? Electronic Performance Monitoring and Employee Job Performance," *Personnel Psychology* 67 (2014), pp. 605–35.

89. R. Silverman, "Managers: Watch Your Language," *Wall Street Journal*, September 20, 2015, p. R9; The Royal Society, "Understanding Unconscious Bias," https://www.youtube.com/watch?v=dVp9Z5k0dEE, accessed November 1, 2016; A. Tversky and D. Kahneman, "Availability: A Heuristic for Judging Frequency and Probability," *Cognitive Psychology* 5 (1973), pp. 207–32.

90. S. Leibowitz, "Stanford University Researchers Analyzed the Language in 125 Performance Reviews from a Tech Company and Found Something Disturbing," *Business Insider*, October 1, 2015.

91. K. Wexley and W. Nemeroff, "Effects of Racial Prejudice, Race of Applicant, and Biographical Similarity on Interviewer Evaluations of Job Applicants," *Journal of Social and Behavioral Sciences* 20 (1974), pp. 66–78.

92. D. Smith, "Training Programs for Performance Appraisal: A Review," *Academy of Management Review* 11 (1986), pp. 22–40.

93. G. Latham, K. Wexley, and E. Pursell, "Training Managers to Minimize Rating Errors in the Observation of Behavior," *Journal of Applied Psychology* 60 (1975), pp. 550–55.

94. J. Bernardin and E. Pence, "Effects of Rater Training: Creating New Response Sets and Decreasing Accuracy," *Journal of Applied Psychology* 65 (1980), pp. 60–66.

95. E. Pulakos, "A Comparison of Rater Training Programs: Error Training and Accuracy Training," *Journal of Applied Psychology* 69 (1984), pp. 581–88; E. Dierdorff, E. Surface, and K. Brown, "Frame-of-Reference Training Effectiveness: Effects of Goal Orientation and Self-Efficacy on Affective, Cognitive, Skill-Based and Transfer Outcomes," *Journal of Applied Psychology* 95 (2010), pp. 1181–1191.

96. H. J. Bernardin, M. R. Buckley, C. L. Tyler, and D. S. Wiese, "A Reconsideration of Strategies in Rater Training," in G. R. Ferris (ed.), *Research in Personnel and Human Resource Management* (Greenwich, CT: JAI Press, 2000), vol. 18, pp. 221–74.

97. Silverman, "Managers: Watch Your Language"; Google, "Making the Unconscious Conscious," https://www.youtube.com/watch?v=NW5s_-Nl3JE, accessed November 1, 2016.

98. J. Sammer, "Calibrating Consistency," *HR Magazine*, January 2008, pp. 73–75.

99. S. W. J. Kozlowski, G. T. Chao, and R. F. Morrison, "Games Raters Play: Politics, Strategies, and Impression Management in Performance Appraisal," in *Performance Appraisal: State of the Art in Practice*, pp. 163–205; C. Rosen, P. Levy, and R. Hall, "Placing Perceptions of Politics in the Context of the Feedback Environment, Employee Attitudes, and Job Performance," *Journal of Applied Psychology* 91 (2006), pp. 211–20.

100. R. Pyrillis, "The Reviews Are In," *Workforce Management*, May 2011, pp. 20–25.

101. K. Wexley, V. Singh, and G. Yukl, "Subordinate Participation in Three Types of Appraisal Interviews," *Journal of Applied Psychology* 58 (1973), pp. 54–57; K. Wexley, "Appraisal Interview," in *Performance Assessment*, ed. R. A. Berk (Baltimore: Johns Hopkins University Press, 1986), pp. 167–85; D. Cederblom, "The Performance Appraisal Interview: A Review, Implications, and Suggestions," *Academy of Management Review* 7 (1982), pp. 219–27; B. D. Cawley, L. M. Keeping, and P. E. Levy, "Participation in the Performance Appraisal Process and Employee Reactions: A Meta-analytic Review of Field Investigations," *Journal of Applied Psychology* 83, no. 3 (1998), pp. 615–63; H. Aguinis, *Performance Management* (Upper Saddle River, NJ: Pearson Prentice Hall, 2007); C. Lee, "Feedback, Not Appraisal," *HR Magazine*, November 2006, pp. 111–14; R. Hanson and E. Pulakos, *Putting the 'Performance' Back in Performance Management* (Alexandria, VA: Society for Human Resource Management, 2015); M. Budworth, G. Latham, and L. Manroop, "Looking Forward to Performance Improvement: A Field Test of the Feedforward Interview for Performance Management," *Human Resource Management* 54 (2014), pp. 45–54; A. Kinicki, K. Jacobson, S. Peterson, and G. Prussia,

"Development and Validation of the Performance Management Behavior Questionnaire," *Personnel Psychology* 66 (2013), pp. 1–45.

102. B. Hite, "Employers Rethink How They Give Feedback," *Wall Street Journal*, October 13, 2008, p. B5.

103. Weinstein, "Annual Review under Review."

104. R. Feintzeig, " Everything Is Awesome! Why You Can't Tell Employees They're Doing a Bad Job," *Wall Street Journal*, February 10, 2015, p. B1; A. Bryant, "A Boss's Challenge: Have Everyone Join the 'In' Group," *New York Times*, March 23, 2013, p. BU2.

105. W. Giles and K. Mossholder, "Employee Reactions to Contextual and Session Components of Performance Appraisal," *Journal of Applied Psychology* 75 (1990), pp. 371–77.

106. E. Locke and G. Latham, *A Theory of Goal Setting and Task Performance* (Englewood Cliffs, NJ: Prentice Hall, 1990).

107. H. Klein, S. Snell, and K. Wexley, "A Systems Model of the Performance Appraisal Interview Process," *Industrial Relations* 26 (1987), pp. 267–80; C. Crossley, C. Cooper, and T. Wernsing, "Making Things Happen Through Challenging Goals: Leader Proactivity, Trust, and Business-Unit Performance," *Journal of Applied Psychology*, 98 (2103), pp. 540–49.

108. E. Kasson, "Plan Your Exits", *HR Magazine* (June 2016):111-117.

109. Cappelli, "Why Managers Should Stop Thinking of A, B, and C Players."

110. *Brito v. Zia Co.*, 478 F.2d 1200 (10th Cir 1973).

111. K. Kraiger and J. Ford, "A Meta-Analysis of Ratee Race Effects in Performance Rating," *Journal of Applied Psychology* 70 (1985), pp. 56–65; S. Needleman, "Monitoring the Monitors: Small Firms Increasingly Are Keeping Tabs on Their Workers, Keystroke by Keystroke," *Wall Street Journal*, August 16, 2010, p. R8.

112. P. Sackett, C. DuBois, and A. Noe, "Tokenism in Performance Evaluation: The Effects of Work Groups Representation on Male–Female and White–Black Differences in Performance Ratings," *Journal of Applied Psychology* 76 (1991), pp. 263–67.

113. "GE Subsidiary MRA Systems to Pay $130,000 to Settle EEOC Age Discrimination Suit," June 3, 2010, news release from www.eeoc.gov, accessed April 29, 2015.

114. "EEOC Sues Wisconsin Plastics for Discrimination against Hmong and Hispanic Employees," June 9, 2014, news release from www.eeoc.gov, accessed April 29, 2015.

115. J. Segal, "That Difficult Conversation," *HR Magazine*, April 2016, pp. 74–75; E. Kasson, "Plan Your Exits," *HR Magazine*, June 2016, pp. 111–117; G. Barrett and M. Kernan, "Performance Appraisal and Terminations: A Review of Court Decisions since *Brito v. Zia* with Implications for Personnel Practices," *Personnel Psychology* 40 (1987), pp. 489–503; H. Field and W. Holley, "The Relationship of Performance Appraisal System Characteristics to Verdicts in Selected Employment Discrimination Cases," *Academy of Management Journal* 25 (1982), pp. 392–406; J. M. Werner and M. C. Bolino, "Explaining U.S. Courts of Appeals Decisions Involving Performance Appraisal: Accuracy, Fairness, and Validation," *Personnel Psychology* 50 (1997), pp. 1–24; J. Segal, "Performance Management Blunders," *HR Magazine*, November 2010, pp. 75–77.

Employee Development

LEARNING OBJECTIVES

After reading this chapter, you should be able to:

LO 9-1 Explain how employee development contributes to strategies related to employee retention, development of intellectual capital, and business growth. *page 382*

LO 9-2 Discuss the steps in the development planning process. *page 385*

LO 9-3 Explain the employees' and company's responsibilities in planning development. *page 385*

LO 9-4 Discuss current trends in using formal education for development. *page 389*

LO 9-5 Relate how assessment of personality type, work behaviors, and job performance can be used for employee development. *page 393*

LO 9-6 Explain how job experiences can be used for skill development. *page 398*

LO 9-7 Develop successful mentoring programs. *page 405*

LO 9-8 Describe how to train managers to coach employees. *page 408*

LO 9-9 Discuss what companies are doing to melt the glass ceiling. *page 409*

LO 9-10 Use the 9-box grid for identifying where employees fit in a succession plan and construct appropriate development plans for them. *page 410*

ENTER THE WORLD OF BUSINESS

Development is 3M's Adhesive for Maintaining a Competitive Advantage

3M has been around for more than 100 years, using science and innovation to provide consumer products including tape, Post-It notes, bandages, sandpaper, and business products such as various types of films, filters, and wound care dressings. 3M considers all employees as leaders and so it provides development opportunities at each stage of their careers. 3M strives to engage all employees by focusing on their career and development desires. In fact, one of 3M's sustainability objectives is that all of its global workforce (90,000 employees in 70 countries) will be actively involved in development opportunities by 2025.

Each year, all employees create or update their development plan, which includes short- and long-term career goals. All employees are encouraged to continuously learn and improve their skills. 3M's tuition reimbursement program encourages employees to seek education in order to meet current job responsibilities and help prepare for career changes or to advance on their chosen career paths. For many functional areas, competency models are available that provide links to relevant training opportunities and development recommendations that can be discussed and agreed upon with the employee's supervisor. Options include growing the competency through on-the-job activities or social learning through a coach or mentor.

Because 3M believes leadership development provides a competitive advantage, it has invested in multiple leadership development programs offered at different stages in an employee's career. Business and leadership courses are available to employees at any level, including online programs available to all of 3M's global employees. 3M emphasizes diversity, collaboration, and inclusion in all of its leadership programs. Leadership programs are based on key leadership behaviors, which are linked to leaders' performance evaluations.

For example, one leadership development program, 3M Leadership Way, has four levels: Spark, Ignite, Amplify, and Catalyst. Spark is targeted to junior 3M leaders who have been identified as having high potential. Ignite participants are new managers who are learning their roles. Training on how to build effective teams is provided using gamification and virtual technology. Managers complete a project to show the impact of learning and applications in their daily work. In Amplify, leaders of multiple teams work on projects, visit customers, and work on their skills for nine months. Catalyst, is a year-long program in which leaders attend leadership meetings; gain exposure to customer and other perspectives outside of 3M; and work on a project that focuses on a challenge issued by top management, a customer-based project to help solve the customer's needs, or a community-based project. All of the levels include self-assessment of competencies as well as 360-degree feedback and coaching.

SOURCES: Based on B. Hassell, "The Best of Both Worlds: Learning through a Marketer's Lens," *Chief Learning Officer,* September 2016, pp. 26, 28, 30; "About" from www.3M.com and "Education and Career Growth," from http://www.3m.com/3M/en_US/sustainability-report/global-challenges/education-and-development/#EducationCareerGrowth, accessed May 22, 2017.

Introduction

As the 3M example illustrates, employee development is a key contributor to a company's competitive advantage by helping employees understand their strengths, weaknesses, and interests and by showing them how new jobs and expanded job responsibilities are available to them to meet their personal growth needs. This helps retain valuable managers who might otherwise leave to join clients or competitors. Development is important for all employees, not just managers. Employee development is a necessary component of a company's efforts to compete in the new economy, to meet the challenges of global competition and social change, and to incorporate technological advances and changes in work design. Employee development is key to ensuring that employees have the competencies necessary to serve customers and create new products and customer solutions. Regardless of the business strategy, development is important for retaining talented employees. Also, because companies (and their employees) must continually learn and change to meet customer needs and compete in new markets, the emphasis placed on both training and development has increased. As we noted in Chapter 1, employee commitment and retention are directly related to how employees are treated by their managers.

©KEN Wolter/123RF

Career development for employees is a key contributor to 3M's continued success across many digital platforms.

This chapter begins by discussing the relationship among development, training, and careers. Choosing an approach is one part of development planning. Before employees choose development activities, the employee and the company must have an idea of the employee's development needs and the purpose of development. Identifying the needs and purpose of development is part of the planning process, which this chapter describes in detail. Employee and company responsibilities at each step of the process are emphasized. The chapter also looks at development approaches, including formal education, assessment, job experiences, and interpersonal relationships, with a focus on the types of skills, knowledge, and behaviors that are strengthened by each development method. The chapter concludes with a discussion of special issues in employee development, including succession planning and using development to help women and minorities move into upper-level management positions (referred to as "melting the glass ceiling").

Development
The acquisition of knowledge, skills, and behaviors that improve an employee's ability to meet changes in job requirements and in client and customer demands.

LO 9-1
Explain how employee development contributes to strategies related to employee retention, development of intellectual capital, and business growth.

The Relationship among Development, Training, and Careers

DEVELOPMENT AND TRAINING

Development refers to formal education, job experiences, relationships, and assessment of personality and abilities that help employees prepare for the future. The 3M example illustrates that although development can occur through participation in planned programs, it often results from performing different types of work. Because it is

	TRAINING	DEVELOPMENT
Focus	Current	Future
Use of work experiences	Low	High
Goal	Preparation for current job	Preparation for changes
Participation	Required	Voluntary

Table 9.1
Comparison between Training and Development

future-oriented, it involves learning that is not necessarily related to the employee's current job.[1] Table 9.1 shows the differences between training and development. Traditionally, training focuses on helping employees' performance in their current jobs. Development prepares them for other positions in the company and increases their ability to move into jobs that may not yet exist.[2] Development also helps employees prepare for changes in their current jobs that may result from new technology, work designs, new customers, or new product markets.

Development is especially critical for talent management, particularly for senior managers and employees with leadership potential (recall our discussion of attracting and retaining talent in Chapter 1). Development is necessary for ensuring that Millennial employees are prepared to take Baby Boomers' leadership roles as they retire. Companies report that the most important talent management challenges they face include developing existing talent and attracting and retaining existing leadership talent.[3] Also, development provides opportunities for all employees to grow their skills and use them in different ways, which has been shown to contribute to high levels of engagement and satisfaction.[4]

Chapter 7 emphasized the strategic role of training. As training continues to become more strategic (i.e., related to business goals), the distinction between training and development will blur. Both training and development will be required and will focus on current and future personal and company needs.

DEVELOPMENT AND CAREERS

Today's careers are known as protean careers.[5] A **protean career** is based on self-direction with the goal of psychological success in one's work. Employees take major responsibility for managing their careers. For example, an engineer may decide to take a sabbatical from her position to work in management at the United Way for a year. The purpose of this assignment could be to develop her managerial skills as well as help her personally evaluate if she likes managerial work more than engineering.

The protean career has several implications for employee development. The goal of the new career is **psychological success**: the feeling of pride and accomplishment that comes from achieving life goals that are not limited to achievements at work (such as raising a family and having good physical health). Psychological success is self-determined rather than determined solely through signals the employee receives from the company (like salary increases and promotions). For example, a 52-year-old woman co-managed a real estate business in California with her husband.[6] She always wanted to work in medicine or health care and took health science classes in college but decided to work in real estate because it provided a good income and flexibility when she was raising her children. After working in real estate for 25 years, she pursued her passion by taking prerequisite classes and applying to nursing school.

Protean career
A career that is changing frequently due to both changes in the person's interests, abilities, and values and changes in the work environment.

Psychological success
The feeling of pride and accomplishment that comes from achieving life goals.

Unfortunately, her husband suffered a debilitating stroke, making her the sole provider for the family. She sold the real estate business, applied and was accepted to nursing school, and managed her husband's care. At age 57, she graduated from nursing school but was unable to find a job in California. She eventually found a job in a hospital in Oklahoma and moved there with her husband. After gaining valuable experience, she moved back to California and now works in a facility for developmentally disabled adults. She is passionate about her new job despite its long and inflexible working hours, and the physical and emotional demands of staying on her feet all day and helping people with many needs.

Employees need to develop new skills rather than rely on a static knowledge base. This has resulted from companies' need to be more responsive to customers' service and product demands. As we emphasized in Chapter 7, learning is continuous, often informal, and involves creating and sharing knowledge.

The emphasis on continuous learning has altered the direction and frequency of movement within careers (known as a *career pattern*).[7] Traditional career patterns consisted of a series of steps arranged in a linear hierarchy, with higher steps related to increased authority, responsibility, and compensation. Expert career patterns involve a lifelong commitment to a field or specialization (such as law, medicine, or management). These types of career patterns will not disappear. Rather, career patterns involving movement across specializations or disciplines (a spiral career pattern) will become more prevalent. These new career patterns mean that developing employees (as well as employees taking control of their own careers) will require providing them with the opportunity to (1) determine their interests, skill strengths, and weaknesses and (2) based on this information, seek appropriate development experiences that will likely involve job experiences and relationships as well as formal courses.

The most appropriate view of today's careers are that they are "boundaryless and often change."[8] A career may include movement across several employers (job hopping) or even different occupations. Studies have found that by age 35, 25% of employees have held five jobs or more, and for employees 55 and older, 20% have held 10 jobs or more.[9] One-third of employers expect job hopping to occur, especially among new college graduates, but 40% believe it becomes less acceptable when employees are in their mid-30s. The reality is that employees will be unlikely to stay at one company for their entire or even a significant part of their career. This means that companies and employees should add value to each other.[10] That is, regardless of how long employees stay, developing them can help the company adapt to changing business conditions and strategies by providing new skill sets and managerial talent. It can help reduce employees' job hopping because they feel less need to change employers to build their skill sets or gain valuable job experiences.

For example, Citigroup has introduced several development programs to recruit and keep its Millennial employees.[11] One program provides the opportunity to work on global projects. A project in Kenya will help small businesses develop growth strategies. Another program allows employees to spend a year working with nonprofits. These Citigroup programs help meet Millennial employees' needs to help others, gives them a break from the long hours and stress of their banking jobs, and helps them develop new skills and gain new perspectives.

"Boundaryless" means that careers may involve identifying more with a job or profession than with the present employer. A career can also be considered boundaryless in the sense that career plans or goals are influenced by personal or family demands and values. One way that employees cope with changes in their personal lives as well as in employment relationships is to rearrange and shift their roles and responsibilities. Employees can change their careers throughout their lives based on awareness of strengths and weaknesses, perceived need to balance work and life, and the need to find stimulating and exciting work.[12] Career success may not be tied to promotions but to achieving goals that are personally meaningful to the employee rather than those set by parents, peers, or the company. As we discuss later in the chapter, careers are best managed through partnerships between employees and their company that create a positive relationship through which employees are committed to the organization but can take personal control for managing their own careers to benefit themselves and the company.

As this discussion shows, to retain and motivate employees, companies need to provide a system to identify and meet employees' development needs. This is especially important to retain good performers and employees who have potential for managerial positions. Such systems are often known as **development planning systems** or career management systems. We discuss these systems in the next section.

> **Development planning system**
> A system to retain and motivate employees by identifying and meeting their development needs (also called *career management systems*).

Development Planning Systems

Companies' development planning systems vary in the level of sophistication and the emphasis they place on different components of the process. Steps and responsibilities in the development planning system are shown in Figure 9.1.

> **LO 9-2**
> Discuss the steps in the development planning process.

SELF-ASSESSMENT

Self-assessment refers to the use of information by employees to determine their career interests, values, aptitudes, and behavioral tendencies. It often involves psychological tests such as the Myers-Briggs Type Indicator (described later in the chapter), the Strong Interest Inventory, and the Self-Directed Search. The Strong Interest Inventory helps

> **LO 9-3**
> Explain the employees' and company's responsibilities in planning development.

Figure 9.1

Steps and Responsibilities in the Development Planning Process

	Self-assessment	Reality check	Goal setting	Action planning
Employee responsibility	Identify opportunities and needs to improve.	Identify what needs are realistic to develop.	Identify goal and method to determine goal progress.	Identify steps and timetable to reach goal.
Company responsibility	Provide assessment information to identify strengths, weaknesses, interests, and values.	Communicate performance evaluation; where employee fits in long-range plans of the company; and changes in industry, profession, and workplace.	Ensure that goal is SMART (specific, measurable, attainable, relevant, and timely); commit to help employee reach the goal.	Identify resources employee needs to reach goal, including additional assesment, courses, work experiences, and relationships.

employees identify their occupational and job interests; the Self-Directed Search identifies employees' preferences for working in different types of environments (like sales, counseling, landscaping, and so on). Tests may also help employees identify the relative values they place on work and leisure activities.

Through the assessment, a development need can be identified. This need can result from gaps between current skills and/or interests and the type of work or position the employee wants. For example, BB&T Corporation provides all of its associates access to a personal communications style assessment.[13] The assessment is used to identify strategies that can help associates to relate more effectively to to their co-workers and clients.

REALITY CHECK

Reality check refers to the information employees receive about how the company evaluates their skills and knowledge and where they fit into the company's plans (potential promotion opportunities, lateral moves). Usually this information is provided by the employee's manager as part of performance appraisal. Some companies also use the 360-degree feedback assessment, which involves employees completing a self-evaluation of their behaviors or competencies while managers, peers, direct reports, and even customers provide smaller evaluations. (360-degree feedback is discussed later in the chapter.) It is not uncommon in well-developed systems for the manager to hold separate performance appraisals and development discussions.

For example, at Michelin North America, the employee, his or her boss, and the employee's career manager make up what is known as the "career triangle."[14] The employee and his or her manager discuss the employee's current position, the skills the employee would like to develop, and possible new roles. These discussions help employees understand the expectations for their current and possible new positions, their current performance, and how they can improve. Michelin has an internal job posting system that members of the career triangle can use to search for next jobs and career interests that match the employees' interests and goals.

GOAL SETTING

Goal setting refers to the process of employees developing short- and long-term development objectives. These goals usually relate to desired positions (e.g., becoming sales manager within three years), level of skill application (using one's budgeting skills to improve the unit's cash flow problems), work setting (moving to corporate marketing within two years), or skill acquisition (learning how to use the company's human resource information system). These goals are usually discussed with the manager and written into a development plan. A sample development plan for a product manager is shown in Figure 9.2. Development plans usually include descriptions of strengths and weaknesses, career goals, and development activities for reaching the career goal. An effective development plan is simple, clear, and realistic, and it focuses on developmental needs that are most relevant to both the individual's career and the organization's strategic objectives.[15]

Consigli Construction provides employees with a online tool that enables them to see possible lateral moves and promotion opportunities.[16] Employees can click on a specific role to see the job description, summary, required experience, performance standards, preferred education, certification or licensing requirements, learning plan, and promotion criteria.

Figure 9.2

Sample Development Plan

Name: _____   **Title:** Project Manager   **Immediate Manager:** _____

Competencies
Please identify your three greatest strengths and areas for improvement.

Strengths
- Strategic thinking and execution (confidence, command skills, action orientation)
- Results orientation (competence, motivating others, perseverance)
- Spirit for winning (building team spirit, customer focus, respect colleagues)

Areas for Improvement
- Patience (tolerance of people or processes and sensitivity to pacing)
- Written communications (ability to write clearly and succinctly)
- Overly ambitious (too much focus on successful completion of projects rather than developing relationships with individuals involved in the projects)

Development Goals
Please describe your overall career goals.
- **Long-term:** Accept positions of increased responsibility to a level of general manager (or beyond). The areas of specific interest include but are not limited to product and brand management, technology and development, strategic planning, and marketing.
- **Short-term:** Continue to improve my skills in marketing and brand management while utilizing my skills in product management, strategic planning, and global relations.

Next Assignments
Identify potential next assignments (including timing) that would help you develop toward your goals.
- Manager or director level in planning, development, product, or brand management. Timing estimated to be Fall 2017.

Training and Development Needs
List both training and development activities that will either help you develop in your current assignment or provide overall development.
- Master's degree classes will allow me to practice and improve my written communications skills. The dynamics of my current position, teamwork, and reliance on other individuals allow me to practice patience and to focus on individual team members' needs along with the success of the projects.

Employee _____   **Date** _____
Immediate Manager _____   **Date** _____
Mentor _____   **Date** _____

ACTION PLANNING

During this phase, employees complete an action plan. An **action plan** is a written strategy that employees use to determine how they will achieve their short- and long-term career goals. Action plans may involve any one or a combination of development approaches such as enrolling in courses and seminars, getting additional assessment, obtaining new job experiences, or finding a mentor or coach (see the section "Approaches

Action plan
A document summarizing what the trainee and manager will do to ensure that training transfers to the job.

to Employee Development").[17] The development approach used depends on the needs and developmental goal. Wells Fargo's online iDevelop site helps employees prioritize their development needs and create development plans.[18] Employees use the site to identify their competencies. They use the competencies they consider as strengths to choose development activities including training programs and online resources.

EXAMPLES OF DEVELOPMENT PLANNING AND CAREER MANAGEMENT SYSTEMS

Effective development planning systems include several important features (see Table 9.2). Consider development planning and career management systems at Procter & Gamble and Genentech.[19] Procter & Gamble's promotion-from-within policy is supported by the career development plans completed by every employee. These plans identify what type of experience the employee needs and what the employee's next job will be as well as what future jobs he or she might hold. Employees post their resumes online to show managers the skills they are building as well as to communicate whether they are willing to take a different job. Employee career paths and resumes are reviewed at monthly meetings for each business unit. The biotechnology company Genentech Inc. developed CareerLab to help employees perform well in their current jobs and to provide opportunities for job enrichment and lateral career moves. CareerLab is a physical and virtual place where employees can consider their skill strengths and weaknesses as well as their interests, and take ownership of their development. CareerLab includes the opportunity to get career advice from consultants, participate in LearningLabs (webinars and class sessions that cover different topics such as networking for career growth and managing your personal brand), receive mentoring, and attend career workshops. CareerLab also provides access to online career resources including assessments that cover personal style, values, skills, strengths, and interests. Genentech has found that employees who use CareerLab have a high level of engagement with their work, better career conversations with their managers, improved productivity, and a greater likelihood of staying with the company.

Table 9.2
Design Features of Effective Development Systems

1. System is positioned as a response to a business need or supports the business strategy.
2. Employees and managers participate in development of the system.
3. Employees are encouraged to take an active role in career management and development.
4. Evaluation is ongoing and used to improve the system.
5. Business units can customize the system for their own purposes (with some constraints).
6. Employees have access to development and career information sources (including advisors and positions available).
7. Senior management and the company culture support the development system.
8. The development system is linked to other human resource practices such as performance management, training, and recruiting systems.
9. A large, diverse talent pool is created.
10. Development plans and talent evaluation information are available and accessible to all managers.

SOURCE: Based on B. Kaye and C. Smith, "Career Development: Shifting from Nicety to Necessity," *T + D*, January 2012, pp. 52–55; M. Weinstein, "Paths to Success: Responsibility vs. Promotion," *Training*, July/August 2014, pp. 52–54; D. Hall, *Careers in and out of Organizations* (Thousand Oaks, CA: Sage, 2002).

Approaches to Employee Development

Four approaches are used to develop employees: formal education, assessment, job experiences, and interpersonal relationships.[20] Many companies use a combination of these approaches. CHG Healthcare Services' leadership development program includes participating in a 360-degree assessment evaluating the extent to which the employees' behavior aligns with the company's culture and core values, formal education through leadership programs, and mentoring.[21] Figure 9.3 shows the frequency of use of different employee development practices. Both high-visibility assignment and stretch opportunities are considered developmental job experiences.

Although much development activity is targeted at managers, all levels of employees may be involved in development. For example, most employees typically receive performance appraisal feedback (a development activity related to assessment) at least once per year. As part of the appraisal process (see Chapter 8), employees are typically asked to complete individual development plans outlining (1) how they plan to change their weaknesses and (2) their future plans (including positions or locations desired and education or experience needed). Next we explore each type of development approach.

FORMAL EDUCATION

Formal education programs include off-site and on-site programs designed specifically for the company's employees, short courses offered by consultants or universities, executive MBA programs, and university programs in which participants live at the university while taking classes. These programs may involve lectures by business experts, business games and simulations, adventure learning, and meetings with customers.

LO 9-4
Discuss current trends in using formal education for development.

Formal education programs
Employee development programs, including short courses offered by consultants or universities, executive MBA programs, and university programs.

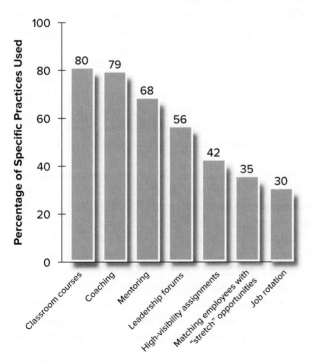

Figure 9.3
Frequency of Use of Employee Development Practices
SOURCE: EFMD, Network of Corporate Academies, Society for Human Resource Management, "Leadership Development: The Path to Greater Effectiveness," 2016, www.shrm.org.

Many companies, such as McDonald's and General Electric, rely primarily on in-house development programs offered by training and development centers or corporate universities, rather than sending employees to programs offered by universities.[22] Companies rely on in-house programs because they can be tied directly to business needs, can be easily evaluated using company metrics, and can get senior-level management involved.

The thousands of restaurant managers and owner-operators who attend McDonald's Hamburger University each year in Oak Brook, Illinois, get classroom training and participate in simulations on how to run a business that delivers consistent service, quality, and cleanliness. They also receive coaching and peer support face-to-face and online. The company's highest-performing executives participate in a nine-month leadership institute at Hamburger U, where they tackle major issues facing the company.

General Electric (GE) has one of the oldest and most widely known management development centers in the world. GE invests approximately $1 billion each year in training and education programs for its employees.[23] Since 2000, the 189 most senior executives in the company spent at least 12 months in training and professional development. GE develops managers at the John F. Welch Leadership Development Center at Crotonville, New York, offering over 1,800 instructor-led and virtual courses and programs.[24] The facility has residence buildings where participants stay while attending programs, as well as classrooms for courses, programs, and seminars. Each year, GE employees—chosen by their managers based on their performance and potential—attend management development programs. The programs include professional skills development and specialized courses in areas such as risk analysis and loan structuring. All of the programs emphasize theory and practical application. Course time is spent discussing business issues facing GE. The programs are taught by in-house instructors, university faculty members, and even CEO Jeff Immelt. GE also offers courses through its global learning centers in Rio de Janeiro, Abu Dhabi, Shanghai, and Bengaluru (in fact, over 70% of in-person sessions are delivered outside the United States).

Examples of management development programs available at GE are shown in Table 9.3. As you can see, GE uses a combination of coursework and job experiences to develop entry-level and top levels of management. Other programs such as the Business Manager Course and the Executive Development Course involve action learning. GE also holds seminars on better understanding customer expectations and leadership conferences designed specifically for African Americans, women, or Hispanic managers to discuss leading and learning.

A number of institutions offer executive education in the United States and abroad, including Harvard University, the Wharton School, the University of Michigan, INSEAD, the International Institute for Management Development (IMD), and the Center for Creative Leadership. At the University of Virginia, the Darden School of Business offers an executive MBA program in which students attend classes on campus once a month (Thursday through Saturday). The on-campus time provides opportunities for students to collaborate on presentations, simulations, and case studies. The school also brings executive MBA students to campus four times for leadership residencies. During each week-long residency, the students use workshops, coaching, and reflection to get better at handling their everyday management challenges. Between the times on campus, the students continue their education with independent study, online classes, and tools for virtual meetings and online exams.[25]

Another trend in executive education is for employers and the education provider to create programs with content and experiences designed specifically for the audience. For example, Duke Corporate Education developed a custom program for Thomson Reuters to increase their managers' skills related to thinking innovatively to help the company

Table 9.3
Examples of Leadership Development Programs at General Electric

PROGRAM	SUMMARY	QUALIFICATIONS TO ATTEND
Commercial Leadership Program	Two-year rotational program focused on development through three or four rotational assignments, education that develops sales competencies, and exposure to leaders. The program prepares individuals for a successful career in sales or sales support. The rotational assignments include projects driven by business priorities. Commercial skills development occurs through business-specific training, coursework, and global training summits.	Bachelor's degree in engineering, or relevant business or science degree. Prior intern or co-op experience, or up to three years' work experience in sales, sales support, or marketing. Strong analytical, communication, interpersonal, and leadership skills. Willingness to relocate.
Experienced Commercial Leadership Program (ECLP): Sales and Marketing	Two-year program includes international training in a variety of locations and leadership opportunities, including change initiatives. Committee participation is encouraged to improve ability to interact with senior business leaders. Every four months, employees complete a self-assessment and review it with managers to identify development needs, career interests, and accomplishments.	An MBA/postgraduate degree with sales and/or marketing experience; demonstrated leadership, and communication and analytical skills; willingness to travel; fluency in English; expertise that is aligned with a particular GE business.

SOURCES: Based on "Commercial Leadership Program Summary," https://www.ge.com/careers/culture/university-students/commercial-leadership-program/global, accessed March 24, 2017; "Experienced Commercial Leadership Program," http://www.ge.com/au/careers/our-programs/eclp/what-you-need-to-know, and http://www.ge.com/au/careers/our-programs/eclp/about-eclp, accessed March 24, 2017.

grow.[26] The Thomson Reuters program sponsor encouraged participants to identify an opportunity or problem with their business that would require innovative thinking. To help the managers develop innovative thinking, Duke used an experiential exercise designed to help managers consider how different global markets can affect their strategies and to understand how consumers' tastes can shift according to where they are located. In the experiential exercise, participants were immersed in a local market to learn how to think about and do business differently. Programs were offered in New York, London, and Shanghai, and involved trips to neighborhoods, businesses, and museums as well as meetings with local leaders to understand the distinctive features of each business market. As a result of the program, participants increased their awareness of how they could be more innovative in their jobs and lead diverse teams. They also gained insights they could directly apply to their business, such as how to use brainstorming techniques to quickly integrate knowledge and ideas.

Managers who attend the Center for Creative Leadership development program take psychological tests; receive feedback from managers, peers, and direct reports; participate in group-building activities (like adventure learning, discussed in Chapter 7); receive counseling; and set improvement goals and write development plans.[27]

Enrollment in executive education programs or MBA programs may be limited to managers or employees identified to have management potential. As a result, many companies also provide tuition reimbursement as a benefit for all employees to encourage them to develop. **Tuition reimbursement** refers to the practice of reimbursing employees' costs for college and university courses and degree programs. Companies that have evaluated tuition reimbursement programs have found that the programs increase employee retention rates and readiness for promotion, and improve job performance.[28]

Tuition reimbursement
The practice of reimbursing employees' costs for college and university courses and degree programs.

INTEGRITY IN ACTION

Development Is More Than Preparing for Promotion

Voya Financial's goal is to be "America's retirement company." It helps customers plan, invest, and protect their savings for retirement. The company serves more than 13 million customers and has received numerous awards for being an ethical company and a desirable place to work. Voya's corporate responsibility pillars include "empowering our people," "serving our clients," "investing in communities," and protecting the environment."

To ensure that Voya is a customer-focused financial company with high ethical standards, the company has taken steps to align its financial strategy with a leadership development strategy that supports its culture of continuous improvement and corporate values. To do so, Voya first identified the core leader behaviors that align with its mission and values. The core leader behaviors included demonstrating integrity, leading with a passion and clarity, and

delivering continuous improvement through talent development and customer service.

Next, considering the core leadership behaviors, Voya designed leadership programs for leaders at all levels of the company. Three courses focus on change management, situational leadership, and performance management. In the performance management course, leaders learn how to identify their personal shortcomings to effective communication and develop skills to help them enhance their ability to provide feedback and coaching, to recognize and reward effective performance, and to create a more inclusive and collaborative culture. Another course covers how to create an environment that demonstrates value, respect, and fair treatment for all customers and employees. The 6P workshop for managers emphasizes how to lead through continuous improvement by using

purpose, people, performance, process, partnership, and problem solving.

To support Voya's development efforts focused on ensuring that leader behaviors align with company values, an equal percentage of managers' performance evaluations are based on how they manage and their success in reaching performance goals. Leaders are terminated if they don't demonstrate Voya's values in how they work.

DISCUSSION QUESTIONS

1. Did Voya support empowerment and ethics through its leader development program? Support your position.
2. Do you think it's necessary or just nice to have employee development support company values? Why or why not?

SOURCES: Based on "Company Overview" and "Corporate Responsibility Pillars," corporate.voya.com, accessed March 22, 2017; S. Gale, "Voya: We Can Always Do Better," *Chief Learning Officer*, January/February 2017, pp. 52–53.

Verizon Wireless invests $26 million annually in a tuition assistance program, in which 23,000 of its employees participate.[29] Employees can receive tuition assistance for attending a university or college or for the costs of the company's on-site program conducted at call centers and corporate offices. The on-site program classes, taught by university faculty, help employees earn degrees by attending classes where they work and when they have free time in their work schedules. They are eligible for tuition reimbursement from the day they are hired and have to make no commitment to stay employed with the company. Their expenses are limited to $8,000 per year for full-time employees and $4,000 for part-time employees. This exceeds the $5,250 annual reimbursement limit that most companies use based on the tax-free maximum established by the IRS. To be eligible for reimbursement, coursework has to relate to the employees' current job or career path within Verizon Wireless. Evaluation of the program has shown that it has resulted in increased morale and helped to attract new and retain current employees.

The "Integrity in Action" box highlights how Voya Financial is using formal education programs to develop ethical company leaders.

ASSESSMENT

Assessment involves collecting information and providing feedback to employees about their behavior, communication style, or skills.[30] The employees, their peers, managers, and customers may provide information. Assessments are used for several reasons. First, assessment is used most frequently to identify employees with managerial potential and to measure current managers' strengths and weaknesses. Assessment is also used to identify managers with the potential to move into higher-level executive positions, and it can be used with work teams to identify the strengths and weaknesses of individual team members and the decision processes or communication styles that inhibit the team's productivity. Assessments can help employees understand their tendencies, their needs, the type of work environment they prefer, and the type of work they might prefer to do.[31] This information, along with the performance evaluations they receive from the company, can help employees decide what type of development goals might be most appropriate for them (e.g., leadership position, increased scope of their current position).

Companies vary in the methods and the sources of information they use in developmental assessment. Many companies use employee performance evaluations. Companies with sophisticated development systems use psychological tests to measure employees' skills, interests, personality types, and communication styles. Self, peer, and managers' ratings of employees' interpersonal styles and behaviors may also be collected. Popular assessment tools include personality tests, assessment center performance appraisal, and 360-degree feedback.

Personality Tests and Inventories

Tests are used to determine if employees have the personality characteristics necessary to be successful in specific managerial jobs or jobs involving international assignments. Personality tests typically measure five major dimensions: extraversion, adjustment, agreeableness, conscientiousness, and openness to experience (see Table 6.3 in Chapter 6).

The **Myers-Briggs Type Inventory (MBTI)** refers to an assessment that is based on Carl Jung's personality type theory. This theory emphasizes that we have a fundamental personality type that shapes and influences how we understand the world, process information, and socialize. The assessment determines which one of 16 personality types fits best. The 16 unique personality types are based on preferences for introversion (I) or extraversion (E), sensing (S) or intuition (N), thinking (T) or feeling (F), and judging (J) or perceiving (P). The assessment tool identifies individuals' preferences for energy (introversion versus extraversion), information gathering (sensing versus intuition), decision making (thinking versus feeling), and lifestyle (judging versus perceiving).[32] Each personality type has implications for work habits and interpersonal relationships. For example, individuals who are introverted, sensing, thinking, and judging (known as ISTJs) tend to be serious, quiet, practical, orderly, and logical. These persons can organize tasks, be decisive, and follow through on plans and goals. ISTJs have several weaknesses because they do not tend to use the opposite preferences: extraversion, intuition, feeling, and perceiving. These weaknesses include problems dealing with unexpected opportunities, appearing too task-oriented or impersonal to colleagues, and making overly quick decisions. Visit the website www.cpp.com for more information on the personality types.

The DiSC assessment measures personality and behavioral style, including dominance (direct, strong-willed, forceful), influence (sociable, talkative), steadiness (gentle

LO 9-5
Relate how assessment of personality type, work behaviors, and job performance can be used for employee development.

Assessment
Collecting information and providing feedback to employees about their behavior, communication style, or skills.

Myers-briggs type inventory (MBTI)
A psychological test used for team building and leadership development that identifies employees' preferences for energy, information gathering, decision making, and lifestyle.

accommodating), and conscientiousness (private, analytical).[33] See www.discprofile.com for more information on DiSC.

For example, CareSource, a Medicaid-managed care provider in Dayton, Ohio, has a defined process for identifying and developing employees who have the potential to be strong leaders and effective managers.[34] Assessment of fit with the organization's values and culture, which emphasize serving the underserved, begins with the recruiting process. The company uses multiple assessment tools to evaluate managers' competencies (recall the discussion of competencies in Chapter 8). These assessments include the Myers-Briggs Type Indicator; Gallup's StrengthsFinder, to identify managers' strengths and develop plans for using their strengths with their employee team; and the Leadership Practices Inventory, which provides managers with an idea of their leadership skills as evaluated by peers, their boss, and their own self-assessment, and is used to build a personal leadership development plan. Also, twice a year, managers are evaluated on competencies and behavior that CareSource believes are characteristics of an effective leader and manager: a service orientation, organizational awareness, teamwork, communications, and organizational leadership. Based on the assessment results, managers with high leadership potential are encouraged to participate in a variety of development activities.

Assessment Center

Assessment center
A process in which multiple raters evaluate employees' performance on a number of exercises.

At an **assessment center**, multiple raters or evaluators (assessors) evaluate employees' performance on a number of exercises.[35] An assessment center is usually at an off-site location such as a conference center. Between 6 and 12 employees usually participate at one time. Assessment centers are used primarily to identify if employees have the personality characteristics, administrative skills, and interpersonal skills needed for managerial jobs. They are also increasingly being used to determine if employees have the necessary skills to work in teams.

Leaderless group discussion
Process in which a team of five to seven employees solves an assigned problem within a certain time period.

The types of exercises used in assessment centers include leaderless group discussions, interviews, in-baskets, and role-plays.[36] In a **leaderless group discussion**, a team of five to seven employees is assigned a problem and must work together to solve it within a certain time period. The problem may involve buying and selling supplies, nominating a subordinate for an award, or assembling a product. In the **interview**, employees answer questions about their work and personal experiences, skill strengths and weaknesses, and career plans. An **in-basket** is a simulation of the administrative tasks of the manager's job. The exercise includes a variety of documents that may appear in the in-basket on a manager's desk. The participants read the materials and decide how to respond to them. Responses might include delegating tasks, scheduling meetings, writing replies, or even ignoring a memo. In a **role-play**, the participant takes the part or role of a manager or another employee. For example, an assessment center participant may be asked to take the role of a manager who has to give a negative performance review to a subordinate. The participant is told about the subordinate's performance and is asked to prepare for and actually hold a 45-minute meeting with the subordinate to discuss the performance problems. The role of the subordinate is played by a manager or other member of the assessment center design team or company. The assessment center might also include interest and aptitude tests to evaluate an employee's vocabulary, general mental ability, and reasoning skills. Personality tests may be used to determine if employees can get along with others, their tolerance for ambiguity, and other traits related to success as a manager.

Interview
Employees are questioned about their work and personal experiences, skills, and career plans.

In-basket
A simulation of the administrative tasks of a manager's job.

Role-play
A participant taking the part or role of a manager or other employee.

Assessment center exercises are designed to measure employees' administrative and interpersonal skills. Skills typically measured include leadership, oral and written communication, judgment, organizational ability, and stress tolerance. Table 9.4 shows an example of the skills measured by the assessment center. Each exercise gives participating employees the opportunity to demonstrate several different skills. For example, the exercise requiring scheduling to meet production demands evaluates employees' administrative and problem-solving ability. The leaderless group discussion measures interpersonal skills such as sensitivity toward others, stress tolerance, and oral communication skills.

Managers are usually used as assessors. The managers are trained to look for employee behaviors that are related to the skills that will be assessed. Typically, each assessor observes and records one or two employees' behaviors in each exercise. The assessors review their notes and rate each employee's level of skills (e.g., 5 = high level of leadership skills, 1 = low level of leadership skills). After all employees have completed the exercises, the assessors discuss their observations of each employee. They compare their ratings and try to agree on each employee's rating for each of the skills.

As we mentioned in Chapter 6, research suggests that assessment center ratings are related to performance, salary level, and career advancement.[37] Assessment centers may also be useful for development because employees who participate in the process receive feedback regarding their attitudes and skill strengths and weaknesses.[38] For example, Steelcase, the office furniture manufacturer based in Grand Rapids, Michigan, has used assessment centers for first-level managers.[39] The assessment center exercises include in-basket, interview simulation, and a timed scheduling exercise requiring participants to fill positions created by absences. Managers are also required to confront an employee on a performance issue, getting the employee to commit to improve. Because the exercises relate closely to what

Table 9.4
Examples of Skills Measured by Assessment Center Exercises

| | | EXERCISES | | | |
	IN-BASKET	SCHEDULING EXERCISE	LEADERLESS GROUP DISCUSSION	PERSONALITY TEST	ROLE-PLAY
SKILLS					
Leadership (dominance, coaching, influence, resourcefulness)	X		X	X	X
Problem solving (judgment)	X	X	X		X
Interpersonal (sensitivity, conflict resolution, cooperation, oral communication)			X	X	X
Administrative (organizing, planning, written communications)	X	X	X		
Personal (stress tolerance, confidence)			X	X	X

NOTE: X indicates skill measured by exercise.

managers are required to do at work, feedback given to managers based on their performance in the assessment center can target specific skills or competencies that they need to be successful managers.

Performance Appraisals and 360-Degree Feedback Systems

As we described in Chapter 8, *performance appraisal* is the process of measuring employees' performance. Performance appraisal information can be useful for employee development under certain conditions.[40] The appraisal system must tell employees specifically about their performance problems and how they can improve their performance. This includes providing a clear understanding of the differences between current performance and expected performance, identifying causes of the performance discrepancy, and developing action plans to improve performance. Managers must be trained in frequent performance feedback. Managers also need to monitor employees' progress in carrying out action plans.

Recall our earlier discussion of how Just Born uses performance appraisals for evaluation and development (see Chapter 8).[41] The appraisal starts with a planning meeting between employee and manager. The department's strategic initiatives and the employee's role are discussed. The employee and the manager agree on four personal objectives that will help the department reach its goals as well as key performance outcomes related to the employee's job description. Competencies the employee needs to reach the personal objectives are identified. The manager and the employee jointly develop a plan for improving or learning the competencies. During the year, the manager and the employee monitor progress toward reaching the performance and personal objectives and achievement of the learning plan. Pay decisions made at the end of each year are based on the achievement of both performance and learning objectives.

A recent trend in performance appraisals for management development is the use of upward feedback and 360-degree feedback. **Upward feedback** refers to appraisal that involves collecting subordinates' evaluations of managers' behaviors or skills. The 360-degree feedback process is a special case of upward feedback. In **360-degree feedback systems**, employees' behaviors or skills are evaluated not only by subordinates but also by peers, customers, their bosses, and the employees themselves. The raters complete a questionnaire asking them to rate the person on a number of different dimensions. Table 9.5 illustrates the types of skills related to management success that are rated in a 360-degree feedback questionnaire. Typically, raters are asked to assess the manager's strength in a particular area or whether development is needed. Raters may also be asked to identify how frequently they observe a competency or skill (e.g., always, sometimes, seldom, never).

The results of a 360-degree feedback system show how the manager was rated on each item. The results also show how self-evaluations differ from evaluations from the other raters. Typically managers review their results, seek clarification from the raters, and set specific development goals based on the identified strengths and weaknesses.[42] Table 9.6 shows the type of activities involved in using 360-degree feedback for development.[43]

The benefits of 360-degree feedback include collecting multiple perspectives of managers' performance, allowing employees to compare their own personal evaluations with the views of others, and formalizing communications about behaviors and skills ratings between employees and their internal and external customers. Several studies have shown that performance improves and behavior changes as a result of participating in upward feedback and 360-degree feedback systems.[44] The most change occurs in individuals who receive lower ratings from others than they gave themselves (overraters).

Upward feedback
A performance appraisal process for managers that includes subordinates' evaluations.

360-degree feedback system
A performance appraisal process for managers that includes evaluations from a wide range of persons who interact with the manager. The process includes self-evaluations as well as evaluations from the manager's boss, subordinates, peers, and customers.

Table 9.5
Skills Related to Managerial Success

Resourcefulness	Can think strategically, engage in flexible problem solving, and work effectively with higher-level management
Doing whatever it takes	Has perseverance and focus in the face of obstacles
Being a quick study	Quickly masters new technical and business knowledge
Building and mending relationships	Knows how to build and maintain working relationships with co-workers and external parties
Leading subordinates	Delegates to subordinates effectively, broadens their opportunities, and acts with fairness toward them
Compassion and sensitivity	Shows genuine interest in others and sensitivity to subordinates' needs
Straightforwardness and composure	Is honorable and steadfast
Setting a developmental climate	Provides a challenging climate to encourage subordinates' development
Confronting problem subordinates	Acts decisively and fairly when dealing with problem subordinates
Team orientation	Accomplishes tasks through managing others
Balance between personal life and work	Balances work priorities with personal life so that neither is neglected
Decisiveness	Prefers quick and approximate actions to slow and precise ones in many management situations
Self-awareness	Has an accurate picture of strengths and weaknesses and is willing to improve
Hiring talented staff	Hires talented people for the team
Putting people at ease	Displays warmth and a good sense of humor
Acting with flexibility	Can behave in ways that are often seen as opposites

SOURCE: Based on C. D. McCauley, M. M. Lombardo, and C. J. Usher, "Diagnosing Management Development Needs: An Instrument Based on How Managers Develop," *Journal of Management* 15 (1989), pp. 389–403.

Table 9.6
Activities Involved in Using 360-Degree Feedback for Development

1. **Understand strengths and weaknesses**
   Review ratings for strengths and weaknesses
   Identify skills or behaviors where self and others' (manager's, peers', customers') ratings agree and disagree
2. **Identify a development goal**
   Choose a skill or behavior to develop
   Set a clear, specific goal with a specified outcome
3. **Identify a process for recognizing goal accomplishment**
4. **Identify strategies for reaching the development goal**
   Establish strategies such as reading, job experiences, courses, and relationships
   Establish strategies for receiving feedback on progress
   Establish strategies for reinforcing the new skill or behavior

Potential limitations of 360-degree feedback include the time demands placed on the raters to complete the evaluations, managers seeking to identify and punish raters who provided negative information, the need to have a facilitator help interpret results, and companies' failure to provide ways that managers can act on the feedback they receive (development planning, meeting with raters, taking courses).

In effective 360-degree feedback systems, reliable or consistent ratings are provided, raters' confidentiality is maintained, the behaviors or skills assessed are job related (valid), the system is easy to use, and managers receive and act on the feedback.[45]

Technology allows 360-degree questionnaires to be delivered online to the raters. This increases the number of completed questionnaires returned, makes it easier to process the information, and speeds feedback reports to managers.

Regardless of the assessment method used, the information must be shared with the employee for development to occur. Along with assessment information, the employee needs suggestions for correcting skill weaknesses and using skills already learned. Suggestions might include participating in training courses or developing skills through new job experiences. Based on the assessment information and available development opportunities, employees should develop action plans to guide their self-improvement efforts.

Blue Cross Blue Shield of Michigan uses 360-degree feedback as part of its team-leader development program.[46] The 360-degree assessment includes a self-evaluation, manager evaluation, staff evaluation, and evaluations from four or five peers or customers. The assessment results are shared with the team leader and the employee's coach, who identify two or three improvement areas, along with metrics to measure achievement.

JOB EXPERIENCES

LO 9-6
Explain how job experiences can be used for skill development.

Job experience
The relationships, problems, demands, tasks, and other features that employees face in their jobs.

Stretch assignments
Job assignments in which there is a mismatch between an employee's skills and past experiences and the skills required for success on the job.

Most employee development occurs through **job experiences**:[47] relationships, problems, demands, tasks, or other features that employees face in their jobs. A major assumption of using job experiences for employee development is that development is most likely to occur when employees are given stretch assignments. **Stretch assignments** refer to assignments in which there is a mismatch between the employee's skills and past experiences and the skills required for success on the job. To succeed in their jobs, employees must stretch their skills—that is, they are forced to learn new skills, apply their skills and knowledge in a new way, and master new experiences.[48] New job assignments help take advantage of employees' existing skills, experiences, and contacts, while helping them develop new ones.[49] For example, VF Corporation, which includes North Face, Vans, and Lee brands, encourages employees to move throughout the organization.[50] This helps the brands located in Silicon Valley compete for Millennial talent against high-tech firms also located there. For example, a supply chain employee who had developed expertise in manufacturing in her first position with VF, took a position in a new plant that was opening in the Dominican Republic. This helped her learn about setting up a new operation and manufacturing, procurement, distribution, and sourcing in an international operation. For job experiences to be effective development activities, they should be tailored to employees' development needs and goals.

Most of what we know about development through job experiences comes from a series of studies conducted by the Center for Creative Leadership.[51] Executives were asked to identify key career events that made a difference in their managerial styles and the lessons they learned from these experiences. The key events included those involving the job assignment (such as fixing a failing operation), those involving interpersonal relationships (getting along with supervisors), and the specific type of transition required (situations in which the executive did not have the necessary background). The job demands and what employees can learn from them are described in Table 9.7.

Table 9.7
Job Demands and
What Employees
Can Learn From
Them

Job Demands	What Employees Can Learn
Transitions	Handling responsibilities that are new, different, or broader than those in previous job
Change	Developing new strategic direction, reorganizing, growing or reducing staff, or responding to rapid change; dealing with poorly performing employees
High Level of Responsibility	Making highly visible and important decisions that impact the business; managing multiple groups, functions, products, or departments; dealing with external stakeholders such as unions, government agencies, local politicians
Nonauthority Relationships	Getting work done by influencing persons over whom you have no direct authority, such as peers, boss, and external stakeholders
Obstacles	Coping and succeeding despite adverse business conditions, a lack of top management or peer support and encouragement, or working with a boss who has poor management skills or a different management style

SOURCES: Based on C. McCauley and M. McCall Jr. (eds.), *Using Experience to Develop Leadership Talent* (San Francisco: Jossey-Bass, 2014); C. D. McCauley, L. J. Eastman, and J. Ohlott, "Linking Management Selection and Development through Stretch Assignments," *Human Resource Management* 84 (1995), pp. 93–115; W. Macaux, "Making the Most of Stretch Assignments," *TD*, June 14, 2010; G. Morris and K. Rogers, "High Potentials Are Still Your Best Bet," *T + D*, February 2013, pp. 58–62.

One concern regarding the use of demanding job experiences for employee development is whether they are viewed as positive or negative stressors. Job experiences that are seen as positive stressors challenge employees to stimulate learning. Job challenges viewed as negative stressors create high levels of harmful stress for employees exposed to them. Recent research findings suggest that all of the job demands, with the exception of obstacles, are related to learning.[52] Managers reported that obstacles and job demands related to creating change were more likely to lead to negative stress than the other job demands. This suggests that companies should carefully weigh the potential negative consequences before placing employees in development assignments that involve obstacles or create change.

Although the research on development through job experiences has focused on executives and managers, line employees can also learn from job experiences. As we noted earlier, for a work team to be successful, its members now need the kinds of skills that only managers were once thought to need (such as dealing directly with customers, analyzing data to determine product quality, and resolving conflict among team members). Besides the development that occurs when a team is formed, employees can further develop their skills by switching work roles within the team.

Figure 9.4 shows the various ways that job experiences can be used for employee development. These include enlarging the current job, job rotation, transfers, promotions, downward moves, and temporary assignments. For companies with global operations (multinationals), employee development sometimes involves international assignments that require frequent travel or relocation. The "Competing through Sustainability" box describes how managers are developing skills through working for nonprofit organizations.

Figure 9.4

How Job
Experiences Are
Used for Employee
Development

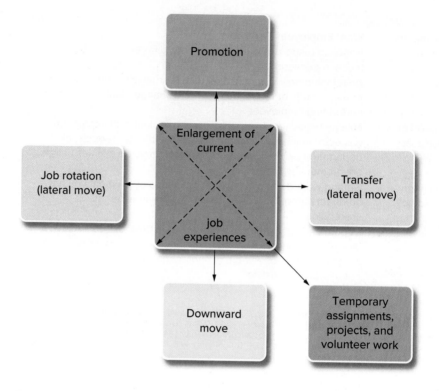

Enlarging the Current Job

Job enlargement refers to adding challenges or new responsibilities to employees' current jobs. This could include special project assignments, switching roles within a work team, or researching new ways to serve clients and customers. For example, an engineering employee may join a task force developing new career paths for technical employees. Through this project work, the engineer may lead certain aspects of career path development (such as reviewing the company's career development process). As a result, the engineer not only learns about the company's career development system but also uses leadership and organizational skills to help the task force reach its goals. Some companies are enlarging jobs by giving two managers the same responsibilities and job title and allowing them to divide the work (two-in-a-box).[53] This helps managers learn from a more experienced employee; helps companies fill jobs that require multiple skills; and, for positions requiring extensive travel, ensures that one employee is always on site to deal with work-related issues. For example, at Cisco Systems, the head of the Cisco routing group, who was trained as an engineer but now works in business development, shared a job with an engineer. Each employee was exposed to the other's skills, which has helped both perform their jobs better.

Job Rotation and Lateral Moves

Job rotation gives employees a series of job assignments in various functional areas of the company or movement among jobs in a single functional area or department. Job rotation involves a planned sequence of jobs that the employee is expected to hold, whereas lateral moves may not necessarily involve a predetermined sequence of jobs or positions. For example, in her 11-year career at AT&T, one manager has held six different positions, and she never had the same title for more than 3 years.[54] In her last position, she was in charge of hiring, reporting to executives, and training and supporting all sellers located in her region. Now, she has taken a position as a director of call centers.

Job enlargement
Adding challenges or new responsibilities to an employee's current job.

Job rotation
The process of systematically moving a single individual from one job to another over the course of time. The job assignments may be in various functional areas of the company, or movement may be between jobs in a single functional area or department.

COMPETING THROUGH SUSTAINABILITY

Serving on Nonprofit Boards Benefits Many

Managers are joining boards of non-profit organizations to help other and the community, gain skills, and advance their careers. Nonprofit board experience helps managers develop their leadership skills and broaden their network. They may get opportunities to have experiences that they won't normally get in their job such as running a fundraising campaign or participating in strategic planning. These experiences helps

strengthen their current skills or develop new skill sets. For example, one manager joined the YMCA board. His experience helping recruit a new YMCA executive helped him conduct better job interviews with potential candidates seeking jobs at his company. He now challenges candidates to see how they handle stressful situations and spends more time discussing with other managers if a candidate would fit well with the

company culture. Nonprofits benefit because they need skilled managers who can help the firm operate more efficiently and effectively.

DISCUSSION QUESTION
1. How could development planning help maximize the benefits received by a manager serving on a nonprofit-board?

SOURCE: Based on J. Lublin, "Nonprofit boards offer career boosts", *Wall Street Journal* (October 5, 2016): B8.

This position has a greater scope and more responsibilities than her previous position (she now oversees about 1,700 employees).

Job rotation helps employees gain an overall appreciation of the company's goals, increases their understanding of different company functions, develops a network of contacts, and increases employees' skills.[55] At Stryker Orthopaedics, the sales department gives employees the opportunity to experience five different functional areas with sales so that employees can decide which areas they might be most interested in working in.[56] Bell and Howell encourages employees to seek positions outside their current functional area.[57] This helps employees develop their skills and personal network and facilitates knowledge sharing throughout the company. Also, job rotation provides the opportunity for another employee to move into the vacated position, creating a system that helps employees to continuously develop skills. Haskell offers job rotation opportunities for all design engineers to gain a broad perspective of package systems engineering.[58] Design engineers rotate into the Systems Analytics group, which involves process improvement and simulation testing for manufacturing systems. This rotation gives engineers the opportunity to learn how to use data for decision making based on simulation tests. Haskell has found that the rotation has resulted in fewer manufacturing design errors, better designs, and reductions in time and costs to complete projects.

Despite the advantages of job rotation, there are several potential problems for both the employee and the work unit. The rotation may cause employees to adopt a short-term perspective when problem solving. Employees' satisfaction and motivation may be adversely affected because they find it difficult to develop functional specialties and they don't spend enough time in one position to receive a challenging assignment. Productivity losses and workload increases may be experienced by both the department gaining a rotating employee and the department losing the employee due to training demands and loss of a resource.

Transfers, Promotions, and Downward Moves

Upward, lateral, and downward mobility is available for development purposes in most companies.[59] In a **transfer**, an employee is assigned a job in a different area of the company. Transfers do not necessarily increase job responsibilities or compensation.

Transfer
The movement of an employee to a different job assignment in a different area of the company.

401

Promotions
Advances into positions with greater challenge, more responsibility, and more authority than the employee's previous job.

Downward move
A job change involving a reduction in an employee's level of responsibility and authority.

They are likely lateral moves (a move to a job with similar responsibilities). **Promotions** are advancements into positions with greater challenges, more responsibility, and more authority than in the previous job. Promotions usually include pay increases.

A **downward move** occurs when an employee is given less responsibility and authority.[60] This may involve a move to another position at the same level (lateral demotion), a temporary cross-functional move, or a demotion because of poor performance. Temporary cross-functional moves to lower-level positions, which give employees experience working in different functional areas, are most frequently used for employee development. For example, engineers who want to move into management often take lower-level positions (like shift supervisor) to develop their management skills.

Because of the psychological and tangible rewards of promotions (such as increased feelings of self-worth, salary, and status in the company), employees are more willing to accept promotions than lateral or downward moves. Promotions are more readily available when a company is profitable and growing. When a company is restructuring or experiencing stable or declining profits—especially if numerous employees are interested in promotions and the company tends to rely on the external labor market to staff higher-level positions—promotion opportunities may be limited.[61]

Transfers, job rotation, promotions, lateral moves, and downward moves may involve relocation within the United States or to another country. This can be stressful not only because the employee's work role changes, but if the employee is in a two-career family, the spouse also must find new employment. In addition, the family has to join a new community. Transfers disrupt employees' daily lives, interpersonal relationships, and work habits.[62] People have to find new housing, shopping, health care, and leisure facilities, and they may be many miles from the emotional support of friends and family. They also have to learn a new set of work norms and procedures; they must develop interpersonal relationships with their new managers and peers; and they are expected to be as productive in their new jobs as they were in their old jobs even though they may know little about the products, services, processes, or employees for whom they are responsible.

Because transfers can provoke anxiety, many companies have difficulty getting employees to accept them. Research has identified the employee characteristics associated with a willingness to accept transfers:[63] high career ambitions, a belief that one's future with the company is promising, and a belief that accepting a transfer is necessary for success in the company. Employees who are not married and not active in the community are generally most willing to accept transfers. Among married employees, the spouse's willingness to move is the most important influence on whether an employee will accept a transfer.

Unfortunately, many employees have difficulty associating transfers and downward moves with development. They see them as punishments rather than as opportunities to develop skills that will help them achieve long-term success with the company. Many employees decide to leave a company rather than accept a transfer. Companies need to successfully manage transfers not only because of the costs of replacing employees but also because of the costs directly associated with them. For example, one estimate is that a full-service relocation for an employee and his or her family is approximately $70,000.[64] To help encourage employees to reduce relocation costs and to give employees control over how to spend relocation allowances to best meet their needs, many companies are providing lump sums for relocation. That is, employees are given a set amount of money to pay for relocation costs. They are typically not required to submit receipts for expenses. Also, some companies provide employees with a network of recommended service providers so that the employees don't feel burdened by identifying responsible vendors.

To ensure that employees accept transfers, promotions, and downward moves as development opportunities, companies can provide

- Information about the content, challenges, and potential benefits of the new job and location
- Involvement in the transfer decision by sending the employees to preview the new location and giving them information about the community
- Clear performance objectives and early feedback about their job performance
- A host at the new location to help them adjust to the new community and workplace
- Information about how the job opportunity will affect their income, taxes, mortgage payments, and other expenses
- Reimbursement and assistance in selling and purchasing or renting a place to live
- An orientation program for the new location and job
- Information on how the new job experiences will support the employee's career plans
- Assistance for dependent family members, including identifying schools and child care and elder care options
- Help for the spouse in identifying and marketing skills and finding employment[65]

Temporary Assignments, Projects, Volunteer Work, and Sabbaticals

Temporary assignments refer to job tryouts such as employees taking on a position to help them determine if they are interested in working in a new role, employee exchanges, sabbaticals, and voluntary assignments. All temporary assignments have a predetermined ending date after which the employees return to their permanent position. For example, Mondelez International, a snack company with 100,000 employees, wanted to help its managers learn about how to market its products using mobile devices. For several days, they sent their managers to nine small mobile-technology companies to help them gain an understanding of their entrepreneurial spirit and how quickly these companies generated ideas and built and tested prototypes of new marketing efforts.[66] An associate brand manager from PepsiCo's New York headquarters spent a week at Airbnb, a San Francisco–based online travel rental business. Managers from the two companies hoped to learn from each other's brand management practices. Both companies have casual, collaborative work environments. But compared to PepsiCo's brand management, Airbnb's brand management is based more on instinct than on data analysis and the ideas of marketing agencies. Marketing managers at Airbnb were interested in learning about how PepsiCo built data sets of market research. To develop a broad understanding of the business, directors at Genentech Inc. spend 10% of their time over six to nine months in a different function working on special projects, participating in task forces, and shadowing business leaders.[67]

Employee exchange is another type of temporary assignment. Procter & Gamble (P&G) and Google have swapped employees.[68] Employees from the two companies participate in each other's training programs and attend meetings where business plans are discussed. Both companies hope to benefit from the employee swap. Procter & Gamble is trying to increase its understanding of how to market laundry detergent, toilet paper, and skin cream products to a new generation of consumers who spend more time online than watching television. Google wants to gain more ad revenue by persuading companies to shift from showcasing their brands on television to video-sharing sites such as YouTube.

Temporary assignments can include a **sabbatical**. A sabbatical refers to a leave of absence from the company for personal reflection, renewal, and skill development. Employees on sabbatical often receive full pay and benefits. Sabbaticals let employees get away from the day-to-day stresses of their jobs and acquire new skills and perspectives.

Temporary assignment
Job tryouts such as employees taking on a position to help them determine if they are interested in working in a new role.

Sabbatical
A leave of absence from the company to renew or develop skills.

Sabbaticals also allow employees more time for personal pursuits such as writing a book or spending more time with young children. Sabbaticals are common in a variety of industries ranging from consulting firms to the fast-food industry.[69] They typically range from 4 to 10 weeks. Sabbaticals can involve travel, finishing a degree or other learning opportunities, donating time to charity, working on research or new product development, or working on a "green" cause. At David Weekley Homes, employees must have worked with the company for at least 10 years before they are eligible to take a paid sabbatical. Employees who choose to take a sabbatical are given a $2,000 grant to use as they see fit.[70]

As part of Dow's leadership development program, Leadership in Action, employees go on global temporary assignments in which they are matched with organizations that need support for sustainable development projects, especially in business growth areas for Dow.[71] High-potential employees are organized in teams. They work with nongovernmental organizations (NGOs) on projects that meet community needs in Ethiopia, Ghana, and other countries where Dow is considering opening businesses. The team members develop skills in solving problems in cultures and communities that are extremely different from their own.

Volunteer assignments can also be used for development. Volunteer assignments may give employees opportunities to manage change, teach, have a high level of responsibility, and be exposed to other job demands (see Table 9.7). For General Mills, volunteer assignments and involvement with community projects is one of the ways the company lives its corporate values.[72] Employees work in a wide variety of charities, with duties ranging from serving meals to the homeless, painting rooms at child care centers, or serving as corporate board members. Besides providing valuable services to community organizations, General Mills believes volunteer assignments help employees improve team relationships and develop leadership and strategic thinking skills.

EVIDENCE-BASED HR

CA Technologies created the Leaders at all Levels (LaaL) program to give employees the tools and resources they need to develop skills in leading themselves, leading the organization, and leading through others. One program in LaaL, the leadership development program, targets mid-level managers and individual contributors. Another program, managing and leading, provides skills for recently hired, promoted, and existing managers. In both programs, learning occurs through experiential learning, social interactions, and face-to-face instruction. To ensure that skills are used on the job, participants meet with their managers to set expectations and managers are provided with a toolkit. The manager toolkit identifies what skills are emphasized in the program, a demonstration of successful use of the skills, and recommendations for how to support and reinforce use of the skills on the job.

Program evaluation included reactions, learning, and results. All participants liked the program and believed it was relevant and meaningful for their personal growth and development. Pre- and post-program self-assessments showed that managers who participated in the program believed they improved their strategic vision and direction for their teams by 68% and had a 22% higher level of confidence in providing performance and development coaching to their team members. Voluntary turnover for program participants was 3% lower than for the overall company. Based on data collected in CA's performance management process, program participants performed at a higher level than employees who did not participate in the program.

SOURCE: Based on J. Castaneda, "Bench Strength," *TD*, June 2015, pp. 30–35.

INTERPERSONAL RELATIONSHIPS

Employees can also develop skills and increase their knowledge about the company and its customers by interacting with a more experienced organization member. Mentoring and coaching are two types of interpersonal relationships that are used to develop employees.

Mentoring

A **mentor** is an experienced, productive senior employee who helps develop a less experienced employee (the protégé). Because of the lack of potential mentors, and recognizing that employees can benefit from relationships with peers and colleagues, some companies have initiated and supported group and peer mentoring.

Most mentoring relationships develop informally as a result of interests or values shared by the mentor and the protégé. Research suggests that employees with certain personality characteristics (like emotional stability, the ability to adapt their behavior based on the situation, and high needs for power and achievement) are most likely to seek a mentor and be an attractive protégé for a mentor.[73] Mentoring relationships can also develop as part of a formal mentoring program, that is, a planned company effort to bring together successful senior employees with less experienced employees. Table 9.8 shows examples of how companies are using formal mentoring programs. Mentoring programs

Mentor
An experienced, productive senior employee who helps develop a less experienced employee.

Table 9.8
Examples of Mentoring Programs

EMC Corporation—The company combines mentoring with instructor-led training for new technical support engineers. The engineers can learn from their peers and discuss concepts from the training with their mentors.

Microsoft—The mentoring program includes career development mentoring and peer mentoring. Career development mentoring focuses on career and professional development through structured, year-long cross-group mentoring. Peer mentoring is less structured and focuses on transfer of work-related knowledge among members of the same work team.

Sodexo—Peer-to-peer mentoring is a program managed directly by Sodexo's Network Groups. Networks are organized around a common dimension of diversity and are created by employees who want to raise awareness in Sodexo of their identity groups. They include network groups based on national origin, race, sexual orientation, military service, and intergenerations. The Spirit of Mentoring Bridge Programs are informal divisional pairings in which newly hired and front-line managers come together to expand professional development opportunities and increase the depth and diversity of Sodexo's management.

Mariner Finance—The company uses technology such as chat functions, video, and specific websites for mentors and protégés to enable more timely communications between themselves as well as between all employees participating in the mentoring program.

Gilbane—The One to One mentoring program pairs leaders with executives outside of their business and geographic area for six months to increase their readiness to take a new position and strengthen their leadership potential. Matching is made on the basis of talent surveys and personality assessments. Mentors and protégés meet once each month to share career advice and company knowledge.

Vistage Worldwide—Teams of 15–20 employees provide opportunities for advice on personal or professional challenges. A trained peer-group facilitator guides the discussion and helps the team listen, paraphrase, and ask probing questions in order to provide new perspectives on the issue and potential solutions.

SOURCES: Based on "*Training* Top 125: Aditya Birla Minacs," *Training*, January/February 2014, p. 101; Sodexo, Inc., website, www.sodexousa.com, accessed March 26, 2017; "*Training* Top 125: Gilbane," *Training*, January/February 2016, 69; "*Training* Top 125: Vistage Worldwide," *Training,* January/February 2017, p. 69; M. Weinstein, "Mentoring in the Digital Age," *Training*, September/October 2016, pp. 28–31; R. Emelo, "Shift Your Focus with Modern Mentoring," *TD*, September 2015, pp. 36–41; R. Emelo, "Conversations with Mentoring Leaders," *T + D*, June 2011, pp. 32–37.

Table 9.9
Characteristics of Successful Formal Mentoring Programs

1. Mentor and protégé participation is voluntary. Relationship can be ended at any time without fear of punishment.
2. The mentor–protégé matching process does not limit the ability of informal relationships to develop. For example, a mentor pool can be established to allow protégés to choose from a variety of qualified mentors.
3. Mentors are chosen on the basis of their past record in developing employees, willingness to serve as a mentor, and evidence of positive coaching, communication, and listening skills.
4. Mentor–protégé matching is based on how the mentor's skills can help meet the protégé's needs.
5. The purpose of the program is clearly understood. Projects and activities that the mentor and protégé are expected to complete are specified.
6. The length of the program is specified. Mentor and protégé are encouraged to pursue the relationship beyond the formal period.
7. A minimum level of contact between the mentor and protégé is specified. Mentors and protégés need to determine when they will meet, how often, and how they will communicate outside the meetings.
8. Protégés are encouraged to contact one another to discuss problems and share successes.
9. The mentor program is evaluated. Interviews with mentors and protégés give immediate feedback regarding specific areas of dissatisfaction. Surveys gather more detailed information regarding benefits received from participating in the program.
10. Employee development is rewarded, which signals to managers that mentoring and other development activities are worth their time and effort.

have many important purposes, including socializing new employees, developing managers, and providing opportunities for women and minorities to share experiences and gain the exposure and skills needed to move into management positions.

Developing Successful Mentoring Programs. One major advantage of formalized mentoring programs is that they ensure access to mentors for all employees, regardless of gender or race. An additional advantage is that participants in the mentoring relationship know what is expected of them.[74] One limitation of formal mentoring programs is that mentors may not be able to provide counseling and coaching in a relationship that has been created artificially.[75] To overcome this limitation, it is important that mentors and protégés spend time discussing work styles, their personalities, and their backgrounds, which helps build the trust needed for both parties to be comfortable with their relationship.[76] Toshiba America Medical Systems doesn't have a formal mentoring program. However, Toshiba encourages informal mentoring from the first day employees are hired. Both managers and HR business partners take the time to help new employees meet their colleagues and show them around the workplace.[77]

Table 9.9 presents the characteristics of a successful formal mentoring program. Mentors should be chosen based on interpersonal and technical skills. They also need to be trained.[78] For mentors, protégés, and the company to get the most out of mentoring, tools and support are needed.[79] A key to successful mentoring programs is that the mentor and protégé be well matched and can interact with each other face-to-face, virtually, or using social media.

Matching systems are available to help match mentors and protégés, track mentors' and protégés' work, help build development plans, and schedule mentor and protégé meetings.[80] The "Competing through Technology" box shows how Cardinal Health is using the cloud to help make mentoring relationships more effective.

The Cloud Keeps Mentoring Going

Cardinal Health adopted a cloud-based system for matching mentors and protégés. To ensure that mentoring relationships were meaningful and to ensure that participants understood the time commitment and expected level of involvement, Cardinal Health adopted a six-month time period for mentoring relationships with the option of renewing for another six months. To serve as a mentor, employees had to work for the company for at least one year and agree to participate if chosen.

The cloud-based system uses mathematical algorithms to match mentors and protégés and provides tools to track and manage their relationship. Employees can enroll in the program using a mobile device or notebook computer. Mentors and potential protégés complete profiles that are entered into the cloud-based system. Mentors' profiles highlight their expertise and what they believe they can offer protégés. Protégés' profiles describe themselves and what they are looking for in a mentor. Protégés can search for a specific mentor or rely on the system to provide a list of potential mentor matches based on the compatibility of their profiles. Each list of matches includes mentors' profiles, mentoring objectives, and a percentage showing how well each mentor matches the protégé's criteria.

Once the matching process is complete, the system allows mentors and protégés to schedule their meetings and to send alerts. Protégés are expected to make contact with their mentor and to use the system to set goals for the relationship and provide meeting agendas. At the end of six months, the system automatically alerts protégés to provide a summary explaining whether they met their goals and if they want to renew the relationship for another six months. The system also tracks protégés' career moves, retention, and whether or not they feel they have met their development goals.

DISCUSSION QUESTION

1. Considering the characteristics of successful formal mentoring relationships shown in Table 9.9, how does the cloud-based system help ensure the effectiveness of mentoring relationships? Explain.

SOURCE: Based on S. Gale, "Mentoring in the Cloud at Cardinal Health," *Chief Learning Officer*, September 2016, pp. 50–51.

Benefits of Mentoring Relationships. Both mentors and protégés can benefit from a mentoring relationship. Research suggests that mentors provide career and psychosocial support to their protégés. **Career support** includes coaching; protection; sponsorship; and providing challenging assignments, exposure, and visibility. **Psychosocial support** includes serving as a friend and a role model, providing positive regard and acceptance, and creating an outlet for the protégé to talk about anxieties and fears. Additional benefits for the protégé include higher rates of promotion, higher salaries, and greater organizational influence.[81] Tamara Trummer summarizes some of the benefits she gained from mentoring relationships: "I found mentors in two of my earlier companies, both male and female managers who 'taught me the ropes' in an informal sense by giving me inside information about the company, certain executives—and even such practical things as how to conduct business travel and handle an expense account."[82] One mentor arranged for her to travel from the remote manufacturing plant where she worked to the corporate office and set up meetings with key employees with whom she would have to work. Her mentors have also included co-workers, peers, and even subordinates who have taught her computer software skills. As a result of her positive experiences as a protégé, Trummer now mentors others employees.

Mentoring relationships provide opportunities for mentors to develop their interpersonal skills and increase their feelings of self-esteem and worth to the organization.

Career support
Coaching, protection, sponsorship, and providing challenging assignments, exposure, and visibility.

Psychosocial support
Serving as a friend and role model, providing positive regard and acceptance, and creating an outlet for a protégé to talk about anxieties and fears.

For individuals in technical fields such as engineering or health services, the protégé may help mentors gain knowledge about important new scientific developments in their field (and therefore prevent them from becoming technically obsolete).

Reverse mentoring refers to mentoring in which younger employees mentor more senior employees. UnitedHealth Group pairs senior executives with emerging Millennial leaders.[83] UnitedHealth hopes the program will help the executives see the business differently, better understand the latest uses of technology and social media, and learn how to create a workplace that will attract, retain, and motivate Millennials and Generation Zers.

Mentoring can also occur between mentors and protégés from different organizations. Websites such as Everwise are available to help find online mentors. For example, Amy Dobler wanted to enhance her career at Jive Software, so she went online and was matched with Edel Keville, a human resources vice president at Levi Strauss & Company.[84] Using Everwise, Dobler completed an online questionnaire about her personality, education, career path, and personal goals. Both women had similar personalities and career paths in human resources and technology. After the online match, an Everwise relationship manager personally introduced the two women. The advice, guidance, and support that Dobler received from Keville in the mentoring relationship over a few months helped her gain confidence needed to present to senior managers, lead international training sessions, and improve her delegation skills.

Reverse mentoring
A business situation in which younger employees mentor more senior employees.

Coaching

LO 9-8
Describe how to train managers to coach employees.

Coach
A peer or manager who works with an employee to motivate the employee, help him or her develop skills, and provide reinforcement and feedback.

A **coach** is a peer or manager who works with employees to motivate them, help them develop skills, and provide reinforcement and feedback. There are three roles that a coach can play.[85] Part of coaching may be one-on-one with an employee (such as giving feedback). Another role is to help employees learn for themselves. This involves helping them find experts who can assist them with their concerns and teaching them how to obtain feedback from others. Third, coaching may involve providing resources such as mentors, courses, or job experiences that employees may not be able to gain access to without the coach's help.

Consider how Edward Jones, United Shore Financial Services, the Bill & Melinda Gates Foundation, and Wide Open West (WOW!) use coaching.[86] Edward Jones provides new financial advisers with trained coaches who provide confidential phone coaching when asked. The goal of the coaches is to retain the new advisers and help them become successful. United Shore Financial Services requires company leaders to conduct monthly coaching sessions with each member of their team. The Gates Foundation uses professionally trained coaches to facilitate sessions with groups of 8–10 people. The topic sessions include authentic leadership, courageous conversations, and developing a global mindset. At WOW! managers have coaching relationships with every employee they supervise in which they provide performance feedback on their daily work. Together they identify learning activities and development plans.

Research suggests that coaching helps managers improve by identifying areas for improvement and setting goals.[87] Getting results from a coaching relationship can take at least six months of weekly or monthly meetings. To be effective, a coach generally conducts an assessment, asks questions that challenge the employee to think deeply about his or her goals and motives, helps the employee create an action plan, and follows up regularly to help the employee stay on track. Employees contribute to the success of coaching when they persevere in practicing the behaviors identified in the action plan.[88]

Special Issues in Employee Development

MELTING THE GLASS CEILING

A major development issue facing companies today is how to get women and minorities into upper-level management positions—how to melt the **glass ceiling**.

Women are underrepresented in all levels of management positions.[89] Although women represent 46% of the workforce, only 37% hold managerial positions, 33% hold senior manager or director roles, 29% are vice presidents, and 19% hold the highest executive positions. Men are promoted at much higher rates than women during their early career stages, and entry-level women are significantly more likely than men to have spent five or more years in the same job.

From a leadership development perspective, companies may be reluctant to treat women differently than men despite acknowledging that women lack executive sponsors or mentors, have insufficient experience, and need better work/life balance. This barrier may be due to stereotypes or company systems that adversely affect the development of women or minorities.[90] The glass ceiling is likely caused by lack of access to training programs, appropriate developmental job experiences, and developmental relationships (such as mentoring).[91]

For example, Mary Barra made history when she became the first woman CEO of global automobile maker General Motors.[92] Prior to becoming CEO, Barra was in a product development job, an operational job critical to the company's success. But 55% of women are in functional roles such as lawyers, chief of finance, or human resources, which may not put them in the career path needed to become a CEO. Women and minorities often have trouble finding mentors because of their lack of access to the "old boy network"; managers' preference to interact with other managers of similar status rather than with line employees; and intentional exclusion by managers who have negative stereotypes about women's and minorities' abilities, motivation, and job preferences.[93]

Research has found no gender differences in access to job experiences involving transitions or creating change.[94] However, male managers receive significantly more assignments involving high levels of responsibility (high stakes, managing business diversity, handling external pressure) and appreciation for their contributions than female managers of similar ability and managerial level. Also, compared to male managers, female managers report experiencing more challenge due to lack of personal support (a type of job demand considered to be an obstacle and related to harmful stress) and lack of appreciation for their contributions. Career encouragement from peers and senior managers does help women advance to higher management levels.[95] Managers making developmental assignments need to carefully consider whether gender biases or stereotypes are influencing the types of assignments given to women versus men.

Many companies are making efforts to melt the glass ceiling.[96] General Electric has emphasized placing women in more powerful roles and including them in leadership meetings. For example, women hold positions leading GE's China health care and transportation businesses and sit on the company's highest management committee. Women account for approximately 25% of GE's executives, an increase of 16% since 2001. The software company SAP SE set a goal for women to hold 25% of all managerial roles by the end of 2017. SAP's Leadership Excellence Acceleration Program (LEAP) includes high-performing women whom managers have identified as ready for promotion. In the program's virtual course, they meet monthly to listen to guest speakers, they complete action assignments, and by the end of the course they are expected to have increased their personal network. So far, the first group of LEAP graduates have become

LO 9-9
Discuss what companies are doing to melt the glass ceiling.

Glass ceiling
A barrier to advancement to higher-level jobs in the company that adversely affects women and minorities. The barrier may be due to lack of access to training programs, development experiences, or relationships (e.g., mentoring).

Table 9.10
Recommendations for Melting the Glass Ceiling

- Make sure senior management supports and is involved in the program.
- Make a business case for change.
- Make the change public.
- Gather data on problems causing the glass ceiling using task forces, focus groups, and questionnaires.
- Create awareness of how gender attitudes affect the work environment.
- Force accountability through reviews of promotion rates and assignment decisions.
- Promote development for all employees.

SOURCES: Based on B. Groysberg and K. Connolly, "Great Leaders Who Make the Mix Work," *Harvard Business Review*, September 2013, pp. 68–76; D. McCracken, "Winning the Talent War for Women," *Harvard Business Review*, November–December 2000, pp. 159–67.

first-level managers and 11% of current managers have moved into director roles. Adobe, American Express, Cisco Systems, and American Electric Power use executive shadowing and coaching programs to help women enhance their visibility and access to top business leaders.

Table 9.10 provides recommendations for melting the glass ceiling and helping retain talented women.

LO 9-10
Use the 9-box grid for identifying where employees fit in a succession plan and construct appropriate development plans for them.

SUCCESSION PLANNING

Succession planning
The identification and tracking of high-potential employees capable of filling higher-level managerial positions.

High-potential employees
Employees the company believes are capable of being successful in high-level management positions.

Bench strength
The business strategy of having a pool of talented employees who are ready when needed to step in to a new position within the organization.

Succession planning refers to the process of identifying and tracking high-potential employees who are capable of moving into different positions in the company resulting from planned or unplanned job openings due to turnover, promotion, or business growth. Succession planning is often discussed when considering company's managers or top leaders, but it is an important consideration for any job. Succession planning helps organizations in several different ways.[97] It requires senior management to systematically review leadership talent in the company. It ensures that top-level managerial talent is available. It provides a set of development experiences that managers must complete to be considered for top management positions; this avoids premature promotion of managers who are not ready for upper management ranks. Succession planning systems also help attract and retain managerial employees by providing them with development opportunities that they can complete if upper management is a career goal for them. **High-potential employees** are those the company believes are capable of being successful in higher-level managerial positions such as general manager of a strategic business unit, functional director (such as director of marketing), or CEO.[98] High-potential employees typically complete an individual development program that involves education, executive mentoring and coaching, and rotation through job assignments. Job assignments are based on the successful career paths of the managers whom the high-potential employees are being prepared to replace. High-potential employees may also receive special assignments, such as making presentations and serving on committees and task forces.

Despite the importance of succession planning, many companies do not do it well. A survey of company directors showed that fewer than half believed they were spending enough time on succession planning and 18% did not agree that their company had adequate bench strength in its talent pipeline.[99] **Bench strength** refers to having a pool of talented employees who are ready when needed.

Table 9.11 shows the process used to develop a succession plan.[100] The first step is to identify what positions are included in the succession plan, such as all management

Table 9.11

The Process of
Developing a
Succession Plan

1. Identify what positions are included in the plan.
2. Identify the employees who are included in the plan.
3. Develop standards to evaluate positions (e.g., competencies, desired experiences, desired knowledge, developmental value).
4. Determine how employee potential will be measured (e.g., current performance and potential performance).
5. Develop the succession planning review.
6. Link the succession planning system with other human resource systems, including training and development, compensation, performance management, and staffing systems.
7. Determine what feedback is provided to employees.
8. Measure the effectiveness of the succession plan.

SOURCES: Based on A. Cremo & T. Bux, "Creating a Vibrant Organizational Leadership Pipeline", *TD* (July 2016): 76-77; W. Rothwell, "The Future of Succession Planning," *T + D*, September 2010, pp. 51–54; B. Dowell, "Succession Planning," in *Implementing Organizational Interventions*, ed. J. Hedge and E. Pulaskos (San Francisco: Jossey-Bass, 2002), pp. 78–109; R. Barnett and S. Davis, "Creating Greater Success in Succession Planning," *Advances in Developing Human Resources* 10 (2008), pp. 721–39.

positions or only certain levels of management. The second step is to identify which employees are part of the succession planning system. For example, in some companies only high-potential employees are included in the succession plan. Third, the company needs to identify how positions will be evaluated. For example, will the emphasis be on competencies needed for each position or on the experiences an individual needs to have before moving into the position? Fourth, the company should identify how employee potential will be measured. That is, will employees' performance in their current jobs as well as ratings of potential be used? Will employees' position interests and career goals be considered? Fifth, the succession planning review process needs to be developed. Typically, succession planning reviews first involve employees' managers and human resources. A talent review could also include an overall assessment of leadership talent in the company, an identification of high-potential employees, based on their performance and potential, and a discussion of plans to keep key managers from leaving the company.

Many companies use the 9-box grid for conducting the succession planning review. The **9-box grid** is a three-by-three matrix used by groups of managers and executives to compare employees within one department, function, division, or the entire company.[101] The 9-box grid is used for analysis and discussion of talent, to help formulate effective development plans and activities, and to identify talented employees who can be groomed for top-level management positions in the company. As shown in Figure 9.5 one axis of the matrix is based on an assessment of job performance. The other axis is typically labeled "potential" or "promotability." Typically, managers' assessment of performance (based on the company's performance management system) and potential influences employees' development plans. For example, as shown in Figure 9.5, "Stars" should be developed for leadership positions in the company.

For example, CHG Healthcare Services' goal was to increase the number of company leaders by 15% and reduce leaders' turnover.[102] CHG used the 9-box to identify potential leaders and develop leadership bench strength. Employees were evaluated based on their performance and potential. Employees who were identified as high performers with high potential were selected to go through a 360-degree assessment of their skills. This assessment was used in a leadership program designed specifically to develop their potential

9-box grid
A three-by-three matrix used by groups of managers and executives to compare employees within one department, function, division, or the entire company.

Figure 9.5

Example of a 9-Box Grid

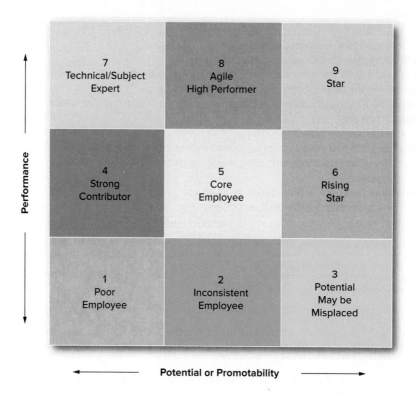

Performance

7 Technical/Subject Expert	8 Agile High Performer	9 Star
4 Strong Contributor	5 Core Employee	6 Rising Star
1 Poor Employee	2 Inconsistent Employee	3 Potential May be Misplaced

Potential or Promotability

and skills to ensure they were ready for promotion. The results have been positive. Leadership turnover has decreased by one-third, internal promotion rates for leaders have increased by nearly 50%, and the leader-to-employee ratio has improved by 24%.

Contrast the development plans of "Stars" with employees in the other areas of the grid. The development plans for "Poor Employees" emphasize performance improvement in their current position rather than getting them challenging new job experiences. If they do not improve in their current position, they are likely to be fired. "Technical/ Subject Experts" are outstanding performers but have low potential for leadership positions. Their development plans likely emphasize keeping their knowledge, skills, and competencies current and getting them experiences to continue to motivate them and facilitate creativity and innovation. "Potential May Be Misplaced" employees may have just taken a new position and haven't had the time to demonstrate high performance, or these employees' knowledge, skills, or competencies might not match their job requirements. Their development plans might emphasize moving them to a position that best matches their skill set or, if they have just moved to the job, ensuring that they get the training and development opportunities and resources necessary to help them attain high performance levels. "Core Employees" are solid but not outstanding performers who have moderate potential. Development plans for these employees will include a mix of training and development designed to help ensure their solid performance continues. Also, their development plans likely include some development experiences that can help grow their skills and determine their interest and ability to perform in positions requiring different skills and/or more responsibility.

Sixth, succession planning is dependent on other human resource systems, including compensation, training and development, and staffing. Incentives and bonuses may be linked to completion of development opportunities. Activities such as training courses, job experiences, mentors, and 360-degree feedback should be part of high-potential

Wanted: Leaders in Growth Markets

Global companies hoping to grow their business by expanding to Africa are having a difficult time finding leaders to run their operations. Companies are trying to recruit leaders, but candidates lack the necessary management skills. Contributing to the problem is the fact that Africa has few high-quality business schools. As a result, especially in Kenya and Nigeria, individuals with interests in management choose to attend schools or work elsewhere and don't want to return to Africa.

Global companies have tried to solve the problem by using expatriates to fill management roles, but relocation is costly and it is only a temporary solution for the lack of local talent.

Companies are trying numerous ways to develop and retain local talent. For instance, McKinsey and Co. invests in training Kenyan professionals in critical thinking, quantitative analysis, and cooperation and team-building skills. Ernst & Young LLP is using rotational programs that send Africans to other countries with plans for them to return to Africa. These rotations provide international experience and help develop leadership skills.

DISCUSSION QUESTIONS

1. In addition to job rotations and formal education, what other types of development activities might help grow leaders for Africa?
2. How might succession planning be useful?

SOURCE: Based on L. Gellman, "Nurturing Talent Is Hard in Africa," *Wall Street Journal*, December 9, 2015, p. B9.

employees' development plans. Companies need to decide, for example, whether they will fill an open management position internally with a less-experienced employee who will improve in the role over time or hire a manager from outside the company who can deliver results immediately. Seventh, employees need to be provided with feedback on future moves, expected career paths, and development goals and experiences. Finally, the succession planning process needs to be evaluated. This includes identifying and measuring appropriate results outcomes (such as reduced time to fill manager positions, increased use of internal promotions) as well as collecting measures of satisfaction with the process (reaction outcomes) from employees and managers. Also, modifications that will be made to the succession planning process need to be identified, discussed, and implemented. The "Competing through Globalization" box describes the challenges companies face in finding local leaders.

Turnover is common in Valvoline Instant Oil Change's industry.[103] This means that succession planning and developing bench strength are critical for all employees. Each month managers rate all their employees on their readiness for promotion to their next job level and provide an overall evaluation of when they are ready, such as "today" or "within six months." Managers work with employees on development plans designed to get them to be ready today. The development plans and evaluations are entered into an online system that allows higher-level managers to identify stores and areas where talent is not available in order to improve succession plans. Managers can identify employees, known as "blockers," who are not willing or able to develop further but are in positions that would be considered as a promotion for other employees. Succession planning has initiated a demand for training across the entire career path to ensure that assistant managers are developed as well as senior technicians who might take their jobs and new technicians who need to be ready to take on more responsibilities. Top-level managers use the online system to identify if talent is available to expand stores in a geographic area. Also, the company includes the number of managers available for promotion on their balanced scorecards, which measure company performance.

Blue Cross Blue Shield of Michigan (BCBSM) identifies and develops the company's next generation of leaders as well as talented employees.[104] Members of the executive team have formal succession plans. At the executive level, potential successors' evaluations include an evaluation of their readiness for a new position, for example, ready today or ready in three-to-five years. This has resulted in the development of considerable bench strength for executive positions. All executive positions have at least one successor identified, and 75% of the successors are evaluated as ready today to take the position. But BCBSM also supports succession planning and talent review at all levels of the organization. BCBSM conducts companywide talent reviews to identify current and future skill strengths and weaknesses. BCBSM uses a 9-box grid to assess performance and potential. Management teams meet to discuss the 9-box results for their employees individually and as a group. Part of the meeting is devoted to ensuring that managers are using similar standards for evaluating employee performance and likelihood of future advancement. After the talent reviews are completed, BCBSM holds talent summits to ensure that managers across all divisions understand the company's talent and its development needs, and are aware of cross-division job openings and talent strengths and weaknesses. Supporting this process, BCBSM conducts an annual talent inventory. Employees are asked to identify their career interests and skills. This information is used in manager–employee discussions of BCBSM's talent needs and their individual development plans, career goals, and development activities.

Paychex bases succession planning on its leadership competency model.[105] Paychex uses the 9-box grid to identify leaders with high performance potential. Potential evaluations are based on agility, ability, and aspiration. Succession candidates participate in two leadership development programs. Each succession candidate develops an individual development plan. The individual development plans are designed to meet business needs and competency gaps through development activities known at Paychex as the 3Es: education, exposure, and experience. A dedicated "leadership developer" works with the employee and his or her manager to provide coaching, help with the individual development plan, and monitor progress. Last year, over 1,700 executives, senior executives, managers, and supervisors completed assessment of their leadership competencies, performance, and potential. The succession planning process has resulted in over 25% of senior managers, managers, and supervisors identified as ready for a promotion to the next level within one to two years, succession plans for all officer and senior manager positions at Paychex, and an increase of 18% in open senior management positions filled with internal candidates.

One of the important issues in succession planning is deciding whether to tell employees if they are on or off the list of potential candidates for higher-level manager positions.[106] There are several advantages and disadvantages that companies need to consider. One advantage of making a succession planning list public or telling employees who are on the list is that they are more likely to stay with the company because they understand they likely will have new career opportunities. Another is that high-potential employees who are not interested in other positions can communicate their intentions. This helps the company avoid investing costly development resources in them and allows the company to have a more accurate idea of its high-potential managerial talent. The disadvantages of identifying high-potential employees are that those not on the list may become discouraged and leave the company or changes in business strategy or the employees' performance could take them off the list. Also, employees might not believe they have had a fair chance to compete for leadership positions if they already know that a list of potential candidates has been established. One way to avoid these problems is to let employees know they are on the list but not discuss a specific position they will likely reach.

Another is to frequently review the list of candidates and clearly communicate plans and expectations. Managers at Midmark Corporation, a medical equipment manufacturer based in Versailles, Ohio, identify successors every six months as part of the company's performance review process and produce a potential list of candidates. Some employees are also labeled as high potential and others are identified as having high potential for leadership positions. Employees with high potential for leadership positions are considered for challenging development assignments involving overseas relocation. Using interviews, the company determines if employees on the succession list are interested in and qualified for leadership positions.

A LOOK BACK

3M's Employee Development Programs

The chapter opener described how 3M uses development plans, competency models, tuition reimbursement, and leadership development program to enhance employees skill and career development in order to maintain and gain a competitive advantage.

QUESTIONS

1. How does development at 3M help the company gain a competitive advantage?
2. Why does 3M emphasize development for all employees rather than just focus on employees with the greatest potential to be company leaders?
3. Which of the development activities provided by 3M is most beneficial for employees and the company? Why?

SUMMARY

Companies use various employee development methods, including formal education, assessment, job experiences, and interpersonal relationships. Most companies use one or more of these approaches to develop employees. Formal education involves enrolling employees in courses or seminars offered by the company or educational institutions. Assessment involves measuring the employee's performance, behavior, skills, or personality characteristics. Job experiences include job enlargement, rotating to a new job, promotions, transfers, or temporary assignments. A more experienced, senior employee (a mentor) can help employees better understand the company and gain exposure and visibility to key persons in the organization. Part of a manager's job responsibility may be to coach employees. Regardless of the development approaches used, employees should have a development plan to identify (1) the type of development needed, (2) development goals, (3) the best approach for development, and (4) whether development goals have been reached. For development plans to be effective, both the employee and the company have responsibilities that need to be fulfilled.

KEY TERMS

Development, 382
Protean career, 383
Psychological success, 383
Development planning system, 385
Action plan, 387
Formal education programs, 389
Tuition reimbursement, 391
Assessment, 393
Myers-Briggs Type Inventory (MBTI), 393
Assessment center, 394
Leaderless group discussion, 394

DISCUSSION QUESTIONS

1. How could assessment be used to create a productive work team?
2. List and explain the characteristics of effective 360-degree feedback systems.
3. Why do companies develop formal mentoring programs? What are the potential benefits for the mentor? For the protégé?
4. Your boss is interested in hiring a consultant to help identify potential managers among current employees of a fast-food restaurant. The manager's job is to help wait on customers and prepare food during busy times, oversee all aspects of restaurant operations (including scheduling, maintenance, on-the-job training, and food purchase), and help motivate employees to provide high-quality service. The manager is also responsible for resolving disputes that might occur between employees. The position involves working under stress and coordinating several activities at one time. She asks you to outline the type of assessment program you believe would do the best job of identifying employees who will be successful managers. What will you tell her?
5. Many employees are unwilling to relocate because they like their current community, and spouses and children prefer not to move. Yet employees need to develop new skills, strengthen skill weaknesses, and be exposed to new aspects of the business to prepare for management positions. How could an employee's current job be changed to develop management skills?
6. Can experiences that managers have outside of the company be beneficial for development? Identify the types of experiences and explain why they are beneficial.
7. What are some examples of sabbaticals, and why are they beneficial?
8. What is coaching? Is there one type of coaching? Explain.
9. Why are many managers reluctant to coach their employees?
10. Why should companies be interested in helping employees plan their development? What benefits can companies gain? What are the risks?
11. What are the manager's roles in a development system? Which role do you think is most difficult for the typical manager? Which is the easiest role? List the reasons why managers might resist involvement in career management.
12. Draw the 9-box grid. How is it useful for succession planning?
13. Nationwide Financial, a 5,000-employee life insurance company based in Columbus, Ohio, found that its management development program contained four types of managers. One type, unknown leaders, have the right skills but their talents are unknown to top managers in the company. Another group, arrogant leaders, believe they have all the skills they need. What types of development program would you recommend for each of these types of managers?

SELF-ASSESSMENT EXERCISE

Additional assignable self-assessments available in Connect.

Go to www.keirsey.com. Complete the Keirsey Temperament Sorter. What did you learn about yourself? How could the instrument you completed be useful for employee development? What might be some disadvantages of using this instrument?

EXERCISING STRATEGY

Leadership Development at HITT Contracting

It is difficult to attract Millennials to the construction industry because of long work hours, hazardous worksites, intense clients, and stressful schedules. But as one of the largest general contractors in the United States, HITT Contracting is providing development and growth opportunities that are making it an attractive employer for the best and brightest talent. For example, HITT's Futures leadership program has four phases: Cornerstone, Foundation, Integration, and Acceleration.

In the Cornerstone phase, construction interns are assigned a sponsor who has three to five years of experience working at HITT. Interns get hands-on experience regardless of whether they are working in the office or at a job site. Sponsors provide the interns with specific tasks and responsibilities. They also participate in social activities and training courses throughout their internship. In the Foundation phase, returning summer interns and new full-time project engineers work on-site and have the site superintendent serve as their mentor. All project engineers are given a curriculum they must complete before they can be promoted. The courses are offered through HITT Institute. HITT also has a generous tuition reimbursement program that project engineers can use to pursue advanced degrees, engineering certifications, and other courses. At the end of their first year, project engineers can choose one of five career paths: project management; site operations; safety; preconstruction; or mechanical, electrical, or plumbing specialties.

The Integration phase involves engineers developing their skills in the track they selected. The engineers often continue to contact their superintendent mentor, and they themselves serve as mentors for construction interns who they are responsible for coaching and training. In the Integration phase, engineers still have opportunities to cross-train through working on new projects or work teams. They also have the opportunity to attend social events where they can network with HITT leaders and industry professionals. In Acceleration, the final phase of the program, engineers have the opportunity to take management and leadership roles. As mid-level managers, they oversee their own projects and supervise other team members.

QUESTIONS

1. Does the Futures leadership program contribute to HITT Contracting's competitive advantage in the construction industry? Why or why not? What important business outcomes are likely influenced by the program?
2. What other types of development activities should HITT Contracting consider for the Futures leadership program? Explain your choice(s)?

SOURCE: Based on J. Dominick, "Break Your Ground with HITT," *TD*, February 2016, pp. 38–42; "Overview" and "HITT Futures Leadership Program," www.hitt.com, accessed March 22, 2017.

MANAGING PEOPLE

Employee Development at ESPN

Entertainment and Sports Programming Network, known as ESPN, is in the global multimedia sports and entertainment business. To remain in its leadership role in the sports and entertainment business, ESPN needs to continue to provide the best live sports programming as well as expand and develop its digital presence through social media. To do so, ESPN recognizes the importance of creating exceptional employee experiences through its commitment to people, partnerships, culture, and excellence. Employee development plays a key role in helping to create exceptional employee experiences at ESPN. But employee development at ESPN faces several challenges. One challenge is the speed at which the global news, broadcasting, and entertainment business operates. This can make it difficult for employees to take the time away from activities such as producing and delivering programming to focus on development activities.

Another challenge is that ESPN has reportedly been asked by its parent company, Disney, to cut as much as $250 million from this year's budget. This likely will result in layoffs for 200–300 employees.

ESPN has taken several steps to ensure that its development efforts overcome these challenges and support employees' career interests and goals, enhance their skills, and grow top leadership talent. ESPN requires every employee to complete an individual development plan (IDP). The IDP helps employees consider where they currently are in their careers, their career goals, and how they plan to reach their career goals. The learning function at ESPN reviews and supports the IDP, which has been completed by over 95% of employees.

Similar to other companies, ESPN uses the 70-20-10 approach to development. This means that most employee development occurs on the job, whereas 20% comes from relationships and informal learning, and 10% from formal courses targeted at specific skills. For example, ESPN has a Leadership GPS, which is a tool used by employees to track their development progress. The Leadership GPS helps employees set development goals. It also provides advice on which types of development activities (such as courses, job shadowing, or experiences) are available and will help them meet their goals. ESPN The University offers courses related to different business areas, which are taught by executives and business leaders. This is important because its gets company leaders from different business areas involved in developing employees. It also helps to provide employees with a greater understanding of the different aspects of ESPN's business such as production, programming, and HR and how they fit together. ESPN Center Court is a development program targeted exclusively to high-potential employees who are on the fast track to future leadership roles in the company. Center Court uses job rotations to give high-potential employees the opportunity to experience different aspects of the business. They also interact with the company's president and top executives. To facilitate development through relationships, ESPN has a mentoring program known as Open Access that is available to all employees. The only requirements are that employees desire to learn from others and want to build relationships to achieve their development goals.

To ensure that development activities support business needs, ESPN has a learning and advisory board, which includes senior leaders and vice presidents from its different businesses. Every major initiative is reviewed and has to receive support from the board before it is implemented. Also, the Employee Learning Council, which includes employees from each of ESPN's business units, provides feedback and helps to plan development programs.

QUESTIONS

1. ESPN requires all employees to complete an individual development plan (IDP). What should be included on an effective development plan?
2. How could ESPN identify employees with the potential for top leadership positions?
3. Do you think ESPN should place less emphasis on developing employees because of the current need for layoffs? Explain your answer.

SOURCES: Based on F. Kalman, "ESPN's Top Play: Learning," Chief Learning Officer, March 2013, pp. 22–25, 47; M. Ingram, "Here's Why ESPN Is Looking at Layoffs Amid a Wave of Cost Cuts," *Fortune,* March 8, 2017; "Learning and Development," http://espncareers.com/working_here/learning_development, accessed March 26, 2017.

HR IN SMALL BUSINESS

How Service Express Serves Employees First

Service Express, Inc. (SEI), headquartered in Grand Rapids, Michigan, provides maintenance for critical computer hardware, such as the servers that run companies' data processing and the storage units that keep data secure but accessible. Its customers include hospitals, universities, banks, manufacturing companies, and other organizations in more than a dozen states, and employees travel to the customers' work sites. This type of work requires people who are dependable, technically skilled, and committed to responsive, fast service.

SEI attracts, equips, and keeps such employees with a vision that is unusual for a business: to "work with our employees to help them achieve their personal, professional, and financial goals." What is unusual is that the company puts the employees' goals first. The perspective goes back to the company's founder, who realized that the value placed on helping employees achieve their goals attracted people with similar values, and they in turn focused on helping customers achieve their goals.

To put the vision into practice, SEI managers hold twice-yearly Vision Talks with each of their employees, starting with the employee's first day on the job. During these meetings, the employee shares or updates his or her goals, working with the manager to identify how the company can enable the employee to achieve the goals. The company trains managers in how to conduct the Vision Talks effectively, recognizing that employees will need to build trust before they start sharing personal goals.

During the talks, managers help the employees shape general ideas into measurable and attainable goals. These become part of a personal development plan, updated quarterly, which also includes objectives for training, project completion, and so on. Occasionally, managers identify goals that can be tied to a business opportunity. For example, an employee who wants to move to another state can be part of a business expansion into that state, or an employee who wants to build something from the ground up can lead a new business line. A dramatic example involves a salesperson who had no interest in management, so he focused on developing sales skills. At one point, the salesperson's manager asked him to help train and coach a newer employee, and the salesperson discovered that he found it satisfying to help another person succeed. He set a new goal to become a manager—and eventually became vice president of sales.

QUESTIONS

1. How does the description of careers at Service Express fit the chapter's description of a protean career? What is the role of employee development in this context?
2. Suppose SEI continues growing and asks you to advise management on how to maintain its focus on employee development. Suggest to SEI two or three development methods from the chapter, and explain why you recommend each.

SOURCES: Service Express, "About SEI," http://www.seiservice.com, accessed March 26, 2017; Service Express, "The SEI Way Is How We Identify Our Unique Company," http://www.seiservice.com, accessed March 26, 2017; Bo Burlingham, "The Best Small Companies in America: 2016," Forbes, January 27, 2016.

NOTES

1. D. Day, *Developing Leadership Talent* (Alexandria, VA: SHRM Foundation, 2007); M. London, *Managing the Training Enterprise* (San Francisco: Jossey-Bass, 1989); C. McCauley and S. Heslett, "Individual Development in the Workplace," in *Handbook of Industrial, Work, and Organizational Psychology*, vol. 1, ed. N. Anderson, D. Ones, H. Sinangil, and C. Viswesveran (London: Sage Publications, 2001), pp. 313–35.
2. R. W. Pace, P. C. Smith, and G. E. Mills, *Human Resource Development* (Englewood Cliffs, NJ: Prentice Hall, 1991); W. Fitzgerald, "Training versus Development," *Training and Development Journal*, May 1992, pp. 81–84; R. A. Noe, S. L. Wilk, E. J. Mullen, and J. E. Wanek, "Employee Development: Issues in Construct Definition and Investigation of Antecedents," in *Improving Training Effectiveness in Work Organizations*, ed. J. K. Ford (Mahwah, NJ: Lawrence Erlbaum, 1997), pp. 153–89.
3. PricewaterhouseCoopers, "Good to Grow: 2014 US CEO Survey," www.pwc.com, accessed February 20, 2015; J. Green, "Chowing Down on Boomers' Brains," *Bloomberg Businessweek*, January 25–31, 2016, pp. 19–20.
4. ATD Staff, "All the Happy People," *TD*, July 2016, p. 15.
5. M. Gubler, J. Arnold, and C. Coombs, "Reassessing the Protean Career Concept: Empirical Findings, Conceptual Components, and Measurement," *Journal of Organizational Behavior* 35 (2014), pp. 23–40; D. T. Hall, "Protean Careers of the 21st Century," *Academy of Management Executive* 11 (1996), pp. 8–16; D. Hall, *Careers in and out of Organizations* (Thousand Oaks, CA: Sage, 2002); J. Greenhaus, G. Callahan, and V. Godshalk, *Career Management*, 4th ed. (Thousand Oaks, CA: Sage, 2010).
6. K. Essick, "From a Job to a Calling," *Wall Street Journal*, March 16, 2015, p. R4.
7. K. R. Brousseau, M. J. Driver, K. Eneroth, and R. Larsson, "Career Pandemonium: Realigning Organizations and Individuals," *Academy of Management Executive* 11 (1996), pp. 52–66.
8. M. Wang and C. Wanberg, "100 Years of Applied Psychology Research on Individual Careers: From Career Management to Retirement," *Journal of Applied Psychology* 102 (2017), pp. 546–63; W. Inn and B. Crowell, "Organizations and Managers Must Reassess How They View Career Development," *TD*, September 2015, pp. 42–46; M. B. Arthur, "The Boundaryless Career: A New Perspective of Organizational Inquiry," *Journal of Organization Behavior* 15 (1994), pp. 295–309; P. H. Mirvis and D. T. Hall, "Psychological Success and the Boundaryless Career," *Journal of Organization Behavior* 15 (1994), pp. 365–80; M. Lazarova and S. Taylor, "Boundaryless Careers, Social Capital, and Knowledge Management: Implications for

Organizational Performance," *Journal of Organizational Behavior* 30 (2009), pp. 119–39; D. Feldman and T. Ng, "Careers: Mobility, Embeddedness, and Success," *Journal of Management* 33 (2007), pp. 350–77.
9. "Nearly One-Third of Employers Expect Workers to Job-Hop," *Career Builder*, www.careerbuilder.com, accessed April 2, 2015; "Is Job Hopping the New Normal?" *T + D*, August 2014, p. 20.
10. J. Lublin, "Job Hopping Is Losing Its Stigma," *Wall Street Journal*, July 27, 2016, p. B8; R. Hoffman, B. Casnocha, and C. Yeh, "Tours of Duty: The New Employer-Employee Compact," *Harvard Business Review*, June 2013, pp. 48–58.
11. C. Rexrode, "Citi to Millennials: Take a Year Off", *Wall Street Journal* (March 17, 2016): C1-C2.
12. L. Mainiero and S. Sullivan, "Kaleidoscope Careers: An Alternative Explanation for the 'Opt-Out' Revolution," *Academy of Management Executive* 19 (2005), pp. 106–23; S. Sullivan and L. Mainiero, "Benchmarking Ideas for Fostering Family-Friendly Workplaces," *Organizational Dynamics* 36 (2007), pp. 45–62.
13. *Training* Top 125, "BB&T Corporation", *Training* (January/February 2016): 73.
14. M. McGraw, "The Michelin Method," *Human Resource Executive*, March 2016, pp. 14–16.
15. P. Asinof, "IDPs: Talent Development's Superglue," *TD*, January 2016, pp. 42–47.
16. *Training* Top 125, "Consigli Construction," *Training*, January/February 2016, p. 87.
17. D. T. Jaffe and C. D. Scott, "Career Development for Empowerment in a Changing Work World," in *New Directions in Career Planning and the Workplace*, ed. J. M. Kummerow (Palo Alto, CA: Consulting Psychologists Press, 1991), pp. 33–60; L. Summers, "A Logical Approach to Development Planning," *Training and Development* 48 (1994), pp. 22–31; D. B. Peterson and M. D. Hicks, *Development First* (Minneapolis, MN: Personnel Decisions, 1995).
18. M. McGraw, "Millennials Take Up the Mantle," *Human Resource Executive*, December 2015, pp. 16–20.
19. *Training* Top 125, "Genentech, Inc.," *Training*, January/February 2016, p. 67; R. Emlo, "The Power of Discovery," *Chief Learning Officer*, January 2015, pp. 38–48; "Genentech, Inc.: Career Lab," *Training*, January/February 2015, pp. 102–3; N. Waller, "How Men and Women See the Workplace Differently," *Wall Street Journal*, September 27, 2016, pp. B1, B2.
20. R. Noe, *Employee Training and Development*, 7th ed. (New York: McGraw-Hill, Irwin, 2015); K. O'Leonard and L. Loew,

"Investing in the Future," *Human Resource Executive*, July/August 2012, pp. 30–34.

21. "CHG Healthcare Services," *Training*, January/February 2017, p. 53.

22. C. Waxer, "Course Review," *Human Resource Executive*, December 2005, pp. 46–48; Pat Galagan, "90,000 Served: Hamburger University Turns 50," *T + D*, April 2011, pp. 46–51; Beth Kowitt, "Why McDonald's Wins in Any Economy," *Fortune*, September 5, 2011.

23. General Electric, "GE Crotonville: The Future of Leadership," https://www.ge.com/sites/default/files/GE_Crotonville_Future_of_Leadership.pdf, accessed March 24, 2017.

24. R. Knight, "GE's Corporate Boot Camp cum Talent Spotting Venue," *Financial Times Business Education*, March 20, 2006, p. 2; J. Durett, "GE Hones Its Leaders at Crotonville," *Training*, May 2006, pp. 25–27.

25. University of Virginia Darden School of Business, "MBA for Executives," www.darden.virginia.edu, accessed March 30, 2012.

26. Duke Corporate Education, "Thomson Reuters Case Study: Innovation," 2012, http://www.dukece.com/clients/documents/ThomsonReutersCaseStudy.pdf, accessed April 3, 2015.

27. Center for Creative Leadership, "Leadership Development Programs," https://www.ccl.org/open-enrollment-programs/leadership-development-program/, accessed March 24, 2017.

28. R. Johnson, "The Learning Curve: The Value of Tuition Reimbursement," *Training*, November 2005, pp. 30–33; G. Benson, D. Finegold, and S. Mohrman, "You Paid for the Skills, Now Keep Them: Tuition Reimbursement and Voluntary Turnover," *Academy of Management Journal* 47 (2004), pp. 315–31.

29. From Verizon, "Frequently Asked Questions: Do You Offer Tuition Reimbursement/Assistance?" www.verizon.com, accessed March 24, 2017; "Top 125 Hall of Fame: Verizon," *Training*, January/February 2014, pp. 58–59.

30. Day, *Developing Leadership Talent*.

31. E. Harrell, "A Brief History of Personality Tests," *Harvard Business Review*, March/April 2017, 63; M. Weinstein, "Personalities & Performance," *Training*, July/August 2008, pp. 36–40.

32. S. K. Hirsch, *MBTI Team Member's Guide* (Palo Alto, CA: Consulting Psychologists Press, 1992); A. L. Hammer, *Introduction to Type and Careers* (Palo Alto, CA: Consulting Psychologists Press, 1993); J. Llorens, "Taking Inventory of Myers-Briggs," *T + D*, April 2010, pp. 18–19.

33. From www.discprofile.com, website for DiSC, accessed February 1, 2012.

34. M. Weinstein, "The X Factor," *Training*, May/June 2011, pp. 65–67.

35. G. C. Thornton III and W. C. Byham, *Assessment Centers and Managerial Performance* (New York: Academic Press, 1982); L. F. Schoenfeldt and J. A. Steger, "Identification and Development of Management Talent," in *Research in Personnel and Human Resource Management*, ed. K. N. Rowland and G. Ferris (Greenwich, CT: JAI Press, 1989), vol. 7, pp. 151–81.

36. Thornton and Byham, *Assessment Centers and Managerial Performance*.

37. B. B. Gaugler, D. B. Rosenthal, G. C. Thornton III, and C. Bentson, "Metaanalysis of Assessment Center Validity," *Journal of Applied Psychology* 72 (1987), pp. 493–511; D. W. Bray, R. J. Campbell, and D. L. Grant, *Formative Years in Business: A Long-Term AT&T Study of Managerial Lives* (New York: Wiley, 1974).

38. R. G. Jones and M. D. Whitmore, "Evaluating Developmental Assessment Centers as Interventions," *Personnel Psychology* 48 (1995), pp. 377–88.

39. J. Schettler, "Building Bench Strength," *Training*, June 2002, pp. 55–58.

40. S. B. Silverman, "Individual Development through Performance Appraisal," in *Developing Human Resources*, pp. 5–120 to 5–151.

41. M. Sallie-Dosunmu, "Born to Grow," *TD*, May 2006, pp. 34–37.

42. J. S. Lublin, "Turning the Tables: Underlings Evaluate Bosses," *Wall Street Journal*, October 4, 1994, pp. B1, B14; D. O'Reilly, "360-Degree Feedback Can Change Your Life," *Fortune*, October 17, 1994, pp. 93–100; J. F. Milliman, R. A. Zawacki, C. Norman, L. Powell, and J. Kirksey, "Companies Evaluate Employees from All Perspectives," *Personnel Journal*, November 1994, pp. 99–103.

43. Center for Creative Leadership, *Skillscope for Managers: Development Planning Guide* (Greensboro, NC: Center for Creative Leadership, 1992); G. Yukl and R. Lepsinger, "360-Degree Feedback," *Training*, December 1995, pp. 45–50.

44. L. Atwater, P. Roush, and A. Fischthal, "The Influence of Upward Feedback on Self- and Follower Ratings of Leadership," *Personnel Psychology* 48 (1995), pp. 35–59; J. F. Hazucha, S. A. Hezlett, and R. J. Schneider, "The Impact of 360-Degree Feedback on Management Skill Development," *Human Resource Management* 32 (1993), pp. 325–51; J. W. Smither, M. London, N. Vasilopoulos, R. R. Reilly, R. E. Millsap, and N. Salvemini, "An Examination of the Effects of an Upward Feedback Program over Time," *Personnel Psychology* 48 (1995), pp. 1–34; J. Smither and A. Walker, "Are the Characteristics of Narrative Comments Related to Improvements in Multirater Feedback Ratings over Time?" *Journal of Applied Psychology* 89 (2004), pp. 575–81; J. Smither, M. London, and R. Reilly, "Does Performance Improve Following Multisource Feedback? A Theoretical Model, Meta-analysis, and Review of Empirical Findings," *Personnel Psychology* 58 (2005), pp. 33–66.

45. D. Bracken, "Straight Talk about Multirater Feedback," *Training and Development*, September 1994, pp. 44–51; K. Nowack, J. Hartley, and W. Bradley, "How to Evaluate Your 360-Feedback Efforts," *Training and Development*, April 1999, pp. 48–52; M. Levine, "Taking the Burn out of the 360-Degree Hot Seat," *T + D*, August 2010, pp. 40–45.

46. M. Weinstein, "BCBSM's Big Picture Focus," *Training*, January/February 2016, pp. 46–50.

47. M. W. McCall Jr., M. M. Lombardo, and A. M. Morrison, *Lessons of Experience* (Lexington, MA: Lexington Books, 1988); L. Dragoni, P. Tesluk, J. Russell, and I. Oh, "Understanding Managerial Development: Integrating Developmental Assignments, Learning Orientation, and Access to Developmental Opportunities in Predicting Managerial Competencies," *Academy of Management Journal* 52 (2009), pp. 731–43.

48. R. S. Snell, "Congenial Ways of Learning: So Near yet So Far," *Journal of Management Development* 9 (1990), pp. 17–23.

49. R. Morrison, T. Erickson, and K. Dychtwald, "Managing Middlescence," *Harvard Business Review*, March 2006, pp. 78–86.

50. McGraw, "Millennials Take Up the Mantle."

51. McCall, Lombardo, and Morrison, *Lessons of Experience*; M. W. McCall, "Developing Executives through Work Experiences," *Human Resource Planning* 11 (1988), pp. 1–11; M. N. Ruderman, P. J. Ohlott, and C. D. McCauley, "Assessing Opportunities for Leadership Development," in *Measures of Leadership*, pp. 547–62; C. D. McCauley, L. J. Estman, and P. J. Ohlott, "Linking Management Selection and Development through Stretch Assignments," *Human Resource Management* 34 (1995), pp. 93–115.

52. S. Courtright, A. Colbert, and D. Choi, "Fired Up or Burned Out? How Developmental Challenge Differentially Impacts Leader Behavior," *Journal of Applied Psychology* 99 (2014), pp. 681–96; C. D. McCauley, M. N. Ruderman, P. J. Ohlott, and J. E. Morrow, "Assessing the Developmental Components of Managerial Jobs," *Journal of Applied Psychology* 79 (1994), pp. 544–60; J. LePine, M. LePine, and C. Jackson, "Challenge and Hindrance Stress: Relationships with Exhaustion, Motivation to Learn, and Learning Performance," *Journal of Applied Psychology* 89 (2004) pp. 883–91.

53. S. Thurm, "Power-Sharing Prepares Managers," *Wall Street Journal*, December 5, 2005, p. B4.

54. E. Short, "Move Around before Moving Up," *Chief Learning Officer*, July 2014, pp. 19–21.

55. M. London, *Developing Managers* (San Francisco: Jossey-Bass, 1985); M. A. Campion, L. Cheraskin, and M. J. Stevens, "Career-Related Antecedents and Outcomes of Job Rotation," *Academy of Management Journal* 37 (1994), pp. 1518–42; M. London, *Managing the Training Enterprise* (San Francisco: Jossey-Bass, 1989).

56. B. Ware, "Stop the Gen Y Revolving Door," *T + D*, May 2014, pp. 58–63.

57. *Training* Top 125, "Bell and Howell," *Training*, January/February 2016, p. 95.

58. *Training* Top 125, "Haskell," *Training*, January/February 2017, p. 67.

59. D. C. Feldman, *Managing Careers in Organizations* (Glenview, IL: Scott Foresman, 1988); D. Hall, *Careers In and Out of Organizations* (Thousand Oaks, CA: Sage, 2002).

60. D. T. Hall and L. A. Isabella, "Downward Moves and Career Development," *Organizational Dynamics* 14 (1985), pp. 5–23.

61. H. D. Dewirst, "Career Patterns: Mobility, Specialization, and Related Career Issues," in *Contemporary Career Development Issues*, ed. R. F. Morrison and J. Adams (Hillsdale, NJ: Lawrence Erlbaum, 1991), pp. 73–108.

62. J. M. Brett, L. K. Stroh, and A. H. Reilly, "Job Transfer," in *International Review of Industrial and Organizational Psychology: 1992*, ed. C. L. Cooper and I. T. Robinson (Chichester, England: Wiley, 1992); D. C. Feldman and J. M. Brett, "Coping with New Jobs: A Comparative Study of New Hires and Job Changers," *Academy of Management Journal* 26 (1983), pp. 258–72.

63. R. A. Noe, B. D. Steffy, and A. E. Barber, "An Investigation of the Factors Influencing Employees' Willingness to Accept Mobility Opportunities," *Personnel Psychology* 41 (1988), pp. 559–80; S. Gould and L. E. Penley, "A Study of the Correlates of Willingness to Relocate," *Academy of Management Journal* 28 (1984), pp. 472–78; J. Landau and T. H. Hammer, "Clerical Employees' Perceptions of Intra-organizational Career Opportunities," *Academy of Management Journal* 29 (1986), pp. 385–405; R. P. Duncan and C. C. Perruci, "Dual Occupation Families and Migration," *American Sociological Review* 41 (1976), pp. 252–61; J. M. Brett and A. H. Reilly, "On the Road Again: Predicting the Job Transfer Decision," *Journal of Applied Psychology* 73 (1988), pp. 614–620.

64. J. Ramirez, "Smart Money," *Human Resource Executive*, January/February 2015, pp. 22–27.

65. J. M. Brett, "Job Transfer and Well-Being," *Journal of Applied Psychology* 67 (1992), pp. 450–63; F. J. Minor, L. A. Slade, and R. A. Myers, "Career Transitions in Changing Times," in *Contemporary Career Development Issues*, pp. 109–20; C. C. Pinder and K. G. Schroeder, "Time to Proficiency Following Job Transfers," *Academy of Management Journal* 30 (1987),

pp. 336–53; G. Flynn, "Heck No—We Won't Go!" *Personnel Journal*, March 1996, pp. 37–43.

66. R. Silverman, "Field Trip: Learning from Startups," *Wall Street Journal*, March 27, 2013, p. B8.

67. C. McCauley, "Make Experience Count," *Chief Learning Officer*, May 2014, p. 50.

68. E. Byron, "A New Odd Couple: Google, P&G Swap Workers to Spur Innovation," *Wall Street Journal*, November 19, 2008, pp. A1, A18.

69. C. J. Bachler, "Workers Take Leave of Job Stress," *Personnel Journal*, January 1995, pp. 38–48; "Types of Sabbaticals," www.yoursabbatical.com, accessed April 17, 2013.

70. L. Shen, "These 19 Great Employers Offer Paid Sabbaticals," *Fortune*, March 7, 2016.

71. Based on K. Everson, "Dow Chemical's New Formula for Global Leaders," *Chief Learning Officer*, April 2015, pp. 42–43, 49; "Mission & Vision," www.dow.com, accessed March 26, 2017; "Leadership in Action: Ethiopia," www.dow.com/en-us/careers/working-at-dow/learning-and-development, accessed March 26, 2017.

72. Company website, "Volunteerism," www.generalmills.com, accessed March26, 2017; M. Weinstein, "Charity Begins @ Work," *Training*, May 2008, pp. 56–58; K. Ellis, "Pass It On," *Training*, June 2005, pp. 14–19.

73. D. B. Turban and T. W. Dougherty, "Role of Protégé Personality in Receipt of Mentoring and Career Success," *Academy of Management Journal* 37 (1994), pp. 688–702; E. A. Fagenson, "Mentoring: Who Needs It? A Comparison of Protégés' and Nonprotégés' Needs for Power, Achievement, Affiliation, and Autonomy," *Journal of Vocational Behavior* 41 (1992), pp. 48–60.

74. A. H. Geiger, "Measures for Mentors," *Training and Development Journal*, February 1992, pp. 65–67.

75. K. E. Kram, *Mentoring at Work: Developmental Relationships in Organizational Life* (Glenview, IL: Scott Foresman, 1985); K. Kram, "Phases of the Mentoring Relationship," *Academy of Management Journal* 26 (1983), pp. 608–25; G. T. Chao, P. M. Walz, and P. D. Gardner, "Formal and Informal Mentorships: A Comparison of Mentoring Functions and Contrasts with Nonmentored Counterparts," *Personnel Psychology* 45 (1992), pp. 619–36; C. Wanberg, E. Welsh, and S. Hezlett, "Mentoring Research: A Review and Dynamic Process Model," in *Research in Personnel and Human Resources Management*, ed. J. Martocchio and G. Ferris (New York: Elsevier Science, 2003), pp. 39–124.

76. E. White, "Making Mentorships Work," *Wall Street Journal*, October 23, 2007, p. B11; E. Holmes, "Career Mentors Today Seem Short on Advice but Give a Mean Tour," *Wall Street Journal*, August 28, 2007, p. B1; J. Sandberg, "With Bad Mentors It's Better to Break Up Than to Make Up," *Wall Street Journal*, March 18, 2008, p. B1.

77. M. Weinstein, "Please Don't Go," *Training*, May/June 2011, pp. 28–34.

78. L. Eby, M. Butts, A. Lockwood, and A. Simon, "Protégés' Negative Mentoring Experiences: Construct Development and Nomo-logical Validation," *Personnel Psychology* 57 (2004), pp. 411–47; M. Boyle, "Most Mentoring Programs Stink—but Yours Doesn't Have To," *Training*, August 2005, pp. 12–15.

79. R. Emelo, "Conversations with Mentoring Leaders," *T + D*, June 2011, pp. 32–37.

80. "Training Top 125: Cartus," *Training*, January/February 2015, p. 87; J. Alsever, "Looking for a Career Mentor You Love? Let Cold Data Be Your Guide, *Fast Company*, www.fastcompany.com,

accessed July 22, 2014; M. Weinstein, "Tech Connects," *Training*, September 2008, pp. 58–59.

81. G. F. Dreher and R. A. Ash, "A Comparative Study of Mentoring among Men and Women in Managerial, Professional, and Technical Positions," *Journal of Applied Psychology* 75 (1990), pp. 539–46; T. D. Allen, L. T. Eby, M. L. Poteet, E. Lentz, and L. Lima, "Career Benefits Associated with Mentoring for Protégés: A Meta-Analysis," *Journal of Applied Psychology* 89 (2004), pp. 127–36; R. A. Noe, D. B. Greenberger, and S. Wang, "Mentoring: What We Know and Where We Might Go," in *Research in Personnel and Human Resources Management*, ed. G. Ferris and J. Martucchio (New York: Elsevier Science, 2002), pp. 129–74; R. A. Noe, "An Investigation of the Determinants of Successful Assigned Mentoring Relationships," *Personnel Psychology* 41 (1988), pp. 457–79; B. J. Tepper, "Upward Maintenance Tactics in Supervisory Mentoring and Nonmentoring Relationships," *Academy of Management Journal* 38 (1995), pp. 1191–205; B. R. Ragins and T. A. Scandura, "Gender Differences in Expected Outcomes of Mentoring Relationships," *Academy of Management Journal* 37 (1994), pp. 957–71.

82. S. Wells, "Tending Talent," *HR Magazine*, May 2009, pp. 53–60.

83. J. Crosby, "Target, UnitedHealth, and Other Companies Turning to Reverse Mentoring to Tap Millennials Knowledge", *Star Tribune* (July 25, 2016) from www.startribune.com accessed March 24, 2017.

84. Alsever, "Looking for a Career Mentor You Love? Let Cold Data Be Your Guide."

85. D. B. Peterson and M. D. Hicks, *Leader as Coach* (Minneapolis, MN: Personnel Decisions, 1996).

86. "*Training* Top 125: Edward Jones," *Training*, January/February 2016, p. 69; "*Training* Top 125: United Shore Financial Services," *Training*, January/February 2016, p. 89; S. Mann and S. Smith, "Expanded Coaching Culture Drives Results," *TD*, June 2015, pp. 36–41; R. Emelo, "Shift Your Focus with Modern Mentoring," *TD*, September 2015, pp. 36–41.

87. J. Smither, M. London, R. Flautt, Y. Vargas, and L. Kucine, "Can Working with an Executive Coach Improve Multisource Ratings over Time? A Quasiexperimental Field Study," *Personnel Psychology* 56 (2003), pp. 23–44.

88. A. Vorro, "Coaching Counsel," *Inside Counsel*, February 2012, Business & Company Resource Center, http://galenet.galegroup.com.

89. LeanIn.Org and McKinsey & Company, "Women in the Workplace 2016," https://womenintheworkplace.com/, accessed March 24, 2017.

90. U.S. Department of Labor, *A Report on the Glass Ceiling Initiative* (Washington, DC: U.S. Department of Labor, 1991).

91. B. Groysberg and K. Connolly, "Great Leaders Who Make the Mix Work," *Harvard Business Review*, September 2013, pp. 68–76; P. J. Ohlott, M. N. Ruderman, and C. D. McCauley, "Gender Differences in Managers' Developmental Job Experiences," *Academy of Management Journal* 37 (1994), pp. 46–67; D. Mattioli, "Programs to Promote Female Managers Win Citations," *Wall Street Journal*, January 30, 2007, p. B7.

92. J. Green, "This Is Not a Trend," *Bloomberg Businessweek*, September 1–September 7, 2014, pp. 19–20.

93. U.S. Department of Labor, *A Report on the Glass Ceiling Initiative*; R. A. Noe, "Women and Mentoring: A Review and Research Agenda," *Academy of Management Review* 13 (1988), pp. 65–78; B. R. Ragins and J. L. Cotton, "Easier Said Than Done: Gender Differences in Perceived Barriers to Gaining a Mentor," *Academy of Management Journal* 34 (1991), pp. 939–51.

94. L. A. Mainiero, "Getting Anointed for Advancement: The Case of Executive Women," *Academy of Management Executive* 8 (1994), pp. 53–67; J. S. Lublin, "Women at Top Still Are Distant from CEO Jobs," *Wall Street Journal*, February 28, 1995, pp. B1, B5; P. Tharenov, S. Latimer, and D. Conroy, "How Do You Make It to the Top? An Examination of Influences on Women's and Men's Managerial Advancement," *Academy of Management Journal* 37 (1994), pp. 899–931.

95. P. Tharenou, "Going Up? Do Traits and Informal Social Processes Predict Advancement in Management?" *Academy of Management Journal* 44 (2001), pp. 1005–17.

96. N. Waller, "How Men and Women See the Workplace Differently", *Wall Street Journal*, September 27, 2016, pp. B1 & B2; J. Lublin, "Group Vows to Advance More Women at Work", *Wall Street Journal*, December 6, 2016; J. Lublin, "GE Engineers New Paths to Promote Women", *Wall Street Journal*, December 14, 2016, p. B5.

97. W. J. Rothwell, *Effective Succession Planning*, 4th ed. (New York: AMACOM, 2010).

98. C. B. Derr, C. Jones, and E. L. Toomey, "Managing High-Potential Employees: Current Practices in Thirty-Three U.S. Corporations," *Human Resource Management* 27 (1988), pp. 273–90.

99. J. Lublin and T. Francis, "Boards Often Fumble CEO Changes," *Wall Street Journal*, June 9, 2016, pp. B1–B2.

100. D. Sims, "Five Ways to Increase Success in Succession Planning," *T + D*, August 2014, pp. 60–63; Rothwell, *Effective Succession Planning*; N. Davis and W. Pina-Ramirez, "Essential Continuity," *T + D*, March 2015, pp. 45–47.

101. K. Tyler, "On the Grid," *HR Magazine*, August 2011, pp. 67–69; D. Day, *Developing Leadership Talent* (Alexandria, VA: SHRM Foundation, 2007).

102. M. Weinstein, "The Heart of CHG Healthcare Services," *Training*, January/February 2015, pp. 44–48.

103. "Valvoline Instant Oil Change: Bench Planning," *Training*, January/February 2014, p. 108.

104. M. Weinstein, "BCBSM's Big Picture Focus," *Training*, January/February 2016, pp. 46–50; M. Weinstein, "BCBSM Empowers Employees," *Training*, January/February 2015, pp. 50–53.

105. J. Grenzer, "Succession Planning," *Training*, May/June 2014, pp. 74–75.

106. "Should You Tell Employees They're Part of a Succession Plan?" *HR Magazine*, January/February 2015, pp. 26–27; M. Steen, "Where to Draw the Line on Revealing Who's Next in Line," *Workforce Management*, June 2011, pp. 16–18.

Employee Separation and Retention

LEARNING OBJECTIVES

After reading this chapter, you should be able to:

LO 10-1 Distinguish between involuntary and voluntary turnover, and discuss how each of these forms of turnover can be leveraged for competitive advantage. *page 427*

LO 10-2 List the major elements that contribute to perceptions of justice and how to apply these in organizational contexts involving discipline and dismissal. *page 431*

LO 10-3 Specify the relationship between job satisfaction and various forms of job withdrawal, and identify the major sources of job satisfaction in work contexts. *page 442*

LO 10-4 Design a survey feedback intervention program, and use this to promote retention of key organizational personnel. *page 450*

There Is Really No Good Answer to the Question, "Rogue Employees or Toxic Culture?"

One of the key strategic pillars to the success and growth of Wells Fargo bank was the idea of cross-selling. *Cross-selling* refers to the practice of getting a current customer (e.g., a checking account holder) to open a new account (e.g., a credit card). Since customers are charged for each account, the more accounts, the merrier, in terms of revenue streams. Wells Fargo set aggressive cross-selling goals for employees: Meeting goals was rewarded with bonuses, and failing to meet them led to terminations. The goal was eight accounts per customer. On average, Wells Fargo customers had 6.3 products, far more than customers at other banks. The only way these goals could be met, however, was by selling customers products without their consent. Indeed, in one of the largest cases of bank fraud in history, the Los Angeles City Attorney's Office proved that Wells Fargo opened over two million deposit and credit accounts without customers' knowledge.

The bank tried to attribute this crime to rogue employees who, against the bank's wishes, engaged in this unlawful behavior of their own free volition. The bank was able to point to internal documents that explicitly stated that "customer consent for each specific solution or service is required every time," and that "splitting a customer deposit and opening multiple accounts for the purpose of increasing potential incentive compensation is considered a sales integrity violation." The company was also able to point to routine purges in which employees were fired for this practice, one of which netted over 5,000 employees in less than one year.

However, the practice of cross-selling without customer consent was so recurrent and widespread that the focus shifted quickly to the organizational culture and leadership as the source of the problem. Employees were told by their supervisors to ignore the ethics guidelines and that they would wind up being terminated anyway if they did not meet their sales goals. The goals were very unrealistic, and, according to CEO John Stumpf, the number eight was chosen "because it rhymed with great." Although one might hope that the company's human resources department would have helped workers deal with this system, instead it was revealed that people who called the HR ethics hotline were fired quickly after making those calls.

Stumpf was eventually called into a congressional hearing on the topic, during which Senator Elizabeth Warren of Massachusetts accused him of exhibiting "gutless leadership." The bank agreed to pay over $185 million in fines for the operations in California alone, with similar fines levied in other states. Although the "gutless leadership" charge may have hurt the CEO, he could take solace in the fact that he did not have to return any of his own pay and bonuses—amounting to over $20 million—the highest compensation for any CEO in the banking industry.

SOURCES: E. Glazer, "How Wells Fargo's High-Pressure Sales Culture Spiraled Out of Control," *Wall Street Journal*, September 16, 2016; M. Corkery and S. Cowley, "Wells Fargo Warned Workers against Sham Accounts, But 'They Needed a Paycheck'," *New York Times*, September 16, 2016; M. Egan, "I Called the Wells Fargo Ethics Line and Was Fired," CNNMoney.com, September 21, 2016; M. Corkery, "Elizabeth Warren Accuses Wells Fargo Chief of Gutless Leadership," *New York Times*, September 20, 2016.

Introduction

Every executive recognizes the need for satisfied, loyal customers. If the firm is publicly held, it is also safe to assume that every executive appreciates the need to have satisfied, loyal investors. Customers and investors provide the financial resources that allow the organization to survive. However, not every executive understands the need to generate satisfaction and loyalty among employees. Yet there is a strong link between employee satisfaction and engagement, on the one hand, and critical organizational outcomes, on the other hand. This may even be the deciding factor when it comes to who wins and who loses in the competitive market because retention rates among employees are related to retention rates among customers.[1] Research has established a direct link between employee retention rates and sales growth, and companies that are cited as one of the "100 Best Companies to Work For" routinely outperform their competition on many other financial indicators of performance. This is especially the case in the service industry, where the direct contact between employees and customers enhances the relationship between employee satisfaction and customer satisfaction.

For example, Costco Wholesale is well known throughout the retail industry for treating its employees better than most of its competitors. Costco pays many of its its hourly workers over $20/hour, compared to the industry average of $12/hour. Costco also provides company-sponsored health insurance to all employees, as well as tuition reimbursement programs that allow employees who start out at the lowest level of the shop floor to climb the corporate ladder. The result is that voluntary turnover within the organization is very low for the retail industry. The turnover rate among employees is less than 5% in a cutthroat industry where the average is closer to 30%. This feeds directly into Costco's business model and strategic plan. Due to Costco's emphasis on low prices, 80% of its profit comes from membership fees. Even though Costco's membership fees are 20% higher than Sam's Club's, over 90% of customers renew each year, providing a stable and predictable source of income. CEO Craig Jelinek notes, "We know it's a lot more profitable in the long term to minimize employee turnover and maximize employee productivity, commitment and loyalty. If you treat consumers with respect and treat employees with respect, good things are going to happen to you."[2]

In addition to holding on to key personnel, another hallmark of successful firms is their ability and willingness to dismiss employees who are engaging in counterproductive behavior. As we saw in the vignette that opened this chapter, Wells Fargo took a significant hit in terms of financial penalties because thousands of employees were opening accounts for customers, and charging them fees for those accounts, without ever asking their consent. Beyond the fines, however, is the reputational damage in the marketplace that these acts caused. If you were a victim of Wells Fargo, would why would you ever bank there again, given all the other alternatives available to you?

It is somewhat ironic that one of the keys to retaining productive employees is ensuring that these people are not being made miserable by supervisors or co-workers who are engaging in unproductive, disruptive, or dangerous behavior. Unfortunately, surveys indicate that many managers—indeed as many as 70%—struggle to give frank and honest feedback to poorly performing subordinates, and then wind up experiencing and tolerating poor performance for long periods.[3]

Thus, to compete effectively, organizations must take steps to ensure that good performers are motivated to stay with the organization, whereas chronically low performers are allowed, encouraged, or, if necessary, forced to leave. Retaining top performers is not always easy, however. Competing organizations are constantly looking to steal top performers, and "poaching talent" is becoming an increasingly common way for organizations to build themselves up, while tearing down their competitors at the same time.[4] It is also not nearly as easy to fire employees as many people think. The increased willingness of people to sue their employers, combined with an unprecedented level of violence in the workplace, has made discharging employees who lack talent legally complicated and personally dangerous. Recent data indicate that more than 25,000 occupational assault injuries occur each year at the hands of employees who claim their stress levels pushed them over the edge.[5] For example, in 2014, a former employee at United Parcel Services shot and killed two supervisors who he believed were responsible for his termination decision.[6]

This chapter focuses on employee separation and retention. The material presented in Chapters 8 and 9 can be used to help establish who are the current effective performers as well as who is likely to respond well to future developmental opportunities. This chapter completes Part Three by discussing what can be done to retain high-performing employees who warrant further development as well as how to manage the separation process for low-performing employees who have not responded well to developmental opportunities.

Since much of what needs to be done to retain employees involves compensation and benefits, this chapter also serves as a bridge to Part Four, which addresses these issues in more detail. The chapter is divided into two sections. The first examines **involuntary turnover**, that is, turnover initiated by the organization (often among people who would prefer to stay). The second deals with **voluntary turnover**, that is, turnover initiated by employees (who the company often would prefer to keep). Although both types of turnover reflect employee separation, they are clearly different phenomena that need to be examined separately.

Managing Involuntary Turnover

Despite a company's best efforts in the area of personnel selection, training, and design of compensation systems, some employees will occasionally fail to meet performance requirements or will violate company policies while on the job. For example, in 2012, Secret Service members responsible for protecting the president of the United States on an upcoming trip to Colombia were caught bringing prostitutes to their hotel rooms. Secret Service work rules forbid bringing *any* foreign national, let alone prostitutes, to a security zone prior to a presidential visit; hence, these employees had to be terminated.[7] However, problems at this agency persisted, and in 2015, the terminations climbed higher into the organizational ranks when four top Secret Service officers were also removed from their jobs following an incident in which a man carrying a knife jumped the White House fence and managed to run all the way into the mansion before being caught. The new top official noted that "change is necessary to gain a fresh perspective on how we conduct business," and this is the rationale behind most such terminations.[8]

Organizations need to invoke a discipline program that could ultimately lead to an individual's discharge. As we saw in the case of Wells Fargo, when problems persist repeatedly over time, people stop thinking that the problem is due to rogue employees and conclude instead that the organization has a much larger underlying problem. To avoid the latter conclusion, organizations have to deal swiftly and decisively with problem employees.

Discharging employees can be a difficult task that needs to be handled with the utmost care and attention to detail. First, legal aspects of this decision can have important repercussions for the organization. Historically, in the absence of a specified contract, either the employer or the employee could sever the employment relationship at any time. The severing of this relationship could be for "good cause," "no cause," or even "bad cause." Over time, this policy has been referred to as the **employment-at-will doctrine**. This employment-at-will

Involuntary turnover
Turnover initiated by the organization (often among people who would prefer to stay).

Voluntary turnover
Turnover initiated by employees (who the company often would prefer to keep).

LO 10-1
Distinguish between involuntary and voluntary turnover, and discuss how each of these forms of turnover can be leveraged for competitive advantage.

Employment-at-will doctrine
The doctrine that, in the absence of a specific contract, either an employer or an employee could sever the employment relationship at any time.

doctrine has eroded significantly over time, however. Today employees who are fired sometimes sue their employers for wrongful discharge.

A *wrongful discharge suit* typically attempts to establish that the discharge either (1) violated an implied contract or covenant (i.e., the employer acted unfairly) or (2) violated public policy (i.e., the employee was terminated because he or she refused to do something illegal, unethical, or unsafe). For example, in July 2014, a United Airlines flight from San Francisco to Hong Kong was close to departing when a team of flight attendants found threatening graffiti scrawled on the plane. The attendant crew refused to allow the plane to take off unless it was given a new, full security check, but company authorities who did not want to delay the flight balked and said the plane had already been cleared once and they were not going to do it twice. The flight attendants stood their ground and the flight was eventually cancelled, but the entire crew was then fired for insubordination. This was deemed a wrongful discharge, however, because the crew was obviously refusing to do something that was potentially unsafe.[9] Returning to the Wells Fargo example, although no one claimed this to be the case, if an employee was explicitly told to open new accounts without customer consent and was fired for failing to do so, then that person would have a strong case for wrongful discharge.

Wrongful discharge suits can also be filed as a civil rights infringement if the person discharged is a member of a protected group. For example, in 2015, 10 African American employees at McDonald's sued the company, alleging that they were fired because of their race. In fact, the manager at the franchise was quoted as saying that he "needed to get the ghetto out of the store." McDonald's Corporation had no intention of defending this manager but tried to argue that this was an issue between the employees and the "franchisee" (i.e., the local manager) not the "franchiser" (i.e., the corporate entity). The National Labor Relations Board did not see it that way and ruled against the corporation.[10]

The number of such "protected groups" is large and includes racial minorities, women, older workers (over 40 years of age), homosexuals, disabled workers (including the obese), whistle-blowers, people who have filed workers compensation claims, and—if one counts reverse discrimination claims—Caucasians. As noted by Lisa Cassilly, a defense attorney for the firm Alston and Bird, "It's difficult to find someone who doesn't have some capacity to claim protected status."[11] This means that in almost any instance when someone is fired for poor performance, the alternative possibility that this person was a victim of discrimination can be raised.

Not surprisingly, this has led to an increase in litigation. Although the research suggests that a plaintiff usually loses a wrongful termination case, the high cost of litigating the case makes some employers reluctant to fire employees, even when they are low performers. When this happens, the employer's short-term emphasis on staying out of court has come into conflict with the long-term need to develop a competitive workforce.

One reaction to this dilemma is to endure long stretches of poor performance in order to create the extensive "paper trail" that would support a negative action. Whereas HR professionals often point the finger of blame at supervisors who have not done a diligent job documenting past performance problems, supervisors often turn around and accuse HR of being "nervous Nellies" who never seem satisfied with the amount of evidence provided by supervisors. Moreover, keeping poor performers in their roles does not directly affect HR professionals every day, as it does supervisors, who have to watch helplessly as the morale of the rest of the workforce erodes. There is nothing more corrosive to team-based structures than wide variability in effort and performance between different members.

Secure in the Closet

How would you feel if you showed up for work one day and found that someone new was hired, and that he or she had the exact same job title as yours? What would you do if soon afterward, your budget was cut to zero, your team was reassigned to a different project, and everyone stopped replying to your e-mails? Would you quit? If you would quit, then you get the concept of *le placard*, which translated from the French refers to "the closet." This is where workers go when they are no longer wanted in a French company but cannot be fired due to laws that protect job security at all costs. The idea is to make the worker so miserable that he or she will quit. As one resident of *le placard* has noted, "You still have to come to work every day, but you have no idea why."

For a whole host of reasons, job security is highly coveted, but there are also downsides to being stuck in a job and being totally unable to escape

because of the inability to land any new job. This is precisely the predicament that faces many French employees. In France, workers either get a *contrat a duree indeterminee* (CDI) or a short-term contract that can be renewed only twice. Although historically, most French workers received CDIs, over the past decade, the awarding of CDIs has almost ceased. Now, most newly hired workers can obtain only short-term contracts. Many employers are just too afraid of hiring full-time workers who can never be let go, even when economic conditions might demand it.

This has led to a 10% unemployment rate in France, which is the highest in the European Union. Even worse, the unemployment rate for people under 25 years of age is 25%. This brings us back to the poor people stuck in the closet. Knowing they can never get a new CDI, and that they are unlikely to get even a short-term contract, they are

stuck in a job where they are bullied to leave, but realistically, they have nowhere to go. Indeed, surveys of French workers show that CDI holders experience more job stress and harassment than those holding short-term contracts and that, like unemployment rates, the levels of job stress in France are the highest in the European Union.

DISCUSSION QUESTIONS

1. Given the negative impact of worker protections on the French economy, why might government officials still stick by these policies?

2. In what ways do efforts to protect workers, other than those examined here, backfire in terms of promoting employee outcomes such as job satisfaction?

SOURCES: P. Druckerman, "The Miserable French Workplace," *New York Times,* May 11, 2016; A. Chassany, "New World of Work: Outsiders Battle in France's Dual Jobs Market," *Financial Times,* August 10, 2015; S. Cypel, "Why French Workers Are So Mad," *New York Times,* June 8, 2016.

For example, Kimberly-Clark was once considered a paternalistic organization that hired people for life. However, increasingly, performance problems associated with certain individuals were seriously harming bottom-line results. One 30-year veteran at the company noted, "We all talk about how having the best team is the most important difference maker in your results, but we didn't have the supporting processes to make that sustainable." In 2015, a new emphasis on performance management helped Kimberly-Clark retain 95% of its top performers while shedding 45% of workers whose performance was rated unacceptable or inconsistent.[12]

Another questionable reaction is to initiate punitive actions short of termination, in an effort to get the employee to quit on his or her own. This reaction is often a result of frustrated supervisors, who, unable to fire someone because of HR, resort to punishing the employee in other ways. This might include giving the person a low-level work assignment, a downsized office, or some other form of undesirable treatment.

©WIN-Initiative/Getty Images

Start-up companies are notorious for terminating employees in a ruthless manner in the early days of their development.

The problem with this approach, however, is that it might be construed as "retaliation," and the employer could be sued for this, even if the original discrimination suit is dismissed. As you can see from the "Competing through Globalization" box, however, there are no such protections in place in France, where attempting to get rid of unwanted people by trying to make them quit on their own has been raised to an art form.

Finally, a third unsustainable reaction is to pay off the employee with thousands of dollars in excess severance pay in return for waiving the right to sue for wrongful dismissal. That is, even if the employer feels the case is unwarranted, in order to avoid litigation, the employer may offer the terminated employee $20,000 or more to waive the right to sue. The problem with this strategy is that it sets the expectation that all poor performers are entitled to compensation on their way out the door, which eventually increases the amount of potential future litigation by rewarding frivolous charges. As defense attorney Mark Dichter notes, "I can design HR policies that can virtually eliminate your risk of facing employment claims, but you'll have a pretty lousy workforce. At the end of the day, you have to run your business."[13]

In some cases, the problem of having "a lousy workforce" eventually gets solved by outside forces. For example, when Warren Buffet teamed up 3G Capital, a private equity firm, to buy ketchup maker Heinz, 90% of the executive management team at the company was ousted in less than one month. 3G eventually cut 20% of the workforce, and one year later, adjusted earnings at Heinz rose by 40%. Although this may seem harsh, Warren Buffet stated bluntly that "efficiency is required over time in capitalism and I really tip my hat to what the 3G people have done.[14]

Zero tolerance for poor performers is a critical element of success, especially for new and small firms when there is a great deal on the line. For example, new start-ups are notorious for terminating workers ruthlessly in the early stages of their development, and firing people after just three days is not uncommon. Yammer, a social networking site for businesses, fired over 30% of its employees in its first few years of doing business. Adam Pisoni, the senior technical chief at Yammer, boasts, "We are just really good about eliminating people whose skills were lacking and brutally honest when it comes to evaluating newcomers."[15] Within this industry, where "failing fast" is considered a virtue, helping an employee move on from a situation where the fit is bad may result in that person moving on to a place where the fit is better. For example, Paul English was fired from one start-up, NetCentric Corporation, and this experience led him back to his roots as a coder. He eventually started his own business, which he later sold for millions of dollars. English's strategy with newcomers at his own start-up—not surprisingly—was equally tough. When it comes to poor performers, English notes, "You've got to cut that tumor out. If you can't fix it, you've got to get rid of it."[16]

The costs associated with letting poor performers stay on within the organization cannot be discounted. Organizations that introduce forced distribution rating systems—where low performers are systematically identified and, where necessary, eliminated from payrolls—often experience quick improvement gains in the range of 40%.[17] Given the critical financial and personal risks associated with employee dismissal, it is easy to see why the development of a standardized, systematic approach to discipline and discharge is critical to all organizations. These decisions should not be left solely to the discretion of individual managers or supervisors. In the next section, we explore aspects of an effective discipline and discharge policy.

PRINCIPLES OF JUSTICE

As we noted in Chapter 8, **outcome fairness** refers to the judgment that people make with respect to the *outcomes received* relative to the outcomes received by other people with whom they identify (referent others). Clearly, a situation in which one person is at risk of losing his or her job while others are not is conducive to perceptions of outcome unfairness on the part of the discharged employee. One area where this consistently manifests itself is with organizations that employ a large number of temporary workers to do jobs that are similar to jobs performed by full-time employees.

For example, at Microsoft, although full-time workers are protected when it comes to job security, the company's thousands of contract workers enjoy no such protections. In fact, even when it came to benefits such as paid sick days, full-time employees were allowed 25 days, compared to 0 for contract workers. In 2015, 40 temporarily employed programmers created their own union—the Temporary Workers of America—and pressured Microsoft to improve the work lives of contract workers who view themselves as "a permanent tier of second-class workers." Although the union was able to get the number of paid sick days up to 15 (from 0), it has had little success increasing job security, and so it is still the case that these workers could lose their jobs with very little notice.[18]

Perhaps, the only thing worse than losing one's job might be losing one's job and then being prevented from seeking a similar job elsewhere. Employers are increasingly asking would-be hires to sign noncompete clauses in their hiring paperwork. A noncompete clause means that if the employee is terminated or voluntarily leaves the job, this person cannot seek new employment at a firm in the same industry. Traditionally, these kinds of clauses were aimed at high-paid jobs such as top-level executives or senior technical personnel who, due to their positions, had access to critical proprietary knowledge about the company's strategy or technology. These contacts were jointly negotiated and were generally considered "fair."

Today, however, these contracts have trickled down to low-paid, entry-level employees where there is little negotiation. For example, Jimmy John's, the ubiquitous sandwich-making franchise, makes all employees sign a noncompete clause as a matter of standard business practice. Although the company has never tried to stop minimum-wage employees from taking all their knowledge to Blimpie's or another chain, the mere fact that they have the clause strikes many observers as unbalanced and unfair.[19] In general, if one is sued, courts rarely support noncompete contracts that are not aimed at protecting proprietary information, trade secrets, or copyrighted formulas. As one legal expert notes, "You are not allowed to get a noncompete just because you don't want the person to quit."[20]

Whereas outcome justice focuses on the ends, procedural and interactional justice focus on means. If methods and procedures used to arrive at and implement decisions that impact the employee negatively are seen as fair, the reaction is likely to be much more positive than if this is not the case. **Procedural justice** focuses specifically on the *methods used to determine the outcomes received*. Table 10.1 details six key principles that determine whether people perceive procedures as being fair. Even given all the negative ramifications of being dismissed from one's job, the person being dismissed may accept the decision with minimum anger if the procedures used to arrive at the decision are consistent, unbiased, accurate, correctable, representative, and ethical. When the

LO 10-2
List the major elements that contribute to perceptions of justice and how to apply these in organizational contexts involving discipline and dismissal.

Outcome fairness
The judgment that people make with respect to the outcomes received relative to the outcomes received by other people with whom they identify.

Procedural justice
A concept of justice focusing on the methods used to determine the outcomes received.

Table 10.1

Six Determinants of
Procedural Justice

1. **Consistency.** The procedures are applied consistently across time and other persons.
2. **Bias suppression.** The procedures are applied by a person who has no vested interest in the outcome and no prior prejudices regarding the individual.
3. **Information accuracy.** The procedure is based on information that is perceived to be true.
4. **Correctability.** The procedure has built-in safeguards that allow one to appeal mistakes or bad decisions.
5. **Representativeness.** The procedure is informed by the concerns of all groups or stakeholders (co-workers, customers, owners) affected by the decision, including the individual being dismissed.
6. **Ethicality.** The procedure is consistent with prevailing moral standards as they pertain to issues like invasion of privacy or deception.

procedures for the decisions are perceived in this fashion, the individual does not feel unfairly singled out, and this helps maintain his or her faith in the system as a whole, even if he or she is unhappy with the specific decision that was triggered by the system.[21]

Lack of bias and informational accuracy are the most critical features of the six, and the potential for subjective judgments to be biased means that employers often have to go beyond simple supervisor evaluations in most cases.[22] In an effort to ensure that they have an airtight case, many employers have turned to private investigators to collect objective evidence where necessary. For example, when a Florida hospital suspected that a worker who claimed she was out with the flu for three days was instead completely healthy, it hired a private investigator to look into the case. In fact, the woman had gone to Universal Studio theme parks those days, and the investigation uncovered photos of her from three different roller coaster rides (which routinely photograph riders and then try to sell the pictures to them), as well as a video showing her volunteering as part of an animal act—all time-stamped and dated. Needless to say, this led to a termination that the worker was not interested in challenging.[23] As you can see from the "Competing through Technology" box, companies today can go to great lengths to monitor employee behavior, and we are entering a new world when it comes to surveillance, all of which is driven by a need to protect the organization's interests.

Interactional justice
A concept of justice referring to the interpersonal nature of how the outcomes were implemented.

Whereas procedural justice deals with how a decision was made, **interactional justice** refers to the *interpersonal nature of how the outcomes were implemented.* For example, in many documented cases, after giving employees the news of their termination, employers immediately have security guards whisk them out of the building with their various personal items haphazardly thrown together in cardboard boxes. This strips people of their dignity, as well as their job, and employees who witness this happen to a co-worker show a drastically lower level of organizational commitment from that day forward.[24] Table 10.2 lists the four key determinants of interactional justice. When the decision is explained well and implemented in a fashion that is socially sensitive, considerate, and

Table 10.2

Four Determinants of
Interactional Justice

1. **Explanation.** Emphasize aspects of procedural fairness that justify the decision.
2. **Social sensitivity.** Treat the person with dignity and respect.
3. **Consideration.** Listen to the person's concerns.
4. **Empathy.** Identify with the person's feelings.

COMPETING THROUGH TECHNOLOGY

The Brave New World of Employee Monitoring

Life in the banking industry has never been the same since the 2008 banking financial crisis. Increased compliance scrutiny and laws like the Dodd-Frank Act have created an environment that does not tolerate mistakes. Since that time, U.S. banks have paid out over $200 billion in fines attributable to employees who engaged in money laundering, market manipulation, and even terrorist financing. In the wake of these events, more and more financial institutions are looking toward technologies that can help them monitor employees and catch problems before it is too late.

One company entering the market to serve this need is InfoWatch. This Moscow-based company has developed technology that allows employers to eavesdrop on employees' mobile phones when they are used on the company's premises. CEO Natalya Kaspersky notes that "these technologies have been used by secret services

and the military in certain countries and our breakthrough is employing them for corporate security." The technology works by amplifying wireless calls inside a building, and then handing off these signals to a broader network outside the building that scans for keywords like "brokerage account" or "initial public offering." If any one phone registers a specific number of hits on any keyword, the information is sent automatically to the company's security department.

Behavox, a London-based company working in the same product market space, takes this approach even further and goes beyond communications to detect a potential problem employee. Behavox employs machine learning algorithms to examine every aspect of a person's time at work, including e-mails, ID card swipes, stress levels in voice recordings, and even trips to the bathroom. The system checks these behaviors against profiles of former

traders who were convicted of crimes over the past 15 years, looking for pattern matches.

Clearly, these technologies create issues associated with worker rights and protections. As is the case with so many aspects of this brave new world, striking the right balance between security and privacy is not going to be easy.

DISCUSSION QUESTIONS

1. If you were working in the banking industry, would you be comfortable having all of this new technology-driven scrutiny designed to ensure compliance aimed at you?

2. What other industries other than banking might be interested in the technology described here and why?

SOURCES: A. Effinger, "The Rise of the Compliance Guru—and Banker Ire," *Bloomberg Markets*, June 25, 2015; I. Khrennikov, "Now the Boss Can Monitor Your Phone," *Businessweek*, June 20, 2016, pp. 31–32; G. Finch and E. Robinson, "Bathroom Three Times Today," *Businessweek*, January 23, 2017, pp. 32–33.

empathetic, this helps defuse some of the resentment that might come about from a decision to discharge an employee.

PROGRESSIVE DISCIPLINE AND ALTERNATIVE DISPUTE RESOLUTION

Except in the most extreme cases, employees should generally not be terminated for a first offense. Rather, termination should come about at the end of a systematic discipline program. Effective discipline programs have two central components: documentation (which includes specific publication of work rules and job descriptions that should be in place prior to administering discipline) and progressive punitive measures. Thus, as shown in Table 10.3, punitive measures should be taken in steps of increasing magnitude, and only after having been clearly documented.

This may start with an unofficial warning for the first offense, followed by a written reprimand for additional offenses. At some point, later offenses may lead to a

INTEGRITY IN ACTION

No Soup for You!

Dalene Bowden is the stereotype of the friendly cafeteria lady. Having worked at the Irving Middle School in Pocatello, Idaho, for three years, she was close to the children and loved her job. When one hungry 12-year-old girl was unable to come up with $1.70 to pay for her lunch during the week before Christmas, Bowden gave her a hot lunch anyway out of human kindness. That was a mistake. Even though Bowden personally offered to pay the $1.70 herself, a supervisor who witnessed the event said the food should have been thrown away, and terminated Bowden's employment contract later that day for "theft of service."

That, too, was a mistake. Within hours of the dismissal, this "Christmas-gone-wrong" story went viral across the country. Headlines in major news outlets decried the event, and phone calls, tweets, and letters poured in from all over the world. Traffic at the middle school's Facebook page got so intense it froze. Thousands of

people signed an online petition in support of Bowden, and for the first time, Pocatello, Idaho, was the center of the media world. The mayor of Pocatello quickly threw the school superintendent under the bus, stating clearly that "the city and the school system are separate entities with no jurisdictional oversight over each other," and that the city "had nothing to do with Ms. Bowden's firing." Unlike the mayor, who was obviously trying to duck the issue, the school superintendent stood by the decision and asserted that the supervisor had acted appropriately in firing Bowden.

This was yet another mistake. The superintendent stated that the district "does not and has never taken negative employment action against any food service worker due to a singular event of this nature." Instead, it turned out that Bowden was a repeat offender who had been issued a verbal warning after giving away a cookie in a separate incident.

Joyfully, like most Christmas stories, this one had a happy ending. In a deal brokered by the mayor, everyone came to their senses. Bowden's job was reinstated, and new procedures were established for dealing with students who didn't have money.

DISCUSSION QUESTIONS

1. Although it easy to identify with the school lunch lady in this story, the fact remains that school districts cannot afford to feed each and every child sent their way for free. What can these schools do to get some control over costs while not creating horror stories like the one reported here?

2. How does the presence of the Internet affect employers in regions like Idaho in a way that perhaps is unprecedented?

SOURCES: A. Dier, "School Lunch Lady Feeds Hungry Kid, Gets Fired," *USA Today*, December 24, 2015; A. Southhall, "Idaho School Worker Fired over Free Lunch Can Have Job Back," *New York Times*, December 24, 2015; E. Izadi, "Lunch Lady Who Was Fired after Giving a Hungry Student a Free Meal Is Offered Job Back," *Washington Post*, December 24, 2015.

Alternative dispute resolution (ADR)
A method of resolving disputes that does not rely on the legal system, often proceeding through the four stages of open-door policy, peer review, mediation, and arbitration.

temporary suspension. Before a company suspends an employee, it may even want to issue a "last chance notification," indicating that the next offense will result in termination. Such procedures may seem exasperatingly slow, and they may fail to meet one's emotional need for quick and satisfying retribution. In the end, however, when problem employees are discharged, the chance that they can prove they were discharged for poor cause has been minimized. As the "Integrity in Action" box illustrates, however, going through the steps too quickly can expose the organization to a wrongful discharge complaint or, at the very least, poor outcomes in the world of public relations.

At various points in the discipline process, the individual or the organization might want to bring in outside parties to help resolve discrepancies or conflicts. As a last resort, the individual might invoke the legal system to resolve these types of conflicts, but to avoid this, more and more companies are turning to **alternative dispute resolution (ADR)**.

OFFENSE FREQUENCY	ORGANIZATIONAL RESPONSE	DOCUMENTATION
First offense	Unofficial verbal warning	Witness present
Second offense	Official written warning	Document filed
Third offense	Second official warning, with threat of temporary suspension	Document filed
Fourth offense	Temporary suspension and "last chance notification"	Document filed
Fifth offense	Termination (with right to go to arbitration)	Document filed

Table 10.3
An Example of a Progressive Discipline Program

Alternative dispute resolution can take on many different forms, but in general, ADR proceeds through the four stages shown in Table 10.4. Each stage reflects a somewhat broader involvement of different people, and the hope is that the conflict will be resolved at earlier steps. However, the last step may include binding arbitration, in which an agreed-upon neutral party resolves the conflict unilaterally if necessary.

The use of ADR is growing rapidly among employers. In 2012, only 16% of employers required workers to sign away their legal rights to sue the employer in exchange for ADR procedures, but by 2014 this figure was up to 43%. Part of this trend is attributable to a 2011 Supreme Court ruling that upheld the legal status of pre-employment-required ADR sign-offs. Prior to this ruling, many lower courts were vacating or striking down ADR judgments, which meant that rather than keeping disputes out of court, ADR just added another layer to the process. The Supreme Court removed this layer and ruled that employees voluntarily signed the agreements. Thus, they were bound to them, even though they could not have been hired had they not signed. This makes ADR very attractive to employers. Litigation costs associated with class action suits dropped by roughly $150 million between 2011 and 2014.[25]

Whereas ADR is effective in dealing with problems related to performance and interpersonal differences in the workplace, many of the problems that lead an organization to

Table 10.4
Stages in Alternative Dispute Resolution

Stage 1: Open-door policy
The two people in conflict (e.g., supervisor and subordinate) attempt to arrive at a settlement together. If none can be reached, they proceed to

Stage 2: Peer review
A panel composed of representatives from the organization that are at the same level of those people in the dispute hears the case and attempts to help the parties arrive at a settlement. If none can be reached, they proceed to

Stage 3: Mediation
A neutral third party from outside the organization hears the case and, via a nonbinding process, tries to help the disputants arrive at a settlement. If none can be reached, the parties proceed to

Stage 4: Arbitration
A professional arbitrator from outside the organization hears the case and resolves it unilaterally by rendering a specific decision or award. Most arbitrators are experienced employment attorneys or retired judges.

want to terminate an individual's employment relate to drug or alcohol abuse. In these cases, the organization's discipline and dismissal program should also incorporate an employee assistance program. Due to the increased prevalence of these programs in organizations, we describe them in detail here.

EMPLOYEE ASSISTANCE AND WELLNESS PROGRAMS

Employee assistance programs (EAPs)
Employer programs that attempt to ameliorate problems encountered by workers who are drug dependent, alcoholic, or psychologically troubled.

An **employee assistance program (EAP)** is a referral service that supervisors or employees can use to seek professional treatment for various problems. EAPs vary widely, but most share some basic elements. First, the programs are usually identified in official documents published by the employer (such as employee handbooks). Supervisors (and union representatives, where relevant) are trained to use the referral service for employees whom they suspect of having health-related problems. Employees are also trained to use the system to make self-referrals when necessary.

Although originally targeted at the use of illegal drugs, many EAPs increasingly have had to deal with employees who have problems attributable to prescription drugs, especially painkillers. The percentage of workers who have tested positive for illegal drugs has decreased steadily from 14% in 1988 to just 3% in 2013. However, positive tests for painkillers such as Oxycontin and Vicodin rose 175% between 2005 and 2013 alone.[26] This problem is particularly acute for white working-class men. A recent study suggests that 11% of this group is unemployed and not seeking work, and that nearly half of them are taking pain medication on a daily basis. Worse yet, those who do work report similar levels of pain medication use as those who do not work.

Obviously, a worker taking a prescription drug may still pose a safety threat to other workers or customers when under the drug's influence. Thus, many organizations have zero-tolerance policies for many prescription drugs that are just as strict as their policies for illegal drugs.[27] Moreover, even if a painkiller is legal in one country where the firm operates, it may not be legal in another country. For example, in 2015, Julie Hamp, the most senior female executive at Toyota, was forced to resign when she was arrested for being in possession of oxycodone—another powerful painkiller—that just happened to be illegal in Japan.[28]

The key to the effectiveness of an EAP is striking the right balance between collecting information that can be used to promote employee health, on the one hand, and the employee's right to privacy, on the other. Many employees are afraid to come forward with information that they think may damage their careers, and so it is in the employer's best interest to support people who do self-refer by keeping their information confidential, and then supporting them through counseling and rehabilitation.[29] However, rehabilitation rates for workers with alcohol or drug addiction are far from 100%, so the employer still has an obligation to monitor progress to make sure that these workers are not a safety threat to others. For example, the EEOC ruled in 2014 that if a worker is part of an EAP and is being treated for alcoholism, a manager who knows this and sees this person drinking alcohol at an office party is obligated to report this to the EAP. Again, this may seem a violation of privacy, but this right has to be weighed against other employees' right to a safe workplace.[30]

Whereas EAPs deal with employees who have developed problems at work because of health-related issues, employee wellness programs take a proactive and preemptive focus on trying to prevent health-related problems in the first place. Employee wellness programs come in many different sizes and varieties, so it is difficult to make general statements about their cost and effectiveness. Some companies just hand out pamphlets on how to maintain better health and call that a wellness program.[31] Other programs have employees use wearable sensors like Fitbits, monitor their health status continuously, provide company-sponsored facilities and medical staff to support better health, and then reward employees financially for accomplishing health-related goals.[32]

Not all employees will respond to positive incentives, however. Hence, some companies take a more punitive approach to wellness. For example, Michelin Tire Company not only collects health-related data from employees but also punishes employees who fail to meet health goals. Michelin employees who have high blood pressure or whose waistlines exceed a certain limit (40 inches for men and 35 inches for women) are forced to pay an extra $1,000 for health care coverage. This might seem unfair for a company whose mascot is the "spare-tired" Michelin Man, but similar penalties have been levied by Miracle-Gro, CVS/caremark, Honeywell, and General Electric. All of these companies have found that people react more strongly to threats of losses than promises of gains. Reward programs at these companies that offered incentives to get healthier simply did not seem to work. By contrast, punishment-based programs definitely get people's attention. These companies have also found that roughly 80% of health care costs are generated by just 20% of workers, and a staggering 1% of workers generate 33% of the costs. Targeting these specific individuals has proven to be an efficient way to get costs under control, but there are legal limits to how far employers can go with these sorts of penalties.[33]

One of the major determinants of how far employee wellness programs can push their employees is how central health is to effectively performing the work. In general, if one defines obesity as having a body mass index (BMI) of 30 or higher, then there is an obesity epidemic in the United States.[34] The obesity rate for Americans doubled between 1993 and 2012, and for some organizations, this is a threat to their ability to accomplish their mission. For example, the Federal Aviation Authority (FAA) passed a new rule in 2013 that any commercial or private pilot with a BMI of 40 or more has to be examined by a sleep specialist to confirm that they do not have sleep apnea. Sleep apnea is highly related to obesity, and the FAA identified over a half-dozen incidents in 2012 where a pilot fell asleep in the cockpit. This included a well-publicized case in which a Bombardier regional jet traveling to Hawaii overflew the airport where it was supposed to land by 30 miles after a 20-minute lapse in radio communication with the tower.[35]

Another organization that is highly concerned about obesity is the U.S. Federal Bureau of Investigation (FBI). In 2015, the director of the agency issued a new requirement that its agents pass a fitness test once a year and that failure to do so will be part of their annual performance evaluation and raise process. At one time, almost all members of the FBI worked in highly active jobs in the field where they were chasing and arresting criminals. However, the threats of terrorism, cybersecurity, and large-scale fraud have pushed many employees into offices, where they sit at computers for long stretches of time. This has had a predictable effect on obesity rates in the agency. To counter the problem, the agency now requires agents to be able to do 24 push-ups without stopping and 35 sit-ups in a minute. It also requires that agents be able to sprint 300 yards in less than a minute and run a mile in under 12 minutes.[36]

OUTPLACEMENT COUNSELING

The permanent nature of an employee termination not only leaves the person angry, but it also leads to confusion as to how to react and in a quandary regarding what happens next. If the person feels there is nothing to lose and nowhere else to turn, the potential for violence or litigation is higher than most organizations are willing to tolerate. Therefore, many organizations provide **outplacement counseling**, which tries to help dismissed employees manage the transition from one job to another. There is a great deal of variability in the services offered via outplacement programs, typically including career counseling, job search support, résumé

Outplacement counseling
Counseling to help displaced employees manage the transition from one job to another.

critiques, job interviewing training, and provision of networking opportunities. Increasingly, these programs are moving online both to reduce costs and in recognition that most job search activity now takes place online. Face-to-face meetings between counselors and clients are largely becoming a thing of the past, being replaced by Web-based tools.[37]

Many observers have criticized the effectiveness of outplacement programs, charging that the companies that offer the services care more about avoiding litigation and bad public relations than about getting former employees new jobs. Many programs take a "one-size-fits-all" approach with standardized training programs not tailored to the specific needs of clients and industries, as well as boilerplate résumé services that send out almost identical documents for different workers. The evidence suggests that 40% of workers offered such services never show up, and another 30% quit using them after one or two sessions.[38] Many employers remain committed to these programs, however, and evidence supports the business case for this activity.

Specifically, when it comes to employee lawsuits, employers that offer outplacement activities have a 10% reduced likelihood of litigation by former employees, relative to companies that fail to provide such services. In addition, roughly 20% of employers that engaged in outplacement activities reported that turnover decreased among employees who remained after the initiation of such programs. Recruitment costs for new employees were also reported to be 24% lower for firms that provided this sort of employee assistance. Finally, 38% of employees that offered outplacement saw an increase in employee satisfaction one year after the downsizing event, compared to just 14% for employers that did not offer services.[39]

At the very least, outplacement counseling can help people realize that losing a job is not the end of the world and that other opportunities exist. For example, when John Morgridge was fired from his job as branch manager at Honeywell, it made him realize that his own assertiveness and need for independence were never going to cut it in a large, bureaucratic institution like Honeywell. Morgridge took his skills and went on to build computer network maker Cisco Systems, which is now worth more than $1 billion.[40] This is a success story for Morgridge, but the fact that a major corporation like Honeywell let his talent go certainly reflects a lost opportunity for the company. Retaining people who can make such contributions is a key to gaining and maintaining competitive advantage. The second half of this chapter is devoted to issues related to retention.

Managing Voluntary Turnover

Earlier in this chapter, our focus was on how to help employees who were not contributing to the organization's goal in a manner that protected the firm's ability to compete, and on how to support former employees' transition into alternative employment. In this section, we focus on the other side of the separation equation—preventing employees who are highly valued by the organization from leaving (and perhaps even joining the competition). At the organizational level, turnover results in lowered work-unit performance, which in turn harms the firm's financial performance.[41] This causal chain is especially strong when the organization is losing its top performers. Research suggests that some of the organization's top performers are up to 300% more productive than average employees, and retaining these workers is especially difficult.[42]

Moreover, an organization that has a reputation for being successful becomes an especially attractive target to external forces that may look to steal talent. For example, because of its positive reputation, Apple has always been a company that has had to work hard to hold on to its valued employees. Tesla Motors has hired over 150 former Apple executives, designers, and engineers in the past few years alone. Part of Tesla's competitive strategy is to exploit the fact that software has gone from providing 10% of the value of a car to 60%; thus, the skills and orientation of former Apple employees are a great fit for Tesla's business model.[43] Although this hiring pattern might be good news for Tesla, it is just the tip of the iceberg when it comes to losing valuable talent. As we saw in Chapter 5, stopping employee attrition was the driving factor behind an illegal agreement between high-tech companies not to recruit from each other.

Employees may be attached to their jobs for any of a number of different reasons, and employers need to recognize this in their efforts to retain workers. For example, pay and job security used to be the primary drivers of retention for older generations of workers, but this is not always the case today. Evidence seems to suggest that younger employees prefer benefits to cash, and they generally want to work in an environment that is fun and collaborative and that provides a great deal of immediate feedback and opportunities for development. This generation of employees has a lot to offer employers, including the fact that they are technically skilled, racially diverse, socially interconnected, and willing to collaborate.

However, the annual rate of voluntary turnover among Millennials tends to be higher than that associated with other generations, which has led some observers to conclude that they are impatient and entitled. For example, according to one recent survey, Millennial employees working in the investment banking industry left their positions after just 17 months on the job. In 1995, those who eventually quit only did so after being on the job for 30 months.[44] Still, as one experienced manager notes, "If they don't feel like they're making a contribution to a company quickly, they don't stay, but if you provide them with the right environment, they'll work forever—around the clock."[45] In this section of the chapter, we examine the job withdrawal process that characterizes voluntary employee turnover, and we illustrate the central role that job satisfaction plays in this process.

PROCESS OF JOB WITHDRAWAL

Job withdrawal is a set of behaviors that dissatisfied individuals enact to avoid the work situation. The right side of Figure 10.1 shows a model grouping the overall set of behaviors into three categories: behavior change, physical job withdrawal, and psychological job withdrawal.

We present the various forms of withdrawal in a progression, as if individuals try the next category only if the preceding is either unsuccessful or impossible to implement. This theory of **progression of withdrawal** has a long history and many adherents.[46] For example, someone who is dissatisfied with the job or organization might not be able to just jump to another job right away but will instead either disengage temporarily

Progression of withdrawal
The theory that dissatisfied individuals enact a set of behaviors to avoid the work situation.

Figure 10.1
An Overall Model of the Job Dissatisfaction–Job Withdrawal Process

(through absenteeism or tardiness) or psychologically (through lower job involvement and organizational commitment) until the right opportunity comes along.[47]

Indeed, a good predictor at this stage of the turnover process is whether the employee is assimilating into the organization's culture, as evidenced by the language the employee uses. A study that examined 10 million e-mail traces of new employees found that newcomers who eventually thrived and stayed with the company were quick to adopt the language patterns of veteran employees when it came to practices like cursing, expressions of positive emotions, and imagery. Employees who were more likely to leave for either voluntary or involuntary reasons tended to maintain the linguistic style they had prior to joining the company.[48]

Others theories have suggested that there is no tight progression in that any one of the categories can compensate for another, and people choose the category that is most likely to redress the specific source of dissatisfaction. Still other theories maintain that turnover is set up by a general level of persistent dissatisfaction that then is triggered abruptly by some single disruptive event at work that either pushes the employee away (such as a dispute with a supervisor or co-worker) or pulls the employee away (an alternative employment opportunity).[49] This model focuses on "the straw that breaks the camel's back" but shares with all the other theories an emphasis on job dissatisfaction as the necessary but insufficient cause of turnover. Regardless of what specific theory one endorses, there is a general consensus that withdrawal behaviors are clearly related to one another, and they are all at least partially caused by job dissatisfaction.[50]

Behavior Change

One might expect that an employee's first response to dissatisfaction would be to try to change the conditions that generate the dissatisfaction. This can lead to supervisor–subordinate confrontation, perhaps even conflict, as dissatisfied workers try to bring about changes in policy or upper-level personnel. Although at first this type of conflict can feel threatening to the manager, on closer inspection, this is really an opportunity for the manager to learn about and perhaps solve an important problem. When properly channeled by a secure and supportive leader, "voicing opportunities" for lower-level employees can often result in substantial organizational improvements and prevent turnover among highly engaged employees.[51]

Whistle-blowing
Making grievances public by going to the media or government.

Less constructively, employees can initiate change through **whistle-blowing** (making grievances public by going to the media).[52] Whistle-blowers are often dissatisfied individuals who cannot bring about internal change and, out of a sense of commitment or frustration, take their concerns to external constituencies. For example, regardless of what others thought of him, in his own mind Edward Snowden was doing the right thing. Concerned that the National Security Agency was increasingly spying on U.S. citizens by collecting information on over 10 million telephone calls, he went public with this information in June 2013. He felt he was doing his civic duty in trying to inspire a national debate on the "security–privacy" trade-off that seemed to be taking place in the United States at that time. He also knew the severity of his actions, noting, "I understand I will be made to suffer for my actions, but I will be satisfied if the federation of secret law, unequal pardon and irresistible executive powers that rule the world that I love are revealed for even an instant."[53]

In the eyes of many people within the U.S. government, Edward Snowden was a traitor. In the effort to thwart global terrorism, the program at the heart of this controversy merely captured data on who was talking to whom, and not the content of any of those conversations. The program was simply trying to lay out the social network of global terrorists, part of which resides within the country's borders. The data could be used to secure a legal warrant for tapping a phone, but no phone was ever tapped illegally. However, by making the program public, Snowden tipped off potential terrorists to heretofore unknown dangers and thus aided and abetted them in the goal of avoiding detection.[54] Whether or not Edward Snowden is a whistle-blower or traitor will be for history to decide, but for ethicists, this example illustrates how the employee has to balance two central trusts: the trust of his employer, who pays him to do specific work under a specific contract he willingly signed; and the trust of the larger society in which he resides to protect its citizens from rogue companies or overreaching branches of government.[55]

Although this type of whistle-blowing activity has always taken place, the advent of websites like Wikileaks has provided a more obvious and convenient outlet for this activity. Wikileaks is most famous for collecting and publishing information provided by government and military sources, but it has also threatened private companies such as Bank of America.[56] This type of whistle-blowing is also on the rise because of a provision of the 2010 Dodd-Frank regulatory overhaul that encourages this behavior by offering 30% of penalties collected by the government to individuals who help unearth illegal actions, in an effort to compensate them for the risks they take.[57]

As you can see from the "Competing th rough Technology" box, companies today go to great lengths to protect themselves from breaches like this by closely monitoring employee behavior though the increased use of technology. Clearly, we are entering a new world when it comes to surveillance, all of which is driven by a need to protect the organization's interests. Because many of these settlements involve multi-million-dollar settlements, this specific incentive can be powerful.

Physical Job Withdrawal

If the job conditions cannot be changed, a dissatisfied worker may be able to solve the problem by leaving the job. This could take the form of an internal transfer if the dissatisfaction is job specific (i.e., the result of an unfair supervisor or unpleasant working conditions). However, if the source of the dissatisfaction relates to organization-wide policies (lack of job security or below-market pay levels), then organizational turnover is likely. As we indicated earlier, there is a negative relationship between turnover rates and organizational performance, and it is generally costly to replace workers—especially high performers in skilled jobs.[58]

Another way of physically removing oneself from the dissatisfying work, short of quitting altogether, is to be absent. Although less financially disruptive relative to having an employee quit his or her job, absenteeism is still costly for many employers, especially small companies, where it is often harder to make up for a single person's absence. The direct cost of employee absenteeism has been estimated to represent roughly 2% of payroll; however, there are also indirect costs of absenteeism. For example, the employer may need to pay a replacement worker or pay other workers overtime to make up for the person who failed to show up. In addition, production might be reduced and customers might have to wait longer for services. When these indirect costs are added to the equation, absenteeism costs closer to 4% of payroll.[59]

Psychological Withdrawal

When dissatisfied employees are unable to change their situation or remove themselves physically from their jobs, they may psychologically disengage themselves from their jobs. Although they are physically on the job, their minds may be somewhere else.

This psychological disengagement can take several forms. First, if the primary dissatisfaction has to do with the job itself, the employee may display a very low level of job involvement. **Job involvement** is the degree to which people identify themselves with their jobs. People who are uninvolved with their jobs consider their work an unimportant aspect of

Job involvement
The degree to which people identify themselves with their jobs.

Organizational commitment
The degree to which an employee identifies with the organization and is willing to put forth effort on its behalf.

their lives. A second form of psychological disengagement, which can occur when the dissatisfaction is with the employer as a whole, is a low level of organizational commitment. **Organizational commitment** is the degree to which an employee identifies with the organization and is willing to put forth effort on its behalf. Individuals who feel they have been treated unjustly by their employer often respond by reducing their level of commitment and are often looking for the first good chance to quit their jobs. In contrast, employees who are involved in their job and committed to their employer are much more likely to respond to problems by speaking up, voicing their concerns, and trying to change what they may consider a bad situation. Most whistle-blowers tend to be people committed to their jobs and organizations, not people who forget about their jobs the moment they leave the workplace.[60]

JOB SATISFACTION AND JOB WITHDRAWAL

LO 10-3
Specify the relationship between job satisfaction and various forms of job withdrawal, and identify the major sources of job satisfaction in work contexts.

As we saw in Figure 10.1, the key driving force behind all the different forms of job withdrawal is **job satisfaction**, which we define as a pleasurable feeling that results from the perception that one's job fulfills or allows for the fulfillment of one's important job values.[61] This definition reflects three important aspects of job satisfaction. First, job satisfaction is a function of *values,* defined as "what a person consciously or unconsciously desires to obtain." Second, this definition emphasizes that different employees have different views of which values are important, and this is critical in determining the nature and degree of their job satisfaction. The third important aspect of job satisfaction is *perception*. An individual's perceptions may not be a completely accurate reflection of reality, and different people may view the same situation differently.

Job satisfaction
A pleasurable feeling that results from the perception that one's job fulfills or allows for the fulfillment of one's important job values.

Frame of reference
A standard point that serves as a comparison for other points and thus provides meaning.

In particular, people's perceptions are often strongly influenced by their frame of reference. A **frame of reference** is a standard point that serves as a comparison for other points and thus provides meaning. For example, a nurse might compare her salary to the salaries of other nurses and her overall satisfaction with pay depends on this comparison as much as the absolute value of pay itself. A female nurse makes, on average, a little over $55,000 a year in salary. This is a healthy salary, and she might be satisfied with this salary until she learns that, on average, a male nurse doing the same work made slightly over $65,000 a year.[62] Since some readers of this book are in an MBA program or may be thinking about applying for MBA programs, you might wonder if there is a gender gap in pay for men versus women who obtained an MBA. The answer to that question is provided in the "Evidence-Based HR" box.

These kinds of frame-of-reference effects are powerful, and many companies try to reduce the impact of social comparisons by making pay levels secret. However, as work becomes more collaborative and team oriented, there is increasing demand for transparency about pay and even for team member input into pay decisions. Balancing team members' need-to-know with privacy concerns, as well as the need to mitigate conflict between team members who disagree about their relative worth, is increasingly a struggle in many business contexts.[63]

SOURCES OF JOB DISSATISFACTION

Many aspects of people and organizations can cause dissatisfaction among employees. Managers and HR professionals need to be aware of these because they are the levers that can raise job satisfaction and reduce employee withdrawal.

Unsafe Working Conditions

Earlier in this chapter, we discussed the employer's role in helping employees stay healthy via employee assistance programs for specific problems like drug addiction and alcohol dependency. Obviously, if employers care this much about the risk employees are

Satisfaction with pay is one of the central dimensions of overall satisfaction that predicts both worker effort and involuntary turnover. However, almost as important as the absolute level of pay is the relative level of pay between an employee and some other person that the employee considers a reference person. Social comparisons play a large role in the process of determining whether one is fairly paid for one's skills and contributions; therefore, people react negatively to pay differences based on factors other than contributions to the work.

For example, some observers have suggested that a pay gap exists between men and women that is attributable to sex bias. A study conducted by *Businessweek* examined this question strictly for men and women who had obtained MBA degrees. According to a survey of over 12,000 individuals who received their MBAs within the past eight years, the evidence suggests that both male and female degree holders start out at close to the same rate of pay, roughly $98,000 for women and $105,000 for men. After eight years, however, that gap widens, with men earning $175,000, compared to $140,000 for women. Men and women tend to work in different industries (men tend to work more in finance), and the nature of the work they do differs (e.g., the survey suggests that, on average, men supervise five people, whereas women supervise three). As a result, it is hard to know if this reflects bias, but it remains a hard social comparison for some women to take.

SOURCE: N. Kitroef and J. Rodkin, "The Pay Gap That Haunts MBAs," *Businessweek*, October 26, 2015, pp. 38–42.

exposed to off the job, then there needs to be an even stronger emphasis on risk exposure that occurs on the job.

Of course, each employee has a right to safe working conditions. In Chapter 3, we reviewed the Occupational Safety and Health Act of 1970 (OSHA), which spells out those rights in detail. We also discussed in that chapter how to develop safety awareness programs that identify and communicate job hazards, as well as how to reinforce safe work practices that would allow one to pass an OSHA inspection. Although in that chapter we primarily emphasized legal compliance, we need to revisit the topic, because OSHA is not the only audience likely to evaluate the safety of jobs. The perception and reaction of the organization's own employees to working conditions has implications for satisfaction, retention, and competitive advantage that go well beyond merely meeting the legal requirements. That is, if applicants or job incumbents conclude that their health or lives are at risk because of the job, then attracting and retaining workers will be impossible.

Not all jobs pose safety risks, but the nature of the work in a whole host of jobs makes managing safety-related perceptions critical. This includes jobs such as fishing boat operators, timber cutters, airline pilots/flight attendants, structural metal workers, garbage collectors, and taxi drivers/chauffeurs, all of which have been identified as jobs where people are most likely to be involved in fatal accidents. In fact, in these job categories alone, close to 1,000 people die annually. Other jobs that rate low in terms of fatal accidents rate higher in nonfatal accidents, and this includes many jobs in eating establishments, hospitals, nursing homes, convenience stores, and the long-haul trucking industry. Still other jobs pose risks in terms of contracting occupational diseases due to exposure to chemicals. Finally, some jobs create health risks simply because of the long hours and high stress associated with them.[64] This was highlighted recently by several cases in the aviation industry, in which air traffic controllers who were working at night were found to be sleeping on the job because of extended hours. For example, in one case, a lone controller was working on less than 2 hours' sleep in the previous 24 hours, and this was a contributing factor in the crash of Comair Flight 191 in Lexington, Kentucky.[65] In general, working at night runs counter to the basic physiology of the human body and disrupts one's natural circadian rhythm, which in turn causes a whole host of physical problems. Thus, working at night has to be considered a safety issue in any job for which this is a task requirement.[66]

Protecting workers and ensuring their safety is particularly challenging when trying to manage overseas operations. For example, in 2013, companies in the fashion industry, such as H&M, Gap, and Zara, were blamed for the deaths of over a thousand garment workers who perished when the old and dilapidated building they worked in collapsed in Bangladesh. In the wake of that disaster, Western companies vowed to help Bangladesh upgrade the safety of its facilities. Yet three years later, 80% of the 1,600 buildings identified as unsafe had not been touched. Kohl Gill, a labor activist notes, "There's been so much attention put on this, it's kind of surprising so little progress has been made."[67]

Personal Dispositions

Because dissatisfaction is an emotion that ultimately resides within the person, it is not surprising that many researchers who have studied these outcomes have focused on individual differences. For example, in Chapter 6, we described the "Big Five" model of personality, and several of these traits have been linked to higher turnover intentions and actual turnover. In general, turnover is more likely to be an issue for employees who are low in emotional stability, low in conscientiousness, and low in agreeableness.[68]

Negative affectivity
A dispositional dimension that reflects pervasive individual differences in satisfaction with any and all aspects of life.

Negative affectivity is a term used to describe a dispositional dimension that reflects pervasive individual differences in satisfaction with any and all aspects of life. Individuals who are high in negative affectivity report higher levels of aversive mood states, including anger, contempt, disgust, guilt, fear, and nervousness across all contexts (work and nonwork). People who are high in negative affectivity tend to focus extensively on the negative aspects of themselves and others. They also tend to persist in their negative attitudes even in the face of organizational interventions, such as increased pay levels, that generally increase the levels of satisfaction of other people.

All of this implies that some individuals tend to bring low satisfaction with them to work. Thus, these people may be relatively dissatisfied regardless of what steps the organization or the manager takes. By contrast, research suggests that people who are positive tend to work harder, are more likely to be committed to the organization, are paid more, and are promoted more often.[69] Like anything, however, one can get too much of a good thing, and if a work group is made up of people who are all high in positive affect, they are often overly optimistic and fail to engage in a sufficient level of critical thinking regarding what might go wrong with plans or projects. Thus, when it comes to team composition, a built-in "devil's advocate" can be a highly valuable member.[70]

The evidence on the linkage between these kinds of traits and job satisfaction suggests the importance of personnel selection as a way of raising overall levels of employee satisfaction. If job satisfaction remains relatively stable across time and jobs because of characteristics like negative affectivity, this suggests that transient changes in job satisfaction will be difficult to sustain in these individuals, who will typically revert to their "dispositional" or adaptation level over time. Thus, some employers try to screen for this when selecting job candidates. For example, at Zappos, the online retailer of shoes and apparel, CEO Tony Hsieh notes, "We do our best to hire positive people and put them where their positive thinking is reinforced."[71]

Tasks and Roles

As a predictor of job dissatisfaction, nothing surpasses the nature of the task itself. Many aspects of a task have been linked to dissatisfaction. Several elaborate theories relating task characteristics to worker reactions have been formulated and extensively tested. We discussed several of these in Chapter 4. In this section, we focus on three primary aspects of tasks that affect job satisfaction: the complexity of the task, the amount of flexibility in where and when the work is done, and, finally, the value the employee puts on the task.

With a few exceptions, there is a strong positive relationship between task complexity and job satisfaction. That is, the boredom generated by simple, repetitive jobs that do not mentally challenge the worker leads to frustration and dissatisfaction.[72] Many observers have attributed much of the recent labor unrest in China to this specific aspect of the work. For example, the Han Hoi riot started as a minor fracas between two young workers but soon escalated into a pitched battle that involved over 2,000 employees and 5,000 paramilitary forces. The two workers, who everyone agrees started the riot, were from different regions and had just finished a stressful 12-hour shift at the factory that makes iPods and iPads. The work was boring and low paid, and frustrations boiled over when a small argument turned into a shoving and pushing match.

Witnesses claim that security workers at the plant overreacted to the incident and began brutally beating the two young people. At that point, hundreds of workers rushed the security personnel and returned the favor. Soon, more and more security personnel were called to the scene, followed by more and more restive workers. A major revolt was under way, and when it was over, 40 people were hospitalized and the facility had to be shut down for days after fires and looting gutted many stretches of the campus that housed close to 80,000 workers.[73] This riot was just one of many that put a spotlight on the tension between Chinese factories that base their business model on low cost-strategies that create low-scope jobs and unpleasant working conditions, and a new generation of Chinese workers who seem less willing to tolerate those conditions.

China is not the only Asian country where issues related to work hours have become a major issue. In 2016, Tadashi Ishii, the CEO of Japan's largest advertising company was forced to resign after labor law violations at the firm came to light after a highly publicized suicide by one of his employees. The worker, Matsuri Takahashi, had logged over 100 hours of forced overtime in the month prior to her death, and her suicide note, posted on her social media page, went viral in Japan. Working conditions in Japan have been challenging for so long, that there is a term—*karoshi*—used to describe "death by overwork."[74]

One of the major interventions aimed at reducing job dissatisfaction by increasing job complexity is *job enrichment*. As the term suggests, this intervention is directed at jobs that are "impoverished" or boring because of their repetitive nature or low scope. Many job enrichment programs are based on the job characteristics theory discussed earlier in Chapter 4. Another task-based intervention is **job rotation**. This is a process of systematically moving a single individual from one job to another over the course of time. Although employees may not feel capable of putting up with the dissatisfying aspects of a particular job indefinitely, they often feel they can do so temporarily.

Job rotation can do more than simply spread out the dissatisfying aspects of a particular job. It can increase work complexity for employees and provide valuable cross-training in jobs so that employees eventually understand many different jobs. This makes for a more flexible workforce and increases workers' appreciation of the other tasks that have to be accomplished for the organization to complete its mission. For example, Walmart recently introduced a new program, called Upskilling, that is a combination of job rotation and job enrichment aimed at developing low-level workers into middle-level managers.[75]

Job rotation
The process of systematically moving a single individual from one job to another over the course of time. The job assignments may be in various functional areas of the company, or movement may be between jobs in a single functional area or department.

Because of the degree to which nonwork roles often spill over and affect work roles, and vice versa, a second critical aspect of work that affects satisfaction and retention is the degree to which scheduling is flexible. To help employees manage their multiple roles, companies have turned to a number of family-friendly policies to both recruit new talent and hold on to the talent they already have. These policies may include provisions for child care, elder care, flexible work schedules, job sharing, telecommuting, and extended maternal and paternal leaves.

When it comes to maternity and paternity leave, however, most employers in the United States do far less than what one sees in the rest of the world. Although the Family and Medical Leave Act requires employers to give parents 12 weeks of leave after having a child, this is an unpaid leave, and many employees cannot afford to go that long without pay—especially after having a baby. In terms of international rankings, the United States ranks last, tied with Liberia, Papua New Guinea, and Suriname, as one of only four countries that does not offer paid leave for new parents.[76]

Many U.S. companies do not necessarily need prodding by the government to improve the work/life balance of their employees.[77] Especially in the field of investment banking, employers are responding to the demands of the Millennial labor force, which seems less than willing to work 80 hours a week in the hope of some big payoff down the line.[78] Indeed, the percentage of business school graduates going into investment banking dropped from 13% to 4% between 2007 and 2015, whereas the percentage going into Silicon Valley–type jobs increased from 7% to 17% over the same period.[79] The belief seems to be that Silicon Valley firms are more worker friendly—although as shown in the "Competing through Sustainability" box—that might not be true in all cases.

Prosocial motivation
The degree to which people are motivated to help other people.

By far, the most important aspect of work in terms of generating satisfaction is the degree to which it is meaningfully related to core values of the worker. The term **prosocial motivation** is often used explicitly to capture the degree to which people are motivated to help other people. When people believe that their work has an important impact on other people, they are much more willing to work longer hours.[80] This form of motivation can also be triggered by recognizing that one's work has a positive impact on those who benefit from one's service, such as customers or clients. In contrast, when one's social needs are thwarted, they often react negatively and in self-defeating ways that drive people away from them.[81]

In addition to prosocial motivation, work may have meaning for people because they see it as a calling that gives their lives purpose. In this case, the exact tasks that go into the work may not even matter. Rather, everything depends on the outcome that results from the work. For example, Michael Pratt, a researcher who has studied meaning at work extensively, often recounts a fable of bricklayers all working at the same site who are asked what they are doing. One sighs and states sadly, "I am putting one brick on top of another." A second says with indifference that that he is "making six pence an hour." The third responds excitedly, exclaiming, "I am building a cathedral!" All three workers are doing the same work, but one person finds meaning in it whereas the others do not, and this makes all the difference when it comes to job satisfaction.[82]

Supervisors and Co-workers

The two primary sets of people in an organization who affect job satisfaction are co-workers and supervisors. Workers may be satisfied with their supervisors for one of two reasons. First, job incumbents may see their supervisors as having "warmth," that is, genuinely caring about the workers and respecting them as people. Thus, being in a culture where people are generally civil and polite makes people feel their own dignity and worth above and beyond their contributions to the work itself. Incivility causes stress, and research shows that people who are treated rudely have a hard time focusing on the task and, instead, ruminate about

Tales of Amazon Warriors

"This is the greatest place I hate to work." These are the words John Rossman, a former Amazon executive, uses in attempting to describe how people working at Amazon feel about the culture. This mixed message seems to perfectly capture the positive and negative sentiments that exist side by side among employees at the company. Certainly, one cannot argue with Amazon's success. In 2015, Amazon surpassed Walmart as the most valuable retailer in the country, with a market valuation of over $250 billion. The company's CEO, Jeff Bezos, was ranked by *Forbes* magazine as the fifth-wealthiest person in the world. He notes, "My main job today? I work hard at helping to maintain the culture."

There are several aspects of Amazon's culture that makes it unique. Bezos believes that there are several forces that sap businesses over time after they become successful, including bureaucracy, excessive spending, and lack of discipline. Employees are empowered to be creative and given wide-ranging autonomy to pursue revolutionary ideas like "package delivering drones." At the same time, they are held to incredibly high standards of accountability, but these are the very factors that explain why some people absolutely thrive and love working for the company.

Above and beyond the three demons of bureaucracy, spending, and discipline, what really makes Amazon most unique is its stance toward conflict. Whereas most organizations try to minimize conflict, Bezos believes that "harmony" is completely overvalued at most work organizations. Amazon employees are encouraged to disagree, debate, and tear one another's ideas to pieces. Instead of polite praise and compromise, the goal is to see whose ideas can survive in a Darwinian battle for the one best solution or innovation. The internal phone directory even provides instructions on how to send anonymous feedback to one another's supervisors. Many employees cannot stand up to this kind of scrutiny, however. Bo Olson, who spent two years in the book marketing branch at Amazon noted, "You walk out of a conference room and you'll see a grown man covering his face— nearly every person I worked with I saw cry at their desk." Still, although many individuals cannot seem to endure the culture for long, Amazon seems to sustain the culture with a never-ending stream of new recruits ready to do battle.

DISCUSSION QUESTIONS

1. If you were working in HR for Amazon, what kinds of individuals would you look for and what kinds would you avoid when it comes to making hiring decisions?
2. Although debate can bring about more refined ideas, can you envision any situations in which public confrontation might escalate in a way that ultimately harms an organization?

SOURCES: J. Kantor and D. Streitfeld, "Inside Amazon: Wrestling Big Ideas in a Bruising Workplace," *New York Times,* August 15, 2015; J. Kantor and D. Streitfeld, "Jeff Bezos and Amazon Employees Join Debate over Its Culture," *New York Times,* August 17, 2015; D. Streitfeld and J. Kantor, "Depiction of Amazon Stirs Debate about Work Culture," *New York Times,* August 18, 2015.

their poor treatment and ways to perhaps get even.[83] Many employers recognize this fact, and the tolerance that organizations once had for tough and cruel bosses is no longer accepted today. For example, in 2014, Jill Abramson, the editor of the *New York Times* was removed from her position because of "her arbitrary decision-making, a failure to consult and bring colleagues with her, inadequate communication, and mistreatment of colleagues."[84]

Second, as just mentioned, people may be satisfied with their supervisors because the supervisors provide support that helps them achieve their own goals. That is, although it is nice to have a supervisor and co-workers who are warm, it is also critical that these people be "competent" in terms of helping workers and their teams get the mission accomplished. In fact, when given a choice between a leader who was warm but incompetent or a leader who was cold but competent, 70% opted for the cold and competent leader.[85]

Still, nothing beats the combination of high warmth and high competence in a leader, and employees led by a supervisor who is viewed as both supportive and competent will work longer hours and delay gratification in terms of rewards, trusting that something good will eventually come to them from all their hard work.

Supervisors are not the only potential source of social warmth and support, and in many cases, abuse by co-workers can have an even more profound negative influence on one's job satisfaction. For example, a 2012 survey indicated that 35% of respondents reported being bullied by co-workers on the job. *Workplace bullying* is defined as repeated health-harming mistreatment by one or more perpetrators at work that takes the form of verbal abuse and offensive conduct that is threatening, humiliating, or intimidating to the point where it prevents work from getting done. Unlike abusive bosses, who often let up once a specific task is accomplished, bullying by co-workers tends to be a constant, unrelenting process. Although it is common for high schools to adopt nonbullying rules, this has not been the case among employers, even though bullies rarely stop being bullies simply because they graduated from high school.[86]

Because a supportive environment reduces dissatisfaction, many organizations foster team building both on and off the job (such as via softball or bowling leagues). The idea is that group cohesiveness and support for individual group members will be increased through exposure and joint efforts. Although management certainly cannot ensure that each stressed employee develops friends, it can make it easier for employees to interact—a necessary condition for developing friendship and rapport.

Pay and Benefits

We should not discount the influence of the job incumbent, the job itself, and the surrounding people in terms of influencing job satisfaction, but for most people, work is their primary source of income and financial security. Pay is also seen as an indicator of status within the organization as well as in society at large. Thus, for many individuals, the standing of their pay relative to those within their organization, or the standing of their pay relative to others doing similar work for other employers, becomes even more important than the level of pay itself. Thus, for some people, pay is a reflection of self-worth, so pay satisfaction takes on critical significance when it comes to retention.[87] The role of pay and benefits is so large that we devote the entire next part of this book to these topics. Within this chapter, we focus primarily on satisfaction with two aspects of pay (pay levels and benefits) and how these are assessed within the organization. Methods for addressing these issues are discussed in Part Four of this book.

One of the main dimensions of pay satisfaction deals with pay levels relative to market wages. When it comes to retention, employees recruited away from one organization by another are often lured with promises of higher pay levels. In fact, exit surveys of high-performing employees who have left their organization indicate "better pay" as the reason in over 70% of the cases, compared to only 33% who indicate "better opportunity." Ironically, when the managers of those same workers are polled, 68% cite "better opportunity" versus the 45% who indicate it was "better pay," suggesting quite a difference of opinion.[88] As labor markets started tightening up in 2015, many employers recognized the need to raise pay levels in order to stop attrition. Even Walmart, which bases its entire business model on cutting costs, boosted the pay of many of its employees to $10/hour in 2015, well above the minimum wage, in order to retain its most experienced personnel and reduce the need to hire and train new workers. CEO Doug McMillon, who initiated the raises, noted, "We want associates who care about the company and are highly engaged about the business."[89]

Satisfaction with benefits is another important dimension of overall pay satisfaction. Because many individuals have a difficult time ascertaining the true dollar value of their benefits package, however, this dimension may not always be as salient to people as pay itself.

To derive competitive advantage from benefits' expenditures, it is critical not only to make them highly salient to employees but also to link them to the organization's strategic direction. For example, Starbucks wanted to attract workers who were smart and valued education but could not necessarily afford to hire people with college educations. As discussed in Chapters 1 and 2, Starbucks started a tuition reimbursement program that would pay for employees who pursued their bachelor's degree at Arizona State University. The cost of the program was roughly $45,000 per employee over the course of the four years, but the company saw this as a great way of attracting and retaining the kind of employee that fit its business model.[90]

MEASURING AND MONITORING JOB SATISFACTION

Most attempts to measure job satisfaction rely on workers' self-reports. There is a vast amount of data on the reliability and validity of many existing scales as well as a wealth of data from companies that have used these scales, allowing for comparisons across firms. Established scales are excellent places to begin if employers wish to assess the satisfaction levels of their employees. An employer would be foolish to "reinvent the wheel" by generating its own versions of measures of these broad constructs. Of course, in some cases, organizations want to measure their employees' satisfaction with aspects of their work that are specific to that organization (such as satisfaction with one particular health plan versus another). In these situations the organization may need to create its own scales, but this will be the exception rather than the rule.

One standardized, widely used measure of job satisfaction is the Job Descriptive Index (JDI). The JDI emphasizes various facets of satisfaction: pay, the work itself, supervision, co-workers, and promotions. Table 10.5 presents several items from the JDI scale. Other scales exist for those who want to get even more specific about different facets of satisfaction. For example, although the JDI assesses satisfaction with pay, it does not break up pay into different dimensions.[91] The Pay Satisfaction Questionnaire (PSQ) focuses on these more specific dimensions (pay levels, benefits, pay structure, and pay raises); thus, this measure gives a more detailed view of exactly what aspects of pay are most or least satisfying.[92]

Although satisfaction surveys used to be a once-a-year affair, increasingly technology is creating opportunities for firms and managers to get more rapid feedback. Pulse surveys are very short questionnaires that go out every day or once a week that focus on a small set of specific questions—perhaps even just one question—which the company

Table 10.5

Sample Items from a Standardized Job Satisfaction Scale (the JDI)

Instructions: Think of your present work. What is it like most of the time? In the blank beside each word given below, write

- Y   for "Yes" if it describes your work
- N   for "No" if it does NOT describe your work
- ?   if you cannot decide

Work Itself		Pay		Promotion Opportunities	
?	Routine	?	Less than I deserve	?	Dead-end job
?	Satisfying	?	Highly paid	?	Unfair policies
?	Good	?	Insecure	?	Based on ability
Supervision				**Co-workers**	
?	Impolite			?	Intelligent
?	Praises good work			?	Responsible
?	Doesn't supervise enough			?	Boring

SOURCE: W. K. Balzar, D. C. Smith, D. E. Kravitz, S. E. Lovell, K. B. Paul, B. A. Reilly, and C. E. Reilly, *User's Manual for the Job Descriptive Index (JDI)* (Bowling Green, OH: Bowling Green State University, 1990).

wants to keep track of over time.[93] The idea behind these quick-fire polls is to uncover issues faster and as they develop rather than wait until the end of the year when the issue may have festered. Also, these surveys tend to avoid long-term memory problems that reduce the value of once-a-year questionnaires. Usually these surveys are anonymous in order to reduce employees' fear of voicing opinions, and organizations try to show demonstrable actions taken soon after issues are raised.[94]

LO 10-4

Design a survey feedback intervention program, and use this to promote retention of key organizational personnel.

SURVEY FEEDBACK INTERVENTIONS

Regardless of what measures are used or how many facets of satisfaction are assessed, a systematic, ongoing program of *employee survey research* should be a prominent part of any HRM strategy for a number of reasons. First, it allows the company to monitor trends over time and thus prevent problems in the area of voluntary turnover before they happen. For example, Figure 10.2 shows the average profile for different facets of satisfaction for a hypothetical company in 2011, 2013, and 2015. As the figure makes clear, the level of satisfaction with promotion opportunities in this company has eroded over time, whereas the satisfaction with co-workers has improved. If there was a strong relationship between satisfaction with promotion opportunities and voluntary turnover among high performers, this would constitute a threat that the organization might need to address via some of the employee development techniques discussed in Chapter 8.

A second reason for engaging in an ongoing program of employee satisfaction surveys is that it provides a means of empirically assessing the impact of changes in policy (such as introduction of a new performance appraisal system) or personnel (e.g., introduction of a new CEO) on worker attitudes. Figure 10.3 shows the average profile for different

Figure 10.2

Average Profile for Different Facets of Satisfaction over Time

Figure 10.3

Average Profile for Different Facets of Satisfaction before and after a Major Event

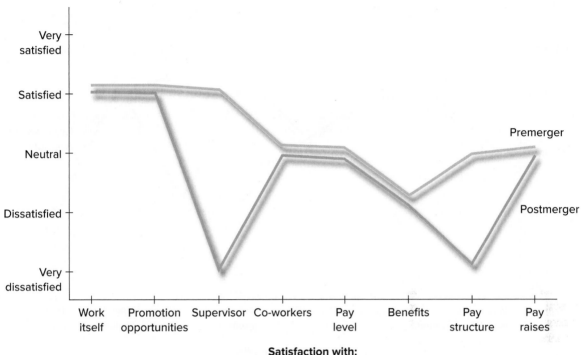

satisfaction facets for a hypothetical organization one year before and one year after a merger. An examination of the profile makes it clear that since the merger, satisfaction with supervision and pay structure has decreased dramatically, and this has not been offset by any increase in satisfaction along other dimensions. Again, this might point to the need for training programs for supervisors (like those discussed in Chapter 7) or changes in the pay system (like those discussed in Chapter 11).

Third, when these surveys incorporate standardized scales like the JDI, they often allow the company to compare itself with others in the same industry along these dimensions. For example, Figure 10.4 shows the average profile for different satisfaction facets for a hypothetical organization and compares this to the industry average. Again, if we detect major differences between one organization and the industry as a whole (on overall pay levels, for example), this might allow the company to react and change its policies before there is a mass exodus of people moving to the competition.

According to Figure 10.4, the satisfaction with pay levels is low relative to the industry, but this is offset by higher-than-industry-average satisfaction with benefits and the work itself. As we showed in Chapter 6, the organization might want to use this information to systematically screen people. That is, the fit between the person and the organization would be best if the company selected applicants who reported being most interested in the nature of the work itself and benefits, and rejected those applicants whose sole concern was with pay levels.

Within the organization, a systematic survey program also allows the company to check for differences between units and, hence, to benchmark "best practices" that might be generalized across units. For example, Figure 10.5 shows the average profile for five different regional divisions of a hypothetical company. The figure shows that satisfaction

Figure 10.4

Average Profile for Different Facets of Satisfaction versus the Industry Average

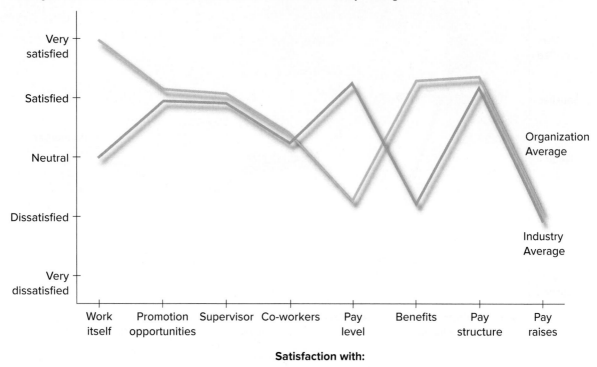

Satisfaction with:

Figure 10.5

Average Profile for Different Facets of Satisfaction for Different Regional Divisions

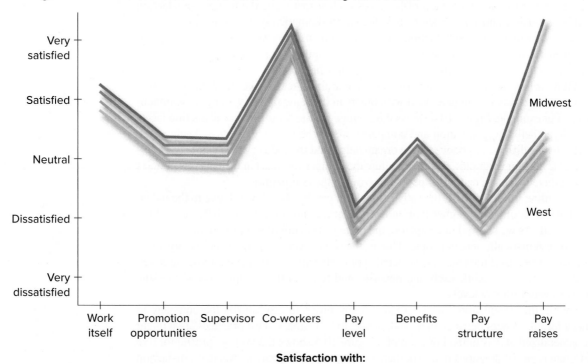

Satisfaction with:

with pay raises is much higher in one of the regions relative to the others. If the overall amount of money allocated to raises was equal through the entire company, this implies that the manner in which raises are allocated or communicated in the Midwest region might be something that the other regions should look in to.

Finally, although the focus in this section has been on surveys of current employees, any strategic retention policy also has to consider surveying people who are about to become ex-employees. Exit interviews with departing workers can be a valuable tool for uncovering systematic concerns that are driving retention problems. If conducted properly, an exit interview can reveal the reasons why people are leaving. For example, results from recent exit interviews among employees show that there are two distinct groups of people who are leaving their jobs—one set of workers who cannot get enough hours and a second set of workers who are working too many hours. This may seem ironic and counterintuitive, but in some ways it makes sense, given the way work is increasingly structured around two distinct classes of workers—hourly and salaried. That is, because they are being paid by the hour, it makes sense for employers to limit the amount of time hourly workers spend on the job. They want to avoid paying any overtime hours (valued at time and a half), but beyond that, they may even try to limit the number of hours to 30 in order to avoid having to pay for mandated health care.[95] Thus, many hourly workers cannot get enough work.[96] In contrast, salaried employees represent a fixed rather than variable cost; hence, there is pressure to make these individuals work very long hours, including nights and weekends. Many of these workers forgo taking vacation days that are provided to them or work while on vacation.[97] Obviously, it would benefit everyone in the workforce to help smooth out some of this over- and under-demand for labor, but this shows the pervasive power of rules regarding pay and pay structure—the topic of Part Four.

A LOOK BACK

Job Satisfaction, Retention, and Wells Fargo

In the story that opened this chapter, we saw how the culture at Wells Fargo seemed to force, or at least enable, employees to engage in unethical and illegal behavior. A key factor influencing the ability of any organization to accomplish its mission is who is leaving and who is staying when it comes to turnover. Organizations need to have policies in place that make it easy and advantageous for low performers or unethical employees to leave (involuntary turnover), but make it difficult and costly for valued contributors to (voluntary turnover). Managing the "flow" of employees thus becomes a critical source of competitive advantage and is often the difference between survival and bankruptcy.

QUESTIONS

1. In what ways does an organizational crisis like that faced by Wells Fargo make it easier for firms to manage involuntary turnover?

2. In what ways does an organizational crisis like that faced by Wells Fargo make it more difficult for firms to manage voluntary turnover?

3. What role can employee attitude surveys play in maintaining a loyal and engaged workforce? What are some of the challenges associated with getting accurate and reliable information from employee surveys, and how might a toxic culture prevent obtaining accurate data?

SUMMARY

This chapter examined issues related to employee separation and retention. Involuntary turnover reflects a separation initiated by the organization, often when the individual would prefer to stay a member of the organization. Voluntary turnover reflects a separation initiated by the individual, often when the organization would prefer that the person stay a member. Organizations can gain competitive advantage by strategically managing the separation process so that involuntary turnover is implemented in a fashion that does not invite retaliation, and voluntary turnover among high performers is kept to a minimum. Retaliatory reactions to organizational discipline and dismissal decisions can be minimized by implementing these decisions in a manner that promotes feelings of procedural and interactional justice. Voluntary turnover can be minimized by using surveys to measure and monitor employee levels of satisfaction with critical facets of the job and the organization, and then addressing any problems identified by such surveys.

KEY TERMS

Involuntary turnover, 427
Voluntary turnover, 427
Employment-at-will
  doctrine, 427
Outcome fairness, 431
Procedural justice, 431
Interactional justice, 432

Alternative dispute resolution
  (ADR), 434
Employee assistance programs
  (EAPs), 436
Outplacement counseling, 437
Progression of withdrawal, 439
Whistle-blowing, 440

Job involvement, 441
Organizational commitment, 442
Job satisfaction, 442
Frame of reference, 442
Negative affectivity, 444
Job rotation, 445
Prosocial motivation, 446

DISCUSSION QUESTIONS

1. The discipline and discharge procedures described in this chapter are systematic but rather slow. In your opinion, should some offenses lead to immediate dismissal? If so, how would you justify this to a court if you were sued for wrongful discharge?
2. Organizational turnover is generally considered a negative outcome, and many organizations spend a great deal of time and money trying to reduce it. What situations would indicate that an increase in turnover might be just what an organization needs? Given the difficulty of terminating employees, what organizational policies might be used to retain high-performing workers and, at the same time, increase attrition among low-performing workers?
3. Three popular interventions for enhancing worker satisfaction are job enrichment, job rotation, and role analysis.

What are the critical differences among these interventions, and under what conditions might one be preferable to the others?
4. If off-the-job stress and dissatisfaction begin to create on-the-job problems, what are the rights and responsibilities of the human resource manager in helping the employee to overcome these problems? Are intrusions into such areas an invasion of privacy, a benevolent and altruistic employer practice, or simply a prudent financial step taken to protect the firm's investment?
5. Discuss the advantages of using published, standardized measures in employee attitude surveys. Do employers ever need to develop their own measures for such surveys? Where would one turn to learn how to do this?

SELF-ASSESSMENT EXERCISE

Additional assignable self-assessments available in Connect.

The characteristics of your job influence your overall satisfaction with the job. One way to be satisfied at work is to find a job with the characteristics that you find desirable. The following assessment is a look at what kind of job is likely to satisfy you.

The following phrases describe different job characteristics. Read each phrase, then circle a number to indicate how much of the job characteristic you would like. Use the following scale: 1 = very little; 2 = little; 3 = a moderate amount; 4 = much; 5 = very much.

1. The opportunity to perform a number of different activities each day　　1 2 3 4 5

2. Contributing something significant to the company　　1 2 3 4 5

3. The freedom to determine how to do my job　　1 2 3 4 5

4. The ability to see projects or jobs through to completion, rather than performing only one piece of the job　　1 2 3 4 5

5. Seeing the results of my work, so I can get an idea of how well I am doing the job　　1 2 3 4 5

6. A feeling that the quality of my work is important to others in the company　　1 2 3 4 5

7. The need to use a variety of complex skills　　1 2 3 4 5

8. Responsibility to act and make decisions independently of managers or supervisors　　1 2 3 4 5

9. Time and resources to do an entire piece of work from beginning to end　　1 2 3 4 5

10. Getting feedback about my performance from the work itself　　1 2 3 4 5

Add the scores for the pairs of items that measure each job characteristic. A higher score for a characteristic means that characteristic is more important to you.

Skill Variety: The degree to which a job requires you to use a variety of skills.

Item 1: _____ + Item 7: _____ = _____

Task Identity: The degree to which a job requires completion of a whole and identifiable piece of work.

Item 4: _____ + Item 9: _____ = _____

Task Significance: The degree to which a job has an impact on the lives or work of others.

Item 2: _____ + Item 6: _____ = _____

Autonomy: The degree to which a job provides freedom, empowerment, and discretion in scheduling the work and determining processes and procedures for completing the work.

Item 3: _____ + Item 8: _____ = _____

Feedback: The degree to which carrying out job-related tasks and activities provides you with direct and clear information about your effectiveness.

Item 5 _____ + Item 10: _____ = _____

SOURCE: Adapted from R. Daft and R. Noe, *Organizational Behavior* (New York: Harcourt, 2001).

EXERCISING STRATEGY

Working at the Internal Revenue Service: A Taxing Experience

Dating all the way to biblical times, being a tax collector has never been a popular occupation. However, one could argue that, at least when it comes to working for the Internal Revenue Service (IRS) in the United States, the job has never been more difficult. The agency has faced five straight years of budget cuts, with the biggest of these—a $346 million cut—implemented in 2015. This cut came as a result of congressional outrage when the agency was charged with politically mishandling requests for tax-exempt status from Tea Party and other Republican- leaning groups. One could argue that these historic cuts came at a time when the complexity of the work—due to passage of the Affordable Care Act, with its complicated set of tax subsidies—was higher than ever.

These cuts have certainly trickled down to the workforce, where morale has never been lower. Salaries at the agency have risen only 2% the past five years and the slashing of secretarial support has left agents with a host of low-level clerical duties that cut into the more substantive parts of the job. Facilities have been allowed to decay, and the computers and software that agents work with are estimated to be three generations behind what one would find in the private sector. Office supplies are nowhere to be found, and workers have to provide their own

pens, paper, and other basic necessities for performing their job. On top of all of this, worker safety is always an issue due to the crazed nature of some taxpayers who feel that the government is stealing their money. Several years ago, one such taxpayer flew a kamikaze mission with a single-engine plane into an IRS facility in Texas, killing one worker and injuring many others.

Not surprisingly, all of this has led to a high rate of voluntary turnover within the worker ranks. Between 2010 and 2015, 15,000 IRS employees quit their jobs, and this is just the tip of a demographic iceberg. The IRS has less than 2,000 employees who are under the age of 30, and half of those are part time. Over 50% of the workforce will be eligible to retire by 2019, and there is little hope that many of these most experienced agents will stick around one day longer than they need to when it comes to retirement.

Clearly, no one enjoys paying their taxes, and, thus, few people are shedding any tears for these workers. However, the government does require money to operate, and many people fear that employee turnover and morale problems are cutting into the agency's ability to accomplish its mission. Audits are at historically low levels, and many criminal investigations of known tax evaders have been delayed or placed on hold. As one IRS veteran noted in despair, "I shouldn't have to say this but the IRS brings in about 93% of the revenue in this country. We're not soldiers but we are serving our country."

QUESTIONS

1. In what ways does an organizational crisis like that faced by the IRS make it easier for firms to manage involuntary turnover?

2. In what ways does an organizational crisis like that faced by the IRS make it more difficult for firms to manage voluntary turnover?

SOURCES: D. Leonard and R. Rubin, "The Taxman Bummeth," *Bloomberg Businessweek*, April 13, 2015, pp. 50-55; D. Kettl, "Why the War on the IRS Makes No Cents," *Excellence in Government*, June 30, 2015; G. Korte, "IRS Tax Collectors, Do Fewer Audits in 2015," *USA Today*, January 13, 2015.

MANAGING PEOPLE

Lights Out for Late-Night Workers

For many employees—and especially for working parents—the best time of the day to get some quality work done comes when they are out of the office and the kids are asleep. This is the new 9–11 p.m. work shift, and although the short-term benefits of leveraging these two hours for work may seem to be in the best interests of employers and employees, new evidence suggests that the long-term problems associated with this practice outweigh its benefits.

In particular, research shows that working right up until it's "lights out for bed" is highly disruptive of sleep, which in turn harms employee engagement and performance the next day. Lack of performance on that next day then prompts even more late-night work, which creates a vicious cycle of sleep deprivation. Indeed, the mere practice of looking at one's smartphone after 9 p.m. has demonstrable negative effects on sleeping patterns. The blue light emitted by a smartphone is the single most disruptive band of light when it comes to inhibiting the sleep-promoting hormone melatonin. Combining this biological reaction with biological reactions caused by workplace stress is a recipe for disaster. As researcher Chris Barnes notes, "Smartphones are almost perfectly designed to disrupt sleep."

The negative effects of sleep deprivation on employee performance and safety are well known, and for some occupations, like airline pilots, there are strict rules that enforce sleep discipline. An airline will routinely ground flights for lack of crew rest, and although the safety and performance implications for most jobs are not quite as critical as those associated with commercial aviation, if the job is worth doing right, it's worth doing right after a good night's sleep.

QUESTIONS

1. Is it fair for an employer to ask people who already put in an eight-hour day to work 9–11 p.m. without overtime pay? Why or why not?

2. If an employer does not require this, but people do it anyway in order to get ahead, should the employer discourage or prevent it in order to promote long-term sustainability? Explain.

SOURCES: B. Stone, "The New Night Shift," *Bloomberg Businessweek*, August 7, 2014, pp. 87-89; C. Barnes, K. Lanaj, and R. Johnson, "Research: Using a Smartphone After 9 PM Leaves Workers Disengaged, *The Harvard Business Review Blog*, January 15, 2014; R. Pyrillis, "Sleep Derailed," *Workforce*, July 2014, pp. 29–31.

HR IN SMALL BUSINESS

Learning to Show Appreciation at Datotel

Datotel is a St. Louis company whose name explains what it does. The name combines the word *data* with the word *hotel,* and it uses its computers to safely store backups of its client companies' data. It's a fast-growing business, and for founder David Brown, one important challenge has been making sure employees know the company appreciates them even as everyone is scrambling to keep up with the demands of expanding a small business.

With about three dozen people to think about, Brown first tried a methodical approach: He created an employee-of-the-month program in which the lucky recipient would receive a thank-you e-mail message, a $25 gift card, and recognition for all employees to see on the company's intranet. Brown saw this program as one he could readily find the time to implement, and he hoped the reward and recognition would inspire high levels of job involvement and organizational commitment.

One advantage of a small company is that you can quickly see people's reactions to your efforts. Unfortunately, what Brown saw on people's faces and heard in their conversations was that recipients of the employee-of-the-month rewards were not exactly excited. The program was just too formulaic and impersonal. If Datotel was to keep employees engaged, it needed a different way to show that their efforts mattered.

So Brown tried a different approach, even though it requires more effort. He committed his eight managers to noticing and reporting employee accomplishments. To implement this, he sets aside part of regular management meetings—part of each daily phone meeting and 15 minutes of each weekly in-person meeting—to discuss employee accomplishments. Whenever a manager notes that an employee has done something extraordinary, Brown asks for one of the managers besides the person's direct supervisor to thank the employee in person. Brown has also made a personal commitment to write thank-you notes. In fact, with e-mail the norm at his technology company, he makes some of the notes stand out by writing them by hand and mailing them to the employees at home.

One employee who thinks the extra effort matters is engineer Stephanie Lewis. One day Lewis returned home to find a note from Brown, observing that he had heard during management meetings that Lewis had done exceptionally well in working with a customer. Brown thanked her for the effort. Lewis's reaction: "It made me feel important to get something so personal and unique" from her company's busy leader.

Just as communicating "thank you" has helped with motivation, going the extra mile to communicate has helped Datotel's managers stay connected with one another and the company's mission. As the company grew and jobs became more specialized, Brown recognized that he would have to bring people together formally to share information about what was happening. He began to call meetings once a quarter, and so that the environment will be positive, he establishes a theme he thinks will get employees thinking and generate some fun. When the theme was "Rumble in the Jungle," the company leaders dressed as boxers, and when

the theme was "Top Gun," they dressed as aviators and met in an airplane hangar.

The effort to allow for fun is interwoven with the company's core values: passion, integrity, fun, teamwork, "superior business value," and "improving the community in which we work." These values aim to unite the employees in a commitment to customer service that gives the company an edge in its industry. The values are also meant to be an advantage for recruiting and retaining the best people. On Datotel's website, the "Inside Datotel" page lists 10 reasons for wanting to work at the company, and the top reason is the core values: "Our Core Values represent everything that we stand for, and we take pride in them."

QUESTIONS

1. Based on the information given, which sources of job satisfaction has Datotel addressed? What other sources might the company address, and how?
2. Suggest several measures Datotel could use to evaluate the success of its employee retention efforts. Be sure these are practical for a company of a few dozen employees.
3. In a company as small as Datotel, losing even one employee can present real difficulties. Suppose one of Datotel's managers begins to have performance problems and seems unwilling or unable to improve. Suggest how you, as an HR consultant, could help David Brown resolve this problem in a way that is fair to everyone involved and that keeps the company moving forward.

SOURCES: Datotel corporate website, www.datotel.com, accessed July 8, 2015; Nadine Heintz, "Building a Culture of Employee Appreciation," *Inc.*, September 2009; Jeremy Nulik, "Never Stop Being a Student of Business," *Small Business Monthly (St. Louis)*, July 2009, www.sbmon.com; Christopher Boyce, "Engineer Finds Solution to Business Problem," *St. Louis Post-Dispatch*, June 12, 2009.

NOTES

1. J. D. Shaw, M. K. Duffy, J. L. Johnson, and D. E. Lockhart, "Turnover, Social Capital Losses, and Performance," *Academy of Management Journal* 48 (2005), pp. 594–606.
2. B. Stone, "How Cheap Is Craig Jelinek?" *Bloomberg Businessweek*, June 6, 2013, pp. 55–60.
3. K. Sulkowicz, "Straight Talk at Review Time," *BusinessWeek*, September 10, 2007, p. 16.
4. F. Hanson, "'Poaching' Can Be Pricey, but Benefits May Outweigh Costs," *Workforce Management*, January 30, 2006, pp. 37–39.
5. B. Haskins, "OSHA Updates Guidance on Preventing Workplace Violence in Health Care, Social Services," *Safety and Health*, April 15, 2017.
6. A. Campos-Flores and L. Stevens, "Ex-UPS Employee in Alabama Kills Two; Self," *Wall Street Journal*, September 23, 2014.
7. E. Perez and D. Molinski, "More Firings at Secret Service," *Wall Street Journal*, April 19, 2012.
8. A. Grossman, "Four Top Secret Service Officials to Be Removed from Posts," *Wall Street Journal*, January 14, 2015.
9. D. Bennet, "United's Quest to Be Less Awful," *Businessweek*, January 14, 2016, pp. 50–56.
10. J. Gershman, "McDonald's Wrongful Termination Lawsuit to Test NLRB Ruling," *Wall Street Journal*, January 22, 2015.
11. M. Orey, "Fear of Firing," *Businessweek*, April 23, 2007, pp. 52–62.
12. L. Weber, "At Kimberly Clark, 'Dead Wood' Workers have No Place to Hide," *Wall Street Journal*, August 21, 2016.
13. Orey, "Fear of Firing."
14. S. Berfield, "Things Are About to Get Ugly at Kraft," *Businessweek*, August 24, 2015, pp. 20.
15. S. Gleason and R. Feintzeig, "Startups Are Quick to Fire," *Wall Street Journal*, December 12, 2013, www.wsj.com.
16. R. Feintzeig, "Once Fired, Now a Founder: How a Tech Leader Rebuilt His Career," *Wall Street Journal*, December 13, 2013.
17. S. E. Scullen, P. K. Bergey, and L. Aimon-Smith, "Forced Distribution Rating Systems and the Improvement of Workforce

Potential: A Baseline Simulation," *Personnel Psychology* 58 (2005), pp. 1–32.

18. J. Eidelson "Dear Microsoft…" *Businessweek*, May 4, 2014, pp. 37–38.

19. N. Irwin, "When the Guy Making Your Sandwich Has a No-Compete Clause," *New York Times*, October 14, 2014.

20. A. Viswanatha, "Noncompete Agreements Hobble Junior Employees," *Wall Street Journal*, February 2, 2016.

21. C. M. Holmvall and D. R. Bobocel, "What Fair Procedures Say about Me: Self-Construals and Reactions to Procedural Fairness," *Organizational Behavior and Human Decision Processes* 105 (2008), pp. 147–68.

22. E. J. Castilla and S. Bernard, "The Paradox of Meritocracy in Organizations," *Administrative Science Quarterly* 55 (2010), pp. 543–76.

23. E. Spitznagel, "The Sick Day Bounty Hunters," *Bloomberg Businessweek*, December 6, 2010, pp. 93–95.

24. H. Y. Li, J. B. Bingham, and E. E. Umphress, "Fairness from the Top: Perceived Procedural Justice and Collaborative Problem Solving in New Product Development," *Organization Science* 18 (2007), pp. 200–16.

25. L. Weber, "More Companies Block Employees from Filing Suits," *Wall Street Journal*, March 31, 2015.

26. L. Weber, "Drug Use on Decline at Work, Except Rx," *Wall Street Journal*, November 18, 2014.

27. A. Campo-Flores, "Drug Use at Work Roils Firms," *Wall Street Journal*, October 12, 2014.

28. Y. Kubota and E. Pfanner, "Arrested Toyota Managing Officer Resigns," *Wall Street Journal*, July 1, 2015.

29. R. Pyrillis, "A Monumental Problem," *Workforce*, September 2014, pp. 45–47.

30. K. Everson, "Dealing with Demons and Deadlines," *Workforce*, April 2015, pp. 29–31.

31. S. Sipek, "Wondering about Wellness," *Workforce*, July 2014.

32. L. Weber, "Wellness Programs Get a Health Check," *Wall Street Journal*, October 7, 2014.

33. L. Kwoh, "When Your Boss Makes You Pay for Being Fat," *Wall Street Journal*, April 5, 2013.

34. S. Sipek, "Observations on Obesity in the Workforce," *Workforce*, September 2014, p. 18.

35. A. Pasztor, "FAA to Evaluate Obese Pilots for Sleep Disorder," *Wall Street Journal*, November 20, 2013.

36. M.S. Schmidt, "Battling Crime and Calories at the FBI," *New York Times*, April 5, 2015.

37. L. Weber and R. Feintzeig, "Assistance to Laid off Workers Gets Downsized," *Wall Street Journal*, February 18, 2014.

38. P. Dvorack and J. S. Lublin, "Outplacement Firms Struggle to Do Job," *Wall Street Journal*, August 20, 2009.

39. B. Lowsky, "Inside Outplacement," *Workforce*, July 2014, pp. 37–38.

40. J. Jones, "How to Bounce Back if You're Bounced Out," *Businessweek*, January 27, 1998, pp. 22–23.

41. J. D. Shaw, N. Gupta, and J. E. Delery, "Alternative Conceptualizations of the Relationship between Voluntary Turnover and Organizational Performance," *Academy of Management Journal* 48 (2005), pp. 50–68.

42. J. Sullivan, "Not All Turnover Is Equal," *Workforce Management*, May 21, 2007, p. 42.

43. T. Higgins and D. Hull, "Apple Induction," *Bloomberg Businessweek*, February 15, 2015, pp. 36–37.

44. D. Huang and L. Gellman, "Millennial Employees Confound Big Banks," *Wall Street Journal*, April 8, 2016.

45. L. Kwoh, "More Firms Bow to Generation Y's Demands," *Wall Street Journal*, August 21, 2012.

46. J. G. Rosse, "Relations among Lateness, Absence and Turnover: Is There a Progression of Withdrawal?" *Human Relations* 41 (1988), pp. 517–31.

47. E. R. Burris, J. R. Detert, and D. S. Chiaburu, "Quitting before Leaving: The Mediating Effects of Psychological Attachment and Detachment on Voice," *Journal of Applied Psychology* 93 (2008), pp. 912–22.

48. J. Lublin, "The Telltale Sign a New Hire Isn't Fitting In," *Wall Street Journal*, June 10, 2017.

49. C. Sablynski, T. Mitchell, T. Lee, J. Burton, and B. Holtom, "Turnover: An Integration of Lee and Mitchell's Unfolding Model and Job Embeddedness Construct and Hulin's Withdrawal Construct," in *The Psychology of Work*, ed. J. Brett and F. Drasgow (Mahwah, NJ: Lawrence Erlbaum Associates, 2002).

50. D. A. Harrison, D. A. Newman, and P. L. Roth, "How Important Are Job Attitudes? Meta-analytic Comparisons of Integrative Behavioral Outcomes and Time Sequences," *Academy of Management Journal* 49 (2006), pp. 305–25.

51. E. J. McClean, E. R. Burris, and J. R. Detert, "When Does Voice Lead to Exit? It Depends on Leadership," *Academy of Management Review*, 56 (2013), pp. 525–48.

52. M. P. Miceli and J. P. Near, "Characteristics of Organizational Climate and Perceived Wrongdoing Associated with Whistle-Blowing Decisions," *Personnel Psychology* 38 (1985), pp. 525–44.

53. D. Barrett and D. Yadron, "Contractor Says He Is Source of NSA Leak," *Wall Street Journal*, June 10, 2013.

54. M. Mukasey, "Leaking Secrets to Terrorists," *Wall Street Journal*, June 9, 2013.

55. D. E. Wittkower, "Are You a Whistleblower or a Snitch?" *Wall Street Journal*, June 17, 2013.

56. H. Son and A. Lee, "B of A Was Unprepared for Wikileaks, Chief Moynihan Says," *Bloomberg Businessweek*, March 23, 2011, p. 23.

57. S. Patterson and J. Strasburg, "Source's Cover Blown by SEC," *Wall Street Journal*, April 25, 2012.

58. T. Y. Park, and J. D. Shaw, "Turnover Rates and Organizational Performance: A Meta-analysis," *Journal of Applied Psychology*, 98 (2013), pp. 268–309.

59. S. E. Needleman, "Sick Time Rules Re-Emerge," *Wall Street Journal*, March 1, 2012.

60. S. Shellenbarger, "When It Comes to Work, Can You Care Too Much?" *Wall Street Journal*, April 29, 2014.

61. E. A. Locke, "The Nature and Causes of Job Dissatisfaction," in *The Handbook of Industrial & Organizational Psychology*, ed. M. D. Dunnette (Chicago: Rand McNally, 1976), pp. 901–69.

62. B. Casselman, "Male Nurses Make More Money," *Wall Street Journal*, February 25, 2013.

63. R. E. Silverman, "Psst . . . This Is What Your Co-worker Is Paid," *Wall Street Journal*, January 29, 2013.

64. F. Jones, D. B. O'Connor, M. Conner, B. McMillan, and E. Ferguson, "Impact of Daily Mood, Work Hours and Isostrain Variables on Self-Reported Health Behaviors," *Journal of Applied Psychology* 92 (2007), pp. 1731–40.

65. J. Jacoby, "Air Traffic Control Staffing under Scrutiny," CNN.com, March 25, 2011.

66. M. Price, "The Risks of Night Work," *Monitor on Psychology*, January 2011, pp. 39–41.

67. V. Vara, "The Toll of Cheap Clothing," *Businessweek*, October 31, 2016.

68. R. D. Zimmerman, "Understanding the Impact of Personality Traits on Individuals' Turnover Decisions: A Meta-analysis," *Personnel Psychology* 61 (2008), pp. 309–48.

69. C. Kenny, "The Economic Power of Positive Thinking," *Bloomberg Businessweek*, January 10, 2015, pp. 8–9.

70. M. McCardle, "Why Negativity Is Really Awesome," *Bloomberg Businessweek*, February 20, 2014, pp. 6–7.

71. J. M. O'Brian, "Zappos Knows How to Kick It," *Fortune*, January 2, 2009, pp. 55–60.

72. L. W. Porter and R. M. Steers, "Organizational, Work and Personal Factors in Employee Absenteeism and Turnover," *Psychological Bulletin* 80 (1973), pp. 151–76.

73. P. Mozur and T. Orlink, "Hon Hoi Riot Undermines Squeeze on Chinese Manufacturers," *Wall Street Journal*, September 24, 2012.

74. P. Landers and A. Martin, "Japan Ad Agency CEO to Resign over 'Death by Overwork' Case," *Wall Street Journal*, December 28, 2016.

75. T. Jacoby, "Walmart Tests Upskilling," *Wall Street Journal*, September 4, 2015.

76. L. Sandler, "How to Love Paid Family Leave," *Wall Street Journal*, July 27, 2014.

77. R. E. Silverman, "High Finance and Family Friendly? KKR Is Trying," *Wall Street Journal*, September, 26, 2016.

78. C. Cain Miller, "More Than Their Mothers, Young Women Plan Career Pauses," *New York Times*, July 22, 2015.

79. J. Surane, "The MBA Dilemma," *Businessweek*, August 10, 2015, pp. 41–42.

80. A. M. Grant, "Relational Job Design and the Motivation to Make a Prosocial Difference," *Academy of Management Review* 32 (2007), pp. 393–417.

81. A. M. Grant, E. M. Campbell, G. Chen, K. Cottone, D. Lapedia, and K. Lee, "Impact and Art of Motivation Maintenance: The Effects of Contact with Beneficiaries on Persistance Behavior," *Organizational Behavior and Human Decision Processes* 103 (2007), pp. 53–67.

82. K. Weir, "More Than Job Satisfaction," *Monitor on Psychology*, December 2013, pp. 39–43.

83. C. Porath, "No Time to Be Nice at Work," *New York Times*, June 19, 2015.

84. M. Korn and R. Feintzeig, "Is the Hard Nosed Boss Obsolete?" *Wall Street Journal*, May 22, 2014.

85. S. Shellenbarger, "When the Boss Works Long Hours, Must We All? *Wall Street Journal*, February 9, 2014.

86. D. Wescot, "Field Guide to Office Bullies," *Bloomberg Businessweek*, November 26, 2012, pp. 94–95.

87. S. C. Currall, A. J. Towler, T. A. Judge, and L. Kohn, "Pay Satisfaction and Organizational Outcomes," *Personnel Psychology* 58 (2005), pp. 613–40.

88. E. White, "Opportunity Knocks, and It Pays a Lot Better," *Wall Street Journal*, November 13, 2006, p. B3.

89. P. Ziobro and E. Morath, "Wal-Mart Raising Wages as Market Gets Tighter," *Wall Street Journal*, February 19, 2015.

90. F. Wilkinson, "Starbucks, Magna Cum Grande," *Bloomberg Businessweek*, June 19, 2014, p. 14.

91. H. G. Heneman and D. S. Schwab, "Pay Satisfaction: Its Multidimensional Nature and Measurement," *International Journal of Applied Psychology* 20 (1985), pp. 129–41.

92. T. Judge and T. Welbourne, "A Confirmatory Investigation of the Dimensionality of the Pay Satisfaction Questionnaire," *Journal of Applied Psychology* 79 (1994), pp. 461–66.

93. R. E. Silverman, "Are You Happy at Work? Bosses Push Weekly Polls," *Wall Street Journal*, December 2, 2014.

94. C. Mims, "Bosses Use Anonymous Networks to Learn What Workers Really Think," *Wall Street Journal*, June 21, 2015.

95. E. Maltby and S. E. Needleman, "Some Small Businesses Opt for the Health-Care Penalty," *Wall Street Journal*, April 7, 2013.

96. S. J. Lambert, "When Flexibility Hurts," *New York Times*, September 19, 2012.

97. P. Coy, "The Leisure Gap," *Bloomberg Businessweek*, July 23, 2012, pp. 8–9.

CHAPTER

11

Pay Structure Decisions

LEARNING OBJECTIVES

After reading this chapter, you should be able to:

LO 11-1 List the main decision areas and concepts in employee compensation management. *page 462*

LO 11-2 Describe the major administrative tools used to manage employee compensation. *page 465*

LO 11-3 Explain the importance of competitive labor market and product market forces in compensation decisions. *page 474*

LO 11-4 Discuss the significance of process issues such as communication in compensation management. *page 478*

LO 11-5 Describe new developments in the design of pay structures. *page 479*

LO 11-6 Explain where the United States stands on pay issues from an international perspective. *page 481*

LO 11-7 Explain the reasons for the controversy over executive pay. *page 486*

LO 11-8 Describe the regulatory framework for employee compensation. *page 488*

Increasing Wages and Salaries: The Role of Labor Market Competition and Business Strategy

Many companies have recently raised wage and salary rates for their employees. Walmart, for example, raised its lowest pay rate recently in steps: first to roughly $9/hour and then to $10/hour. (Previously, employees in some states could earn as little as $7.25/hour, the mandated federal minimum wage.) It has also increased opportunities for pay growth internally through changes to its pay raise and promotion systems. Walmart reports that its average pay for full-time employees who are not managers increased to $13.69/hour an increase of 16% from two years ago. Other retailers like Target and Gap made similar moves. McDonald's also raised its wages. Starbucks announced not only a wage increase for full-time employees in company-operated stores, but also that it will double the size of company stock awards to employees having two or more years of service. Depending on the worker, the combined effect will be a 5–15% increase in compensation. Starbucks is also revising its benefits programs and dress code.

The reasons these companies have given for compensation increases and changes vary. One reason is that it is a necessary response to the tightening of labor markets (i.e., there is more competition for workers). The U.S. national unemployment rate peaked at 10% in late 2009 and stayed above 9% until late 2011. Now, however, the unemployment rate is 4.5%, making it more challenging for employers competing in the labor market to hire not only enough workers but also workers of the necessary quality. Employee wages and benefits are a major share of total costs at these companies, and they traditionally seek to keep a tight rein on such costs to keep their product prices low for consumers and to generate profits for shareholders.

Walmart is certainly known as a cost-conscious company. So, why did the company raise its pay rates? Part of the decision was driven by the tightening of the labor market. Another driver for Walmart, however, was business strategy. By some accounts, "relentless" labor cost-cutting over many years was driving shoppers away from Walmart as they experienced long waits in the check-out line, empty shelves, and no employees to help them. As one analyst put it, "If an item is not on the shelf, you cannot sell it." Walmart had been cutting labor costs not only by keeping wages and benefits low but also by keeping employee headcount low. That approach was perhaps no longer working. Less than 20% of stores were hitting their customer experience targets. Same-store sales had dropped for five straight quarters. Walmart decided that it needed more and better employees to turn things around. Some evidence indicated that Walmart had become not an employer of choice, but one of last choice. That had consequences for employee quality and commitment to helping the company succeed (e.g., in creating a good customer experience). The tightening of the labor market made things even worse.

So Walmart decided to pay its employees better. According to one estimate, it will cost $2.7 billion per year to do so. Will it prove to be a good investment? Walmart U.S. Chief Operating Officer Judith McKenna says that the pay increases and other changes to improve Walmart as a place to work are expected to help improve customer service and store performance. Consistent with that, Walmart reports that about 75% of its stores are now hitting customer experience targets and that sales are back on an upward trajectory. The impact on profits will take more time and analysis to evaluate.

CONTINUED

SOURCES: S. Nassauer, "Wal-Mart to Adjust Policies on Employee Pay Increases," *Wall Street Journal*, January 26, 2017; N. Irwin, "How Did Walmart Get Cleaner Stores and Higher Sales? It Paid Its People More," *New York Times*, October 15, 2016; C. Isidore and P. Harlow, "Starbucks Baristas Get Big Raises: 5% or More," CNNMoney.com, July 11, 2016; S. Strom, "McDonald's to Raise Pay at Outlets It Operates," *New York Times*, April 2, 2015, p. B1; P. Zorro, "Target Says It Will Raise Wages, Too," *Wall Street Journal*, March 19, 2015, p. B3; M. Krantz, "Walmart's Wages Get CEO's Attention," *USA Today*, March 2, 2015, p. 2B; A. Matthews and T. Francis, "Aetna Sets Wage Floor: $16 an Hour," *Wall Street Journal*, January 13, 2015, p. B1.

Introduction

LO 11-1

List the main decision areas and concepts in employee compensation management.

From the employer's point of view, pay is a powerful tool for furthering the organization's strategic goals. First, pay has a large impact on employee attitudes and behaviors. It influences the kind of employees who are attracted to (and remain with) the organization. In the chapter opener, Walmart decided to change its pay level in an effort to attract a workforce more in line with what it needed to execute its business strategy (including creating the desired customer experience). Pay can also be a powerful motivational tool for aligning current employees' interests with those of the broader organization (an issue we address more fully in Chapter 12). Second, employee compensation is typically a significant organizational cost and thus requires close scrutiny. As Table 11.1 shows, the cost of total compensation (cash and benefits) is 9% to 46% of revenues, depending on the industry.

For Walmart and other companies, competing by keeping prices low for customers has traditionally translated into paying low wages and raising them only when pressure from labor market competition (and perhaps from other sources, as we saw in the chapter opener) becomes sufficiently strong, such as now, with growth in the economy and lower unemployment rates. However, as we also saw in Walmart's case, keeping wages and employee headcount too low to control costs can get in the way of executing the business strategy (e.g., by undermining the customer experience), resulting in decreased revenues and profits. The economic cycle means economic activity and labor market competition will eventually slow. When things slow down for companies, they often cut labor costs by reducing headcount or reducing variable aspects of compensation (e.g., profit-sharing bonuses or 401k retirement plan contributions). But every company should plan ahead for how they will have an efficient workforce in place and ready to go when the demand for their products picks up again. For example, when Toyota paused automobile assembly at U.S. plants due to slow sales, it did not lay off workers. It did offer a voluntary buyout plan under which workers signing up received 10 weeks of salary plus 2 weeks' salary for every year worked. Employees who remained worked 36-hour rather than

Table 11.1

Total Compensation as a Percentage of Revenues, Median by Industry

INDUSTRY	TOTAL COMPENSATION/REVENUES
Health care	44%[a]
Manufacturing/engineering	21%[a]
Utilities	18%[a]
All industries	30%[b]

SOURCE: PwC, *Trends in HR Effectiveness: With Excerpts from 2016 PwC Saratoga Benchmarks*, November 2016, http://www.pwc.com/us/en/hr-management/publications/assets/pwc-trends-in-hr-effectiveness-final.pdf; PwC, *Trends in HR Effectiveness: With Excerpts from 2015 PwC Saratoga Benchmarks*, November 2015, http://www.pwc.com/us/en/hr-management/publications/assets/pwc-trends-in-the-workforce-2015.pdf.
[a]Based on November 2016 report.
[b]Based on November 2015 report.

40-hour weeks and reallocated their time to receive increased training and look for new ways to reduce costs.

From the employees' point of view, policies having to do with wages, salaries, and other earnings affect their overall income and thus their standard of living. Both the level of pay and its seeming fairness compared with others' pay are important. Pay is also often considered a sign of status and success. Employees attach great importance to pay decisions when they evaluate their relationship with the organization. Therefore, pay decisions must be carefully managed and communicated.

Total compensation, as noted, consists of cash compensation (salary, merit increases, bonuses, stock options, and other incentives) and benefits (e.g., health insurance, paid vacation, unemployment compensation). In this chapter, we focus on salary levels. In Chapter 12, we address merit increases and incentive issues. In Chapter 13, we examine benefits decisions. Total rewards, total returns, and inducements are concepts that include not only total compensation but also any other (nonmonetary) rewards (interesting or fulfilling work, good co-workers, development opportunities, recognition) that are associated with the employment relationship. These nonmonetary rewards are discussed in Chapters 4, 5, and 10. An organization must choose to what degree its total rewards strategy depends on monetary rewards (compensation) and what mix of compensation components will be used.

Salary level decisions can be broken into two areas: pay structure and individual pay. In this chapter, we focus on **pay structure**, which in turn entails a consideration of pay level and job structure. **Pay level** is defined here as the average pay (including wages, salaries, and bonuses) of jobs in an organization. (Benefits also matter, but these are discussed separately in Chapter 13.) **Job structure** refers to the relative pay of jobs in an organization. Consider the same two jobs in two different organizations. In Organization 1, jobs A and B are paid an annual average compensation of $40,000 and $60,000, respectively. In Organization 2, the pay rates are $45,000 and $55,000, respectively. Organizations 1 and 2 have the same pay level ($50,000), but the job structures (relative rates of pay) differ.

Both pay level and job structure are characteristics of organizations and reflect decisions about jobs rather than about individual employees. This chapter's focus is on why and how organizations attach pay policies to jobs. In Chapter 12, we look within jobs to discuss the different approaches that can determine the pay of individual employees as well as the advantages and disadvantages of these different approaches.

Why is the focus on jobs in developing a pay structure? As the number of employees in an organization increases, so too does the number of human resource management decisions. In determining compensation, for example, each employee must be assigned a rate of pay that is acceptable in terms of external, internal, and individual equity (defined later) and in terms of the employer's cost. Although each employee is unique and thus requires some degree of individualized treatment, standardizing the treatment of similar employees (those with similar jobs) can help greatly to make compensation administration and decision making more manageable and more equitable. Thus, pay policies are often attached to particular jobs rather than tailored entirely to individual employees.

Pay structure
The relative pay of different jobs (job structure) and how much they are paid (pay level).

Pay level
The average pay, including wages, salaries, and bonuses, of jobs in an organization.

Job structure
The relative pay of jobs in an organization.

Equity Theory and Fairness

In discussing the consequences of pay decisions, it is useful to keep in mind that employees often evaluate their pay relative to that of other employees. Equity theory suggests that people evaluate the fairness of their situations by comparing them with those of other people.[1] Equity is not equality. Equal pay for two workers with unequal contributions (*inputs* in equity theory) would likely be perceived as unfair if this information is known, especially by the worker making the stronger contributions to the organization. According to equity theory, a person (p) compares her own ratio of perceived outcomes O (pay, benefits, working conditions) to perceived inputs I (effort, ability, experience) to the ratio of a comparison other (o).

$$O_p/I_p <, >, \text{or} = O_o/I_o?$$

If p's ratio (O_p/I_p) is smaller than the comparison other's ratio (O_o/I_o), then *underreward inequity* results. If p's ratio is larger, then *overreward inequity* results, although evidence suggests that this type of inequity is less likely to occur and less likely to be sustained because p may rationalize the situation by reevaluating her outcomes less favorably or inputs (self-worth) more favorably.[2]

The consequences of p's comparisons depend on whether equity is perceived. If equity is perceived, no change is expected in p's attitudes or behavior. In contrast, perceived inequity may cause p to restore equity. Some ways of restoring equity are counterproductive, including (1) reducing one's own inputs (not working as hard), (2) increasing one's outcomes (such as by theft), or (3) leaving the situation that generates perceived inequity (leaving the organization or refusing to work or cooperate with employees who are perceived as overrewarded).

Equity theory's main implication for managing employee compensation is that, to an important extent, employees evaluate their pay by comparing it with what others get paid, and their work attitudes and behaviors are influenced by such comparisons. For example, consider one provision of the contract that former Texas Ranger and New York Yankee shortstop Alex Rodriguez signed years ago. It stated that during the the first several years of his contract, his base compensation had to be at least $2 million higher than any other shortstop in major league baseball. A second provision permitted Rodriguez to void seasons in the latter years of his contract unless his base compensation was at least $1 million higher than any position player in major league baseball. Otherwise, Rodriguez would be free to leave his current team. These provisions that pegged Rodriguez's pay to other players' pay provide a compelling example of the importance of being paid well in *relative* terms.

Another implication is that employee perceptions are what determine their evaluation. The fact that management believes its employees are paid well compared with those of other companies does not necessarily translate into employees' beliefs. Employees may have different information or make different comparisons than management. For example, Toyota recently set a goal to move from using wages in the U.S. auto industry as the standard of comparison to using the (lower) prevailing wages in the state where each plant is located. To do so, however, Toyota recognizes its challenge is to educate team members (employees) and managers to help them understand and accept the change.

Two types of employee social comparisons of pay are especially relevant in making pay level and job structure decisions. (See Table 11.2.) First, *external equity* pay comparisons focus on what employees in other organizations are paid for doing the same general job. Such comparisons are likely to influence the decisions of applicants to accept job offers as well as the attitudes and decisions of employees about whether to stay with an organization or take a job elsewhere. (See Chapters 5 and 10.) The organization's choice of pay level influences its employees' external pay comparisons and their consequences. A market pay survey is the primary administrative tool organizations use in choosing a pay level.

Table 11.2
Pay Structure Concepts and Consequences

PAY STRUCTURE DECISION AREA	ADMINISTRATIVE TOOL	FOCUS OF EMPLOYEE PAY COMPARISONS	CONSEQUENCES OF EQUITY PERCEPTIONS
Pay level	Market pay surveys	External equity	External employee movement (attraction and retention of quality employees); labor costs; employee attitudes
Job structure	Job evaluation	Internal equity	Internal employee movement (promotion, transfer, job rotation); cooperation among employees; employee attitudes

Second, *internal equity* pay comparisons focus on what employees within the same organization are paid. Employees make comparisons with lower-level jobs, jobs at the same level (but perhaps in different skill areas or product divisions), and jobs at higher levels. These comparisons may influence general attitudes of employees; their willingness to transfer to other jobs within the organization; their willingness to accept promotions; their inclination to cooperate across jobs, functional areas, or product groups; and their commitment to the organization. The organization's choice of job structure influences its employees' internal comparisons and their consequences. Job evaluation is the administrative tool organizations use to design job structures.

In addition, employees make internal equity pay comparisons with others performing the same job. Such comparisons are most relevant to Chapter 12, which focuses on using pay to recognize individual contributions and differences.

We now turn to ways to choose and develop pay levels and pay structures, the consequences of such choices, and the ways two administrative tools—market pay surveys and job evaluation—help in making pay decisions.

Developing Pay Levels

MARKET PRESSURES

Any organization faces two important competitive market challenges in deciding what to pay its employees: product market competition and labor market competition.[3]

LO 11-2
Describe the major administrative tools used to manage employee compensation.

Product Market Competition

First, organizations must compete effectively in the product market. In other words, they must be able to sell their goods and services at a quantity and price that will bring a sufficient return on their investment. Organizations compete on multiple dimensions (quality, service, and so on), and price is one of the most important dimensions. An important influence on price is the cost of production.

An organization that has higher labor costs than its product market competitors will have to charge higher average prices for products of similar quality. Thus, for example, if labor costs are 30% of revenues at Company A and Company B, but Company A has labor costs that are 20% higher than those of Company B, we would expect Company A to have product prices that are higher by $(0.30 \times 0.20) = 6\%$. At some point, the higher price charged by Company A will contribute to a loss of its business to competing companies with lower prices (like Company B). Until recently, in the automobile industry, hourly labor cost (including not only wages but also retiree and active worker benefits such as health care) in assembly plants averaged $75 for the U.S. Big Three (Chrysler, General Motors, Ford), compared to $52 for Toyota and Honda plants in the United States. On average, it takes roughly 30 hours to assemble a car. So, the labor cost to assemble for the Big Three was $30 \times \$75 = \$2,250$, compared to $30 \times \$52 = \$1,560$ for Toyota and Honda. That labor cost disadvantage had to have been offset by superior vehicle quality, performance, and so forth for the Big Three to make a profit. The bankruptcies at Chrysler and General Motors indicate that was not possible. More recently, the U.S. Big Three have reduced their labor costs to $47/hour at Chrysler, $55/hour at General Motors, and $57/hour at Ford, primarily by hiring new workers at lower wages and by reducing benefits costs.[4] That is a major change, now putting them much closer to the roughly $49/hour labor cost at Honda and Toyota. As a result, the Big Three have become much more competitive and their financial performance has improved dramatically. Toyota's labor costs have risen over time in the United States due to the inevitable aging of its workforce and the associated increased health care and retiree benefits. In a sense, it is going through the same life cycle as the Big Three did.

In contrast, a newly opened plant, such as the Volkswagen plant in Chattanooga, Tennessee, is estimated to have hourly labor costs of $27 initially.[5] That $27/hour cost to build Volkswagen Passats in Tennessee is much lower than Volkswagen's hourly labor cost to build cars in Germany, which had been estimated as high as nearly $100 (when the euro was at its strongest against the U.S. dollar). A more recent estimate of Volkswagen's hourly labor cost in Chattanooga is $38/hour.[6] Due to this labor cost saving (and due to lower costs for parts, transportation, and so forth), Volkswagen expected to be able to reduce the price of a Passat from $28,000 (when it was built in Germany) to $20,000 when it was first built in Tennessee. Lower labor costs can be found in Mexico (and even lower labor costs than in Mexico in other parts of the world). Thus, although Audi, Honda, Mazda, and Nissan have all announced plans to open new North American plants, all will be built in Mexico. Only recently, for the first time in many years, did an automobile company (Chinese-owned Volvo) announce plans to build a new plant in the United States, specifically in South Carolina, which has the lowest rate of unionization of any U.S. state.[7]

The cost of labor is directly reflected in the price of the car. Therefore, *product market competition* places an *upper bound* on labor costs and compensation. This upper bound is more constrictive when labor costs are a larger share of total costs and when demand for the product is affected by changes in price (i.e., when demand is *elastic*). Unless higher labor costs are offset by higher worker productivity or desirable product features that allow a higher product price, it will be difficult to sustain these relatively high costs in a competitive product market. As we have noted, Volkswagen will be able to lower the price of its Passat by producing it in the United States, where its labor costs will be lower than in Germany and lower than those of U.S. competitors. The search for lower labor costs is a continuous process. As companies move production to low-wage countries, wages there eventually rise, sometimes causing companies to move production to countries with still lower wages.

What components make up labor costs? A major component is the average cost per employee. This is made up of both direct payments (such as wages, salaries, and bonuses) and indirect payments (such as health insurance, Social Security, and unemployment compensation). A second component of labor costs is the staffing level (number of employees). Not surprisingly, financially troubled organizations often seek to cut costs by focusing on one or both components. Staff reductions, hiring freezes, wage and salary freezes, and sharing benefits costs with employees are several ways of making the organization's labor costs more competitive in the product market.

Labor Market Competition

A second important competitive market challenge is *labor market competition*, which reflects the number of workers available relative to the number of jobs available. Shortages and surpluses influence pay levels. For example, as we saw in the chapter-opening story, a shortage of workers will put upward pressure on wages and salaries, as organizations must pay to compete against other companies that hire similar employees. These labor market competitors typically include not only companies that have similar products but also those in different product markets that hire similar types of employees. If an organization is not competitive in the labor market, it will fail to attract and retain employees of sufficient numbers and quality. For example, even if a computer manufacturer offers newly graduated electrical engineers the same pay as other computer manufacturers, if automobile manufacturers and other labor market competitors offer salaries $5,000 higher, the computer company may not be able to hire enough qualified electrical engineers. Labor market competition places a *lower bound* on pay levels.

EMPLOYEES AS A RESOURCE

Because organizations have to compete in the labor market, they should consider their employees not just as a cost but also as a resource in which the organization has invested and from which it expects valuable returns.[8] Although controlling costs directly affects an organization's ability to compete in the product market, the organization's competitive position can be compromised if costs are kept low at the expense of employee productivity and quality. Having higher labor costs than your competitors is not necessarily a concern if you also have the best and most effective workforce, one that produces products more efficiently and with better quality (see our earlier example of WalMart).

Pay policies and programs are one of the most important human resource tools for encouraging desired employee behaviors and discouraging undesired behaviors. Therefore, they must be evaluated not just in terms of costs but also in terms of the returns they generate—how they attract, retain, and motivate a high-quality workforce. For example, if the average revenue per employee in Company A is 20% higher than in Company B, it may not be important that the average pay in Company A is 10% higher than in Company B.

DECIDING WHAT TO PAY

Although organizations face important external labor and product market pressures in setting their pay levels, a range of discretion remains.[9] How large the range is depends on the particular competitive environment the organization faces. Where the range is broad, an important strategic decision is whether to pay above, at, or below the market average. The advantage of paying above the market average is the ability to attract and retain the top talent available and help generate positive job attitudes (e.g., satisfaction), all of which can translate into a highly effective and productive workforce. The disadvantage, of course, is the added cost.[10]

Under what circumstances do the benefits of higher pay outweigh the higher costs? According to **efficiency wage theory**, one circumstance is when organizations have

Efficiency wage theory
A theory stating that wages influence worker productivity.

technologies or structures that depend on highly skilled employees. For example, organizations that emphasize decentralized decision making may need higher-caliber employees. Another circumstance in which higher pay may be warranted is when an organization has difficulties observing and monitoring its employees' performance. It may therefore wish to provide an above-market pay rate to ensure the incentive to put forth maximum effort. The theory is that employees who are paid more than they would be paid elsewhere will be reluctant to shirk because they wish to retain their good jobs.[11] Interestingly, some companies (e.g., Zappos, Amazon) have decided that it sometimes makes sense to pay employees to leave if they are staying only because of the money and despite being a better fit elsewhere.[12]

MARKET PAY SURVEYS

Benchmarking
Comparing an organization's practices against those of the competition.

To compete for talent, organizations use **benchmarking**, a procedure in which an organization compares its own practices against those of the competition. In compensation management, benchmarking against product market and labor market competitors is typically accomplished through the use of one or more pay surveys, which provide information on going rates of pay among competing organizations.

The use of pay surveys requires answers to several important questions:[13]

1. Which employers should be included in the survey? Ideally, they would be the key labor market and product market competitors.
2. Which jobs are included in the survey? Because only a sample of jobs is ordinarily used, care must be taken that the jobs are representative in terms of level, functional area, and product market. Also, the job content must be sufficiently similar.
3. If multiple surveys are used, how are all the rates of pay weighted and combined? Organizations often have to weight and combine pay rates because different surveys are often tailored toward particular employee groups (labor markets) or product markets. The organization must decide how much relative weight to give to its labor market and product market competitors in setting pay.

Several factors affect decisions on how to combine surveys.[14] Product market comparisons that focus on labor costs are likely to deserve greater weight when (1) labor costs represent a large share of total costs, (2) product demand is elastic (it changes in response to product price changes), (3) the supply of labor is inelastic, and (4) employee skills are specific to the product market (and will remain so). In contrast, labor market comparisons may be more important when (1) attracting and retaining qualified employees is difficult and (2) the costs (administrative, disruption, and so on) of recruiting replacements are high.

As this discussion suggests, knowing what other organizations are paying is only one part of the story. It is also necessary to know what those organizations are getting in return for their investment in employees. To find that out, some organizations examine ratios such as revenues/employees and revenues/labor costs. The first ratio includes the staffing component of employee cost but not the average cost per employee. The second ratio, however, includes both. Note that comparing these ratios across organizations requires caution. For example, different industries rely on different labor and capital resources. So comparing the ratio of revenues to labor costs of a petroleum company (capital intensive, high ratio) to a hospital (labor intensive, low ratio) would be like comparing apples and oranges. But within industries, such comparisons can be useful. Besides revenues, other return-on-investment data might include product quality, customer satisfaction, and potential workforce quality (such as average education and skill levels).

Rate Ranges

As the preceding discussion suggests, obtaining a single "going rate" of market pay is a complex task that involves a number of subjective decisions; it is both an art and a science. Once a market rate has been chosen, how is it incorporated into the pay structure? Typically—especially for white-collar jobs—it is used for setting the midpoint of pay ranges for either jobs or pay grades (discussed next). Market survey data are also often collected on minimum and maximum rates of pay as well. The use of **rate ranges** permits a company to recognize differences in employee performance, seniority, training, and so forth in setting individual pay (discussed in Chapter 12). For some blue-collar jobs, however, particularly those covered by collective bargaining contracts, there may be a single rate of pay for all employees within the job.

Rate ranges
Different employees in the same job may have different pay rates.

Key Jobs and Nonkey Jobs

In using pay surveys, it is necessary to make a distinction between two general types of jobs: key jobs and nonkey jobs. **Key jobs** (also known as benchmark jobs) have relatively stable content and—perhaps most important—are common to many organizations. Therefore, it is possible to obtain market pay survey data on them. Note, however, that to avoid too much of an administrative burden, organizations may not gather market pay data on all such jobs. In contrast to key jobs, **nonkey jobs** are, to an important extent, unique to organizations (and/or have content different from jobs in other organizations having the same title). Thus, by definition, they cannot be directly valued or compared through the use of market surveys. Therefore, they are treated differently in the pay-setting process.

Key jobs
Benchmark jobs, used in pay surveys, that have relatively stable content and are common to many organizations.

Nonkey jobs
Jobs that are unique to organizations and that cannot be directly valued or compared through the use of market surveys.

DEVELOPING A JOB STRUCTURE

Although external comparisons of the sort we have been discussing are important, employees also evaluate their pay using internal comparisons. So, for example, a vice president of marketing may expect to be paid roughly the same amount as a vice president of information systems because they are at the same organizational level, with similar levels of responsibility and similar impacts on the organization's performance. A job structure can be defined as the relative worth of various jobs in the organization, based on these types of internal comparisons. We now discuss how such decisions are made.

Job Evaluation

One typical way of measuring internal job worth is to use an administrative procedure called **job evaluation**. A job evaluation system is composed of compensable factors and a weighting scheme based on the importance of each **compensable factor** to the organization. Simply stated, compensable factors are the characteristics of jobs that an organization values and chooses to pay for. These characteristics may include job complexity, working conditions, required education, required experience, and responsibility. Most job evaluation systems use several compensable factors. Job analysis (discussed in Chapter 4) provides basic descriptive information on job attributes, and the job evaluation process that assigns values to these compensable factors.

Job evaluation
An administrative procedure used to measure internal job worth.

Compensable factors
The characteristics of jobs that an organization values and chooses to pay for.

Scores can be generated in a variety of ways, but they typically include input from a number of people. A job evaluation committee commonly generates ratings. Although there are numerous ways to evaluate jobs, the most widely used is the point-factor system, which yields job evaluation points for each compensable factor.[15]

Table 11.3
Example of a
Three-Factor Job
Evaluation System

JOB TITLE	COMPENSABLE FACTORS			
	EXPERIENCE	EDUCATION	COMPLEXITY	TOTAL
Computer tech	40	30	40	110
Programmer analyst	40	50	65	155
Systems analyst	65	60	85	210

The Point-Factor System

After generating scores for each compensable factor on each job, job evaluators often apply a weighting scheme to account for the differing importance of the compensable factors to the organization. Weights can be generated in two ways. First, *a priori* weights can be assigned, which means factors are weighted using expert judgments about the importance of each compensable factor. Second, weights can be derived empirically based on how important each factor seems in determining pay in the labor market. (Statistical methods such as multiple regression can be used for this purpose.) For the sake of simplicity, we assume in the following example that equal *a priori* weights are chosen, which means that the scores on the compensable factors can simply be summed.

Table 11.3 shows an example of a three-factor job evaluation system applied to three jobs. Note that the jobs differ in the levels of experience, education, and complexity required. Summing the scores on the three compensable factors provides an internally oriented assessment of relative job worth in the organization. In a sense, the programmer analyst job is worth 41% (155/110 − 1) more than the computer tech job, and the systems analyst job is worth 91% (210/110 − 1) more than the computer tech job. Whatever pay level is chosen (based on benchmarking and competitive strategy), we would expect the pay differentials to be somewhat similar to these percentages. The internal job evaluation and external survey-based measures of worth can, however, diverge.

DEVELOPING A PAY STRUCTURE

In the example provided in Table 11.4, there are 15 jobs, 10 of which are key jobs. For these key (also known as benchmark) jobs, both pay survey and job evaluation data are available. For the five nonkey jobs, by definition, no survey data are available, only job evaluation information. Note that, for simplicity's sake, we work with data from only two pay surveys and we use a weighted average that gives twice as much weight to survey 1. Also, our example works with a single structure. Many organizations have multiple structures that correspond to different job families (like clerical, technical, and professional) or product divisions.

How are the data in Table 11.4 combined to develop a pay structure? First, it is important to note that both internal and external comparisons must be considered in making compensation decisions. However, because the pay structures suggested by internal and external comparisons do not necessarily converge, employers must balance them carefully. Studies suggest that employers may differ significantly in the degree to which they place priority on internal- or external-comparison data in developing pay structures.[16]

At least three pay-setting approaches, which differ according to their relative emphasis on external or internal comparisons, can be identified: (1) using market survey data, (2) using the pay policy line, and (3) using pay grades.[17]

Table 11.4

Job Evaluation and Pay Survey Data

JOB	KEY JOB?	JOB TITLE	JOB EVALUATION	SURVEY 1 (S1)	SURVEY 2 (S2)	SURVEY COMPOSITE (2/3*S1 + 1/3*S2)
A	y	Computer tech	110	$3,219	$2,770	$3,070
B	y	Engineering tech I	115	3,530	3,053	3,370
C	y	Programmer analyst	155	4,666	4,142	4,491
D	n	Industrial engineer	165	—	—	—
E	n	Compensation analyst	170	—	—	—
F	y	Accountant	190	5,781	4,958	5,507
G	y	Systems analyst	210	6,840	6,166	6,614
H	n	Director of personal	225	—	—	—
I	y	Software engineer	245	7,971	7,210	7,717
J	y	Systems analyst—senior	255	8,328	6,832	7,829
K	y	Accounting manager	270	9,389	9,043	9,274
L	y	Electrical engineer—senior	275	8,794	7,670	8,419
M	n	Accounting director	315	—	—	—
N	y	Director of engineering	320	11,242	10,515	11,000
O	n	Chief scientist	330	—	—	—

SOURCES: Adapted from S. Rynes, B. Gerhart, G. T. Milkovich, and J. Boudreau, *Current Compensation Professional Institute* (Scottsdale, AZ: American Compensation Association, 1988); G. T. Milkovich and B. Gerhart, *Cases in Compensation,* Version 11.1e (2013). Reprinted with permission.

Market Survey Data

The approach with the greatest emphasis on external comparisons (market survey data) is achieved by basing pay directly on market surveys that cover as many key jobs as possible. For example, the rate of pay for job A in Table 11.5 would be $3,070; for job B, $3,370; and for job C, $4,491. For nonkey jobs (jobs D, E, H, M, and O), however, pay survey information is not available, and we must proceed differently. Basically, we develop a market **pay policy line** based on the key jobs (for which both job evaluation and market pay survey data are available). As Figure 11.1 shows, the data can be plotted with a line of best fit estimated. This line can be generated using a statistical procedure (regression analysis). Regressing the data from the "Survey Composite" column in Table 11.4 on the data from the "Job Evaluation" column in Table 11.4 (using only rows without missing data) yields the following equation:

Pay policy line
A mathematical expression that describes the relationship between a job's pay and its job evaluation points.

$$-\$1{,}058 + \$36.30 \times \text{job evaluation points}$$

In other words, the predicted monthly salary (based on fitting a line to the key job data) is obtained by plugging the number of job evaluation points into this equation. Thus, for example, job M, a nonkey job, would have a predicted monthly salary of $-\$1058 + \$36.30 \times 315 = \$10{,}377$.

As Figure 11.1 also indicates, it is not necessary to fit a straight line to the job evaluation and pay survey data. In some cases, a pay structure that provides increasing monetary rewards to higher-level jobs may be more consistent with the organization's goals or with the external market. For example, nonlinearity may be more appropriate if higher-level jobs are especially valuable to organizations and the talent to perform such jobs is rare. The curvilinear function in Figure 11.1 is obtained in the same way as above, except that the salary survey data are first transformed using the natural logarithm before being regressed on job evaluation points. The predicted monthly salaries are then

Table 11.5

Pay Midpoints under Different Approaches

JOB	KEY JOB?	JOB TITLE	JOB EVALUATION	(1) SURVEY + POLICY	(2) PAY POLICY	(3) GRADES
A	y	Computer tech	110	$3,070	$2,936	$3,480
B	y	Engineering tech I	115	3,370	3,117	3,480
C	y	Programmer analyst	155	4,491	4,570	5,296
D	n	Industrial engineer	165	4,933	4,933	5,296
E	n	Compensation analyst	170	5,114	5,114	5,296
F	y	Accountant	190	5,507	5,840	5,296
G	y	Systems analyst	210	6,614	6,566	7,110
H	n	Director of personnel	225	7,110	7,110	7,110
I	y	Software engineer	245	7,717	7,837	7,110
J	y	Systems analyst—senior	255	7,828	8,200	8,926
K	y	Accounting manager	270	9,274	8,744	8,926
L	y	Electrical engineer—senior	275	8,419	8,926	8,926
M	n	Accounting director	315	10,378	10,378	10,741
N	y	Director of engineering	320	11,000	10,560	10,741
O	n	Chief scientist	330	10,922	10,922	10,741

SOURCES: Adapted from S. Rynes, B. Gerhart, G. T. Milkovich, and J. Boudreau, *Current Compensation Professional Institute* (Scottsdale, AZ: American Compensation Association, 1988); G. T. Milkovich and B. Gerhart, *Cases in Compensation,* Version 11.1e (2013). Reprinted with permission.

Figure 11.1

Pay Policy Lines, Linear and Natural Logarithmic Functions

transformed back into dollars (e.g., using the EXP function in Excel). The resulting equation using this approach is as follows:

$$\text{Natural logarithm of pay} = \$7.446 + (0.006 \times \text{job evaluation points})$$

Pay Policy Line

A second pay-setting approach that combines information from external and internal comparisons is to use the pay policy line to derive pay rates for both key and nonkey jobs. This approach differs from the first approach in that actual market rates are no longer used for key jobs. This approach introduces a greater degree of internal consistency into the structure because the pay of all the jobs is linked directly to the number of job evaluation points.

Pay Grades

A third approach is to group jobs into a smaller number of pay classes, pay ranges, or **pay grades**. Table 11.6 (see also Table 11.5, last column), for example, demonstrates one possibility: a five-grade structure. Each job within a grade would have the same rate range (i.e., would be assigned the same midpoint, minimum, and maximum). The advantage of this approach is that the administrative burden of setting separate rates of pay for hundreds (even thousands) of different jobs is reduced. It also permits greater flexibility in moving employees from job to job without raising concerns about, for example, going from a job having 230 job evaluation points to a job with 215 job evaluation points. What might look like a demotion in a completely job-based system is often a nonissue in a grade-based system. Note that the **range spread** (the distance between the minimum and maximum) is larger at higher levels, in recognition of the fact that performance differences are likely to have more impact on the organization at higher job levels. (See Figure 11.2.)

The disadvantage of using grades is that some jobs will be underpaid and others overpaid. For example, job C and job F both fall within the same grade (Pay Grade 2). The midpoint for job C under a grade system is $5,296 per month, or about $700 to $800 or so more than under the two alternative pay-setting approaches in Table 11.5. Obviously, this will contribute to higher labor costs and potential difficulties in competing in the product market. Unless there is an expected return to this increased cost, the approach is questionable. Job F, by contrast, is paid roughly $200 to $500 less per month under the

Pay grades
Jobs of similar worth or content grouped together for pay administration purposes.

Range spread
The distance between the minimum and maximum amounts in a pay grade.

Table 11.6
Sample Pay Grade Structure

PAY GRADE	JOB EVALUATION POINTS RANGE		MONTHLY PAY RATE RANGE		
	MINIMUM	MAXIMUM	MINIMUM	MIDPOINT	MAXIMUM
1	100	150	$2,784	$3,480	$4,176
2	150	200	4,237	5,296	6,354
3	200	250	5,688	7,110	8,533
4	250	300	7,141	8,926	10,710
5	300	350	8,592	10,741	12,906

Figure 11.2

Sample Pay Grade
Structure

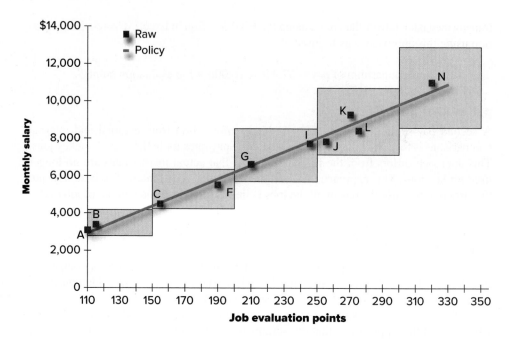

grades system than it would be otherwise. Therefore, the company may find it more difficult to compete in the labor market.

CONFLICTS BETWEEN MARKET PAY SURVEYS AND JOB EVALUATION

LO 11-3

Explain the importance of competitive labor market and product market forces in compensation decisions.

An examination of Table 11.5 suggests that the relative worth of jobs is quite similar overall, whether based on job evaluation or pay survey data. However, some inconsistencies typically arise, and these are usually indicated by jobs whose average survey pay is significantly below or above the pay policy line. The closest case in Table 11.5 is job L, for which the average pay falls significantly below the policy line. One possible explanation is that a relatively plentiful supply of people in the labor market are capable of performing this job, so the pay needed to attract and retain them is lower than would be expected given the job evaluation points. Another kind of inconsistency occurs when market surveys show that a job is paid higher than the policy line (like job K). Again, this may reflect relative supply and demand, in this case driving pay higher.

How are conflicts between external and internal equity resolved, and what are the consequences? The example of the vice presidents of marketing and information technology may help illustrate the type of choice faced. The marketing VP job may receive the same number of job evaluation points, but market survey data may indicate that it typically pays less than the information technology VP job, perhaps because of tighter supply for the latter. Does the organization pay based on the market survey (external comparison) or on the job evaluation points (internal comparison)?

Emphasizing the internal comparison would suggest paying the two VPs the same. In doing so, however, either the VP of marketing would be "overpaid" or the VP of information technology would be "underpaid." The former drives up labor costs (product market problems); the latter may make it difficult to attract and retain a quality VP of information technology (labor market problems).

Another consideration has to do with the strategy of the organization. In some organizations (like Pepsi and Nike), the marketing function is critical to success. Thus, even though the market for marketing VPs is lower than that for information technology VPs, an organization may choose to be a pay leader for the marketing position (pay at the 90th percentile, for example) but only meet the market for the information technology position (perhaps pay at the 50th percentile). In other words, designing a pay structure requires careful consideration of which positions are most central to dealing with critical environmental challenges and opportunities in reaching the organization's goals.[18]

What about emphasizing external comparisons? Two potential problems arise. First, the marketing VP may be dissatisfied because she expects a job of similar rank and responsibility to that of the information technology VP to be paid similarly. Second, it becomes difficult to rotate people through different VP positions (for training and development) because going to the marketing VP position might appear as a demotion to the VP of information technology.

There is no one right solution to such dilemmas. Each organization must decide which objectives are most essential and choose the appropriate strategy. However, there has been a shift over time such that most organizations now emphasize external comparisons/market pricing, perhaps because of increasing competitive pressures over time.[19]

MONITORING COMPENSATION COSTS

Pay structure influences compensation costs in a number of ways. Most obviously, the pay level at which the structure is pegged influences these costs. However, this is only part of the story. The pay structure represents the organization's intended policy, but actual practice may not coincide with it. Take, for example, the pay grade structure presented earlier. The midpoint for grade 1 is $3,480, and the midpoint for grade 2 is $5,296. Now, consider the data on a group example of individual employees in Table 11.7. One frequently used index of the correspondence between actual and intended pay is the **compa-ratio**, computed as follows:

Compa-ratio
An index of the correspondence between actual and intended pay.

$$\text{Grade compa-ratio} = \text{Actual average pay for grade/Pay midpoint for grade}$$

The compa-ratio directly assesses the degree to which actual pay is consistent with the pay policy. A compa-ratio less than 1.00 suggests that actual pay is lagging behind the policy, whereas a compa-ratio greater than 1.00 indicates that pay (and costs) exceeds that of the policy. Although there may be good reasons for compa-ratios to differ from 1.00, managers should also consider whether the pay structure is allowing costs to get out of control.

Table 11.7
Compa-Ratios for Two Grades

EMPLOYEE	JOB	PAY	MIDPOINT	EMPLOYEE COMPA-RATIOS
	Grade 1			
1	Engineering tech I	$3,690	$3,480	1.06
2	Computer tech	3,306	3,480	.95
3	Engineering tech I	4,037	3,480	1.16
4	Engineering tech I	3,862	3,480	1.11
			Mean	**1.07**
	Grade 2			
5	Programmer analyst	6,250	5,296	1.18
6	Accountant	6,037	5,296	1.14
7	Accountant	5,878	5,296	1.11
			Mean	**1.15**

GLOBALIZATION, GEOGRAPHIC REGION, AND PAY STRUCTURES

As Figure 11.3 shows, market pay structures can differ substantially across countries both in terms of their level and in terms of the relative worth of jobs. Compared with cities in China, India, and Mexico, the labor markets in U.S. and German cities provide

Geographic location is an important factor for HR departments to consider when establishing a pay structure. Living in New York City is more expensive than other places, and employers need to factor in living costs when deciding on salaries so that they can hire a strong workforce.

©GRANT V. Faint/Photodisc/Getty Images RF

Figure 11.3

Net Earnings (after Taxes and Social Security Contributions) in Selected Occupations, Six World Cities

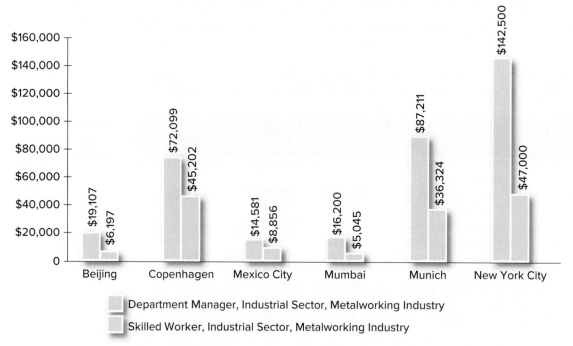

SOURCE: UBS, "Prices and Earnings 2015: A Comparison of Purchasing Power around the Globe," September 2015, Zurich, Switzerland.

much higher levels of pay overall and also different payoffs to skill, education, and advancement. These differences create a dilemma for global companies. For example, should a German manager posted to Beijing be paid according to the standard in Germany or China? If the Germany standard is used, a sense of inequity is likely to exist among local Chinese peers in Beijing. If the China market standard is used, it may be all but impossible to find a German engineer willing to accept an assignment in Beijing. Typically, expatriate pay and benefits (like housing allowance and tax equalization) continue to be linked more closely to the home country. However, this link appears to be slowly weakening and now depends more on the nature and length of the assignment.[20]

Within the United States, Runzheimer International reports that most companies have either a formal or an informal policy that provides for pay differentials based on geographic location.[21] These differentials are intended to prevent inequitable treatment of employees who work in more expensive parts of the country. For example, according to Salary.com, the cost of living index for New York City is roughly 83% higher than in Madison, Wisconsin. Therefore, an employee receiving annual pay of $50,000 in Madison would require annual pay of $91,500 in New York City to retain the same purchasing power. The most common company approach is to move an employee higher in the pay structure to compensate for higher living costs. However, the drawback of this approach is that it may be difficult to adjust the salary downward if costs in that location fall or if the employee moves to a lower-cost area. Thus, some companies choose to pay an ongoing supplement that changes or disappears in the event of such changes.

EVIDENCE-BASED HR

Walmart is legendary for its attention to (some would say, obsession with) cost control so that it can pass lower prices on to customers, making it difficult for other retailers to compete. However, as we saw in the chapter opener, Walmart seems to have metrics-based evidence that it perhaps has pushed labor cost control too far, reducing workforce quality and motivation, to the detriment of the customer experience, sales, and profits. That evidence was based on the company's own internal data. External benchmarking data suggest a similar story. Walmart is currently in last place out of 15 companies in its category (department and discount stores) on the American Customer Satisfaction Index, and one has to go back to 2006 to find a year in which it was not in last place. As we also saw in the chapter opener, Walmart has recently taken steps to increase employee pay in hopes of better executing its business strategy and turning things around.

In contrast to Walmart, Costco is first out of 26 companies in its category (specialty retail stores) on the American Customer Satisfaction Index, and since 2006 there have been only two years when another company in its category ranked higher. That difference may be due in part to Costco's traditionally following a different strategy than Walmart, paying higher wages and covering more of its employees with health insurance, requiring them to pay smaller health insurance premiums, and contributing more to their retirement plans. As we saw, Walmart raised its lowest wage to $9.25/hour. Costco's lowest wage is $13.00/hour.

Some major retailers experience 100% turnover each year, and the associated costs (for hiring, orienting, training, and replacing employees) can add up. One retailer with 50,000 employees found the annual turnover cost was more than $150 million. Thus, "saving money" by paying lower wages perhaps didn't ultimately save money. Another

CONTINUED

retailer known for its high wages and its commitment to "conscious capitalism" is The Container Store, which sells shelving systems, storage containers, and other products to help organize the house and garage. It pays front-line workers about $50,000 per year, even more than Costco pays workers with several years of experience (around $44,000 per year) and significantly more than Walmart pays such workers. Then-CEO and Container Store founder Kip Tindell explained the company's high wage this way: "One great person can easily do the business productivity of three good people," and it is necessary to pay well "particularly if you are trying to attract and keep really good people."

However, even companies committed to the high-wage business model may need to step back at times. The Container Store recently announced that, in response to slower sales, it would reduce labor costs by reducing the number of employees (by leaving open positions unfilled) and by freezing wages and 401k (retirement) contributions. Employee pay will still lead the market, but until evidence indicates that sales are improving and/or that cutting labor costs is worsening employee turnover, customer service, and sales, even The Container Store will retrench to a degree on employee-related costs.

SOURCES: "The Container Store Bucks the Wage-Hiking Trend," Investopedia.com, April 27, 2016; M. Armental, "Container Store Plans to Cut Payroll, Freeze Wages," Marektwatch.com, April 25, 2016; A. Garcia, "Costco's Entry-Level Workers Are Getting a Raise," CNNMoney.com, March 3, 2016; H. Tabuchi, "Walmart Lifts Its Wage Floor to $9 an Hour," *New York Times*, February 20, 2015, p. A1; R. Feintzeig, "Container Store Bets on $50,000 Retail Worker," *Wall Street Journal*, October 15, 2014, p. B6; C. DeRose and N. Tichy, "Are You Spending More by Paying Your Employees Less?" *Forbes*, April 29, 2013; W. F. Cascio, "The High Cost of Low Wages," *Harvard Business Review*, December 2006, p. 23; The American Customer Satisfaction Index, http://www.theacsi.org.

The Importance of Process: Participation and Communication

LO 11-4

Discuss the significance of process issues such as communication in compensation management.

Compensation management has been criticized for following the simplistic belief that "if the right technology can be developed, the right answers will be found."[22] In reality, however, any given pay decision is rarely obvious to the diverse groups that make up organizations, regardless of the decision's technical merit or basis in theory. Of course, it is important when changing pay practices to decide which program or combination of programs makes the most sense, but how such decisions are made and how they are communicated also matter.[23]

PARTICIPATION

Employee participation in compensation decision making can take many forms. For example, employees may serve on task forces charged with recommending and designing a pay program. They may also be asked to help communicate and explain its rationale. This is particularly true in the case of job evaluation as well as many of the programs discussed in Chapter 12. To date, for what are perhaps obvious reasons, employee participation in pay-level decisions remains fairly rare.

It is important to distinguish between participation by those affected by policies and those who must actually implement the policies. Managers are in the latter group (and often in the former group at the same time). As in other areas of human resource management, line managers are typically responsible for making policies work. Their intimate involvement in any change to existing pay practices is, of course, necessary.

COMMUNICATION

A dramatic example of the importance of communication was found in a study of how an organization communicated pay cuts to its employees and the effects on theft rates and perceived equity.[24] Two organization units received 15% across-the-board pay cuts. A third unit received no pay cut and served as a control group. The reasons for the pay cuts were communicated in different ways to the two pay-cut groups. In the "adequate explanation" pay-cut group, management provided a significant amount of information to explain its reasons for the pay cut and also expressed significant remorse. In contrast, the "inadequate explanation" group received much less information and no indication of remorse. The control group received no pay cut (and thus no explanation).

The control group and the two pay-cut groups began with the same theft rates and equity perceptions. After the pay cut, the theft rate was 54% higher in the "adequate explanation" group than in the control group. But in the "inadequate explanation" condition, the theft rate was 141% higher than in the control group. In this case, communication had a large, independent effect on employees' attitudes and behaviors.

Communication is likely to have other important effects. We know, for example, as emphasized by equity theory, that not only actual pay but also the comparison standard influence employee attitudes.[25] Under two-tier wage plans, employees doing the same jobs are paid two different rates, depending on when they were hired. Moreover, the lower-paid employees do not necessarily move into the higher-paying tier. Common sense might suggest that the lower-paid employees would be less satisfied, but this is not necessarily true. In fact, a study by Peter Cappelli and Peter Sherer found that the lower-paid employees were more satisfied on average.[26] Apparently, those in the lower tier used different (lower) comparison standards than those in the higher tier. The lower-tier employees compared their jobs with unemployment or lower-paying jobs they had managed to avoid. As a result, they were more satisfied, despite being paid less money for the same work. This finding does not mean that two-tier wage plans are likely to be embraced by an organization's workforce. It does, however, support equity theory through its focus on the way employees compare their pay with other jobs and the need for managers to take this into consideration. Employees increasingly have access to salary survey information, which is likely to result in more comparisons and thus a greater need for effective communication.

Managers play the most crucial communication role because of their day-to-day interactions with their employees.[27] Therefore, they must be prepared to explain why the pay structure is designed as it is and to judge whether employee concerns about the structure need to be addressed with changes to the structure. One common issue is deciding when a job needs to be reclassified because of substantial changes in its content. If an employee takes on more responsibility, he or she will often ask the manager for assistance in making the case for increased pay for the job.

Challenges

PROBLEMS WITH JOB-BASED PAY STRUCTURES

The approach taken in this chapter, that of defining pay structures in terms of jobs and their associated responsibilities, remains the most widely used in practice. However, job-based pay structures have a number of potential limitations.[28] First, they may encourage bureaucracy. The job description sets out specific tasks and activities for which the incumbent is responsible and, by implication, those for which the incumbent is not responsible. Although this facilitates performance evaluation and control by the

LO 11-5
Describe new developments in the design of pay structures.

manager, it can also encourage a lack of flexibility and a lack of initiative on the part of employees: "Why should I do that? It's not in my job description." Second, the structure's hierarchical nature reinforces a top-down decision making and information flow as well as status differentials, which do not lend themselves to taking advantage of the skills and knowledge of those closest to production. Third, the bureaucracy required to generate and update job descriptions and job evaluations can become a barrier to change because wholesale changes to job descriptions can involve a tremendous amount of time and cost. Fourth, the job-based pay structure may not reward desired behaviors, particularly in a rapidly changing environment where the knowledge, skills, and abilities needed yesterday may not be very helpful today and tomorrow. Fifth, the emphasis on job levels and status differentials encourages promotion-seeking behavior but may discourage lateral employee movement because employees are reluctant to accept jobs that are not promotions or that appear to be steps down.

RESPONSES TO PROBLEMS WITH JOB-BASED PAY STRUCTURES
Delayering and Banding

In response to the problems caused by job-based pay structures, some organizations have implemented **delayering**, or reducing the number of job levels to achieve more flexibility in job assignments and in assigning merit increases. Pratt and Whitney, for example, changed from 11 pay grades and 3,000 job descriptions for entry-level through middle-management positions to 6 pay grades and several hundred job descriptions.[29] These broader groupings of jobs are also known as *broad bands*. Table 11.8 shows how banding might work for a small sample of jobs.

IBM greatly reduced the bureaucratic nature of the system, going from 5,000 job titles and 24 salary grades to a simpler 1,200 jobs and 10 bands. Within their broad bands, managers were given more discretion to reward high performers and to choose pay levels that were competitive in the market for talent.

One possible disadvantage of delayering and banding is a reduced opportunity for promotion. Therefore, organizations need to consider what they will offer employees instead. In addition, to the extent that there are separate ranges within bands, the new structure may not represent as dramatic a change as it might appear. These distinctions can easily become just as entrenched as they were under the old system. Broad bands, with their greater spread between pay minimums and maximums, can also lead to weaker budgetary control and rising labor costs. Alternatively, the greater spread can permit managers to better recognize high performers with high pay. It can also permit the organization to reward employees for learning.

Paying the Person: Pay for Skill, Knowledge, and Competency

A second, related response to job-based pay structure problems has been to move away from linking pay to jobs and toward building structures based on individual

Delayering
Reducing the number of job levels within an organization.

Table 11.8
Example of Pay Bands

TRADITIONAL STRUCTURE		BANDED STRUCTURE	
GRADE	**TITLE**	**BAND**	**TITLE**
10	Senior Engineer	5	Senior Engineer
8	Engineer II	4	Engineer
6	Engineer I		

characteristics such as skills or knowledge.[30] Competency-based pay is similar but usually refers to a plan that covers exempt employees (such as managers). The basic idea is that if you want employees to learn more skills and become more flexible in the jobs they perform, you should pay them to do it. (See Chapter 7 for a discussion of the implications of skill-based pay systems on training.) According to Gerald Ledford, however, it is "a fundamental departure" because employees are now "paid for the skills they are capable of using, not for the job they are performing at a particular point in time."[31]

Skill-based pay systems seem to fit well with the increased breadth and depth of skill that changing technology continues to bring.[32] Indeed, research demonstrates that workforce flexibility is significantly increased under skill-based pay.[33] For example, in a production environment, workers might be expected not only to operate machines but also to take responsibility for maintenance and troubleshooting, quality control, and even modifying computer programs.[34] Toyota concluded years ago that "none of the specialists [e.g., quality inspectors, many managers, and foremen] beyond the assembly worker was actually adding any value to the car. What's more . . . assembly workers could probably do most of the functions of specialists much better because of their direct acquaintance with conditions on the line."[35]

Skill-based pay
Pay based on the skills employees acquire and are capable of using.

In other words, an important potential advantage of skill-based pay is its contribution to increased worker flexibility, which in turn facilitates the decentralization of decision making to those who are most knowledgeable. It also provides the opportunity for leaner staffing levels because employee turnover or absenteeism can now be covered by current employees who are multiskilled.[36] In addition, multiskilled employees are important in cases where different products require different manufacturing processes or where supply shortages or other problems call for adaptive or flexible responses—characteristics typical, for example, of many newer so-called advanced manufacturing environments (like flexible manufacturing and just-in-time systems).[37] More generally, it has been suggested that skill-based plans also contribute to a climate of learning and adaptability and give employees a broader view of how the organization functions. Both changes should contribute to better use of employees' know-how and ideas. Consistent with the advantages just noted, a field study found that a change to a skill-based plan led to better quality and lower labor costs in a manufacturing plant.[38]

Of course, skill-based and competency-based approaches also have potential disadvantages.[39] First, although the plan will likely enhance skill acquisition, the organization may find it a challenge to use the new skills effectively. Without careful planning, it may find itself with large new labor costs but little payoff. In other words, if skills change, work design must change as quickly to take full advantage. Second, if pay growth is based entirely on skills, problems may arise if employees "top out" by acquiring all the skills too quickly, leaving no room for further pay growth. (Of course, this problem can also afflict job-based systems.) Third, and somewhat ironically, skill-based plans may generate a large bureaucracy—usually a criticism of job-based systems. Training programs need to be developed. Skills must be described, measured, and assigned monetary values. Certification tests must be developed to determine whether an employee has acquired a certain skill. Finally, as if the challenges in obtaining market rates under a job-based system were not enough, there is almost no body of knowledge regarding how to price combinations of skills (versus jobs) in the marketplace. Obtaining comparison data from other organizations will be difficult until skill-based plans become more widely used.

CAN THE U.S. LABOR FORCE COMPETE?

We often hear that U.S. labor costs are simply too high to allow U.S. companies to compete effectively with companies in other countries. The average hourly labor costs

LO 11-6
Explain where the United States stands on pay issues from an international perspective.

Table 11.9
Average Hourly
Labor Cost (Cash
and Benefits) for
Production Workers
in Manufacturing by
Country and Year, in
U.S. Dollars

	1985	1990	1995	2000	2005	2010	2015
Industrialized							
Canada	$10.95	$15.95	$16.10	$16.04	$26.81	$34.60	$30.94
Czech Republic				2.83	7.28	11.61	10.29
Germany[a]	9.57	21.53	30.26	23.38	38.18	43.83	42.42
Japan	6.43	12.64	23.82	22.27	25.56	31.75	23.60
United States	13.01	14.91	17.19	19.76	29.74	34.81	37.71
Newly industrialized							
Brazil				4.38	5.05	11.08	7.97
China					0.83	1.98	4.93[b]
Korea, Republic of	1.25	3.82	7.29	8.19	15.13	17.73	22.68
Mexico	1.60	1.80	1.51	2.08	5.36	6.14	5.90
Taiwan	1.49	3.90	5.85	7.30	7.93	8.37	9.51

[a] West Germany for 1985 and 1990 data.

[b] Most recent Conference Board data was $4.12 (in 2013) for China. The 2015 estimate for China was obtained by inflating the Conference Board estimates based on wage inflation data from the National Bureau of Statistics of China.

SOURCES: Data from 1985–2010 are from the Bureau of Labor Statistics, U.S. Department of Labor, "International Comparisons of Hourly Compensation Costs in Manufacturing," various years. Data from post-2010 are from the Conference Board, "International Comparisons of Hourly Compensation Costs in Manufacturing, 2015," December 2016.

(cash and benefits) for manufacturing production workers in the United States and in other advanced industrialized and newly industrialized countries are given in Table 11.9 in U.S. dollars.

As we saw in Chapter 5 and in this chapter, companies continue to monitor labor costs and other factors in deciding where to locate production. Based solely on a cost approach, it would perhaps make sense to try to shift many types of production from a country like Germany to other countries, particularly the newly industrialized countries. Would this be a good idea? Not necessarily. There are several factors to consider.

Instability of Country Differences in Labor Costs

First, note that relative labor costs are very unstable over time. For example, Table 11.9 shows that in 1985, U.S. labor costs were 36% greater than those of (West) Germany. But by 1990, the situation was reversed, with (West) German labor costs exceeding those of the United States by 44%, and remaining higher. Did German employers suddenly become more generous while U.S. employers clamped down on pay growth? Not exactly. Because our figures are expressed in U.S. dollars, currency exchange rates influence such comparisons, and these exchange rates often fluctuate significantly from year to year. For example, in 1985, when German labor costs were 74% of those in the United States, the U.S. dollar was worth 2.94 German marks. But in 1990 the U.S. dollar was worth 1.62 German marks. If the exchange rate in 1990 were still 1 to 2.94, the average German hourly wage in U.S. dollars would have been $11.80, or about 80% of the U.S. average in 1990 rather than the actual $21.53, or 144% of the U.S. average.

In any event, relative to countries like Germany, U.S. labor costs during many of the years shown in Table 11.9 have been lower. This explains, in part, decisions by German companies like BMW, Mercedes-Benz, and Volkswagen to locate production facilities in South Carolina, Alabama, and Tennessee, respectively, where labor costs are substantially lower than in Germany. Proximity to the large U.S. market and currency exchange hedging are other factors. More recently, as noted earlier, German automakers (and those from other countries) have been building new North American plants in Mexico for these reasons and because of Mexico's low labor costs. Finally, we see in Table 11.9 that from 2010 to 2015 labor costs have seemingly declined in a number of countries. Again, however, that is a function in many cases of the costs being expressed in U.S. dollars and fluctuating currency exchange rates, not a decline in labor costs in local currency. For example, in 2010, one Canadian dollar was worth 0.97 U.S. dollars, but by 2015, one Canadian dollar was worth only 0.78 U.S. dollars, a decline in value of roughly 20%. As such, when expressed in Canadian dollars (using Conference Board data not shown in the table), labor costs in the local currency grew in Canada from 35.46 in 2010 to 39.58 in 2015, an increase of roughly 12%.[40]

On the other side of the world, Foxconn (Hon Hai Precision), is a Taiwanese company that assembles Apple products such as the iPhone, mostly in plants in China, where it has roughly one million employees, including over 200,000 employees on its Longhua and Guanlan campuses in Shenzhen. Foxconn is said to be considering building a $7 billion plant (to provide display panels for Sharp) in the United States that would create a significant number of jobs.[41] However, by one estimate, the labor cost component of an iPhone assembled in Shenzhen, China, is less than one-quarter of what it would cost if assembled at a U.S. facility.[42] Some estimates are that the labor cost difference would be much larger, more consistent with the difference shown in Table 11.9.[43] Additionally, the supply chain (with suppliers having similarly lower labor costs) for Apple products is well established in Asia. Thus, moving any significant part of the production of Apple products to the United States would be a challenge. It is perhaps most likely in the case where shipping costs are high (e.g., display panels versus iPhones) and where political pressures and/or tariffs point to locating at least some production in such markets.

Skill Levels

Second, the quality and productivity of national labor forces can vary dramatically. This is an especially important consideration in comparisons between labor costs in industrialized countries like the United States and developing countries like Mexico. For example, the high school graduation rate in the United States is 77% versus 44% in Mexico.[44] Thus, lower labor costs may reflect the lower average skill level of the workforce; certain types of skilled labor may be less available in low-labor-cost countries. By contrast, any given company needs only enough skilled employees for its own operations. Some companies have found that low labor costs do not necessarily preclude high quality.

As we have seen, many automakers have chosen Mexico for new plants to serve markets in North America. In Europe, countries such as Poland, Slovakia, and the Czech Republic have many skilled workers and lower labor costs than countries such as Germany, which has resulted in the expansion of production there and is also used as a bargaining chip when seeking more productive work rules at home.

Productivity

Third, and most directly relevant, are data on comparative productivity and unit labor costs, essentially meaning labor cost per hour divided by productivity per hour worked. One indicator of productivity is gross domestic product (or total output of the economy)

Figure 11.4

Gross Domestic Product (GDP) per Person, Adjusted for Purchasing Power Differences, U.S. dollars

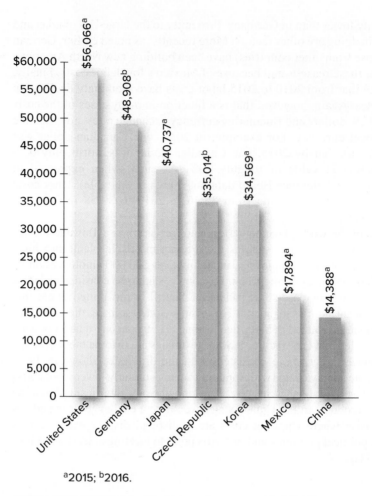

[a]2015; [b]2016.

SOURCE: OECD, OECD Statistics, http://stats.oecd.org, accessed April 19, 2017.

per person. On this measure, the United States fares well. (See Figure 11.4.) The combination of lower labor costs and higher productivity translates, at least on average, into lower unit labor costs in the United States than in Japan and western Europe.

Considerations Other Than Labor Cost

Fourth, any consideration of where to locate production cannot be based on labor cost considerations alone. For example, although the average hourly labor cost in Country A may be $15 versus $10 in Country B, if labor costs are 30% of total operating costs and nonlabor operating costs are roughly the same, then the total operating costs might be $65 ($50 + $15) in Country A and $60 ($50 + $10) in Country B. Although labor costs in Country B are 33% less, total operating costs are only 7.7% less. This may not be enough to compensate for differences in skills and productivity, customer wait time, transportation costs, taxes, and so on. Further, the direct labor component of many products, particularly high-tech products (such as electronic components), may often be 5% or less. Therefore, the effect on product price-competitiveness may be less significant.[45]

Where to Manufacture? Balancing Labor Costs, Production Costs, and Customer Needs

As Table 11.9 shows, average hourly labor cost (wages and benefits) in China ($4.93) remains much lower than in the United States ($37.71). That means that China continues to offer large cost advantages for some manufacturers, such as those for which the cost of labor is a substantial component of total cost (or would be a large component of cost if produced in another country). However, over the past decade, labor costs in China have increased more than 400%, whereas in the United States, the increase is closer to 25%. Further, wages in China are higher near the coast, where the supply chains are most developed, thus making production there more efficient. Land and electricity prices have also increased substantially in China.

Increases in labor (and other) costs and the prospect of large increases going forward is one factor that has led some companies to develop production capacity elsewhere. For example, Adidas is opening its first factory in 30 years in its home country of Germany (in Ansbach, Bavaria). One way the company will address Germany's higher labor costs ($42.42/hour) is through the extensive use of automation

to manufacture shoes. A major reason for moving a small amount of production to Germany is to improve the speed and flexibility with which the company can respond to changing customer preferences. Being close to customers allows a better feel for what customers there want, and also allows companies to have less of a delay in shipping what customers want. They can also lower their costs of carrying inventory when the product is made closer to the customer. For companies that manufacture products that are expensive to transport, that too encourages production closer to customers. Nike and Apple are taking similar steps.

But it is not just consumer goods companies that need to be close to customers. Jabil manufactures circuit boards for companies such as Apple and Electolux SA. They too foresee increasing demands by their customers to customize their products and to do so with short lead times. Chinese firms too are setting up new production overseas, including in the United States. Again, this move is driven not only by labor and other costs but also by the customer. In the case of domestic Chinese firms, they may feel the need to look

elsewhere for opportunities to grow revenues if the Chinese market has matured. Another factor is contingency planning, in case proposals to raise trade barriers (e.g., increasing tariffs on imported goods from countries such as China) come to fruition.

DISCUSSION QUESTIONS

1. Have labor costs in China increased enough that it is a major factor in firms moving production elsewhere? If they are moving, is it more likely to be to Germany or the United States, or to a country with lower labor costs than China?
2. Summarize factors other than labor costs that firms consider when making decisions. Does the importance of these factors depend on the firm (e.g., small firm versus large firm)? Explain.
3. Under what circumstances is a firm most likely to emphasize low labor costs versus other factors in locating production? Is one factor the nature of the product? Do firms have some products that are more mass market and some that are more customized?

SOURCES: N. Trentmann, "For More Chinese Firms, It Pays to Make It in the U.S.A.," *Wall Street Journal*, February 26, 2017; K. Chu and E. E. Jervell, "At Western Firms Like Adidas, Rise of the Machines Is Fueled by Higher Asia Wages, "*Wall Street Journal*, June 9, 2016.

Thus, the decision on where to locate production depends on labor costs but also on other factors. Being close to where customers are matters a great deal. Product development speed may be greater when manufacturing is physically close to the design group. Quick response to customers (as when making a custom replacement product) is difficult when production facilities are on the other side of the world. Inventory levels can be reduced dramatically through the use of manufacturing methods such as just-in-time production, but suppliers need to be in close physical proximity. The "Competing through Globalization" box provides some examples of recent decisions by companies that reflect these considerations.

On the other hand, some firms are aggressively offshoring jobs (including professional or knowledge worker jobs) primarily to reduce labor costs. For example, financial services firms like Goldman Sachs and Citigroup now have significant numbers of employees in India doing statistical and research work at much lower pay levels.[46] As another example, IBM began to move thousands of programmer jobs overseas to countries such as China, where the hourly cost at the time was $12.50/hour versus $56/hour in the United States, potentially saving more than $100 million per year.[47] In some cases, companies using low-cost labor overseas have decided that those workers are paid too little and pay more than would be necessary simply to attract and retain enough workers. For example, a few years ago, European garment retailers including H&M and Zara wrote to the prime minister of Cambodia "pledging" to pay owners of Cambodian garment suppliers more so that they could pay their workers more. Subsequently, the garment industry wage increased by over 50%.[48]

EXECUTIVE PAY

LO 11-7
Explain the reasons for the controversy over executive pay.

The issue of executive pay has been given widespread attention in the press. In a sense, the topic has received more coverage than it deserves because there are very few top executives and their compensation often accounts for a small share of an organization's total labor costs. However, top executives have a disproportionate ability to influence organization performance, so decisions about their compensation are critical. They can also be symbolic. During the global financial crisis of 2007–2008, the U.S. government, as part of the Troubled Asset Relief Program (TARP), decided it was appropriate to further regulate executive pay in firms receiving government "bailout" money.

Top executives also help set the tone or culture of the organization. If, for example, the top executive's pay seems unrelated to the organization's performance, with pay staying high even when business is poor, employees may not understand why some of their own pay is at risk and fluctuates (not only up, but also down), depending on how the organization is performing.

How much do executives make? Table 11.10 provides some data. Long-term compensation, typically in the form of stock plans, is the major component of CEO pay, which means that CEO pay varies with the performance of the stock market (see the "Annual Change in S&P 500" column). Table 11.11 shows that some CEOs are paid well above the medians/averages shown in Table 11.10.

As Table 11.10 shows, the ratio of top-executive pay to that of an average worker was 280 for the most recent year. (The ratio is much higher in some earlier years, usually because in those years average rather than median CEO pay was measured. Average pay is always higher than median pay for CEOs.) The ratio in the United States is higher than in the other largest world economies (China, Japan, Germany, United Kingdom).[49] Such comparisons, however, typically do not adjust for the fact that U.S. CEOs lead larger companies than those in comparison countries. Large companies pay more.

This ratio (or differential) has been described as creating a "trust gap"—that is, in employees' minds, a "frame of mind that mistrusts senior management's intentions, doubts its competence, and resents its self-congratulatory pay." The issue becomes more

Table 11.10
Realized CEO Compensation

YEAR	CEO PAY						ANNUAL CHANGE IN CEO PAY	ANNUAL CHANGE IN S&P 500	WORKER PAY*	CEO PAY/ WORKER PAY**
	SALARY	BONUS	SALARY PLUS BONUS	STOCK OPTIONS	STOCK GRANTS***	TOTAL PAY				
2015	$1.1 million	2.0 million	$3.1 million	$1.1 million	$5.1 million	$10.4 million	1%	1%	$37,186	280
2014	1.1 million	2.1 million	3.2 million	1.2 million	4.7 million	10.3 million	1%	14%	36,455	283
2013	1.1 million	2.0 million	3.1 million	1.4 million	4.2 million	10.2 million	11%	32%	35,555	287
2012	1.0 million	1.9 million	2.9 million	1.3 million	3.8 million	9.2 million	4%	16%	34,519	269
2011	1.0 million	2.0 million	3.0 million	1.7 million	3.3 million	8.9 million	****	2%	33,800	263
2010			3.0 million	3.0 million	2.5 million	8.5 million	−29%	15%	33,119	258
2009			3.0 million	3.3 million	5.8 million	12.1 million	−14%	26%	32,093	377
2008			3.6 million	3.6 million	6.9 million	14.1 million	−18%	−37%	31,617	446
2007			4.0 million	4.9 million	8.2 million	17.1 million	34%	5%	30,682	558
2006			3.8 million	2.4 million	6.5 million	12.7 million	3%	16%	29,529	431
2005			3.7 million	2.1 million	6.6 million	12.4 million	—	—	28,305	438
2000			2.9 million	4.5 million	7.0 million	14.3 million	—	—	25,013	573
1995			2.0 million	0.7 million	0.7 million	3.3 million	—	—	20,804	160
1990			1.6 million	0.3 million	0.7 million	2.6 million	—	—	18,187	144

*Worker pay (annual) is based on establishment survey data on earnings of production and nonsupervisory workers on private nonfarm payrolls, U.S. Bureau of Labor Statistics, *Employment & Earnings Online, Establishment Data from the Current Employment Statistics Survey* (CES), National, Table B-8a, https://www.bls.gov/opub/ee/archive.htm. The December average weekly earnings number is multiplied by 52 to obtain worker pay (annual).

**Ratio of CEO pay to hourly employee pay.

***Through 2010, "other" compensation is included in this category. In most cases, the value of stock grants accounts for most of pay in this category.

****Not computed due to change in definition of total compensation from a mean to a median.

NOTE: Through 2010, the three pay category averages of salary plus bonus, stock awards, and stock options add up to equal average total pay. Beginning in 2011, the pay categories do not add up to total pay because some compensation categories (non-equity incentive plan compensation, change in pension value and nonqualified deferred compensation earnings, all other compensation) reported in the Summary Compensation Table of company proxy statements are excluded and because medians are used.

SOURCES: Through 2010, CEO pay data are *averages* from *Forbes* magazine. Through 1999 (1995 here), *Forbes* data pertain to the 800 largest companies. Beginning with year 2000 through 2010, *Forbes* data pertain to the 500 largest U.S. companies (S&P 500). Beginning in 2011, CEO pay data pertain to the 500 largest U.S. companies (S&P 500) and are *medians* (versus averages) from Equilar, *CEO Pay Trends 2016*, https://www.meridiancp.com/wp-content/uploads/Equilar-CEO-Pay-Trends-Report.pdf.

Table 11.11
Highest-Paid
Executives

	TOTAL COMPENSATION
Sundar Pichai, Alphabet, Inc. (Google)	$100.5 million
Thomas M. Rutledge, Charter Comm., Inc.	$98.5 million
Dara Khosrowshahi, Expedia, Inc.	$94.6 million
Leslie Moonves, CBS	$69.6 million

SOURCE: R. Lightner and T. Francis, "How Much Do Top CEOs Make?" *Wall Street Journal*, April 20, 2017.

salient when many of the same companies with high executive pay simultaneously engage in layoffs or other forms of employment reduction. Employees might ask, "If the company needs to cut costs, why not cut executive pay rather than our jobs?"[50] The issue is one of perceived fairness. One study, in fact, reported that business units with higher pay differentials between executives and rank-and-file employees had lower customer satisfaction, which was speculated to result from employees' perceptions of inequity coming through in customer relations.[51] An important factor to consider in assessing how much executives are paid is how they are paid (i.e., whether their pay is performance based). This is an issue we return to in Chapter 12.

Government Regulation of Employee Compensation

We discuss equal employment opportunity, as well as minimum wage, overtime, and prevailing wage laws here. We also discuss regulation of executive compensation in Chapter 12.

EQUAL EMPLOYMENT OPPORTUNITY

LO 11-8
Describe the regulatory framework for employee compensation.

Equal employment opportunity (EEO) regulation (such as Title VII of the Civil Rights Act) prohibits sex- and race-based differences in employment outcomes such as pay, unless justified by business necessity (like pay differences stemming from differences in job performance). In addition to regulatory pressures, organizations must deal with changing labor market and demographic realities. At least two trends are directly relevant in discussing EEO.[52] First, whereas women represented 33% of all employees in 1960, they now make up 46% of the labor force. Second, since 1960, the percentage of Whites among all employees has dropped from 90% to 79%. White men now account for 43% of all U.S. employment, and that percentage will probably continue to decline, making attention to EEO issues in compensation even more important.

Is there equality of treatment in pay determination? Typically, the popular press focuses on raw earnings ratios. For example, among full-time workers, the ratio of female-to-male weekly median earnings is .81, the ratio of black-to-white earnings is .77, and the ratio of Hispanic/Latino-to-white earnings is .72.[53] These percentages have generally risen over the past two to three decades, but significant differences in pay clearly remain.[54] In contrast, Asian Americans earn 19% more than whites. Among executives, women appear to have lower pay than men, partly due to women being less likely to receive performance-based (e.g., stock and bonus-related) pay.[55]

The usefulness of raw percentages is limited, however, because some portion of earnings differences arises from differences in legitimate factors: education, labor market experience, and occupation. Adjusting for such factors reduces earnings differences based on sex and race or ethnicity, but significant differences remain. With few exceptions, such adjustments rarely account for more than half of the earnings differential.[56]

What aspects of pay determination are responsible for such differences? In the case of women, it is suggested that their work is undervalued. Another explanation rests on the "crowding" hypothesis, which argues that women were historically restricted to entering a small number of occupations. As a result, the supply of workers far exceeded demand, resulting in lower pay for such occupations. If so, market surveys would only perpetuate the situation.

Comparable worth (or pay equity) is a public policy that advocates remedies for any undervaluation of women's jobs. The idea is to obtain equal pay, not just for jobs of equal content (already mandated by the Equal Pay Act of 1963) but also for jobs of equal value or worth, on the basis of Title VII of the Civil Rights Act. Typically, job evaluation is used to measure worth. Table 11.12, which is based on Washington state data from one of the first comparable worth cases years ago, compares measures of worth based on internal comparisons (job evaluation) and external comparisons (market surveys).[57] Disagreements between the two measures are apparent. Internal comparisons suggest that women's jobs are underpaid, whereas external comparisons are less supportive of this argument. For example, although the licensed practical nurse job receives 173 job evaluation points and the truck driver position receives 97 points, the market rate (and thus the state of Washington employer rate) for the truck driver position is $1,493 per month versus only $1,030 per month for the nurse. The truck driver is paid 26.6% more than the pay policy line would predict, whereas the nurse is paid only 75.3% of the pay policy line prediction. Based on job evaluation points, the value of the nurse is 78.3% (173/97 − 1) higher, not 31.0% (1 − $1,030/$1,493) lower as is seen in the market pay.

Comparable worth
A public policy that advocates remedies for any undervaluation of women's jobs (also called *pay equity*).

Table 11.12

Job Evaluation Points, Monthly Prevailing Market Pay Rates, and Proportion of Incumbents in Job Who Are Female

BENCHMARK JOB TITLE	JOB EVALUATION POINTS	MARKET PAY	MARKET PAY AS PERCENTAGE OF PREDICTED PAY	PERCENT FEMALE IN JOB
Warehouse worker	97	$1,286	109.1%	15.4%
Truck driver	97	1,493	126.6	13.6
Licensed practical nurse	173	1,030	75.3	89.5
Maintenance carpenter	197	1,707	118.9	2.3
Civil engineer	287	1,885	116.0	0.0
Registered nurse	348	1,368	76.3	92.2
Senior computer systems analyst	384	2,080	113.1	17.8

NOTE: Predicted salary is based on regression of prevailing market rate on job evaluation points $2.43 × Job evaluation points + 936.19, r = 0.77.

One potential problem with using job evaluation to establish worth independent of the market is that job evaluation procedures were never designed for this purpose.[58] Rather, as demonstrated earlier, their major use is in helping to capture the market pay policy and then applying that to nonkey jobs for which market data are not available. In other words, job evaluation has typically been used to help apply the market pay policy, quite the opposite of replacing the market in pay setting.

As with any regulation, there are also concerns that EEO regulation obstructs market forces, which, according to economic theory, provide the most efficient means of pricing and allocating people to jobs. In theory, moving away from a reliance on market forces would result in some jobs being paid too much and others too little, leading to an over-supply of workers for the former and an undersupply for the latter. In addition, some empirical evidence suggests that a comparable worth policy would not have much impact on the relative earnings of women in the private sector.[59] One limitation of such a policy is that it targets single employers, ignoring that men and women tend to work for different employers.[60] To the extent that segregation by employer contributes to pay differences between men and women, comparable worth would not be effective. In other words, to the extent that sex-based pay differences are the result of men and women working in different organizations with different pay levels, such policies will have little impact.

Perhaps most important, despite potential problems with market rates, the courts have consistently ruled that using the going market rates of pay is an acceptable defense in comparable worth litigation suits.[61] The rationale is that organizations face competitive labor and product markets. Paying less or more than the market rate will put the organization at a competitive disadvantage. Thus, there is no comparable worth legal mandate in the U.S. private sector.

However, by the early 1990s, almost half of the states had begun or completed comparable worth adjustments to public-sector employees' pay. In addition, in 1988 the Canadian province of Ontario mandated comparable worth in both the private and public sectors. Further, although comparable worth is not mandated in the U.S. private sector, the Department of Labor (Office of Federal Contracts Compliance), which enforces Executive Order 11246, put into place enforcement standards and guidelines in 2006 that prohibit race- or sex-based "systemic compensation discrimination," which it defines as a situation "where there are statistically significant compensation disparities (as established by a regression analysis) between similarly situated employees, after taking into account the legitimate factors which influence compensation, such as: education, prior work experience, performance, productivity, and time in the job."[62] Further, passage of the 2009 Lilly Ledbetter Fair Pay Act means that employers may face claims in situations where a discriminatory decision (e.g., too small of a pay raise) was made many years earlier, but the effect (lower pay) continues into the more current period.

Some work has focused on pinpointing where women's pay falls behind that of men. One finding is that the pay gap is wider where bonus and incentive payments (not just base salary) are examined. Other evidence indicates that women lose ground at the time they are hired and actually do better once they are employed for some time.[63] One interpretation is that when actual job performance (rather than the limited general qualification information available on applicants) is used in decisions, women may be less likely to encounter unequal treatment. If so, more attention needs to be devoted to ensuring fair treatment of applicants and new employees.[64] However, a "glass ceiling" is believed to exist in some organizations that allows women (and minorities) to come within sight of the top echelons of management, but not advance to them (see "Melting the Glass Ceiling" in Chapter 9.

Automation, Technology, and the Demand for Employees

Labor cost, which is a function of cost per employee (wages and benefits) × number of employees, is a major expense for many firms. Thus, firms must decide on an ongoing basis not only how much to pay employees but also how many employees to have. One factor involved in these decisions is the availability of technology. Labor (employees) and capital (e.g., technology such as computers, machinery, robots, and automation) can be complements or substitutes in production. If complements, use of more capital requires use of more labor in production. If substitutes, use of more capital requires less use of labor in production (i.e., fewer employees).

When labor and capital are substitutes, an increase in the price of labor and/or a decrease in the cost of capital will generally result in the use of fewer employees in production. A caveat is that as production becomes more efficient, allowing lower prices for the product, resulting increases in demand for the product may result in an increase in the number of at least some types of employees (called the scale effect), even as the role of labor in production declines relative to the role of capital. As we saw in the "Competing through Globalization" box, some firms are expanding production in countries with high labor costs but are controlling costs by using more robots and automation to reduce the number of employees they need.

Looking forward, some occupations appear to be especially at risk. One example is the job of driver. The reason? The development of self-driving technology. Consider that there are estimated to be 600,000 Uber drivers, 180,000 taxi drivers, and 3.5 million truck drivers in the United States. To maximize profits, firms will be evaluating the relative costs and benefits of replacing drivers with self-driving vehicles. Of course, some new jobs will be created by the many firms working to develop self-driving technology, a product for which demand may be substantial. For example, General Motors has announced plans to hire 1,163 workers in San Francisco, where it will create a new center for research and development of autonomous and connected vehicles. The company anticipates that the average salary for these employees will be $116,000 and that the minimum salary will be $59,000. The jobs will be in areas such as software development, street vehicle testing, and human resources.

The job of cashier is also vulnerable to automation. If all goes as planned, shoppers will soon be able to walk into an Amazon Go grocery, do their shopping, and then simply walk out. Sensors will detect what products they have taken, and they will be billed automatically. It is not just in these relatively low-skill, modestly paid occupations where capital may substitute for employees. It was recently reported that BlackRock, Inc., the world's largest asset manager, would begin to rely more heavily on "robots" (computer models), and less on human money managers, to choose investments. The reason for this shift is that there is increasingly slim evidence that asset managers can generate better returns than computer models. Yet the cost of employing asset managers is significant. BlackRock's customers (investors), as in the broader investment industry, are increasingly pushing back on paying investment fees that they feel may be out of line with investment returns. Low-cost, passive investing (e.g., index-based mutual funds) is a competing investment model that appeals to many customers. Initially, several dozen employees, including seven stock portfolio managers, are expected to depart as part of this transition to greater use of computer models in asset management.

DISCUSSION QUESTIONS

1. What factors make it more likely that employers will substitute technology for employees?

CONTINUED

It is likely, however, that organizations will differ in terms of where women's earnings disadvantages arise. For example, advancement opportunities for women and other protected groups may be hindered by unequal access to the "old boy" or informal network. This, in turn, may be reflected in lower rates of pay. Mentoring programs have been suggested as one means of improving access. Indeed, one study found that mentoring was successful, having a significant positive effect on the pay of both men and women, with women receiving a greater payoff in percentage terms than men.[65]

MINIMUM WAGE, OVERTIME, AND PREVAILING WAGE LAWS

Fair labor standards act (FLSA)
The 1938 law that established the minimum wage and overtime pay.

Minimum wage
The lowest amount that employers are legally allowed to pay; the 1990 amendment of the Fair Labor Standards Act permits a subminimum wage to workers under the age of 20 for a period of up to 90 days.

For covered ("nonexempt") employees, the 1938 **Fair Labor Standards Act (FLSA)** establishes a **minimum wage** for jobs, which now stands at $7.25/hour. State laws may specify higher minimum wages. The FLSA also permits a subminimum training wage that is approximately 85% of the minimum wage, which employers are permitted to pay most employees under the age of 20 for a period of up to 90 days.

The FLSA also requires that nonexempt employees be paid at a rate of one and a half times their hourly rate for each hour of overtime worked beyond 40 hours in a week. The hourly rate includes not only the base wage but also other components such as bonuses and piece-rate payments. The FLSA requires overtime pay for any hours beyond 40 in a week that an employer "suffers or permits" the employee to perform, regardless of whether the work is done at the workplace or whether the employer explicitly asked or expected the employee to do it. If the employer knows the employee is working overtime but neither moves to stop it nor pays time and a half, a violation of the FLSA may have occurred. A department store was the target of a lawsuit that claimed employees were "encouraged" to, among other things, write thank-you notes to customers outside of scheduled work hours but were not compensated for this work. Although the company denied encouraging this off-the-clock work, it reached an out-of-court settlement to pay between $15 million and $30 million in back pay (plus legal fees of $7.5 million) to approximately 85,000 sales representatives it employed over a three-year period.[66]

Technology has helped create a sharing economy. With a touch of your smartphone, you can hail a car from Uber or schedule a housekeeper from Handy to clean your home or fix something in it. However, technology has also exposed gaps in employment law and raised challenges for workers and companies. Because these workers are often independent contractors, rather than employees, they are not covered by standard employment laws. Several sharing-economy companies have faced lawsuits by workers contending they should be treated as employees and thus be covered by FLSA requirements such as for overtime and a minimum wage. Although Uber's own study reported that its drivers make an average of $19/hour, that is before expenses. Drivers, especially those making less than $19/hour (gross) may not have a net wage that reaches the

INTEGRITY IN ACTION

Some Firms Decide to Go Ahead with Pay Increases (Even Though Now They May Not Have To)

As described in this chapter, the overtime provision of the FLSA requires that employees be paid at a rate of one and a half times their hourly rate for each hour of overtime worked beyond 40 hours in a week. One criterion for determining whether employees are covered by the overtime provision (nonexempt employees are covered; exempt employees are not) is that their salary is below a certain level. That "salary test" had been $455/week ($23,660/year) for many years. In May 2016, under the Obama administration, the U.S. Department of Labor's Wage and Hour Division issued a revision that increased the salary test to $970/week ($47,476/year).

In response, some employers informed employees who were exempt under the old salary test but not under the new one (i.e., those being paid an annual salary between $23,660 and $47,476) that they would be reclassified from exempt to nonexempt hourly. Other employers, like the Kroger grocery chain, took a different approach, developing a plan to increase the pay of about 4,500 managerial and supervisory employees to $47,476 or more to maintain their exempt status (no overtime pay required) under the new salary test.

Then, two major events took place. First, a federal district court judge issued a temporary injunction that blocked the new salary test rule from taking place nationwide. Second, Donald Trump was elected president. The result is that employers are uncertain about what the salary test for

determining exempt status (overtime coverage) will be. President Trump's Secretary of Labor (head of the Department of Labor), Alex Acosta, suggested in testimony to Congress that the salary test may be "somewhere around $33,000" per year.

In the meantime, Kroger has decided to move forward with its plan to increase salaries. Kroger's executive vice president and chief financial officer, Mike Schlotman explained it this way: It would be "a direct violation of our core values" to tell employees we were going to increase their pay "and then not do it because the law changed." Another company, Brand Value Accelerator LLC, an e-commerce marketing company, also plans to follow through on its plan to increase salaries of 13 of its 59 employees to keep them exempt. Its chief executive, Dylan Whitman, says that "I would have a slimy feeling going back to them" and telling them we changed our mind.

Other companies will take more of a wait-and-see attitude. Tammy McCutchen, former head of the Department of Labor's Wage and Hour Division under George W. Bush and part of Trump's transition team, suggested that employers might wish to "slow down" salary increases that had been planned in expectation of an increase in the salary test. She also proposed what she described as a "radical" approach: "ask employees . . . if they'd prefer the flexibility that goes with exempt status—which many also see as a

symbol of achievement—or if they'd prefer the overtime pay." Of course, employers will ultimately need to evaluate how wage increases will influence their ability to compete in both the product market and the labor market. If employers' labor costs are higher than those of their competitors, then these employers must get something in return, such as employees of higher quality or those who are more motivated and committed. Otherwise, higher costs risk decreasing the demand for the employers' products, which typically translates into fewer jobs for employees.

DISCUSSION QUESTIONS

1. Does it make sense for employers to give pay raises to employees when they are no longer "necessary"? In addressing this issue, think of the nature of the employment relationship or psychological contract between employers and employees. Perhaps you can use the analogy of personal relationships. What is the role of creating good will?

2. Check the recent news to get an update on what, if any, changes have been made to the salary test. How much did it change? Does it seem like an appropriate number? Why or why not?

SOURCES: S. Mills, "What's Next for Employers under the FLSA Overtime Rule?" Society for Human Resource Management, March 15, 2017, www.shrm.org; R. Simon and R. E. Silverman, "Some Employers Stick with Raises Despite Uncertainty on Overtime Rule," *Wall Street Journal*, December 20, 2016.

Changes in the Nature of Work and Employment: The Gig Economy

Ryan Heenan is a songwriter who works "whenever, wherever." He writes customized jingles and videos (digitally) for clients all over the world. For him, such work is "really a dream come true" because it gives him "freedom" to choose when and how much he works. He says all he needs is an Internet connection.

Ariana Baseman works in a traditional, full-time job, but in her spare time, she is a rideshare driver in Detroit, Michigan. She likes that she can "log on and work when I want." The freedom and flexibility and (sometimes) the opportunity to make extra money are a few of the positive aspects of the gig economy. Potential downsides are a lack of benefits and uncertain income flows. Rideshare driver Baseman observes, "Sometimes you're not making any money because you're not getting any work" and "that part's not really in your control." Songwriter Heenan says in looking back at his former full-time regular job working at a school, "I took things like health insurance for granted.... When you freelance, you have to find those things on your own, and it's expensive."

These are examples of gig economy workers. A definition used by the U.S. Bureau of Labor Statistics is that "a gig describes a single project or task for which a worker is hired, often through a digital marketplace, to work on demand." A gig can be a short-term job as an employee, and some gigs can be self-employment. The Bureau of Labor Statistics notes that gigs are not new, but that "companies connecting workers with these jobs through websites or mobile applications (more commonly known as apps) is a more recent development." Uber, Lyft, Airbnb, Amazon Flex, and Freelancer are some of the better known examples.

For organizations that need to get work done, there has always been a choice of whether to use their own employees, to use workers employed by other organizations, or to use independent contractors (self-employed) workers. (We will talk more about that choice in Chapter 13.) Now, due to a confluence of factors that include a preference on the part of both some workers and some organizations for more flexibility along with the technology to allow them to better find and match each others' needs, these new gig work arrangements have changed how organizations acquire and pay for human capital. Organizations that wish to sustain their competitiveness over time, particularly in certain industries, will need to evolve their approach.

Consider the case of James Knight, who recently left his full-time job as a programmer at Google to do freelance programming. That meant leaving behind Google's famously extensive benefits package and a secure job and income. He was willing to do that because he believes he can earn twice as much money writing code for dating and other apps while having the flexibility to "travel to Spain and hopscotch across Europe."

Martin Langhoff, 39, was formerly a chief technology officer for an organization. He grew tired of the "bureaucracy and endless meetings" that some people view as part of the deal for employees of big companies and wanted to have more flexibility and be able to focus more on writing code. Now, his services are available through 10X, and he can sometimes be found writing code aboard his a 41-foot sailboat that, in line with the sharing economy, he shares with other owners. He recently helped develop a security product for a large U.S. company. Langhoff says he earns 50% more than when he had a traditional job. Anne Adams left Bank of America Merrill Lynch to freelance through TopTal. She is currently writing software for a large U.S. insurance company. Even though these are high-paying gigs, there is still "definitely a level of stress" that comes from not having the security of a traditional job. James Knight, who left Google, says that is a good thing for him because "I have motivation issues if I don't think my pay check is on the line."

McKinsey estimates that roughly 70% of gig workers ("free agents" and "casual earners") prefer that arrangement, whereas the remaining 30% ("reluctants"

CONTINUED

and "financially strapped") would choose traditional full-time jobs if available. In the case of the freelance programmers we discussed here, the gig route seems to be their preference. That is an important fact for organizations to recognize as they think about how to sustain their access to human capital in the long run and what its cost will be, especially where it is valuable and/or scarce. For other types of employees with less valuable and/or scarce human capital (and thus with less leverage to choose whether to be a gig worker or not), organizations will need to consider whether the potential cost savings and flexibility of such a model outweigh what may be lost in terms of employee commitment and development of uniquely valuable organization-specific skills. Organizations will also need to consider how evolving regulation of the gig economy and workers may affect their choices going forward.

DISCUSSION QUESTIONS

1. From the point of view of a worker, what are the pros and cons of being a gig worker versus being an employee?
2. From the point of view of an organization, what are the pros and cons of using gig workers?
3. Should employment laws be revised to better cover workers in the sharing economy? Who would benefit? Would anyone lose?
4. Would you prefer to be an employee or a gig worker? Explain. Can you foresee your preference shifting in the future? Explain.

SOURCES: E. Torpey and A. Hogan, "Working in a Gig Economy," U.S. Bureau of Labor Statistics, Career Outlook, May 2016, https://www.bls.gov/careeroutlook/2016/article/what-is-the-gig-economy.htm; S. Wang, "Why an Ex-Google Coder Makes Twice as Much Freelancing," *Bloomberg*, January 19, 2016; J. Manyika, S. Lund, J. Bughin, K. Robinson, J. Mischke, and D. Mahajan, "Independent Work: Choice, Necessity, and the Gig Economy," McKinsey Global Institute, October 2016.

(federal) minimum wage of $7.25/hour, given that they supply their own vehicles and thus pay for expenses, including depreciation of their vehicles.[67]

Executive, professional, administrative, outside sales, and certain "computer employees" occupations are **exempt** from FLSA coverage. *Nonexempt* occupations are covered and include most hourly jobs. Exempt status depends on job responsibilities and salary. All exemptions (except for outside sales) require that an employee be paid no less than $455/week. Near the end of President Obama's administration, the Wage and Hour Division of the U.S. Department of Labor proposed increasing this salary "test" to $970/week, which would greatly increase the number of U.S. employees who are nonexempt (i.e., covered by FLSA overtime provisions).[68] However, the Trump administration seems likely to halt the change. It may propose a higher (than $455) salary test, but that has not yet occurred. In any case, some employers had already taken steps to comply with what they thought would be a $970/week salary test (including by giving pay increases to some employees to keep them exempt). As the "Integrity in Action" box describes, rather than go back on those pay increases, some employers have decided to keep them.

The job responsibility criteria vary. For example, the executive exemption is based on whether two or more people are supervised; whether there is authority to hire and fire (or whether particular weight is given to the employee's recommendations); and whether the employee's primary duty is managing the enterprise, recognized department, or subdivision of the enterprise. The Wage and Hour Division (www.dol.gov/whd/), U.S. Department of Labor, and its local offices can provide further information on these definitions. (The exemptions do *not* apply to police, firefighters, paramedics, and other first responders.)

Two pieces of legislation—the Davis-Bacon Act of 1931 and the Walsh-Healey Public Contracts Act of 1936—require federal contractors to pay employees no less than the prevailing wages in the area. Davis-Bacon covers construction contractors receiving federal money of more than $2,000. Typically, prevailing wages have been based on relevant union contracts, partly because only 30% of the local labor force is required to be used in establishing the prevailing rate. Walsh-Healey covers all government contractors receiving $10,000 or more in federal funds.

Exempt
Employees who are not covered by the Fair Labor Standards Act. Exempt employees are not eligible for overtime pay.

Finally, employers must take care in deciding whether a person working on their premises is classified as an employee or an independent contractor. We address this issue in Chapter 13. The "Competing through Sustainability" box addresses how this issue relates to the developing "gig economy" and the ongoing decisions and challenges created for organizations regarding gig workers.

 A LOOK BACK

Pay Levels, Labor Costs, and Pay Strategy

We began this chapter with a look at some companies that have recently increased their pay levels. Although controlling compensation costs is important, it is especially important for some of these companies (e.g., Walmart) to be able to compete on price in their product markets. They also need to pay more to compete in their labor markets, which have become more competitive in recent years as the economy has recovered and grown. Not doing so would make it more difficult to recruit and retain the quality of workforce needed. In the case of Walmart, contributing to its decision to increase pay levels was labor market competition as well as the need to better execute its business strategy, including improving the customer experience, which required better workforce quality. We also saw in this chapter how companies such as automobile makers continue to use relative labor cost as an important decision in where they locate production plants. Thus, pay level and pay structure decisions influence the success of strategy execution by influencing not only labor costs but also workforce quality, as well as employee perceptions of equity. Different pay structures can also vary in the degree to which they provide flexibility and incentives for employees to learn and be productive.

QUESTIONS

1. What types of changes have the companies discussed in this chapter made to their pay levels and pay structures to support execution of their business strategies?
2. Would other companies seeking to better align their pay structures with their business strategies benefit from imitating the changes made at these companies?

SUMMARY

Equity theory suggests that social comparisons are an important influence on how employees evaluate their pay. Employees make external comparisons between their pay and the pay they believe is received by employees in other organizations. Such comparisons may have consequences for employee attitudes and retention. Employees also make internal comparisons between what they receive and what they perceive others within the organization are paid. These types of comparisons may have consequences for internal movement, cooperation, and attitudes (like organization commitment). Such comparisons play an important role in the controversy over executive pay, as illustrated by the focus of critics on the ratio of executive pay to that of lower-paid workers.

Pay benchmarking surveys and job evaluation are two administrative tools widely used in managing the pay level and job structure components of the pay structure, which influence employee social comparisons. Pay surveys also permit organizations to benchmark their labor costs against other organizations. Globalization is increasing the need for organizations to be competitive in both their labor costs and productivity. The nature of pay structures is undergoing fundamental changes in many organizations, including the move to fewer pay levels to reduce labor costs and bureaucracy, and a shift by some employers from paying employees for narrow jobs to giving them broader responsibilities and paying them to learn the necessary skills. How a new compensation program is decided on, designed, implemented, and communicated is perhaps just as important as its core characteristics.

KEY TERMS

Pay structure, 463
Pay level, 463
Job structure, 463
Efficiency wage theory, 467
Benchmarking, 468
Rate ranges, 469
Key jobs, 469

Nonkey jobs, 469
Job evaluation, 469
Compensable factors, 469
Pay policy line, 471
Pay grades, 473
Range spread, 473
Compa-ratio, 475

Delayering, 480
Skill-based pay, 481
Comparable worth, 489
Fair Labor Standards Act
   (FLSA), 492
Minimum wage, 492
Exempt, 495

DISCUSSION QUESTIONS

1. You have been asked to evaluate whether your organization's current pay structure makes sense in view of what competing organizations are paying. How would you identify the organizations with which to compare your organization? Why might your organization's pay structure differ from those in competing organizations? What are the potential consequences of having a pay structure that is out of line relative to those of your competitors?

2. Top management has decided that the organization is too bureaucratic and has too many layers of jobs to compete effectively. You have been asked to suggest innovative alternatives to the traditional "job-based" approach to employee compensation and to list the advantages and disadvantages of these new approaches.

3. If major changes of the type mentioned in Question 2 are to be made, what types of so-called process issues need to be considered? Of what relevance is equity theory in helping to understand how employees might react to changes in the pay structure?

4. Are executive pay levels unreasonable? Why or why not?

5. Your company plans to build a new manufacturing plant but is undecided where to locate it. What factors would you consider in choosing in which country (or state) to build the plant?

6. You have been asked to evaluate whether a company's pay structure is fair to women and minorities. How would you go about answering this question?

SELF-ASSESSMENT EXERCISE

Mc Graw Hill Education **connect**

Additional assignable self-assessments available in Connect.

Consider your current job or a job you had in the past. For each of the following pay characteristics, indicate your level of satisfaction by using the following scale: 1 = very dissatisfied; 2 = somewhat dissatisfied; 3 = neither satisfied nor dissatisfied; 4 = somewhat satisfied; 5 = very satisfied.

_____ 1. My take-home pay
_____ 2. My current pay
_____ 3. My overall level of pay
_____ 4. Size of my current salary
_____ 5. My benefit package
_____ 6. Amount the company pays toward my benefits
_____ 7. The value of my benefits

_____ 8. The number of benefits I receive
_____ 9. My most recent raise
_____ 10. Influence my manager has over my pay
_____ 11. The raises I have typically received in the past
_____ 12. The company's pay structure
_____ 13. Information the company gives about pay issues of concern to me
_____ 14. Pay of other jobs in the company
_____ 15. Consistency of the company's pay policies
_____ 16. How my raises are determined
_____ 17. Differences in pay among jobs in the company
_____ 18. The way the company administers pay

These 18 items measure four dimensions of pay satisfaction. Find your total score for each set of item numbers to measure your satisfaction with each dimension.

Pay Level
Total of items 1, 2, 3, 4, 9: _____
Benefits
Total of items 5, 6, 7, 8: _____
Pay Structure and Administration
Total of items 12, 13, 14, 15, 17, 18: _____

Pay Raises
Total of items 10, 11, 16: _____
Considering the principles discussed in this chapter, how could your company improve (or how could it have improved) your satisfaction on each dimension?

SOURCE: Based on H. G. Heneman III and D. P. Schwab, "Pay Satisfaction: Its Multidimensional Nature and Measurement," *International Journal of Psychology* 20 (1985), pp. 129–41.

EXERCISING STRATEGY

Gravity Payments: Raising Minimum Worker Pay to $70K

A few years ago, Dan Price, CEO of Gravity Payments, which processes credit card transactions for businesses, announced that the minimum employee annual pay would be increased by the end of 2017 to $70,000. He also announced that as part of the plan to fund the pay increase for employees, he would reduce his own annual compensation from roughly $1 million to $70,000, at least until profits increased enough for him to feel he should be paid more. The new pay policy would result in 70 out of the company's then 120 employees receiving a pay increase. Price's rationale for the pay increase was "so people who are giving their blood, sweat and tears for our clients can live a normal life and pay their bills." To put it mildly, Price's announcement drew a lot of attention and generated conflicting opinions.

QUESTIONS
1. Conduct your own research using the sources listed below and other sources you find. Describe more fully the rationale given by Dan Price for the pay increase.
2. What additional data (e.g., on which outcomes) would you like to have to evaluate whether the pay increase was a good idea?
3. What is your overall assessment of whether raising (minimum) pay for all employees to $70,000 per year was a good idea?

SOURCES: C. Sailor, "No Regrets for Dan Price: CEO Who Put $70K Minimum Wage in Place Is Here to Stay," Tacoma *News Tribune*, February 11, 2017; "P. Davidson, Does a $70,000 Minimum Wage Work?" *USA Today*, May 26, 2016; S. Kim, "Gravity Payments CEO Will Live on $70,000 Worker Wage, Thinks His Life Will Be Luxe Enough," ABCNews.go.com, April 14, 2015.

MANAGING PEOPLE

Reporting the Ratio of Executive Pay to Worker Pay: Is it Worth the Trouble?

Section 953(b) of the 2010 Dodd-Frank Wall Street Reform and Consumer Protection Act requires covered companies to report the ratio of annual total compensation of the chief executive officer (or any equivalent position) to the median of the annual total compensation of all other employees. In August 2015, the Securities and Exchange Commission (SEC) provided rules for companies to follow in computing and reporting the ratio.[69] However, following President Trump's election, on February 6, 2017, the acting chairman of the SEC stated "I have . . . directed the staff to reconsider the implementation of the rule" until the SEC receives further public input. As such, the future of the rule is uncertain.

Supporters of the rule, such as the AFL-CIO labor organization, argue that reporting the ratio will help rein in what it sees as exorbitant (and growing) levels of executive pay, especially when compared to what has happened to worker

pay. According to an analysis of S&P 500 firms by the AFL-CIO, the ratio of CEO pay to typical U.S. worker pay rose from 42 in 1980 to 380 more recently.

The AFL-CIO and other supporters of the rule hope it will also encourage boards of directors to consider whether worker pay, which has grown more slowly than inflation (and as indicated above, much more slowly than CEO pay), should be higher. The AFL-CIO also argues that research shows that larger pay differentials between CEOs and rank-and-file workers lead to poorer firm performance due to perceptions of inequity and the negative effects that has on worker morale and productivity. There is also a feeling that when CEOs get paid as much as they do, too much credit goes to them for a firm's success and not enough to other employees.

Many companies see things differently. David Hirschmann, head of the U.S. Chamber of Commerce's Center for Capital

Markets, says the ratio is not meaningful or helpful to investors and will instead be used as "a political tool to attack companies." Companies argue that with a global workforce and different payroll systems in different countries, computing the ratio is much more difficult than it would seem. For example, the consulting firm Accenture has 246,000 employees in 120 countries and a variety of payroll systems (and definitions of pay in different countries). Jill Smart, head of human resources at Accenture, says that the work required to compute the ratio of CEO to worker pay would be "quite incredible."

Other companies, however, are already doing it and have done so for years. They say it is not that difficult or costly. Whole Foods, for example, capped the ratio of executive to front-line worker pay at 19 about a decade ago. Mark Ehrnstein, a vice president there, says that it does not take months,

but rather a few days, and that it does not cost "millions of dollars" to calculate the ratio.

QUESTIONS

1. Do you believe it is an undue burden on companies to compute and report the ratio of chief executive compensation to employee compensation? Why or why not?
2. Do you believe reporting this ratio will result in changes that benefit companies, employees, or society? Explain.

SOURCES: U.S. Securities and Exchange Commission, "SEC Adopts Rule for Pay Ratio Disclosure," Press Release 2015-160 (Washington, DC: Author, August 5, 2015), http://www.sec.gov/news/pressrelease/2015-160.html; G. Morgenson, "Despite Federal Regulation, C.E.O–Worker Pay Gap Data Remains Hidden," *New York Times*, April 10, 2015; Leslie Kwoh, "Firms Resist New Pay-Equity Rules," *Wall Street Journal*, June 26, 2012; Elliot Blair Smith and Phil Kuntz, "CEO Pay 1,795-to-1 Multiple of Wages Skirts U.S. Law," www.bloomberg.com, April 29, 2013.

HR IN SMALL BUSINESS

Changing the Pay Level at Eight Crossings

Based in Sacramento, California, Eight Crossings provides transcription services for physicians, lawyers, hospitals, and authors. Its employees also answer phones, edit documents, and transcribe legal documents. The company's employees work either at the service center in Sacramento or in their homes, where they receive audio or text files via the Internet. In this way, Eight Crossings' employees can work in their specialty as needed without tying up a doctor's or attorney's office space.

Initially, the ease of sending files electronically was an advantage that enabled Eight Crossings to grow at a tremendous pace. But it has also opened up the company to competition from similar services provided from low-wage locations such as India. In addition, as voice recognition software has improved, automation could take over some of the processes that have been handled by skilled, experienced transcribers.

In that situation, Eight Crossings CEO Patrick Maher felt the pressure when clients began to ask him for a lower rate. Most of the costs of running Eight Crossings are related to labor. Overhead and materials are minimal for this type of work. Consequently, for Maher to offer his clients a better price, he would have to cut what he paid employees or stop earning a profit.

The pay level at Eight Crossings had been about 5% above the average for the industry. Maher believed that this pay strategy gave his company an advantage in recruiting and keeping the best transcribers. Pay was calculated per line of text at a rate that varied according to the complexity of the material being transcribed. Depending on how many hours

they worked and how complex the jobs they took, each transcriber earned between $20,000 and $70,000 a year.

In looking for ways to trim expenses, Maher considered that part of most documents included sections of boilerplate text. These are generated automatically by transcribers' software but were included in the number of lines for which the transcribers were paid. Maher concluded these amounted to a 5% bonus paid for each assignment. Maher decided he could cut transcribers' pay by 5% and in effect still pay them the same rate for what they were actually transcribing (but without the "bonus").

That pay cut would bring pay levels at Eight Crossings down to the market rate. Would that mean employees would leave for greener pastures? Maher guessed not, considering that his company was receiving résumés from experienced transcribers looking for work.

Maher's next challenge was how to communicate the pay cut to employees working in 22 locations, many working from home and communicating with the office electronically. He began by discussing the situation with the company's eight supervisors, who check the transcribers' work for quality. This prepared them to address employees' concerns. Next, he sent an e-mail to the transcribers, explaining the reasons for the change and inviting questions.

Maher's fears about the pay cut were not realized. Employees expressed understanding of the move and appreciation for his commitment to continue sending work to U.S. workers. And because Eight Crossings is paying the market rate, moving to another company would not offer employees an advantage in terms of pay.

QUESTIONS

1. How did the change in pay level at Eight Crossings affect its ability to attract and retain a high-quality workforce?

2. Do you think the company's pay structure was better suited to its objectives before or after the reduction in pay level? Why?

3. How would you evaluate the company's method of communicating the change in pay level? What improvements to that process can you suggest?

SOURCES: Darren Dahl, "Special Financial Report: Employee Compensation," *Inc.*, July 2009; Eight Crossings, corporate website, www.eightcrossings.com, accessed May 30, 2015, and "Company Profile: No. 609, Eight Crossings," Inc. 500/5000 (2000), www.inc.com.

NOTES

1. J. S. Adams, "Inequity in Social Exchange," in *Advances in Experimental Social Psychology*, ed. L. Berkowitz (New York: Academic Press, 1965); P. S. Goodman, "An Examination of Referents Used in the Evaluation of Pay," *Organizational Behavior and Human Performance* 12 (1974), pp. 170–95; C. O. Trevor and D. L. Wazeter, "A Contingent View of Reactions to Objective Pay Conditions: Interdependence among Pay Structure Characteristics and Pay Relative to Internal and External Referents," *Journal of Applied Psychology* 91 (2006), pp. 1260–1275; M. M. Harris, F. Anseel, and F. Lievens, "Keeping Up with the Joneses: A Field Study of the Relationships among Upward, Lateral, and Downward Comparisons and Pay Level Satisfaction," *Journal of Applied Psychology* 93, no. 3 (May 2008), pp. 665–73; Gordon D. A. Brown, Jonathan Gardner, Andrew J. Oswald, Jing Qian, "Does Wage Rank Affect Employees' Well-being?" *Industrial Relations* 47, no. 3 (July 2008), p. 355; D. Card, M. Alexandre, E. Moretti, and E. Saez, "Inequality at Work: The Effect of Peer Salaries on Job Satisfaction," *American Economic Review* 102 (2012), pp. 2981–3003; E. Della Torre, M. Pelagatti, and L. Solari, "Internal and External Equity in Compensation Systems, Organizational Absenteeism, and the Role of the Explained Inequalities," *Human Relations* 68 (2015), pp. 409–40.

2. J. B. Miner, *Theories of Organizational Behavior* (Hinsdale, IL: Dryden Press, 1980); B. Gerhart and S. L. Rynes, *Compensation: Theory, Evidence, and Strategic Implications* (Thousand Oaks, CA: Sage, 2003).

3. B. Gerhart and G. T. Milkovich, "Employee Compensation: Research and Practice," in *Handbook of Industrial and Organizational Psychology*, 2nd ed., ed. M. D. Dunnette and L. M. Hough (Palo Alto, CA: Consulting Psychologists Press, 1992); G. T. Milkovich, J. M. Newman, and B. Gerhart, *Compensation*, 11th ed. (New York: McGraw-Hill/Irwin, 2014).

4. M. Martinez, "Ford: Labor Costs Up about 1.5% Yearly after UAW Deal," *Detroit News*, November 30, 2015; B. Snavely, "Chrysler Has Lowest per Worker Labor Costs," *Detroit Free Press*, March 23, 2015; D. Barkholz, "Can UAW Fix Tier 2 Disparity? Return to Pattern Bargaining Unlikely," *Automotive News*, March 8, 2015; K. Naughton, "Detroit Worker Bonuses Approach Records on Rising Profits," *Bloomberg Businessweek*, February 13, 2015.

5. Mike Ramsey, "VW Chops Labor Costs in U.S.," *Wall Street Journal*, May 23, 2011, http://online.wsj.com/article/SB100 01424052748704083904576335501132396440.html; Mark Guarino, "Lower Wages Now at Big Three Automakers, But New Hires Aren't Whining," *Christian Science Monitor*, May 7, 2013.

6. Snavely, "Chrysler Has Lowest per Worker Labor Costs"; J. D. Stoll, "Volvo to Open Plant in U.S., State to Be Chosen in a Month; Car Maker Says Labor Rates Are Just Part of It," *Wall Street Journal*, March 30, 2015.

7. Ibid; Diana T. Kurylko, "Volvo's Catch-Up Game: South Carolina's European Supply Base Makes Things Easier for Automaker," *Automotive News*, August 1, 2016.

8. C. Chadwick, "Towards a More Comprehensive Model of Firms' Human Capital Rents," *Academy of Management Review*, November 12, 2015, doi:10.5465/amr.2013.0385; W. F. Cascio and J. W. Boudreau, *Investing in People: Financial Impact of Human Resource Initiatives*, 2nd ed. (Upper Saddle River, NJ: Pearson Financial Times Press, 2010); I. S. Fulmer and R. E. Ployhart, "Our Most Important Asset: A Multidisciplinary/Multilevel Review of Human Capital Valuation for Research and Practice," *Journal of Management*, November 12, 2013; I. S. Fulmer, B. Gerhart, and K. S. Scott, "Are the 100 Best Better? An Empirical Investigation of the Relationship between Being a 'Great Place to Work' and Firm Performance," *Personnel Psychology* 56 (2003), pp. 965–93; A. Edmans, "Does the Stock Market Fully Value Intangibles? Employee Satisfaction and Equity Prices," *Journal of Financial Economics* 101 (3), pp. 621–40.

9. B. Gerhart and G. T. Milkovich, "Organizational Differences in Managerial Compensation and Financial Performance," *Academy of Management Journal* 33 (1990), pp. 663–91; E. L. Groshen, "Why Do Wages Vary among Employers?" *Economic Review* 24 (1988), pp. 19–38; Gerhart and Rynes, *Compensation*.

10. J. D. Shaw, "Pay Levels and Pay Changes," in *Handbook of Industrial, Work and Organizational Psychology* (2014), Thousand Oaks, CA: Sage; A. L. Heavey, J. A. Holwerda, and J. P. Hausknecht, "Causes and Consequences of Collective Turnover: A Meta-Analytic Review," *Journal of Applied Psychology* 98, no. 3 (2013), p. 412; M. L. Williams, M. A. McDaniel, N. T. Nguyen, "A Meta-Analysis of the Antecedents and Consequences of Pay Level Satisfaction," *Journal of Applied Psychology* 91 (2006), pp. 392–413; M. C. Sturman, C. O. Trevor, J. W. Boudreau, and B. Gerhart, "Is It Worth It to Win the Talent War? Evaluating the Utility of Performance-Based Pay," *Personnel Psychology* 56 (2003), pp. 997–1035; B. Klaas and J. A. McClendon, "To Lead, Lag or Match: Estimating the Financial Impact of Pay Level Policies," *Personnel Psychology* 49 (1996), pp. 121–41; S. C. Currall, A. J. Towler, T. A. Judge, and L. Kohn, "Pay Satisfaction and Organizational Outcomes," *Personnel Psychology* 58 (2005), pp. 613–40; M. P. Brown, M. C. Sturman, and M. J. Simmering, "Compensation Policy

and Organizational Performance: The Efficiency, Operational, and Financial Implications of Pay Levels and Pay Structures," *Academy of Management Journal* 46 (2003), pp. 752–62; Eric A. Verhoogen, Stephen V. Burks, and Jeffrey P. Carpenter, "Fairness and Freight-Handlers: Local Labor Market Conditions and Wage-Fairness Perceptions in a Trucking Firm," *Industrial & Labor Relations Review* 60, no. 4 (July 2007), p. 477; T. A. Judge, R. F. Piccolo, N. P. Podsakoff, J. C. Shaw, and B. L. Rich, "The Relationship between Pay and Job Satisfaction: A Meta-Analysis of the Literature," *Journal of Vocational Behavior* 77 (2010), pp. 157–67; M. Subramony, N. Krause, J. Norton, and G. N. Burns, "The Relationship between Human Resource Investments and Organizational Performance: A Firm-Level Examination of Equilibrium Theory," *Journal of Applied Psychology* 93 (2008), pp. 778–88; J. P. Hausknecht and C. O. Trevor, "Collective Turnover at the Group, Unit, and Organizational Levels: Evidence, Issues, and Implications," *Journal of Management* 37 (2011), pp. 352–88; A. L. Heavey, J. A. Holwerda, and J. P. Hausknecht, "Causes and Consequences of Collective Turnover: A Meta-Analytic Review," *Journal of Applied Psychology* 98 (2013), pp. 412–53.

11. G. A. Akerlof, "Gift Exchange and Efficiency-Wage Theory: Four Views," *American Economic Review* 74 (1984), pp. 79–83; J. L. Yellen, "Efficiency Wage Models of Unemployment," *American Economic Review* 74 (1984), pp. 200–5.

12. J. McGregor, "Zappos to Employees: Get Behind Our 'No Bosses' Approach, or Leave with Severance," *Washington Post*, March 31, 2015; Kim Peterson, "Why Amazon Pays Employees $5,000 to Quit," CBS Moneywatch, April 11, 2014, http://www.cbsnews.com/news/amazon-pays-employees-5000-to-quit/.

13. S. L. Rynes and G. T. Milkovich, "Wage Surveys: Dispelling Some Myths about the Market Wage," *Personnel Psychology* 39 (1986), pp. 71–90; R. J. Greene, "Compensation Surveys: The Rosetta Stones of Market Pricing," *World at Work*, 2014, 1st Quarter, pp. 23–31.

14. B. Gerhart and G. T. Milkovich, "Employee Compensation: Research and Practice," in *Handbook of Industrial and Organizational Psychology*, 2nd ed., ed. M. D. Dunnette and L. M. Hough (Palo Alto, CA: Consulting Psychologists Press, 1992).

15. Milkovich, Newman, and Gerhart, *Compensation*, 11th ed.

16. B. Gerhart, G. T. Milkovich, and B. Murray, "Pay, Performance, and Participation," in *Research Frontiers in Industrial Relations and Human Resources*, ed. D. Lewin, O. S. Mitchell, and P. D. Sherer (Madison, WI: IRRA, 1992).

17. C. H. Fay, "External Pay Relationships," in *Compensation and Benefits*, ed. L. R. Gomez-Mejia (Washington, DC: Bureau of National Affairs, 1989).

18. J. P. Pfeffer and A. Davis-Blake, "Understanding Organizational Wage Structures: A Resource Dependence Approach," *Academy of Management Journal* 30 (1987), pp. 437–55; M. A. Carpenter and J. B. Wade, "Micro-level Opportunity Structures as Determinants of Non-CEO Executive Pay," *Academy of Management Journal* 45 (2002), pp. 1085–103.

19. M. Bidwell, F. Briscoe, I. Fernandez-Mateo, and A. Sterling, "The Employment Relationship and Inequality: How and Why Changes in Employment Practices Are Reshaping Rewards in Organizations," *Academy of Management Annals* 7, no. 1 (2013), pp. 61–121; G. E. Ledford, "The Changing Landscape of Employee Rewards: Observations and Prescriptions," *Organizational Dynamics* 43, no. 3 (2014), pp. 168–79; Milkovich, Newman, and Gerhart, *Compensation*, 11th ed.

20. C. M. Solomon, "Global Compensation: Learn the ABCs," *Personnel Journal*, July 1995, p. 70; R. A. Swaak, "Expatriate

Management: The Search for Best Practices," *Compensation and Benefits Review*, March–April 1995, p. 21.

21. *1997–1998 Survey of Geographic Pay Differential Policies and Practices* (Rochester, WI: Runzeimer International).

22. E. E. Lawler III, *Pay and Organizational Development* (Reading, MA: Addison-Wesley, 1981).

23. R. Folger and M. A. Konovsky, "Effects of Procedural and Distributive Justice on Reactions to Pay Raise Decisions," *Academy of Management Journal* 32 (1989), pp. 115–30; H. G. Heneman III and T. A. Judge, "Compensation Attitudes," in S. L. Rynes and B. Gerhart, eds., *Compensation in Organizations* (San Francisco: Jossey-Bass, 2002), pp. 61–103; J. Greenberg, "Determinants of Perceived Fairness of Performance Evaluations," *Journal of Applied Psychology* 71 (1986), pp. 340–42; H. G. Heneman III, "Pay Satisfaction," *Research in Personnel and Human Resource Management* 3 (1985), pp. 115–39.

24. J. Greenberg, "Employee Theft as a Reaction to Underpayment of Inequity: The Hidden Cost of Pay Cuts," *Journal of Applied Psychology* 75 (1990), pp. 561–68.

25. Adams, "Inequity in Social Exchange"; C. J. Berger, C. A. Olson, and J. W. Boudreau, "The Effect of Unionism on Job Satisfaction: The Role of Work-Related Values and Perceived Rewards," *Organizational Behavior and Human Performance* 32 (1983), pp. 284–324; P. Cappelli and P. D. Sherer, "Assessing Worker Attitudes under a Two-Tier Wage Plan," *Industrial and Labor Relations Review* 43 (1990), pp. 225–44; R. W. Rice, S. M. Phillips, and D. B. McFarlin, "Multiple Discrepancies and Pay Satisfaction," *Journal of Applied Psychology* 75 (1990), pp. 386–93.

26. Cappelli and Sherer, "Assessing Worker Attitudes."

27. S. Marasi and R. J. Bennett, "Pay Communication: Where Do We Go from Here?" *Human Resource Management Review* 26 (2016), pp. 50–58; I. S. Fulmer and Y. Chen, "How Communication Affects Employee Knowledge of and Reactions to Compensation Systems," in V. Miller and M. Gordon, eds., *Meeting the Challenge of Human Resource Management: A Communication Perspective* (New York: Routledge/Taylor & Francis, 2014), pp. 167–78; I. Caron, A. K. Ben-Ayed, and C. Vandenberghe, "Collective Incentive Plans, Organizational Justice and Commitment," *Relations Industrielles/Industrial Relations* 68, no. 1 (2013).

28. R. M. Kanter, *When Giants Learn to Dance* (New York: Simon & Schuster, 1989); E. E. Lawler III, *Strategic Pay* (San Francisco: Jossey-Bass, 1990); "Farewell, Fast Track," *BusinessWeek*, December 10, 1990, pp. 192–200; R. L. Heneman, G. E. Ledford, Jr., and M. T. Gresham, "The Changing Nature of Work and Its Effects on Compensation Design and Delivery," in S. L. Rynes and B. Gerhart, eds., *Compensation in Organizations*.

29. P. R. Eyers, "Realignment Ties Pay to Performance," *Personnel Journal*, January 1993, p. 74.

30. Lawler, *Strategic Pay*; G. Ledford, "3 Cases on Skill-Based Pay: An Overview," *Compensation and Benefits Review*, March–April 1991, pp. 11–23; G. E. Ledford, "Paying for the Skills, Knowledge, Competencies of Knowledge Workers," *Compensation and Benefits Review*, July–August 1995, p. 55; Heneman et al., "The Changing Nature of Work"; G. Ledford, "Factors Affecting the Long-term Success of Skill-based Pay," *WorldatWork Journal*, First Quarter (2008), pp. 6–18; J. Canavan, "Overcoming the Challenge of Aligning Skill-based Pay Levels to the External Market," *WorldatWork Journal*, First Quarter (2008), pp. 18–24; E. C. Dierdorff and E. A. Surface, "If You Pay for Skills, Will They Learn? Skill Change and Maintenance Under a Skill-Based Pay System," *Journal of Management* 34 (2008), pp. 721–43.

31. Ledford, "3 Cases."

32. Heneman et al., "The Changing Nature of Work."

33. A. Mitra, N. Gupta, and J. D. Shaw. "A Comparative Examination of Traditional and Skill-Based Pay Plans," *Journal of Managerial Psychology* 26 (2011), pp. 278–96.

34. T. D. Wall, J. M. Corbett, R. Martin, C. W. Clegg, and P. R. Jackson, "Advanced Manufacturing Technology, Work Design, and Performance: A Change Study," *Journal of Applied Psychology* 75 (1990), pp. 691–97.

35. J. P. Womack, D. T. Jones, D. Roos, and D. S. Carpenter, *The Machine That Changed the World: Based on the Massachusetts Institute of Technology 5-Million Dollar 5-Year Study on the Future of the Automobile* (New York: Rawson Assoc., 1990), p. 56.

36. Lawler, *Strategic Pay.*

37. Ibid.; Gerhart and Milkovich, "Employee Compensation."

38. B. C. Murray and B. Gerhart, "An Empirical Analysis of a Skill-Based Pay Program and Plant Performance Outcomes," *Academy of Management Journal* 41, no. 1 (1998), pp. 68–78.

39. Ibid.; N. Gupta, D. Jenkins, and W. Curington, "Paying for Knowledge: Myths and Realities," *National Productivity Review*, Spring 1986, pp. 107–23; J. D. Shaw, N. Gupta, A. Mitra, and G. E. Ledford, "Success and Survival of Skill-Based Pay Plans," *Journal of Management* 31 (2005), pp. 28–49.

40. *The Conference Board International Labor Comparisons, Manufacturing Hourly Compensation Costs, Data 1996– 2015*, https://www.conference-board.org/ilcprogram/index.cfm?id=18777.

41. M. Snider, "Foxconn May Build $7B Plant in U.S.," *USA Today*, January 23, 2017, https://www.usatoday.com/story/tech/news/2017/01/23/foxconn-may-build-7b-plant-us/96945414/.

42. M. Lau, "Would US Workers Really Want the Jobs That Have Gone to China?" *South China Morning Post*, January 29, 2017, http://www.scmp.com/news/china/policies-politics/article/2059590/would-us-workers-really-want-jobs-have-gone-china.

43. R. Jennings, "Foxconn May Follow, If Trump Pulls US Tech Companies Back to America," *South China Morning Post*, December 29, 2016, http://www.scmp.com/business/article/2057959/foxconn-may-follow-if-trump-pulls-us-tech-companies-back-america.

44. *Education at a Glance—OECD Indicators* 2010, www.OECD.org.

45. M. Hayes, "Precious Connection: Companies Thinking about Using Offshore Outsourcing Need to Consider More than Just Cost Savings," *Information Week*, October 20, 2003; Harold L. Sirkin et al., "Made in America Again," Boston Consulting Group, August 2011; K. Chu, "Not Made in China," *Wall Street Journal*, May 1, 2013; Y. Zhang, "China Begins to Lose Edge as World's Factory Floor," *Wall Street Journal*, January 17, 2013; A. Fox, "America, Inc.: More U.S. Manufacturers Are Making a U-turn on Offshoring," *HR Magazine*, May 2013, pp. 45–48.

46. Heather Timmons, "Cost-Cutting in New York, but a Boom in India," *New York Times*, August 12, 2008, p. C1. Reprinted with permission of PARS International.

47. William Bulkeley, "IBM Documents Give Rare Look at Sensitive Plans on 'Offshoring,'" *Wall Street Journal*, January 19, 2004; David Wessel, "Big U.S. Firms Shift Hiring Abroad," *Wall Street Journal*, April 19, 2011.

48. C. Larson, "Cambodia's Wages Rise, Orders Don't. A year after garment worker strikes, pay is up 63 percent," *Bloomberg Businessweek*, February 5, 2015; T. Wright, "Stores Propose Higher Wages in Asia," *Wall Street Journal*, October 15, 2014, p. B8; J. Hookway and S. Narin, "Cambodia Sets Minimum Wage below Union Demands," *Wall Street Journal*, November 12, 2014.

49. W. Liu and A. Melin, "The Best and Worst Countries to Be a Rich CEO," *Businessweek*, November 16, 2016.

50. A. Farnham, "The Trust Gap," *Fortune*, December 4, 1989, pp. 56ff; Scott McCartney, "AMR Unions Express Fury," *Wall Street Journal*, April 17, 2003; AFL-CIO, "Dodd-Frank Section 953(b): Why CEO-to-Worker Pay Ratios Matter For Investors," www.aflcio.org/content/download/1090/9807/version/1/file/Why-CEO-to-Worker-Pay-Ratios-Matter-For-Investors.pdf, accessed May 16, 2013.

51. D. M. Cowherd and D. I. Levine, "Product Quality and Pay Equity between Lower-Level Employees and Top Management: An Investigation of Distributive Justice Theory," *Administrative Science Quarterly* 37 (1992), pp. 302–20.

52. U.S. Bureau of Labor Statistics. Women in the labor force: A databook. April 2017. Report 1065.

53. U.S. Bureau of Labor Statistics, *Highlights of Women's Earnings in 2015*, Report No. 1064. Washington, DC: Author, November 2016.

54. Ibid.

55. C. Kulich, G. Trojanowski, M. K. Ryan, S. A. Haslam, and L. D. R. Renneboog, "Who Gets the Carrot and Who Gets the Stick? Evidence of Gender Disparities in Executive Remuneration," *Strategic Management Journal* 32 (2011), pp. 301–21; F. Munôz-Bullón, "Gender-Level Differences among High-Level Executives," *Industrial Relations* 49 (2010), pp. 346–70.

56. B. Gerhart, "Gender Differences in Current and Starting Salaries: The Role of Performance, College Major, and Job Title," *Industrial and Labor Relations Review* 43 (1990), pp. 418–33; G. G. Cain, "The Economic Analysis of Labor-Market Discrimination: A Survey," in *Handbook of Labor Economics*, ed. O. Ashenfelter and R. Layard (New York: North-Holland, 1986), pp. 694–785; F. D. Blau and L. M. Kahn, "The Gender Pay Gap: Have Women Gone as Far as They Can?" *Academy of Management Perspectives*, February 2007, pp. 7–23.

57. Helen Remick, "The Comparable Worth Debate," *Public Personnel Management*, Winter 1981.

58. D. P. Schwab, "Job Evaluation and Pay-Setting: Concepts and Practices," in *Comparable Worth: Issues and Alternatives*, ed. E. R. Livemash (Washington, DC: Equal Employment Advisory Council, 1980).

59. B. Gerhart and N. El Cheikh, "Earnings and Percentage Female: A Longitudinal Study," *Industrial Relations* 30 (1991), pp. 62–78; R. S. Smith, "Comparable Worth: Limited Coverage and the Exacerbation of Inequality," *Industrial and Labor Relations Review* 61 (1988), pp. 227–39.

60. W. T. Bielby and J. N. Baron, "Men and Women at Work: Sex Segregation and Statistical Discrimination," *American Journal of Sociology* 91 (1986), pp. 759–99.

61. Rynes and Milkovich, "Wage Surveys"; and G. T. Milkovich, J. M. Newman, and B. Gerhart, *Compensation*, 10th ed. (New York: McGraw-Hill/Irwin, 2010).

62. U.S. Department of Labor website, at www.dol.gov/esa/regs/compliance/ofccp/faqs/comstrds.htm.

63. Gerhart, "Gender Differences in Current and Starting Salaries"; B. Gerhart and G. T. Milkovich, "Salaries, Salary Growth, and Promotions of Men and Women in a Large, Private Firm," in *Pay Equity: Empirical Inquiries*, ed. R. Michael, H. Hartmann, and B. O'Farrell (Washington, DC: National Academy Press, 1989); K. W. Chauvin and R. A. Ash, "Gender Earnings Differentials in Total Pay, Base Pay, and Contingent Pay," *Industrial and Labor Relations Review* 47 (1994), pp. 634–49; M. M. Elvira and M. E. Graham, "Not Just a Formality: Pay System Formalization and Sex-Related Earnings Effects," *Organization Science* 13 (2002), pp. 601–17.

64. Gerhart, "Gender Differences in Current and Starting Salaries"; B. Gerhart and S. Rynes, "Determinants and Consequences of Salary Negotiations by Graduating Male and Female MBAs," *Journal of Applied Psychology* 76 (1991), pp. 256–62.

65. G. F. Dreher and R. A. Ash, "A Comparative Study of Mentoring among Men and Women in Managerial, Professional, and Technical Positions," *Journal of Applied Psychology* 75 (1990), pp. 539–46.

66. G. A. Patterson, "Nordstrom Inc. Sets Back-Pay Accord on Suit Alleging 'Off-the-Clock' Work," *Wall Street Journal*, January 12, 1993, p. A2; for additional information on overtime legal issues, see A. Weintraub and J. Kerstetter, "Revenge of the Overworked Nerds," *Businessweek*, www.businessweek.com, December 8, 2003.

67. L. Weber and R. E. Silverman, "On-Demand Workers: 'We Are Not Robots'," *Wall Street Journal*, January 28, 2015, p. B1.

68. U.S. Department of Labor, "Fact Sheet: Proposed Rulemaking to Update the Regulations Defining and Delimiting the Exemptions for 'White Collar' Employees," http://www.dol.gov/whd/overtime/NPRM2015/factsheet.htm.

69. After waiting several years to issue a proposed rule and then providing time for groups to comment, the U.S. Securities and Exchange Commission (SEC) issued its final rule in August 2015. Rule details are provided in SEC press release 2015-160 available at www.sec.gov.

12 Recognizing Employee Contributions with Pay

LEARNING OBJECTIVES

After reading this chapter, you should be able to:

LO 12-1 Discuss how pay influences individual employees, and describe three theories that explain the effect of compensation on individuals. *page 506*

LO 12-2 Describe the fundamental pay programs for recognizing employees' contributions to the organization's success. *page 512*

LO 12-3 List the advantages and disadvantages of the pay programs. *page 514*

LO 12-4 Describe how organizations combine incentive plans in a balanced scorecard. *page 525*

LO 12-5 Discuss issues related to performance-based pay for executives. *page 526*

LO 12-6 Explain the importance of process issues such as communication in compensation management. *page 530*

LO 12-7 List the major factors to consider in matching the pay strategy to the organization's strategy. *page 532*

Employers Raise Pay but Keep an Eye on Fixed Costs

According to the Employment Cost Index, U.S. Bureau of Labor Statistics, employer costs (per employee) for wages and benefits combined grew 2.2% last year in private industry. In recent years, it has hovered around 2.0%, up from a low of 1.3% in 2009, the year in which the unemployment rate peaked at a 25-year-high of 10%. The growth in pay, albeit modest, reflects the tightening of labor markets that we discussed in Chapter 11. Breaking out costs indicates that wages and salaries grew 2.3% and benefits grew 1.8%. Over that same period, shareholders of U.S. companies (according to the Russell 3000 Index) earned almost a 13% return on their investments and over the most recent five years earned an average annual return on their investments of nearly 15%. During the same five-year period, employer costs for compensation grew an average of 2.0% per year. The last time annual growth in compensation costs grew as much as 3.0% was in 2007.

Aon Hewitt reports, based on a survey of larger companies, that merit pay increases are expected to average 3.0% in 2017. The survey also reports that, at least among white-collar professionals, bonuses of 12.8% of salary on average are available in a large number of companies. Ken Abosch of Aon Hewitt notes, however, that "the unfortunate reality is that's still a limited segment of the workforce" with relatively few hourly workers eligible for such bonuses. Abosch observes that the lack of larger increases to base pay is "a little counterintuitive" given how the economy has strengthened and how competition for workers has intensified. In his opinion, "it's indicative of the pressure organizations are under to keep the lid on fixed costs." Using bonuses, a form of variable pay, makes cost containment more possible in future years if business turns downward. In contrast, Barry Gerhart of the University of Wisconsin–Madison notes, "If you put the money into salary, it's there forever. If you give out money in terms of a bonus, people get it that year and have to re-earn it the following year."

In the same vein, the Big Three U.S. automakers have moved to better control fixed labor costs by using profit sharing payments (which are similar to bonuses but often depend more on company performance and less on individual performance) in place of base pay increases, which have been absent for many years for Big Three workers and will average only about 1.5% per year over the next four years. In lieu of base pay increases, there will also be some lump sum bonuses not linked to profits and profit sharing payments. This is in the context of seeking to control already high wage and benefits costs. On the profit sharing front, Ford Motor will pay an average $9,000 to each full-time unionized worker for 2016, the highest in its history. The average payout at Fiat Chrysler is $5,000 and at General Motors, it is $11,000. As long as the automakers continue to have strong profits, workers will perhaps not focus on the uncertainty of some of their income stream. When profits decline, the Big Three U.S. automakers will, by design, see their labor costs also decline, making it more feasible to remain viable. But, of course, those savings will come at a cost to workers.

SOURCES: C. Dawson, C. Rogers, and J. D. Stoll, "Workers Benefit as Auto Sales Rise," *Wall Street Journal*, January 27, 2017; U.S. Bureau of Labor Statistics, U.S. Department of Labor, *Employment Cost Index Summary*, January 31, 2017, www.bls.gov; J. McGregor, "Holding Out Hope for a Bigger Raise or Bonus in 2017?" *Washington Post*, September 27, 2016; M. Colias, "GM, UAW Reach Tentative Labor Pact with 'Significant' Wage Gains," *Automotive News*, October 26, 2015; Dan Gorenstein, "Why You've Been Getting Bonuses, Not Raises, Lately," *Marketplace*, August 29, 2014, www.marketplace.org.

Introduction

As the chapter opening illustrates, organizations must pay competitive salaries and benefits to compete in the labor market, which has tightened recently with unemployment rates dropping. At the same time, however, organizations must control labor costs (which influence product price) to compete in the product market. Employers have also learned to be especially careful about taking on fixed labor costs.

Chapter 11 discussed setting pay for jobs. In this chapter we focus on setting pay for individual employees. We examine how to use pay to recognize and reward employees' contributions to the organization's success. Employees' pay does not depend solely on the jobs they hold. Instead, differences in performance (individual, group, or organization), seniority, skills, and so forth are used as a basis for differentiating pay among employees.[1] In some cases, large amounts of compensation can be at stake.

Several key questions arise in evaluating different pay programs for recognizing contributions. First, what are the costs of the program? Second, what is the expected return (in terms of influences on attitudes and behaviors) from such investments? Third, does the program fit with the organization's human resource strategy and its overall business strategy? Fourth, what might go wrong with the plan in terms of unintended consequences? For example, will the plan encourage managers and employees to pay more attention to some objectives (e.g., short-term sales) than to some others (e.g., customer service, long-term customer satisfaction, and long-term sales)?

Organizations have a relatively large degree of discretion in deciding how to pay, especially compared with the pay level decisions discussed in Chapter 11. The same organizational pay level (or "compensation pie") can be distributed (shared) among employees in many ways. Whether each employee's share is based on individual performance, profits, seniority, or other factors (the "how" to pay decision), the size of the pie (and thus the cost to the organization, the "how much" to pay decision) can remain the same.

Regardless of cost differences, different pay programs can have very different consequences for productivity and return on investment. Indeed, a study of 150 organizations found not only that the largest differences between organizations had to do with how (rather than how much) they paid but also that these differences resulted in different levels of profitability.[2]

How Does Pay Influence Individual Employees?

LO 12-1
Discuss how pay influences individual employees, and describe three theories that explain the effect of compensation on individuals.

Incentive effect
The effect a pay plan has on the behaviors of current employees.

Pay plans are typically used to energize, direct, sustain, or control the behavior of current employees. We refer to the effect of pay plans on current employees as an **incentive effect**. (Later, we will introduce the concept of a sorting effect, which is how pay influences employee behaviors by how pay shapes the composition of the workforce.) Equity theory, described in Chapter 11, is relevant here as well. Most employees compare their own pay with that of others, especially those in the same job. Perceptions of inequity may cause employees to take actions to restore equity. Unfortunately, some of these actions (like quitting, reduced effort, or lack of cooperation) may not help the organization.

Three additional theories also help explain the effects of compensation: reinforcement, expectancy, and agency theories.

REINFORCEMENT THEORY

E. L. Thorndike's law of effect states that a response followed by a reward is more likely to recur in the future. The implication for compensation management is that high employee performance followed by a monetary reward will make future high performance more likely. By the same token, high performance not followed by a reward will make it less likely in the future. The theory emphasizes the importance of a person's actual experience of a reward.

EXPECTANCY THEORY

Although **expectancy theory** also focuses on the link between rewards and behaviors, it emphasizes expected (rather than experienced) rewards. In other words, it focuses on the effects of incentives. Behaviors (job performance) can be described as a function of ability and motivation. In turn, motivation is hypothesized to be a function of expectancy, instrumentality, and valence perceptions. Compensation systems differ according to their impact on these motivational components. Generally speaking, the main influence of compensation is on instrumentality: the perceived link between behaviors and pay. In other words, as an employee, will my outcomes be better (e.g., higher pay, faster promotions, more autonomy) if I perform well or is performance simply not very relevant to my outcomes? The "Competing through Technology" box describes how Kimberly-Clark has used technology to support its shift to a stronger emphasis on pay for performance (i.e., instrumentality). Valence of pay outcomes should remain the same under different pay systems. Expectancy perceptions (the perceived link between effort and performance) often have more to do with employee selection, job design, and training than with pay systems. A possible exception would be skill-based pay, which directly influences employee training and thus expectancy perceptions.

> **Expectancy theory**
> The theory that says motivation is a function of valence, instrumentality, and expectancy.

Intrinsic and Extrinsic Motivation

Although expectancy theory implies that linking an increased amount of rewards to performance will increase motivation and performance, some authors have used cognitive evaluation theory to question this assumption, arguing that monetary rewards may increase extrinsic motivation but decrease intrinsic motivation. Extrinsic motivation depends on rewards (such as pay and benefits) controlled by an external source, whereas intrinsic motivation depends on rewards that flow naturally from work itself (like performing interesting work).[3] In other words, the concern would be that paying a child to read books may diminish the child's natural interest (intrinsic motivation) in reading, and the child may in the future be less likely to read books in the absence of monetary incentives.

Although monetary incentives may reduce intrinsic motivation in some settings (such as education), the evidence suggests that such effects are small and probably not very relevant to most work settings, where monetary payment is the norm.[4] A meta-analytic review of field research found that intrinsic motivation was actually higher, not lower, when extrinsic incentives were in place. One reason that extrinsic incentives may not have an adverse effect on intrinsic motivation in the workplace is the sorting process (discussed shortly) in the labor market, which matches people, over time, to jobs that fit their preferences, including reward preferences (e.g., for intrinsic and/or extrinsic motivators).[5] Further, evidence indicates that incentive pay has significant positive effects on performance, which is a function of both intrinsic and extrinsic motivation.[6] Scholars in the study of creativity (thought to be an increasingly important organization capability) in organizations have proposed a revised model in which pay for performance can have positive synergistic effects with intrinsic motivation on creativity.[7] Therefore, although money is not the only effective way to motivate behavior and monetary rewards will not always solve motivation problems, monetary rewards do not appear to run much risk of compromising intrinsic motivation in most work settings.[8] And, as we will see, although pay for performance has its risks, there may be more risk in not using it in terms of foregone performance.

AGENCY THEORY

Agency theory focuses on the divergent interests and goals of the organization's stakeholders and the ways that employee compensation can be used to align these interests and goals. We cover agency theory in some depth because it provides especially relevant implications for compensation design.

An important characteristic of the modern corporation is the separation of ownership from management (or control). Unlike the early stages of capitalism, in which owner and manager were often the same, today, with some important exceptions (mostly smaller companies), most stockholders are far removed from the day-to-day operation of companies. Although this separation has important advantages (like mobility of financial capital and diversification of investment risk), it also creates agency costs—the interests of the **principals** (owners) and their **agents** (managers) may no longer converge. What is best for the agent, or manager, may not be best for the owner.

Principal
In agency theory, a person (e.g., the owner) who seeks to direct another person's behavior.

Agent
In agency theory, a person (e.g., a manager) who is expected to act on behalf of a principal (e.g., an owner).

Agency costs can arise from two factors. First, principals and agents may have different goals (goal incongruence). Second, principals may have less than perfect information about the degree to which the agent is pursuing and achieving the principal's goals (information asymmetry).

Consider three examples of agency costs that can occur in managerial compensation.[9] First, although shareholders seek to maximize their wealth, management may spend money on things such as perquisites (corporate jets, for example) or "empire building" (making acquisitions that do not add value to the company but may enhance the manager's prestige or pay). Second, managers and shareholders may differ in their attitudes toward risk. Shareholders can diversify their investments (and thus their risks) more easily than managers (whose only major source of income may be their jobs), so managers are typically more averse to risk. They may be less likely to pursue projects or acquisitions with high potential payoff. It also suggests a preference on the part of managers for relatively little risk in their pay (high emphasis on base salary, low emphasis on uncertain bonuses or incentives). Indeed, research shows that managerial compensation in manager-controlled firms is more often designed in this manner.[10] Third, decision-making horizons may differ. For example, if managers change companies more than owners change ownership, managers may be more likely to maximize short-run performance (and pay), perhaps at the expense of long-term success.

Agency theory is also of value in the analysis and design of nonmanagers' compensation. In this case, interests may diverge between managers (now in the role of principals) and their employees (who take on the role of agents).

In designing either managerial or nonmanagerial compensation, the key question is, How can such agency costs be minimized? Agency theory says that the principal must choose a contracting scheme that helps align the interests of the agent with the principal's own interests (that is, it reduces agency costs). These contracts can be classified as either behavior oriented (such as merit pay) or outcome oriented (stock options, profit sharing, commissions, and so on).[11]

At first blush, outcome-oriented contracts seem to be the obvious solution. If profits are high, compensation goes up. If profits drop, compensation goes down. The interests of "the company" and employees are aligned. An important drawback, however, is that such contracts also increase the agent's risk. And because agents are averse to risk, they may require higher pay (a compensating wage differential) to make up for it.[12] Thus, a trade-off between risk and incentives must be considered. Outcome-oriented contracts are, for example, typically a major component of executive compensation.[13]

Behavior-based contracts, on the other hand, do not transfer risk to the agent and thus do not require a compensating wage differential. However, the principal must be able to overcome the information asymmetry issue. To do so the principal must either invest in monitoring (e.g., add more supervisors) and information or else revert, at least in part, to structuring the contract so that pay is linked at least partly to outcomes.[14]

Which type of contract should an organization use? It depends partly on the following factors:[15]

- *Risk aversion.* Risk aversion among agents makes outcome-oriented contracts less likely.
- *Outcome uncertainty.* Profit is an example of an outcome. Agents are less willing to have their pay linked to profits to the extent that there is a risk of low profits. They would therefore prefer a behavior-oriented contract.
- *Job programmability.* As jobs become less programmable (less routine), outcome-oriented contracts become more likely because monitoring becomes more difficult.[16]
- *Measurable job outcomes.* When outcomes are more measurable, outcome-oriented contracts are more likely.[17]
- *Ability to pay.* Outcome-oriented contracts contribute to higher compensation costs because of the risk premium.
- *Tradition.* A tradition or custom of using (or not using) outcome-oriented contracts will make such contracts more (or less) likely.

In summary, the reinforcement, expectancy, and agency theories all focus on the fact that behavior–reward contingencies can shape behaviors. However, agency theory is of particular value in compensation management because of its emphasis on the risk–reward trade-off, an issue that needs close attention when companies consider variable pay plans, which can carry significant risk.

How Do Pay Sorting Effects Influence Labor Force Composition?

Traditionally, using pay to recognize employee contributions has been thought of as a way to influence the behaviors and attitudes of current employees, whereas pay level and benefits have been seen as a way to influence so-called membership behaviors: decisions about whether to join or remain with the organization. However, it is now recognized that individual pay programs may also affect the nature and composition of an organization's workforce.[18] For example, it is possible that an organization that links pay to performance may attract more high performers than an organization that does not link the two. There may be a similar effect with respect to job retention.[19] This effect on workforce composition is sometimes referred to as a **sorting effect**.

Continuing the analysis, different pay systems appear to attract people with different personality traits and values.[20] Organizations that link pay to individual performance may be more likely to attract individualistic and risk-oriented employees, whereas organizations relying more heavily on team rewards are more likely to attract team-oriented employees. The implication is that the design of compensation programs needs to be

Sorting effect
The effect a pay plan has on the composition of the current work-force (the types of employees attracted and retained).

COMPETING THROUGH TECHNOLOGY

Helping Firms to Better Assess (and Reward) Employee Performance

In the past, a job at Kimberly-Clark, the maker of Kleenex, was for life and paid above-market wages. There was little pressure to perform. You could "hide in the weeds." Things have changed. The company is now focused on rewarding top performers and "managing out dead wood" rather than allowing them to remain and be paid as though their performance was high. In recent years, the company has retained 95% of its top performers. In the case of employees who get low performance scores, 44% left the company, voluntarily or otherwise. Liz Gottung, the chief human resources officer, is "pretty pleased" that turnover of low performers has increased.

Companies such as Kimberly-Clark use technology in the form of software from providers such as WorkDay, Inc., SAP SE, and Cornerstone, not only to track salaried employee performance against goals but also to ask for and give feedback to others. The software also estimates the risk that an employee will leave the company using factors such as job title, current rate of pay, and how long it has been since the employee was promoted. The software can also suggest proactive actions (e.g., a pay increase, finding a promotion opportunity) that are likely to help retain high performers.

DISCUSSION QUESTIONS
1. Compare the "old" Kimberly-Clark and the "new" Kimberly-Clark in terms of the degree to which desirable incentive and sorting effects are likely.
2. Why do you think Kimberly-Clark made a major change to its emphasis on performance? You may wish to do some research on the paper industry and how the size of the industry and competition have changed over time. Be sure to consider changes in technology.

SOURCES: T. Greenwald, "How AI Is Transforming the Workplace," *Wall Street Journal*, March 10, 2017; L. Weber, "Nowhere to Hide for 'Dead Wood' Workers," *Wall Street Journal*, August 22, 2016.

carefully coordinated with the organization and human resource strategy. Increasingly, both in the United States and abroad, employers are seeking to establish stronger links between pay and performance.

Pay-for-Performance Programs
DIFFERENTIATION IN PERFORMANCE AND PAY

Many organizations seek to use pay to differentiate between employees (i.e., create pay dispersion) based on their performance, especially in jobs (e.g., higher job levels) where the consequences of good versus average versus poor performance become more important to organization performance.[21] Some evidence suggests that high performers can generate a disproportionate amount of value.[22] If so, paying high performers an amount they feel is equitable (see Chapter 11) to motivate them (i.e., achieve positive incentive effects), as well as to attract and retain them (i.e., achieve positive sorting effects), becomes increasingly important. Conventional wisdom sometimes says that differentiation among individuals is ill advised in certain contexts (e.g., teams, collectivistic cultures, where creativity/innovation are critical), but the evidence does not support such simple claims and, indeed, differentiation/pay for individual performance can be important for success in these contexts also.[23] What we can say is that employees will pay close attention to why different employees get paid differently and how fair those differences are, and their perceptions of fairness will drive their behaviors.[24] The amount of

Japanese Companies Shift Emphasis from Seniority to Performance

In the traditional Japanese employment system, seniority is a major determinant of how much an employee is paid. Performance has not been emphasized as strongly in Japan as in countries like the United States. Some Japanese companies have sought in past years to shift to a greater emphasis on performance. A renewed commitment is being made to that effort by some companies, including Toyota, Hitachi, Sony, and Panasonic, partly in response to a call by Prime Minister Shinzō Abe to improve company efficiency as part of his effort to increase economic growth and wage growth in Japan.

Over the past 10 years, the rate of economic growth in Japan comes in last among the world's other largest economies (United States, China, Germany, France, United Kingdom). So the idea of looking at how companies in better-performing economies pay their employees and using some of those practices is perhaps overdue. The plan is to increase the importance of not only performance but also job responsibility in setting employee pay. The change may start primarily with younger employees, as companies are reluctant to modify the nature of the accepted relationship with older, more senior employees.

In addition to providing stronger performance incentives for current employees, these companies hope to gain an edge in recruiting younger employees, who would welcome working for a company where, rather than wait until they are older to make more money, they would have the opportunity to be paid well now if their contributions to the company prove to be valuable.

DISCUSSION QUESTIONS

1. What is wrong with paying for seniority instead of performance?
2. Why is the prime minister of Japan interested in how companies pay?
3. If you were choosing between a company that paid for seniority and a company that paid for performance, which would you choose? What about 20 years from now? Would you make the same choice? Explain.

SOURCES: M. Oi, "Japan Seeks Alternatives to Its Pay System," BBC News, Japan. March 22, 2016; K. Inagaki, "Japan Inc Shuns Seniority in Favour of Merit-Based Pay," *Financial Times*, January 27, 2015; Y. Hagiwara and C. Trudell, "Toyota Plans Overhaul to Seniority-Based Pay," Bloomberg.com, January 26, 2015.

---

differentiation that makes sense will depend on the level of interdependence and cooperation desired in a particular context.[25] See the "Competing through Globalization" box for an example of a country, Japan, where companies are striving to emphasize pay for performance more strongly.

DIFFERENTIATION STRENGTH/INCENTIVE INTENSITY: PROMISE AND PERIL

A key decision in designing pay-for-performance plans concerns *incentive intensity,* the strength of the relationship between performance and pay (i.e., how strongly we differentiate in performance and pay). For example, if I increase (decrease) my performance by 20%, by what percent will my pay increase (decrease)? The larger the change in pay, the stronger the incentive intensity. For jobs in which objective, results-based measures of performance are available (e.g., sales, executives, stock brokers, investment bankers, investment portfolio managers, loan officers), incentive intensity tends to be higher, compared to jobs in which more subjective, behavior-based (e.g., performance ratings) must be used (e.g., staff jobs in human resources, accounting). It is generally more of a challenge to credibly link big differences in pay to subjective measures.

An important principle is that the stronger the incentive intensity, the stronger the motivation but also the greater the chance for unintended, undesirable consequences.[26] For instance, we can link the pay of an automobile repair shop manager to sales and that will likely drive higher sales. We hope the higher sales result from efficiency and innovation in customer service, but we have to acknowledge the risk that higher sales may be driven by fixing things on customers' cars that do not need fixing. Likewise, paying mortgage loan officers based on the mortgage revenue they create can generate more revenue, it is hoped again through outstanding customer service, but the risk is that loans will be given to people who cannot afford them, which can become a problem for the bank in the future. Similarly, we can pay teachers based in part on how well their students perform on standardized tests. But we need to safeguard against the possibility that some teachers may look for ways to increase scores through means other than better teaching. Finally, if a financial institution's top executives believe the government will decide the institution is "too big to fail," they may be likely to take larger investment risks ("excessive risk taking" to the government that subsequently decides it must bail out the firm if the risks go bad and to the shareholders who lose if bankruptcy ensues). This is especially a risk if the executives do not have the same downside risk faced by shareholders. We will see other risks of pay for performance in this chapter as well and also steps that companies and regulators have taken to avoid such risks (e.g., caps on bonuses, clawback provisions, balanced scorecards).

When one hears stories of what can go wrong with pay for performance, it may be tempting to choose a weaker incentive intensity to avoid such problems. That may be wise in some cases. However, one must be careful not to weaken incentive intensity too much, else the reward for high performance can become too weak to motivate employees. And if a competitor provides a pay-for-performance environment with stronger incentive intensity, your strong performers may decide to work there instead (i.e., a negative sorting result). So, as we have noted, there is also a risk to weakening incentive intensity/pay for performance too much.

TYPES OF PAY FOR PERFORMANCE: AN OVERVIEW

LO 12-2
Describe the fundamental pay programs for recognizing employees' contributions to the organization's success.

Table 12.1 classifies pay programs for recognizing employee contributions on the basis of three dimensions. First, programs differ depending on whether payouts become part of base pay (merit pay, skill-based pay), are a fixed cost, or are variable. Second, some programs (merit pay and merit bonuses) measure performance using primarily subjective measures, whereas others (e.g., incentive pay) rely on more objective performance measures. Third, performance can be measured at the individual level (e.g., merit pay) or at the unit (gainsharing) or organization level (profit sharing, ownership).

In compensating employees, an organization does not have to choose one program over another. Instead, a combination of programs is often the best solution. For example, one program may foster teamwork and cooperation but not enough individual initiative. Another may do the opposite. Used in conjunction, a balance may be attained. Such balancing of objectives, combined with careful alignment with the organization and human resource strategy, may help increase the probability that a pay-for-performance program has its intended effects and reduce the probability of unintended consequences and problems.[27] The balanced scorecard, which we discuss later in this chapter, is an example of a structured approach to balancing objectives. The fundamental principle is that we care about financial results, but we also care about *how* they are achieved and also how nonfinancial measures can be used, tracked, and influenced to achieve better future financial results. So, it also helps avoid too much short-term focus.[28]

Table 12.1

Programs for Recognizing Employee Contributions

	MERIT PAY	MERIT BONUS	INCENTIVE PAY	PROFIT SHARING	STOCK OWNERSHIP/ STOCK OPTIONS	GAINSHARING	SKILL BASED
Design features							
Fixed (becomes part of base salary) or variable	Fixed	Variable (bonus)	Variable (bonus)	Variable (bonus)	Variable (equity changes)	Variable (bonus)	Fixed
Performance measure (subjective or objective)	Subjective (usually supervisor rating)	Subjective (usually supervisor rating), but higher-level jobs may include objective components also	Objective (e.g., productivity)	Objective (profit)	Objective (stock price/returns)	Objective (e.g., productivity, safety, rework, customer satisfaction)	Objective and/or subjective (certifying which skills are acquired)
Performance measure (individual or collective)	Individual	Individual, but higher-level jobs may include unit and/or organization outcomes.	Individual	Collective (organization)	Collective (organization)	Collective (unit)	Individual

Merit Pay (and Merit Bonuses)

LO 12-3
List the advantages and disadvantages of the pay programs.

Merit pay
Traditional form of pay in which base pay is increased permanently.

Merit bonus
Merit pay paid in the form of a bonus, instead of a base pay increase.

Merit increase grid
A grid that combines an employee's performance rating with his or her position in a pay range (i.e., compa-ratio) to determine the size and frequency of his or her pay increases.

In traditional **merit pay** programs, annual base pay increases are usually linked to performance appraisal ratings. (See Chapter 8.) Some type of merit pay program exists in almost all organizations.[29] In some cases, employers have moved toward a form of merit pay that relies on bonuses rather than increases to base pay. One reason for the widespread use of merit pay, or **merit bonuses**, a form of variable pay, is its ability to define and reward a broad range of performance dimensions. (See Table 12.2 for an example.) Indeed, given the pervasiveness of merit pay programs, we devote a good deal of attention to them here.[30]

Basic Features. Many merit pay programs work off of a **merit increase grid**. As Table 12.3 indicates, the size and frequency of pay increases are determined by two factors. The first factor is the individual's performance rating (better performers receive higher pay). The second factor is position in range (that is, an individual's compa-ratio). So, for example, an employee with a performance rating that exceeds expectations and a compa-ratio of 120 would receive a pay increase of roughly 3%. By comparison, an employee with a performance rating of exceeds expectations and a compa-ratio of 85 would receive an increase of around 7%. (Note that the general magnitude of increases in such a table is influenced by inflation rates.) One reason for factoring in the compa-ratio is to control compensation costs and maintain the integrity of the pay structure. If a person with a compa-ratio of 120 received a merit increase of 7%, she would soon exceed the pay range maximum. Not factoring in the compa-ratio would also result in uncontrolled growth of compensation costs for employees who continue to perform the same job year after year. Instead, some organizations think in terms of assessing where the employee's pay is now and where it should be,

Table 12.2
Sample Performance Dimensions

1. Knows Job
2. Takes Initiative
3. Exercises Good Judgment
4. Inspires and Develops Others
5. Demonstrates Interpersonal and Teaming Skills
6. Produces Results

Table 12.3
Merit Increase Grid

RECOMMENDED SALARY INCREASES BY PERFORMANCE RATING AND COMPA-RATIO		
	COMPA-RATIO[a]	
	80–90%	91–110%	111–120%
Performance rating			
Exceeds expectations	7%	5%	3%
Meets expectations	4%	3%	2%
Below expectations	2%	0%	0%

[a]Employee salary/midpoint of their salary range.

PERFORMANCE RATING	COMPA-RATIO TARGET
Exceeds expectations	111–120
Meets expectations	91–110
Below expectations	Below 91

Table 12.4
Performance Ratings and Compa-Ratio Targets

given a particular performance level. Consider Table 12.4. An employee who consistently performs at the highest level is targeted to be paid at 111–120% of the market (that is, a compa-ratio of 111–120). To the extent that the employee is far from that pay level, larger and more frequent pay increases are necessary to move the employee to the correct position. However, if the employee is already at that pay level, smaller pay increases will be needed. The main objective in the latter case would be to provide pay increases that are sufficient to maintain the employee at the targeted compa-ratio.

In controlling compensation costs, another factor that requires close attention is the distribution of performance ratings. (See Chapter 8.) In many organizations, 60–70% of employees fall into the top two (out of four to five) performance rating categories.[31] This means tremendous growth in compensation costs because most employees will eventually be above the midpoint of the pay range, resulting in compa-ratios well over 100. To avoid this, some organizations provide guidelines regarding the percentage of employees who should fall into each performance category, usually limiting the percentage that can be placed in the top two categories. These guidelines are enforced differently, ranging from true guidelines to strict forced-distribution requirements.[32]

In general, merit pay programs have the following characteristics. First, they identify individual differences in performance, which are assumed to reflect differences in ability or motivation. By implication, system constraints on performance are not seen as significant. Second, the majority of information on individual performance is collected from the immediate supervisor. Peer and subordinate ratings are rare, and where they exist, they tend to receive less weight than supervisory ratings.[33] Third, there is a policy of linking pay increases to performance appraisal results.[34] Fourth, the feedback under such systems tends to occur infrequently, often once per year at the formal performance review session. Fifth, the flow of feedback tends to be largely unidirectional, from supervisor to subordinate.

Criticisms of Traditional Merit Pay Programs. Criticisms of this process have been raised. For example, W. Edwards Deming, a leader of the total quality management movement, argued that it is unfair to rate individual performance because "apparent differences between people arise almost entirely from the system that they work in, not from the people themselves."[35] Examples of system factors include coworkers, the job, materials, equipment, customers, management, supervision, and environmental conditions. These are believed to be largely outside the worker's control, instead falling under management's responsibility. Deming argued that the performance rating is essentially "the result of a lottery."[36] Although that may be true for some jobs, for others (attorneys, consultants, investment bankers, athletes, salespeople, managers), there can be major differences in individual performance.[37]

Deming also argued that the individual focus of merit pay discourages teamwork: "Everyone propels himself forward, or tries to, for his own good, on his own life preserver. The organization is the loser."[38] As an example, if people in the purchasing department are evaluated based on the number of contracts negotiated, they may have little interest in materials quality, even though manufacturing is having quality problems.

Deming's solution was to eliminate the link between individual performance and pay. This approach reflects a desire to move away from recognizing individual contributions. What are the consequences of such a move? It is possible that fewer employees with individual-achievement orientations would be attracted to and remain with the organization. One study of job retention found that the relationship between pay growth and individual performance over time was weaker at higher performance levels. As a consequence, the organization lost a disproportionate share of its top performers.[39] In other words, too little emphasis on individual performance may leave the organization with average and poor performers.[40]

Thus, although Deming's concerns about too much emphasis on individual performance are well taken, one must be careful not to replace one set of problems with another. Instead, there needs to be an appropriate balance between individual and group objectives. At the very least, ranking and forced-distribution performance-rating systems need to be considered with caution, lest they contribute to behavior that is too individualistic and competitive.

Another criticism of merit pay programs is the way they measure performance. If the performance measure is not perceived as being fair and accurate, the entire merit pay program can break down. One potential impediment to accuracy is the almost exclusive reliance on the supervisor for providing performance ratings, even though peers, subordinates, and customers (internal and external) often have information on a person's performance that is as good as or better than that of the supervisor. A 360-degree performance feedback approach (discussed in Chapter 9) gathers feedback from each of these sources. To date, however, organizations have mainly used such data for development purposes and have been reluctant to use these multisource data for making pay decisions.[41]

In general, process issues, including communication, expectation setting, and credibility/fairness, are important in administering merit pay and pay-for-performance.[42] In any situation where rewards are distributed, employees appear to assess fairness along two dimensions: distributive (based on how much they receive) and procedural (what process was used to decide how much).[43] Some of the most important aspects of procedural fairness, or justice, appear in Table 12.5. These items suggest that employees desire clear and consistent performance standards, as well as opportunities to provide input, discuss their performance, and appeal any decision they believe to be incorrect.

Perhaps the most basic criticism is that merit pay does not really exist. High performers, it is argued, are not paid significantly more than mediocre or even poor performers in most cases.[44] For example, consider the data in Table 12.6 from a WorldatWork survey. It shows that high performers received an average merit increase of 4.8%, compared to 2.6% for average performers. On a salary of $50,000 per year, that is a difference of $1,100 per year, or $21.15 per week (before taxes). Critics of merit pay point out that this difference is probably not significant enough to influence employee behaviors or attitudes. Indeed, as Table 12.7 indicates, the majority of employees do not believe there is much payoff to higher levels of performance in their organizations. Whether that view varies among high, average, and low performers is not known.

In fact, however, small differences in pay can accumulate into large differences over time. Consistently receiving 4.8% increases (versus 2.6%) over 30 years with a starting salary of $50,000 would translate into a career salary advantage (before taxes) of roughly $1,000,000 (net present value of roughly $600,000, assuming a discount rate of 2.5%).[45] Whether employees think in these terms is open to question. But even if they do not, nothing prevents an organization from explaining to employees that what may appear to be small differences in pay can add up to large differences over time.

Employees' Belief That in Evaluating Their Performance, Their Supervisor...
- Was honest and ethical and tried to be fair
- Considered your input
- Used consistent standards
- Provided feedback
- Took the time to become familiar with your role and performance, including factors beyond your control
- After a merit pay decision was made, was receptive to discussion of how the decision was made (and/or an appeal) and working together to develop an action plan going forward

Table 12.5
Examples of Procedural Justice in Merit Pay Decisions

SOURCE: Adapted from R. Folger and M. A. Konovsky, "Effects of Procedural and Distributive Justice on Reactions to Pay Raise Decisions," *Academy of Management Journal* 32 (1989), p. 115.

	PERCENT OF WORKFORCE	AVERAGE BASE PAY INCREASE
Highest-rated	8%	4.8%
Next highest-rated	28	3.7
Middle-rated	57	2.6
Low-rated	7	0.9
Lowest-rated	2	0.1

Table 12.6
Distribution of Performance Rating and Average Base Pay Increase as a Function of Performance (United States)

Note: Based on companies with a five-point rating scale.
SOURCE: Mercer, *2014/2015 US Compensation Planning Survey*, www.mercer.com.

	% WHO AGREE
When I do a good job, my performance is rewarded.	40%
My organization does an adequate job of matching pay to performance.	46%

Table 12.7
Pay and Performance, Employee Perceptions

SOURCE: Mercer, *What's Working™ Survey, United States*, www.mercer.com.

Of course, the accumulation effect just described can also be seen as a drawback if it contributes to an entitlement mentality. Here the concern is that a big merit increase given early in an employee's career remains part of base salary "forever." It does not have to be re-earned each year, and the cost to the organization grows over time, perhaps more than either the employee's performance or the organization's profitability would always warrant. Merit bonuses (payouts that do not become part of base salary, a form of variable pay), are thus increasingly used by organizations in lieu of or in addition to merit increases. In fact, merit bonuses (see Table 12.8), in the companies that use them and for the employee groups they use them for, are now larger than traditional pay increases. Preliminary evidence suggests that merit bonuses may have a larger positive impact (compared to traditional merit increases) on future performance.[46] If that result proves to be robust across organizations, it, together with the merit bonus advantage in terms of controlling fixed costs, likely goes far toward explaining the greater use of merit bonuses. The payoff to high performance that comes from merit bonuses adds to the payoff from merit increases.

Table 12.8
Merit Bonus as a
Percentage of Salary,
by Employee Group

HOURLY UNION NONEXEMPT	SALARIED NONEXEMPT	SALARIED EXEMPT
6.2%	7.1%	13.0%

SOURCE: Ken Abosch. "The Shifting Landscape of Variable Pay." *Workspan*, April 2017, 6042-47.

Finally, high-performing employees are also more likely to be promoted (into higher-paying jobs) and are also more likely to have higher-paying opportunities at alternative employers. Indeed, these are the major pathways through which employees increase their salaries (and earnings overall, including through bonus and stock plans) over the course of their careers, not through pay increases received within the same jobs.[47] Unless one believes that employees rise to higher job and pay levels over time primarily due to some other factor (chance, seniority), it seems likely that performance differences are largely responsible and determinative over time. All these factors can be communicated to employees to help them see the payoff to high performance. And the higher the performance, the more likely it is one can keep the job (and salary).[48]

Individual Incentives

Like merit pay, individual incentives reward individual performance, but with two important differences. First, payments are not rolled into base pay. They must be continuously earned and re-earned. Second, performance is usually measured as physical output (such as number of water faucets produced) rather than by subjective ratings. Individual incentives have the potential to significantly increase performance. Locke and his colleagues found that monetary incentives increased production output by a median of 30%—more than any other motivational device studied.[49]

Nevertheless, individual incentives, at least in their purest form, are relatively rare, covering roughly 7% of all U.S. workers and less than 4% of those outside of sales occupations. In fact, the amount of attention received by individual incentives in research (and the popular press) is arguably out of proportion with their (limited) presence in the workplace, especially relative to merit pay.[50] Why is that the case? First, most jobs (like those of many managers and professionals) have, strictly speaking, no physical output measure. Instead, they involve what might be described as "knowledge work." There may or may not be alternative objective measures of performance available (e.g., financial and/or operational), which are needed to use individual incentives. The balanced scorecard gives a good flavor of what objective performance outcomes for managers often look like when they are available. Second, even in jobs where physical output measures are available, potential administrative problems (such as setting and maintaining acceptable standards) often prove intractable.[51] Third, individual incentives may do such a good job of motivating employees that they do whatever they get paid for and nothing else. (For example, one Dilbert cartoon showed employees celebrating when told they would be paid for every software error they found and fixed. The implication was that they would deliberately write errors into the software and then fix them to earn as much money as possible.) Fourth, as the name implies, individual incentives, again if used in their purest/simplest form, typically do not fit well with a team approach. Fifth, they may be inconsistent with the goals of acquiring multiple skills and proactive problem solving. Learning new skills often requires employees to slow or stop production. If the employees are paid based on production volume, they may not want to slow down or stop. Sixth, some incentive plans, if not designed carefully, reward output volume at the expense of quality or customer service. Seventh, especially for lower-paid employees, the risk of a variable pay plan like incentive pay not paying off, perhaps because of factors beyond the employee's control, is difficult to manage and/or may undermine motivation or cause unintended consequences such as gaming the system to protect income.

Therefore, although individual incentives carry potential advantages and, in fact, can have large positive effects, they are not likely to contribute to a flexible, proactive, quality-conscious, problem-solving workforce unless they can be designed to avoid the potential pitfalls described here.[52] Incorporating a broader range of objectives beyond physical output alone is one common step toward that end.

Profit Sharing and Ownership

Profit Sharing. At the other end of the individual–group continuum are profit sharing and stock ownership plans. Under **profit sharing**, payments are based on a measure of organization performance (profits), and the payments do not become part of the base salary. Profit sharing has two potential advantages. First, it may encourage employees to think more like owners, taking a broad view of what needs to be done to make the organization more effective. Thus, the sort of narrow self-interest encouraged by individual incentive plans (and perhaps also by merit pay) is presumably less of an issue. Instead, increased cooperation and citizenship are expected. Second, because payments do not become part of base pay, but instead are variable pay, labor costs are automatically reduced during difficult economic times, and wealth is shared during good times. Consequently, organizations may not need to rely on layoffs as much to reduce costs during tough times.[53]

Profit sharing
A compensation plan in which payments are based on a measure of organization performance (profits) and do not become part of the employees' base salary.

Does profit sharing contribute to better organization performance? The evidence is not clear. Although there is consistent support for a correlation between profit sharing payments and profits, questions have been raised about the direction of causality.[54] For example, Ford, Chrysler, and GM all have profit sharing plans in their contracts with the United Auto Workers (UAW). (See Table 12.9 for provisions of the GM–UAW plan.) Years ago, under an older profit sharing plan, the average profit sharing payment at Ford one year was $4,000 per worker versus an average of $550 per worker at GM and $8,000 at Chrysler. Given that the profit sharing plans used were very similar, it seems unlikely that the profit sharing plans (through their effects on worker motivation) caused Ford and Chrysler to be more profitable. Rather, it would appear that profits were higher at Ford for other reasons (e.g., better cars), resulting in higher profit sharing payments.

This example also helps illustrate the fundamental drawback of profit sharing. Why should automobile workers at GM receive profit sharing payments that are only 1/15 the size received by those doing the same type of work at Chrysler? Is it because Chrysler UAW members performed 15 times better than their counterparts at GM that year? Probably not. Rather, workers are likely to view top management decisions regarding products, engineering, pricing, and marketing as more important. As a result, with the exception of top (and perhaps some middle) managers or plans that cover a small number of employees (i.e., in small companies), most employees are unlikely to see a strong connection between what they do and what they earn under profit sharing. This means that performance motivation is likely to change very little under profit sharing. Consistent with expectancy theory, motivation depends on a strong link between behaviors and valued consequences such as pay (instrumentality perceptions).

Another factor that reduces the motivational impact of profit sharing plans is that most plans are of the deferred type. Roughly 16% of full-time employees in medium-size

Table 12.9
Profit Sharing in the
General Motors—
United Auto Workers
Contract

PROFITS $BILLIONS			MAXIMUM $PAYOUT	PROFITS $BILLIONS			MAXIMUM $PAYOUT
–	<	1.25	0	6.50	<	6.75	6,500
1.25	<	1.50	1,250	6.75	<	7.00	6,750
1.50	<	1.75	1,500	7.00	<	7.25	7,000
1.75	<	2.00	1,750	7.25	<	7.50	7,250
2.00	<	2.25	2,000	7.50	<	7.75	7,500
2.25	<	2.50	2,250	7.75	<	8.00	7,750
2.50	<	2.75	2,500	8.00	<	8.25	8,000
2.75	<	3.00	2,750	8.25	<	8.50	8,250
3.00	<	3.25	3,000	8.50	<	8.75	8,500
3.25	<	3.50	3,250	8.75	<	9.00	8,750
3.50	<	3.75	3,500	9.00	<	9.25	9,000
3.75	<	4.00	3,750	9.25	<	9.50	9,250
4.00	<	4.25	4,000	9.50	<	9.75	9,500
4.25	<	4.50	4,250	9.75	<	10.00	9,750
4.50	<	4.75	4,500	10.00	<	10.25	10,000
4.75	<	5.00	4,750	10.25	<	10.50	10,250
5.00	<	5.25	5,000	10.50	<	10.75	10,500
5.25	<	5.50	5,250	10.75	<	11.00	10,750
5.50	<	5.75	5,500	11.00	<	11.25	11,000
5.75	<	6.00	5,750	11.25	<	11.50	11,250
6.00	<	6.25	6,000	11.50	<	11.75	11,500
6.25	<	6.50	6,250	11.75	<	12.00	11,750
				>		= 12.0	12,000

Note: Employees working 1,850 or more hours per year receive the maximum payout. Those working fewer hours receive a prorated payout based on their hours worked. Profits are defined as operating income (earnings before interest and taxes) for North America (only).

SOURCE: https://uaw.org/app/uploads/2015/10/64171_UAW-GM-Hourly-Highlights-Revp-11-final.pdf

and large private establishments participate in profit sharing plans, but only 1% of employees overall (about 6% of those in profit sharing plans) are in cash plans where profits are paid to employees during the current time period.[55]

Not only may profit sharing fail to increase performance motivation, but employees may also react very negatively when they learn that such plans do not pay out during business downturns.[56] First, they may not feel they are to blame because they have been performing their jobs well. Other factors are beyond their control, so why should they be penalized? Second, what seems like a small amount of at-risk pay for a manager earning $80,000 per year can be very painful to someone earning $15,000 or $20,000. As such, one theoretical advantage of profit sharing—that it makes labor costs variable and more in line with ability to pay—may not always be realized. A caveat is that making labor costs more variable (including downward) may be more feasible in companies that have been under financial duress and face serious long-term competitive challenges. An example would be the automobile industry. As we saw in the chapter opening, their recent performance has been strong, which has translated into high profit-sharing payments for employees. However, as we have also seen, salary increases (which become fixed costs) at the automobile companies have been rare in recent years.

Consider the case of the Du Pont Fibers Division, which had a plan that linked a portion of employees' pay to division profits.[57] After the plan's implementation, employees' base salary was about 4% lower than similar employees in other divisions unless 100% of the profit goal (a 4% increase over the previous year's profits) was reached. Thus, there was what might be called downside risk. However, there was also considerable upside opportunity: If 100% of the profit goal was exceeded, employees would earn more than similar employees in other divisions. For example, if the division reached 150% of the profit goal (6% growth in profits), employees would receive 12% more than comparable employees in other divisions.

Initially, the plan worked fine. The profit goal was exceeded, and employees earned slightly more than employees in other divisions. In the following year, however, profits were down 26%, and the profit goal was not met. Employees received no profit sharing bonus; instead, they earned 4% less than comparable employees in other divisions. Profit sharing was no longer seen as a very good idea. Du Pont management responded to employee concerns by eliminating the plan and returning to a system of fixed base salaries with no variable (or risk) component. This outcome is perhaps not surprising from an agency theory perspective, which suggests that employees must somehow be compensated to assume increased risk.

One solution some organizations choose is to design plans that have upside but not downside risk. In such cases, when a profit sharing plan is introduced, base pay is not reduced. Thus, when profits are high, employees share in the gain, but when profits are low, they are not penalized. Such plans largely eliminate what is purported to be a major advantage of profit sharing: reducing labor costs during business downturns. During business upturns, labor costs will increase. Given that the performance benefits of such plans are not assured, an organization runs the risk under such plans of increasing its labor costs with little return on its investment.

In summary, although profit sharing may be useful as one component of a compensation system (to enhance identification with broad organizational goals), it may need to be complemented with other pay programs that more closely link pay to outcomes that individuals or teams can control (or "own"), particularly in larger companies. In addition, profit sharing runs the risk of contributing to employee dissatisfaction or higher labor costs, depending on how it is designed. However, moving beyond concerns about its motivation impact, profit sharing does have the major advantage of making labor costs more variable, a major advantage when sales and profits decline.

Ownership (including stock options). Recent data show that in the neighborhood of 20 million Americans own stock in the companies for which they work.[58] Employee ownership is similar to profit sharing in some key respects, such as encouraging employees to focus on the success of the organization as a whole. In fact, with ownership, this focus may be even stronger. Like profit sharing, ownership may be less motivational the larger the organization. And because employees may not realize any financial gain until they actually sell their stock (typically upon leaving the organization), the link between pay and performance may be even less obvious than under profit sharing. Thus, from a reinforcement theory standpoint (with its emphasis on actually experiencing rewards), the effect on performance motivation may be limited.[59]

One way of achieving employee ownership is through **stock options**, which give employees the opportunity to buy stock at a fixed price. Say the employees receive options to purchase stock at $10 per share in 2016, and the stock price reaches $30 per share in 2021. They have the option of purchasing stock ("exercising" their stock options) at $10 per share in 2021, thus making a tidy return on investment if the shares are then sold. If the stock

Stock options
An employee ownership plan that gives employees the opportunity to buy the company's stock at a previously fixed price.

price goes down to $8 per share in the year 2021, however, there will be no financial gain. Therefore, employees are encouraged to act in ways that will benefit the organization.

For many years, stock options had typically been reserved for executives in larger, established companies. Then, there was a trend for some years toward pushing eligibility farther down in the organization.[60] In fact, many companies, including PepsiCo, Merck, McDonald's, Walmart, and Procter & Gamble, began granting stock options to employees at all levels. Among start-up companies like those in the technology sector, these broad-based stock option programs have long been popular and companies like Microsoft and Cisco Systems attribute much of their growth and success to these option plans. Some studies suggest that organization performance is higher when a large percentage of top and mid-level managers are eligible for long-term incentives such as stock options, which is consistent with agency theory's focus on the problem of encouraging managers to think like owners.[61] However, it is not clear whether these findings would hold up for lower-level employees, particularly in larger companies, who may see much less opportunity to influence overall organization performance. Another issue with options is whether executives and employees place sufficient value on them, given their cost.[62]

The Golden Age of stock options has faded some. Investors have long questioned the historically favorable tax treatment of employee stock options. In 2004, the Financial Accounting Standards Board (FASB) issued FAS 123R, a landmark change, requiring companies to expense options on their financial statements, which reduces reported net income, dramatically in some cases. Microsoft decided to eliminate stock options in favor of actual stock grants. This is partly in response to the new accounting standards and partly in recognition of the fact that Microsoft's stock price is not likely to grow as rapidly as it once did, making options less effective in recruiting, retaining, and motivating its employees. It appears that many companies are cutting back on stock options overall, and especially for nonexecutive employees.

Those companies that continue to use broad-based stock options have encountered difficulties in keeping employees motivated during years when there has been a steep decline in stock prices. For example, in 2009 Google's stock price dropped to $306, down from $741 in 2007, putting many employee stock options "underwater" (i.e., the stock price was under the option/exercise price), meaning that employees were not able to make any gain from exercising their options. Google's answer to this situation was an option exchange where employees turned in their underwater options in return for options having an exercise price equal to the current (lower) stock price. The hope was that employee motivation and retention would be reinvigorated.[63] The "Competing through Sustainability" box describes more recent examples of the use of stock option exchanges. As another example of the challenge in using stock-based compensation, one estimate was that (nonexecutive) employees of Facebook and of Zynga experienced declines in the value of their company stock and stock options of $7.2 billion and $1.4 billion, respectively, after initial public offerings of stock.[64] (Now, some years later, it seems like things have worked out OK for them!)

Employee stock ownership plan (ESOP)
An employee ownership plan that provides employers certain tax and financial advantages when stock is granted to employees.

Employee stock ownership plans (ESOPs), under which employers give employees stock in the company, are the most common form of employee ownership, with the number of employees in such plans increasing from 4 million in 1980 to about 14 million in 2017 in the United States.[65] Including non-ESOP stock option, stock purchase, and stock-based retirement plans, it is estimated that about 28 million U.S. employees own some portion of the companies for which they work, controlling about 8% of U.S. corporate equity. In Japan, most companies listed on Japanese stock markets have an ESOP, and these companies appear to have higher average productivity than non-ESOP companies.[66] ESOPs raise a number of unique issues. On the negative side, they can carry

COMPETING THROUGH SUSTAINABILITY

Using Stock Option Exchanges to Sustain Employee Motivation

During the dot.com bust in the early 2000s and again during the financial crisis of 2009, widespread drops in company stock market prices resulted in some investors losing a lot of money. It also resulted in employees in such companies seeing the value of their stock options plummet. As explained in this chapter, an employee stock option allows an employee to purchase stock in the company in the future at the option price, which is fixed, typically equal to the share price when the options are granted. For example, if the current share price is $100 and thus the option price is fixed at $100/share and the actual share price then later goes up to $150/share, an employee can sell each vested option and realize a gain of $150 − $100 = $50 on each share. The idea is that the employee will be motivated to do whatever he or she can to help the company succeed because the larger the ensuing increase in stock price, the more money the employee will make by exercising the option to buy the stock at the fixed price of $100.

However, the stock price does not go up in all companies, even when the overall stock market is doing well, as in recent years. In fact, the stock price in some companies will go down. When that happens, the ability of stock options to motivate employees also goes down. As a result, each year, some companies reprice employee stock options and/or use a stock option exchange where they sell their underwater

options (i.e., those where the option price is above the current stock price) and/or exchange them for new stock options having lower option prices and/or actual stock share ownership, which offer a better prospect to employees receiving gains from future increases in the stock price. Relying on underwater stock options is a particularly unsustainable compensation strategy in small companies, which tend to have lower base pay, which they offset with the prospect of employees making substantial gains through stock option programs. If the possibility of such gains disappears, so too may employees (to other firms that have higher salaries and/or better prospects for stock-based compensation gains).

For example, the stock price of Jive Software Inc. peaked at $27.16 in 2012. But several years later the stock price had fallen all the way to below $4. The result was that about one-quarter of employee stock options were underwater. Further, for employees holding options issued in 2012, the option price in some cases would be around $27. It is likely that an employee holding such options would not be terribly motivated by the possibility that the stock price would rise about $27 in the foreseeable future. As a consequence, Jive asked shareholders to approve an employee stock option exchange program.

Bryan LeBlanc, Jive's chief financial officer, put it this way: "We were looking for ways wherever we could to help the people who

were staying with Jive be as incented and motivated as possible." Understandably, shareholders may wonder why they don't get to have stock they bought at $27 a share that is now at $4 a share "repriced." Nevertheless, the majority of Jive's shareholders approved the exchange. As a result, nearly 80% of employee stock options were exchanged for restricted stock units that would vest over a two- year time period. The hope is that employees will once again be motivated to help the company succeed, resulting in the stock price going higher, something that would pay off for both employees and (other) shareholders.

DISCUSSION QUESTIONS

1. Given that employees can make a lot of money on stock options if the stock price increases (a large upside potential), shouldn't employees as part of that deal have to accept the downside risk (options that lose much of their value) when the stock price decreases? Explain.

2. What about nonemployee shareholders and options holders? Are there stock option (and/or stock) exchange programs to protect them from declines in the stock price? As an option or shareholder, how would you feel about a stock option exchange for employees?

SOURCE: A. Stewart, "More Firms Move to Reprice Options," *Wall Street Journal*, September 13, 2016.

significant risk for employees. An ESOP must, by law, invest at least 51% of assets in its company's stock, resulting in less diversification of investment risk (in some cases, no diversification). Consequently, when employees buy out companies in poor financial condition to save their jobs, or when the ESOP is used to fund pensions, employees risk serious financial difficulties if the company does poorly.[67] This is not just a concern for employees, because, as agency theory suggests, employees may require higher pay to offset increased risks of this sort.

ESOPs can be attractive to organizations because they have tax and financing advantages and can serve as a takeover defense (under the assumption that employee owners will be "friendly" to management). ESOPs give employees the right to vote their securities (if registered on a national exchange).[68] As such, some degree of participation in a select number of decisions is mandatory, but overall participation in decision making appears to vary significantly across organizations with ESOPs. Some studies suggest that the positive effects of ownership are larger in cases where employees have greater participation,[69] perhaps because the "employee–owner comes to psychologically experience his/her ownership in the organization."[70]

Gainsharing, Group Incentives, and Team Awards

Gainsharing
A form of group compensation based on group or plant performance (rather than organization-wide profits) that does not become part of the employee's base salary.

Gainsharing. **Gainsharing** programs offer a means of sharing productivity gains with employees. Although sometimes confused with profit sharing plans, gainsharing differs in two key respects. First, instead of using an organization-level performance measure (profits), the programs measure group or plant performance, which is likely to be seen as more controllable by employees. Second, payouts are distributed more frequently and not deferred. In a sense, gainsharing programs represent an effort to combine the best features of organization-oriented plans like profit sharing and individual-oriented plans like merit pay and individual incentives. Like profit sharing, gainsharing encourages pursuit of broader goals than individual-oriented plans do. But, unlike profit sharing, gainsharing can motivate employees much as individual plans do because of the more controllable nature of the performance measure and the frequency of payouts. Studies indicate that gainsharing improves performance.[71]

One type of gainsharing, the Scanlon plan (developed in the 1930s by Joseph N. Scanlon, president of a local union at Empire Steel and Tin Plant in Mansfield, Ohio), provides a monetary bonus to employees (and the organization) if the ratio of labor costs to the sales value of production is kept below a certain standard. Table 12.10 shows a modified (i.e., costs in addition to labor are included) Scanlon plan. Because actual costs ($850,000) were less than allowable costs ($907,500) in the first and second periods, there is a gain of $57,500. The organization receives 45% of the savings, and the employees receive the other 55%, although part of the employees' share is set aside in the event that actual costs exceed the standard in upcoming months (as Table 12.10 shows did occur).

Gainsharing plans like the Scanlon plan and pay-for-performance plans in general often encompass more than just a monetary component. There is often a strong emphasis on taking advantage of employee know-how to improve the production process through problem-solving teams and suggestion systems.[72] A number of recommendations have been made about the organization conditions that should be in place for gainsharing to succeed. Commonly mentioned factors include (1) management commitment, (2) a need to change or a strong commitment to continuous improvement, (3) management's acceptance and encouragement of employee input, (4) high levels of cooperation and interaction, (5) employment security, (6) information sharing on productivity and costs, (7) goal setting, (8) commitment of all involved parties to the process of change and

ITEMS	AVERAGE OF 1ST AND 2ND PERIODS	AVERAGE OF 2ND AND 3RD PERIODS
1. Sales in dollars	$1,000,000	$1,000,000
2. Inventory change and work in process	100,000	100,000
3. Sales value of production	1,100,000	1,100,000
4. Allowable costs (82.5% × 3 above)	907,500	907,500
5. Actual costs	850,000	917,500
6. Gain (4–5 above)	57,500	−10,000
7. Employee share (55% of 6 above)	31,625	−5,500
8. Monthly reserve (20% of 7 above)*	6,325	−5,500
9. Bonus to be distributed (7–8)	25,300	0
10. Company share (45% of 6 above)	25,875	−4,500
11. Participating payroll	132,000	132,000
12. Bonus percentage (9/11)	19.2%	0.0%
13. Monthly reserve (8 above)	$6,325	−$5,500
14. Reserve at the end of last period	0	6,325
15. Year-end reserve to date	6,325	825

Table 12.10
Example of Gainsharing (Modified Scanlon Plan) Report

*If no bonus, 100% of 7 above
SOURCE: From *Gainsharing and Goalsharing: Aligning Pay and Strategic Goals,* by K. Mericle and D. O. Kim. Reproduced with permission of Greenwood Publishing Group via Copyright Clearance Center.

improvement, and (9) agreement on a performance standard and calculation that is understandable, seen as fair, and closely related to managerial objectives.[73]

Group Incentives and Team Awards. Whereas gainsharing plans are often plant-wide, group incentives and team awards typically pertain to a smaller work group.[74] Group incentives (like individual incentives) tend to measure performance in terms of physical output, whereas team award plans may use a broader range of performance measures (like cost savings, successful completion of product design, or meeting deadlines). As with individual incentive plans, these plans have a number of potential drawbacks. Competition between individuals may be reduced, but it may be replaced by competition between groups or teams. Also, consistent with our earlier discussion of pay effects on workforce composition, any plan that does not adequately recognize differences in individual performance risks demotivating top performers or losing them. Finally, as with any incentive plan, a standard-setting process must be developed that is seen as fair by employees, and these standards must not exclude important dimensions such as quality.

Balanced Scorecard

As the preceding discussion indicates, every pay program has advantages and disadvantages. Therefore, rather than choosing one program, some companies find it useful to design a mix of pay programs, one that has just the right chemistry for the situation at hand. Relying exclusively on merit pay or individual incentives may result in high levels

LO 12-4
Describe how organizations combine incentive plans in a balanced scorecard.

Table 12.11

Illustration of Balanced Scorecard Incentive Concept

PERFORMANCE MEASURE	TARGET INCENTIVE	INCENTIVE SCHEDULE		ACTUAL PERFORMANCE	INCENTIVE EARNED
		PERFORMANCE	% TARGET		
Financial • Return on capital employed	$100	20% + 16–20 12–16 Below 12	150 100 50 0	18%	$100
Customer • Product returns	$ 40	1 in: 1,000 + 900–999 800–899 Below 800	150 100 50 0	1 in 876	$ 20
Internal • Cycle time reduction (%)	$ 30	9% + 6–9 3–6 0–3	150 100 50 0	11%	$ 45
Learning and growth • Voluntary employee turnover	$ 30	Below 5% 5–8 8–12	150 100 50	7%	$ 30
Total	$200				$195

SOURCE: From F. C. McKenzie and M. P. Shilling, "Avoiding Performance Traps: Ensuring Effective Incentive Design and Implementation," *Compensation and Benefits Review,* July–August 1998, pp. 57–65. *Compensation and Benefits Review by American Management Association.* Reproduced with permission of Sage Publications, Inc. via Copyright Clearance Center.

of work motivation but unacceptable levels of individualistic and competitive behavior and too little concern for broader plant or organization goals. Relying too heavily on profit sharing and gainsharing plans may increase cooperation and concern for the welfare of the entire plant or organization, but it may reduce individual work motivation to unacceptable levels. However, a particular mix of merit pay, gainsharing, and profit sharing could contribute to acceptable performance on all these performance dimensions.

One approach that seeks to balance multiple objectives is the balanced scorecard (see Chapter 1), which Kaplan and Norton describe as a way for companies to "track financial results while simultaneously monitoring progress in building the capabilities and acquiring the intangible assets they would need for future growth."[75]

Table 12.11 shows how a mix of measures might be used by a manufacturing firm to motivate improvements in a balanced set of key business drivers. We will also see shortly a scorecard used by Merck.

Managerial and Executive Pay

LO 12-5
Discuss issues related to performance-based pay for executives.

Because of their significant ability to influence organization performance, top managers and executives are a strategically important group whose compensation warrants special attention, including its competitiveness in the labor market.[76] In Chapter 11 we discussed how much this group is paid. Here we focus on the issue of how their pay is determined.

Business magazines such as *Forbes* and *Bloomberg Businessweek* often publish lists of top executives who did the most for their pay and those who did the least. The latter group has been the impetus for much of the attention to executive pay. The problem seems to be that in some companies, top executive pay is high every year, regardless of profitability or stock market performance. One study, for example, found that CEO pay changes by $3.25 for every $1,000 change in shareholder wealth. Although this relationship was interpreted to mean that "the compensation of top executives is virtually independent of corporate performance," later work demonstrates, to the contrary, that executive pay, in most companies, is significantly aligned with shareholder return.[77]

How can executive pay be linked to organization performance? From an agency theory perspective, the goal of owners (shareholders) is to encourage the agents (managers and executives) to act in the best interests of the owners. This may mean less emphasis on noncontingent pay, such as base salary, and more emphasis on outcome-oriented "contracts" that make some portion of executive pay contingent on the organization's profitability or stock performance.[78] Among mid-level and top managers, it is common to use both short-term bonus and long-term incentive plans to encourage the pursuit of both short- and long-term organization performance objectives. Indeed, the bulk of executive compensation comes from restricted stock, stock options, and other forms of long-term compensation. Putting pay "at risk" in this manner can be a strong incentive. However, agency theory suggests that while too little pay at risk may weaken the incentive effect, too much pay at risk can also be a problem if executives take excessive risks with firm assets.[79] The banking and mortgage industry problems of late provide an example.

Organizations use such pay-for-performance plans, and what are their consequences? Research suggests that organizations vary substantially in the extent to which they use both long-term and short-term incentive programs. Further, greater use of such plans among top and mid-level managers is associated with higher subsequent levels of profitability. As Table 12.12 indicates, greater reliance on short-term bonuses and long-term incentives (relative to base pay) resulted in substantial improvements in return on assets.[80] For top executives, aligning compensation with past shareholder return is associated with his or her future shareholder returns.[81]

Earlier, we saw how the balanced scorecard approach could be applied to paying manufacturing employees. It is also useful in designing executive pay. Table 12.13 shows how the choice of performance measures can be guided by a desire to balance shareholder, customer, and employee objectives. Financial results can be seen as a lagging

Table 12.12
The Relationship between Managerial Pay and Organization Return on Assets

BONUS/BASE RATIO	LONG-TERM INCENTIVE ELIGIBILITY	PREDICTED RETURN ON ASSETS %	PREDICTED RETURN ON ASSETS $[a]
10%	28%	5.2%	$250 million
20	28	5.6	269 million
10	48	5.9	283 million
20	48	7.1	341 million

[a]Based on the assets of the average *Fortune* 500 company in 1990.
SOURCE: B. Gerhart and G. T. Milkovich, "Organizational Differences in Managerial Compensation and Financial Performance," *Academy of Management Journal* 33 (1990), pp. 663–91.

Table 12.13
Merck Performance (Balanced) Scorecard, Chief Executive Officer

	TARGET POINTS
Financial Revenue vs. plan Earnings per share vs. plan Value of growth (e.g., ROI vs. plan)	60
Customer Merck customer service level (% orders delivered on time) Merck Trust & Value Customer Survey	14
Key Business Drivers Cost structure (operating expense vs. plan) Revenue growth in high-priority areas	16
Culture (high performance, sustainable) Employee Culture Survey	10
Total	100

SOURCE: Proxy Statement, Merck & Co., Inc., April 14, 2014, www.merck.com/finance/proxy/pr2014.pdf.

indicator that tells the company how it has done in the past, whereas customer and employee metrics like those in Table 12.13, used by Merck, are leading indicators that tell the company how its financial results will be in the future. Importantly, empirical research should be conducted in each company to validate these or other hypothesized leading indicators of financial performance.[82]

As we saw in the global financial crisis, a focus on only (aggressive) financial goals, without also considering how those goals are achieved, raises the danger that executives and others will take too great a risk and/or engage in unethical behavior to achieve those objectives. These behaviors can do great harm to the company over time. A scorecard used by Citigroup for its top 50 executives had a weight of 70% toward financial objectives (profitability, expense management, use of capital, risk) and 30% toward nonfinancial (in the short-term) objectives (setting strategic direction; having strong risk and controls management and strong personnel management; enhancing relations with external stakeholders, including shareholders). The highest possible performance score was 100%, whereas the lowest was minus 40%. The hope is that by linking pay incentives to this broader set of performance objectives, not just to financial goals as in the past, Citigroup will achieve better financial performance over time and achieve it in a less risky manner. Nobody wants to go through another financial industry meltdown, and this is one part of the plan to avoid that. Similarly, but using more pointed language, Volkswagen recently changed the way it pays its executives in response to a major (and costly) scandal that it hopes to avoid repeating in the future. (See the "Integrity in Action" box.)

Finally, there is pressure from regulators and shareholders to better link pay and performance. The U.S. Securities and Exchange Commission (SEC) requires companies to report compensation levels for the five highest-paid executives and the company's performance relative to that of competitors over a five-year period. In 2006, the SEC put additional rules into effect that require better disclosure of the value of executive perquisites and retirement benefits. In 2010, the Dodd-Frank Wall Street Reform and Consumer Protection Act was signed into law in the United States. Although its focus is primarily on financial institutions, Dodd-Frank added Section 14A to the Securities and Exchange, which added new requirements for public companies

INTEGRITY IN ACTION

Volkswagen Changes How It Pays

Volkswagen (VW) has an integrity problem. Volkswagen was discovered to have installed software that sensed when an engine was being tested for emissions and (temporarily) reduced emissions to a level that would pass the test. In actual driving conditions, however, VW diesel engines emitted emissions up to 40 times the legal limit. VW's marketing campaign had emphasized the wonder of the diesel engine's performance combined with environmental benefits, even though it was not true. That campaign in turn was a vital part of VW's Strategy 2018 growth plan to bypass General Motors and Toyota to become the world's largest automaker. Employees were subjected to tremendous pressure and intimidation from the top cascading down to every level to do whatever was necessary to achieve this growth goal (and keep their jobs). This apparently included engineers "willing to commit crimes to defraud the public."

As a result of this scandal, multiple legal actions have been brought against the company. VW has entered into settlements of civil lawsuits brought by drivers who found themselves stuck with noncompliant vehicles. This includes the largest U.S. class action settlement ever. The company has also paid criminal fines that together total nearly $25 billion (so far).

In an effort to avoid such problems in the future and to "quell investor ire" that executives earned large bonuses (despite their role in the scandal and large VW losses), the company is changing the way it pays. No bonuses will be paid in the future if certain financial objectives are not met. Base salary will be increased 30%, but the total amount of base salary plus bonus that an executive can receive will now be capped at $10 million for the CEO and $5.5 million for other board members. Also, for the

first time, executives will be given company stock, presumably in an effort to better align their interests with those of shareholders. It appears that this stock-based compensation is not subject to the caps. Thus, if shareholders do well, executives can still do quite well.

DISCUSSION QUESTIONS

1. What caused the Volkswagen scandal? What can you infer about the nature of its former pay strategy and the role it may have played?
2. Consider Volkswagen's revised pay strategy. How well do you think it will succeed going forward? Do you have suggestions for other changes? Explain.

SOURCES: W. Boston, "VW Revamps Pay, Imposes Caps," *Wall Street Journal*, February 25/26, 2017; S. Randazzo, "U.S. Court Gives Initial Approval to Volkswagen Vehicle Emissions Settlement," *Wall Street Journal*, February 14, 2017; J. Rothfeder, "The Volkswagen Settlement: How Bad Management Leads to Big Punishment," *The New Yorker*, July 1, 2016.

broadly.[83] For example, it requires that shareholders have a "say on pay," meaning that they have the right to a (nonbinding) vote on executive pay plans. Dodd-Frank also requires that firms disclose the ratio of the pay of the top executive to that of rank-and-file employees. Companies, under pressure from regulators and investors, have also increasingly adopted policies that allow them to clawback (i.e., get back) compensation paid to executives who are later found to have increased their pay by engaging in behaviors detrimental to companies and the economy.

Regulators in a number of countries have also sought to limit the size of bonus payments in hopes of reducing the incentive to engage in behaviors such as excessive risk taking, which have proved detrimental in the past.[84] Large retirement fund investors such as TIAA-CREF and CalPERS have proposed guidelines to better ensure that boards of directors act in shareholders' best interests when making executive pay decisions, rather than being beholden to management. Some of the governance practices believed to be related to director independence from management (Dodd-Frank has similar provisions)

Table 12.14
Guidelines for Board of Directors Independence and Leadership

1. **Majority of independent directors:** At a minimum, a majority of the board consists of directors who are independent. Boards should strive to obtain board composition made up of a substantial majority of independent directors.
2. **Independent executive session:** Independent directors meet periodically (at least once a year) alone in an executive session, without the CEO. The independent board chair or lead (or presiding) independent director should preside over this meeting.
3. **Independent director definition:** Each company should disclose in its annual proxy statement the definition of "independence" relied upon by its board.
4. **Independent board chairperson:** The board should be chaired by an independent director. The CEO and chair roles should only be combined in very limited circumstances; in these situations, the board should provide a written statement in the proxy materials discussing why the combined role is in the best interest of shareowners, and it should name a lead independent director to fulfill duties that are consistent with those provided in other company material.
5. **Examine separate chair/CEO positions:** When selecting a new chief executive officer, boards should reexamine the traditional combination of the "chief executive" and "chair" positions.
6. **Board role of retiring CEO:** Generally, a company's retiring CEO should not continue to serve as a director on the board and at the very least be prohibited from sitting on any of the board committees.
7. **Board access to management:** The board should have a process in place by which all directors can have access to senior management.
8. **Independent board committees:** Committees that perform the audit, director nomination, and executive compensation functions should consist entirely of independent directors.
9. **Board oversight:** The full board is responsible for the oversight function on behalf of shareowners. Should the board decide to have other committees (e.g., executive committee) in addition to those required by law, the duties and membership of such committees should be fully disclosed.
10. **Board resources:** The board, through its committees, should have access to adequate resources to provide independent counsel advice, or other tools that allow the board to effectively perform its duties on behalf of shareowners.

SOURCE: The California Public Employees Retirement System, "Global Principles of Accountable Corporate Governance," August 18, 2008.

are shown in Table 12.14. More detailed analyses of board governance practices are available from Institutional Shareholder Services.[85] In addition, when a firm's future is at risk, the board may well need to demonstrate its independence from management by taking dramatic action, which may include removing the chief executive.

Process and Context Issues

LO 12-6
Explain the importance of process issues such as communication in compensation management.

In Chapter 11 we discussed the importance of process issues such as communication and employee participation. Earlier in the present chapter we discussed the importance of fairness, both distributive and procedural. Significant differences in how such issues are handled can be found both across and within organizations, suggesting that organizations have considerable discretion in this aspect of compensation management.[86] As such, it represents another strategic opportunity to distinguish one's organization from the competition.

EMPLOYEE PARTICIPATION IN DECISION MAKING

Consider employee participation in decision making and its potential consequences. Involvement in the design and implementation of pay policies has been linked to higher pay satisfaction and job satisfaction, presumably because employees have a better understanding of and greater commitment to the policy when they are involved.[87]

What about the effects on productivity? Agency theory provides some insight. The delegation of decision making by a principal to an agent creates agency costs because employees may not act in the best interests of top management. In addition, the more agents there are, the higher the monitoring costs.[88] Together, these issues suggest that delegation of decision making can be very costly.

However, agency theory suggests that monitoring would be less costly and more effective if performed by employees because they have knowledge about the workplace and behavior of fellow employees that managers do not have. As such, the right compensation system might encourage self-monitoring and peer monitoring.[89] Researchers have suggested that two general factors are critical to encouraging such monitoring: monetary incentives (outcome-oriented contracts in agency theory) and an environment that fosters trust and cooperation. This environment, in turn, is a function of employment security, group cohesiveness, and individual rights for employees—in other words, respect for and commitment to employees.[90]

In any case, a survey of organizations found that only 11% of employees always or often participated in compensation design teams. Participation by managers was better, but still the exception (32%).[91]

COMMUNICATION

Another important process issue is communication.[92] Earlier, we spoke of its importance in the administration of merit pay, both from the perspective of procedural fairness and as a means of obtaining the maximum impact from a merit pay program.[93] More generally, a change in any part of the compensation system is likely to give rise to employee concerns. Rumors and assumptions based on poor or incomplete information are always an issue in administering compensation, partly because of its importance to employee economic security and well-being. Therefore, in making any changes, it is crucial to determine how best to communicate reasons for the changes to employees. Some organizations rely on video messages from the chief executive officer to communicate the rationale for major changes. Brochures and/or websites that include scenarios for typical employees are sometimes used, as are focus group sessions in which small groups of employees are interviewed to obtain feedback about concerns that can be addressed in later communication programs. Ultimately, however, most pay-related communications come through individual discussions with one's supervisor, still ahead of the company website, e-mail, and discussions with the human resource department.[94]

PAY AND PROCESS: INTERTWINED EFFECTS

The preceding discussion treats process issues such as participation as factors that may facilitate the success of pay programs. At least one commentator, however, has described an even more important role for process factors in determining employee performance:

> Worker participation apparently helps make alternative compensation plans . . . work better—and also has beneficial effects of its own . . . . It appears that changing the way workers are treated may boost productivity more than changing the way they are paid.[95]

This suggestion raises a broader question: How important are pay decisions, per se, relative to other human resource practices? Although it may not be terribly useful to attempt to disentangle closely intertwined programs, it is important to reinforce the notion that human resource programs, even those as powerful as compensation systems, do not work alone.

Consider gainsharing programs. As described earlier, pay is often only one component of such programs. (See Table 12.10.) How important are the nonpay components?[96] There is ample evidence that gainsharing programs that rely almost exclusively on the monetary component can have substantial effects on productivity.[97] However, a study of an automotive parts plant found that adding a participation component (monthly meetings with management to discuss the gainsharing plan and ways to increase productivity) to a gainsharing pay incentive plan raised productivity. In a related study, employees were asked about the factors that motivated them to engage in active participation (such as suggestion systems). Employees reported that the desire to earn a monetary bonus was much less important than a number of nonpay factors, particularly the desire for influence and control in how their work was done.[98] A third study reported that both productivity and profitability were enhanced by the addition of employee participation in decisions, beyond the improvement derived from monetary incentives such as gainsharing.[99]

Organization Strategy and Compensation Strategy: A Question of Fit

LO 12-7
List the major factors to consider in matching the pay strategy to the organization's strategy.

Although much of our focus has been on the general, or average, effects of different pay programs, it is also useful to think in terms of matching pay strategies to organization strategies.[100] To take an example from medicine, using the same medical treatment regardless of the symptoms and diagnosis would be odd. Likewise, in choosing a pay strategy, one must consider how effectively it will further the organization's overall business strategy. Consider again the findings reported in Table 12.12. The average effect of moving from a pay strategy with below-average variability in pay to one with above-average variability is an increase in return on assets of almost two percentage points (from 5.2% to 7.1%). But in some organizations, the increase could be smaller. In fact, greater variability in pay could contribute to a lower return on assets in some organizations. In other organizations, greater variability in pay could contribute to increases in return on assets of greater than two percentage points. Obviously, being able to tell where variable pay works and where it does not could have substantial consequences.

Of course, as this chapter and Chapter 11 suggest, certain best practices may be of benefit to all or at least most organizations. Returning to our medical analogy, scientific consensus seems to be that certain behaviors (e.g., exercise, good nutrition) enhance health, whereas others (e.g., smoking, drugs, alcohol) harm health. So, too, there may be best practices when it comes to compensation strategy. Examples include choosing a pay level that balances the ability to compete in the product market and in the labor market, paying for performance to obtain positive incentive and sorting effects, paying attention to both distributive (e.g., equity theory) and procedural justice issues, and complying with regulatory requirements.

Returning to how to approach the issue of fit, recall that in Chapter 2 we discussed directional business strategies, two of which were growth (internal or external) and concentration ("sticking to the knitting"). How should compensation strategies differ according to whether an organization follows a growth strategy or a concentration strategy? Table 12.15 provides some suggested matches. Basically, a growth strategy's emphasis

PAY STRATEGY DIMENSIONS	ORGANIZATION STRATEGY	
	CONCENTRATION	GROWTH
Risk sharing (variable pay)	Low	High
Time orientation	Short term	Long term
Pay level (short run)	Above market	Below market
Pay level (long-run potential)	Below market	Above market
Benefits level	Above market	Below market
Centralization of pay decisions	Centralized	Decentralized
Pay unit of analysis	Job	Skills

Table 12.15
Matching Pay Strategy and Organization Strategy

SOURCES: L. R. Gomez-Mejia and D. B. Balkin, *Compensation, Organizational Strategy, and Firm Performance* (Cincinnati, OH: South-Western, 1992), Appendix 4b; and L. R. Gomez-Mejia, P. Berrone, and M. Franco-Santos. *Compensation and Organizational Performance* (Armonk, NY: M.E. Sharpe 2010), Appendix 3.2.

on innovation, risk taking, and new markets is linked to a pay strategy that shares risk with employees but also gives them the opportunity for high future earnings by having them share in whatever success the organization has.[101] This means relatively low levels of fixed compensation in the short run but the use of bonuses and stock options, for example, that can pay off handsomely in the long run. Stock options have been described as the pay program "that built Silicon Valley," having been used by companies such as Apple, Microsoft, and others.[102] When such companies become successful, everyone from top managers to secretaries can become millionaires if they own stock. Growth organizations are also thought to benefit from a less bureaucratic orientation, in the sense of having more decentralization and flexibility in pay decisions and in recognizing individual skills, rather than being constrained by job or grade classification systems. By contrast, concentration-oriented organizations are thought to require a very different set of pay practices by virtue of their lower rate of growth, more stable workforce, and greater need for consistency and standardization in pay decisions. As noted earlier, Microsoft has eliminated stock options in favor of stock grants to its employees, in part because it is not the growth company it once was.

 A LOOK BACK

Pay for Performance: Balancing Objectives (and Risks)

In this chapter, we discussed the potential advantages and disadvantages of different types of incentive or pay-for-performance plans. We saw that these pay plans can have both intended and unintended consequences. We also saw that some organizations have paid a big price for not realizing the problems with their pay plans until it was too late and only then did they change them. (See also "Exercising Strategy" at the end of the chapter.) Designing a pay-for-performance strategy typically seeks to balance the pros and cons of different plans and reduce the chance of unintended consequences. To an important degree, pay strategy will depend on the particular goals and strategy of the organization and its units. At the beginning of this chapter, we saw that many organizations are working to link pay to performance and reduce fixed labor costs.

QUESTIONS

1. Does money motivate? Use the theories and examples discussed in this chapter to address this question.
2. Think of a job that you have held. Design an incentive plan. What would be the potential advantages and disadvantages of your plan? If your money was invested in the company, would you adopt the plan?

SUMMARY

Our focus in this chapter has been on the design and administration of programs that recognize employee contributions to the organization's success. These programs vary as to whether they link pay to individual, group, or organization performance. Often, it is not so much a choice of one program or the other as it is a choice between different combinations of programs that seek to balance individual, group, and organization objectives.

Wages, bonuses, and other types of pay have an important influence on an employee's standard of living. This carries at least two important implications. First, pay can be a powerful motivator. An effective pay strategy can substantially promote an organization's success; conversely, a poorly conceived pay strategy can have detrimental effects. Second,

the importance of pay means that employees care a great deal about the fairness of the pay process. A recurring theme is that pay programs must be explained and administered in such a way that employees understand their underlying rationale and believe they are fair.

The fact that organizations differ in their business and human resource strategies suggests that the most effective compensation strategy may differ from one organization to another. Although benchmarking programs against the competition is informative, what succeeds in some organizations may not be a good idea for others. The balanced scorecard suggests the need for organizations to decide what their key objectives are and use pay to support them.

KEY TERMS

Incentive effect, 506
Expectancy theory, 507
Principal, 508
Agent, 508
Sorting effect, 509

Merit pay, 514
Merit bonus, 514
Merit increase
   grid, 514
Profit sharing, 519

Stock options, 521
Employee stock ownership plan
   (ESOP), 522
Gainsharing, 524

DISCUSSION QUESTIONS

1. To compete more effectively, your organization is considering a profit sharing plan to increase employee effort and to encourage employees to think like owners. What are the potential advantages and disadvantages of such a plan? Would the profit sharing plan have the same impact on all types of employees? Is the size of your organization an important consideration? Why? What alternative pay programs should be considered?
2. Gainsharing plans have often been used in manufacturing settings but can also be applied in service organizations. How could performance standards be developed for

gainsharing plans in hospitals, banks, insurance companies, and so forth?
3. Your organization has two business units. One unit is a long-established manufacturer of a product that competes on price and has not been subject to many technological innovations. The other business unit is just being started. It has no products yet, but it is working on developing a new technology for testing the effects of drugs on people via simulation instead of through lengthy clinical trials. Would you recommend that the two business units have the same pay programs for recognizing individual contributions? Why?

4. Throughout the chapter, we have seen many examples of companies making changes to how they pay for performance. Do you believe the changes at these companies make sense? What are the potential payoffs and pitfalls of their new pay strategies?

SELF-ASSESSMENT EXERCISE

connect

Additional assignable self-assessments available in Connect.

Pay is only one type of incentive that can motivate you to perform well and contribute to your satisfaction at work. This survey will help you understand what motivates you at work. Consider each aspect of work and rate its importance to you, using the following scale: 5 = very important, 4 = somewhat important, 3 = neutral, 2 = somewhat unimportant, 1 = very unimportant.

Work environment	1	2	3	4	5
Level of independence in job	1	2	3	4	5
Level of teamwork required for job	1	2	3	4	5
Other (enter your own):					
_____	1	2	3	4	5
_____	1	2	3	4	5
_____	1	2	3	4	5

Salary or wages	1	2	3	4	5
Cash bonuses	1	2	3	4	5
Boss's management style	1	2	3	4	5
Location of workplace	1	2	3	4	5
Commute	1	2	3	4	5
Job security	1	2	3	4	5
Opportunity for advancement	1	2	3	4	5

Which aspects of work received a score of 5? A score of 4? These are the ones you believe motivate you to perform well and make you happy in your job. Which aspects of work received a score of 1 or 2? These are least likely to motivate you. Is pay the only way to motivate you?

SOURCE: Based on the "Job Assessor" found at www.salarymonster.com, accessed August 2002.

EXERCISING STRATEGY

Pay and Strategy Execution at Wells Fargo: Incentives Gone Awry

Wells Fargo has been ordered to pay a fine of $185 million to the U.S. government and the City and County of Los Angeles for creating "fake" accounts for customers who did not ask for the accounts. As we saw in the opening of our earlier Chapter 10, that was an unintended consequence of the push by Wells Fargo to grow revenue by cross-selling (e.g., getting a checking account holder to take a new credit card). It also reached a settlement, perhaps the first of many, of $110 million with Wells Fargo customers over the same issues. It appears that the fake accounts were created so that Wells Fargo employees could meet their sales targets. That, in turn, would allow them to keep their jobs and in some cases earn large bonuses.

As we saw in the case of Volkswagen, these unethical actions appear to have been a result of pressure from the top to grow the company. One employee described the culture at the bank as "cross-sell, cross-sell, cross-sell." Cross-selling refers to the practice of asking existing customers to open another account (e.g., a checking account, a new credit card, a home loan, or a line of credit). During one big push to increase sales called "Jump into January," employees were pressured to sell 20 products a day. The environment was described as "soul crushing" and one in which everyone was "miserable." If you did not sell enough, you would be fired. Another employee said that managers did not directly ask him to deceive customers but instead would repeatedly ask, "Where are you at? How are you gonna get there?" But, if you hit your numbers, you did not get those questions. Some former employees reported that one way to hit your numbers was to include extra forms in a transaction to open a requested account. For example, if a customer was applying for a home loan, the banker would include a form for a line of credit and hope the customer would not notice when signing all the papers.

According to New York Federal Reserve President Bill Dudley, the "widespread fraud" at Wells Fargo shows the "powerful role—for good or bad—that incentives can play." He compared what happened at Wells Fargo to how compensation systems helped cause the mortgage crisis and financial crisis of several years ago. Wells Fargo reports that it is now changing its compensation plan away from a focus on cross-selling as many banking products as possible to a focus on customer service, customer usage, and growth in primary balances.

QUESTIONS

1. Have you experienced cross-selling as a bank customer? What was your reaction? What would your reaction be if the bank opened a line of credit for you that you did not want?
2. How is what happened at Wells Fargo similar to what happened at Volkswagen? (See the "Integrity in Action" box, earlier in this chapter.)
3. What caused the problems at Wells Fargo, and how can they be fixed? How helpful will the new compensation plan be in fixing things? Why?

SOURCES: E. Glazer, "Wells Fargo to Roll Out New Compensation Plan to Replace Sales Goals: Bankers Say Previous Lofty Goals Pushed Them to Open Accounts without Customers' Knowledge," *Wall Street Journal,* January 6, 2017; B. Chappell, "Wells Fargo Fined $185 Million over Creation of Fake Accounts for Bonuses," National Public Radio. September 8, 2016; M. Egan. "Wells Fargo Customers in $110 Million Settlement over Fake Accounts," CNNMoney.com, March 29, 2017; C. Arnold, "Former Wells Fargo Employees Describe Toxic Sales Culture, Even at HQ," National Public Radio, October 4, 2016; M. Egan, "Top Fed Official Likens Wells Fargo Fraud to Mortgage Crisis," CNNMoney.com, March 21, 2017.

MANAGING PEOPLE

ESOPs: Who Benefits?

Mandy Cabot wants to make sure the shoemaking business that she and her husband built over the past 20 years remains in good hands after they're gone. The 58-year-old co-founder of Dansko, a West Grove, PA, company with more than $150 million in annual sales, says she fears that selling to a competitor, or a private-equity firm, would result in layoffs or other cost-cutting measures.

So last February, the couple transferred ownership of the business to its 180 employees. By "keeping it in the family" and giving workers a real stake in its future, Ms. Cabot says she hopes the company will keep going strong for years to come. "This is our baby, but at some point we have to cease being parents and become grandparents," she adds.

Ms. Cabot, who launched Dansko in 1990 by selling shoes from the back of a Volvo station wagon, says the tax benefits associated with employee stock ownership enabled the S corporation to manage the long-term debt of buying out the couple's ownership stake. But, she adds, "It's not some tax dodge."

Known as employee stock-ownership plans, or ESOPs, the move is being embraced by smaller firms, especially those struggling to find buyers during the weak economy. Under typical plans, an owner's interest in a business is bought out, in part or in whole—often through a bank loan—with the stock being held in trust. Employees then cash in their shares as they retire.

Michael Keeling, president of the ESOP Association, a Washington lobby group, argues, "A company's success isn't just driven by the brilliance of the CEO, but also by its employees, and more owners feel [their employees] deserve something more for that."

This week, a bipartisan group of lawmakers introduced a bill to encourage employee-ownership plans. But critics of the plans say owners who are looking for an easy exit are simply spreading the risks of business ownership by convincing employees to gamble their retirement savings. Andrew Stumpff, University of Michigan, says it's bad enough to risk your retirement savings in a single company. But it's even worse if that company is your employer, he says. "If the company fails, you lose your savings and your job." That risk is very real, he adds, citing Enron, WorldCom and Lehman Brothers as examples of high-profile failures at shared-ownership companies, especially Enron Corp. where workers lost their savings.

The real attraction for owners, opponents say, is generous tax breaks that shelter capital gains and dividends tied to the plans.

As of 2011, there were an estimated 10,900 employee-owned businesses across the country, a 12% increase from 2007 and a record high dating back to the mid-1970s, when the plans first appeared, according to the National Center for Employee Ownership. Nearly all of the employee-owned businesses have fewer than 500 workers. Some 10 million employees are currently enrolled in these plans, representing more than $860 billion in assets, the group estimates.

Norman Stein, Drexel University, says employee ownership under the ESOP model causes more harm than good. Many of the plans are based on a bloated assessment of the value of the businesses. Many workers who are participating in the plans are left holding overvalued shares, long after the original owner has cashed out: "I'm not against employees owning some stock in their employer, but not if it's tied to a retirement plan," he says. "It's a troubling trend."

Separate studies by Harvard University and Rutgers, as well as by the National Bureau of Economic Research, have found that businesses with shared-ownership plans fared better during the recession than more traditionally structured firms, including fewer layoffs, higher productivity and stronger employee loyalty.

Dawn Huston, 31, started working at Dansko 11 years ago, sorting shoes for delivery. Now a warehouse processor, she says the idea of owning a piece of the company made her nervous at first—though she wasn't worried about her retirement savings, since the company offers a separate 401(k) plan, she adds. Over the past year, she's begun referring to Dansko as "our company." "I feel like they consider us family and it feels like a family," she says of the switch to employee ownership.

Adele Connors, 60, co-founder of Adworkshop, a Lake Placid, NY, marketing agency, says a move to employee ownership "really changed the culture of our company" with workers now being "more engaged." Kelly Frady, 43, an account supervisor at Adworkshop, says the agency's employee-ownership plan has fostered a team spirit among its staff. "Everyone knows that you do well and your stock will rise," she says. "It's a driving factor in making the company succeed in the long term."

Kim Jordan, who co-founded the New Belgium Brewing Co. with her husband in 1991, says employee ownership ensures that the company's values and culture will remain intact—including its commitment to sustainable farming and an environmentally friendly production process. In December, she extended full ownership of the Fort Collins, CO, brewery to its 480 employees.

"We've always tried to involve our people in the running of the business," she says. The goal, she says, isn't just to reward employees, but also to foster innovation by creating a company culture where workers think more like entrepreneurs.

QUESTIONS

1. Is an ESOP good for employees? Why or why not?
2. Does an ESOP motivate employees "better"? Explain the reasons for your answer.
3. What happens to employees' retirement income if they are at an ESOP company that runs into financial problems? What happens to the same employees, if instead, they work at a non-ESOP company that runs into financial problems?

SOURCE: Angus Loten, "Founders Cash Out, but Do Workers Gain?" *Wall Street Journal*, April 17, 2013.

HR IN SMALL BUSINESS

Employees Own Bob's Red Mill

Headquartered in Portland, Oregon, Bob's Red Mill Natural Foods sells a variety of whole-grain flours and mixes, specializing in gluten-free products. The "Bob" of the company's name is Bob Moore, the founder and president. In 2010, more than 30 years after he started the business, Moore called his 200 employees together and announced that he was giving them the company. As a retirement plan for them, he had set up an employee stock ownership plan, placing the company's stock in a trust fund. All employees who had been with the company at least three years were immediately fully vested in the plan. As employees retire, they will receive cash for their shares.

Watching the company's stock rise in their retirement plan is not the only financial incentive for employees of Bob's Red Mill. In the mid-1990s, the company established a profit sharing plan. The chief financial officer gives employees a weekly sales update, which they can use to estimate profits and determine their share.

The numbers have been mostly good during the past two decades. When John Wagner, chief financial officer, joined the company in 1993, there were just 28 employees generating sales of $3.2 million. Under Wagner's guidance, the company began participating in trade shows, attracting the interest of health food stores, food distributors, and later on, supermarket chains. The company's market expanded from a few states to cover North America and some international markets. The company reports that its revenues have grown at rates between 20% and 30% in the years since 2004.

Along the way, Moore and his employees have been unwavering in their dedication to the company and its mission of providing foods that make America healthier. Ten years after the business started, a fire caused by arson destroyed the mill, but Moore had it rebuilt, and the company now runs a 15-acre production facility, operating in three shifts, six days a week.

Why did Moore give his company to his employees on his 81st birthday rather than selling it to one of the many parties who have expressed an interest in buying? For Moore, the answer is all about his employees and their commitment to the company. He told a reporter, "These people are far too good at their jobs for me to just sell [the business]." Employees return the praise. For example, Bo Thomas, maintenance superintendent, said, "It just shows how much faith and trust Bob has in us. For all of us, it's more than just a job."

QUESTIONS

1. Which types of incentive pay are described in this case? Are these based on individual, group, or company performance?
2. Would you expect the motivational impact of stock ownership or profit sharing to be different at a small company like Bob's Red Mill than in a large corporation? Explain.
3. Suppose Bob's Red Mill brought you in as a consultant to review the company's total compensation. Explain why you would or would not recommend that the company add other forms of incentive pay, and identify any additional forms of compensation you would recommend for the company's employees.

SOURCES: Corporate website, "About Us," www.bobsredmill.com; Karen E. Klein, "ESOPs on the Rise among Small Businesses," *Bloomberg Businessweek*, April 26, 2010; Dana Tims, "Founder of Bob's Red Mill Natural Foods Transfers Business to Employees," *Oregon Live*, February 16, 2010, http://blog.oregonlive.com; and Christine Brozyna, "American Heart: Owner of Multi-Million Dollar Company Hands Over Business to Employees," *ABC News*, February 18, 2010, http://abcnews.go.com.

NOTES

1. We draw freely in this chapter on several literature reviews: B. Gerhart and G. T. Milkovich, "Employee Compensation: Research and Practice," in *Handbook of Industrial and Organizational Psychology*, vol. 3, 2nd ed., ed. M. D. Dunnette and L. M. Hough (Palo Alto, CA: Consulting Psychologists Press, 1992); B. Gerhart and S. L. Rynes, *Compensation: Theory, Evidence, and Strategic Implications* (Thousand Oaks, CA: Sage, 2003); B. Gerhart, "Compensation Strategy and Organization Performance," in S. L. Rynes and B. Gerhart, eds., *Compensation in Organizations: Current Research and Practice* (San Francisco: Jossey-Bass, 2000), pp. 151–94; B. Gerhart, S. L. Rynes, and I. S. Fulmer, "Compensation," *Academy of Management Annals* 3 (2009); and B. Gerhart and M. Fang, "Pay for (Individual) Performance: Issues, Claims, Evidence and the Role of Sorting Effects," *Human Resource Management Review*, 24 (2014), pp. 41–52.

2. B. Gerhart and G. T. Milkovich, "Organizational Differences in Managerial Compensation and Financial Performance," *Academy of Management Journal* 33 (1990), pp. 663–91.

3. E. Deci and R. Ryan, *Intrinsic Motivation and Self-Determination in Human Behavior* (New York: Plenum, 1985); A. Kohn, "Why Incentive Plans Cannot Work," *Harvard Business Review*, September–October 1993.

4. B. Gerhart and M. Fang, "Pay, Intrinsic Motivation, Extrinsic Motivation, Performance, and Creativity in the Workplace: Revisiting Long-Held Beliefs," *Annual Review of Organizational Psychology and Organizational Behavior* 2 (2015), pp. 489–521; R. Eisenberger and J. Cameron, "Detrimental Effects of Reward: Reality or Myth?" *American Psychologist* 51 (1996), pp. 1153–66; S. L. Rynes, B. Gerhart, and L. Parks, "Personnel Psychology: Performance Evaluation and Compensation," *Annual Review of Psychology*, 56 (2005), pp. 571–600; M. Fang and B. Gerhart, "Does Pay for Performance Diminish Intrinsic Interest? A Workplace Test Using Cognitive Evaluation Theory and the Attraction-Selection-Attrition Model," *International Journal of Human Resource Management*, 23 (2012), pp. 1176–96; M. Gagné and E. L. Deci, "Self-Determination Theory and Work Motivation," *Journal of Organizational Behavior* 26, pp. 331–62; G. E. Ledford, Jr., M. Fang, and B. Gerhart, "Negative Effects of Extrinsic Rewards on Intrinsic Motivation: More Smoke Than Fire," *World at Work Journal* 16, no. 2 (2013), pp. 17–29; K. Byron, and S. Khazanchi, "Rewards and Creative Performance: A Meta-analytic Test of Theoretically Derived Hypotheses," *Psychological Bulletin*, 138 (2012), pp. 809–30.

5. P. C. Cerasoli, J. M. Nicklin, and M. T. Ford, "Intrinsic Motivation and Extrinsic Incentives Jointly Predict Performance: A 40-Year Meta-analysis," *Psychological Bulletin* 140 (2014), pp. 980–1008; M. Fang and B. Gerhart, "Does Pay for Performance Diminish Intrinsic Interest? A Workplace Test Using Cognitive Evaluation Theory and the Attraction-Selection-Attrition Model," *International Journal of Human Resource Management* 23 (2012), pp. 1176–96; A. A. Grandey, N. W. Chi, and J. A. Diamond, "Show Me the Money! Do Financial Rewards for Performance Enhance or Undermine the Satisfaction from Emotional Labor?" *Personnel Psychology* 66, no. 3 (2013), pp. 569–612.

6. Y. Garbers and U. Konradt, "The Effect of Financial Incentives on Performance: A Quantitative Review of Individual and Team-Based Financial Incentives," *Journal of Occupational and Organizational Psychology* 87 (2014), pp. 102–37; D. G. Jenkins, Jr., A. Mitra, N. Gupta, and J. D. Shaw, "Are Financial Incentives Related to Performance? A Meta-analytic Review of Empirical Research," *Journal of Applied Psychology*, 83 (1998), pp. 777–87; Gerhart and Fang, "Pay for (Individual) Performance: Issues, Claims, Evidence and the Role of Sorting Effects."

7. T. M. Amabile and M. G. Pratt, "The Dynamic Componential Model of Creativity and Innovation in Organizations: Making Progress, Making Meaning," *Research in Organizational Behavior* 36 (2016), pp. 157–83.

8. For an alternative view, see E. L. Deci, A. H. Olafsen, and R. M. Ryan, "Self-Determination Theory in Work Organizations: The State of a Science," *Annual Review of Organizational Psychology and Organizational Behavior* 4 (2017), pp. 19–43. For a workplace study that claims to find that financial incentives "crowded out" (reduced) intrinsic motivation, see T. Gubler, I. Larkin, and L. Pierce, "Motivational Spillovers from Awards: Crowding Out in a Multitasking Environment," *Organization Science* 27 (2016), pp. 286–303. A study that concludes that pay for performance has a net negative effect on work effort is B. Kuvaas, R. Buch, M. Gagné, A. Dysvik, and J. Forest, "Do You Get What You Pay For? Sales Incentives and Implications for Motivation and Changes in Turnover Intention and Work Effort," *Motivation and Emotion* 40 (2016), 667–80. However, when I compute total effects of pay for performance on work effort using their Figure 3, I find a positive net effect.

9. D. R. Dalton, M. A. Hitt, S. T. Certo, and C. M. Dalton, "The Fundamental Agency Problem and Its Mitigation: Independence, Equity, and the Market for Corporate Control," *Academy of Management Annals* 1 (2007), pp. 1–64; R. A. Lambert and D. F. Larcker, "Executive Compensation, Corporate Decision Making, and Shareholder Wealth," in *Executive Compensation*, ed. F. Foulkes (Boston: Harvard Business School Press, 1989), pp. 287–309.

10. L. R. Gomez-Mejia, H. Tosi, and T. Hinkin, "Managerial Control, Performance, and Executive Compensation," *Academy of Management Journal* 30 (1987), pp. 51–70; H. L. Tosi Jr. and L. R. Gomez-Mejia, "The Decoupling of CEO Pay and Performance: An Agency Theory Perspective," *Administrative Science Quarterly* 34 (1989), pp. 169–89.

11. K. M. Eisenhardt, "Agency Theory: An Assessment and Review," *Academy of Management Review* 14 (1989), pp. 57–74.

12. R. E. Hoskisson, M. A. Hitt, and C. W. L. Hill, "Managerial Incentives and Investment in R&D in Large Multiproduct Firms," *Organizational Science* 4 (1993), pp. 325–41; M. Bloom and G. T. Milkovich, "Relationships among Risk, Incentive Pay, and Organizational Performance," *Academy of Management Journal* 41 (1998), pp. 283–97.

13. A. J. Nyberg, I. S. Fulmer, B. Gerhart, and M. A. Carpenter, "Agency Theory Revisited: CEO Return and Shareholder Interest Alignment," *Academy of Management Journal* 53 (2010), pp. 1029–49.

14. Eisenhardt, "Agency Theory."

15. Ibid.; E. J. Conlon and J. M. Parks, "Effects of Monitoring and Tradition on Compensation Arrangements: An Experiment with Principal–Agent Dyads," *Academy of Management Journal* 33 (1990), pp. 603–22; K. M. Eisenhardt, "Agency- and

Institutional-Theory Explanations: The Case of Retail Sales Compensation," *Academy of Management Journal* 31 (1988), pp. 488–511; Gerhart and Milkovich, "Employee Compensation"; J. Devaro and F. A. Kurtulus, "An Empirical Analysis of Risk, Incentives and the Delegation of Worker Authority," *Industrial and Labor Relations Review* 63 (2010), pp. 641–61.

16. G. T. Milkovich, J. Hannon, and B. Gerhart, "The Effects of Research and Development Intensity on Managerial Compensation in Large Organizations," *Journal of High Technology Management Research* 2 (1991), pp. 133–50; J. Devaro and F. A. Kurtulus, "An Empirical Analysis of Risk, Incentives and the Delegation of Worker Authority," *Industrial and Labor Relations Review*, 63 (2010), pp. 641–61.

17. V. Brenĉiĉ and J. B. Norris, "On-the-Job Tasks and Performance Pay: A Vacancy-Level Analysis," *Industrial and Labor Relations Review* 63 (2010), pp. 511–44. See also the discussion of performance reliability in B. Gerhart and S. L. Rynes, *Compensation* (2003).

18. G. T. Milkovich and A. K. Wigdor, *Pay for Performance* (Washington, DC: National Academy Press, 1991); Gerhart and Milkovich, "Employee Compensation"; Gerhart and Rynes, *Compensation: Theory, Evidence, and Strategic Implications*; A. Nyberg, "Retaining Your High Performers: Moderators of the Performance-Job Satisfaction-Voluntary Turnover Relationship," *Journal of Applied Psychology* 95 (2010), pp. 440–53; C. O. Trevor, G. Reilly, and B. Gerhart, "Reconsidering Pay Dispersion's Effect on the Performance of Interdependent Work: Reconciling Sorting and Pay Inequality," *Academy of Management Journal* 55 (2012), pp. 585–610; S. Carnahan, R. Agarwal, and B. A. Campbell, "Heterogeneity in Turnover: The Effect of Relative Compensation Dispersion of Firms on the Mobility and Entrepreneurship of Extreme Performers," *Strategic Management Journal*, 33 (2012), pp. 1411–30; J. D. Shaw, "Pay Dispersion, Sorting, and Organizational Performance," *Academy of Management Discoveries* 1(2015), pp. 165–79.

19. C. Trevor, B. Gerhart, and J. W. Boudreau, "Voluntary Turnover and Job Performance: Curvilinearity and the Moderating Influences of Salary Growth and Promotions," *Journal of Applied Psychology* 82 (1997), pp. 44–61; C. B. Cadsby, F. Song, and F. Tapon, "Sorting and Incentive Effects of Pay-for-Performance: An Experimental Investigation," *Academy of Management Journal* 50 (2007), pp. 387–405; A. Salamin and P. W. Hom, "In Search of the Elusive U-Shaped Performance-Turnover Relationship: Are High Performing Swiss Bankers More Liable to Quit?" *Journal of Applied Psychology* 90 (2005), pp. 1204–16; J. D. Shaw, and N. Gupta, "Pay System Characteristics and Quit Patterns of Good, Average, and Poor Performers," *Personnel Psychology* 60 (2007), pp. 903–28; J. D. Shaw, B. R. Dineen, R. Fang, R. F. Vellella, "Employee-Organization Exchange Relationships, HRM practices, and Quit Rates of Good and Poor Performers," *Academy of Management Journal*, 52 (2009), pp. 1016–1033.

20. B. D. Blume, R. S. Rubin, and T. T. Baldwin, "Who Is Attracted to an Organization Using a Forced Distribution Performance Management System?" *Human Resource Management Journal* 23, no. 4 (2013), pp. 360–78; T. Dohmen and A. Falk, "Performance Pay and Multidimensional Sorting: Productivity, Preferences, and Gender," *American Economic Review* 101, no. 2 (2011), pp. 556–90; R. D. Bretz, R. A. Ash, and G. F. Dreher, "Do People Make the Place? An Examination of the Attraction–Selection–Attrition Hypothesis," *Personnel Psychology* 42 (1989), pp. 561–81; T. A. Judge and R. D. Bretz, "Effect of

Values on Job Choice Decisions," *Journal of Applied Psychology* 77 (1992), pp. 261–71; D. M. Cable and T. A. Judge, "Pay Performances and Job Search Decisions: A Person–Organization Fit Perspective," *Personnel Psychology* 47 (1994), pp. 317–48.

21. G. T. Milkovich, J. M. Newman, and B. Gerhart, *Compensation*, 11th ed. (New York: McGraw-Hill/Irwin, 2014); K. Abosch and B. Gerhart, "The Case for Differentiated Pay for Performance," World at Work Total Rewards Conference & Exhibition, 2013.

22. E. H. O'Boyle and H. Aguinis, "The Best and the Rest: Revisiting the Norm of Normality of Individual Performance," *Personnel Psychology* 65 (2012), pp. 79–119; H. Aguinis and E. O'Boyle, "Star Performers in Twenty-First Century Organizations," *Personnel Psychology* 67, no. 2 (2014), pp. 313–50; H. Aguinis, E. O'Boyle, E. Gonzalez-Mulé, and H. Joo, "Cumulative Advantage: Conductors and Insulators of Heavy-Tailed Productivity Distributions and Productivity Stars," *Personnel Psychology*, 2014; K. F. Hallock, *Pay: Why People Earn What They Earn and What You Can Do Now to Make More* (Cambridge: Cambridge University Press, 2012). A key part of the argument is that performance is not normally distributed. For an alternative view of the evidence questioning whether the performance distribution is nonnormal, see J. W. Beck, A. S. Beatty, and P. R. Sackett, "On the Distribution of Job Performance: The Role of Measurement Characteristics in Observed Departures from Normality," *Personnel Psychology* 67 (2014), pp. 531–66.

23. Gerhart and Fang, "Pay for (Individual) Performance: Issues, Claims, Evidence and the Role of Sorting Effects."

24. J. D. Shaw, "Pay Dispersion," *Annual Review of Organizational Psychology and Organizational Behavior* 1, no. 1 (2014), pp. 521–44; P. E. Downes and D. Choi, "Employee Reactions to Pay Dispersion: A Typology of Existing Research," *Human Resource Management Review* 24, no. 1 (2014), pp. 53–66; C. O. Trevor, G. Reilly, and B. Gerhart, "Reconsidering Pay Dispersion's Effect on the Performance of Interdependent Work: Reconciling Sorting and Pay Inequality," *Academy of Management Journal* 55 (2012), pp. 585–610; A. Bucciol, N. J. Foss, and M. Piovesan, "Pay Dispersion and Performance in Teams," *PloS ONE* 9, no. 11 (2014), e112631.

25. W. He, L. R. Long, and B. Kuvaas, "Workgroup Salary Dispersion and Turnover Intention in China: A Contingent Examination of Individual Differences and the Dual Deprivation Path Explanation," *Human Resource Management* 55 (2015), pp. 301–320; S. H. Moon, S. E. Scullen, and G. P. Latham, "Precarious curve ahead: The effects of forced distribution rating systems on job performance," *Human Resource Management Review* 26, no. 2 (2016), pp. 166–179; N. Gupta, S. A. Conroy, and J. E. Delery, "The many faces of pay variation," *Human Resource Management Review* 22, no. 2 (2012), pp. 100–115; J. D. Shaw, "Pay dispersion," *Annual Review of Organizational Psychology and Organizational Behavior* 1, no. 1 (2014), pp. 521–544; S. A. Conroy, and N. Gupta, "Team pay-for-performance: The devil is in the details," *Group & Organization Management* 41, no. 1 (2016), pp. 32–65; W. Huang, "Responsible pay: managing compliance, organizational efficiency and fairness in the choice of pay systems in China's automotive companies," *The International Journal of Human Resource Management* 27, no. 18 (2016), pp. 2161–2181.

26. B. Gerhart, "Incentives and Pay for Performance in the Workplace," *Advances in Motivation Science* 4 (2017), pp. 91–140; B. Gerhart and M. Fang, "Competence and Pay for Performance," in *Handbook of Competence and Motivation,* 2nd ed., ed. A. J. Elliot, C. S. Dweck, and D. S. Yeager (New York: Guilford, 2017); D. Pohler and J. A. Schmidt, "Does Pay–for–Performance Strain

the Employment Relationship? The Effect of Manager Bonus Eligibility on Nonmanagement Employee Turnover," *Personnel Psychology* 69 (2015), pp. 395–429.

27. E. E. Lawler III, *Strategic Pay* (San Francisco: Jossey-Bass, 1990); Gerhart and Milkovich, "Employee Compensation"; Gerhart and Rynes, *Compensation: Theory, Evidence, and Strategic Implications*; B. Gerhart, C. Trevor, and M. Graham, "New Directions in Employee Compensation Research" in *Research in Personnel and Human Resources Management,* ed. G. R. Ferris (London: JAI Press, 1996), pp. 143–203; M. Beer and M. D. Cannon, "Promise and Peril in Implementing Pay-for-Performance," *Human Resource Management* 43 (2004), pp. 3–20.

28. In some cases, under exceptional circumstances, an organization may, at least temporarily, design an incentive plan to focus everyone's attention on one critical objective. For example, after the oil spill and worker fatalities in the Gulf of Mexico, BP temporarily revised its compensation program to make safety the sole factor in determining pay raises. (See G. Chazan and D. Mattioli, "BP Links Pay to Safety in Fourth Quarter," *Wall Street Journal*, October 19, 2010.) But having a single objective is not typically advisable.

29. R. D. Bretz, G. T. Milkovich, and W. Read, "The Current State of Performance Appraisal Research and Practice," *Journal of Management* 18 (1992), pp. 321–52; R. L. Heneman, "Merit Pay Research," *Research in Personnel and Human Resource Management* 8 (1990), pp. 203–63; Milkovich and Wigdor, *Pay for Performance*; Rynes, Gerhart, and Parks, "Personnel Psychology: Performance Evaluation and Compensation." Some evidence suggests that merit pay may be more effective when reinforced by other aspects of the pay strategy and/or by leadership of supervisors. See J. H. Han, K. M. Bartol, and S. Kim, "Tightening Up the Performance–Pay Linkage: Roles of Contingent Reward Leadership and Profit-Sharing in the Cross-Level Influence of Individual Pay-for-Performance," *Journal of Applied Psychology* 100 (2014), pp. 417–30. Other evidence suggests that merit pay may be more effective with certain employee personality profiles, consistent with our earlier discussion of sorting. See I. S. Fulmer and W. J. Walker, "More Bang for the Buck? Personality Traits as Moderators of Responsiveness to Pay-for-Performance," *Human Performance* 28, no. 1 (2015), pp. 40–65.

30. Gerhart ("Incentives and Pay for Performance in the Workplace") states that merit pay is likely used in virtually 100% of private-sector U.S. organizations based on the following: WorldatWork, the professional association for compensation professionals, as one of its activities, conducts surveys of compensation practices in organizations. It reports that 94% have merit pay programs (*Compensation Programs and Practices;* Scottsdale, AZ: WorldatWork, 2016). Given that 22% of responding organizations were in the nonprofit, not-for-profit, or public sectors, where we know that the use of pay for performance is considerably lower, as is its intensity when it is used (WorldatWork, *Compensation Programs and Practices*; Scottsdale, AZ: WorldatWork, 2012), it seems likely that merit pay is used in essentially all private-sector organizations in the United States.

31. Bretz et al., "Current State of Performance Appraisal."

32. B. D. Blume, T. T. Baldwin, and R. S. Rubin, "Reactions to Different Types of Forced Distribution Performance Evaluation Systems," *Journal of Business and Psychology* 24 (2009), pp. 77–91.

33. Bretz et al., "Current State of Performance Appraisal."

34. Ibid.

35. W. E. Deming, *Out of the Crisis* (Cambridge, MA: Center for Advanced Engineering Study, Massachusetts Institute of Technology, 1986), p. 110.

36. Ibid.

37. E. O'Boyle Jr. and H. Aguinis, "The Best and the Rest: Revisiting the Norm of Normality of Individual Performance," *Personnel Psychology* 65 (2012), pp. 79–119; C. O. Trevor, G. Reilly, and B. Gerhart, "Reconsidering Pay Dispersion's Effect on the Performance of Interdependent Work: Reconciling Sorting and Pay Inequality," *Academy of Management Journal*, 55 (2012), pp. 585–610.

38. Deming, *Out of the Crisis.*

39. Trevor et al., "Voluntary Turnover."

40. Gerhart and Rynes, *Compensation: Theory, Evidence, and Strategic Implications.*

41. Rynes, Gerhart, and Parks, "Personnel Psychology: Performance Evaluation and Compensation."

42. J. Schaubroeck, J. D. Shaw, M. K. Duffy, "An Under-Met and Over-Met Expectations Model of Employee Reactions to Merit Raises," *Journal of Applied Psychology* 93 (2008) pp. 424–34; S. Kepes, J. Delery, and N. Gupta, "Contingencies in the Effects of Pay Range on Organizational Effectiveness," *Personnel Psychology* 62 (2009), pp. 497–531; M. S. Chien, J. S. Lawler, and J. F. Uen, "Performance-Based Pay, Procedural Justice and Job Performance for RD Professionals: Evidence from the Taiwanese High-Tech Sector," *International Journal of Human Resource Management* 21 (2010), pp. 2234–48; P. Bamberger and E. Belogolovsky, "The Impact of Pay Secrecy on Individual Task Performance," *Personnel Psychology* 63 (2010), pp. 965–96.

43. R. Folger and M. A. Konovsky, "Effects of Procedural and Distributive Justice on Reactions to Pay Raise Decisions," *Academy of Management Journal* 32 (1989), pp. 115–30; J. Greenberg, "Determinants of Perceived Fairness of Performance Evaluations," *Journal of Applied Psychology* 71 (1986), pp. 340–42.

44. Rynes, Gerhart, and Parks, "Personnel Psychology: Performance Evaluation and Compensation."

45. B. Gerhart and S. Rynes, "Determinants and Consequences of Salary Negotiations by Graduating Male and Female MBAs," *Journal of Applied Psychology* (1991), pp. 256–62; Gerhart and Rynes, *Compensation: Theory, Evidence, and Strategic Implications.*

46. A. J. Nyberg, J. R. Pieper, and C. O. Trevor, "Pay-for-Performance's Effect on Future Employee Performance: Integrating Psychological and Economic Principles toward a Contingency Perspective," *Journal of Management* 42, no. 7 (2016). However, a different study reports no effect of merit bonuses but does find a positive effect of merit pay on subsequent performance. See S. Park and M. C. Sturman, "Evaluating Form and Functionality of Pay-for-Performance Plans," *Human Resource Management* 55, no. 4 (2016), pp. 697–719. Both the Nyberg et al. and Park and Sturman studies are of single organizations. Different pay-for-performance strategies may work in different organizations.

47. Gerhart and Fang, "Pay for (Individual) Performance"; Gerhart, "Incentives and Pay for Performance in the Workplace."

48. J. C. Dencker, "Why Do Firms Lay Off and Why?" *Industrial Relations*, 51 (2012), pp. 152–69.

49. E. A. Locke, D. B. Feren, V. M. McCaleb, K. N. Shaw, and A. T. Denny, "The Relative Effectiveness of Four Methods of Motivating Employee Performance," in *Changes in Working*

Life, ed. K. D. Duncan, M. M. Gruenberg, and D. Wallis (New York: Wiley, 1980), pp. 363–88; D. G. Jenkins Jr., A. Mitra, N. Gupta, and J. D. Shaw, "Are Financial Incentives Related to Performance? A Meta-analytic Review of Empirical Research," *Journal of Applied Psychology*, 83 (1998), pp. 777–87; for a summary of additional evidence, see also Gerhart and Rynes, *Compensation: Theory, Evidence, and Strategic Implications*.

50. Gerhart and Milkovich, "Employee Compensation"; Gerhart, "Incentives and Pay for Performance in the Workplace."

51. D. Roy, "Quota Restriction and Goldbricking in a Machine Shop," *American Journal of Sociology* 57, no. 5 (1952), pp. 427–42.

52. A recent study, for example, found that in using a monthly incentive/commission with health care providers, performance was better if an occasional exception was made to prevent providers' income from dropping as much as the formula would determine in months when their sales were low. M. Maltarich, A. J. Nyberg, G. Reilly, D. Abdulsalam, and M. Martin, "Pay-for-Performance, Sometimes: An Interdisciplinary Approach to Integrating Economic Rationality with Psychological Emotion to Predict Individual Performance," *Academy of Management Journal*, in press.

53. This idea has been referred to as the "share economy." See M. L. Weitzman, "The Simple Macroeconomics of Profit Sharing," *American Economic Review* 75 (1985), pp. 937–53. For supportive empirical evidence, see the following studies: J. Chelius and R. S. Smith, "Profit Sharing and Employment Stability," *Industrial and Labor Relations Review* 43 (1990), pp. 256S–73S; B. Gerhart and L. O. Trevor, "Employment Stability under Different Managerial Compensation Systems," working paper (Ithaca, NY: Cornell University Center for Advanced Human Resource Studies, 1995); D. L. Kruse, "Profit Sharing and Employment Variability: Microeconomic Evidence on the Weitzman Theory," *Industrial and Labor Relations Review* 44 (1991), pp. 437–53.

54. Gerhart and Milkovich, "Employee Compensation"; M. L. Weitzman and D. L. Kruse, "Profit Sharing and Productivity," in *Paying for Productivity*, ed. A. S. Blinder (Washington, DC: Brookings Institution, 1990); D. L. Kruse, *Profit Sharing: Does It Make a Difference?* (Kalamazoo, MI: Upjohn Institute, 1993); M. Magnan and S. St-Onge, "The Impact of Profit Sharing on the Performance of Financial Services Firms," *Journal of Management Studies* 42 (2005), pp. 761–91.

55. "GM/UAW: The Battle Goes On," *Ward's Auto World,* May 1995, p. 40; E. M. Coates III, "Profit Sharing Today: Plans and Provisions," *Monthly Labor Review,* April 1991, pp. 19–25.

56. Gerhart and Rynes, *Compensation: Theory, Evidence, and Strategic Implications.*

57. American Management Association, *CompFlash*, April 1991, p. 3.

58. "New Data Show Widespread Employee Ownership in U.S.," National Center for Employee Ownership, www.nceo.org/library/widespread.html.

59. Indeed, a recent study found that the correlation between use of broad-based stock and/or stock option plans and firm performance was small (r = .04). E. H. O'Boyle, P. C. Patel, and E. Gonzalez–Mulé, "Employee Ownership and Firm Performance: A Meta–analysis," *Human Resource Management Journal* 26, no. 4 (2016), pp. 425–48.

60. "Executive Compensation: Taking Stock," *Personnel* 67 (December 1990), pp. 7–8; "Another Day, Another Dollar Needs Another Look," *Personnel* 68 (January 1991), pp. 9–13;

J. Blasi, D. Kruse, and A. Bernstein, *In the Company of Owners* (New York: Basic Books, 2003).

61. Gerhart and Milkovich, "Organizational Differences in Managerial Compensation."

62. K. F. Hallock, *Pay: What People Earn and What They Can Do to Earn More* (Cambridge: Cambridge University Press, 2012).

63. S. Thurm, J. S. Lublin, and J. E. Vascellaro, "Google's 'One-to-One' Exchange Could Prompt Others to Follow," *Wall Street Journal*, January 23, 2009.

64. S. Ovide and S. Thurm, "Silicon Valley's Stock Funk," *Wall Street Journal*, October 6–7, 2012.

65. National Center for Employee Ownership, *ESOP (Employee Stock Ownership Plan) Facts,* www.esop.org, retrieved June 2, 2017.

66. D. Jones and T. Kato, "The Productivity Effects of Employee Stock Ownership Plans and Bonuses: Evidence from Japanese Panel Data," *American Economic Review* 185 (1995), pp. 391–414. At the time of the study, 91% of Japanese companies had an ESOP.

67. "Employees Left Holding the Bag," *Fortune,* May 20, 1991, pp. 83–93; M. A. Conte and J. Svejnar, "The Performance Effects of Employee Ownership Plans," in Blinder, *Paying for Productivity*, pp. 245–94.

68. Conte and Svejnar, "Performance Effects of Employee Ownership Plans."

69. Ibid.; T. H. Hammer, "New Developments in Profit Sharing, Gainsharing, and Employee Ownership," in *Productivity in Organizations*, ed. J. P. Campbell, R. J. Campbell and Associates (San Francisco: Jossey-Bass, 1988); K. J. Klein, "Employee Stock Ownership and Employee Attitudes: A Test of Three Models," *Journal of Applied Psychology* 72 (1987), pp. 319–32.

70. J. L. Pierce, S. Rubenfeld, and S. Morgan, "Employee Ownership: A Conceptual Model of Process and Effects," *Academy of Management Review* 16 (1991), pp. 121–44.

71. D. C. Jones, P. Kalmi, and A. Kauhanen, "Teams, Incentive Pay, and Productive Efficiency: Evidence from a Food-Processing Plant," *Industrial and Labor Relations Review* 63 (2010), pp. 606–26; R. T. Kaufman, "The Effects of Improshare on Productivity," *Industrial and Labor Relations Review* 45 (1992), pp. 311–22; M. H. Schuster, "The Scanlon Plan: A Longitudinal Analysis," *Journal of Applied Behavioral Science* 20 (1984), pp. 23–28; M. M. Petty, B. Singleton, and D. W. Connell, "An Experimental Evaluation of an Organizational Incentive Plan in the Electric Utility Industry," *Journal of Applied Psychology* 77 (1992), pp. 427–36; W. N. Cooke, "Employee Participation Programs, Group-Based Incentives, and Company Performance: A Union–Nonunion Comparison," *Industrial and Labor Relations Review* 47 (1994), pp. 594–609; J. B. Arthur and L. Aiman-Smith, "Gainsharing and Organizational Learning: An Analysis of Employee Suggestions over Time," *Academy of Management Journal* 44 (2001), pp. 737–54; J. B. Arthur and G. S. Jelf, "The Effects of Gainsharing on Grievance Rates and Absenteeism over Time," *Journal of Labor Research* 20 (1999), pp. 133–45.

72. Jerry L. McAdams, "Design, Implementation, and Results: Employee Involvement and Performance Reward Plans," *Compensation and Benefits Review*, March–April 1995, pp. 45–55.

73. T. L. Ross and R. A. Ross, "Gainsharing: Sharing Improved Performance," in *The Compensation Handbook*, 3rd ed., ed. M. L. Rock and L. A. Berger (New York: McGraw-Hill, 1991).

74. T. M. Welbourne and L. R. Gomez-Mejia, "Optimizing Team Incentives in the Workplace," in *The Compensation Handbook*, 3rd ed. (New York: McGraw-Hill, 2000), pp. 275–290; E. Siemsen, S. Balasubramanian, and A. V. Roth, "Incentives That Induce Task-Related Effort, Helping, and Knowledge Sharing in Workgroups," *Management Science* 10 (2007), pp. 1533–50.

75. R. S. Kaplan and D. P. Norton, "Using the Balanced Scorecard as a Strategic Management System," *Harvard Business Review*, January–February 1996, pp. 75–85.

76. I. S. Fulmer, "The Elephant in the Room: Labor Market Influences on CEO Compensation," *Personnel Psychology* 62 (2009), pp. 659–95.

77. M. C. Jensen and K. J. Murphy, "Performance Pay and Top-Management Incentives," *Journal of Political Economy* 98 (1990), pp. 225–64. A stronger relationship between CEO pay and performance was found by R. K. Aggarwal and A. A. Samwick, "The Other Side of the Trade-off: The Impact of Risk on Executive Compensation," *Journal of Political Economy* 107 (1999), pp. 65–105; A. J. Nyberg, I. S. Fulmer, B. Gerhart, and M. A. Carpenter, "Agency Theory Revisited: CEO Returns and Shareholder Interest Alignment," *Academy of Management Journal* 53 (2010), pp. 1029–49. Also, these observed relationships translate into significant changes in CEO pay in response to modest changes in financial performance of a company, as made clear by Gerhart and Rynes, *Compensation: Theory, Evidence, and Strategic Implications*; B. Gerhart, S. L. Rynes, and I. S. Fulmer, "Pay and Performance: Individuals, Groups, and Executives," *Academy of Management Annals* 3 (2009), pp. 251–315.

78. M. C. Jensen and K. J. Murphy, "CEO Incentives—It's Not How Much You Pay, but How," *Harvard Business Review* 68 (May–June 1990), pp. 138–53. The definitive resource on executive pay is B. R. Ellig, *The Complete Guide to Executive Compensation*, 2nd ed. (New York: McGraw-Hill, 2007); B. Gerhart, S. L. Rynes, and I. S. Fulmer, "Pay and Performance: Individuals, Groups, and Executives," *Academy of Management Annals* 3 (2009), pp. 251–315.

79. C. E. Devers, A. A. Cannella, G. P. Reilly, and M. E. Yoder, "Executive Compensation: A Multidisciplinary Review of Recent Developments," *Journal of Management* 33 (2007), pp. 1016–72; W. G. Sanders and D. C. Hambrick, "Swinging for the Fences: The Effects of CEO Stock Options on Company Risk Taking and Performance," *Academy of Management Journal* 50 (2007), pp. 1055–78; Gerhart, Rynes, and Fulmer, "Pay and Performance."

80. Gerhart and Milkovich, "Organizational Differences in Managerial Compensation."

81. M. Hanlon, S. Rajgopal, and T. Shevlin, "Are Executive Stock Options Associated with Future Earnings?" *Journal of Accounting and Economics* 36 (2003), pp. 3–43; A. J. Nyberg, I. S. Fulmer, B. Gerhart, and M. Carpenter "Agency Theory Revisited: CEO Return and Shareholder Interest Alignment," *Academy of Management Journal* 53 (2010), pp. 1029–49.

82. See A. J. Rucci, S. P. Kirn, and R. T. Quinn, "The Employee-Customer-Profit Chain at Sears," *Harvard Business Review*, January-February 1998, pp. 82–97; C. D. Ittner and D. F. Larcker, "Coming Up Short on Nonfinancial Performance Measurement," *Harvard Business Review*, November 2003, pp. 88–95.

83. J. E. Bachelder III, *New York Law Journal*, March 21, 2014.

84. L. Noonan, "UK's Top 5 Banks Slash Bonus Pools by More Than £1 Billion," *Financial Times,* April 6, 2015; D. Wighton, "Many More EU Firms Face Caps on Bonuses," *Wall Street Journal,* March 5, 2015, p. C3; B. Moshinsky, "Too-Big-to-Fail May Lead to U.S. Bank Pay Rules: Hoenig," *Bloomberg Business,* December 9, 2014.

85. Institutional Shareholder Services, *ISS Governance QuickScore 2.0,* http://www.issgovernance.com/file/files/ISSGovernanceQuickScore2.0.pdf.

86. J. Cutcher-Gershenfeld, "The Impact on Economic Performance of a Transformation in Workplace Relations," *Industrial and Labor Relations Review* 44 (1991), pp. 241–60; Irene Goll, "Environment, Corporate Ideology, and Involvement Programs," *Industrial Relations* 30 (1991), pp. 138–49.

87. L. R. Gomez-Mejia and D. B. Balkin, *Compensation, Organizational Strategy, and Firm Performance* (Cincinnati: South-Western, 1992); G. D. Jenkins and E. E. Lawler III, "Impact of Employee Participation in Pay Plan Development," *Organizational Behavior and Human Performance* 28 (1981), pp. 111–28.

88. D. I. Levine and L. D. Tyson, "Participation, Productivity, and the Firm's Environment," in Blinder, *Paying for Productivity.*

89. T. Welbourne, D. Balkin, and L. Gomez-Mejia, "Gainsharing and Mutual Monitoring: A Combined Agency–Organizational Justice Interpretation," *Academy of Management Journal* 38 (1995), pp. 881–99.

90. Ibid.

91. D. Scott and T. McMullen, *The Impact of Rewards Programs on Employee Engagement* (Scottsdale, AZ: WorldatWork, June 2010).

92. I. S. Fulmer and Y. Chen, "How Communication Affects Employee Knowledge of and Reactions to Compensation Systems," in *Meeting the Challenge of Human Resource Management: A Communication Perspective,* ed. V. Miller and M. Gordon (New York: Routledge/Taylor & Francis, 2014).

93. A. Colella, R. L. Paetzold, A. Zardkoohi, and M. J. Wesson, "Exposing Pay Secrecy," *Academy of Management Review* 32 (2007), pp. 55–71; J. Schaubroeck et al., "An Under-Met and Over-Met Expectations Model of Employee Reactions to Merit Raises," *Journal of Applied Psychology* 93 (March 2008), pp. 424–34; S. Marasi and R. J. Bennett, "Pay Communication: Where Do We Go From Here?" *Human Resource Management Review* 26 (2016), pp. 50–58.

94. I. Caron, A. K. Ben-Ayed, and C. Vandenberghe, "Collective Incentive Plans, Organizational Justice and Commitment," *Relations Industrielles/Industrial Relations* 68, no. 1 (March 2013); WorldatWork, *Compensation Programs and Practices* (Scottsdale, AZ: WorldatWork, 2012).

95. Blinder, Paying for Productivity.

96. Hammer, "New Developments in Profit Sharing"; Milkovich and Wigdor, *Pay for Performance*; D. J. B. Mitchell, D. Lewin, and E. E. Lawler III, "Alternative Pay Systems, Firm Performance and Productivity," in Blinder, *Paying for Productivity.*

97. Kaufman, "The Effects of Improshare on Productivity"; M. H. Schuster, "The Scanlon Plan: A Longitudinal Analysis," *Journal of Applied Behavioral Science* 20 (1984), pp. 23–28; J. A. Wagner III, P. Rubin, and T. J. Callahan, "Incentive Payment and Nonmanagerial Productivity: An Interrupted Time Series Analysis of Magnitude and Trend," *Organizational Behavior and Human Decision Processes* 42 (1988), pp. 47–74.

98. C. R. Gowen III and S. A. Jennings, "The Effects of Changes in Participation and Group Size on Gainsharing Success: A Case Study," *Journal of Organizational Behavior Management* 11 (1991), pp. 147–69.

99. L. Hatcher, T. L. Ross, and D. Collins, "Attributions for Participation and Nonparticipation in Gainsharing-Plan Involvement Systems," *Group and Organization Studies* 16 (1991), pp. 25–43; Mitchell et al., "Alternative Pay Systems."

100. L. R. Gomez-Mejia, P. Berrone, and M. Franco-Santos, *Compensation and Organizational Performance* (Armonk, NY: M. E. Sharpe, 2010).

101. B. R. Ellig, "Compensation Elements: Market Phase Determines the Mix," *Compensation and Benefits Review* 13 (3) (1981), pp. 30–38; L. R. Gomez-Mejia and D. B. Balkin, *Compensation, Organizational Strategy, and Firm Performance* (Cincinnati, OH: South-Western Publishing, 1992); M. K. Kroumova and J. C. Sesis, "Intellectual Capital, Monitoring, and Risk: What Predicts the Adoption of Employee Stock Options?" *Industrial Relations* 45 (2006), pp. 734–52; Y. Yanadori and J. H. Marler, "Compensation Strategy: Does Business Strategy Influence Compensation in High-Technology Firms?" *Strategic Management Journal* 27 (2006), pp. 559–70; B. Gerhart, "Compensation Strategy and Organizational Performance" in *Compensation in Organizations,* ed. S. L. Rynes and B. Gerhart (San Francisco: Jossey-Bass, 2000).

102. A. J. Baker, "Stock Options—a Perk That Built Silicon Valley," *Wall Street Journal*, June 23, 1993, p. A20.

13 Employee Benefits

LEARNING OBJECTIVES

After reading this chapter, you should be able to:

LO 13-1 Discuss the growth in benefits costs and the underlying reasons for that growth. *page 547*

LO 13-2 Explain the major provisions of employee benefits programs. *page 550*

LO 13-3 Discuss how employee benefits in the United States compare with those in other countries. *page 559*

LO 13-4 Describe the effects of benefits management on cost and workforce quality. *page 563*

LO 13-5 Explain the importance of effectively communicating the nature and value of benefits to employees. *page 573*

LO 13-6 Describe the regulatory constraints that affect the way employee benefits are designed and administered. *page 577*

Work (and Family?) in Tech and Finance

Recent statistics from the Organization for Economic Cooperation and Development show that the average American works 1,790 hours each year. By comparison, for the two largest economies in Europe, Germany and France, the corresponding numbers are 1,371 and 1,482. In other words, if the workweek is roughly 40 hours, workers in Germany and France work 8 to 10 weeks less per year than do those in the United States. Even in Japan, the largest developed economy in Asia (and second largest overall after China), which has wrestled with the problem of "death by overwork," workers work fewer hours per year (1,719) than those in the United States. The United States is sometimes referred to as "the no vacation nation." The United States is also one of the very few advanced economies that does not require employers to provide paid sick leave or paid maternity leave.

The norm of working many hours is even more pronounced in certain parts of the U.S. economy, such as the tech sector. Several years ago, Facebook co-founder and chief executive Mark Zuckerberg said, "We may not own a car. We may not have a family. Simplicity in life allows us to focus on what's important." There are other models, however. SAS Institute, a software company in North Carolina, has been on the Great Places to Work Institute/*Fortune* list of 100 Best Companies to Work For in each of the 20 years the list has been published. In describing SAS, the 100 Best list states that "the data analytics firm pulls out the stops to make employees stress less" and that is "the key to innovation" at SAS. For example, SAS has long had a policy of a 35-hour workweek. SAS also provides 90 days of fully paid maternity leave and 20 days of fully paid paternity leave. And, unlike some companies, where employees seem to be reluctant to take the leave, at SAS the average maternity leave is 61 days and the average paternity leave is 9 days.

Like the tech industry, the finance industry has also been a place to work long hours. The career formula on Wall Street has always been "grind out years of marathon workweeks" of up to 100 hours "and marathon tasks in exchange" for later opportunities to do deals and make millions. However, that formula seems not to be what some new hires want these days. In 1995, the average stay of a newly hired associate was 30 months. Now, it is 17 months. Firms are working to stem turnover by redesigning associate work to be less menial and to help associates advance more quickly to jobs with more responsibility. Another initiative is to reduce work hours, as well as to allow associates some time to pursue other things important to them. For example, J.P. Morgan has begun an initiative called "Pencils Down" that encourages investment bankers to take weekends off. But the initiative comes with the caveat that if bankers are doing a deal, putting their pencils down may not be advisable. The bank is also now limiting hours of summer interns, requiring them to stay away from the office between midnight and 7:00 a.m. Citigroup recently announced that incoming analysts could choose to work for one year at a nonprofit before beginning their career at Citigroup and that it would pay 60% of their starting salary during that year. Both Citigroup and Moelis have also initiated a program that allows young bankers to go to Kenya to work for four weeks on a microfinance project. Of course, not all more senior employees are enthused, especially with the moves to limit workweek hours because the amount of work to be done has not necessarily changed and it is frustrating when a "younger analyst isn't available as they want them to be." However, one executive opined that "just

CONTINUED

SOURCES: "100 Best Companies to Work For 2017," *Fortune,* March 9, 2017, www.beta.fortune.com/best-companies; C. Rexrod, "Citigroup to Millennial Bankers: Take a Year Off," *Wall Street Journal*, March 16, 2016; C. C. Miller, "Silicon Valley's Struggle Adapting to Families," *New York Times,* April 8, 2015, p. A3; L. Gellman and Justin Baer, "Goldman Sachs Sweetens Deal for Young Bankers," *Wall Street Journal*, November 5, 2015; D. Huang and L. Gellman, "Millennial Employees Confound Big Banks," *Wall Street Journal*, April 8, 2016.

Introduction

If we think of benefits as a part of total employee compensation, many of the concepts discussed in Chapters 11 and 12 apply here as well. This means, for example, that both cost and behavioral objectives are important. The cost of benefits adds an average of 46.3% to every dollar of payroll, thus accounting for 31.6% of the total employee compensation package. Controlling labor costs is not possible without controlling benefits costs. Similarly, achieving the objective of labor costs being variable and moving in the same direction of revenues and profits (rather than being fixed costs) is also not possible without careful attention to benefits strategy. On the behavioral side, benefits seem to influence whether potential employees come to work for a company, whether they stay, when they retire—perhaps even how they perform (although the empirical evidence, especially for the latter point, is surprisingly limited).[1] Although employers continue to be focused on cost control, different employees look for different types of benefits and, as the chapter opener indicates, cost considerations are giving some way in the pursuit of attracting employees. As we will see, benefits can (also) be used to differentiate an employer from competitors, allowing it to tap into what in some cases may be a valuable, but underutilized, part of the pool of human capital.

Although it makes sense to think of benefits as part of total compensation, benefits have unique aspects. First, there is the question of legal compliance. Although direct compensation is subject to government regulation, the scope and impact of regulation on benefits is far greater. Some benefits, such as Social Security, are mandated by law. Others, although not mandated, are subject to significant regulation or must meet certain criteria to achieve the most favorable tax treatment; these include pensions and savings plans. The heavy involvement of government in benefits decisions reflects the central role benefits play in maintaining economic security.

A second unique aspect of benefits is that organizations offer them so commonly that they have come to be institutionalized. Providing medical and retirement benefits of some sort remains almost obligatory for many (e.g., large) employers. A large employer that did not offer such benefits to its full-time employees would be highly unusual, and the employer might well have trouble attracting and retaining a quality workforce.

A third unique aspect of benefits, compared with other forms of compensation, is their complexity. It is relatively easy to understand the value of a dollar as part of a salary but not as part of a benefits package. The advantages and disadvantages of different types of medical coverage, pension provisions, disability insurance, and investment options for retirement funds are often difficult to grasp, and their value (beyond a general sense that they are good to have) is rarely as clear as the value of one's salary. Most fundamentally, employees may not even be aware of the benefits available to them; and if they are aware, they may not understand how to use them. When employers spend large sums of money on benefits but employees do not understand the benefits or attach much value to them, the return on employers' benefits investment will be fairly dismal.[2] One reason for giving more responsibility to employees for retirement planning and other benefits is to increase their understanding of the value of such benefits.

Reasons for Benefits Growth

In thinking about benefits as part of total compensation, a basic question arises: Why do employers choose to channel a significant portion of the compensation dollar away from cash (wages and salaries) into benefits? Economic theory tells us that people prefer a dollar in cash over a dollar's worth of any specific commodity because the cash can be used to purchase the commodity or something else.[3] Cash is less restrictive. Several factors, however, have contributed to less emphasis on cash and more on benefits in compensation. To understand these factors, it is useful to examine the growth in benefits over time and the underlying reasons for that growth.

Figure 13.1 gives an indication of the overall growth in benefits. Note that in 1929, on the eve of the Great Depression, benefits added an average of only 3% to every dollar of payroll. By 1955 this figure had grown to 17%, and it has continued to grow, now accounting for 46.3 cents on top of every payroll dollar.

Many factors contributed to this tremendous growth.[4] First, during the 1930s several laws were passed as part of Franklin Roosevelt's New Deal, a legislative program aimed at buffering people from the devastating effects of the Great Depression. The

LO 13-1
Discuss the growth in benefits costs and the underlying reasons for that growth.

Figure 13.1

Growth of Employee Benefits, Percentage of Wages and Salaries and of Total Compensation, 1929–2017, Civilian Workers

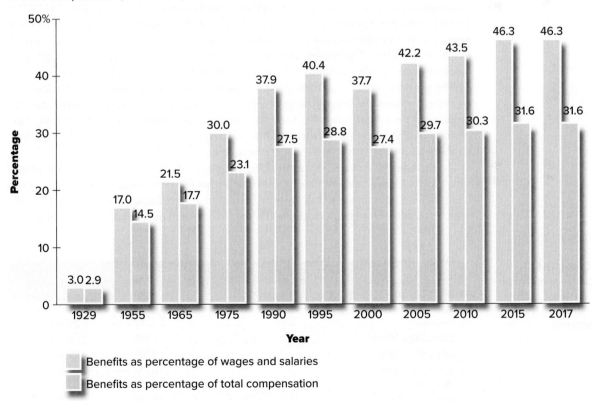

Benefits as percentage of wages and salaries

Benefits as percentage of total compensation

SOURCES: Data through 1990, U.S. Chamber of Commerce Research Center, *Employee Benefits 1990, Employee Benefits 1997, Employee Benefits 2000* (Washington, DC: U.S. Chamber of Commerce, 1991, 1997, and 2000). Data from 1995 onward, "Employer Costs for Employee Compensation," www.bls.gov.

Social Security Act and other legislation established legally required benefits (such as the Social Security retirement system) and modified the tax structure in such a way as to effectively make other benefits—such as workers' compensation (for work-related injuries) and unemployment insurance—mandatory. Second, wage and price controls instituted during World War II, combined with labor market shortages, forced employers to think of new ways to attract and retain employees. Because benefits were not covered by wage controls, employers channeled more resources in this direction. Once institutionalized, such benefits tended to remain even after wage and price controls were lifted.

Marginal tax rate
The percentage of an additional dollar of earnings that goes to taxes.

Third, the tax treatment of benefits programs is often more favorable for employees than the tax treatment of wages and salaries, meaning that a dollar spent on benefits has the potential to generate more value for the employees than the same dollar spent on wages and salaries. The **marginal tax rate** is the percentage of additional earnings that goes to taxes. Consider the hypothetical employee in Table 13.1 and the effect on take-home pay of a $1,000 increase in salary. The total effective marginal tax rate is higher for higher-paid employees and also varies according to state and city. (The state of New York and New York City have among the highest marginal tax rates.) A $1,000 annual raise for the employee earning $80,000 per year would increase net pay $596.70 ($1,000 × [1 − 0.4033]). In contrast, an extra $1,000 put into benefits would lead to an increase of $1,000 in "take-home benefits."

Employers, too, realize tax advantages from certain types of benefits. Although both cash compensation and most benefits are deductible as operating expenses, employers (like employees) pay Social Security and Medicare tax on salaries up to a limit ($128.200 for 2017) and Medicare tax on the entire salary, as well as other taxes like workers' compensation and unemployment compensation. However, no such taxes are paid on most employee benefits. The bottom line is that the employer may be able to provide more value to employees by spending the extra $1,000 on benefits instead of salary.

The tax advantage of benefits also takes another form. Deferring compensation until retirement allows the employee to receive cash, but at a time (retirement) when the employee's tax rate is sometimes lower because of a lower income level. More important, perhaps, is that investment returns on the deferred money typically accumulate tax free, resulting in much faster growth of the investment.

A fourth factor that has influenced benefits growth is the cost advantage that groups typically realize over individuals. Organizations that represent large groups of employees can purchase insurance (or self-insure) at a lower rate because of economies of scale, which spread fixed costs over more employees to reduce the cost per person. Insurance

Table 13.1
Example of Marginal Tax Rates for an Employee Salary of $80,000

	NOMINAL TAX RATE	EFFECTIVE TAX RATE
Federal	25.00%	25.00%
State (New York)	6.65	4.99
City (New York)	3.59	2.69
Social Security	6.20	6.20
Medicare	1.45	1.45
Total tax rate	42.89	40.33

Note: State and city taxes are deductible on the federal tax return, reducing their effective tax rate.

risks can be pooled more easily in large groups, and large groups can also achieve greater bargaining power in dealing with insurance carriers or medical providers.

A fifth factor influencing the growth of benefits was the growth of organized labor from the 1930s through the 1950s. This growth was partly a result of another piece of New Deal legislation, the National Labor Relations Act, which greatly enhanced trade unions' ability to organize workers and negotiate contracts with employers. Benefits were often a key negotiation objective. (Indeed, they still are. Benefits issues continue to be a common reason for work stoppages.) Unions were able to successfully pursue their members' interests in benefits, particularly when tax advantages provided an incentive for employers to shift money from cash to benefits. For unions, a new benefit such as medical coverage was a tangible success that could have more impact on prospective union members than a wage increase of equivalent value, which might have amounted to only a cent or two per hour. Also, many nonunion employers responded to the threat of unionization by implementing the same benefits for their own employees, thus contributing to benefits growth.

Finally, employers may also provide unique benefits as a means of differentiating themselves in the eyes of current or prospective employees. In this way, employers communicate key aspects of their culture that set them apart from the rest of the pack. Patagonia, an outdoor clothing company, prides itself on its commitment to the "triple bottom line": Do well by shareholders, but also by employees and the community/environment. When it comes to shareholders and employees, Patagonia makes sure its employees get outside and test its gear. (To make that easier, the company allows employees to set their own hours.) That is something its employees enjoy, and it also helps the company design and redesign products so that they are attractive to customers, which makes money for shareholders. It is only fitting for employees located in Ventura, California, that the title of founder Yvon Chouinard's memo is "Let My People Go Surfing."[5] Table 13.2 shows some additional examples.

Table 13.2
Differentiating via Benefits

Offers up to five free nights each year at any of the company's hotels (plus meals for half-price during those stays)	Four Seasons
Gives expectant mothers four weeks of leave at 100% pay *prior* to the birth of a child (and six to eight weeks' leave at 100% pay after giving birth)	Genentech
Gives employees an annual stipend of $2,000 to travel and stay in Airbnb lodgings anywhere in the world	Airbnb
Provides a 1,200-acre camping and recreational area for employee use	Steelcase
Shuts down the entire company for one week in December and one week over the summer	Adobe
Offers a free Double-Double burger and fries during each shift	In-N-Out Burger
Provides a rooftop dog park	Zynga

SOURCES: P. Mosendz, "These 20 Companies Offer Incredible (and Unusual) Benefits," *Bloomberg,* February 7, 2017, https://www.bloomberg.com/news/articles/2017-02-07/these-20-companies-offer-incredible-and-unusual-benefits; Zynga company website, "Benefits," https://www.zynga.com/careers/benefits; R. Hackett, "5 Great Reasons to Work for Four Seasons," *Fortune,* February 1, 2015, http://fortune.com/2015/02/01/perks-four-seasons/; Great Place to Work Institute, Genentech, http://reviews.greatplacetowork.com/genentech; L. Dishman, "These Are the Best Employee Benefits and Perks," FastCompany, February 3, 2016, https://www.fastcompany.com/3056205/these-are-the-best-employee-benefits-and-perks.

Benefits Programs

LO 13-2
Explain the major
provisions of employee
benefits programs.

Most benefits fall into one of the following categories: social insurance, private group insurance, retirement, pay for time not worked, and family-friendly policies.[6] Table 13.3, based on Bureau of Labor Statistics (BLS) data, provides an overview of the prevalence of specific benefits programs. As the table shows, the percentage of employees covered by these benefits programs increases with establishment size. Likewise, as shown in Table 13.4, benefits (and total compensation) costs also increase with establishment size.

SOCIAL INSURANCE (LEGALLY REQUIRED)
Social Security

Among the most important provisions of the Social Security Act of 1935 was the establishment of old-age insurance and unemployment insurance. The act was later amended to add survivor's insurance (1939), disability insurance (1956), hospital insurance (Medicare Part A, 1965), and supplementary medical insurance (Medicare Part B, 1965) for the elderly. Together these provisions constitute the federal Old Age, Survivors, Disability, and Health

Table 13.3
Percentage of Full-Time Workers in U.S. Private Industry with Access to Selected Benefits Programs, by Establishment Size

		ESTABLISHMENT SIZE	
	ALL	1–99 EMPLOYEES	500 OR MORE EMPLOYEES
Medical care	67%	55%	88%
Short-term disability insurance	40	29	63
Long-term disability insurance	33	23	60
All retirement	66	52	90
Defined benefit pension	18	9	43
Defined contribution plan	62	49	82
Life insurance	55	40	85
Paid leave			
Sick	64	55	80
Vacation	76	68	89
Personal	40	28	62
Family	13	9	23

SOURCE: U.S. Bureau of Labor Statistics, *National Compensation Survey: Employee Benefits in the United States,* March 2016, Bulletin 2785, September 2016, https://www.bls.gov/ncs/ebs/.

Table 13.4
Total Hourly Compensation and Benefits Costs, U.S. Private Industry, by Establishment Size

		ESTABLISHMENT SIZE	
	ALL	1–99 EMPLOYEES	500 OR MORE EMPLOYEES
Total compensation	$32.76	$27.71	$48.34
Wages and salaries	22.83	20.11	31.56
Benefits	9.83	7.60	16.78

SOURCE: *Employer Costs for Employee Compensation—December 2016. News Release.* March 17, 2017. USDL-17-0321, https://www.bls.gov/news.release/pdf/ecec.pdf.

Insurance (OASDHI) program. More than 90% of U.S. employees are covered by the program, the main exceptions being railroad and federal, state, and local government employees, who often have their own plans. Note, however, that an individual employee must meet certain eligibility requirements to receive benefits. To be fully insured typically requires 40 quarters of covered employment and minimum earnings ($1,300 in 2017) per quarter. However, the eligibility rules for survivors' and disability benefits are somewhat different.

Social Security retirement (old-age insurance) benefits for fully insured workers begin at age 65 years and 6 months (full benefits) or age 62 (at a permanent reduction in benefits) for those born in 1940. The full retirement age now rises with birth year, reaching age 67 for those born in 1960 or later. Although the amount of the benefit depends on one's earnings history, benefits do not go up after reaching a certain earnings level. Thus high earners help subsidize benefit payments to low earners. In 2017, the maximum benefit at full retirement age is $2,687/month ($32,244/year). Cost-of-living increases are provided each year that the consumer price index increases. The age at which you retire matters. If retiring at age 62 (i.e., before full retirement age), the maximum benefit in 2017 is $2,153/month ($25,836/year). But, if you waited until age 70, the maximum retirement benefit in 2015 is $3,538/month ($42,456/year). There is no further benefit to retiring after age 70. There is also a spousal benefit of up to 50% of the primary recipient's benefit (if larger than the spouse's own benefit).

An important attribute of the Social Security retirement benefit is that for those at full retirement age, it is free from state tax in about half of the states and free from federal tax if no other income is received or if that other income falls below a certain level (recently, $25,000 for single tax return filers, $32,000 for married/joint filers). Additionally, the federal tax code has an earnings test for those who are still earning wages (and not yet at full retirement age). In 2017, beneficiaries (who must be 62 or older) below the full retirement age were allowed to make $16,920; in the year an individual reaches full retirement age, the earnings test is $44,880. If these amounts are exceeded, the Social Security benefit is reduced $1 for every $2 in excess earnings for those under the full retirement age and $1 for every $3 in the year a worker reaches the full retirement age. These provisions are important because of their effects on the work decisions of those between age 62 and full retirement age. The earnings test increases a person's incentive to retire (otherwise, full Social Security benefits are not received), and if she continues to work, the incentive to work part time rather than full time increases. A major change made in January 2000 is that there is no earnings test once full retirement age is reached. Therefore, these workers no longer incur any earnings penalty (and thus have no tax-related work disincentive).

How are retirement and other benefits financed? Both employers and employees are assessed a payroll tax of 7.65% (a total of 15.3%) on the first $127,200 (as of 2017) of the employee's earnings. Of the 7.65%, 6.2% funds OASDHI and 1.45% funds Medicare (Part A). Unlike the OASDHI tax, the 1.45% Medicare tax is assessed on all earnings. (The self-employed pay a 12.4% OASDHI tax plus a 2.9% Medicare tax.) In addition, as of 2013, the Affordable Care Act added what the Social Security Administration calls a High Income Tax and what the Internal Revenue Service calls the Additional Medicare Tax, which is 0.9% on adjusted gross income above $200,000 for single filers and $250,000 for married filers. This tax is paid only by individuals. Employers do not pay this tax.

What are the behavioral consequences of Social Security benefits? Because they are legally mandated, employers do not have discretion in designing this aspect of their benefits programs. However, Social Security does affect employees' retirement decisions. The eligibility age for benefits and any tax penalty for earnings influence retirement decisions. The elimination of the tax penalty on earnings for those at full retirement age should mean a larger pool of older workers in the labor force for employers to tap into.

Unemployment Insurance

Established by the 1935 Social Security Act, this program has four major objectives: (1) to offset lost income during involuntary unemployment, (2) to help unemployed workers find new jobs, (3) to provide an incentive for employers to stabilize employment, and (4) to preserve investments in worker skills by providing income during short-term layoffs (which allows workers to return to their employer rather than start over with another employer).

The unemployment insurance program is financed largely through federal and state taxes on employers. Although, strictly speaking, the decision to establish the program is left to each state, the Social Security Act created a tax incentive structure that quickly led every state to establish a program. The federal tax rate is currently 0.6% on the first $7,000 of wages. Many states have a higher rate or impose the tax on a greater share of earnings. Currently, Washington state has the maximum covered (taxable) earnings of any state at $44,000.[7]

An important feature of the unemployment insurance program is that no state imposes the same tax on every employer. Instead, the size of the tax depends on the employer's experience rating. Employers that have a history of laying off a large share of their workforces pay higher taxes than do those that do not. In some states, an employer that has had very few layoffs may pay no state tax. In contrast, an employer with a poor experience rating could pay a tax as high as 5–10%, depending on the state.[8]

Unemployed workers are eligible for benefits if they (1) have a prior attachment to the workforce (often 52 weeks or four quarters of work at a minimum level of pay); (2) are available for work; (3) are actively seeking work (including registering at the local unemployment office); and (4) were not discharged for cause (such as willful misconduct), did not quit voluntarily, and are not out of work because of a labor dispute.

Benefits also vary by state, but they are typically about 50% of a person's earnings and last for 26 weeks. Extended benefits for up to 13 weeks are also available. A state must, for example, pay extended benefits if the insured unemployment rate for the previous 13 weeks is at least 5% and is 120% of the rate for the same 13-week period in the two previous years.[9] Emergency extended (federal) benefits are also sometimes funded by Congress. All states have minimum and maximum weekly benefit levels. In contrast to Social Security retirement benefits, unemployment benefits are taxed as ordinary income.

Because unemployment insurance is, in effect, legally required, management's discretion is limited here, too. Management's main task is to keep its experience rating low by avoiding unnecessary workforce reductions (e.g., by relying on the sorts of actions described in Chapter 5).

Workers' Compensation

Workers' compensation laws cover job-related injuries and death.[10] Prior to enactment of these laws, workers suffering work-related injuries or diseases could receive compensation only by suing for damages. Moreover, the common-law defenses available to employers meant that such lawsuits were not usually successful. In contrast, these laws operate under a principle of no-fault liability, meaning that an employee does not need to establish gross negligence by the employer. In return, employers receive immunity from lawsuits. (One exception is the employer who intentionally contributes to a dangerous workplace.) Employees are not covered when injuries are self-inflicted or stem from intoxication or "willful disregard of safety rules."[11] Approximately 90% of all U.S. workers are covered by state workers' compensation laws, although again there are differences among states, with coverage ranging from 70% to more than 95%.

Workers' compensation benefits fall into four major categories: (1) disability income, (2) medical care, (3) death benefits, and (4) rehabilitative services.

Disability income is typically two-thirds of predisability earnings, although each state has its own minimum and maximum. In contrast to unemployment insurance benefits, disability benefits are tax free. The system is financed differently by different states, some having a single state fund, most allowing employers to purchase coverage from private insurance companies. Self-funding by employers is also permitted in most states. The cost to the employer is based on three factors. The first factor is the nature of the occupations and the risk attached to each. Premiums for low-risk occupations may be less than 1% of payroll; the cost for some of the most hazardous occupations may be as high as 100% of payroll. The second factor is the state where work is located. For example, in the 50 U.S. states, the maximum compensation a worker can receive for loss of an arm averages $169,878, but it ranges from a minimum of $48,840 in Alabama to a maximum of $859,634 in Nevada.[12] The third factor is the employer's experience rating.

The experience rating system again provides an incentive for employers to make their workplaces safer. Dramatic injuries (like losing a finger or hand) are less prevalent than minor ones, such as sprains and strains. Back strain is the most expensive benign health condition in developed countries. Each year in the United States, 3–4% of the population is temporarily disabled and 1% is permanently and totally disabled.[13] Many actions can be taken to reduce workplace injuries, such as work redesign and training, and to speed the return to health, and thus to work (e.g., exercise).[14] Some changes can be fairly simple (such as permitting workers to sit instead of having them bend over). It is also important to hold managers accountable (in their performance evaluations) for making workplaces safer and getting employees back to work promptly following an injury. With the passage of the Americans with Disabilities Act, employers came under even greater pressure to deal effectively and fairly with workplace injuries. See the discussion in Chapter 3 on safety awareness programs for some of the ways employers and employees are striving to make the workplace safer.

One challenge is managing pain from workplace injuries effectively and efficiently and avoiding prescription painkiller abuse. Some firms and insurers have moved toward using data better to assess high-risk workers. In such cases, employees are assigned a case worker right from the start. The case worker closely monitors the employee's situation. If, for example, a case worker sees that a worker with a broken ankle continues taking opioids longer than two weeks, an alert may be issued. The idea is to intervene so that a broken ankle or a minor lower-back injury does not turn into a lifetime problem with prescription painkiller addiction. Companies can also use analytics from Rising (Rising Medical Solutions) and similar companies to benchmark their workers' compensation cases against those of other companies in the same industry or geographic location as a way to compare the risk of fraud and abuse to that faced by other companies, which can help them decide how much of a problem they have.

PRIVATE GROUP INSURANCE

As we noted earlier, group insurance rates are typically lower than individual rates because of economies of scale, the ability to pool risks, and the greater bargaining power of a group. This cost advantage, together with tax considerations and a concern for employee security, helps explain the prevalence of employer-sponsored insurance plans. We discuss two major types: medical insurance and disability insurance. Note that these programs are not legally required; rather, they are offered at the discretion of employers.

Medical Insurance

Not surprisingly, public opinion surveys indicate that medical benefits are by far the most important benefit to the average person.[15] As Table 13.3 indicates, most full-time employees have medical insurance, especially in larger workplaces. Three basic types of medical expenses are typically covered: hospital expenses, surgical expenses, and physicians' visits. Other benefits that employers may offer include dental care, vision care, birthing centers, and prescription drug programs. Perhaps the most important issue in benefits management is the challenge of providing quality medical benefits while controlling costs, a subject we return to in a later section. We also discuss the Affordable Care Act in a later section.

Consolidated Omnibus Budget Reconciliation Act (COBRA)
The 1985 act that requires employers to permit employees to extend their health insurance coverage at group rates for up to 36 months following a qualifying event, such as a layoff.

The **Consolidated Omnibus Budget Reconciliation Act (COBRA)** of 1985 requires employers to permit employees to extend their health insurance coverage at group rates for up to 36 months following a "qualifying event" such as termination (except for gross misconduct), a reduction in hours that leads to the loss of health insurance, death, and other events. The beneficiary (whether the employee, spouse, or dependent) must have access to the same services as employees who have not lost their health insurance. Note that the beneficiaries do not get free coverage. Rather, they receive the advantage of purchasing coverage at the employer rather than the individual rate.

Disability Insurance

Two basic types of disability coverage exist.[16] As Table 13.3 indicates, only in larger workplaces are most employees covered by short-term and long-term disability insurance. Short-term plans typically provide benefits for six months or less, at which point long-term plans take over, potentially covering the person for life. The median and modal salary replacement rate is 60%, although short-term plans sometimes have higher rates. There are typically (in 88% of plans) caps on the amount (median = $8,000) that can be paid each month.[17] Federal income taxation of disability benefits depends on the funding method. Where employee contributions completely fund the plan, there is no federal tax. Benefits based on employer contributions are taxed. Finally, disability benefits, especially long-term ones, need to be coordinated with other programs, such as Social Security disability benefits.

RETIREMENT

Earlier we discussed the old-age insurance part of Social Security, a legally required source of retirement income. This remains the largest single component of the elderly's overall retirement income (35%). Other sources of income are pensions (17%), earnings from assets (savings and other investments like stocks and bonds, 11%), earnings (34%), and other sources (3%).[18]

Employers have no legal obligation to offer private retirement plans, but many do. As we note later, if a private retirement plan is provided, it must meet certain standards set forth by the Employee Retirement Income Security Act.

Defined Benefit

A *defined benefit plan* guarantees ("defines") a specified retirement benefit level to employees based typically on a combination of years of service and age as well as on the employee's earnings level (e.g., the three to five highest earnings years). For instance, an organization might guarantee a monthly pension payment of $1,500 to an employee retiring at age 65 with 30 years of service and an average salary over the final 5 years of

$40,000. As Table 13.3 indicates, full-time employees in 18% of all workplaces, 43% of large workplaces, are covered by such plans. (Defined benefit coverage has fallen by half since 1980.)[19]

Defined benefit plans insulate employees from investment risk, which is borne by the company. In the event of severe financial difficulties that force the company to terminate or reduce employee pension benefits, the **Pension Benefit Guaranty Corporation (PBGC)** provides some protection of benefits. Established by the **Employee Retirement Income Security Act (ERISA)** of 1974, the PBGC guarantees a basic benefit, not necessarily complete pension benefit replacement, for employees who were eligible for pensions at the time of termination. It insures the retirement benefits of 41 million workers in more than 24,000 plans. In 2016, PBGC paid benefits of $5.7 billion to 840,000 retirees from more than 4,700 failed single-employer plans. (Of those, 46,000 employees from 76 failed single-employer plans were newly covered by the PBGC in 2016.)[20] The maximum annual benefit for single-employer plans is limited to the lesser of an employee's annual gross income during a PBGC-defined period or $28,994 at age 55, $41,881 at age 60, $64,432 at age 65, $106,957 at age 70, and $195,873 at age 75 for plans terminated in 2017.[21] Thus, higher-paid employees, who would have received higher pensions under the company plan, can experience major cuts in pensions if the PBGC must take over the plan. Payouts are not adjusted for cost-of-living changes. The PBGC is funded by an annual premium of $64 per (single-employer) plan participant in 2016, plus an additional variable-rate premium for underfunded plans.[22] Note that the PBGC does not guarantee health care benefits.

Pension Benefit Guaranty Corporation (PBGC) The agency that guarantees to pay employees a basic retirement benefit in the event that financial difficulties force a company to terminate or reduce employee pension benefits.

Employee Retirement Income Security Act (ERISA) The 1974 act that increased the fiduciary responsibilities of pension plan trustees, established vesting rights and portability provisions, and established the Pension Benefit Guaranty Corporation (PBGC).

Defined Contribution

Unlike defined benefit plans, *defined contribution plans* do not promise a specific benefit level for employees upon retirement. Rather, an individual account is set up for each employee with a guaranteed size of contribution. The advantage of such plans for employers is that they shift investment risk to employees and present fewer administrative challenges because there is no need to calculate payments based on age and service and no need to make payments to the PBGC. As Table 13.3 indicates, defined contribution plans are especially preferred in smaller companies, perhaps because of small employers' desire to avoid long-term obligations or perhaps because small companies tend to be younger, often being founded since the trend toward defined contribution plans. Some companies have both defined benefit and defined contribution plans.

There is a wide variety of defined contribution plans, a few of which are described briefly here. One of the simplest is a money purchase plan, under which an employer specifies a level of annual contribution (such as 10% of salary). At retirement age, the employee is entitled to the contributions plus the investment returns. The term *money purchase* stems from the fact that employees often use the money to purchase an annuity rather than taking it as a lump sum. Profit-sharing plans and employee stock ownership plans are also often used as retirement vehicles. Both permit contributions (cash and stock, respectively) to vary from year to year, thus allowing employers to avoid fixed obligations that may be burdensome in difficult financial times. Section 401(k) plans (named after the tax code section) permit employees to defer compensation on a pretax basis. Annual contributions in 2017 are limited to $18,000.[23] For those age 50 or over, an additional $6,000 per year in catch-up contributions is also permitted. Additionally, many employers (80%) match some portion (mean = 4.7%) of employee contributions.[24] A final incentive is tax based. For example, based on Table 13.1, $10,000 contributed to a 401(k) plan would only be worth $(1 - 0.4333) \times \$10,000 = \$5,667$ if taken in salary.

Defined contribution plans continue to grow in importance, while, as we saw earlier, defined benefit plans have become less common. An important implication is that defined contribution plans put the responsibility for wise investing squarely on the shoulders of the employee. Several factors affect the amount of income that will be available to an employee upon retirement. First, the earlier the age at which investments are made, the longer returns can accumulate. As Figure 13.2 shows, an annual investment of $3,000 made between ages 21 and 29 will be worth much more at age 65 than a similar investment made between ages 31 and 39. Second, different investments have different historical rates of return. Between 1928 and 2016 the average annual return was 9.53% for stocks, 5.18% for bonds, and 3.46% for cash (e.g., short-term Treasury bills or bank savings accounts). As Figure 13.2 shows, *if* historical rates of return were to continue, an investment in a mix of 60% stock, 30% bonds, and 10% cash between the ages of 21 and 29 would be worth about four times as much at age 65 as would the same amount kept in the form of cash. A third consideration is the need to counteract investment risk by diversification because stock and bond prices can be volatile in the short run. Although stocks have the greatest historical rate of return, that is no guarantee of future performance, particularly over shorter time periods. (This fact becomes painfully obvious during the dramatic drops in stock market values that are experienced every so often, most recently a drop of 38% in the S&P 500 in 2008.) Thus some investment advisers recommend a mix of stock, bonds, and cash, as shown in Figure 13.2, to reduce investment risk. Younger investors may wish to have more stock, while those closer to retirement age typically have less stock in their portfolios.

Figure 13.2

The Relationship of Retirement Savings to Age When Savings Begins and Type of Investment Portfolio

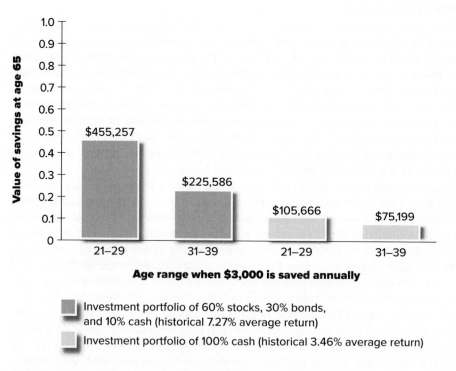

Note: Historical rates of return, geometric averages, 1928–2016: stocks (S&P 500), 9.53%; bonds (10-year U.S. Treasury Bond), 5.18%; cash (3-month U.S. Treasury Bill), 3.46%.

SOURCE: A. Damodaran, "Annual Returns on Stock, T. Bonds and T. Bills: 1928–Current," http://people.stern.nyu.edu/adamodar/New_Home_Page/datafile/histretSP.html.

It's also important—indeed, extraordinarily important—not to invest too heavily in any single stock.[25] Some Enron employees had 100% of their 401(k) assets in Enron stock. When the price dropped from $90 to less than $1 and Enron entered bankruptcy, their retirement money was gone. Employees at Bear Stearns, a storied Wall Street firm, also learned the hard way what can happen when you put all your eggs in one basket—company stock. When the stock price fell from its peak of $160 to $2 and Bear was purchased by JP Morgan Chase, the value of employee-owned shares fell from $6.3 billion to $79 million, a loss of 99%. Risk is compounded further by risk of job loss when one's employer struggles financially. So, repeat several times: *Always diversify,* and don't put all your retirement eggs in one basket.[26]

The Pension Protection Act (PPA) of 2006 requires defined contribution plans holding publicly traded securities to provide employees with (1) the opportunity to divest employer securities and (2) at least three investment options other than employer securities. The PPA also allows employers to enroll workers in their 401(k) plan automatically and to increase a worker's 401(k) contribution automatically to coincide with a raise or a work anniversary. Workers can decline, but the onus is on them to do so. Since the PPA, automatic enrollment (50% of plans) and automatic escalation (44%) have become common, thus helping increase worker retirement contributions.[27]

According to the U.S. Department of Labor's Employee Benefits Security Administration, ERISA requires that employers "meet fiduciary responsibilities." That includes acting solely in the interest of plan participants in managing the retirement plan, carrying out these management duties prudently, following plan documents, diversifying plan investments, and paying only reasonable plan expenses. Companies can be sued for any breach of these fiduciary responsibility duties. As an example, Lockheed reached a $62 million settlement in 2015 of a lawsuit that alleged its 401(k) plan was not prudently managed (e.g., because it charged excessive fees to participants). Toward the end of the Barack Obama's presidency, the Department of Labor issued a new fiduciary rule, which would have required any financial professional working with retirement plans and/or who provides retirement planning advice to meet the fiduciary standard described here. Under Donald Trump's administration, the fiduciary rule has been put on hold and is under review by the Department of Labor. In the meantime, most financial professionals will continue to be held to the lesser "suitability standard," which means they are required to provide investment recommendations suitable for their clients but not necessarily in the best interest of their clients.

Cash Balance Plans

One way to combine the advantages of defined benefit plans and defined contribution plans is to use a **cash balance plan**. This type of retirement plan consists of individual accounts, as in a 401(k) plan. But in contrast to a 401(k), all the contributions come from the employer. Usually, the employer contributes a percentage of the employee's salary, say, 4% or 5%. The money in the cash balance plan earns interest according to a predetermined rate, such as the rate paid on U.S. Treasury bills. Employers guarantee this rate as in a defined benefit plan. This arrangement helps employers plan their contributions and helps employees predict their retirement benefits. If employees change jobs, they generally can roll over the balance into an individual retirement account.

Organizations switching from traditional defined benefit plans to cash balance plans should consider the effects on employees as well as on the organization's bottom line. Defined benefit plans are most generous to older employees with many years of service, and cash balance plans are most generous to young employees who will have many years

Cash balance plan
A retirement plan in which the employer sets up an individual account for each employee and contributes a percentage of the employee's salary; the account earns interest at a predetermined rate.

ahead in which to earn interest. For an organization with many experienced employees, switching from a defined benefit plan can produce great savings in pension benefits. In that case, the older workers are the greatest losers, unless the organization adjusts the program to retain their benefits.

Funding, Communication, and Vesting Requirements

ERISA does not require organizations to have pension plans, but those that are set up must meet certain requirements. In addition to the termination provisions discussed earlier, plans must meet certain guidelines on management and funding. For example, employers are required to make yearly contributions that are sufficient to cover future obligations. (As noted previously, underfunded plans require higher premiums.) ERISA also specifies a number of reporting and disclosure requirements involving the IRS, the Department of Labor, and employees.[28] Employees, for example, must receive within 90 days after entering a plan a **summary plan description (SPD)** that describes the plan's funding, eligibility requirements, risks, and so forth. Upon request, an employer must also make available to an employee an individual benefit statement, which describes the employee's vested and unvested benefits. Obviously, employers may wish to provide such information on a regular basis anyway as a means of increasing employees' understanding and the value employees attach to their benefits.

> **Summary plan description (SPD)**
>
> A reporting requirement of the Employee Retirement Income Security Act (ERISA) that obligates employers to describe the plan's funding, eligibility requirements, risks, and so forth within 90 days after an employee has entered the plan.

ERISA guarantees employees that when they become participants in a pension plan and work a specified minimum number of years, they earn a right to a pension upon retirement. These are referred to as *vesting rights*.[29] Vested employees have the right to their pension at retirement age, regardless of whether they remain with the employer until that time. Employee contributions to their own plans are always completely vested. The vesting of employer-funded pension benefits must take place under one of two schedules. Employers may choose to vest employees after five years; until that time, employers can provide zero vesting if they choose. Alternatively, employers may vest employees over a three- to seven-year period, with at least 20% vesting in the third year and each year thereafter. These two schedules represent minimum requirements; employers are free to vest employees more quickly. These are the two choices relevant to the majority of employers. However, so-called top-heavy plans, where pension benefits for "key" employees (like highly paid top managers) exceed a certain share of total pension benefits, require faster vesting for nonkey employees. On the other hand, multiemployer pension plans need not provide vesting until after 10 years of employment.

These requirements were put in place to prevent companies from terminating employees before they reach retirement age or before they reach their length-of-service requirements in order to avoid paying pension benefits. Transferring employees or laying them off as a means of avoiding pension obligations is not legal either, even if such actions are motivated partly by business necessity.[30] Employers are, however, free to choose whichever of the two vesting schedules is most advantageous. For example, an employer that experiences high quit rates during the fourth and fifth years of employment may choose five-year vesting to minimize pension costs.

The traditional defined benefit pension plan discourages employee turnover or delays it until the employer can recoup the training investment in employees.[31] Even if an employee's pension benefit is vested, it is usually smaller if the employee changes employers, mainly because the size of the benefit depends on earnings in the final years with an employer. Consider an employee who earns $30,000 after 20 years and $60,000 after 40 years.[32] The employer pays an annual retirement benefit equal to 1.5% of final earnings times the number of years of service. If the employee stays with the employer for 40 years, the annual benefit level upon retirement would be $36,000 (0.015 × $60,000 × 40). If, instead, the employee changes employers after 20 years (and has the same earnings progression), the retirement benefit from the first employer would be $9,000 (0.015 × $30,000 × 20). The annual benefit from the second employer would be $18,000 (0.015 × $60,000 × 20). Therefore, staying with one employer for 40 years would yield an annual retirement benefit of $36,000, versus a combined annual retirement benefit of $27,000 ($9,000 + $18,000) if the employee changes employers once. It has also been suggested that pensions are designed to encourage long-service employees, whose earnings growth may eventually exceed their productivity growth, to retire. This is consistent with the fact that retirement benefits reach their maximum at retirement age.[33]

The fact that in recent years many employers have sought to reduce their workforces through early retirement programs is also consistent with the notion that pensions are used to retain certain employees while encouraging others to leave. One early retirement program approach is to adjust years-of-service credit upward for employees willing to retire, resulting in a higher retirement benefit for them (and less monetary incentive to work). These workforce reductions may also be one indication of a broader trend toward employees becoming less likely to spend their entire careers with a single employer.[34] On one hand, if more mobility across employers becomes necessary or desirable, the current pension system's incentives against (or penalties for) mobility may require modification. On the other hand, perhaps increased employee mobility will reinforce the continued trend toward defined contribution plans [like 401(k)s], which have greater portability (ease of transfer of funds) across employers.[35]

PAY FOR TIME NOT WORKED

At first blush, paid vacation, holidays, sick leave, and so forth may not seem to make economic sense. The employer pays the employee for time not spent working, receiving no tangible production value in return. Therefore, some employers may see little direct advantage. Perhaps for this reason, a minimum number of vacation days (20) is mandated by law in the European Community. As many as 30 days of vacation is not uncommon for relatively new employees in Europe. By contrast, there is no legal minimum in the United States, but 10 days is typical for large companies. U.S. workers must typically be with an employer for 20 to 25 years before they receive as much paid vacation as their western European counterparts.[36]

Sick leave programs in the United States, among employers that provide them, often provide full salary replacement for a limited period of time, usually not exceeding 26 weeks. The amount of sick leave is often based on length of service, accumulating with service (one day per month, for example). Sick leave policies need to be carefully structured to avoid providing employees with the wrong incentives. For example, if sick leave days disappear at the end of the year (rather than accumulate), a "use it or lose it" mentality may develop among employees, contributing to greater absenteeism. Organizations have developed a number of measures to counter this.[37] Some allow sick days to accumulate, then pay employees for the number of sick days when they retire or resign. Employers may also attempt to communicate to their employees that accumulated sick leave is better saved to use as a bridge to long-term disability, because the replacement rate (the ratio of sick leave or disability payments to normal salary) for the former is typically higher. Sick leave payments may equal 100% of usual salary, whereas the typical replacement ratio for long-term disability is 60%, so the more sick leave accumulated, the longer an employee can avoid dropping to 60% of usual pay when unable to work.

LO 13-3
Discuss how employee benefits in the United States compare with those in other countries.

Figure 13.3

Normal Annual Hours Worked Relative to United States

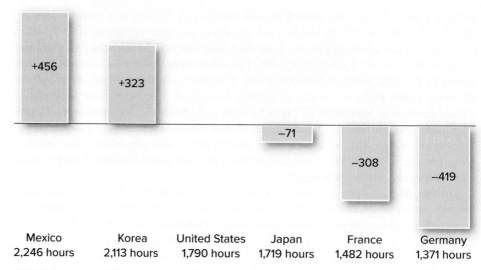

Mexico	Korea	United States	Japan	France	Germany
+456	+323		−71	−308	−419
2,246 hours	2,113 hours	1,790 hours	1,719 hours	1,482 hours	1,371 hours

SOURCE: Organization for Economic Cooperation and Development. Data for 2015. http://stats.oecd.org/Index.aspx? Section on Labour, Subsection on Labour Force Statistics. Accessed April 15, 2017.

Microsoft recently required its contractors and vendors to provide paid sick leave for their employees.[38] In 2015, President Obama signed an executive order requiring companies that contract with the federal government to provide paid sick leave. Other companies pay for time that employees devote to charity. For example, employees in General Electric's high-potential program can be paid for a week doing charitable work. One recent example was volunteering with BuildOn, a charity that has built more than 660 schools in impoverished areas of the world.[39]

Although vacation and other paid leave programs help attract and retain employees, there is a cost to providing time off with pay, especially in a global economy. The fact that vacation and other paid leave practices differ across countries contributes to the differences in labor costs described in Chapter 11. Consider that, on average, in manufacturing, German workers work 419 fewer hours per year than their U.S. counterparts. (See Figure 13.3.) In other words, German workers are at work approximately 10.2 fewer weeks per year than their U.S. counterparts. It is perhaps not surprising then that German manufacturers have looked outside Germany for alternative production sites. (However, you might consider what you could do with the equivalent of an extra 10 plus weeks away from work.)

FAMILY-FRIENDLY POLICIES

To ease employees' conflicts between work and nonwork, organizations may use *family-friendly policies* (also known as policies that help balance work and family) such as family leave policies and child care.[40] Although the programs discussed here would seem to be targeted to a particular group of employees, these programs often have "spillover effects" on other employees, who see them as symbolizing a general corporate concern for human resources, thus promoting loyalty even among employee groups that do not use the programs and possibly resulting in improved organizational performance.[41] Evidence suggests that firms using family-friendly policies have better quality management practices overall that are positively associated with organization performance.[42]

COMPETING THROUGH SUSTAINABILITY

Ikea Provides Parental Leave (to All Employees)

There are only so many hours in a week and no prospect of that changing. Employees want to have careers and earn enough money to live the lives they want. But fitting in earning and living each week can be a challenge. That is especially true when a new child arrives. As we note elsewhere in this chapter, paid family leave is required by law in many developed countries, but the United States is not one of them. Therefore, it falls to individual employers to decide whether to offer paid family leave to provide a more sustainable model to balance work, family, and life. In the chapter opener, we saw that the SAS Institute is one of the leaders in this area. However, SAS employs mostly well-paid, highly-skilled employees and the competition for those jobs is fierce.

What about an example of a company in the United States that has primarily lower-paid, hourly employees, even those who are part time, and provides paid family leave? Well, one example is Ikea, a furniture company headquartered in, not the United States, but in Sweden. It recently announced a new paid family leave policy of 12–16 weeks, depending on how long employees have been with the company. The policy will cover roughly 13,000 of its 15,000 U.S. employees and the policy will apply to mothers and fathers and to births, adoptions, and foster children. Employees with at least one year of tenure will receive 12 weeks, with 100% of their salary paid for the first 6 weeks and 50% of their salary paid for the remaining 6 weeks. Employees with at least three years of tenure will receive 16 weeks, with 8 weeks of 100% pay and the remaining 8 weeks at 50% of pay. Even employees who work only 10 hours a week would be eligible. Ikea's plan is to use interim assignments to do the work and to encourage managers, one-half of whom are women, to use the program themselves as part of its strategy to make hourly workers comfortable using it. In addition to helping provide a more sustainable approach to balancing work and nonwork spheres, Ikea, like many companies, especially retailers, is also facing a tightening labor market, as we discussed in Chapter 11. As such, Ikea also recently increased its minimum hourly wage to nearly $12/hour.

DISCUSSION QUESTIONS
1. How unique is Ikea's policy? Explain.
2. What factors have contributed to Ikea's adoption of this policy? Will both employees and Ikea benefit from this policy? What about shareholders? Explain.

SOURCES: B. Lam, "Ikea's Leave Policy Actually Includes Most of Its Workers," *The Atlantic*, December 6, 2016; A. D'Innocenzio, "As Workforce Tightens, Ikea Expands Parental Leave," *Milwaukee Journal Sentinel*, December 6, 2016.

Since 1993 the **Family and Medical Leave Act** requires organizations with 50 or more employees within a 75-mile radius to provide as much as 12 weeks of unpaid leave after childbirth or adoption; to care for a seriously ill child, spouse, or parent; or for an employee's own serious illness. Employees are guaranteed the same or a comparable job on their return to work. Employees with less than one year of service or who work less than 25 hours per week or who are among the 10% highest paid are not covered.

Many employers had already taken steps to deal with this issue, partly to help attract and retain key employees. Less than 10% of American families fit the image of a husband working outside the home and a wife who stays home to take care of the children.[43]

The United States still offers significantly less unpaid leave than most western European countries and Japan. Moreover, paid family leave remains rare in the United States (13% of employees are eligible, according to Table 13.3), in even sharper contrast

Family and Medical Leave Act
The 1993 act that requires employers with 50 or more employees to provide up to 12 weeks of unpaid leave after childbirth or adoption; to care for a seriously ill child, spouse, or parent; or for an employee's own serious illness.

to western Europe and Japan, where it is typically mandated by law.[44] Until the passage of the Americans with Disabilities Act, the only applicable law was the Pregnancy Discrimination Act of 1978, which requires employers that offer disability plans to treat pregnancy as they would any other disability. The "Competing through Sustainability" box provides an example of a (Swedish) company that provides paid leave in the United States, notably even for low-paid employees.

Experience with the Family and Medical Leave Act suggests that a majority of those opting for this benefit fail to take the full allotment of time. This is especially the case among female executives. Many of these executives find they do not enjoy maternity leave as much as they expected they would and miss the challenges associated with their careers. Others fear that their careers would be damaged in the long run by missing out on opportunities that might arise while they are out on leave.[45]

Child Care

U.S. companies increasingly provide some form of child care support to their employees. This support comes in several forms that vary in their degree of organizational involvement.[46] The lowest level of involvement, offered by 38% of companies, is when an organization supplies and helps employees collect information about the cost and quality of available child care. At the next level, organizations provide vouchers or discounts for employees to use at existing child care facilities (2% of companies). At the highest level, firms provide child care at or near their worksites (7% of companies). Toyota's Child Development Program provides 24-hour-a-day care for children of workers at its Georgetown, Kentucky, plant. This facility is designed to meet the needs of employees working evening and night shifts who want their children to be on the same schedule. In this facility, the children are kept awake all night. At the end of the night shift, the parents pick up their children and the whole family goes home to bed.[47]

An organization's decision to staff its own child care facility should not be taken lightly. It is typically a costly venture with important liability concerns. Moreover, the results, in terms of reducing absenteeism and enhancing productivity, are often mixed.[48] One reason for this is that many organizations are "jumping on the day care bandwagon" without giving much thought to the best form of assistance for their specific employees.

As an alternative example, Memphis-based First Tennessee Bank, which was losing 1,500 days of productivity a year because of child care problems, considered creating its own on-site day care center. Before acting, however, the company surveyed its employees. This survey indicated that the only real problem with day care occurred when the parents' regular day care provisions fell through because of sickness on the part of the child or provider. Based on these findings, the bank opted to establish a sick-child care center, which was less costly and smaller in scope than a full-time center and yet still solved the employees' major problem. As a result, absenteeism dropped so dramatically that the program paid for itself in the first nine months of operation.[49]

©Lexington Herald-Leader/Getty Images

Toyota employees check in on their kids at the Georgetown location on-site child care.

Managing Benefits: Employer Objectives and Strategies

Although the regulatory environment places some important constraints on benefits decisions, employers retain significant discretion and need to evaluate the payoff of such decisions.[50] As discussed earlier, however, this evaluation needs to recognize that employees have come to expect certain things from employers. Employers who do not meet these expectations run the risk of violating what has been called an "implicit contract" between the employer and its workers. If employees believe their employers feel little commitment to their welfare, they can hardly be expected to commit themselves to the company's success.

Clearly, there is much room for progress in the evaluation of benefits decisions.[51] Despite some of the obvious reasons for benefits—group discounts, regulation, and minimizing compensation-related taxes—organizations do not do as well as they could in spelling out what they want their benefits package to achieve and evaluating how well they are succeeding. Research suggests that most organizations do not have written benefits objectives.[52] Obviously, without clear objectives to measure progress, evaluation is difficult (and less likely to occur). Table 13.5 provides the most highly ranked benefits objectives across U.S. companies.[53]

LO 13-4
Describe the effects of benefits management on cost and workforce quality.

SURVEYS AND BENCHMARKING

As with cash compensation, an important element of benefits management is knowing what the competition is doing. Survey information on benefits packages is available from private consultants, the U.S. Chamber of Commerce, and the Bureau of Labor Statistics (BLS).[54] BLS data of the sort in Table 13.3 and the more detailed information on programs and provisions available from consultants are useful in designing competitive benefits packages. To compete effectively in the product market, cost information is also necessary. A good source is again the BLS, which provides information on benefits costs for specific categories as well as breakdowns by industry, occupation, union status, and organization size. (See Figure 13.4.)

COST CONTROL

In thinking about cost control strategies, it is useful to consider several factors. First, the larger the cost of a benefit category, the greater the opportunity for savings. Second, the growth trajectory of the benefit category is also important: even if costs are currently acceptable, the rate of growth may result in serious costs in the future. Third, cost containment efforts can work only to the extent that the employer has significant discretion in choosing how much to spend in a benefit category. Much of the cost of legally required benefits (like Social Security) is relatively fixed, which constrains cost reduction efforts. Even with legally required benefits, however, employers can take actions to limit costs

Increase employee productivity
Increase employee satisfaction
Increase employee loyalty
Attract employees
Help employees make better financial decisions

Table 13.5
The Five Most Highly Ranked Benefits Objectives for Employers

SOURCE: *MetLife's 15 Annual U.S. Employee Benefits Trends Study,* 2017, https://benefittrends.metlife.com/media/1382/2017-ebts-report_0320_exp0518_v2.pdf.

Figure 13.4

Employee Benefits Cost by Category, Private-Sector Workers

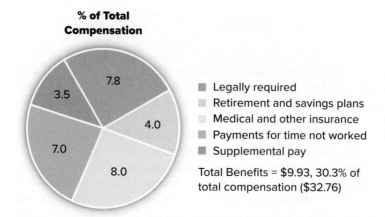

% of Total Compensation

- Legally required
- Retirement and savings plans
- Medical and other insurance
- Payments for time not worked
- Supplemental pay

Total Benefits = $9.93, 30.3% of total compensation ($32.76)

SOURCE: U.S. Department of Labor, "Employer Costs for Employee Compensation—December 2016," March 17, 2017, News Release USDL-17-0321.

because of "experience ratings," which impose higher taxes on employers with high rates of unemployment or workers' compensation claims.

One benefit—medical and other insurance—stands out as a target for cost control for two reasons. Costs are high and growth in costs has typically been high, even in the face of determined efforts to control the growth of costs. Second, employers have many options for attacking costs and improving quality, and the Affordable Care Act makes these issues even more salient for employers.

Health Care: Controlling Costs and Improving Quality

As Table 13.6 indicates, the United States spends more on health care than any other country in the world, which helps explain why there is so much focus on controlling health care costs. U.S. health care expenditures have gone from roughly 5% of gross domestic product (GDP) in 1960 (about $27 billion) to roughly 17% (which works out to

Table 13.6

Health Care Costs and Outcomes in Various Countries

	LIFE EXPECTANCY AT BIRTH, FEMALE	INFANT MORTALITY RATE (PER 1,000)	HEALTH EXPENDITURES AS A PERCENTAGE OF GDP
Canada	84	4	10%
France	86	4	11
Germany	84	3	11
Japan	87	2	11
Korea	86	3	7
Mexico	78	11	6
United Kingdom	83	4	10
United States	81	6	17

SOURCES: Organization for Economic Cooperation and Development, *OECD Health Statistics 2016*, www.OECD.org, and World Bank, http://data.worldbank.org/, accessed April 20, 2017.

	CENTERS FOR DISEASE CONTROL AND PREVENTION, ALL AGES		GALLUP–HEALTHWAYS, 18 AND OLDER
YEAR	MILLIONS	%	%
2000	41.3	14.9	
2005	41.2	14.2	
2010	48.6	16.0	16.4
2011	46.3	15.1	17.0
2012	45.5	14.7	16.8
2013	44.8	14.4	17.1[a]
2014	36.0	11.5	12.9[a]
2015	28.6	9.1	11.9[a]
2016			10.9[a]

Table 13.7
Number and Percentage of People without Health Insurance, United States

[a]Fourth quarter of year.

SOURCES: Z. Auter, "US Uninsured Rate Holds at Low of 10.9% in Fourth Quarter," Gallup, January 19, 2017, http://www.gallup.com/poll/201641/uninsured-rate-holds-low-fourth-quarter.aspx; J. Levy, "In U.S., Uninsured Rate Dips to 11.9% in First Quarter," http://www.gallup.com/poll/182348/uninsured-rate-dips-first-quarter.aspx; J. S. Schiller, B. W. Ward, and G. Freeman, "Early Release of Selected Estimates Based on Data from the 2013 National Health Interview Survey," June 2014, Centers for Disease Control and Prevention, http://www.cdc.gov/nchs/data/nhis/earlyrelease/earlyrelease201406.pdf; B. W. Ward, T. C. Clarke, C. N. Nugent, and J. S. Schiller, "Early Release of Selected Estimates Based on Data from the 2015 National Health Interview Survey," Centers for Disease Control and Prevention, May 2016, https://www.cdc.gov/nchs/data/nhis/earlyrelease/earlyrelease201605.pdf.

about $3.1 trillion) more recently. Yet the percentage of full-time workers receiving job-related health benefits had declined over the same period, peaking at 16–17%, or almost 50 million uninsured (see Table 13.7).[55] As Table 13.6 shows, the United States also trails Japan and western Europe on measures of life expectancy and infant mortality. The United States recently made progress on health insurance coverage (see Table 13.7), apparently due to the Affordable Care Act.[56]

Unlike workers in most western European countries, who have nationalized health systems, the majority of Americans receiving health insurance get it through their (or a family member's) employer.[57] Consequently, health insurance, like pensions, discourages employee turnover because not all employers provide health insurance benefits.[58]

One trend in plan design has been to shift costs to employees through the use of (higher) deductibles, coinsurance, exclusions and limitations, and maximum benefits.[59] These costs can be structured such that employees act on incentives to shift to less expensive plans.[60] Another trend has been to focus on reducing, rather than shifting, costs through such activities as preadmission testing and second surgical opinions. The use of alternative providers like **health maintenance organizations (HMOs)** and **preferred provider organizations (PPOs)** has also increased. HMOs differ from more traditional providers by focusing on preventive care and outpatient treatment, requiring employees to use only HMO services, and providing benefits on a prepaid basis. Many HMOs pay physicians and other health care workers a flat salary instead of using the traditional fee-for-service system, under which a physician's pay may depend on the number of patients seen. Paying on a salary basis is intended to reduce incentives for physicians to schedule more patient visits or medical procedures than might be necessary. (Of course, there is the risk that incentives will be reduced too much, resulting in inadequate access to medical procedures and specialists.) PPOs are essentially groups of health care providers that contract with employers, insurance companies, and so forth to provide health care at a

Health Maintenance Organization (HMO)
A health care plan that provides benefits on a prepaid basis for employees who are required to use only HMO medical service providers.

Preferred Provider Organization (PPO)
A group of health care providers who contract with employers, insurance companies, and so forth to provide health care at a reduced fee.

reduced fee. They differ from HMOs in that they do not provide benefits on a prepaid basis and employees often are not required to use the preferred providers. Instead, employers may provide incentives for employees to choose, for example, a physician who participates in the plan. In general, PPOs seem to be less expensive than traditional delivery systems but more expensive than HMOs.[61]

Another trend in employers' attempts to control costs has been to vary required employee contributions based on the employee's health and risk factors rather than charging each employee the same premium. Some companies go further, refusing to employ people with certain risk factors such as smokers.

Some employers now offer a "Medical tourism" benefit, which means sending patients to other countries where medical procedures can sometimes be done much more cheaply. For example, under a program at Hannaford Brothers, a Maine-based grocery chain, the company would pay for an employee (and significant other) to travel to Singapore for a knee or hip replacement. Doing so saved the company roughly $30,000 to $40,000 and saved the employee about $3,000 in out-of-pocket costs (i.e., the deductible). And, the employee and travel companion get to experience another country.[62] Telemedicine is another approach to reducing costs (see the "Competing through Technology" box).

Employee Wellness Programs. Employee wellness programs (EWPs) focus on changing behaviors both on and off work time that could eventually lead to future health problems. EWPs are preventive in nature; they attempt to manage health care costs (and workers' compensation costs) by decreasing employees' needs for services. Typically, these programs aim at specific health risks such as high blood pressure, high cholesterol levels, smoking, and obesity. They also try to promote positive health influences such as physical exercise and good nutrition. Johnson & Johnson estimated a return of $2.71 for every $1.00 spent on employee wellness programs.[63] However, not all companies have found such positive returns.[64] Thus, each company should bring evidence to bear to evaluate its own return, which will likely depend on the program design, the nature of the workforce, and other contextual factors.

EWPs are either passive or active. Passive programs use little or no outreach to individuals, nor do they provide ongoing support to motivate them to use the resources. Active wellness centers assume that behavior change requires not only awareness and opportunity but also support and reinforcement.

One example of a passive wellness program is a health education program that aims to raise awareness of the importance of good health and how to achieve it. In these programs, a health educator usually conducts classes or lunchtime lectures (or coordinates outside speakers). The program may also have various promotions (like an annual mile run or a "smoke-out") and include a newsletter that reports on current health issues.

Another kind of passive employee wellness program is a fitness facility. In this kind of program, the company sets up a center for physical fitness equipped with aerobic and muscle-building exercise machines and staffed with certified athletic trainers. The facility is publicized within the organization, and employees are free to use it on their own time. Aetna, for example, has created five state-of-the-art health clubs that serve more than 7,500 workers.[65] Northwestern Mutual Life's fitness facilities are open 24 hours a day to its 3,300 employees.[66] Health education classes related to smoking cessation and weight loss may be offered as well.

One kind of active wellness center is the outreach and follow-up model. This type of wellness center contains all the features of a passive model, but it also has counselors who handle one-on-one outreach and provide tailored, individualized programs for

Telemedicine

With the advent of faster Internet connections and ever-increasing access to digital technology (i.e., via smartphones, webcams, and other devices), more health care providers are relying on electronic communications to interact with patients. Outside of St. Louis, doctors and nurses work 24/7 in a "hospital without beds" to provide remote support for 38 small hospitals across several states, many of which do not have a doctor on-site 24/7. In the intensive care unit, doctors use large video monitors that report data on remote patients and also have access via a high-resolution, two-way camera.

Employers also are providing a telemedicine option to their employees. One survey found that 70% of large employers offer the option, but only about 3% of employees at those companies had used it. Companies face an ongoing challenge of controlling health care costs and improving worker productivity. Telemedicine can assist in this regard, by helping workers to miss less work time to take care of health issues. One estimate is

that a typical telemedicine visit costs about $50. That compares to in-person visits, which are estimated to be $110 to a primary care provider, $150 for urgent care, and $865 for an emergency room visit. The employee also saves the time ordinarily needed to travel to and from an appointment plus the time spent waiting to see a provider.

Telemedicine typically works as follows: A patient requests a consultation with a provider by phone or online. Medical histories are taken on the phone and/or submitted by the patient online. A doctor or other health care provider then contacts the patient to discuss his or her symptoms. The provider can recommend treatment (including ordering a prescription) or advise the patient to make an appointment for an in-person visit.

So, why don't more employees use available telemedicine services? One reason is that some medical conditions are (or could be) too serious. Employees may also

prefer to see their regular doctor. There are also issues with how well treatment is coordinated with the employee's primary doctor and, relatedly, obtaining access to patient health records may be a challenge. For now, some employees find the service valuable, and time will tell whether telemedicine—through improvements in technology, integration, and other aspects—becomes a larger part of health care delivery and one part of addressing cost control and productivity goals.

DISCUSSION QUESTIONS

1. As an employee, how would you feel about using the telemedicine option? Explain.
2. Think about (and try to estimate) how much it costs for an employee to travel to see a healthcare provider during working hours. Be sure to include the cost of time.

SOURCES: L. Schencker, "More Employers Are Offering Telemedicine, but Why Aren't Workers Using It?" *Chicago Tribune*, October 7, 2016; M. Beck, "How Telemedicine Is Transforming Health Care," *Wall Street Journal*, June 26, 2016.

---

employees. Typically, tailored programs obtain baseline measures on various indicators (weight, blood pressure, lung capacity, and so on) and measure individuals' progress relative to these indicators over time. The programs set goals and provide small, symbolic rewards to individuals who meet their goals. Of course, stronger incentives are available and these could be paired with a wellness program.

This encouragement provided under an active wellness center needs to be particularly targeted to employees in high-risk categories (like those who smoke, are overweight, or have high blood pressure) for two reasons. First, a small percentage of employees create a disproportionate amount of health care costs; therefore, targeted interventions are more efficient. Second, research shows that those in high-risk categories are the most likely to perceive barriers (like family problems or work overload)[67] to participating in company-sponsored fitness programs. Thus, untargeted interventions are likely to miss the people that most need to be included.

Research on these different types of wellness centers leads to several conclusions.[68] First, the costs of health education programs are significantly less than those associated with either fitness facility programs or the follow-up model. Second, all three models are effective in reducing the risk factors associated with cardiovascular disease (obesity, high blood pressure, smoking, and lack of exercise). However, the follow-up model is significantly better than the other two in reducing the risk factors.

Somewhat ironically, well-meaning employers sometimes do things that work at cross-purposes—for example, providing employees with easy access to good food, while also wanting employees to be fit. Google decided to keep its good food, but it also decided it needed to change the way it presented food to employees. Its research found that people tend to load up on the first food they see. So, Google changed the cafeteria line so that the first thing employees now see is something healthy: the salad bar. Desserts weren't taken away but were banished to the far corner of the cafeteria (and serving size reduced). Google also focused on communicating to employees which foods were low in calories (green tags) and which ones (those higher in calories) were best taken in smaller portions (red tags).[69]

Health Care Costs and Quality: Ongoing Challenges. In 2016, the average annual premium for family coverage was $18,142, up 3.4% from the previous year, with employers paying $12,865 (71%) and employees paying $5,277 (29%) on average. For single coverage, the average premium was $6,435, with employers paying $5,306 (82%) and employees paying $1,129 (18%).[70] (These numbers pertain only to employers that provide health care benefits.)

Two important phenomena are often encountered in cost control efforts. First, piecemeal programs may not work well because steps to control one aspect (such as medical cost shifting) may lead employees to "migrate" to other programs that provide medical treatment at no cost to them (like workers' compensation). Second, there is often a so-called Pareto group, which refers to a small percentage (perhaps 20%) of employees being responsible for generating the majority (often 80%) of health care costs. Obviously, cost control efforts will be more successful to the extent that the costs generated by the Pareto group can be identified and managed effectively.[71]

Although cost control will continue to require a good deal of attention, there is a growing emphasis on monitoring health care quality, which has been described as "the next battlefield." A major focus is on identifying best medical practices by measuring and monitoring the relative success of alternative treatment strategies using large-scale databases and research.[72] "Big data" can be used to move beyond intuition to make better decisions, including helping organizations to provide quality health care coverage for employees, while controlling costs.

At Caesars Entertainment Corporation (which operates casinos), health insurance claim data on its 65,000 employees and their covered family members is analyzed as part of meeting this challenge. Among the thousands of variables that can be tracked are how much different medical services are used, the degree to which employees use name-brand versus (less expensive) generic prescription drugs, and the number of emergency room (ER) visits, which cost over $1,200 on average (for outpatient visits). By contrast, a visit to the doctor's office or to an urgent care facility is much less expensive (e.g., between $100 and $200). As an example, when Caesars looked at its Harrah's property in Philadelphia, it discovered that only about 11% of emergencies were being treated at urgent care facilities versus 34% across all of Caesars. To encourage employees to use the less expensive urgent care option more and emergency rooms less, Harrah's initiated a campaign to remind employees of how expensive ER visits are and provided them with a list of urgent care and alternative facilities that they were encouraged to use. Two years later, 17% of emergencies (up from 11%) were going to urgent care. Further, multiple ER visits by individual employees fell from 40% to 30%. Overall, on a companywide basis, in the first few years since beginning to track ER visits, Caesars employees had 10,000 fewer ER visits, replacing them with less expensive alternatives, resulting in a savings of $4.5 million.[73] In addition, employers increasingly cooperate with one another to develop "report cards" on health care

EVIDENCE-BASED HR

The new Health Transformation Alliance, a collaboration of 38 companies employing 6 million workers (including American Express and Johnson & Johnson), will use data and technology to improve the quality and cost of health care for its employees. The Alliance hopes to save as much as $600 million on drug spending, representing a reduction of approximately 15%. Part of the savings comes from the Alliance's bargaining power. However, another part of the plan is to change how care is delivered for conditions like diabetes, hip and knee replacements, and lower back pain. One element involves doctors' pay more strongly reflecting meeting objectives such as patient recovery time, with less incentive to prescribe more drugs or perform more tests and procedures. The Alliance will also use IBM's Watson software to "help" select drugs (and doctors) that provide the best value for the money and to predict which employees are most likely to develop conditions such as diabetes so as to take preventive action sooner. To perform these analyses, the goal is to use four years of data on pharmacy and insurance claims and electronic employee health records from each company.

Other companies are taking similar steps, sometimes focusing on particular issues that are most critical to them. For example, engine maker Cummins, Inc. is devoting considerable attention to the misuse of prescription opioid painkillers and is working to find alternative pain control methods for employees. Cummins notes the need for caution as most pain medication is legally prescribed and control of pain is critical. At the same time, use of such medication raises safety issues on the job and also can imperil employees' long-term health. According to one estimate, annual medical expenses for opioid abusers are about twice as high as the employer cost for other employees. Cummins relies on programs that use drug-test data and work with a pharmacy-benefits manager to track data on opioid prescriptions and attempt to detect pill-shopping. The company recently opened a new facility at its headquarters that provides services such as massage, acupuncture, physical therapy, and a full-time pharmacist, all in the interest of finding better and safer ways to control pain. Cummins has also trained supervisors on how to identify employees who may be having problems with painkillers and has trained plant managers on how to triage employees having an overdose.

SOURCES: J. Walker, "Alliance of Companies Unveil First Steps Aimed at Cutting Health-Care Costs," *Wall Street Journal*, March 7, 2017; R. E. Silverman, "One Employer Fights against Prescription-Drug Abuse," *Wall Street Journal*, November 15, 2016.

provider organizations to facilitate better choices by the employers and to receive improved health care. General Motors, Ford, and Chrysler, for example, have developed this type of system and made it web accessible.[74]

When we discuss the Affordable Care Act later in this chapter, we will see that the act allows employers to use larger incentives (and penalties) than previously to encourage employee wellness, and some companies are making changes accordingly. We have provided a number of examples in this chapter of how employers use these tools. We now provide a few more. The state of Maryland will penalize employees as much as $450 per year for not undergoing required screenings or for not following up on treatment plans for chronic conditions. At pharmacy company CVS Health, an employee who does not complete the annual health assessment will have to pay $600 more per year for insurance coverage. (On the incentive side, JetBlue employees can receive as much as $400 per year in their health savings or reimbursement accounts for signing up for a variety of activities including smoking cessation.) Survey evidence indicates that most employees don't approve of such programs. Nevertheless, use seems to be increasing as employers seek to control health care costs.[75]

Staffing Responses to Control Benefits Cost Growth

Employers may change staffing practices to control benefits costs. First, because benefits costs are fixed (in that they do not usually increase with hours worked), the benefits cost per hour can be reduced by having employees work more hours. However, there are drawbacks to having employees work more hours. The Fair Labor Standards Act (FLSA), introduced in Chapter 11, requires that nonexempt employees be paid time-and-a-half for hours in excess of 40 per week. Yet the decline in U.S. work hours tapered off in the late 1940s; work hours have increased since then. Thus, even with the time-and-a-half cost of overtime, employers may prefer employees to work more hours, given the level of fixed benefits costs (and the fact that hiring additional workers would further increase fixed benefits costs in addition to increasing recruiting and training costs).[76]

A second possible effect of FLSA regulations (although this is more speculative) is that organizations will try to have their employees classified as exempt whenever possible (although such attempts may run afoul of FLSA law). The growth in the number of salaried workers (many of whom are exempt) may also reflect an effort by organizations to limit the benefits cost per hour without having to pay overtime. A third potential effect is the growth in part-time employment and the use of temporary workers, which may be a response to rising benefits costs. Part-time workers are less likely to receive benefits than full-time workers, although labor market shortages in recent years have reduced this difference.[77] Benefits for temporary workers are also usually quite limited.

Fourth, employers may be more likely to classify workers as independent contractors rather than employees, which eliminates the employer's obligation to provide legally required employee benefits. However, the Internal Revenue Service (IRS) scrutinizes such decisions carefully, as Microsoft and other companies have discovered. Microsoft was compelled to reclassify a group of workers as employees (rather than as independent contractors) and to grant them retroactive benefits. Uber, which competes with taxis by providing ride-sharing, is one of many companies currently facing legal action challenging its classification of workers (drivers in the Uber case) as contractors rather than as employees. The IRS looks at several factors, including the permanency of the relationship between employer and worker, how much control the employer exercises in

INTEGRITY IN ACTION

Hiring Contractors or Employees?

One investment banker described the thinking of many companies regarding hiring employees as follows: "Can I automate it? If not, can I outsource it? If not, can I give it to an independent contractor or freelancer?" In other words, adding an employee is "a last resort." Virgin Atlantic's chief executive tells investors that "we will outsource every job that we can that is not customer-facing." So far, that includes baggage delivery, reservations, catering, and heavy maintenance. Google, which is regularly ranked by *Fortune* as one of the best places to work, is thought to have equal numbers of outsourced workers and employees. Uber, of course, relies on independent contractors. We saw that some gig workers prefer this model. However, some do not because of uncertain work and income and the lack of benefits.

The *New York Times* editorial board observed that the idea of the gig economy can sound good, enabling (often with technology) workers to follow their entrepreneurial dreams and freeing workers from the "drudgery of 9 to 5 jobs." However, it then went on to say that "there is no utopia at companies like Uber, Lyft, Instacart, and Handy," where it says workers are "manipulated into

working long hours for low pay" and where "companies have discovered they can use technology to engage in "old fashioned worker exploitation."

Some companies that operate in industries where the gig model is common are taking a different course by hiring workers as employees, whether because of integrity, efficiency reasons, or both. They are doing so in part because of the problems other companies have experienced using the gig model. For example, Uber and similar companies continue to face a slew of lawsuits arguing that workers should be classified as employees, thus making them eligible for benefits. Another issue is whether the cost of acquiring and retaining workers who are not employees is beginning to eat up the theoretical cost savings of the gig model. For example, Managed by Q, which provides office and cleaning services, hires employees. Homer, a food delivery and logistics company in New York, hires its couriers as employees and pays $15 an hour. Homer believes that this has created a "culture of retention," which saves on recruiting and turnover costs and also makes for consistently better customer service. Similarly, Eden, a company in the Bay Area that helps

manage offices, uses "wizards" (employees) to clean and fix things for its clients. It says that the employee model means that its costs are 30% higher, but this approach works for Eden because its employees also "stay 30% longer."

DISCUSSION QUESTIONS

1. Is doing something that is good for workers and costs money always bad for business (win-lose, zero-sum), or can it be good for business and workers (win-win)?

2. How are the workers described here different from other gig workers (e.g., software developers)? Do the groups have similar or different preferences and leverage? Does one group need more protection than the other group? Explain.

3. Do you feel it is better to leave decisions about the relationship with workers in the hands of employers, or do you see the need for a larger role of government? Explain.

SOURCES: The Editorial Board, "The Gig Economy's False Promise," *New York Times*, April 10, 2017; A. Griswold, "Startups Have a Crazy New Idea for Saving Money: Be Nice to Workers," *Quartz*, October 20, 2016; L. Weber, "The End of Employees," *Wall Street Journal*, February 3, 2017.

directing the worker, and whether the worker offers services to only that employer. Permanency, control, and dealing with a single employer are viewed by the IRS as suggestive of an employment relationship. The "Integrity in Action" box provides examples of companies that have moved toward using more employees rather than more independent contractors.

Western Firms Design the Workplace and Benefits to Attract and Retain Indian Women

In India, about 27% of women are in the labor force, compared to 50% worldwide and compared to over 60% labor force participation in China, another large emerging economy. In India, even women's clothing stores are said to have primarily male employees. However, at the new Mall of India in suburban Dehli, one-half of employees at food and fashion establishments are women. Although one goal is diversity, several executives expressed their belief that "women are great for business" because they are seen as "more hygienic, customer-friendly," and less likely to leave. Another executive says that "people in the U.S. won't believe the kinds of things we do" to attract and retain female employees in India.

One issue is that quick-serve food businesses like KFC serve meat, which is "blasphemous for most Hindus." One mother wanted to make sure "it wouldn't corrupt her daughter." The mother looked in the window. When she saw other women working there, she felt it would be a "safe place" for her and gave her daughter permission to work there. McDonald's invites family members to visit its stores to see the work environment for women. Burger King teaches its female employees self-defense. KFC, Pizza Hut, and others offer a mentorship program that helps develop women to become managers. Some stores employ only women. Other stores schedule women only for morning shifts so that they can finish before dark. McDonald's assigns "a female confidant" in each store so that they have someone they can talk to about personal or family issues, things they may be hesitant to discuss with a male supervisor or coworker. It also provides flexible hours to mothers and tries to transfer them to another store if they move to live with their husbands. McDonald's also changed its uniforms in response to reluctance of families to let their daughters wear trousers. They make the trousers looser and permitted women to leave their shirts untucked. In combination, that helped make uniforms more similar to traditional Indian clothing. The father of one young woman had initially resisted allowing his daughter to work at McDonald's but agreed once he became comfortable that she would be safe at work. He died recently, making his daughter the family's only wage-earner. Her mother does not work. She just switched to a new job at Wendy's for an increase in pay, and she says that "I can take care of everything now."

DISCUSSION QUESTIONS

1. Why is it a challenge in India to attract and retain women as employees?
2. To what extent are the strategies used in India applicable elsewhere?

SOURCES: P. Rana, "Fast-Food Chains in India Cultivate Untapped Workforce: Women," *Wall Street Journal*, December 27, 2016.

NATURE OF THE WORKFORCE

Although general considerations such as cost control and "protection against the risks of old age, loss of health, and loss of life" are important, employers must also consider the specific demographic composition and preferences of their current workforces in designing their benefits packages. The "Competing through Globalization" box provides examples of how some companies have tailored their policies to attract and retain women employees in India.

At a broad level, basic demographic factors such as age and sex can have important consequences for the types of benefits employees want. For example, an older workforce is more likely to be concerned about (and use) medical coverage, life insurance, and pensions. A workforce with a high percentage of women of childbearing age may care more about disability leave. Young, unmarried men and women often have less interest in benefits generally, preferring higher wages and salaries.

Although some general conclusions about employee preferences can be drawn based on demographics, more finely tuned assessments of employee benefit preferences need to be done. One approach is to use marketing research methods to assess employees' preferences the same way consumers' demands for products

©Stan Honda/Getty Images

and services are assessed.[78] Methods include personal interviews, focus groups, and questionnaires. Relevant questions might include the following:

- What benefits are most important to you?
- If you could choose one new benefit, what would it be?
- If you were given *x* dollars for benefits, how would you spend it?

As with surveys generally, care must be taken not to raise employee expectations regarding future changes. If the employer is not prepared to act on the employees' input, surveying may do more harm than good.

The preceding discussion may imply that the current makeup of the workforce is a given, but this is not the case. As discussed earlier, the benefits package may influence the composition of the workforce. For example, a benefits package that has strong medical benefits and pensions may be particularly attractive to older people or those with families. An attractive pension plan may be a way to attract workers who wish to make a long-term commitment to an organization.[79] Where turnover costs are high, this type of strategy may have some appeal. On the other hand, a company that has lucrative health care benefits may attract and retain people with high health care costs. Sick leave provisions may also affect the composition of the workforce. Organizations need to think about the signals their benefits packages send and the implications of these signals for workforce composition. In this vein, Table 13.8 shows the benefits used by Google, a company that regularly tops *Fortune*'s list of "100 Best Companies to Work For," to attract and retain its desired workforce.

COMMUNICATING WITH EMPLOYEES AND MAXIMIZING BENEFITS VALUE
Employees Typically Underestimate the Value of their Benefits

Effective communication of benefits information to employees is critical if employers are to realize sufficient returns on their benefits investments. Research makes it clear that current employees and job applicants often have a very poor idea of what benefits provisions are already in place and the cost or market value of those benefits. One study asked employees to estimate both the amount contributed by the employer to their medical

LO 13-5
Explain the importance of effectively communicating the nature and value of benefits to employees.

Table 13.8
Employee Benefits at
Google

- Sleep pods
- Up to $8,000/year in tuition reimbursement
- On-site perks include medical and dental facilities; oil change and bike repair; valet parking; free washers and dryers; and free breakfast, lunch, and dinner on a daily basis at 11 gourmet restaurants
- Seven-acre sports complex, which includes a roller hockey rink; courts for basketball, bocce, and shuffle ball; and horseshoe pits
- Unlimited sick leave
- 27 days of paid time off after one year of employment
- Global Education Leave program, enabling employees to take a leave of absence to pursue further education for up to 5 years and $150,000 in reimbursement
- Free shuttles equipped with WiFi from locations around the Bay Area to headquarter offices
- Fuel-efficiency vehicle incentive program ($5,000 incentive to purchase a hybrid car)
- A climbing wall
- Classes on a variety of subjects from estate planning and home purchasing to foreign language lessons in French, Spanish, Japanese, and Mandarin
- The ability to bring your dog to work
- When an employee dies, the spouse receives 50% of salary for 10 years and children each receive $12,000 per year until age 19 (age 23 if full-time students)
- Paid maternity (and paternity) leave: 5 months for mothers, 3 months for fathers

SOURCES: "100 Best Companies to Work For 2017," *Fortune*, http://beta.fortune.com/best-companies/; M. Garner, "Google Employees' Favorite Perks—Here's 8 of the Best," *The Street*, January 18, 2016, https://www.thestreet.com/story/13420255/4/google-employees-favorite-perks-here-s-8-of-the-best.html; J. Bort, "These 18 Tech Companies Offer the Best Benefits, According to Employees," *Business Insider*, May 1, 2015; J. D'Onfro and K. Smith, "Google Employees Reveal Their Favorite Perks about Working for the Company," *Business Insider*, July 1, 2014.

insurance and what it would cost the employees to provide their own health insurance. Employees significantly underestimated both the cost and market value of their medical benefits. In the case of family coverage, employee estimates of what it costs their employer to provide coverage for them were, on average, 62% below the actual cost.[80] As we saw earlier, the average employer today providing health care benefits spends $12,865 per year for family coverage. In the absence of effective communication, the just-discussed study would imply that a typical employee today might credit employers with only providing a benefit worth $4,889 (i.e., 0.38 × $12,865)—again, a very poor return on the employer's investment.

Research suggests that the situation with job applicants is no better. One study of MBAs found that 46% believed that benefits added 15% or less on top of direct payroll. Not surprisingly, perhaps, benefits were dead last on the applicants' priority lists in making job choices.[81] A study of undergraduate business majors found similar results, with benefits ranked 15th (out of 18) in importance in evaluating jobs. These results must be interpreted with caution, however. Some research suggests that job attributes can be ranked low in importance, not because they are unimportant per se, but because all employers are perceived to be about the same on that attribute. If some employers offered noticeably poorer benefits, the importance of benefits could become much greater.

Organizations can help remedy the problem of applicants' and employees' lack of knowledge about benefits. One study found that employees' awareness of benefits information was significantly increased through several media, including memoranda,

	PERCENTAGE
Enrollment materials (online or paper)	84%
Group employee benefits communications with an organizational representative	65
One-to-one employee benefits counseling with an organizational representative	51
Internet	48
Direct mail to home/residence	41
Newsletters (online or paper)	39
Benefit fairs	26
Virtual education	13
Social media	4
Group employee benefits communications with your vendor	3
Other	2

Table 13.9
Benefits Communication Methods Used by Organizations

Note: Survey of 447 organizations.
SOURCE: Employee Benefits Communication Methods, Adapted from "SHRM Survey Findings: State of Employee Benefits in the Workplace—Communicating Benefits," © SHRM 2012 (series), p. 15.

question-and-answer meetings, and detailed brochures. The increased awareness, in turn, contributed to significant increases in benefits satisfaction. Another study suggests, however, that increased employee knowledge of benefits can have a positive or negative effect, depending on the nature of the benefits package. For example, there was a negative, or inverse, correlation between cost to the employee and benefits satisfaction overall, but the correlation was more strongly negative among employees with greater knowledge of their benefits.[82] The implication is that employees will be least satisfied with their benefits if their cost is high and they are well informed.

One thing an employer should consider with respect to written benefits communication is that it has been estimated that tens of millions of employees in the United States may be functionally illiterate. Of course, there are many alternative ways to communicate benefits information. (See Table 13.9.) Nevertheless, most organizations spend little to communicate information about benefits, and much of this is spent on general written communications. Considering that Bureau of Labor Statistics data cited earlier indicate that U.S. employers spend a large amount of money on benefits ($9.83/hour or about $20,446/year) and that large employers spend even more ($16.78/hour or about $34,902/year), together with the complex nature of many benefits and the poor understanding of most employees, the typical communication effort may be inadequate.[83]

On a more positive note, organizations are increasingly using online tools to personalize and tailor communications to individual employees. Online tools have also enabled many organizations to eliminate benefits-related jobs now that employees can get answers to many benefits questions on their own. In addition, effective use of traditional approaches (e.g., booklets) can have a large effect on employee awareness.[84] Survey data (see Table 13.10) indicate that both traditional and online methods are seen as effective by employees, although one suspects that will continue to evolve over time. The table also indicates that although most employees are happy with the current frequency of benefits communication from their employers, a sizable minority would like more.

Table 13.10

Percentage of
Employees
Preferring Amount
and Types of
Benefits
Communication

Frequency of Communication Preferred
Happy with current frequency: 55%
Prefer more frequently: 31%
No opinion: 10%
Prefer less frequently: 4%
Type of Communication Preferred
Work e-mail: 47%
Personal e-mail: 28%
Online avatar that recommends benefits to meet individual needs: 19%
Group meetings: 19%
Individual one-on-one meetings: 18%

SOURCES: Frequency preferences: Prudential Group Insurance, *Ninth Study Of Employee Benefits: Today & Beyond,* 2016, http://research.prudential.com/documents/rp/benefits_and_beyond_2016.pdf. Based on *N* = 969 employees, ages 22 or older, who work full time for a company with at least 50 employees. Type preferences: Prudential Group Insurance, *Eighth Annual Study of Employee Benefits: Today & Beyond,* 2014, http://research.prudential.com. Based on *N* = 1,000 employees, ages 22 or older, who work full time for a company with at least 25 employees.

Flexible Benefits Plans

Rather than a single standard benefits package for all employees, flexible benefit plans (flex-plans or cafeteria-style plans) permit employees to choose the types and amounts of benefits they want for themselves. The plans vary according to such things as whether minimum levels of certain benefits (such as health care coverage) are prescribed and whether employees can receive money for having chosen a "light" benefits package (or have to pay extra for more benefits). One example is vacation, where some plans permit employees to give up vacation days for more salary or, alternatively, purchase extra vacation days through a salary reduction.

What are the potential advantages of such plans?[85] In the best case, almost all of the objectives discussed previously can be positively influenced. First, employees can gain a greater awareness and appreciation of what the employer provides them, particularly with plans that give employees a lump sum to allocate to benefits. Second, by permitting employee choice, there should be a better match between the benefits package and the employees' preferences. As just one example of heterogeneous employee preferences, one study looked at how much salary employees would be willing to give up to have certain benefits. In the case of work schedule flexibility, females, those above median pay, and those age 57 or older would give up 23%, 30%, and 28% more base pay (compared to other groups), respectively, for greater flexibility.[86] Matching benefits to different employee preferences should improve employee attitudes and retention and perhaps performance.[87] Third, employers may achieve overall cost reductions in their benefits programs. Cafeteria plans can be thought of as similar to defined contribution plans, whereas traditional plans are more like defined benefit plans. The employer can control the size of the contribution under the former, but not under the latter, because the cost and utilization of benefits is beyond the employer's control. Costs can also be controlled by designing the choices so that employees have an incentive to choose more efficient options. For example, in the case of a medical flex-plan, employees who do not wish to take advantage of the (presumably more cost-effective) HMO have to pay significant deductibles and other costs under the alternative plans. Choice and resulting better matches might also lower costs by reducing spending on benefits that few employees value.

One drawback of cafeteria-style plans is their administrative cost, especially in the initial design and start-up stages. However, software packages and standardized flex-plans developed by consultants offer some help in this regard. Another possible drawback to these plans is adverse selection. Employees are most likely to choose benefits that they expect to need the most. Someone in need of dental work would choose as much dental coverage as possible. As a result, employer costs can increase significantly as each employee chooses benefits based on their personal value. Another result of adverse selection is the difficulty in estimating benefits costs under such a plan, especially in small companies. Adverse selection can be controlled, however, by limiting coverage amounts, pricing benefits that are subject to adverse selection higher, or using a limited set of packaged options, which prevents employees from choosing too many benefits options that would be susceptible to adverse selection.

Flexible Spending Accounts

A flexible spending account permits pretax contributions of up to $2,600 to an employee account that can be drawn on to pay for uncovered health care expenses (like deductibles or copayments). A separate account of up to $5,000 per year is permitted for pretax contributions to cover dependent care expenses. The federal tax code requires that funds in the health care and dependent care accounts be earmarked in advance and spent during the plan year. Remaining funds revert to the employer. Therefore, the accounts work best to the extent that employees have predictable expenses. The major advantage of such plans is the increase in take-home pay that results from pretax payment of health and dependent care expenses. Consider again the hypothetical employee with an effective total marginal tax rate of 40.33% from Table 13.1. The take-home pay from an additional $10,000 in salary with and without a flexible dependent care account is as follows:

	NO FLEXIBLE SPENDING CARE ACCOUNT	FLEXIBLE SPENDING CARE ACCOUNT
Salary portion	$10,000	$10,000
Pretax dependent care contribution	0	−2,600
Taxable salary	10,000	7,400
Tax (40.33%)	−4,033	−2,984
After-tax cost of dependent care	−2,600	0
Take-home pay	$ 3,367	$ 4,415

Therefore, the use of a flexible spending account saves the employee just over $1,000 ($4,415–$3,367 = $1,048) per year.

General Regulatory Issues

Although we have already discussed a number of regulatory issues, some additional ones require attention.

LO 13-6
Describe the regulatory constraints that affect the way employee benefits are designed and administered.

AFFORDABLE CARE ACT

The Affordable Care Act (ACA), signed into law in 2010, has several provisions that will have a major impact on employers as they are implemented through the year 2018. As we go to press, the future of the law is not clear. So far, there has been much discussion about the repeal or revision of the ACA, but no legislation has been passed. In the meantime, employers are subject to its provisions, which are summarized in Table 13.11.

NONDISCRIMINATION RULES, QUALIFIED PLANS, AND TAX TREATMENT

As a general rule, all benefits packages must meet certain rules to be classified as qualified plans. What are the advantages of a qualified plan? Basically, it receives more favorable tax treatment than a nonqualified plan. In the case of a qualified retirement plan, for example, these tax advantages include (1) an immediate tax deduction for employers for their contributions to retirement funds, (2) no tax liability for the employee at the time of the employer deduction, and (3) tax-free investment returns (from stocks, bonds, money markets, or the like) on the retirement funds.[88]

What rules must be satisfied for a plan to obtain qualified status? Each benefit area has different rules. It would be impossible to describe the various rules here, but some general observations are possible. Taking pensions as an example again, vesting requirements must be met. More generally, qualified plans must meet so-called nondiscrimination rules. Basically, this means that a benefit cannot discriminate in favor of "highly compensated employees." One rationale behind such rules is that the tax benefits of qualified benefits plans (and the corresponding loss of tax revenues for the U.S. government) should not go disproportionately to the wealthy.[89] Rather, the favorable tax treatment is designed to encourage employers to provide important benefits to a broad spectrum of employees. The nondiscrimination rules discourage owners or top managers from adopting plans that benefit them exclusively.

SEX, AGE, AND DISABILITY

Beyond the Pregnancy Discrimination Act's requirements discussed earlier in the chapter, a second area of concern for employers in ensuring legal treatment of men and women in the benefits area has to do with pension benefits. Women tend to live longer than men, meaning that pension benefits for women are more costly, all else being equal. However, in its 1978 *Manhart* ruling, the Supreme Court declared it illegal for employers to require women to contribute more to a defined benefit plan than men: Title VII protects individuals, and not all women outlive all men.[90]

Two major age-related issues have received attention under the Age Discrimination in Employment Act (ADEA) and later amendments such as the Older Workers Benefit Protection Act (OWBPA). First, employers must take care not to discriminate against workers over age 40 in the provision of pay or benefits. As one example, employers cannot generally cease accrual (stop the growth) of retirement benefits at some age (like 65) as a way of pressuring older employees to retire.[91] Second, early retirement incentive programs need to meet the following standards to avoid legal liability: (1) The employee is not coerced to accept the incentive and retire, (2) accurate information is provided regarding options, and (3) the employee is given adequate time (is not pressured) to make a decision.

Employers also have to comply with the Americans with Disabilities Act (ADA), which went into effect in 1992. The ADA specifies that employees with disabilities must have "equal access to whatever health insurance coverage the employer provides other employees." However, the act also notes that the terms and conditions of health insurance can be based on risk factors as long as this is not a subterfuge for denying the benefit to those with

Table 13.11
The Affordable Care Act: Impact on Employers

PENALTIES FOR NOT PROVIDING HEALTH BENEFITS

The health reform law does not require employers to provide health benefits. However, it does impose penalties in some cases on larger employers (those with 50 or more full-time workers or 50 or more full-time equivalents [FTE]) that do not provide insurance to their workers or that provide coverage that is unaffordable.

Larger employers that do not provide coverage are assessed a penalty if any one of their workers receives a tax credit when buying insurance on their own in a health insurance exchange. Workers with income up to 400% of the poverty level are eligible for tax credits. The employer penalty is equal to $2,000 multiplied by the number of workers in the business in excess of 30 workers (with the penalty amount increasing over time).

In some instances, larger employers that offer coverage could be subject to penalties as well. If the coverage does not have an actuarial value of at least 60%—meaning that on average it covers at least 60% of the cost of covered services for a typical population—or the premium for the coverage would exceed 9.5% of a worker's income, then the worker can obtain coverage in an exchange and be eligible for a tax credit. For each worker receiving a tax credit, the employer will pay a penalty up to a maximum of $2,000 times the number of workers in excess of 30 workers.

Businesses with fewer than 25 FTEs and average annual wages of less than $50,000 that pay at least half of the cost of health insurance for their employees are eligible for a tax credit.

TAXES*

The law increases the Medicare Hospital Insurance (Part A) payroll tax on earnings for higher-income taxpayers (more than $200,000/individual and $250,000/couple) by 0.9 percentage points, from 1.45% to 2.35%. Employers will be responsible for withholding these taxes.

The law creates a new tax on so-called "Cadillac" insurance plans provided by employers. Beginning in 2018, plans valued at $10,200 or more for individual coverage or $27,500 or more for family policies will be subject to an excise tax of 40% on the value of the plan that exceeds these thresholds. The tax will be levied on insurers and self-insured employers, not directly on employees. The threshold amounts will be increased for inflation beginning in 2020, and may be adjusted upward if health care costs rise more than expected prior to implementation of the tax in 2018. The thresholds are also adjusted upward for retired individuals age 55 and older who are not eligible for Medicare, for employees engaged in high-risk professions, and for firms that may have higher health care costs because of the age or gender of their workers.

COVERAGE OF DEPENDENTS

The ACA requires plans and issuers that offer dependent coverage to make the coverage available until a child reaches the age of 26. Both married and unmarried children qualify for this coverage. This rule applies to all plans in the individual market and to new employer plans. It also applies to existing employer plans unless the adult child has another offer of employer-based coverage (such as through his or her job). Children up to age 26 can stay on their parent's employer's plan even if they have another offer of coverage through their own employer.

WELLNESS PROGRAMS

Employers can provide rewards to employees of up to 30% of the total plan premium as part of a wellness program incentive, up from the previous limit of 20%. Under the law, the Secretary of Health and Human Services may increase this limit to 50% if deemed appropriate. Wellness programs must be "reasonably designed to promote health or prevent disease." The law also creates a five-year grant program to encourage small employers that do not currently have wellness programs to establish them. The program would offer $200 million in fiscal years 2011–2015 to employers with fewer than 100 employees who work 25 hours or more per week.

*Two new taxes do not directly involve employers. First, there is a 2.3% medical device excise tax on the sale of any taxable medical device by its manufacturer, producer, or importer. Second, there is (another) additional Medicare payroll tax of 3.8% on investment income for singles earning $200,000 or more and couples earning $250,000 or more.

SOURCES: Internal Revenue Service, "Questions and Answers on Employer Shared Responsibility Provisions Under the Affordable Care Act," www.irs.gov, accessed May 5, 2015; The Henry J. Kaiser Family Foundation, http://kff.org/health-reform/faq/health-reform-frequently-asked-questions/and http://kff.org/quiz/health-reform-quiz/, accessed May 22, 2013; UC-Berkeley Labor Center, "Affordable Care Act Summary of Provisions Affecting Employer-Sponsored Insurance," April 2013, http://laborcenter.berkeley.edu/healthpolicy/ppaca12.pdf, accessed May 22, 2013; National Association of Manufacturers, "Affordable Care Act Provisions Affecting Employers, 2013 and Beyond," www.nam.org/~/media/DB85A8CD0C174B6A8BC9077850FE6AC9/AffordableCareActEmployers_11_2_12.pdf, accessed May 22, 2013; U.S. Department of Labor, Employee Benefits Security Administration, "Young Adults and the Affordable Care Act: Protecting Young Adults and Eliminating Burdens on Businesses and Families," www.dol.gov/ebsa/faqs/faq-dependentcoverage.html.

disabilities. Employers with risk-based programs in place would be in a stronger position, however, than employers who make changes after hiring employees with disabilities.[92]

MONITORING FUTURE BENEFITS OBLIGATIONS

Financial Accounting Statement (FAS) 106
The rule issued by the Financial Accounting Standards Board in 1993 requiring companies to fund benefits provided after retirement on an accrual rather than a pay-as-you-go basis and to enter these future cost obligations on their financial statements.

Financial Accounting Statement (FAS) 106, issued by the Financial Accounting Standards Board, became effective in 1993. This rule requires that any benefits (excluding pensions) provided after retirement (the major one being health care) can no longer be funded on a pay-as-you-go basis. Rather, they must be paid on an accrual basis, and companies must enter these future cost obligations on their financial statements. The effect on financial statements can be substantial.

Increasing retiree health care costs (and the change in accounting standards) have also led some companies to require white-collar employees and retirees to pay insurance premiums for the first time in history and to increase copayments and deductibles. Survey data indicate that some companies are ending retiree health care benefits altogether. GM, for example, recently eliminated retiree health care benefits for white-collar workers. Union contracts prevented GM from eliminating the blue-collar plan.

However, as part of its bankruptcy proceeding, GM reached a settlement with the United Automobile Workers (UAW) union to create a voluntary employee benefit association (VEBA) trust. GM agreed to contribute roughly $35 billion to fund the VEBA. Ford ($13.2 billion) and Chrysler ($7.1 billion) also reached agreements to set up VEBAs. By one estimate, the VEBAs moved $100 billion in retiree health care obligations off the financial statements of the three U.S. automakers, playing a major role in reducing labor cost per vehicle produced. Also, the VEBAs, like defined contribution plans, make the cost for the companies certain. After paying to set up the VEBAs, they have no future obligations to cover retiree health care. It is up to the UAW to administer the VEBA.[93]

Other companies have reduced benefits or increased retiree contributions. Obviously, such changes hit the elderly hard, especially those with relatively fixed incomes. Not surprisingly, legal challenges have arisen. The need to balance the interests of shareholders, current employees, and retirees in this area will be one of the most difficult challenges facing managers in the future.

Although use of defined benefit (pension) plans has declined significantly over time in the United States, tens of millions of people are covered by ongoing plans (and/or frozen plans—those not open to new participants). Two factors, in particular, influence employer costs. First, the Pension Benefit Guaranty Corporation, which insures pensions, regularly increases the premium paid by employers. As noted earlier, the PBGC raised its annual premium to $64/worker by 2016, up from $42/worker in 2014, a 53% increase in cost to employers. Second, the Society of Actuaries revised its mortality tables for the first time since 2000. Life expectancy for a 65-year-old has been revised upward from 85.2 to 88.8 for women and from 82.6 to 86.6 for men, again substantially increasing the cost obligation to employers.[94]

A LOOK BACK

Employee Benefits: More Responsibility for Workers

We have seen that many organizations have become less paternalistic in their employee benefits strategies. Employees now have more responsibility, and sometimes more risk, regarding their benefits choices. ("Gig" workers, who are typically independent contractors, have even more responsibility, because they have no employer and thus no employer-provided benefits.) One change has been in the area of retirement income plans, where employers have moved toward greater reliance on defined contribution plans. Such plans require employees to understand investing; otherwise, their retirement years may not be so happy. The risk to employees is especially great when defined contribution plans invest a substantial portion of their assets in company stock. One reason companies do this is because they wish to move away from an entitlement mentality and instead link benefits to company performance. However, if the company has financial problems, employees risk losing not only their jobs but also their retirement money. Another change has been in the area of health care benefits. Employees are being asked to pay an increased proportion of the costs and also to use data on health care quality to make better choices about health care. Of course, different companies have different benefits strategies. We saw at the beginning and throughout the chapter that some companies (and not just those in the tech industry) are not primarily in the mode of reducing benefits and/or passing on more costs to employees. Rather, they are looking for ways to make their benefits packages more attractive to help them compete in the labor market for valuable human capital.

QUESTIONS

1. Why do employers offer benefits? Is it because the law requires it, because it makes good business sense, or because it is the right thing to do?
2. How much responsibility should employers have for the health and well-being of their employees? Take the perspective of both a shareholder and an employee in answering this question.
3. If you were advising a new company on how to design its health care plan, what would you recommend?

SUMMARY

Effective management of employee benefits is an important means by which organizations compete successfully. Benefits costs are substantial and continue to grow rapidly in some areas, most notably health care. Control of such costs is necessary to compete in the product market. At the same time, employers must offer a benefits package that permits them to compete in the labor market. Beyond investing more money in benefits, the attraction and retention of quality employees can be helped by better communication of the value of the benefits package and by allowing employees to tailor benefits to their own needs through flexible benefits plans.

Employers continue to be a major source of economic security for employees, often providing health insurance, retirement benefits, and so forth. Changes to benefits can have a tremendous impact on employees and retirees. Therefore, employers carry a significant social responsibility in making benefits decisions. At the same time, employees need to be aware that they will increasingly become responsible for their own economic security. Health care benefit design is changing to encourage employees to be more informed consumers, and retirement benefits will depend more and more on the financial investment decisions employees make on their own behalf.

KEY TERMS

Marginal tax rate, 548
Consolidated Omnibus Budget
    Reconciliation Act
    (COBRA), 554
Pension Benefit Guaranty Corporation
    (PBGC), 555

Employee Retirement Income Security
    Act (ERISA), 555
Cash balance plan, 557
Summary plan description (SPD),
    558
Family and Medical Leave Act, 561

Health maintenance organization
    (HMO), 565
Preferred provider organization
    (PPO), 565
Financial Accounting Statement
    (FAS) 106, 580

DISCUSSION QUESTIONS

1. The chapter opener described how some companies are reducing their expectations of employees to work long hours each week. Why are these employers changing their expectations? Explain what the consequences are for employers and employees and whether you think such changes are a good idea.
2. Employers are shifting more responsibility to employees in the area of employee benefits. Describe specific examples of this trend. What are the likely consequences of this change? Where does the social responsibility of employers end, and where does the need to operate more efficiently begin?
3. Your company, like many others, is experiencing substantial increases in health care costs. What suggestions can you offer that may reduce the rate of cost increases?
4. Why is communication so important in the employee benefits area? What sorts of programs can a company use to communicate more effectively? What are the potential positive consequences of more effective benefits communication?
5. What are the potential advantages of flexible benefits and flexible spending accounts? Are there any potential drawbacks?
6. Although benefits account for a large share of employee compensation, many people feel there is little evidence on whether an employer receives an adequate return on the benefits investment. One suggestion has been to link benefits to individual, group, or organization performance. Explain why you would or would not recommend this strategy to an organization.

SELF-ASSESSMENT EXERCISE

Additional assignable self-assessments available in Connect.

One way companies determine which types of benefits to provide is to use a survey asking employees which types of benefits are important to them. Read the following list of employee benefits. For each benefit, mark an X in the column that indicates whether it is important to you or not.

Benefit	Important to Have	Not Important to Have	% Employers Offering
Dependent-care flexible spending account	_____	_____	70%
Flextime	_____	_____	64
Ability to bring child to work in case of emergency	_____	_____	30
Elder-care referral services	_____	_____	21
Adoption assistance	_____	_____	21
On-site child care center	_____	_____	6
Gym subsidy	_____	_____	28
Vaccinations on site (e.g., flu shots)	_____	_____	61
On-site fitness center	_____	_____	26
Casual dress days (every day)	_____	_____	53
Organization-sponsored sports teams	_____	_____	39
Food services/subsidized cafeteria	_____	_____	29
Travel-planning services	_____	_____	27
Dry-cleaning services	_____	_____	15
Massage therapy services at work	_____	_____	12
Self-defense training	_____	_____	6
Concierge services	_____	_____	4

Compare your importance ratings for each benefit to the corresponding number in the right-hand column that indicates the percentage of employers that offer the benefit. Are you likely to find jobs that provide the benefits you want? Explain.

SOURCE: Based on Figure 2, "Percent of Employers Offering Work/Life Benefits (by Year)," in *Workplace Visions* 4 (2002), p. 3, published by the Society for Human Resource Management.

EXERCISING STRATEGY

Small Businesses React in Different Ways to Health Care Coverage

When the Affordable Care Act was enacted in 2010, many small firms feared that the cost of providing health care to their employees under the employer mandate could put them out of business. Jeff Salter, chief executive of Caring Senior Service, continues to worry about the employer mandate cost. He says his company of 1,800 employees is not big enough or profitable enough to cover all of its employees. Of the company's 60 locations, 7 are large enough to be subject to the employer mandate. In those locations, 23 out of 208 eligible employees have signed up for coverage. The cost of covering each of those employees is $360/month. Yet, he is not certain he would eliminate coverage if the employer mandate went away. One reason may be as we have seen previously, the tightening labor market. At Bonanno Concepts in Denver, which has 10 restaurants, about 175 of 250 eligible employees have signed up for the health insurance plan Bonnano was required to put in place under the employer mandate. Frank Bonanno says that "I don't like the cost, but it also makes us super-competitive when we are hiring." The company offers employees three tiers of coverage, with costs of $135 to $186 a month for individuals and $703 to $856 for families. David deParrie, a bartender, who had had no health insurance for about a decade, chose the lowest-cost option. He says that "the coverage isn't that great, but it gives me peace of mind." Rick Levi, the chief executive of a company in Des Moines that employs 300 food-service workers that work in a variety of locations across 11 states, thought about paying the employer penalty instead of providing health insurance to its employees. He said that "we had a lot of gnashing of teeth but then decided it was the right thing to do." Nevertheless, Mr. Levi closely monitors employee hours so as to keep a lid on the number of full-time employees, who qualify for the health benefits.

QUESTIONS

1. Why does offering health coverage make Frank Bonanno's restaurant company "super-competitive" in recruiting employees?
2. How do you think Bonanno's view on being required to provide health care coverage to employees might change if the unemployment rate rises in the future?
3. Over the long run, what are some ways that employers may choose to respond to higher labor costs?
4. What changes have been made recently to the Affordable Care Act? How will those changes affect employees and employers?

SOURCE: R. Simon, "Small Businesses Change Tune on Health-Insurance Coverage," *Wall Street Journal*, February 15, 2017.

MANAGING PEOPLE

Some Companies Want Employees (back) at the Office

Roughly one in five U.S. workers perform some work from home or some other remote location and this remote work group averages about three hours of remote work per day. There are a variety of reasons why some companies allow (some) employees to work remotely. In the case of IBM, it reported at one point that about 40 percent of its employees worked remotely, allowing it to reduce its office space by almost 80 million square feet, saving it about $100 million per year. Giving employees the flexibility to balance work, family, and other non-work issues, as well as the improvements in technology (and its falling cost), contributed to companies adopting remote work policies. Some employees (and perhaps their supervisors) also felt that they would be more productive if given this flexibility. Other well-known companies that were prominent adopters of remote work included Aetna, Bank of America, Best Buy, Honeywell, IBM, and Yahoo.

What do these companies and IBM have in common now? The answer is that all have since either ended or curtailed programs that allow employees to work remotely, rather than at the company office. IBM, for example, recently gave remote working employees the choice of returning to work at the office or applying for a new position. Presumably, some will not wish to choose either option and will look for another job and/or retire. Why have these companies changed their view on remote work? The commonly stated reasons are that more work is done by teams and that face-to-face interaction between team members is thought to be more effective in identifying business problems to solve and business opportunities to exploit, developing creative solutions/strategies to do so, and executing them well.

QUESTIONS

1. Do these companies that have scaled back or ended remote work have anything in common? For example, are these companies with strong revenue, profit, and market value growth? Are they in similar or different industries/businesses? To the degree they have something in

common, are these companies likely representative of what other companies are doing, or will do in terms of how much they permit remote working?

2. Summarize the advantages and disadvantages of remote work. Are there particular types of companies where remote work is more/less likely to be effective?

3. How do you think employees will react to changes (such as those at IBM) in remote work policies? What will be the short-run and long-run consequences?

SOURCE: John Simons. The Boss Wants You Back in the Office. *Wall Street Journal*, July 25, 2017. https://www.wsj.com/articles/the-boss-wants-you-back-in-the-office-1500975001?tesla=y?mod=djem_jiewr_HR_domainid; Sarah Kesler. IBM, remote-work pioneer, is calling thousands of employees back to the office. Quartz, March 21, 2017. https://qz.com/924167/ibm-remote-work-pioneer-is-calling-thousands-of-employees-back-to-the-office/; John Simons. IBM, a Pioneer of Remote Work, Calls Workers Back to the Office *Wall Street Journal*, May 18, 2017. https://www.wsj.com/articles/ibm-a-pioneer-of-remote-work-calls-workers-back-to-the-office-1495108802

HR IN SMALL BUSINESS

Babies Welcomed at T3

T3 is an independent advertising agency launched by Gay Warren Gaddis in Austin, Texas, in 1989. It has grown rapidly, thanks to Gaddis's ability to stay in front of tumultuous change in the advertising and marketing industry. Traditional agencies have approached their work by thinking about ads to be placed on the air or in newspapers and magazines. In contrast, Gaddis and her staff have specialized in developing integrated campaigns that harness all the ways to communicate about a brand, including communication via the Internet.

Innovation continues to be a company value. The company's careers web page says T3 looks for "Great thinkers. Individuals with curious, open minds. Relentless problem-solvers constantly looking for new, often unconventional, solutions." The company is structured without the boundaries that have traditionally separated functions in the advertising world, so that employees can bring their perspectives together to solve client problems.

That innovative spirit hasn't been limited to advertising. Gaddis also thinks creatively about managing her firm's human resources. Six years after starting T3, Gaddis observed that four of her key employees were all pregnant at about the same time. If they all proceeded in the traditional way, taking a few months' leave, Gaddis would be scrambling to keep her agency running without them. So Gaddis decided to try something unusual: She told the four employees they were welcome to bring their babies to work. While some big companies establish on-site day care, Gaddis simply counted on the employees to work flexibly in the presence of their children.

Many people would assume that babies at work would create a distracting environment, but in fact, the new program was a success. T3 kept the policy in place and even gave it a name: T3 and Under. So far, 80 babies have come to work at one point or another. Gaddis says parents are so appreciative that they try extra hard to make the arrangement work. One such parent, Emily Dalton, feels reassured by being able to just swivel her chair when she wants to check on her baby: "You're not worrying," she told a newspaper reporter, "You're being spit up on, but you're not . . . calling somewhere to check on your child." She admits that she has to be extra flexible when her baby, Annie, is awake but adds, "I powerhouse when she sleeps." When the babies reach nine months or start to crawl, the parents are expected to make arrangements for day care.

Bringing babies to work is, of course, only one employee benefit. T3, which now has offices in New York and San Francisco as well as the one in Austin, offers medical, dental, and vision insurance; various life insurance policies; disability insurance; a 401(k) plan; paid time for vacations, holidays, and sick leave; and discounts on gym memberships and cell phone plans. There are also some other unusual benefits: breakfast on Mondays, candy on Fridays, a book club, and a "bring your dog to work" policy. As for this last policy, the T3 website comments, "While we don't have hard metrics on what [dogs] do for our creativity or productivity, we do believe they play a part in adding balance to what can be a very unbalanced business."

Advertising may be an "unbalanced" business, but so far, T3 seems to be coping well enough. And T3's fearless leader, Gay Warren Gaddis, was named Ernst and Young's Entrepreneur of the Year for central Texas in 2014.

QUESTIONS

1. Of the employee benefits mentioned in this case, which do you think are important for keeping a creative workforce engaged at T3?

2. What are some of the advantages of the agency's T3 and Under policy? What are some of the risks? How can the company address those risks?

3. At what other kinds of companies, if any, do you think a "bring your baby to work" policy might be effective as an employee benefit? Why?

SOURCES: Josh Spiro, "Where Every Day Is Take Your Baby to Work Day," *Inc.*, December 9, 2009; Eric Aasen, "Babies-at-Work Programs Let New Parents Stay Close to Their Kids," *Dallas Morning News*, March 26, 2008; T3, "Careers" and "Company," corporate website, www.t-3.com, accessed July 21, 2014.

NOTES

1. J. H. Dulebohn, J. C. Molloy, S. M. Pichler, and B. Murray, "Employee Benefits: Literature Review and Emerging Issues," *Human Resource Management Review* 19 (2009), pp. 86–103; J. J. Martocchio, *Employee Benefits*, 2nd ed. (New York: McGraw-Hill, 2006).

2. H. W. Hennessey, "Using Employee Benefits to Gain a Competitive Advantage," *Benefits Quarterly* 5, no. 1 (1989), pp. 51–57; B. Gerhart and G.T. Milkovich, "Employee Compensation: Research and Practice," in *Handbook of Industrial and Organizational Psychology*, vol. 3, 2nd ed., ed. M. D. Dunnette and L. M. Hough (Palo Alto, CA: Consulting Psychologists Press, 1992); J. Swist, "Benefits Communications: Measuring Impact and Value," *Employee Benefit Plan Review*, September 2002, pp. 24–26.

3. R. Ehrenberg and R. S. Smith, *Modern Labor Economics: Theory and Public Policy*, 7th ed. (Upper Saddle River, NJ: Addison Wesley Longman, 2000).

4. B. T. Beam Jr. and J. J. McFadden, *Employee Benefits*, 6th ed. (Chicago: Dearborn Financial Publishing, 2000).

5. J. Murphy, "At Patagonia, Trying New Outdoor Adventures Is a Job Requirement," *Wall Street Journal,* March 9, 2015; B. Schulte, "A Company That Profits as It Pampers Workers," *Washington Post*, October 25, 2014.

6. The organization and description in this section draws heavily on Beam and McFadden, *Employee Benefits*.

7. U.S. Department of Labor, Employment and Training Administration, "Comparison of State Unemployment Laws," https://workforcesecurity.doleta.gov/unemploy/comparison2016.asp; Employment Security Department, Washington State, "Taxable Wage Base," http://www.esd.wa.gov/uitax/taxreportsandrates/fileandpaytaxes/taxable-wage-base.php.

8. J. A. Penczak, "Unemployment Benefit Plans," in *Employee Benefits Handbook*, 3rd ed., ed. J. D. Mamorsky (Boston: Warren, Gorham & Lamont, 1992).

9. U.S. Department of Labor, "Unemployment Compensation: Federal-State Partnership," Office of Unemployment Insurance, Division of Legislation, April 2013.

10. J. V. Nackley, *Primer on Workers' Compensation* (Washington, DC: Bureau of National Affairs, 1989).

11. Beam and McFadden, *Employee Benefits*, p. 81.

12. L. Groeger, M. Grabell, and C. Cotts, "Workers' Comp Benefits: How Much Is a Limb Worth?" *ProPublica*, accessed May 4, 2015, http://projects.propublica.org; see also: www.dol.gov/esa.

13. A. H. Wheeler, "Pathophysiology of Chronic Back Pain," 2002, www.emedicine.com.

14. J. R. Hollenbeck, D. R. Ilgen, and S. M. Crampton, "Lower Back Disability in Occupational Settings: A Review of the Literature from a Human Resource Management View," *Personnel Psychology* 45 (1992), pp. 247–78; J. J. Martocchio, D. A. Harrison, and H. Berkson, "Connections between Lower Back Pain, Interventions, and Absence from Work: A Time-Based Meta-Analysis," *Personnel Psychology* (2000), p. 595.

15. Employee Benefit Research Institute, "Value of Employee Benefits Constant in a Changing World," March 28, 2002, www.ebri.org.

16. Beam and McFadden, *Employee Benefits*.

17. U. S. Bureau of Labor Statistics, *National Compensation Survey: Employee Benefits in the United States, 2014*, Bulletin 2779, September 2014, USDL-15-0386, www.bls.gov.

18. Social Security Administration, "Fast Facts and Figures about Social Security, 2014," published September 2014, http://www.ssa.gov/policy/docs/chartbooks/fast_facts/2014/fast_facts14.html#page5

19. Barbara A. Butrica, Howard M. Iams, Karen E. Smith, and Eric J. Toder, "The Disappearing Defined Benefit Pension and Its Potential Impact on the Retirement Incomes of Baby Boomers," U.S. Social Security Administration, Social Security Bulletin, Vol. 69, No. 3, 2009.

20. Pension Benefit Guaranty Corporation, *Annual Report, 2016*, www.pbgc.gov.

21. Pension Benefit Guaranty Corporation, Maximum Monthly Guarantee Tables, https://www.pbgc.gov/wr/benefits/guaranteed-benefits/maximum-guarantee.html, accessed June 6, 2017.

22. Ibid.

23. www.irs.gov. Those age 50 and over have higher contribution limits.

24. "PSCA Releases Results of 59th Annual Survey of Profit Sharing and 401(k) Plans," https://www.psca.org/psca-releases-results-of-59th-annual-survey-of-profit-sharing-and-401-k-plans; PSCA's *57th Annual Survey of Profit Sharing and 401(k) Plans*, 2014.

25. J. Fierman, "How Secure Is Your Nest Egg?" *Fortune*, August 12, 1991, pp. 50–54.

26. A. R. Sorking, "JP Morgan Pays $2 a Share for Bear Stearns," *New York Times*, March 17, 2008; P. Lattman and J. Strasburg, "We Are All in a Daze, Says One Employee, Life Savings Wiped Out," *Wall Street Journal*, March 18, 2008; D. Maxey, J. L. Pessin, and I. Salisbury, "The Job/Stock Double Whammy: Bear Saga Shows Perils of Loading Up on Employer Equity," *Wall Street Journal*, March 18, 2008.

27. *PSCA's 57th Annual Survey of Profit Sharing and 401(k) Plans*.

28. Beam and McFadden, *Employee Benefits*.

29. B. J. Coleman, *Primer on Employee Retirement Income Security Act*, 3rd ed. (Washington, DC: Bureau of National Affairs, 1989).

30. *Continental Can Company v. Gavalik*, summary in *Daily Labor Report* (December 8, 1987): "Supreme Court Lets Stand Third Circuit Ruling That Pension Avoidance Scheme Is ERISA Violation," No. 234, p. A-14.

31. A. L. Gustman, O. S. Mitchell, and T. L. Steinmeier, "The Role of Pensions in the Labor Market: A Survey of the Literature," *Industrial and Labor Relations* 47 (1994), pp. 417–38.

32. D. A. DeCenzo and S. J. Holoviak, *Employee Benefits* (Englewood Cliffs, NJ: Prentice Hall, 1990).

33. E. P. Lazear, "Why Is There Early Retirement?" *Journal of Political Economy* 87 (1979), pp. 1261–84; Gustman et al., "The Role of Pensions."

34. P. Cappelli, *The New Deal at Work: Managing the Market-Driven Workforce* (Boston: Harvard Business School Press, 1999).

35. S. Dorsey, "Pension Portability and Labor Market Efficiency," *Industrial and Labor Relations* 48, no. 5 (1995), pp. 276–92.

36. Commission of the European Communities, European Community Directive 93/104/EC, issued November 23, 1993, and amended June 22, 2000, by Directive 2000/34/EC, http://europa/eu.int/comm/index_en.htm.

37. DeCenzo and Holoviak, *Employee Benefits*.

38. C. C. Miller, "Microsoft Tells Its Partners to Provide Paid Sick Leave," *New York Times,* March 26, 2015, p. A3.

39. N. Knox and M. Murphy, "Charity as a Recruiting Tool," *Wall Street Journal*, September 2, 2014, p. B4.

40. J. H. Wayne, M. M. Butts, W. J. Casper, and T. D. Allen, "In Search of Balance: A Conceptual and Empirical Integration of Multiple Meanings of Work–Family Balance,"*Personnel Psychology* 70 (2016), pp. 167–210; A. Huffman and L. T. Eby, *The Oxford Handbook of Work and Family* (Oxford, UK: Oxford University Press, 2016); T. D. Allen, R. C. Johnson, K. M. Kiburz, and K. M. Shockley, "Work–Family Conflict and Flexible Work Arrangements: Deconstructing Flexibility,"*Personnel Psychology* 66 (2013), pp. 345–76; A. Mandeville, J. Halbesleben, and M. Whitman, "Misalignment and Misperception in Preferences to Utilize Family–Friendly Benefits: Implications for Benefit Utilization and Work–Family Conflict,"*Personnel Psychology* 69 (2016), pp. 895–929; R. S. Gajendran, D. A. Harrison, and K. Delaney–Klinger, "Are Telecommuters Remotely Good Citizens? Unpacking Telecommuting's Effects on Performance Via I–Deals and Job Resources, *Personnel Psychology* 68 (2015), pp. 353–93; T. L. Dumas and J. Sanchez-Burks, "The Professional, the Personal, and the Ideal Worker: Pressures and Objectives Shaping the Boundary between Life Domains," *Academy of Management Annals* 9 (2015), pp. 803–43; G. M. Spreitzer, L. Cameron, and L. Garrett, "Alternative Work Arrangements: Two Images of the New World of Work," *Annual Review of Organizational Psychology and Organizational Behavior* 4 (2017), pp. 473–99.

41. S. L. Grover and K. J. Crooker, "Who Appreciates Family Responsive Human Resource Policies: The Impact of Family-Friendly Policies on the Organizational Attachment of Parents and Non-parents," *Personnel Psychology* 48 (1995), pp. 271–88; T. J. Rothausen, J. A. Gonzalez, N. E. Clarke, and L. L. O'Dell, "Family-Friendly Backlash: Fact or Fiction? The Case of Organizations' On-Site Child Care Centers," *Personnel Psychology* 51 (1998), p. 685; M. A. Arthur, "Share Price Reactions to Work–Family Initiatives: An Institutional Perspective," *Academy of Management Journal* 46 (2003), p. 497; J. E. Perry-Smith and T. Blum, "Work–Family Human Resource Bundles and Perceived Organizational Performance," *Academy of Management Journal* 43 (2000), pp. 1107–17.

42. N. Bloom, T. Kretschmer, and J. Van Reenen, "Are Family-Friendly Workplace Practices a Valuable Firm Resource?" *Strategic Management Journal* 32 (2011), pp. 343–67.

43. "The Employer's Role in Helping Working Families." For examples of child care arrangements in some well-known companies (e.g., AT&T, Apple, Exxon, IBM, Merck), see "A Look at Child-Care Benefits," USA *Today*, March 14, 1989, p. 4B; U.S. Census Bureau, "America's Families and Living Arrangements," June 2001, www.census.gov.

44. J. Waldfogel, "International Policies toward Parental Leave and Child Care," *Future of Children* 11, no. 1 (2001), pp. 99–111.

45. P. Hardin, "Women Execs Should Feel at Ease about Taking Full Maternity Leave," *Personnel Journal*, September 1995, p. 19.

46. Families and Work Institute, "2012 National Study of Employers," http://familiesandwork.org/site/research/reports/main.html. Nationally representative survey of 1,126 employers with 50 or more employees.

47. J. Fierman, "It's 2 a.m..: Let's Go to Work," *Fortune*, August 21, 1995, pp. 82–88.

48. E. E. Kossek, "Diversity in Child Care Assistance Needs: Employee Problems, Preferences, and Work-Related Outcomes," *Personnel Psychology* 43 (1990), pp. 769–91.

49. "A Bank Profits from Its Work/Life Program," *Workforce*, February 1997, p. 49.

50. R. Broderick and B. Gerhart, "Nonwage Compensation," in *The Human Resource Management Handbook*, ed. D. Lewin, D. J. B. Mitchell, and M. A. Zadi (San Francisco: JAI Press, 1996).

51. Dulabohn et al., "Employee Benefits."

52. Hennessey, "Using Employee Benefits to Gain a Competitive Advantage."

53. One study, conducted in Spain, reports that employee perceptions of benefits level (amount, value, and number of benefits) correlate .42 with their organization commitment and – .32 with their turnover intention. J. M. de la Torre-Ruiz, M. D. Vidal-Salazar, and E. Cordón-Pozo, "Employees Are Satisfied with Their Benefits, but So What? The Consequences of Benefit Satisfaction on Employees' Organizational Commitment and Turnover Intentions," *International Journal of Human Resource Management,* April 7, 2017, pp. 1–24. In their review of other studies on the correlation between benefits level and turnover intention, the authors state that these studies "have not reached definitive conclusions," but the majority of studies they review reported, consistent with their own findings, that employee intention to leave was reduced when benefits were higher and/or perceived as higher.

54. U.S. Bureau of Labor Statistics, "Employer Cost for Employee Compensation," www.bls.gov; U.S. Chamber of Commerce Research Center, Employee Benefits Study, annual (Washington, D.C.: U.S. Chamber of Commerce).

55. www.census.gov.

56. S. Armour, "Uninsured Rate Down Sharply Since Health Law Was Enacted," *Wall Street Journal*, March 16, 2015, www.wsj.com.

57. Employee Benefit Research Institute, *EBRI's Fundamentals of Employee Benefit Programs*, 6th ed. (Washington, DC: Author, 2009).

58. A. C. Monheit and P. F. Cooper, "Health Insurance and Job Mobility: The Effects of Public Policy on Job-Lock," *Industrial and Labor Relations Review* 48 (1994), pp. 86–102.

59. R. Lieber, "New Way to Curb Medical Costs: Make Employees Feel the Sting," *Wall Street Journal*, June 23, 2004, p. A1.

60. M. Barringer and O. S. Mitchell, "Workers' Preferences among Company-Provided Health Insurance Plans," *Industrial and Labor Relations Review* 48 (1994), pp. 141–52.

61. Beam and McFadden, *Employee Benefits.*

62. Jared Shelly, "Transformation Vacation," *Human Resource Executive*, November 1, 2008.

63. L. Berry, A. Mirabito, and W. Baun, "What's the Hard Return on Employee Wellness Programs?" *Harvard Business Review*, December 2010, pp. 104–12.

64. Rand Corporation, *Do Workplace Wellness Programs Save Employers Money?* 2004, http://www.rand.org/content/dam/rand/pubs/research_briefs/RB9700/RB9744/RAND_RB9744.pdf. The return to $1 spent on disease management was estimated as $3.80 for disease management, but only $0.50 for lifestyle management (eating, smoking, exercise).

65. S. Tully, "America's Healthiest Companies," *Fortune*, June 12, 1995, pp. 98–106.

66. G. Flynn, "Companies Make Wellness Work," *Personnel Journal*, February 1995, pp. 63–66.

67. D. A. Harrison and L. Z. Liska, "Promoting Regular Exercise in Organizational Fitness Programs: Health-Related Differences in Motivational Building Blocks," *Personnel Psychology* 47 (1994), pp. 47–71.

68. J. C. Erfurt, A. Foote, and M. A. Heirich, "The Cost-Effectiveness of Worksite Wellness Programs for Hypertension Control, Weight Loss, Smoking Cessation and Exercise," *Personnel Psychology* 45 (1992), pp. 5–27.

69. J. Chang and M. Marsh, "The Google Diet: Search Giant Over-hauled Its Eating Options to 'Nudge' Healthy Choices," *ABC News,* January 25, 2013.

70. Henry J. Kaiser Family Foundation, *2016 Employer Health Benefits Survey,* September 14, 2016, http://kff.org/report-section/ehbs-2016-summary-of-findings/; Henry J. Kaiser Family Foundation, *Premiums and Worker Contributions among Workers Covered by Employer-Sponsored Coverage, 1999–2016,* September 14, 2016, http://kff.org/interactive/premiums-and-worker-contributions/#/?coverageGroup=family.

71. H. Gardner, unpublished manuscript (Cheyenne, WY: Options & Choices, 1995); The Henry J. Kaiser Family Foundation and Health Research and Educational Trust, http://kff.org/health-costs/slide/concentration-of-health-care-spending-in-the-u-s-population-2010/, accessed May 20, 2013.

72. H. B. Noble, "Quality Is Focus for Health Plans," *New York Times,* July 3, 1995, p. A1; J. D. Klinke, "Medicine's Industrial Revolution," *Wall Street Journal,* August 21, 1995, p. A8.

73. S. Rosenbush and M. Totty, "How Big Data Is Changing the Whole Equation for Business," *Wall Street Journal,* March 8, 2013; S. Kliff, "An Average ER Visit Costs More than an Average Month's Rent," *Washington Post,* March 2, 2013; A. W. Mathews, "Same Doctor Visit, Double the Cost," *Wall Street Journal,* August 27, 2012.

74. J. B. White, "Business Plan," *Wall Street Journal,* October 19, 1998, p. R18.

75. L. Weber, "A Health Check for Wellness Programs," *Wall Street Journal,* October 8, 2014, p. B1.

76. J. Schor, *The Overworked American: The Unexpected Decline of Leisure* (New York: Basic Books, 1991); U.S. Bureau of Labor Statistics, "Workers Are on the Job More Hours over the Course of a Year," *Issues in Labor Statistics,* February 1997.

77. Hewitt Associates. www.hewitt.com.

78. Beam and McFadden, *Employee Benefits.*

79. One study found that having a supplemental defined contribution retirement plan improved safety among truck drivers and that this effect was larger in smaller companies. One possible explanation provided is that older workers are safer drivers and more likely to be attracted to (and stay with) a company that offers better retirement benefits. S. Werner, C. S. Kuiate, T. R. Noland, and A. J. Francia, "Benefits and Strategic Outcomes: Are Supplemental Retirement Plans and Safer Driving Related in the US Trucking Industry?" *Human Resource Management* 55 (2015), pp. 885–900.

80. M. Wilson, G. B. Northcraft, and M. Neale, "The Perceived Value of Fringe Benefits," *Personnel Psychology* 38 (1985), pp. 309–20.

81. R. Huseman, J. Hatfield, and R. Robinson, "The MBA and Fringe Benefits," *Personnel Administrator* 23, no. 7 (1978), pp. 57–60. See summary in H. W. Hennessey Jr., "Using Employee Benefits to Gain a Competitive Advantage," *Benefits Quarterly* 5, no. 1 (1989), pp. 51–57.

82. Hennessey et al., "Impact of Benefit Awareness"; the same study found no impact of the increased awareness and benefits

satisfaction on overall job satisfaction. G. F. Dreher, R. A. Ash, and R. D. Bretz, "Benefit Coverage and Employee Cost: Critical Factors in Explaining Compensation Satisfaction," *Personnel Psychology* 41 (1988), pp. 237–54.

83. M. C. Giallourakis and G. S. Taylor, "An Evaluation of Benefit Communication Strategy," *Employee Benefits Journal* 15, no. 4 (1991), pp. 14–18; Employee Benefits Research Institute, "How Readable Are Summary Plan Descriptions for Health Care Plans," *EBRI Notes,* October 2006, ebri.org.

84. J. Abraham, R. Feldman, and C. Carlin, "Understanding Employee Awareness of Health Care Quality Information: How Can Employers Benefit?" *Health Services Research* 39 (2004), pp. 1799–1816; J. H. Marler, S. L. Fisher, and W. Ke, "Employee Self-Service Technology Acceptance: A Comparison of Pre-Implementation and Post-Implementation Relationships," *Personal Psychology* 62 (2009), pp. 327–58.

85. Beam and McFadden, *Employee Benefits*; M. W. Barringer and G. T. Milkovich, "A Theoretical Explanation of the Adoption and Design of Flexible Benefit Plans: A Case of Human Resource Innovation," *Academy of Management Review* 23 (1998), pp. 305–24.

86. T. Eriksson and N. Kristensen, "Wages or Fringes? Some Evidence on Trade-Offs and Sorting," *Journal of Labor Economics* 32, no. 4 (2014), pp. 899–928.

87. For supportive evidence, see A. E. Barber, R. B. Dunham, and R. A. Formisano, "The Impact of Flexible Benefits on Employee Satisfaction: A Field Study," *Personnel Psychology* 45 (1992), pp. 55–75; E. E. Lawler, *Pay and Organizational Development* (Reading, MA: Addison-Wesley, 1981); J. C. Dencker, A. Joshi, and J. J. Martocchio, "Employee Benefits as Context for Intergenerational Conflict," *Human Resource Management Review* 17 (2007), pp. 208–20; A. Caza, M. W. McCarter, and G. B. Northcraft, "Performance Benefits of Reward Choice: A Procedural Justice Perspective," *Human Resource Management Journal* 25 (2015), 184–199. Caza et al. also found a positive effect of benefits choice on performance in a library study where performance was measured by how well undergraduate students were able to combine words into compound words.

88. Beam and McFadden, *Employee Benefits.*

89. Ibid.

90. *Los Angeles Dept. of Water & Power v. Manhart,* 435 US SCt 702 (1978), 16 EPD, 8250.

91. S. K. Hoffman, "Discrimination Litigation Relating to Employee Benefits," *Labor Law Journal,* June 1992, pp. 362–81.

92. Ibid., p. 375.

93. S. J. Sacher and J. Day, "The New VEBAs," *BNA Pension and Benefits* blog, June 1, 2010, http://pblog.bna.com; P. C. Borzi, "Retiree Health VEBAs: A New Twist on an Old Paradigm. Implications for Retirees, Unions, and Employers," The Henry J. Kaiser Family Foundation, March 2009.

94. V. Monga, "Pension Plans Brace for a One–Two Punch," *Wall Street Journal,* March 25, 2014, p. B1.

CHAPTER

14 Collective Bargaining and Labor Relations

LEARNING OBJECTIVES

After reading this chapter, you should be able to:

LO 14-1 Describe what is meant by collective bargaining and labor relations. *page 590*

LO 14-2 Identify the labor relations goals of society, management, and labor unions. *page 592*

LO 14-3 Explain the legal environment's impact on labor relations. *page 603*

LO 14-4 Describe the major labor–management interactions: organizing, contract negotiations, and contract administration. *page 606*

LO 14-5 Describe new, less adversarial approaches to labor–management relations. *page 623*

LO 14-6 Explain how changes in competitive challenges (e.g., product market competition and globalization) are influencing labor–management interactions. *page 630*

LO 14-7 Explain how labor relations in the public sector differ from labor relations in the private sector. *page 634*

ENTER THE WORLD OF BUSINESS

Collective Action by Nonunion Workers and Supporters

The National Labor Relations Act protects "concerted activity" (collectively discussing or taking action to address work conditions) by workers, whether they are represented by a union or not. Increasingly, low-wage, nonunion workers have taken concerted activity to raise wages for themselves and others. A major goal is to create a national movement to raise hourly wages to $15/hour (the "Fight for 15") to help workers make ends meet. A primary target has been McDonald's. In recent years, workers and supporters took part in rallies, including at McDonald's locations in New York, Boston, and Philadelphia. Additionally, McDonald's has had to close its headquarters outside of Chicago the last three years in a row due to protests surrounding its shareholders' meeting. McDonald's did later increase its lowest wage rates to be at least $1 above the applicable mandated minimum wage, which nationally is $7.25 and higher in New York. Although protesters believed their actions played a major role, McDonald's did not attribute the wage increase to the protests, but rather said it was due to tightening labor market competition. And, the wage remained well below $15. In any case, the workers who participated in lawful rallies for a higher wage were protected from discipline for protesting, despite not being members of a union, because their participation constitutes concerted activity.

In another example, three employees at a Hyundai plant in Alabama were scheduled to work from 6:00 a.m. to 2:00 p.m. on the last day before a holiday break. Two days before that, a supervisor told them they would instead work from 6:30 a.m. to 3:00 p.m. The workers, nevertheless punched out and left at 2:00. They were subsequently informed that they had "voluntarily resigned" by leaving at 2:00 and would no longer be employed at Hyundai. A National Labor Relations Board (NLRB) judge ruled that the company had violated the employees' rights and ordered it to reinstate the employees, pay them back pay (lost wages) and expenses, and post a notice stating that the NLRB had determined that the company "violated Federal labor law."

Concerted activity among nonunion employees and its legal protections is not something that only large companies need to understand. For example, employees at an urgent care center in Minnesota sent an anonymous letter to the owner, a doctor, who had announced a plan to cut wages by 10%. They suggested alternative ways to save money. Shortly thereafter, two employees who wrote the letter—one, a radiation technologist, and the other, a physician's assistant—were fired. One of the fired employees filed a charge with the NLRB regional office in Minneapolis. After an investigation, a complaint was issued alleging the owner's actions were unlawful. A trial was held before an administrative law judge, who concurred. He ordered the employees reinstated with back pay (for the period of time they missed work due to being fired). The owner appealed the judge's decision to the full NLRB in Washington, D.C. A panel of three members of the board unanimously decided to uphold the judge's decision.

SOURCES: B. Harper, "NLRB Rules against Hyundai in Holiday Plant Walkout," *USA Today*, March 10, 2017; National Labor Relations Board, Protected Concerted Activity, www.nlrb.gov, accessed April 15, 2017; P. Davidson, "Fast-Food Workers Strike, Seeking $15 Wage, Political Muscle," *USA Today*, November 10, 2015; R. L. Swarns, "McDonald's Workers, Vowing a Fight, Say Raises Are Too Little for Too Few," *New York Times*, April 6, 2015; S. Greenhouse, "A Broader Strategy on Wages," *New York Times*, March 31, 2015; J. Young and J. Madden, "Hundreds Protest in Downpour at Shut McDonald's Headquarters," Reuters, May 26, 2016.

Introduction

In the chapter opener, we saw workers taking collective action to change terms and conditions of employment but without any formal union representation and without being members of a union. The National Labor Relations Act protects such "concerted activity" for everyone, whether union members or not. In this case, workers and their supporters, similar to unionized workers, hope to bring pressure to bear on McDonald's (and others) to improve wages and other aspects of the job. Unions can help achieve important worker goals, including not only higher wages but also worker protection and giving workers a say in their workplaces. A main source of negotiating leverage for unions is the ability to strike, which interrupts production, sales, and profits. In the end, however, such conflicts must be balanced against the common interests that bind workers and companies together. Worker jobs and income, as well as company profits, depend on the two parties being able to cooperate to ensure the company's ability to be competitive and survive.

The Labor Relations Framework

LO 14-1
Describe what is meant by collective bargaining and labor relations.

John Dunlop, former secretary of labor and a leading industrial relations scholar, suggested in the book *Industrial Relations Systems* (1958) that a successful industrial relations system consists of four elements: (1) an environmental context (technology, market pressures, and the legal framework, especially as it affects bargaining power); (2) participants, including employees and their unions, management, and the government; (3) a "web of rules" (rules of the game) that describe the process by which labor and management interact and resolve disagreements (such as the steps followed in settling contract grievances); and (4) ideology.[1] For the industrial relations system to operate properly, the three participants must, to some degree, have a common ideology (e.g., acceptance of the capitalist system) and must accept the roles of the other participants. Acceptance does not translate into convergence of interests, however. To the contrary, some degree of worker–management conflict is inevitable because, although the interests of the two parties overlap (e.g., survival of the firm and thus survival of workers' jobs and investors' profits), they also diverge in key respects (such as how to divide the economic profits between workers and investors).[2]

Therefore, according to Dunlop and other U.S. scholars of like mind, an effective industrial relations system does not eliminate conflict. Rather, it provides institutions (and a web of rules) that resolve conflict in a way that minimizes its costs to management, employees, and society. The collective bargaining system is one such institution, as are related mechanisms such as mediation, arbitration, and participation in decision making. These ideas formed the basis for the development in the 1940s of schools and departments of industrial and labor relations to train labor relations professionals who, working in both union and management positions, would have the skills to minimize costly forms of conflict such as strikes (which were reaching record levels at the time) and maximize integrative (win–win) solutions to such disagreements.

A more recent industrial relations model, developed by Harry Katz and Thomas Kochan, is particularly helpful in laying out the types of decisions management and unions make in their interactions and the consequences of such decisions for attainment of goals in areas such as wages and benefits, job security, and the rights and responsibilities of unions and managements.[3] According to Katz and Kochan, these choices occur at three levels.

First, at the strategic level, management makes basic choices such as whether to work with its union(s) or to devote its efforts to developing nonunion operations. Environmental factors (or competitive challenges) offer both constraints and opportunities in implementing strategies. For example, if public opinion toward labor unions becomes negative during a particular time period, some employers may see that as an opportunity to rid themselves of unions, whereas other employers may seek a better working relationship with their unions. Similarly, increased competition may dictate the need to increase productivity or reduce labor costs, but whether this is accomplished by shifting work to nonunion facilities or by working with unions to become more competitive is a strategic choice that management faces.

Although management has often been the initiator of change in recent years, unions face a similar choice between fighting changes to the status quo and being open to new labor–management relationships (like less adversarial forms of participation in decision making, such as labor–management teams).

Katz and Kochan suggest that labor and management choices at the strategic level in turn affect the labor–management interaction at a second level, the functional level, where contract negotiations and union organizing occur, and at the final workplace level, the arena in which the contract is administered. The relationships between labor and management at each of the three levels are somewhat interdependent, but the relationship at the three levels may also differ. For example, whereas management may have a strategy of building an effective relationship with its unions at the strategic level, there may be significant day-to-day conflicts over work rules, grievances, and so forth at any given facility or bargaining unit (workplace level).

The labor relations framework depicted in Figure 14.1 incorporates many of the ideas discussed so far, including the important role of the environment (the competitive challenges); union, management, and societal goals; and a separation of union–management

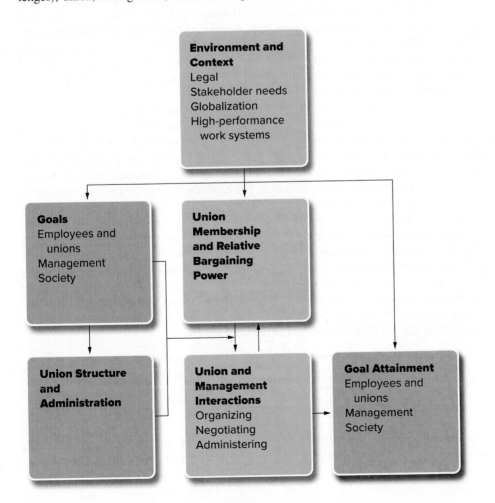

Figure 14.1

A Labor Relations Framework

interactions into categories (union organizing, contract negotiation, contract administration) that can have important influences on one another but may also be analyzed somewhat independently. The model also highlights the important role that relative bargaining power plays in influencing goals, union–management interactions, and the degree to which each party achieves its goals. Relative bargaining power, in turn, is significantly influenced by the competitive environment (legal, social, quality, high-performance work systems, and globalization competitive challenges) and the size and depth of union membership.[4]

We now describe the components of this model in greater depth. The remainder of the chapter is organized into the following sections: the goals and strategies of society, management, and unions; union structure (including union administration and membership); the legal framework, perhaps the key aspect of the competitive environment for labor relations; union and management interactions (organizing, contract negotiation, contract administration); and goal attainment. Environmental factors (other than legal) and bargaining power are discussed in the context of these sections. In addition, two special topics, international comparisons and public-sector labor relations, are discussed.

Goals and Strategies

LO 14-2

Identify the labor relations goals of society, management, and labor unions.

SOCIETY

In one sense, labor unions, with their emphasis on group action, do not fit well with the individualistic orientation of U.S. capitalism. However, industrial relations scholars such as Beatrice and Sidney Webb and John R. Commons argued in the late 1800s and early 1900s that individual workers' bargaining power was far smaller than that of employers, who were likely to have more financial resources and the ability to easily replace workers.[5] Effective institutions for worker representation (like labor unions) were therefore seen as a way to make bargaining power more equal.

Labor unions' major benefit to society is the institutionalization of industrial conflict, which is therefore resolved in the least costly way. Although disagreements between management and labor continue, it is better to resolve disputes through discussion (collective bargaining) than by battling in the streets. As an influential group of industrial relations scholars put it in describing the future of advanced industrial relations around the world, "Class warfare will be forgotten. The battles will be in the corridors instead of the streets, and memos will flow instead of blood."[6] In this sense, collective bargaining not only has the potential to reduce economic losses caused by strikes but also may contribute to societal stability. For this reason, industrial relations scholars have often viewed labor unions as an essential component of a democratic society.[7] These were some of the beliefs that contributed to the enactment of the National Labor Relations Act (NLRA) in 1935, which sought to provide an environment conducive to collective bargaining and has since regulated labor and management activities and interactions.

Even Senator Orrin Hatch, described by *Bloomberg BusinessWeek* as "labor's archrival on Capitol Hill," has spoken of the need for unions:

> There are always going to be people who take advantage of workers. Unions even that out, to their credit. We need them to level the field between labor and management. If you didn't have unions, it would be very difficult for even enlightened employers not to take advantage of workers on wages and working conditions, because of [competition from] rivals. I'm among the first to say I believe in unions.[8]

Although an industrial relations system based on collective bargaining has drawbacks, so too do the alternatives. Unilateral control by management sacrifices workers' rights.

Extensive involvement of government and the courts can result in conflict resolution that is expensive, slow, and imposed by someone (a judge) with much less firsthand knowledge of the circumstances than either labor or management.

MANAGEMENT

One of management's most basic decisions is whether to encourage or discourage the unionization of its employees. It may discourage unions because it fears higher wage and benefit costs, the disruptions caused by strikes, and an adversarial relationship with its employees or, more generally, greater constraints placed on its decision-making flexibility and discretion. Historically, management has used two basic strategies to avoid unionization.[9] It may seek to provide employment terms and conditions that employees will perceive as sufficiently attractive and equitable so that they see little gain from union representation. Or it may aggressively oppose union representation, even when there is significant employee interest. Use of the latter strategy has increased significantly over the past several decades.

If management voluntarily recognizes a union or if employees are already represented by a union, the focus is shifted from dealing with employees as individuals to employees as a group. Still, certain basic management objectives remain: controlling labor costs and increasing productivity (by keeping wages and benefits in check) and maintaining management prerogatives in important areas such as staffing levels and work rules. Of course, management always has the option of trying to decertify a union (that is, encouraging employees to vote out the union in a decertification election) if it believes that the majority of employees no longer wish to be represented by the union.

LABOR UNIONS

Labor unions seek, through collective action, to give workers a formal and independent voice in setting the terms and conditions of their work. Table 14.1 shows typical provisions negotiated by unions in collective bargaining contracts. Labor unions attempt to represent their members' interests in these decisions. Without adequate union representation, not only workers' wages, but also their safety and welfare, are more likely to be put at risk. This is particularly true in low-wage economies where regulatory protection may also be lacking.

Just before more than 1,100 workers perished in the Rana Plaza eight-story factory building collapse in Bangladesh in April 2013, workers on the third floor were startled by what sounded like an explosion. They also saw cracks in the walls. An engineer was brought in to examine the cracks, and he found that they were structural. He recommended immediate evacuation of the building. Workers evacuated but were ordered back to work. If they did not go back, they would lose their pay, which, at $38/month, they likely did not feel they could afford.

The question was how could such a tragedy be prevented from happening again? One response has been for companies that buy from garment suppliers in Bangladesh to develop and enforce worker safety and treatment standards. (See the "Integrity in Action" box for more details on this effort.) Another response is: What if the workers at Rana Plaza had been represented by a labor union? Perhaps the workers, if unionized, could have refused to follow the order to return to work. As one response to the tragedy, the Bangladesh government stated that it would begin to allow the country's 4 million garment workers to form trade unions and do so without first obtaining permission from factory owners. Labor unions can provide protection for workers and also help negotiate

Table 14.1
Typical Provisions in Collective Bargaining Contracts

Establishment and administration of the agreement	**Wage determination and administration**	**Plant operations**
Bargaining unit and plant supplements	General provisions	Work and shop rules
Contract duration and reopening and renegotiation provisions	Rate structure and wage differentials	Rest periods and other in-plant time allowances
Union security and the checkoff	Allowances	Safety and health
Special bargaining committees	Incentive systems and production bonus plans	Plant committees
Grievance procedures	Production standards and time studies	Hours of work and premium pay practices
Arbitration and mediation	Job classification and job evaluation	Shift operations
Strikes and lockouts	Individual wage adjustments	Hazardous work
Contract enforcement	General wage adjustments during the contract period	Discipline and discharge
Functions, rights, and responsibilities	**Job or income security**	**Paid and unpaid leave**
Management rights clauses	Hiring and transfer arrangements	Vacations and holidays
Plant removal	Employment and income guarantees	Sick leave
Subcontracting	Reporting and call-in pay	Funeral and personal leave
Union activities on company time and premises	Supplemental unemployment benefit plans	Military leave and jury duty
Union–management cooperation	Regulation of overtime, shift work, etc.	**Employee benefit plans**
Regulation of technological change	Reduction of hours to forestall layoffs	Health and insurance plans
Advance notice and consultation	Layoff procedures; seniority; recall	Pension plans
	Worksharing in lieu of layoff	Profit-sharing, stock purchase, and thrift plans
	Attrition arrangements	Bonus plans
	Promotion practices	**Special groups**
	Training and retraining	Apprentices and learners
	Relocation allowances	Workers with disabilities and older workers
	Severance pay and layoff benefit plans	Women
	Special funds and study committees	Veterans
		Union representatives
		Nondiscrimination clauses

SOURCE: From Harry Katz, Thomas Kochan, and Alexander Colvin, *An Introduction to Collective Bargaining and Industrial Relations* 4e, 2008. Reproduced with permission of The McGraw-Hill Companies, Inc.

higher wages to give workers a better standard of living. Of course, these potential advantages will be weighed against the potential consequence of higher labor costs and/or lost working time due to strikes (and thus less competitive product prices, which could reduce sales and employment). In the best case scenario, an effective labor–management relationship can bring more efficient organization of workers in the production process, and higher wages can allow more selectivity in hiring and a more productive workforce.

A major goal of labor unions is bargaining effectiveness, because with it comes the power and influence to make the employees' voices heard and to effect changes in the workplace.[10]

INTEGRITY IN ACTION

The Alliance for Bangladesh Worker Safety

According to the website of the Alliance for Bangladesh Worker Safety, it was established to improve workplace safety in Bangladesh's garment factories in the aftermath of factory tragedies there such as the collapse of the Rana Plaza building. The Alliance reports that its accomplishments in its first year included the following:

- Developed and implemented Bangladesh's first integrated fire safety and structural integrity standard
- Inspected all 587 factories used by Alliance members as sources for their garments
- Provided fire safety training to roughly 1 million workers and managers employed in these factories

The Alliance's first annual report also provided the following case study of its actions at a local company called RSI Apparels Limited. It reported that an inspection revealed a building structural problem that posed an immediate risk to worker safety. Production at the factory was stopped and safety upgrades made. The Alliance paid one-half of the salaries of workers who were not able to work during that time period and the owner of the factory paid the other half.

The Alliance's third report, two years later, includes a comparison of fire safety in Bangladesh garment factories in 2012, prior to establishment of the Alliance, and 2016. There were 250 garment factory fires in Bangladesh in 2012, which claimed 115 lives.

In contrast, in 2016, there were 30 fires and no lives lost. Fire safety training is a continued emphasis. The Alliance reports that 1.2 million workers have now been trained and another 800,000 have received a refresher course. The Alliance also reports that it has "suspended" (i.e., removed from the Alliance-compliant list) 97 factories "for failure to make progress on repairs that address safety concerns." That does not prevent such factories from operating, but if there is loss of life in one of those factories, the companies using them will have to answer for their decision.

SOURCE: Alliance for Bangladesh Worker Safety, *Third Annual Report: Protecting and Empowering Bangladesh Garment Workers,* September 2016; *First Annual Report: Protecting the Lives and Livelihoods of Bangladesh's Garment Workers,* July 2014, www.bangladeshworkersafety.org.

The right to strike is one important component of bargaining power. In turn, the success of a strike (actual or threatened) depends on the relative magnitude of the costs imposed on management versus those imposed on the union. A critical factor is the size of union membership. More members translate into a greater ability to halt or disrupt production and also into greater financial resources for continuing a strike in the face of lost wages.

Union Structure, Administration, and Membership

A necessary step in discussing labor–management interactions is a basic knowledge of how labor and management are organized and how they function. Management has been described throughout this book. We now focus on labor unions.

NATIONAL AND INTERNATIONAL UNIONS

Most union members belong to a national or international union. In turn, most national unions are composed of multiple local units, and most are affiliated with the American Federation of Labor and Congress of Industrial Organizations (AFL-CIO).

Table 14.2
Largest Labor Unions
in the United States

ORGANIZATION	NUMBER OF MEMBERS
1. National Education Association	2,968,722
2. Service Employees International Union	1,901,161
3. American Federation of Teachers	1,544,143
4. American Federation of State, County, and Municipal Employees	1,346,739
5. International Brotherhood of Teamsters	1,273,695
6. United Food and Commercial Workers International Union	1,256,441
7. International Brotherhood of Electrical Workers	666,602
8. Laborers	581,477
9. United Steel, Paper and Forestry, Rubber, Manufacturing, Energy, Allied Industrial, and Service Workers International Union	571,179
10. Machinists	563,314
11. United Brotherhood of Carpenters and Joiners	445,870
12. United Automobile, Aerospace, and Agricultural Implement Workers of America International Union	415,963
13. International Union of Operating Engineers	377,263
14. United Association of Journeymen and Apprentices of the Plumbing and Pipe Fitting Industry of the United States and Canada	336,021
15. Police	321,922
16. Firefighters	303,112

SOURCE: U.S. Department of Labor, Office of Labor-Management Standards, Online Public Disclosure Room, Union Search [search on "Membership"], https://www.dol.gov/olms/regs/compliance/rrlo/lmrda.htm, accessed April 23, 2017.

The largest national unions are listed in Table 14.2. The National Education Association, which is not affiliated with the AFL-CIO, is the largest union, with almost 3 million members. An important characteristic of a union is whether it is a craft or industrial union. The electrical workers' and carpenters' unions are craft unions, meaning that the members all have a particular skill or occupation. Craft unions often are responsible for training their members (through apprenticeships) and for supplying craft workers to employers. Requests for carpenters, for example, would come to the union hiring hall, which would decide which carpenters to send out. Thus craft workers may work for many employers over time, their constant link being to the union. A craft union's bargaining power depends greatly on the control it can exercise over the supply of its workers.

In contrast, industrial unions are made up of members who are linked by their work in a particular industry (such as steelworkers and autoworkers). Typically they represent many different occupations. Membership in the union is a result of working for a particular employer in the industry. Changing employers is less common than it is among craft workers, and employees who change employers remain members of the same union only if they happen to move to other employers covered by that union. Whereas a craft union may restrict the number of, say, carpenters to maintain higher wages, industrial unions try to organize as many employees in as wide a range of skills as possible.

LOCAL UNIONS

Even when a national union plays the most critical role in negotiating terms of a collective bargaining contract, negotiation occurs at the local level as well as over work rules and other issues that are locally determined. In addition, administration of the contract is carried out largely at the local union level. Consequently, the bulk of day-to-day interaction between labor and management takes place at the local union level.

The local of an industrial-based union may correspond to a single large facility or to a number of small facilities. In a craft-oriented union, the local may cover a city or a region. The local union typically elects officers (like president, vice president, treasurer). Responsibility for contract negotiation may rest with the officers, or a bargaining committee may be formed for this purpose. Typically the national union provides assistance, ranging from background data about other settlements and technical advice to sending a representative to lead the negotiations.

Individual members' participation in local union meetings includes the election of union officials and strike votes. However, most union contact is with the shop steward, who is responsible for ensuring that the terms of the collective bargaining contract are enforced. The shop steward represents employees in contract grievances. Another union position, the business representative, performs some of the same functions, especially where the union deals with multiple employers, as is often the case with craft unions.

AMERICAN FEDERATION OF LABOR AND CONGRESS OF INDUSTRIAL ORGANIZATIONS (AFL-CIO)

The AFL-CIO is not a labor union but rather an association that seeks to advance the shared interests of its member unions at the national level, much as the Chamber of Commerce and the National Association of Manufacturers do for their member employers. As Figure 14.2 indicates, there are 55 affiliated national and international unions and thousands of locals. An important responsibility of the AFL-CIO is to represent labor's interests in public policy issues such as civil rights, economic policy, safety, and occupational health. It also provides information and analysis that member unions can use in their activities: organizing new members, negotiating new contracts, and administering contracts.

UNION SECURITY

The survival and security of a union depends on its ability to ensure a regular flow of new members and member dues to support the services it provides. Therefore, unions typically place high priority on negotiating two contract provisions with an employer that are critical to a union's security or viability: checkoff provisions and union membership or contribution. First, under a **checkoff provision**, the employer, on behalf of the union, automatically deducts union dues from employees' paychecks.

A second union security provision focuses on the flow of new members (and their dues). The strongest union security arrangement is a **closed shop**, under which a person must be a union member (and thus pay dues) before being hired. A closed shop is, however, illegal under the NLRA. A **union shop** requires a person to join the union within a certain amount of time (30 days) after beginning employment. An **agency shop** is similar to a union shop but does not require union membership, only that dues be paid. **Maintenance of membership** rules do not require union membership but do require that employees who choose to join must remain members for a certain period of time (such as the length of the contract).

Under the 1947 **Taft-Hartley Act** (an amendment to the NLRA), states may pass so-called **right-to-work laws**, which make union shops, maintenance of membership, and agency shops illegal. The idea behind such laws is that compulsory union membership

Checkoff provision
A union contract provision that requires an employer to deduct union dues from employees' paychecks.

Closed shop
A union security provision requiring a person to be a union member before being hired. Illegal under NLRA.

Union shop
A union security provision that requires a person to join the union within a certain amount of time after being hired.

Agency shop
A union security provision that requires an employee to pay union membership dues but not to join the union.

Maintenance of membership
Union rules requiring members to remain members for a certain period of time (e.g., the length of the union contract).

Taft-hartley act
The 1947 act that outlawed unfair union labor practices.

Right-to-work laws
State laws that make union shops, maintenance of membership, and agency shops illegal.

Figure 14.2
AFL-CIO
Organization Chart

```
┌─────────────────────────┐
│    55 Affiliated        │
│    National Unions      │
└─────────────────────────┘
            │
┌─────────────────────────┐
│    Executive Council    │
│    55 Vice Presidents   │
│                         │
│    President            │
│    Secretary-Treasurer  │
│    Executive Vice President │
└─────────────────────────┘
            │
┌─────────────────────────┐
│   AFL-CIO Departments   │
│  • Accounting           │
│  • Campaigns            │
│  • Civil, Human and Women's Rights │
│  • Digital Strategies   │
│  • Facilities Management│
│  • Government Affairs    │
│  • Human Resources      │
│  • Information Technology│
│  • International        │
│  • Meetings and Travel  │
│  • Office of General Counsel │
│  • Office of Investment │
│  • Organizing           │
│  • Policy               │
│  • Political            │
│  • Public Affairs       │
│  • Support Services     │
├─────────────────────────┤
│  Trade and Industrial   │
│      Departments        │
│  • Building and Construction │
│    Trades               │
│  • Maritime Trades      │
│  • Metal Trades         │
│  • Professional Employees │
│  • Transportation Trades│
│  • Union Label and Service Trades │
└─────────────────────────┘
            │
┌─────────────────────────┐
│ Thousands of affiliated local │
│ unions and 12.5 million │
│      members            │
│                         │
│  51 State Federations   │
└─────────────────────────┘
```

SOURCE: AFL-CIO, http://afl-cio.org/About/What-the-AFL-CIO-Does, accessed April 29, 2017.

(or making employees pay union dues) infringes on the employee's right to freedom of association. From the union perspective, a big concern is "free riders," employees who benefit from union activities without belonging to a union. By law, all members of a bargaining unit, whether union members or not, must be represented by the union. If the union is required to offer service to all bargaining unit members, even those who are not union members, it may lose its financial viability.

UNION MEMBERSHIP AND BARGAINING POWER

At the strategic level, management and unions meet head-on over the issue of union organizing. Increasingly, employers are actively resisting unionization in an attempt to control costs and maintain their flexibility. Unions, by contrast, must organize new members and hold on to their current members to have the kind of bargaining power and financial resources needed to achieve their goals in future organizing and to negotiate and administer contracts with management. For this reason we now discuss trends in union membership and possible explanations for those trends.

Since the 1950s, when union membership rose to 35% of employment, membership has consistently declined as a percentage of employment. It now stands at 11.1% of all employment and 6.4% of private-sector employment.[11] As Figure 14.3 indicates, this decline shows no indication of reversing.[12]

What factors explain the decline in union membership? Several have been identified.[13]

Figure 14.3

Union Membership Density among U.S. Wage and Salary Workers, 1973–2016

SOURCE: From B. T. Hirsch and D. A. MacPherson, *Union Membership and Earnings Data Book 2001* (Washington, DC: The Bureau of National Affairs, Inc., 2001). Reprinted with permission. Data for 2001 to 2016 obtained from U.S. Bureau of Labor Statistics, www.bls.gov.

Structural Changes in the Economy

At the risk of oversimplifying, we might say that unions have traditionally been strongest in urban workplaces (especially those outside the South) that employ middle-aged men in blue-collar jobs. However, much recent job growth has occurred among women and youth in the service sector (in contrast to the manufacturing sector) of the economy. Although unionizing such groups is possible, unions have so far not had much success organizing these groups in the private sector. Despite the importance of structural changes in the economy, studies show that they account for no more than one-quarter of the overall union membership decline.[14]

Increased Employer Resistance

Almost one-half of large employers in a survey reported that their most important labor goal was to be union-free. This contrasts sharply with 60 years ago, when Jack Barbash wrote that "many tough bargainers [among employers] prefer the union to a situation where there is no union. Most of the employers in rubber, basic steel and the automobile industry fall in this category." The idea then was that an effective union could help assess and communicate the interests of employees to management, thus helping management make better decisions. But product-market pressures, such as foreign competition and deregulation (e.g., trucking, airlines, telecommunications), have contributed to increasing employer resistance to unions.[15] These changes in the competitive environment have contributed to a change in management's perspective and goals.[16]

In the absence of significant competition from foreign producers, unions were often able to organize entire industries. For example, the UAW organized all four major producers in the automobile industry (GM, Ford, Chrysler, and American Motors). The UAW usually sought and achieved the same union–management contract at each company. As a consequence, a negotiated wage increase in the industry could be passed on to the consumer in the form of higher prices. No company was undercut by its competitors because the labor cost of all major producers in the industry was determined by the same union–management contract, and the U.S. public had little option but to buy U.S.-made cars. However, the onset of foreign competition in the automobile market changed the competitive situation as well as the UAW's ability to organize the industry.[17] U.S. automakers were slow to recognize and respond to the competitive threat from foreign producers, resulting in a loss of market share and employment.

Competitive threats have contributed to increased employer resistance to union organizing and, in some cases, to an increased emphasis on ridding themselves of existing unions. Unionized workers receive, on average, 26% higher wages, and this advantage is still estimated to be 10–15% when observable characteristics of union and nonunion workers are equated. The compensation advantage is still larger if benefits are also included. Many employers have decided that they can no longer compete with these higher labor costs, and union membership has suffered as a result.[18] One measure of increased employer resistance is the dramatic increase in the late 1960s in the number of unfair employer labor practices (violations of sections of the NLRA such as section 8(a)(3), which prohibits firing employees for union organizing, as we discuss later) even though the number of elections held did not change much. (See Figure 14.4.) The use of remedies such as back pay for workers also grew, but the costs to employers of such penalties does not appear to have been sufficient to prevent the growth in employer unfair labor practices. Not surprisingly, the union victory rate in representation elections decreased from almost 59% in 1960 to below 50% by 1975. Although the union victory rate in elections during the two most recent years has actually been higher (64%), the

Figure 14.4

Employer Resistance to Union Organizing, 1950–2016

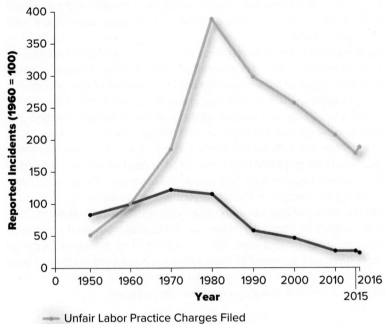

- Unfair Labor Practice Charges Filed
- Representation Elections Held

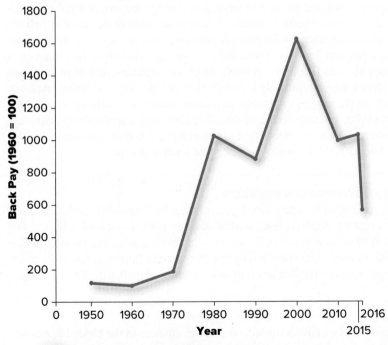

- Back Pay Received by Workers as Remedy to Unfair
  Labor Practice (2016 dollars)

SOURCE: Adapted and updated from R. B. Freeman and J. L. Medoff, *What Do Unions Do?* (New York: Basic Books, 1984). Data for from www.nlrb.gov. Graphs and Data.https://www.nlrb.gov/news-outreach/graphs-data.

number of elections has declined precipitously (77%) between 1970 and 2016. Moreover, decertification elections have come to represent a larger share of all elections in recent years.[19] Given the significant decline in both elections and union membership percentage (see Figure 14.3), the increases in the number of unfair labor practice charges and back pay awards is all the more notable.

Finally, even if a union wins the right to represent employees, its ability to successfully negotiate a contract with the employer is not guaranteed. Indeed, refusal to bargain by the employer is the unfair labor practice most frequently filed (over half of all charges) against employers. One study examined 22,000 organizing drives by unions in the United States over a six-year period. Only about one-seventh of these drives eventually resulted in a union contract, either because the election was lost (or challenged) or because, after a win, a contract could not be obtained with the employer. Further, this success rate was lower still (by 30%) in cases where the employer filed an unfair labor practice against the union.[20]

At a personal level, some managers may face serious consequences if a union successfully organizes a new set of workers or mounts a serious organizing drive. One study indicated that 8% of the plant managers in companies with organizing drives were fired, and 10% of those in companies where the union was successful were fired (compared with 2% in a control group).[21] Furthermore, only 3% of the plant managers facing an organizing drive were promoted, and none of those ending up with a union contract were promoted (compared with 21% of the managers in the control group). Therefore, managers are often under intense pressure to oppose unionization attempts.

Substitution with HRM

A major study of the human resource management strategies and practices among large, nonunion employers found that union avoidance was often an important employee relations objective.[22] Top management's values in such companies drive specific policies such as promotion from within, an influential personnel–human resource department, and above-average pay and benefits. These policies, in turn, contribute to a number of desirable outcomes such as flexibility, positive employee attitudes, and responsive and committed employees, which ultimately lead to higher productivity and better employee relations. In other words, employers attempt to remain nonunion by offering most of the things a union can offer, and then some, while still maintaining a productivity advantage over their competitors. Of course, one aspect of union representation that employers cannot duplicate is the independent employee voice that a union provides.

Substitution by Government Regulation

Since the 1960s, regulation of many employment areas has increased, including equal employment opportunity, pensions, and worker displacement. Combined with existing regulations, this increase may result in fewer areas in which unions can provide worker rights or protection beyond those specified by law. Yet western European countries generally have more regulations and higher levels of union membership than the United States.[23]

Worker Views

Industrial relations scholars have long argued that the absence in the United States of a history of feudalism and of strong class distinctions found in western Europe have contributed to a more pragmatic, business-oriented (versus class-conscious) unionism. Although this may help explain the somewhat lower level of union membership in the United States, its relevance in explaining the downward trend is not clear. Further, when U.S. workers are asked about their interest in joining a union, interest is substantial.[24]

Union Actions and Industry Structure

In some ways, unions have hurt their own cause. First, corruption in unions such as the Teamsters may have had a detrimental effect. Second, questions have been raised about how well unions have adapted to recent changes in the economic structure. Employee groups and economic sectors with the fastest growth rates tend to have the lowest rates of unionization.[25] Women are slightly less likely to be in unions than men (10.2% vs. 11.2%), and nonmanufacturing industries such as finance, insurance, and real estate have a lower union representation (2.3%) than does transportation and utilities (18.9%) or manufacturing (8.8%). The South is also less heavily organized than the rest of the country, with, for example, South Carolina having a unionization rate of 1.6%, compared with 23.6% in New York.[26] For example, none of the foreign-owned automobile assembly plants (e.g., BMW, Mercedes-Benz, Toyota, Volkswagen, Nissan) located in the South are unionized (although they would be in their home countries). One reason for the smaller union presence in southern states is the existence of right-to-work laws (see our earlier discussion) in such states. (We should note, however, that since 2012, Indiana, Michigan, and Wisconsin, traditional union strongholds, have all become right-to-work states.)

Legal Framework

Although competitive challenges have a major impact on labor relations, the legal framework of collective bargaining is an especially critical determinant of union membership and relative bargaining power and, therefore, of the degree to which employers, employees, and society are successful in achieving their goals. The legal framework also constrains union structure and administration and the manner in which unions and employers interact. Perhaps the most dramatic example of labor laws' influence is the 1935 passage of the Wagner Act (also known as the National Labor Relations Act or NLRA), which actively supported collective bargaining rather than impeding it. As a result, union membership nearly tripled, from 3 million in 1933 (7.7% of all employment) to 8.8 million (19.2% of employment) by 1939.[27] With increased membership came greater union bargaining power and, consequently, more success in achieving union goals.

Before the 1930s, the legal system was generally hostile to unions. The courts generally viewed unions as coercive organizations that hindered free trade. Unions' focus on collective voice and collective action (strikes, boycotts) did not fit well with the U.S. emphasis on capitalism, individualism, freedom of contract, and property rights.[28]

The Great Depression of the 1930s, however, shifted public attitudes toward business and the free-enterprise system. Unemployment rates as high as 25% and a 30% drop in the gross national product between 1929 and 1933 focused attention on employee rights and on the shortcomings of the system as it existed then. The nation was in a crisis, and President Franklin Roosevelt responded with dramatic action, the New Deal. On the labor front, the 1935 NLRA ushered in a new era of public policy for labor unions, enshrining collective bargaining as the preferred mechanism for settling labor–management disputes.

The introduction to the NLRA states:

> It is in the national interest of the United States to maintain full production in its economy. Industrial strife among employees, employers, and labor organizations interferes with full production and is contrary to our national interest. Experience has shown that labor disputes can be lessened if the parties involved recognize the legitimate rights of each in their relations with one another. To establish these rights under the law, Congress enacted the National Labor Relations Act. Its purpose is to define and protect the rights of employees and employers, to encourage collective bargaining, and to eliminate certain practices on the part of labor and management that are harmful to the general welfare.[29]

LO 14-3

Explain the legal environment's impact on labor relations.

Table 14.3

Are You Excluded from the NLRA's Coverage?

The NLRA specifically excludes from its coverage individuals who are
- Employed as a supervisor
- Employed by a parent or spouse
- Employed as an independent contractor
- Employed in the domestic service of any person or family in a home
- Employed as agricultural laborers
- Employed by an employer subject to the Railway Labor Act
- Employed by a federal, state, or local government
- Employed by any other person who is not an employer as defined in the NLRA

SOURCE: National Labor Relations Board, Basic Guide to the National Labor Relations Act (Washington, DC: U.S. Government Printing Office, 1997). Available at www.nlrb.gov. Accessed June 20, 2017.

The rights of employees are set out in Section 7 of the act, including the "right to self-organization, to form, join, or assist labor organizations, to bargain collectively through representatives of their own choosing, and to engage in other concerted activities for the purpose of collective bargaining. The act also gives employees the right to refrain from any or all of such activities except [in cases] requiring membership in a labor organization as a condition of employment."[30] Examples of protected activities include

- Union organizing
- Joining a union, whether it is recognized by the employer or not
- Going out on strike to secure better working conditions
- Refraining from activity on behalf of the union[31]

Although the NLRA has broad coverage in the private sector, Table 14.3 shows that there are some notable exclusions.

UNFAIR LABOR PRACTICES—EMPLOYERS

The NLRA prohibits certain activities by both employers and labor unions. Unfair labor practices by employers are listed in Section 8(a) of the NLRA. Section 8(a)(1) prohibits employers from interfering with, restraining, or coercing employees in exercising their rights to join or assist a labor organization or to refrain from such activities. Section 8(a)(2) prohibits employer domination of or interference with the formation or activities of a labor union. Section 8(a)(3) prohibits discrimination (e.g., firing employees engaged in union organizing) in any aspect of employment that attempts to encourage or discourage union-related activity. Section 8(a)(4) prohibits discrimination against employees for providing testimony relevant to enforcement of the NLRA. Section 8(a)(5) prohibits employers from refusing to bargain collectively with a labor organization that has standing under the act. Examples of employer unfair labor practices are listed in Table 14.4.

UNFAIR LABOR PRACTICES—LABOR UNIONS

Originally the NLRA did not list any union unfair labor practices. These were added through the 1947 Taft-Hartley Act. The 1959 Landrum-Griffin Act further regulated unions' actions and their internal affairs (like financial disclosure and conduct of elections). Section 8(b)(1)(a) of the NLRA states that a labor organization is not to "restrain or coerce employees in the exercise of the rights guaranteed in Section 7" (described earlier). Table 14.5 provides examples of union unfair labor practices.

Table 14.4
Examples of Employer Unfair Labor Practices

- Threatening employees with loss of their jobs or benefits if they join or vote for a union
- Threatening to close down a plant if organized by a union
- Questioning employees about their union membership or activities in a manner that restrains or coerces them
- Spying or pretending to spy on union meetings
- Granting wage increases that are timed to discourage employees from forming or joining a union
- Taking an active part in organizing a union or committee to represent employees
- Providing preferential treatment or aid to one of several unions trying to organize employees
- Discharging employees for urging other employees to join a union or refusing to hire applicants because they are union members
- Refusing to reinstate workers when job openings occur because the workers participated in a lawful strike
- Ending operation at one plant and opening the same operation at another plant with new employees because employees at the first plant joined a union
- Demoting or firing employees for filing an unfair labor practice or for testifying at an NLRB hearing
- Refusing to meet with employees' representatives because the employees are on strike
- Refusing to supply the employees' representative with cost and other data concerning a group insurance plan covering employees
- Announcing a wage increase without consulting the employees' representative
- Failing to bargain about the effects of a decision to close one of employer's plants

SOURCE: National Labor Relations Board, *Basic Guide to the National Labor Relations Act* (Washington, DC: U.S. Government Printing Office, 1997). Available at www.nlrb.gov. Accessed June 20, 2017.

Table 14.5
Examples of Union Unfair Labor Practices

- Mass picketing in such numbers that nonstriking employees are physically barred from entering the plant
- Acts of force or violence on the picket line or in connection with a strike
- Threats to employees of bodily injury or that they will lose their jobs unless they support the union's activities
- Fining or expelling members for crossing a picket line that is unlawful
- Fining or expelling members for filing unfair labor practice charges or testifying before the NLRB
- Insisting during contract negotiations that the employer agree to accept working conditions that will be determined by a group to which it does not belong
- Fining or expelling union members for the way they apply the bargaining contract while carrying out their supervisory responsibilities
- Causing an employer to discharge employees because they spoke out against a contract proposed by the union
- Making a contract that requires an employer to hire only members of the union or employees "satisfactory" to the union
- Insisting on the inclusion of illegal provisions in a contract
- Terminating an existing contract and striking for a new one without notifying the employer, the Federal Mediation and Conciliation Service, and the state mediation service (where one exists)
- Attempting to compel a beer distributor to recognize a union (the union prevents the distributor from obtaining beer at a brewery by inducing the brewery's employees to refuse to fill the distributor's orders)
- Picketing an employer to force it to stop doing business with another employer who has refused to recognize the union (a "secondary boycott")

SOURCE: National Labor Relations *Board, A Guide to Basic Law and Procedures under the National Labor Relations Act* (Washington, DC: U.S. Government Printing Office, 1997). Available at www.nlrb.gov. Accessed June 20, 2017.

ENFORCEMENT

Enforcement of the NLRA rests with the National Labor Relations Board, which is composed of a five-member board, the general counsel, and 33 regional offices. The basis for the NLRA is the commerce clause of the U.S. Constitution. Therefore, the NLRB's jurisdiction is limited to employers whose operations affect commerce generally and interstate commerce in particular. In practice, only purely local firms are likely to fall outside the NLRB's jurisdiction. Specific jurisdictional standards (nearly 20) that vary by industry are applied. Two examples of businesses that are covered (and the standards) are retail businesses that had more than $500,000 in annual business and newspapers that had more than $200,000 in annual business.

The NLRB's two major functions are to conduct and certify representation elections and prevent unfair labor practices. In both realms, it does not initiate action. Rather, it responds to requests for action. The NLRB's role in representation elections is discussed in the next section. Here we discuss unfair labor practices.

Unfair labor practice cases begin with the filing of a charge, which is investigated by a regional office. A charge must be filed within six months of the alleged unfair practice, and copies must be served on all parties. (Registered mail is recommended.) If the NLRB finds the charge to have merit and issues a complaint, there are two possible actions. It may defer to a grievance procedure agreed on by the employer and union. Otherwise, a hearing is held before an administrative law judge. The judge makes a recommendation, which can be appealed by either party. The NLRB has the authority to issue cease-and-desist orders to halt unfair labor practices. It can also order reinstatement of employees, with or without back pay. In one recent year, for example, $110 million in back pay was awarded. Note, however, that the NLRA is not a criminal statute, and punitive damages are not available. If an employer or union refuses to comply with an NLRB order, the board has the authority to petition the U.S. Court of Appeals. The court can choose to enforce the order, remand it to the NLRB for modification, change it, or set it aside altogether.

Union and Management Interactions: Organizing

LO 14-4
Describe the major labor–management interactions: organizing, contract negotiations, and contract administration.

To this point we have discussed macro trends in union membership. Here we shift our focus to the more micro questions of why individual employees join unions and how the organizing process works at the workplace level.

WHY DO EMPLOYEES JOIN UNIONS?

Virtually every model of the decision to join a union focuses on two questions.[32] First, is there a gap between the pay, benefits, and other conditions of employment that employees actually receive versus what they believe they should receive? Second, if such a gap exists and is sufficiently large to motivate employees to try to remedy the situation, is union membership seen as the most effective or instrumental means of change? The outcome of an election campaign hinges on how the majority of employees answer these two questions.

THE PROCESS AND LEGAL FRAMEWORK OF ORGANIZING

The NLRB is responsible for ensuring that the organizing process follows certain steps. At the most general level, the NLRB holds a union representation election if at least 30% of employees in the bargaining unit sign authorization cards (see Figure 14.5). If more than 50% of the employees sign authorization cards, the union may request that the

YES, I WANT THE IAM

I, the undersigned employee of

_____
(Company)

authorize the International Association of Machinists and Aerospace Workers (IAM) to act as my collective bargaining agent for wages, hours and working conditions. I agree that this card may be used either to support a demand for recognition or an NLRB election, at the discretion of the union.

Name (print) _____ Date _____

Home Address _____ Phone _____

City _____ State _____ Zip _____

Job Title _____ Dept. _____ Shift _____

Sign Here X_____

Note: This authorization to be SIGNED and DATED in employee's own handwriting.
YOUR RIGHT TO SIGN THIS CARD IS PROTECTED BY FEDERAL LAW.

RECEIVED BY (Initial) _____

Figure 14.5
Authorization Card

employer voluntarily recognize it. If 50% or fewer of the employees sign, or if the employer refuses to recognize the union voluntarily, the NLRB conducts a secret-ballot election. The union is certified by the NLRB as the exclusive representative of employees if more than 50% of employees vote for the union. If more than one union appears on the ballot and neither gains a simple majority, a runoff election is held. Once a union has been certified as the exclusive representative of a group of employees, no additional elections are permitted for one year. After the negotiation of a contract, an election cannot be held for the contract's duration or for three years, whichever comes first. The parties to the contract may agree not to hold an election for longer than three years, but an outside party cannot be barred for more than three years.

As mentioned previously, union members' right to be represented by leaders of their own choosing was expanded under the Taft-Hartley Act to include the right to vote an existing union out—that is, to decertify it. The process follows the same steps as a representation election. A decertification election is not permitted when a contract is in effect. Research indicates that when decertification elections are held, unions typically do not fare well, losing the majority of the time.[33]

The NLRB also is responsible for determining the appropriate bargaining unit and the employees who are eligible to participate in organizing activities. A unit may cover employees in one facility or multiple facilities within a single employer, or the unit may cover multiple employers. In general, employees on the payroll just prior to the ordering of an election are eligible to vote, although this rule is modified in some cases where, for example, employment in the industry is irregular. Most employees who are on strike and who have been replaced by other employees are eligible to vote in an election (such as a decertification election) that occurs within 12 months of the onset of the strike.

As shown in Table 14.3, the following types of employees cannot be included in bargaining units: agricultural laborers, independent contractors, supervisors, and managers. Beyond this, the NLRB attempts to group together employees who have a community of interest in their wages, hours, and working conditions. In many cases this grouping will be sharply contested, with management and the union jockeying to include or exclude certain employee subgroups in the hope of influencing the outcome of the election.

During the Obama administration, the NLRB issued a number of important rulings. One ruling, referred to by the U.S. Chamber of Commerce as the "ambush election rule," is designed to streamline and speed representation elections, presumably in hopes of helping unions be more successful in organizing new workers.[34] Specific changes include allowing unions to file election petitions electronically rather than requiring them to be submitted by mail, requiring businesses to give unions personal e-mail addresses (in addition to telephone numbers) of workers if they have them on file (within two days), and making it more difficult for employers to challenge elections until after they are conducted. The changes are intended to shorten the time between the call for a vote and actual election to 25 days or less, nearly 2 weeks less than the previous median of 38 days and 3.5 weeks less than the median of 59 days in cases where employers contest the holding or other aspects of an election. Evidence suggests that the rules have had the intended effect of shortening time to elections.[35]

A second ruling, Browning-Ferris, which may have even larger ramifications, appears to make it more likely that in a case where Company A contracts with a staffing firm (Company B) to provide it with workers, Company A could be held responsible (depending on the amount of control it exercises over workers, directly and/or indirectly) as a joint employer (along with Company B) for employment practices, rather than such responsibility falling exclusively to Company B.[36] As such, a union now has a better chance of being able to negotiate directly with Company A, making it more difficult for Company A to avoid dealing with the union.

Another ruling also moves toward making a company responsible for workers who are not its employees, in this case, employees of its franchises. This case involved McDonald's. Some workers brought a complaint against McDonald's for retaliating against workers who went out on strike to join the "Fight for 15" protests for higher wages. Importantly, the NLRB ruled in the case that McDonald's, which owns only 10% of McDonald's stores, is a joint employer with its franchisees, which own and operate, and employ workers in, the other 90% of stores. The NLRB stated that "through its franchise relationship and its use of tools, resources, and technology," McDonald's "engages in sufficient control over its franchisees' operations." The ruling poses a threat to McDonald's and other companies that use a franchise model. McDonald's could become at least partly responsible for (including for the cost of litigation-related expenses) any labor and/or employment law violations committed by its franchisees, and there are many (14,000) of them in far-flung places. The Service Employees International Union (SEIU) hopes the ruling will put pressure on large companies like McDonald's to take more responsibility for the actions of its franchisees, leading to better treatment of workers.[37]

The bigger picture is that a change in presidential administration will eventually influence how pro-labor versus pro-business the NLRB is, as the terms of current board members expire and the new president has the opportunity to appoint new board members for fixed terms. The expectation is that Trump appointees to the NLRB will be more pro-business (or less pro-labor, depending on one's perspective).

A 2016 NLRB ruling, though having a much narrower effect and outside the for-profit business sector, may be of interest to current or future graduate students reading this book. The NLRB ruled that teaching assistants and research assistants at private universities are employees under the NLRA, thus giving them the right to organize and join a union. (At public universities, state laws apply.)[38]

Organizing Campaigns: Management and Union Strategies and Tactics

Tables 14.6 and 14.7 list common issues that arise during most campaigns.[39] Unions attempt to persuade employees that their wages, benefits, treatment by employers, and opportunity to influence workplace decisions are not sufficient and that the union will be

UNION ISSUES	PERCENTAGE OF CAMPAIGNS
Union will prevent unfairness and will set up a grievance procedure and seniority system.	82%
Union will improve unsatisfactory wages.	79
Union strength will give employees voice in wages, working conditions.	79
Union, not outsider, bargains for what employees want.	73
Union has obtained gains elsewhere.	70
Union will improve unsatisfactory sick leave and insurance.	64
Dues and initiation fees are reasonable.	64
Union will improve unsatisfactory vacations and holidays.	61
Union will improve unsatisfactory pensions.	61
Employer promises and good treatment may not be continued without union.	61
Employees choose union leaders.	55
Employer will seek to persuade or frighten employees to vote against union.	55
No strike without vote.	55
Union will improve unsatisfactory working conditions.	52
Employees have legal right to engage in union activity.	52

Table 14.6
Most Common Issues Raised by Unions in Representation Election Campaigns

SOURCE: J. Getman, S. Goldberg, and J. B. Herman, *Union Representation Elections: Law and Reality* (New York: Russell Sage Foundation, 1976), Table 4–3; N = 33 representation election campaigns.

COMPANY ISSUES	PERCENTAGE OF CAMPAIGNS
Improvements not dependent on unionization.	85%
Wages good, equal to, or better than under union contract.	82
Financial costs of union dues outweigh gains.	79
Union is outsider.	79
Get facts before deciding; employer will provide facts and accept employee decision.	76
If union wins, strike may follow.	70
Loss of benefits may follow union win.	67
Strikers will lose wages; lose more than gain.	67
Unions not concerned with employee welfare.	67
Strike may lead to loss of jobs.	64
Employer has treated employees fairly and/or well.	60
Employees should be certain to vote.	54

Table 14.7
Most Common Issues Raised by Companies in Representation Election Campaigns

SOURCES: J. Fossum, *Labor Relations: Development, Structure and Processes*, 5th ed., 1992. Reprinted with permission of The McGraw-Hill Companies, Inc. Original data from J. Getman, S. Goldberg, and J. B. Herman, *Union Representation Elections: Law and Reality* (New York: Russell Sage Foundation, 1976), Table 4-2; N = 33 representation election campaigns.

effective in obtaining improvements. Management emphasizes that it has provided a good package of wages, benefits, and so on. It also argues that, whereas a union is unlikely to provide improvements in such areas, it will likely lead to certain costs for employees, such as union dues and the income loss resulting from strikes.

Table 14.8
Percentage of Firms Using Various Methods to Oppose Union-Organizing Campaigns

Survey of employers	
Consultants used	41%
Unfair labor practice charges filed against employer	24
Survey of union organizers	
Consultants and/or lawyers used	70
Unfair labor practices by employer	
Charges filed	36
Discharges or discriminatory layoffs	42[a]
Company leaflets	80
Company letters	91
Captive audience speech	91[b]
Supervisor meetings with small groups of employees	92
Supervisor intensity in opposing union	
Low	14
Moderate	34
High	51

[a]This percentage is larger than the figure for charges filed because it includes cases in which no unfair labor practice charge was actually filed against the employer.

[b]Refers to management's requiring employees to attend a session on company time at which the disadvantages of union membership are emphasized.

SOURCE: R. B. Freeman and M. M. Kleiner, "Employer Behavior in the Face of Union Organizing Drives," *Industrial and Labor Relations Review* 43, no. 4 (April 1990), pp. 351–65. © Cornell University.

As Table 14.8 indicates, employers use a variety of methods to oppose unions in organizing campaigns, some of which may go beyond what the law permits, especially in the eyes of union organizers. This perception is supported by our earlier discussion, which noted a significant increase in employer unfair labor practices since the late 1960s. (See Figure 14.4.)

Why would employers increasingly break the law? Fossum suggests that the consequences (like back pay and reinstatement of workers) of doing so are "slight."[40] His review of various studies suggests that discrimination against employees involved in union organizing decreases union-organizing success significantly and that the cost of back pay to union activists reinstated in their jobs is far smaller than the costs that would be incurred if the union managed to organize and gain better wages, benefits, and so forth.

Still, the NLRB attempts to maintain a noncoercive atmosphere under which employees feel they can exercise free choice. It will set aside an election if it believes that either the union or the employer has created "an atmosphere of confusion or fear of reprisals."[41] Examples of conduct that may lead to an election result being set aside include the following:

- Threats of loss of jobs or benefits by an employer or union to influence votes or organizing activities
- A grant of benefits or a promise of benefits as a means of influencing votes or organizing activities
- An employer or union making campaign speeches to assembled groups of employees on company time less than 24 hours before an election
- The actual use or threat of physical force or violence to influence votes or organizing activities[42]

Table 14.9
What Supervisors Should and Should Not Do to Stay Union-Free

WHAT TO DO:

Report any direct or indirect signs of union activity to a core management group.

Deal with employees by carefully stating the company's response to pro-union arguments. These responses should be coordinated by the company to maintain consistency and to avoid threats or promises.

Take away union issues by following effective management practice all the time:

  Deliver recognition and appreciation.

  Solve employee problems.

  Protect employees from harassment or humiliation.

  Provide business-related information.

  Be consistent in treatment of different employees.

  Accommodate special circumstances where appropriate.

  Ensure due process in performance management.

  Treat all employees with dignity and respect.

WHAT TO AVOID:

Threatening employees with harsher terms and conditions of employment or employment loss if they engage in union activity.

Interrogating employees about pro-union or anti-union sentiments that they or others may have or reviewing union authorization cards or pro-union petitions.

Promising employees that they will receive favorable terms or conditions of employment if they forgo union activity.

Spying on employees known to be, or suspected of being, engaged in pro-union activities.

SOURCE: From J. A. Segal, *HR Magazine*. Reproduced with permission of Society for Human Resource Management (www.shrm.org), Alexandria, VA, publisher of *HR Magazine*.

Supervisors have the most direct contact with employees. Thus, as Table 14.9 indicates, it is critical that they be proactive in establishing good relationships with employees if the company wishes to avoid union-organizing attempts. It is also important for supervisors to know what not to do (Threatening, Interrogating, Promising, Spying—TIPS) should a drive take place.

In response to organizing difficulties, the union movement has tried alternative approaches. **Associate union membership** is not linked to an employee's workplace and does not provide representation in collective bargaining. Instead the union provides other services, such as discounts on health and life insurance or credit cards.[43] In return, the union receives membership dues and a broader base of support for its activities. Associate membership may be attractive to employees who wish to join a union but cannot because their workplace is not organized by a union. Other types of (nonunion) employee representation models are evolving. The "Competing through Sustainability" box provides and example of a model agreed upon by Uber and the International Association of Machinists union.

Supervisors and their employers must also recognize that social media is increasingly used as a tool in union-organizing drives and understand how to effectively and legally respond to such communications. Workers' concerted activity protections under the NLRA apply here.

Associate union membership
A form of union membership by which the union receives dues in exchange for services (e.g., health insurance, credit cards) but does not provide representation in collective bargaining.

COMPETING THROUGH SUSTAINABILITY

A Unique Approach to Representing Nonunion Employees in the Gig Economy

Uber recently entered into an agreement with the International Association of Machinists and Aerospace Workers (IAM) to create an association, the Independent Drivers Guild, for drivers in New York to provide a mechanism for dialogue with the company and to put in place some limited benefits and protections in lieu of forming a traditional union, which is not feasible as long as drivers are independent contractors, not employees. The guild founder is James Conigliaro Jr., assistant director and general counsel at the IAM's District 15. Mr. Conigliaro said, "It's important to have immediate assistance in the industry and this is the structure that provides that."

Uber has been beset by lawsuits and other actions that stem from its model of treating drivers as contractors rather than employees, a model that helps Uber keep costs low and gives it flexibility. As non-employees, drivers are not covered by laws such as the Fair Labor Standards Act, which requires minimum wage and overtime payments or by the NLRA, which provides the right to join and organize a labor union. As one example of a costly lawsuit, Uber agreed to pay up to $100 million to drivers

who argued they should be classified as employees. The settlement does not include that provision. But, in addition to the $100 million in payments, Uber has agreed to put less pressure on drivers to accept all requested rides. The agreement with the IAM to deal with the Independent Drivers Guild is perhaps another sign of Uber's desire to find a more sustainable model to manage its relationship with its drivers going forward.

The Independent Drivers Guild agreement is for five years, and it includes monthly meetings between guild members and Uber management. The agreement also includes an appeal mechanism for drivers who feel they have been treated unfairly. Drivers will also have access to discounted legal services and discounted insurance. However, unlike a traditional union, guild members will not be able to negotiate a contract, which would set fares, benefits, and discipline procedures. Although Uber will receive input from the guild, it will, importantly, retain final say on those matters. Two other differences from a traditional union stand out: The Guild is partially funded by Uber, and it will not be able to ask the NLRB

to intervene if it feels the company is violating the agreement. The IAM union has also pledged to refrain from trying to organize drivers and from encouraging them to strike during the term of the agreement.

Some people are under-whelmed by the agreement. For example, Abdoul Diallo, who founded a different drivers' association in New York said the new guild seemed "bogus" and that it would be better to have a real union. Accordingly, he will continue to encourage drivers to sign authorization cards asking that the Amalgamated Transit Union represent them.

DISCUSSION QUESTIONS
1. How is the Independent Drivers Guild different from a labor union?
2. Why did Uber agree to work with the guild? Why did the IAM union agree to this model?
3. How well do you think this guild model will work over time? Do you think it will serve as a model for other companies? Explain.

SOURCES: N. Scheiber and M. Isaac, "Uber Recognizes New York Drivers' Group, Short of a Union," *New York Times,* May 10, 2016; J. Cao and E. Newcomer, "Uber and Union Agree to Form Drivers Guild in New York City," Bloomberg.com, May 10, 2016.

One challenge is that, unlike the days of discussions around the water cooler, when employees go online to criticize their company or supervisor, such complaints can now reach millions of people, including customers and clients.[44] Companies have sought to prevent such actions by developing policies for use of social media and to protect against disparagement. Such policies are likely to be less subject to challenge to the extent that they are not overly broad (i.e., such that they prohibit almost any topics or any concerted action) and allow discussion of clearly legitimate topics such as wages, hours, and working conditions. Employers may (though it depends on the circumstances) prohibit the use of social media (for any purpose) by employees when they are scheduled to be working. Employers can also prohibit harassment of colleagues.

Employers also need to be aware that the NLRB recently changed its rules on employee use of employer e-mail systems for the purpose of labor organizing. Its new rule states that use of e-mail for union-related communications must be permitted by employers in cases where employers allow employees general access to the employer's e-mail system. Although the board said a total ban was possible, it also stated that "it will be the rare case." As such, in general, the board stated that employees are permitted to use e-mail to engage in "statutorily protected discussions about the terms and conditions of their employment while on nonworking time." The board also stated that employees had the right to use the employer e-mail system for "an initial organizational campaign" when attempting to form a union. Although technically this activity is not to be done during working time, as a practical matter it may be difficult to tell whether an employee was on work time or break time when the e-mail was sent. Finally, it should be noted that an employer is typically permitted to monitor employee e-mail communications as long as it does not increase the intensity of such monitoring in response to union-related activity. Given the power of technology and how it can be used for union-organizing purposes, it is perhaps no surprise that some companies are cautious about encouraging employees to use certain types of electronic communication tools. See the "Competing through Technology" box for more on this point.

Corporate campaigns seek to bring public, financial, or political pressure on employers during the organizing (and negotiating) process.[45] For example, the Building and Construction Trades Department of the AFL-CIO successfully lobbied Congress to eliminate $100 million in tax breaks for a Toyota truck plant in Kentucky until Toyota agreed to use union construction workers and pay union wages.[46] The Amalgamated Clothing and Textile Workers Union (ACTWU) corporate campaign against J. P. Stevens during the late 1970s was one of the first and best known. The ACTWU organized a boycott of J. P. Stevens products and threatened to withdraw its pension funds from financial institutions where J. P. Stevens officers acted as directors. J. P. Stevens subsequently agreed to a contract with the ACTWU.[47]

> **Corporate campaigns**
> Union activities designed to exert public, financial, or political pressure on employers during the union-organizing process.

Unions also hope to use their financial assets to influence companies. Unions directly control billions in pension funds and share control with employers of billions more. All told, unions may have an influence over about $3 trillion in such investments.[48]

In some success stories, unions have eschewed elections in favor of strikes and negative publicity to pressure corporations to accept a union. Several years ago, the Hotel Employees and Restaurant Employees (HERE) union organized 9,000 workers, with 80% of these memberships resulting from pressure on employers rather than a vote. The Union of Needletrades, Industrial, and Textile Employees (UNITE) also succeeded with this approach. After losing an election by just two votes among employees of Up-to-Date Laundry, which cleans linens for Baltimore hotels and hospitals, UNITE decided to try other tactics, including a corporate campaign. It called a strike to demand that Up-to-Date recognize the union. It also persuaded several major customers of the laundry to threaten to stop using the laundry's services, shared claims of racial and sexual harassment with state agencies and the National Association for the Advancement of Colored People (NAACP), and convinced the Baltimore city council to require testimony from Up-to-Date. Eventually, the company gave in, recognized the union, and negotiated a contract that raised the workers' $6/hour wages and gave them better benefits. A final

Apps and Worker Organizing

The United Food and Commercial Workers (UFCW) union has tried for years without success to organize Walmart employees in hopes of negotiating higher pay and benefits and other standard contractual terms (e.g., a grievance procedure). Recently, a group called OUR Walmart separated from the UFCW union and is now seeking to be an advocate for Walmart employees. Part of its strategy involves using social media, and it recently developed a smartphone app called WorkIt, which it has asked employees to download. The app collects employee-related information including name, e-mail address, telephone number, and zip code. Of course, such information is essential in any organizing attempt. The app also provides a way for employees to communicate with one another, including comparing notes about working at Walmart. The app uses artificial intelligence, as well as "a peer network of experts," to answer employee questions about working at Walmart,

including those having to do with their legal rights.

What is Walmart's response? "Don't' download" it. The *Wall Street Journal* reports that Walmart has directed store managers to tell employees the app was not developed by Walmart and to describe it as an OUR Walmart "scheme" to get employees to hand over personal information to the union "by using deceptive and slick looking social media and apps."

In other companies, employees use apps like Shyft to swap work shifts with other employees. An employee at Buffalo Wild Wings says her supervisor asked her to download and use the app. By contrast, a Starbucks spokesman said the company is aware of such apps but that it "encourage[s] our partners to involve their managers" when adjusting their work schedules. Some employers are said to be "wary" of such apps because it makes it so much easier for employees to share information, not so different

perhaps from the WorkIt app developed by OUR Walmart.

Clearly, technology allows employees to communicate with each other and for union organizers to communicate with employees. Thus, employers will need to think through their own social media strategies for getting their message across to employees.

DISCUSSION QUESTIONS

1. From a union's perspective, what are some advantages of using social media for its communications?
2. From a company's perspective, what are the risks of encouraging employees' use of social media to communicate with one another?
3. Looking ahead, how will the role of apps at the workplace change, and what are the implications of those changes?

SOURCES: L. Weber, "Apps Empower Workers, Ease Scheduling," *Wall Street Journal,* January 3, 2017; S. Nassauer, "Wal-Mart Tells Workers: Don't Download Labor Group's Chat App," *Wall Street Journal,* November 15, 2016.

example would be the "Fight for 15," which involved holding rallies and demonstrations by nonunion workers at companies such as McDonald's and Walmart to pressure businesses to raise their minimum hourly wage to $15/hour (and to call for increases in state, local, and federal minimum wages to $15 as well). Although these and other companies did raise their minimum hourly wage, they did not raise it to $15 and it is difficult to know whether it was the "Fight for 15" campaign or a tightening labor market that was the cause (or perhaps both played a role). In any case, by one estimate, the SEIU has spent $19 million in supporting this effort.[49]

Another advantageous union-organizing strategy is to negotiate employer neutrality and card-check provisions into a contract. Under a *neutrality provision*, the employer pledges not to oppose organizing attempts elsewhere in the company. A *card-check provision* is an agreement that if a certain percentage—by law, at least a majority—of employees sign an authorization card, the employer will recognize their union representation. An impartial outside agency, such as the American Arbitration Association, counts the cards. The Communication Workers of America negotiated these provisions in its dispute with Verizon. Evidence suggests that this strategy can be very effective for unions.

However, unions must avoid running afoul of the Racketeer Influenced and Corrupt Organizations Act (RICO). For example, the SEIU waged a corporate campaign beginning in 2009 against Sodexo, a French-owned food service company operating in the United States. The SEIU's campaign, "Clean Up Sodexo," focused on bringing to the public's attention food safety and other concerns at Sodexo, something that could damage its business. Sodex sued the SEIU, claiming the campaign was an attempt to conspire to extort Sodexo with the threat of financial damage unless Sodexo agreed to a card-check provision for recognizing the union (rather than requiring that workers vote in a secret-ballot election). Sodexo alleged that the SEIU engaged in blackmail, vandalism, and other prohibited actions in an effort to prevent Sodexo from winning food contracts. In 2011, a legal settlement was reached before trial, under which the SEIU agreed to end its campaign against Sodexo.[50]

Union and Management Interactions: Contract Negotiation

The majority of contract negotiations take place between unions and employers that have been through the process before. In most cases, management has come to accept the union as an organization that it must work with. But when the union has just been certified and is negotiating its first contract, the situation can be very different. In fact, unions are unable to negotiate a first contract in 27–37% of the cases.[51] As noted previously, more than half of all unfair labor practice charges filed against employers pertain to the refusal to negotiate.

Labor–management contracts differ in their bargaining structures—that is, the range of employees and employers that are covered. As Table 14.10 indicates, the contracts differ, first, according to whether narrow (craft) or broad (industrial) employee interests are

Table 14.10
Types and Examples of Bargaining Structures

EMPLOYEE INTERESTS COVERED	EMPLOYEE INTERESTS COVERED		
EMPLOYEE INTERESTS COVERED	MULTIEMPLOYER (CENTRALIZED)	SINGLE-EMPLOYER— MULTIPLANT	SINGLE-EMPLOYER— SINGLE PLANT (DECENTRALIZED)
Craft (Narrow)	Construction trades Interstate trucking Longshoring Hospital association	Airline Teacher Police Firefighters Railroad	Craft union in small manufacturing plant Hospital
Industrial or Multiskill (Broad)	Coal mining (underground) Basic steel (pre-1986) Hotel association	Automobiles Steel (post-1986) Farm equipment State government Textile	Industrial union in small manufacturing plant

SOURCE: From H. C. Katz and T. A. Kochan, *An Introduction to Collective Bargaining and Industrial Relations* 4e, 2008. Reprinted with permission of The McGraw-Hill Companies, Inc.

covered. Second, they differ according to whether they cover multiple employers or multiple plants within a single employer. (A single employer may have multiple plants, some union and some nonunion.) Different structures have different implications for bargaining power and the number of interests that must be incorporated in reaching an agreement.

THE NEGOTIATION PROCESS

Distributive bargaining

The part of the labor–management negotiation process that focuses on dividing a fixed economic "pie."

Integrative bargaining

The part of the labor–management negotiation process that seeks solutions beneficial to both sides.

Attitudinal structuring

The aspect of the labor–management negotiation process that refers to the relationship and level of trust between the negotiators.

Intraorganizational bargaining

The part of the labor–management negotiation process that focuses on the conflicting objectives of factions within labor and management.

Richard Walton and Robert McKersie suggested that labor–management negotiations could be broken down into four subprocesses: distributive bargaining, integrative bargaining, attitudinal structuring, and intraorganizational bargaining.[52] **Distributive bargaining** focuses on dividing a fixed economic "pie" between the two sides. A wage increase, for example, means that the union gets a larger share of the pie, management a smaller share. It is a win–lose situation. **Integrative bargaining** has a win–win focus; it seeks solutions beneficial to both sides. So if management needs to reduce labor costs, it could reach an agreement with the union to avoid layoffs in return for the union agreeing to changes in work rules that might enhance productivity.

Attitudinal structuring refers to the relationship and trust between labor and management negotiators. Where the relationship is poor, it may be difficult for the two sides to engage in integrative bargaining because each side hesitates to trust the other side to carry out its part of the deal. For example, the union may be reluctant to agree to productivity-enhancing work-rule changes to enhance job security if, in the past, it has made similar concessions but believes that management did not stick to its assurance of greater job security. Thus the long-term relationship between the two parties can have a very important impact on negotiations and their outcomes.

Intraorganizational bargaining reminds us that labor–management negotiations involve more than just two parties. Within management, and to an even greater extent within the union, different factions can have conflicting objectives. High-seniority workers, who are least likely to be laid off, may be more willing to accept a contract that has layoffs (especially if it also offers a significant pay increase for those whose jobs are not at risk). Less senior workers would likely feel very differently. Thus negotiators and union leaders must simultaneously satisfy both the management side and their own internal constituencies. If they do not, they risk the union membership's rejecting the contract, or they risk being voted out of office in the next election. Management, too, is unlikely to be of one mind about how to approach negotiations. Some will focus more on long-term employee relations, others will focus on cost control, and still others will focus on what effect the contract will have on stockholders.

MANAGEMENT'S PREPARATION FOR NEGOTIATIONS

Clearly, the outcome of contract negotiations can have important consequences for labor costs and labor productivity and, therefore, for the company's ability to compete in the product market. Adapting Fossum's discussion, we can divide management preparation into the following seven areas, most of which have counterparts on the union side:[53]

1. *Establishing interdepartmental contract objectives:* The employer's industrial relations department needs to meet with the accounting, finance, production, marketing, and other departments and set contract goals that will permit each department to meet its responsibilities. As an example, finance may suggest a cost figure above which a contract settlement would seriously damage the company's financial health. The bargaining team needs to be constructed to take into account these various interests.

2. *Reviewing the old contract:* This step focuses on identifying provisions of the contract that might cause difficulties by hindering the company's productivity or flexibility or by leading to significant disagreements between management and the union.

3. *Preparing and analyzing data:* Information on labor costs and the productivity of competitors, as well as data the union may emphasize, needs to be prepared and analyzed. The union data might include cost-of-living changes and agreements reached by other unions that could serve as a target. Data on employee demographics and seniority are relevant for establishing the costs of such benefits as pensions, health insurance, and paid vacations. Finally, management needs to know how much it would be hurt by a strike. How long will its inventory allow it to keep meeting customer orders? To what extent are other companies positioned to step in and offer replacement products? How difficult would it be to find replacement workers if the company decided to continue operations during a strike?

4. *Anticipating union demands:* Recalling grievances over the previous contract, having ongoing discussions with union leaders, and becoming aware of settlements at other companies are ways of anticipating likely union demands and developing potential counterproposals.

5. *Establishing the cost of possible contract provisions:* Wages have not only a direct influence on labor costs but often an indirect effect on benefit costs (such as Social Security and paid vacation). Recall that benefits add about 46 cents to every dollar's worth of wages. Also, wage or benefit increases that seem manageable in the first year of a contract can accumulate to less manageable levels over time.

6. *Preparing for a strike:* If management intends to operate during a strike, it may need to line up replacement workers, increase its security, and figure out how to deal with incidents on the picket line and elsewhere. If management does not intend to operate during a strike (or if the company will not be operating at normal levels), it needs to alert suppliers and customers and consider possible ways to avoid the loss of their business. This could even entail purchasing a competitor's product in order to have something to sell to customers.

7. *Determining strategy and logistics:* Decisions must be made about the amount of authority the negotiating team will have. What concessions can it make on its own, and which ones require it to check with top management? On which issues can it compromise, and on which can it not? Decisions regarding meeting places and times must also be made.

NEGOTIATION STAGES AND TACTICS

Negotiations go through various stages.[54] In the early stages, many more people are often present than in later stages. On the union side, this may give all the various internal interest groups a chance to participate and voice their goals. This, in turn, helps send a message to management about what the union feels it must do to satisfy its members, and it may also help the union achieve greater solidarity. Union negotiators often present an extensive list of proposals at this stage, partly to satisfy their constituents and partly to provide themselves with issues on which they can show flexibility later in the process. Management may or may not present proposals of its own; sometimes it prefers to react to the union's proposals.

During the middle stages, each side must make a series of decisions, even though the outcome is uncertain. How important is each issue to the other side? How likely is it that disagreement on particular issues will result in a strike? When and to what extent should one side signal its willingness to compromise on its position?

In the final stage, pressure for an agreement increases as the deadline for a strike approaches. Public negotiations may be only part of the process. Negotiators from each side may have one-on-one meetings or small-group meetings where public relations pressures are reduced. In addition, a neutral third party may become involved, someone who can act as a go-between or facilitator. In some cases, the only way for the parties to convince each other of their resolve (or to convince their own constituents of the other party's resolve) is to allow an impasse to occur.

Various books suggest how to avoid impasses by using mutual gains or integrative bargaining tactics. For example, *Getting to Yes*, by Roger Fisher and William Ury, describes four basic principles:[55]

1. Separate the people from the problem.
2. Focus on interests, not positions.
3. Generate a variety of possibilities before deciding what to do.
4. Insist that the results be based on some objective standard.

BARGAINING POWER, IMPASSES, AND IMPASSE RESOLUTION

Employers' and unions' conflicting goals are resolved through the negotiation process just described. An important determinant of the outcome of this process is the relative bargaining power of each party, which can be defined as the "ability of one party to achieve its goals when faced with opposition from some other party to the bargaining process."[56] In collective bargaining, an important element of power is the relative ability of each party to withstand a strike. Although strikes in the United States are rare, the threat of a strike often looms large in labor–management negotiations. The relative ability to take a strike, whether one occurs or not, is an important determinant of bargaining power and, therefore, of bargaining outcomes.

MANAGEMENT'S WILLINGNESS TO TAKE A STRIKE

Management's willingness to take a strike comes down to two questions:

1. *Can the company remain profitable over the long run if it agrees to the union's demands?* The answer is more likely to be yes to the extent that higher labor costs can be passed on to consumers without losing business. This, in turn, is most likely when the price increase is small because labor costs are a small fraction of total costs or there is little price competition in the industry. Low price competition can result from regulated prices, from competition based on quality (rather than price), or from the union's organizing all or most of the employers in the industry, which eliminates labor costs as a price factor.

   Unions share part of management's concern with long-term competitiveness because a decline in competitiveness can translate into a decline in employment levels. However, the majority of union members may prefer to have higher wages, despite employment declines, particularly if a minority of the members (those with low seniority) suffer more employment loss and the majority keep their employment with higher wages.

2. *Can the company continue to operate in the short run despite a strike?* Although "hanging tough" on its bargaining goals may pay off for management in the long run, the short-run concern is the loss of revenues and profits from production being disrupted. The cost to strikers is a loss of wages and possibly a permanent loss of jobs.

Under what conditions is management most able to take a strike? The following factors are important:[57]

1. *Product demand:* Management is less able to afford a strike when the demand for its product is strong because that is when more revenue and profits are lost.

2. *Product perishability:* A strike by certain kinds of employees (farm workers at harvest time, truckers transporting perishable food, airline employees at peak travel periods) will result in permanent losses of revenue, thus increasing the cost of the strike to management.

3. *Technology:* An organization that is capital intensive (versus labor intensive) is less dependent on its employees and more likely to be able to use supervisors or others as replacements. Telephone companies are typically able to operate through strikes, even though installing new equipment or services and repair work may take significantly longer than usual.

4. *Availability of replacement workers:* When jobs are scarce, replacement workers are more available and perhaps more willing to cross picket lines. Using replacement workers to operate during a strike raises the stakes considerably for strikers who may be permanently replaced. Most strikers are not entitled to reinstatement until there are job openings for which they qualify. If replacements were hired, such openings may not occur for some time (if at all). In some cases, companies can use managers to temporarily replace striking workers. For example, decades ago, the third author of this text recalls his father, a manager at Ohio Bell in Cleveland, going to New York Bell in New York state to cover for jobs left open by striking workers. (Years before that, he was walking the picket line on strike before he got promoted.) More recently, Caterpillar prepared for a possible strike by "training managerial and support staff for production jobs" at one of its plants.[58]

5. *Multiple production sites and staggered contracts:* Multiple sites and staggered contracts permit employers to shift production from the struck facility to facilities that, even if unionized, have contracts that expire at different times (so they are not able to strike at the same time). For decades, Boeing's production of key aircraft was limited to its unionized Seattle location. It subsequently opened a second production facility in South Carolina, the state with the lowest union membership. Boeing has been successful in its goal of keeping the second production facility non-union and it can now use it as leverage in negotiations with its unionized workers in Seattle.[59]

6. *Integrated facilities:* When one facility produces something that other facilities need for their products, the employer is less able to take a strike because the disruption to production goes beyond that single facility. The just-in-time production system, which provides very little stockpiling of parts, further weakens management's ability to take a strike.

7. *Lack of substitutes for product:* A strike is more costly to the employer if customers have a readily available alternative source from which to purchase the goods or services the company provides.

©Andrew Resek/McGraw-Hill

Management has several factors to consider before taking a strike. Most negotiations do not result in a strike since it is often not in the best interests of either party.

Bargaining outcomes also depend on the nature of the bargaining process and relationship, which includes the types of tactics used and the history of labor relations. The vast majority of labor–management negotiations do not result in a strike because a strike is typically not in the best interests of either party. Furthermore, both the union and management usually realize that if they wish to interact effectively in the future, the experience of a strike can be difficult to overcome. When strikes do occur, the conduct of each party during the strike can also have a lasting effect on labor–management relations. Violence by either side or threats of job loss by hiring replacements can make future relations difficult.

IMPASSE RESOLUTION PROCEDURES: ALTERNATIVES TO STRIKES

Given the substantial costs of strikes to both parties, procedures that resolve conflicts without strikes have arisen in both the private and public sectors. Because many public-sector employees do not have the right to strike, alternatives are particularly important in that arena. In the private sector, alternatives may be used to avoid a strike or to help settle an ongoing dispute and end a strike.

Mediation

A procedure for resolving collective bargaining impasses by which a mediator with no formal authority acts as a facilitator and go-between in the negotiations.

Three often-used impasse resolution procedures are mediation, fact finding, and arbitration. All of them rely on the intervention of a neutral third party, most typically provided by the Federal Mediation and Conciliation Service (FMCS), which must be notified 60 days prior to contract expiration and 30 days prior to a planned change in contract terms (including a strike). Each year, the FMCS's annual report describes its activities in avoiding disputes and in settling ongoing disputes.[60] **Mediation** is the least formal but most widely used of the procedures (in both the public and private sectors). One survey found it was used by nearly 40% of all large private-sector bargaining units.[61] A mediator has no formal authority but, rather, acts as a facilitator and go-between in negotiations.

Fact finder

A person who reports on the reasons for a labor–management dispute, the views and arguments of both sides, and a nonbinding recommendation for settling the dispute.

A **fact finder**, most commonly used in the public sector, typically reports on the reasons for the dispute, the views and arguments of both sides, and (in some cases) a recommended settlement, which the parties are free to decline. That these recommendations are made public may give rise to public pressure for a settlement. Even if a fact finder's settlement is not accepted, the hope is that he or she will identify or frame issues in such a way as to facilitate an agreement. Sometimes, for the simple reason that fact finding takes time, the parties reach a settlement during the interim.

Arbitration

A procedure for resolving collective bargaining impasses by which an arbitrator chooses a solution to the dispute.

The most formal type of outside intervention is **arbitration,** under which a solution is actually chosen by an arbitrator (or arbitration board). In some instances the arbitrator can fashion a solution (conventional arbitration). In other cases the arbitrator must choose either the management's or union's final offer (final offer arbitration) on either the contract as a whole or on an issue-by-issue basis. Traditionally, arbitrating the enforcement or interpretation of contract terms (rights arbitration) has been widely accepted, whereas arbitrating the actual writing or setting of contract terms (interest arbitration, our focus here) has been reserved for special circumstances. These include some public-sector negotiations, where strikes may be especially costly (such as those by police or firefighters) and a very few private-sector situations, where strikes have been especially debilitating to both sides (the steel industry in the 1970s).[62] One reason for avoiding greater use of interest arbitration is a strong belief that the parties closest to the situation (unions and management, not an arbitrator) are in the best position to effectively resolve their conflicts.

Union and Management Interactions: Contract Administration

GRIEVANCE PROCEDURE

Although the negotiation process (and the occasional resulting strike) receive the most publicity, the negotiation process typically occurs only about every three years, whereas contract administration goes on day after day, year after year. The two processes—negotiation and administration—are linked, of course. Vague or incomplete contract language developed in the negotiation process can make administration of the contract difficult. Such difficulties can, in turn, create conflict that can spill over into the next negotiation process.[63] Furthermore, events during the negotiation process—strikes, the use of replacement workers, or violence by either side—can lead to management and labor difficulties in working successfully under a contract.

A key influence on successful contract administration is the grievance procedure for resolving labor–management disputes over the interpretation and execution of the contract. During World War II, the War Labor Board helped institutionalize the use of arbitration as an alternative to strikes to settle disputes that arose during the term of the contract. The soon-to-follow Taft-Hartley Act further reinforced this preference. Today the great majority of grievance procedures have binding arbitration as a final step, and only a minority of strikes occur during the term of a contract. (Most occur during the negotiation stage.) Strikes during the term of a contract can be especially disruptive because they are more unpredictable than strikes during the negotiation phase, which occur only at regular intervals.

Beyond its ability to reduce strikes, a grievance procedure can be judged using three criteria.[64] First, how well are day-to-day contract questions resolved? Time delays and heavy use of the procedure may indicate problems. Second, how well does the grievance procedure adapt to changing circumstances? For example, if the company's business turns downward and the company needs to cut costs, how clear are the provisions relating to subcontracting of work, layoffs, and so forth? Third, in multiunit contracts, how well does the grievance procedure permit local contract issues (like work rules) to be included and resolved?[65]

From the employees' perspective, the grievance procedure is the key to fair treatment in the workplace, and its effectiveness rests both on the degree to which employees feel they can use it without fear of recrimination and whether they believe their case will be carried forward strongly enough by their union representative. The **duty of fair representation** is mandated by the NLRA and requires that all bargaining unit members, whether union members or not, have equal access to and representation by the union in the grievance procedure. Too many grievances may indicate a problem, but so may too few. A very low grievance rate may suggest a fear of filing a grievance, a belief that the system is not effective, or a belief that representation is not adequate.

As Table 14.11 suggests, most grievance procedures have several steps prior to arbitration. Moreover, the majority of grievances are settled during the earlier steps of the process, which is desirable both to reduce time delays and to avoid the costs of arbitration. If the grievance does reach arbitration, the arbitrator makes the final ruling in the matter. A series of Supreme Court decisions in 1960, commonly known as the Steelworkers' Trilogy, established that the courts should essentially refrain from reviewing the merits of arbitrators' decisions and, instead, limit judicial review to the question of whether the issue was subject to arbitration under the contract.[66] Furthermore, unless

Duty of fair representation
The National Labor Relations Act requirement that all bargaining unit members have equal access to and representation by the union.

Table 14.11

Steps in a Typical Grievance Procedure

Employee-initiated grievance

Step 1

a. Employee discusses grievance or problem orally with supervisor.
b. Union steward and employee may discuss problem orally with supervisor.
c. Union steward and employee decide (1) whether problem has been resolved or (2) if not resolved, whether a contract violation has occurred.

Step 2

a. Grievance is put in writing and submitted to production superintendent or other designated line manager.
b. Steward and management representative meet and discuss grievance. Management's response is put in writing. A member of the industrial relations staff may be consulted at this stage.

Step 3

a. Grievance is appealed to top line management and industrial relations staff representatives. Additional local or international union officers may become involved in discussions. Decision is put in writing.

Step 4

a. Union decides on whether to appeal unresolved grievance to arbitration according to procedures specified in its constitution and/or bylaws.
b. Grievance is appealed to arbitration for binding decision.

Discharge grievance

a. Procedure may begin at step 2 or step 3.
b. Time limits between steps may be shorter to expedite the process.

Union or group grievance

a. Union representative initiates grievance at step 1 or step 2 on behalf of affected class of workers or union representatives.

SOURCE: From H. C. Katz, T. A. Kochan, and A. J. S. Colvin, *An Introduction to Collective Bargaining and Industrial Relations*, 4e, 2008. Reprinted with permission of The McGraw-Hill Companies, Inc.

the contract explicitly states that an issue is not subject to arbitration, it will be assumed that arbitration is an appropriate means of deciding the issue. Giving further strength to the role of arbitration is the NLRB's general policy of deferring to arbitration.

What types of issues most commonly reach arbitration? Data from the FMCS on a total of 2,473 grievances show that discharge and disciplinary issues topped the list with 913 cases.[67] Other frequent issues include the use of seniority in promotion, layoffs, transfers, work assignments, and scheduling (309 cases); wages (178); and benefits (127).

What criteria do arbitrators use to reach a decision? In the most common case—discharge or discipline—the following due process questions are important:[68]

1. *Did the employee know what the rule or expectation was and what the consequences of not adhering to it were?*
2. *Was the rule applied in a consistent and predictable way?* In other words, are all employees treated the same?
3. *Are facts collected in a fair and systematic manner?* An important element of this principle is detailed record keeping. Both employee actions (such as tardiness) and management's response (verbal or written warnings) should be carefully documented.
4. *Does the employee have the right to question the facts and present a defense?* An example in a union setting is a hearing with a shop steward present.

5. *Does the employee have the right to appeal a decision?* An example is recourse to an impartial third party, such as an arbitrator.
6. *Is there progressive discipline?* Except perhaps for severe cases, an arbitrator will typically look for evidence that an employee was alerted as early as possible that behavior was inappropriate and the employee was given a chance to change prior to some form of severe discipline, such as discharge.
7. *Are there unique mitigating circumstances?* Although discipline must be consistent, individuals differ in terms of their prior service, performance, and discipline record. All of these factors may need to be considered.

COOPERATIVE LABOR–MANAGEMENT STRATEGIES

Jack Barbash described the nature of the traditional relationship between labor and management (during both the negotiation and administration phases) as follows:

> Bargaining is a love–hate, cooperation–conflict relationship. The parties have a common interest in maximizing the total revenue which finances their respective returns. But they take on adversarial postures in debating how the revenue shall be divided as between wages and profits. It is the adversarial posture which has historically set the tone of the relationship.[69]

LO 14-5
Describe new, less adversarial approaches to labor–management relations.

Although there had always been exceptions to the adversarial approach, one reading is that there has been a general trend toward less adversarial workplace relations (at least where the union's role is accepted by management).[70] This transformation has two basic objectives: (1) to increase the involvement of individuals and work groups in overcoming adversarial relations and increasing employee commitment, motivation, and problem solving and (2) to reorganize work so that work rules are minimized and flexibility in managing people is maximized. These objectives are especially important for companies that need to be able to shift production quickly in response to changes in markets and customer demands. The specific programs aimed at achieving these objectives include employee involvement in decision making, self-managing employee teams, labor–management problem-solving teams, broadly defined jobs, and sharing of financial gains and business information with employees. Examples include the labor–management relationships at Ford, Harley-Davidson, and Chrysler's engine plant in Dundee, Michigan.[71]

The Dundee engine plant is not only an example of a new approach to labor relations. It also has the blessing of the UAW. Why? According to the president of the UAW local, "It's a question of survival." Hourly workers at the plant are highly educated and skilled and rotate through different jobs to provide skill flexibility to support production flexibility, engage workers, and reduce repetitive motion injuries. Unlike a traditional plant where there can be scores of hourly job classifications/titles, the Dundee plant has only two: team member and team leader. There are no supervisors. Team leaders, rather than only observing, work alongside teams of six team members. The guiding principles are captured by what are called the "four As": "anyone can do anything anytime, anywhere." That is much different from the more typical idea of "if it's not in my job description, I don't have to do it, I won't do it, and if I did do it, I would probably get in trouble." The UAW was concerned at first with the "four As" approach because without narrow job descriptions, management has more discretion, and workers less discretion, in what workers do each day. As the UAW put it, it could allow management to "pull out anybody, anytime." However, the need for flexibility in production is so central to the success of the plant in a global competitive environment and to Chrysler being willing to make future investments (the key to jobs) in the plant that the UAW leadership agreed. The team approach, job rotation, and flexibility expectations translate into higher skill and education requirements. Hourly workers at the plant must have a two-year technical degree, hold a skilled journeyman's card, or have had several years of experience in advanced manufacturing.[72]

Union resistance to such programs has often been substantial, precisely because the programs seek to change workplace relations and the role that unions play. Without the union's support, these programs are less likely to survive and less likely to be effective if they do survive.[73] Union leaders have often feared that such programs will weaken unions' role as an independent representative of employee interests. Indeed, according to the NLRA, to "dominate or interfere with the formation or administration of any labor organization or contribute financial or other support to it" is an unfair labor practice. An example of a prohibited practice is "taking an active part in organizing a union or committee to represent employees."[74]

One case that has received much attention is that of Electromation, a small electrical parts manufacturer. In 1992 the NLRB ruled that the company had violated Section 8(a)(2) of the NLRA by setting up worker–management committees (typically about six workers and one or two managers) to solve problems having to do with absenteeism and pay scales.[75] The original complaint was filed by the Teamsters union, which was trying to organize the (nonunion) company and felt that the committees were, in effect, illegally competing with them to be workers' representatives. Similarly, Polaroid dissolved an employee committee that had been in existence for over 40 years in response to the U.S. Department of Labor's claim that it violated the NLRA. The primary functions of the employee committee had been to represent employees in grievances and to advise senior management on issues such as pay and company rules and regulations. In a third case, the NLRB ruled in 1993 that seven worker–management safety committees at DuPont were illegal under the NLRA because they were dominated by management. The committee members were chosen by management and their decisions were subject to the approval of the management members of the committees. Finally, the committees made decisions about issues that were mandatory subjects of bargaining with the employees' elected representative—the chemical workers' union.[76] The impact of such cases will be felt both in nonunion companies, as union organizers move to fill the worker representation vacuum, and in unionized companies, as managers find they must deal more directly and effectively with their unions.

Employers must take care that employee involvement meets the legal test, but the NLRB has clearly supported the legality of involvement in important cases. For example, in a 2001 ruling, the NLRB found that the use of seven employee participation committees at a Crown Cork & Seal aluminum can manufacturing plant did not violate federal labor law. The committees in question make and implement decisions regarding a wide range of issues, including production, quality, training, safety, and certain types of worker discipline. The NLRB determined that these committees were not employer-dominated labor organizations, which would have violated federal labor law. Instead of "dealing with" management in a bilateral manner where proposals are made that are either rejected or accepted by management, the teams and committees exercise authority, delegated by management, to operate the plant within certain parameters. Indeed, the NLRB noted that rather than "dealing with management," the evidence indicated that within delegated areas of authority, the teams and committees "are management." This authority was found to be similar to that delegated to a first-line supervisor. Thus the charge that the teams and committees did not have final decision-making authority (and so were not acting in a management capacity) did not weigh heavily with the NLRB, which noted, "Few, if any, supervisors in a conventional plant have authority that is final and absolute." Instead, it was noted that managers typically make recommendations that move up through "the chain of command."[77] Table 14.12 summarizes factors that may indicate a team or committee is in violation of national labor law.

Although there are legal concerns to address, some evidence suggests that these new approaches to labor relations—incorporating greater employee participation in decisions,

Table 14.12
When Teams May Be Illegal

Primary factors to look for that could mean a team violates national labor law:	
Representation	Does the team address issues affecting nonteam employees? (Does it represent other workers?)
Subject matter	Do these issues involve matters such as wages, grievances, hours of work, and working conditions?
Management involvement	Does the team deal with any supervisors, managers, or executives on any issue?
Employer domination	Did the company create the team or decide what it would do and how it would function?

SOURCE: From *BusinessWeek*, January 25, 1993.

using employee teams, multiskilling, rotating jobs, and sharing financial gains—can contribute significantly to an organization's effectiveness,[78] as well as to workers' wages and job satisfaction.[79] Indeed, these practices are now often referred to as *high-performance work systems.* One study, for example, compared the features of traditional and transformational approaches to labor relations at Xerox.[80] As Table 14.13 indicates, the transformational approach was characterized by better conflict resolution, more shop-floor cooperation, and greater worker autonomy and feedback in decision making. Furthermore, compared with the traditional approach, transformational labor relations were found to be associated with lower costs, better product quality, and higher productivity. Several years ago, a presidential commission concluded that the evidence is "overwhelming that employee participation and labor–management partnerships are good for workers, firms, and the national economy." National survey data also indicate that most employees want more influence in workplace decisions and believe that such influence leads to more

Table 14.13
Patterns in Labor–Management Relations Using Traditional and Transformational Approaches

	PATTERN	
DIMENSION	**TRADITIONAL**	**TRANSFORMATIONAL**
Conflict resolution		
Frequency of conflicts	High	Low
Speed of conflict resolution	Slow	Fast
Informal resolution of grievances	Low	High
Third- and fourth-step grievances	High	Low
Shop-floor cooperation		
Formal problem-solving groups (such as quality, reducing scrap, employment security)	Low	High
Informal problem-solving activity	Low	High
Worker autonomy and feedback		
Formal autonomous work groups	Low	High
Informal worker autonomous activity	Low	High
Worker-initiated changes in work design	Low	High
Feedback on cost, quality, and schedule	Low	High

SOURCE: Adapted from J. Cutcher-Gershenfeld, "The Impact on Economic Performance of a Transformation in Work-place Relations," *Industrial and Labor Relations Review* 44 (1991), pp. 241–60. Reprinted with permission.

effective organizations.[81] Further evidence (see the "Evidence-Based HR" box) suggests that these high-performance work systems work well across countries.

EVIDENCE-BASED HR

A recent study provided a review of the effect of high-performance work systems (HPWSs) on business performance at the level of the plant and the firm. HPWSs are human resource practices (e.g., selective hiring, strong training/development, worker involvement in decision, pay for performance) that aim to increase worker contributions to business performance. Conventional wisdom is that these practices are best suited to the United States or perhaps a few other countries (e.g., the United Kingdom) whose organizations are seen as having an "Anglo-Saxon" approach to management and are not likely to work as well in other countries due to the greater strength of unions, different legal frameworks, and/or cultural differences. However, many global companies standardize their employment policies despite these differences and feel that they can be successful. That is not to say that policies are executed in the exact same manner in all countries, but the broad policies are consistent. For example, a company may involve workers in decisions, but in Germany it may be mandated in certain sectors of the economy, whereas in the United States it is not but instead is done according to the employer's choice.

So, what does the evidence from the study say? The following table reports the mean correlation, mean r, between use of HPWSs and business performance, as well as the number of studies conducted in each country, K, and the number of firms/establishments included, N, in those K studies in each country. The 95% confidence interval is also reported. Results for the four countries with the largest K outside of the United States are reported separately.

COUNTRY OR REGION	K	N	MEAN r	95% CONFIDENCE INTERVAL FOR MEAN r
United States	48	11,309	.23	.20 to .26
Non-United States	108	24,458	.22	.18 to .26
China	16	3,692	.35	.26 to .43
Korea	8	1,899	.26	.17 to .36
Spain	13	3,430	.20	.14 to .26
United Kingdom	13	2,758	.16	.06 to .26

These countries differ significantly in terms of national culture (see Chapter 15) and in terms of union strength. (For example, in Spain, 70% of employees are covered by collective bargaining agreements versus 13% in the United States.) In looking at this pattern of results, ask yourself the following questions: (1) Is the mean r different in the United States versus outside the United States? (2) Is the mean r negative in any country? (3) Does the confidence interval include .00 for any country? Keeping in mind the caveat that policies can (and sometimes must) be implemented differently in different countries, what do these results say about the claim that policies must be tailored to the country?

SOURCE: T. Rabl, M. Jayasinghe, B. Gerhart, and T. M. Kühlmann, "A Meta-Analysis of Country Differences in the High-Performance Work System–Business Performance Relationship: The Roles of National Culture and Managerial Discretion," *Journal of Applied Psychology* 99, no. 6 (2014), pp. 1011–41.

Labor Relations Outcomes

The effectiveness of labor relations can be evaluated from management, labor, and societal perspectives.[82] Management seeks to control costs and enhance productivity and quality. Labor unions seek to raise wages and benefits and exercise control over how employees spend their time at work (such as through work rules). Each of the three parties typically seeks to avoid forms of conflict (like strikes) that impose significant costs on everyone. In this section we examine several outcomes.

STRIKES

Table 14.14 presents data on strikes in the United States that involved 1,000 or more employees. Of the 15 large strikes in 2016, four were in health care (nurses) and three were in education (teachers in two cases, university faculty in the other), and two were among county government employees. The remaining work stoppages were among longshoremen, cleaners, communication workers (at Verizon and AT&T), painting and decorating employees, and transport workers. So most of the strikes involved white-collar employees. None were in manufacturing. Because strikes are more likely in large units, the lack of data on smaller units is probably not a major concern, although such data would, of course, raise the figure on the estimated time lost to strikes. For example, for the 1960s, this estimate is 0.12% using data on strikes involving 1,000 or more employees versus 0.17% for all strikes. Although strikes impose significant costs on union members, employers, and society, it is clear from Table 14.14 that strikes are the exception rather than the rule. Very little working time is lost to strikes in the United States (with annual work hours of 1,800, less than 6 minutes per worker and less than one hour per unionized worker in 2016) and their frequency in recent years is generally low by historical standards. Does this mean that the industrial relations system is working well? Not necessarily. Those who believe labor should be

YEAR	STOPPAGES	NUMBER OF WORKERS (THOUSANDS)	PERCENTAGE OF TOTAL WORKING TIME LOST
1950	424	1,698	0.26%
1955	363	2,055	0.16
1960	222	896	0.09
1965	268	999	0.10
1970	381	2,468	0.29
1975	235	965	0.09
1980	187	795	0.09
1985	54	324	0.03
1990	44	185	0.02
1995	31	192	0.02
2000	39	394	0.06
2005	22	100	0.01
2010	11	45	<0.005
2015	12	47	<0.005
2016	15	99	<0.005

Table 14.14
Work Stoppages Involving 1,000 or More Workers

SOURCE: U.S. Bureau of Labor Statistics, *Major Work Stoppages in 2016,* Economic News Release, USDL-17-0180, February 9, 2017, https://www.bls.gov/news.release/pdf/wkstp.pdf.

strong to represent its members would view the low number (by historical standards) of strikes as another sign that labor is too weak to do so.

WAGES AND BENEFITS

Table 14.15 compares wages and benefits of union members to nonunion members using both a survey of working individuals (CPS) and a survey of employers/establishments (NCS). Private-sector unionized workers received, on average, wages 19–24% higher than their nonunion counterparts, depending on the survey.[83] Based on the employer survey data, the effect of unions on total compensation is even higher because of an even larger effect of unions on benefits.[84] However, these are raw differences. To assess the net effect of unions on wages more accurately, adjustments must be made.[85] We now briefly highlight a few of these.

The union wage effect is likely to be overestimated to the extent that unions can more easily organize workers who are already highly paid or who are more productive. The gap is

Table 14.15

Compensation, Union versus Nonunion Employees, United States, Worker Survey and Employer Survey

	MEDIAN WEEKLY EARNINGS BY UNION REPRESENTATION AND % IN UNION, FULL-TIME WORKERS[a] (WORKER SURVEY)		
		MEDIAN WEEKLY EARNINGS	
	% IN UNION	**UNION REPRESENTED**	**NONUNION**	**UNION/ NONUNION**
All	10.7[b]	$ 995	$ 802	1.24
Men	11.2	1,042	890	1.17
Women	10.2	942	723	1.30
Management and professional	11.6	1,159	1,197	0.97
Service	9.6	753	505	1.49
Sales and office	6.6	804	686	1.17
Production, transportation, and material moving	13.7	876	631	1.39
Private sector	6.4	932	789	1.18
Public sector	34.4	1,055	900	1.17
	HOURLY WAGES/SALARIES, BENEFITS, AND TOTAL COMPENSATION (EMPLOYER SURVEY)		
		UNION MEMBERS	**NONUNION**	**UNION/ NONUNION**
Total compensation		$47.82	$31.31	1.53
Wages and salaries		$26.61	$22.27	1.19
Benefits		$19.21	$ 9.04	2.13

[a]Part-time workers (5.7%) are less likely than full-time workers (11.8%) to be union members.

[b]The percentage of all employees represented by unions is 12.0%.

SOURCES: Median weekly earnings and percentages in union data based on the Current Population Surveys: U.S. Bureau of Labor Statistics, *Union Members—2016*, News Release, USDL-17-0107, January 26, 2017; wages/salaries, benefits, and total compensation data, based on a survey of employers, are from U.S. Bureau of Labor Statistics, National Compensation Survey (NCS), *Employer Costs for Employee Compensation—December 2016*, News Release USDL-17-0321, March 17, 2017; the worker survey includes civilian (private-sector and public-sector) employees. The employer survey includes private-sector employees only.

likely to be underestimated to the extent that nonunion employers raise wages and benefits in response to the perceived "union threat" in the hope that their employees will then have less interest in union representation. When these and other factors are taken into account, the net union advantage in wages, though still substantial, is reduced by as much as one-half. The union benefits advantage is also reduced, but it remains larger than the union wage effect, and the union effect on total compensation is therefore larger than the wage effect alone.[86]

Beyond differences in pay and benefits, unions typically influence the way pay and promotions are determined. Whereas management often seeks to deal with employees as individuals, emphasizing performance differences in pay and promotion decisions, unions seek to build group solidarity and avoid the possibly arbitrary treatment of employees. To do so, unions focus on equal pay for equal work. Any differences among employees in pay or promotions, they say, should be based on seniority (an objective measure) rather than on performance (a subjective measure susceptible to favoritism). It is very common in union settings for there to be a single rate of pay for all employees in a particular job classification.

Although wages and benefits are higher for union members, job satisfaction is lower, on average.[87] Reasons include less positive perceptions of supervision, promotion opportunities, and the interest and discretion in their work. Given that dissatisfaction is an important driver of union activity, it may be that unionization is part consequence (workers in worse jobs are more likely to organize), as well as part cause of job dissatisfaction.

PRODUCTIVITY

There has been much debate regarding the effects of unions on productivity.[88] Unions are believed to decrease productivity in at least three ways: (1) The union pay advantage causes employers to use less labor and more capital per worker than they would otherwise, which reduces efficiency across society; (2) union contract provisions may limit permissible workloads, restrict the tasks that particular workers are allowed to perform, and require employers to use more employees for certain jobs than they otherwise would; and (3) strikes, slowdowns, and working-to-rule (slowing down production by following every workplace rule to an extreme) result in lost production.[89]

On the other hand, unions can have positive effects on productivity.[90] Employees, whether members of a union or not, communicate to management regarding how good a job it is doing by either the "exit" or "voice" mechanisms. "Exit" refers to simply leaving the company to work for a better employer. "Voice" refers to communicating one's concerns to management without necessarily leaving the employer. Unions are believed to increase the operation and effectiveness of the voice mechanism.[91] This, in turn, is likely to reduce employee turnover and its associated costs. More broadly, voice can be seen as including the union's contribution to the success of labor–management cooperation programs that make use of employee suggestions and increased involvement in decisions. A second way that unions can increase productivity is (perhaps ironically) through their emphasis on the use of seniority in pay, promotion, and layoff decisions. Although management typically prefers to rely more heavily on performance in such decisions, using seniority has a potentially important advantage— namely, it reduces competition among workers. As a result, workers may be less reluctant to share their knowledge with less senior workers because they do not have to worry about less senior workers taking their jobs. Finally, the introduction of a union may have a "shock effect" on management, pressuring it into tightening standards and accountability and paying greater heed to employee input in the design and management of production.[92]

Although there is evidence that unions have both positive and negative effects on productivity, most studies have found that union workers are more productive than nonunion workers. Nevertheless, it is generally recognized that most of the findings on this issue are open to a number of alternative explanations, making any clear conclusions difficult. For example, if unions raise productivity, why has union representation of employees declined over time, even within industries?[93] A related concern is that unionized establishments are more likely to survive where there is some inherent productivity advantage unrelated to unionism that actually offsets a negative impact of unionism. If so, these establishments would be overrepresented, whereas establishments that did not survive the negative impact of unions would be underrepresented. Consequently, any negative impact of unions on productivity would be underestimated.

PROFITS AND STOCK PERFORMANCE

Even if unions do raise productivity, a company's profits and stock performance may still suffer if unions raise costs (such as wages) or decrease investment by a greater amount. Evidence shows that unions have a large negative effect on profits and that union coverage tends to decline more quickly in firms experiencing lower shareholder returns, suggesting that some firms become more competitive partly by reducing union strength.[94] Similarly, one study found that each dollar of unexpected increase in collectively bargained labor costs resulted in a dollar reduction in shareholder wealth. Another study estimated that if policies were changed to encourage the unionization rate in the United States to double, the value of shareholder equity in newly organized firms would be decreased by 4.3%.[95] Other research suggests that investment in research and development is lower in unionized firms.[96] Strikes, although infrequent, lower shareholder returns in both the struck companies and firms (like suppliers) linked to those companies.[97] These research findings describe the average effects of unions. The consequences of more innovative union–management relationships for profits and stock performance are less clear.

The International Context

LO 14-6
Explain how changes in competitive challenges (e.g., product market competition and globalization) are influencing labor–management interactions.

Except for China, Russia, and Ukraine, the United States has more union members than any other country. (If one were to include only countries where workers can freely elect union leaders of their own choosing, then the United States would arguably rank first in union membership.) Yet, as Table 14.16 indicates, aside from France and Korea, the United States has the lowest unionization rate (union density) of any country in the table. Even more striking are differences in union coverage, the percentage of employees whose terms and conditions of employment are governed by a union contract. (See Table 14.16.) In the European Union, the union coverage rate is 62%, and as high as 98% in France, meaning that the influence of labor unions far outstrips what would be implied by their membership levels.[98] Why are the unionization rate and coverage comparatively low in the United States? One explanation is that the United States does not have as strong a history of deep class-based divisions in society as other countries do. For example, labor and social democratic political parties are commonplace in western Europe, and they are major players in the political process. Furthermore, the labor movement in western and northern Europe is broader than that in the United States. It extends not just to the workplace but—through its own or closely related political parties—directly into the national political process.

What is the trend in union membership rates and coverage? In the United States, we saw earlier that the trend is clearly downward, at least in the private sector. Although there have also been declines in membership rates in many other countries, coverage rates have stayed high in many of these countries. In the United States, deregulation and competition from foreign-owned companies have forced companies to become more efficient. Combined with the fact that the union wage premium in the United States is substantially larger than in other advanced industrialized countries, it is not surprising that management opposition

COUNTRY	MEMBERSHIP PERCENTAGE OF EMPLOYMENT (DENSITY)	COVERAGE PERCENTAGE OF EMPLOYMENT
United States	11	13
Canada	26	29
Japan	18	17
Korea	10	12
Australia	16	6
European Union	28	62
Germany	18	58
Netherlands	18	85
France	8	98
United Kingdom	25	30
Czech Republic	13	47

Table 14.16
Union Membership and Union Coverage, Selected Countries

SOURCES: OECD Library, *Economic Policy Reforms 2016, Going for Growth Interim Report,* February 26, 2016. Coverage rates of collective bargaining agreements and trade union density rates. [Choose "XLS" link.], http://www.oecd-ilibrary.org/economics/economic-policy-reforms-2016_growth-2016-en;jsessionid=3snafpifhok2.x-oecd-live-02. Original data from OECD estimates and J. Visser, ICTWSS Database, version 5.0. Amsterdam: Amsterdam Institute for Advanced Labour Studies AIAS, October 2015, accessed April 29, 2017.

would be higher in the United States than elsewhere.[99] This, in turn, may help explain why the decline in union influence has been especially steep in the United States.

It seems likely that—with the growing globalization of markets—labor costs and productivity will continue to be key challenges. The European Union (EU) added 10 new member countries in 2004, 2 more in 2007, and 1 more in 2013, bringing its total to 28 countries and more than 500 million people, or about 63% larger than the United States. The newer EU countries (e.g., Bulgaria, Croatia, the Czech Republic, Poland, Romania, Slovakia) have much lower wages than the existing EU countries. Closer to home, we have the North American Free Trade Agreement among the United States, Canada, and Mexico. These common market agreements mean that goods, services, and production will continue to move more freely across international borders. Where substantial differences in wages, benefits, and other costs of doing business (such as regulation) exist, there will be a tendency to move to areas that are less costly, unless skills are unavailable or productivity is significantly lower there. Unless labor unions can increase their productivity sufficiently or organize new production facilities, union influence is likely to decline.

In addition to membership and coverage, the United States differs from western Europe in the degree of formal worker participation in decision making. Works' councils (joint labor–management decision-making institutions at the enterprise level) and worker representation on supervisory boards of directors (codetermination) are mandated by law in countries such as Germany. The Scandinavian countries, Austria, and Luxembourg have similar legislation. German works' councils make decisions about changes in work or the work environment, discipline, pay systems, safety, and other human resource issues. The degree of codetermination on supervisory boards depends on the size and industry of the company. For example, in German organizations having more than 2,000 employees, half of the board members must be worker representatives. (However, the chairman of the board, a management representative, can cast a tie-breaking vote.) In contrast, worker representation on boards of directors in the United States is still rare.[100]

The works' councils exist in part because collective bargaining agreements in countries such as Germany tend to be oriented toward industrywide or regional issues, with less emphasis on local issues. However, competitive forces have led employers to increasingly opt out of centralized bargaining, even in the countries best known for centralized bargaining, like Sweden and Germany.[101]

What happens when a company from a country with low union strength operates in a country with high union strength? In the case of Amazon, an American company operating in Germany, the answer for now is that it is following its American strategy toward unions in Germany. Amazon has a works council (required by German law), and it deals with worker representatives "directly" (i.e., without the presence of a union). Verdi, a major German labor union, has been trying to change that, saying that Amazon has "a culture that we see as foreign." Amazon similarly says that, "Verdi and Amazon do not go together." Amazon and its "U.S. way of doing business" are sometimes referred to as using a "Wild West" approach to management. (This is not meant as a compliment but rather indicates the belief that there is a lack of concern for worker welfare.) Verdi has called on workers to strike. So far, those actions do not appear to have interrupted Amazon's deliveries to customers in Germany, and Amazon continues to hold to its no-union policy in Germany (as in the United States).[102]

Another interesting example is Volkswagen, a German company operating an automobile production plant in Chattanooga, Tennessee, in the United States. It has a strong, formal relationship with unions in Germany but has no union in the United States. Volkswagen has not actively opposed unionization at its U.S. plant (in contrast to the opposition unions would face from many U.S. companies). The UAW did not receive the necessary 50% + 1 votes in a recent representation election to become the sole representative of workers at VW's Chattanooga plant. Subsequently, Volkswagen, it is said under pressure from its unions in Germany, announced a new labor policy for its Chattanooga plant. Any labor group that receives (based on an independent outside audit) support from at least 15% of workers can have on-site space to post announcements and hold regular meetings with the plant's human resource department. Any group that receives support from at least 45% of workers would additionally be able to meet every two weeks with plant managers. Note that, unlike in Germany, Volkswagen is thought to be unable to use a works council at the Chattanooga plant because under U.S. labor law, it might be deemed an employer-dominated labor organization. (See our earlier discussion of the Electromation case and the closely related Table 14.12.)[103] A more recent development is that the UAW, after losing the plantwide election, did win an organizing vote (108 for, 44 against) to represent a group of skilled tradesmen at Volkswagen's Chattanooga plant. Although the group is a very small portion of the plant's 1,450 manufacturing employees (and 2,500 employees overall), this is the first time any organizing drive at a foreign-owned plant in the U.S. South has been successful. An important caveat, however, is that the UAW has not yet been able to negotiate a first contract with Volkswagen, which, as we have seen, is a step where unions often fail, even after winning an organizing vote.[104]

China is now the world's second largest economy and one of its fastest growing. Workers increasingly want to share in economic growth through higher wages and more purchasing power. That means collective action can be expected to increase. Indeed, recent research finds that the level of strike activity and labor unrest has increased dramatically in China. Moreover, strikes, which were once predominantly defensive or reactive (to protect what workers already had), have become increasingly offensive or proactive (with the aim of achieving new gains for workers, such as higher wages). In some sense, China, on its economic development path, may be now going through what the U.S. economy and labor relations went through many decades ago.[105] Interestingly, as the "Competing through Globalization" box demonstrates, some Chinese companies are gaining experience with the challenges of labor relations in the United States.

Companies from China Meet Labor Unions in the United States

Chinese companies' direct investments in the United States, including acquisitions and new facilities, last year totaled a record $15.7 billion. That is up from just over $4 billion as recently as 2011 and less than $1 billion per year in the 2006–2009 time period. An example of an acquisition is China-based Haier's purchase of GE's appliance business for $5.6 billion. That includes five manufacturing plants in Appliance Park in Louisville, Kentucky, where the IUE-CWA union represents about 4,000 employees.

Haier is looking overseas for growth opportunities. Profit margins on appliances like refrigerators and washing machines in its domestic market of China are "razor-thin" as a result of stiff competition. There is also a slowdown in people buying new homes in China, which depresses demand for appliances. Another important reason for building its presence in the United States is that the company avoids import tariffs, which drive up costs and make it more difficult to price appliances competitively. Like many companies, as we have seen, Haier also wants to be geographically closer to its customers so as to better understand their particular appliance preferences and to be able to react to changes more quickly than can competitors overseas. Haier will also be able to use the GE brand for its appliances for 40 years, which will be important in competing for customers who respect the GE brand and are unsure about a Chinese company such as Haier. The U.S. appliance market is also competitive and, at present, the Appliance Park plants are estimated to be losing "hundreds of millions" of dollars per year. Therefore, Haier is looking to reduce costs, including labor costs, and improve efficiency.

Haier's first contract offer to the union was voted down by employees. One reason was an attempt by Haier to improve efficiency by limiting bumping rights, which allow a more senior worker whose job is being eliminated to bump (replace) a less senior worker in another job. That begins a cascade of bumps, which causes disruption and inefficiency. A second contract offer was approved, which limited bumping rights but not as greatly. The approved contract will also start new full-time employees at $14/hour, down from the previous starting rate of $15.50/hour. The contract also creates a new category of "flexible" part-time workers who will start at $12/hour. Haier says it still has work to do on reducing costs and plans to "get our wage structure right over the course of time" as more senior workers, some of whom earn $25– $40/hour, leave and are replaced by lower-paid, less senior workers.

One reason given for why labor costs "grew out of proportion to competitors" is that GE's appliance business was "hidden" as part of GE's conglomerate structure. Other GE business units that were doing better reached contract agreements that covered IUE-CWA workers, but those same terms were negotiated or extended to GE Appliance employees represented by IUE-CWA, despite differences in profitability of the business units. In any case, it is now up to Haier to turn things around at Appliance Park.

An example of a new facility built in the United States by a Chinese company is the new Golden Dragon Precise Copper Tube Group. The $120 million plant created 290 jobs for locals in Wilcox County, Alabama, one of the poorest counties in the country. Golden Dragon makes copper pipes used in air conditioning machinery. State and local governments gave Golden Dragon a variety of incentives such as free land, infrastructure, money to train workers, and a grant of $20 million. Another reason said to influence Golden Dragon's decision to choose Alabama as the location of its new plant is that it is generally a much less union-friendly environment than in most other states, especially those in the Northeast, Midwest, and Northwest (although those differences in some cases have narrowed). Thus, Golden Dragon was "taken aback" when workers, who wanted higher pay and reported "difficulties in communicating with Chinese bosses," undertook a union-organizing drive shortly after the

CONTINUED

plant opened. That was not expected in Alabama. Indeed, Robert Bentley, the governor of Alabama, sent letters to employees urging them to vote against the union. However, by a narrow vote, certified by the NLRB, employees chose to be represented by the United Steelworkers Union.

One example of a difference in culture might be a banner that hangs inside the factory. It says "One Quality escape erases All the good you have done in the past." Some workers describe its tone as "hectoring." Golden Dragon also brought 70 employees, or "advisers," from China to help start up and run the plant. They live in prefabricated housing immediately adjacent to the plant, which is away from town surrounded by woods. Many do not speak English. They have a Chinese chef who feeds them. That expatriates like these Chinese advisers have their own living area separate from locals is something seen around the world, with Americans often known for such arrangements. Now, the roles are reversed. In any case, one can imagine the challenge in solving communication problems. A more tangible issue is that the starting wage is currently $11/hour. Current U.S. Bureau of Labor Statistics data indicate that the average wage in U.S. manufacturing ("goods-producing industries") is $25.92/hour.

Of course, in addition to the government incentives and the reputation of Alabama as a less friendly environment for labor unions, another factor in locating the plant in Wilcox County was its low wages and high unemployment, meaning good availability of low-cost workers. Now, however, Golden Dragon finds itself in a more complex and challenging situation than perhaps it anticipated. The company is unlikely to have had any experience with union activity of the sort encountered in Alabama, as unions in China work much differently, typically in close coordination with the Communist Party.

As a final note, the fact that employees at Golden Dragon in Alabama voted to join a union is only one step toward achieving employee goals. The next step, which is to successfully negotiate a contract with the company, is also necessary. That is far from automatic. One of the main sources of leverage for a union in negotiating a new contract is its ability to go on strike. So, things are yet to be resolved.

DISCUSSION QUESTIONS

1. How did Haier enter the U.S. market? How else could it have entered? Why did it choose the method it did?
2. What changes is Haier trying to make at the plants in Kentucky? Why?
3. How did Golden Dragon enter the U.S. market? What are the pros and cons of its approach, compared to Haier's approach?
4. Why did Golden Dragon choose to locate in Alabama? What unexpected challenges has it encountered? What advice would you give the company?

SOURCES: T. Mann, "China's Haier Group Focuses on Costs at Louisville's Appliance Park," *Wall Street Journal*, January 12, 2017; J. Haggerty, "A Clash of Cultures at Alabama Factory," *Wall Street Journal*, February 28, 2016; C. Harlan and X. Jing, "A Grim Bargain," *Washington Post*, December 1, 2015; Y. Yang, "China's Housing Boom Ends as Prices Fall in Top Cities," *Financial Times,* January 18, 2017.

The Public Sector

LO 14-7

Explain how labor relations in the public sector differ from labor relations in the private sector.

Unlike the private sector, union membership in the public sector grew in the 1960s and 1970s and remained fairly stable through the 1980s. As we saw earlier in Figure 14.3, 34.4% of government employees (versus 6.4% of private- sector employees) are currently union members. Like the NLRA in the private sector, changes in the legal framework contributed significantly to union growth in the public sector. One early step was the enactment in Wisconsin of collective bargaining legislation in 1959 for its state employees.[106] (However, things change. A few years ago, Wisconsin's governor signed a bill that stripped most state and local employees of most of their collective bargaining rights.) Executive Order 10988 provided collective bargaining rights for federal employees in 1962. By the end of the 1960s, most states had passed similar laws. The Civil Service Reform Act of 1978, Title VII, later established the Federal Labor Relations Authority (modeled after the NLRB). Many states have similar administrative agencies to administer their own laws.

An interesting aspect of public-sector union growth is that much of it has occurred in the service industry and among white-collar employees—groups that have traditionally been viewed as difficult to organize. Indeed, as we saw earlier in Table 14.2, of the four currently largest labor unions in the United States, two represent teachers, and the other two represent service workers and public-sector workers.

In contrast to the private sector, strikes are illegal at the federal level of the public sector and in most states. At the local level, all states prohibit strikes by police (Hawaii being a partial exception) and firefighters (Idaho being the exception). Teachers and state employees are somewhat more likely to have the right to strike, depending on the state. In 2016, of the 15 work stoppages involving 1,000 or more workers, 7 were in the public sector (primarily local government—teachers, and health care workers).

Nonunion Representation Systems

With unions now representing just 11.1% of U.S. workers, the question is to what degree are forms of nonunion representation operating to cover the remaining 88.9% of workers? Table 14.17 indicates that in one survey, about one-third (274 of 823) of nonunion workers were covered by a representation system established by management. In other words, more workers in this survey (274) were covered by nonunion representation systems than were covered by union–management collective bargaining contracts (170). In addition, the perceptions of workers regarding how strongly worker representatives "stand up" for them and how actively they consult with them about their ideas and concerns were remarkably similar under both management-established systems and union collective bargaining agreements. That, of course, does not mean that a nonunion representation system, which ordinarily does not have the same independence and leverage as an elected labor union, is equivalent to having a collective bargaining agreement and union. But, clearly, nonunion representation systems play an important role in the workplace.[107]

Table 14.17
Worker Representation Systems, Union and Nonunion

	COLLECTIVE BARGAINING AGREEMENT (N = 170)	NO COLLECTIVE BARGAINING AGREEMENT (N = 823)	
		MANAGEMENT ESTABLISHED SYSTEM[a] (N = 274)	NO SYSTEM (N = 549)
Representatives can be counted on to stand up for workers, even if it means disagreeing with management[b]	84%	84%	NA
Representatives actively consult with workers about their ideas and concerns[b]	77	89	NA
Representatives actively consult with management over wages and benefits	100[c]	77	NA

N = 993 U.S. workers
[a]Covered by a "nonunion, management established system, where worker representatives meet with management."
[b]Sum of those responding either "To Some Extent" or "To a Great Extent."
[c]Estimated.
SOURCE: J. Godard and C. Frege, "Labor Unions, Alternative Forms of Representation, and the Exercise of Authority Relations in U.S. Workplaces," *Industrial and Labor Relations Review* 66 (2013), pp. 142–68.

A LOOK BACK

Labor Union Strength Continues Its Decline in the United States, but Remains a Factor in Certain Sectors

The membership rate, and thus influence, of labor unions in the United States and in many other long-industrialized countries has been on the decline in the private sector. However, even in the United States, there continue to be companies in certain sectors (e.g., automobile manufacturers, health care, education, airlines) where labor unions represent a large share of employees and thus play a major role in the operation and success of those companies. In each of these situations, effective labor relations are crucial for both companies and workers, as well as for society. In non-union companies, employers that do not have effective employee relations are more likely to face union organizing efforts. Also, as we saw in the chapter opener, workers can take collective action without formal union representation as a possible means of improving their jobs.

QUESTIONS

1. Many people picture labor union members as being men in blue-collar jobs in manufacturing plants. Is that accurate? Are there certain types of jobs where an employer can be fairly certain that employees will not join a union? Give examples.
2. Why do people join labor unions? Would you be interested in joining a labor union if given the opportunity? Why or why not? As a manager, would you prefer to work with a union, or would you prefer that employees not be represented by a union? Explain.
3. What led to a change in labor relations at Chrysler's Dundee engine plant? What was the nature of the change, and do you think it is an important and sustainable change?
4. What role do (or can) labor unions play in low-wage countries such as Bangladesh?

SUMMARY

Labor unions seek to represent the interests of their members in the workplace. Although this may further the cause of industrial democracy, management often finds that unions increase labor costs while setting limits on the company's flexibility and discretion in decision making. As a result, the company may witness a diminished ability to compete effectively in a global economy. Not surprisingly, management in nonunion companies often feels compelled to actively resist the unionization of its employees. This, together with a host of economic, legal, and other factors, has contributed to union losses in membership and bargaining power in the private sector. There are some indications, however, that management and unions are seeking new, more effective ways of working together to enhance competitiveness while giving employees a voice in how workplace decisions are made.

KEY TERMS

Checkoff provision, 597
Closed shop, 597
Union shop, 597
Agency shop, 597
Maintenance of membership, 597
Taft-Hartley Act, 597

Right-to-work laws, 597
Associate union membership, 611
Corporate campaigns, 613
Distributive bargaining, 616
Integrative bargaining, 616
Attitudinal structuring, 616

Intraorganizational
   bargaining, 616
Mediation, 620
Fact finder, 620
Arbitration, 620
Duty of fair representation, 621

DISCUSSION QUESTIONS

1. Why do employees join unions?
2. What has been the trend in union membership in the United States, and what are the underlying reasons for the trend?
3. What are the consequences for management and owners of having a union represent employees?
4. What are the general provisions of the National Labor Relations Act, and how does it affect labor–management interactions?

5. What are the features of traditional and nontraditional labor relations? What are the potential advantages of the "new" nontraditional approaches to labor relations?
6. How does the U.S. industrial and labor relations system compare with systems in other countries, such as those in western Europe?

SELF-ASSESSMENT EXERCISE

Additional assignable self-assessments available in Connect.

Would you join a union? Each of the following phrases expresses an opinion about the effects of a union on employees' jobs. For each phrase, circle a number on the scale to indicate whether you agree that a union would affect your job as described by the phrase.

Having a union would result in . . .	Strongly Disagree				Strongly Agree
1. Increased wages	1	2	3	4	5
2. Improved benefits	1	2	3	4	5
3. Protection from being fired	1	2	3	4	5
4. More promotions	1	2	3	4	5

5. Better work hours	1	2	3	4	5
6. Improved productivity	1	2	3	4	5
7. Better working conditions	1	2	3	4	5
8. Fewer accidents at work	1	2	3	4	5
9. More interesting work	1	2	3	4	5
10. Easier handling of employee problems	1	2	3	4	5
11. Increased work disruptions	5	4	3	2	1
12. More disagreements between employees and management	5	4	3	2	1
13. Work stoppages	5	4	3	2	1

Add up your total score. The highest score possible is 65; the lowest, 13. The higher your score, the more you see value in unions, and the more likely you would be to join a union.

SOURCE: Based on S. A. Youngblood, A. S. DeNisi, J. L. Molleston, and W. H. Mobley, "The Impact of Work Environment, Instrumentality Beliefs, Perceived Union Image, and Subjective Norms on Union Voting Intentions," *Academy of Management Journal* 27 (1984), pp. 576–90.

EXERCISING STRATEGY

Boeing Employees in South Carolina Vote "No" on Union Representation

Employees at Boeing's aircraft production plants near Charleston, South Carolina, recently voted against joining the International Association of Machinists (IAM) union. The plants assemble 787 Dreamliner jets and are the sole location where the new 787-10, the largest jet in the Dreamliner family, is assembled. Boeing first purchased existing plants from other companies in 2004, 2008, and 2009. It then built two new aircraft production facilities that began producing planes in 2012 and 2016, respectively. The IAM claimed that Boeing employees in South Carolina make 36% less, on average, than Boeing's unionized employees building 787 aircraft in its main facility in Everett, Washington, just outside of Seattle. An IAM organizer said, "We are disheartened" that employees will

continue to work in "a system that suppresses wages, fosters inconsistency and awards only a chosen few." Apparently, however, employees for the most part did not agree, as 74% voted against having the IAM union represent them. The vote perhaps reflects a general discomfort in South Carolina about the likely effect of unions on future economic development. For example, Senator Lindsey Graham and former governor Nikki Haley, both advised Boeing employees not to support a union. Senator Graham said that while he respected the right of employees at Boeing to decide what was in their best interests, he argued that what was best for South Carolina was if "Boeing stays here and grows" and that "if you destroy the business model that led Boeing to come to South Carolina, we all lose."

Presumably Boeing came to South Carolina in part because its level of unionization, according to the U.S. Bureau of Labor Statistics, is the lowest of all 50 states, with 1.6% of employees being union members. By comparison, in Washington state, where Boeing has produced aircraft for many years, 17.4% of employees are union members. Hope Wroblewski, a manufacturing technician in South Carolina who voted against the union, said that she did not want to be pressured by the union to pay union dues (which are not mandatory in South Carolina, a right-to-work state) and she did not want to be accused by the union of being a scab if she crossed the picket line when union members were on strike. She is also happy with her wages and benefits, which a Boeing spokesman says are set to be consistent with wages in local markets.

A check of Occupational Employment Statistics from the Bureau of Labor Statistics indicates the mean hourly wage in production occupations is $22.50 in the Seattle area versus $19.88 in the Charleston area, a difference of 13%. So, perhaps differences in local markets do not fully explain the difference in wages. It would, however, add to the business case for Boeing to produce planes in the Charleston area, in addition to (or perhaps instead of, over time) in the Seattle area, as lower costs, all else equal, translate into larger profits.

And the lack of a union and the unlikely prospect of a union in the future stands in contrast to its plants in Seattle, "which are heavily unionized and have a history of strife between labor and management." One way that strife shows itself is through strikes, which slow or stop production. It is, of course, hard to make a profit selling planes when planes are not being produced.

QUESTIONS

1. Explain Boeing's reasons for wanting to have an alternative (to Seattle) to produce aircraft. Explain why it chose South Carolina.
2. Do you feel Boeing employees in South Carolina made a decision in their own best interests by voting against union representation? Why or why not?
3. If you were an employee at Boeing in South Carolina, would you have voted for or against the union? Explain.
4. If you were an employee at Boeing in Seattle, would you support continued union representation? Explain.

SOURCES: D. Cameron, "Boeing Workers in South Carolina Vote against Joining Union," *Wall Street Journal*, February 15, 2017; M. Ehrenfreund, "Boeing Workers in South Carolina Vote against Union," *Washington Post*, February 15, 2017.

MANAGING PEOPLE

Twinkies, HoHos, and Ding Dongs: No Treat for Labor Unions

Let's talk about Twinkies, HoHos and Ding Dongs. They have long been found in the snack food aisle and have even been described as having "a legendary history." One fun fact: The cream inside a Twinkie was banana flavored for many years. But when World War II brought rationing, including of bananas, Hostess changed the flavor of the cream to vanilla. OK, one more fun fact: Although there is an urban legend that Twinkies never go bad, it seems that the reality is they have a shelf life of about 25 days. That is considered quite a long shelf life for a baked good product. What is the secret? It may be that Twinkies lack any dairy products.

Unfortunately, whatever the flavor of the "cream" inside or the shelf life of a Twinkie, the company that makes them, Hostess Brands, recently declared bankruptcy. However, Metropoulos & Co. and Apollo purchased Hostess Brands, which reopened four bakery/plants, coming to the rescue of Twinkie-deprived consumers (Hostess Brands was subsequently sold again to The Gores Group).

One thing Hostess will not do going forward after reopening plants is to use union workers. The 86-year-old company closed down and entered bankruptcy, in part, due to a nationwide strike by one of its unions. Chief executive C. Dean Metropoulos said $60 million in capital investments will be spent on the plants and that the plan is to hire at least 1,500 workers. But Mr. Metropoulos in an interview made his views on the role of unions clear: There will be no role.

Hostess Brands Inc. once employed 19,000 workers. Of those, 15,000 were represented by unions. The Teamsters union, which represented the largest share of Hostess Brands workers, after difficult negotiations agreed to a new collective bargaining contract following the bankruptcy trial in court. In contrast, the second-largest union, the Bakery, Confectionery, Tobacco Workers & Grain Millers International Union, began a nationwide work stoppage after failing to agree on a contract with the company, which led to the company imposing a new, less favorable contract on the union. The resulting strike, according to the company, crippled its operations, ultimately leading the company to shut down.

The company and the bakers union expressed different views on the importance of the unionized bakers. The president of the Bakers union, David Durkee, stated that because only members of the bakers union knew how to run the equipment in the plants used to bake snacks, the bakers union members would be hired back to work. In contrast, the new owners of Hostess have said that they will be able to find capable nonunion workers in the areas where plants are reopening, all located in areas where unemployment is high. Prior to bankruptcy, Hostess plants had been running at less than 50% of capacity. Going forward, the plants are expected to run at 85–90% capacity, making production much more efficient and, presumably, allowing the company to make an adequate profit. Of course, if the nonunion workers to be used going forward are also less costly, that will further bring costs down and profits up. The caveat is that it remains to be seen whether new nonunion bakers can quickly learn how to efficiently do the work in the plants. To avoid hiring Teamsters as drivers, Hostess plans to outsource driving/delivery and related tasks. It will also outsource sales.

QUESTIONS

1. Why did Hostess Brands Inc. go into bankruptcy?
2. Did unions act in the best interests of the workers they represented? Did the two unions involved follow the same strategy?
3. Will the new company, Hostess Brands LLC, perform better? Why or why not?

SOURCES: R. Feintzeig, "New Twinkie Maker Shuns Union Labor," *Wall Street Journal*, April 24, 2013; A. Kleinman, "Twinkie Facts: 12 Things You Didn't Know about the Beloved Snack," *Huffington Post,* November 16, 2012, www.huffingtonpost.com/2012/11/16/twinkie-facts-12-things_n_2144143.html; "Twinkies Shelf Life," www.snopes.com/food/ingredient/twinkies.asp.

HR IN SMALL BUSINESS

Republic Gets Serious

When Serious Materials acquired Republic Windows and Doors, union–management relations got a much-needed breath of fresh air. Republic had nearly vanished amidst economic meltdown and accusations of mismanagement and corruption. Serious Materials, by contrast, is a firm with a high-minded business strategy and a commitment to fair-mindedness.

The problems became public when workers at Republic staged a six-day sit-in at the Chicago factory, which had been one of the largest window-glass factories in the United States. When orders from construction companies stopped coming in, management, after just three days' warning, closed the plant without granting workers any severance pay or giving the legally required 60 days' notice, and filed for bankruptcy. Bowing to public pressure, the company's lenders, including Bank of America, reached an agreement to give the workers $6,000 apiece in severance pay.

But that wasn't the end. The workers turned to the National Labor Relations Board with another complaint. They said Republic's owner, Richard Gillman, had secretly begun transferring the company's machinery to a (nonunion) window-manufacturing facility he bought in Iowa just before closing the Chicago factory. In fact, all the equipment would have been gone, they said, except that their six-day occupation of the factory interfered with the plan—they wouldn't allow Gillman to enter. Employees also followed trucks carrying machinery to learn where it was being taken. The union demanded that the machinery be returned to the Chicago plant, so a new owner could operate it.

Meanwhile, a hero arrived on the scene: Kevin Surace, founder and chief executive of Serious Materials, a maker of eco-friendly building products, including energy-efficient windows. Surace saw acquisition of the Republic facility as a chance to expand into the Chicago region with a ready-made plant and equipment, not to mention trained people eager to work.

When he decided to make an offer, Surace did something unusual: Instead of talking first to the firms' main creditors, he made his first visit to the employees' union, the United Electrical, Radio, and Machine Workers of America. He met with the union's president, Carl Rosen, as well as several Republic workers. Rosen recalled that Surace's reasoning was that for the deal to work, he needed a skilled workforce. The parties agreed that Serious Materials would make the facility a union shop, and employees would be paid their former salaries and receive credit for their seniority at Republic. Only then did Surace approach Bank of America. The bank initially wasn't interested, so Surace went to General Electric, owner of the lease on the equipment, and bought out the lease, a coup that convinced the bank to sell. Surace announced plans to reopen the plant and rehire the 300 employees who had been laid off when Republic closed its doors. The resulting publicity quickly brought in inquiries and even some paying customers.

Since the acquisition, the Republic story may be nearing its end. County prosecutors brought charges against Gillman for looting the business and stealing machinery for the Iowa enterprise (which also failed, less than two months after it launched). Because Republic had been in bankruptcy, the equipment was not Gillman's but belonged to his creditor, GE. State's Attorney Anita Alvarez said, "Just two weeks before Christmas, in a dire economy, the company shut the doors of their business and deserted their workers and all of their families." Gillman denied the charges.

A sign of Surace's very different attitude toward his workforce came a few months after the acquisition by Serious Materials, when Vice President Joe Biden came to visit the Chicago facility. Biden was there to represent how the Obama administration's economic stimulus plan was supporting "green" initiatives. Surace noticed that onstage for the press conference were various dignitaries but no representatives of the workers. In spite of the Secret Service's reluctance to add last-minute guests, Surace insisted that workers have a face at the press conference. By the time the TV cameras were rolling, the cast of dignitaries included Armando Robles, a maintenance worker and the president of the employees' union.

QUESTIONS

1. Richard Gillman attempted to stay in business by transferring work to a nonunion facility, and Kevin Surace plans to make the operation profitable as a union shop. Do you think the decision to rely on union or nonunion labor spells the difference between the success and failure of this enterprise? Why or why not?

2. How (if at all) do you think Kevin Surace's initial approach to the union when acquiring the company will influence the business success of the window factory?

3. Imagine that Serious Materials has hired you as an HR consultant for the Chicago window factory. Suggest how the company can build on its initial goodwill with workers to create positive labor relations and a highly motivated workforce for the long run.

SOURCES: R. Mitchum, "Republic Workers File Labor Charges," *Chicago Tribune*, January 7, 2009; R. Mitchum, "Former Republic Workers Find Hope," *Chicago Tribune*, January 15, 2009; A. Sweeney and M. Walberg, "Tables Turn on Man Who Shut Republic Windows," *Chicago Tribune*, September 11, 2009; L. Buchanan, "Entrepreneur of the Year: Kevin Surace of Serious Materials," *Inc.*, December 2009.

NOTES

1. J. T. Dunlop, *Industrial Relations Systems* (New York: Holt, 1958).
2. C. Kerr, "Industrial Conflict and Its Mediation," *American Journal of Sociology* 60 (1954), pp. 230–45.
3. T. A. Kochan, *Collective Bargaining and Industrial Relations* (Homewood, IL: Richard D. Irwin, 1980), p. 25; H. C. Katz and T. A. Kochan, *An Introduction to Collective Bargaining and Industrial Relations*, 3rd ed. (New York: McGraw-Hill, 2004).
4. Katz and Kochan, *An Introduction to Collective Bargaining*.
5. S. Webb and B. Webb, *Industrial Democracy* (London: Longmans, Green, 1897); J. R. Commons, *Institutional Economics* (New York: Macmillan, 1934).
6. C. Kerr, J. T. Dunlop, F. Harbison, and C. Myers, "Industrialism and World Society," *Harvard Business Review*, February 1961, pp. 113–26.
7. T. A. Kochan and K. R. Wever, "American Unions and the Future of Worker Representation," in *The State of the Unions*, ed. G. Strauss et al. (Madison, WI: Industrial Relations Research Association, 1991).
8. "Why America Needs Unions, but Not the Kind It Has Now," *BusinessWeek*, May 23, 1994, p. 70.
9. Katz and Kochan, *An Introduction to Collective Bargaining*.
10. J. Barbash, *The Elements of Industrial Relations* (Madison: University of Wisconsin Press, 1984).
11. U.S. Bureau of Labor Statistics, www.bls.gov.
12. J. T. Bennett and B. E. Kaufman, *The Future of Private Sector Unionism in the United States* (Armonk, NY: M. E. Sharpe, 2002).
13. Katz and Kochan, *An Introduction to Collective Bargaining*. Katz and Kochan in turn build on work by J. Fiorito and C. L. Maranto, "The Contemporary Decline of Union Strength," *Contemporary Policy Issues* 3 (1987), pp. 12–27.
14. G. N. Chaison and J. Rose, "The Macrodeterminants of Union Growth and Decline," in *The State of the Unions*, ed. George Strauss et al. (Madison, WI: Industrial Relations Research Association, 1991).
15. D. L. Belman and K. A. Monaco, "The Effects of Deregulation, Deunionization, Technology, and Human Capital on the Work and Work Lives of Truck Drivers," *Industrial and Labor Relations Review* 54 (2001), pp. 502–24.
16. T. A. Kochan, R. B. McKersie, and J. Chalykoff, "The Effects of Corporate Strategy and Workplace Innovations in Union Representation," *Industrial and Labor Relations Review* 39 (1986), pp. 487–501; Chaison and Rose, "The Macrodeterminants of Union Growth"; J. Barbash, *Practice of Unionism* (New York: Harper, 1956), p. 210; W. N. Cooke and D. G. Meyer, "Structural and Market Predictors of Corporate Labor Relations Strategies," *Industrial and Labor Relations Review* 43 (1990), pp. 280–93; T. A. Kochan and P. Cappelli, "The Transformation of the Industrial Relations and Personnel Function," in *Internal Labor Markets*, ed. P. Osterman (Cambridge, MA: MIT Press, 1984); J. Logan, "The Union Avoidance Industry in the United States," *British Journal of Industrial Relations* 44 (2006), pp. 651–75.
17. Kochan and Cappelli, "The Transformation of the Industrial Relations and Personnel Function."
18. The 27% difference is based on 2012 data from www.bls.gov. S. B. Jarrell and T. D. Stanley, "A Meta-Analysis of the Union–Nonunion Wage Gap," *Industrial and Labor Relations Review* 44 (1990), pp. 54–67; P. D. Linneman, M. L. Wachter, and W. H. Carter, "Evaluating the Evidence on Union Employment and Wages," *Industrial and Labor Relations Review* 44 (1990), pp. 34–53; L. Mischel and M. Walters, "How Unions Help All Workers," Economic Policy Institute Briefing Paper (2003).
19. National Labor Relations Board annual reports.
20. J. P. Ferguson, "The Eyes of the Needles: A Sequential Model of Union Organizing Drives, 1999–2004," *Industrial and Labor Relations Review* 62, no. 3 (2008), pp. 3–21.
21. R. B. Freeman and M. M. Kleiner, "Employer Behavior in the Face of Union Organizing Drives," *Industrial and Labor Relations Review* 43 (1990), pp. 351–65.
22. F. K. Foulkes, "Large Nonunionized Employers," in *U.S. Industrial Relations 1950–1980: A Critical Assessment*, ed. J. Steiber et al. (Madison, WI: Industrial Relations Research Association, 1981).
23. Katz and Kochan, *An Introduction to Collective Bargaining*.
24. R. B. Freeman and J. Rogers, *What Workers Want* (Ithaca, NY: Cornell University Press, 1999).
25. E. E. Herman, J. L. Schwarz, and A. Kuhn, *Collective Bargaining and Labor Relations* (Englewood Cliffs, NJ: Prentice Hall, 1992), p. 32.

26. www.bls.gov; AFL-CIO website.

27. Herman et al., *Collective Bargaining*, p. 33.

28. Kochan, *Collective Bargaining and Industrial Relations*, p. 61.

29. National Labor Relations Board, *A Guide to Basic Law and Procedures under the National Labor Relations Act* (Washington, DC: U.S. Government Printing Office, 1991).

30. Ibid.

31. Ibid.

32. H. N. Wheeler and J. A. McClendon, "The Individual Decision to Unionize," in *The State of the Unions*.

33. National Labor Relations Board annual reports, www.nlrb.gov.

34. M. Trottman, "New Rules Adopted for Union Elections," *New York Times*, December 13–14, 2014, p. B4.

35. M. Trottman. "New Labor-Board Rule Speeds Union Votes. Average election time has fallen 40% since NLRB regulation took effect in April." *Wall Street Journal*. August 26, 2015.

36. Melanie Trottman, "Ruling Clears Way for Unions," *Wall Street Journal*, August 27, 2015; M. Bultman, "One Year after Browning-Ferris, Employers Decry Uncertainty," Law360, August 16, 2016, https://www.law360.com/articles/828691/one-year-after-browning-ferris-employers-decry-uncertainty.

37. "Obama's Union McDouble" [editorial], *Wall Street Journal*, December 22, 2014; M. Trottman and J. Jargon, "NLRB Names McDonald's as 'Joint-Employer' at Its Franchisees," *Wall Street Journal*, December 19, 2014.

38. D. Douglas-Gabriel, "Are They Students? Or Are They Employees?" *Washington Post*, August 23, 2016.

39. J. G. Getman, S. B. Goldberg, and J. B. Herman, *Union Representation Elections: Law and Reality* (New York: Russell Sage Foundation, 1976).

40. J. A. Fossum, *Labor Relations*, 8th ed. (New York: McGraw-Hill, 2002), p. 149.

41. National Labor Relations Board, *A Guide to Basic Law*, p. 17.

42. Ibid.

43. Herman et al., *Collective Bargaining*; P. Jarley and J. Fiorito, "Associate Membership: Unionism or Consumerism?" *Industrial and Labor Relations Review* 43 (1990), pp. 209–24.

44. W. Welkowitz, "Social Media: The New Big Tool for Union Organizing," Labor and Employment Blog, *Bloomberg BNA*, February 3, 2015, www.bna.com; T. Puckett, "NLRB Rulings Have Far-Reaching Impact on Employers and Policies," *Oklahoma Employment Law Letter*, February 4, 2015, www.hrhero.com.

45. Katz and Kochan, *An Introduction to Collective Bargaining*; R. L. Rose, "Unions Hit Corporate Campaign Trail," *Wall Street Journal*, March 8, 1993, p. B1.

46. P. Jarley and C. L. Maranto, "Union Corporate Campaigns: An Assessment," *Industrial and Labor Relations Review* 44 (1990), pp. 505–24.

47. Katz and Kochan, *An Introduction to Collective Bargaining*.

48. A. McFellin, "Labor Unions in the New Economy," *Common Dreams*, March 24, 2013, www.heartlandnetwork.org/newsroom/10-in-the-news/63-labor-unions-in-the-new-economy-2.

49. T. Devaney, "SEIU Spent $19M on Fight for $15," *The Hill*, April 3, 2017, http://thehill.com/regulation/labor/327011-seiu-spent-19m-on-fight-for-15.

50. K. Maher, "SEIU to End Sodexo Campaign," *Wall Street Journal*, September 15, 2011.

51. Chaison and Rose, "The Macrodeterminants of Union Growth."

52. R. E. Walton and R. B. McKersie, *A Behavioral Theory of Negotiations* (New York: McGraw-Hill, 1965).

53. Fossum, *Labor Relations*. See also C. S. Loughran, *Negotiating a Labor Contract: A Management Handbook*, 2nd ed. (Washington, DC: Bureau of National Affairs, 1990).

54. C. M. Steven, *Strategy and Collective Bargaining Negotiations* (New York: McGraw-Hill, 1963); Katz and Kochan, *An Introduction to Collective Bargaining*.

55. Roger Fisher and William Ury, *Getting to Yes* (New York: Penguin Books, 1991).

56. Kochan, *Collective Bargaining and Industrial Relations*.

57. Fossum, *Labor Relations*.

58. J. R. Haggerty, "Caterpillar Girds for a Strike," *Wall Street Journal*, March 2–3, 2013, p. B3.

59. J. Ostrower, "Union Cancels Boeing Vote," *Wall Street Journal*, April 18–19, 2015, p. B3; J. Ostrower, "New Dreamliner to Be Built at Nonunion Plant," *Wall Street Journal*, July 31, 2014; J. Ostrower, "New Boeing Pact Wins Cost Controls," *Wall Street Journal*, January 5, 2014, p. B3.

60. Federal Mediation and Conciliiation Service, *Annual Report for Fiscal Year 2016*, January 13, 2017, https://www.fmcs.gov/wp-content/uploads/2017/01/AnnualReport2017Jan13.pdf.

61. Kochan, *Collective Bargaining and Industrial Relations*, p. 272.

62. Herman et al., *Collective Bargaining*.

63. Katz and Kochan, *An Introduction to Collective Bargaining*.

64. Kochan, *Collective Bargaining and Industrial Relations*, p. 386.

65. Alternative criteria would be efficiency, equity, and worker voice. J. W. Budd and A. J. S. Colvin, "Improved Metrics for Workplace Dispute Resolution Procedures: Efficiency, Equity, and Voice," *Industrial Relations* 47, no. 3 (July 2008), p. 460.

66. *United Steelworkers v. American Manufacturing Co.*, 363 U.S. 564 (1960); *United Steelworkers v. Warrior Gulf and Navigation Co.*, 363 U.S. 574 (1960); *United Steelworkers v. Enterprise Wheel and Car Corp.*, 363 U.S. 593 (1960).

67. Original data from U.S. Federal Mediation and Conciliation Service, *Fiftieth Annual Report, Fiscal Year 2006* (Washington, DC: U.S. Government Printing Office, 2006); www.fmcs.gov.

68. J. R. Redecker, *Employee Discipline: Policies and Practices* (Washington, DC: Bureau of National Affairs, 1989).

69. Barbash, *The Elements of Industrial Relations*, p. 6.

70. T. A. Kochan, H. C. Katz, and R. B. McKersie, *The Transformation of American Industrial Relations* (New York: Basic Books, 1986), chap. 6; J. B. Arthur, "The Link between Business Strategy and Industrial Relations Systems in American Steel Minimills," *Industrial and Labor Relations Review* 45 (1992), pp. 488–506; M. Schuster, "Union Management Cooperation," in *Employee and Labor Relations*, ed. J. A. Fossum (Washington, DC: Bureau of National Affairs, 1990); E. Cohen-Rosenthal and C. Burton, *Mutual Gains: A Guide to Union–Management Cooperation*, 2nd ed. (Ithaca, NY: ILR Press, 1993); T. A. Kochan and P. Osterman, *The Mutual Gains Enterprise* (Boston: Harvard Business School Press, 1994); E. Applebaum and R. Batt, *The New American Workplace* (Ithaca, NY: ILR Press, 1994).

71. J. Marquez, "Streamlined Model: Engine of Change," *Workforce Management*, July 17, 2006, pp. 1, 20–30; B. Visnic, "Harbour-Topping Chrysler JV Engine Plant Attracting Foreign Attention," *Edmunds Auto Observer*, July 20, 2008, www.autoobserver.com; J. McCracken, "Desperate to Cut Costs, Ford Gets Union's Help," *Wall Street Journal*, March 2, 2007, p. A1; M. Oneal, "Model Partnership: Automakers, Labor Could Learn from Harley-Davidson's Kansas City Operation," *Columbus Dispatch*, May 27, 2006 (original article in *Chicago Tribune*).

72. L. P. Vellequette. FCA's Dundee Engine Plant achieves silver designation for productivity. Automotive News, May 15, 2015.

73. A. E. Eaton, "Factors Contributing to the Survival of Employee Participation Programs in Unionized Settings," *Industrial and Labor Relations Review* 47, no. 3 (1994), pp. 371–89.

74. National Labor Relations Board, *A Guide to Basic Law*.

75. A. Bernstein, "Putting a Damper on That Old Team Spirit," *BusinessWeek*, May 4, 1992, p. 60.

76. Bureau of National Affairs, "Polaroid Dissolves Employee Committee in Response to Labor Department Ruling," *Daily Labor Report*, June 23, 1992, p. A3; K. G. Salwen, "DuPont Is Told It Must Disband Nonunion Panels," *Wall Street Journal*, June 7, 1993, p. A2.

77. "NLRB 4-0 Approves Crown Cork & Seal's Use of Seven Employee Participation Committees," *HR News*, September 3, 2001.

78. Kochan and Osterman, *Mutual Gains*; J. P. MacDuffie, "Human Resource Bundles and Manufacturing Performance: Organizational Logic and Flexible Production Systems in the World Auto Industry," *Industrial and Labor Relations Review* 48, no. 2 (1995), pp. 197–221; W. N. Cooke, "Employee Participation Programs, Group-Based Incentives, and Company Performance: A Union–Nonunion Comparison," *Industrial and Labor Relations Review* 47, no. 4 (1994), pp. 594–609; C. Doucouliagos, "Worker Participation and Productivity in Labor-Managed and Participatory Capitalist Firms: A Meta-Analysis," *Industrial and Labor Relations Review* 49, no. 1 (1995), pp. 58–77; L. W. Hunter, J. P. MacDuffie, and L. Doucet, "What Makes Teams Take? Employee Reactions to Work Reforms," *Industrial and Labor Relations Review* 55 (2002), pp. 448–72; S. J. Deery and R. D. Iverson, "Labor-Management Cooperation: Antecedents and Impact on Organizational Performance," *Industrial and Labor Relations Review* 58 (2005), pp. 588–609; James Combs, Yongmei Liu, Angela Hall, and David Ketchen, "How Much Do High-Performance Work Practices Matter? A Meta-Analysis of Their Effects on Organizational Performance," *Personnel Psychology* 59, no. 3 (2006), pp. 501–28; T. Rabl, M. Jayasinghe, B. Gerhart, and T. M. Köhlmann, "How Much Does Country Matter? A Meta-Analysis of the HPWP Systems-Business Performance Relationship," *Academy of Management Annual Meeting Proceedings*, August 2011.

79. R. D. Mohr and C. Zoghi, "High-Involvement Work Design and Job Satisfaction," *Industrial and Labor Relations Review* 61, no. 3 (April 2008), pp. 275–96; P. Osterman, "The Wage Effects of High Performance Work Organization in Manufacturing," *Industrial and Labor Relations Review* 59 (2006), pp. 187–204.

80. J. Cutcher-Gershenfeld, "The Impact of Economic Performance of a Transformation in Workplace Relations," *Industrial and Labor Relations Review* 44 (1991), pp. 241–60.

81. R. B. Freeman and J. Rogers, *Proceedings of the Industrial Relations Research Association*, 1995. A survey of workers represented by the United Autoworkers at six Chrysler manufacturing plants found generally positive worker reactions to the implementation of work teams, streamlined job classifications, and skill-based pay. See L. W. Hunter, J. P. MacDuffie, and L. Doucet, "What Makes Teams Take? Employee Reactions to Work Reforms," *Industrial and Labor Relations Review* 55 (2002), p. 448. A study of the airline industry, moreover, concludes that relational factors, such as conflict and workplace culture, also play an important role in firm performance. See J. H. Gittell, A. vonNordenflycht, and T. A. Kochan, "Mutual Gains or Zero Sum? Labor Relations and Firm Performance in the Airline Industry," *Industrial and Labor Relations Review* 57 (2004), p. 163.

82. H. Doucouliagos, R. B. Freeman, and P. Laroche, *The Economics of Trade Unions: A Study of a Research Field and Its Findings* (London: Routledge, 2017).

83. U.S. Bureau of Labor Statistics, *Employer Costs for Employee Compensation (ECEC)*, http://stats.bls.gov.

84. Ibid.

85. P. E. Gabriel and S. Schmitz, "A Longitudinal Analysis of the Union Wage Premium for US Workers," *Applied Economics Letters* 21 (2014), pp. 487–89; M. L. Blackburn, "Are Union Wage Differentials in the United States Falling?" *Industrial Relations* 47, no. 3 (July 2008), p. 390.

86. Jarrell and Stanley, "A Meta-Analysis"; R. B. Freeman and J. Medoff, *What Do Unions Do?* (New York: Basic Books, 1984); L. Mishel and M. Walters, "How Unions Help All Workers," *Economic Policy Institute Briefing Paper*, August 2003, www.epinet.org.

87. C. P. Green and J. S. Heywood, Dissatisfied union workers: sorting revisited. *British Journal of Industrial Relations* 53, no. 3 (2015), pp. 580–600; T. H. Hammer and A. Augar, "The Impact of Unions on Job Satisfaction, Organizational Commitment, and Turnover," *Journal of Labor Research* 26 (2005), pp. 241–66; B. Artz "The Impact of Union Experience on Job Satisfaction," *Industrial Relations: A Journal of Economy and Society* 49 (2010), pp. 387–405.

88. J. T. Addison and B. T. Hirsch, "Union Effects on Productivity, Profits, and Growth: Has the Long Run Arrived?" *Journal of Labor Economics* 7 (1989), pp. 72–105; H. Doucouliagos and P. Laroche, "Unions and Innovation: New Insights From the Cross–Country Evidence." *Industrial Relations* 52, no. 2 (2013), pp. 467–91.

89. R. B. Freeman and J. L. Medoff, "The Two Faces of Unionism," *Public Interest* 57 (Fall 1979), pp. 69–93.

90. Ibid.; L. Mishel and P. Voos, *Unions and Economic Competitiveness* (Armonk, NY: M. E. Sharpe, 1991); M. Ash and J. A. Seago, "The Effect of Registered Nurses' Unions on Heart-Attack Mortality," *Industrial and Labor Relations Review* 57 (2004), p. 422; C. Doucouliagos and P. Laroche, "What Do Unions Do to Productivity? A Meta-Analysis," *Industrial Relations* 42 (2003), pp. 650–91.

91. Freeman and Medoff, "Two Faces."

92. S. Slichter, J. Healy, and E. R. Livernash, *The Impact of Collective Bargaining on Management* (Washington, DC: Brookings Institution, 1960); Freeman and Medoff, "Two Faces."

93. R. B. Freeman and J. L. Medoff, *What Do Unions Do?* (New York: Basic Books, 1984); Herman et al., *Collective Bargaining*; Addison and Hirsch, "Union Effects on Productivity"; Katz and Kochan, *An Introduction to Collective Bargaining*; Lineneman et al., "Evaluating the Evidence."

94. B. E. Becker and C. A. Olson, "Unions and Firm Profits," *Industrial Relations* 31, no. 3 (1992), pp. 395–415; B. T. Hirsch and B. A. Morgan, "Shareholder Risks and Returns in Union and Nonunion Firms," *Industrial and Labor Relations Review* 47, no. 2 (1994), pp. 302–18. Hristos Doucouliagos and Partice Laroche, "Unions and Profits: A Meta-Regression Analysis," *Industrial Relations* 48, no. 1 (January 2008), p. 146.

95. D. S. Lee and A. Mas, "Long-Run Impacts of Unions on Firms: New Evidence from Financial Markets, 1961–1999," *Quarterly Journal of Economics*, 127 (2012), pp. 333–78.

96. Addison and Hirsch, "Union Effects on Productivity." See also B. T. Hirsch, *Labor Unions and the Economic Performance of Firms* (Kalamazoo, MI: W. E. Upjohn Institute, 1991); J. M. Abowd, "The Effect of Wage Bargains on the Stock Market Value of the Firm," *American Economic Review* 79 (1989), pp. 774–800; Hirsch, *Labor Unions*.

97. B. E. Becker and C. A. Olson, "The Impact of Strikes on Shareholder Equity," *Industrial and Labor Relations Review* 39,

no. 3 (1986), pp. 425–38; O. Persons, "The Effects of Automobile Strikes on the Stock Value of Steel Suppliers," *Industrial and Labor Relations Review* 49, no. 1 (1995), pp. 78–87.

98. C. Brewster, "Levels of Analysis in Strategic HRM: Questions Raised by Comparative Research," Conference on Research and Theory in HRM, Cornell University, October 1997.

99. C. Chang and C. Sorrentino, "Union Membership in 12 Countries," *Monthly Labor Review* 114, no. 12 (1991), pp. 46–53; D. G. Blanchflower and R. B. Freeman, "Going Different Ways: Unionism in the U.S. and Other Advanced O.E.C.D. Countries" (Symposium on the Future Role of Unions, Industry, and Government in Industrial Relations. University of Minnesota), cited in Chaison and Rose, "The Macrodeterminants of Union Growth," p. 23.

100. J. P. Begin and E. F. Beal, *The Practice of Collective Bargaining* (Homewood, IL: Richard D. Irwin, 1989); T. H. Hammer, S. C. Currall, and R. N. Stern, "Worker Representation on Boards of Directors: A Study of Competing Roles," *Industrial and Labor Relations Review* 44 (1991), pp. 661–80; Katz and Kochan, *An Introduction to Collective Bargaining*; H. Gunter and G. Leminsky, "The Federal Republic of Germany," in *Labor in the Twentieth Century*, ed. J. T. Dunlop and W. Galenson (New York: Academic Press, 1978), pp. 149–96.

101. "Adapt or Die," *The Economist*, July 1, 1995, p. 54; G. Steinmetz, "German Firms Sour on Stem That Keeps Peace with Workers: Centralized Bargaining, a Key to Postwar Gains, Inflates Costs, Companies Fear," *Wall Street Journal*, October 17, 1995, p. A1; H. C. Katz, W. Lee, and J. Lee, *The New Structure of Labor Relations: Tripartism and Decentralization* (Ithaca, NY: ILR Press/Cornell University, 2004).

102. E. Thomasson and M. Potter, "Union Calls New Strikes at Amazon's German Warehouses," Reuters, December 21, 2016; N. Wingfield, "Amazon Proves Infertile Soil for Unions, So Far," *New York Times,* May 16, 2016; S. Sloat, "In Germany, Amazon Keeps Unions at Bay," *Wall Street Journal,* September 24, 2014, p. A1.

103. A. Young, "UAW Welcomes Volkswagen Policy Shift After Years of Failing to Gain Traction in Anti-Union South," *International Business Times*, November 12, 2014.

104. C. Brooks, "Chattanooga Auto Workers to Host Strike Meeting," Labor Notes, January 6, 2017, www.labornotes.com; M. Ramsey, "UAW Wins Vote at VW Chattanooga Plant as Some Workers Vote to Unionize," *New York Times,* December 7, 2015.

105. M. Elfstrom and S. Kuruvilla, "The Changing Nature of Unrest in China," *Industrial and Labor Relations Review* April 2014, pp. 453–80.

106. J. F. Burton and T. Thomason, "The Extent of Collective Bargaining in the Public Sector," in *Public Sector Bargaining*, ed. B. Aaron, J. M. Najita, and J. L. Stern (Washington, DC: Bureau of National Affairs, 1988).

107. J. Godard and C. Frege, "Labor Unions, Alternative Forms of Representation, and the Exercise of Authority Relations in U.S. Workplaces," *Industrial and Labor Relations Review* 66 (2013), pp. 142–68; P. J. Gollan and D. Lewin, "Employee Representation in Non-Union Firms: An Overview," *Industrial Relations* 52 (2013), pp. 173–93.

LEARNING OBJECTIVES

After reading this chapter, you should be able to:

LO 15-1   Identify the recent changes that have caused companies to expand into international markets. *page 647*

LO 15-2   Discuss the four factors that most strongly influence HRM in international markets. *page 649*

LO 15-3   List the different categories of international employees. *page 658*

LO 15-4   Identify the four levels of global participation and the HRM issues faced within each level. *page 659*

LO 15-5   Discuss the ways companies attempt to select, train, compensate, and reintegrate expatriate managers. *page 662*

ENTER THE WORLD OF BUSINESS

GM's U.S.–Mexico Challenge

As markets have become more globalized, many companies have created global supply chains, sourcing and manufacturing all across the world. With the passage of the North American Free Trade Agreement, Mexico became a prime target for automobile manufacturers to build *maquiladora* plants where Mexican workers provide a substantial labor cost advantage over U.S.-based United Automobile Workers (UAW) union members. In addition, the products assembled in Mexico are shipped not just to the United States but all around the world. In fact, GM recorded a record profit in its North American market resulting in UAW workers receiving $12,000 in profit sharing. General Motors assembles about 20% of its highly profitable trucks in Mexico and until recently had plans to move much of its sport-utility vehicle production there, as a way to further reduce costs and increase profits.

However, the election of Donald Trump as president of the United States has put a wrinkle in those plans. In an effort to keep companies from moving production outside the United States, Trump has

©Bloomberg/getty Images

proposed a border tax of as much as 35% on any products coming to the United States from Mexico. However, even a more modest tax of 20% is estimated to wipe out a quarter of GM's profit in the region.

SOURCE: J. Stoll and M. Colias, "Mexico Is Key Cog in GM's Profit Machine," *Wall Street Journal*, February 8, 2017, https://www.wsj.com/articles/gm-says-it-supports-tax-reform-but-border-tax-is-complicated-1486473480.

Introduction

The environment in which business competes is rapidly becoming globalized. More and more companies are entering international markets by exporting their products overseas, building plants in other countries, and entering into alliances with foreign companies. In the mid-1980s, 61 of the top 100 organizations had their headquarters in the United States. By 2004 that number had dropped to 35, and Table 15.1 shows the world's 25 largest companies in 2016, and of those only 10 were headquartered in the United States, 8 in Asia, and 7 in Europe. As you can see from the table, whereas General Motors used to dominate the globe in market share, Volkswagen, Toyota, and Daimler all had greater sales than GM in 2016.

Forbes magazine lists its top 2,000 global companies and identifies a subset that exhibit exceptional growth rates, which they dub "Global High Performers." In 2011, 69 of the 130 high-performer companies (those standing out from their peers in growth, return to investors, and future prospects) were headquartered outside of the United States.[1]

Most organizations now function in the global economy. U.S. businesses are entering international markets at the same time that foreign companies are entering the U.S. market.

Table 15.1
2016 *Fortune* Global 500

RANK	COMPANY	REVENUES ($ MILLIONS)	PROFITS ($ MILLIONS)
1	Wal-Mart Stores	482,130	14,694
2	State Grid	329,601	10,201
3	China National Petroleum	299,271	7,091
4	Sinopec Group	294,344	3,595
5	Royal Dutch Shell	272,156	1,939
6	Exxon Mobil	246,204	16,150
7	Volkswagen	236,600	−1,520
8	Toyota Motor	236,592	19,264
9	Apple	233,715	53,394
10	BP	225,982	−6,482
11	Berkshire Hathaway	210,821	24,083
12	McKesson	192,487	2,258
13	Samsung Electronics	177,440	16,532
14	Glencore	170,497	−4,964
15	Industrial and Commercial Bank of China	167,227	44,098
16	Daimler	165,800	9,345
17	United Health Group	157,107	5,813
18	CVS Health	153,290	5,237
19	Exor Group	152,591	825
20	General Motors	152,356	9,687
21	Ford Motor	149,558	7,373
22	China Construction Bank	147,910	36,303
23	AT&T	146,801	13,345
24	Total	143,421	5,087
25	Hon Hai Precision Industries (Foxconn)	141,213	4,627

SOURCE: From *Fortune.* © 2016 Time Inc. Used under license.

In addition, cross-border mergers (e.g., Merck/Schering-Plough, New York Stock Exchange/Deutsche Börse) are increasing. In fact, in 2016, three of the five biggest mergers dealt with companies headquartered in different countries.[2]

What is behind the trend toward expansion into global markets? Companies are attempting to gain a competitive advantage, which can be provided by international expansion in a number of ways. First, these countries are new markets with large numbers of potential customers. For companies that are producing below their capacity, expansion provides a means of increasing sales and profits. Second, many companies are building production facilities in other countries as a means of capitalizing on those countries' lower labor costs for relatively unskilled jobs. For example, many of the Mexican *maquiladora* plants provide low-skilled labor at considerably lower cost than in the United States. In 2015 the average hourly manufacturing wage in Mexico was $3.47, versus $23.04 in the United States.[3] Third, the rapid increase in telecommunications and information technology enables work to be done more rapidly, efficiently, and effectively around the globe. With the best college graduates available for $2.00 an hour in India versus $12–$18 an hour in the United States, companies can hire the best talent (resulting in better work) at a lower cost. And because their day is our night, work done in the United States can be handed off to those in India for a 24/7 work process.[4]

The End of Employment?

Technological advancements always have displaced workers. The ATM allowed customers to carry out bank transactions without having to go to a teller, thus eliminating the need for as many tellers. In the face of rising labor costs, many fast food restaurants have cut back on cashiers in favor of kiosks. However, until recently, most technological innovations displaced low-skilled and manual workers.

The advent of artificial intelligence (AI) may soon do the same to higher-skilled jobs such as computer programmers, civil engineers, and musicians, according to Vinod Khosla, one of the world's most influential venture capitalists. He predicts that 80% of the workforce may be replaced by AI-based automation in as little as 20 years. In a *Forbes* article, he wrote, "It seems likely that the top 10 to 20-percent of any profession... will continue to do well. What happens to the bottom 20-percent or even 80-percent, if that is the delineation? Will the bottom 80-percent be able to compete effectively against computer systems that are superior to human intelligence?"

Before you get too scared, remember that such dire predictions are not new. One economist wrote about technological unemployment that is "unemployment due to our discovery of means of economizing the use of labour outrunning the pace at which we can find new uses for labour." That economist was John Maynard Keynes writing in 1930.

DISCUSSION QUESTION

1. Do you think these technological advances will have such a profound negative impact on jobs? Why or why not?

SOURCE: I. Wladawsky-Berger, "The Emerging Unpredictable Age of AI," *Wall Street Journal*, February 10, 2017, http://blogs.wsj.com/cio/2017/02/10/the-emerging-unpredictable-age-of-ai/

While this process has moved jobs from the United States overseas, technological advances may make the disappearance of jobs a global phenomenon. The "Competing through Technology" box discusses this potential challenge.

Deciding whether to enter foreign markets and whether to develop plants or other facilities in other countries, however, is no simple matter, and many human resource issues surface.

This chapter discusses the human resource issues that must be addressed to gain competitive advantage in a world of global competition. This is not a chapter on international human resource management (the specific HRM policies and programs companies use to manage human resources across international boundaries).[5] The chapter focuses instead on the key factors that must be addressed to strategically manage human resources in an international context. We discuss some of the important events that have increased the global nature of business over the past few years. We then identify some of the factors that are most important to HRM in global environments. Finally, we examine particular issues related to managing expatriate managers. These issues present unique opportunities for firms to gain competitive advantage.

Current Global Changes

Several recent social and political changes have accelerated the movement toward international competition. The effects of these changes have been profound and far reaching. Many are still evolving. In this section we discuss the major developments that have accentuated the need for organizations to gain a competitive advantage through effectively managing human resources in a global economy.

LO 15-1
Identify the recent changes that have caused companies to expand into international markets.

EUROPEAN UNION

European countries have managed their economies individually for years. Because of the countries' close geographic proximity, their economies have become intertwined. This created a number of problems for international businesses; for example, the regulations of one country, such as France, might be completely different from those of another country, such as Germany. In response, most of the European countries agreed to participate in the European Economic Community (EEC), which began in 1992. The EEC is a confederation of most of the European nations that agree to engage in free trade with one another, with commerce regulated by an overseeing body called the European Commission (EC). Under the EEC, legal regulation in the participating countries has become more, although not completely, uniform. Assuming that the EEC's trend toward free trade among members continues, Europe has become one of the largest free markets in the world. In addition, as of 1999, all of the members of the EEC share a common currency, the euro. This ties the members' economic fates even more closely with one another. In addition to the previous 15 EU states, as of May 1, 2004, 12 EU accession states—Bulgaria, Cyprus, the Czech Republic, Estonia, Hungary, Latvia, Lithuania, Malta, Poland, Romania, Slovakia, and Slovenia—were added to the EU, expanding the economic zone covered by the European Union. In 2013, Croatia was added to the EU, and Iceland, Macedonia, Montenegro, Serbia, and Turkey are candidates to be admitted into the EU.

The EU has recently been threatened by the exit of the United Kingdom. This "Brexit" stemmed from a slim majority of U.K. voters deciding that they no longer wanted to be governed largely from a bureaucracy located in Brussels, Belgium. Britain and the EU are currently negotiating the terms of this separation, but many observers predict that, at least in the short term, this exit will have a negative impact on the British economy.

NORTH AMERICAN FREE TRADE AGREEMENT

The North American Free Trade Agreement (NAFTA) is an agreement among Canada, the United States, and Mexico that has created a free market even larger than the European Economic Community. The United States and Canada already had a free trade agreement since 1989, but NAFTA brought Mexico into the consortium. The agreement was prompted by Mexico's increasing willingness to open its markets and facilities in an effort to promote economic growth.[6] As previously discussed, the *maquiladora* plants exemplify this trend. In addition, some efforts have been made to expand the membership of NAFTA to other Latin American countries, such as Chile.

NAFTA has increased U.S. investment in Mexico because of Mexico's substantially lower labor costs for low-skilled employees. This has had two effects on employment in the United States. First, many low-skilled jobs went south, decreasing employment opportunities for U.S. citizens who lack higher-level skills. Second, it has increased employment opportunities for Americans with higher-level skills.[7]

As mentioned in the chapter opening, Donald Trump's election has created uncertainty for companies making their location decisions. The president campaigned on renegotiating NAFTA and has frequently berated companies seeking to build plants in Mexico, particularly when it entails closing plants in the United States.

THE GROWTH OF ASIA

An additional global market that is of economic consequence to many firms lies in Asia. Whereas Japan has been a dominant economic force for over 20 years, countries such as Singapore, Hong Kong, and Malaysia recently have become significant economic forces.

More important, China, with its population of more than 1 billion and trend toward opening its markets to foreign investors, presents a tremendous potential market for goods. In fact, some observers predict that China's economy will soon be larger than that of the United States.

GENERAL AGREEMENT ON TARIFFS AND TRADE

The General Agreement on Tariffs and Trade (GATT) is an international framework of rules and principles for reducing trade barriers across countries around the world. It currently consists of more than 100 member-nations. The most recent round of GATT negotiations resulted in an agreement to cut tariffs (taxes on imports) by 40%, reduce government subsidies to businesses, expand protection of intellectual property such as copyrights and patents, and establish rules for investing and trading in services. It also established the World Trade Organization (WTO) to resolve disputes among GATT members.

These changes—the European Union, NAFTA, the growth of Asia, and GATT—all exemplify events that are pushing companies to compete in a global economy. These developments are opening new markets and new sources of technology and labor in a way that has never been seen in history. However, this era of increasing international competition accentuates the need to manage human resources effectively to gain competitive advantage in a global marketplace. This requires understanding some of the factors that can determine the effectiveness of various HRM practices and approaches.

Factors Affecting HRM in Global Markets

Companies that enter global markets must recognize that these markets are not simply mirror images of their home country. Countries differ along a number of dimensions that influence the attractiveness of direct foreign investment in each country. These differences determine the economic viability of building an operation in a foreign location, and they have a particularly strong impact on HRM in that operation. Researchers in international management have identified a number of factors that can affect HRM in global markets, and we focus on four factors, as depicted in Figure 15.1: culture, education–human capital, the political–legal system, and the economic system.[8] The "Competing through Globalization" box provides an example of the kinds of things firms must address before deciding whether or not to set up operations in parts of Africa.

LO 15-2

Discuss the four factors that most strongly influence HRM in international markets.

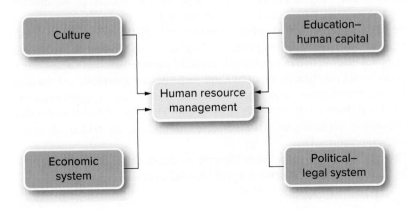

Figure 15.1

Factors Affecting Human Resource Management in International Markets

COMPETING THROUGH GLOBALIZATION

Risks and Rewards of Doing Business in Africa

One reason companies expand internationally is to escape the slowing economies of their home country and to capture some of the profits available in rapid-growth regions. Companies in Africa know this particularly well. Companies that have enjoyed the developed and wealthier economy of South Africa now complain of its slow (2.2%) GDP growth and seek opportunities in the faster-growing, less-developed countries of Nigeria (5.5%) and Angola (6.6%).

There are risks to doing business in these regions, such as insurgent attacks by Boko Haram, and rapidly declining currencies. Nigeria, Africa's largest economy, is highly dependent on oil, so that when global oil prices dropped, so did its currency. A lack of existing infrastructure and the presence of militant groups make continued growth difficult and dangerous. Yet the old adage states, "more risk, more reward."

The search for this reward and the need for growth to power increased profitability is what has encouraged Nampak Ltd., a packaging company, to buy a $300 million factory in Nigeria and to build a $180 million factory in Angola. Africa's economy as a whole is growing at 5%, not far behind China and India. As more of the continent's population enters the middle class, they will demand and be able to afford more goods and services. With so much to gain, avoiding these countries may be the riskier option.

DISCUSSION QUESTION

1. What risks and opportunities should a company weigh when deciding whether it should expand into another country?

SOURCE: M. Stevis and P. McGroarty, "Businesses Seek Out New African Frontiers," *Wall Street Journal,* March 31, 2015.

CULTURE

By far the most important factor influencing international HRM is the culture of the country in which a facility is located. Culture is defined as "the set of important assumptions (often unstated) that members of a community share."[9] These assumptions consist of beliefs about the world and how it works and the ideals that are worth striving for.[10]

Culture is important to HRM for two reasons. First, it often determines the other three factors affecting HRM in global markets. Culture can greatly affect a country's laws, in that laws are often the codification of right and wrong as defined by the culture. Culture also affects human capital, because if education is greatly valued by the culture, then members of the community try to increase their human capital. Finally, as we discuss later, cultures and economic systems are closely intertwined.[11]

However, the most important reason culture is important to HRM is that it often determines the effectiveness of various HRM practices. Practices found to be effective in the United States may not be effective in a culture that has different beliefs and values.[12] For example, U.S. companies rely heavily on individual performance appraisal, and rewards are tied to individual performance. In Japan, however, individuals are expected to subordinate their wishes and desires to those of the larger group. Thus, individual-based evaluation and incentives are not nearly as effective there and, in fact, are seldom observed among Japanese organizations.[13]

In this section we examine a model that attempts to characterize different cultures. This model illustrates why culture can have a profound influence on HRM.

Hofstede's Cultural Dimensions

In a classic study of culture, Geert Hofstede identified four dimensions on which various cultures could be classified.[14] In a later study he added a fifth dimension that aids in characterizing cultures.[15] The relative scores for 10 major countries are provided in Table 15.2. **Individualism–collectivism** describes the strength of the relation between an individual and other individuals in the society—that is, the degree to which people act as individuals rather than as members of a group. In individualist cultures, such as the United States, Great Britain, and the Netherlands, people are expected to look after their own interests and the interests of their immediate families. The individual is expected to stand on her own two feet rather than be protected by the group. In collectivist cultures, such as Colombia, Pakistan, and Taiwan, people are expected to look after the interest of the larger community, which is expected to protect people when they are in trouble.

The second dimension, **power distance**, concerns how a culture deals with hierarchical power relationships—particularly the unequal distribution of power. It describes the degree of inequality among people that is considered to be normal. Cultures with small power distance, such as those of Denmark and Israel, seek to eliminate inequalities in power and wealth as much as possible, whereas countries with large power distances, such as India and the Philippines, seek to maintain those differences.

Differences in power distance often result in miscommunication and conflicts between people from different cultures. For example, in Mexico and Japan individuals are always addressed by their titles (Señor Smith or Smith-san, respectively). Individuals from the United States, however, often believe in minimizing power distances by using first names. Although this is perfectly normal, and possibly even advisable in the United States, it can be offensive and a sign of disrespect in other cultures.

The third dimension, **uncertainty avoidance**, describes how cultures seek to deal with the fact that the future is not perfectly predictable. It is defined as the degree to which people in a culture prefer structured over unstructured situations. Some cultures, such as those of Singapore and Jamaica, have weak uncertainty avoidance. They socialize individuals to accept this uncertainty and take each day as it comes. People from these cultures tend to be rather easygoing and flexible regarding different views. Other cultures, such as

Individualism–collectivism
One of Hofstede's cultural dimensions; describes the strength of the relation between an individual and other individuals in a society.

Power distance
One of Hofstede's cultural dimensions; concerns how a culture deals with hierarchical power relationships—particularly the unequal distribution of power.

Uncertainty avoidance
One of Hofstede's cultural dimensions; describes how cultures seek to deal with an unpredictable future.

Table 15.2
Cultural Dimension Scores for 10 Countries

	PD[a]	ID	MA	UA	LT
United States	40 L[b]	91 H	62 H	46 L	29 L
Germany	35 L	67 H	66 H	65 M	31 M
Japan	54 M	45 M	95 H	92 H	80 H
France	68 H	71 H	43 M	86 H	30[c] L
Netherlands	38 L	80 H	14 L	53 M	44 M
Hong Kong	68 H	25 L	57 H	29 L	96 H
Indonesia	78 H	14 L	46 M	48 L	25[c] L
West Africa	77 H	20 L	46 M	54 M	16 L
Russia	95[c] H	50[c] M	40[c] L	90[c] H	10[c] L
China	80[c] H	20[c] L	50[c] M	60[c] M	118 H

[a]PD = power distance; ID = individualism; MA = masculinity; UA = uncertainty avoidance; LT = long-term orientation.
[b]H = top third; M = medium third; L = bottom third (among 53 countries and regions for the first four dimensions; among 23 countries for the fifth).
[c]Estimated.
SOURCE: From Geert Hofstede, "Cultural Constraints in Management Theories," *Academy of Management Executive,* February 1993, Vol. 7, No. 1, p. 91. Reproduced with permission of Academy of Management, via Copyright Clearance Center.

those of Greece and Portugal, socialize their people to seek security through technology, law, and religion. Thus, these cultures provide clear rules as to how one should behave.

Masculinity–femininity dimension
One of Hofstede's cultural dimensions; describes the division of roles between the sexes within a society.

The **masculinity–femininity dimension** describes the division of roles between the sexes within a society. In "masculine" cultures, such as those of Germany and Japan, what are considered traditionally masculine values—showing off, achieving something visible, and making money—permeate the society. These societies stress assertiveness, performance, success, and competition. "Feminine" cultures, such as those of Sweden and Norway, promote values that have been traditionally regarded as feminine, such as putting relationships before money, helping others, and preserving the environment. These cultures stress service, care for the weak, and solidarity.

Long-term–short-term orientation
One of Hofstede's cultural dimensions; describes how a culture balances immediate benefits with future rewards.

Finally, the fifth dimension comes from the philosophy of the Far East and is referred to as the **long-term–short-term orientation**. Cultures high on the long-term orientation focus on the future and hold values in the present that will not necessarily provide an immediate benefit, such as thrift (saving) and persistence. Hofstede found that many Far Eastern countries such as Japan and China have a long-term orientation. Short-term orientations, by contrast, are found in the United States, Russia, and West Africa. These cultures are oriented toward the past and present and promote respect for tradition and for fulfilling social obligations.

The current Japanese criticism of management practices in the United States illustrates the differences in long-term–short-term orientation. Japanese managers, traditionally exhibiting a long-term orientation, engage in 5- to 10-year planning. This leads them to criticize U.S. managers, who are traditionally much more short-term in orientation because their planning often consists of quarterly to yearly time horizons.

These five dimensions help us understand the potential problems of managing employees from different cultures. Later in this chapter we will explore how these cultural dimensions affect the acceptability and utility of various HRM practices. However, it is important to note that these differences can have a profound influence on whether a company chooses to enter a given country. One interesting finding of Hofstede's research was the impact of culture on a country's economic health. He found that countries with individualist cultures were more wealthy. Collectivist cultures with high power distance were all poor.[16] Cultures seem to affect a country's economy through their promotion of individual work ethics and incentives for individuals to increase their human capital.

Implications of Culture for HRM

Cultures have an important impact on approaches to managing people. As we discuss later, the culture can strongly affect the education–human capital of a country, the political–legal system, and the economic system. As Hofstede found, culture also has a profound impact on a country's economic health by promoting certain values that either aid or inhibit economic growth.

More important to this discussion, however, is that cultural characteristics influence the ways managers behave in relation to subordinates, as well as the perceptions of the appropriateness of various HRM practices. First, cultures differ strongly on such things as how subordinates expect leaders to lead, how decisions are handled within the hierarchy, and (most important) what motivates individuals. For example, in Germany, managers achieve their status by demonstrating technical skills, so employees look to them to assign their tasks and resolve technical problems. In the Netherlands, by contrast, managers focus on seeking consensus among all parties and must engage in an open-ended exchange of views and balancing of interests.[17] Clearly, these methods have different implications for selecting and training managers in the different countries.

Second, cultures may influence the appropriateness of HRM practices. For example, as discussed previously, the extent to which a culture promotes an individualistic versus a collectivist orientation will impact the effectiveness of individually oriented HRM systems. In the United States, companies often focus selection systems on assessing an individual's technical skill and, to a lesser extent, social skills. In collectivist cultures, by contrast, companies focus more on assessing how well an individual will perform as a member of the work group.

Culture often influences how employees value certain aspects of their work environment. In an interesting study comparing call center workers in India (a collectivist culture) and the United States (an individualistic culture), researchers found that in the United States person–job fit was the stronger predictor of turnover relative to India, where person–organization fit, links to the organization, and links to the community were the stronger predictors of turnover.[18]

Similarly, cultures can influence compensation systems. Individualistic cultures such as those found in the United States often exhibit great differences between the highest- and lowest-paid individuals in an organization, with the highest-paid individual often receiving 200 times the salary of the lowest. Collectivist cultures tend to have much flatter salary structures, with the top-paid individual receiving only about 20 times the overall pay of the lowest-paid one.

Cultural differences can affect the communication and coordination processes in organizations. Collectivist cultures, as well as those with less of an authoritarian orientation, value group decision making and participative management practices more highly than do individualistic cultures. When a person raised in an individualistic culture must work closely with those from a collectivist culture, communication problems and conflicts often appear. Much of the emphasis on "cultural diversity" programs in organizations focuses on understanding the cultures of others in order to better communicate with them.

EVIDENCE-BASED HR

Although national culture is important, research suggests that its importance may be overstated. Researchers reexamining Hofstede's original work found that, in addition to differences across nations, significant cultural differences also existed within nations. They further found that the differences in cultures across organizations within countries was larger than the differences across countries. Their results imply that although one cannot ignore national culture, one must not think that certain HR practices may not be effective simply based on a regard for national culture. People of varying cultural backgrounds within a nation will be drawn to organizations whose cultures better match their individual, as opposed to national, value systems.

In addition, many observers have suggested that the effectiveness of high-performance work systems (HPWS) depends on the cultural or institutional constraints, such that they may be ineffective in cultures that exhibit high power distance or high collectivism. However, a meta-analysis revealed that the effects of HPWS on firm performance were positive in all cultures, and contrary to expectations, if anything, higher in the cultures where the cultural hypothesis suggested they would be lower.

SOURCES: T. Rable, M. Jayasinghe, B. Gerhart, and T. Kuhlmann, "A Meta-Analysis of Country Differences in the High-Performance Work System–Business Performance Relationship: The Roles of National Culture and Managerial Discretion," *Journal of Applied Psychology* 99, no. 6 (2014), pp. 1011–41; B. Gerhart and M. Fang, "National Culture and Human Resource Management Assumptions and Evidence," *International Journal of Human Resource Management* 16, no. 6 (June 2005), pp. 971–86.

EDUCATION—HUMAN CAPITAL

A company's potential to find and maintain a qualified workforce is an important consideration in any decision to expand into a foreign market. Thus, a country's human capital resources can be an important HRM issue. *Human capital* refers to the productive capabilities of individuals—that is, the knowledge, skills, and experience that have economic value.[19]

A country's human capital is determined by a number of variables. A major variable is the educational opportunities available to the labor force. In the Netherlands, for instance, government funding of school systems allows students to go all the way through graduate school without paying.[20] Similarly, the free education provided to citizens in the former Soviet bloc resulted in high levels of human capital, in spite of the poor infrastructure and economy that resulted from the socialist economic systems. In contrast, some developing countries, such as Nicaragua and Haiti, have relatively low levels of human capital because of a lack of investment in education.

A country's human capital may profoundly affect a foreign company's desire to locate there or enter that country's market. Countries with low human capital attract facilities that require low skills and low wage levels. This explains why U.S. companies desire to move their currently unionized low-skill–high-wage manufacturing and assembly jobs to Mexico, where they can obtain low-skilled workers for substantially lower wages. Similarly, Japan ships its messy, low-skill work to neighboring countries while maintaining its high-skill work at home.[21] Countries like Mexico, with relatively low levels of human capital, might not be as attractive for operations that consist of more high-skill jobs.

Countries with high human capital are attractive sites for direct foreign investment that creates high-skill jobs. In Ireland, for example, more than 25% of 18 year olds attend college, a rate much higher than in other European countries. In addition, Ireland's economy supports only 1.1 million jobs for a population of 3.5 million. The combination of high education levels, a strong work ethic, and high unemployment makes the country attractive for foreign firms because of the resulting high productivity and low turnover. The Met Life insurance company set up a facility for Irish workers to analyze medical insurance claims. It has found the high levels of human capital and the high work ethic provide such a competitive advantage that the company is currently looking for other work performed in the United States to be shipped to Ireland. Similarly, as already discussed, the skills of newly graduated technology workers in India are as high as or higher than those found among their counterparts in the United States. In addition, because jobs are not as plentiful in India, the worker attitudes are better in many of these locations.[22]

POLITICAL—LEGAL SYSTEM

The regulations imposed by a country's legal system can strongly affect HRM. The political–legal system often dictates the requirements for certain HRM practices, such as training, compensation, hiring, firing, and layoffs. In large part, the legal system is an outgrowth of the culture in which it exists. Thus, the laws of a particular country often reflect societal norms about what constitutes legitimate behavior.[23] Many countries allow (or even expect) that payoffs be made to decision makers, be they procurement employees or politicians. However, the Foreign Corrupt Practices Act prohibits any American companies from doing so, even if they are doing so in another country. The "Integrity in Action" box shows how Las Vegas Sands got into trouble doing business in China.

Did They Know, or Not Want to Know?

The casino company Las Vegas Sands has settled allegations of violations of antibribery laws to the tune of $6.96 million. The Foreign Corrupt Practices Act bans bribery of state officials, and a company internal review board concluded it had likely violated the act because it did not have appropriate accounting controls. The allegations surround its hiring of a Chinese consultant who was a former government official and paying him $5.8 million although there was no "discernible legitimate business purpose."

Sands wanted to buy a Chinese basketball team as a way to promote its casinos in Macau but were precluded from doing so because they are a gambling entity. They arranged for the consultant to buy the team, but then employees questioned suspicious irregularities in the accounting. In addition, $3.6 million was wired to the consultant's companies from companies controlled by Sands for a building lease. However, the consultant was unable to show that he had purchased the building. A Sands employee and an outside lawyer raised questions about the irregularities. They were then removed and replaced with less experienced employees by a Sands executive in China.

As part of the settlement agreement, Sands no longer employs any of the implicated individuals and has completed extensive remedial measures to ensure compliance in the future.

DISCUSSION QUESTIONS

1. Do you think the company knew what was going on?
2. How should Sands have handled this situation instead?

SOURCE: C. Kirkham and A. Berzon, "Sands to Pay $6.96 Million to Settle U.S. Investigation," *Wall Street Journal,* January 20, 2017, https://www.wsj.com/articles/sands-to-pay-6-96-million-to-settle-u-s-investigation-1484891654.

For example, the United States has led the world in eliminating discrimination in the workplace. Because of the importance this has in our culture, we also have legal safeguards such as equal employment opportunity laws (discussed in Chapter 3) that strongly affect the hiring and firing practices of firms. As a society, we also have strong beliefs regarding the equity of pay systems; thus, the Fair Labor Standards Act (discussed in Chapter 11), among other laws and regulations, sets the minimum wage for a variety of jobs. We have regulations that dictate much of the process for negotiation between unions and management. These regulations profoundly affect how human resources are managed in the United States.

Similarly, the legal regulations regarding HRM in other countries reflect their societal norms. For example, in Germany employees have a legal right to "codetermination" at the company, plant, and individual levels. At the company level, a firm's employees have direct influence on the important decisions that affect them, such as large investments or new strategies. This is brought about through having employee representatives on the supervisory council *(Aufsichtsrat).* At the plant level, codetermination exists through works councils. These councils have no rights in the economic management of the company, but they can influence HRM policies on such issues as working hours, payment methods, hirings, and transfers. Finally, at the individual level, employees have contractual rights, such as the right to read their personnel files and the right to be informed about how their pay is calculated.[24]

The European Economic Community provides another example of the effects of the political–legal system on HRM. The EEC's Community Charter of December 9, 1989, provides for the fundamental social rights of workers. These rights include freedom of movement, freedom to choose one's occupation and be fairly compensated, guarantee of

COMPETING THROUGH SUSTAINABILITY

Company Solutions to the Refugee Crisis

Turmoil all over the Middle East, Northern Africa, and elsewhere has resulted in millions of people who have been displaced from their homes and often their home countries. This refugee issue has created challenges for countries that want to accept them but need to have some assurances that these individuals will not become a strain on social welfare programs. Enter a number of companies in the United States that have committed to helping these refugees.

Approximately 50 companies joined the Partnership for Refugees, created by Barack Obama's administration. This group sought to expand work opportunities for refugees both in the United States and around the globe. However, with the Trump administration's decision to put a hold on refugees, many of these companies decided to continue their efforts on their own. Funded by Chobani's chief executive officer Hamdi Ulukaya, a Turkish immigrant, the coalition of companies such as LinkedIn, MasterCard, and TripAdvisor met to discuss how they could help. For instance, over the next five years Starbucks has committed to hiring 10,000 refugees across its operations in 75 countries. TripAdvisor earmarked $5 million to aid refugees over the next three years, and Airbnb committed $4 million to resettlement agencies going forward. TripAdvisor spokesperson Desiree Fish described the coalition well, saying, "Even though many of us in the partnership are competitors, at the end of the day we're all fighting to do the right thing."

DISCUSSION QUESTIONS

1. Many of these companies have been criticized for giving jobs that Americans could do to refugees.
2. Do you think this is a good idea? Why or why not?

SOURCE: K. Gee, "Big Employers Go It Alone in Push to Help Refugees," *Wall Street Journal*, February 7, 2017, https://www.wsj.com/articles/big-employers-go-it-alone-in-push-to-help-refugees-1486479600.

social protection via social security benefits, freedom of association and collective bargaining, equal treatment for men and women, and a safe and healthful work environment, among others.

The recent instability and fighting in Syria and other areas has created a refugee crisis as millions of people flee their home countries for other countries that may provide a safe environment. The European Union states have accepted a number of these refugees, far more than the United States, where refugee immigration has been capped by the Trump administration at 50,000. However, a number of companies have stepped up to try to help those refugees who do gain entry to the United States, as described in the "Competing through Sustainability" box.

ECONOMIC SYSTEM

A country's economic system influences HRM in a number of ways. As previously discussed, a country's culture is tied integrally to its economic system, and these systems provide many of the incentives for developing human capital. In socialist economic systems there are ample opportunities for developing human capital because the education system is free. However, under these systems, there is little economic incentive to develop human capital because there are no monetary rewards for increasing human capital. In addition, in former Soviet bloc countries, an individual's investment in human capital did not always result in a promotion. Rather, it was investment in the Communist Party that led to career advancements.

In capitalist systems the opposite situation exists. There is less opportunity to develop human capital without higher costs. (You have probably observed tuition increases at U.S. universities.) However, those who do invest in their individual human capital, particularly through education, are more able to reap monetary rewards, thus providing more incentive for such investment. In the United States, individuals' salaries usually reflect differences in human capital (high-skill workers receive higher compensation than low-skill workers). In fact, research estimates that an individual's wages increase by between 10% and 16% for each additional year of schooling.[25]

In addition to the effects of an economic system on HRM, the health of the system can have an important impact. For example, we referred earlier to lower labor costs in India. In developed countries with a high level of wealth, labor costs tend to be quite high relative to those in developing countries. Although labor costs are related to the human capital of a country, they are not perfectly related, as shown by Figure 15.2. This chart provides a good example of the different hourly labor costs for manufacturing jobs in various countries.

An economic system also affects HRM directly through its taxes on compensation packages. Thus, the differential labor costs shown in Figure 15.2 do not always reflect the actual take-home pay of employees. Socialist systems are characterized by tax systems that redistribute wealth by taking a higher percentage of a person's income as he or she moves up the economic ladder. Capitalist systems attempt to reward

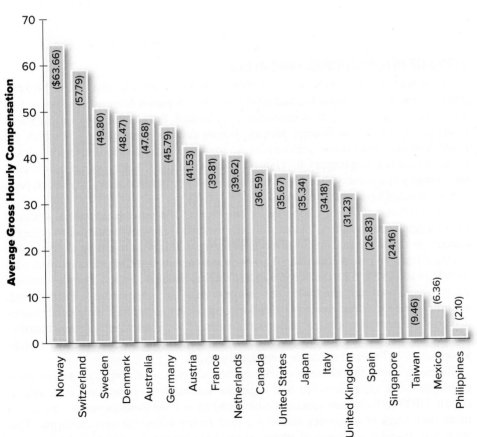

Figure 15.2

Hourly Compensation Costs in Manufacturing, U.S. Dollars, 2012

SOURCE: U.S. Bureau of Labor Statistics, www.bls.gov/news.release/pdf/ichcc.pdf.

individuals for their efforts by allowing them to keep more of their earnings. Companies that do business in other countries have to present compensation packages to expatriate managers that are competitive in take-home, rather than gross, pay. HRM responses to these issues affecting expatriate managers will be discussed in more detail later in this chapter.

These differences in economies can have a profound impact on pay systems, particularly among global companies seeking to develop an international compensation and reward system that maintains cost controls while enabling local operations to compete in the war for talent. One recent study examining how compensation managers design these systems indicates that they look at a number of factors including the global firm strategy, the local regulatory and political context, institutions and stakeholders, local markets, and national culture. While they try to learn from the best practices that exist globally, they balance these approaches with the constraints imposed by the local environment.[26]

In conclusion, every country varies in terms of its culture, education–human capital, poltical–legal system, and economic system. These variations directly influence the types of HRM systems that must be developed to accommodate the particular situation. The extent to which these differences affect a company depends on how involved the company is in global markets. In the next section we discuss important concepts of global business and various levels of global participation, particularly noting how these factors come into play.

Managing Employees in a Global Context
TYPES OF INTERNATIONAL EMPLOYEES

Before discussing the levels of global participation, we need to distinguish between parent countries, host countries, and third countries. A **parent country** is the country in which the company's corporate headquarters is located. For example, the United States is the parent country of General Motors. A **host country** is the country in which the parent country organization seeks to locate (or has already located) a facility. Thus, Great Britain is a host country for General Motors because GM has operations there. A **third country** is a country other than the host country or parent country, and a company may or may not have a facility there.

There are also different categories of employees. The term **expatriate** is generally used for employees sent by a company in one country to manage operations in a different country. With the increasing globalization of business, it is now important to distinguish among different types of expatriates. **Parent-country nationals (PCNs)** are employees who were born and live in the parent country. **Host-country nationals (HCNs)** are those employees who were born and raised in the host, as opposed to the parent, country. Finally, **third-country nationals (TCNs)** are employees born in a country other than the parent country and host country but who work in the host country. Thus, a manager born and raised in Brazil employed by an organization located in the United States and assigned to manage an operation in Thailand would be considered a TCN.

Research shows that countries differ in their use of various types of international employees. One study revealed that Japanese multinational firms have more ethnocentric HRM policies and practices (they tend to use Japanese expatriate managers more than local host-country nationals) than either European or U.S. firms. This study also found that the use of ethnocentric HRM practices is associated with more HRM problems.[27]

Parent country
The country in which a company's corporate headquarters is located.

Host country
The country in which the parent-country organization seeks to locate or has already located a facility.

Third country
A country other than a host or parent country.

LO 15-3
List the different categories of international employees.

Expatriate
Employee sent by his or her company to manage operations in a different country.

Parent-country nationals (PCNs)
Employees who were born and live in a parent country.

Host-country nationals (HCNs)
Employees born and raised in a host, not parent, country.

Third-country nationals (TCNs)
Employees born in a country other than a parent or host country.

LEVELS OF GLOBAL PARTICIPATION

We often hear companies referred to as "multinational" or "international." However, it is important to understand the different levels of participation in international markets. This is especially important because as a company becomes more involved in international trade, different types of HRM problems arise. In this section we examine Nancy Adler's categorization of the various levels of international participation from which a company may choose.[28] Figure 15.3 depicts these levels of involvement.

Domestic

Most companies begin by operating within a domestic marketplace. For example, an entrepreneur may have an idea for a product that meets a need in the U.S. marketplace. This individual then obtains capital to build a facility that produces the product or service in a quantity that meets the needs of a small market niche. This requires recruiting, hiring, training, and compensating a number of individuals who will be involved in the production process, and these individuals are usually drawn from the local labor market. The focus of the selection and training programs is often on the employees' technical competence to perform job-related duties and to some extent on interpersonal skills. In addition, because the company is usually involved in only one labor market, determining the market rate of pay for various jobs is relatively easy.

As the product grows in popularity, the owner might choose to build additional facilities in different parts of the country to reduce the costs of transporting the product over large distances. In deciding where to locate these facilities, the owner must consider the attractiveness of the local labor markets. Various parts of the country may have different cultures that make those areas more or less attractive according to the work ethics of the potential employees. Similarly, the human capital in the different areas may vary greatly because of differences in educational systems. Finally, local pay rates may differ. It is for these reasons that the U.S. economy in the past 10 years has experienced a movement of jobs from northern states, which are characterized by strong unions and high labor costs, to the Sunbelt states, which have lower labor costs and are less unionized.

LO 15-4
Identify the four levels of global participation and the HRM issues faced within each level.

Figure 15.3
Levels of Global Participation

Incidentally, even domestic companies face problems with cultural diversity. In the United States, for example, the representation of women and minorities is increasing within the workforce. These groups come to the workplace with worldviews that differ from those of the traditional white male. Thus, we are seeing more and more emphasis on developing systems for managing cultural diversity within single-country organizations, even though the diversity might be on a somewhat smaller scale than the diversity of cultures across national boundaries.[29]

In a meta-analysis of the effects of cultural diversity on the functioning of multicultural work groups, Stahl and colleagues found that cultural diversity leads to process losses through increased task conflict and decreased social integration. At the same time, it leads to process gains through increasing creativity and satisfaction.[30]

It is important to note that companies functioning at the domestic level face an environment with very similar cultural, education–human capital, political–legal, and economic situations, although some variation might be observed across states and geographic areas.

International

As more competitors enter the domestic market, companies face the possibility of losing market share; thus, they often seek other markets for their products. This usually requires entering international markets, initially by exporting products but ultimately by building production facilities in other countries. The decision to participate in international competition raises a host of human resource issues. All the problems regarding locating facilities are magnified. One must consider whether a particular location provides an environment where human resources can be successfully acquired and managed.

Now the company faces an entirely different situation with regard to culture, education–human capital, the political–legal system, and the economic system. For example, the availability of human capital is of utmost importance, and there is a substantially greater variability in human capital between the United States and other countries than there is among the various states in the United States.

A country's legal system may also present HRM problems. For example, France has a relatively high minimum wage, which drives up labor costs. In addition, regulations make it extremely difficult to fire or lay off an employee. In Germany companies are legally required to offer employees influence in the management of the firm. Companies that develop facilities in other countries have to adapt their HRM practices to conform to the host country's laws. This requires the company to gain expertise in the country's HRM legal requirements and knowledge about how to deal with the country's legal system, and it often requires the company to hire one or more host-country nationals. In fact, some countries legally require companies to hire a certain percentage of HCNs for any foreign-owned subsidiary.

Finally, cultures have to be considered. To the extent that the country's culture is vastly different from that of the parent organization, conflicts, communication problems, and morale problems may occur. Expatriate managers must be trained to identify these cultural differences, and they must be flexible enough to adapt their styles to those of their host country. This requires an extensive selection effort to identify individuals who are capable of adapting to new environments and an extensive training program to ensure that the culture shock is not devastating.

Multinational

Whereas international companies build one or a few facilities in another country, they become multinational when they build facilities in a number of different countries, attempting to capitalize on lower production and distribution costs in different locations.

The lower production costs are gained by shifting production from higher-cost locations to lower-cost locations. For example, some of the major U.S. automakers have plants all over the world. They continue to shift their production from the United States, where labor unions have gained high wages for their members, to *maquiladora* facilities in Mexico, where the wages are substantially lower. Similarly, these companies minimize distribution and labor costs by locating facilities in central and eastern European countries such as Poland, Hungary, and the Slovak Republic for manufacturing and assembling automobiles to sell in the European market.

The HRM problems multinational companies face are similar to those international companies face, only magnified. Instead of having to consider only one or two countries' cultural, education–human capital, political–legal, and economic systems, the multinational company must address these differences for a large number of countries. This accentuates the need to select managers capable of functioning in a variety of settings, give them necessary training, and provide flexible compensation systems that take into account the different market pay rates, tax systems, and costs of living.

Multinational companies now employ many "inpatriates"—managers from different countries who become part of the corporate headquarters staff. This creates a need to integrate managers from different cultures into the culture of the parent company. In addition, multinational companies now take more expatriates from countries other than the parent country and place them in facilities of other countries. For example, a manager from Scotland, working for a U.S. company, might be assigned to run an operation in South Africa. This practice accentuates the need for cross-cultural training to provide managerial skills for interaction with individuals from different cultures.

Global

Many researchers now propose a fourth level of integration: global organizations. Global organizations compete on state-of-the-art, top-quality products and services and do so with the lowest costs possible. Whereas multinational companies attempt to develop identical products distributed worldwide, global companies increasingly emphasize flexibility and mass customization of products to meet the needs of particular clients. Multinational companies are usually driven to locate facilities in a country as a means of reaching that country's market or lowering production costs, and the company must deal with the differences across the countries. Global firms, by contrast, choose to locate a facility based on the ability to effectively, efficiently, and flexibly produce a product or service and attempt to create synergy through the cultural differences.

This creates the need for HRM systems that encourage flexible production (thus presenting a host of HRM issues). These companies proactively consider the cultures, education–human capital, political–legal systems, and economic systems to determine where production facilities can be located to provide a competitive advantage. Global companies have multiple headquarters spread across the globe, resulting in less hierarchically structured organizations that emphasize decentralized decision making. This results in the need for human resource systems that recruit, develop, retain, and use managers and executives who are competent transnationally.

A transnational HRM system is characterized by three attributes.[31] **Transnational scope** refers to the fact that HRM decisions must be made from a global rather than a national or regional perspective. This creates the need to make decisions that balance the need for uniformity (to ensure fair treatment of all employees) with the need for flexibility (to meet the needs of employees in different countries). **Transnational representation** reflects the multinational composition of a company's managers. Global participation does not necessarily ensure that

Transnational scope
A company's ability to make HRM decisions from an international perspective.

Transnational representation
Reflects the multinational composition of a company's managers.

each country is providing managers to the company's ranks. This is a prerequisite if the company is to achieve the next attribute. **Transnational process** refers to the extent to which the company's planning and decision-making processes include representatives and ideas from a variety of cultures. This attribute allows for diverse viewpoints and knowledge associated with different cultures, increasing the quality of decision making.

These three characteristics are necessary for global companies to achieve cultural synergy. Rather than simply integrating foreigners into the domestic organization, a successful transnational company needs managers who will treat managers from other cultures as equals. This synergy can be accomplished only by combining selection, training, appraisal, and compensation systems in such a way that managers have a transnational rather than a parochial orientation. However, a survey of 50 companies in the United States and Canada found that global companies' HRM systems are far less transnational in scope, representation, and process than the companies' strategic planning systems and organizational structures.[32]

In conclusion, entry into international markets creates a host of HRM issues that must be addressed if a company is to gain competitive advantage. Once the choice has been made to compete in a global arena, companies must seek to manage employees who are sent to foreign countries (expatriates and third-country nationals). This causes the need to shift from focusing only on the culture, education–human capital, political–legal, and economic influences of the host country to examining ways to manage the expatriate managers who must be located there. Selection systems must be developed that allow the company to identify managers capable of functioning in a new culture. These managers must be trained to identify the important aspects of the new culture in which they will live as well as the relevant legal–political and economic systems. Finally, these managers must be compensated to offset the costs of uprooting themselves and their families to move to a new situation vastly different from their previous lives. In the next section we address issues regarding management of expatriates.

MANAGING EXPATRIATES IN GLOBAL MARKETS

We have outlined the major macro-level factors that influence HRM in global markets. These factors can affect a company's decision whether to build facilities in a given country. In addition, if a company does develop such facilities, these factors strongly affect the HRM practices used. However, an important issue recognized over the past few years is the set of problems inherent in selecting, training, compensating, and reintegrating expatriate managers.

According to a study by the National Foreign Trade Council (NFTC), there were 250,000 Americans on assignments overseas and that number was expected to increase. In addition, the NFTC estimates that the average one-time cost for relocating an expatriate is $60,000.[33] The importance to the company's profitability of making the right expatriate assignments should not be underestimated. Expatriate managers' average compensation package is approximately $250,000,[34] and the cost of an unsuccessful expatriate assignment (that is, a manager returning early) is approximately $100,000.[35] The failure rate for expatriate assignments among U.S. firms had been estimated at between 15% and 40%. However, more recent research suggests that the current figure is much lower. Some recent studies of European multinationals put the rate at 5% for most firms. Although the failure rate is generally recognized as higher among U.S. multinationals, it is doubtful that the proportion reaches the 15–40% range.[36]

In the final section of the chapter, we discuss the major issues relevant to the management of expatriate managers. These issues cover the selection, training, compensation, and reacculturation of expatriates.

Selection of Expatriate Managers

One of the major problems in managing expatriate managers is determining which individuals in the organization are most capable of handling an assignment in a different culture. Expatriate managers must have technical competence in the area of operations; otherwise, they will be unable to earn the respect of subordinates. However, technical competence has been almost the sole variable used in deciding who to send on overseas assignments, despite the fact that multiple skills are necessary for successful performance in these assignments.[37]

According to Brookfield Global Relocation Services's 2016 Global Mobility Trends report, almost 80% of companies do not formally assess international assignment candidates in terms of their adaptability, and only 20% use a candidate's self-assessment of their adaptability. Also, 48% are unsure if the attrition rate of their expatriates is higher than the attrition rate in the rest of their workforce.

A successful expatriate manager must be sensitive to the country's cultural norms, flexible enough to adapt to those norms, and strong enough to make it through the inevitable culture shock. In addition, the manager's family must be similarly capable of adapting to the new culture. These adaptive skills have been categorized into three dimensions:[38] (1) *the self dimension* (the skills that enable a manager to maintain a positive self-image and psychological well-being), (2) *the relationship dimension* (the skills required to foster relationships with the host-country nationals), and (3) *the perception dimension* (those skills that enable a manager to accurately perceive and evaluate the host environment). One study of international assignees found that they considered the following five factors to be important, in descending order of importance: family situation, flexibility and adaptability, job knowledge and motivation, relational skills, and extracultural openness.[39] Table 15.3 presents a series of considerations and questions to ask potential expatriate managers to assess their ability to adapt to a new cultural environment.

One construct that has been emerging in the expatriate literature is cultural intelligence (CQ). This characteristic refers to an individual's ability to adapt across cultures through sensing the different cues regarding appropriate behavior across cultural settings or in multicultural settings. In fact, one set of researchers found that CQ was related to cultural adjustment and task performance among a sample of international executives.[40]

Little evidence suggests that U.S. companies have invested much effort in attempting to make correct expatriate selections. One researcher found that only 5% of the firms surveyed administered any tests to determine the degree to which expatriate candidates possessed cross-cultural skills.[41] More recent research reveals that only 35% of firms choose expatriates from multiple candidates and that those firms emphasize only technical job-related experience and skills in making these decisions.[42] These findings glaringly demonstrate that U.S. organizations need to improve their success rate in overseas assignments. As discussed in Chapter 6, the technology for assessing individuals' knowledge, skills, and abilities has advanced. The potential for selection testing to decrease the failure rate and productivity problems of U.S. expatriate managers seems promising. For instance, research has examined the "Big Five" personality dimensions as predictors of expatriate success (remember these from Chapter 6). For instance, one study distinguished between expatriate success as measured by not terminating the assignment and success as measured by supervisory evaluations of the expatriate. The researcher found that agreeableness, emotional stability, and extraversion were negatively related to the desire to terminate the assignment (i.e., they wanted to stay on the assignment longer), and conscientiousness was positively related to supervisory evaluations of the expatriate.[43]

A final issue with regard to expatriate selection is the use of women in expatriate assignments. For a long time, U.S. firms believed that women would not be successful managers in countries where women have not traditionally been promoted to management positions (such

Table 15.3
Select Topics for Assessing Candidates for Overseas Assignments

Motivation
- What are the candidate's reasons and degree of interest in wanting an overseas assignment?
- Does the candidate have a realistic understanding of what is required in working and living overseas?
- What is the spouse's attitude toward an overseas assignment?

Health
- Are there any health issues with the candidate or family members that might impact the success of the overseas assignment?

Language ability
- Does the candidate have the potential to learn a new language?
- Does the candidate's spouse have the ability to learn a new language?

Family considerations
- How many moves has the family made among different cities or parts of the United States? What problems were encountered?
- What is the spouse's goal in this move overseas?
- How many children are in the family, and what are their ages? Will all the children move as part of the overseas assignment?
- Has divorce or its potential, or the death of a family member, had a negative effect on the family's cohesiveness?
- Are there any adjustment problems the candidate would expect, should the family move overseas?

Resourcefulness and initiative
- Is the candidate independent and capable of standing by his or her decisions?
- Is the candidate able to meet objectives and produce positive results with whatever human resources and facilities are available regardless of challenges that might arise in a foreign business environment?
- Can the candidate operate without a clear definition of responsibility and authority?
- Will the candidate be able to explain the goals of the company and its mission to local managers and workers?
- Does the candidate possess sufficient self-discipline and self-confidence to handle complex problems?
- Can the candidate operate effectively in a foreign country without normal communications and supporting services?

Adaptability
- Is the candidate cooperative, open to the opinions of others, and able to compromise?
- How does the candidate react to new situations and efforts to understand and appreciate cultural differences?
- How does the candidate react to criticism, constructive or otherwise?
- Will the candidate be able to make and develop contacts with peers in a foreign country?
- Does the candidate demonstrate patience when dealing with problems? Is he or she resilient and able to move forward after setbacks?

Career planning
- Does the candidate consider the assignment more than a temporary overseas trip?
- Is the overseas assignment consistent with the candidate's career development and one that was planned by the company?
- What is the candidate's overall attitude toward the company?
- Is there any history or indication of interpersonal problems with this candidate?

Financial
- Are there any current financial and/or legal considerations that might affect the assignment (e.g., house or car purchase, college expenses)?
- Will undue financial pressures be put upon the candidate and his or her family as a result of an overseas assignment?

SOURCES: P. Caligiuri, *Cultural Agility: Building a Pipeline of Successful Global Professionals* (San Francisco: Jossey-Bass, 2012); P. Caligiuri, D. Lepak, and J. Bonache, *Managing the Global Workforce* (West Sussex, United Kingdom: John Wiley & Sons, 2010); M. Shaffer, D. Harrison, H. Gregersen, S. Black, and L. Ferzandi, "You Can Take It with You: Individual Differences and Expatriate Effectiveness," *Journal of Applied Psychology* 91 (2006), pp. 109–25; P. Caligiuri, "Developing Global Leaders," *Human Resource Management Review* 16 (2006), pp. 219–28; P. Caligiuri, M. Hyland, A. Joshi, and A. Bross, "Testing a Theoretical Model for Examining the Relationship between Family Adjustment and Expatriates' Work Adjustment," *Journal of Applied Psychology* 83 (1998), pp. 598–614; David M. Noer, *Multinational People Management: A Guide for Organizations and Employees* (Arlington, VA: Bureau of National Affairs, 1975).

as in Japan and other Asian countries). However, recent evidence indicates that this is not true. Robin Abrams, an expatriate manager for Apple Computer's Hong Kong office, states that nobody cares whether "you are wearing trousers or a skirt if you have demonstrated core competencies." In fact, some women believe that the novelty of their presence among a group of men increases their credibility with locals. In fact, some research suggests that male and female expatriates can perform equally well in international assignments, regardless of the country's cultural predispositions toward women in management. However, female expatriates self-rate their adjustment lower in countries that have few women in the workforce.[44] Research has shown that female expatriates were perceived as being effective regardless of the cultural toughness of the host country.[45] The fact is that female expatriates feel more strongly than their supervisors that prejudice does not limit women's ability to be successful.[46]

Training and Development of Expatriates

Once an expatriate manager has been selected, it is necessary to prepare that manager for the upcoming assignment. Because these individuals already have job-related skills, some firms have focused development efforts on cross-cultural training. A review of the cross-cultural training literature found support for the belief that cross-cultural training has an impact on effectiveness.[47] Even so, cross-cultural training is hardly universal. According to one survey, 69% of the 150 respondent companies offered cultural training for their outbound employees.[48]

What exactly is emphasized in cross-cultural training programs? The details regarding these programs were discussed in Chapter 7. Most programs attempt to create an appreciation of the host country's culture so that expatriates can behave appropriately.[49] This entails emphasizing a few aspects of cultural sensitivity. First, expatriates must be clear about their own cultural background, particularly as it is perceived by the host nationals. With an accurate cultural self-awareness, managers can modify their behavior to accentuate the effective characteristics while minimizing those that are dysfunctional.[50]

Second, expatriates must understand the particular aspects of culture in the new work environment. Although culture is an elusive, almost invisible phenomenon, astute expatriate managers must perceive the culture and adapt their behavior to it. This entails identifying the types of behaviors and interpersonal styles that are considered acceptable in both business meetings and social gatherings. For example, Germans value promptness for meetings to a much greater extent than do Latin Americans. Table 15.4 displays some ways body language conveys different messages in different countries.

Table 15.4
International Body Language

COUNTRY	NONVERBAL MESSAGES
Argentina	If the waiter approaches pointing to the side of his head and making a spinning gesture with his finger, don't think he's lost it—he's trying to say you have a phone call.
Bangladesh	Bursting to go to the toilet? Hold it. It is considered very rude to excuse yourself from the table to use the bathroom.
Bolivia	Don't make "the sign of the fig" (thumb protruding between index and middle finger), historically a sign that you couldn't care less—it is very insulting.
Bulgaria	Bulgarians nod the head up and down to mean no, not yes. To say yes, a Bulgarian nods the head back and forth.

(continued)

Table 15.4

International Body Language (*concluded*)

COUNTRY	NONVERBAL MESSAGES
China	In Eastern culture, silence really can be golden. So don't panic if long periods of silence form part of your meeting with Chinese clients. It simply means they are considering your proposal carefully.
Egypt	Because across the Arab world the left hand is unclean, use your right to accept business cards and to greet someone. Use only your right hand for eating.
Fiji	To show respect to your Fijian hosts when addressing them, stand with your arms folded behind your back.
France	The French don't like strong handshakes, preferring a short, light grip or air kissing. If your French colleague is seen to be playing an imaginary flute, however, it means he thinks you are not being truthful.
Germany	When Germans meet across a large conference table and it is awkward to reach over and shake hands, they will instead rap their knuckles lightly on the table by way of a greeting.
Greece	Beware of making the okay sign to Greek colleagues as it signifies bodily orifices. A safer bet is the thumbs-up sign. The thumbs-down, however, is the kind of gesture reserved for when a Greek motorist cuts you off on the highway.
Hong Kong	When trying to attract someone's attention, don't use your index finger with palm extended upward. This is how the Cantonese call their dogs.
India	Beware of whistling in public—it is the height of rudeness here.
Japan	Japan is a real minefield for Western businesspeople, but one that always gets to them is the way the Japanese heartily slurp their noodles at lunch. Far from being rude, it actually shows appreciation of the food in Japanese culture.
Jordan	No matter how hungry you are, it is customary to refuse seconds from your host twice before finally accepting a third time.
Lebanon	Itchy eyebrow? Don't scratch it. Licking your little finger and brushing it across your eyebrow is provocative.
Malaysia	If you find a Malaysian standing with hands on hips before you, you've clearly said something wrong. It means he's livid.
Mexico	Mexicans are very tactile and often perform a bizarre handshake whereby, after pressing together the palms, they will slide their hands upward to grasp each other's thumbs.
Netherlands	The Dutch may seem open-minded, but if Dutch people tap the underside of their elbow, it means they think you're unreliable.
Pakistan	The overt display of a closed fist is an incitement to war.
Philippines	The "Roger Moore" is a common greeting here—a quick flash of the eyebrows supersedes the need for handshakes.
Russia	The Russians are highly tactile meet and greeters, with bear hugs and kisses directly on the lips commonplace. Don't take this habit to nearby Uzbekistan, however. They'd probably shoot you.
Saudi Arabia	If a Saudi man takes another's hand on the street, it's a sign of mutual respect.
Samoa	When your new Samoan host offers you a cup of the traditional drink, kava, make sure to deliberately spill a few drops on the ground before taking your first sip.
Turkey	Be careful not to lean back on your chair and point the sole of your foot at anyone in a meeting in Istanbul. Pointing with the underside of the foot is highly insulting.

SOURCES: K. Elkins and M. Nudelman, "The Shocking Differences in Basic Body Language Around the World," *Business Insider,* March 17, 2015, http://www.businessinsider.com/body-language-around-the-world-2015-3; R. Axtell, *Gestures: The Dos and Taboos of Body Language Around the World,* (New York: Wiley, 1991); P. Harris and R. Moran, *Managing Cultural Differences,* 3rd ed. (Houston, TX: Gulf Publishing, 1991); R. Linowes, "The Japanese Manager's Traumatic Entry into the United States: Understanding the American-Japanese Cultural Divide," *Academy of Management Executive* 7, no. 4 (1993), p. 26; D. Doke, "Perfect Strangers," *HR Magazine*, December 2004, pp. 62–68.

Table 15.5
Expatriate Adjustment
Factors

Work Environment (the employees, culture, and climate where the expatriate works)

Language (the ability of the expatriate to communicate effectively)

Job or Task Characteristics (the expatriate's freedom, autonomy and variety in how they work)

Leisure Time (opportunities to engage in sports, hobbies and other leisure activities)

Urbanity (pollution, traffic, and beauty of the location)

Work-Life Balance (ability to balance time spent at work and with family)

Living Quarters (size and type of living accommodations)

Family Life (family cohesion and harmony with partner)

Local Friendships (number and depth of local friendships)

Contact to Those Left Behind (ability to maintain relationships with family and friends in the home country)

SOURCE: Hippler, T., Caligiuri, P., Johnson, J., Baytalskaya, N. (2014). The development and validation of a theory-based expatriate adjustment scale. *International Journal of Human Resource management, 25*(14), 1938-1959.

Finally, expatriates must learn to communicate accurately in the new culture. Some firms attempt to use expatriates who speak the language of the host country, and a few provide language training. However, most companies simply assume that the host-country nationals all speak the parent-country's language. Although this assumption might be true, seldom do these nationals speak the parent-country language fluently. Thus, expatriate managers must be trained to communicate with others when language barriers exist.

Recent research has validated some of the most important expatriate adjustment factors. These are listed in Table 15.5.

Effective cross-cultural training helps ease an expatriate's transition to the new work environment. It can also help avoid costly mistakes, such as the expatriate who attempted to bring two bottles of brandy into the Muslim country of Qatar. The brandy was discovered by customs; not only was the expatriate deported, but the company also was "disinvited" from the country.[51]

Compensation of Expatriates

One of the more troublesome aspects of managing expatriates is determining the compensation package. As discussed previously, these packages average $250,000, but it is necessary to examine their exact breakdown. Most use a balance sheet approach to determine the total package level. This approach entails developing a total compensation package that equalizes the purchasing power of the expatriate manager with that of employees in similar positions in the home country and provides incentives to offset the inconveniences incurred in the location. Purchasing power includes all of the expenses associated with the expatriate assignment. Expenses include goods and services (food, personal care, clothing, recreation, and transportation), housing (for a principal residence), income taxes (paid to federal and local governments), reserve (savings, payments for benefits, pension contributions), and shipment and storage (costs associated with moving and/or storing personal belongings). A typical balance sheet is shown in Figure 15.4.

As you can see from this figure, the employee starts with a set of costs for taxes, housing, goods and services, and reserve. However, in the host country, these costs are significantly higher. Thus, the company must make up the difference between costs in the home and those in the host country, and then provide a premium and/or incentive for the employee to go through the trouble of living in a different environment.

Figure 15.4

The Balance Sheet for Determining Expatriate Compensation

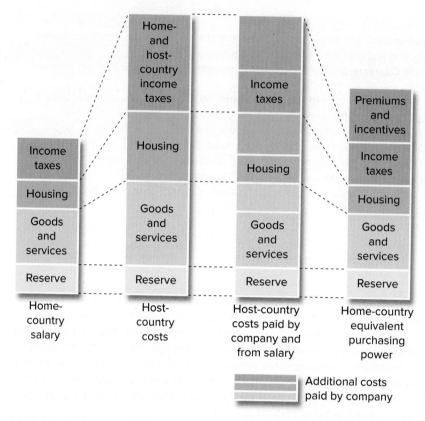

SOURCE: From C. Reynolds, "Compensation of Overseas Personnel," in J. J. Famulari, ed., *Handbook of Human Resource Administration,* 2nd ed., 1986. Copyright © 1986. Reproduced with permission of The McGraw-Hill Companies, Inc.

Total pay packages have four components. First, there is the base salary. Determining the base salary is not a simple matter, however. Fluctuating exchange rates between countries may make an offered salary a raise some of the time, a pay cut at other times. In addition, the base salary may be based on comparable pay in the parent country, or it may be based on the prevailing market rates for the job in the host country. Expatriates are often offered a salary premium beyond that of their present salary as an inducement to accept the expatriate assignment.

Tax equalization allowances are a second component. They are necessary because of countries' different taxation systems in high-tax countries. For example, a senior executive earning $100,000 in Belgium (with a maximum marginal tax rate of 70.8%) could cost a company almost $1 million in taxes over five to seven years.[52] Under most tax equalization plans, the company withholds the amount of tax to be paid in the home country, then pays all of the taxes accrued in the host country.

A third component, benefits, presents additional compensation problems. Most of the problems have to do with the transportability of the benefits. For example, if an expatriate contributing to a pension plan in the United States is moved to a different country, does the individual have a new pension in the host country, or should the individual be allowed to contribute to the existing pension in her home country? What about health care systems located in the United States? How does the company ensure that expatriate employees have equal health care coverage? For example, in one company, the different health care plans available resulted in situations where it might cost significantly less to have the

CITY, COUNTRY	WCOL INDEX	RANK	RANK MOVEMENT (SINCE 2016)
Singapore, Singapore	129	1	0
Paris, France	126	2	0
Oslo, Norway	124	3	0
Zurich, Switzerland	121	4	0
Sydney, Australia	120	5	0
Melbourne, Australia	118	6	0
Geneva, Switzerland	116	7	−1
Copenhagen, Denmark	115	8	2
Hong Kong, Hong Kong	113	9	4
Seoul, South Korea	113	9	6

Table 15.6
The 10 Most Expensive Cities (New York = 100)

SOURCE: Economist Intelligence Unit (2015), "Worldwide Cost of Living 2015." www.eiu.com.

employee fly to the United States to have a procedure performed rather than to have it done in the host country. However, the health plans did not allow this alternative.

Finally, allowances are often offered to make the expatriate assignment less unattractive. Cost-of-living allowances are payments that offset the differences in expenditures on day-to-day necessities between the host country and the parent country. For instance, Table 15.6 shows the differences in cost of living among some of the larger international cities. Housing allowances ensure that the expatriate can maintain the same home-country living standard. Education allowances reimburse expatriates for the expense of placing their children in private English-speaking schools. Relocation allowances cover all the expenses of making the actual move to a new country, including transportation to and from the new location, temporary living expenses, and shipping and/or storage of personal possessions. Figure 15.5 illustrates a typical summary sheet for an expatriate manager's compensation package.

The cost of a U.S. expatriate working in another country is approximately three to four times that of a comparable U.S. employee.[53] In addition, "about 38% of multinational companies surveyed by KPMG LLP for its 2006 Global Assignment Policies and Practices say overseas assignment programs are 'more generous than they need to be'."[54] These two facts combined have put pressure on global organizations to rethink their tax equalization strategy and expatriate packages.

Reacculturation of Expatriates

A final issue of importance to managing expatriates is dealing with the reacculturation process when the managers reenter their home country. Reentry is no simple feat. Culture shock takes place in reverse. The individual has changed, the company has changed, and the culture has changed while the expatriate was overseas. According to one source, 60–70% of expatriates did not know what their position would be upon their return, and 46% ended up with jobs that gave them reduced autonomy and authority.[55] Twenty percent of workers want to leave the company when they return from an overseas assignment, and this presents potentially serious morale and productivity problems.[56] In fact, the most recent estimates are that 25% of expatriate managers leave the company within one year of returning from their expatriate assignments.[57] If these repatriates leave, the company has virtually no way to recoup its substantial investment in human capital.[58]

Figure 15.5

International
Assignment
Allowance Form

John H. Doe			1 October 2017	
Name			**Effective date**	
Singapore			Manager, SLS./Serv. AP/ME	
Location of assignment			**Title**	

Houston, Texas	1234	202	202
Home base	**Emp. no.**	**LCA code**	**Tax code**

Reason for Change: International Assignment

	Old	New
Monthly base salary	_____	$5,000.00
Living cost allowance	_____	$1,291.00
Foreign service premium	_____	$ 750.00
Area allowance	_____	-0-
Gross monthly salary	_____	$7,041.00
Housing deduction	_____	$ 500.00
Hypothetical tax	_____	$ 570.00
Other	_____	_____
Net monthly salary	_____	$5,971.00

Prepared by _____   **Date** _____

Vice President, Human Resources _____   **Date** _____

Companies are increasingly making efforts to help expatriates through reacculturation. Two characteristics help in this transition process: communication and validation.[59] *Communication* refers to the extent to which the expatriate receives information and recognizes changes while abroad. The closer the contact with the home organization while abroad, the more proactive, effective, and satisfied the expatriate will be upon reentry. *Validation* refers to the amount of recognition received by the expatriate upon return home. Expatriates who receive recognition from their peers and their bosses for their foreign work and their future potential contribution to the company have fewer troubles with reentry compared with those who are treated as if they were "out of the loop." Given the tremendous investment that firms make in expatriate employees, usually aimed at providing global experience that will help the company, firms certainly do not want to lose expatriates after their assignments have concluded.

A research study noted the role of an expatriate manager's expectations about the expatriate assignment in determining repatriation adjustment and job performance. This study found that managers whose job expectations (constraints and demands in terms of volume and performance standards) and nonwork expectations (living and housing conditions) were met exhibited a greater degree of repatriation adjustment and higher levels of job performance.[60] Monsanto has an extensive repatriation program that begins long before the expatriate returns. The program entails providing extensive information regarding the potential culture shock of repatriation and information on how family members, friends, and the office environment might have changed. Then, a few months after returning, expatriate managers hold "debriefing" sessions with several colleagues to help work through difficulties. Monsanto believes that this program provides them with a source of competitive advantage in international assignments.[61]

In sum, a variety of HR practices can support effective expatriation. In general, the selection system must rigorously assess potential expatriates' skills and personalities and even focus on the candidate's spouse. Training should be conducted prior to and during the expatriate assignment, and the assignment itself should be viewed as a career development experience. Effective reward systems must go beyond salary and benefits, and while keeping the employee "whole" and even offering a monetary premium, should also provide access to career development and learning opportunities. Finally, serious efforts should be made to manage the repatriation process.[62] A summary of the key points is provided in Table 15.7.

Table 15.7
Human Resource Practices That Support Effective Expatriation

Staffing and Selection
- Communicate the value of international assignments for the company's global mission.
- Ensure that those with the highest potential move internationally.
- Provide short-term assignments to increase the pool of employees with international experience.
- Recruit employees who have lived or who were educated abroad.

Training and Career Development
- Make international assignment planning a part of the career development process.
- Encourage early international experience.
- Create learning opportunities during the assignment.
- Use international assignments as a leadership development tool.

Performance Appraisal and Compensation
- Differentiate performance management based on expatriate roles.
- Align incentives with expatriation objectives.
- Tailor benefits to the expatriate's needs.
- Focus on equality of opportunities, not cash.
- Emphasize rewarding careers rather than short-term outcomes.

Expatriation and Repatriation Activities
- Involve the family in the orientation program at the beginning and the end of the assignment.
- Establish mentor relationships between expatriates and executives from the home location.
- Provide support for dual careers.
- Secure opportunities for the returning manager to use knowledge and skills learned while on the international assignment.

SOURCE: From P. Evans, V. Pucik, and J. Barsoux, *The Global Challenge: Framework for International Human Resource Management*, 2002. Reproduced with permission of The McGraw-Hill Companies, Inc.

⟩⟩⟩ A LOOK BACK

GM's US-Mexico Challenge

GM's dilemma resembles that of many other companies seeking to compete in a globalized market. To move more production to Mexico would increase profits and benefit U.S. UAW workers with larger profit-sharing checks but would likely reduce the number of workers receiving those checks. Keeping more production in the United States would maintain or grow the number of workers there but would likely reduce the amount of money they would receive in profit sharing.

QUESTIONS

1. What do you think is more important: fewer workers with higher pay, or more workers with lower pay?
2. How might the border tax impact Mexican workers and what responsibility does GM have to them? Should a global company care more about its home-country workers than host-country workers?
3. How do you think GM should handle this decision and why?

SUMMARY

Today's organizations are more involved in international commerce than ever before, and the trend will continue. Recent historic events such as the development of the European Union, NAFTA, the economic growth of Asia, and GATT have accelerated the movement toward a global market. Companies competing in the global marketplace require top-quality people to compete successfully. This requires that managers be aware of the many factors that significantly affect HRM in a global environment, such as culture, education–human capital, the political–legal system, and the economic system, and that they understand how these factors come into play in the various levels of global participation. Finally, it requires that they be adept at developing HRM systems that maximize the effectiveness of all human resources, particularly with regard to expatriate managers. Managers cannot overestimate the importance of effectively managing human resources to gain competitive advantage in today's global marketplace.

KEY TERMS

Individualism–collectivism, 651
Power distance, 651
Uncertainty avoidance, 651
Masculinity–femininity dimension, 652
Long-term–short-term orientation, 652

Parent country, 658
Host country, 658
Third country, 658
Expatriate, 658
Parent-country nationals (PCNs), 658

Host-country nationals (HCNs), 658
Third-country nationals (TCNs), 658
Transnational scope, 661
Transnational representation, 661
Transnational process, 662

DISCUSSION QUESTIONS

1. What current trends and/or events (besides those mentioned at the outset of the chapter) are responsible for the increased internationalization of the marketplace?
2. According to Hofstede (in Table 15.2), the United States is low on power distance, high on individuality, high on masculinity, low on uncertainty avoidance, and low on long-term orientation. Russia, by contrast, is high on power distance, moderate on individuality, low on masculinity, high on uncertainty avoidance, and low on long-term orientation. Many U.S. managers are transplanting their own HRM practices into Russia while companies seek to develop operations there.

How acceptable and effective do you think the following practices will be and why? (a) Extensive assessments of individual abilities for selection? (b) Individually based appraisal systems? (c) Suggestion systems? (d) Self-managing work teams?

3. The chapter notes that political–legal and economic systems can reflect a country's culture. The former Eastern bloc countries seem to be changing their political–legal and economic systems. Is this change brought on by their cultures, or will culture have an impact on the ability to change these systems? Why?

4. Think of the different levels of global participation. What companies that you are familiar with exhibit the different levels of participation?
5. Think of a time when you had to function in another culture (on a vacation or job). What were the major obstacles you faced, and how did you deal with them? Was this a stressful experience? Why? How can companies help expatriate employees deal with stress?
6. What types of skills do you need to be able to manage in today's global marketplace? Where do you expect to get those skills? What classes and/or experiences will you need?

SELF-ASSESSMENT EXERCISE

connect

Additional assignable self-assessments available in Connect.

The following list includes a number of qualities that have been identified as being associated with success in an expatriate assignment. Rate the degree to which you possess each quality, using the following scale:

1 = very low
2 = low
3 = moderate
4 = high
5 = very high

_____ Resourcefulness/resilience
_____ Adaptability/flexibility
_____ Emotional stability
_____ Ability to deal with ambiguity/uncertainty/differences
_____ Desire to work with people who are different

_____ Cultural empathy/sensitivity
_____ Tolerance of others' views, especially when they differ from your own
_____ Sensitivity to feelings and attitudes of others
_____ Good health and wellness

Add up your total score for the items. The higher your score, the greater your likelihood of success. Qualities that you rated low would be considered weaknesses for an expatriate assignment. Keep in mind that you will also need to be technically competent for the assignment, and your spouse and family (if applicable) must be adaptable and willing to live abroad.

SOURCE: Based on "Rating Scale on Successful Expatriate Qualities," from P. R. Harris and R. T. Moran, *Managing Cultural Differences*, 3rd ed. (Houston: Gulf, 1991), p. 569.

EXERCISING STRATEGY

Walmart's Global Strategy

Walmart's international division has an important job. With 80% of the retail industry's growth coming from outside of the United States, Walmart's $137 billion in international sales in 2014—29% of sales overall—is a key driver of overall revenue growth. To drive this performance, David Cheesewright, CEO of Walmart's international division, is focusing on current operations in growth markets and e-commerce. Shopping trends indicate that what customers buy is changing fast, and that they are quickly switching to online shopping platforms. After decades of work trying to develop a foundation in the Chinese market, Walmart is consolidating its portfolio of stores in that country, closing nonperforming retail stores and investing in successful ones. To enter the Chinese e-grocery market, Walmart holds a 51% stake in Yihaodian, which has posted triple-digit growth—twice the market rate. The company's operations in

Brazil and Mexico are experiencing slowing growth, in part a result of economic cycles and their brand's life cycle, but they still offer the opportunity to develop strong, mature businesses. International expansion comes with country-specific challenges. After experiencing too many regulatory difficulties in India, Walmart canceled plans to open retail stores there. Instead, Walmart India is focusing on business-to-business sales.

Although Walmart has successfully dominated the U.S. market, it has found that expanding its reach across the globe does not always fit with its strengths. In addition, navigating the variety of economic and regulatory requirements across different countries adds significant complexity to the company's operations. Finally, gaining access to and managing workforces with different values, cultures, and languages present tremendous challenges.

QUESTIONS

1. What criteria should a company use to determine which countries it should expand into?
2. How can a company assess how cultural and economic differences might impede its ability to succeed in different countries?
3. What things can companies do to manage a global workforce more effectively?

SOURCE: S. Banjo, "Wal-Mart's Strategy to Jump Start Growth in China," *Wall Street Journal,* August 5, 2014.

MANAGING PEOPLE

Huawei's Culture

What is the world's third largest smartphone maker by shipments? Chinese telecommunications company Huawei Technologies Co. has earned that spot over the past five years while doubling revenues to almost $60 billion. But the bigger question is, to what has the company attributed its success? The answer is, its hard-driving culture.

Chief Executive Officer (CEO) Ren Zhengfei was a former People's Liberation Army engineer, and his military background clearly has influenced the culture. He has been quoted as saying "In victory, we raise glasses to celebrate together. In defeat, we risk our lives to rescue each other."

That may sound hokey, but in the midst of the Ebola outbreak in 2014, the Chinese workers stayed in the affected areas to maintain production even while other companies were evacuating. In Huawei's 2015 annual report Chairwoman Sun Yafang wrote "When a crisis occurs, you will find Huawei employees heading toward it."

Examples of employee sacrifice have become part of the history of the company. Stories are told of employees in Siberia building telecom networks in sub-zero temperatures, of expatriates in Germany living in dormitories and sharing bathrooms, and of engineers in Shenzhen keeping mattresses under their desks to pull all-nighters.

But as CEO Zhengfei nears retirement, two questions have emerged. First, can such a sacrificial corporate culture continue to exist, particularly in an industry known for its war for talent? Second, can Mr. Zhengfei's successor lead the company with the same level of authority as he?

QUESTIONS

1. Would you want to work in a company with a culture like Huawei's? Why or why not?
2. Do you think it is possible to sustain such a culture as leaders change? Why or why not?

SOURCE: https://www.wsj.com/articles/huaweis-founder-casts-a-long-shadow-over-telecom-giant-1480715055

HR IN SMALL BUSINESS

Is Translating a Global Business?

One field in which small businesses have recently enjoyed rapid growth is in the business of providing translations. As barriers to international business continue to fall, more and more people are encountering language differences in the people they work with, sell to, and buy from. At the same time, advances in technology are providing avenues to deliver translations over the phone and over the Internet.

TransPerfect is one of the success stories. The company, based in New York City, started out when founder Steve Iverson, a French teacher, began translating documents for clients. Satisfied customers returned, looking for translations of patents and annual reports—even for court reporting in foreign languages. The company now provides translations in over 170 languages. It has offices in more than 90 cities spread over six continents.

CETRA Language Solutions is headquartered in Elkins Park, Pennsylvania. It started with a lawsuit: while founder Jiri Stejskal was working on his doctorate degree in Slavic languages and literature, a Philadelphia law firm asked him to translate thousands of pages of documents related to a case. Stejskal brought in all the Czech translators he could find, and his company was born. Now CETRA's employees and hundreds of consultants serve the federal government plus companies involved in law, marketing research, and life sciences. The company's freelance translators and interpreters are located throughout the world.

LinguaLinx, based in Troy, New York, handles more than words. It converts documents, websites, and multimedia into almost 150 languages. The company not only has to find qualified translators, but it also needs experts in technology to make state-of-the-art presentations. To recruit employees, LinguaLinx emphasizes interesting work experiences, rather than fancy perks. The company's careers website describes opportunities to work with a diverse, multicultural group, including clients at leading corporations and nonprofit organizations.

QUESTIONS

1. What kinds of challenges would be involved in recruiting and selecting people to translate documents from Spanish, Polish, and French into English?

2. Would those challenges be easier to meet by recruiting within the United States or by looking for talent overseas? Explain.

3. Suppose a small translation business asked you to advise the company on how to overcome cultural barriers among a staff drawn from three countries. Suggest a few ways the company could use training and performance management to achieve this goal.

SOURCES: Tanisha A. Sykes, "Growth in Translation," *Inc.*, August 4, 2009; Joel Dresang, "Iverson Language Associates Acquired by N.Y. Firm," *Millwaukee Journal Sentinel*, December 2, 2008; Business & Company Resource Center, http://galenet.galegroup.com; TransPerfect corporate website, www.transperfect.com, accessed June 19, 2015; CETRA Language Solutions corporate website, www.cetra.com, accessed June 19, 2015, and LinguaLinx corporate website, www.lingualinx.com, accessed June 19, 2015.

NOTES

1. "The World's Biggest Companies," *Forbes*, April 26, 2011, www.wistv.com/Global/story.asp?S=14514970&clienttype=printable.
2. L. Shen, "Here Are the 5 Biggest M&A Deals of 2016," *Fortune*, December 28, 2016, http://fortune.com/2016/12/28/mergers-and-acquisitions-donald-trump/
3. The Conference Board, "International Comparisons of Hourly Compensation Costs in Manufacturing, 2015 - Summary Tables," April 12, 2016, https://www.conference-board.org/ilcprogram/index.cfm?id=38269
4. D. Kirkpatrick, "The Net Makes It All Easier—Including Exporting U.S. Jobs," *Fortune*, May 2003, www.fortune.com/fortune/print/0,15935,450755,00.html.
5. R. Schuler, "An Integrative Framework of Strategic International Human Resource Management," *Journal of Management* (1993), pp. 419–60.
6. L. Rubio, "The Rationale for NAFTA: Mexico's New 'Outward Looking' Strategy," *Business Economics* (1991), pp. 12–16.
7. H. Cooper, "Economic Impact of NAFTA: It's a Wash, Experts Say," *Wall Street Journal*, June 17, 1997.
8. R. Peiper, *Human Resource Management: An International Comparison* (Berlin: Walter de Gruyter, 1990).
9. V. Sathe, *Culture and Related Corporate Realities* (Homewood, IL: Richard D. Irwin, 1985).
10. M. Rokeach, *Beliefs, Attitudes, and Values* (San Francisco: Jossey-Bass, 1968).
11. L. Harrison, *Who Prospers? How Cultural Values Shape Economic and Political Success* (New York: Free Press, 1992).
12. N. Adler, *International Dimensions of Organizational Behavior*, 2nd ed. (Boston: PWS-Kent, 1991).
13. R. Yates, "Japanese Managers Say They're Adopting Some U.S. Ways," *Chicago Tribune*, February 29, 1992, p. B1.
14. G. Hofstede, "Dimensions of National Cultures in Fifty Countries and Three Regions," in *Expectations in Cross-Cultural Psychology*, eds. J. Deregowski, S. Dziurawiec, and R. C. Annis (Lisse, Netherlands: Swets and Zeitlinger, 1983).
15. G. Hofstede, "Cultural Constraints in Management Theories," *Academy of Management Executive* 7 (1993), pp. 81–90.
16. G. Hofstede, "The Cultural Relativity of Organizational Theories," *Journal of International Business Studies* 14 (1983), pp. 75–90.
17. G. Hofstede, "Cultural Constraints in Management Theories."
18. A. Ramesh, and M. Gelfland, "Will They Stay or Will They Go? The Role of Job Embeddedness in Predicting Turnover in Individualistic and Collectivistic Cultures," *Journal of Applied Psychology* 95, no. 5 (2010), pp. 807–23.
19. S. Snell and J. Dean, "Integrated Manufacturing and Human Resource Management: A Human Capital Perspective," *Academy of Management Journal* 35 (1992), pp. 467–504.
20. N. Adler and S. Bartholomew, "Managing Globally Competent People," *The Executive* 6 (1992), pp. 52–65.
21. B. O'Reilly, "Your New Global Workforce," *Fortune*, December 14, 1992, pp. 52–66.
22. A. Hoffman, "Are Technology Jobs Headed Offshore?" Monster.com, http://technology.monster.com/articles/offshore.
23. J. Ledvinka and V. Scardello, *Federal Employment Regulation in Human Resource Management* (Boston: PWS-Kent, 1991).
24. P. Conrad and R. Peiper, "Human Resource Management in the Federal Republic of Germany," in *Human Resource Management: An International Comparison*, ed. R. Peiper (Berlin: Walter de Gruyer, 1990).
25. R. Solow, "Growth with Equity through Investment in Human Capital," The George Seltzer Distinguished Lecture, University of Minnesota.
26. M. Bloom, G. Milkovich, and A. Mitra, "Toward a Model of International Compensation and Rewards: Learning from How Managers Respond to Variations in Local Host Contexts," working paper 00-14 (Ithaca, NY: Cornell University Center for Advanced Human Resource Studies, 2000).
27. R. Kopp, "International Human Resource Policies and Practices in Japanese, European, and United States Multinationals," *Human Resource Management* 33 (1994), pp. 581–99.
28. Adler, *International Dimensions of Organizational Behavior*.
29. S. Jackson and Associates, *Diversity in the Workplace: Human Resource Initiatives* (New York: Guilford Press, 1991).
30. G. Stahl, M. Maznevski, A. Voight, and K. Jonsen, "Unraveling the Effects of Cultural Diversity in Teams: A Meta-Analysis of

Research on Multicultural Work Groups," *Journal of International Business Studies* 41 (2010), pp. 690–709.

31. Adler and Bartholomew, "Managing Globally Competent People."

32. Ibid.

33. S. Dolianski, "Are Expats Getting Lost in the Translation?" *Workforce*, February 1997.

34. L. Copeland and L. Griggs, *Going International* (New York: Random House, 1985).

35. K. F. Misa and J. M. Fabriacatore, "Return on Investments of Overseas Personnel," *Financial Executive* 47 (April 1979), pp. 42–46.

36. N. Forster, "The Persistent Myth of High Expatriate Failure Rates: A Reappraisal," *International Journal of Human Resource Management* 8, no. 4 (1997), pp. 414–34.

37. M. Mendenhall, E. Dunbar, and G. R. Oddou, "Expatriate Selection, Training, and Career-Pathing: A Review and Critique," *Human Resource Management* 26 (1987), pp. 331–45.

38. M. Mendenhall and G. Oddou, "The Dimensions of Expatriate Acculturation," *Academy of Management Review* 10 (1985), pp. 39–47.

39. W. Arthur and W. Bennett, "The International Assignee: The Relative Importance of Factors Perceived to Contribute to Success," *Personnel Psychology* 48 (1995), pp. 99–114.

40. K. Ng and C. Earley, "Culture and Intelligence: Old Constructs, New Frontiers," *Group and Organization Management* 31 (2006), pp. 4–19; S. Ang, L. Van Dyne, C. Koh, K. Y. Ng, K. J. Templer, C. Tay, and N. A. Chandrasekar, "Cultural Intelligence: Its Measurement and Effects on Cultural Judgment and Decision Making, Cultural Adaptation, and Task Performance," *Management and Organization Review* 3 (2007), pp. 335–71.

41. R. Tung, "Selecting and Training of Personnel for Overseas Assignments," *Columbia Journal of World Business* 16, no. 2 (1981), pp. 68–78.

42. Moran, Stahl, and Boyer, Inc., *International Human Resource Management* (Boulder, CO: Moran, Stahl, & Boyer, 1987).

43. P. Caligiuri, "The Big Five Personality Characteristics as Predictors of Expatriates' Desire to Terminate the Assignment and Supervisor Rated Performance," *Personnel Psychology* 53 (2000), pp. 67–88.

44. P. Caligiuri and R. Tung, "Comparing the Success of Male and Female Expatriates from a U.S.-based Multinational Company," *International Journal of Human Resource Management* 10, no. 5 (1999), pp. 763–82.

45. L. Stroh, A. Varma, and S. Valy-Durbin, "Why Are Women Left at Home? Are They Unwilling to Go on International Assignments?" *Journal of World Business* 35, no. 3 (2000), pp. 241–55.

46. A. Harzing, *Managing the Multinationals: An International Study of Control Mechanisms* (Cheltenham, UK: Edward Elgar, 1999).

47. J. S. Black and M. Mendenhall, "Cross-Cultural Training Effectiveness: A Review and Theoretical Framework for Future Research," *Academy of Management Review* 15 (1990), pp. 113–36.

48. B. Fitzgerald-Turner, "Myths of Expatriate Life," *HR Magazine* 42, no. 6 (June 1997), pp. 65–74.

49. P. Dowling and R. Schuler, *International Dimensions of Human Resource Management* (Boston: PWS-Kent, 1990).

50. Adler, *International Dimensions of Organizational Behavior.*

51. Dowling and Schuler, *International Dimensions of Human Resource Management.*

52. R. Schuler and P. Dowling, *Survey of ASPA/I Members* (New York: Stern School of Business, New York University, 1988).

53. C. Joinson, "No Returns: Localizing Expats Saves Companies Big Money and Can Be a Smooth Transition with a Little Due Diligence by HR," *HR Magazine* 11, no. 47 (2002), p. 70.

54. J. J. Smith, "Firms Say Expats Getting Too Costly, but Few Willing to Act" (2006), *SHRM*, retrieved March 9, 2007, www.shrm.org/global/library_published/subject/nonIC/CMS_018300.asp.

55. C. Solomon, "Repatriation: Up, Down, or Out?" *Personnel Journal* (1995), pp. 28–37.

56. "Workers Sent Overseas Have Adjustment Problems, a New Study Shows," *Wall Street Journal*, June 19, 1984, p. 1.

57. J. S. Black, "Repatriation: A Comparison of Japanese and American Practices and Results," *Proceedings of the Eastern Academy of Management Bi-annual International Conference* (Hong Kong, 1989), pp. 45–49.

58. J. S. Black, "Coming Home: The Relationship of Expatriate Expectations with Repatriation Adjustment and Job Performance," *Human Relations* 45 (1992), pp. 177–92.

59. Adler, *International Dimensions of Organizational Behavior.*

60. Black, "Coming Home."

61. C. Solomon, "Repatriation: Up, Down, or Out?"

62. P. Evans, V. Pucik, and J. Barsoux, *The Global Challenge: International Human Resource Management* (New York: McGraw-Hill, 2002), p. 137.

16 Strategically Managing the HRM Function

LEARNING OBJECTIVES

After reading this chapter, you should be able to:

LO 16-1 Describe the roles that HRM plays in firms today and the categories of HRM activities. *page 680*

LO 16-2 Discuss how the HRM function can define its mission and market. *page 683*

LO 16-3 Explain the approaches to evaluating the effectiveness of HRM practices. *page 687*

LO 16-4 Describe the new structures for the HRM function. *page 693*

LO 16-5 Describe how outsourcing HRM activities can improve service delivery efficiency and effectiveness. *page 695*

LO 16-6 Relate how process reengineering is used to review and redesign HRM practices. *page 696*

LO 16-7 Discuss the types of new technologies that can improve the efficiency and effectiveness of HRM. *page 699*

LO 16-8 List the competencies the HRM executive needs to become a strategic partner in the company. *page 706*

Cisco is Rewiring HR

Fran Katsoudas assumed the chief people officer role at Cisco with the goal of challenging the way that the company had done HR. She called it "breaking HR."

Cisco was there at the creation of the Internet and has become a $49 billion technology company with 70,000 employees working at 372 locations across 92 countries. Managing employees across such a large geographic footprint requires thinking innovatively about processes and rigorously about values and culture.

One innovation in HR process was the decision to eliminate performance ratings. Many firms that have done this studied the elimination of performance ratings, rolled out pilot programs, evaluated them, made changes, and then rolled out a new approach to performance management. Cisco did away with the performance reviews before it had developed the replacement. Katsoudas says, "We announced we were moving away from performance ratings before we knew what we were moving to. We're betting on our managers to have the right type of conversation with their employees." This approach allows them to better involve employees in the design of the new approach.

That leads to the emphasis on values and culture. Based on employee input, Katsoudas developed the "People Manifesto," which lays out how Cisco treats employees and what Cisco expects from employees. This manifesto identifies three foundational principles:

- *Connect Everything:* Cisco connects employees with the people, information, and opportunities they need to succeed, and it expects employees to connect with peers to deliver the best outcomes and results.
- *Innovate Everywhere:* Cisco provides an open and agile environment to help employees explore ideas, challenge norms, and develop skills, and it expects employees to pursue a better, smarter, and faster tomorrow.
- *Benefit Everyone:* Cisco hires the best and the brightest, develops them, and recognizes their contributions, and it expects employees to live the values and believe in winning together.

Katsoudas's efforts have been driving significant change at Cisco. She certainly has been "breaking HR."

SOURCE: M. Wylie, "Cisco's chief people officer is 'breaking HR'," *BizWomen,* March 10, 2016, http://www.bizjournals.com/bizwomen/news/profiles-strategies/2016/03/san-jose-cisco-s-chief-people-officer-is-breaking.html.

Introduction

Throughout this book we have emphasized how human resource management practices can help companies gain a competitive advantage. We identified specific practices related to managing the internal and external environment; designing work and measuring work outcomes; and acquiring, developing, and compensating human resources. We have also discussed the best of current research and practice to show how they may contribute to a company's competitive advantage.

As we said in Chapter 1, the role of the HRM function has been evolving over time. As we see in this chapter's opening story, it has now reached a crossroads. Although it began as a purely administrative function, most HR executives now see the function's major role as being much more strategic. However, this evolution has resulted in a misalignment between the skills and capabilities of members of the function and the new requirements placed on it. Virtually every HRM function in top companies is going through a transformation process to create a function that can play this new strategic role while successfully fulfilling its other roles. This transformation process is also going on globally. Managing this process is the subject of this chapter. First we discuss the various activities of the HRM function. Then we examine how to develop a market- or customer-oriented HRM function. We then describe the current structure of most HRM functions. We discuss some of the software applications used by the HR function. We examine the competencies that will be needed in the future for HR professionals. Finally, we provide a specific analysis of the role that the Chief HR Officer plays in making companies more successful.

Activities of HRM

LO 16-1
Describe the roles that HRM plays in firms today and the categories of HRM activities.

To understand the transformation going on in HRM, one must understand HRM activities in terms of their strategic value. One way of classifying these activities is depicted in Figure 16.1. Transactional activities (the day-to-day transactions such as benefits administration, record keeping, and employee services) are low in their strategic value. Traditional activities such as performance management, training, recruiting, selection,

Figure 16.1

Categories of HRM Activities and Percentages of Time Spent on Them

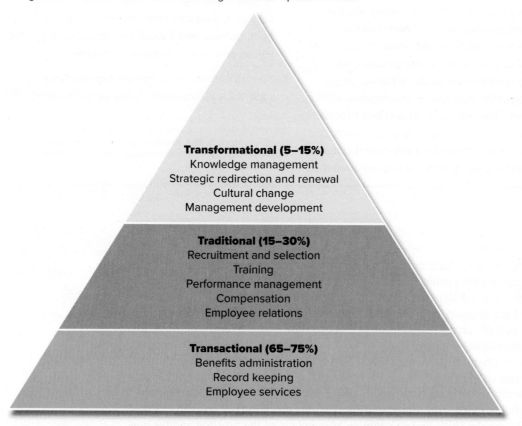

Transformational (5–15%)
Knowledge management
Strategic redirection and renewal
Cultural change
Management development

Traditional (15–30%)
Recruitment and selection
Training
Performance management
Compensation
Employee relations

Transactional (65–75%)
Benefits administration
Record keeping
Employee services

SOURCE: P. Wright, G. McMahan, S. Snell, and B. Gerhart, *Strategic Human Resource Management: Building Human Capital and Organizational Capability.* Technical report. Cornell University, 1998.

compensation, and employee relations are the nuts and bolts of HRM. These activities have moderate strategic value because they often form the practices and systems to ensure strategy execution. For instance, one role of HR is often to set policies regarding the legitimate activities that salespeople can engage in to make sales in foreign countries. Transformational activities create long-term capability and adaptability for the firm. These activities include knowledge management, management development, cultural change, and strategic redirection and renewal. Obviously, these activities comprise the greatest strategic value for the firm.

As we see in the figure, most HRM functions spend the vast majority of their time on transactional activities, with substantially less on traditional and very little on transformational activities. However, virtually all HRM functions, in order to add value to the firm, must increase their efforts in the traditional and transformational activities. To do this, however, requires that HR executives (1) develop a strategy for the HRM function, (2) assess the current effectiveness of the HRM function, and (3) redesign, reengineer, or outsource HRM processes to improve efficiency and effectiveness. These issues will be discussed in the following sections.

Strategic Management of the HRM Function

In light of the various roles and activities of the HRM function, it is highly unlikely that any function can (or should) effectively deliver on all roles and all activities. Although this is a laudable goal, resource constraints in terms of time, money, and head count require that the HR executive make strategic choices about where and how to allocate these resources for maximum value to the firm.

Chapter 2 explained the strategic management process that takes place at the organization level and discussed the role of HRM in this process. HRM has been seen as a strategic partner that has input into the formulation of the company's strategy and develops and aligns HRM programs to help implement the strategy. However, for the HRM function to become truly strategic in its orientation, it must view itself as a separate business entity and engage in strategic management in an effort to effectively serve the various internal customers.

In this respect, one recent trend within the field of HRM, consistent with the total quality management philosophy, is for the HR executive to take a customer-oriented approach to implementing the function. In other words, the strategic planning process that takes place at the level of the business can also be performed with the HRM function. HR executives in more progressive U.S. companies have begun to view the HRM function as a strategic business unit and have tried to define that business in terms of their customer base, their customers' needs, and the technologies required to satisfy customers' needs (Figure 16.2). For example, Joe Ruocco, the former chief HR officer at Goodyear, encouraged his HR function to take a customer-centric approach. As you can see in Figure 16.3, Goodyear views the business (line clients) and the employees (associates) as its main customers. The figure provides examples of the different tools and processes at the company's disposal to meet those customer needs.

A customer orientation is one of the most important changes in the HRM function's attempts to become strategic. It entails first identifying customers. The most obvious example of HRM customers are the line managers who require HRM services. In addition, the strategic planning team is a customer in the sense that it requires identification, analysis, and recommendations regarding people-oriented

Figure 16.2
Customer-Oriented
Perspective of the
HRM Function

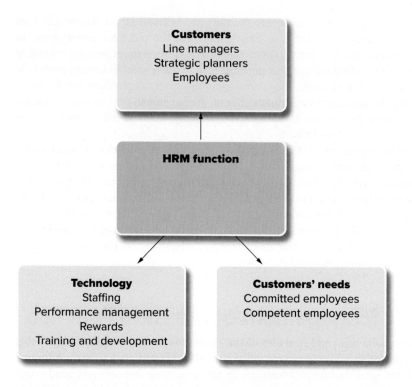

Figure 16.3
Goodyear's
Customer-Centric
View of HR

SOURCE: Courtesy of former Goodyear chief HR officer Joe Ruocco.

business problems. Employees are also HRM customers because the rewards they receive from the employment relationship are determined or administered by the HRM department.

In addition, the products of the HRM department must be identified. Line managers want to have high-quality employees committed to the organization. The strategic planning team requires information and recommendations for the planning process as well as programs that support the strategic plan once it has been identified. Employees want compensation and benefit programs that are consistent, adequate, and equitable, and they want fair promotion decisions. At Southwest Airlines, the "People" department administers customer surveys to all clients as they leave the department to measure how well their needs have been satisfied.

Finally, the technologies through which HRM meets customer needs vary depending on the need being satisfied. Selection systems ensure that applicants selected for employment have the necessary knowledge, skills, and abilities to provide value to the organization. Training and development systems meet the needs of both line managers and employees by giving employees development opportunities to ensure they are continually increasing their human capital and, thus, providing increased value to the company. Performance management systems make clear to employees what is expected of them and assure line managers and strategic planners that employee behavior will be in line with the company's goals. Finally, reward systems similarly benefit all customers (line managers, strategic planners, and employees). These systems assure line managers that employees will use their skills for organizational benefit, and they provide strategic planners with ways to ensure that all employees are acting in ways that will support the strategic plan. Obviously, reward systems provide employees with an equitable return for their investment of skills and effort.

Building an HR Strategy

THE BASIC PROCESS

How do HR functions build their HR strategies? Research has examined how HR functions go about the process of building their HR strategies that should support the business strategies. Conducting case studies on 20 different companies, Wright and colleagues describe the generic approach as somewhat consistent with the process for developing a business strategy.[1]

LO 16-2
Discuss how the HRM function can define its mission and market.

As depicted in Figure 16.4, the function first scans the environment to determine the trends or events that might have an impact on the organization (e.g., future talent shortage, increasing immigrant population, aging of the workforce).

It then examines the strategic business issues or needs (e.g., is the company growing, expanding internationally, needing to develop new technologies?). For

Figure 16.4

Basic Process for HR Strategy

Figure 16.5

Goodyear's Strategic
Business Priorities

instance, Figure 16.5 displays Goodyear's major business strategy priorities. As can be seen in this example, a clear strategic priority is the attraction, motivation, and retention of talent.

From these issues, the HR strategy team needs to identify the specific people issues that will be critical to address in order for the business to succeed (a potential leadership vacuum, lack of technological expertise, lack of diversity, etc.). All of this information is used in designing the HR strategy, which provides a detailed plan regarding the major priorities and the programs, policies, and processes that must be developed or executed. Finally, this HR strategy is communicated to the relevant parties, both internal and external to the function. Again, Goodyear's talent management strategy, depicted in Figure 16.6, shows how Goodyear seeks to differentiate itself in the labor market as well as the major priority areas that the HR strategy seeks to address.

Thus, the HR strategy is a framework that guides individuals in HR by helping them understand where and how they will impact the company. At Google this four-pronged People Operations strategy consists of the following elements:

1. "Find them, Grow them, Keep them." The idea is to find great people to work for Google, grow and develop their skills, and do everything possible to keep them at Google.
2. "Put our users first." This goal echoes what Google does as a company, also illustrating how those in HR should think about the users of people operations, which are all the other Google employees.
3. "Put on your own oxygen mask before assisting others." The thinking behind this goal is that in many organizations HR is doing all this work in the company for others and they forget to grow and develop their own people. Eventually this

Figure 16.6

Goodyear's Global Talent Management Process

cripples the function's ability to serve the rest of the organization because the very best, most talented people get recruited out of HR to go be heads of HR at other companies.

4. "This space intentionally left blank." In Google's environment, things change very, very quickly and that creates a lot of uncertainty. Uncertainty causes people to put less discretionary effort into their work, to be less satisfied, less collaborative, more competitive with fellow employees as well as making them more likely to leave the company. Hence, this goal is an attempt to explicitly recognize the dynamic nature of Google's internal and external environment.[2]

INVOLVING LINE EXECUTIVES

This generic process provides for the potential to involve line executives in a number of ways. Because the HR strategy seeks to address business issues, involving those in charge of running the business can increase the quality of information from which the HR strategy is created. This involvement can occur in a few ways. First, line executives could simply provide input, through surveys or interviews about the business challenges and strategy. Second, they could be members of the team that actually develops the HR strategy. Third, once the strategy is developed, they could receive communications with the HR strategy information. Finally, they could have to formally approve the strategy, in essence "signing off" that the HR strategy fully supports the business strategy. The most progressive organizations use all four forms of involvement, asking a large group of executives for input, having one or two executives on the team, communicating the HR strategy broadly to executives, and having the senior executive team formally approve it.

CHARACTERIZING HR STRATEGIES

As you can see in Figure 16.7, a study of 20 companies revealed the variety of ways that HR strategies can be generated to create a linkage to the business.

First, at the most elementary level, "HR-focused" HR functions articulate people outcomes that stem more from an analysis of what their functions currently do than from an understanding of how those people outcomes relate to the larger business. Second, "people-linked" functions have clearly identified, articulated, and aligned their HR activities around people issues and outcomes, but not business issues and outcomes. Third, "business-linked" HR functions begin with an assessment of what HR is doing, then identify the major people outcomes they should focus on, and, in a few cases, how those might translate into positive business outcomes. Finally, "business-driven" functions have fully developed HR strategies that begin by identifying the major business needs and issues, consider how people fit in and what people outcomes are necessary, and then build HR systems focused on meeting those needs. For example, as Kroger sought to develop a new strategy for competing in the retail grocery store market, it required a different approach to leadership. Figure 16.8 shows the leadership competencies necessary to execute the strategy. The larger focus is on leaders who have a passion for people and a passion for results, with a number of more specific competencies making up each.

The HR strategy must help address the issues the business faces that will determine its success. As finding, attracting, and retaining talent has become a critical issue, virtually every HR function is addressing this as part of the HR strategy.

Figure 16.7

Approaches to Developing an HR Strategy

An Outside-In Perspective

Business-Driven (5 cases)

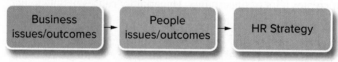

3 Different Inside-Out Stages

Business-Linked (5 cases)

People-Linked (7 cases)

HR-Focused (3 cases)

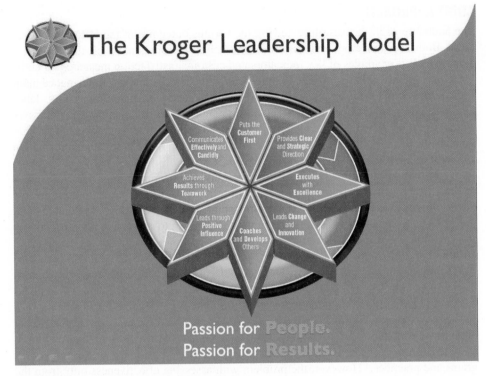

Figure 16.8
Kroger's Leadership Model

SOURCE: Courtesy of Kroger chief HR officer Katy Barclay.

Measuring HRM Effectiveness

The strategic decision-making process for the HRM function requires that decision makers have a good sense of the effectiveness of the current HRM function. This information provides the foundation for decisions regarding which processes, systems, and skills of HR employees need improvement. Often HRM functions that have been heavily involved in transactional activities for a long time tend to lack systems, processes, and skills for delivering state-of-the-art traditional activities and are thoroughly unable to contribute in the transformational arena. Thus, diagnosis of the effectiveness of the HRM function provides critical information for its strategic management.

In addition, having good measures of the function's effectiveness provides the following benefits:[3]

- *Marketing the function:* Evaluation is a sign to other managers that the HRM function really cares about the organization as a whole and is trying to support operations, production, marketing, and other functions of the company. Information regarding cost savings and benefits is useful to prove to internal customers that HRM practices contribute to the bottom line. Such information is also useful for gaining additional business for the HRM function.
- *Providing accountability:* Evaluation helps determine whether the HRM function is meeting its objectives and effectively using its budget.

Two approaches are commonly used to evaluate the effectiveness of HRM practices: the audit approach and the analytic approach.

LO 16-3
Explain the approaches to evaluating the effectiveness of HRM practices.

AUDIT APPROACH

Audit approach

Type of assessment of HRM effectiveness that involves review of customer satisfaction or key indicators (e.g., turnover rate, average days to fill a position) related to an HRM functional area (e.g., recruiting, training).

The **audit approach** focuses on reviewing the various outcomes of the HRM functional areas. Both key indicators and customer satisfaction measures are typically collected. Table 16.1 lists examples of key indicators and customer satisfaction measures for staffing, equal employment opportunity, compensation, benefits, training, performance management (employee appraisal and development), succession planning, safety, labor relations, and overall effectiveness. The development of electronic employee databases and information systems has made it much easier to collect, store, and analyze the functional key indicators (more on this later in the chapter) than in the past, when information was kept in file folders.

We previously discussed how HRM functions can become much more customer oriented as part of the strategic management process. If, in fact, the function desires to be more customer focused, then one important source of effectiveness data can be the customers. Just as firms often survey their customers to determine how effectively the customers feel they are being served, the HRM function can survey its internal customers.

One important internal customer is the employees of the firm. Employees often have both direct contact with the HRM function (through activities such as benefits administration and payroll) and indirect contact with the function through their involvement in activities such as performance appraisals, pay raises, and training programs. Many organizations such as AT&T, Motorola, and General Electric use their regular employee attitude survey as a way to assess the employees as users/customers of the HRM programs and practices.[4] However, the problem with assessing effectiveness only from the employees' perspective is that often they are responding not from the standpoint of the good of the firm but rather from their own individual perspective. For example, employees notoriously and consistently express dissatisfaction with pay level (who doesn't want more money?), but to simply ratchet up pay across the board would put the firm at a serious labor cost disadvantage.

Table 16.1

Examples of Key Indicators and Customer Satisfaction Measures for HRM Functions

KEY INDICATORS	CUSTOMER SATISFACTION MEASURES
Staffing	
Average days taken to fill open requisitions	Anticipation of personnel needs
Ratio of acceptances to offers made	Timeliness of referring qualified workers to line supervisors
Ratio of minority/women applicants to representation in local labor market	Treatment of applicants
Per-capita requirement costs	Skill in handling terminations
Average years of experience/education of hires per job family	Adaptability to changing labor market conditions
Equal employment opportunity	
Ratio of EEO grievances to employee population	Resolution of EEO grievances
Minority representation by EEO categories	Day-to-day assistance provided by personnel department in implementing affirmative action plan
Minority turnover rate	Aggressive recruitment to identify qualified women and minority applicants

(Continued)

KEY INDICATORS	CUSTOMER SATISFACTION MEASURES
Compensation Per-capita (average) merit increases Ratio of recommendations for reclassification to number of employees Percentage of overtime hours to straight time Ratio of average salary offers to average salary in community	Fairness of existing job evaluation system in assigning grades and salaries Competitiveness in local labor market Relationship between pay and performance Employee satisfaction with pay
Benefits Average unemployment compensation payment (UCP) Average workers' compensation payment (WCP) Benefit cost per payroll dollar Percentage of sick leave to total pay	Promptness in handling claims Fairness and consistency in the application of benefit policies Communication of benefits to employees Assistance provided to line managers in reducing potential for unnecessary claims
Training Percentage of employees participating in training programs per job family Percentage of employees receiving tuition refunds Training dollars per employee	Extent to which training programs meet the needs of employees and the company Communication to employees about available training opportunities Quality of introduction/orientation programs
Employee appraisal and development Distribution of performance appraisal ratings Appropriate psychometric properties of appraisal forms	Assistance in identifying management potential Organizational development activities provided by HRM department
Succession planning Ratio of promotions to number of employees Ratio of open requisitions filled internally to those filled externally	Extent to which promotions are made from within Assistance/counseling provided to employees in career planning
Safety Frequency/severity ratio of accidents Safety-related expenses per $1,000 of payroll Plant security losses per square foot (e.g., fires, burglaries)	Assistance to line managers in organizing safety programs Assistance to line managers in identifying potential safety hazards Assistance to line managers in providing a good working environment (lighting, cleanliness, heating, etc.)
Labor relations Ratio of grievances by pay plan to number of employees Frequency and duration of work stoppages Percentage of grievances settled	Assistance provided to line managers in handling grievances Efforts to promote a spirit of cooperation in plant Efforts to monitor the employee relations climate in plant
Overall effectiveness Ratio of personnel staff to employee population Turnover rate Absenteeism rate Ratio of per-capita revenues to per-capita cost Net income per employee	Accuracy and clarity of information provided to managers and employees Competence and expertise of staff Working relationship between organizations and HRM department

SOURCE: Reprinted with permission. Excerpts from Chapter 15, "Evaluating Human Resource Effectiveness," pp. 187–222, by Anne S. Tsui and Luis R. Gomez-Mejia, from *Human Resource Management: Evolving Roles and Responsibilities*, edited by Lee Dyer. Copyright © 1988 by The Bureau of National Affairs, Inc., Washington, DC, 20037. To order BNA publications call toll free 1-800-960-1220.

Figure 16.9

Comparing HR and Line Executives' Evaluations of the Effectiveness of HRM Roles

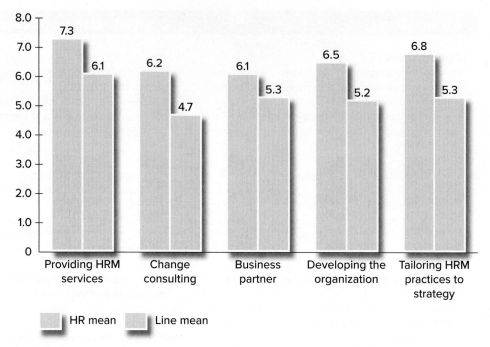

SOURCE: P. Wright, G. McMahan, S. Snell, and B. Gerhart, "Comparing Line and HR Executives' Perceptions of HR Effectiveness: Services, Roles, and Contributions," CAHRS (Center for Advanced Human Resource Studies) working paper 98-29, School of ILR, Cornell University, Ithaca, NY.

Thus, many firms have gone to surveys of top line executives as a better means of assessing the effectiveness of the HRM function. The top-level line executives can see how the systems and practices are impacting both employees and the overall effectiveness of the firm from a strategic standpoint. This can also be useful for determining how well HR employees' perceptions of their function's effectiveness align with the views of their line colleagues. For example, a study of 14 firms revealed that HR executives and line executives agreed on the relative effectiveness of HR's delivery of services such as staffing and training systems (that is, which were most and least effectively delivered) but not on the absolute level of effectiveness. As Figure 16.9 shows, HR executives' ratings of their effectiveness in different roles also diverged significantly from line executives'. In addition, line executives viewed HRM as being significantly less effective with regard to HRM's actual contributions to the firm's overall effectiveness, as we see in Figure 16.10.[5]

THE ANALYTIC APPROACH

Analytic approach

Type of assessment of HRM effectiveness that involves determining the impact of, or the financial costs and benefits of, a program or practice.

The **analytic approach** focuses on either (1) determining whether the introduction of a program or practice (like a training program or a new compensation system) has the intended effect, (2) estimating the financial costs and benefits resulting from an HRM practice, or (3) using analytic data to increase organizational effectiveness. For example, in Chapter 7 we discussed how companies can determine a training program's impact on learning, behavior, and results. Evaluating a training program is one strategy for determining whether the program works. Typically, in an overall evaluation of

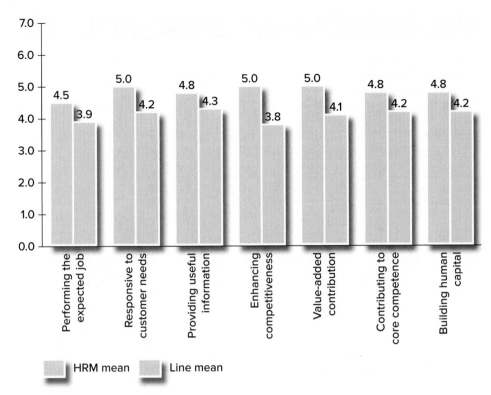

SOURCE: P. Wright, G. McMahan, S. Snell, and B. Gerhart, "Comparing Line and HR Executives' Perceptions of HR Effectiveness: Services, Roles, and Contributions," CAHRS (Center for Advanced Human Resource Studies) working paper 98-29, School of ILR, Cornell University, Ithaca, NY.

Figure 16.10

Comparing HR and Line Executives' Evaluations of the Effectiveness of HRM Contributions

effectiveness, we are interested in determining the degree of change associated with the program.

The second strategy involves determining the dollar value of the training program, taking into account all the costs associated with the program. Using this strategy, we are not concerned with how much change occurred but rather with the dollar value (costs versus benefits) of the program. Table 16.2 lists the various types of cost–benefit

Table 16.2

Types of Cost–Benefit Analyses

Human resource accounting
- Capitalization of salary
- Net present value of expected wage payments
- Returns on human assets and human investments

Utility analysis
- Turnover costs
- Absenteeism and sick leave costs
- Gains from selection programs
- Impact of positive employee attitudes
- Financial gains of training programs

SOURCE: Based on A. S. Tsui and L. R. Gomez-Mejia, "Evaluating HR Effectiveness," in *Human Resource Management: Evolving Roles and Responsibilities*, ed. L. Dyer (Washington, DC: Bureau of National Affairs, 1988), pp. 1–196.

Table 16.3

Effectiveness and Cost-Effectiveness of Two Wellness Programs for Four Cardiovascular Disease Risk Factors

	SITE C	SITE D
Annual direct program costs, per employee per year	$30.96	$38.57
Percentage of cardiovascular disease risks[a] for which risk was moderately reduced or relapse prevented	48%	51%
Percentage of preceding entry per annual $1 spent per employee	1.55%	1.32%
Amount spent per 1% of risks reduced or relapse prevented	$.65	$.76

[a]High blood pressure, overweight, smoking, and lack of exercise.

SOURCE: J. C. Erfurt, A. Foote, and M. A. Heirich, "The Cost-Effectiveness of Worksite Wellness Programs," *Personnel Psychology* 45 (1992), p. 22.

analyses that are done. The human resource accounting approach attempts to place a dollar value on human resources as if they were physical resources (like plant and equipment) or financial resources (like cash). Utility analysis attempts to estimate the financial impact of employee behaviors (such as absenteeism, turnover, job performance, and substance abuse).

For example, wellness programs are a popular HRM program for reducing health care costs through reducing employees' risk of heart disease and cancer. One study evaluated four different types of wellness programs. Part of the evaluation involved determining the costs and benefits associated with the four programs over a three-year period.[6] A different type of wellness program was implemented at each site. Site A instituted a program involving raising employees' awareness of health risks (distributing news articles, blood pressure testing, health education classes). Site B set up a physical fitness facility for employees. Site C raised awareness of health risks and followed up with employees who had identified health risks. Site D provided health education and follow-up counseling and promoted physical competition and health-related events. Table 16.3 shows the effectiveness and cost-effectiveness of the Site C and Site D wellness models.

The analytic approach is more demanding than the audit approach because it requires the detailed use of statistics and finance. A good example of the level of sophistication that can be required for cost–benefit analysis is shown in Table 16.4. This table shows the types of information needed to determine the dollar value of a new selection test for entry-level computer programmers.

Finally, HR analytics can be used by the function to increase the effectiveness of the firm. For instance, Google's analytic approach to HR has revealed which backgrounds and capabilities are correlated with high performance as well as the leading cause of attrition—an employee's feeling that he or she is underused at the company. It also discovered that the ideal number of recruiting interviews is 5, down from a previous average of 10.

In addition, Project Oxygen was aimed at developing great managers (named because good management, like oxygen, keeps the company alive). The analytics team poured through performance management scores, employee surveys, and other data on group managers based on two dimensions: their task performance and their people performance. They then conducted a double-blind study focusing on those who were top (or bottom) on both dimensions, in order to identify eight behaviors that characterized good managers.[7]

Table 16.4
Example of Analysis
Needed to
Determine the Dollar
Value of a Selection
Test

Cost–benefit information

Current employment	4,404
Number separating	618
Number selected	618
Average tenure	9.69 years

Test information

Number of applicants	1,236
Testing cost per applicant	$10
Total test cost	$12,360
Average test score	0.80 SD
Test validity	0.76
SD_y (per year)[a]	$10,413

Computation

Quantity = Average tenure × Applicants selected
= 9.69 years × 618 applicants
= 5,988 person-years

Quality = Average test score × Test validity × SD_y
= 0.80 × 0.76 × $10,413
= $6,331 per year

Utility = (Quantity × Quality) – Costs
= (5,988 person-year × $6,331 per year) – $12,360
= $37.9 million

[a]SD_y = Dollar value of one standard difference in job performance. Approximately 40% of average salary.
SOURCES: From J. W. Boudreau, "Utility Analysis," in *Human Resource Management: Evolving Roles and Responsibilities*, ed. L. Dyer (Washington, DC: Bureau of National Affairs, 1988), p. 150; F. L. Schmidt, J. E. Hunter, R. C. McKenzie, and T. W. Muldrow, "Impact of Valid Selection Procedures on Work-Force Productivity," *Journal of Applied Psychology* 64 (1979), pp. 609–26.

Improving HRM Effectiveness

LO 16-4
Describe the new
structures for the HRM
function.

Once a strategic direction has been established and the effectiveness of HRM evaluated, leaders of the HRM function can explore how to improve its effectiveness in contributing to the firm's competitiveness. Returning briefly to Figure 16.1, which depicted the different activities of the HRM function, often the improvement focuses on two aspects of the pyramid. First, within each activity, HRM needs to improve both the efficiency and effectiveness in performing each of the activities. Second, often there is a push to eliminate as much of the transactional work as possible (and some of the traditional work) to free up time and resources to focus more on the higher-value-added transformational work. Redesign of the structure (reporting relationships) and processes (through outsourcing and information technology) enables the function to achieve these goals simultaneously. Figure 16.11 depicts this process.

RESTRUCTURING TO IMPROVE HRM EFFECTIVENESS

Traditional HRM functions were structured around the basic HRM subfunctions such as staffing, training, compensation, appraisal, and labor relations. Each of these areas had a director who reported to the VP of HRM, who often reported to a VP of finance and administration. However, for the HRM function to truly contribute strategically to firm effectiveness, the senior HR person must be part of the top management team (reporting

Figure 16.11

Improving HRM Effectiveness

directly to the chief executive officer), and there must be a different structural arrangement within the function itself.

A generic structure for the HRM function is depicted in Figure 16.12. As we see, the HRM function effectively is divided into three divisions: the centers for expertise, the field generalists, and the service center.[8] The centers for expertise usually consist of the functional specialists in the traditional areas of HRM such as recruitment, selection, training, and compensation. These individuals ideally act as consultants in the development of state-of-the-art systems and processes for use in the organization. The field generalists consist of the HRM generalists who are assigned to a business unit within the firm. These individuals usually have dual reporting relationships to both the head of the line business and the head of HRM (although the line business tends to take priority). They ideally take responsibility for helping the line executives in their business to strategically address people issues, and they ensure that the HRM systems enable the business to execute its strategy. Finally, the service center consists of individuals who ensure that the transactional activities are delivered throughout the organization. These service centers often leverage information technology to efficiently deliver employee services. For example, organizations such as Chevron have created call-in service centers where employees can dial a central number where service center employees are available to answer their questions and process their requests and transactions.

Figure 16.12
Old and New
Structures for the
HRM Organization

Historical HRM organization structure

New HRM organization structure

SOURCE: P. Wright, G. McMahan, S. Snell, and B. Gerhart, *Strategic Human Resource Management: Building Human Capital and Organizational Capability,* technical report (Ithaca, NY: Cornell University, 1998).

Such structural arrangements improve service delivery through specialization. Center for expertise employees can develop current functional skills without being distracted by transactional activities, and generalists can focus on learning the business environment without having to maintain expertise in functional specializations. Finally, service center employees can focus on efficient delivery of basic services across business units.

OUTSOURCING TO IMPROVE HRM EFFECTIVENESS

Restructuring the internal HRM function and redesigning the processes represent internal approaches to improving HRM effectiveness. However, increasingly HR executives are seeking to improve the effectiveness of the systems, processes, and services the function delivers through outsourcing. **Outsourcing** entails contracting with an outside vendor to provide a product or service to the firm, as opposed to producing the product using employees within the firm.

Outsourcing
An organization's use of an outside organization for a broad set of services.

LO 16-5
Describe how outsourcing HRM activities can improve service delivery efficiency and effectiveness.

Why would a firm outsource an HRM activity or service? Usually this is done for one of two reasons: Either the outsourcing partner can provide the service more cheaply than it would cost to do it internally, or the partner can provide it more effectively than it can be performed internally. Early on, firms resorted to outsourcing for efficiency reasons. Why would using an outsourced provider be more efficient than having internal employees provide a service? Usually it is because outsourced providers are specialists who are able to develop extensive expertise that can be leveraged across a number of companies.

For example, consider a relatively small firm that seeks to develop a pension system for employees. To provide this service to employees, the HRM function would need to learn all of the basics of pension law. Then it would need to hire a person with specific expertise in administering a pension system in terms of making sure that employee contributions are withheld and that the correct payouts are made to retired employees. Then the company would have to hire someone with expertise in investing pension funds. If the firm is small, requirements of the pension fund might not fill the time (80 hours per week) of these two new hires. Assume that it takes only 20 total hours a week for these people to do their jobs. The firm would be wasting 60 hours of employee time each week. However, a firm that specializes in providing pension administration services to multiple firms could provide the 20 hours of required time to that firm and three other firms for the same cost as if the firm had performed this activity internally. Thus, the specialist firm could charge the focal firm 50% of what it would cost the small firm to do the pensions internally. Of that 50%, 25% (20 hours) would go to paying direct salaries and the other 25% would be profit. Here the focal firm would save 50% of its expenses while the provider would make money.

Now consider the aspect of effectiveness. Because the outsourced provider works for a number of firms and specializes in pensions, its employees develop state-of-the-art knowledge of running pension plans. They can learn unique innovations from one company and transfer that learning to a new company. In addition, employees can be more easily and efficiently trained because all of them will be trained in the same processes and procedures. Finally, with experience in providing constant pension services, the firm is able to develop a capability to perform these services that could never be developed by two individuals working 25% of the time on these services. This is known as *scale,* which refers to larger companies being better able to allocate human resources efficiently. The "Competing through Globalization" box shows how Hershey's sacrificed the opportunity for global scale by being acquired by Mondelez in order to maintain its presence and impact on Hershey, Pennsylvania.

What kind of services are being outsourced? Firms primarily outsource transactional activities and services of HRM such as pension and benefits administration as well as payroll. However, a number of traditional and some transformational activities have been outsourced as well.

Reengineering
Review and redesign of work processes to make them more efficient and improve the quality of the end product or service.

LO 16-6
Relate how process reengineering is used to review and redesign HRM practices.

IMPROVING HRM EFFECTIVENESS THROUGH PROCESS REDESIGN

In addition to structural arrangements, process redesign enables the HRM function to more efficiently and effectively deliver HRM services. Process redesign often uses information technology, but information technology applications are not a requirement. Thus, we will discuss the general issue of process reengineering and then explore information technology applications that have aided HRM in process redesign.

Reengineering is a complete review of critical work processes and redesign to make them more efficient and able to deliver higher quality. Reengineering is especially critical to ensuring that the benefits of new technology can be realized. Applying new technology

Hershey's Rebuffs Mondelez's Takeover Offer

Recently Hershey's, the candy company, rebuffed an offer to be acquired by Mondelez International Inc. Modelez, a huge global food company, offered lots of money, to make the merged company named "Hershey's," and to keep the chocolate headquarters in Hershey, Pennsylvania. Usually companies that receive offers like that would give up control to an acquirer with such global scale, but Hershey's is no usual company.

Hershey's, the maker of Hershey's kisses and Reese's peanut butter cups, was founded by Milton Hershey over a century ago and the company grew wildly successful. Mr. Hershey and his wife had no children of their own, but they did have a passion to help needy children. They created the Milton Hershey School, which provides free education, food, clothes, and housing to underprivileged children. When the Hersheys passed away, they left their fortune to the Hershey Trust Co. The Trust is run by 10 members who make decisions regarding the $12 billion endowment, an amusement park, the Milton Hershey School, a resort and spa, and even a real estate company. Needless to say, one cannot imagine what Hershey, Pennsylvania, would be without Hershey's, and that is the

main reason that Hershey's, the company, decided to remain independent. As John Foley, a member of the town's board of supervisors (and a graduate of the Milton Hershey School) says, "They should never sell it. Even if the headquarters stayed here, we'd lose our power."

DISCUSSION QUESTION

1. Do you think that Hershey's was right in its decision to turn down Mondelez's acquisition offer? Why or why not?

SOURCE: A. Gasparo, "Hershey, Pa., Is the Town That Chocolate Built," *Wall Street Journal*, August 15, 2016, www.wsj.com/articles/hershey-pa-is-the-town-that-chocolate-built-1471301344.

to an inefficient process will not improve efficiency or effectiveness. Instead, it will increase product or service costs related to the introduction of the new technology.

Reengineering can be used to review the HRM department functions and processes, or it can be used to review specific HRM practices such as work design or the performance management system. The reengineering process involves the four steps shown in Figure 16.13: identify the process to be reengineered, understand the process, redesign the process, and implement the new process.[9]

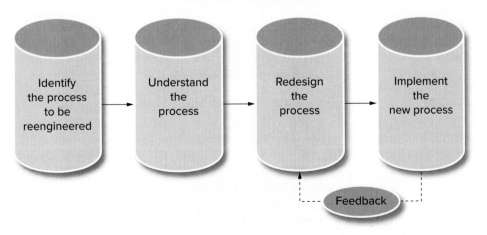

Figure 16.13
The Reengineering Process

Identifying the Process

First, the company should identify the process they want to reengineer and the individuals who are part of that process. Managers who control the process or are responsible for functions within the process (sometimes called "process owners") should be identified and asked to be part of the reengineering team. Team members should include employees involved in the process (to provide expertise) and those outside the process, as well as internal or external customers who see the outcome of the process.

Understanding the Process

Several things need to be considered when evaluating a process:

- Can jobs be combined?
- Can employees be given more autonomy? Can decision making and control be built into the process through streamlining it?
- Are all the steps in the process necessary?
- Are data redundancy, unnecessary checks, and controls built into the process?
- How many special cases and exceptions have to be dealt with?
- Are the steps in the process arranged in their natural order?
- What is the desired outcome? Are all of the tasks necessary? What is the value of the process?

Various techniques are used to understand processes. Data-flow diagrams are useful to show the flow of data among departments. Figure 16.14 shows a data-flow diagram for

Figure 16.14

A Data-Flow Diagram for Payroll Data

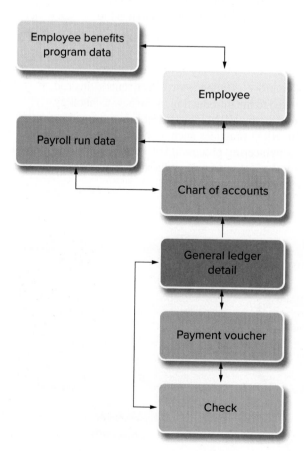

payroll data and the steps in producing a paycheck. Information about the employee and department are sent to the general account. The payroll check is issued based on a payment voucher that is generated from the general accounting ledger. Data-entity relationship diagrams show the types of data used within a business function and the relationship among the different types of data. In scenario analysis, simulations of real-world issues are presented to data end users. The end users are asked to indicate how an information system could help address their particular situations and what data should be maintained to deal with those situations. Surveys and focus groups collect information about the data collected, used, and stored in a functional area, as well as information about time and information-processing requirements. Users may be asked to evaluate the importance, frequency, and criticality of automating specific tasks within a functional area. For example, how critical is it to have an applicant tracking system that maintains data on applicants' previous work experience? Cost–benefit analyses compare the costs of completing tasks with and without an automated system or software application. For example, the analysis should include the costs in terms of people, time, materials, and dollars; the anticipated costs of software and hardware; and labor, time, and material expenses.[10]

Redesigning the Process

During the redesign phase, the team develops models, tests them, chooses a prototype, and determines how to integrate the prototype into the organization.

Implementing the Process

The company tries out the process by testing it in a limited, controlled setting before expanding companywide. For example, J. M. Huber Corporation, a New Jersey–based conglomerate that has several operating divisions scattered throughout the United States, used reengineering to avoid installing new software onto inefficient processes.[11] HR staff began by documenting and studying the existing work flow and creating a strategy for improving efficiency. Top management, mid-level managers, and HR staff worked together to identify the processes they most wanted to improve. They determined that the most critical issue was to develop a client–server system that could access data more easily than the mainframe computer they were currently using. Also, the client–server system could eliminate many of the requisitions needed to get access to data, which slowed down work. The HRM department's efforts have streamlined record-keeping functions, eliminated redundant steps, and automated manual processes. The fully automated client–server system allows employees to sign up and change benefits information using an interactive voice-response system that is connected to the company's database. In addition, managers have easier access to employees' salary history, job descriptions, and other data. If an employee is eligible for a salary increase and the manager requests a change and it is approved, the system will process it (without entry by a clerical worker), and the changes will be seen on the employee's paycheck. Results of the reengineering effort are impressive. The redesigned processes have reduced the number of problems that HRM has to give to other departments by 42%, cut work steps by 26%, and eliminated 20% of the original work. Although the company is spending more than $1 million to make the technology work, it estimates that the investment should pay for itself in five years.

LO 16-7
Discuss the types of new technologies that can improve the efficiency and effectiveness of HRM.

Improving HRM Effectiveness through New Technologies—E-HRM

Since the mid-1990s, as HRM functions sought to play a more strategic role in their organizations, the first task was to eliminate transactional tasks in order to free up time to focus on traditional and transformational activities. Part of building a strategic HR function requires moving much of the transactional work away from being done by HR employees so that they can have time available to work on strategic activities. Consequently, the use of technology can make HR more strategic and by doing so increase the value that HR adds to the business.[13] As indicated in Figure 16.11, outsourcing of many of these activities provided one mechanism for reducing this burden. However, more relevant today is the focus on the use of information technology to handle these tasks. Early on this was achieved by the development and implementation of information systems that were run by the HRM function but more recently have evolved into systems that allow employees to serve themselves. As described earlier, employees can access the system and make their benefit enrollment, changes, or claims online. Clearly, technology has freed HRM functions from transactional activities to focus on more strategic actions.

However, the speed requirements of e-business force HRM functions to explore how to leverage technology for the delivery of traditional and transformational HRM activities. This does not imply that over time all of HRM will be executed online, but rather a number of HRM activities currently delivered via paper or face-to-face communications can be delivered electronically with no loss (and even gains) in effectiveness and efficiency. This is illustrated by Figure 16.15. We explore some examples next. The "Competing through Technology" box illustrates how Charity: Water has been using technology to link donors to how their contributions are being used.

Figure 16.15

Change in Delivery

E-Enabled Delivery of HRM

Traditional face-to-face delivery

Electronic delivery

Tranformational (25–35%)
Knowledge management
Strategic redirection and renewal
Cultural change
Management development

Traditional (25–35%)
Recruitment and selection
Training
Performance management
Compensation
Employee relations

Transactional (15–25%)
Benefits administration
Record keeping
Employee services

Outsourcing

Process redesign, information technology

COMPETING THROUGH TECHNOLOGY

Charity: Water Connects Donors with Beneficiaries through Technology

At a recent fundraising gala, former nightclub promoter Scott Harrison provided preloaded locked iPads to each table with pictures of a single resident of Adi Etot, Ethiopia, a town in great need of clean water. After giving some background information on life in Adi Etot, Harrison gave attendees the password to see more photos as he asked them to donate $30 in honor of that person. Then, after almost everyone had donated, the attendees saw a real-time image of the people whom they had just seen, surrounding a well as the sun rose. As the drill used to make the well was turned on 6,500 miles away, it unleashed a huge stream, spraying water over the villagers.

Harrison started Charity: Water after traveling around the globe on a Mercy Ship and seeing thousands of people in the developing world who suffered from waterborne sicknesses. The charity guarantees that 100% of donations go to providing clean water in the developing world. To provide maximum transparency to donors, Charity: Water worked with Google maps to map every well it has helped to drill. In addition, it received a $5 million grant from Google to install sensors on wells so that they can be monitored remotely, and it uses machine learning to identify when wells are beginning to function erratically.

Although providing clean water reduces illnesses, almost more important is the time these wells save. Women and children often have to walk three or four hours each way to get water, which can prevent girls from attending school. As wells are drilled closer to a village, young women regain that time and gain an education as a result.

Charity: Water helps to provide clean water that villagers can access more easily, helping to reduce illness and improve the education of villagers. It uses technology to connect donors to these beneficiaries, to help donors feel confident that they are helping real people in real places.

DISCUSSION QUESTION

1. Would being able to see where Charity: Water wells are drilled and how they are functioning make you more confident that your contributions are being well spent? Why or why not?

SOURCE: B. Paynter, "How Charity: Water Uses Data to Connect Donors and the People They Are Helping," *Fast Company*, March 20, 2017, https://www.fastcompany.com/3068686/how-charity-water-uses-data-to-connect-donors-and-the-people-theyre-helping.

In a world dominated by social media, companies like Google are now using it for internal purposes. Google developed "Grow," an internal platform that makes it easy for Googlers to find learning opportunities, jobs, one-on-one advice, and other development resources to suit their needs and interests. Grow unifies myriad learning, development, and job search tools into a one-stop shop for Googlers to manage and act on their development. It suggests courses, opportunities, advisors, and more based on what the company knows about the Googler (e.g., role, level, location) and the data a Googler provides within the tool (e.g., skills he or she wants to develop). Not surprisingly, given Google's search capability, this system allows employees to search for learning resources or jobs of interest.

Grow is an inherently social platform, and every Googler has a customizable profile that is visible to others. Figure 16.16 displays the Grow profile of Sunil Chandra, Google's VP of staffing and operations. As you can see, Googlers can tag skills they have (e.g., consulting, people management, and coaching for Sunil) and those they want to develop (e.g., entrepreneurship and prioritization) in their profile. Skills listed in Grow help the system get to know the user and offer more personalized job recommendations. Googlers can also indicate if they would like to advise others on a particular skill. If

Figure 16.16

Personal Web Page for Sunil Chandra

©Google, Inc.

Sunil tags himself as a "Skill Advisor" on a topic (e.g., leadership), he will appear in Grow's search results, and other Googlers can view his skills and contact him for advice. He can select the option to "teach other Googlers," as well, which would connect him to Google's g2g (or "Googlers-to-Googlers") program, an internal volunteer teaching network that allows employees to teach their peers on a variety of subjects.

As mentioned earlier, Grow also allows Googlers to list skills they would like to develop. They can add up to 10 skills, and Grow will use these inputs to further customize their learning recommendations. To help Googlers get started, Grow suggests a number of skills on the right-hand side of the page (culled from a multiyear study of the skills that make Googlers effective in their roles). In Sunil's case, he has already added all of his suggested skills directly to his profile, which is why the tool reflects "no suggested skills." Sunil's profile also includes his picture, job title, location, and a link to his internal employee page to help his fellow Googlers get to know him.

In sum, Grow profiles are a great way for Googlers to teach the tool about their skills and development areas, and get better learning and job recommendations in the process. It also helps Googlers connect with their peers as advisors, mentors, or internal teachers, in addition to providing a host of other learning and development resources.

Recruitment and Selection

Traditional recruitment and selection processes have required considerable face-to-face communications with recruitment firms and potential employees, labor-intensive assessment devices, and significant monitoring of managerial decisions to ensure that hiring patterns and decisions do not run afoul of regulatory requirements. However, technology has transformed these processes.

For example, online recruiting accounts for one of every eight hires according to kforce.com's poll of 300 U.S. companies. IBM employees now fill out forms on the web to identify contract help they need, and that information is immediately sent to 14 temp agencies. Within an hour, agencies respond with résumés for review, allowing IBM to cut hiring time from 10 days to 3 and to save $3 million per year.

Finally, technology has enabled firms to monitor hiring processes to minimize the potential for discriminatory hiring decisions. For example, Home Depot was accused of forcing female applicants into cashier jobs while reserving the customer service jobs for males. While not admitting guilt, as part of its consent decree Home Depot uses technology to identify people who have skills for jobs they are not applying for based on key words in their résumés. In addition, the technology forces managers to interview diverse candidate sets before making decisions.

Compensation and Rewards

Compensation systems in organizations probably reflect the most pervasive form of bureaucracy within HRM. In spite of the critical role they play in attracting, motivating, and retaining employees, most systems consist of rigid, time-consuming, and ineffective processes. Managers fill out what they believe to be useless forms, ignore guidelines, and display a general disdain for the entire process.

Leveraging technology may allow firms to better achieve their compensation goals with considerably less effort. For example, one problem many merit or bonus pay plans face is that managers refuse to differentiate among performers, giving everyone similar pay increases. This allows them to spend less time thinking about how to manage (rate and review) performance as well as minimizes the potential conflict they might face. Thus, employees do not see linkages between performance and pay, resulting in lower motivation among all employees and higher turnover among top performers (and possibly lower turnover among bottom performers). To minimize this, Cypress Semiconductors requires managers to distinguish between equity and merit and forces distributions with regard to both concepts.[14] For example, equity means that the top-ranked performer in any group of peers should make 50% more than the lowest-ranked performer, and people with comparable performance should receive comparable salaries. With regard to merit, there must be at least a 7% spread between the lowest and highest pay raises (if the lowest raise is 3%, then the highest must be at least 10%). If ratings and raises are input into a system, the firm can monitor and control the rating process to ensure that adequate differentiations are made consistent with the policy.

Training and Development

Exploring different vehicles for delivering training (PC, video, and the like) certainly is not a new concept. In addition, a number of firms have begun delivering training via the web. Their experience suggests that some types of training can be done effectively via the Internet or an intranet, whereas others might not. For example, companies such as IBM and Dell both boast that they have developed Internet-based training for some parts of their workforce.

Interestingly, the challenge of speedy delivery of HRM services brings the concept of Internet-based training to the forefront. In today's competitive environment, firms compete to attract and retain both customers and talented employees. How well a firm develops and treats existing employees largely determines how well it achieves these outcomes. Yet the challenges of speed, project focus, and changing technology create environments that discourage managers from managing their people, resulting in a situation where employees may not feel respected or valued.

This presents a challenge to firms to provide both the incentive and the skills for managers to treat employees as assets rather than commodities. Consider how Internet-based training might facilitate this. Assume that you work for Widget.com, a fast-growing, fast-paced e-business. You arrive at work Monday morning, and your e-mail contains a high-priority message with either an attachment or a link to a URL. It is your Monday morning challenge from the CEO, and you know that the system will track whether you link and complete this challenge. When you link to it, you see a digital video of your CEO telling you how people are Widget.com's competitive advantage, and that when they don't feel valued, they leave. Thus, his challenge to you is to make your employees feel valued today. To do so, you will in the next 10 minutes learn how to express appreciation to an employee. You receive six learning points; you observe a digitized video model performing the learning points; you review the learning points again and take a quiz. You then see the CEO giving you the final challenge: that in the next 15 minutes you are to take one of your employees aside and express your appreciation using the skill you just developed.

Notice the advantages of this process. First, it was not time consuming, like most three-day or one-week training programs. The entire process (training and demonstration with a real employee) took less than 30 minutes; you have developed a skill; and an employee now probably feels better about the organization. It communicated a real organizational value or necessary competency. It didn't require any travel expenses to a training facility. It did not overwhelm you with so much information that you would be lucky to remember 10% of what you were exposed to. Finally, it was a push, rather than pull, approach to training. The firm did not wait for you to realize you had a deficiency and then go search and sign up for training. It pushed the training to you.

Technology allows firms to deliver training and development for at least some skills or knowledge faster, more efficiently, and probably more effectively. It can quickly merge training, communication, and immediate response to strategic contingencies.

Creating and nurturing a committed workforce presents a tremendous challenge to firms today. According to a survey conducted by Monster.com, 61% of Americans consider themselves overworked and 86% are not satisfied with their jobs.[15] Such findings suggest that firms need to find ways to monitor commitment levels, identify potential obstacles to commitment, and respond quickly to eliminate those obstacles. In large part, attitude surveys have constituted the platform from which these activities were managed in the past.

Consider the traditional attitude survey. Surveys are administered to employees over a period of four to six weeks. The data are entered and analyzed, requiring another six to eight weeks. A group interprets the results to identify the major problem areas, and task forces are formed to develop recommendations; this process easily takes another four to six months. Finally, decisions must be made about implementing the task force recommendations. In the end, employees might see responses to their concerns at best 12–18 months after the survey—and then the survey administrators cannot understand why employees think that completing the survey is a waste of time.

Now consider how technology can shorten that cycle. E-pulse represents one attempt to create a platform for almost real-time attitude surveys. Developed by Theresa Welbourne at the University of Alabama, E-pulse is a scalable survey device administered online. Normally three questions are asked regarding how employees feel about work, but more questions can be added to get feedback on any specific issue. The survey goes out online, and when employees complete it, the data are immediately entered and analyzed. In essence, the part of the process that took four months in the past has been reduced to a day.

Next the firm can decide how it wants to use the information. For example, it could be broken down by business, site, or work unit, with the relevant information going to the leader of the chosen unit of analysis. In essence, a supervisor could receive almost immediate feedback about the attitudes of his or her work group, or a general manager about his or her business unit. The supervisor or manager can respond immediately, even if only to communicate that she or he realizes a problem exists and will take action soon.

Although technology provides for faster HRM, only a more systemic approach will ensure better and smarter HRM. For example, using technology to disseminate information to supervisors and managers may be faster, but unless those individuals possess good problem-solving and communication skills, they may either ignore the information or, worse yet, exacerbate the problem with inappropriate responses. As we noted with regard to training, this systemic approach requires knocking down traditional functional walls to deliver organizational solutions rather than functional programs. Thus, the challenge is to view the technology not as a panacea or even as a functional tool but rather as a catalyst for transforming the HRM organization.

Improving HRM Effectiveness through New Technologies—HRM Information Systems

Several new and emerging technologies can help improve the effectiveness of the HRM function. **New technologies** are current applications of knowledge, procedures, and equipment that have not been used previously. New technology usually involves automation—that is, replacing human labor with equipment, information processing, or some combination of the two.

In HRM, technology has already been used for three broad functions: transaction processing, reporting, and tracking; decision support systems; and expert systems.[12] **Transaction processing** refers to computations and calculations used to review and document HRM decisions and practices. This includes documenting relocation, training expenses, and course enrollments and filling out government reporting requirements (such as EEO-1 reports, which require companies to report information to the government regarding employees' race and gender by job category). **Decision support systems** are designed to help managers solve problems. They usually include a "what if" feature that allows users to see how outcomes change when assumptions or data change. These systems are useful, for example, for helping companies determine the number of new hires needed based on different turnover rates or the availability of employees with a certain skill in the labor market. **Expert systems** are computer systems incorporating the decision rules of people deemed to have expertise in a certain area. The system recommends actions that the user can take based on the information provided by the user. The recommended actions are those that a human expert would take in a similar situation (such as a manager interviewing a job candidate).

Predictive Analytics

The more recent use of technology and data has been in the area of predictive analytics. Earlier in the chapter we discussed how HR functions can analytically evaluate their performance through either tracking certain metrics or surveying internal customers. Although such a backward-looking approach can help the function to pinpoint areas for improvement, more recent effort has been devoted to trying to identify problems before they happen.

Predictive analytics refers to the use of data to make predictions about actions or outcomes in the future. For example, many technology companies hate to see good employees leave because they are so hard to replace. Looking at data to identify indicators that an employee is about to leave would be helpful for organizations if they want to intervene. For instance, Adobe Systems has found that a strong predictor of an employee's desire to leave is when the employee begins to update his or her LinkedIn profile. Google has developed sophisticated algorithms looking at a number of variables and uses these algorithms to identify which employees are likely to leave.

New technologies
Current applications of knowledge, procedures, and equipment that have not been previously used. Usually involves replacing human labor with equipment, information processing, or some combination of the two.

Transaction processing
Computations and calculations used to review and document HRM decisions and practices.

Decision support systems
Problem-solving systems that usually include a "what-if" feature that allows users to see how outcomes change when assumptions or data change.

Expert systems
Computer systems incorporating the decision rules of people recognized as experts in a certain area.

EVIDENCE-BASED HR

How can predictive analytics help solve real company problems? No firm wants to lose valued high-performing employees, but often they do not know the employees are thinking about leaving until it is too late. A recent study by Gardner, Van Iddekinge, and Hom found that employees often shows behaviors predictive of quitting. The extensive validation study across a number of different employee groups identified the following behaviors as signs that an employee may be thinking about leaving the organization:

1. Their work productivity has decreased more than usual.
2. They have acted less like a team player than usual.
3. They have been doing the minimum amount of work more frequently.
4. They have been less interested in pleasing their manager than usual.
5. They have been less willing to commit to long-term timelines than usual.
6. They have exhibited a negative change in attitude.
7. They have exhibited less effort and work motivation than usual.
8. They have exhibited less focus on job-related matters than usual.
9. They have expressed dissatisfaction with their current job more frequently than usual.
10. They have expressed dissatisfaction with their supervisor more frequently than usual.
11. They have left early from work more frequently than usual.
12. They have lost enthusiasm for the mission of the organization.
13. They have shown less interest in working with customers than usual.

SOURCE: T. M. Garder, C. H. Van Iddekinge, & P. W. Hom, "If You've Got Leavin' on Your Mind: The Identification and Validation of Pre-quitting Behaviors," *Journal of Management.* Published online August 29, 2016.

Customization

Finally, the vast increases in technological capability and data has a number of companies looking to better customize an employee's experience with the organization. In the past, many companies allowed "cafeteria" benefit plans that allowed employees to choose the benefits they most desired. However, today some firms allow employees to customize their pay mix (e.g., take lesser or greater amounts of fixed versus variable pay, or varying the type of variable pay such as bonuses versus stock). Also, companies can proactively approach employees who may want to think about changing benefits based on changes in life events (e.g, when an employee adds a child as a beneficiary, the company can suggest putting money into life insurance or into educational savings accounts). In all these cases, companies are not forcing changes onto employees but rather are using the information they have about employees to help those employees better manage their work and personal lives.

LO 16-8
List the competencies the HRM executive needs to become a strategic partner in the company.

The Future for HR Professionals

The future for careers in the human resource profession seems brighter than ever. An increasing number of successful companies such as Microsoft have made the top HR job a member of the senior management team, reporting directly to the chief executive officer. CEOs recognize the importance of their workforce in driving competitive success. Firms need to seek the balance between attracting, motivating, and retaining the very best talent and keeping labor and administrative costs as low as possible. Finding such a balance requires HR leaders who have a deep knowledge of the business combined with a deep knowledge of HR issues, tools, processes, and technologies.

For a reader who is just getting a first glimpse of the HRM function, to portray what a vastly different role HRM must play today compared to 20 or even 10 years ago is impossible. As noted earlier, HRM has traditionally played a largely administrative role—simply processing paperwork plus developing and administering hiring, training, appraisal, compensation, and benefits systems—and all of this has been unrelated to the strategic direction of the firm. In the early 1980s, HRM took on more of a one-way linkage role, helping to implement strategy. Now strategic decision makers are realizing the importance of people issues and so are calling for HRM to become the "source of people expertise" in the firm.[16] This requires that HR managers possess and use knowledge of how people can and do play a role in competitive advantage as well as the policies, programs, and practices that can leverage the firm's people as a source of competitive advantage. This leads to an entirely new set of competencies for today's strategic HR executive.[17]

In the future, HR professionals will need four basic competencies to become partners in the strategic management process.[18] First, they will need "business competence"—knowing the company's business and understanding its economic financial capabilities. This calls for making logical decisions that support the company's strategic plan based on the most accurate information possible. Because in almost all companies the effectiveness of decisions must be evaluated in terms of dollar values, the HR executive must be able to calculate the costs and benefits of each alternative in terms of its dollar impact.[19] In addition, the nonmonetary impact needs to be considered. The HR executive must be fully capable of identifying the social and ethical issues attached to HRM practices. HR professionals must often act as the conscience of the organization in all aspects. The "Competing through Sustainability" box describes how Citigroup has hired a seminary professor to help act as the conscience of the organization.

Second, HR professionals will need "professional–technical knowledge" of state-of-the-art HRM practices in areas such as staffing, development, rewards, organizational design, and communication. New selection techniques, performance appraisal methods, training programs, and incentive plans are being developed continually. Some of these programs can provide value, whereas others may be no more than the products of today's HRM equivalent of snake oil. HR executives must be able to critically evaluate the new techniques offered as state-of-the-art HRM programs and use only those that will benefit the company.

Third, they must be skilled in the "management of change processes," such as diagnosing problems, implementing organizational changes, and evaluating results. Every time a company changes its strategy in even a minor way, the entire company has to change. These changes result in conflict, resistance, and confusion among the people who must implement the new plans or programs. The HR executive must have the skills to oversee the change in a way that ensures its success. In fact, one survey of *Fortune* 500 companies found that 87% of the companies had their organization development/change function as part of the HR department.[20]

Finally, these professionals must also have "integration competence," meaning the ability to integrate the three other competencies to increase the company's value. This means that, although specialist knowledge is necessary, a generalist perspective must be taken in making decisions. This entails seeing how all the functions within the HRM area

Saving Citigroup

Given the financial crisis and the criticism of the banking industry throughout the 2016 presidential campaign, bankers do not have a great reputation. The general public often sees them as greedy and unethical. In fact, Michael Corbat, CEO of Citigroup states, "If you look today at what the poll numbers say, what the general population says, there is a distrust of banks." Because of that, Citigroup has made an interesting hire: a seminarian.

Dr. David Miller is a professor at Princeton University and runs the university's "Faith and Work Initiative" focused on helping people of faith to integrate that faith with their careers. However, he has not always been a professor, nor a saint. He graduated in business from Bucknell University, where he helped organize fraternity parties. From there he entered into a career in business working for companies like IBM and State Street. Now he consults with companies like Citigroup to help them build cultures that drive more ethical decision making.

Mr. Corbat, at a meeting of managing directors, suggested that in potentially risky situations, they ask Dr. Miller's 4 Ms: "What would your mother, your mentor, the media, and—if you are inclined—your maker think?"

Dr. Miller's influence is increasingly seen within Citigroup. Citi executives have developed three questions that they want to become integral to their culture and that have become part of its mission statement: Is it in our clients' interest, does it create economic value, and is it systemically responsible? Those, along with the 4 Ms, may be great questions for business students to think about.

DISCUSSION QUESTION
1. Do you think it is a good idea to have a seminary professor help executives make better ethical decisions? Why or why not?

SOURCE: C. Rexrode, "The Banker-Turned-Seminarian Trying to Save Citigroup's Soul," *Wall Street Journal,* March 17, 2017, www.wsj.com/articles/the-banker-turned-seminarian-trying-to-save-citigroups-soul-1489743006.

fit together to be effective and recognizing that changes in any one part of the HRM package are likely to require changes in other parts of the package.

Google has sought to achieve this integration with what it calls the "three-thirds" staffing model. This consist of the following groups of people with complimentary skill sets:

1. *One-third traditional HR people:* subject matter experts in benefits, compensation, employee relations, learning, and recruiting. Their expertise, pattern recognition, and emotional intelligence serve as the foundation for developing services and programs.
2. *One-third consultants:* high-end strategy experts with a background in management consulting who thrive on solving big, amorphous problems and bring a deliberate, business approach to people issues.
3. *One-third analytics professionals:* master's and doctoral-level folks who measure, analyze, and provide insight into all that the people operations function does, and to prove what really works. They have a healthy appetite for the impossible and drive experimentation to ensure that Google is as innovative on the people side as it is on the product side.

This staffing model has enabled Google to build the required skill base and integrate the various people needed to build a world-class HR organization.[21]

The Role of the Chief Human Resource Officer

Having discussed the increasing importance of HR and the new strategic role of HR professionals, in closing we examine the role of the leader of the HR function. These chief human resource officers (CHROs) bear the responsibility for leading the HR function as well as ensuring that HR systems and processes deliver value to the company. Only recently have researchers attempted to examine what these HR leaders do and how they affect the business.

A recent survey identified seven roles that CHROs have to play to one degree or another, and then asked *Fortune* 150 CHROs to identify how they spend their time across those roles. As can be seen in Figure 16.17, CHROs reported spending the second most time (21%) as a **strategic advisor** to the executive team. This role entails sharing the people expertise as part of the decision-making process, as well as shaping how the firm's human capital fits into its strategy. This also was the role that was most frequently cited as having the greatest impact on the firm. One CHRO described the importance of the strategic advisor role as:

> HR is critical, but it's a tool in the firm's portfolio. First, to truly impact the success of the firm, the CHRO needs to have a broad credibility that only comes from understanding every facet of the business at a level deep enough to be able to add business value in discussions with every leader. That means understanding the firm's economics, customer behavior, products, technology, etc. at a level deep enough to steer and shape decisions in these areas. From that flows the trust and credibility to counter the "conventional wisdom" on how best to manage people and shape the firm's talent agenda. Without this broader credibility, the CHRO can talk about talent, but risks not having sufficient context to make the right decisions. Second, from the CEO's perspective, the most useful thing is the integration of the people strategy with every other part of the firm's operations. The only way to truly integrate these areas is to be actively involved in the broader discussions as well.[22]

The role of **talent architect** also sees a significant portion of time spent (17%) and was also frequently cited as the role in which the CHRO has the greatest impact on the

Strategic advisor A role of the CHRO that focuses on the formulation and implementation of the firm's strategy.

Talent architect A role of the CHRO that focuses on building and identifying the human capital critical to the present and future of the firm.

What percent of your time would you say you spend in each of the following roles?

Firm representative 5% Other 0%
Workforce sensor 8%
Functional leader 22%
Strategic advisor 21%
Executive coach 17%
Talent architect 17%
Board liaison 10%

Figure 16.17

Percentage of Time CHROs Spend in Each Role

INTEGRITY IN ACTION

Uber's CEO Needs CHRO Help

Following the claims of a former engineer about how women were not treated fairly at Uber and CEO Travis Kalanick's being caught on video verbally abusing an Uber driver, the mercurial CEO stated that he "needed leadership help." Consequently, Uber has begun interviewing a number of well-known operating executives to serve as his number 2. Certainly, this would be helpful, however, would it be enough?

First, if Kalanick displays narcissistic behavior, he is not alone. Recent research revealed that between 5–16% of CEOs may be considered narcissists. This research also showed that narcissistic CEOs have teams that do not get along, nor do they have much respect for the CEO.

Who is the best positioned member of the leadership team to help a CEO who struggles with weaknesses in terms of leadership style? In fact, in most cases the CHRO serves this role. CHROs are able (and expected) to have hard conversations with CEOs, often confronting them when the CEO has displayed ineffective or possibly offensive behaviors.

DISCUSSION QUESTION

1. In part, because of his leadership deficiencies, Kalanick resigned as CEO in June, 2017. If you had been Uber's CHRO, how would you have tried to counsel him so that his resignation might not have been necessary

SOURCE: G. Bensiger, G. Morris, and G. Wells, "Uber Interviews Heavyweights for a Crucial Job: Handling Travis Kalanick," *Wall Street Journal*, April 27, 2017, www.wsj.com/articles/uber-interviews-heavyweights-for-a-crucial-job-handling-travis-kalanick-1493304051.

---

business. Playing the role of talent architect requires that CHROs help the executive team see the importance of talent, identify present and future talent gaps, and come to own the talent agenda. One CHRO described the importance of this role this way:

> Keeping the senior team focused on the strategic talent needs of the business allows proper identification of talent gaps and future needs, thus allowing time to develop best talent and design appropriate experiential assignments.[23]

Counselor/confidante/coach
A role of the CHRO that focuses on counseling or coaching team members or resolving interpersonal or political conflicts among team members.

CHROs report spending as much time in the role of **counselor/confidante/coach** as they do in the talent architect role (17%), and a number of CHROs listed this role as one of the roles with the greatest impact. This role seemingly is a broad one, and it can entail anything from behavioral or performance counseling to being the personal sounding board for the CEO. Perhaps as pressure mounts on CEOs from investors and analysts, the CHRO is the most trusted advisor that can be counted on to give personal advice or simply to listen to the CEO's problems. Sometimes CEOs may tend to behave dysfunctionally, and the CHRO may be the one to help point that out. The "Integrity in Action" box describes how Uber's CEO may need a good CHRO to play this role. Consider the following poignant comment regarding this role:

> If I do my job right, I am the copper wire that connects all the outlets of the firm together effectively. This includes Organization Development work (which some might put in the strategic advisor category), performance counseling and relationship building, business consulting and the strategic elements of talent acquisition and planning.[24]

Often this counselor/confidante/coach role entails coaching senior leaders regarding their communication style, and particularly warning them when their messages might be misinterpreted by those lower in the organizations.

Table 16.5
Roles of the CHRO

Strategic advisor to the executive team: activities focused specifically on the formulation and implementation of the firm's strategy.

Counselor/confidante/coach to the executive team: activities focused on counseling or coaching team members or resolving interpersonal or political conflicts among team members.

Liaison to the board of directors: preparation for board meetings, phone calls with board members, attendance at board meetings.

Talent architect: activities focused on building and identifying the human capital critical to the present and future of the firm.

Leader of the HR function: working with HR team members regarding the development, design, and delivery of HR services.

Workforce sensor: activities focused on identifying workforce morale issues or concerns.

Representative of the firm: activities with external stakeholders, such as lobbying, speaking to outside groups, etc.

The **leader of the HR function** is the role in which CHROs spent the most time (22%), but it is not seen as one that has the greatest impact. This role deals with ensuring that the HR function is aligning its activities and priorities toward the needs of the business, and it usually entails meeting with direct reports to provide guidance and check on progress. However, CHROs increasingly rely on their direct reports to design and deliver HR services while they shift their attention to advising and counseling the top executive team.

Liaison to the board of directors entails all of the activities in which CHROs engage with the board of directors, including discussions of executive compensation, CEO performance, CEO succession, and performance of other members of the executive leadership team. This role is increasing in importance, although it has a long way to go before equaling the strategic advisor, talent architect, and counselor/confidante/coach roles.

Finally, CHROs to some extent become the face of the organization to outside constituents such as labor unions, nongovernmental organizations, and the press. They spend the least amount of time in the **representative of the firm** role (see Table 16.5).

The new strategic role for HRM presents both opportunities and challenges. HRM has the chance to profoundly impact the way organizations compete through people. But with this opportunity comes serious responsibility and accountability.[25] HRM functions of the future must consist of individuals who view themselves as businesspeople who happen to work in an HRM function, rather than as HRM people who happen to work in a business.

Leader of the HR function
A role of the CHRO that focuses on working with HR team members regarding the development, design, and delivery of HR services.

Liaison to the board of directors
A role of the CHRO that focuses on preparation for board meetings, phone calls with board members, and attendance at board meetings.

Representative of the firm
A role of the CHRO that focuses on activities with external stakeholders, such as lobbying, speaking to outside groups, etc.

A LOOK BACK

Rewiring HR at Cisco

Fran Katsoudas has made a number of innovative moves with regard to how to manage HR at Cisco. The history of HR at Cisco had been focused on risk and compliance, but the emphasis has shifted to people, culture, and employee experience. In an interview with *Hispanic Executive*, Katsoudas said that her emphasis for 2017 was as follows:

- Creating a culture where employees can experience one company, many careers through job changes, continuous skills development, and stretch assignments
- Building the best teams and creating an environment of safety and trust, which will enable innovation
- Continuing to move to "one size fits one" offerings so that employees can create and experience their own journey

This is what today's HR function works on. Rather that focus on administrative tasks, modern HR functions help to build business success by building the human capabilities firms need to succeed.

QUESTIONS

1. In light of what you have read in this chapter, do you think that Cisco is innovating? Why or why not?
2. What do you think Katsoudas means by the term "one size fits one?"

SOURCE: K. C. Forsythe, "Breaking HR at Cisco," *Hispanic Executive*, 2017, http://hispanicexecutive.com/2017/breaking-hr-at-cisco/.

SUMMARY

The roles required of the HRM function have changed as people have become recognized as a true source of competitive advantage. This has required a transformation of the HRM function from focusing solely on transactional activities to an increasing involvement in strategic activities. In fact, according to one study, 64% of HR executives said that their HRM function is in a process of transformation.[26] The strategic management of the HRM function will determine whether HRM will transform itself to a true strategic partner or simply be blown up.

In this chapter we explored the various changing roles of the HRM function. HRM today includes the roles of administrative expert, employee advocate, change agent, and strategic partner. The function must also deliver transactional, traditional, and transformational services and activities to the firm, and it must be both efficient and effective. HR executives must strategically manage the HRM function just as the firm must be strategically managed. This requires that HRM develop measures of the function's performance through customer surveys and analytic methods. These measures can form the basis for planning ways to improve performance. HRM performance can increase through new structures for the function, through using reengineering and information technology, and through outsourcing.

KEY TERMS

Audit approach, 688
Analytic approach, 690
Outsourcing, 695
Reengineering, 696
New technologies, 705

Transaction processing, 705
Decision support systems, 705
Expert systems, 705
Strategic advisor, 709
Talent architect, 709

Counselor/confidante/coach, 710
Leader of the HR function, 711
Liaison to the board of directors, 711
Representative of the firm, 711

DISCUSSION QUESTIONS

1. Why have the roles and activities of the HRM function changed over the past 20–30 years? What has been driving this change? How effectively do you think HRM has responded?
2. How can the processes for strategic management discussed in Chapter 2 be transplanted to manage the HRM function?
3. Why do you think that few companies take the time to determine the effectiveness of HRM practices? Should a company be concerned about evaluating HRM practices? Why? What might people working in the HRM function gain by evaluating the function?
4. How might imaging technology be useful for recruitment? For training? For benefits administration? For performance management?
5. Employees in your company currently choose and enroll in benefits programs after reading brochures, completing enrollment forms, and sending them to their HR rep. A temporary staff has to be hired to process the large amount of paperwork that is generated. Enrollment forms need to be checked, sorted, batched, sent to data entry, keypunched, returned, and filed. The process is slow and prone to errors. How could you use process reengineering to make benefits enrollment more efficient and effective?
6. Some observers argue that outsourcing an activity is bad because the activity is no longer a means of distinguishing the firm from competitors. (All competitors can buy the same service from the same provider, so it cannot be a source of competitive advantage.) Is this true? If so, why would a firm outsource any activity?

SELF-ASSESSMENT EXERCISE

Additional assignable self-assessments available in Connect.

How ethical are you? Read each of the following descriptions. For each, circle whether you believe the behavior described is ethical or unethical.

1. A company president found that a competitor had made an important scientific discovery that would sharply reduce the profits of his own company. The president hired a key employee of the competitor in an attempt to learn the details of the discovery.   Ethical   Unethical
2. To increase profits, a general manager used a production process that exceeded legal limits for environmental pollution.   Ethical   Unethical
3. Because of pressure from her brokerage firm, a stockbroker recommended a type of bond that she did not consider to be a good investment.   Ethical   Unethical
4. A small business received one-fourth of its revenues in the form of cash. On the company's income tax forms, the owner reported only one-half of the cash receipts.   Ethical   Unethical
5. A corporate executive promoted a loyal friend and competent manager to the position of divisional vice president in preference to a better qualified manager with whom she had no close ties.   Ethical   Unethical
6. An employer received applications for a supervisor's position from two equally qualified applicants. The employer hired the male applicant because he thought some employees might resent being supervised by a female.   Ethical   Unethical
7. An engineer discovered what he perceived to be a product design flaw that constituted a safety hazard. His company declined to correct the flaw. The engineer decided to keep quiet, rather than taking his complaint outside the company.   Ethical   Unethical
8. A comptroller selected a legal method of financial reporting that concealed some embarrassing financial facts. Otherwise, those facts would have been public knowledge.   Ethical   Unethical
9. A company paid a $350,000 "consulting" fee to an official of a foreign country. In return, the official promised to help the company obtain a contract that should produce a $10 million profit for the company.   Ethical   Unethical
10. A member of a corporation's board of directors learned that her company intended to announce a stock split and increase its dividend. On the basis of this favorable information, the director bought additional shares of the company's stock. Following the announcement of the information, she sold the stock at a gain.   Ethical   Unethical

Now score your results. How many actions did you judge to be unethical?

All of these actions are unethical. The more of the actions you judged to be unethical, the better your understanding of ethical business behavior.

SOURCE: Based on S. Morris et al., "A Test of Environmental, Situational, and Personal Influences on the Ethical Intentions of CEOs," *Business and Society* 34 (1995), pp. 119–47.

EXERCISING STRATEGY

The Need for HR at Tech Start-Ups

Marc Andreessen, one of Netscape's founders and a venture capitalist in the Silicon Valley, tweeted his version of the Top 10 ways that start-ups can damage themselves. One way was "Refuse to take HR seriously: allow terrible internal manager & employee behavior to catalyze into catastrophic ethical and legal crisis."

The San Francisco–based software start-up GitHub exemplifies this potential issue. On an anonymous messaging app, an unnamed user posted, "The self proclaimed Queen of GitHub is leaving her throne. The masses cheer." Julie Ann Horvath, the subject of the post, responded with a flurry of online allegations regarding gender harassment at the company. A month later, company president and cofounder Tom Preston-Werner stepped down, in spite of the fact that he was not associated with the post. He did acknowledge that he had made errors in judgment in how he handled the situation.

The situation exemplifies the problems that often plague a free-wheeling start-up company. The lack of rules and structure create a culture where people can innovate, but sometimes rules exist for a reason. An absence of rules combined with young people inexperienced in office politics and used to a say-whatever-you-want mindset with regard to social media can create a cauldron in which conflict brews.

The company brought in an investigator to explore the substance of the gender harassment and hostile work environment claims. The investigator found no evidence supporting the claims but did find that a culture that blurred personal and professional boundaries exacerbated the conflict between Mr. Preston-Werner and Ms. Horvath. In addition, with the lack of a substantive HR function, the company seemed ill-equipped to deal with the conflict.

Tech start-up GitHub has been forced to grow up, and the 250-person company seems to have taken Mr. Andreessen's advice to heart when it comes to HR. The company now has almost a dozen people devoted to developing leadership training programs, organizational design, and conflict resolution. It also employs an individual formally trained in conflict resolution. In addition, the company has begun developing a formal organizational structure with clear reporting relationships and distinct managerial predictions.

Start-up tech firms often resist such moves for fear that the rules, structures, and job descriptions will stifle innovation and cost too much money. However, as the GitHub story shows, such costs often serve as necessary investments to build a successful company over the long term.

QUESTIONS

1. Why is it important for start-ups to pay attention to people issues?
2. How can having a good HR function help start-ups to grow profitably?
3. How do you think HR differs in large companies like IBM or Goodyear, compared to start-ups like GitHub?

SOURCE: E. Rusli. "Torment Claims Make GitHub Grow Up." *The Wall Street Journal*, July 17, 2014. www.wsj.com

MANAGING PEOPLE

Well Fargo's Recovery?

The power of incentives cannot be underestimated, and if you are looking for an example, look no further than Wells Fargo. The bank recently took a significant reputational and financial hit as illegal and unethical practices on the part of the banks employees came to light. The scandal resulted in a $185 million fine and enforcement action associated with employees opening as many as 2.1 million customer accounts without their knowledge.

The scandal can be traced back to the bank desiring to increase the number of customer accounts. For instance, a customer who has multiple checking and savings accounts, an auto loan, and a mortgage is much more profitable for a bank than someone with just a savings and/or checking account. So, the goal itself made sense as part of the bank's growth strategy.

However, a poorly designed incentive scheme took a legitimate goal but encouraged people to achieve it in ways that were both unethical and illegal. For instance, branch employees who hit their targets for new accounts might earn bonuses from $500 to $2000 each quarter and district managers could earn bonuses from $10,000 to $20,000 each year.

The pressure began with a "Jump into January" push where the retail banking head communicated lofty goals for branches and employees. These lofty goals and the associated bonuses with achieving them led many employees to display improper behavior.

When these practices came to light, Wells Fargo fired 5,300 lower level staff who had engaged in improper sales practices over the previous 5 years. However, remaining staff felt skeptical as the senior level executives had not faced discipline. However, that has begun to change. The board clawed back

from the CEO and head of retail banking tens of millions of dollars in equity. Neither was fired, but both left the company shortly thereafter. More recently, the board discussed eliminating bonuses for both the current CEO and CFO. The bank has now fired a number of executives below the c-suite.

QUESTIONS

1. Do you think Wells Fargo has done enough to punish those responsible for this scandal? Why or why not?
2. Why do you think the board would not fire the CEO and head of retail banking, but rather let them leave voluntarily?

SOURCE: https://www.wsj.com/articles/wells-fargo-fires-four-executives-following-probe-of-sales-practices-scandal-1487704642

HR IN SMALL BUSINESS

Employees Make a Difference at Amy's Ice Creams

One of the bright spots for hungry people in Austin, Texas, is Amy's Ice Creams—its factory on Burnet Road or one of several Amy's stores. Founder Amy Miller, who dropped out of medical school to start the business, figures it is just another way to "make a difference in people's lives," offering customers a fun place to celebrate or cheer up.

Miller had been paying for med school with a job at Steve's Ice Cream, but when the company was sold, she thought the new owners were too stodgy, so she opened her own ice cream shop. Given the motivation to strike out on her own, it's not surprising that her goal is to manage her employees in a different way, one that combines informal fun with care for others.

The spirit of fun is defined by the employee selection process Miller invented. When interviewing candidates, Miller hands them a white paper bag with the instruction to "make something creative" and show her later. One applicant used it to make a hot-air balloon. Another put food in a bag, gave it to a homeless person, took a photo of the gift, and put the photo in the bag to return as the creative offering.

Job design also plays up the fun. Amy's prized employees don't just scoop up ice cream but also come up with ways to create a playful atmosphere. The company encourages workers to juggle shakers or give away a scoop of ice cream to a customer who is willing to sing and dance.

While the two painted concrete cows that sit in front of the Amy's factory are an emblem of the company's commitment to fun, its commitment to caring has a more uplifting sign: Amy's Ice Creams funded the construction of a room in a local children's cancer care center. The room resembles an ice cream shop and includes freezers stocked with ice cream—a treat that patients can share with visiting family members.

Service to the community is also connected to employee engagement. At Amy's, the employees choose the charities

the company will support. At a prom hosted by Amy's every year, the company selects a King and Queen to honor based on which employees did the most company-sponsored charitable work. In this way, employee rewards are tied to the company's value.

Fun and community service aren't just a way to be nice; they also have made Amy's Ice Creams a company ice cream lovers care to buy from. The company reaps millions of dollars in sales and has expanded the number of locations to meet growing demand in Austin as well as in Houston and San Antonio. Still, it's not just about the revenues. Co-owner (and Amy's husband) Steve Simmons told a reporter, "We never want to be a mega-company. When we don't know employees' names, there's a problem."

QUESTIONS

1. Which elements of a customer-oriented HRM perspective does Amy's Ice Creams seem to have? (See Figure 16.2.)
2. Suppose Amy's hired you as a consultant to evaluate whether the company has an effective HRM function. Which outcomes would you look for? How would you measure them?
3. Generally, a small ice cream shop such as Amy's cannot afford to pay store workers very high wages. How well do you think the company can achieve high employee satisfaction without high pay? What can it do to foster satisfaction besides the efforts described here? How could e-HRM support these efforts?

SOURCES: Amy's Ice Creams corporate website, www.amysicecreams.com, accessed June 19, 2015; Janine Popick, "GrowCo.: Growth by Involvement at Amy's Ice Creams," *Inc.*, March 16, 2010; Renuka Rayasam, "Sweet Success," *Ausin American-Stateman*, September 29, 2005; Business & Company Resource Center, http://galenet.galegroup.com; and Michael Malone, "Chain Founder; Amy Miller, Amy's Ice Creams," *Restaurant Business*, March 1, 2003, www.allbusiness.com

NOTES

1. P. Wright, S. Snell, and P. Jacobsen, "Current Approaches to HR Strategies: Inside-Out vs. Outside-In," *Human Resource Planning* 27 (2004), pp. 36–46.
2. Personal communication, June 2010.
3. A. S. Tsui and L. R. Gomez-Mejia, "Evaluating HR Effectiveness," in *Human Resource Management: Evolving Roles and Responsibilities*, ed. L. Dyer (Washington, DC: Bureau of National Affairs, 1988), pp. 1-187–1-227.
4. D. Ulrich, "Measuring Human Resources: An Overview of Practice and a Prescription for Results," *Human Resource Management* 36, no. 3 (1997), pp. 303–20.
5. P. Wright, G. McMahan, S. Snell, and B. Gerhart, "Comparing Line and HR Executives' Perceptions of HR Effectiveness: Services, Roles, and Contributions," working paper 98-29 (Ithaca, NY: Cornell University Center for Advanced Human Resource Studies, 1998).
6. J. C. Erfurt, A. Foote, and M. A. Heirich, "The Cost-Effectiveness of Worksite Wellness Programs," *Personnel Psychology* 15 (1992), p. 22.
7. T. H. Davenport, J. Haris, and J. Shapiro, "Competing on Talent Analytics," *Harvard Business Review*, October 2010, pp. 52–59.
8. P. Wright, G. McMahan, S. Snell, and B. Gerhart, *Strategic HRM: Building Human Capital and Organizational Capability*, technical report (Ithaca, NY: Cornell University, 1998).
9. T. B. Kinni, "A Reengineering Primer," *Quality Digest*, January 1994, pp. 26–30; "Reengineering Is Helping Health of Hospitals and Its Patients," *Total Quality Newsletter*, February 1994, p. 5; R. Recardo, "Process Reengineering in a Finance Division," *Journal for Quality and Participation*, June 1994, pp. 70–73.
10. L. Quillen, "Human Resource Computerization: A Dollar and Cents Approach," *Personnel Journal*, July 1989, pp. 74–77.
11. S. Greengard, "New Technology Is HR's Route to Reengineering," *Personnel Journal*, July 1994, pp. 32c–32o.
12. R. Broderick and J. W. Boudreau, "Human Resource Management, Information Technology, and the Competitive Edge," *Academy of Management Executive* 6 (1992), pp. 7–17.
13. S. Shrivastava and J. Shaw, "Liberating HR through Technology," *Human Resource Management* 42, no. 3 (2003), pp. 201–17.
14. C. O'Reilly and P. Caldwell, *Cypress Semiconductor (A): Vision, Values, and Killer Software* (Stanford University Case Study, HR-8A, 1998).
15. "61 Percent of Americans Consider Themselves Overworked and 86 Percent Are Not Satisfied with Their Job, According to Monster's 2004 Work/Life Balance Survey," *Business Wire*, August 3, 2004.
16. G. McMahan and R. Woodman, "The Current Practice of Organization Development within the Firm: A Survey of Large Industrial Corporations," *Group and Organization Studies* 17 (1992), pp. 117–34.
17. B. Becker, M. Huselid, and D. Ulrich, *The HR Scorecard: Linking People, Strategy, and Performance* (Cambridge, MA: HBS Press, 2001).
18. D. Ulrich and A. Yeung, "A Shared Mindset," *Personnel Administrator*, March 1989, pp. 38–45.
19. G. Jones and P. Wright, "An Economic Approach to Conceptualizing the Utility of Human Resource Management Practices," *Research in Personnel/Human Resources* 10 (1992), pp. 271–99.
20. R. Schuler and J. Walker, "Human Resources Strategy: Focusing on Issues and Actions," *Organizational Dynamics*, Summer 1990, pp. 5–19.
21. Company documents.
22. P. Wright, "Strategies and Challenges of the Chief Human Resource Officer: Results of the First Annual Cornell/CAHRS Survey of CHROs," technical report (Ithaca, NY: Cornell University, 2009).
23. Ibid.
24. Ibid.
25. J. Paauwe, *Human Resource Management and Performance: Unique Approaches for Achieving Long-Term Viability* (Oxford: Oxford University Press, 2004).
26. L. Csoka and B. Hackett, *Transforming the HR Function for Global Business Success* (New York: Conference Board, 1998), Report 1209-19RR.

GLOSSARY

9-box grid   A three-by-three matrix used by groups of managers and executives to compare employees within one department, function, division, or the entire company.

360-degree feedback system   A feedback process for managers that includes evaluations from a wide range of persons who interact with the manager. The process includes self-evaluations as well as evaluations from the manager's boss, subordinates, peers, and customers. This can be used for performance appraisal or development.

Acceptability   The extent to which a performance measure is deemed to be satisfactory or adequate by those who use it.

Action learning   Training in which teams work on an actual business problem, commit to an action plan, and are accountable for carrying out the plan.

Action plan   A document summarizing what the trainee and manager will do to ensure that training transfers to the job.

Action steps   The part of a written affirmative action plan that specifies what an employer plans to do to reduce underutilization of protected groups.

Adventure learning   Learning focused on the development of teamwork and leadership skills by using structured outdoor activities.

Agency shop   A union security provision that requires an employee to pay union membership dues but not to join the union.

Agent   In agency theory, a person (e.g., a manager) who is expected to act on behalf of a principal (e.g., an owner).

Alternative dispute resolution (ADR)   A method of resolving disputes that does not rely on the legal system, often proceeding through the four stages of open-door policy, peer review, mediation, and arbitration.

Americans with Disabilities Act (ADA)   A 1990 act prohibiting individuals with disabilities from being discriminated against in the workplace.

Analytic approach   Type of assessment of HRM effectiveness that involves determining the impact of, or the financial costs and benefits of, a program or practice.

Appraisal politics   A situation in which evaluators purposefully distort a rating to achieve personal or company goals.

Apprenticeship   A work-study training method with both on-the-job and classroom training.

Arbitration   A procedure for resolving collective bargaining impasses by which an arbitrator chooses a solution to the dispute.

Artificial intelligence   Technology that can think like a human.

Assessment   Collecting information and providing feedback to employees about their behavior, communication style, or skills.

Assessment center   A process in which multiple raters evaluate employees' performance on a number of exercises.

Associate union membership   A form of union membership by which the union receives dues in exchange for services (e.g., health insurance, credit cards) but does not provide representation in collective bargaining.

Attitudinal structuring   The aspect of the labor–management negotiation process that refers to the relationship and level of trust between the negotiators.

Audit approach   Type of assessment of HRM effectiveness that involves review of customer satisfaction or key indicators (e.g., turnover rate, average days to fill a position) related to an HRM functional area (e.g., recruiting, training).

Avatars   Computer depictions of humans that can be used as imaginary coaches, co-workers, and customers in simulations.

Balanced scorecard   A means of performance measurement that gives managers a chance to look at their company from the perspectives of internal and external customers, employees, and shareholders.

Benchmarking   Comparing an organization's practices against those of the competition.

Bench strength   The business strategy of having a pool of talented employees who are ready when needed to step in to a new position within the organization.

Big data   Information merged from a variety of sources, including HR databases, corporate financial statements, and employee surveys, to make evidence-based HR decisions and show that HR practices can influence the organization's bottom line.

Blended learning Delivering content and instruction with a combination of technology-based and face-to-face methods.

Bona fide occupational qualification (BFOQ) A job qualification based on race, sex, religion, and so on that an employer asserts is a necessary qualification for the job.

Calibration meetings A way to discuss employees' performance with the goal of ensuring that similar standards are applied to their evaluations.

Career support Coaching, protection, sponsorship, and providing challenging assignments, exposure, and visibility.

Cash balance plan A retirement plan in which the employer sets up an individual account for each employee and contributes a percentage of the employee's salary; the account earns interest at a predetermined rate.

Centralization The degree to which decision-making authority resides at the top of the organizational chart.

Change The adoption of a new idea or behavior by a company.

Checkoff provision A union contract provision that requires an employer to deduct union dues from employees' paychecks.

Closed shop A union security provision requiring a person to be a union member before being hired. Illegal under NLRA.

Cloud computing A computing system that provides information technology infrastructure over a network in a self-service, modifiable, and on-demand model.

Coach A peer or manager who works with an employee to motivate the employee, help him or her develop skills, and provide reinforcement and feedback.

Cognitive ability tests Tests that include three dimensions: verbal comprehension, quantitative ability, and reasoning ability.

Communities of practice Groups of employees who work together, learn from each other, and develop a common understanding of how to get work accomplished.

Comparable worth A public policy that advocates remedies for any undervaluation of women's jobs (also called *pay equity*).

Compa-ratio An index of the correspondence between actual and intended pay.

Compensable factors The characteristics of jobs that an organization values and chooses to pay for.

Competencies Sets of skills, knowledge, and abilities and personal characteristics that enable employees to perform their jobs.

Competency model Identifies and provides a description of competencies that are common for an entire occupation, organization, job family, or specific job.

Competitiveness A company's ability to maintain and gain market share in its industry.

Concentration strategy A strategy focusing on increasing market share, reducing costs, or creating and maintaining a market niche for products and services.

Concurrent validation A criterion-related validity study in which a test is administered to all the people currently in a job and then incumbents' scores are correlated with existing measures of their performance on the job.

Consolidated Omnibus Budget Reconciliation Act (COBRA) The 1985 act that requires employers to permit employees to extend their health insurance coverage at group rates for up to 36 months following a qualifying event, such as a layoff.

Content validation A test-validation strategy performed by demonstrating that the items, questions, or problems posed by a test are a representative sample of the kinds of situations or problems that occur on the job.

Continuous learning A learning system that requires employees to understand the entire work process and expects them to acquire new skills, apply them on the job, and share what they have learned with other employees.

Coordination training Training a team in how to share information and decision-making responsibilities to maximize team performance.

Corporate campaigns Union activities designed to exert public, financial, or political pressure on employers during the union-organizing process.

Counselor/confidante/coach A role of the CHRO that focuses on counseling or coaching team members or resolving interpersonal or political conflicts among team members.

Criterion-related validity A method of establishing the validity of a personnel selection method by showing a substantial correlation between test scores and job-performance scores.

Cross-cultural preparation The process of educating employees (and their families) who are given an assignment in a foreign country.

Cross-training Training in which team members understand and practice each other's skills so that members are prepared to step in and take another member's place should he or she temporarily or permanently leave the team.

Decision support systems Problem-solving systems that usually include a "what-if" feature that allows users to see how outcomes change when assumptions or data change.

Delayering Reducing the number of job levels within an organization.

Departmentalization The degree to which work units are grouped based on functional similarity or similarity of work-flow.

Development The acquisition of knowledge, skills, and behaviors that improve an employee's ability to meet changes in job requirements and in client and customer demands.

Development planning system A system to retain and motivate employees by identifying and meeting their development needs (also called *career management systems*).

Direct applicants People who apply for a job vacancy without prompting from the organization.

Disparate impact A theory of discrimination based on facially neutral employment practices that disproportionately exclude a protected group from employment opportunities.

Disparate treatment A theory of discrimination based on different treatment given to individuals because of their race, color, religion, sex, national origin, age, or disability status.

Distributive bargaining The part of the labor–management negotiation process that focuses on dividing a fixed economic "pie."

Diversity training Refers to learning efforts that are designed to change employees' attitudes about diversity and/or develop skills needed to work with a diverse workforce.

Downsizing The planned elimination of large numbers of personnel, designed to enhance organizational effectiveness.

Downward move A job change involving a reduction in an employee's level of responsibility and authority.

Due process policies Policies by which a company formally lays out the steps an employee can take to appeal a termination decision.

Duty of fair representation The National Labor Relations Act requirement that all bargaining unit members have equal access to and representation by the union.

Efficiency wage theory A theory stating that wages influence worker productivity.

E-learning Instruction and delivery of training by computers through the Internet or company intranet.

Employee assistance programs (EAPs) Employer programs that attempt to ameliorate problems encountered by workers who are drug dependent, alcoholic, or psychologically troubled.

Employee engagement The degree to which employees are fully involved in their work and the strength of their job and company commitment.

Employee Retirement Income Security Act (ERISA) The 1974 act that increased the fiduciary responsibilities of pension plan trustees, established vesting rights and portability provisions, and established the Pension Benefit Guaranty Corporation (PBGC).

Employee stock ownership plan (ESOP) An employee ownership plan that provides employers certain tax and financial advantages when stock is granted to employees.

Employment-at-will doctrine The doctrine that, in the absence of a specific contract, either an employer or an employee could sever the employment relationship at any time.

Employment-at-will policies Policies stating that either an employer or an employee can terminate the employment relationship at any time, regardless of cause.

Empowering Giving employees the responsibility and authority to make decisions.

Equal employment opportunity (EEO) The government's attempt to ensure that all individuals have an equal opportunity for employment, regardless of race, color, religion, sex, age, disability, or national origin.

Equal Employment Opportunity Commission (EEOC) The government commission established to ensure that all individuals have an equal opportunity for employment, regardless of race, color, religion, sex, age, disability, or national origin.

Ergonomics The interface between individuals' physiological characteristics and the physical work environment.

Ethics The fundamental principles of right and wrong by which employees and companies interact.

Evidence-based HR Demonstrating that HR practices have a positive influence on the company's bottom line or key stakeholders (employees, customers, community, shareholders).

Exempt Employees who are not covered by the Fair Labor Standards Act. Exempt employees are not eligible for overtime pay.

Expatriate Employee sent by his or her company to manage operations in a different country.

Expectancy theory The theory that says motivation is a function of valence, instrumentality, and expectancy.

Experiential programs Training programs in which trainees gain knowledge and theory, participate in behavioral simulations, analyze the activity, and connect the theory and activity with on-the-job situations.

Expert systems Computer systems incorporating the decision rules of people recognized as experts in a certain area.

Explicit knowledge Knowledge that is well documented and easily transferred to other persons.

External analysis Examining the organization's operating environment to identify strategic opportunities and threats.

External growth strategy An emphasis on acquiring vendors and suppliers or buying businesses that allow a company to expand into new markets.

External labor market Persons outside the firm who are actively seeking employment.

Fact finder A person who reports on the reasons for a labor–management dispute, the views and arguments of both sides, and a nonbinding recommendation for settling the dispute.

Fair labor standards act (FLSA) The 1938 law that established the minimum wage and overtime pay.

Family and Medical Leave Act The 1993 act that requires employers with 50 or more employees to provide up to 12 weeks of unpaid leave after childbirth or adoption; to care for a seriously ill child, spouse, or parent; or for an employee's own serious illness.

Financial Accounting Statement (FAS) 106 The rule issued by the Financial Accounting Standards Board in 1993 requiring companies to fund benefits provided after retirement on an accrual rather than a pay-as-you-go basis and to enter these future cost obligations on their financial statements.

Forecasting The attempts to determine the supply of and demand for various types of human resources to predict areas within the organization where there will be future labor shortages or surpluses.

Formal education programs Employee development programs, including short courses offered by consultants or universities, executive MBA programs, and university programs.

Formal training Training and development programs and courses that are developed and organized by the company.

Four-fifths rule A rule that states that an employment test has disparate impact if the hiring rate for a minority group is less than four-fifths, or 80 %, of the hiring rate for the majority group.

Frame of reference A standard point that serves as a comparison for other points and thus provides meaning.

Gainsharing A form of group compensation based on group or plant performance (rather than organization-wide profits) that does not become part of the employee's base salary.

General duty clause The provision of the Occupational Safety and Health Act that states an employer has an overall obligation to furnish employees with a place of employment free from recognized hazards.

Generalizability The degree to which the validity of a selection method established in one context extends to other contexts.

Gig economy Companies who rely primarily on non-traditional employment to meet service and product demands

Glass ceiling A barrier to advancement to higher-level jobs in the company that adversely affects women and minorities. The barrier may be due to lack of access to training programs, development experiences, or relationships (e.g., mentoring).

Goals What an organization hopes to achieve in the medium- to long-term future.

Goals and timetables The part of a written affirmative action plan that specifies the percentage of women and minorities that an employer seeks to have in each job group and the date by which that percentage is to be attained.

Group- or team-building methods Training methods that help trainees share ideas and experiences, build group identity, understand the dynamics of interpersonal relationships, and get to know their own strengths and weaknesses and those of their co-workers.

Hands-on methods Training methods that require the trainee to be actively involved in learning.

Health Maintenance Organization (HMO) A health care plan that provides benefits on a prepaid basis for employees who are required to use only HMO medical service providers.

High-performance work systems Work systems that maximize the fit between employees and technology.

High-potential employees Employees the company believes are capable of being successful in high-level management positions.

Host country The country in which the parent-country organization seeks to locate or has already located a facility.

Host-country nationals (HCNs) Employees born and raised in a host, not parent, country.

HR dashboard HR metrics such as productivity and absenteeism that are accessible by employees and managers through the company intranet or human resource information system.

HR or workforce analytics The practice of using data from HR databases and other data sources to make evidence-based HR decisions.

Human resource information system (HRIS) A system used to acquire, store, manipulate, analyze, retrieve, and distribute information related to human resources.

Human resource management (HRM) The policies, practices, and systems that influence employees' behavior, attitudes, and performances.

Human resource recruitment The practice or activity carried on by the organization with the primary purpose of identifying and attracting potential employees.

In-basket A simulation of the administrative tasks of a manager's job.

Incentive effect The effect a pay plan has on the behaviors of current employees.

Inclusion Creating an environment in which employees share a sense of belonging, mutual respect, and commitment with others so they can perform their best work.

Individualism–collectivism One of Hofstede's cultural dimensions; describes the strength of the relation between an individual and other individuals in a society.

Informal learning Learning that is learner initiated, involves action and doing, is motivated by an intent to develop, and does not occur in a formal learning setting.

Intangible assets A type of company asset that includes human capital, customer capital, social capital, and intellectual capital.

Integrative bargaining The part of the labor–management negotiation process that seeks solutions beneficial to both sides.

Interactional justice A concept of justice referring to the interpersonal nature of how the outcomes were implemented.

Internal analysis The process of examining an organization's strengths and weaknesses.

Internal growth strategy A focus on new market and product development, innovation, and joint ventures.

Internal labor force Labor force of current employees.

Internship On-the-job learning sponsored by an educational institution, or part of an academic program.

Interview Employees are questioned about their work and personal experiences, skills, and career plans.

Intraorganizational bargaining The part of the labor–management negotiation process that focuses on the conflicting objectives of factions within labor and management.

Involuntary turnover Turnover initiated by the organization (often among people who would prefer to stay).

ISO 9000:2015 A series of quality assurance standards developed by the International Organization for Standardization in Switzerland and adopted worldwide.

Job analysis The process of getting detailed information about jobs.

Job description A list of the tasks, duties, and responsibilities (TDRs) that a job entails.

Job design The process of defining the way work will be performed and the tasks that will be required in a given job.

Job enlargement Adding challenges or new responsibilities to an employee's current job.

Job evaluation An administrative procedure used to measure internal job worth.

Job experience The relationships, problems, demands, tasks, and other features that employees face in their jobs.

Job hazard analysis technique A breakdown of each job into basic elements, each of which is rated for its potential for harm or injury.

Job involvement The degree to which people identify themselves with their jobs.

Job redesign The process of changing the tasks or the way work is performed in an existing job.

Job rotation The process of systematically moving a single individual from one job to another over the course of time. The job assignments may be in various functional areas of the company, or movement may be between jobs in a single functional area or department.

Job satisfaction A pleasurable feeling that results from the perception that one's job fulfills or allows for the fulfillment of one's important job values.

Job specification A list of the knowledge, skills, abilities, and other characteristics (KSAOs) that an individual must have to perform a job.

Job structure The relative pay of jobs in an organization.

Kaizen Practices participated in by employees from all levels of the company that focus on continuous improvement of business processes.

Key jobs Benchmark jobs, used in pay surveys, that have relatively stable content and are common to many organizations.

Knowledge management The process of enhancing company performance by designing and using tools, systems, and cultures to improve creation, sharing, and use of knowledge.

Knowledge workers Employees who own the intellectual means of producing a product or service.

Leader of the HR function A role of the CHRO that focuses on working with HR team members regarding the development, design, and delivery of HR services.

Leaderless group discussion Process in which a team of five to seven employees solves an assigned problem within a certain time period.

Leading indicator An objective measure that accurately predicts future labor demand.

Lean thinking A way to do more with less effort, equipment space, and time, but still provide customers what they need and want.

Learning management system (LMS) Technology platform that automates the administration, development, and delivery of a company's training program.

Learning organization An organization whose employees are continuously attempting to learn new things and apply what they have learned to improve product or service quality.

Liaison to the board of directors A role of the CHRO that focuses on preparation for board meetings, phone calls with board members, and attendance at board meetings.

Long-term–short-term orientation One of Hofstede's cultural dimensions; describes how a culture balances immediate benefits with future rewards.

Maintenance of membership Union rules requiring members to remain members for a certain period of time (e.g., the length of the union contract).

Malcolm Baldrige National Quality Award An award established in 1987 to promote quality awareness, to recognize quality achievements of U.S. companies, and to publicize successful quality strategies.

Manager support The degree to which trainees' managers emphasize the importance of attending training programs and stress the application of training content to the job.

Managing diversity and inclusion The process of creating an environment that allows all employees to contribute to organizational goals and experience personal growth.

Marginal tax rate The percentage of an additional dollar of earnings that goes to taxes.

Masculinity–femininity dimension One of Hofstede's cultural dimensions; describes the division of roles between the sexes within a society.

Massive open online courses (MOOCs) Online learning designed to enroll large numbers of learners who have access to the Internet and composed of interactive coursework including video lectures, discussion groups, wikis, and assessment quizzes.

Mediation A procedure for resolving collective bargaining impasses by which a mediator with no formal authority acts as a facilitator and go-between in the negotiations.

Mentor An experienced, productive senior employee who helps develop a less experienced employee.

Merit bonus Merit pay paid in the form of a bonus, instead of a salary increase.

Merit increase grid A grid that combines an employee's performance rating with his or her position in a pay range to determine the size and frequency of his or her pay increases.

Merit pay Traditional form of pay in which base pay is increased permanently.

Minimum wage The lowest amount that employers are legally allowed to pay; the 1990 amendment of the Fair Labor Standards Act permits a subminimum wage to workers under the age of 20 for a period of up to 90 days.

Mobile devices Equipment such as smartphones and tablet computers that provide employees with anytime, anywhere access to HR applications and other work-related information.

Motivation to learn The desire of the trainee to learn the content of a training program.

Myers Briggs Type Inventory (MBTI) A psychological test used for team building and leadership development that identifies employees' preferences for energy, information gathering, decision making, and lifestyle.

Needs assessment The process used to determine if training is necessary.

Negative affectivity A dispositional dimension that reflects pervasive individual differences in satisfaction with any and all aspects of life.

New technologies Current applications of knowledge, procedures, and equipment that have not been previously used. Usually involves replacing human labor with equipment, information processing, or some combination of the two.

Nonkey jobs Jobs that are unique to organizations and that cannot be directly valued or compared through the use of market surveys.

Nontraditional employment Includes the use of independent contractors, freelancers, on-call workers, temporary workers, and contract company workers.

Occupational Safety and Health Act (OSHA) The 1970 law that authorizes the federal government to establish and enforce occupational safety and health standards for all places of employment engaging in interstate commerce.

Offshoring A special case of outsourcing, in which the jobs that move leave one country and go to another.

Onboarding Refers to the process of helping new hires adjust to social and performance aspects of their new jobs.

On-the-job training (OJT)   Peers or managers training new or inexperienced employees who learn the job by observation, understanding, and imitation.

Opportunity to perform   The trainee is provided with or actively seeks experience using newly learned knowledge, skills, or behavior.

Organizational analysis   A process for determining the business appropriateness of training.

Organizational commitment   The degree to which an employee identifies with the organization and is willing to put forth effort on its behalf.

Outcome fairness   The judgment that people make with respect to the outcomes received relative to the outcomes received by other people with whom they identify.

Outplacement counseling   Counseling to help displaced employees manage the transition from one job to another.

Outsourcing   An organization's use of an outside organization for a broad set of services.

Parent country   The country in which a company's corporate headquarters is located.

Parent-country nationals (PCNs)   Employees who were born and live in a parent country.

Pay grades   Jobs of similar worth or content grouped together for pay administration purposes.

Pay level   The average pay, including wages, salaries, and bonuses, of jobs in an organization.

Pay policy line   A mathematical expression that describes the relationship between a job's pay and its job evaluation points.

Pay structure   The relative pay of different jobs (job structure) and how much they are paid (pay level).

Pension Benefit Guaranty Corporation (PBGC)   The agency that guarantees to pay employees a basic retirement benefit in the event that financial difficulties force a company to terminate or reduce employee pension benefits.

Performance appraisal   The process through which an organization gets information on how well an employee is doing his or her job.

Performance feedback   The process of providing employees information regarding their performance effectiveness.

Performance improvement plan (PIP)   A plan that describes the performance changes that a poorly performing employee needs to make in a specified time period or face termination.

Performance management   The means through which managers ensure that employees' activities and outcomes are congruent with the organization's goals.

Performance support systems   Computer applications that can provide (as requested) skills training, information access, and expert advice.

Person analysis   A process for determining whether employees need training, who needs training, and whether employees are ready for training.

Power distance   One of Hofstede's cultural dimensions; concerns how a culture deals with hierarchical power relationships—particularly the unequal distribution of power.

Predictive validation   A criterion-related validity study that seeks to establish an empirical relationship between applicants' test scores and their eventual performance on the job.

Preferred Provider Organization (PPO)   A group of health care providers who contract with employers, insurance companies, and so forth to provide health care at a reduced fee.

Presentation methods   Training methods in which trainees are passive recipients of information.

Principal   In agency theory, a person (e.g., the owner) who seeks to direct another person's behavior.

Procedural justice   A concept of justice focusing on the methods used to determine the outcomes received.

Profit sharing   A compensation plan in which payments are based on a measure of organization performance (profits) and do not become part of the employees' base salary.

Progression of withdrawal   The theory that dissatisfied individuals enact a set of behaviors to avoid the work situation.

Promotions   Advances into positions with greater challenge, more responsibility, and more authority than the employee's previous job.

Prosocial motivation   The degree to which people are motivated to help other people.

Protean career   A career that is changing frequently due to both changes in the person's interests, abilities, and values and changes in the work environment.

Psychological success   The feeling of pride and accomplishment that comes from achieving life goals.

Psychosocial support   Serving as a friend and role model, providing positive regard and acceptance, and creating an outlet for a protégé to talk about anxieties and fears.

Quantitative ability   Refers to the speed and accuracy with which one can solve arithmetic problems of all kinds.

Range spread   The distance between the minimum and maximum amounts in a pay grade.

Rate ranges Different employees in the same job may have different pay rates.

Readiness for training Employee characteristics that provide them with the desire, energy, and focus necessary to learn from training.

Reasonable accommodation Making facilities readily accessible to and usable by individuals with disabilities.

Reasoning ability Refers to a person's capacity to invent solutions to many diverse problems.

Recruitment The process of seeking applicants for potential employment.

Reengineering Review and redesign of work processes to make them more efficient and improve the quality of the end product or service.

Referrals People who are prompted to apply for a job by someone within the organization.

Reliability The consistency of a performance measure; the degree to which a performance measure is free from random error.

Repatriation The preparation of expatriates for return to the parent company and country from a foreign assignment.

Representative of the firm A role of the CHRO that focuses on activities with external stakeholders, such as lobbying, speaking to outside groups, etc.

Repurposing Directly translating instructor-led training online.

Reshoring Moving jobs from overseas to the United States.

Return on investment Refers to the estimated dollar return from each dollar invested in learning.

Reverse mentoring A business situation in which younger employees mentor more senior employees.

Right-to-work laws State laws that make union shops, maintenance of membership, and agency shops illegal.

Role behaviors Behaviors that are required of an individual in his or her role as a jobholder in a social work environment.

Role-play A participant taking the part or role of a manager or other employee.

Sabbatical A leave of absence from the company to renew or develop skills.

Safety awareness programs Employer programs that attempt to instill symbolic and substantive changes in the organization's emphasis on safety.

Sarbanes-Oxley Act of 2002 A congressional act passed in response to illegal and unethical behavior by managers and executives. The act sets stricter rules for business, especially related to accounting practices—including requiring more open and consistent disclosure of financial data and the CEO's assurance that the data are completely accurate—and provisions that affect the employee–employer relationship (e.g., development of a code of conduct for senior financial officers).

Selection The process by which an organization attempts to identify applicants with the necessary knowledge, skills, abilities, and other characteristics that will help it achieve its goals.

Self-service Giving employees online access to human resources information.

Serious games Games in which the training content is turned into a game but has business objectives.

Shared service model A way to organize the HR function that includes centers of expertise or excellence, service centers, and business partners.

Simulation A training method that represents a real-life situation, allowing trainees to see the outcomes of their decisions in an artificial environment.

Situational interview An interview procedure where applicants are confronted with specific issues, questions, or problems that are likely to arise on the job.

Six Sigma process A system of measuring, analyzing, improving, and controlling processes once they meet quality standards.

Skill-based pay Pay based on the skills employees acquire and are capable of using.

Social networking Websites and blogs that facilitate interactions between people.

Social performance management Social media and microblogs similar to Facebook, LinkedIn, and Yammer that allow employees to quickly exchange information, talk to each other, provide coaching, and receive feedback and recognition in the form of electronic badges.

Sorting effect The effect a pay plan has on the composition of the current workforce (the types of employees attracted and retained).

Specificity The extent to which a performance measure gives detailed guidance to employees about what is expected of them and how they can meet these expectations.

Stakeholders The various interest groups who have relationships with and, consequently, whose interests are tied to the organization (e.g., employees, suppliers, customers, shareholders, community).

Standard deviation rule A rule used to analyze employment tests to determine disparate impact; it uses the difference between the expected representation for minority groups and the actual representation to determine whether the difference between the two is greater than would occur by chance.

Stock options   An employee ownership plan that gives employees the opportunity to buy the company's stock at a previously fixed price.

Strategic advisor   A role of the CHRO that focuses on the formulation and implementation of the firm's strategy.

Strategic choice   The organization's strategy; the ways an organization will attempt to fulfill its mission and achieve its long-term goals.

Strategic congruence   The extent to which the performance management system elicits job performance that is consistent with the organization's strategy, goals, and culture.

Strategic human resource management (SHRM)   A pattern of planned human resource deployments and activities intended to enable an organization to achieve its goals.

Strategy formulation   The process of deciding on a strategic direction by defining a company's mission and goals, its external opportunities and threats, and its internal strengths and weaknesses.

Strategy implementation   The process of devising structures and allocating resources to enact the strategy a company has chosen.

Stretch assignments   Job assignments in which there is a mismatch between an employee's skills and past experiences and the skills required for success on the job.

Succession planning   The identification and tracking of high-potential employees capable of filling higher-level managerial positions.

Summary plan description (SPD)   A reporting requirement of the Employee Retirement Income Security Act (ERISA) that obligates employers to describe the plan's funding, eligibility requirements, risks, and so forth within 90 days after an employee has entered the plan.

Support network   Trainees who meet to discuss their progress in using learned capabilities on the job.

Sustainability   The ability of a company to make a profit without sacrificing the resources of its employees, the community, or the environment. Based on an approach to organizational decision making that considers the long-term impact of strategies on stakeholders (e.g., employees, shareholders, suppliers, community).

Tacit knowledge   Knowledge based on personal experience that is difficult to codify.

Taft-hartley act   The 1947 act that outlawed unfair union labor practices.

Talent architect   A role of the CHRO that focuses on building and identifying the human capital critical to the present and future of the firm.

Talent management   Attracting, retaining, developing, and motivating highly skilled employees and managers.

Task analysis   The process of identifying the tasks, knowledge, skills, and behaviors that need to be emphasized in training.

Team leader training   Training of the team manager or facilitator.

Technique of operations review (TOR)   Method of determining safety problems via an analysis of past accidents.

Teleconferencing   Synchronous exchange of audio, video, or text between individuals or groups at two or more locations.

Temporary assignment   Job tryouts such as employees taking on a position to help them determine if they are interested in working in a new role.

Third country   A country other than a host or parent country.

Third-country nationals (TCNs)   Employees born in a country other than a parent or host country.

Total quality management (TQM)   A cooperative form of doing business that relies on the talents and capabilities of both labor and management to continually improve quality and productivity.

Training   A planned effort to facilitate the learning of job-related knowledge, skills, and behavior by employees.

Training design process   A systematic approach for developing training programs.

Training outcomes   A way to evaluate the effectiveness of a training program based on cognitive, skill-based, affective, and results outcomes.

Transaction processing   Computations and calculations used to review and document HRM decisions and practices.

Transfer   The movement of an employee to a different job assignment in a different area of the company.

Transfer of training   The use of knowledge, skills, and behaviors learned in training on the job.

Transitional matrix   A matrix showing the proportion or number of employees in different job categories at different times.

Transnational process   The extent to which a company's planning and decision-making processes include representatives and ideas from a variety of cultures.

Transnational representation Reflects the multinational composition of a company's managers.

Transnational scope A company's ability to make HRM decisions from an international perspective.

Tuition reimbursement The practice of reimbursing employees' costs for college and university courses and degree programs.

Uncertainty avoidance One of Hofstede's cultural dimensions; describes how cultures seek to deal with an unpredictable future.

Unconscious bias A judgment outside of our consciousness that affects decisions based on background, culture, and personal experience.

Union shop A union security provision that requires a person to join the union within a certain amount of time after being hired.

Upward feedback A performance appraisal process for managers that includes subordinates' evaluations.

Utility The degree to which the information provided by selection methods enhances the effectiveness of selecting personnel in real organizations.

Utilization analysis A comparison of the race, sex, and ethnic composition of an employer's workforce with that of the available labor supply.

Validity The extent to which a performance measure assesses all the relevant—and only the relevant—aspects of job performance.

Verbal comprehension Refers to a person's capacity to understand and use written and spoken language.

Virtual reality Computer-based technology that provides trainees with a three-dimensional learning experience. Trainees operate in a simulated environment that responds to their behaviors and reactions.

Virtual teams Teams that are separated by time, geographic distance, culture, and/or organizational boundaries and rely exclusively on technology for interaction between team members.

Voluntary turnover Turnover initiated by employees (who the company often would prefer to keep).

Webcasting Classroom instruction provided online via live broadcasts.

Whistle-blowing Making grievances public by going to the media or government.

Workforce utilization review A comparison of the proportion of workers in protected subgroups with the proportion that each subgroup represents in the relevant labor market.

NAME AND COMPANY INDEX

SUBJECT INDEX